# THE OFFICIAL HISTORY
## OF PRIVATISATION

This first volume of the Official History studies the background to UK privatisation, and the privatisations that took place from May 1979 to June 1987. First commissioned by the then Prime Minister, Tony Blair, as an authoritative history, this volume addresses a number of key questions:

- To what extent was privatisation a clear policy commitment within the Thatcher Governments of the 1980s – or did Government simply stumble on the idea?
- Why were particular public corporations sold early in the 1980s and other sales delayed until well into the 1990s?
- What were the privatisation objectives and how did they change over time, if at all?
- How was each privatisation planned and executed, how were different City advisers appointed and remunerated, what precise roles did they play?
- How was each privatisation administered; in what ways did the methods evolve and change and why? How were sale prices determined?
- Which government departments took the lead role; what was the input of the Treasury and Bank of England; what was the relationship between Ministers and civil servants?

The study draws heavily from the official records of the British Government, to which the author was given full access, and from interviews with leading figures involved in each of the privatisations – including ex-Ministers, civil servants, business and City figures, as well as academics who have studied the subject. This new official history will be of much interest to students of British political history, economics and business studies.

**David Parker** is Research Professor in Privatisation and Regulation in the School of Management, Cranfield University, UK. He has researched privatisation for over 25 years, and has acted as a consultant on privatisation internationally. Previous publications include co-authoring *The International Handbook on Privatization*.

D1612485

# WHITEHALL HISTORIES: GOVERNMENT OFFICIAL HISTORY SERIES

ISSN: 1474–8398

The Government Official History series began in 1919 with wartime histories, and the peacetime series was inaugurated in 1966 by Harold Wilson. The aim of the series is to produce major histories in their own right, compiled by historians eminent in the field, who are afforded free access to all relevant material in the official archives. The Histories also provide a trusted secondary source for other historians and researchers while the official records are not in the public domain. The main criteria for selection of topics are that the histories should record important episodes or themes of British history while the official records can still be supplemented by the recollections of key players; and that they should be of general interest, and, preferably, involve the records of more than one government department.

### THE UNITED KINGDOM AND THE EUROPEAN COMMUNITY
Vol. I: The Rise and Fall of a National Strategy, 1945–1963
*Alan S. Milward*

### SECRET FLOTILLAS
Vol. I: Clandestine Sea Operations to Brittany, 1940–1944
Vol. II: Clandestine Sea Operations in the Mediterranean, North Africa and the Adriatic, 1940–1944
*Sir Brooks Richards*

### SOE IN FRANCE
*M. R. D. Foot*

### THE OFFICIAL HISTORY OF THE FALKLANDS CAMPAIGN:
Vol. I: The Origins of the Falklands War
Vol. II: War and Diplomacy
*Sir Lawrence Freedman*

### THE OFFICIAL HISTORY OF BRITAIN AND THE CHANNEL TUNNEL
*Terry Gourvish*

### CHURCHILL'S MYSTERY MAN: DESMOND MORTON AND THE WORLD OF INTELLIGENCE
*Gill Bennett*

### THE OFFICIAL HISTORY OF PRIVATISATION
Vol. I: The Formative Years 1970–1987
*David Parker*

# THE OFFICIAL HISTORY OF PRIVATISATION

Volume I:
The formative years 1970–1987

*David Parker*

Routledge
Taylor & Francis Group

LONDON AND NEW YORK

First published 2009
by Routledge
2 Park Square, Milton Park, Abingdon, Oxon, OX14 4RN

Simultaneously published in the USA and Canada
by Routledge
270 Madison Avenue, New York, NY 10016

*Routledge is an imprint of the Taylor & Francis Group, an informa business*

Typeset in Times New Roman by
Florence Production Ltd, Stoodleigh, Devon
Printed by the MPG Books Group
in the UK

*British Library Cataloguing in Publication Data*
A catalogue record for this book is available from the British Library

*Library of Congress Cataloging in Publication Data*
Parker, David, 1949 Sept. 28–.
The official history of privatisation/David Parker.
p. cm. – (Whitehall histories: government official history series; ISSN 1474-8398)
Includes bibliographical references and index.
1. Privatization – Great Britain – History.  2. Great Britain – Economic policy –
20th century.  3. Great Britain – Economic conditions – 20th century.  I. Title.
II. Title: Official history of privatization.
HD4148.P368 2009
338.941'05 – dc22          2008036925

ISBN10: 0–415–46916–3 (hbk)
ISBN10: 0–203–88152–4 (ebk)

ISBN13: 978–0–415–46916–6 (hbk)
ISBN13: 978–0–203–88152–1 (ebk)

The author has been given full access to official documents. He alone is responsible for the statements made and the views expressed.

# CONTENTS

CONTENTS

# ABBREVIATIONS

| | |
|---|---|
| ABP | Associated British Ports |
| ADR | American Depository Receipts |
| AGM | Annual General Meeting |
| APS | Assistant Private Secretary |
| ASI | Adam Smith Institute |
| AUEW | Amalgamated Union of Engineering Workers |
| BA | British Airways Corporation later PLC |
| BAA | British Airports Authority later BAA PLC |
| BAe | British Aerospace Corporation later PLC |
| BBC | British Broadcasting Corporation |
| BCal | British Caledonian airline |
| BEA | British European Airways |
| BGC | British Gas Corporation later British Gas PLC |
| BL | British Leyland PLC |
| BNOC | British National Oil Corporation |
| BOAC | British Overseas Airways Corporation |
| BP | British Petroleum PLC |
| BR | British Rail |
| BRINDEX | The Association of British Independent Oil Exploration Companies |
| BS | British Shipbuilders Corporation |
| BSC | British Steel Corporation later British Steel PLC |
| BSI | British Standards Institute |
| BT | British Telecommunications Corporation later PLC |
| BTDB | British Transport Docks Board |
| BTG | British Technology Group |
| CAA | Civil Aviation Authority |
| C&W | Cable and Wireless PLC |
| CBI | Confederation of British Industry |
| CC | Competition Commission |
| CCA | Current cost accounting |
| CEO | Chief Executive Officer |
| CORGI | Corporation of Registered Gas Installers |
| CPRS | Central Policy Review Staff |
| CPS | Centre for Policy Studies |
| CUP | Central Unit on Purchasing |

| | |
|---|---|
| DG | Director General |
| DGGS | Director General Gas Supply (alternative title of DGOFGAS) |
| DGOFGAS | Director General of the Office of Gas Supply (also see DGGS) |
| DGOFT | Director General of the Office of Fair Trading |
| DGOFTEL | Director General Office of the Office of Telecommunications (also see DGT) |
| DGT | Director General of Telecommunications (alternative title of DGOFTEL) |
| DLO | Direct labour organisation |
| DOI | Department of Industry |
| DSH | Drake and Scull Holdings |
| DTI | Department of Trade and Industry |
| EEC/EC/EU | European Economic Community later European Community later European Union |
| EFL | External Financing Limit |
| ERDF | European Regional Development Fund |
| FCC | Federal Communications Commission (USA) |
| FCO | Foreign and Commonwealth Office |
| FT | Financial Times newspaper, London |
| GCHQ | General Communications Headquarters |
| GDP | Gross Domestic Product |
| GEC | General Electric Company Ltd |
| GLC | Greater London Council |
| GMBATU | General and Municipal Boilermakers and Allied Trade Union |
| GPO | General Post Office |
| GUC | Gas Users Council (later Gas Consumers' Council) |
| H&W | Harland and Wolff shipyard |
| HCA | Historic cost accounting |
| IEA | Institute of Economic Affairs |
| IFR | Investment and Financing Review |
| IMF | International Monetary Fund |
| IPO | Initial Public Offering (initial stock market flotation) |
| IRC | Industrial Reorganisation Corporation |
| JPPC | Joint Privatisation Promotion Committee (sale of British Gas) |
| LNG | Liquid natural gas |
| LPTB | London Passenger Transport Board |
| MEBO | Management and employee buy out |
| MMC | Monopolies and Mergers Commission |
| MoD | Ministry of Defence |
| MORI | Market & Opinion Research International Ltd |
| MP | Member of Parliament |
| MTFS | Medium Term Financial Strategy |
| n/a | not available/not applicable |
| NALGO | National and Local Government Officers' Association |
| NAO | National Audit Office |
| NBC | National Bus Company |
| NCB | National Coal Board |
| NCL | National Carriers Ltd (subsidiary of the NFC) |

| | |
|---|---|
| n.d. | no date |
| NDLS | National Dock Labour Scheme |
| NEB | National Enterprise Board |
| NEDC | National Economic Development Council |
| NEDO | National Economic Development Office |
| NESL | North Eastern Shipbuilders Ltd |
| NFC | National Freight Corporation |
| NGCC | National Gas Consumer Council |
| NHS | National Health Service |
| NLF | National Loans Fund |
| NPV | Net present value |
| NUM | National Union of Mineworkers |
| OFCOM | Office of Communications |
| OFGAS | Office of Gas Supply |
| OFGEM | Office of Gas and Electricity Markets |
| OFT | Office of Fair Trading |
| OFTEL | Office of Telecommunications |
| OPA | Oil and Pipelines Agency |
| OPEC | Organisation of the Petroleum Exporting Countries |
| ORPL/ORPT | Output-related profit levy/output-related profit tax |
| PABX | Private Automatic Branch Exchange |
| PAC | Public Accounts Committee of the House of Commons |
| PCN | Personal Communications Network |
| P/E | Price earnings ratio (the price of the share in relation to the earnings per share) |
| PEAU | Public Enterprises Analytical Unit (HM Treasury) |
| PM | Prime Minister |
| PO | Post Office/Post Office Corporation |
| POEU | Post Office Engineering Union |
| POUNC | Post Office Users National Council |
| PPS | Parliamentary Private Secretary |
| PRT | Petroleum Revenue Tax |
| PS | Private Secretary |
| PSA | Property Services Agency |
| PSBR | Public Sector Borrowing Requirement |
| PTA | Passenger Transport Authority |
| PTE | Passenger Transport Executive |
| R&D | Research and development |
| RO | Royal Ordnance/Royal Ordnance factories |
| RPI | Retail price index |
| RR | Rolls-Royce PLC |
| SBG | Scottish Bus Group |
| SBGI | Society of British Gas Industries |
| SERPS | State Earnings Related Pension Scheme |
| STG | Scottish Transport Group |
| TEMA | Telecommunications Engineering and Manufacturing Association |
| TGWU | Transport and General Workers Union |

| | |
|---|---|
| TH | Trafalgar House PLC |
| TRC | The Radio Chemical Centre Ltd |
| TSB | Trustee Savings Banks later TSB PLC |
| TUC | Trades Union Congress |
| TUPE | Transfer of Undertakings (Protection of Employment) Regulations 1981 |
| UK | United Kingdom |
| UKCS | United Kingdom Continental Shelf |
| US/USA | United States of America |
| USH | United Scientific Holdings |
| VANS | Value added network services (in telecommunications) |
| VAT | Value added tax |
| VSEL | Vickers Shipbuilding and Engineering Employee Consortium |
| YTS | Youth Training Scheme |
| £M3 | Sterling M3 – a broad measure of the money supply |

# LIST OF FIGURES, TABLES AND PLATES

## Figures

## Tables

## Plates

The following plates appear between pp.282 and 283.

# ACKNOWLEDGEMENTS

The author and publishers are grateful to the following sources for permission to reproduce illustrations: BT Archives, plate 8; Fred Mott/Hulton Archive/Getty Images plate 1; Peter Jordan/Time and Life Pictures/Getty Images, plate 11; The History of Advertising Trust (www.hatads.org.uk), plates 6 and 9; PA Photos, plates 3 and 4; Sir Peter Thompson, plate 2; The Press and Journal, Aberdeen Journals Ltd, plate 5.

# PREFACE

In September 2004 I was appointed by the then Prime Minister Tony Blair to write the history of Privatisation in Britain as part of the programme of Official Histories managed by the Cabinet Office. I had worked as an economist researching privatisation internationally since the 1980s. Therefore I was delighted to be given the opportunity to prepare this Official History. My brief was to review the evolution of the privatisation programme from May 1979 to May 1997 or during the years of the Conservative Governments. I was also asked to review the years leading up to 1979 and especially from 1970 to better understand the programme's origins and context. I chose to concentrate upon the privatisations involving the sale of public corporations, including the nationalised industries and their subsidiaries. However, I have not entirely ignored the policies introduced that put public services out to competitive tender.

It soon became clear during the writing of this Official History that to do full justice to the wealth of information available in Government records and from interviews with those involved in implementing the privatisations, and to provide a truly authoritative account, two published volumes would be needed. This volume, Volume 1, studies the background to privatisation and the privatisations of the first two Conservative Governments led by Margaret Thatcher, from May 1979 to June 1987. Volume 2, to follow, will cover the privatisations undertaken during the third Thatcher Government from June 1987 to November 1990 and those undertaken by the Major Governments. John Major succeeded Margaret Thatcher as Prime Minister and headed two Governments, from November 1990 to April 1992 and from April 1992 to the beginning of May 1997. However, any division of Government policy into such discrete historical periods is to a degree arbitrary and throws up difficulties for the historian. In particular, in a number of cases the sales of second and third tranches of shares in privatised businesses were completed a number of years after the initial share flotation. It seemed most appropriate to discuss these later sales in the chapter or chapters concerned with the original share disposal. Equally some privatisations were planned under one Government but completed under another. In general my treatment is to discuss these privatisations when discussing the privatisation programme of the Government in which the shares were sold, unless there were good reasons not to do so. The main exceptions are the privatisations relating to the oil industry and to shipbuilding, which in each case are grouped together. This means, for example, that the privatisation of the British Airports Authority is studied in Volume 2. The planning for the disposal of BAA began well before the 1987 General Election, but the Election interrupted the final advertising campaign and the sale was not completed until afterwards.

The privatisation programme that began in Britain after the election of the Conservative Government led by Margaret Thatcher in May 1979 was strongly opposed by the Opposition

Labour Party in Parliament and treated with some hostility mixed with indifference by the smaller Social Democrat-Liberal Alliance, later renamed the Liberal Democrats. A number of economists and journalists also heavily criticised the policy at the time. They labelled it economically flawed, badly administered, unfair in terms of its wealth redistribution effects and largely irrelevant to reversing Britain's economic problems that had become so apparent in the 1970s. Needless to say the trade unions were strongly opposed to each of the privatisations in turn. And yet privatisation has not been reversed. Since May 1997 Labour Governments have continued to put public services into the private sector, albeit under the banner of public-private partnerships rather than privatisation. I was not asked to review privatisation policy under the post-1997 Labour Government and therefore leave this task to future scholars.

On embarking on this Official History a number of questions were uppermost in my mind. Notably, to what extent was privatisation a clear policy commitment within the Thatcher Governments of the 1980s – or did Government simply stumble on the idea? The Conservatives' 1979 Election Manifesto neither used the word "privatisation" nor heralded a major denationalisation programme. But this is not to say that behind the public façade such a policy was not taking shape.

Another question concerned what determined the sequencing of the privatisations: why were particular public corporations sold early in the 1980s and other sales delayed until well into the 1990s? Related to this, what were the privatisation objectives and how did they change over time, if at all? There is also the question of how each privatisation was planned and executed, how the different City advisers were appointed and remunerated, what precise roles they played and how the sale prices were determined. Complementing this theme, how was each privatisation administered, in what ways did the methods evolve and change and why? Which government departments took the lead role, what was the input of the Treasury and Bank of England, and what was the relationship between Ministers and civil servants?

The British Civil Service is known for its political impartiality, but were any alarm bells rung within the administration that led the politicians to change direction and perhaps even policy? Finally, how did the industries' managements respond and to what extent did they influence the content and timing of the privatisations?

The study draws heavily from the official records of the British Government to which I was given full access and from interviews with leading figures involved in each of the privatisations, including ex-Ministers, civil servants, business and City figures, as well as academics that have studied the subject. The official records are extensive and it was necessary to be selective if the Official History was ever to be completed. Heavy use has been made of the Prime Minister's papers held in the Cabinet Office, Cabinet minutes and memoranda and the minutes and memoranda of relevant Cabinet committees, along with departmental papers and HM Treasury papers, especially relating to the larger privatisations. In addition, the published autobiographies and memoirs of ex-Ministers and nationalised industry management proved useful in terms of corroborating certain facts and providing useful background information and sometimes a different perspective.

A large number of academic papers and books, many appraising the consequences of privatisation for economic performance, have been published since the 1980s and in preparing this Official History their content has not been neglected. However, my purpose was not to re-plough existing land but rather to capitalise on my privileged access to the official papers and those involved to provide a new insight into the UK's privatisation experiment. Incidentally, the careful reader will already have noticed that I have used the terms Britain and the UK seemingly interchangeably. This is the approach I adopt throughout the text, although some purists might criticise me for doing so. When writing the text, in terms of readability, sometimes the term Britain (or British) and sometimes the term the UK seemed the more appropriate.

In terms of interview material I would particularly like to thank those below for giving me the benefit of their insights. In addition, I would like to thank Andrew Riley of Churchill College, Cambridge, for arranging a most useful conference on 5 December 2006 which he kindly invited me to chair and which brought together many of the major players within Government, the City and management involved in the privatisation of British Telecommunications. Those who spoke at that conference and who in a number of cases subsequently provided me with further information are also listed here. My thanks go to the following: Malcolm Argent, Lord Kenneth Baker, Tim Barker, Peter Benson, Lord John Biffen, John Blundell, Sir Samuel Brittan, Sir Richard Broadbent, Sir Patrick Brown, Sir Ian Byatt, Sir Bryan Carsberg, Professor Martin Cave, Julian Cazalet, Kenneth Clarke, Sir David Clementi, Jeremy Colman, Roy Croft, Peter Cropper, Geoff Dart, Roger Davis, Jeannie Drake, Dr David Evans, Kit Farrow, Sir Christopher Foster, Lord Norman Fowler, Lord Ian Gilmour, Colin Green, Gerry Grimstone, Sir John R S Guinness, Giles Henderson, Lord Michael Heseltine, Mark Higson, Sir John Hoskyns, Lord Geoffrey Howe, Lord David Howell, Howard Hyman, Sir George Jefferson, Lord Patrick Jenkin, Professor John Kay, Bruce Laidlaw, Lord Norman Lamont, Lord Nigel Lawson, Peter Lilley, Simon Linnett, Professor Stephen Littlechild, Sir Callum McCarthy, Alastair Macdonald, Lord John MacGregor, Peter Meinertzhagen, John Michell, Nicholas Monk, Lord John Moore, Sir John Nott, Bill Paine, Lord Cecil Parkinson, Michael Parr, Lord James Prior, John Redwood, Michael Reidy, John Rhodes, John Rickard, Jonathan Rickford, Sir Adam Ridley, Sir Malcolm Rifkind, Professor Colin Robinson, Sir Steve Robson, Sir Denis Rooke, Sir Michael Scholar, Adam Scott, Tom Sharp, Sir Alfred Sherman, Victor Smith, Rupert Steele, Lord Jeffrey Sterling, Sir Keith Stuart, Lord Norman Tebbit, Sir Peter Thompson, Michael Valentine, Lord Iain Vallance, Sir John Vickers, Anna Walker, Lord Peter Walker, Laurie Young, Lord David Young.

I would also especially like to acknowledge the access provided by Sir Adam Ridley to his collection of Conservative Party Research Department papers.

Of course, none of the above is responsible for the final content of this Official History. Also, as some of those with whom I had the privilege of interesting discussion did not wish to have their comments attributed, I have chosen not to identify separately material that draws from these discussions in the Official History. However, it is quite proper to confirm that without the insights of those involved in each of the privatisations, this Official History would have been much less rich.

A further tranche of acknowledgements is due to those who assisted me in my research and preparation of the final text. In particular, I must thank Tessa Stirling, Sally Falk and Chris Grindall of the Histories, Openness and Records Unit of the Cabinet Office who administered this project and responded with enthusiasm to my requests to obtain government files and assisted in obtaining access to ex-Ministers and civil servants. Equally, I am most indebted to my Project Board chaired by Tessa Stirling, Head of the Histories, Openness and Records Unit, and including Tony Baker, Christopher Clarke, Gina Coulson, Peter Fish, Arthur Pryor, Irene Ripley, Stephen Twigge and Phillip Wood. Their advice at meetings and by correspondence and their careful reading and correction of draft chapters were invaluable.

Grateful thanks are also due to Eve Hussey and later Rosemary Cockfield and Dawn Richardson at Cranfield University, where I am based, for help in setting up interviews, tracing and ordering inter-library loans, preparing tables and undertaking editing corrections. In addition, I would like to acknowledge my sincere appreciation to the Department for Business, Enterprise and Regulatory Reform (formerly the Department of Trade and Industry) for providing access to their library and various departmental records, HM Treasury for providing access to their records, and to Cranfield University library and especially Helen Wetherill for responding speedily and accurately to my requests for statistical data. Thanks are also due to Cranfield University for supporting this study by relieving me of many of the teaching and other academic duties normally expected of a University Professor. Last but not least I must thank my family and especially my wife, Megan, for tolerating the mood swings and long periods of absence in my study that always accompany the preparation of a major piece of research.

On 8 December 1986 at a meeting of the Bow Group at Westminster the then Secretary of State for Trade and Industry, the Rt Hon Paul Channon, commented with great prescience:

"When, in many years time, the history of Mrs Thatcher's Government comes to be written, it will be hard to single out any one thing as being our greatest and most lasting achievement. Already such changes as the taming of the trade union militants, the conquest of inflation and the re-establishment of Britain's reputation in the world have had a profound and far-reaching effect on the nation's future But there is one other policy which must also be a strong challenger for the title and in the longer term, may prove even more significant. That is privatisation."

The British privatisation experience is still widely admired and emulated across the globe. This Official History is intended to be useful and informative not only to academic students of privatisation and public policy, but to politicians and civil servants in Britain and overseas grappling with how best to privatise and keen to learn from the UK's pioneering programme.

*David Parker*
*Research Professor, Privatisation and Regulation*
*Cranfield School of Management*
*Cranfield University, Bedfordshire, UK*
*July 2008*

# 1

# NATIONALISATION TO PRIVATISATION

## 1945–79 – The genesis of a policy idea

The term "privatisation" has common public currency from the early 1980s. Prior to this date the description "denationalisation" was preferred when referring to the sale of state-owned industries. It is not entirely clear who first coined the term privatisation. The writer on management, Peter Drucker, claims to have used the word as early as 1969,[1] but there are other claimants. A number of Conservative Ministers in the first Thatcher Government attribute the term to their shadow Cabinet colleague in the 1970s, David Howell, which suggests that Howell initiated the use of it within the Conservative leadership.[2] Margaret (later Baroness) Thatcher, the Prime Minister from 1979 to 1990, is on record as disliking the word – "Not a word I'm particularly fond of. In fact a dreadful bit of jargon to inflict on the language of Shakespeare".[3] But it was used in Cabinet and Cabinet Committees after 1979 and in the two volumes of her autobiography.[4]

Whatever the origins of the term and its possible detrimental effects on the English language, the years from 1979 to 1997 saw a large movement of assets in Britain from state to private ownership, now referred to as "privatisation". The programme involved a complex set of interacting policy initiatives including public flotations and trade sales of nationalised industries, divestments and asset sales, and competitive tendering and contracting out in central and local government and the National Health Service (NHS). In addition, privatisation cannot be separated completely from other economic policy initiatives at the time, notably monetarism and controlling public expenditure, tax reductions and other "supply side" reforms. Sometimes the whole set of economic policies is labelled "Thatcherism".

This opening chapter considers the origins of privatisation as policy from 1979. The starting point is a discussion of nationalisation. The chapter then turns to consider some developments in economic theory during the 1960s and 1970s which formed an intellectual underpinning for the privatisations that occurred later. The aim is to address why, by the late 1970s, privatisation was seen as being both a desirable and a feasible policy option by a growing number of economists. The extent to which privatisation was policy in the Conservative Party by 1979 is the subject of chapter 2.

## The origins of state ownership

In 1776 Adam Smith published his seminal study of the market economy, *The Wealth of Nations*. In this treatise on capitalism, Smith commented: "Great nations are never impoverished by private, though they sometimes are by public prodigality and misconduct. The whole, or almost the whole public revenue, is in most countries employed in maintaining unproductive hands."[5] The message seemed clear enough: government enterprises are more likely to destroy the wealth of nations than create it. Although Smith acknowledged that some state provision would be needed for public works that would not be profitable for private enterprise to supply or where wider public benefits existed, normally economic activity was best pursued by competitive private enterprise. The success of the industrial revolution in Britain was founded firmly on Smith's principles of private enterprise, private property and free trade.

However, from the late nineteenth century state enterprises slowly increased in number and state regulation expanded. In spite of the dominance of "laissez-faire" economics in the nineteenth century, forms of state intervention developed to tackle perceived market failure. In some cases state intervention took the form of state regulation of private business. The railways were an example. Built by private capital, as early as the 1840s there was a demand that the railways be brought under state control because of their economic importance in terms of moving passengers and freight. This was reflected in the powers given to the Government under The Railways Act of 1844. This Act empowered the state to purchase all railways constructed after the passage of the Act and that were in existence after 21 years. Although these powers were never used, during the nineteenth century the railways became heavily state-regulated, especially in terms of the charges they could levy.

In gas, electricity, the water supply and tram (and later bus) transport, state intervention went further. A mixture of state-regulated private enterprise and municipally-owned enterprises resulted.[6] In the face of rapid urbanisation and the associated overcrowding and lack of sanitation in cities, during the nineteenth century municipal enterprises were established to provide water, gas and later electricity and public transport systems, often alongside state-regulated private sector operators. For example, the cholera outbreaks of the 1830s and 1840s were instrumental in leading councils to seek to improve water supplies and sanitation. This development is often referred to in the history books as the period of "gas and water socialism" or "municipal socialism". However, as most of the councils in the nineteenth century were dominated by ratepayers and businessmen, it is misleading to label the development "socialist". Rather it was a reflection of the social and economic needs of the time and the conclusion that the unregulated private sector was unable to supply adequate public services and that these services should be a function of the state, albeit at this time at the local rather than national level.

Between 1845 and the early 1870s there was a large growth in the number of statutory water undertakings, with 250 systems run by local government by the end of the period. There was also a similarly large spurt in local authority generation of electricity later in the century. Between 1895 and 1900 the number of statutory electricity undertakings in Britain rose from 91 to 229, of which 71 per cent were owned by municipalities. In the 1900s there was a comparable growth in tramways with the number of undertakings increasing to 311 in 1905, of which one half were municipally owned. In gas supply the most rapid growth of provision was from the 1850s to the 1880s, by which time local councils accounted for 39 per cent of gas supplies. The fact that these "public utilities" needed to seek compulsory purchase orders from Parliament to obtain rights of way to build their systems encouraged the movement towards state ownership.

The spread of municipally-owned enterprises was paralleled by a growth in state regulation of the private sector operators of public services. Charges and outputs for gas, water, electricity and tram transport became regulated by various state bodies. Arguments about the fair level of charges and the adequacy of services were not uncommon.[7] Study of the development of municipal enterprises draws attention to the extent to which regulatory failures in the nineteenth and early twentieth centuries made public ownership increasingly popular. It sometimes proved difficult to regulate the private sector operators effectively.[8] Also, research suggests that municipalisation may have been an economic solution to supplying public services. A number of municipally-owned gas and electricity suppliers may have performed no worse in terms of costs of production than their privately-owned counterparts.[9]

By the First World War, alongside the municipally-owned enterprises there existed a small number of businesses controlled by central government. The Royal Mail had been a Crown activity since the sixteenth century and in 1868 the Post Office took over the operation of the country's telegraph system. The Port of London became publicly owned in 1908 and the telephone system came under the control of the Post Office in 1912 (with the exception of the service in Kingston-upon-Hull, where the municipality mounted a successful campaign against central government control). At the outbreak of the First World War, in 1914, the then First Lord of the Admiralty, Winston Churchill, took the Anglo-Persian oil company into state hands to protect oil supplies for the Royal Navy. Later renamed British Petroleum (BP), some of the company's shares would be sold off by government in 1977 to raise revenue for the Exchequer, anticipating the start of large-scale privatisation in Britain after the General Election of 1979.

In the years between the two World Wars economic recession and the resulting unemployment led to mounting criticism of private enterprise. This period saw significant lobbying for nationalisation. For example, there were critical reports on the running of the coal mines in 1919 and electricity in 1926. These led to recommendations to establish bigger undertakings to replace the numerous private sector collieries and private and municipal electricity providers, respectively. Before the Sankey Commission in 1919 the miners' union proposed the transfer of the ownership of the mines and mineral rights to a Mining Council, a half of the membership of which would be appointed by the Crown and a half by the union.[10] The Commission only narrowly rejected the introduction of state ownership. In 1926 the Government established a state-owned national grid under a new Central Electricity Board to rationalise and develop electricity transmission across the country, thereby beginning the nationalisation of electricity supply. In the same year public wireless broadcasting was effectively nationalised with the establishment of the British Broadcasting Corporation (BBC). This was followed, in 1933, by the setting up of the London Passenger Transport Board (LPTB) in a bid to rationalise and improve public transport in the capital. Commercial air travel also came under state influence during the interwar years. In 1924 the Government encouraged the creation of Imperial Airways out of four private airlines and in 1935 British Airways was established. Imperial Airways and British Airways were nationalised in 1939 and the state-owned British Overseas Airways Corporation (BOAC) was created.[11]

## The public corporation

The Labour politician Herbert Morrison was the chief architect of the LPTB and would play a prominent role in the nationalisations after 1945 by the post-war Labour Government. In his book *Socialisation and Transport* published in 1933, Morrison set out his vision for state enterprise: "We are seeking a combination of public ownership, public accountability, and business management for public ends."[12] In this vision the boards of the state enterprises would be independent of government, in the sense that Ministers would not interfere in their decision making except on matters where specific legal duties were imposed on them. This was intended to address the criticism that politicians and government departments were not appropriate managers of commercial enterprises. Later the role of Ministers would be restricted in the nationalisation statutes largely to powers to give "general directions" to the boards on matters that affected the national interest. In effect, the board of the public corporation would be the state sector equivalent of the board of a private sector joint stock company. The boards would have a high degree of independence, subject to being accountable not to shareholders but to the public through Ministers for the operation of their businesses.

In 1918, the young Labour Party had adopted a new constitution including Clause 4. Clause 4 pledged the Party to "the common ownership of the means of production, distribution and exchange". This commitment anticipated the socialisation of the economy: however it was unclear at the time what precise form "common ownership" should take. During the second half of the nineteenth century the nascent labour movement had supported the spread of municipal enterprises. The early part of the twentieth century saw the left wing of the labour movement flirt with syndicalism and control of industry through worker councils, especially around the time of the First World War. But in the interwar years the majority of the labour movement, including the major trade unions, backed away from such radical ideas in favour of the public corporation.[13] In part this was because of concerns about the impact on economic efficiency of worker control and in part because of the unions' anxiety about the possible effect on their role. The trade unions had been set up to negotiate pay and working conditions with employers rather than manage industries. What would be their raison d'être if workers actually ran the enterprises? In further part it arose because of the economic advantages of controlling industries such as electricity and the railways nationally rather than at the local or small-scale level. Worker-controlled enterprises, like municipal undertakings, were likely to remain small in size. They were unlikely to tackle the rationalisation of industries such as coal, gas and electricity, as recommended in the reports of various official inquiries in the interwar years.

The public board appeared to offer an alternative to bureaucratic control of industry by government departments. Whereas civil servants had little or no training in, or experience of, running businesses and Ministers rarely stayed long enough in one department to build up expertise in the activities of any industry, the boards would be filled with professionals with a long-term interest in their industries. During the drafting of the London Passenger Transport Bill it had been suggested that the Board should contain representatives of the former shareholders, of local government and of the workers. Morrison had successfully resisted this, stressing instead the case for appointments solely on the basis of ability. Professional, experienced management on public boards would mirror the professional management increasingly in control of companies in the private sector.

There was some concern at the time that representation of the labour movement in the running of state enterprises might be lost. Nevertheless, the appointment to state enterprises of management according to ability and experience rather than to represent sectional interests was endorsed by a Trades Union Congress (TUC) report in 1932; although the report did go on to suggest that Advisory Committees should be created alongside the boards to represent particular interests, including the trade unions. A subsequent joint statement by the General Council of the TUC and the Executive Committee of the Labour Party confirmed that day-to-day administration of businesses was a matter for "trained business administrators".[14] This and other Labour Party and TUC reports in the 1930s recommended that trade unions should remain independent of the management of public corporations, so as to be able to continue to undertake their traditional role of representing workers in negotiations over pay and working conditions. While this was not considered to rule out some board representation for the unions, the stance taken meant that there was to be no union or worker control of state industries. In 1945 a report of the TUC General Council confirmed that both the Labour Party and the TUC desired public control of industry but not workers' control, and that board appointments should be on the basis of ability so as to promote the efficient working of the industries.[15]

In a book extolling the virtues of the public corporation published in 1938, Lincoln Gordon of Harvard University wrote: "Perhaps no feature in recent thought in applied economics in this country is more striking than the rapidity with which it [the public corporation] has gained favour among almost all sections of opinion."[16] In the USA the Emergency Housing Corporation, the Electric Home and Farm Authority, the Inland Waterways Corporation and, best known of all, the Tennessee Valley Authority were just some of a number of public corporations created in the interwar years. In other words, the growing popularity in Britain of the public corporation form of state ownership mirrored a wider, international development.

By 1945 state ownership of a number of major industries in the form of the public corporation was accepted Labour Party policy and only the extent to which the trade unions should be represented on public boards remained to be settled.[17] Nor in Britain was the public corporation simply Labour Party policy; by 1945 it had won considerable cross-party support. The public board had been endorsed by an Industrial Inquiry for the Liberal Party in 1928[18] and by leading interwar economists such as A.C. Pigou and J.M. Keynes, the inspiration for post-war Keynesian economics. The Conservatives had created the Central Electricity Board and the BBC in the mid-1920s as public corporations.

Also, there was cross-party agreement that a number of the industries that were nationalised after 1945 needed major restructuring. The successful development of a national electricity grid in the late 1920s and 1930s by the Central Electricity Board seemed to vindicate government planning, but concerns continued about the state of the remainder of the electricity industry, as evidenced by the proceedings of the McGowan Committee in 1936. Only the War prevented the introduction of legislation to rationalise the distribution of electricity. Similar concerns were expressed in the Heyworth Report on gas supply.[19] Reporting just after the 1945 General Election, the Committee recommended rationalisation of the industry under public ownership. Turning to coal mining and transport, the Coal Mines Act of 1930 established a Coal Mines Reorganisation Commission with a view to amalgamating the collieries into larger and more viable units and in 1931 a Royal Commission considered how best to achieve co-ordination of the country's transport. While its report did not recommend nationalisation, neither did it formally reject it.[20] In March 1945 the Reid Committee criticised the continued fragmented structure of the coal industry involving a large number of small and inefficient pits. In July 1942 a confidential report for the Ministry of War Transport recommended unification of the country's transport system under a national Transport Corporation. This Corporation would, with certain exceptions, have an entire monopoly of internal transport by road, rail, canal and air.[21]

In other words, a momentum had built up by 1945 on the need for centralised control and planning of the outputs and inputs of a number of the industries that would be nationalised by the Government elected that year. The momentum towards centralised state ownership had been encouraged by wartime planning. During the Second World War, electricity, gas and parts of the transport system came partially under state ownership and coal mining and iron and steel production were heavily state-regulated.[22] State control of these industries during the War was used to justify continued state planning afterwards. Also, a number of the industries were in poor shape by 1945 so that their future under private ownership was uncertain. A neglect of investment as resources were diverted into maximising war production meant that the industries were in need of investment at the end of the War on a scale that private capital might be reluctant to provide, especially where prices and outputs remained state-regulated. Only from the late 1940s were wartime controls including rationing lifted in Britain. The railways and coal mining caused particular concern. The Railways Act of 1921 had provided for the compulsory amalgamation of the existing 119 companies into four regional companies as an alternative to nationalisation. But motor transport had continued to eat into the railways' markets in freight and passenger conveyance in the interwar years, and the competitiveness of the railways had deteriorated further during the War. By 1945 the economic position of the coal mines was at least as bad; coal production had actually declined during the War reflecting a lack of investment and the working out of the most easily mined coal seams.[23]

## The 1945 Labour Government

The Labour Party's 1945 General Election Manifesto proposed the public ownership of the Bank of England, the fuel and power industries including coal mining, inland transport, and iron and steel. In the case of the coal industry the rationale was to bring "great economies in operation" by amalgamating the multitude of privately-owned collieries and modernising production methods. Public ownership of gas and electricity was expected to "lower charges, prevent competitive waste, open the way for co-ordinated research and development and lead to the reforming of uneconomic areas of distribution". Nationalisation of inland transport would provide for co-ordination of rail, road, air and canal transport; while in the case of iron and steel, the high prices and inefficient plants kept open under private ownership would be rationalised after nationalisation.[24] As the Official Historian of Nationalisation, Sir Norman Chester, concludes: "one feature common to most of the industries and services in the Labour Party's programme was the claim, supported in many instances by impartial reports, that some form of Government action was needed in the interests of promoting greater efficiency."[25]

The election in 1945 of the first Labour Government with a majority of MPs over all other parties led to the nationalisation of a number of industries, as summarised in Table 1.1. The Bank of England was taken into state ownership in 1946. The following year saw the nationalisation of the coal industry.[26] Coal proved to be a particularly complicated nationalisation because it involved the acquisition of the assets of 750 to 800 concerns rather than the nationalisation of entire companies.[27] The other nationalisations involved the take-over of companies. In 1948–9 the railways and electricity and gas supplies were brought into state ownership including, in the case of electricity and gas, the municipal undertakings. In 1949 the iron and steel industry was to be nationalised; however its transfer to the state sector had not been completed by the time of the election of a Conservative Government in 1951. This brought the nationalisation of iron and steel to a halt. After 1951 the Conservative Government transferred most of the industry back into private hands. Alongside these nationalisations, in 1945 two new public corporations were created for the state airlines to complement the existing BOAC, one for European and domestic air routes (British European Airways, BEA) and the other for South American routes (British South American Airways

*Table 1.1* The main industries taken into state ownership 1945–51

| Industry | Date of state takeover | Numbers employed at the time |
|---|---|---|
| Bank of England | 1 March 1946 | 6,700 |
| Civil aviation | 1 August 1946 | 23,300 |
| Coal | 1 January 1947 | 765,000 |
| Cable and Wireless | 1 January 1947 | 9,500 |
| Railways and subsidiary transport businesses | 1 January 1948 | 888,000 |
| Electricity | 1 April 1948 | 176,000 |
| Gas | 1 April 1949 | 143,500 |
| Iron and steel | 15 February 1951 | 292,000 |

*Source*: Based on Childs, 2001, p.14.

Corporation). In 1949 BOAC and the British South American Airways Corporation were merged. Another state takeover involved Cable and Wireless Ltd, the operator of telecommunication services in a number of Commonwealth countries. This company was taken into public ownership after the War following a meeting of Commonwealth Governments in May 1944. The meeting decided that a public corporation should be created for telecommunications in each of the Commonwealth countries, each owned by the government of the country but linked to the UK company.

In total, the 1945–51 nationalisations transferred over 2.3 million employees from the private to the public sector. In terms of sheer size, the nationalisations of coal, railways, electricity, gas and iron and steel were the most important, accounting for over two million employees and 20 per cent of the country's fixed capital formation.[28] Subsequently the Conservatives denationalised some parts of road transport, as well as iron and steel, but otherwise the nationalisations remained in place.[29]

Each of the nationalisations necessitated a separate piece of legislation to give the Government the power to take over the enterprises and establish a public corporation, much as later each of the major privatisations of the 1980s and 1990s would be anticipated by legislation to establish an enterprise under the Companies Act.[30] Compensation was paid to the previous owners. Usually the appropriate amounts of compensation due were disputed, with owners arguing that they deserved more; an exception was coal nationalisation where the purchase terms were successfully agreed with the owners. The compensation terms for the railways were strongly criticised. The Government used Stock Exchange quotations and the shareholders of the railway companies argued that market quotations were not directly related to the value of the assets and their earning potential. The shares traded daily were a small proportion of the total capital involved.[31] The discontent over the amounts paid to nationalise the industries was mirrored in the 1980s by the controversy over the amounts the private sector paid to reacquire them.

The public corporations created had a number of similarities to companies in the private sector. They were given their own corporate legal status, their own separate accounts, appointed their own employees (who were not civil servants) and could sue and be sued in their own right. However, the nationalised industries were to have more complex objectives than making profits. Each board was given objectives that were a mixture of commercial aims and wider economic and social goals, which were categorised as "public interest objectives". For example, under the Coal Industry Nationalisation Act 1946, the National Coal Board (NCB) was required to make supplies of coal available "of such qualities and sizes, in such quantities and at such prices, as may seem to them best calculated to further the public interest in all respects, including the avoidance of any undue or unreasonable preference or advantage".[32]

The nationalised industries were expected to operate efficiently and economically, setting reasonable charges without price discrimination between consumers. This would later lead to some difficulty when the industries came under pressure to set prices according to the costs of supply. They were also expected to promote the development of production and good labour relations. No direct control over pricing was retained by government departments or in the form of a government price tribunal, as it was felt that pricing was a matter for the boards, perhaps subject to occasional Ministerial advice. The partial exception was the railways where prices had been state regulated since the nineteenth century.[33]

## Early difficulties

Although in the Labour Party the public board was the accepted form of state ownership by 1945, there had been no real consideration of the constitutional, administrative and financial arrangements under which the boards should operate. In his book *Socialisation and Transport* Morrison had devoted a chapter to "The Management of Socialised Industries", but this was mainly given over to a discussion of the advantages and disadvantages of public corporations. This meant that a number of important organisational issues were left to be addressed later. In a number of cases this led to significant restructuring of the industries during the 1950s and 1960s.[34]

Monopoly positions in markets plus access to public funds threatened to remove the pressure to operate efficiently. The British public corporation was not the equivalent of a private sector joint stock company. To begin with it did not have shareholders and nor did it have a profit maximising objective, although it was expected that the public corporations would not make long-term losses. The boards of public corporations were in no sense "residual risk bearers". Risk fell ultimately on the taxpayer or on consumers through higher prices. Equally, members of public boards had no rights to any financial surpluses earned and they received fixed salaries rather than performance-related pay.

The result was very different corporations in the public and private sectors.[35] To a degree this was recognised at the time: Morrison applied the phrase "high custodian of the public interest" to the new boards. The assumption was that because the industries were state-owned they would be managed efficiently in the public interest. At the same time, the scope for conflict over what was the public interest was already evident in the expectations of the trade unions. The unions supported nationalisation in 1945 in the anticipation that their members would receive much more favourable treatment in terms of wages and working conditions than had been the case under private ownership. The implications of this for the management and finances of the nationalised industries were, again, left to be sorted out later.

Nor had the Labour Party in 1945 a clear view about the board structure for the new public corporations. The only issue that had been addressed in any real detail was the extent of worker representation on the boards, although even this had not been entirely settled. In each of the new public corporations, boards were created including non-executive directors, alongside executive directors, appointed by Ministers to represent the public interest.

Later it became common to have a token board member from a relevant trade union. The board members were both full-time and part-time appointees, usually for three or five year periods.

The issue of the appropriate level of pay for board members caused particular difficulty. The salaries were to be paid by the board and not the Treasury, in part because it was felt that Treasury-determined salaries were unlikely to attract people of the right calibre to the new boards. However, this did not stop the Permanent Secretary at the Treasury, on hearing that salaries of £15,000 to £20,000 were being talked about for the Chairman of the new National Coal Board, writing a letter of complaint to the Chancellor of the Exchequer. He warned that if salaries of that order were paid to the middle and upper staff of the corporations, civil servants who could be ill-spared would be tempted away from government departments. In spite of such protests, the Labour Government continued to take the view that a failure to pay market salaries would condemn the industries to being less efficiently managed. At the same time, and less publicly, some Ministers feared that the case for high salaries would not be understood by the Party's supporters and would be unpopular in the country – they were also likely to be above the amount normally paid to Ministers. In the end the Minister of Fuel and Power was asked to try and appoint the Chairman and other members of the NCB at salaries that fell short of what the Minister thought would be needed, although still above Civil Service norms.[36]

The appropriate mechanism for setting pay in the nationalised industries, at all levels, would remain a festering sore with disputes erupting from time to time. Periodic government intervention to reduce wage settlements in the public corporations as an example to the rest of the workforce produced a negative effect on labour relations. This came to a head during the 1970s when a number of the nationalised industries were plagued by strikes and it proved increasingly difficult to recruit high calibre management.[37] By the 1970s top salaries in the public corporations lagged well behind the norm for similar jobs in the private sector.

The emphasis at nationalisation was on creating large and highly centralised corporations to gain economies of scale and remove the inefficiencies highlighted in interwar official reports. Even where district management or area boards were established, the key strategic decision making was placed largely or wholly at the centre. The resulting businesses were much bigger than any existing government organisation. For example, the Post Office was an atypically large state body in 1945, employing 250,000. By contrast, the nationalised coal industry would employ 760,000 and went from having around 800 management units prior to nationalisation to one, the NCB.[38] In electricity the number of management units was 561 before nationalisation and 15 afterwards, and in gas 1,000 before and 13 after nationalisation. In road haulage the planned concentration was even more dramatic, with the industry post-nationalisation controlled by a single body, the British Transport Commission, reflecting the belief at the time in the virtues of a centrally planned transport system. In the event this arrangement quickly proved unsatisfactory, centralisation was never really accomplished, and the Commission was eventually disbanded.

Establishing highly centralised organisations had the advantage of achieving quicker nationalisations. Vesting the assets in one or a small number of state-owned bodies was administratively simpler than vesting them in large numbers of independent units. But the result was management structures and organisations that would prove problematic in the following years. The main exception to all of this was the iron and steel industry. A new Corporation was established in 1951 to oversee the operations of a number of publicly-owned companies and this meant that, in contrast to the other nationalised industries, the structure created was potentially decentralised.[39] In principle, the companies would have been able to compete for business and this could have had advantages in terms of promoting efficiency. However, the Corporation's creation was quickly overshadowed by the arrival of a new Conservative administration and denationalisation of the industry, and therefore the structure was never really tested.

Alongside inadequate consideration of the appropriate organisational structures for the nationalised industries other than the penchant for centralisation, there was insufficient attention paid to the future of the industries' finances. When the Coal Industry Nationalisation Bill was introduced, the Minister of Fuel and Power made it clear that the industry was not necessarily expected to pay its way each year, and should build up reserves to cover any deficits in later years (at this time a shortage of fuel seemed to rule out losses in the industry, for the foreseeable future at least). Therefore, in the draft Bill revenues were to be sufficient to meet all outgoings properly chargeable to revenue account "on an average of good and bad years". This phrase "on an average of good and bad years" was at first copied by the Ministry of Transport when drafting the Transport Bill, but the wording was later changed to "taking one year with another". This wording was then used in the Electricity, Gas and Iron and Steel Bills. The idea was that the public corporations should finance their operating and capital expenses without becoming a burden on the taxpayer and that where they competed with private sector firms there should not be unfair competition due to state subsidies. At the time, the Treasury was more concerned with avoiding the industries becoming a burden on the taxpayer than with making a particular level of profit.[40]

For this reason the Treasury had initially been hostile to the idea that it should guarantee the capital of the nationalised industries. However, when the Treasury guarantee became agreed Government policy, the Treasury's efforts switched to ensuring that there should be no concealed subsidy in the form of the corporations failing to make payments on their loans. Except in the cases of the Bank of England and the coal industry, at nationalisation Ministerial and Treasury opinion favoured the boards issuing stock in their own right rather than borrowing from the Treasury. Loans from the Treasury would make the Exchequer a direct creditor of the industry and it was felt that this might create an expectation of taxpayer funding. However, the boards soon experienced difficulty in selling the large amounts of new stock they wished to issue. As a result, a succession of issues was partly taken up by the Bank of England's Issue Department. It was therefore decided in 1956 to suspend direct stock issues and to finance future borrowings through the Treasury.[41] Henceforth, the borrowings of the nationalised industries for investment occurred through the National Loans Fund with an implicit government guarantee.[42]

The protection of consumers received little attention during the drafting and passage of the nationalisation legislation, in spite of the fact that a number of giant monopolies were being created. Consumer committees were set up in the industries to represent the consumer viewpoint such as the Coal Advisory Committee which provided advice to the Minister, [43] but without an obvious ability to influence the industries' strategies significantly. The corporations were subject to Ministerial oversight, but the concern at the time was not to place Ministers in a position where they might come under political pressure to intervene in pricing.[44] Hence, the Coal Bill did not give the Minister any power to control the prices charged by the NCB. Leaving the management with discretion over pricing and service levels was not considered to be a serious defect at the time because of the view that exploitation of the consumer resulted from the pursuit of profits for shareholders. The new public boards did not have a profit objective or shareholders and therefore this problem was removed.

Moreover, the public corporations were expected to operate the industries for the public benefit and were therefore, if anything, expected to perform more efficiently than the former private enterprises in the sense of supplying adequate outputs at low prices.

The precise responsibilities of Ministers towards the industries varied under the different nationalisation statutes. But in general the boards were given the main statutory duties, functions and responsibilities and Ministers only a few specific powers.[45] These powers related to the appointment and dismissal of Board members and approval of the investment programmes drawn up by the boards. Other powers related to agreeing programmes of research and development, approving the form of accounts and controlling each industry's borrowings subject to a ceiling approved by Parliament, and to issuing "general directions" to the boards in the national interest.

During the Second Reading of the Coal Industry Nationalisation Bill, the left-wing Labour MP Emanuel Shinwell asked, "Who are better fitted to judge [the public interest] than the people who are running the industry?" There was a belief, in retrospect naive, that the boards would necessarily act in the national interest. Reflecting this, the power of Ministers under the Acts to give general directives to the industries was not intended to provide wide scope for Ministerial interference in their management. Ministers were not given powers to issue "specific directives" to the boards. It seems that at the time the legal advice within Government was that the taking of specific powers, for example over output decisions or the use of particular assets, would tend to be regarded by the courts as a limitation on, rather than an enhancement of, the powers contained in the right to give general directions.[46] However, the phrase "matters appearing to the Minister to affect the national interest", introduced during the drafting of the Coal Bill, might have appeared to give Ministers considerable discretion when issuing general directives, but in a memorandum in July 1947 the Lord President stated that, "It is generally agreed that there should be as few general directions as possible issued by Ministers to Boards." In March 1948 a Ministerial Committee noted that it was "accepted policy that general directions should only be issued in exceptional circumstances . . . It would never be possible to control a recalcitrant board by issuing a stream of general directions".[47]

In the event no general directions were issued by the 1945–51 Labour Governments. The first was issued by the subsequent Conservative administration in its first few weeks in office, to limit the actions of the Iron and Steel Corporation ahead of the industry's denationalisation.[48] However, the restriction on Ministers' formal powers to intervene in the management of the nationalised industries would not prove a deterrent to Ministers and civil servants from using influence behind the scenes to get their way – and without becoming directly responsible for any mistakes. The formal division of powers between the boards and the Ministers would also mean that Ministers would be able to duck Parliamentary questions on matters of operational management that were legally the prerogative of the boards. In place of formal directions, Ministers and their civil servants tended to develop close channels of communication with the Chairmen and their boards through day-to-day contacts. As a result, in the public corporations informal rather than formal Ministerial influence evolved.[49]

Day-to-day intervention in the management of the industries by Ministers was supposed to be ruled out, but in reality it proved difficult to separate a Minister's responsibility for the future of an industry from operational decisions. Hence, a main reason for the adoption of the public corporation form – public accountability without political interference in the running of the industries – was compromised by the informal control process that evolved. This would become particularly obvious in the 1970s when Ministers interfered in the details of pricing decisions, wage settlements and investment projects.[50] But early signs of tension appeared immediately after nationalisation. By the end of the 1940s Ministers had become heavily involved in the details of the industries' pension schemes because of the implications for the industries' costs and the pensions payable to other public sector employees. Also, Ministers had considered it necessary to get involved in production and pay decisions in the industries.[51] In 1947 a national coal shortage compounded by a particularly harsh winter led the Government to press the NCB for six day working in the mines, to raise the output of coal, while at the same time avoiding a substantial rise in miners' earnings. No general direction was given. The Government preferred to express its views informally so as to "assist the Board in reaching a decision which would achieve the objective desired".[52] Later, Governments would intervene in management decisions especially when an industry faced financial difficulties or when large investment programmes were at stake or where major redundancies or strikes threatened.

Clearly there were inherent weaknesses in the form that nationalisation took after 1945, particularly in relation to organisational structures, finances, management and public accountability. Signs of dissatisfaction were already mounting by the late 1940s. In April 1947 an internal committee set up by the Prime Minister expressed concern about the increasing burden of administrative work placed on government departments by the nationalised industries, contrary to the expectation that the public corporation would avoid departmental bureaucracy. The committee also expressed concern about the growing size of the industries' administrations. The nationalised industries were not proving to be efficient, lean animals. By 1950 the Lord President was complaining about the large increase in staff in the electricity industry.[53] Although an important rationale for nationalisation had been improved economic efficiency, Ministers were already expressing worries about efficiency levels.

## Growing disillusionment

By the early 1950s the unions and workers were already showing signs of disillusionment. The nationalisation legislation had left most of the managers, officials and supervisors still in charge. Unions complained that there seemed to have been little change in the attitude of management or in the status of workers. Nor was it obvious that there had been significant improvements in pay and working conditions. A sub-committee of a Ministerial Committee tasked to look into this matter acknowledged in May 1951 that there was a good deal of frustration and disappointment about the results of nationalisation. There was particular criticism of red tape and bureaucracy in the industries and extravagance in terms of official cars and other perks for top management. At the 1949 National Union of Mineworkers' annual conference there were more resolutions on nationalisation than any other matter.[54]

The growing discontent about the performance of the nationalised industries was reflected in the Labour Party's Election Manifesto in 1950. This stated that, "Labour will not be content until each public enterprise is a model of efficiency and social responsibility."[55] It was by now clear that the Government of the day would still be held accountable for the performance of the industries no matter what the legislation might say about the division of responsibilities between Ministers and Boards. On the doorstep at the General Election that year the public held Government answerable for service failures.[56] This would continue. The performance of the nationalised industries would remain a recurring embarrassment for governments and this played a part in convincing some politicians by 1979 that Government would be much better off without them.

Concern about the performance of the industries particularly surfaced whenever their finances deteriorated. In the late 1940s only the nationalised airlines needed subsidies and there was no call on the Treasury guarantee of debt.[57] But once the post-war years of shortage ended, in the 1950s, the finances of the coal and railway industries deteriorated sharply. They would become perennial loss makers. Both industries were subject to periodic capital restructuring involving subsidies and debt write-offs, but which reversed their financial position only temporarily. Periodically the performance of the other nationalised industries attracted unfavourable comment, due to their finances or because of poor services. For example, by the 1960s the long waiting list for telephones was a particular source of public discontent.

In addition to concerns in political circles about the finances of the nationalised industries, there was increasing criticism of the relationship between the Boards and Ministers. In an introduction to an influential Fabian Society study in 1963, Roy Jenkins, who later became Home Secretary and then Chancellor of the Exchequer during the 1964–70 Labour Governments, catalogued a number of the mounting problems of the nationalised industries.[58] Many of the difficulties, he argued, could be attributed to Conservative Governments since 1951 mismanaging the industries. But on the relationship between Boards and Ministers Jenkins recognised a more fundamental problem: "The creators of the nationalised industries in the post-war Labour Government do not seem to have anticipated the uneasy relationship that has grown up between ministers and the chairmen of the boards of the nationalized industries, for which the ministers are responsible."[59]

In an endeavour to improve Parliamentary scrutiny of the industries, in 1952 the House of Commons established the Select Committee on Nationalised Industries, which went on to publish a series of highly critical reports. For example, in 1967 the Committee examined the issue of "ministerial control" and diagnosed a series of problems related to "an underlying confusion touching all elements in the system, but centring on the sponsoring Departments. Sometimes this has revealed itself as a confusion about purposes . . . Sometimes it has been seen as a confusion about policies . . . Sometimes it has been a confusion about methods . . . But mainly it has been a confusion of responsibilities . . .".[60]

With disillusionment growing about nationalisation both inside and outside Parliament, financial performance targets were proposed in a White Paper in 1961. Until then the industries had operated under the "break even" requirement "taking one year with another" laid down in their nationalisation statutes. The 1961 White Paper stressed that "although the industries have obligations of a national and non-commercial kind, they are not, and ought not, to be regarded as social services absolved from economic and commercial justification."[61] From 1961 other financial objectives than "break even" were set for each of the industries separately, usually in terms of rates of return on assets or on sales over five year periods (major exceptions to this were the loss-making NCB, which was required simply to break even after interest and depreciation, and British Rail, which was asked to reduce its deficit and break even as soon as possible). The industries still lacked guidance, however, on how to set prices and determine investment levels. If prices were set too low and investments were not appraised using adequate return on capital tests then resource misallocation would occur. Resources would be diverted away from the private to the public sector even though they would have earned a higher economic return in the private sector.

In broad terms, decisions on resource allocation made by nationalised industries should approximate as closely as possible to those that would occur in a competitive market.[62] This means marginal cost pricing, minimised production costs and normal profits (equivalent to the cost of raising capital in a competitive capital market).[63] Reality was very different. Most of the nationalised industries were statutory monopolies and there was evidence that costs were not minimised. Profitability was low and sometimes well below the private sector cost of capital, despite the setting of financial targets from 1961. Some of the nationalised industries, such as electricity, telephones, airways and, especially after the substitution of natural gas from the North Sea for town gas, the gas industry, operated in expanding sectors of the economy. Others operated in relatively stagnant or declining markets, notably the Post Office, bus services, railways and the coal industry. The different market conditions determined differences in economic performance. A number of industries, notably public transport, also carried the burden of significant social objectives, such as keeping open bus and rail routes that were not financially viable.

In 1967 another Government White Paper established economic, performance targets.[64] Now the nationalised industries were expected to adopt marginal cost pricing and to use a test discount rate for investment appraisal, set at ten per cent from 1969. The aim was to achieve allocative efficiency and avoid the use of resources in the nationalised industries that would provide a higher economic return in private business. The fact that attaining these performance objectives might not be compatible with the financial targets set under the 1961 White Paper was, at least in public, largely sidestepped by Government. However, although the introduction of guidance on economic pricing and investment was a move forward, events in the nationalised industries were quickly overtaken by a severe deterioration in their finances. A war broke out in the Middle East in October 1973 and in the following months world oil prices quadrupled. In Britain this added to the economic pressures on the industries resulting from a deteriorating domestic economy. The result was a combination of rising inflation and rising unemployment, sometimes described at the time by the term "stagflation". A number of the nationalised industries were badly affected because oil was an important input, for example in road transport and electricity. Also, to protect their members' real wages from the effects of inflation, the industries' unions submitted large wage claims. The result was a significant rise in production costs. Moreover, Government responded to rising inflation by postponing or reducing the price increases demanded by the industries' managements to reflect their higher costs.[65] This started in April 1971 when the steel industry's proposed price rise of 14 per cent was trimmed to 7 per cent by the Government. The result was a serious decline in the financial position of the nationalised sector. This led to the setting up of an inquiry into the industries by the National Economic Development Office (NEDO).[66]

The NEDO inquiry reported in 1976 and looked in detail at four of the nationalised industries. It found that in no cases were prices based on marginal costs, despite the recommendations of the 1967 White Paper.[67] In contrast, the financial targets that originated in the earlier 1961 White Paper were taken more seriously by management, although Government intervention in the industries meant that managements were struggling to achieve the targets set. The NEDO report stressed that there was no effective system for measuring the performance of the industries or for assessing managerial competence. It also confirmed that the confusion in the roles of Boards, Ministers and Parliament, which had existed since the 1940s, was continuing to blur accountability for the performance of the industries. The report concluded that there was no systematic framework for reaching agreement on long-term objectives and strategy. In response, NEDO recommended changes to the governance of the state industries so as to address what it saw as a lack of trust and mutual understanding between those who ran the industries and Ministers and civil servants. In particular, it recommended that Policy Councils should be established to operate alongside the corporations' Boards with these Councils responsible for strategy and the existing Boards for executive authority.

The NEDO inquiry was followed by another government White Paper on the nationalised industries, in 1978.[68] This paper confirmed the importance of financial targets, usually set as a return on average net assets employed in each industry, and introduced a new "required rate of return" which the industries would be expected to achieve on their new investment (set at 5 per cent in real terms before tax). Otherwise, each industry was to be left "to work out the details of its prices with regard to its markets and its overall objectives, including its financial targets".[69] Given that a number of the industries were monopolies, it was not clear how this instruction would guarantee economic efficiency. Other recommendations in the White Paper included the publication of more performance indicators, some governance changes, and changes in consumer representation and reporting requirements. However, a primary recommendation of the NEDO inquiry, the creation of Policy Councils, was firmly rejected by Government. It was felt that this would merely add a further tier of complexity to what was already a difficult relationship between the Government and the corporation management.

Also new at the time were External Financing Limits (EFLs). EFLs were introduced from 1976/77 in response to concerns about the growing level of government debt and were limits on the annual borrowings of the nationalised industries. The lower the EFL, the more an industry would have to finance its investment plans out of its own resources and if set as a negative figure, a net repayment of loans would be due from the industry to the Exchequer. The introduction of EFLs would mean that prices in the nationalised industries would now be set with achieving the EFL target uppermost in mind. This added a further complication to the management of the industries when set alongside achieving financial targets and the requirements of the 1978 White Paper.

## A dismal performance?

By the late 1970s the nationalised industries dominated strategic sectors of the economy and accounted for around 10 per cent of Britain's GDP, 14 per cent of total investment and 8 per cent of employment, employing around 1.5 million people. The largest investors were the British Steel Corporation, the Electricity Board and the Post Office, accounting in 1975 for some 9.4 per cent of gross domestic fixed capital formation. However, it was clear to many observers that the industries suffered from confused management leading to poor economic performance.[70] On average the nationalised industries earned financial surpluses in the 1950s, albeit not sufficiently large to meet the total interest payments on their debts. Net income (after depreciation at historic cost but before interest) as a proportion of total assets was generally less than 5.6 per cent but with some of the corporations, such as BEA, occasionally doing much better. In British manufacturing industry comparable rates of return were in the region of 16 per cent.[71] In the 1960s financial performance in the nationalised sector improved with the surpluses rising to four per cent of net fixed assets, which was just about the level needed to meet the interest costs on the industries' loan capital.[72] In a background paper accompanying its 1975 report into the nationalised industries, NEDO produced labour and total factor productivity figures for ten of the major nationalised industries and for manufacturing as a whole. It found wide disparities in the performance of each of the state-owned industries over the period 1960 to 1975.[73] There were also significant differences in performance in terms of output growth and employment (Table 1.2).

*Table 1.2* Nationalised Industry Growth Rates 1960–75 (average percentage per annum)

| Authority | Period | Output (%) | Employment | Output per head (%) |
|---|---|---|---|---|
| British Airways | 1960–74 | 11.0 | 3.6 | 7.1 |
| British Gas | 1960–75 | 7.4 | –1.4 | 8.9 |
| British Rail | 1963–75 | 0.0 | –5.5 | 5.8 |
| British Steel Corporation | 1958–75 | –3.9 | –2.5 | –4.4 |
| Electricity | 1960–75 | 4.7 | –1.6 | 6.3 |
| National Coal Board | 1960–75 | –4.3 | –5.9 | 1.7 |
| Post Office (Postal) | 1960–75 | 0.5 | 0.1 | 0.4 |
| Post Office (Telecommunications) | 1960–75 | 5.9 | 2.1 | 7.7 |
| National Bus | 1969–75 | –2.2 | –3.4 | 1.1 |
| Total manufacturing industry | 1960–75 | 2.7 | –0.7 | 3.4 |

Source: NEDO (1976) *A Study of the UK Nationalised Industries: their role in the economy and control in the future: A report to the Government from the National Economic Development Office*, London: HMSO, Table 1.2, p.16.

The economist Richard Pryke, in a detailed study of the relative performance of nationalised industries and private sector manufacturing companies, published in 1971, concluded that in terms of labour and capital productivity, on average the nationalised industries had performed relatively well especially in the 1960s.[74] Nevertheless, in terms of profitability and most other financial indicators the nationalised industries certainly performed badly.[75]Moreover, the financial performance of a number of the nationalised industries deteriorated during the mid and late 1970s as a result of rising input costs and the price restraint imposed by governments as part of their counter-inflation policies. Table 1.2 gives details of nationalised industry growth rates and average labour productivity growth between the early 1960s and the mid-1970s. Some industries performed well compared with British manufacturing industry as a whole. However, Table 1.3 provides profit figures for each year from 1970 to 1985 for the public corporations and private sector industrial and commercial companies. Throughout the entire period the differences were huge.[76] Two later studies by Richard Pryke, published in 1981 and 1982 and covering the nationalised industries in the period from when his previous study ended, the late 1960s, confirmed a major deterioration in economic performance in the 1970s. This failure Pryke blamed largely on a combination of poor management and government policy.[77]

Comparisons of the performance of particular state and private sector industries in Britain are limited by the fact that many of the nationalised industries were monopolies and had no obvious comparators in the private sector. At the same time, what seems clear is that in terms of profitability, in particular, on average the nationalised industries repeatedly underperformed compared to the private sector down to the 1970s, and profitability deteriorated further during that decade. There was also evidence of distorted investment in "prestige projects", such as the promotion of British nuclear technology in the electricity industry, occurring alongside under-investment in other areas. The financial consequences were painful. Taking the whole 30 years after 1954, accumulated government subsidies, capital write-offs and other payments to the nationalised industries totalled nearly £8 billion. Of course, profitability and sound finances may not be appropriate indicators of performance if state enterprises pursue legitimate non-profit goals in the public interest and it is the case that in terms of labour

*Table 1.3* Profitability of public corporations and industrial and commercial companies, 1970–85 (percentages)

| Year | Public corporations | | Industrial and commercial companies[c] (%) |
|------|-----------|-----------|-----------|
| | [a] (%) | [b] (%) | |
| 1970 | 6.4 | 5.6 | 16.8 |
| 1971 | 6.0 | 5.3 | 16.8 |
| 1972 | 6.2 | 4.6 | 18.5 |
| 1973 | 6.2 | 4.3 | 18.7 |
| 1974 | 4.9 | 2.4 | 17.2 |
| 1975 | 4.9 | 3.1 | 14.6 |
| 1976 | 6.2 | 4.8 | 15.6 |
| 1977 | 6.2 | 4.9 | 17.8 |
| 1978 | 5.7 | 4.4 | 17.1 |
| 1979 | 5.0 | 3.6 | 18.3 |
| 1980 | 4.7 | 3.4 | 16.1 |
| 1981 | 5.6 | 4.0 | 16.0 |
| 1982 | 6.6 | 4.8 | 16.7 |
| 1983 | 6.8 | 4.8 | 19.4 |
| 1984 | 6.3 | 3.4 | 20.6 |
| 1985 | 5.1 | 2.6 | 21.3 |

*Notes*:

a   Gross trading surplus as a percentage of net capital stock at replacement cost

b   Gross trading surplus, net of subsidies, as a percentage of net capital stock at replacement cost.

c   Gross trading profit as a percentage of net capital stock at replacement cost

*Source*: *National Income and Expenditure* (various editions); Vickers and Yarrow (1988), p.143.

productivity the industries seem to have performed much better, at least until the late 1960s. Nevertheless, at best the performance of the industries was patchy. The belief of a growing number of commentators that the nationalised industries had much scope to improve their performance would be reinforced after 1980 when the Government permitted the Monopolies and Mergers Commission (MMC) to investigate the nationalised industries for the first time. The Commission's Reports of the early 1980s on the letter post, gas appliance retailing, electricity generation and coal mining, revealed a catalogue of deficiencies.[78]

## "We cannot go on like this"

By the late 1970s there was considerable dissatisfaction with the state of the nationalised industries, the source of which can be traced back to the weaknesses inherent in the public corporation form of ownership. There was particular concern that the industries were out of control and "that something needed to be done" and that "we cannot go on like this".[79] Sir Geoffrey Howe, Chancellor of the Exchequer in the first Thatcher Government, concluded in May 1981: "The Morrisonian constitution grants our nationalised corporations a degree of autonomy which is probably unique in the Western world. In the strict sense of the word, they are constitutionally 'irresponsible'".[80] Howe's conclusion is in harmony with the view that even when Ministers did intervene in the management of the nationalised industries, the Boards' almost complete monopoly of technical expertise limited the effectiveness of their intervention. This is not inconsistent with the view that the industries suffered from excessive ministerial interference. In general, the Boards of the nationalised industries suffered from the worst of both worlds. They neither had sufficient independence from Government to operate fully commercially, especially where they were dependent on Government for their finances, nor were they properly accountable to Government for their actions; for example, it was almost impossible to remove Board members before their contracts expired. Moreover, the industries were often statutory monopolies and lacked the efficiency incentives resulting from competition. As a result, and despite the expectation in the 1940s that nationalisation would lead to higher economic efficiency by cutting out wasteful private sector competition, the economic performance of a number of the nationalised industries had been at best mixed and at worst downright poor. Notably bad performers in the 1970s were the coal industry, the railways and road freight transport. At the same time, it is wrong to suppose that all of the nationalised industries were consistently poor performers, even in the 1970s; this was not the case. For example, the gas industry had an enviable reputation for investment and technological development.

Successive governments had attempted to improve the performance and accountability of the industries with major initiatives launched in 1961, 1967 and 1978; but with seemingly limited effect. The Select Committee on Nationalised Industry in 1967 followed by the major inquiry into the industries by NEDO in the mid-1970s confirmed that the arm's length relationship between Ministers and Boards was failing and that numerous inefficiencies had arisen in terms of managing the industries. Such concerns had not prevented a Labour Government in 1967 from renationalising the steel industry and a subsequent Labour Government in 1974 from taking British Leyland (the country's largest vehicle manufacturer but in serious financial difficulty) into state ownership. This Government had also set up the National Enterprise Board to inject public money into industry and had established the British National Oil Corporation to invest in the North Sea oil fields. In 1977 Labour nationalised the country's aerospace and shipbuilding industries consolidating 31 companies into two new state corporations, British Aerospace and British Shipbuilding. Hence it would be a gross exaggeration to conclude that state ownership was in retreat before 1979. Indeed, Conservative Governments had occasionally expanded state ownership too, notably in 1971 when the Health administration rescued Rolls-Royce from bankruptcy. Nevertheless, within the Conservative Party by the late 1970s there was no enthusiasm for further nationalisation and there was a desire to find some way of reducing the size of the existing state sector. In the Labour Party there were those who favoured more state ownership, particularly on the left of the Party. But even here the suggestion was that it might take some form other than the public corporation. As Denis Healey, the Labour Chancellor of the Exchequer in the second half of the 1970s has since commented: "The public corporation which was chosen by the Attlee Government [after 1945] as the form of nationalisation, is now generally recognised to have failed to meet the nation's needs; it failed even to satisfy the aspirations of those who worked in the nationalised industries themselves."[81]

## Privatisation: the economic rationale

The intellectual roots of privatisation can be traced back to Adam Smith and probably before.[82] However, "neoclassical economics", the dominant paradigm in economics in the twentieth century, with its origins in the theorising of economists such as Stanley Jevons, Alfred Marshall and Leon Walras in the nineteenth century, was primarily concerned with the importance of competitive markets in goods and services rather than ownership. Economic efficiency depended upon giving consumers plenty of choice. The development of neo-classical economics with its interest in modelling market equilibria under varying competitive conditions occurred at more or less the same time as the development of the joint stock company as an institution controlling resources in the economy. The joint stock company introduced a division of ownership and control in business or what would much later be called an "agency" relationship. The resulting arrival of "professional management" in the private sector seemed to blur the distinction between the private and public sectors.

In neoclassical economics, competition matters more than ownership. However, there were dissenters: Marxist economists certainly emphasised the importance of property ownership and from the opposite ideological perspective so did the so-called Austrian economists. During the formative years of neoclassical economics certain theorists, notably Carl Menger and Friedrich von Wieser and later Ludwig von Mises and Friedrich von Hayek, established an alternative approach to economics. This later became known as the Austrian school; a term which reflects its origins. Instead of studying competition in terms of market equilibria, the Austrian school preferred to view competition as a process of innovation and discovering new profit opportunities. There was renewed interest in Austrian economics in the 1970s, and an interest in certain other economic theories that came together to present a powerful critique of state ownership, namely public choice theory, agency theory, the new economics of regulation, and monetarism.

### *Austrian economics*

In Austrian economics the crucial importance of the competitive market economy lies in its flexibility to respond to market signals. As one of the leading exponents of this view, Hayek, a student of Mises, wrote in 1948 (p.79): "The really central problem of economics . . . is how the spontaneous interaction of a number of people, each possessing only bits of knowledge, brings about a state of affairs . . . which could be brought about by deliberate direction only by somebody who possesses the combined knowledge of all these individuals".[83] According to Austrian economics, private enterprise seeks out new markets and production methods through a discovery process. By contrast, because of the absence of the profit motive and private property rights, state-owned enterprises lack the incentive and ability to respond similarly to changes in demand and supply. Moreover, even if politicians and civil servants were minded to try and mimic private markets, they would lack the information to do so. In the absence of competitive market signals reflecting resource costs under private ownership, decision makers cannot know what decisions to take to maximise economic efficiency. In other words, in Austrian analysis private property is a precondition for efficient exchange in the market. Austrian economists also equate private enterprise and competitive markets with human action and therefore individual freedom. State ownership is considered to be incompatible with individual freedom. In this tradition ownership certainly matters.

In 1945 Hayek had published an apocalyptic warning about the growth of the state and its impact on individual freedom and enterprise in his book *The Road to Serfdom*, from which Winston Churchill, the Conservative Party leader, had quoted to no avail during the 1945 General Election.[84] Hayek had followed this up with other publications critical of big govern-ment including *Individualism and Economic Order* in 1948. Margaret Thatcher met Hayek in 1975 and would later credit him with influencing her economic thinking.[85] She wrote to him in 1989 after ten years as Prime Minister, acknowledging that: "There is of course still so much to do. But none of it would have been possible without the values and beliefs to set us on the right road and provide the right sense of direction. The leadership and inspiration that your work and thinking gave us were absolutely crucial."[86] Thatcher's introduction to Hayek was achieved through the good offices of the Institute of Economic Affairs (IEA) in London. Established by Ralph Harris and Arthur Seldon in 1957, the IEA trod an isolated path in the 1960s as a promoter of small government and private enterprise at a time when state intervention was in the ascendancy, especially under the Labour Governments of 1964–70. Hayek had been instrumental in founding the IEA and the IEA would become a populariser of Austrian economics. It published a number of Hayek's essays including in the 1970s *Full Employment at Any Price* (1975) and *Denationalisation of Money* (1976). Thatcher attended its lunches and seminars after she became Conservative Party leader and in 1979 Ralph Harris was created a life peer in the first honours list of the new Thatcher Government.[87]

### Public choice theory

In addition to Austrian economics, the IEA was a promoter of public choice theory. Public choice theory draws upon neoclassical economics and especially the notion of individual utility maximisation. Some of its earliest exponents were James Buchanan, Gordon Tullock and William Niskanen.[88] Public choice theory applies market economic principles to the study of political decision making – hence its alternative title, "the economics of politics". Central to public choice theory is the notion that government employees may pursue self-interest when making economic policy and taking political decisions. Niskanen equated this with the pursuit of "salary, perquisites of the office, public regulation, power, patronage, output of the bureau, ease of making changes, and ease in managing the bureau".[89] All but the last two relate to the size of the bureau and hence this led to Niskanen's claim that public sector outputs would be greatly oversupplied. For politicians, individual utility maximisation would take the form of maximising the chances of remaining in office by focusing on vote-winning programmes and courting influential pressure groups and potential sources of political funding. While the resulting policies might be promoted as being in the "public interest", the reality is government spending and intervention that advances the utility of particular interests both inside and outside government. The taxpayer acquiesces in the rising cost of funding public programmes because each individual taxpayer notices only a small incremental rise in their tax burden on each occasion that public spending rises. By contrast, the beneficiaries of public spending are more concentrated, gain more individually, and therefore lobby even harder for more spending on their causes.

From this theoretical perspective, state ownership makes the allocation of resources dependent on political rather than market forces.[90] In public choice theory state ownership is associated with empire building, gold plating of public investments, union restrictive practices and other economic waste. The theory had a powerful influence on economic thinking during the 1970s and 1980s. It was popularised in Britain through the publications and meetings of the IEA and, after its foundation in 1977, by another free market "think tank" based in London, the Adam Smith Institute (ASI) directed by Madsen Pirie. Public choice theory has been criticised for an over-emphasis on self-seeking over other, possibly altruistic, behaviour within government.[91] Nevertheless, it provided a sobering antidote in the 1970s to the Morrisonian view that nationalised industry boards would necessarily be the "high custodian of the public interest". The more cynical view of motivation within government encapsulated within public choice theory seemed more consistent with the experiences of nationalisation in Britain at the time, especially the actions of the industries' trade unions, who seemed determined to raise the wages of their members no matter the costs to the public at large. Public choice theory would go on to influence later theorising on privatisation in the 1980s and 1990s.[92]

### Agency theory

Public choice theory was joined in the 1970s by a new interest in the role of property rights and agency relationships. In the 1970s the term property rights theory was commonly used, but today the description agency theory is more prominent in the literature. The theory of agency is applied to both the public and private sectors and differences in the efficacy of monitoring and controlling agent behaviour in the two sectors are contrasted.[93] In joint stock companies the principals are the shareholders who appoint boards of directors as agents to manage their assets. In state enterprises the public are the principals and through the political process officials are appointed as agents to manage the resources.

The starting point is the contention that if complete contracts could be written by principals (i.e. shareholders in the private sector and the public or taxpayer in the state sector) covering all possible contingencies during the contract period so as to determine agent behaviour, and agent behaviour could be costlessly monitored, the precise form of ownership should not matter. This conclusion about the neutrality of ownership relies on very strong assumptions, however, the main ones being information and the ability of principals to enter into complete contracts.

In reality incomplete contracts are the norm in owner-manager relationships.[94] Also, because of information asymmetries, principals may not be able to monitor agent behaviour at low cost. In particular, it is often difficult for principals to know if management failures are due to the behaviour of the management or to other variables such as the effects of the business cycle or macroeconomic policy (sometimes summarised in the literature as "states of nature"). In this situation, property rights and the different governance structures that exist in the private and public sectors do matter. When only incomplete contracts are feasible, in theory the form of ownership, or more specifically managerial incentives, can dramatically affect a firm's economic performance.

In the absence of complete contracts and costless monitoring of agents, principals must arrange for governance schemes to encourage the management behaviour they prefer. In the opinion of a number of economists, in the private sector corporate governance regimes have evolved that encourage through profit-related pay, stock options and the like, and because of the ever present threat of takeover by new management, management to drive out waste and maximise profitability.[95] By contrast, in the state sector such incentives are considered to be absent or at least attenuated.[96] Certainly in the post-war period the managers of public corporations in Britain tended to have fixed salaries, no stock options (there was no publicly quoted stock in the nationalised industries) and there was no credible takeover threat. In addition, state industries were rarely, if ever, allowed to fail. Sanctions against poor performance were more evident in the private sector than in the public sector.[97]

Like Austrian economics and public choice theory, agency theory leads to the conclusion that state enterprises will be managed less efficiently than private enterprises and will be less responsive to changes in consumer demand and input costs. However, like public choice theory, the conclusions from agency theory for ownership are open to challenge. There is an obvious incentive for the sole trader to maximise profit and without doubt Margaret Thatcher's views on individual responsibility were weaned by her upbringing in her father's grocery store. But it is less clear that a similar incentive exists in large joint stock companies, which are the real alternative to nationalised industries.[98]

In the agency literature much weight is placed on the existence of the takeover threat facing publicly-quoted joint stock companies, in which, if a company's share price is depressed because shareholders lose confidence in the management, the firm becomes vulnerable to a hostile takeover bid. In the same literature the common conclusion that large-scale industry in the private sector performs more efficiently than in the state sector, relies heavily on the existence of a well-functioning market for corporate control. Yet studies of the capital market in Britain suggest that takeovers are not necessarily a reliable vehicle for policing management behaviour; in particular, research shows that it is by no means always the worst performing firms that become takeover targets.[99] Also, there is now a voluminous literature that provides conflicting evidence on whether mergers improve the economic and financial performance of the companies involved.[100] To complicate matters further, stock markets may suffer from a free-rider problem so that investors will not necessarily dispose of their shares when a firm's performance is disappointing. It may be rational behaviour on the part of an individual shareholder to hold on to his or her shares and not sell when the share price falls, in the anticipation that the share price will recover particularly if there is a takeover bid.[101] Moreover, both public and private sector firms are likely to perform better when they operate in competitive product markets because competition for consumers weeds out the underperformers irrespective of ownership. Consistent with most of neoclassical economics, this suggests that the product market may be more important in terms of creating efficiency incentives than the market for corporate control.[102]

Nevertheless, alongside Austrian economics and public choice theory, agency theory provided a powerful theoretical rationale for privatisation from the 1970s.[103] All these theories have in common the conclusion that state-owned and privately-owned firms differ in behaviour and performance because of differences in (a) information and incentives, (b) objectives, and (c) constraints on managerial behaviour. The theories lead to predictions of both overmanning and wasteful investment in nationalised industries, conclusions that appear consistent with the record of the British nationalised industries.

### *The new economics of regulation*

Another important intellectual development in the 1970s occurred in the economics of regulation. In welfare economics a competitive private enterprise economy can produce what is known as a Pareto efficient outcome or a "Pareto equilibrium".[104] A Pareto equilibrium occurs when no reallocation of resources can occur to make at least one individual in society better off without making another individual worse off. However, for a competitive economy to produce this outcome a number of strong assumptions are needed. In practice, these conditions are too restrictive to be taken as an adequate determinant of public policy. "Market failure" exists in the form of external costs and benefits from market transactions, information asymmetries, monopoly provision and inequalities in income and wealth.

In tackling market failure, the government might choose to manipulate consumer demands and firms' supplies through the use of taxes and subsidies. An alternative is for the state to regulate the output of private sector firms, for example by requiring permission to produce and by controlling prices and outputs. This is the approach that was adopted in Britain for some utility services in the nineteenth century and by government for the privatised monopolies in the 1980s. A further possibility is state ownership and direct provision of goods and services or nationalisation.

From the 1940s in a number of countries nationalisation was the preferred option for tackling the market failure associated with "natural monopoly". A natural monopoly occurs when economies of scale or scope mean that it is more cost-efficient for the output to be supplied by one firm than by two or more competing firms, as is usually the case where duplicating networks of pipes, rails or cables would be economically inefficient. But from the 1970s the idea of private ownership with state regulation became more popular. Instead of government owning the monopolist to prevent the abuse of market dominance, there was new interest in the prospects for private sector ownership with the state regulating prices and outputs.[105] In this way monopoly profits might be avoided without removing the incentive for firms to be efficient. By restoring private ownership, the agency problem inherent in public ownership would be avoided.

A perfectly operating state regulator should be able to set prices and outputs so as to prevent monopoly abuse and achieve allocative efficiency, while private property rights encourage maximum productive efficiency or production at least cost. The problem is that perfectly operating regulators do not exist. The advances in economic thinking on regulation in the 1960s and 1970s concentrated on this and three main sets of arguments resulted. Most, if not all, of the relevant research related to regulation as practised in the USA, where there was a history of privately-owned but state-regulated provision of public services such as transport, telecommunications, energy supplies and water. Firstly, there were advances in the understanding of the motivation for regulation. A number of studies from the early 1970s proposed that regulation will be captured by special interests. This "regulatory capture" literature suggested that regulation is designed to benefit the public interest, but over time is distorted to serve the interests of the regulated industries, for example by preventing new competitors entering the industry.[106] An especially strong form of the thesis argued that from the outset regulation is shaped by special interest groups to their own advantage. The result, which received much attention in the 1970s and 1980s, was a new impetus in public policy in favour of deregulation and market liberalisation. Competitive markets have always been preferred by economists. What the "regulatory capture" literature did was to add weight to the argument that government should strive to make industries more competitive so as to remove the need for regulation.[107]

The second set of advances in the economics of regulation concerned the understanding of regulatory decisions and their impact on private sector resource allocation. Regulators have imperfect information about the markets they regulate, including the economically efficient level of prices and outputs. In this environment, state regulators risk introducing economic distortions that lead to inferior performance. In the 1970s the literature particularly emphasised the likelihood of over-investment in industries where the rate of return was regulated, or the so-called "Averch-Johnson effect".[108] But other possible outcomes were also highlighted depending upon the precise form regulation takes, including over-employment and a reduced (or inflated) quality of service.[109] The outcome was renewed interest in the 1970s on how best to structure regulation to avoid monopoly abuse, while maintaining efficiency incentives. This was evident in the early 1980s during the planning of the privatisation of British Telecom with the development of "price cap" in place of rate of return regulation (see chapter 12).

Thirdly, new research into "contestable markets" published at the time of the first Thatcher Government underlined that even where a monopoly exists, provided that there are no appreciable barriers to entry into or exit from the market, the monopolist will have to price outputs *as if* the industry is competitive.[110] Prices above the levels set in competitive markets would stimulate new entry and lower prices. This in turn created interest in removing barriers to entry in monopoly industries such as telecommunications and subjecting remaining monopoly activities to periodic competitive tendering. An extension to the logic of contestable market theory was periodic competition for contracts, which provided an economic rationale for the Government's policies in the 1980s of "contracting out" public services.[111] Under what became known as a "Chadwick-Demsetz auction", the winning bidder would agree to provide the public service at least cost.[112]

## *Monetarism*

Finally, during the second half of the 1970s monetarism challenged Keynesianism as the dominant force in macroeconomics. The impact of this is difficult to exaggerate. Under the influence of Keynesian economics, governments in the post-war period had felt obliged to intervene in the economy by "pump priming" aggregate demand whenever a recession threatened. In 1936 in his *The General Theory of Employment, Interest and Money*, Keynes had suggested that governments could reverse general unemployment by stimulating demand using their tax and spending powers.[113] A classic application of this was the action of the Heath Government in 1971/72 when faced with the threat of one million unemployed. The administration reduced taxes and raised public spending. Through fiscal (tax and public spending) and sometimes monetary policy (interest rate and bank reserve asset) changes, successive post-war governments in Britain boosted demand to avoid recession and attempted to cut demand whenever the economy began to "overheat" and prices rose, leading to "stop-go" cycles. By contrast, the central tenet of monetarism was that inflation was the result of monetary expansion or, more simply, "printing too much money". Inflation would only be brought back under control and the conditions for more real jobs created by controlling the money supply, and in turn this necessitated restraint in government borrowing. Through the banking system the issuing of government debt tended to expand the money supply. Also, whereas Keynesian economics involved government management of demand in the economy, monetarists preferred to leave economic adjustments to the free market. Politically inspired demand adjustments were judged to distort market adjustment, resulting in inflation.[114]

Monetarist economics would be important in determining budgetary policy after 1979. During the second half of the 1970s the Conservative Party leadership embraced monetarism and in turn the need to restrict public borrowing. This was something Conservatives were ideologically disposed to favour anyway. It is not therefore too surprising that a number of leading Conservatives endorsed monetary restraint to curb inflation. Although monetarism did not necessarily imply privatisation, its leading proponent at the time, Professor Milton Friedman at the University of Chicago, was certainly a free marketeer.[115] He was also a believer in low taxes and deregulation. Lower taxes would provide the conditions for entre-preneurial activity and higher investment. When in 1976 two Oxford University academics, Bacon and Eltis, published a study which suggested that Government in Britain was "crowding out" private sector employment and investment through excessive spending and borrowing, the conclusion was consistent with the monetarist notion that public spending must be reigned back. The concept of "crowding out" achieved widespread favourable media coverage in Britain in the mid-1970s.[116] The search for ways of restraining public borrowing both to free up funding for tax cuts and to reduce monetary expansion would, after the 1979 General Election, be an important stimulus for a privatisation programme.

*  *  *

Economic theory provided an important intellectual underpinning for privatisation. Without the change in economic thinking brought about by monetarism and the intellectual arguments of public choice theory and agency theory, regarding the workings of government and the effects of ownership on economic performance, it is probable that there would have been less momentum for privatisation both within and outside government. Equally, without the insights of economists researching regulation from the 1960s, it is possible that deregulation and market liberalisation policies would not have evolved as they did and that private ownership with state regulation would not have been seen as an appropriate response to monopoly instead of nationalisation. Even though there was widespread disenchantment with nationalisation by the late 1970s, it was developments in economic theory that provided the intellectual rationale for Thatcher's privatisations; they provided the policy with an economic legitimacy.

Of course, there is a risk that economists over-emphasise the importance of economic theory in changing public opinion and shaping public policy: this notwithstanding Keynes' oft-quoted remark that "Practical men, who believe themselves to be quite exempt from any intellectual influences, are usually the slaves of some defunct economist." Possibly no Minister in the Thatcher Cabinets of the 1980s that introduced the privatisations had read many or possibly any of the original theoretical papers (Sir Keith Joseph is the most likely exception). Almost certainly, therefore, they were unaware of their assumptions and limitations. With the exception of monetarism and a fleeting reference to "supply side" reforms, Thatcher's autobiographies make no mention of economic theories. However, this does not detract from the fact that theoretical developments favourable to privatisation helped to alter attitudes towards state ownership. At the time when there was real disillusionment with the performance of state enterprises, a growing number of economists were producing theoretical contributions explaining why state ownership failed. Moreover, the meetings and publications of organisations like the IEA and ASI helped to popularise the ideas beyond the world of academic economics. Newspaper and magazine articles began to appear with the content reflecting the theoretical developments. The change in editorial policy of *The Economist*, during the 1970s for example, reflected this trend. Explanations appeared for the poor performance of the nationalised industries, where the solution lay not in their reform but their abolition.

Without the developments in economic theory, privatisation would have been simply a matter of political ideology with no persuasive economic underpinnings. In 1986 John Kay and David Thompson published an article in *The Economic Journal* titled "Privatisation: a policy in search of a rationale". Kay and Thompson's title derives from their view that the Conservative Party's privatisation programme had a number of not always well-articulated objectives some of which were potentially inconsistent. As they comment: "the reality behind the apparent multiplicity of objectives is not that the policy has a rather sophisticated rationale, but rather that it is lacking any clear analysis of purpose or effects; and hence any objective which seems achievable is seized as justification."[117] Arguably, however, this is misleading, for by the late 1970s there were economic theories clearly supportive of privatisation and growing in popularity – privatisation had a rationale. What was less clear was whether the new Conservative Government had the political will to bring it about.

By the late 1970s the high hopes for nationalisation that had existed in the mid-1940s had been dashed. The public corporation form of state ownership had revealed a number of serious, perhaps fatal, organisational weaknesses and the economic record of the nationalised industries had not been such as to fulfil the Morrisonian belief that the management would act as "high custodian of the public interest". Nationalisation was increasingly criticised. However, this is not to say that the Conservative Government elected in May 1979 was necessarily committed to large-scale privatisation. In public policy it is one thing to acknowledge a problem, it is quite another to do something about it.

# 2

# THE CONSERVATIVE PARTY, NATIONALISATION AND THE 1979 GENERAL ELECTION

Apart from the iron and steel industry and road haulage which were denationalised after 1951, the Conservative Governments of the 1950s and 1960s accepted the nationalisations of the 1945–51 Labour administrations, albeit grudgingly. Harold Macmillan, Prime Minister and Leader of the Conservative Party from 1957 to 1963, like many of his generation had been deeply affected by the unemployment of the 1930s. In 1938 he had published a volume called *The Middle Way* setting out a policy agenda between free market liberalism and the socialist state, in which he advocated policies such as compulsory industrial reorganisation and a National Investment Board.[1] Macmillan kept the nationalisations that had occurred immediately after the War, although like others in his Party he opposed any extension of state ownership. The Party's rank and file at annual Party conferences might criticise the state-owned industries but large-scale denationalisation seemed beyond practical politics. A Party Policy Committee on the Nationalised Industries, established in 1956 to examine the position of the nationalised industries in the economy and make recommendations, produced no major policy proposals.

Prior to the 1970s there was a broad consensus between the main political parties in Britain on the need for a "mixed economy". This consensus is reflected in the term often used at the time, "Butskellism" – a word composed from the names of Hugh Gaitskell, Labour Chancellor of the Exchequer in 1950, and Rab Butler,[2] the first Chancellor of the Exchequer after the Conservative's election victory of 1951. This is not to say that the consensus that reigned was always an easy one. In January 1958 Peter Thorneycroft, Conservative Chancellor of the Exchequer, and two junior Ministers in the Treasury, Enoch Powell and Nigel Birch, resigned from the Government rather than accept higher public spending. In 1958 Denzil Freeth, one of the first MPs from the Bow Group wing of the Conservative Party,[3] broke the virtual silence in the Parliamentary Party on denationalisation by advocating it in the House of Commons. However, these events did not alter the general disposition within the leadership of the Conservative Party that the mixed economy should not – perhaps could not – be challenged.

Edward Heath became leader of the Conservative Party in 1965, after the Conservatives' General Election defeat of October 1964. In opposition the Party, as political parties do, re-examined its policies including its attitude towards public spending, taxation and state ownership. The re-examination of nationalisation was carried out by a group led by Nicholas Ridley, who would go on to become a leading activist for privatisation in the Conservative Governments after 1979. The Nationalised Industries Policy group presented its preliminary report in November 1967 and a final report in early 1968. The report concluded that, "The public sector of industry is a millstone round our necks ... We have a built-in system of misallocation of capital in our economy." The group recommended a gradual dismantling of the public sector and flagged the advantages of using asset sales to spread share ownership, something the Thatcher Governments would take up with enthusiasm over a decade later. A number of state enterprises were singled out for sale to the private sector, including the steel industry, which had only recently been renationalised by Labour, in 1967, and the BEA and BOAC airlines. The report also recommended the disposal of government shareholdings in the Northern Ireland aircraft manufacturer Short Brothers and Upper Clyde Shipbuilders, of British Rail's shipping and hovercraft services, and of Thomas Cook the travel agent business. However, the report acknowledged that at least for the immediate future, larger-scale denationalisation was unrealistic – it would be difficult to undertake (some of the industries were huge), there would be trade union opposition, and possibly a lack of public support. Indeed, the remainder of the Ridley report was largely taken up with how to manage the nationalised industries better, by detaching the industries from political pressures and introducing clearer guidelines on how the industries should operate.

The report received a mixed reception within the Conservative Party. In particular, the sections on denationalisation did not meet with much enthusiasm amongst most senior Conservatives, including Heath and, more surprisingly given later events, Sir Keith Joseph, the shadow Trade spokesman.[4] On the recommendation that the nationalised industries should be run on commercial lines and maximise profits, Heath considered that the suggestion was naïve given the industries' monopoly powers. Margaret Thatcher is reported to have sided with Heath declaring that public utilities "could never be run on straight commercial lines. One could not have two rival enterprises seeking to sell electricity in competition one with another". Joseph took the opportunity of the interest aroused within the leadership of the party by the Ridley report "to give another outing to his current hobby-horse, a state holding company in the mould of the IRC (Industrial Reorganisation Corporation)".[5] The IRC had been established by the Labour administration in 1967 to assist the restructuring of industry. At a later meeting of the Party's Nationalised Industries Policy group he predicted that it would not be possible in the short term to sell off the recently renationalised steel industry.[6] In his memoirs Ridley claims that the recommendations of his group "Suitably disguised . . . went into the Manifesto".[7] This is a considerable exaggeration.

Under the slogan "A Better Tomorrow", the Conservative Party's Election Manifesto emphasised the importance of a vigorous competition policy and lower taxes and less state intervention.[8] But it offered, at best, only a gradual reduction in the role of the nationalised industries in the economy. The Manifesto promised to "stop further nationalisation" including the nationalisation of the ports, as threatened by Labour,[9] and to "progressively reduce the involvement of the State in the nationalised industries, for example in the steel industry, so as to improve their competitiveness". The Manifesto offered "An increasing use of private capital . . . to reduce the burden on the taxpayer, get better investment decisions, and ensure more effective use of total resources". This would include partnerships with private enterprise in shipping lines, hotels, parking facilities, catering services and the development of vacant land. The Manifesto stopped well short of providing a definite commitment on denationalisation. In 1970 the Conservative Party was still wedded to the mixed economy. While the Party did not wish to see an extension of nationalisation, nor was there much evidence of a determination to reduce the size of the nationalised sector significantly. The new Conservative administration was not committed to a radical free market agenda.[10]

At the same time, the Conservatives were keen to stop, and if possible reverse, what seemed to be the remorseless rise in the share of the economy accounted for by government expenditure. Government spending as a percentage of GDP had risen from 44 per cent when Labour took office in 1964 to 50 per cent by 1969. In January 1970, and in anticipation of the pending General Election, the leadership of the Conservative Party met to review its policies at the Selsdon Park Hotel in Surrey. The broad thrust of the policy programme has been described as "reducing the role of government in the life of the citizen, and on increasing the scope and responsibility of the individual".[11] One result of the meeting was the invention of the label "Selsdon man" by the Labour Prime Minister, Harold Wilson, in an attempt to portray the Conservatives as prehistoric reactionaries.[12] However, although this label stuck, the meeting at Selsdon Park did not signal a fundamental shift in Conservative thinking on the "middle way", but rather a tidying up of loose ends in Conservative policies ahead of the election.[13] This was widely misunderstood at the time.[14] As Norman Tebbit, a Government Minister in the 1980s, records in his memoirs: "At the time of the election [in 1970] I naively assumed that the conversion of both Ted Heath and the Party to the Selsdon programme was one of deeply rooted conviction. In doing so I overestimated Ted Heath's conviction and I underestimated the resistance to new thinking and change within the establishment of the Party."[15]

The General Election on 18 June 1970 produced a surprising victory for the Conservatives. Labour had been ahead in the opinion polls when the election was called, but in the event the Conservatives won 330 seats to Labour's 287. At the first Party Conference after the Election, in Blackpool the following October, Heath set out what he saw as the main challenges for his Government. These took the form of reviewing all government expenditure and cutting costs wherever waste was identified, reducing taxation and "to bring our fellow citizens to recognise that they must be responsible for the consequences of their actions" – he had in mind especially those workers who demanded unreasonable pay awards.[16] But there was to be no major programme of denationalisation.

## The Heath Government, 1970–4

Under Heath, government policy initially followed the more market-oriented approach signalled in the Party's Election Manifesto. In particular, in the House of Commons John Davies, the Secretary of State for Trade and Industry, confirmed that the new Government would not support failing industries. Davies had only recently been elected an MP and was a former director-general of the employers' body the Confederation of British Industry (CBI). Also, on 27 October 1970 the Chancellor of the Exchequer, Tony Barber, was able to inform the House of Commons that public spending cuts of £330 million had been agreed for 1971–72. These cuts included the ending of school milk for older primary age children by the Education Secretary, Margaret Thatcher.[17] The October Budget also cut income tax and corporation tax, raised prescription charges and the price of school meals, introduced admission charges for museums and cut back industrial grants and subsidies in favour of tax allowances. In the same month and after some initial hesitation the IRC was axed. The Government judged its existence to be inconsistent with the aim of reducing state intervention in the economy. Interestingly, Sir Keith Joseph, who would from the mid-1970s champion the rolling back of state intervention in the economy, believed that some of the IRC's activities could be useful and opposed its abolition.

In 1970 the Heath Government was against direct state involvement in the setting of prices and wages. In addition to the ending of the IRC, the first months of the new Government saw the National Board for Prices and Incomes closed. The Conservatives opposed the use of prices and incomes policies and the Board had been at the centre of the previous administration's counter-inflation policy.[18] The Consumer Council and the Shipbuilding Industry Board were also abolished and Labour's Industrial Expansion Act with its state enabling powers was repealed. Although the National Economic Development Council established in 1962 as a tripartite (government, employers and unions) forum to discuss economic strategy survived, Heath decided not to chair its meetings. Under previous governments the Prime Minister had normally been in the chair.

Also some modest denationalisations were announced. In June 1971 the Government agreed to sell off the state-run brewery and public houses in Carlisle, taken into state-ownership during the First World War in an attempt to reduce drunkenness amongst munitions workers.[19] In addition the travel agency business Thomas Cook was lined up for sale. It had come under state ownership following the nationalisation of the railway companies in 1948. The Government also decided to introduce legislation to hive off some of the non-mining activities of the NCB including brick-making, which led Lord Robens to refuse a further term as Chairman of the NCB. The Government also flirted with selling off the gas and electricity boards' showrooms which retailed appliances and handled the payment of consumers' bills, although in the event this came to nothing.[20] The more radical recommendations of the Ridley group were not taken up and the iron and steel industry, whose renationalisation in 1967 the Conservatives had vigorously opposed, was not listed for denationalisation.

Heath in his memoirs blames the failure to pursue more denationalisations firmly on employers:

"We were advised by employers' organisations that the programme should go no further at this stage. British capitalism was at such a low ebb that no one would have taken over the major concerns which, on paper at least, might one day look like attractive candidates for privatisation. In some instances, notably that of the steel industry, which ideologues on both left and right in those days regarded as a totem, we were dissuaded by the management from causing any further upheaval. It was agreed that a more extensive programme should wait until our second term. Everyone in the Cabinet saw the need for delay. Even the Thatcher government, ten years later, waited a full parliament to elapse before privatising British Steel."[21]

In effect, Heath excuses the lack of progress on denationalisation on the short time he was Prime Minister, while taking a swipe at the later Thatcher privatisations:

"The 1970–4 government never implemented a full-scale programme of privatisation, because only three and three quarter years in power did not permit it, not least because any lasting settlement of the public-private debate would have to be planned and introduced gradually over many years if it was to be sound. The profiteering behaviour of privatised utilities [in the 1990s] was a major factor in public disenchantment with the Conservative Party."[22]

This is a most extraordinary account and implies that Thatcher stole Heath's clothes. If only he had been given a second term as Prime Minister he might have out-Thatchered Thatcher. This stretches credibility. In 1970 the Conservative Party and the country were much less prepared for a radical shake-up of the "middle way" than would be the case by the end of the decade. Denationalisation had to await the public disenchantment with the performance of state enterprises and with the performance of the British economy as a whole that occurred during the 1970s.

The decline of confidence in nationalisation which certainly existed by 1979 has to be seen within the wider crisis of confidence about the British economy by that time. From 1971 the Heath Government was increasingly diverted into dealing with a rapidly deteriorating economic situation. In 1970 the economy was buoyed up by expanding consumption and government expenditure on goods and services, partially reflecting Labour's pre-election spending. However, investment faltered in 1971 and exports began to suffer from the end of that year. Meanwhile, hourly wage rates were rising by around 9.4 per cent in the second quarter of 1970 and 15.6 per cent by the second quarter of 1973. The Government also had to face a series of economically damaging industrial disputes. As early as July 1970 the Government felt forced to declare a state of emergency in the face of a dock strike. This was settled after the appointment of a court of inquiry.[23] The court of inquiry decided to grant an expensive pay settlement and this openly encouraged other unions to press home their wage claims. The Government was then embroiled in what became known as the "dirty-jobs dispute". This dispute involved refuse collectors and certain other local government employees. An inquiry under Sir Jack Scamp triggered another inflationary pay settlement. This was quickly followed by a work to rule on the part of the power workers. They went back to work after Lord Wilberforce was brought in to arbitrate and a further large pay increase was conceded.[24]

In late 1971 a serious dispute erupted in the coal mines. The miners' dispute proved to be particularly bitter and spilled over into heavy secondary picketing, especially at the Saltley cokeworks in Birmingham where the mine workers were successful in preventing the release of coal stocks to the power stations. With electricity supplies greatly disrupted the result was yet another official inquiry, in February 1972, again under Lord Wilberforce, and yet another high pay offer, this time of 22 per cent. This was a little less than the union had demanded but still well above the rate of inflation.[25]

The previous Labour Government had been troubled by a rising number of man-days lost through official and unofficial union strike action. In January 1969 it had published proposals to reform industrial relations in the shape of a White Paper titled *In Place of Strife*. The proposed legislation included fines on trade unions which refused to hold strike ballots or to agree to a 28 day "cooling off" period before strikes were called, and the setting up of a new Industrial Board that would have statutory powers to impose settlements in industrial disputes. The proposals had split the Labour Party and had been ditched ahead of the General Election.

In the face of the continued rise in industrial conflict, the Conservative Government now took up the baton of reforming industrial relations. The Industrial Relations Act was passed at the end of the Government's first parliamentary session, in 1971. However, the Act was quickly discredited when striking dockers received jail sentences and the Amalgamated Union of Engineering Workers (AUEW) had its assets sequestrated. The legislation provoked a rash of strikes and the Government caved in.[26]

This was not the only setback. The Government had also begun to reverse its stance on state aid for industry. Early in the life of the Government John Davies had mockingly used the phrase "lame ducks" in a speech in the House of Commons to describe industries with little prospect of recovery.[27] The Government would not be willing to pour public money into propping up such industries. Towards the end of 1970 the Mersey Docks and Harbour

Board ran out of money after suffering a debilitating combination of weak management and militant unions. The Cabinet refused to make a loan to save the Board, which went into liquidation. But it did agree to provide public money for port improvements and a 30 per cent capital write-down, subject to the appointment of a new chairman.[28]

The liquidation of the Board could be presented as a product of the Government's stated stance on lame ducks, although financial assistance had been given. In his memoirs Heath confirms that it was the Government's instinct not to provide financial help but that there was an overwhelming political necessity at the time to do so.[29] However, soon afterwards John Davies's earlier promises on lame ducks definitely began to have an empty ring. In the face of rising unemployment and evidence of widespread lack of international competitiveness in British industry, the Government was drawn into more and more direct intervention in industry. The financial meltdown of the Mersey Docks and Harbour Board was immediately followed by the more economically decisive collapse of Rolls-Royce. In March 1968 Rolls-Royce had negotiated a fixed price contract with Lockheed, the American aircraft manufacturer, to supply a new and technologically demanding engine, the RB211, for its planned L-1011 Tri-star aircraft. The Labour Government had enthusiastically supported Rolls-Royce's bid to win the work, viewing the ultimate success as an important international endorsement of the UK's technological prowess. In consequence, perhaps the company discounted the prospect of financial failure believing that government would provide financial assistance whenever necessary. Whatever the truth, due to large cost overruns in developing the new engine, by 1970 the company faced a financial crisis.

It seems that the Government first became aware of the scale of the company's financial difficulties only in July 1970.[30] Given that the banks were reluctant to provide more funding, in November the Government offered financial support. However, on 22 January 1971 Rolls-Royce management revealed that the scale of the financial hole in the company was even larger than previously anticipated. It appears that the Rolls-Royce Board had only recently become fully aware of the true size of the financial losses now forecast. On 3 February the Cabinet decided to allow Rolls-Royce to go into bankruptcy with the Government agreeing to take over responsibility for the aero-engine, marine engine and industrial divisions of the business. The company was not converted into a public corporation – therefore technically it was not nationalised – and Heath notes in his autobiography that this was intentional so that it "could be rapidly sold off again to private investors when conditions were right".[31] Rolls-Royce motors, the car division, was quickly sold off just over a year later, but the conditions for the disposal of the remainder of Rolls-Royce would not prove to be right for a further 15 years.

The saving of Rolls-Royce was widely supported within the Government and Parliament even though it ran counter to the Government's proclaimed hostility towards saving failing businesses. Rolls-Royce was one of the most prestigious of British manufacturing names and the PM believed that closure of the business would have serious consequences for domestic and international confidence in British manufacturing as a whole.[32] There was also the question of jobs; the company employed around 80,000, some in areas of high unemployment. But perhaps above all were the implications for the defence sector and relations with the US Government. Rolls-Royce was seen as being critical to the country's defence capability and failure to deliver the RB211 engine would have soured relations with the Americans. The British Government had lobbied hard to win the contract only a few years earlier and the Lockheed company was dependent for its future on the success of its new aircraft, which in turn depended on delivery of the new engine. Margaret Thatcher comments in her memoirs that it was important on defence grounds to maintain Rolls-Royce's aero manufacturing capability.[33] The free market Minister in the Governments of the 1980s, Norman Tebbit, reminisces in his autobiography, equally defensively, "I persuaded myself, as did many Conservatives, that Rolls was a special case. The defence and international considerations were paramount, and the bail out was inevitable, even if unpalatable."[34]

Rolls-Royce may not have been a true "lame duck" for it was at the forefront of techno-logical development and without the costs of developing the RB211 engine the company was financially viable. But that could not be said for the next enterprise that challenged the Government's industrial policy, Upper Clyde Shipbuilders. The merchant shipbuilder became insolvent in June 1971, which threatened the loss of 15,000 jobs concentrated around Glasgow, a region that already had higher than national unemployment. The workers staged a work-in to save the four yards from closure. As tensions mounted between police and strikers, the Chief Constable of Glasgow reported that he could not promise to maintain public order with the police resources available to him.[35] On 24 February 1972 the Government backed down. The administration agreed that it would provide £35 million to save three of the four yards, effectively rescinding the earlier closure decision.

In hindsight Heath concludes that the Government was wrong to bail out the yards because of the message it transmitted about the Government's willingness to save other private sector companies in financial difficulty.[36] In her memoirs Mrs Thatcher refers similarly to the saving of the Upper Clyde Shipbuilders as "a small but memorably inglorious episode . . . I was deeply troubled", although she seems to have kept these reservations to herself at the time.[37] In the country the saving of the Upper Clyde Shipbuilders was seen for what it was, a major Government "U-turn".[38]

By 1972 the economic situation was deteriorating rapidly and the energy of the Govern-ment was progressively channelled into reducing first unemployment and then rampant inflation. On 20 January, for the first time since 1947, unemployment threatened to rise to over one million. In relation to the unemployment figures of the later 1970s and the 1980s the figure was comparatively low. But it was high compared with the very low levels of unemployment achieved during the 1950s and 1960s and which were the benchmark at the time. Government and much of the media considered one million unemployed a suicidal figure politically. The Government responded by introducing a programme of reflation. This began with a mini-budget in July 1971 and the setting of an annual economic growth target of 4.5 per cent; a figure that was self-evidently ambitious in the light of the economy's growth trend in recent years of between two and three per cent.

The reflationary package worked – indeed it worked too well. By 1973 GDP was growing at a record breaking 7.9 per cent, a rate that was well above the economy's growth potential and therefore clearly unsustainable. What became known as the "Barber boom", after Tony Barber the Chancellor of the Exchequer, involved a dash for growth that culminated in a secondary banking crisis, a stock exchange crash and rocketing inflation. The inflationary pressures in the domestic economy were compounded by steeply rising world commodity prices, made worse in Britain by the decision to abandon the fixed exchange rate and float the pound on 23 June 1972. The pound subsequently depreciated. The decision to float followed heavy speculation against sterling in the foreign exchange markets.

On 1 January 1973 the UK entered the European Common Market. Heath had successfully negotiated Britain's entry after a number of false starts and attention now turned to how well Britain would be able to compete in Europe. The Prime Minister was of the view that if British industry was to thrive, major investment and restructuring were needed.[39] It seems that Heath and some of his colleagues were influenced by what they saw as the seemingly more co-operative attitude between government and industry in mainland Europe and now attempted to emulate this in Britain. The Conservative Government would still oppose state intervention in principle, but principle was now confronted by the need to ensure Britain's competitiveness.

This shifting of position became most obvious with the passage of a new Industry Act in 1972, which reflected the Government's frustration with the slowness of private industry to change.[40] It greatly increased the scope for state funding of industry.[41] In addition to extending regional development grants and new grants to merchant shipbuilding, the legislation provided for financial assistance to any industry anywhere where the Secretary of State for Trade and Industry was satisfied that this would be of likely benefit to the economy. After back-bench criticism of this carte blanche spending power, the Government accepted an amendment to the Bill under which Parliamentary approval for individual amounts exceeding £5 million would be required. Also, an Industrial Development Advisory Board including captains of industry was established to advise the Secretary of State. Nevertheless, there could be no hiding the fact that the Act dramatically reversed the Government's earlier stance against state intervention in the economy. It was described by Tony Benn, Labour's shadow Industry spokesman, as "a massive measure of intrusion".[42] Heath later described its passage less dramatically as "a sensible, pragmatic and practical response to a disappointing state of affairs . . . If investment is simply failing to happen when it is most needed, then the pragmatist does what he can to help and stimulates it. Conservatism at its best is always empirical, not dogmatic".[43]

In effect, the Industry Act empowered the Government to both "pick winners" and save "losers" or "lame ducks". The new powers in the Act enabled the Government to help both high-tech companies such as the computer firm ICL, which subsequently received £25.8 million in launch aid, and companies in traditional industries such as the Mersey Docks and Harbour Board and the Govan and Cammell Laird shipyards, which in return for government grants were expected to introduce programmes of modernisation. The Government also created a new Office of Fair Trading to oversee competition policy and a Consumer Protection Advisory Committee, which seemed to revive some of the work of the Consumer Council that the Government had abolished as unnecessary in 1970.

Towards the end of 1972, Peter Walker, who was a known interventionist and firmly of the "middle way" persuasion, replaced John Davies as Secretary of State for Trade and Industry. At the 1973 Conservative Party conference Walker spoke enthusiastically about the creation of a "'new capitalism' . . . harnessing . . . economic growth to the creation of a civilised society". By the summer of 1973 the design of a new Companies Bill was underway which would have provided for even greater powers of state intervention in business. However, its introduction was overtaken by a strike by the country's coal miners and a resulting General Election.

The "U-turn" on state intervention in industrial restructuring was now complete. At the Department of Trade and Industry Walker instituted breakfast meetings with industrialists in which he encouraged them to invest and restructure. Heath made a speech in which he described the company Lonrho, headed by the buccaneering Tiny Rowland, as the "unacceptable face of capitalism"[44] and the Cabinet agreed, in the face of opposition from the Treasury, to support the British Steel Corporation's ten year strategy to expand and modernise steel making capacity. British Steel was not to be denationalised. Instead, there would now be extra public funding, initially of some £570 million to concentrate production in five giant steel plants.[45] The NCB also benefited from new state largesse, securing £1.1 billion of additional financing, in an attempt (yet again) to establish a financially viable coal mining industry. The Government went further, it also created two new state enterprises. In 1972 British Nuclear Fuels Ltd was set up with the state owning the share capital and the British Gas Corporation was established to unify the gas industry in response to the introduction of "natural gas" from the North Sea. Previously this nationalised industry had been organised under regional boards.

Meanwhile the macroeconomic environment continued to deteriorate. In September 1971 the Government had abolished credit controls, freeing the banks to expand lending. There was an immediate rise in the money supply. Bank lending to the private sector rose by 48 per cent in 1972 and 43 per cent in 1973.[46] The first product was a sharp rise in house prices. The depreciation in the value of sterling on the foreign exchanges plus the start of an international oil crisis after the outbreak of the Yom Kippur war in the Middle East, in the autumn of 1973, added to a growing public perception of incompetence in the Government's economic management. In 1973–74 oil prices more than quadrupled as the Organisation of the Petroleum Exporting Countries (OPEC) flexed its muscles and capitalised on the high world demand for oil. By early 1974 inflation was above 11 per cent and in 1975 it would peak at over 25 per cent (Figure 2.1). The Government's response to rising inflation was another apparent "U-turn", this time on prices and incomes policy, to complement the U-turn on industrial intervention. Elected on a Manifesto that blamed inflation on Labour's high taxation and devaluation of the currency in 1967, and which shunned prices and incomes policies, the devaluation in June 1972 was followed by a prices and incomes policy announced on 26 September. After an abortive attempt to agree a voluntary policy in tripartite talks, the policy was made statutory in November 1972 and a 90 day freeze on prices, wages, rents and dividends was enforced.[47] The introduction of the prices and incomes policy saw the creation of two new official bodies, a Price Commission and a Pay Board, in effect resurrecting the National Board for Prices and Incomes that the Government had scrapped only two years' earlier.

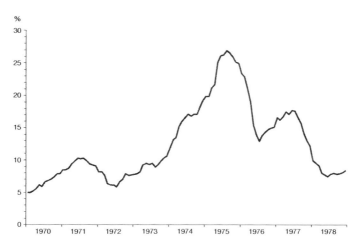

*Figure 2.1* UK inflation 1970–78
*Source*: Office for National Statistics.

The reintroduction of a prices and incomes policy was heavily criticised by some Conservatives and notably Enoch Powell and Nicholas Ridley on the right of the Party.[48] Ridley had left the Government in April 1972. Heath's memoirs suggest that he was pushed out;[49] Ridley maintains that he resigned because of disillusionment with the direction Government policy was taking.[50] There were also some misgivings amongst other Ministers. However, in the event the Cabinet endorsed the policy in the absence of any more appealing way of stemming inflation without creating mass unemployment. In his memoirs, Kenneth Baker, a junior Minister involved in implementing the prices and incomes policy, comments that: "Others, like Margaret Thatcher, Keith Joseph, John Nott and myself, suppressed any misgivings in the hope that it would work in the short term."[51]

In the short term the prices and incomes policy did succeed in moderating inflation and the Stage 1 freeze was followed by a Stage 2 announced in January 1973 with pay rises limited to £1 a week plus four per cent with a maximum annual increase of £250.[52] But prices and incomes policies do not address the root causes of inflation: rather they suppress the inflationary pressures. Unions may be willing to restrain wage demands to the policy "norms" for a while but are unlikely to continue to do so if their members' living standards decline. This came to a head after the announcement of a Stage 3 on 8 October 1973. Stage 3 allowed for a seven per cent norm in wage increases, a figure that was below the rate of inflation at that time. Its introduction also coincided with renewed trouble in the nationalised coal mines.

The leadership of the National Union of Mineworkers (NUM) had been invigorated by their success in extracting major concessions from the Government in the industrial dispute of the previous year. In clear breach of Stage 3 the union now submitted a pay claim, way above the seven per cent norm, that amounted to a 35 per cent wage rise. In support of its demand the union ordered an overtime ban to take effect from 12 November. With the adequacy of coal stocks at power stations at risk, five days later the Government declared a state of emergency and controls on electricity supplies were introduced. With coal stocks continuing to fall and in order to make further savings in electricity consumption, the Government took the unprecedented step on 13 December of ordering a three-day working week across the economy, to commence on 1 January. An industrial dispute was thereby turned into a major political crisis.

Electricity was largely generated from domestic coal supplies and the NUM implemented secondary picketing of the power stations to prevent new coal supplies arriving, in a repeat of its successful strategy during the dispute of 1972. On 5 February the union dramatically escalated the dispute by voting for an all-out strike. In response Heath decided to take the matter to the country. A General Election followed on 28 February which the Government attempted to fight on the issue of "Who governs Britain?". Inevitably the Election became a judgement on the Government's whole economic record.

The result was a minority Labour administration. The Conservatives won almost 230,000 more votes than Labour but because of the vagaries of Britain's "first past the post" electoral system, four fewer MPs. A few months later, in October 1974, the Labour Prime Minister, Harold Wilson, called a further General Election in the hope of attaining a clear Parliamentary majority. The strategy was only partially successful with Labour achieving an overall majority of just three seats. Heath fought the second election on the theme of "national unity" and "one nation" Toryism and it was an even bigger disaster for the Conservatives than the first. Their share of the popular vote fell from 37.9 per cent in February to 35.8 per cent in October.

## Margaret Thatcher and "The Right Approach"

The foolhardy decision to take the matter of who runs the country to the electorate in response to a strike and his failure to win the two ensuing elections effectively ended Heath's leadership of the Conservative Party. Although he wished to stay on as head of the Party, he was forced to accept a leadership contest. When Sir Keith Joseph and Edward du Cann, Chairman of the Party's backbench 1922 Committee and an anti-Heathite, stepped aside as leadership contenders, the latter because of concerns that his business dealings would be subjected to critical scrutiny, Margaret Thatcher announced her candidature. After the loss of the February 1974 Election Heath had moved Thatcher from Education to be shadow spokesperson on the environment and on Treasury matters. She was asked to deputise for Robert Carr, the shadow Chancellor, and was given special responsibility to lead the opposition to Labour's Finance Bill. Her highly effective assault on Labour's economic policies helped to bolster her standing within the Parliamentary Party. Nevertheless, at the time of the contest the front runner in the Conservative Party to win against Heath was William Whitelaw, who was the Party's Deputy Leader. Out of loyalty to Heath Whitelaw chose not to run against him in the first ballot on 4 February 1975 but entered the second, decisive round a week later. In the first ballot Thatcher beat Heath, ending any hope that he still had that he would be able to cling to the leadership.[53] Heath withdrew from the contest before the second ballot. Although Whitelaw was expected to win in the second round of voting,[54] on 11 February the Party's MPs chose Margaret Thatcher, by a vote of 146 to 76.

It is almost certain that Thatcher would not have run against Sir Keith Joseph.[55] Joseph was her economics mentor and friend, but he withdrew from the leadership race following a speech in Birmingham where he appeared to suggest that births amongst the lowest social classes threatened "our human stock". This was reported and exaggerated by sections of the media and the resulting criticism unsettled him. Another reason for his failure to stand was his "inordinate self-doubt and agonizing bouts of indecision".[56] Certainly, Joseph's indecision would sully his periods as a Cabinet Minister in the 1980s. But this personality flaw should not be allowed to detract from his importance in the reshaping of Conservative economic policy in a free market direction after the two Heath election defeats. He and Thatcher always remained close.

In the 1960s Joseph had frequented meetings of the Institute of Economic Affairs. Even so his later "free market" posture had not been evident during his stint as Secretary of State for Health and Social Security in the Heath administration. Here he had headed one of the Government's biggest spending departments and had defended his department's budget against Treasury-inspired cuts. Also, and as already mentioned, he was much against the abolition of Labour's interventionist Industrial Reorganisation Corporation in 1970. In his autobiography Heath comments caustically that after the first 1974 election defeat: "Keith Joseph apparently expected to be promoted to Treasury spokesman, but the arguments against that were overwhelming. At a time when we were sure to be pressing for tough government measures, it would have been absurd to entrust the shadow Chancellorship to one of the biggest spenders of our period in government."[57]

Immediately after the February election defeat Joseph did undergo something of a spectacular conversion. He quickly became the leading advocate of free markets and smaller government within the shadow Cabinet. In a series of speeches he began to set out an alternative economic and social strategy to that pursued by the Heath Government, which he now largely disowned. Initially he labelled the strategy "the social market" after the policies adopted on the Continent and especially in West Germany, but later this title was dropped because it sounded too "collectivist". In his speeches Joseph argued for self-help to tackle social problems, monetarism to control inflation, and lower public expenditure and reduced taxation to stimulate private enterprise. Particularly influential in setting the stage was a speech given at Preston in September 1974 where Joseph confirmed his rejection of prices and incomes policy and Keynesian economics. He maintained that a government commitment to keeping full employment at all times was mistaken and that governments could not guarantee work. Attempts to do so would mean more government borrowing and printing money, which would simply lead to higher inflation.[58]

The speech was clearly a repudiation of the macroeconomic policies adopted by the Heath Government and an endorsement of monetarism. It is said to have "emotionally hurt and annoyed" Heath.[59] However, the speech appears to have had an energising effect on Thatcher, who as Education Minister in the Heath Government had also headed a big spending department. Kenneth Baker, a minister in the later Thatcher Governments, claims that "it was this speech which persuaded Margaret Thatcher that a wholly new approach to economic policy was necessary."[60] In fact, it is unlikely that one speech on its own was so influential. Thatcher was already adjusting her public position on the economy following the removal of the constriction of being a government minister. She would later write on the ending of the Heath Government: "I had given little thought to the future. But I knew in my heart that it was time not just for a change in government but for a change in the Conservative Party."[61] Joseph's Preston speech signalled the direction in which economic policy would evolve under Thatcher's leadership of the Conservative Party. Later Thatcher would acknowledge "I could not have become Leader of the Opposition, or achieved what I did as Prime Minister, without Keith."[62]

Margaret Thatcher had entered Parliament in 1959 as the Member for Finchley in North London and had gained office as Parliamentary Secretary to the Minister of Pensions and National Insurance in October 1961. In an article in the *Daily Telegraph* on 28 March 1969 she had set out her views on the need for a smaller state and had advocated extensive denationalisation. However, her views were not always consistent and some of her early statements against public spending have to be set against her record during her four years as Education Secretary in the Heath Government. Thatcher proved to be a stout defender of her department's large budget and successfully championed extra public spending in the form of the building of more primary schools and the raising of the minimum school leaving age. She would never entirely shake off criticism for ending free school milk for eight to eleven year olds, captured in the taunt "Margaret Thatcher, milk snatcher", but conceded to this cut in the face of Treasury pressure for expenditure reductions in return for preserving her school building programme. She reversed the previous Labour Government's policy of compulsory comprehensive schooling, yet at the same time oversaw the creation of more comprehensive schools than any other Education Secretary. She also reprieved the Open University created by the previous Labour administration and which had been scheduled for closure by the Conservatives before it had enrolled its first students.[63] As she later reminisced:

"On the whole I got what I wanted. I got the primary school building programme, and there was no further postponement of the date for raising the school leaving age . . . . I took the view that most parents are able to pay for milk for their children, and that the job of the Government was to provide such things in education which they couldn't pay for, like new primary schools . . . The important thing was to protect education, and that's what we did. Indeed, we expanded it."[64]

At the same time, Thatcher had demonstrated from her earliest days in politics an opposition, in principle at least, to large government. During her early period as a Parliamentary candidate in the late 1940s and early 1950s, she had made clear her belief in individual responsibility, lower taxes, sound money and freedom from state controls.[65] Some have attempted to associate her stance on the individual and society with her upbringing in semi-rural Grantham in Lincolnshire: "From her secure family background come the values of self reliance, hard work, thrift, the family, and belief in just deserts and not looking to the 'nanny state'."[66] Others have suggested similarly that her economic liberalism owed "less to political theorists than to her upbringing in her father's grocery shop"[67] or to "homespun political wisdom".[68]

One of her biographers, John Campbell, argues that as a shadow Cabinet Minister in the late 1960s responsible for power and later transport, Thatcher was already "developing ever more clearly the conviction that public ownership was economically, politically and morally wrong".[69] Also, in addition to her instinctive belief in individual effort and free enterprise, she had made clear the importance to her of Britain's success as a nation. She was already by instinct a nationalist at heart and, as Campbell also argues, "The tension between liberalism and nationalism persisted throughout her career."[70] Indeed, she would prove to be every bit as much a nationalist as an economic liberal when Prime Minister in the 1980s.

Equally, it would be wrong to conclude that by 1974 Thatcher believed in the set of policies which would later be termed "Thatcherism". In addition to being a high spending Minister between 1970 and 1974, she had been a member of the Party's Economic Policy Committee that had considered and rejected the Ridley group report on nationalised industries.[71] While Thatcher's belief in individual liberty, private property and the family were deeply ingrained, during the Heath administration she never chose to put her Ministerial position at risk by openly opposing the "U-turns" that the Government introduced. In particular, Thatcher did not express public opposition to the prices and incomes policy, to joining the European Community or to saving Rolls-Royce.[72] In her autobiography Thatcher pays tribute to the few Conservatives who did criticise the Heath Government's policies, conceding: "Although my reservations grew, I was not at this stage among them."[73] Later Thatcher became known as a "conviction politician", but some of those who worked with her in Government in the 1980s reveal a more pragmatic and compromising figure than this popular one, which she herself did much to cultivate.[74] For example, Lord Carrington, Foreign Secretary in the first Conservative Government until the Falklands War in 1982, describes her as "a woman of integrity, [who] could weigh evidence, perceive (no doubt often with irritation) what course could turn out best and, against natural impulse, decide to follow it". In other words, "her heart was generally compelled by her to yield, albeit grudgingly, to her highly intelligent head."[75]

Thatcher's views on self-help and the free market were reinforced and recast after the election defeats of 1974 and the ignominy of political failure by a swelling tide of unease in the Conservative Party and the country about the trajectory of the British economy. This was matched by scepticism about the ability of existing policies to bring about a reversal in the country's economic and social decline, as evidenced by the failure of the Heath administration and the policies now being pursued by the new Labour Government. The "British disease" may have been exaggerated, but at the time it was perceived to be real nonetheless[76] and not least by Thatcher. Between 1950 and 1970 the British economy had grown at only half the rate of its Western European neighbours and its performance in the 1970s proved to be particularly poor. Sterling would lose over one-third of its value against a basket of international currencies between 1972 and 1978 due to inflation and a loss of international confidence in Britain. Unemployment passed the politically significant one million mark in the third quarter of 1975 and in the same year inflation hit 25 per cent. Output per head grew by only 1.2 per cent between 1973 and 1976 compared with 9 per cent in France and 10 per cent in Germany.[77]

While Margaret Thatcher was settling into her new role as leader of the Conservative Party, the Labour Government elected in October 1974 struggled to tackle the combination of rising inflation and unemployment. In the autumn of 1976 a sterling crisis led the Government to seek a large International Monetary Fund (IMF) loan, which came with deflationary strings attached. Resorting to the IMF for emergency funding was widely interpreted as a national humiliation and in return for the loan the IMF insisted on a programme of big public spending cuts. This in turn led to cash limits on government departments and what became known as external financing limits (EFLs) for the nationalised industries.[78] Divisions within the Labour Party over the direction of economic policy became more acute as departmental budgets suffered. At the Labour Party Conference in September 1976 the Prime Minister, James Callaghan, had seemingly dumped Keynesian economics, warning his Party, "We used to think that you could spend your way out of a recession and increase employment by cutting taxes and boosting Government spending. I tell you in all candour that the option no longer exists."[79] The speech was not well received especially by those Labour activists who had begun to line up behind Tony Benn, the Secretary of State for Energy, who was now ploughing a thoroughly socialist furrow in his public speeches. Probably it was only Callaghan's fear that Benn on the back benches would be even more disruptive than Benn in Cabinet that prevented him from being sacked. Keynesianism with its emphasis on counter-cyclical fiscal policies to maintain full employment had dominated thinking on British macroeconomic policy from the 1940s. In its place – or perhaps more correctly alongside it – the Labour Government introduced monetary targets and sharp reductions in public expenditure, despite deep reservations within the Parliamentary Party. By 1979 the seeds of monetarism had been laid within Government. In particular, the Treasury was already proving to be fertile ground for monetarist ideas given the parlous state of the British economy and the apparent failure of "big government".

From 1975 monetarism and economic liberalism took a hold of the leadership of the Conservative Party, but only gradually. This development was reinforced by a belief extending well beyond the Party that the British economic disease could only be dealt with by tackling what were popularly seen as the two main culprits – the unions and high taxation. In the keynote speech to her first Conservative Party Conference as leader, Thatcher put the case for less government and for individual freedom. But not too much was read into this by most commentators since previous Party leaders, including Heath, had made similar speeches in Opposition.[80] Also, Thatcher had to tread carefully as practically the whole of her shadow Cabinet had supported someone other than herself during the leadership election and the majority of its members were still unrepentant Heathites. Heath had been rejected because he had lost two General Elections rather than on ideological grounds and Thatcher was well aware of this. As the mercurial Conservative Minister of the 1980s, Alan Clark, observed, "When on the evening of 13 February 1975 Margaret Thatcher took her seat, at the centre of the table in the Leader's Room, and watched her colleagues troop in to their assigned places she could have been pardoned for taking an informal head count of her supporters. It would not have taken long. The name was Keith Joseph."[81] Nor was her position especially secure in the Parliamentary Party despite her victory in the leadership contest.

It has been suggested that after 1975 perhaps two-thirds of Conservative MPs would have preferred someone other than Thatcher as Party Leader.[82]

As a consequence, Thatcher could not have attempted to create a shadow Cabinet in her own image, even if her own position on economic matters was certain, which was not obviously the case. One of her first acts as Leader was to appoint Lord Peter Thorneycroft, the Chancellor who had resigned in 1958 when the Macmillan Government had refused to cut public spending, as Party Chairman. This appointment was consistent with the general direction she wanted to take the Party, although Thorneycroft would prove to be a troublesome ally during the 1979 General Election[83] and was replaced by Cecil Parkinson in 1981. Another of her significant appointments was William Whitelaw whom Margaret Thatcher had beaten in the second ballot for the Party leadership. He was reappointed Deputy Leader and in subsequent years would become a close confidant of Thatcher, but could not be accurately described as a Thatcherite even if by then the term had been invented. Whitelaw was solidly within the "middle way" Conservative tradition. Other appointees were Sir Geoffrey Howe, who was made shadow Chancellor replacing Robert Carr. Howe had joined the Heath Cabinet as Minister for Trade and Consumer Affairs in November 1972 having cut his mark as an ideas man in the Conservative Party in the Bow Group. He had proved to be a prolific pamphleteer and went on to chair an important Party committee on economic policy after 1975, the Economic Reconstruction Committee. However, neither could Howe be described as a Thatcherite in 1975. He had been for a time the Cabinet Minister directly responsible for price control during the ill-fated prices and incomes policy of the Heath Government.

Other than these changes, Thatcher replaced few of the shadow Ministers she inherited from the Heath era. The only heavyweight dismissed was Peter Walker and amongst the more junior ranks Paul Channon – both would come back as Ministers in her Governments after 1979. Heath did not join the shadow Cabinet. According to Thatcher she asked him to – albeit very half-heartedly – and he refused.[84] His animosity towards her for what he saw as her "betrayal in the extreme" of standing against him for the Party leadership would never wane.

As the historians Anthony Seldon and Daniel Collings comment: "The balance in Mrs Thatcher's 'shadow Cabinet' was undoubtedly 'wet' . . . Very few were subscribers to the new thinking."[85] Members of the shadow Cabinet such as John Biffen and John Nott and, of course, Joseph were of a monetarist persuasion and they controlled some of the economic policy jobs. But others, notably Howe and Nigel Lawson, were seen as Heath men and became converts to full-blooded monetarism only later.[86] Lawson, a student of Roy Harrod at Oxford and subsequently a journalist, went from being a Keynesian to a sophisticated monetarist during the second half of the 1970s. Howe would be Thatcher's first Chancellor of the Exchequer and Lawson her second.

The search for new policies under Thatcher resulted from the perceived failure of the earlier ones during the Heath Government. These new policies came from various sources. Undoubtedly influential was the Institute of Economic Affairs, whose meetings Thatcher, Joseph, Howe and other leading figures in the later privatisations, such as Patrick Jenkin, Jock Bruce-Gardyne and Rhodes Boyson,[87] attended during the 1970s.[88] The IEA promoted policies such as removing rent controls, contracting out and charging for public services, freer labour markets and lower taxes and public spending, along with the ditching of Keynesian economics and its replacement by monetarism, all of which the later Conservative Governments would pursue. Others influenced by the IEA who were later involved in the privatisation programme of the 1980s included Sir John Hoskyns, the first head of the Downing Street Policy Unit after the 1979 General Election, and Adam Ridley a director of a new Conservative think tank, the Centre for Policy Studies.[89] Milton Friedman, the leading proponent of monetary economics in the 1970s, is on record as claiming, "Without the IEA, I doubt very much whether there would have been a Thatcherite revolution."[90] Others are less sure: Patrick Cosgrave, a long standing friend and adviser to Thatcher, stresses in his early biography of her published in 1978, "it would be wrong, in looking back on her career, to exaggerate the extent of her involvement with ideas of what has come to be known as the New Right."[91] As already discussed, Thatcher's faith in markets was the result of a deep-seated and conditional instinct in favour of individual endeavour. The meetings of the IEA she attended served as useful confirmation of her innate sympathy for private over state enterprise, while not reversing her reservations about what might be politically possible. The same was probably true for others in the shadow Cabinet. Sir Keith Joseph observed in an interview in 1987 that he had reached his views "with the help of friends", while he suspected that Thatcher had relied on "her own common sense and instinct".[92]

Alongside the IEA there were a number of other bodies that fed ideas into the Conservative Party after 1975. These included Aims of Industry (later Aims), the National Association of Freedom, the Selsdon Group,[93] the Conservative Philosophy Group and the Salisbury Group. Thatcher gave particular support to the National Association for Freedom (later renamed the Freedom Association) founded by Norris McWhirter in 1975. Another influential body was the Economic Dining Club established by Nicholas Ridley in 1972, which Thatcher joined and of which she became a frequent attendee.[94] Also important was the Economic Reconstruction Committee reporting to the shadow Cabinet, headed by Geoffrey Howe and including the future Conservative Ministers David Howell, Nigel Lawson, Peter Rees, Nicholas Ridley, John Biffen and John Nott.[95] This group oversaw the Party's economic policy making. Also worthy of acknowledgement is the Adam Smith Institute in London, which from its foundation in 1977 became an influential exponent of the economic case for privatisation.

Sections of the press, business and academia were instrumental too in changing the political environment in favour of what later would be called Thatcherism.[96] In the newspapers, particularly the journalists Samuel Brittan writing in the *Financial Times*, Woodrow Wyatt the former Labour MP writing in the *Sunday Mirror*, and William Rees-Mogg and Peter Jay at *The Times* were converts to monetarism and smaller government. Jay was the son-in-law of the Labour Prime Minister James Callaghan and helped write the September 1975 Conference speech when Callaghan suggested that government could not spend its way out of recession. From the business world John Hoskyns, Norman Strauss an employee of Unilever, and Alfred Sherman were just a few of the businessmen who became involved with Party policy committees in the second half of the 1970s. Turning to academia, Alan Walters, Peter Bauer, Patrick Minford and David Laidler were particularly influential in shaping the shadow Cabinet's approach to macroeconomics. A Professor of Economics at the LSE, Walters had been seconded to Whitehall briefly during the Heath Government but had made no headway in getting his monetarist beliefs accepted.[97] After the ascendancy of Thatcher to the leadership, Walters helped promote monetarism within the Conservative ranks, for example he was particularly active in the Selsdon Group. He would go on to become a confidant to Thatcher on economic policy between 1981 and 1984 and again in 1989.

Both Walters and Hoskyns were involved with the new Centre for Policy Studies (CPS). This had been established by Sir Keith Joseph immediately after the February 1974 General

Election defeat. Funded mainly by sympathetic businessmen, ostensibly the objective of the CPS was to draw lessons from successful social market economies in Europe, particularly West Germany. It was in this guise that Heath agreed to its creation. However, it quickly became a new right of centre "think tank" for the Party, rivalling the longer-established Conservative Research Department as a forum for new ideas on economic and social issues. Joseph was its first chairman and Margaret Thatcher its vice-chairman.[98] Alfred Sherman became the Centre's second Director of Studies. Sherman, a former communist but now an outspoken economic liberal, helped write a number of Joseph's speeches including the important September 1974 speech at Preston and quickly emerged as the driving force within the CPS. He later described the role of the CPS grandly as follows: "Our job was to question the unquestioned, think the unthinkable, blaze new trails."[99] Under the influence of Walters and Sherman at the CPS, Thatcher's enthusiasm for monetarism grew and with it the need to rein back public spending.[100] The Centre was soon providing a platform to transfer the ideas of the IEA and other free market pressure groups into political action. The CPS published wide-ranging and speculative policy documents during the second half of the 1970s attacking post-war economic management and the centre ground.[101] Also, it brought into the Party persons such as David Young, who became a frequent caller at the CPS and who would become another early proponent of privatisation in the Thatcher Governments of the 1980s.[102]

Under the influence of these various think tanks, discussion groups and personae from the media, business and academia, the policies of the Conservative Party began to change. Views were also changing outside the Party as the "middle way" was assailed by the new economic theories discussed earlier, in chapter 1, and by the evidence of economic failure. As one Conservative put it at the time, "The world has changed. There is now no middle ground to seek. Nothing less will suffice than a major reversal of the trends which ever since 1945 Labour has promoted and Conservatives have accepted."[103]

Thatcher gave the job of reformulating economic policy particularly to Sir Keith Joseph who "pursued his remit with enthusiasm" through numerous study groups.[104] The Party set out its new economic and social agenda in policy papers, the most important of which were *The Right Approach – a Statement of Conservative Aims* published in October 1976 and *The Right Approach to the Economy* published the following year. The former document was written by Angus Maude and Chris Patten, head of the Conservative Research Department, and set out policy goals on lower taxation, lower public spending and borrowing, and less state interference. The 1977 policy document was intended to help shape the Party's Manifesto for the next general election and was edited by Maude and authored by Howe, Joseph and David Howell from the economic right and Jim Prior from the left of the Party. The document advocated firm monetary and fiscal policies and "realistic and responsible" collective bargaining.

Together the two policy documents attempted to project a consensus within the Conservative Party around value for money in public spending, free enterprise, wider ownership and the rule of law. In particular, the importance of controlling both trade union power and the money supply to bring down inflation was evident. However, while the documents did suggest some movement to the right politically, there was no suggestion of a seismic shift. For example, there was no unequivocal rejection of pay policy. It was accepted that under a future Conservative Government there might be some need for consultation with employers and unions on pay. Cuts in public expenditure seemed essential if monetary stability and enterprise were to be restored, but the leadership of the Party proved reluctant to identify precisely where the cuts would fall. While some, notably Thatcher, were disposed to be anti-union, others in the shadow Cabinet, and notably Jim Prior, were more conciliatory and believed that confrontation with the trade unions would risk another "Who rules Britain?" election. The documents therefore used imprecise wording acceptable to both camps.

Thatcher is known to have been less than happy with the content of especially the 1977 document, *The Right Approach to the Economy*, and particularly its leaning towards some kind of economic forum to settle disputes between employers and the unions. At the time this was being canvassed by Howe in the Party's Economic Reconstruction Committee.[105] Equally, she remained cautious about the extent of radical change that would be acceptable within her shadow Cabinet and the Party at large. In particular, in the mid-1970s the Conservative Party was far from being a Party of privatisation. For example, John Redwood, who later became a leading advocate, wrote in 1976: "It is neither possible nor desirable to return to a free market economy. There would be too much upheaval involved in dismantling the large State and private monopolies currently operating in the economy."[106] *The Right Approach – a Statement of Conservative Aims* merely states "The Government has nationalised great sections of industry, which it has subsequently mismanaged" and "The precise limits that should be placed on intervention by the State are reasonably the subject of debate within the Conservative Party, as are the proper boundaries between state and private provision."[107]

Presumably the debate was ongoing. The only firm commitments on state ownership in the document were to repeal the 1975 Industry Act and its product the National Enterprise Board, established to channel public funding into manufacturing industry, and reverse the nationalisation of shipbuilding and aerospace currently under way. Hidden away on page 33 of the document was the brief comment: "In some cases it may also be appropriate to sell back to private enterprise assets or activities where willing buyers can be found."[108] The only case named where this might occur was in the oil sector, where another new state enterprise, the British National Oil Corporation, was to have its "financial privileges" ended and "where appropriate" its assets were to be sold "to willing buyers at reasonable prices". Instead, the emphasis in this document was on making the nationalised industries perform better by re-establishing commercial and financial discipline, by setting clear financial objectives and encouraging them to recruit top quality management. The 1977 policy document was only a little more explicit about the desire to introduce private capital into the nationalised industries, concluding: "The long term aim must be to reduce the preponderance of state ownership and widen the basis of ownership in our community. Ownership by the state is not the same as ownership by the people. It is the very opposite."[109] No new commitments were made on denationalisation.

## Uncertain direction and the 1979 General Election

In its two Election Manifestos in 1974 Labour had pledged to take the shipbuilding, ship repairing and marine engineering industries, along with aircraft industries, into public ownership. This was justified on the grounds that the industries concerned received government financial assistance and were heavily dependent on government contracts, although in shipbuilding in particular the unions also hoped that state ownership would reverse the threat of job losses. The shipbuilding industry was facing growing foreign competition. In 1975 the nationalisation legislation was presented and duly opposed by the Conservatives. During its passage it faced a number of legal challenges. The compensation terms under the state takeover proved to be especially controversial. The Labour Government used Stock Exchange valuations as the basis for the compensation paid to shareholders, even though critics argued that the stock market prices were depressed by the threat of nationalisation with inadequate compensation.[110] The Nationalisation Bill received royal assent on 17 March 1977, but only after the Government dropped the provisions relating to ship repairing. The Conservative Party made clear that it was committed to early denationalisation of the shipbuilding and aerospace industries once returned to power. The arguments over the compensation terms for the former owners would linger on into the 1980s.

In addition, on 31 January 1975 Labour introduced into Parliament a new Industry Bill. The Bill established the National Enterprise Board (NEB) and planning agreements between major companies and the Government. The Conservatives committed themselves to early abolition of the legislation including the NEB, which they associated with propping up "lame ducks" and a futile attempt by Government "to pick winners". In 1976 the British National Oil Corporation (BNOC) was created to increase state control over oil extraction from the North Sea. In the following four years, including during the 1979 General Election campaign, the Conservatives' privatisation plans would be largely limited to reversing the nationalisation of the shipbuilding and aerospace industries and scrapping the NEB.[111] Their attitude towards the future of BNOC remained uncertain. Although the 1976 policy document had raised the prospect of some sell-off of BNOC's assets, the 1979 Election Manifesto simply commented that "We shall take a complete review of all of the activities of the British National Oil Corporation as soon as we take office."

Meanwhile the shadow Cabinet was still far from united on economic policy. Michael Heseltine was the shadow Secretary of State for Trade and Industry and his action in seizing the mace in the House of Commons and brandishing it towards the Labour benches during a debate on the nationalisation of shipbuilding and aerospace was widely reported. However, Heseltine like some others in the shadow Cabinet did not share the extent of his leader's passion for reducing state intervention in the economy. In his autobiography he emphasises the gap between Thatcher and some of her colleagues, a gap that would continue into the early 1980s:

> "'Getting off people's backs', 'tearing up forms' and 'untying the red tape' are great rallying cries for audiences of small businessmen. And with much justification. But it's not the whole story. Where one comes face to face with major industrial sectors, dependent upon government for much of their development underpinning and procurement, engaged in the international search for market places in fierce competition with other similarly interdependent industries, a rather more realistic understanding of what the world is about rapidly sets in. Or that is how matters seemed to the shadow Secretary of State for Trade and Industry of the time – though evidently not to his more purist, fundamentalist leader."[112]

A particularly serious clash occurred between Heseltine and Thatcher at the time of the collapse of the country's main vehicle manufacturer British Leyland (BL). In 1974 the finances of BL were in a perilous state and the newly elected Labour Government instructed Sir Don Ryder to prepare a report. In March 1975 the report was delivered recommending that the company be saved through state ownership. The vast majority of BL's shares were then purchased by the Government and the Government appointed Ryder, who also became Chairman of the new National Enterprise Board (NEB), to vet all decisions regarding the running of the company. BL was Britain's only surviving large-scale, domestically-owned vehicle manufacturer and the closure of the company threatened large-scale redundancies, especially in the West Midlands. However, Thatcher preferred that BL be put into liquidation and pressed her shadow Secretary of State for Trade and Industry to pursue this line. Heseltine refused, believing that to advocate liquidation of BL would be political folly, especially as the West Midlands included many of the Parliamentary seats the Conservatives would need to win to achieve victory in the next general election. Heseltine prevailed, no doubt because Thatcher realised that her views were in a distinct minority within the shadow Cabinet and perhaps in the Party. Conservative MPs in the West Midlands welcomed the state rescue and even Sir Keith Joseph defended a £400 million loan to the company.[113] In November 1976 Heseltine was summarily demoted from Trade and Industry by Thatcher to become shadow Environment spokesman.[114]

The row between Heseltine and Thatcher over saving BL was a particularly acute example of differences that existed in the shadow Cabinet over economic policy in the second half of the 1970s. The Conservative leadership and Party were far from united around a monetarist and free market agenda,[115] albeit that tensions in the shadow Cabinet were usually suppressed by the desire to maintain unity to defeat Labour. Adam Ridley, who had been appointed to the new CPS from the Conservative Research Department, complained in July 1978 that "our programme of publications seems to be in a state of constant flux and some of the shadow Cabinet seem unaware of what is going on."[116] Penny Junor in her biography of Thatcher suggests that she believed she "was surrounded by mealy-mouthed moderates, who were so terrified of rocking the boat and losing support that they didn't have the guts to do what had to be done".[117]

Reality was more complex than this. Many in the Party remained loyal to the "one nation" concept of Conservatism, promoted by Heath in the two 1974 General Elections, and regarded the free market views of Joseph and others such as John Biffen and Nicholas Ridley as dangerous dogmatism. In the majority view the Conservative Party was fundamentally pragmatic in nature not dogmatic. A lurch to free markets and monetarism was viewed as an overly simplistic, overly ideological response to the country's economic problems, and one likely to lead to unacceptable levels of unemployment and social division. Such "one-nation" Toryism was represented in the shadow Cabinet by Jim Prior, Francis Pym and Norman St. John Stevas in particular, all of whom would have prominent roles in the 1979 Conservative Government.[118] Whatever Thatcher's true feelings, she understood the political necessity of maintaining Party unity.

The shadow Cabinet remained, therefore, up to the 1979 Election an uneasy coalition, which held together by reflecting differing views in the Conservative Party about the appropriate direction of economic policy.[119] Moreover, it is far from obvious that Thatcher herself was yet clear in 1979 about which policies to adopt. As the Party chairman, Lord Thorneycroft, commented around this time, Thatcher was "A complex compound of faith and caution".[120] Practical politics and the overwhelming desire to become Prime Minister continued to outweigh innate ideological convictions, just as her determination to remain a Government Minister had done during the earlier Heath administration. Hence the shadow Cabinet did not categorically drop the idea of using pay policies, which were a form of direct intervention in labour markets and which many saw as the root cause of the collapse of the Heath Government. Thatcher appears to have feared, like many of her colleagues including Howe, that completely abandoning the option of using pay policy would be seen by the electorate as leaving the Conservatives with nothing to confront union wage demands. The possibility that an electorate deeply disenchanted with a Labour Government might still vote

Labour, believing that it was the only political party able to tame the unions, haunted the Conservative leadership.[121] The differences of opinion between so-called "wets" (one-nation Tories) and "dries" (the monetarist evangelists) would spill over into conflict within Cabinet during the early months of the 1979 Conservative Government.

Moreover, the downplaying of prices and incomes policy as a means of tackling inflation probably owed as much to the belief that the Conservatives would be unable to negotiate an agreement with the unions as it did to the leadership's new fondness for monetarism. Joseph had recruited the two businessmen, John Hoskyns and Norman Strauss to assist the Party in revising its policies and they wrote an important Party document in 1977 called *Stepping Stones*. This argued for a gradual, staged approach to economic reform, but saw the success of a future Conservative Government as particularly dependent upon seeing off trade union opposition. Therefore, a central recommendation was the ending of the powers and privileges of the unions. However, up until the industrial disputes during the winter of 1978–79 which sealed the fate of the Labour Government, Conservative policy towards the unions remained extremely cautious.[122] The only legislation flagged involved taking powers to introduce postal ballots for union elections. In 1977 the so-called Grunwick Dispute, involving a film-reprocessing plant in London which refused to accept a closed shop agreement with the union, provoked ugly and violent scenes between pickets and police that infuriated the Conservative leadership. Nevertheless, not until the industrial anarchy during the winter of 1978–79 did more elements of the *Stepping Stones* document become Conservative Party policy.

Facing rising inflation, in July 1975 the Labour Government had abandoned its hostility to wage controls and had introduced yet another prices and incomes policy, starting with a universal pay rise limit of £6 per week and a freeze for those on incomes of over £8,500 a year. The policy went through various iterations or "stages" during the following years and in July 1978 a new stage was announced involving a limit of five per cent on pay rises unless justified by higher productivity. Serious industrial unrest followed during the winter of 1978–79, which became known as "the Winter of Discontent". It began with a short but successful strike at the Ford Motor Company that led to the award of wage increases ranging from 15 per cent to 17 per cent, well above the Government's five per cent limit. Then the road haulage drivers struck, demanding a 25 per cent pay rise and this dispute was followed by industrial action by oil tanker drivers. Public sector workers also waded in. Ambulance staff, school caretakers, refuse collectors, water workers and others struck for a £60 minimum wage. By mid-winter the industrial unrest was reaching crisis proportions with the non-treatment of hospital patients, uncollected refuse, and difficulties in arranging burials in Liverpool after the grave diggers struck. This action received particularly prominent media coverage. The press reported angry scenes of violence on picket lines and it seemed for a time that the unions were leading the country into chaos. On 22 January 1979 1.5 million workers joined a national Day of Action, leading to the biggest stoppage of workers since the 1926 General Strike.

The strikes damaged industrial production and caused much disruption. But the sustained impact of the Winter of Discontent was political rather than economic. Whereas in the autumn of 1978 Labour had been tipped to win a general election, the wave of industrial unrest condemned the Labour Government to defeat. Labour had staked its reputation on delivering moderate wage demands in return for government polices sympathetic to the working class, such as more spending on health and social services and employment laws that permitted most types of strike actions, under what was termed the "Social Contract" with the unions. The industrial chaos ended any remaining confidence in the existence of a preferential relationship between Labour and the trade unions. This was confirmed in the autumn by the Trades Union Congress (TUC) voting against a renewal of the "Social Contract" and the Labour Party Conference voting to reject all pay controls. Thatcher later acknowledged the importance of the Winter of Discontent to her subsequent election victory and in shaping her policies during the 1980s: "Appalling as the scenes of the winter of 1978/79 turned out to be, without them and without their exposure of the true nature of socialism, it would have been far more difficult to achieve what was done in the 1980s."[123]

In a television interview on 14 January 1979 Thatcher called on the PM to restore the authority of government and introduce, with all party agreement, a curb on the unions including an end to secondary picketing and secret ballots before strikes were called. The Labour Government chose to respond by conceding pay rises well above the pay limit of five per cent to bring the strikers back to work and negotiating a "Concordat" with the TUC to replace the Social Contract. Under the "Concordat" the union leadership agreed to provide a voluntary code of behaviour to deal with strikes, picketing, strike ballots and the closed shop. This won the Government some breathing space but few friends, and no one was under any illusion about the fragility of the new arrangement and the extent to which the Government had been publicly humiliated by the unions. Harris exaggerates a little when he says in his biography of Thatcher, "the public sector unions elected Mrs Thatcher to power in 1979"; but undoubtedly they greatly assisted.[124]

The Labour Government had been elected with a slender majority in October 1974 and from March 1977, after a series of by-election defeats, only a deal with the Liberal Party had kept the Government in power. In August 1978 the pact with the Liberals, the so-called "Lib-Lab pact", dissolved and the Government became reliant on support from Scottish and Welsh nationalist MPs. These MPs had their own agenda, to promote the devolution of powers to Scottish and Welsh parliaments with a view to eventual separation from England and "home rule". After the Scottish Nationalist MPs deserted the Government over its policy on devolution, on 28 March 1979 Labour lost a confidence vote in Parliament. A general election was called.

"Rolling back the frontiers of the state" was the title of paragraph 5 of the Conservatives' 1983 Campaign Guide dealing with the record of the Government between 1979 and 1983. It has come to symbolise the economic essence of Thatcherism. However, the 1979 Conservative Election Manifesto did not herald such a programme. In her Foreword to the Manifesto, Thatcher stated that the aim was to set out "a broad framework for the recovery of our country, based not on dogma, but on reason, on common sense, above all on the liberty of our people under the law".[125]The Manifesto was drafted by Adam Ridley and Chris Patten – Patten was on the moderate wing of the Party, Ridley, connected to the Centre for Policy Studies, was more radical – and edited by Angus Maude. Seldon and Collings correctly describe the Manifesto as being "high on general principle, but light on specific commitments."[126]

The Manifesto stressed five key tasks for a Conservative Government: "to restore the health of our economic and social life", "to restore incentives so that hard work pays", "to uphold Parliament and the rule of law", "to support family life" and "to strengthen Britain's defences". The measures to be taken against the unions had been reinforced as a result of the winter's strikes with new proposals to limit secondary picketing and to reform the closed shop,[127] alongside the earlier policy promise of postal ballots for union elections. There was also a commitment to cut income tax at all levels. But in a number of other policy areas the promises were much weaker. For example, on public spending the Manifesto promised to cut the expenditure of the hated National Enterprise Board and other "Socialist programmes"; beyond that the commitment was restricted to reducing "waste, bureaucracy and over-government" through unspecified reforms. Patrick Jenkin, the shadow Health Secretary, had earlier undertaken work on encouraging private health insurance and cutting the automatic link between pensions and earnings. Little of this found its way into the Party's Manifesto. Jenkin promised during the election campaign that Labour's planned increases in spending on the NHS would be honoured.[128]

The Manifesto did provide a commitment to give council house tenants a legal right to buy their homes at a discount and after 1979 the Government pursued this policy with gusto. The idea had first appeared as a proposal in the Conservative Party's October 1974 Election Manifesto and appears to have originated with Peter Walker.[129] Initially Walker seems to have wanted to transfer all council homes to their tenants free of charge. But transferring homes without charge was something that the shadow Cabinet considered a step too far.[130] Interestingly, Thatcher was suspicious at the outset of the whole idea of selling council homes at a discount. She feared that the policy would alienate "bedrock Conservative voters" who lived in privately-owned residences with mortgages and who would object to the Government's munificence.[131] But Walker eventually got his way. The sale of council homes would become one of the most popular policies of the first Thatcher administration.

In other respects the Manifesto was not dissimilar to the 1970 Manifesto.[132] As Jim Prior, a Minister in the first Thatcher Government, has since commented: "Our commitments made in the 1979 manifesto were not all that different from those made in 1970. In fact, the 1979 manifesto was reassuringly moderate in content and tone . . .".[133] Another leading Conservative, Lord Hailsham, has observed similarly that: "We fought, and won, the 1979 election on virtually the same platform as that which had carried Edward Heath to victory in 1970. Those who talk about Thatcherism and suggest that Margaret Thatcher revolutionized the thinking or ideology (if there is one) of the Conservative Party should, I believe, ponder this fact."[134] In 1979 the Conservatives fought the General Election on a platform of sound money, trade union reform and income tax cuts. These objectives were not far removed from those of former Conservative Governments.

The Manifesto's commitments on denationalisation were particularly limited. A volume published in 1976 on *The Conservative Opportunity* had reviewed the problems in the nationalised sector including low profitability, high pay rises and overmanning, but surprisingly had concluded that these results were "not attributable to nationalisation as such".[135] In the same volume John Redwood, who would after 1979 become a firebrand for privatisation within the Party and No.10, had simply recommended that "the nationalised industries should be left to their own devices in running the services awarded to them" and that dismantling the state monopolies would involve "too much upheaval".[136] In 1978 Aims, the free enterprise organisation, had called for "the State to withdraw from direct participation in business and commerce".[137] But when an updated version of the earlier Ridley report was leaked to *The Economist* in May 1978, it was immediately disowned by the Conservative leadership. Sir Keith Joseph had asked Ridley to lead a small group to look at denationalisation, although Ridley later noted that at the time he had been sceptical, "I told him that I had done this once before for Ted Heath and that nothing had happened." Although Joseph replied that it would be different this time, Ridley was unsure whether to believe him. Moreover, Ridley did not suppose that a Conservative Government would implement such a programme.[138] The report did go to the Party's Economic Reconstruction Committee, but it had little impact and was quietly shelved.

Nigel Lawson states in his memoirs that he and colleagues such as Joseph, Howe, John Nott and David Howell did see privatisation as an important part of the economic policies of a future Conservative government in 1979.[139] However, this was not the Party's official position. An internal Party Campaign Guide for Parliamentary candidates included criticism of the performance of the nationalised industries and especially the taking into public ownership of aerospace and shipbuilding, but little else.[140] Certainly, as we have seen, the Party's economic policy documents of 1976 and 1977 had been somewhat circumspect on the future of state industries and the election Manifesto shunned any radicalism on ownership. The term privatisation was not used in the Manifesto and nor was the word "denationalisation." The Manifesto simply repeated the Party's commitment to "offer to sell back to private ownership the recently nationalised aerospace and shipbuilding concerns, giving their employees the opportunity to purchase shares", to dispose of the National Freight Corporation, "restrict the powers of the National Enterprise Board", amend the 1975 Industry Act, and promote private bus services. Apart from this, the nationalised industries would be expected to raise their productivity and would be given "a clearer financial discipline in which to work" and there would be less government interference in their management. The emphasis was on avoiding ploughing even more public funding into the nationalised industries. A number of former Ministers in this first Thatcher Government have confirmed that there was still much uncertainty within the Party leadership in 1979 about the public's likely response to privatisation and this restricted the extent to which the policy was championed publicly. But even if this had not been the case, they stress there could not have been a longer shopping list of privatisations in the Manifesto. It was important first to get into government to establish what could be achieved.

The Conservatives' advertising campaign in 1979 is best remembered for the Saatchi and Saatchi agency's "Labour isn't working" poster with its picture of a long dole queue. The election was fought on the economic record of the Labour Government rather than on the policies that might be introduced by a Conservative administration, which the electorate probably did not expect to be much different from those under Callaghan and Heath. The campaign built on a public sentiment following the Winter of Discontent that Labour had deserted the common man and that there was a need for change. During the election Thatcher portrayed herself as both a "conviction politician" and an "ordinary housewife", all rolled into one. She promoted herself as a working mum with the normal concerns of a housewife about the cost of the weekly shop. This was quite an achievement given her atypically wealthy circumstances, but it was an image sustained by the press, much of which was deeply disillusioned with Labour.

At a press conference the day before the voters went to the poll Thatcher commented: "We entered the campaign very much with the theme it is time for change. We have not swerved from that theme."[141] Nevertheless, throughout the election campaign Thatcher voiced moderation as far as state ownership was concerned so as to avoid alienating voters especially in key marginal seats; for example, she agreed that industrial subsidies to British Leyland should not be suddenly ended, in spite of her earlier opposition to bailing out BL.[142] When in March 1978 Howe had suggested that a Conservative Government might sell some of its shareholding in BP, repeating the share sale undertaken by Labour the previous year to raise funds for the Exchequer, Thatcher had firmly denied any such intention.[143] She again strenuously repudiated any such intention the day before voting.[144] Thatcher harboured concerns that selling shares in BP would reduce government control over the energy sector at a time of great difficulties in the world energy market. This would continue during her first months as Prime Minister.[145]

The General Election was held on 3 May 1979 and the Conservatives achieved a majority of 70 seats over Labour and 43 seats over the other parties combined. The election produced the largest voting swing in British post-war elections up to that time, of 5.2 per cent nationally and 7.7 per cent in the South of the country. The swing was a more modest but no less significant 4.2 per cent in the North, where much of the country's heavy industry was situated. The Conservative victory owed much to a desertion of Labour by those voters Labour could usually rely upon. Labour managed to win only a half of the votes of trade unionists and 45 per cent of the working class vote. The swing to the Conservatives amongst unskilled workers was 9 per cent and amongst skilled workers even larger, at 11.5 per cent.

\* \* \*

In her first speech in Parliament after the Election Mrs Thatcher called the results a watershed. *The Economist* concluded that "the British people have voted for change" and the left-leaning *New Statesman* that the election was "not a defeat, a disaster".[146] However, it was unclear both in the country and the Conservative Party what the arrival of the new Government would really mean. As one commentator has observed, "neither the majority of the electorate nor the majority of the Cabinet quite knew what they were letting themselves in for."[147] In particular, it was by no means clear that there was a mandate for wide economic reform.[148] The Conservatives' share of the vote, at 43.9 per cent, was the lowest percentage support for any post-war government with the exception of the elections of 1974. As a detailed analysis of the election later showed, the result was more down to the discredited Labour Government than to widespread public support for the Conservatives' policies.[149]

Conservative Party policy under Thatcher's leadership from 1975 had taken on a more free market flavour with an emphasis on monetarism, lower taxes and lower public spending, but there was still much uncertainty about what Conservative policy would actually be when elected.[150] Thatcher was nervous about the possible public reaction to denationalisation and the subject had barely surfaced as an issue in the general election campaign. She was also, understandably, particularly worried about the possible response of the trade unions. The unions had brought down the Conservative Government in 1974 and had now fatally damaged the chances of the re-election of a Labour Government. Would it be possible to denationalise a major industry if the unions opposed it? Also, one of her leading free market Ministers in the 1980s, Nicholas Ridley, concedes that even the policies of the new Government that had been agreed were not well thought out, despite the work of research organisations, numerous study groups and policy committees, established when in Opposition: "Thus, the full nature of 'Thatcherism' was not known to the electorate in 1979. Nor was it fully understood within the parliamentary party."[151] This was certainly true of what came to be known as "privatisation". Few expected that Thatcher would prove to be as radical in government as she had sometimes seemed in Opposition. Many simply saw her as an infuser of traditional Conservative values with new fervour. In particular, there was no serious expectation that the new Prime Minister would oversee the almost entire dismantling of nationalisation in Britain – which she did.

# 3

# BALANCING THE BOOKS

## Privatisation and the 1979–83 Government

In a speech in Paris on 15 December 1988 the Chancellor of the Exchequer, Nigel Lawson, commented on the UK's privatisation experience that while the techniques and methods of privatisation had changed during the 1980s to reflect the different types of businesses privatised, the objective had remained the same, namely "to improve the industry's efficiency and its service to the customer". By contrast, he stated, "The money that is raised, while useful, has always been a second-order question."[1]

That the money raised was of secondary importance may have been true by 1988, but especially in the first two to three years of the new Conservative Government the pressure to meet the public sector borrowing requirement (PSBR) targets set by the Chancellor dominated much of the thinking within the Treasury and to a degree within the Government as a whole. In 1980 the "Medium Term Financial Strategy" (MTFS) was published, which confirmed that control of the money supply was the keystone of the Government's policy to control inflation. Although there is no necessary link between the PSBR and a growth in the money supply, because the critical factor is how the PSBR is financed, the Treasury feared that high government borrowing would lead to faster monetary growth and therefore higher prices. The priority, therefore, was to find a means of holding down the PSBR at a time when it was threatening to rise quickly due to the economic recession triggered by higher oil prices and public sector wage demands resulting from the Clegg awards. The Labour Government had established the Clegg Commission to enquire into public sector pay in an endeavour to placate the unions during the "Winter of Discontent". During the election campaign Margaret Thatcher agreed to comply with its findings – a decision she and her Treasury Ministers would soon regret.[2] In May 1979 inflation was around ten per cent, two years later it had doubled, standing at 21.9 per cent. Meanwhile, between 1979 and 1981 real GDP fell by 3.6 per cent and manufacturing output by some 14 per cent. The sale of state assets or what became known as privatisation, offered a means of closing the gap between government spending and taxation without having to raise taxes further. Even so, this Government elected on a tax cutting agenda saw taxation as a percentage of GDP rise from around 36 per cent in 1979/80 to 40 per cent in 1982/3 and taxation rose as a proportion of earnings.[3] Public expenditure as a share of GDP also increased and the Government struggled to keep a cap on the PSBR in its first two years in office, as the figures in Tables 3.1 and 3.2 confirm.

The convention in British public sector accounting was to treat privatisation receipts as a reduction in the total of public spending. This chapter discusses how the idea of privatisation evolved within the Government after May 1979. It establishes the economic context and especially the macroeconomic difficulties that faced the first Thatcher Government and which

*Table 3.1* Income tax and National Insurance contributions as a percentage of gross earnings 1979/80 and 1982/3

| Taxation as a percentage of: | Half average earnings | Average earnings | Twice average earnings |
|---|---|---|---|
| 1979/80 | 16.4 | 28.0 | 31.6 |
| 1981/2 | 21.1 | 29.4 | 32.4 |
| 1982/3 (forecast) | 21.3 | 30.0 | 32.5 |

*Source*: C(83)5, "Economic Strategy Memorandum by the Chancellor of the Exchequer", 1 February 1983.

*Table 3.2* Public expenditure, taxation and the PSBR 1979/80 to 1982/3

| | % GDP | | | |
|---|---|---|---|---|
| | *1979/80* | *1980/1* | *1981/2* | *1982/3* |
| Public expenditure | 41 | 43 | 44.5 | 44 |
| Taxation (including NIC) | 36 | 37.5 | 40.5 | 40 |
| PSBR | 5 | 6 | 4 | 3 |

*Note*: NIC = National Insurance (social security) contributions.
*Source*: C(83)5.

played an important part in pushing privatisation up the list of the Government's priorities. It considers the time sequence for the development of the overall policy and discusses the main issues and problems that arose. Details of each of the important privatisations during the first Thatcher Government is left over to the following three chapters.

## The first hesitant steps

The extent to which a Conservative Government under Margaret Thatcher's leadership would pursue a privatisation programme had been unclear both before and during the general election campaign. The Manifesto commitments were limited in scope and the composition of the new Cabinet was such that those who might have been expected to be keen, notably Joseph, Howe and Thatcher herself,[4] were counterbalanced by those who could be expected to adopt a more cautious approach, perhaps adopting even a sceptical stance, such as Walker, St. John-Stevas, Gilmour and Prior. Indeed, until a Ministerial reshuffle in September 1981, within the Cabinet the economic doves outnumbered the economic hawks.[5] Nigel Lawson, who joined the Cabinet as a result of this reshuffle, suggests in his memoirs that privatisation was policy in May 1979, but at the same time acknowledges "that little detailed work had been done on the subject in Opposition". He also comments that Thatcher had reservations, notably her "understandable fear of frightening the floating voter".[6] However, most other Ministers in the first Thatcher Government disagree and argue that large-scale privatisation was not policy when the Government was elected.[7] Addressing the perilous state of the economy and the power of the trade unions were more obvious priorities for Government in May 1979 than the ownership of nationalised industries. The Conservative Party was ideologically committed to private enterprise, but in 1979 it was not committed to widespread

53

denationalisation. Dossiers drawn up within the Conservative Party for Ministers entering their departments made little or no mention of possible denationalisation. The Treasury dossier was concerned with improving the financial controls over the nationalised industries. The Transport dossier mentioned a "partial" denationalisation of the National Freight Corporation but only once the enterprise was returned to profitability. Legislation to sell off the Corporation was considered not to be an immediate priority.[8]

The Conservatives' 1979 Election Manifesto had committed the Party to the denationalisation of aerospace and shipbuilding nationalised by the Labour Government in 1977, introducing private capital into the National Freight Corporation, winding down the National Enterprise Board and some liberalisation of bus transport – but nothing more. In addition, in the Queen's Speech on the Opening of Parliament there was only a passing reference to denationalisation. The emphasis was on bringing forward proposals "to amend the Industry Act 1975 and to restrict the activities of the National Enterprise Board", along with an indistinct reference to reducing public ownership "by providing opportunities for members of the public and employees to participate through the purchase of shares". [9] Other relevant proposals included the promise of measures to assist the purchase by local authority and new town tenants of their homes. There was no commitment to an extensive programme of what became known later as "privatisation".

However, from the first days in office, government departments were put under pressure by the Treasury to sell assets to help "balance the books". From May 1979 the determination of Treasury Ministers to improve the public finances and bring down the PSBR led to privatisation becoming a policy priority when otherwise there might have been insufficient interest within the Cabinet. The first use of the term "privatisation" by the new Government may have been in Cabinet Sub-Committee on 20 June and then 4 October 1979.[10] But in the early months of the new Government the terms "disposals" and "special asset sales" were more commonly used. The Prime Minister appears to have used the term privatisation publicly for the first time in July 1981.[11]

Within days of the election victory the Government discussed the possibility of asset disposals. In a paper to the Cabinet, the Chief Secretary to the Treasury, John Biffen, outlined possible savings in public spending totalling £750 million to £800 million in the current financial year. This was felt to be insufficient to keep the PSBR under control.[12] He therefore made it clear that "we need to look also at the possibility of selling off assets to reduce the borrowing requirement".[13] He announced that the Treasury was planning to raise £750 million to £1 billion from disposals that year. Early candidates for sale that the Treasury identified were surplus public sector land, council houses, oilfield assets of the BNOC and BP shares. The sale of some of the Government's shareholding in BP would repeat a step undertaken by Labour in 1977 to raise cash following the exchange rate crisis that led to IMF intervention. The sale of council houses fulfilled a Manifesto commitment and the Conservatives had opposed the setting up of BNOC in 1975. The disposal of surplus land was something governments did as a matter of routine, although the Chief Secretary was signalling that the pace of sales ought to rise. Interestingly, a sale of BP shares had been ruled out by Thatcher both before and during the election campaign (see chapter 2, p.50). There is no evidence, however, that at this time she attempted to block the proposal, probably because there were no obvious alternative disposals on offer. The PM would, nonetheless, continue to worry about the effect of selling oil assets on security of supplies in Britain at a time of world oil shortages. These concerns would surface from time to time over the following months.

The PM found the expenditure savings proposed by Treasury Ministers disappointing and sent them back to the Treasury to find at least another £500–600 million in cuts.[14] The Financial Secretary, Nigel Lawson, followed this up with a letter asking Departments to identify assets for disposal. He also requested that any approaches from financial institutions to help with sales should be co-ordinated through the Treasury. Although the bulk of the work on each privatisation would be undertaken by the sponsoring department (the department responsible for the nationalised industry), from as early as 23 May 1979 the Treasury put down a marker that it should be in overall control of the privatisation programme.[15] The aim was to ensure that financial targets were met and that disposals were staggered so as not to put an undue strain on the financial markets. Any stretching of the capacity of the financial markets could have serious consequences for the sales of government debt in particular. Also, in these early days of the Government there was uncertainty about the legality of selling state assets in the absence of enabling legislation. There was some discussion about introducing "an omnibus Bill" to provide the necessary legal authority.[16] However, the Government concluded that each sale would need its own special measures. Like nationalisation before it, privatisation in Britain would occur mainly using separate, dedicated legislation for each enterprise, except, exceptionally, where Ministers were confident that they already had the necessary legal powers to sell assets.

On 31 May 1979 the Cabinet agreed to cuts in public spending of £1.365 billion and asset sales of £1.2 billion for the current financial year.[17] The Treasury had gone some way towards meeting the PM's request for bigger spending cuts and a more ambitious sales target. The disposals target had been raised by £200 million on the maximum figure suggested two weeks earlier. A half of the new targeted amount would come from selling part of the Government's holding of BP shares and £500 million from the disposal of oil assets held by BNOC and also by the British Gas Corporation (BGC). The remaining £100 million would come from a sale of NEB shareholdings in various enterprises built up since the 1975 Industry Act.[18] Lawson confirmed that in his view this sum could be achieved without the passage of special legislation, which would have delayed progress. Later this would prove to be partially mistaken. Over the following weeks the Government found that it had adequate legal powers to sell government land and buildings, but usually could only ensure the sale of the assets of a nationalised industry when the industry's board agreed to sell, unless the Minister took the draconian, and perhaps politically embarrassing, decision to issue the board with a Direction.[19] At this meeting it was agreed to couple asset sales with a commitment to widening property ownership. In Opposition the Chancellor of the Exchequer, Sir Geoffrey Howe, had been a leading proponent of using denationalisation to spread share ownership. His aim met with general approval; the Cabinet agreed that assets should be disposed of "in such a way which would secure the widest possible spread of ownership". In an interesting portent of things to come, it was suggested that in due course this might occur through the creation of equity interests in some of the nationalised industries.[20]

Economic matters were sometimes discussed in meetings of the full Cabinet, especially at the final decision stage, but otherwise much of the debate went on in Cabinet committee. There were two committees particularly concerned with the disposals programme: the Cabinet Ministerial Committee on Economic Strategy, known as "E" Committee (later, in June 1983, this Committee would be renamed "E(A)" Committee[21]) and its Sub-Committee on Disposals, labelled E(DL).[22] E Committee would normally be chaired by the PM and E(DL) by the Chancellor of the Exchequer (for a time during the first Conservative Government E(DL) was chaired by the Secretary of State for Industry, Sir Keith Joseph).

The brief of E(DL) was "to consider the whole question of the disposal of public sector assets and to keep the operation under regular review". Its creation was early confirmation of the importance that the new Government attached to the disposal of state property, although not at this time necessarily the sale of major nationalised industries.[23]

The first meeting of E Committee on 14 May 1979 abolished the Price Commission, established by the previous Labour administration to police its ill-fated prices and incomes policy.[24] The Conservatives had made clear their opposition to government control of prices and incomes both before and during the election campaign. However, this was not intended to signal a free-for-all on wages. Alarmed by the prospect of higher inflation and a repeat of the Heath Government's slide into prices and incomes policy and confrontation with the unions, on 17 July the Committee imposed tight cash limits on the public sector to hold down Government expenditure and pay rises. Although there was to be no state intervention in wage settlements in the private sector, the Government was sending a clear signal that there should be no expectation of large wage increases in the public services including the nationalised industries.[25] In September it was agreed that "cash limits" introduced for Government expenditure generally by Labour in July 1976, would continue to control the level of permitted annual borrowing by the nationalised industries and when set as a negative figure would require a net repayment of borrowings to the Exchequer. These limits, known as External Financing Limits (EFLs), would be announced ahead of the start of the annual pay negotiations.[26] If public sector unions then insisted on demanding larger pay rises, they would have to accept the consequence of lost jobs.

Important to the Government's macroeconomic strategy was controlling the power of the trade unions. The Heath Government had been brought down by the National Union of Mineworkers and the new Conservative Government, and especially the Prime Minister, lived in persistent fear of a repeat of this experience. At least for those nationalised industries that were not monopolies, it was felt that "a cash limit with a required rate of return on capital should provide an adequate discipline" during wage negotiations.[27] However, for the state monopolies the unions would always be mindful that higher wage costs could be passed on to customers in higher prices. The Government concluded, therefore, that union power could only be effectively addressed by removing, wherever possible, the industries' monopolies.[28] However, at this stage there was no clarity on how to bring this about.

In September 1979 the EFLs were set on the basis that labour costs per unit of output should rise by less than inflation, as represented by the retail price index (RPI). This implied a tight squeeze on the nationalised industries' finances, especially since the trade unions were unlikely to concede a reduction in the real wages of their members.[29] Alternatively, the EFLs implied that if the industries agreed wage rises over and above the current inflation rate, they would have to compensate for this through increasing productivity. However, there was the equal and real possibility that the industries would simply divert funding intended for investment into financing pay.[30] Whatever the outcome, it was clear that the nationalised industries faced a difficult future. The struggle to protect capital investment in the industries at a time of high pay settlements became an enduring challenge to Government throughout the first Conservative administration. It played no small part in reinforcing opposition within the Cabinet to nationalisation. If the industries were privatised they would have free access to the external capital market. This advantage also proved influential amongst the senior management of the nationalised industries, many of whom proved lukewarm at first to the prospect of their industries being sold off, but who became increasingly frustrated by what they saw as an artificial borrowing constraint imposed on their investment programmes.

In spite of agreement in Cabinet to the Chancellor's targets for asset sales, during the first meeting of E(DL) Sub-Committee on 5 June 1979 it became clear that reaching the target would prove difficult. It was one thing for the Treasury to set a target, it was quite another to get spending departments to deliver. The Chancellor had identified the sale of oil assets as the primary candidate for raising cash, but at this meeting the Secretary of State for Energy, David Howell, pointed to a number of difficulties he and his officials had identified. While it was agreed that the sale of shares in BP, which were held by the Treasury, should not raise any particular problems, the sale of BGC's oil interests was quite another matter. In preliminary discussions, Sir Denis Rooke, Chairman of BGC, had made it patently clear that in his view the oil interests were essential to the Corporation's ability to supply gas in the medium to longer term. The Board would vigorously oppose any attempt to dispose of them. Howell's conclusion, therefore, was that there could be no guarantee that the sale of any of BGC's oil assets would go through in the current financial year, as Treasury Ministers had intended. To help meet the Chancellor's financial target, he reported that Sir Denis "had offered to find politically acceptable savings" of £100 million in the operations of the Corporation if the Government withdrew the proposal for the sale of its oil assets.[31] Understandably, this suggestion led to some consternation. The offer suggested that the Corporation wished to bargain with the Government.

On the disposal of BNOC assets, Howell reported that this was more straightforward. The required sum of £300 million could be raised by selling the Corporation's stake in the Ninian field in the North Sea. However, once again he disappointed by stating that there could be no guarantee that the sale would be completed in the current financial year because it would take time to organise. Instead, Howell suggested that the Government might consider raising funds by bringing forward Exchequer receipts from BNOC's oil royalties.[32] Other possibilities for the quick raising of cash offered by the Department of Energy included obtaining more oil-related revenues by having a further round of exploration licences or by arranging for BNOC to sell off some of its existing exploration rights.

At the second meeting of E(DL), on 20 June, the possible disposal of BNOC and BGC oil interests dominated the agenda. At this meeting Howell defended his position by arguing that there was "a balance to be struck between on the one hand the desirability of early sales, and on the other the need for security of oil supplies . . . and of leaving BNOC with enough assets to make a success of privatisation at a later date". By avoiding dismembering of the Corporation now, the Government would achieve larger sale receipts in the long run: "the price which might be obtained for them now, on what would inevitably be a cautious assess-ment of their worth, might be well below their current value in two or three years' time."[33] This became the Secretary of State's consistent position over the next few months for both the oil assets of BNOC and BGC, and one that the Treasury could not accept. It was clear already that the Chancellor's ambition to raise substantial amounts from selling the oil assets of BNOC and BGC in the current financial year was at serious risk.

Progress with the sale of the NEB's investments also proved slow. The Secretary of State for Industry, Sir Keith Joseph, was the Government's champion of free market economics and arrived at the Department of Industry with an impressive reading list of 29 works by free market thinkers for his officials to read. But on a number of occasions at the Department of Industry, Joseph would find his ideological preferences compromised by the realities of running a major department of state responsible for large sectors of the economy and many jobs.[34] For example, in the spring of 1980 he submitted a memo on the high-tech company Inmos which had been promised £50 million in aid by Labour. The first £25 million had been paid and Joseph canvassed making a further payment. It is said that the paper was returned by the PM with a handwritten note saying "Really, Keith!"[35] During his first two years as Secretary of State for Industry his department's spending rose by 50 per cent.[36] In September 1982 he was moved to arguably a less challenging role as Secretary of State for Education.[37]

When in Opposition, Joseph had been particularly critical of the 1975 Industry Act and especially the creation of the NEB, which, like many in his Party, he equated with creeping nationalisation. Nevertheless, at the first meeting of E(DL) he reported that the figure of £100 million proposed for NEB disposals in the current year by the Treasury might not be met.[38] He believed that the Chairman of the NEB, Sir Leslie Murphy, would oppose large-scale sales and might argue that they were incompatible with the NEB's statutory duty. Therefore, the Government would have to take new statutory powers. While Joseph offered to include powers to force through sales in a new Industry Bill that he was planning to introduce in the November to amend Labour's Industry Act, awaiting passage of the Bill would delay any disposals. He had come to the conclusion that the best way forward might be to replace the NEB Chairman but again this would take time. In November a new chairman was appointed, Sir Leslie Knight, after resignations from the NEB following a decision on the ownership of Rolls-Royce. Rolls-Royce was removed from the NEB and put under the direct supervision of the Department of Industry without any discussion with the Board.[39] Later British Leyland (BL) was also transferred from the NEB to the Department of Industry. But these changes did not produce a disposal of NEB assets to the private sector in the 1979/80 financial year. The reason Rolls-Royce, along with BL, was transferred from the NEB to the Department of Industry, was partly the Government's hostility towards the NEB and an early desire to cut it down to size and partly the desire of the management of these enterprises to have more independence of decision making outside the umbrella of the NEB. At the time there was no serious prospect of privatising either firm in the short to medium term. BL was making large losses. Rolls-Royce was a more realistic candidate for the introduction of private capital in some form, but any change would need careful planning given the importance of the company to national defence. Only when the company's position strengthened in the mid-1980s did privatisation become a reality.

In his first Budget on 12 June 1979, the Chancellor cut the top rate of tax from 83 per cent to 60 per cent and announced a higher threshold for investment income taxation and a cut in Development Land Tax. However, the Government's finances were such that there was precious little room for overall tax reductions. In compensation, VAT was raised to 15 per cent, there were some other tax rises and prescription charges were also increased. Public spending was cut by £3.5 billion and an ambitious programme for the progressive reduction in public expenditure to 1983/4 was announced. The Budget also confirmed the target for asset sales in the current year would be £1 billion, slightly down on the figure contemplated in Cabinet on 31 May. The Chancellor commented "that the scope for the sale of assets is substantial" but was coy in his Budget speech about how this sum would be raised: "So far as this year's disposals are concerned, we must obviously retain flexibility on timing and on the precise mix of assets in order to ensure a fair price. I do not, therefore, propose to announce the details today."[40] But it later became clear that the arithmetic involved raising £650 million from the disposal of shares in BP, £30 million from land and property disposals, £200 million plus from sales of BNOC's or BGC's oil interests, and some £100 million for the sale of NEB holdings. The bracketing together of BNOC's and BGC's oil interests and the sharp reduction in the total amount to be raised from these sources compared to the figure discussed earlier in Cabinet, was almost certainly a response to the Secretary of State for

Energy's concerns about his ability to force through disposals in the face of opposition from the Corporations. Even so, of the disposals mentioned, a reduction in the Government's shareholding in BP and modest land and building sales were the only ones that seemed a safe prospect, bearing in mind also Joseph's reservations about achieving the NEB disposals target.[41] This was concealed during the Budget debate.

The motivation for selling BP shares was clearly financial, as it had been in 1977 when the Government's holding had been reduced from 68.3 per cent of the company's issued share capital to 51 per cent. Around the time of the Budget, David Hunter of the City firm L. Messel & Co wrote to the Chancellor suggesting that he should consider the use of a ten year convertible bond rather than a direct equity sale for a company such as BP. His argument was that a large share sale would deflate the share price and reduce the proceeds. The suggestion received short shrift from the Chancellor, on the grounds that the use of convertible bonds would contribute to financing of the PSBR but would not reduce it.[42] Also at this time, there was no attempt to suggest that selling the Government's shareholding in BP would make the company more efficient. BP had always operated at arm's length from government and was profitable. In the first months of the new Government, reducing the PSBR and widening the ownership of industry were the two main reasons given for privatisation. For example, both the financial and widening property ownership objectives were referred to in the Chancellor's Budget speech and in a memorandum to E(DL) Sub-Committee on 18 June 1979 by Lawson.[43] Also, on 17 July Lawson had responded to a request from Howell for more clarity on the objectives by stating that they were those consistent with the principles set down by the Chancellor in his Budget speech, namely helping to reduce the PSBR and promoting wider share ownership. The reliance on private finance to "strengthen market discipline" was mentioned as simply a further objective.[44] In his memoirs Howe acknowledges that the need to rein back public expenditure, "gave an early and non-doctrinaire shove to the privatization process".[45] Kenneth Baker, a Minister of State at the Department of Trade who was involved in managing the sale of Cable and Wireless and the later planning of the disposal of British Telecom, comments in his memoirs: "In all the talks I had with Treasury Ministers the only thing they were interested in was the proceeds that would go to the Exchequer."[46]

Nor was it apparent at this early stage in the life of the new Government that privatisation would develop into a major economic strategy. When, following a meeting on the Government's economic plans, Ministers were asked to send in individual lists of desirable policy initiatives that should be undertaken, the replies included suggestions to improve labour skills, work incentives and labour relations, the case for a stronger competition policy, and fiscal reform to promote investment. There were few suggestions relating to state enterprises and no suggestion that a major programme of denationalisation should be pursued.[47]

On 19 June 1979 the Financial Secretary asked Ministers for details of the likely proceeds from the sale of businesses and property and an indication of any changes in the law that would be needed to bring them about. The Treasury was already beginning to assess the prospects for asset sales in the following as well as the current financial year.[48] The replies from departments mentioned a hotchpotch of possible small sales of land and buildings but major disposals of only two state enterprises were included, British Airways (BA) and the British Steel Corporation (BSC), and then only in the next financial year, 1980/1. The catalyst in the case of BA was the Corporation's forecast that it would need £1 billion in new financing for aircraft purchases.[49] British Airways also featured because the Secretary of State for Trade, John Nott, favoured denationalisation as a solution to the airline's financial problems. However, Nott's intention at the time was for the Department of Trade to retain at least a

51 per cent shareholding in BA, while agreeing not to involve itself in the operations of the company.[50] A majority or complete sale of the airline was considered a step too far, removing the Government's power to veto major strategic decisions relating to the future of the airline. Also, in these early weeks of the new Government there was a lack of clarity about what size of private sector shareholding would be needed to change the classification of a company from the public to the private sector, especially for PSBR purposes.[51] A sale of BA shares was authorised under the Civil Aviation Bill 1980 and the Corporation was keen to be transferred to the private sector as soon as possible, but the subsequent recession in airline travel, and later a legal dispute involving the collapsed competitor Laker airways, meant that the privatisation of BA would not occur until February 1987 (for more details see chapter 9, p.196). The delay in selling BSC proved to be even longer, with the sale not occurring until 1988. In both cases deteriorating revenues and rising costs during the early 1980s economic recession meant that the prospects for an early sale quickly receded.

## The search for assets to sell

With an early division having opened up between the Secretary of State for Energy and Treasury Ministers over the fast sale of oil assets and uncertainty over other asset sales, a meeting of E(DL) in July 1979 was chaired by the PM in an attempt to find a way forward. The Sub-Committee had before it a memorandum from the Financial Secretary detailing the options to achieve the Chancellor's target, as well as submissions from the Secretary of State for Energy on future arrangements for state involvement in the oil industry. By now the merits of an early sale of BP shares was also being questioned, on the grounds that this disposal might be worth more if undertaken later.[52]

During the summer discussion continued within the Government on how best to achieve the Chancellor's planned disposals of £1 billion in the current financial year. The possible disposal of NEB assets continued to be a source of friction between Treasury Ministers and the Secretary of State for Industry. On 12 June 1979 Joseph wrote to Lawson suggesting that the Government should treat each of the NEB sales "on its merits" and that each disposal would need to be carefully planned and should not be rushed.[53] It was evident that disposals from the NEB's portfolio would not make up for any delay in selling oil assets.

A memorandum by the Financial Secretary in July, reviewing progress in achieving the disposals target, mentioned that the PM was cautious about an early large sale of BP stock.[54] It seems that the PM's concerns at the time of the election about the selling of BP shares when there was an international oil shortage had now resurfaced. More encouraging was evidence that the Department of Industry might be able to raise £100 million from the NEB holdings after all. It also seemed that £30 million might be raised from the disposal of surplus land and buildings and £20 million or more from the sale of the Government's share holding in the Suez Finance Company, although the timing of this could not be guaranteed.[55] Other assets that were now under active consideration for disposal included New Town properties, the Government's shares in the British Sugar Corporation[56] and an office block at Nine Elms owned by the Covent Garden Market Authority. Lawson was hopeful that together these sales might produce up to £180 million.

To make up for some of the expected financial shortfall, Lawson concluded that it would be necessary to bring forward into the 1979/80 financial year disposals that had so far been under consideration within departments to meet the sales target for 1980/81.[57] The sales target for that year had now been set at £500 million in 1979 prices or £630 million in cash terms, only a half of the level for 1979/80. This was testimony in itself to the difficulties the Government was already facing in finding an adequate number of candidates for disposal. The asset sales that might be brought forward, Lawson suggested, included selling shares in Cable and Wireless (C&W), British Aerospace (BAe) and BA. But in all of these three cases legislation would be needed, although he had been advised that this might not be necessary if the disposals were limited to some of the enterprises' subsidiary activities.[58] To sidestep the delay that would inevitably be caused by waiting for the passage of new legislation, particular consideration was given to hiving off and selling BAe's profitable Dynamics Group concerned with the production of guided weapons. However, in all of the nationalised industries, including BAe, it was expected that the boards would oppose the dismemberment of their empires.

One other possible sale that surfaced early on was the Atomic Energy Authority's subsidiary, The Radio Chemical Centre Ltd (TRC) – later renamed Amersham International. TRC produced radio chemical products for health and other sectors. The Department of Energy felt that there might be no need for special legislation to effect the sale of this enterprise if only 49 per cent or less of the company was sold. However, the Treasury concluded that where the Government retained a majority holding this could mean that the borrowings of the companies would remain part of the PSBR because the Government would still be seen to control the business. As the Treasury's objective was to remove industries' borrowings from the PSBR this would not be a satisfactory outcome. Lawson erred on the safe side and was against the Government retaining any share holding in TRC.[59] The desire to ensure the removal of an industry's borrowings from the PSBR would be an enduring consideration during the planning of all industry privatisations.

Another candidate for early privatisation was the National Freight Corporation (NFC). The denationalisation of NFC had been promised at the election, but it was by now clear that a sale would need careful planning and legislation and was most unlikely to contribute funds to the Exchequer during the current financial year. Another option that had begun to be considered within the Department of Transport involved putting pressure on British Rail (BR) to dispose of surplus land and sell its ferry operation, Sealink, and some of its hotels. However, the Department was aware that such proposals were likely to be strongly resisted by the BR Board, and also by the rail unions.[60] Primary legislation might be required, especially if the Board opposed selling. In mid-July questions were raised about the precise legal position should the Minister intervene and require asset sales in the face of opposition from the boards of public corporations.[61] In any event, the Department of Transport did not hold out much hope that the amounts raised from sales, even if achievable, would contribute much to the Chancellor's disposals target.

In the face of all of this disappointing news the Treasury's pressure on departments to find candidates for disposal intensified. An early Treasury initiative involved departments identifying surplus land and buildings that might be sold off quickly. The sale of land and buildings was a relatively soft target unlikely to arouse fierce opposition. The idea won the strong backing of the PM after a meeting with the economist Gordon Pepper, then a partner in the stockbroking firm of W. Greenwell, who proposed it to her, especially the sale of New Town properties.[62] In subsequent months the Financial Secretary, Nigel Lawson, took this initiative under his wing as part of his responsibility for co-ordinating public sector asset sales.

In a letter of 4 June 1979 Lawson asked the Secretary of State for the Environment, Michael Heseltine, to undertake an examination of the scope for land and building sales both in the short and medium term. He also set in train a review of the measures needed to streamline the sales process, including speeding up local authority planning procedures and securing sales by New Town Corporations.[63] Heseltine took up the initiative with enthusiasm. On 6 June he replied that he would seek to achieve land disposals of £40 million in the current financial year.[64] This produced a grateful letter of thanks from the Chancellor.[65] However, the Treasury was under no illusion. The selling off of land and buildings would not raise large amounts for the Exchequer quickly.[66]

The National Health Service was a huge owner of land and buildings but under existing arrangements proceeds from land sales did not accrue to the hospital but to the regional or district health authority. This reduced the incentive for hospitals to identify land that was surplus to requirements. On 15 June 1979 the PM noted to one of her Private Secretaries, Michael Pattison: "What they have now seems a thoroughly unsatisfactory system." This led Pattison to write to the Department of Health and Social Security asking for the matter to be reviewed.[67] In the autumn, during a visit to the Department, the PM returned to the issue demanding to know what could be done to ensure that local hospitals disposing of property benefited directly from the proceeds. This motivated the Department to issue amendments to the *NHS Handbook on Land Transactions*. These changes provided for hospitals to benefit financially in whole or part from disposals. However, there is no evidence that the initiative transformed attitudes in the NHS to the release of surplus properties. The result led the PM to comment sardonically, "at least they tried and took some action".[68]

Difficulties had also arisen regarding the sale of land and buildings owned by local authorities and the nationalised industries. While government departments had well documented land holdings and were under a duty to dispose of surplus land, this was not true of local authorities and public corporations. On 16 July 1979 Heseltine suggested that the Government should require local authorities and nationalised industries to set up a similar scheme. This would help expose land not in full beneficial use and indicate to developers whether it was available for purchase. He also suggested that the Government should be empowered to direct disposals and that there should, in particular, be a new power for public bodies and bona fide developers to challenge continued public ownership of sites.[69] In E(DL) it was agreed that Ministers should be granted authority to direct the sales of public land. It was also agreed that the idea of a land register for local authorities should be pursued, although only experimentally in the first instance. On 26 July Ministers were asked to consider the appropriate approach that should be adopted to achieve more nationalised industry land sales.[70]

Heseltine was also busy advancing the sale of New Town assets at the instigation of the PM.[71] In August Heseltine commissioned Healey & Baker, a leading firm of estate agents, to advise on the disposals. New Town commercial and industrial properties were an attractive prospect for the disposals programme because of the amounts that might be raised and also because the New Town Corporations were borrowers from the National Loans Fund therefore adding to public sector borrowing. An initial estimate had suggested that the value of the relevant property might amount to around £2 billion, although this was later toned down to nearer £1 billion. Also, to raise close to the sum of £1 billion would require the co-operation of the New Town Corporations. Heseltine estimated that some £70 million could be raised without legislation, reflecting the extent to which he could "twist the arms" of Chairmen of the Corporations. But beyond that he felt that the prospects were far more uncertain unless he was given legal powers to require New Towns to sell.[72] The PM intervened by suggesting that planning should start "on the assumption that we do legislate".[73]

In mid-September 1979 Healey & Baker reported that some £256 million worth of New Town property seemed suitable for sale, although not all of it could be sold at once. In addition, a further £117 million worth of property would become available in 1980/1 as rent reviews were completed. On the basis of this report, Heseltine advised E(DL) on 30 October that he now planned £140 million of sales of land and buildings in the current year and £200 million in 1980/1.[74] This plan was disrupted, however, when local authorities got wind that New Town assets might be up for sale. In December Stevenage Borough Council attempted to promote a Private Bill in Parliament to acquire the assets of the Stevenage New Town Development Corporation. The Bill was killed off in Parliament at the second reading stage, but the local authority action did introduce some uncertainty for a few weeks.[75] Also, when Lawson wrote in the summer to George Younger, the Secretary of State for Scotland, asking for consideration of a major programme of New Town sales in Scotland,[76] Younger replied offering disposals of only £5 million, on the grounds that the possibilities were much fewer in Scotland because of the less developed nature of its New Towns.[77]

As part of the review of government land holdings, discussions had begun on the future of the Forestry Commission. The Commission was the largest owner of woodlands in Britain and a government agency. Lawson was keen that the Commission should be pressed to sell surplus land and that there should be a change of policy to stop further investment in land acquisition and new planting. He also called for the establishment of a target date by which the Commission would cease to be dependent on Exchequer finance.[78] However, much of the Commission's woodlands were in remote parts of Scotland where Younger believed that the scope for large-scale land sales was very limited. Much of the Commission's land holdings were tenanted and of comparatively poor quality. Younger was also wary of the social impact of land sales in terms of employment in the Scottish Highlands. In any event, he explained, to achieve such sales unless voluntarily undertaken by the Commission would require an amendment to the Forestry Act. This would be an unpopular Bill in Scotland.[79] Nicholas Edwards at the Welsh Office responded similarly.[80] However, there was less opposition to the sale of other productive woodland and of the Forestry Commission's land awaiting afforestation. It was considered that these sales might be worth pursuing and the possibility of legislation to smooth the sales later received the PM's support.[81] But difficulties in the country's paper and board industries, which were major customers of the woodlands, meant that on 31 July 1980 a decision was taken to defer a substantive statement on the matter, although the drafting of the legislation was to continue.[82] In the event, later in the year the possible sale of substantial Forestry Commission assets would be further postponed. The Commission remained (and to this day remains) state-owned.

By the autumn of 1979 it was clear that very little progress had been made in achieving the Chancellor's target of £1 billion of disposals. The only sales that were firm were disposals of around £100 million from the NEB (and these sales would be subject to the passage of an Industry Bill unless the NEB could be persuaded to divest voluntarily) and £185 million from miscellaneous sources (land and buildings, the Market Towers property managed by the Covent Garden Market Authority, the British Sugar Corporation and the Government's shares in the Suez Finance company). In addition, there might be around £30 million from the sale of the TRC, but only if the necessary legislation could be secured in time, which seemed unlikely.[83] A disposal that had been agreed involved the mechanical and electrical engineering contractors Drake and Scull Holdings (DSH). This enterprise had been rescued from bankruptcy by the Labour Government in 1976 and was now trading profitably. Its Chairman had made a formal request to the Labour Government for a return to private ownership immediately before the general election.[84] However, the sale would raise only around £1 million. Interestingly, a management suggestion that the sale should be framed in such a way as to promote employee shareholdings was rejected by the Government because of the likely costs, confirming that in the pecking order of Government objectives at this time, maximising sale receipts could outweigh spreading property ownership.[85]

## More early difficulties

In addition to the delays caused by opposition from corporation boards and the need in a number of cases for legislation before sales could go ahead, in these early days of the new Government the disposal process suffered from a lack of experience within government departments. There had been no previous large-scale sale of public assets in Britain and there was no "plan" or "guidance" on selling state industries on departmental shelves on which to draw. Departments were reporting a lack of clarity about how best to proceed with a sell-off of public sector assets, especially so as to best benefit the PSBR. They were particularly unclear as to the status of partial share disposals: would they count?

On 18 July 1979 the Treasury issued written guidance prepared in conjunction with the Central Statistical Office.[86] This made the point that partial share disposals were likely to reduce the PSBR, "only . . . if the Government as an act of deliberate policy ceases to exercise control over the corporations in question and no longer provides them with financial support". In other cases the sale receipts would be treated merely as financing the PSBR. The guidance confirmed "that an existing public corporation should undergo a fundamental change in its ownership and control before it can be reclassified to the private sector". While access to a government guarantee of borrowings was not on its own enough to classify a firm as being in the public sector, "it would make it harder to accept that the situation had changed enough to justify excluding it from the public sector (and the PSBR) . . . where the Government intends to retain 51 per cent or more of the shares, the reclassification is an act of faith".

However, the guidance accepted that the rules were not unambiguous. The borrowings of BP had never been classified as part of public sector borrowing, yet the Government owned a majority of the company's shares. Equally, the debts of Rolls-Royce, BL and C&W were excluded from the PSBR (again they were companies where the Government owned all or most of the shares rather than being public corporations). In addition, in the case of these companies the Government retained the power to intervene in management decisions.[87] Clearly there was some arbitrariness in determining which borrowings were classified as public sector debt. This led to some confusion and complaints about Treasury rulings. In 1980 and 1982 the Treasury firmed up its guidance, suggesting that to safely remove a firm from the public sector, the Government should give up all control including agreeing not to intervene in the company, although it might retain a minority share holding.[88] Nevertheless some uncertainty over the status of disposals of share capital held by government in privatised companies would resurface during the planning for the flotations of British Aerospace, C&W, TRC (Amersham International) and the British Transport Docks Board.

A related difficulty involved the government guarantees to purchasers and suppliers customarily provided by the nationalised industries. A brief attempt was made to standardise the treatment to be applied when industries were sold off. However, the industries had developed different practices; for example BA had made significant use of formal Treasury guarantees and BAe had issued letters of comfort using the implied government guarantee inherent in nationalised industry status should the business be wound up. The NFC's position was different again. There was only one specific guarantee operating, which related to temporary borrowing. Initially, the Chancellor of the Exchequer wanted to see a common approach adopted towards these guarantees when private capital was introduced. He was particularly concerned to ensure that as far as possible there should be no continuing government financial liability following a share sale.[89] However, at E(DL) on 17 October 1979 the Chancellor conceded that it had not proved possible to find a common approach because of the different terms of the guarantees. It was agreed that the planning for sales should continue with Ministers adopting different approaches, as necessary.[90]

Shortly after the Budget, discussion started on departmental public spending bids for 1980/1. On 12 July 1979 the Cabinet was informed that because of the deteriorating economic situation cuts of £6.5 billion in public expenditure plans were needed for 1980/1 to meet the Chancellor's PSBR target. Even with such cuts, the Chief Secretary to the Treasury, John Biffen, warned there would be no scope for significant tax cuts in the next Budget.[91] This prediction provoked the first split in the Cabinet over the direction of macroeconomic policy. While Treasury Ministers argued that it was essential to reduce public expenditure if inflation was to be conquered, particularly if space for promised tax cuts were to be found, a number of other Ministers contended that "the Government's strategy, as developed in Opposition and exemplified in the first Budget, had been overtaken by events." In their view there needed to be more flexibility on public spending and borrowing in the face of an economic recession. So began the division in the Cabinet on the direction of economic policy between the so-called "wets" (notably Peter Walker, Norman St. John-Stevas, Ian Gilmour, Francis Pym and Jim Prior) and the "dries" (most obviously Sir Geoffrey Howe, Sir Keith Joseph, John Biffen and the Prime Minister). This polarisation of views should not be exaggerated because Ministers moved from side to side on different issues. Also, the key economic committees, E and E(DL), were mainly reserved by the PM for those on whom she could rely to push forward with a reforming agenda. The only "wets" on E Committee were Prior and Walker (Lord Soames, who was removed from the Cabinet in the September 1981 reshuffle, was also on E Committee but is not commonly listed as a "wet"). There was only one "wet" on E(DL) Sub-Committee, Walker. Nevertheless, on a number of occasions over the following two years Cabinet and Cabinet Committee meetings were often fraught, with some Ministers sceptical about the whole direction of economic policy.[92] Prior has since commented: "We must have been the most divided Conservative Cabinet ever."[93]

Debate on the appropriate spending targets for the following years continued into the autumn. By then the focus had turned to the prospects for net debt repayments from some of the nationalised industries. As the Chief Secretary emphasised: "Given the need for substantial reductions in the public expenditure plans we have inherited . . . it is essential that the nationalised industries be pressed to make the maximum possible contribution."[94] One consequence of this was an agreement to raise nationalised industry prices especially for gas and electricity, as well as the cancellation of a number of proposed new investments.[95] The higher prices would bring in higher revenues.[96] Even so, in total the nationalised industries proved to be substantial borrowers, as evidenced by the figures in Table 3.3. In 1981/2 the five biggest loss-makers would record a total deficit of £1.5 billion. This occurred even though the prices charged by the nationalised industries rose faster than inflation.[97] Between January 1979 and September 1982 nationalised industry prices rose on average by 82.9 per cent. The RPI rose over the same period by 55.8 per cent. The losses incurred by some of the nationalised industries in spite of sharp price rises gradually hardened opinion

*Table 3.3* Nationalised industry financing 1980/1 to 1982/3

| | £m | |
| --- | --- | --- |
| | Contribution to capital spending from internal resources | Total external financing |
| **1980/81** | | |
| March '80 Budget | | |
| Forecast | 4043 | 2196 |
| Outturn | 2626 | 2900 |
| **1981/82** | | |
| March '81 Budget | | |
| Forecast | 4694 | 2390 |
| Outturn | 3593 | 2960 |
| **1982/83** | | |
| March '82 Budget | | |
| Forecast | 5002 | 2739 |

*Source: Public Expenditure White Paper,* Cmnd. 8494–11, pp.74–8.

within Government that there was no solution to the industries' problems other than their eventual privatisation.

Nevertheless, in the autumn of 1979 resistance was forming within some government departments against rushed asset sales. For example, the British Sugar Corporation had been identified as an early privatisation candidate; but Peter Walker at the Ministry of Agriculture, Fisheries and Food, made clear that he attached "considerable importance" to retaining influence over the Corporation until "a viable solution to the current problems of UK sugar policy" were worked out.[98] On 7 September 1979 at E Committee the Chancellor reported that sales so far agreed still amounted to only around one-third of the amount he needed.[99] In spite of the Financial Secretary asking Ministers to check whether additional realisations could be made in the current financial year following E Committee on 24 July,[100] only the Secretary of State for the Environment had responded, with an offer of land sales. Even if the Secretary of State for Energy achieved sales of BNOC and BGC assets to yield a net £400 million, which was seriously in doubt, this would still leave a balance of £285 million yet to find to meet this year's disposals target. He concluded that the sale of BP shares would now have to make up much of this gap. No doubt mindful of the PM's wavering on the subject, he reminded Ministers that the sale of BP shares had been specifically mentioned in his Budget speech. The City was prepared for the share sale and therefore, in his view: "Abandonment of our plans for the sale . . . would run the risk of being taken as a sign of weakness and indecision."[101] In the end the sale went ahead. In November, 80 million shares in BP representing five per cent of the issued share capital were offered for sale in the stock market at a fixed price of 363p per share, raising a net £283 million and therefore substantially less than the £650 million forecast at the time of the Budget. The modest size of the sale reflected the PM's continuing nervousness about selling oil assets at a time of world oil shortages.

At a meeting of E(DL) on 19 December 1979 the Financial Secretary, Nigel Lawson, reported the current expected sales that would be achieved in 1979/80 and the "fairly firm" and more tentative plans for asset sales in 1980/1 (Tables 3.4 and 3.5).[102] Lawson conceded that the Treasury's target of £150 million from New Town asset sales in 1980/81 was possibly too high. The power to enable the Secretary of State to order the disposal of assets had been included in a new Local Government Planning and Land Bill, but this was unlikely to become law before the summer of 1980. It seems that Heseltine had now revised down his earlier

*Table 3.4* 1979/80 planned disposals in December 1979

| | £m at 1979/80 outturn prices |
|---|---|
| BP shares | 283 |
| BNOC advance payment for oil sales | 600 |
| New Towns | 120 |
| Suez Finance Company shares | 22 |
| British Steel's subsidiaries & property | 15 |
| Property Sources Agency (land and buildings) | 5 |
| Regional Water Authorities' assets (land and buildings) | 3 |
| NEB's shareholdings | 35–85 |
| British Sugar shares | 20 |

*Source*: E(DL)(79)18; "Disposals in 1980/81: Memorandum by the Financial Secretary, Treasury", 14 December 1979.

*Table 3.5* 1980/1 planned disposals in December 1979

| | £m at 1979/80 outturn prices |
|---|---|
| *a) Fairly firm* | |
| New Towns – land & buildings | |
| in England & Wales | 150 |
| in Scotland | 5 |
| British Aerospace shares (about 50%) | 100 |
| Motorway service areas | 40–50 |
| Market Towers | 15 |
| Property Services Agency (land & buildings) | 4 |
| | 314–324 |
| *b) Other (non-hydrocarbon)* | |
| NEB's shareholdings | 25–75 |
| British Steel's shareholdings | 0–50 |
| Cable & Wireless shareholding in Hong Kong subsidiary | 65 |
| The Radiochemical Centre | 20 |
| NCB's shares in its Sankey subsidiary | 10–20 |
| | 120–230 |
| *c) Hydrocarbons* | |
| BNOC ("Operating") shares (25%) | 225 |
| BGC (interest in Wytch Farm oilfield or "alternative contribution") | 100, say |
| | 325 |

*Source*: E(DL)(79)18.

optimistic figures for New Town property sales. Certain other disposals listed by the Chancellor were also considered to be at best speculative by the Ministers of the departments concerned. A number were expected to encounter delays. For example, the planning for the disposal of TRC was proceeding but legislation was still needed. Regarding the disposal of National Coal Board (NCB) subsidiaries that the Treasury was now demanding, and especially a 60 per cent holding in Sankey a coal-fired heating appliance supplier, the NCB's Board was strongly against any sales; while the opposition of the Boards of BNOC and BGC to a disposal of their oil assets continued.

Nor were other Ministers much more positive. Joseph explained that the sale of shares in the Government-owned international telecommunications operator C&W was in some difficulty and progress awaited the appointment of a new Chairman of the company. Norman Fowler, Minister for Transport, had announced on 23 October 1979 that he would open discussions with operators of motorway services regarding disposal of Motorway Service Areas owned by the Government. This sale did not require legislation. But the discussions were still very much at an early stage and no firm price had yet been put on the relevant properties. The Covent Garden Market Authority had now agreed to sell Market Towers, but only subject to certain conditions which were still being explored. More positively, Joseph was able to report that the disposal of the NEB's assets identified earlier could now go ahead as planned. However, the recent fall in share prices meant that the yield was likely to be much less in 1979/80 than the £100 million originally estimated.

In the Treasury the news on disposals was received with great disappointment. The Chancellor still faced a gap of around £200 million between the "fairly firm" disposal plans for 1980/1 on offer from departments and the published target of £500 million in 1979/80 outturn prices. Nor was there any serious prospect of getting close to the £1 billion Budget target for 1979/80 without the BNOC sales, given that only three months of the year remained. Fortunately oil revenues had come to the Chancellor's rescue. On 10 September 1979 E Committee had authorised forward oil sales from BNOC to close the funding gap.[103] In December the Financial Secretary was able to report that oil sales during the current year had produced more money than originally envisaged because of higher oil prices; this had helped make up for the failure to achieve the planned disposals announced in the Budget. In 1979/80, excluding oil royalties, only £370 million was raised from disposals with over three-quarters of that coming from the sale of BP shares. This compares with the Budget target for disposals of £1 billion.

## "The lady's not for turning"

During the autumn of 1979 tense and difficult bilateral discussions between spending departments and the Treasury over future public expenditure had led eventually to agreement in Cabinet, in early November, to further cuts totalling £3 billion. The details were finalised the following January. The reduction was still somewhat less than the sum the Treasury had demanded.[104] The Clegg pay awards, higher interest rates on government debt, economic recession and the nationalised industry deficits were by now seriously undermining the Conservatives' Manifesto commitment to control public spending and provide space for tax cuts.[105] Also, the Conservatives had committed themselves during the Election to raising defence spending, protecting the NHS from cuts, and increasing old age pensions and the pay of the police and armed forces.[106] This further reduced the scope for overall government economies. On 15 November 1979 the Chancellor informed the Cabinet that the economic situation was continuing to worsen and reported poor PSBR, money supply and trade figures. He revealed that he would be announcing that day a sharp rise in the Bank of England's Minimum Lending Rate to 17 per cent with the aim of reigning back monetary growth. The Chancellor blamed this decision on the Cabinet's failure to achieve the Treasury's proposed public expenditure cuts.[107] In the light of the deteriorating economic outlook, at the start of 1980 the Treasury was again reviewing departmental spending plans.

In June 1979 the forecast had been for a PSBR of £8.3 billion in 1980/1. This had now been revised upwards to £10 billion, rising to around £13 billion by 1981/2. To avoid even higher interest rates with their potential damage to economic activity resulting from more government borrowing, in January 1980 the Chancellor recommended a further £1 billion reduction in public spending for 1980/1 and £2 billion for each of the subsequent three years.[108] Increases in nationalised industry charges, particularly for electricity and gas, had already been agreed the previous October.[109] On 17 January 1980 further rises were discussed with the aim of increasing the payments from the industries to the Exchequer, although they were to be justified in public by the need to reduce energy demand.[110] At the end of January the Cabinet confirmed further cuts in the growth of public spending of around £800 million for 1980/1 and between £1.75 billion and £2.2 billion in subsequent years, which would be announced in the Budget in March. This was again somewhat less than the Chancellor had hoped for, but far more than some Ministers were happy to countenance.[111] Cutting public spending when the economy was going into recession conflicted with the principles of Keynesian economics, under which governments pumped money into the economy to reverse rising unemployment, and with the political instincts of some Ministers. In the March 1980 Budget the Chancellor revealed his monetarist Medium Term Financial Strategy (MTFS), including targets for public sector borrowing and the money supply for the financial years up to and including 1983/4. The target rate of monetary growth was to be halved by 1984 to around six per cent with the aim of bringing inflation firmly under control.[112]

The MTFS was announced as the economy deteriorated. During 1980 adult unemployment rose more quickly than in any single year since 1930; by November it had reached 2.1 million. The British economy was caught in a vice between rising costs of production due to inflation and a rising exchange rate, in part reflecting the higher interest rates. Between early 1980 and early 1981 the real exchange rate rose by some 15 per cent as a result of monetary conditions, exacerbated by Britain's new position as a net oil exporter. A further factor was the unexpected decision of the Chancellor of the Exchequer immediately after the May 1979 Election to suspend the use of exchange controls. This meant that domestic monetary aggregates were more likely to be affected by inflows and outflows of money.[113] Monetary growth was overshooting the target set in the MTFS the previous March despite high interest rates. By July 1980 the Chancellor was complaining that the PSBR was coming in significantly higher than estimated, worsened by increased nationalised industry and local authority borrowing.[114] Continuing losses in the coal, steel and shipbuilding industries, a product of recession and wage rises, and the need to continue to subsidise railway services to keep many of them open, were now posing a significant challenge to the Government's economic and financial strategy.[115]

On 3 July 1980 the Cabinet was addressed by Professor Terry Burns, the Chief Economic Adviser Howe had brought into the Treasury, on the country's economic prospects. Burns reiterated that there was no alternative to maintaining the current monetary targets if inflation was to be brought down. The sharp rise in unemployment since the general election was blamed on excessive pay settlements at a time of monetary restraint.[116] However, divisions within the Cabinet over economic strategy were not suppressed by a lecture from the Chief Economic Adviser. When a week later the Chancellor threatened further public spending cuts, a number of Ministers pleaded for more flexibility to prevent permanent damage to British industry.[117] Such was the strength of feeling that there should be more help for British industry through the recession, that the PM agreed to invite the Chancellor to consider options for further measures of industrial support and report back.

By now Treasury Ministers faced great pressure within Government and outside to reverse course, cut interest rates and allow more government spending and borrowing, especially in support of industry.[118] At a by-election in March 1980 in what would normally be a safe Conservative seat, Southend, the Conservatives only just scraped in. At the Confederation of British Industry (CBI) annual conference in the autumn, Terence Beckett, its newly appointed director-general, called for a "bare-knuckle fight" with the Government on economic policy in the face of a sharp decline in manufacturing orders.[119] At the annual Conservative Party Conference in Brighton in October there were criticisms of the Government's economic strategy, including from the Government Minister St. John-Stevas who reputedly talked about the dangers of "theoreticians living in an abstract world".[120] It was at this Conference that the PM responded to her critics by warning: "To those waiting with bated breath for that favourite media catchphrase, the "U-turn," I have one thing to say. You turn if you want to. The Lady's not for turning."[121] These were brave (and memorable) words, but they could not hide the internal divisions that had opened up on economic policy.[122] The divisions were so great that there was growing speculation that Thatcher would be unseated as PM before the next general election.

In November 1980 disagreement again broke out in Cabinet over public spending. Treasury Ministers pressed for a further reduction of £1.61 billion as a necessary step towards bringing public expenditure back to the level agreed in Cabinet the previous March.[123] The Treasury was particularly looking for a £500 million cut in the defence budget and £600 million from a reduction in the uprating of social security benefits. However, Francis Pym, the Defence Secretary, threatened to resign and the Secretary of State for Health and Social Security, Patrick Jenkin, reminded the Cabinet of the PM's undertakings at the time of the election to maintain the purchasing power of welfare benefits. The Treasury was unable to push these cuts through.[124] In the end the Treasury achieved savings of a little over £1 billion in total, significantly less than what it had sought.[125] To fill the widening gap in the Government's finances, on 24 November 1980 the Chancellor announced a rise in employees' national insurance contributions and a new Supplementary Petroleum Duty on North Sea oil to raise tax revenues.[126] Early the following year, in January 1981, the PM instituted her first Cabinet reshuffle, removing Pym from the Ministry of Defence (MoD) and sacking St. John-Stevas as Leader of the House. Also, John Biffen was replaced as Chief Secretary to the Treasury by Leon Brittan. Biffen had "dry" credentials but had recently shown some lack of enthusiasm for the direction of the Government's economic strategy.[127]

## A lack of progress

In addition to the difficult negotiations over public spending, the programme for disposals was still not going well. At a meeting of E(DL) on 19 December 1979 Ministers had been invited to bring forward urgently proposals for additional asset sales in 1980/1.[128] However, the response was lacklustre. On 28 January 1980 the Chancellor of the Exchequer wrote to

E(DL) members noting: "I am concerned that no proposals have come forward. The need to prepare plans is very pressing".[129] Joseph then responded, but was able to confirm disposals of only about £70 million from the NEB's asset portfolio. He also pointed out that the sale of C&W remained uncertain and he remained gloomy about being able to find any other candidates for sale that year.[130] Heseltine at Environment offered nothing beyond the New Town asset sales already agreed.[131] David Howell at Energy continued to play down the prospects for selling the oil assets of BNOC and BGC and subsidiaries of the NCB in the near term. A letter from the Chancellor to Howell on the same day referred to the need for urgent reconsideration of the prospects for disposals of BGC assets and of NCB subsidiaries. In reply, Howell merely offered the possibility of an early paper on the future of the TRC.[132] The Chancellor's disappointment must have been compounded when the Secretary of State for Transport reported "unexpected difficulties" in the negotiations with motorway service operators relating to a sale of the businesses using long leases. While he was still hopeful that he could make a contribution to the disposals target in 1980/1, he concluded: "I am not yet in a position to be precise about the timing of the exercise and the capital realisation."[133]

Frustrated at the failure of his Ministerial colleagues to offer anything new, the Chancellor requested a meeting with the PM.[134] This occurred on 6 March 1980, in conjunction with a discussion on the forthcoming Budget. At the meeting the Chancellor warned that his target figure for disposals in 1980/1 was already in danger. The main possibilities to fill the gap were the sale of BGC's interest in the on-shore Wytch Farm oilfield, a joint venture with BP, and the disposal of C&W. As in his view "The Secretary of State for Energy was proving difficult on the former . . . [he] hoped he could have the Prime Minister's support in putting pressure on Mr. Howell".[135] The PM gave her support agreeing that the disposal of Wytch Farm should be "pursued vigorously". It was also agreed that the Secretary of State for Industry should "bring forward firm proposals for the sale of Cable and Wireless" and that the Secretary of State for Energy should advance the sale of some of the NCB's non-coal businesses.[136]

The meeting with the PM and a follow-up memorandum from the Chancellor of the Exchequer[137] led to a note from No.10 to the Principal Private Secretary at the Department of Energy. It made clear the importance the PM attached to meeting the disposals target for the year.[138] However, Howell simply responded offering the eventual privatisation of BNOC, but not so speedily that receipts would necessarily flow in 1980/1. No commitments were given on Wytch Farm. Within the Department existed a profound commitment to protect the security of the country's energy supplies, inherited from the years of Labour Government. Officials believed that privatisation might put this at risk and must therefore be approached most cautiously. In other words, there seems to have been limited sympathy within the Department in these early months of the new Government that things could be arranged differently quickly.[139] In any case under the 1972 Gas Act the Secretary of State could direct BGC to cease activities and dispose of assets, but only if he was satisfied that this would not impede the proper discharge of the Corporation's duties. Moreover, even if he felt able to proceed with a Directive to the Board, it was not clear that the Board would automatically have to pass the resulting proceeds to the Exchequer.[140] Nor was Howell optimistic about the prospects for the disposal of NCB subsidiaries, labelling them "a rag bag, many of which are unsaleable or saleable for insignificant amounts". Regarding an early sale of the TRC, he now reported that for "technical reasons this is much more an outside than an inside possibility".[141] The Department of Energy's financial advisers considered that it would be preferable to defer the sale until 1981/2 when the amount that could be realised might be twice as high. The PM reacted angrily, scribbling the following note on her copy of Howell's memorandum: "Very negative. It isn't that they *can't* do these things, it's just that they won't."[142]

At a meeting of the Ministerial Group on Nationalised Industry policy on 13 February 1980, Joseph had agreed to oversee the preparation of a paper on disposals in consultation with other Ministers responsible for state-owned industries. The aim was to ensure that the necessary legislation was planned so that disposals were "not delayed to the point when they may be jeopardised by the prospect of an impending General Election". The paper was completed by early May and tabled at an E(DL) meeting on the 12th.[143] It listed those industries where it had been agreed that privatisation Bills would be included in the 1980/1 legislative programme, namely British Airways, British Aerospace and the National Freight Corporation. Also included was Telecommunications, where a Bill was planned to separate telecommunications from the postal services and "pave the way for introducing private capital into some telecommunications activities, in particular by providing for the new corporation to supply some of its services through part-privatised subsidiaries or associates" – however, full privatisation of British Telecommunications (BT) was not contemplated at this time. In addition, the paper mentioned C&W, where a Bill would authorise a part disposal of shares, legislation to release BNOC's oilfield operating assets, a disposal of TRC, and flotation of the British Transport Docks Board. Also listed were a restructuring of British Steel, which by now was making huge losses; disposal of British Rail's interests in hotels, shipping, harbours and property "and possibly hovercraft"; and disposal of the Heavy Goods Vehicle Testing service, by transferring responsibility for testing to the private sector. In addition, the paper detailed other possibilities for future legislation including British Shipbuilders, electricity (involving relaxation of the present restrictions on private generation as a main activity), gas (reducing BGC's monopsony of North Sea gas purchases), coal (raising the statutory limit on the size of privately-owned coal mines), water ("privatisation of some water authorities or their takeover by water companies") and the National Bus Company (introduction of private capital into inter-urban services – although the Secretary of State for Transport reported that there was no real scope for introducing private capital into the rest of the National Bus Company).

This was an ambitious list of possible privatisations and the paper went further setting out other albeit longer-term possibilities for disposal, including telecommunications ("privatisation, possibly by regions"), steel ("privatisation of BSC or break-up into privatised companies") and coal ("worker co-operatives; conversion of NCB into competing companies subject to central supervision of safety; licensing of coal exploration by private companies"). The paper also noted that, "The question of the gas and electricity boards' retailing and contracting activities, and whether, for instance, these might be hived off or disposed of, should be considered further when the current Monopolies and Mergers Commission (MMC) inquiry into retailing gas appliances was concluded." Under the Competition Act 1980 the Government extended the remit of the MMC to enquire into the efficiency of the nationalised industries and anti-competitive practices. Interestingly, the paper suggested that "We may also want to return at a later stage to the question of introducing some private capital into gas and electricity supply, possibly in selected regions." However, it went on to stress that "at present we are unable to identify any workable options." Other possibilities included the introduction of private capital to help finance the British Airports Authority's (BAA) capital investment programme and disposal of a number of the Scottish Transport Group's investments, mainly in buses and ferries.

The paper provides an impressively large list of reforms and might be interpreted as contradicting the proposition that the Government had no prior programme for large-scale privatisation when elected. Certainly many of the possibilities mentioned developed into actual policies during the 1980s and 1990s. However, the content was very much a "wish list" at this time. It had been generated in the first part of 1980 by trawling departments for ideas when the departments were under considerable pressure to come up with proposals to placate the Treasury. Most of the ideas listed were just that, "ideas", or were still at a very early stage of development. Also, Joseph was an obvious proponent of privatisation, but even he doubted how many of the sales listed could actually be carried out and some of his Ministerial colleagues lacked his enthusiasm even to try. As confirmation, at the same meeting of E(DL), a Memorandum from the Financial Secretary on progress towards achieving the £630 million sales target for the current financial year reported that so far only around £412 million to £452 million of the sales identified were "fairly firm" (Table 3.6).[144] This was only a slight improvement on the figures provided the previous December (Table 3.5 above).

Nevertheless, the paper is important in the evolution of privatisation as policy because it indicates how, under Treasury pressure, departments had begun to investigate various possible ways to slim the state sector. A privatisation programme was beginning to take shape and there was recognition that if it was to achieve real momentum it would have to move

*Table 3.6* 1980/1 planned disposals in May 1980

|  | £m |
| --- | --- |
| TARGET | 630 |
| *a) Fairly firm* | |
| New Towns (England & Wales) (assumes cash carryover of £95m) | 260 |
| NEB shareholdings | 70–100 |
| Motorway Service Areas | 40 |
| British Sugar Corporation | 20 |
| Market Towers | 15 |
| PSA | 4 |
| Scottish Smallholdings | 3 |
|  | 412–452 |
| GAP | 218–178 |
| *b) Other possibilities* | |
| North Sea (7th Round Licences)* | 30–100 |
| British Aerospace (about 50 per cent) | 100 (less than) |
| Cable and Wireless | 65 |
| The Radiochemical Centre | 20 |
| NCB Subsidiaries (at least) | 10–20 |
| BGC (interest in Wytch Farm Oilfield) | 100 |

*Note*: * Size uncertain

*Source*: E(DL) (80) 5, "Disposals in 1980/81. Memorandum by the Financial Secretary, HM Treasury", 7 May 1980.

from the selling-off of surplus land and buildings and other miscellaneous small-scale assets to achieving the privatisation of a number of the major nationalised industries or at least some of their subsidiary businesses. However, it was still far from clear that this jump would be made. To assist, Joseph suggested the introduction of a short enabling Bill to give the industries clear legal powers to establish subsidiaries and sell them and to enable Ministers to direct a corporation to exercise that power. However, nothing came of the suggestion, although it would be raised once again during the second Thatcher Government.

At its meeting on 5 August 1980 E(DL) Sub-Committee requested the Secretariat of the Cabinet Office to provide a report on likely asset sales in the following financial year, 1981/2. On 20 October the Secretaries presented their report with a best estimate of disposals yielding slightly more than the disposals target for 1980/1. But of this only about £180 million was regarded as firm.[145] By December 1980 the Secretaries in the Cabinet Office were reporting that the sales of BGC's oil interests and C&W were now definitely deferred into 1981/2 making the achievement of the 1980/1 disposals target virtually impossible.[146]

On 23 January 1981 Nigel Lawson sent a memorandum to members of E(DL) suggesting that in addition to agreeing a disposal target for 1981/2, "On a longer time scale, we ought to consider more radical structural changes in the industries if we are to take privatisation beyond the pool of obvious candidates we have so far identified." Allowing for uncertainties about timing and estimated receipts, the Financial Secretary proposed that the target for the following year, 1981/2, should remain the same at £500 million in 1979/80 prices.[147] However, as before, much uncertainty attached to the main sources of the proceeds.[148] Heseltine was now arguing that it was proving more difficult than expected to sell New Town assets at realistic prices. He proposed no contribution from such sales in 1981/2. Shortly afterwards a paper by the Financial Secretary on the prospects for selling the Royal Mint and the Bank of England's printing works rejected their sale. It was considered too risky to privatise the Mint because of the potential damage to its export business, given that some governments were statutorily required to buy their currency from a Government mint and others chose to do so. Regarding the printing works, it was discovered that these were already classified as being in the private sector in official statistics, which from the perspective of the Treasury largely defeated the object of an early sale. Also, the Bank of England opposed any change in ownership.[149] A memorandum from the Minister of State at the Foreign and Commonwealth Office, Neil Marten, also scotched any early prospect of privatising the Crown Agents, who were responsible for providing procurement, personnel, engineering, financial and some administrative services to overseas government and public bodies.[150] In 1980/81, leaving aside sales of oil and North Sea oil licences, the Government would achieve disposals of assets totalling only £210 million, less than half the target set for the year. This was an even worse performance than in the previous year, which itself had disappointed.

## The 1981 Budget and its aftermath

Serious tensions in the Cabinet over economic policy were about to reach boiling point. The Treasury had failed in the autumn of 1980 to get the spending cuts it felt were needed and by the end of the financial year, in March 1981, the Budget deficit had turned out to be £13.5 billion, almost 60 per cent above the amount originally forecast under the MTFS. From within No. 10 the PM's economic adviser, Professor Alan Walters, who had taken up post in early January on secondment from Johns Hopkins University in Baltimore, called for a loosening of monetary conditions including lower interest rates and a tightening of fiscal policy to take pressure off industry and the exchange rate.[151] In the 1981 Budget the Chancellor responded by cutting the PSBR to £10.5 billion through higher taxation. In particular, tax thresholds and allowances were not raised in line with prices and duties on tobacco, alcohol and petrol were increased at twice the rate of inflation. There were also additional contributions from national insurance, North Sea oil and a tax on bank profits. Walters and Hoskyns within No. 10 favoured a rise in the basic rate of income tax but this was ruled out by the PM and the Chancellor.[152] The total increase in taxation was around £5 billion. Also, announced was an agreement made in Cabinet in February that in future public spending figures would be set in constant prices rather than cash terms.[153] The intention was that wage and other cost rises should now be less easy for departments to pass on to the Treasury.[154] However, demand-driven spending, which accounted for over 60 per cent of public expenditure, for example on unemployment and social security benefits, would not be constrained by this decision. The overall effect on future public spending, therefore, turned out to be much more limited than intended.

The Budget was spectacularly controversial. Thatcher referred to it as "unpopular but crucial".[155] Prior reminisces: "I couldn't say anything bad enough about it . . . I felt so desperately about it that I was willing to chuck in my hand . . . I came very close to resigning".[156] It seems that its content had been revealed to the full Cabinet only on Budget day. [157] Had it been discussed in advance, it is likely that a number of Ministers would have required changes. The Budget was attacked within Parliament and outside.[158] Most memorable was a letter to *The Times* from 364 economists including five former Chief Economic Advisers protesting that it would deflate demand, "deepen the depression, erode the industrial base of our economy and threaten its social and political stability . . . The time has come to reject monetarist policies".[159] It has been suggested that the Budget was about restoring the credibility of the MTFS after the failure to meet the PSBR target.[160] In fact, the Government's favoured monetary aggregate sterling M3 (£M3)[161] was scarcely mentioned in the Budget. The MTFS had proven simplistic, especially in terms of targeting a particular definition of the money supply £M3.[162] The target for £M3 was 7–11 per cent in 1980/1, 6–10 per cent in 1981/2 and 5–9 per cent in 1982/3. The actual outturns were around 16 per cent, 13 per cent and 11 per cent respectively. The target range for 1982 was revised upwards in the Budget but only illustrative figures were given for the following years. From 1981 monetary policy would be implemented more pragmatically. In particular, the previous autumn's cuts in public spending and then the Budget tax rises allowed for a slackening of the monetary squeeze, which over the previous eighteen months or so had badly damaged private sector industry. In November 1980 interest rates had been cut from 16 per cent to 14 per cent. The Budget led to a further reduction by two per cent (although in the autumn the cut had to be reversed temporarily when sterling fell in value by more on the foreign exchanges than the Government thought wise in terms of reducing inflation).

By the spring of 1981 opinion polls were confirming Mrs Thatcher to be the most unpopular Prime Minister since the War.[163] Early in the year the NCB had informed the Government of its plan to close uneconomic pits. At first the Secretary of State for Energy sided with the decision, but in the face of threatened strike action by the miners against the closures the Government backed down. The PM was fearful that there were inadequate coal stocks at power stations to win any dispute, leading to a possible rerun of the power cuts and political debacle of the last months of the Heath Government. The about-turn did little to bolster the Government's standing or Mrs Thatcher's given her promise only weeks earlier not to undertake U-turns. Ian Gow, Parliamentary Private Secretary (PPS) to the PM, reported to her on 27 February that the decision to save the pits, combined with serious doubts about the Government's entire economic strategy, had led to "a noticeable deterioration in the morale of our backbenchers".[164] Matters got worse. Starting in April 1981 in Brixton in South London and spreading in July to the run-down inner-city areas of Liverpool, Birmingham, Manchester, Blackburn, Bradford, Leeds, Derby, Wolverhampton and Leicester, rioting broke out.[165] It seemed for a time that the country, or at least its big towns and cities suffering from high unemployment, might be becoming ungovernable.[166] At the Party annual conference at Blackpool in September 1981 the Government was openly criticised. Former Ministers, St. John-Stevas and Gilmour, held critical fringe meetings and Lord Carrington, the Foreign Secretary, is said to have gone around "asking any Treasury Minister he met what damage they had inflicted on the economy in the previous 24 hours".[167]

However, slowly and imperceptibly during 1981 the economy actually began to recover. Some have attributed this to the tough Budget,[168] although with the benefit of hindsight some signs of recovery had appeared before March. The slowly changing economic tide did not prevent continuing disagreements within the Cabinet on public spending.[169] On 23 July 1981 there was a first meeting of the Cabinet on the next year's spending plans, where Ministers both "wet" and "dry" dutifully tabled their department's budget proposing increases totalling more than £6.5 billion, some £2.5 billion relating to the nationalised industries. The Treasury proposed cuts of £5 billion. The result was a sharp difference of views between Ministers of spending departments and Treasury Ministers. John Nott, the Defence Secretary, and John Biffen, the Secretary of State for Trade, who could usually be relied upon to back the Chancellor of the Exchequer joined those who more predictably voiced opposition to the cuts. Nott was anxious to protect the MoD's budget having taken over at the Ministry of Defence from Pym in January. This left the Chancellor, the Chief Secretary, Joseph, the Home Secretary William Whitelaw and the PM in the minority.[170] Thatcher later described the clash as "one of the bitterest arguments on the economy, or any subject, that I can ever recall taking place at Cabinet during my premiership".[171] When it became obvious that she and her Chancellor were largely isolated, the PM adjourned the discussion until after the summer.

In September 1981 the PM undertook a major Cabinet reshuffle. Michael Heseltine was one of those against the spending cuts who survived. Others were less fortunate. In his view the September Cabinet changes were clear "retaliation" for what had happened in Cabinet in July. The result, he concluded, "tipped the balance of the Cabinet in favour of the "dries" and ensured that it was extremely unlikely that she [the PM] would lose on a major issue again".[172] In February 1979 in an interview with Kenneth Harris of *The Observer* newspaper, Margaret Thatcher had commented on the making of a Cabinet: "One way is to have in it people who represent all the different viewpoints within the Party . . . . The other way is to have in it only people who want to go in the direction in which every instinct tells me we have to go . . . As Prime Minister I couldn't waste time having any internal arguments . . . It must be a 'conviction' Cabinet."[173] In the September reshuffle she removed those she saw as the chief time wasters and lacking in conviction. Gilmour was dismissed and Prior was despatched, much against his better judgement, to the Northern Ireland Office – Mark Carlisle, Lord Soames and Lord Thorneycroft, Chairman of the Party, were also casualties.[174] In came Cecil Parkinson as new Party Chairman[175] and Norman Tebbit as Employment Minister in place of Prior, both committed "Thatcherites". Jock Bruce-Gardyne and Nicholas Ridley, also notorious "dries", moved to the Treasury to support the Chancellor and Lawson moved from the post of Financial Secretary to replace David Howell at Energy. This change reflected the PM's growing frustration with Howell and the Department of Energy over the slow pace of disposing of oil assets.[176] Also, Thatcher seems to have held him at least partially responsible, fairly or not, for the Government's U-turn on pit closures.

The reshuffle placed Lawson, with a determination to see wide-scale privatisation, in the Cabinet. Also, the reshuffle meant that the PM now had a Cabinet team more in tune with her thinking. Lawson writes in his memoirs: "in September 1981, two years and four months after taking office as Prime Minister, Margaret Thatcher at last secured a Cabinet with a Thatcherite majority."[177] Prior retained his seat on E Committee but would now be too busy in Northern Ireland to play an effective blocking role. The dominance of the Committee by Treasury views was strengthened. In October and November 1981 the Cabinet reconvened to discuss public spending and after discussion the proposed cuts were largely agreed,[178] although Nott was still able to protect most of the defence budget.[179]

## A new momentum

In March 1981 the Chancellor of the Exchequer had called for a more ambitious privatisation strategy to be developed. One possibility he proposed was to look for new ways of involving private capital and management in activities closely linked with the industries.[180] The other, and his main suggestion, involved reducing the monopoly powers of the big state utilities by privatising them: "We should not take it for granted that any industry, however basic or monopolistic or however essential the service it provides, should necessarily remain in public ownership." He recognised, however, that "These are not easy issues. Nor can we expect help in resolving them from the Chairmen, management or unions of the industries concerned." To advance his ideas he recommended that he should take over the chairman-ship of E(DL), which he had vacated during the previous year, so as to harness "the sources of information more easily available to a central Department to challenge the objections of sponsor Ministers". The Secretary of State for Industry, Sir Keith Joseph, had been chairing E(DL) in the meantime and the implication was clear – there had been inadequate progress.

On the particular issue of privatising the monopoly utilities, the Chancellor suggested the arranging of "a brains trust or seminar" to include himself and a number of other Ministers most directly involved with the nationalised industries. However, Sir Robert Armstrong, the Cabinet Secretary, while welcoming the Chancellor's initiative introduced a note of caution. Even if some of the nationalised industries could be privatised he argued that this was a policy for the medium term. In any event he concluded, it seemed "likely that there would remain some industries which for one reason or another could not be transformed in this way and would have to remain in public ownership." Armstrong favoured asking the Head of the Central Policy Review Staff (CPRS), Sir Robin (J.R.) Ibbs, to consider the future relationship between government and the nationalised industries in consultation with the sponsoring departments, the Treasury and the No. 10 Policy Unit.[181]

The Chancellor's and Sir Robert's suggestions won the support of John Hoskyns in the No. 10 Policy Unit and the PM decided to discuss the matter with relevant Ministers.[182] In a separate meeting between the PM and the Chancellor on the evening of the 18 March 1981, the Chancellor pressed Thatcher to confirm that the study of the nationalised industries would involve the Treasury, to which the PM agreed provided that the CPRS retained the lead role.[183] However, the Chancellor's request to take over the chair of E(DL) ran into some resistance within No.10, as it was expected that Sir Keith Joseph would not take well to being replaced.[184] It was therefore only in November 1981 that Howe resumed the chairmanship of E(DL), after the matter had been smoothed over with Joseph.

The "brains trust" seminar on the possibility of privatising monopoly industries was held on 29 June 1981 and included the Chancellor of the Exchequer, the Chief Secretary, the Financial Secretary, and the Secretaries of State for Industry, Transport and Energy. Also a number of junior ministers and representatives from the nationalised industries were present. Two academics attended, Professors Michael Beesley and Christopher Foster. During the proceedings it was suggested that businesses currently making losses due to the recession, but that were normally profitable, might be sold by direct trade sale even if a public flotation was not attractive. But the main discussion centred on the "monopoly utilities". Strong arguments were made for breaking them up into regional entities, "some or all of which might be privatised" and "subjecting them to a new regulatory regime, independent of Government". In a note to the PM the Chancellor concluded that the meeting had led him to believe:

"that we need a careful study of the idea of a combined regional structure and regulatory regime [for the monopoly nationalised industries]. There is a large literature and plenty of experience – both good and bad – in this and other countries. It would need to cover a number of difficult issues, not only the scope of regulation (over pricing, return on capital, investment, extent of monopolies) and the appropriate criteria but also how far it should be independent of Government and how this would impinge on our ability to implement particular policies e.g. on energy prices. The consumer dimension would need to be brought in and the means of making it democratically accountable and sufficiently flexible".[185]

In a follow up note from Sir Robin Ibbs the CPRS offered its services to undertake the study after it had completed one that it had already begun on the relationship between government and the nationalised industries.[186] The PM agreed to defer a study of regionalisation and regulation until after the CPRS's report.[187]

At a talk to the Selsdon Group in the Carlton Club on 1 July 1981, Howe explained that it had been experience in government that had moved privatisation to the forefront of politics, in particular the difficulties of controlling the nationalised industries' finances.[188] From 1979 the nationalised industries had been expected to observe their published EFLs even though the Government was well aware that higher inflation and wage settlements would severely test the limits.[189] In subsequent months the growing deficits of the nationalised industries, in spite of the granting of large price rises, had irritated Treasury Ministers and the PM and had encouraged a search for ways of removing the industries' borrowings from the PSBR.[190] In 1980/1 the EFL outturn was £704 million above forecast and in 1981/2 £570 million above forecast. Another serious irritant was poor labour relations in the industries. In 1980 and 1981 seven out of ten days lost through strikes occurred in the public sector with a strike in the steel industry from January to April 1980 being particularly long and acrimonious.[191]

On 20 February 1980 a meeting had taken place between Ministers and the Nationalised Industries Chairmen's Group,[192] where the industries had pressed for their borrowings to be placed outside the PSBR so as to enable them to invest in profitable activities without the EFL constraint. This request was opposed by the Chancellor of the Exchequer and the Chief Secretary, although it is clear that it received some support from some Ministers. For example, Howell at Energy and Younger at the Scottish Office argued that the Treasury needed to be more flexible.[193] On 16 January 1981 the Chancellor tabled in response proposals for the management of the nationalised industries on which the CPRS was asked for comments. A week later, Sir Robin Ibbs responded, broadly agreeing with the Chancellor that there was "no painless way of financing nationalised industry borrowing". He noted that tight EFLs risked restricting desirable investment but doubted that new sources of borrowing could make anything more than a marginal contribution.[194] It was difficult to see how nationalised industry borrowing could be detached from government guarantees. The CPRS concluded that privatisation was the only real way forward. The PM agreed, observing in a scribbled note "The real answer is there aren't any solutions to nationalised industries' problems except to remove the problem by denationalising."[195]

In June 1981 a National Economic Development Office working party under the chairmanship of Sir William Ryrie (then second Permanent Secretary in the Treasury) was set up reflecting concern inside and outside Government that EFLs were frustrating nationalised industry investment and a belief that higher investment would benefit the economy.[196] There was a wide perception that investment in the nationalised industries had been overly suppressed by coming last in the Government's public expenditure priorities. The working party reported in September 1981. It recommended that private finance be introduced into the nationalised industries, provided that this occurred in circumstances of fair competition for funds with private sector borrowers. The resulting investments should provide benefits in terms of improved efficiency and an economic return commensurate with the cost of raising private capital. However, the working party's recommendations received a cool response in the Government, which was intent upon holding down public sector borrowing. Effectively this ended any hope of privatising the financing rather than the ownership of the nationalised industries. Under what became known as the "Ryrie rules", a public sector investment funded by private capital was expected to earn a return sufficient to cover the extra cost of private over public sector funding (government being able to borrow more cheaply than the private sector because of the lower risk of default).[197] It was against this background that the CPRS was asked to write its report on the nationalised industries. The report was completed in July 1981 ahead of the NEDO report. It pointed to weaknesses in the management of the industries and of expertise within government departments to monitor their performance adequately.[198] It confirmed that there was a lack of clear and agreed objectives for the industries and concluded that this lay at the heart of the problem of managing the nationalised industries.[199] To tackle these problems, a principal recommendation in the report was the setting by Government of clear strategic objectives for the corporations. Effectiveness against the objectives would provide a basis for judging management performance.

Other main recommendations were a clearer framework of financial controls, smaller industry boards with a majority of non-executive directors from outside, efficiency audits,[200] and business groups to help set the financial targets and objectives. The business groups concept and the re-composition of boards met with a sceptical response from Government. However, on 19 November 1981 a new Cabinet Sub-Committee on Nationalised Industries (E(NI)) agreed that in future each of the nationalised industries should publish draft objectives and that sponsor departments should report to it annually on performance and prospects against the objectives and on strategic options requiring collective consideration. The setting up of this Sub-committee of E Committee to oversee the nationalised industries was a recommendation of the CPRS and was agreed at a meeting of Ministers on 4 August 1981. The reports on objectives and strategic options would then feed into the industries' annual investment and financing reviews and, thereafter, to the autumn settlement of EFLs and investment approvals. However, the decision to publish objectives for each of the nationalised industries met with a mixed response amongst Ministers, with Lawson particularly critical of the whole value of the exercise and favouring privatisation instead. Lawson was right to be sceptical. Hoskyns in the No. 10 Policy Unit later wrote to the PM, on 20 April 1982, concluding: "The draft objectives proposed so far are scarcely worth the paper they are written on. There is no chance that they will concentrate the minds of the top management to produce different attitudes or performance."[201] By November the Official Committee on Nationalised Industry Policy based in the Treasury reported that the resulting performance reviews and corporate plans varied greatly in quality and value.[202] Like earlier efforts to improve the performance and accountability of the nationalised industries, this initiative seems to have largely failed to produce anything close to the intended benefits.

Following its report on nationalised industries, the PM requested the CPRS to carry out the study requested by the Chancellor of the Exchequer of the nationalised monopolies. On 6 April 1982 Howe wrote to the PM with copies to members of E(NI) welcoming the study that was now underway "as one of the most important in the CPRS current work programme . . . There is a need to think hard and creatively about means of reducing monopoly and increasing competition, by privatisation where we can but by other means where we cannot".[203] The report, which was completed in October 1982, was a profound document, since surprisingly overlooked, which set out a basis on which the monopoly state utilities might best be privatised.

## The CPRS Report on regulating privatised monopolies

The CPRS report on the nationalised monopolies began by carrying out brief reviews of the coal, electricity, water and telecommunications industries, based on discussions with departmental officials, outsiders and a review of published material and practice overseas, notably in the USA and Germany.[204] It concluded that in the UK many state monopolies supplied products and services "which are not strictly 'natural monopoly' products, defined as those where a second supplier would face prohibitively high costs (including costs of entry), because of the nature of the market and technical economies of scale". Rather, many monopolies had simply been created by statute that prohibited competition. Falling into this latter category the CPRS listed electricity generation, telecommunications services, coal production, local bus transport, collection of water, sewage treatment and disposal, and postal services. Activities "which it is less easy to envisage being duplicated by other suppliers" included those involving expensive investment in networks, notably transmission and distribution of water, gas and electricity, sewerage, and "possibly the provision and maintenance of railway tracks". But overall the CPRS review concluded that "the list of genuine 'natural monopoly' activities is not a long one and it is shrinking."

The report suggested that at least some of the state monopolies could and should in time be privatised. Particularly discussed were telecommunications, electricity and gas. The first step would be to remove the statutory barrier to market entry by competing suppliers, backed up by appropriate regulation. Regulation would be needed to protect the emerging competition from cross-subsidisation and predatory pricing on the part of the existing state monopolies. It would also need to protect consumers from monopoly abuse until competition fully developed. The CPRS was aware of the possibility of regulatory failure and considered US regulation "too bureaucratic and legalistic . . . hearings are too formal and applications for price increases too burdensome"; there were often regulatory delays and "agency capture" had occurred, under which the regulator concentrated on producer rather than consumer interests.[205] The report suggested, therefore, that privatisation in Britain would require the development of a different type of regulatory system and one with "a maximum degree of independence from Government".

The report did not favour regulatory powers remaining after privatisation with the sponsoring departments, commenting: "In principle the Sponsor Department may be in a good position to back Government assurances by detailed supervision of the state industry's behaviour. But in practice we consider that Sponsor Departments are likely to be less effective in this role than an independent regulatory agency."[206] The report went on to point out that in addition to other advantages of a regulator separate from government departments, an independent regulatory agency would be able to recruit professional staff and would be less constrained by civil service terms of employment and remuneration. The recommendation was therefore for an agency managed by a small number of members who would be full-time appointees of government with terms of office of at least five years "with cyclical rotation in order to minimise political interference". To further minimise the risks of political interference, it was suggested that there might be a right of appeal against the regulator's decisions to the Monopolies and Mergers Commission, which had experience of examining public interest questions. On regulating profits it was considered that permitted rates of return should be established by the agency (or the MMC as appellate) rather than by Ministers with major reviews taking place only periodically, "for example every 4 or 5 years" to reduce regulatory costs. In the short term, price restraint could be used where maximum rates of return were likely to be exceeded.[207] Left for further consideration was whether there should be a separate regulatory agency for each of the industries or one covering all of the privatised monopolies.[208]

The report recommended that as far as possible the existing state-owned monopolies should be broken up to create competition before being privatised. To this end it concluded that functional separation into different activities was possible, as was regional separation. Functional separation would assist the development of competition, while the breaking up of national monopolies into separate regional companies would lead to benefits in terms of bringing the industries closer to their consumers, promoting innovation and regional wage bargaining. It would also permit the regulatory agency to undertake regional comparisons of efficiency (what later became known as "benchmarking" or "yardstick competition"). Moreover, where monopoly provision continued, the report concluded that there could be scope for introducing "competition for the field" through franchising and contracting out the monopoly activities.

At the time the report was submitted, the Department of Industry was already planning the sale of British Telecommunications and had begun to discuss establishing an Office of Telecommunications as a regulatory body outside the Department. So it is not the case that the CPRS report anticipated the details of the regulation of BT. Rather, it paralleled them, reflecting a growing recognition inside and outside Government that monopoly utilities did not necessarily need to be state-owned and that establishing new regulatory agencies that worked well was not necessarily overly problematic. Importantly, the report confirmed that even the large state monopolies could be successfully privatised with consumers protected by an independent regulator thereby extending the scope of privatisation dramatically.

The CPRS report is an impressive document both in terms of intellectual content and because it so closely predicted, although it may not have designed, both the regulatory policies introduced for the privatised utilities under later Conservative Governments and developments in competitive tendering for public services. The report reflected the developments in the economic theory of regulation briefly reviewed in chapter 2, pp.22–4. Following the

81

report's circulation the Conservative Research Department felt confident enough to declare that "the Government . . . does not accept that state ownership is the only solution for the so-called natural monopolies."[209] Much earlier, in 1979, the Official Committee on Nationalised Industry Policy, based in the Treasury but with representatives from sponsor departments, had suggested that where regulatory agencies would have to be set up if an industry was transferred to the private sector, there might be no decrease in bureaucracy. It had also concluded that if "natural monopolies" were sold, "The process would take some years and might be of doubtful benefit" given the need to create new regulatory bodies.[210] The CPRS report confirmed, therefore, a substantial step forward in Government thinking. Previously the idea that the monopoly utilities should remain state-owned had received almost total cross-party support; for example, the Ridley Report on the future of the nationalised industries produced when the Conservatives were in Opposition had dismissed the idea of privatising the "natural monopolies".[211] The CPRS report set out a framework for privatising the monopolies and establishing new regulatory structures, anticipating the regulatory bodies set up in the 1980s and 1990s when telecommunications, gas, water, airports, electricity and the railways were privatised.

## A privatisation programme takes shape

By the time of the May 1983 General Election a privatisation programme had begun to take shape and attention had even turned to how the monopoly nationalised industries might be sold successfully. Early in the life of the Government the state of the public finances, exacerbated by the sharp economic recession, had stimulated a search for state assets to sell, but by 1983 privatisation had taken on a stronger rationale in its own right. In November 1981 Lawson remarked in the House of Commons: "No industry should remain under State ownership unless there is a positive and overwhelming case for it so doing."[212] In the same month he had reported to E(DL) that the unpublished gross disposals target of £600 million for 1981/2 would be achieved, provided that there was no significant slippage in the planned disposals.[213]

During 1982 the economic situation had continued to improve. In January the Chancellor of the Exchequer commented that "All the signs are that our efforts to restore the economy to health are succeeding. Inflation is coming down; output is going up; the rate of increase in unemployment is slacking." The PSBR for the current year was planned to be £10.5 billion and the Government was on course to achieve it.[214] The PSBR which was around six per cent of GDP in 1980/1 would fall to three per cent by 1982/3. By the time of the 1983 Budget the Government's fiscal situation had improved sufficiently that the Chancellor was able to raise tax thresholds by nearly three times what was required to reflect inflation and announce other tax savings.[215] In the autumn of 1981 inflation had begun to fall again, having declined sharply between the summers of 1980 and 1981. It would continue to fall for the next 18 months, until it was around four per cent by the time of the 1983 General Election (see Figure 3.1). The value of the pound against the dollar fell from $2.40 to $1.50, helping industrial competitiveness.

With this more favourable economic background, in July 1982 the Chief Secretary to the Treasury was able to give for the first time an upbeat assessment of public spending with the Government on target to keep to the planning totals of £120.5 billion in 1983/4 and £127.7 billion in 1984/5, as agreed the previous autumn.[216] On 2 November 1982 he was able to report to Cabinet that good progress had been made on next year's public expenditure

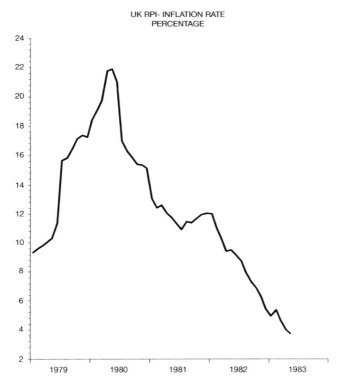

UK RPI- INFLATION RATE
PERCENTAGE

*Figure 3.1* UK RPI inflation rate 1979–83.

*Source*: Office for National Statistics.

in discussions with departmental Ministers and that the expenditure totals would be at or within the previously published planning totals. This was the first time this had been achieved since 1977, and in that year the result was the product of intervention by the IMF. Overall, there was now likely to be a *shortfall* in the planned PSBR for 1982/3 and this provided scope for increases in departmental expenditures, for example in the areas of housing, health and law and order.[217] It also reduced the pressure within Government to sell state assets simply to raise cash. At the same time in 1982/3 the Government paid out £4.6 billion to the nationalised industries to sustain capacity and protect employment and a further £3.46 billion to hold down prices.[218] The nationalised industries were still perceived to be a drain on the Exchequer, which Treasury Ministers were keen to see end.

In February 1981 the first tranche of shares in BAe had been sold successfully. This had been followed by a disposal of shares in C&W in October. In February 1982 TRC was floated in the stock market, under its new name of Amersham International. In the same month NFC was sold through a management-employee buyout and in February 1983 the British Transport Docks Board, renamed Associated British Ports, was privatised through a public flotation. Also, the arrival of Lawson as Secretary of State for Energy in place of Howell in the September 1981 Cabinet changes, saw the privatisation of BNOC's and BGC's oil interests accelerate. A full discussion of the privatisations involving oil assets and of British Aerospace, C&W, Amersham International and the British Transport Docks Board is provided in the next three chapters.

There had also been progress in making some noteworthy smaller disposals, which is summarised here. The 1981 Transport Act, which had authorised the sale of the British Transport Docks Board, also smoothed the way for private investment in subsidiaries of British Rail. The first result was the disposal of 23 British Rail hotels, many of which were run-down and in need of new investment, and some railway catering services. The hotels were sold off from March 1983.[219] By then the planning was advanced for the sale of BR's Sealink ferry service.[220] The disposal of Sealink was completed in July 1984 through a private sale. There were also a number of other specialist asset sales including shares in the Suez Finance Company and motorway service leases in 1979 and 1980, the Government's shares in the British Sugar Corporation in July 1981, the disposal of British Steel subsidiaries in 1982/3, and the sale of the Computer Aided Design Centre, the Hydraulics Research Station and the National Maritime Laboratory in the same period.[221] The Government's 24 per cent shareholding in British Sugar was placed with institutional investors. The BSC assets hived off were Redpath Dorman Long Ltd, Unit Inspection Company, Scunthorpe Open Cast and Bitmac Ltd. In addition, by April 1983 there had been four management buyouts, involving Victaulic Ltd, Britflex, Orkot Engineering Plastics Ltd and Hamilton Foundry. British Steel had also entered into joint ventures with the private sector and had sold certain overseas interests. In the case of the Hydraulics Research Station the Treasury raised concerns about the organisation's business plan and the need for further public funding to enable the privatisation to progress. Nevertheless, after discussion with the Secretary of State for the Environment the sale went ahead.[222] Also, the NEB's investments in a number of companies were gradually unwound. By the spring of 1983 holdings in 35 companies had been sold; prominent amongst these were shares in ICL in December 1979[223] and Ferranti and Fairey in the June and July of 1980. The responsibility for British Leyland and Rolls-Royce had already been transferred to the Department of Industry, as mentioned earlier. What was then left of the NEB was merged with the National Research and Development Corporation to form the British Technology Group.[224] Where state-owned enterprises sold subsidiary businesses the receipts usually remained in the corporations. However, there was an indirect gain to the Exchequer insofar as the corporation's EFL could then be adjusted to reflect the additional receipts.

In addition to all of these sales, there had also been disposals of assets by a number of other government bodies including the Crown Agents, the Forestry Commission, the Government's Property Services Agency and the New Towns, totalling £175 million, and British Leyland had begun to dispose of some of its smaller subsidiaries.[225] The BL businesses sold were Avis, Prestcold and Coventry Climax, together with the company's tractor production assets at Bathgate. In addition, there were two small management buyouts, at Rearsby Components and Goodwin Barsby. One of the first state-owned enterprises where a share sale was authorised had been British Airways, under the Civil Aviation Bill 1980. Economic and legal problems meant that the sale had to be postponed, but in March 1983 International Aeradio, which provided computer and aviation communication services and airport management services, was successfully divested from BA and transferred through a private sale to Standard Telephone and Cable.

In the summer of 1982 the Chancellor had requested that government departments consider the scope for contracting out more of their activities to the private sector and had followed this up with a paper on the subject.[226] The initiative had been warmly welcomed in No. 10 and had won the backing of the Cabinet.[227] Contracting out in central government including government agencies such as research and development establishments was under review by May 1983, possibly as a prelude to a full transfer to the private sector. By the end of 1982 civil service employment had fallen by 14 per cent compared with the level in 1979, but mainly due to the spending squeeze rather than contracting out.[228]

The Government had also acted to promote competitive tendering in the nationalised industries and the NHS; while Michael Heseltine at the Department of the Environment had been active in promoting contracting out by local authorities. The 1980 Local Government Planning and Land Act gave him the power to oblige local authorities to release unused or underused local authority land for sale. The same Act required local authorities to open up construction and maintenance work to competitive tendering. As a result, local authority direct labour organisations now competed with the private sector for construction and maintenance work. The country also saw the beginnings of a transfer of refuse collection and street cleaning services to private firms, with Conservative councils in Southend and Wandsworth leading the way.[229] The Audit Commission was established in 1982 to monitor and improve the performance of local administration in England and Wales and would in subsequent years help to promote privatisation in the form of competitive tendering, which the Government was keen to encourage.[230] Later its brief was extended to include audits of spending by the NHS. Paralleling this development, the Comptroller and Auditor-General's department was converted into a new National Audit Office in 1983 with a remit to "follow public money wherever it goes". In the following years the NAO would provide an important oversight of central government spending and of privatisations.

Alongside these initiatives aimed at reducing costs and raising efficiency in government, immediately after the 1979 Election the PM had established an Efficiency Unit within No. 10, headed by Sir Derek Rayner the Managing Director of the successful retailer Marks & Spencer.[231] This had been commissioned to root out inefficiencies in central government. From 1982 Rayner's Financial Management Initiative was extended across all government departments.[232] Within the Department of the Environment Michael Heseltine championed a complementary management project called MINIS (Management Information System for Ministers).[233] The aim was to cut out waste and identify activities that might be done better in the private sector.

There had also been some notable market liberalisation measures during the first Thatcher Government. A law was passed in 1981 to allow the Post Office's monopoly of mail delivery to be suspended and to permit private operators to supply express mail and parcel services. In addition, the Government acted to reduce the public sector monopoly in electricity supply, permitting private electricity generation. This was authorised by the Energy Act 1983. There had also been a similar reform in the gas sector under the Oil and Gas (Enterprise) Act 1982, with British Gas required to provide a common carrier facility to any other enterprise which wished to supply gas. However, a lack of private sector interest in investing, given the entrenched position of the state-owned electricity and gas suppliers, meant that there would be little private investment in electricity and gas until the industries were fully privatised, which came later.[234]

More successful was the opening up of express coach services to competition. The 1980 Transport Act made it easier for private sector operators to be licensed for bus services and established three trial areas where private bus companies could operate a local service without first obtaining a licence. The Act also opened up the provision of long-distance coach services to competition. This led to a large increase in the number of coach services and with it a fall in prices. However, the opening up to competition of other bus services would not occur until the next Conservative Government (chapter 10). Perhaps most important of all, BT had been split from the Post Office, a new fixed-line competitor had been licensed and legislation had been introduced to privatise BT. In 1981 the Telecommunications Bill provided the Secretary of State with powers to liberalise the telecommunications industry.[235] On 5 July 1981 at supper with Sir Keith Joseph, Kenneth Baker, Minister of State for Information Technology, and David Young, Joseph's special adviser on privatisation in the Department of Industry, obtained Joseph's agreement to proceed with the planning of legislation to privatise BT. This was an important moment in the history of British privatisation. BT would be the first domestic state-owned monopoly to be privatised. Given its importance, the privatisation of BT is discussed in detail in chapters 11 to 13 below.

Finally, there had been a large-scale disposal of public sector housing. Previously local authorities had the option whether to offer council homes for sale to their tenants. Most did not promote purchase and by 1974 no more than seven per cent of the council housing stock had been sold. During the 1974–79 Labour Government sales were not encouraged. In the mid-1970s Heseltine had persuaded Margaret Thatcher, after some initial resistance, to commit a future Conservative Government to sell council homes to tenants at a sharp price discount to encourage purchase. The resulting "right to buy" policy was included in the Conservatives' 1979 Election Manifesto. In the 1980 Housing Act council home tenants of three or more years' standing were given the right to purchase their homes at two-thirds of the market value with a further one per cent discount for each year of tenancy (up to a total discount of 50 per cent). The measure was fiercely opposed by the Labour Party. When some councils continued to put barriers in the way of purchasing through delays in respond-ing to tenants' applications, by trying to dissuade tenants from buying and by imposing conditions on a sale, legal action ensued and the Government won.[236] By May 1983 half a million homes had been bought from councils or other public bodies such as New Town development corporations. In addition, some 200,000 applications to purchase were in the pipeline.[237] In 1982/3 alone over £750 million was raised from house sales, with the receipts staying with councils. Local authorities were permitted to spend 50 per cent of the capital receipts on building new homes, but given the discounted price of the housing sold plus having in many cases to offer mortgages to tenants so that they could buy, the real amount available to councils to reinvest in housing from home sales was often less than ten per cent.[238]

As a result of the Act, between 1979 and 1983 more public sector homes passed into private ownership than in all of the years since 1945. Also, because the sale was not matched by building replacement council homes, there was an overall privatisation of the country's housing stock. In terms of the volume of homes sold in the 1980s and the total receipts, arguably housing was the largest single privatisation of the Thatcher years. It became a flagship Conservative Party policy at elections and did much to create the ethos of a "property owning democracy" that the Party craved. Also, there was evidence that tenants who had purchased their properties were more likely to vote Conservative, which was an added political bonus for the Government. On the downside, it was tenants in public sector houses rather than flats and away from "sink" estates who were the keenest to buy. Consequently, the quality as well as the quantity of the remaining public sector housing stock declined, leaving less choice for low income families. The result in time was fewer housing for those on low incomes. Unfazed, in 1983 Heseltine proposed legislative amendments to extend the right to buy by reducing the qualifying period before a tenant could purchase and increasing the price discount.

The area of public policy which remained out of bounds for privatisation during the first Thatcher Government was the welfare state, leaving aside council home sales and some extension of competitive tendering. This would remain true of later Conservative Governments too. Privatisation of the welfare state raised affordability issues that did not obviously apply to the outputs of the nationalised industries.

Some work had been undertaken by Patrick Jenkin, then shadow Health Secretary, on private health insurance and pensions while in Opposition. However, in the May 1979 General Election campaign Conservative spokesmen steered well clear of controversy on the welfare state by promising, in particular, to maintain expenditure on the National Health Service. The Education Act 1980 widened parental choice of schools and set up the Assisted Places Scheme, under which independent secondary schools could offer places to children from poorer families with Government contributing to the fees. Legislation in the same year introduced some changes to social security including restricting payments to strikers. But these were modest measures.[239]

In July 1981 Jenkin, now at the Department of Health and Social Security, set up a departmental working group to study alternative funding options for the NHS. Also, the Chancellor of the Exchequer was known to be keen to see some radical ideas put forward so as to reduce the cost of the welfare state and provide more room for tax cuts.[240] However, deliberation within Government was effectively halted when in September 1982 a report by the CPRS was leaked to *The Economist* magazine. The document set out proposals for a major dismantling of the welfare state, including the scrapping of state-funding of higher education, de-linking benefits and old age pensions from inflation and a private insurance-based health service. *The Economist* claimed that the document had the backing of the Treasury;[241] but the Government quickly acted to distance itself from the content.[242]

To minimise the potential political damage the PM disowned the document, later calling the uproar it created in the media "the greatest nonsense".[243] At the Conservative Party Annual Conference the following month she attempted to smooth ruffled feathers by proclaiming "let me make one thing absolutely clear. The National Health Service is safe with us".[244] Ian Gilmour's comment that "A whiff of excessive protestation was detectable in the Government's pronouncements" rings true.[245] Thatcher's instincts were to see more private provision in all areas of the economy including welfare services and this was also true of some of her Ministerial colleagues, especially Sir Keith Joseph. But the PM had acute political antennae, believing that privatisation of health and education in particular would be unacceptable to voters. There was also the point that while organisations such as the Institute of Economic Affairs promoted denationalisation of industry, and were winning over more economists to the idea, there had been much less consideration of alternatives to the welfare state by right-wing think tanks. There was certainly little guidance on how best to privatise welfare in a politically acceptable way.[246]

The PM's conference pledge on the NHS effectively ruled out any significant changes to welfare provision and especially with the principle of "free" health care while she remained PM. At the same time, Thatcher's claims of innocence did not stop the Labour Party and the Alliance Party (recently created by a combination of Liberal and Social Democrat MPs newly defected from Labour) making much of the Government's obvious discomfort on the issue during the 1983 Election campaign. Immediately after the 1983 Election the PM punished the CPRS for the embarrassment it had caused her by abolishing it.[247] On announcing her decision at a Cabinet meeting in July 1983 the PM commented, in a thinly veiled reference to the report on the welfare state: "The CPRS had been a valuable organisation in the early years after the 1979 General Election, but studies of the kind the CPRS had recently undertaken needed firm political direction and would be better carried out in the planning units which had now been set up in a number of Departments."

\*    \*    \*

From 1979 to 1981 under pressure from the Treasury, Ministers had scratched around for public assets to sell in the pursuit of quick cash rather than an agreed economic agenda. From 1981 this had started to change and privatisation had become less a financial imperative and more a matter of principle – not that the financial case for privatisation ever entirely disappeared, so far as the Treasury was concerned at least. The Queen's Speech on the Opening of the last Parliament of the first Thatcher administration, on 3 November 1982, referred to measures being brought forward "to permit private investment in British Telecommunications, to establish a telecommunications regulatory body and to reform the Telegraph Acts, to encourage private undertakings to generate and supply electricity, and to facilitate the introduction of private capital into British Shipbuilders".[248] In July the PM had sent a minute to Ministers about the need to sustain the momentum of the privatisation programme commenting: "Suitable candidates institutions *and* functions need to be identified. And subsequent preparations for privatisation need to be pursued as vigorously as possible."[249] In October 1982 the Financial Secretary responded by suggesting regular six-monthly reviews of progress in selling state assets to create a momentum.[250] Each department would now be asked to provide a list of its privatisation candidates on a regular basis. The privatisation programme was now well underway and although the sales so far had not raised large amounts – £493 million in 1981/2 and £455 million in 1982/3[251] – this was all about to change. By the time of the May 1983 General Election a number of privatisations had already been completed or were being planned. The Government had come a long way in four years. Earlier reservations within the administration about both the desirability and practicality of privatisation had faded, except in relation to the welfare state. The Conservatives' Election Manifesto in May 1983 promised a radical privatisation agenda.

Under the second Conservative administration between May 1983 and June 1987 over £10 billion of state assets would be privatised, including a number of major state-owned industries, amongst them telecommunications and gas. The groundwork for this was laid, sometimes painfully, during the first Thatcher Government. The next three chapters look in detail at each of the main privatisations during the first Thatcher administration, namely the oil production assets of the British National Oil Corporation and British Gas, British Aerospace, Cable and Wireless, Amersham International, the National Freight Corporation and Associated British Ports. Each of the privatisations provides useful insights into how privatisation policy evolved from a standing start in May 1979, as well as the difficulties faced.

# 4

# PRIVATISING OIL

The previous chapter recounted how privatisation developed as policy during the first Conservative Government. In this and the following two chapters the main privatisations initiated between May 1979 and June 1983 are discussed in detail. Specifically, this chapter considers the disposal of British Petroleum (BP) shares and the British National Oil Corporation's and the British Gas Corporation's oil production interests. The other two chapters look at the privatisation of British Aerospace and Cable and Wireless and then Amersham International, the National Freight Corporation and Associated British Ports. They were the big privatisations of the first Thatcher Government and their successful transfer to the private sector provided the platform for the privatisations that came later, after the Conservatives were returned to power in May 1983. The experience gained and mistakes made during these initial privatisations are summarised and analysed in chapter 7. A number of the industries covered were transferred to the private sector through a series of shares sales. For convenience, in each case not only are the tranches of shares sold during the 1979–83 Government covered in these chapters but also the subsequent tranches, even though they occurred under later Governments. This is intended to assist those studying the history of particular privatisations. A similar policy is adopted for the privatisations discussed in subsequent chapters.

## The beginnings

The previous Labour Government had sold 17 per cent of the issued share capital of BP plc in June 1977, reducing the Government's holding down to 51 per cent of the shares. However, this was not seen as a precedent for future disposals. The Labour Government had sold the shares only under extreme financial pressure and during the May 1979 Election campaign Margaret Thatcher had denied any intention of selling BP shares. Nevertheless, oil assets, including shares in BP and the oil and gas field interests of the British National Oil Corporation (BNOC) and the British Gas Corporation (BGC), were early candidates for disposal in 1979 identified by the Treasury.

Their sale quickly ran into difficulties. In particular, Lord Kearton, the Chairman of BNOC, and Sir Denis Rooke, the Chairman of BGC, both opposed the sales. Also, the Secretary of State for Energy, David Howell, had strong reservations about a quick disposal and canvassed against a Government confrontation with the boards. While agreeing with the idea of widening the ownership of state-owned industries, he believed that selling oil and gas assets too quickly "could lead to damaging accusations of bad business practice, benefiting the investor at the expense of the taxpayer. It could discredit and undermine the Government's whole approach to the unwinding of the public sector".[1] Howell believed that the Government should delay a sale of oil assets because they would be more valuable in the future and because he favoured the sale of oil enterprises rather than particular oilfields. He also argued that it would be politically difficult to justify a sale of oil assets at a time when oil supplies were in short supply on world markets.

Howell seems to have concluded that annual budgetary constraints should not control the pace and shape of disposals and decisions on method of sale and that decisions on sales should "only be taken after full consultation with the Chairman and the Board of the industry concerned".[2] In the early months of the new Government the Department of Energy adopted a cautious approach to oil asset sales, to the frustration of Treasury Ministers. The Department may have had understandable concerns about a precipitous and ill-considered disposal of the assets. But more serious as an obstacle to a quick sell-off was the opposition of the BNOC and BGC Boards.

The nationalised oil assets were controlled by BGC and BNOC. BGC had been reliant on town gas produced from coal, supplemented by imports of liquefied natural gas, until the discovery in the late 1960s of natural gas in the North Sea. During the 1970s the Corporation built up interests in North Sea gas exploration, of which a by-product was oil, and began to develop onshore oilfields, of which the most important was Wytch Farm in Dorset, developed jointly with BP. BNOC was set up in 1975 by the Labour Government, to ensure the security of oil supplies to the UK from the North Sea fields under development by private sector oil companies. In Opposition the Conservatives had opposed its creation, seeing it as simply another example of wasteful state intervention. By 1979 the enterprise had become a large-scale oil producer in partnership with private sector oil companies and was also the country's primary oil trader. Its oil trading role arose mainly by virtue of its rights to royalties in kind through participation agreements in field developments with other oil companies and because of a preferred position in licensing rounds for new North Sea oil developments. For example, in April 1978 it was given nine new blocks to develop. By May 1979 BNOC had interests in the Thistle, Ninian, Dunlin, Marchinson, Statfjord and smaller fields. Therefore, while it produced only seven per cent of North Sea oil, it had the right to buy and sell a large proportion of the rest. By 1979 BNOC was entitled to purchase up to 51 per cent of the country's oil from the UK Continental shelf (UKCS). The company also had a statutory role as adviser to the Government on North Sea oil matters and an entitlement to a seat on every operating committee managing the North Sea fields, pipelines and terminals. In addition, BNOC effectively had first refusal whenever an interest in North Sea oil was assigned between companies. After the election the Government moved quickly to reduce BNOC's preferred position in North Sea oil developments, its preferential tax treatment and its special status as adviser to the Government on North Sea oil matters.[3]

The disposal of shares in BP along with the oil assets of BNOC and BGC was announced in the Chancellor's Budget in June 1979. Indeed, the sale of oil assets accounted for the largest single part of the Chancellor's £1 billion disposals target for the financial year 1979/80. The sums to be raised were £200 million from the sale of BNOC or BGC assets and £650 million from the sale of shares in BP. The PM seems initially to have leant in favour of BP purchasing all of BNOC's exploration, development and production assets, a proposition that, unsurprisingly, BP found attractive.[4] A sale to BP appeared to be a simple solution to disposing of BNOC's production interests, which had the merit, importantly for the PM, of transferring them to a British company.[5] A number of other companies operating in the North Sea were American and could be expected to bid for BNOC's assets in a public sale. However, BNOC was opposed to the proposal.

At the same time the Treasury demanded the selling of some of BNOC's oilfield investments to achieve the Chancellor of the Exchequer's target. But complicating any quick sale was the oilfield participation agreements that BNOC had entered into to meet the Labour Government's objective of ensuring state control over North Sea exploration and production. These agreements meant that it would normally be necessary to get the consent of BNOC's partners to any disposal of the oilfield assets. Pre-emption rights also existed under the agreements so that the partner oil companies would have the option of making a first bid in any sale. Alternatively, the rights would have to be negotiated away with each of the companies involved in the oilfields in which BNOC had an interest, of which there were 35.[6] Clearly this would be a very time-consuming exercise and there was uncertainty as to its outcome. If some of the companies refused to sign away their rights, which was felt to be quite likely, then the Department of Energy considered that it was probable that the partner companies would insist on acquiring the assets sold off. Some of the partners were British companies (i.e. Burmah, ICI, BP, Shell, LASMO, Charterhouse and P&O), but other partners were from the US. The Treasury concluded that selling to them could produce "presentational problems" and advised that, "it should be possible, though no doubt with some ill feelings, to turn down any bids from them, though perhaps at the expense of failing to realise the best price."[7] A competitive bidding process would produce the largest revenues, although with the risk of disposal to a foreign purchaser. The PM made it quite clear already that she was against oil from the UKCS falling into foreign hands. Nigel Lawson comments in his memoirs that proposals to privatise BNOC faced "Margaret's acute sensitivity that privatisation . . . implied that Britain would somehow lose control of part of her oil".[8]

The future of the Government's oil assets was discussed in early meetings of the Cabinet Sub-Committee on disposals (E(DL)) and the Cabinet's economic strategy committee (E Committee) during the early summer of 1979. At the time the preference of the Secretary of State for Energy was for BNOC's oil production assets to be transferred to a new subsidiary company, which could at a later date issue shares to the public but where the Government might retain a majority shareholding. In his view this had the advantage of giving the British public the opportunity to invest, while protecting national oil interests. Also, it would not close off the option of a later sale of the new subsidiary to BP should this turn out to be the best option.[9] However, the proposal had disadvantages, notably the time it would take to arrange such a disposal. Proceeding down this route would mean that BNOC would contribute nothing in the 1979/80 financial year and nor possibly in 1980/1 to the Chancellor of the Exchequer's targets for annual disposals. Unsurprisingly, therefore, Howell's plan did not meet with an enthusiastic response from the Treasury.[10] The Chancellor was also concerned that if the Government retained a majority shareholding in any company created, the company's borrowings would remain part of the PSBR. This would scuttle much of the logic behind privatisation as seen from the perspective of a Treasury desperate to reduce public sector borrowing.[11] A further potential problem related to a $675 million loan raised by BNOC through a forward oil sale. The terms of the loan agreement seemed to give the banks concerned a right to demand immediate repayment of the loan if the Corporation's assets were sold. However, there was a possibility that the banks would not invoke this right.

## A faltering start

In E(DL) on 20 June 1979 the Financial Secretary, Nigel Lawson, put forward proposals for the sale of BP shares. The proposals involved the Government selling 16 per cent of the shares, thus lowering its holding from 51 per cent to 35 per cent of the issued stock.[12] This holding was considered to be the minimum consistent with maintaining the present arrangement of having two Government Directors on the Board of BP. Lawson's intention was that the issue should give preference to small shareholders and to the company's employees, thereby "promoting the widest possible participation by the people in the ownership of British industry".[13] BP wanted to see preference given to the existing shareholders, but the Treasury was not sympathetic as this would not widen share ownership and would simply benefit the large City institutions with current holdings in BP. In Opposition Sir Geoffrey Howe had championed the spread of property ownership. As Chancellor of the Exchequer, like the Financial Secretary, he was keen that wherever possible Government asset disposals should offer a means of increasing small shareholding amongst the public at large. The objective of widening share ownership was part of privatisation planning from the outset. Lawson also recommended that a minority of the shares, perhaps 20 per cent to 25 per cent, should be sold in New York, and possibly in another European centre such as Frankfurt. This was expected to increase the sale proceeds by as much as 3–5 per cent and reduce "the risk of crowding out the UK equity market and to some the extent the gilt edged market too".[14] That it was feared that the proposed sale of BP shares might "crowd out" the stock market is testimony to the uncertainties that surrounded the ability of Government to attract sufficient investor interest in privatisation issues in these early days. The planned issue was comparatively modest compared to the large privatisation issues that came later.

Although the Chancellor of the Exchequer was committed to selling shares in BP, it seems that the PM was more hesitant to sanction an early sale, especially if it might involve a foreign purchaser.[15] Her concerns related to the state of the international oil market and retaining national influence over North Sea oil assets. On hearing of the terms of the 16 per cent share sale agreed in E(DL), she requested that alternative assets for sale be found "so that the number of BP shares to be sold can be kept to a minimum".[16] She was not alone. Howell had reservations too and on 24 June the Secretary of State for Trade, John Nott, telephoned the PM to state that he felt like "a renegade on this issue".[17] Another Minister, Peter Walker, also expressed doubts about the desirability of selling oil assets given the current energy crisis.[18] The PM responded by saying that she had not realised "that the disposal was to be tackled with such speed". By telegram during a trip to Tokyo in late June, she made it known that she did not want to see any further preparations made for the sale of BP shares until her return.[19] The PM's prevarication on an early sale of BP equity meant that a hole was immediately blown in the Chancellor's Budget arithmetic.[20] In response, the Treasury became even more convinced that there would have to be an immediate sale of some of BNOC's oil assets.

Both the Treasury and the Department of Energy shared the view that BNOC's oil trading role should be retained in the state sector to protect North Sea oil flows for the UK economy at a time of shortages in world markets.[21] No doubt this would also be necessary to placate the PM. The Government's aim was also to take BNOC's regulatory functions relating to North Sea oilfield development into the Department of Energy.

The issue was the wisdom of disposing of BNOC's exploration, development and production facilities. As a minute within No. 10 commented at the time, "'Knowledge is power' and to some extent the ability of the Government to achieve security of supply (and an adequate tax take) depends on its knowledge of what is going on in the oil and gas fields . . . Membership of the Operating Committees of each field [through BNOC] is a very important source of information which cannot be achieved by keeping a purely trading function."[22]

The Conservatives' Election Manifesto had merely promised to "undertake a complete review of all the activities of the British National Oil Corporation as soon as we take office"[23] and there was no consensus within the Conservative Party as to the best way forward. In particular, there was no commitment to denationalise. For example, John Redwood, a critic of nationalisation and from January 1984 head of the No. 10 Policy Unit, wrote in the mid-1970s on the future of BNOC: "BNOC has built a wide range of oil interests rapidly and the rapid escalation in the oil price has underwritten its profitability. Any or all of its assets are readily saleable: it is a fine political judgement as to whether they should be sold."[24] While it was a Labour creation, Redwood recognised that BNOC did serve a useful purpose in achieving greater government control of oil extraction from the North Sea.

In July 1979 Howell wrote to the PM confirming that BP was definitely interested in acquiring all the exploration, development and production activities of BNOC. To overcome the difficulty of pre-emption rights, he suggested that the assets could be transferred first to a new subsidiary company of BNOC and then BP would buy the shares of this company. However, in spite of the apparent attractions of the proposal in terms of simplicity and retaining British ownership, Howell was now not in favour. He advised that the scheme "would be a very high risk course" given the need to get a fair price for the business and the significant market share that BP would then have of UKCS oil production (approaching 22 per cent of reserves and 24 per cent of licensed territory). There was also the likelihood that BP would choose to finance the acquisition using a rights issue, which would require the Government to buy more BP shares or see its shareholding in the company diluted. It was unlikely the Treasury would welcome additional spending on buying BP shares.[25]

In E Committee on 24 July 1979 Howell put forward three alternative options as a way forward: (1) that it might be possible to sell all or most of BNOC's upstream assets to BP in a single package; (2) to sell around £600 million of BP shares, together with a smaller scale disposal of around £200 million of BNOC's and possibly BGC's oil assets; and (3) to sell fewer BP shares but more of BNOC's and possibly BGC's assets.[26] However, it was clear that the PM's support for a quick sale of BNOC could not be relied upon. There was also growing uncertainty as to whether a sale of BNOC's exploration and production facilities to BP would necessarily overcome the pre-emption rights issue. There was also the opposition of the BNOC Board to a disposal to consider, and it was felt in the Department of Energy that a sale exclusively to BP might weaken the Government's future negotiating stance in respect of future UKCS exploration licences, given BP's resulting dominant position in the North Sea.[27] This brought the Committee to the third alternative. Under this option the Government would sell about eight per cent of its holding of BP shares, raising around £350 million. The remaining £400 million needed to meet the Chancellor's target would then be found by selling assets of BNOC, and probably BGC as well. After discussion, on balance the Chancellor of the Exchequer backed this course, which "would leave BNOC as a realistic operation, without prejudging the eventual introduction of private capital into the Corporation's remaining activities".

Howell was requested by E Committee to consult with BNOC, BGC and BP to arrange the sales needed to yield the Treasury's disposals target. BP would be allowed to bid for BNOC's and possibly BGC's oil assets but with no guarantee of winning. Also, for this proposal to succeed the corporations would need to persuade their oilfield partners to forego or sell their pre-emption rights. Still concerned about the security of the country's oil supplies, the PM stressed that if BP did not purchase all of the assets, "the remaining purchases must be by British companies".[28]

With a decision having been taken on BP and BNOC, attention turned to BGC. On 4 September Howell wrote separately to the Chancellor of the Exchequer and the Financial Secretary stressing that an early sale of BGC assets, including the Corporation's onshore oilfield Wytch Farm in Dorset, would be problematic because of difficulty in valuing the relevant assets. Howell also noted that he might need to take legal enabling powers to complete a sale given the opposition of the Board.[29] One possibility would be for the Secretary of State to issue the Board with a Direction. But the issuing of a Direction was far from problem-free. The Gas Act 1972 gave the Secretary of State for Energy power to direct BGC to sell its oilfield interests, although not necessarily the power to direct the Corporation as to whom to sell to.[30] This was a stumbling block given the PM's aim of keeping oil assets British, especially since BGC's partners in the offshore fields were American oil companies and could be expected to be keen bidders. However, the sale of the profitable onshore Wytch Farm field, which represented roughly half of the total value of BGC's oilfield interests, did not pose this problem. BGC's partner in this venture was BP, which could be expected to buy BGC's share.[31]

At E Committee on 10 September 1979 Howell reported that he had decided not to recommend the option of the sale of any part of BGC in 1979/80 because this "could not readily be done in the time available". BGC's management were likely to continue to oppose a sale with the consequence that he would need to resort to a formal Direction to the Board. It was to be expected that this would be "fiercely contested". He was also of the view that the best asset to sell eventually would be Wytch Farm, but considered that there was no point in selling that asset at the present moment because its valuation was so uncertain.[32] Instead, Howell preferred to focus on the disposal of some of BNOC's oil interests. He suggested that £400 million could be found for the Treasury through the sale of BNOC's interests in the Viking and adjacent gasfields in the North Sea and its investments in part of the Statfjord field, preferably to BP. If these sales fell short of £400 million, Lord Kearton, Chairman of BNOC, had now agreed, albeit reluctantly, to the additional sale of interests in another North Sea field, Dunlin, raising perhaps £150–170 million. However, in all cases it would take time to value the fields accurately and negotiate with partners over contractual rights. Also, Howell anticipated considerable continuing opposition to the sales within BNOC and a possible need for legislation to force a sale. He warned that at best BNOC would only be persuaded to accept these sales "provided no further disposals were in prospect".[33] It was clear that BNOC management regarded any sale as a bad business decision. The management argued that the likely disposal value would be low compared to the cash inflows that would accrue, at a time of rising oil prices, from the assets in future years. After discussion the Treasury agreed not to pursue the sale of BNOC's exploration, development and production interests in the current financial year.[34] It would not be possible to force through a sale in the face of a lack of enthusiasm from the Secretary of State for Energy and the outright opposition of the Chairman of BNOC.

To bridge the gap between the amount that was now likely to be raised from the sale of oil and gas assets in 1979/80 and the Chancellor of the Exchequer's Budget target of £1 billion, Howell recommended that BNOC be authorised to sell oil for future delivery in return for cash now. It was expected that this might yield over £400 million, although with the disadvantage that the action, effectively an advance payment for oil, would have to be rolled forward in future years if a negative impact on the Government's finances in a later year was to be avoided.[35] Although the Chancellor of the Exchequer was unhappy with this proposal, in the absence of progress with the sale of oilfields he reluctantly agreed. With no prospect of a disposal of BNOC assets in the current financial year, the Chancellor's funding gap would now be met largely through forward oil sales.[36] The Government would be paid for a large part of the oil sold through BNOC at the beginning of each financial year. In return the oil companies would be guaranteed North Sea oil for refining to a guaranteed value.[37] Although the resulting sums would be included in the Government's figures for disposals revenues (Table 3.4 above), these were not privatisation revenues at all. There was more bad news for the Treasury. With the PM and a number of other Ministers still anxious about the proposed sale of even eight per cent of BP shares, at the same meeting of E Committee on 10 September 1979 it was decided that the plan should be further scaled back and only around five per cent of the total share capital should be disposed of. The share sale went ahead in November, when 80 million BP shares were sold. The BP offer was oversubscribed 1.5 times and dealings in the shares opened at a small price premium. The net proceeds from the sale were £276 million after the costs of the sale.[38] The Government retained 46 per cent of BP's issued shares, and the right to appoint two directors to the BP Board and the power to veto any Board resolution. The sale was handled by the Bank of England, which was responsible for the appointment of the underwriting banks, the brokers, receiving banks and solicitors to the offer. However, after the BP share sale, the Bank largely withdrew from this form of privatisation and future privatisations (except for future sales of BP shares) were handled by the firm's sponsor department in conjunction with the Treasury.[39] The Bank continued to advise on the timing of sales and related issues in the capital market to prevent a privatisation flotation clashing with and disrupting other new issues.

The Government was keen for BP's employees to be encouraged to buy shares and had pressed BP for a scheme involving loans to employees to purchase shares directly from the company through a trust fund. The Conservatives believed that employee shareholding would improve industrial relations by giving workers a bigger stake in the companies for which they worked. But the BP Board rejected the proposal on a mixture of cost and tax grounds, preferring a matching share scheme.[40] Under the scheme implemented, each BP employee was allowed to apply for up to 137 shares representing a value of around £497. If the shares were then allocated to trustees of the BP Group Participating Share Scheme, an equal number of shares were allocated free of charge to the Scheme for the benefit of that employee.[41]

The sale was a "privatisation" insofar as it reduced the state's shareholding in BP to under 50 per cent. However, the sale of this modest number of BP shares – Labour had sold a much larger 17 per cent of the share capital in 1977 – provided a diffident start to the Government's privatisation programme. Also BP had always operated independently of government.[42] Therefore, there could be no question of the privatisation reducing political interference in the company and increasing efficiency within BP and this was never raised as a motive for the sale. The motive for selling BP shares in November 1979 was purely financial. In September 1983 another 130 million shares in BP were sold through the stock market for £566 million, reducing the Government's holding to 32 per cent. [43]The remainder of the Government's shareholding in BP was similarly disposed of in October 1987.

## An uncertain future for BNOC

E Committee returned to the subject of the future of BNOC on 26 November 1979.[44] At this meeting Howell set out two options for eventual private sector participation in BNOC's upstream activities: (1) to separate the upstream assets into a subsidiary company, "BNOC Operating", and to sell off part of the Government's interest, leaving a minimum 25 per cent public sector stake in the oil trading side of BNOC, "BNOC Trading", to protect the national interest; or (2) to retain a unitary BNOC "with a continuing Government interest" so as to protect BNOC's trading activities and the Government's influence over the disposal of North Sea oil. His preference was for the first alternative because it would raise more funds for the Treasury and would be consistent with the Government's aim of denationalising much of BNOC. He ruled out selling all of the oil trading operations because no investor would believe a commitment from the Government not to interfere in oil trading in the future. The total flotation value of BNOC Operating was expected to be in the region of £1.5 billion, based on a preliminary assessment of its gross assets. Howell believed that a public issue could be made in two or more stages, starting "if possible" in late 1980. However, he went on to explain that he would like to keep open the option of disposing of some shares through a free issue to the general public. It seems that he was quite taken at this time by a government issue made in British Columbia.[45] Under the British Columbia scheme, citizens were entitled to apply for five free shares and up to 5,000 shares at a price of C$6 in a British Columbia resources company.

The proposal for free shares was fiercely contested in E Committee, no doubt by Treasury Ministers.[46] It was labelled "administratively complicated and expensive even if confined to a small section of the general public" and it was considered to "involve a significant loss of revenue". With the early privatisation programme heavily influenced by the Chancellor's Budget sums, giving away or heavily discounting the price of shares to the public could be expected to hold little attraction. Interestingly, this and related exchanges on the British Columbia scheme seem to be the only ones of substance recorded in Cabinet papers on providing the public with free shares. In a meeting with the PM on 14 November 1979 Howell had expressed his interest in the British Columbia scheme and the PM had made it known she was not in favour. Her position was summarised by her Private Secretary in the following words: "Too many people, if simply given shares in the North Sea, would not appreciate them."[47] Giving away free shares in the nationalised industries to the public, which was also advocated at the time by Samuel Brittan, an economist and journalist at the *Financial Times*, was not at all attractive to Treasury Ministers or the PM. There was no chance that it would be adopted.

At the meeting on 26 November 1979 some opposition to a sale of BNOC was voiced because it was felt it would involve a loss of control over the Corporation's interests in the North Sea oilfields. Under Howell's plan the Government might retain a minority 25 per cent of the voting rights in the company, as a deterrent to foreign ownership of BNOC. Would this be sufficient? Also, there was a suggestion that any sale of shares in BNOC should occur gradually over up to three years to take advantage of a rising market for oil assets.[48] Regarding the type of share flotation, Howell endorsed a recommendation by his financial advisers, Samuel Montagu, to use an underwritten fixed price offer for sale. An underwritten offer for sale was the method also adopted for the BP share disposal the following month. The alternative of a sale by tender was rejected because "A tender issue could well fail to achieve a satisfactory balance between the two important (and potentially conflicting) objectives of maximising receipts and maximising the spread of [share] holders." Moreover, in his view there was no guarantee that a sale by tender would produce higher receipts as there was risk of setting too high a reserve price leading to under-subscription.[49]

Under a fixed price offer for sale, investors apply for shares knowing the price they will have to pay, but the price is not adjustable to reflect the number of applications made for the shares on offer. Under a sale by tender, by contrast, bids are invited for shares at a price at or above a minimum tender price. The final sale price, known as the "striking price", then reflects demand for the shares in relation to the supply on offer. A sale by tender is therefore more likely to maximise the selling price and minimise over-subscription. The main disadvantage of the method is that it is less attractive to small investors because of its additional complexity, notably the uncertainty over the final, striking price. In addition, a fixed price offer was normal practice for larger share flotations and tended to be favoured by City investors.

An objective of the BNOC disposal included widening share ownership, which told in favour of a fixed price offer. At the same time, there was concern in the Department of Energy that if large numbers of small investors were attracted to the issue there could be difficulties in administering the company's share register. Also, share purchases by individuals "could well be financed in a counter-productive fashion through the encashment of National Savings Certificates and similar widely held investments".[50] This might have an unwelcome offsetting effect on the Treasury's task of funding the PSBR. The tentative view at this stage was that it might be possible to resolve some of the administrative difficulties "by providing that the people will hold their interest not directly in the form of shares but indirectly in the form of units in a trust which would be the registered holder of the people's share in Operating". Voting rights would then be exercised by the trustees. The idea of holding shares indirectly in a trust also surfaced during the early planning of the sale of British Telecom in 1982/3. However, it was eventually rejected because of the inherent complexities of trust share-holdings. The idea was also quietly dropped for BNOC.

Although the eventual disposal of BNOC had been favourably discussed in E Committee, in the spring of 1980 many of the details had yet to be thrashed out. Also, a sceptical note had been introduced into the deliberations in the form of a memorandum from the Central Policy Review Staff within the Cabinet Office. The CPRS memorandum raised concerns about the selling of BNOC assets because of the Corporation's large positive contribution each year to the PSBR.[51] In 1980/1 BNOC contributed £205 million to the Exchequer through a negative EFL. BNOC was profitable and the CPRS warned that, "Privatising BNOC and selling £1 billion of BNOC's assets benefits the PSBR in the years in which the assets are sold, but the £1 billion gained is purchased at a high price in terms of PSBR benefits stretching out into the future." Also, consistent with the view taking shape in the Department of Energy, the CPRS concluded that oil assets "are almost certain to rise in price in the years ahead". Their opinion was that it might be better to sell some of BNOC's oil interest so as to achieve the Chancellor's funding target while retaining the Corporation in the public sector. But if the sale of the business was to go ahead, they believed that to get the best price it would be sensible to stagger the sale into the future. This advice from the CPRS cannot have been welcomed in the Treasury, where there was a keenness to get on with the sale.

It seems that the CPRS intervention had some effect. BNOC's future was discussed again on 12 December 1979, when the Secretary of State for Energy reported that discussions with Ministers since the meeting on 26 November had not led to a material change to his proposals.[52] The plan remained to separate BNOC into two companies, permitting 100 per cent government control over the oil trading operations and the establishment of a separate "upstream" operating function, in which some of the shares would then be sold. However, after discussion the PM concluded that no final decision should be taken pending "full information about the effects of the various available courses on the PSBR" to be investigated by the CPRS and officials from the Treasury and the Department of Energy. In the following weeks further consideration of the appropriate structure for BNOC's privatisation took place, often under the PM's chairmanship, reflecting her concerns about UK oil supplies and the sale price.

At E Committee on 11 March 1980 Howell again confirmed that he intended to restructure BNOC into separate trading and operating companies. However, although he was able to state that progress had been made in drafting the necessary legislation, he revealed that "it was now clear that it would not be ready in time for introduction in the present Session."[53] In addition, even if preparation of the Bill could be completed, in his view to rush it through in what remained of this session of Parliament would mean "an extremely compressed Committee Stage, and probably with a need for a substantial spill-over into the recess".[54] In discussion it was agreed that the Secretary of State should make a statement to Parliament confirming his disposal plans, but that the statement should not go into too much detail given the continuing uncertainties about the best way forward. In the Department of Energy and at the Treasury there were still concerns at this time about the implications of the disposal for BNOC's participation agreements with private sector oil companies. There remained other legal difficulties, including the implications of a sale favouring British purchasers, as preferred by the PM, given the European Treaty rules on discriminating against nationals of other member states. The statement would not, therefore, set out a timetable for the disposal or go into the proportion of private capital that might be introduced.

Events then took a further turn. On 23 April 1980 Howell called on the PM and announced that he had changed his mind on selling a majority shareholding in BNOC Operating. In the light of rising oil prices, the contribution of profits from BNOC to reducing the PSBR and, he claimed, some restlessness in the Conservative Party about selling oil assets, he now favoured proceeding with greater caution and not selling a majority of the business at the present time. It is also clear that he was conscious of the need to maintain the country's security of supply and was genuinely sceptical of the soundness of the Treasury's preference to split up the Corporation.[55] He explained that EEC obligations limited the extent to which the Government could direct private sector oil supplies to the UK, whereas by owning BNOC this could be done more easily. He suggested that the idea of selling a majority shareholding should be deferred and revisited in three years' time. Interestingly, the PM agreed that it would be best to postpone the majority privatisation of BNOC Operating.[56]

## Continuing delays, the BNOC Revenue Bond and the Lazard Report

By the spring of 1980 little progress had been made on the disposal of oil assets apart from the sale of BP shares. In a memorandum to the PM on 12 March the Chancellor of the Exchequer vented his frustration at the slow pace of the disposals programme. He pressed the PM to pressure Howell to accelerate the sale of BGC's onshore oil interests and especially Wytch Farm. At this time Howell was raising as an objection to the early sale of this oil asset a recently discovered oil reservoir below the existing one. In his view this made valuing the Wytch Farm field too difficult at the present time. There was also his lack of legal powers to force a disposal in the face of opposition from the BGC Board. The Chancellor did not believe that the new oil find should be an impediment to a sale and suggested that if Howell felt that his legal powers were not sufficient to force through a sale, then the necessary legislative authority could be included in a Bill, the Petroleum and Submarine Pipelines (Amendment) Bill, which was currently going through Parliament.[57] The prime purpose of the Bill was to amend earlier legislation regulating activities in the North Sea and notably

*Table 4.1* BGC's main oil interests 1980

| Field | % interest | Net present value (£m) (1980 prices) |
|---|---|---|
| Beryl A&B | 10 | 70–100 |
| Fulmar | 4 | 35–45 |
| Montrose | 31 | 45–60 |
| NW Hutton | 26 | 60–110 |
| Wytch Farm | 50 | 90–130 |

*Source*: E(80)81.

the Petroleum and Submarine Pipelines Act 1975, but the legal powers could be tagged on. The result of this memorandum was a note from the PM's office requesting the Secretary of State for Energy to put forward definite proposals to E(DL) on the future of Wytch Farm.[58]

In the summer of 1980 the sale of Wytch Farm was expected to yield about £100 million and the Treasury felt that this could be achieved in the current financial year, 1980/1. The alternative of establishing a separate company into which all of BGC's oil assets would be placed, which would then be floated leaving the Corporation with only a minority interest, would take longer than selling off Wytch Farm separately. At this time BGC's main oil with associated gas interests were in four North Sea fields and Wytch Farm (Table 4.1). The Treasury was keen that Wytch Farm should be sold independently and quickly thereby contributing to the Government's £630 million disposals target set for 1980/1. The remainder of BGC's oil assets could then be grouped together in a separate subsidiary, to be sold off later, perhaps in the following year.[59] However, because in his view BGC was dragging its heels on disposals, the Chancellor of the Exchequer was not at all confident that a sale of a new subsidiary company would actually occur in 1981/2.[60]

Howe was right to be cautious. Before E(DL) on 13 June 1980 the Secretary of State for Energy confirmed his preference for placing all of BGC's oil interests, including Wytch Farm, in a separate company and floating or placing the majority of the shares on the market.[61] However, the smooth creation of a separate oilfields company would require the support of the BGC Board and it was far from clear that the Board would comply. Alongside this, there were now doubts about the validity of a Direction under the 1972 Gas Act from the Secretary of State to BGC to sell off its oil assets, although it was judged that a Direction on the sale of Wytch Farm alone might contain fewer legal difficulties. Howell was reluctant to make a Direction. He warned that a Direction on Wytch Farm would have to be contained in an Order laid before Parliament for 40 days and during this period there would be "ample opportunity for political opposition to be mounted".[62] Nevertheless, on 24 June, E(DL) concluded, in the face of continued opposition from Howell, that he should make it clear to the BGC Board that he would resort to a forced sale of Wytch Farm if this proved necessary.[63]

On 24 July 1980 the Secretary of State for Energy confirmed that, following further discussions with BGC, the Board had rejected the idea of grouping their oil assets into a subsidiary to be sold off. While he was not suggesting that this was necessarily the Corporation's last word on the subject, winning them around to this proposal would take time. Equally, he advised that he could not recommend a forced sale of Wytch Farm because of the likely consequences for his Department's future relations with the BGC Board, leaving aside any legal difficulties; he reiterates this in a memorandum to E Committee.[64] Instead, he wished to continue negotiations with the Board with the intention of reaching an agreed solution, perhaps by the end of March 1981. At the same time, he conceded that he was not optimistic that this deadline would be met.[65]

This conclusion met with a very frosty response from the Chancellor of the Exchequer, who refused to abandon the idea of an early disposal of Wytch Farm.[66] Shortly afterwards Howe wrote a confidential note to the PM complaining again about the Secretary of State's behaviour: "David Howell has over the past year been repeatedly pressed for progress on a contribution from Wytch Farm (or other BGC disposals) to our asset disposals programme. Having got it accepted that it need not be sold to bring proceeds for the 1979/80 programme, his aim now seems to be to talk it out until proceeds are impossible this year . . . I feel strongly that E should confirm E(DL)'s conclusion, and ask David Howell to stop fighting this result and work full out for the achievement of the 1980–81 proceeds from a Wytch Farm sale."[67]

There was to be further disappointment for the Chancellor when E Committee reconvened to discuss the future of BNOC, on 4 August 1980, and Howell confirmed his new position that the trading and upstream activities should remain combined and BNOC should remain under government control for the time being.[68] To help meet the Government's disposals target, he suggested that the Government might instead consider selling revenue bonds aimed especially at small savers, "which would give holders a right to a specified proportion of BNOC's revenues from defined oilfield interests".

Unsurprisingly, this proposal, which risked stopping the planning of the privatisation of BNOC in its tracks, produced a testy rejoinder from the Treasury. The idea of a revenue bond was considered a non-starter because it would be "a more expensive form of financing overall"[69]. Nevertheless, the Committee asked the Secretary of State and the Chancellor of the Exchequer to prepare a detailed report on its feasibility. The PM favoured exploring the idea. The result was put to E Committee on 10 September 1980.[70] Two possible schemes were tabled under which interest on a "revenue bond" would be linked to specified oil revenues of BNOC.[71] In discussion considerable concern was expressed that the Secretary of State's plan involved a backing away from privatisation in favour of what was, in effect, a national savings scheme with BNOC's revenues as a yardstick for interest payments. However, there was some support for the idea.[72] Summing up, the PM gave tentative backing to the proposal, provided that enabling powers were taken to permit future equity participation. The Secretary of State and the Chancellor were asked to undertake further work on the details of what became known as BNOC oil bonds. The proposal was a serious one and was announced at the Conservative Party Annual Conference in Brighton in October 1980 and mentioned in the Chancellor of the Exchequer's 1981 Budget speech. But in the event, after detailed consideration, the idea was dropped. The Treasury continued to be unenthusiastic, as was the Bank of England (both judged that it would be a more expensive way of raising funding than traditional sales of government stock), and the Secretary of State for Energy was persuaded to continue discussions on a disposal of BNOC Operating instead.[73] On 14 May 1981 Howell confirmed that he would now like to proceed again with the planning of the sale of "a substantial Government stake, say 49 per cent" of BNOC Operating with the oilfield participation agreements staying in BNOC Trading to protect security of supply. He stressed that there would be a need to prevent BNOC Operating falling under foreign control.[74] The PM agreed.

The BGC Board had met on 16 July 1980 to consider the Government's request to set up a subsidiary company embracing the Corporation's offshore oil interests and then dispose of a majority interest in it to the private sector. But the Board had confirmed its view that the proposal was inconsistent with its statutory responsibilities under the 1972 Gas Act to behave in the best interests of the Corporation.[75] Oil was found with gas deposits and this was the reason BGC had developed oil exploration and development activities in co-operation with private sector oil companies. To reverse this would mean reneging on the joint agreements and there would be damage to the Corporation's ability to partake in future exploration work. BGC was opposed to having only a minority interest in any new oil exploration and development company.[76] The Board was also of the view that it would be difficult to effect a disposal on proper commercial terms because of the difficulty of valuing the oil reserves.

Howell responded in a letter to Sir Denis Rooke on 14 August 1980 making clear his disappointment. He did not accept that the difficulties of valuing the oil reserves prevented progress nor, he commented, did he understand the Board's opposition to its having a minority interest in the company, given that its interests in the oilfields concerned were already usually of a minority or non-controlling interest form. In the letter he continued to hope that the Board would co-operate with the Government, but threatened that if necessary he would issue a Direction to bring about the disposal of the Wytch Farm oilfield in particular.[77] At an E Committee meeting on 6 August the Secretary of State had been requested to conclude his discussions with BGC in time for a Direction to be issued for the sale of Wytch Farm before the summer recess. However, this deadline was missed.[78]

On 27 August 1980 Sir Denis Rooke replied to Howell's letter adopting a more concili-atory tone and stating that "The Board felt that your letter indicated some misunderstanding of their position, particularly . . . where you refer to the scope for cooperation with the Government . . ." He emphasised that the Minister's proposal had "received consideration of the deepest and most serious kind". Nevertheless, it was still his view that "you wish us to part with productive assets without any real commercial justification as far as the Corpora-tion is concerned." The Board remained opposed to a sale. Rooke also confirmed that a disposal of the Corporation's share of Wytch Farm was particularly unacceptable because Wytch Farm reflected the Corporation's "original thinking and perseverance of the Corpora-tion's staff against the strong trend of traditional oil industry thinking" against onshore exploration. It also provided a base for training and developing new staff in exploration and development techniques onshore.[79]

Following this difficult exchange of views and continuing discussion between Department of Energy officials and the Corporation, BGC relented slightly. It agreed to commission Lazard Brothers & Co in the City to advise on how the Board could meet the Government's objective while still meeting its statutory responsibilities. An interim report and the Corporation's resulting proposals were to be ready by the end of the first week in October 1980. However, the Board made clear that even if the Lazard report favoured a sale, implementation would take some time – in other words, the Board could not be expected to pursue it with any enthusiasm. Nevertheless, Howell was of the view that the Corporation's response should be welcomed, "Otherwise, we would only exacerbate an already difficult position and we would at best forfeit BGC's co-operation in some of the other difficulties that lie ahead." At the same time, under continuing pressure from Treasury Ministers, he agreed that should there not be a positive response from BGC to the Lazard proposal, he would proceed with a draft Direction under the Gas Act.[80] On 15 September 1980 E Committee agreed to await the Lazard report.[81]

The BGC Board considered the interim report from Lazard, which was delivered to time, at a special meeting on 3 October. In this document Lazard envisaged an outcome under which the onshore and offshore oil interests would be placed in a new subsidiary company and then 60 per cent of the shares in the new company would be sold to the private sector. An important factor in achieving an acceptable market price for the shares would be the continuation of the management of the assets by BGC under a contract. Outstanding issues still to be resolved were tax liabilities, the pre-emptive rights of other companies, and the future exploration position of BGC. The Board asked Lazard to continue their work. In a note to the PM on hearing this news, Howell remarked that the development was "encouraging . . . BGC are now adopting a constructive attitude to the disposal of their oil assets". He asked for the PM's support for the Lazard's proposal in preference to preparing a separate sale of Wytch Farm, as favoured by the Treasury.[82]

On 16 October 1980 the Financial Secretary, Nigel Lawson, wrote to the PM with copies to relevant Ministers putting the Treasury's opposite view. With the Chancellor of the Exchequer already facing great difficulty in meeting the 1980/1 target for disposals, he stressed that it was important that some contribution was made in the current financial year from the sale of BGC's oil assets. This would require the sale of Wytch Farm unless a flotation of shares in a new oil company hived off from BGC could be achieved in the current finan-cial year. This was felt to be most unlikely and therefore Lawson pressed once again for the Department of Energy to issue a Direction to force BGC to dispose of Wytch Farm. E Committee had asked Howell to conclude his discussions with BGC in time for a Direction to be laid for a sale before the summer recess, and as this had not occurred, Lawson requested that there should now be no further delay. The BGC Board should be given only to the end of the first week in November to produce a proposal to dispose of Wytch Farm. If it failed to do so, a Direction should then be issued to bring about a forced sale.[83]

The Lazard proposal had also raised another concern in the Treasury. It seemed that BGC expected to retain any sales receipts from the disposal of its oil assets rather than pay them over to the Exchequer. This could not be permitted, because it would mean the Government finances received no immediate benefit from the disposal. Regarding the sale of 60 per cent of the shares, Lawson responded that certainly no lower percentage should be agreed. Based on the Secretary of State's own figures "each additional 10 per cent of shares sold would raise some £30m, which would provide a useful contribution to reducing the PSBR in a very difficult year." The Lazard proposal had included the use of a management contract between the new company and BGC, under which BGC would continue to manage the assets after they were hived off. Lawson was also suspicious of this suggestion, as was the Secretary of State for Industry[84] and the PM.[85] He stressed that it would be necessary to ensure that the contract was "freely negotiated on an arms length basis . . . Nor could the contract be for an indefinite period if the new company is to be completely independent of BGC and outside its control and therefore legitimately in the private sector". An initial contract of two years should be sufficient. This was important if the Government was to claim convincingly that the proceeds of a sale should count as a PSBR reduction rather than simply as a contribution to the financing of the PSBR, on which the Treasury placed great store. This required Government giving up control of the assets, a condition which might be difficult to fulfil if the state-owned BGC continued to manage them.[86]

Howell responded in a note to the PM on 22 October 1980. In it he rejected Lawson's view that there was a reasonable chance of securing receipts in the current financial year from a forced sale of BGC's share in Wytch Farm. He also felt that it was "quite unreasonable" to set the Corporation a deadline of early November to come up with a plan for its disposal. However, in a conciliatory gesture he offered to ensure that the Corporation was aware of the need to plan for a sale of its oil interests in 1981/2 with the revenue coming to the Government and not remaining within the Corporation.[87] Advice from within No. 10 to the PM on 24 October confirmed that it was likely that the disposals target for 1980/1 would be missed, but that achieving a forced sale of Wytch Farm "would undoubtedly be risky because BGC might well drag its feet at all stages and there could be problems in getting a good (and defensible) price in a sale conducted on such a tight timescale". This provoked a handwritten comment in the margin of the memorandum by the PM stating: "I have every sympathy with Mr Lawson's minute in view of the way DoE [Department of Energy] have constantly dragged their feet always saying – it will be better next year. This year is last year's next year and DoE hasn't delivered. Nevertheless, I will give one *last* chance" (emphasis in the original). The PM was therefore reluctantly prepared to accept Howell's plan to sell shares in a company containing BGC's onshore and offshore oil interests including Wytch Farm in the financial year 1981/2, even though this might mean that the disposals target for the current year would not be met. But this agreement came with a clear warning that there must be no further delay.[88]

Planning for the sale of BGC's oil assets went on in the Department of Energy but progress continued to be slow. In part this was because the Department considered that hiving them off and establishing a new company needed to be carefully planned. The Department of Energy had overseen the expansion of state control over energy supplies during the 1974–79 Labour administration and maintaining security of supply was part of the departmental culture. But more importantly, the delay was a product of foot-dragging on the part of the BGC Board. Officials in the Department of Energy endeavoured to speed matters up by appointing their own advisers and holding weekly progress meetings, but BGC continued to procrastinate. On 27 April 1981 Howell had to advise the PM that the Board had now considered the final report from Lazard on the disposal of a majority holding of their oil interests. They had rejected it, concluding that they could not voluntarily set up a subsidiary company containing their oil interests and then agree to its sale. In response, Howell stressed that he remained of the view that a new North Sea oil company based on BGC's existing interests was the best way forward. He therefore concluded that he was left with no alternative but to resort to a Direction to the Board, although he would need to consult before proceeding.[89] Nearly nine months had gone by since Lawson had demanded a directive so that a sale would occur. Meanwhile, the Board of BGC had played for time while awaiting the Lazard report.

## The disposal of Wytch Farm and Enterprise Oil

The PM had given Howell and the BGC Board the benefit of the doubt the previous autumn and now her frustration was clearly evident.[90] The Treasury too decided that there should be no further prevarication. Lawson suggested that powers might be taken to force the sale of *all* of BGC's oil interests in a Bill that would abolish BGC's gas purchase monopsony and possibly require the disposal of its appliance retailing business: "if, as I hope, it is agreed to implement something like the radical option put forward in the recent Monopolies and Mergers Commission Report to reduce BGC's dominance in the retailing of gas appliances. Such a Bill . . . could be politically attractive and could be presented as an important step in our privatisation programme".[91] The MMC, the Government's competition authority, had recently published a highly critical report on the performance of BGC's appliance retailing business. Following this report the Government flirted for a time with the idea of hiving off BGC's gas showrooms.[92] The plan never came to anything, as discussed further in chapter 14.

The Department of Energy now acted and on 13 October 1981 a Direction to BGC's Board to dispose of Wytch Farm came into force, despite the Board's protests. In the following months the planning of this sale and of the remainder of BGC's oil interests proceeded, in spite of opposition from the Board. However, the sale of Wytch Farm continued to be a protracted affair. Delay resulted particularly during the bidding stage for the field. BGC was slow in releasing the information needed for companies to decide whether to bid or not and how much to bid. As Lawson later commented, "The detailed information . . . had to be supplied by British Gas; and extracting this proved very much more difficult than extracting the gas itself."[93] Eventually bidding for Wytch Farm opened in July 1982 and closed in October and three bids were submitted. However, none was considered acceptable based on the Department of Energy's valuation of the field.[94] Lawson was the new Secretary of State for Energy, having moved from the Treasury in the September 1981 Government reshuffle, and was keen to prevent the sale falling through. Howell had been despatched to the Department of Transport. His hesitant performance during the planning of the sale of the oil and gas assets contributed to the move.[95] Lawson now met with the bidders to explore the scope for improved bids and revised bids were submitted. But this resulted in a further loss of time.

In March 1983 Lawson concluded that an acceptable bid had come from the Dorset Group, a consortium of five oil companies including BP, and instructed the BGC Board to negotiate with Dorset.[96] BGC complied reluctantly arguing that the amount they were likely to receive would be about a half of the true asset value. Lawson disputed the Board's analysis.[97] Department of Energy officials produced a detailed document on the bid values to put pressure on BGC to proceed. This culminated in Lawson calling the whole BGC Board to a meeting to be presented with the Department's analysis, which was apparently heard in silence. The result was that negotiations were strung out over a number of further months as BGC questioned the ultimate amount that Dorset should be expected to pay under staged payments. Then towards the end of 1983 discussions stalled on who should bear the risk of planning agreements being refused or delayed relating to a future expansion of the field. The new Secretary of State for Energy following the 1983 General Election, Peter Walker, pressed BGC to complete the sale and absorb the risk;[98] but the Board replied curtly that its view was that the October 1981 Direction did not empower the Secretary of State to intervene in the negotiations with Dorset.[99]

By early 1984 a deal seemed near to completion. It was now derailed by changes to taxation introduced by the Chancellor of the Exchequer in his spring Budget. BGC maintained that the change to Corporation Tax in the Budget had a materially favourable effect on the value of the assets to be transferred. Dorset agreed as a consequence to raise the amount to be paid, but not by enough to satisfy the BGC Board.[100] Meanwhile, Sir Denis Rooke, seems to have decided that if BGC had to agree to a sale of Wytch Farm it should do so to a buyer of its own choosing. He is said to have urged the chairman of RTZ plc, the international mining group, to lodge a rival bid. One of the members of the Board of BGC was a Director of RTZ, which had been one of the unsuccessful bidders against Dorset earlier. Rooke wrote to Walker stating that BGC had been required to enter into negotiations with the Dorset Group against its will and that the deal was non-commercial given the tax change. RTZ followed this up on 29 March 1984 with a bid for Wytch Farm that was substantially higher than that made by Dorset.

Within Government this development was seen as yet a further example of BGC attempting to frustrate a sale. Moreover, to terminate the Dorset purchase now would create considerable difficulties. It was expected that the Dorset Group would argue that their bid had already been accepted in principle and that failure to complete the sale was contrary to good faith. Also, they would have grounds for arguing that they had foregone other commercial opportunities during the months of negotiating the purchase and incurred considerable costs. The costs were likely to be around £2 million. The amount that Dorset might seek in compensation in the courts could be much larger. The Government was also keen to avoid the matter leaking to the press and creating political embarrassment.

In early April 1984 Walker asked for an urgent meeting with the PM to discuss tactics. One option would be to issue BGC with a new Direction to sell to the Dorset Group. But BGC would be able to mount a defence that this was contrary to the Board's legal requirement to obtain the best price for its assets. There could also be criticism from the House of Commons' Public Accounts Committee on the grounds that the Government had not achieved the best price from the sale of Wytch Farm. Another possibility to circumvent BGC opposition, if Dorset was unwilling to match the RTZ bid, would be first to transfer Wytch Farm from BGC to the Department of Energy which then would be the seller.[101] However, it was felt that it would not overcome accusations of bad faith from Dorset unless the asset was then sold to them and on the terms already agreed.

It seems that within No. 10 sympathy did not lie entirely with the Secretary of State for Energy. It was suggested that the current Secretary of State and his predecessor, Nigel Lawson, were striving to avoid criticism of the earlier bidding process and subsequent negotiations falling on them: "A large part of the difficulty lies in the wish of each to so manoeuvre that they do not incur criticism."[102] It was suggested that the new offer from RTZ should be considered on its merits and Dorset be given an opportunity to produce a revised bid. An argument of bad faith by Dorset was felt to be less than justified because a failure to complete purchase deals was a normal commercial risk. Equally, a strongly held view at the time within No. 10 was that "The Prime Minister should never have become involved in this issue. Departments are making a great fuss over an easily resolvable question."[103]

Given that the 1981 Direction required BGC to sell Wytch Farm for the best price and the Dorset bid no longer represented the highest bid, BGC continued to argue that it was therefore no longer obliged to sell to Dorset. In consequence, the Department of Energy did give serious consideration to a transfer of Wytch Farm to Enterprise Oil, the new company it had by now set up to absorb the other oil exploration and production assets of BGC, by providing the company with sufficient funds to purchase at a price slightly above the RTZ offer.[104] On 9 April 1984 the PM held a meeting with the Secretary of State for Energy in the presence of the Chancellor of the Exchequer and the Cabinet Secretary, Robert Armstrong, to discuss the difficulties that had arisen with the sale. Various options were explored but none seemed ideal. A transfer to Enterprise Oil could delay the latter's flotation scheduled for June and would not overcome criticism by Dorset of bad faith on the part of the Government. Sale to RTZ would inevitably be opposed by Dorset and asking Dorset to rebid would not necessarily end the matter. To ask both Dorset and RTZ for new sealed bids would probably mean that the Government would need to reopen bidding to any other interested parties, creating further delay. It was finally agreed that the Secretary of State and the Chancellor should take merchant bank advice and should continue to search for a solution that would not significantly postpone Wytch Farm's sale.[105]

The eventual outcome, following advice from S.G. Warburg & Co in the City and with the PM's agreement, was an offer to the Dorset Group to improve their bid. The Government was advised that it was not unreasonable for it to take this course following the Corporation Tax changes in the Budget.[106] As a result, the Dorset Group was persuaded to increase the amount offered to reflect the Budget benefits. This seemed to protect the Secretary of State from any possible Parliamentary criticism of his decision not to agree to the sale to RTZ.[107] The Dorset Group responded with an offer £4 million above that of RTZ and close to the value of the benefits obtained from the tax changes.[108] With no remaining excuses not to proceed with the sale, the BGC Board grudgingly backed down and accepted Dorset's revised bid.

Disposal of Wytch Farm took place in May 1984, almost five years after the beginning of negotiations with BGC. The eventual terms of the sale to Dorset involved an initial payment of £80 million, followed by a second payment of £130 million when specified production levels were reached. This was expected to occur in 1987/8. The PM noted that she was "delighted" by the outcome.[109] BGC was not. The Department of Energy had persevered in the face of strong opposition from BGC, but a sale that was expected to benefit the Exchequer in 1980/1 eventually produced funds four years later, in 1984/5. By 1984/5 raising revenue from government disposals was no longer the pressing priority that it had been in 1980/1. Also, by now both the Corporation and the Department had bigger fish to fry. Planning was underway for the complete privatisation of the remainder of BGC.

Some time before Wytch Farm was eventually sold the Government had completed its sale of BGC's other oil assets. BGC's oil production interests in the Beryl, Montrose, Fulmar and NW Hutton North Sea oilfields and certain other interests, were transferred on 1 May 1983 to a new subsidiary company of BGC named British Gas North Sea Oil Holdings Ltd, following a Direction under the Oil and Gas (Enterprise) Act 1982.[110] No doubt mindful of BGC's continued opposition to the sale and its successful stalling on the disposal of Wytch Farm, the Secretary of State for Energy was keen to remove Holdings speedily from BGC's control. The decision was taken to transfer the company temporarily to the ownership of the Department of Energy, which would then manage its disposal.[111] BGC had already been slow in providing the detailed legal, tax and accounting information needed to allow the sale to be completed. The intention was to prevent further delay. The transfer had to be deferred until after the 1983 General Election, but the assets came under direct government ownership on 1 September 1983.[112]

The Department of Energy's City adviser for the sale was Kleinwort, Benson (henceforth Kleinworts).[113] Kleinworts was appointed after competition for the work or what was known in the City as a "beauty contest". As with other privatisations, the winning bidder was chosen on the basis of the Government's judgement of its competence to undertake the work and the fees quoted. The bank concluded that the proceeds from a future disposal would be maximised if Holdings was floated in the stock market, as against the alternatives of a trade sale or disposal separately of the individual oilfields.[114] However, the option of a sale to a corporate purchaser was retained in case a flotation became impracticable. Another alternative of floating Holdings as an investment company was ruled out, on the grounds that this concept would be unfamiliar to investors. Also, the view was taken that the threat of litigation over pre-emption rights by Holdings' partners in the various oilfields would be minimised if the enterprise was floated as a separate oil company.[115]

In September 1983 Holdings was renamed Enterprise Oil Ltd. A Memorandum of Understanding agreed between the company and the Government restricted the company from entering into major financial commitments, including new financing, ahead of a share sale, a restriction the Treasury insisted upon in other privatisations.[116] Prior to flotation a new management was recruited because there was no permanent management in place when Holdings transferred from BGC. The estimate was that about 20 or so people would be needed initially. To get the calibre of recruit desired, the Secretary of State requested permission to offer "full market rates" of pay. The Treasury agreed.[117] But the agreement came with an expression of concern over the level of the intended payment to one of the appointees.[118] At the time the Treasury had privately conceded that nationalised industry board salaries were typically some 25 per cent to 50 per cent too low compared to the level of responsibility involved, but saw no prospect in the current economic climate of Ministers agreeing to rectify this. A large rise in management pay would have to await privatisation. The issue of the appropriate pay level for management in privatised enterprises would remain a bone of contention during a number of subsequent nationalised industry sell-offs, frequently surfacing in the media and in Parliament.

The plan to privatise Enterprise Oil was finalised in early June 1984, although a decision on whether to sell through a tender (with the price set depending on the bids made) or a fixed price offer was postponed until the last minute.[119] The Secretary of State for Energy's preference was for a tender so as to deflect criticism, now mounting, that the Government was selling off state assets too cheaply. Small shareholders would be encouraged to apply by permitting striking price applications, which was considered simpler.[120] Small investors would be able to make applications at the striking price, whatever this turned out to be. Also a number of difficulties had to be addressed before the flotation could proceed, in addition to the normal ones of designing a sale prospectus and a marketing campaign, including tax issues arising from the transfer of the fields from BGC to the new company.[121]

The Government's advisers on the pricing of the Enterprise Oil issue were Kleinworts. It was normal practice in the City for the lead merchant bank advising on a flotation to be the issuing house (marketing and distributing the shares in association with the brokers to the issue) and lead underwriter. In this case Kleinworts acted as the main underwriter.[122] Following discussion with Kleinworts, the Treasury and the Department for Energy decided that 212 million shares, representing all of the issued share capital, should be sold by tender with the Government retaining a "special share" until at least 31 December 1988. This would protect for a time, through a condition in the company's Articles of Association against unwelcome, including foreign, takeover bids. The special share would then be redeemable by the company at par value. It was felt that by December 1988 "the company should be sufficiently well established to fend for itself."[123] The special share or what became known alternatively as a "golden share" would be used in a number of the privatisations of the 1980s where the Government judged that the national interest was best served by allowing the Government to veto unwelcome takeover bids. In the case of Enterprise Oil the special share effectively outvoted all other shares if a person or connected persons was to obtain more than 50 per cent of the voting rights in the company. The terms were slightly different to those used for the special shares introduced during the privatisations of Amersham International and Britoil earlier, reflecting uncertainty about their precise legal standing and how special share protections would work in practice.

The introduction of a special share caused some nervousness within the Foreign and Commonwealth Office in particular. The FCO warned that the provision might be challenged as contrary to obligations under the EEC Treaties not to discriminate between nationals of other Member States. This was the first privatisation since the EEC Admissions Directive had been brought into force in the UK so there was considerable uncertainty. A special share was also introduced in the case of Britoil, discussed below, but in that case the risks of a challenge were reduced by drafting the company's Articles of Association in such a way as, on the face of it, to make them compatible with EEC obligations.[124] In the event there was no challenge. Special shares went on to be used in privatisations elsewhere in Europe, although by the late 1990s they were being challenged by the European Commission on the grounds that they limited the free movement of capital.

A sale by tender rather than a fixed price offer was chosen for the flotation of Enterprise Oil because of the recent underpricing of privatisation issues. Kleinworts initially recommended a fixed price offer, but moved towards recommending a tender offer given uncertainties in the oil and financial markets and in recognition of the Government's desire to price this issue in such a way as to clear the market at the highest possible price. The minimum tender price for Enterprise Oil shares was set at 185p with payment due in two instalments (100p on application and 85p on 12 September 1984).[125] Payment in instalments reduced the amount of capital that would need to be set aside by investors at the time of the flotation and was expected to encourage applications. It was a method used in a number of later privatisations. But in the case of tender issues it had further merit in that investors could submit cheques with their applications for the first instalment payment even though they did not know the actual price of the shares, which would be set according to the striking price. The Enterprise Oil issue was not specifically targeted at small investors but a total of 12,442 did apply. Applications for up to 2,500 shares were satisfied at the striking price. Employees could also apply at the striking price and had a higher upper limit, of 13,500 shares each.[126]

Application lists opened and closed on 27 June 1984. In the event, even though the flotation initially received encouraging press coverage with the minimum tender price considered to be sound by financial commentators,[127] a weakening in the days leading up to the issue of the stock market and the spot price for oil, on which the company's revenues heavily depended, meant that the flotation proved to be a disappointment. A further factor was the City's preference for fixed price over tender issues because of the greater scope for making capital gains.[128] Applications were received for just over 66 per cent of the shares on offer. A Department of Energy report on the sale commented, "One can only speculate on whether a fixed price offer might have been better received."[129] To add to the Government's displeasure, the international mining company RTZ disclosed that it had applied for 49.5 per cent of the shares through a variety of nominees. Apparently, RTZ had been minded to subscribe for 51 per cent of the shares, but had been persuaded to reduce its bid slightly to below an obvious controlling interest by its financial advisers, NM Rothschild (Rothschilds).[130] Had RTZ purchased 50 per cent or more of the shares then the Government would have been able to invoke the terms of its "special share".

Subtracting the bids by RTZ's nominees meant that only around 17 per cent of the shares on offer had been bought by other shareholders. In effect, the indirect share applications from RTZ had saved the Government (and the underwriters) from a complete flotation disaster. However, in the Chancellor of the Exchequer's words, the large RTZ holding was clearly "incompatible with the Government's repeatedly declared policy of safeguarding the independence of Enterprise Oil." The transfer of such a large part of the company to RTZ was not the sort of privatisation the Government had in mind when it had planned the sale.

The Government had decided to float Enterprise Oil rather than arrange a trade sale, such as to RTZ, even though the latter might have raised more revenue because it wanted to create an independent exploration and production company in the North Sea.

The special share was ineffective to block the purchase because RTZ acquired slightly under 50 per cent of the equity. But under the terms of the offer for sale agreed with the underwriters, the Government had taken powers to control the allocation of shares "in order to further protect the independence of the company." The Government now chose to exercise this power and reject the nominees' bids. Initially the decision was taken to restrict the allocation of shares to RTZ to ten per cent of the equity. However, by scaling back the RTZ purchase to such an extent a very large number of additional shares would have been left with the underwriters. This was likely to have the effect of depressing the price of Enterprise Oil shares when trading in them began and the underwriters reduced their holdings. This raised fears in the Department of Trade and Industry that this outcome would dampen City enthusiasm for the forthcoming British Telecom issue, in which planning was now well advanced.[131] Kleinworts was also the merchant bank advising the Department on the BT sale. It warned, "that to reduce the allocation of shares in Enterprise Oil to RTZ below 20 per cent was likely to have serious adverse implications for the flotation of BT". On 28 June 1984 in Cabinet, the Secretary of State for Trade and Industry responsible for the BT sale, Norman Tebbit, counselled against limiting the RTZ holding to as low as ten per cent.[132] Indeed, on the evening of the 27th the possibility of selling the whole business to RTZ was briefly considered, although dismissed. The Chancellor particularly took exception to the way RTZ had behaved and wanted to find some way of preventing the company achieving a coup. Eventually it was agreed that the limit on the RTZ holding should be raised from 10 per cent to 20 per cent.[133]

The result was that Enterprise Oil had been sold but at the minimum tender price of 185p per share and with 63 per cent of the issued shares remaining with the underwriters and sub-underwriters.[134] The Government raised £392 million from the sale with costs of sale to the Government put at some £10 million and to the company at £2 million. Part of the costs included the total underwriters' commission of 1.55 per cent, which on this occasion had been earned.[135] A number of the underwriting firms in the City approached the Secretary of State for Energy, Peter Walker, to be freed from the indemnity commitment following the failure of the flotation, but Walker refused and threatened to denounce them if they reneged on their underwriting agreement.

Following the sale, RTZ became a major shareholder in Enterprise Oil finally holding 29.9 per cent of the company's shares, but never took majority ownership. Enterprise Oil was eventually acquired by Shell plc in May 2002.

## Britoil

The discussion now turns back in time to consider the disposal of BNOC Operating. Britoil was the name of the company hived off from BNOC in 1982 and which was essentially BNOC Operating in the Department of Energy's earlier planning. It took over the oil and gas exploration and production interests of BNOC. The new company therefore gained extensive interests in gas related fields and blocks in the North Sea, including the Victor, Viking, Ninian, Thistle, Murchinson and Statfjord fields, holding about six per cent of the UKCS's remaining known recoverable reserves of oil.[136] It provided BGC with around five per cent of its UKCS gas supplies.[137]

On paper the enterprise seemed to be an attractive proposition for private investors, albeit that it proved difficult to value the oilfields given the inevitable uncertainties about the future value of oil extractions (valuations were avoided in the sale prospectus).[138] However, the disappointing sale of shares in Enterprise Oil was mirrored by experience during the Britoil disposal. Outline plans for the privatisation of BNOC's exploration and production interests were announced by the Secretary of State for Energy on 19 October 1981 and the necessary legal powers were contained in the Oil and Gas (Enterprise) Act 1982. Advisers on the flotation to the Government were S.G.Warburg & Co (Warburgs) and to the company NM Rothschild & Son (Rothschilds).[139] As was becoming the norm already for privatisations, the sale was controlled by the sponsor Department, in this case the Department of Energy, with a small group of civil servants working wholly, or at one time or another, on the task. The Department consulted regularly with the Treasury and the Bank of England, as well as BNOC and the financial advisers.

Committees and working groups were set up to manage the preparation of the sale prospectus, accounting and taxation matters, legal issues, specialist petroleum problems, and the sale mechanics, and these included civil servants from the Department of Energy and the Treasury and representatives from the various advisers, including legal advisers.[140] The working of these groups was overseen by a co-ordinating group to ensure that the sale timetable was met. Other privatisations, including the Enterprise Oil sale, were similarly organised. Within the Department of Energy officials drove the privatisation through to a tight timetable, overcoming a number of problems on the way, including a late discovery that some of Britoil's contracts might not be legally valid. During the preparation of the sale, Rothschilds, on behalf of the company, called for an effective cash injection into Britoil before sale so as to avoid high gearing and to achieve a dividend yield of eight per cent. Warburgs, by contrast, recommended a cash extraction, higher gearing and a lower dividend yield, of 5.89 per cent (at the time the average yield for oil majors was 6.7 per cent). After some haggling, the result was a compromise.

The sale of Britoil occurred in November 1982. Employees were offered preferential purchase terms during the flotation, including receiving £60 worth of free shares, one free share for every share purchased up to 186 shares per employee and preferential rights to apply for up to 11,500 additional shares per head at the striking price.[141] The intention was to win over employees to the sale in the face of trade union opposition. The management canvassed for a more generous scheme on the grounds of the high profit earned per employee in the company, but the Government was unwilling to move from the terms of the employee schemes now set up under earlier privatisations. In 1980 the Treasury laid down guidelines that employee schemes should not cost more than five per cent of the expected sales receipts and free shares should be limited to £50 per head. The £60 allowed for Britoil employees reflected the inflation that had occurred since 1980. At flotation 92 per cent of eligible employees accepted the free shares and 79 per cent took up the matching shares available.[142]

The Government introduced a special share to protect against a future takeover bid for Britoil that the Government considered undesirable. Amongst other things this gave the Government temporary majority voting rights if any person obtained over 50 per cent control of the company. It also restricted the winding up or dissolution of the company without Government sanction and permitted the Government to appoint two directors to the Britoil Board.[143] The terms were not dissimilar to those adopted later during the Enterprise Oil sale, except that the Britoil special share was redeemable at any time at the Government's request. In addition, during the sale an active attempt was made to attract small investors; for example, prospectuses and application forms were made available through the Post Office and some bank branches. The sale used a tender offer, but investors applying for up to 2,000 shares were permitted to apply for them at the striking price.[144] Also, the sale price was paid in two instalments, on application and on 6 April 1983, with the first instalment at the fixed price of 100p. To encourage small investors to retain their shares until 30 November 1985, for the first time a "loyalty bonus" of one free share for every ten shares held was introduced.[145] The idea of a loyalty bonus was put forward by Warburgs, the solicitors to the offer (Freshfields) and the Department of Energy in an effort to dissuade small investors from quickly selling their shares after issue – small shareholders selling quickly for a profit, as had occurred following the sale of British Aerospace, was beginning to prove politically embarrassing and was contrary to the Government's stated policy of widening property ownership. There was also a feeling in Government that having lots of long-term small shareholders would provide an effective barrier to nationalisation of Britoil by a future Labour administration.[146] The idea of a loyalty bonus was received with some initial scepticism within No. 10[147] but would be developed further and play an important role in a number of later privatisations, especially during the privatisation of British Telecom in November 1984.

The issue of having a fixed price offer or a sale by tender, or some combination of the two, was discussed between the Secretary of State for Energy Nigel Lawson, the Financial Secretary and financial advisers between May and August 1982. Lawson, smarting from criticism of the huge share premium during the flotation of Amersham International in February 1982, discussed in chapter 6, favoured a tender so that the share price would reflect market bidding. He later recorded: "Whatever happened I could not afford a second Amersham."[148] The financial advisers, Warburgs, argued that there was a real possibility that the market reception to a sale by tender would not be good. However, the Treasury was keen to avoid criticism from the Public Accounts Committee (PAC) of underpricing of privatisation issues and the views of the Financial Secretary prevailed.[149] Another result of criticism from the PAC was that Britoil was the first privatisation where the Government appointed an independent adviser on pricing of the issue, to provide a second opinion to that provided by Warburgs on the correct share price. [150] Independent advisers would be appointed in future privatisations.

The financial advisers' fears that the tender might be unenthusiastically received in the City proved to be correct. In November 1982 the Government floated 51 per cent of the issued shares in Britoil at a minimum tender price of 215p per share. Only 27 per cent of the shares were purchased, the balance being left with the underwriters.[151] It was clearly proving difficult to price initial public offerings in privatised companies correctly. The failure of the Britoil issue in part reflected a decline in oil prices and therefore a change in sentiment towards oil investments during the offer period, from 10 to 19 November. But in addition, Britoil's sale by tender was the largest to date in the stock market and the result was always likely to be uncertain. Sections of the media were sceptical that the flotation would be a success, which did not help and depressed interest in the offer amongst small investors.[152] The City would have preferred a fixed price offer and also shunned the shares.

The sale of Britoil on 10 November 1982 produced gross receipts to the Government of £549 million with costs totalling £13 million. In addition, there were sale costs to the company of some £4 million. With the sale of BNOC Operating as Britoil, in spring 1985 an Oil and Pipelines Agency (OPA) was set up to absorb the trading activities of BNOC.[153] A few months later BNOC was dissolved. The oil trading activities of OPA came to an end in the second half of 1988 when the Government decided to cease taking royalty payments from the North Sea in kind. The participation agreements with oil companies were phased out from 1989. The remainder of the shares held by the Government in Britoil, apart from the "special share", were sold in August 1985. On this occasion a fixed price offer was used and the shares were ten times oversubscribed.

\*　\*　\*

In December 1987 BP bid for Britoil. The Government chose not to use its special share to block the takeover, although it was able to use the threat of blocking the bid to negotiate with BP to keep Britoil's head office in Scotland and to transfer some research and development work there. The existence of the special share had a potential political if not an economic dividend in Scotland for the Government at a time when the Conservative vote there was evaporating. BP's offer to purchase BNOC's exploration, development and production activities had been rejected in 1979. Eight years later BP took over the successor company, Britoil. Like Enterprise Oil, Britoil had only a brief sojourn as an independent company.

# 5

# PRIVATISING BRITISH AEROSPACE AND CABLE AND WIRELESS

By the time of the completion of the sales of Wytch Farm, Britoil and Enterprise Oil, a number of other privatisations had made their way on to the statute books already. The first two to be completed were British Aerospace and Cable and Wireless.

## British Aerospace

The aerospace industry in Britain had been nationalised by Labour in 1977 and the Conservative Election Manifesto in 1979 had committed the new Government to its denationalisation. However, although a Manifesto commitment, there was much hesitancy within Government, including the Treasury, about the desirability of a sale, given the considerable state financial support provided in the form of "launch aid" for new aircraft and BAe's heavy reliance on defence contracts. In particular, BAe had agreed to participate in the European Airbus project and here the extent of the Government's on-going financial commitment was very much a live issue in May 1979.

A plan for the disposal of BAe was put to E(DL) by the Secretary of State for Industry, Sir Keith Joseph, as early as July 1979, within just over two months of the election. BAe was organised into two groups dealing, respectively, with civil and military aircraft and with guided weapons. The Secretary of State's preferred option was the sale of BAe as one organisation but he felt that this might prove unattractive to investors.[1] The Corporation was currently making profits but was rebuilding its position in the civil aircraft business by launching three new aircraft – the BAe 146, Jetsteam and the A310 version of the Airbus, the result of the pan-European Airbus Industrie partnership. Hence, the aircraft business was expected to require a very large injection of cash, possibly amounting to £400 million over the following five years.[2] It was possible, therefore, that selling a company incorporating all of BAe's activities might not be practicable unless the Government offered commitments to support these and perhaps other projects financially. It was not to be expected that this prospect would appeal to the Treasury. Instead, the Secretary of State tentatively suggested that the Government should maintain the option of separately offering for sale shares in the guided weapons business conducted by the Dynamics Group within BAe. This division of BAe was profitable and had a sound cash flow and therefore would be attractive to investors. In his view, therefore, the safest approach would be to pass legislation that left open the option of selling shares in all or only part of the Corporation.

In the early months of the new Government the aim was to retain a major government shareholding in BAe, so as to ensure continued government influence over the management of the business through appointments to the Board. The Corporation's importance to national defence and frequent Government financial contributions to new aircraft development seemed to rule out a 100 per cent privatisation. Also, at the time there was concern that the Government would need to clarify its future relationship with a private sector company before any disposal could go ahead, especially given the state financing of new aircraft projects. Joseph noted that: "This will require careful thought . . . We want to ensure that the company is distanced from Government as far as is reasonable. But we must recognise a number of special factors which will inevitably limit the extent of maximum withdrawal." The Secretary of State had yet to receive expert City advice on the options for disposal and the likely valuation of a sale, but in the summer of 1979 the Department of Industry expected that a partial disposal might yield around £100 million. The Secretary of State's outline proposals were approved. The Chancellor accepted the plan "provided satisfactory agreement could be reached on the definition of the future relationship between the Government and the company, which would ensure that disposals would contribute to the reduction of the PSBR".[3] The proposals included provision for employees to have "a special opportunity" to purchase shares in any flotation.[4]

The decision to denationalise BAe was announced in the House of Commons on 23 July 1979. The Government suggested, purposely vaguely, that it would retain around a half of the issued share capital. Opposing the decision, John Silkin from the Labour benches accused the Secretary of State of permitting the run down of the British aerospace industry so that we would "become merely sub-contractors to the Americans". He also warned that "the question of restoring these assets to public ownership, and on what basis, will be the subject of urgent consideration by the Labour Party in the coming months". Left-wingers Eric Heffer and Dennis Skinner from the Labour benches went further, threatening renationalisation without compensation.[5]

During the summer instructions were given to Parliamentary Counsel to prepare the necessary Bill to sell shares in all or parts of BAe. There had been some suggestion from the Conservatives at the time of nationalisation that a future Conservative Government would favour selling back BAe to its previous owners.[6] However, this would have required fragmenting BAe into at least some of its original constituent companies and this was never considered a serious prospect after May 1979. On 2 October 1979 the Secretary of State circulated a memorandum to members of E(DL) Sub-Committee with the aim of clarifying the relationship between the Government and the company once a private sector shareholding had been established.[7] The memorandum made clear that to promote satisfactory management of the company, attract investors, and to remove the company's borrowings from the PSBR, it would be necessary for the Government to agree not to intervene in commercial decision making after a share disposal. At the same time, the memorandum made it clear that the Government would retain special obligations after a share sale relating to Airbus Industrie (especially in relation to the development costs of the A310 aircraft) and existing financial guarantees to BAe customers. As was not uncommon in nationalised industry, the Corporation's management had reassured those entering into contracts to purchase from BAe, that the Government stood behind the Corporation in the event of any threat to its financial viability.[8] The Department of Industry believed that all of the liabilities and obligations of a privatised BAe would have to be guaranteed by the Government in the event of a future liquidation. The note also acknowledged that the Government would remain BAe's largest customer after a sale, accounting for about one-third of its revenues. BAe sold a large part of its output to the Ministry of Defence (MoD). This also implied a major continuing government interest in the company's fortunes after a sale. However, Joseph concluded that none of this should be allowed to deflect from the desirability of introducing private capital.

Kleinwort, Benson (Kleinworts) was the financial adviser for the sale to the Department of Industry and British Aerospace. In almost all subsequent privatisations the role of adviser to the Government and to the Corporation would be split, with each appointing its own adviser.[9] The experience of the sale of BAe revealed that the interests of government and the industry might diverge, for example on the appropriate capital restructuring; hence the wisdom of having separate advice. It was expected that from time to time there would be some disagreements between the two sets of advisers, but on balance positive results in terms of improved privatisation planning. Having different advisers certainly created a (usually constructive) tension in privatisation sales.

Kleinworts suggested that retaining a government shareholding of between 40 per cent and 60 per cent in BAe should be sufficient to protect the Government's interests. The Secretary of State considered introducing further protection through a power of veto relating to matters of national defence, but concluded that drafting a clause to distinguish defence from commercial concerns would be too difficult. Instead, he proposed to include in the Articles of Association of the new company set up to replace the Corporation, power to appoint two non-executive directors, who would rank equally alongside the other directors of the company and have the same duties. There would also be a provision in the company's Articles to limit and possibly to prevent foreign ownership. To be compliant with obligations under the EEC treaty aimed at preventing discrimination between Member States, such a provision would need to be drafted to make clear that its purpose was to protect national defence interests as permitted under Article 223 of the Treaty of Rome.[10]

However, by the October it had become clear that no sale of BAe could occur before the late spring of the following year, at the earliest.[11] Preparing a successful disposal of the Corporation would take time and planning. Moreover, at E(DL) on 4 October 1979 concerns were expressed that if the Government were to retain a majority shareholding, as under the Secretary of State's current thinking, BAe's borrowings might have to remain part of the PSBR because the Government retained effective control of the company, even if it should choose not to exercise it. At the same time, there was general acceptance of the case for keeping a large shareholding because of the special status of the Corporation as the country's key defence supplier.[12] There was also concern about a proposal from the Department of Industry to guarantee all of the Corporation's inherited liabilities in the event of the company being wound up, to reflect the financial guarantees given in the past. This was likely to reinforce the conclusion that the new company should be classified as remaining in the public sector, even if a majority of the shares were sold. It was agreed that the Treasury and the Department of Industry would need to give further consideration to this issue. There was also the problem of arranging a flotation when a review of public spending, including defence spending, was now underway as part of the Chancellor's autumn review of bids from spending departments. BAe relied heavily on defence orders and the Treasury was locked in difficult bilateral discussions with spending Ministers including the Secretary of State for Defence. Finally, by early 1980 a legal dispute over the terms under which the aerospace firms that made up BAe had been nationalised threatened to further derail an early share flotation. On 23 April 1980 the Chairman of Vickers Ltd wrote to No. 10, suggesting that there should be no sale of shares in BAe until the dispute was settled. As far as he was concerned, Vickers had not been adequately compensated for the loss of its aerospace business at nationalisation.[13] Another factor delaying a sale of BAe in early 1980 was certain tax matters that needed to be sorted out.

The Treasury proved lukewarm towards this privatisation believing that it would raise little revenue and might prove impossible because of the Airbus and other contingent liabilities. Concerns had also surfaced in the City. After the election the Bank of England had volunteered to act as the issuing house for the BAe and other flotations involving the disposal of state assets. The Bank acted as principal adviser on the sale of BP shares in November 1979, including the setting of the share price and along with Kleinworts did some early work on introducing private capital into BAe including exploring the possibility of a bond issue. However, the Bank now signalled that it wanted to withdraw, in part because of a rethink on its appropriate role in privatisations, but also because of particular reservations over aspects of the BAe sale. The Bank feared that the sale might fail, damaging its reputation. Unsurprisingly, within Government this was considered to be "markedly incon-venient" and a potentially serious embarrassment. However, the view was taken that it could be accommodated provided the Bank agreed not to link in public its withdrawal to the BAe flotation.[14]

The Bank seems to have been nervous about the BAe 146 aircraft project, which was expected to absorb considerable future government funds.[15] The Department of Industry's financial adviser, Kleinworts, had indicated that the BAe flotation would be worth much more without it. But to force the management to abandon the project would be strongly resisted by the BAe Board and the aerospace unions. Also, there was concern about BAe's potential liabilities as a partner in the Airbus Industrie joint venture.[16] In March 1980 it became clear that BAe would shortly report its first ever loss due to difficulties in the airlines market. Moreover, in the summer the Government received disappointing news from the City about the expected valuation of the sale. This had now been reduced to £75 million. In spite of this, there was agreement within the Government that it was still important to press ahead with the disposal because of the "political imperative" of doing so.[17] The denationalisation of BAe had been promised in the Conservatives' Election Manifesto. It was felt that a failure to see it through would deal a severe blow to the Government's credibility, whatever the financial merits of a sale.

The British Aerospace Bill containing the necessary powers to sell BAe received its royal assent on 1 May 1980.[18] On 14 October 1980 in E(DL) the Secretary of State for Industry sought agreement to the vesting of the business of BAe in a successor company on 2 November. Vesting day would be the day when the functions and assets of the public corporation were transferred to the new company.[19] Kleinworts advised that the market conditions for a sale might be better then than they would be in early 1981. Preparations to float the Corporation in November 1980 were now advanced and sentiment had moved within Government in favour of a majority share sale if possible. Kleinworts now favoured a majority sale to remove the business from government control and encourage investors to buy the shares. However, whether a sale of any shares in the new company would be possible in November was still questionable. Uncertainties remained over the accounts of Airbus Industrie and the prospects of flotation would also depend on the profit forecasts for the company to go into the sale prospectus, which had yet to be completed. The Stock Exchange required that an offer for sale must be based on audited accounts for a period ending not more than six months before the flotation. BAe drew up its accounts to 31 December each year. Another serious hitch had arisen because of the defence expenditure review under-way and the possible scale of the cuts in defence spending that might be proposed. As the defence equipment budget amounted to about 40 per cent of the MoD's total spending, it was not unreasonable to expect that the cuts would have an appreciable effect on BAe's order book.[20]

As seller, the Government was under a legal requirement to disclose its intentions towards BAe, including planned changes in public spending which might impact on the company even though they had not been publicly announced. Advice within Government was that this would require "full disclosure [of this matter] to our advisers and appropriate disclosure thereafter to the prospectus". But the Cabinet would not be taking a final decision on future public expenditure levels until the end of the month, at the earliest. Reluctantly, therefore, the Secretary of State for Industry concluded that the plan for a November flotation would probably have to be abandoned. In an attempt to prevent the postponement, on 17 October 1980 Joseph saw the Chancellor of the Exchequer to discuss whether the defence programme could be exempted from the planned public expenditure cuts. The Chancellor was able to give no such assurance. Nor was the MoD willing to provide an upper figure on the damage that the reductions, if agreed, might have on its procurement programme so that this could be given in the flotation prospectus. The Secretary of State had been advised that this might be just sufficient to allow the flotation to go ahead. The Chancellor confirmed that the Treasury was looking for cuts of £500 million per annum in defence spending and that this was a bigger priority for the Treasury than the planned sale of 50 per cent of the shares in BAe, which would generate much less.[21]

Meanwhile, Kleinworts warned the Secretary of State that early 1982 was almost certainly the last chance of bringing about a flotation within the life of this Parliament. A later date would be too close to the next general election and "the risk of re-nationalisation without compensation [now a possible threat if there was a future Labour Government] will loom ever larger in investors' minds." Six days later the Secretary of State wrote to the PM with copies to the Chancellor of the Exchequer, the Secretary of State for Defence, Francis Pym, and other members of E(DL), complaining that arguments over the future defence budget were now seriously prejudicing any prospect of a flotation of BAe.[22]

By the end of October 1980 the Department of Industry was planning for a new vesting day of 1 January 1981, with possible flotation in January or February. However, a number of Ministers were sceptical that flotation would be possible early in the New Year. In E(DL) there was agreement simply to return to the matter "in due course when further facts were available".[23] Meanwhile, the Defence Secretary used the BAe flotation as ammunition in his battle with the Treasury over the defence budget. He wrote to the Secretary of State for Industry to garner support, registering his concerns about the way in which the BAe flotation was being undermined "by what I regard as wholly unrealistic [Treasury] assumptions about changes in the future level of defence spending".[24] Joseph replied, while not directly criticising the proposed defence cuts, acknowledging that the Treasury's actions were putting the BAe flotation in jeopardy.[25]

In November 1980 the public spending plans were finalised in Cabinet with the defence budget suffering a smaller reduction than the Treasury had been seeking. However, this still did not clear the way for a flotation of BAe. On 24 November Pym notified Joseph that, while it might now be possible by the New Year to provide details of the likely impact on BAe of MoD procurement cuts in 1981/2, it was unlikely that the effects in later years could be estimated so quickly.[26] The defence spending cuts would still prevent the finalisation of a sale prospectus. Also, while some of the other impediments to a flotation had now been removed, including much of the dispute over the compensation paid during nationalisation and the sums BAe would get from the Airbus Industrie project, the issue of the BAe 146 civil aircraft had still not been settled.[27] Kleinworts had concluded that the BAe 146 aircraft development might not be an obstacle to flotation provided the company had an adequate capital base. But the Department of Industry remained unsure.

Shortly after the 1979 Election the Department of Industry had come close to cancelling the 146 project, which had been started before nationalisation. However, Joseph had decided that to do so would involve a row with the BAe Board which could prejudice the Corporation's sale.[28] The project was first launched in 1973 but a decision on its future was put on ice between 1974 and 1978, reflecting early government concern about its financial viability. On 18 December 1980, having become aware that Kleinworts was advising that the market value of BAe would be higher without the 146 project, John Biffen, Chief Secretary to the Treasury, wrote to Joseph arguing that the project should be urgently reconsidered. The Treasury's understanding was that it was likely to have a substantial negative net present value given the current expectations for sales of the aircraft. Indeed, the financial figures were such that Biffen could not understand why the BAe Board was continuing to proceed with the project. Moreover, he was worried that should the Board cancel the aircraft after a flotation thereby removing the liability, the BAe share price would rise provoking criticism of the Government over the amount raised from the sale; "those who bought shares might appear to benefit at the taxpayer's expense."[29]

Adam Butler, Minister of State in the Department of Industry, replying in Joseph's absence explained that the BAe Board had regularly reviewed the project since its inception and still considered that it was "of strategic importance to their business". The Board had considered the latest financial forecast that had indeed suggested the project might have a negative return, but believed that: "there is almost an equally good chance of the project producing a positive return on future investment". Butler also pointed out that the 146 project was not one which needed government approval to continue. It might therefore be difficult to force a cancellation in the face of Board opposition. Moreover, if cancellation occurred there would be serious job losses and possibly the closure of BAe's Hatfield and Scottish plants. Combining this consideration with the strategic importance of the project and cancellation costs, the Board and the Department were of the view that the project should still proceed. Also, the BAe Chairman gave an assurance that regular reviews would continue to take place and, if it were to become clear that cancellation should be preferred, he would respond "as a matter of commercial judgement".[30]

In other words, both BAe and the Department of Industry took the view that a flotation of shares should not be prejudiced at this late stage by attempting a review of the 146 aircraft project. This position was supported by Kleinworts, who advised that the sale might still go ahead even with the 146 costs, provided that the company's capital base was strengthened first. When Kleinworts consequently recommended a capital injection into BAe of £100 million to be funded from the flotation receipts, there was consternation within the Treasury because of the effect on the economics of the sale.[31] Kleinworts advised that it would be important to structure the company's finances so as to ensure that BAe would be able to pay satisfactory dividends to the new shareholders.[32] Once the financial restructuring was in place, Kleinworts expected that the company would be valued in the stock market at between £250 million to £275 million, compared to its earlier estimate of £275 million to £300 million made before the defence cuts. However, after deducting the capital injection, the costs of concessionary terms for employee shares and the cost of the issue, "we should anticipate the net proceeds from the flotation to be in the range of £15–£30 million, with the stock market valuation of the Government's remaining half share at about £130 million." These net proceeds of sale were significantly lower than originally planned. In an attempt to placate the Treasury, the Secretary of State stressed that there would also be a reduction to the PSBR in the current year of £80 million and major benefits in the order of £400 million over the next five years once BAe's borrowings did not form part of the PSBR. But it is far from clear that the Treasury's concerns were assuaged; the Treasury found the figures most disappointing. By January 1981 the future of the sale really did hang in the balance.

In E(DL) on 11 December 1980 concerns were voiced about the likely political and media criticism of the low sale receipts.[33] Compensation paid to the previous owners following nationalisation in 1977 and subsequent interest on the related government debt amounted to £215 million. Also, there had been public investment in BAe since nationalisation equivalent to £140 million at current prices, and now there was the proposal for a further £100 million as a new capital injection. Therefore, the total of public money put into BAe by privatisation would amount to some £450 million, against an estimated total market value for the company of about £250 million to £275 million. The proceeds seemed comparatively low and it could be argued that "the Company was being sold at a time when its market value was depressed." The PM was clearly concerned about the figures and especially the need to inject £100 million to strengthen the company, no doubt conscious of likely adverse comment by the Public Accounts Committee, and asked the Chancellor to investigate. At the same time, she was aware that there remained a political imperative to sell; denationalisation of BAe was a Manifesto commitment.

With continuing uncertainty about BAe's future MoD orders, the prospects for a flotation before the spring or summer of 1981 now seemed poor and to make matters worse there was the possibility that net receipts then might be even lower than the figure estimated for a sale in February. Also, the Chancellor of the Exchequer and the Chief Secretary were of the view that to sell 50 per cent of BAe for only some £15 million to £30 million net would lead to sharp criticism and could "risk discrediting the manifesto commitment to privatisation".[34] In E(DL) it was suggested that the decision to float in early 1981 should be reassessed, "since if it were cancelled this might well improve the prospects for sale of the Company in, say, 1982". However, it was recognised that cancellation would involve financial and political costs and the decision would be strongly opposed by the BAe Board. It would also bring the sale perilously close to a next general election.

Meanwhile, the Treasury continued to question the desirability of BAe continuing the 146 development, arguing that if it were to be cancelled now the £100 million capital injection might be avoided and a much larger net sum from the sale of BAe would result. The Treasury proposed that the project be axed. The Chancellor also had concerns about vesting on 1 January 1981 given the likelihood of a postponed flotation. His officials had drawn attention to two problems if the gap between vesting day and flotation was protracted. First, there might be criticism of the loss of interest on the Corporation's commencing capital, given that this capital would be extinguished before vesting.[35] Second, the British Aerospace Act 1980, as passed, had not considered the possibility of a delay and there was no provision for interim financing. The bank loans that BAe had negotiated were on terms appropriate in the private sector, but were considered by the Treasury to be "inappropriately onerous for a public sector company". The result would be likely criticism from the House of Commons' Public Accounts Committee. It was the Chancellor's view that the Department of Industry should accept that if flotation was delayed by more than six months after vesting, more satisfactory financing provisions would need to be introduced.[36]

As a result, a memorandum of understanding to cover the period from vesting day to flotation was drawn up between the Department of Industry, the Treasury and BAe. The Government had already agreed a similar arrangement for the National Freight Corporation (NFC), whose privatisation was now also delayed by economic conditions (chapter 6). The privatisation of NFC was planned at the same time as the sale of BAe but from within the Department of Transport. The terms of the memorandum enabled the Government to exercise the same measure of control over BAe after vesting day until flotation as it exercised over BAe as a nationalised industry. It was also agreed that it would be "reasonable and politically sensible" for the Government to seek an amount in respect of dividends on its shares between vesting and the sale to replace interest lost on cancelled debt. However, there were others who thought, "it is important that BAe's business should not be put at any financial disadvantage as a result of this transaction. It would be particularly harmful during the period of the Company's ownership by Government, which will be critical for the success of the eventual flotation, if BAe were to be restricted by lack of funds in a way that prevented it from pursuing its business vigorously."[37] Nevertheless, the memorandum was agreed.

At E(DL) on 11 December 1980 Ministers confirmed that 1 January 1981 should be the vesting day for BAe with flotation in February if possible.[38] A statement to the House of Commons announcing the vesting day and a capital reconstruction consisting of debt write-offs was made on 17 December 1980, by way of a written answer.[39] Treasury officials were nervous about a sentence in the statement that the Government would stand behind the Company and fully guarantee it financially until the beginning of the offer for sale, given continuing uncertainty as to when that might be. But the PM had agreed to its inclusion. The Department of Industry saw this commitment as necessary so as to clarify the situation for those businesses which dealt with BAe.[40]

By early January the PM had been advised that no action could be taken on the 146 project unless a delay in the flotation was to occur.[41] Lawson had come to a similar conclusion, albeit reluctantly. While believing that it was unsatisfactory that there was no real assessment of the viability of the 146 project, given its potential impact on the sale price of BAe and its importance in determining the size of the Government's capital injection into the company, he agreed that to obtain a proper assessment now would prevent a flotation in February.[42] Equally, the Chancellor of the Exchequer had decided to end discussion on the future of the 146 aircraft given the political need to complete the privatisation of BAe quickly.[43]

However, this still left the thorny issue of finalising the estimates of the impact of the new MoD budget on the future revenues of BAe. The MoD was still signalling considerable opposition to being forced into what it saw as an over speedy commitment to future procurement expenditures. In a memorandum to the PM on 16 January 1981, John Nott, the new Secretary of State for Defence, acknowledged "the great political importance of flotation for our objectives as a Government" and for the future of the UK's aerospace sector. But he protested that "the conditions for a flotation now would create difficulties for me in conducting the sort of fundamental look at defence commitments, roles and capabilities which even a few days in office has convinced me is necessary . . . If flotation proceeds, therefore, it must be on the understanding that my freedom to act is not constrained. Whether flotation can legitimately proceed on that understanding must be open to some doubt." [44]

Nott's memorandum, which suggested a continuation in MoD thinking following the departure of Pym in the minor Cabinet reshuffle a few days earlier, led to a riposte from Joseph that much clearer and precise information would need to be given to potential investors than the statement envisaged by the Secretary of State for Defence.[45] February 1981 was considered the last month possible for a flotation based on BAe's most recent audited results, which were for the period to June 1980. Even so the Government needed to obtain a special dispensation from the Stock Exchange to relax the normal rule that a sale prospectus should contain audited results for a period ending not less than six months before the offer for sale. If the February deadline was missed, the next time that a flotation could occur would be from the end of April. However, Kleinworts' view was that after February it was very doubtful that a flotation could occur at all. This was because of the threat of renationalisation by an incoming Labour Government, which would deter investors. A general election was likely in 1983. Also, BAe's Chairman, Sir Austin Pearce, had informed the Minister that he could not expect his colleagues and staff to devote themselves to another round of preparations for a sale after February, albeit that the senior management were keen to see privatisation occur.

On 19 January 1981 the PM held an urgent meeting with the Secretary of State for Industry, the Foreign and Commonwealth Secretary, the Chancellor of the Exchequer, the Secretary of State for Defence and the Attorney General in an attempt to end the impasse. At this meeting Nott requested permission to make a statement on defence expenditure the next day.[46] At the meeting it was agreed that, with a view to facilitating the BAe flotation, wording for a Parliamentary statement by the Secretary of State for Defence would be drafted that satisfied the Secretary of State for Industry's need for some precision as to the impact of the MoD cuts on the company. With the uncertainty of the future defence budget now seemingly removed, or at least papered over, the flotation could proceed. However, Nott was still worried that the MoD might need to claw back in the next financial year a cash overspend in the current year and if this happened "the defence programme would be brought to a halt . . . [and] . . . the effects on defence industry would be disastrous."

In this still uncertain environment the sale of BAe went ahead, following a statement from the Defence Secretary intended to soothe investor nervousness. Shares in BAe were sold in February 1981 using a fixed price offer for sale at 150p per share, payable in full on application. The sale price was set by Kleinworts in discussion with the Government and brokers. A former senior civil servant in the Department of Industry at the time has acknowledged that in this early privatisation officials were rather "green" and tended to accept with insufficient questioning City advice. Just over a half of the company's shares were sold, 51.7 per cent, and the sale grossed £148.6 million. After selling costs, about £43 million went to the Exchequer and £100 million to the company to strengthen its balance sheet.[47] This was somewhat better than Kleinworts' dire prediction in early December, but still less than expected when privatisation planning had begun. The £100 million injection took the form of a payment to the company for new shares; however the Government also agreed to forego about £55 million in dividends outstanding on the cancelled public dividend capital. Kleinworts advised that if the Government insisted on receiving this payment, the company's distributable reserves would be reduced and with it the attractiveness of the share offer to investors. The arrangement was later questioned by the Public Accounts Committee (PAC), which concluded that "the final result was a cash deficit of £12 million to the Exchequer." The Committee also drew attention to the amounts the Government had invested in BAe since nationalisation, something that E(DL) on 11 December 1980 had feared might attract critical attention.[48] On the other hand, if the outstanding dividends had been paid and the Government had not injected capital into the company, the amount raised from the flotation would have been less and perhaps the sale would not have been possible at all. The PAC's criticism of a cash deficit to the Exchequer was therefore arguably harsh.

A total of £5.6 million was spent by the Government on the share issue, the major component being commission to the underwriters, sub-underwriters and brokers.[49] The flotation of BAe involved four main underwriters, Kleinwort Benson, Hill Samuel & Co, Morgan Grenfell and J.Henry Schroder Wagg.[50] The PAC also criticised the Department of Industry's decision to both price the shares keenly to ensure a successful flotation and underwrite the issue, concluding: "we doubt whether . . . it was necessary to underwrite the issue at a cost of £2.6 million in order to guarantee receipt of the proceeds of the fixed price offer".[51] The Treasury, however, defended the decision on the grounds that "underwriting made an important contribution to the Government's primary objective, which was to achieve a successful flotation . . . to get the Government's programme of share sales off to a good start."[52] In addition, the PAC expressed concerns about continuing Government financial commitments relating to the Airbus Industrie project. The Government had accepted an unquantified liability to stand behind BAe should it have difficulty in financing its agreed share of the Airbus project development costs.[53]

The offer for sale was oversubscribed 3.5 times and dealings in the shares opened at a premium of some 13 per cent over the offer price. Each eligible employee was offered 33 free shares worth approximately £50 and matching shares equivalent to the number they chose to buy, subject to a limit of 600 shares per employee. These shares were held by the trustees of an especially created British Aerospace Employee Share Ownership Scheme, to take advantage of privileged tax treatment of the benefits under the 1978 Finance Act. It had been BAe management who had suggested the use of free and matching shares and some in the Government saw it as a useful way of deflecting union criticism of the privatisation and reducing the prospect of future re-nationalisation. The management wanted a more generous scheme, but Treasury Ministers initially opposed the whole idea of free and matching shares, principally, it seems, because of the impact on the sales receipts.[54] In the end the Treasury relented. Nevertheless, the Chancellor of the Exchequer placed an effective cost ceiling for this and future privatisations to encourage employee shareholdings, of five per cent of the expected gross sale proceeds with free share offers not to exceed £50 per head.[55] While the Government favoured encouraging employee shareholdings to motivate workers, the Chancellor was at pains to stress: "the arrangements must be secured at a cost to the Exchequer which is reasonable in terms of preserving the benefits to the PSBR of the flotation . . . Without it we risk a considerable part of the disposal receipts being swallowed up, especially where employee numbers are large in relation to the expected value of the equity . . . I think we must accept that any free offer [during the BAe flotation] will set a precedent which it will be difficult to avoid in subsequent cases."[56]

The Articles of Association of the new company restricted foreign ownership to 15 per cent of the voting shares and the Government gave an undertaking in the sale prospectus to retain around 48 per cent of the issued shares "for the foreseeable future", so as to alleviate investors' fears of a further quick large-scale sale that might depress the share price. The Government also made it clear that it intended to retain a permanent shareholding conferring more than 25 per cent of the voting rights to prevent an alteration to the provisions of the company's Articles of Association relating to UK control and to the continuation of two Government appointed non-executive directors.[57] With the success of the flotation, Joseph called a small party to thank those in his department who had made the sale possible.[58]

The undertaking not to sell more shares in "the foreseeable future" was taken to mean within Government not before February 1983 at the earliest. After some consideration, the Government was advised that the commitment in the sale prospectus should be interpreted as binding for at least two years. In March 1983 a further sale was ruled out by the Secretary of State for Industry because of the rationalisation of BAe plants underway, including closures.[59] So it was not until November 1984 that the Department of Trade and Industry (DTI)[60] obtained advice from merchant bankers, Lazard, on the disposal of at least some of its residual holding. Lazard advised that a disposal could take place through a "placing" of 23.3 per cent of the shares, leaving the Government with the blocking 25 per cent holding it had committed itself to retaining, or an offer for sale of the entire 48 per cent the Government still held.[61] The Treasury favoured a public offer for all of the Government's remaining holding, both to advance the privatisation programme and because there was a shortfall in the annual disposals target for 1984/5 due to a delay to the sale of British Airways. The Treasury's preference was for a share sale to occur in mid-February 1985 "to help fill the financing gap", but it soon became clear that this was not practicable.[62] The impact day was therefore scheduled for 1 May. Although the DTI was initially hesitant about reneging on the commitment to retain 25 per cent of the shares indefinitely, it later gave its full backing. Norman Tebbit, the new Secretary of State for Trade and Industry, was keen to get the Government out of its earlier commitment. The sale of the Government's remaining shareholding was announced in Parliament on 15 January 1985. The Government waived aside objections to reversing its position on retaining a sizeable shareholding, principally from the Labour Opposition in Parliament.[63]

In the second share issue of BAe in May 1985 the share price became payable in two instalments with an initial payment of £2. Fifty-five per cent of the offer was "placed firm" with City institutions (the same percentage as had applied during the sale of British Telecom shares the previous November, see chapter 13). The price of the shares was set towards the bottom of the expected price range, at 375p, but still netted for the Government around £363 million.[64] The offer was oversubscribed 5.4 times.[65] Approximately 264,000 applications were received from the general public and the Government applied a priority allocation to small investors. Applications for up to 20,000 shares were allocated a minimum of 100 shares and a maximum of 275, larger applications received none. About 2,500 employees out of BAe's workforce of 79,000 also applied for shares, although being a secondary offer no financial incentives were provided to encourage employee share ownership, over and above a commitment to give preferential consideration to employee applications.[66]

At the time of the sale there was City speculation that other companies might be interested in acquiring BAe. The second flotation occurred after the British companies Thorn-EMI and GEC had both, during the early summer of 1984, expressed some interest in buying the company.[67] There was concern that this interest might spark a bid from a foreign investor. To address the threat of a possible foreign takeover once the Government's shareholding was removed, a 15 per cent limit was placed on foreign shareholdings in the Articles of Association and a requirement that all directors of the company must be British nationals was entrenched.[68] In addition, the Government was empowered to continue to nominate one director. As an extra safeguard, a "special share" was created, to be retained by the Government, which would ensure that the Government's consent was required before the provisions in the Articles could be amended. The Government reasoned that the creation of the special share made the earlier commitment to continue to hold at least 25 per cent of the issued shares redundant.[69]

As Norman Tebbit, Secretary of State for Trade and Industry at the time of the disposal of the Government's remaining shares in BAe, comments in his memoirs: "In many ways it was the BAe flotation which first proved that the socialist rachet could be reversed."[70]

The flotations in February 1981 and then again in May 1985 saw Labour's nationalisation of aerospace in 1977 completely reversed. The immediate motivation for the privatisation of BAe was primarily political not economic, reflecting a commitment made when the industry had been nationalised. The Exchequer received little immediate benefit from the first share sale. Nevertheless, BAe was now free from government financial controls and dependent for its future success on the private capital market, raising finance on a normal commercial basis. From the management's perspective this was a major step forward.

## Cable and Wireless

In October 1944 an official Committee on Empire Telecommunications Services had concluded against operating telecommunications outside Britain through the Post Office. Within the Commonwealth at this time there was a broad consensus that the ownership and operation of international telecommunications ought not to be left in private hands. Therefore, Cable and Wireless (C&W) was established as a state-owned company under the Companies Act, in 1946.[71] Like British Leyland and Rolls-Royce, legally it was not a public corporation and the management always had a large measure of freedom to operate commercially.[72] The company's origins lay in the nineteenth century and the first transatlantic electric telegraph, although the name Cable and Wireless was not adopted until 1934.[73] On 1 April 1950 almost all of the assets in Britain of C&W, which were external telegraph services, were transferred to the Post Office, leaving the company as an operator of telecommunications services overseas. The Government's shareholding was held by the Treasury.[74]

By the early 1980s C&W employed around 10,000 people, some 8,000 outside the UK, and operated in 37 territories around the world through franchising agreements and the provision of services to independent providers of telecommunication systems. The operating franchises in Hong Kong and Bahrain were of particular importance to the company. Table 5.1 provides a breakdown of turnover and profits in different parts of the world; 99 per cent of revenues were earned outside the UK. In the year ending 31 March 1981 turnover and

*Table 5.1* Cable and Wireless: geographical breakdown of turnover and profits

| *Year ended 31 March 1981* | *Pro forma* | |
|---|---|---|
| | *Turnover* *£000s* | *Profit (loss)* *£000s* |
| Far East and South Pacific | 78,397 | 39,319 |
| Middle East and Africa | 34,562 | 6,582 |
| Bermuda, Caribbean and Central and South America | 29,762 | 8,161 |
| Atlantic and Indian Oceans | 6,851 | 493 |
| Europe, including central projects and cableships | 89,581 | 4,346 |
| United States of America | 15,642 | (899) |
| Sundry income, excluding interest | — | 4,551* |
| Total pro forma turnover and profit before unallocated central corporate expenses, interest and taxation | 254,795 | 62,553 |

*Note*: * No part of the turnover of associated companies was shown, only the attributable profit.
*Source*: Cable and Wireless Offer for Sale document, p.7.

profit before tax were around £255 million and £62 million, respectively. Both turnover and profit were rising. Turnover had been £71.8 million in 1975 and pre-tax profit £21.5 million.

The possible sale of some of the Government's shareholding in C&W was first mooted in the summer of 1979 when the Treasury was hunting for assets to sell to lower the PSBR.[75] Early discussion centred on a sale of 49 per cent of the shares, which it was believed might raise somewhere between £60 million and £120 million. However, this review of the ownership of C&W came at a very sensitive time in the company's history. Over the following months planning for a sale would be heavily constrained by difficulties with negotiations over the future of the Bahrain, and more especially the Hong Kong, operating concessions. The Hong Kong concession was scheduled to expire in 1987 and in the colony there was pressure from business interests for local control of C&W's telecommunications interests. The Hong Kong Governor made it clear that there could be agreement on new ownership arrangements for C&W only on condition that the UK Government retained strategic control of the company, otherwise there was a high risk that C&W's operations in Hong Kong would be taken over by local interests. In Bahrain, C&W's concession would expire in July 1982 and the Bahrain Government had indicated that they too attached considerable importance to the UK Government retaining a dominant influence in the company.[76] How the Government should best retain effective control of C&W would therefore have to be decided before a share sale could proceed in Britain.

Barings Bank was the Department's initial choice of adviser on a sale, but in August 1980 Kleinworts took the leading role. NM Rothschild & Sons (Rothschilds) was also involved for a time.[77] The immediate challenge was to consider how best to approach a disposal of C&W. In addition to the concession negotiations, which would have to be handled with great sensitivity, under a new Telecommunications Bill (designed to split British Telecom from the Post Office and encourage competition in some areas of the domestic telecommunications market) another mainline operator in the UK was to be licensed. C&W had been identified as this operator. By 1981 C&W was busy planning a high-speed digital network in conjunction with BP and Barclays. This became Mercury Communications; later BP and Barclays withdrew from the venture. This major development made the valuing of C&W more difficult.

A feasibility study commissioned from Barings by the Department of Industry confirmed that it would be desirable if the negotiation of the Hong Kong concession was completed before an attempt was made to sell shares in C&W. Negotiation had started and initially the proposal was for an extension of the concession by 25 years. However, lobbying within Hong Kong introduced a condition that C&W should set up a separate subsidiary company to run the Hong Kong operations. Some of the directors of the subsidiary would be nominees of the Governor of Hong Kong and a majority would be British nationals ordinarily resident in the colony. The Department's financial adviser was of the view that apprehension in Hong Kong about a sale of the Government's shareholding in C&W would be reduced if shares were sold first in a Hong Kong subsidiary. However, C&W management was fearful that through the creation of a subsidiary, the Hong Kong Government was preparing the way to exercise local control over the running of the Hong Kong operations, in the event of the British Government ceasing to exercise control of C&W following a sale of shares. Also, setting up a separate subsidiary could have damaging implications for negotiations on the company's other concessions, notably the one in Bahrain. In these circumstances, there was a commercial incentive for C&W not to hurry a conclusion of the negotiations on the setting up of a subsidiary. Soon C&W began to question whether it was really necessary to finalise discussions on the Hong Kong concession before a flotation of the main company's shares occurred.

Within the Government there was concern that the Chairman of C&W, Lord Glenmara, formerly the Labour MP Ted Short, was dragging his feet over planning a flotation of the company, and that little could be done before the appointment of a new Chairman.[78] Meanwhile, Parliamentary Counsel had been busy drafting the necessary legislative provisions to permit a share flotation as part of the drafting of the Telecommunications Bill, but with a view to placing the relevant sections within a short separate Bill should this be required. The Government hoped that a decision on the best way to privatise C&W could be made by the early autumn.[79] However, at E(DL) on 5 August 1980 the Sub-Committee acknowledged the concerns of overseas governments and agreed that a further paper should be prepared by the Department of Industry, in consultation with the Foreign and Commonwealth Office and other interested departments, before any final decision on a disposal was made.[80]

The paper was circulated to E(DL) members on 21 October 1980.[81] The Minister of State at the Department of Industry, Adam Butler, was able to report several developments, including the appointment of a new Chairman, Eric Sharp, formerly Chairman of Monsanto, to replace Lord Glenmara. He was believed to be "generally supportive of the government's intentions" and it was judged that his appointment would bring "a welcome, fresh outlook on C&W's problems". However, it was also felt that "he will have difficulty in overcoming some of the entrenched views of other members of the Court." The Court was the main decision making body of C&W, including one government and two Post Office appointed directors, and equivalent to the board of a private sector company. Set against the positive development of the appointment of a new Chairman keen to pursue privatisation, the path to formal renegotiation of the concession in Hong Kong was now obstructed by a dispute that had broken out between C&W and the Hong Kong Telephone Company (Telco), an independent private enterprise. The dispute had arisen over revenue sharing. This had now developed into a legal action by C&W to recover sums from Telco. The Hong Kong Government was keen to help settle the matter and Butler arranged to discuss the dispute with the Governor when he visited the UK in early November. But in the meantime the matter interrupted the planning of a smooth disposal.[82]

Meanwhile the Government had commissioned a feasibility study on a share flotation for C&W from Kleinworts. Kleinworts had drawn up a possible timetable leading to a sale of shares in C&W in the current financial year, 1980/1. Work to ensure that this option was kept open was underway, including the undertaking of an interim audit of the company. However, like Barings earlier, Kleinworts concluded that the future of the Hong Kong concession was critical to the feasibility and timing of any sale of shares in the main company or in a Hong Kong subsidiary. The bank also advised that an early January deadline on negotiations would be necessary if there was to be a public offer of shares before 31 March 1981. Moreover, the Governor of Hong Kong was now advising that the Hong Kong Government definitely wanted to see the establishment of a locally accountable subsidiary in return for a new concession, although he reported that this could simply be the starting point for negotiation.[83]

On becoming Chairman Eric Sharp found weaknesses in the management of C&W in terms of financial control, corporate planning and management succession and reported to the Government that this would take time to put right.[84] If they were not put right the weaknesses would need to be reported in the flotation prospectus. Given this development, and other difficulties, including that the Telecommunications Bill was not now expected to receive royal assent before the summer, Kleinworts concluded that an offer for sale would have to be put back to September 1981. This would rule out the Government earning sales receipts in the 1980/1 financial year. Regarding the form that a disposal should eventually take, Kleinworts confirmed that selling of shares in a Hong Kong subsidiary first would produce the maximum short-term financial advantage to the Government. The subsidiary was likely to obtain a high valuation because of its profitability and the low rate of profit tax in the colony. Shares in the main company could then be sold later. The Hong Kong operation could be transformed into a local subsidiary company on 1 April 1983 with the Hong Kong Government given the opportunity to purchase a 20 per cent holding. Kleinworts advised that this plan was feasible provided the necessary preparations began no later than the beginning of February 1981.[85]

However, there were unresolved differences between the new Chairman and some of the other C&W directors about the merits of a subsidiary structure for Hong Kong. In particular, it seems that Sharp was not against the establishment and sale of a subsidiary, but the majority of the Court were opposed because of the possible implications for the company's operations in other countries. They also feared attenuating the company's control over the vital Hong Kong revenues. In addition, there was disagreement within C&W over the timing of a share sale in the main company and about the desirability of a sale of shares in the main company to overseas governments. Kleinworts agreed that allowing particular overseas governments to acquire shares in C&W would be unwise because this might encourage demands from other territories in which C&W operated for similar terms. Moreover, the resulting ownership might create uncertainties amongst overseas governments about C&W's independence. But in any case, the Department of Industry, the Foreign and Commonwealth Office and the Ministry of Defence were against foreign ownership. The MoD was particularly opposed because of the possible implications for the control of C&W's international telecommunications at the time of a national emergency.[86]

To address some of these difficulties, thought was given at this time to placing shares with City institutions instead of a public offer or to the sale of C&W to another company. However, it was decided that the former would be unlikely to speed up a sale because the same issues in terms of the Hong Kong concession would arise. It was also probable that the sale receipts would be lower than from a public flotation. It was also decided that selling C&W to another company would not necessarily overcome the problem of the Hong Kong concession, unless the Government was willing to accept a lower valuation to reflect uncertainty about the outcome of the negotiations.

The Chairman and the Court did not dismiss out of hand the idea of a merger or partnership with another company. The telecoms equipment manufacturer GEC showed some interest in the possibility, although C&W was cautious because it considered that linking with GEC would undermine its reputation for impartiality in the purchase of equipment. Sharp was more attracted to a possible link with BP. It was felt that the oil company could bring important management skills and financial resources to C&W. BP was believed to be interested in C&W as a partner to diversify into business telecommunications. Indeed, BP became an early joint investor in Mercury, C&W's planned fixed line operation in Britain. However, any such arrangement might require a separate Bill to provide legal authorisation. It was also felt within the Department of Industry, with justification, that it would be difficult to place an accurate value on C&W in the absence of a market flotation.[87]

More generally, it had become clear that the disposal receipts would very much depend upon the terms negotiated for the Hong Kong concession, irrespective of the method of sale. At an E(DL) meeting on 23 October 1980 the Minister, Adam Butler, revealed that based on Kleinworts' figures the Government now hoped that the eventual sale of C&W might raise around £300 million to £335 million, although this could fall to £240 million to £300 million in a private placing.[88] However, it was conceded that "there is very little prospect indeed of achieving a successful sale of C&W shares to the public in this financial year. We should therefore decide to give up this as our objective and not incur the expenditure necessary if it were maintained." Also, the Department of Industry had concluded that it would be impossible to achieve a separate sale of a Hong Kong subsidiary in 1980/1. Even if Sharp was able to win the Court around to the idea, there would be tax and contract issues to settle along with the current dispute with Telco in Hong Kong. The only way of assisting the Chancellor of the Exchequer to meet his PSBR target for the year would be to sell C&W to another company; but it was judged that "even this appears to offer a remote prospect for realisation this year and could in any event lead to some awkward practical and policy difficulties for us".[89]

The Department of Industry concluded that the best way forward would be to plan for a public offer of shares in C&W around September 1981 and after the renegotiation of the Hong Kong concession had hopefully been completed. However, the final decision on whether first to sell shares in a Hong Kong subsidiary and then in the main company or simply shares in the main company was left to be resolved later. Treasury Ministers continued to press for a share sale in the main company in the current financial year, 1980/1. It was also their view that if this did not prove possible, it would be better from the point of view of monetary control if the sale happened early in the 1981/2 financial year rather than in September. At the meeting of E(DL) on 23 October 1980 it was agreed that all possible options should be retained. It was also agreed that Adam Butler should approach the Chancellor of the Duchy of Lancaster for approval to draft a separate bill alongside the Telecommunications Bill to enable a sale of C&W to be completed in 1980/1, should it prove necessary, and to make arrangements for its early introduction into Parliament. The Chancellor of the Duchy of Lancaster and QL Committee (the Queen's Speeches and Future Legislation Committee) were responsible for the scheduling of the Government's legislative programme. In addition, discussions continued to assess the degree of interest of other companies, including BP, in buying C&W.[90] The Minister was also asked to ensure that there would be no competition policy obstacles to the sale of C&W to another company. Clearly, all options were still open. However, subsequently the decision was taken to proceed with taking legal powers to sell C&W in the Telecommunications Bill rather than a separate bill, which would have taken up more Parliamentary time and would not necessarily have guaranteed a sale in the current financial year.

News was received around this time on C&W's dispute with Telco. This was settled by arbitration as a result of an initiative taken by C&W's new Chairman with support from the Governor of Hong Kong. This development removed one potential barrier to a successful flotation, but at the cost of raising the proportion of the company's local revenues going to Telco from 22 per cent to 40 per cent. The dispute also left a legacy of ill feeling in Hong Kong towards the company. As a result, the Governor now advised that the setting up of a local subsidiary should be deferred for at least two years. Also, the Court of C&W was firmly of the view that the company should be permitted to take advantage of a transitional period to adjust to the new situation in the colony. This would have the benefit of strengthening

C&W's case for requesting a similar transitional period in the negotiations over the renewal of the Bahrain concession. The Bahrain Government was known to be in favour of taking over 60 per cent of C&W's local operation and C&W was understandably keen to prevent this happening. Kleinworts advised that it would be desirable to settle the future of C&W's operation in Bahrain before any shares in C&W were sold.[91]

On 2 December 1980 the House of Commons was informed that a clause would be included in the Telecommunications Bill to empower the Government to dispose of shares in C&W. The following month the new Minister of State at the Department of Industry, Kenneth Baker, reviewed the options. With the company's dispute with Telco now settled, the target was to sell just under 50 per cent of C&W's shares by the end of September 1981. The plan now had the full support of the C&W Court. The previous suggestion, to maximise sales receipts by selling shares in a Hong Kong subsidiary of C&W followed by a sale of shares in the entire Group, was no longer open to the Government following the Governor of Hong Kong's advice. Baker also explained that the possibility of selling shares in C&W to a trade purchaser was now very doubtful. C&W had opposed a link with a telecommunications equipment manufacturer such as GEC and while BP had shown early interest in buying shares, the company had now withdrawn its interest, preferring to explore the possibility of joint ventures.[92]

Before E Committee on 5 March 1981 the Secretary of State for Industry reported that he had decided to relinquish management responsibility for the company while retaining majority ownership. Consultation with overseas governments had confirmed that their opposition to the sale of C&W to the private sector would only be assuaged if the Government retained majority control. Nevertheless, the intention was that the company should be reclassified as part of the private sector. This was an important goal for the Treasury. To support this, the Government would agree to there being no intervention in the company's commercial decisions, except where this was considered necessary to protect the interest of overseas governments in relation to the company's responsibilities under their concessions.[93] The aim was to make a share offering by the end of September in London and Hong Kong. It was also agreed, in conformance with the Government's widening ownership agenda, that there should be arrangements for employees of C&W to acquire shares.

However, the Secretary of State's conclusion that the sale of C&W should only proceed with the Government retaining a majority shareholding met with a frosty reception in No. 10 and in the Treasury. In February the PM demanded to know why the Secretary of State for Industry was planning to sell less than 50 per cent of the Government's shares, when in her view retaining only 33 per cent would be sufficient to give the Government effective control of C&W.[94] On receiving the Minister's proposed draft statement to the House on the future of the company, the PM repeated her concerns.[95] The Treasury responded with a proposal to sell around 66 per cent of C&W's shares. The difference between a sale of less than 50 per cent and 66 per cent was about £50 million and the Treasury was keen to get its hands on this money.[96] The Treasury was also concerned to ensure that the company's future borrowings fell outside the PSBR, which it now argued was doubtful if the Government retained a majority shareholding. The Department of Industry was disappointed by this view given the Secretary of State's assurances on future non-intervention in the management of the company and the fact that in the past C&W's borrowings had never been treated as public borrowing.[97] The PM insisted that the matter be discussed in E Committee.[98] In the meantime, a statement to the House was postponed.

It remained the case that the Department of Industry believed that if the Government were to relinquish a majority of the shares there was a real risk that overseas governments would begin moves to take over C&W's local operations including in Hong Kong. In the Department of Industry David Young, special adviser to the Secretary of State on privatisation, was asked to go out to Hong Kong in February 1981 to help with negotiations. On 2 March, on returning, he sent a hastily drafted letter to No. 10 confirming that the Government needed to retain a majority share ownership in C&W to secure renewal of the concession. Also, he was able to confirm that the Ruler of Bahrain had "expressed concern at our privatisation proposals and it was only our assurance that we would maintain strategic control that won the day".[99] Joseph also weighed in explaining that he wanted to see C&W privatised in full, "But we have to take account of what is practicable and what will give us the best price."[100] The Department of Industry protested that a change in the plan to sell a minority shareholding might create a pretext for foreign governments to start nationalising their C&W concessions, leading to "a widespread domino effect".[101]

The threat was real. On 21 April 1981 George Chambers, Prime Minister of Trinidad and Tobago, wrote to the PM asking whether it was correct that the UK Government intended to divest approximately one-half of its shareholding in C&W. If this was so he wrote: "my Government would wish to have the assurance that early negotiations may be possible so as to give the Trinidad and Tobago Government first option to purchase the shares of Cable and Wireless (West Indies Ltd.)." The Department of Industry was unclear whether the request resulted from a misunderstanding as to the nature of the proposed sale, that the Government of Trinidad and Tobago believed that a sale of C&W would involve selling shares in the West Indies subsidiary company separately, and drafted a reply for the PM on this assumption. This assured the PM of Trinidad and Tobago that no such sale was contemplated. However, there was also concern in the Department that the Government of Trinidad and Tobago might be attempting to take advantage of a share sale in C&W to take control of the Trinidad and Tobago operations.[102]

Kleinworts had already advised that as an alternative to the Government retaining a majority shareholding in C&W, the option of providing a Government veto over decisions made by the Court of C&W through some blocking provisions in the Articles of Association would depress the value of the shares sold.[103] Eric Sharp also favoured the Government retaining a majority holding.[104] But probably particularly influential in terms of not changing the plan at this stage was an argument from the Foreign and Commonwealth Office that if the current plans were changed the Government would have to go back to foreign governments to explain the new position. This "would take time, and could lose goodwill and arouse suspicions" and might be met with particular hostility in Bahrain.[105] Around the same time, Sir Robin Ibbs, the head of the Central Policy Review Staff in the Cabinet Office, gave support to the plan to dispose of less than a majority interest in C&W, on the grounds that this was essential for a successful flotation while avoiding difficulties with overseas governments.[106]

After discussion, on 5 March 1981 E Committee agreed to the Secretary of State's proposal. To placate the PM and Treasury Ministers, the Secretary of State assured the Committee that additional shares in the company would be sold "as soon as this could be arranged consistently with securing the future of the Company's overseas operations". This might occur when overseas governments became confident of the new ownership structure. Nevertheless, although the PM felt forced to back down on a majority disposal, she did so on the understanding that the share sale would leave the Government with a bare majority holding only (just over 50 per cent) and that "in contrast to the arrangements made for British Aerospace, nothing should be said or done that would fetter the Government's freedom to sell further shares in the Company at a later date should a suitable opportunity arise." The Department of Industry was now of the view that around 49 per cent of the shares might be sold. As we have seen, in the case of BAe the Government had given a commitment not to sell further shares for "the foreseeable future", which had been interpreted as meaning for at least two years. It was judged that the same would apply to C&W shares. The Minister of State was sanctioned to make an oral statement to the House on Monday 9 March on the Government's intentions.[107] This statement was subject to some input by the PM to ensure that there could be no suggestion that the Government was committed long term to maintaining majority ownership of C&W.[108]

The decision that in the future the Government would dispose of a majority shareholding necessitated the design of terms to prevent a possible unwelcome takeover of C&W, given the strategic importance of the company's international telecommunications network. Also, there were continuing concerns from some overseas governments, including the Government of Hong Kong, that a major manufacturer of telecommunications equipment might seek to gain control over the company. On 17 July 1981 the Minister of State set out further details of the sale to E(DL), including that, subject to the approval of the Stock Exchange, in the Company's Articles of Association there would be a 15 per cent limit on individual shareholdings (other than that of the Government and trustees of a share scheme to be set up for employees), so as to provide against "undesirable influence over C&W and takeovers" once, in the future, a majority of the shares were sold. This requirement was added because the company's existing Articles of Association, dating from 1929, gave the Directors the power to force the sale of foreign shareholdings in excess of 25 per cent of the issued share capital. But advisers had now concluded that this protection might be contrary to the Treaty of Rome. At the same time, Kleinworts recommended that to prevent the threat of a quick sale of the remainder of the Government's shareholding depressing the share price on flotation, the Government should use the same or similar wording as appeared in the BAe Prospectus, effectively committing not to sell further shares for at least two years.[109]

This re-ignited the concerns of the Treasury. In E(DL) on 23 July 1981 the Chief Secretary to the Treasury complained that any such limitation, alongside an initial minority share sale might well mean that the Company would be classified as in the public sector for some time. In which case, he concluded, "it was questionable whether it was worth proceeding with privatisation." There was a real possibility that before a second tranche of shares could be sold a general election would have removed the Conservative Government, which was politically very unpopular at this time. A majority of C&W shares might not then ever be sold. When E(DL) was unable to resolve the issue of the appropriate percentage of shares to sell, the Chief Secretary and the Minister of State at the Department of Industry were asked to find words for inclusion in the sale prospectus, "which would indicate that these were not intended to be permanent provisions, but without necessitating the re-opening of negotiations with foreign governments".[110] The final wording chosen stated: "HM Government, which is empowered under the British Telecommunications Act 1981 to acquire or dispose of shares in the Company at any time, intends to maintain a majority shareholding for the foreseeable future."[111] The juxtaposition of "at any time" and "for the foreseeable future" was seemingly intentionally ambiguous to leave freedom of manoeuvre. Following this decision, the Treasury relented and decided that C&W's borrowings would not need to be included in the PSBR following the sale of a first tranche of 49 per cent of the shares.

Around the same time settlements were reached with the authorities in the critical Bahrain and Hong Kong markets. On 1 July 1981 the business in Bahrain was transferred to a new company in which C&W had a 40 per cent shareholding, the remainder being held by the Government of Bahrain. On 1 October 1981 a newly formed company was established in Hong Kong with a 20 year exclusive franchise to operate external telecommunications. The Hong Kong Government purchased a 20 per cent shareholding with the rest held by C&W. Following these successful renegotiations the final barriers to a share flotation were removed. The sale of C&W went ahead in London in October 1981 alongside a simultaneous issue of shares in Hong Kong, and with the sale prospectus published in Chinese as well as English, to head off possible lingering criticism of the flotation in the colony.

The sale proved to be bigger by half as much again as the earlier BAe flotation. The share price was set at 168p and the offer was oversubscribed by about 5.6 times.[112] Owing to the oversubscription, applications for over 900 shares were rationed under a formula that depended upon the size of the application.[113] Priority was also given to applications from employees; 2,300 C&W employees applied for shares and received their allocation in full. In addition, 285,833 shares were made available free of charge to trustees of an employees' share scheme.[114] The reason for including an employee share scheme was, as in the case of the BAe flotation, to win over employee support for the privatisation in the face of union opposition and to fulfil the Government's objective of widening share ownership. Once again the management was very much in favour of the proposal.

The Government raised about £224 million from the sale; of this £35 million was passed to the company for new investment and some £7 million was set aside to meet the cost of the flotation.[115] The net proceeds of around £182 million were substantially larger than the Government had expected to raise when the prospects for flotation had been discussed as recently as six months earlier. In part this reflected the company's successful renegotiation of the vital concessions in Hong Kong and Bahrain and on better terms than some had feared might be the case. Also, the success of the flotation may have reflected growing investor interest in the telecommunications sector and in C&W's Mercury project in particular. However, as the issue of C&W's application for a licence to build an alternative telecommunications network was "still an extremely sensitive subject in view of its implications for BT", references in the prospectus to Mercury were kept to a minimum.[116] Dealings in the shares opened at a premium of some 17 per cent over the issue price.

The Secretary of State for Industry, Patrick Jenkin, shrugged off any suggestion that the oversubscription implied that the sale price was set too low, "Those who understand these matters will know that any such inference is superficial."[117] The Chancellor of the Exchequer agreed; but privately did observe that "the initial premium was a large one. . . . It will I think be important to reflect on whether there are lessons to be learned from the flotation which will help us in getting the best results in similar future cases."[118] The PM wrote to Jenkin commenting upon "how impressed I was by the way in which the Cable and Wireless flotation was handled . . . I hope that future flotations and disposals are as well handled as C&W's".[119] No mention was made of the oversubscription or the opening share price premium.

Following the sale in October 1981, and after deducting the shares committed for issue to the employee share scheme established, the Government retained 50 per cent of the company's issued share capital plus one ordinary share. The Government had been requested by the governments of the countries in which C&W operated to retain a majority holding and had agreed to "for the foreseeable future". The PM's and the Treasury's opposition to this had not prevailed, except that the majority holding retained was a bare one. Also, at the time of the privatisation it was hoped that foreign governments could be quickly won around to a future further share sale by demonstrating that a privatised C&W was no threat to their local telecommunications systems. Certainly the PM and the Treasury were keen that the period should not be lengthy.

In the event, a further share sale was announced exactly two years later. The timing of the decision in part resulted from a delay in selling Enterprise Oil and the resulting hole created in the Chancellor's disposals target for 1983/4. On 27 October 1983 the Financial Secretary to the Treasury, John Moore, confirmed that the Government was considering a further sale of C&W shares as part of its continuing privatisation programme. Two days earlier the Chancellor of the Exchequer had written to the PM informing her that soundings with overseas governments, including the Government of Hong Kong suggested that they would raise no objections.[120] The Government's privatisation programme was now more widely understood than had been the case two years earlier and it appears that the previous opposition to a reduction of state ownership in the countries in which C&W operated had declined sharply.

On 25 November 1983 the sub-underwriting for the sale of a further 22 per cent of the shares in C&W was successfully completed and in December 1983 a further 100 million shares, representing 22 per cent of the issued share capital, were offered for sale. So as not to deflate the share price, the prospectus for the second sale provided a commitment that the Government would not sell any more of its shares for a further two years. In March 1983 the company had issued 30 million new shares, to which the Government had waived any entitlement.[121] This event had already reduced the Government's shareholding from 51 per cent to 45 per cent. The sale in December 1983 left the Government with 23 per cent of the issued ordinary share capital and one special share.[122] The special share was issued by the company on 23 November 1983 and prevented a change in the company's Articles of Association drafted before the first share sale, which limited any one person from having over a 15 per cent shareholding in the company, without the Government's agreement. The Articles also required that the chief executive be a British citizen and prevented a voluntary winding up of the company, any material disposal of assets and the creation of further shares with different rights to the issued ordinary shares, to prevent circumventing the veto of the special share.[123] In effect, the use of a special share in privatisations was now sufficiently well-established to remove the need for Government to retain a majority share ownership in a former state enterprise even when there were obvious strategic issues at stake.

The sale was by way of a tender with a minimum tender price of 275p, which was set at a discount to the previous day's closing price in the stock market for C&W shares, of 293p. However, in spite of this and the inclusion of special terms for small investors and employees, like the Britoil and Enterprise Oil tenders for sale (chapter 4), this one was also undersubscribed, by 30 per cent. Small investors and employees were enticed to bid by allowing applications of up to 1,000 shares to be made at the striking price and around 275,000 applications were received from small investors. The undersubscription reflected a lack of institutional interest in the offer. The reluctance of the City to take up the issue was attributed primarily to a dislike of tender issues and concern that there would be only a small or no share premium when dealing in the shares began.[124]

The Government's remaining holding in C&W (excluding the special share) was sold in December 1985 using a fixed price offer for sale at 587p per share. In his Budget speech earlier that year the Chancellor of the Exchequer announced the Government's intention to sell its remaining minority holdings in privatised companies when circumstances permitted. The decision to sell C&W shares was made in late August.[125] The offer involved roadshows to drum up interest in the issue, the establishment of a nationwide network of brokers to co-ordinate regional marketing of the issue, and sophisticated TV, press and poster advertising. Shares were also offered simultaneously in Japan and Canada. All of this drew on the experiences learnt during earlier privatisations and especially that of British Telecom (BT) in November 1984. Also, for the first time in the UK an underwriting syndicate for the offer was created following a competitive tender to determine the underwriting commissions. This resulted in a lower commission rate than paid in earlier privatisations. Also, some shares were placed with City institutions ahead of the main sale, again reflecting experience gained during earlier privatisations. Some of these shares were provisionally placed and were subject to clawback if the public offer was over-subscribed by about four times. That is to say, the shares could be reallocated from the institutions to the public if the public's demand for the shares was exceptionally high. This approach to the placing of shares would be used in a number of subsequent privatisation issues. But in the event of the C&W offer, the clawback was not triggered. Table 5.2 summarises the commissions paid compared to those paid during the earlier sales of BAe and Britoil shares.[126] The final sale of C&W shares was valued at £933 million (including new shares issued by the company), which made it, after BT, the largest equity offer ever mounted in the UK or elsewhere in the world.[127]

The offer was twice oversubscribed and again Government was criticised for getting the share price wrong. Setting a correct share price on flotation so as to attract a sufficiently large number of applications for shares, but without the opportunity for large "stagging" gains, would continue to prove a challenge during all of the Government's privatisation flotations.

*Table 5.2* Commission structures: British Aerospace, Britoil and Cable and Wireless

| | Per cent | | |
| --- | --- | --- | --- |
| | British Aerospace | Britoil | Cable and Wireless |
| Broking | 0.125 | 0.125 | 0.05 |
| Primary underwriting | 0.3 | 0.3 | 0.3* 0.225 } 0.2625 |
| Sub-underwriting | 1.25 | 1.25 | 1.25 |
| Commitment shares (shares placed firm with City institutions immediately before the public offer) | 1.5 | 1.5 | 0.5** |
| Aggregate commission | 1.8125 | 1.8 | 1.3125 |

*Notes*:
* 0.3 per cent paid to sponsors of the offer: 0.225 per cent paid to other syndicate members. 0.2625 is the resulting average payment.
** Provisionally placed shares subject to clawback carried a commission rate of 1.25 per cent.

*Source*: Cable and Wireless Share Sale 1985: Points of General Interest. Note by HM Treasury, Annex D, 18 December 1985, NIP(85)18, HM Treasury Papers A/06. Note: these figures differ slightly from those in Table 16.5, p.423, due to different bases of calculation.

As David Young comments in his memoirs about criticism of the C&W sale price from Labour MPs: "That was the first time that I discovered the great facility that the Opposition had with the exercise of hindsight!"[128] In public the Government shrugged off criticism, although behind the scenes the Treasury was prompted to explore new ways of selling shares in privatised businesses.

\* \* \*

During the 1980s Government Ministers would cite C&W as one of its great privatisation successes. Between 1981 and 1986 the turnover of C&W rose from £255 million to £907 million and profit before tax from £62 million to £242.3 million.[129] There was also heavy investment in the business; the value of the company's fixed assets more than trebled over the same period. The fact that the first tranche of C&W shares was priced at the end of the first day of stock market trading at 197p and that a little over four years later the last tranche could be sold at 587p per share is in itself testament to the company's success in the private sector. However, it is important to acknowledge that turnover and profit had also been rising in the years before privatisation. The sale of C&W involved the flotation of an already successful business, which in the first few years under private ownership continued to succeed.

# 6

# PRIVATISING AMERSHAM INTERNATIONAL, THE NATIONAL FREIGHT CORPORATION AND ASSOCIATED BRITISH PORTS

The next major privatisations following the successful disposals of the first tranches of British Aerospace and Cable and Wireless shares involved Amersham International, the National Freight Corporation (NFC) and Associated British Ports (ABP). The Amersham sale resulted in the largest mis-pricing of a privatisation issue during the first Thatcher Government and the NFC sale was nearly abandoned because of a lack of investor interest. The disposal of ABP also involved a string of problems which delayed the flotation until February 1983, immediately before a general election.

## Amersham International

Amersham International was the name adopted immediately before privatisation for The Radiochemical Centre (TRC), which had been established in 1940 as part of the war effort. Like Cable and Wireless, TRC was a company, not a public corporation, with 100 per cent of its shares publicly owned. It was a specialist producer of radioactive chemicals and was initially part of the state-owned atomic energy industry. From 1971 it was run as an independently managed company, while retaining some close operating links with its former parent, the UK Atomic Energy Authority. It employed around 2,000 people. Of these 1,000 worked at its head office and manufacturing site at Amersham in Buckinghamshire and 400 in Cardiff, which contained about a half of the manufacturing operations. The remainder were employed at subsidiaries in the US, Germany, France, Australia, the Netherlands and Belgium.

The Centre operated in the internationally competitive manufacture of radio-isotopes for use in medicine, industry and research, exporting around 80 per cent of its output. The main customers were hospitals and pharmaceutical companies and certain other specialist manufacturers in Europe and America. Sales growth was typically around 30 per cent per annum and turnover in 1980/1 was over £60 million. The enterprise achieved profit margins in the region of 15–23 per cent.[1] In the words of the Parliamentary Under-Secretary of State at the Department of Energy, John Moore, TRC "was an extremely successful organisation".[2] It was an obvious candidate for privatisation being likely to prove attractive to private investors. It was not considered to be inefficiently run in the state sector.

The disposal of TRC had not been mentioned in the Conservatives' Election Manifesto and the possibility of selling it surfaced during the Chancellor's urgent pursuit of state assets to sell during the summer and autumn of 1979. On 12 May 1980 E(DL) recommended the disposal of TRC.[3] During 1980 and 1981 a plan for the privatisation of TRC took shape and the legal power to privatise the company was included in the Atomic Energy (Miscellaneous Provisions) Bill. The objectives of keeping the firm independent and of allowing employees to buy shares in the company told in favour of a public flotation rather than a trade sale. The Government acknowledged that the company had a dedicated, high quality staff "and that the continued independence of the Company will be a key factor in its future prosperity".[4]

However, initially the method of disposal was left open. After the sale of BAe and C&W it had been decided to appoint separate advisers to the Government and the company so as to minimise any potential conflicts of interest in the advice presented. For the sale of TRC the financial adviser to the Department of Energy (the TRC's sponsor department) was N.M. Rothschild & Co (Rothschilds) and to the company Morgan Grenfell, both selected after a competition. Rothschilds considered TRC to be "a highly attractive investment proposition, likely to command a good price".[5] Its early estimate put the probable proceeds from the sale at between £17 million and £20 million. But by the autumn of 1981 the advice was that a 100 per cent offer for sale might now raise between £40 million and £50 million, while a UK corporate buyer might pay up to £10 million more, and a foreign investor would possibly offer an even larger amount. However, within Government a foreign purchase was considered to be undesirable given the nature of TRC's business.[6]

By November 1981 the Secretary of State for Energy was able to confirm a plan to sell TRC in the current financial year, preferably in February or March 1982.[7] Rothschilds advised that there was no reason to expect greater sale receipts if the disposal was postponed until later in the year and the management suggested that delay could lead to staff unrest. As usual the trade unions were lobbying employees against a sale. The Secretary of State recommended to his colleagues a public flotation as against a trade sale because a trade sale would be likely to damage staff commitment. He also recommended that provisions be included in the company's Articles of Association to limit the size of individual shareholdings and to deter an early takeover of the company. The Government would retain initially a 25 per cent holding to block changes in the Articles – at this time the option of introducing a special share to block changes had not advanced within Government. The Secretary of State considered that a takeover of the business would be embarrassing if it happened soon after the flotation and gave shareholders a large capital gain. The Government's residual share holding might be sold later, to the staff, as part of an employee shareholding scheme.

However, mindful of the Government's target for revenue raising through disposals, the Financial Secretary, Nigel Lawson, confirmed at the same meeting of E(DL) on 27 November 1981 that the Treasury preferred a sale to a corporate buyer. In his opinion a trade sale was likely to raise more money and would more clearly break all links between the company and the Government.[8] In addition, a sale to the right corporate buyer would bring TRC the advantages of a large corporate group including research facilities, finance and strengthened management. Lawson also opposed introducing safeguards to protect the company from a takeover, should there be a public flotation, arguing: "it is not our role to protect this company from the market forces under which we expect other companies to operate. In practice it seems bound to lead to continuing pressures to intervene and would give a future Government a foot in the door to renationalise the Company."[9]

The Secretary of State for Energy could not agree. In his opinion to go down the trade sale route would endanger a serious loss of staff morale in the company.[10] Also, he informed the meeting that the Department of Health and Social Security would be especially concerned if the company was sold abroad because TRC was one of only three companies in Britain in the field of medical diagnostics. In addition, it was the only British supplier of radio-chemicals and radio-pharmaceuticals: "Sale to an American bidder . . . would very significantly strengthen the American grip in this high technology area, and this might result in an increase in prices to UK customers." After discussion the Secretary of State prevailed over the Financial Secretary. It was agreed that the disposal of the company should be undertaken through a public flotation. However, as a concession to the Treasury, instead of the Government retaining 25 per cent of the shares to ward off a foreign takeover, consideration would be given to the creation of a class of preference share with a controlling vote in the event of an unwelcome bid. This share or shares would be held by the Secretary of State for Energy. Later this option was refined as the Government retaining a "special share". It was decided in E(DL) that this "would both constitute a more effective safeguard against a takeover and limit clearly and narrowly the Government's continuing involvement in TRC. It would also bring in immediately perhaps £10 million more by way of sale proceeds than would the offer for sale of only 75 per cent of the shares". On these terms, E(DL) agreed to the disposal of TRC in the current financial year.[11] What became Amersham International was the first privatisation in which a "special share" was used. Nigel Lawson has claimed the credit for coming up with the idea, as an alternative to the Government retaining a sizeable shareholding.

Fifty million shares, representing all of the share capital in what had now been renamed Amersham International, except the special share, were sold on 11 February 1982.[12] The shares were floated using a fixed price offer set at 142p per share, payable in full on application. This price was set after advice from Rothschilds and the stockbroker to the offer, Cazenove & Co.[13] However, arguably Amersham leant itself towards a tender offer because no one in Government was sure how to value it and there was a distinct difference of opinion between the advisers and the Treasury. Nicholas Ridley in his memoirs reveals that as Financial Secretary and prior to the sale he threatened a meeting of bankers and underwriters to pull the flotation of Amersham unless they agreed to a higher share price. In September 1981 Lawson had moved from the Treasury to become Secretary of State for Energy and Ridley had taken his place. Ridley notes that the City called his bluff, "I had to return shamefacedly to the table!"[14] Given the uncertainty over the value of Amersham, he would have preferred a sale by tender. But Lawson opposed the idea on the grounds that a tender would deter small investors because of the uncertainty as to the price they would have to pay.[15] The advisers – Rothschilds and Morgan Grenfell – were also divided on the matter. The Chancellor of the Exchequer, Sir Geoffrey Howe, was asked to adjudicate and came down in favour of a fixed price offer.

The sale grossed £71 million, of which £6 million was absorbed in restructuring costs including debt repaid. There were also sale costs of around £3 million to the Government and £700,000 to the company. The underwriters earned £887,000 in fees and the Labour Party made much of the cost given the large oversubscription. The offer was oversubscribed 24 times with a total of 264,000 applications for shares received. Due to the oversubscription shares were allotted by ballot with, in the end, 65,000 investors receiving shares. A number of investors sold quickly to benefit from a capital gain and perhaps because the allocations received were too small to be retained in an actively managed asset portfolio. In a very acrimonious debate in the House of Commons on 16 March 1982 following the sale, which focused on the over-subscription, the Government was accused by the Labour Party of benefiting their friends in the City and financial speculators and of cheating the British public:

"The Government should not perpetrate the lie on the British public that they are giving wider share ownership by putting up these companies for private grabs."[16]

The sale price for privatisation issues was a matter for negotiation between the Government, its financial advisers and the large City investors – a process where there was scope for brinkmanship and miscalculation on both sides. When the Press Association on 26 February reported that there would be "a top level Government inquiry" ordered by the PM into the sale of Amersham, No. 10 tried to play down the matter. The PM's Press Secretary, Bernard Ingham, a straight-talking Yorkshireman, responded with a caustic letter to David Chipp, Editor in Chief at the Association, stating: "I feel bruised, especially as my people tried at least twice with you to get it put right." The Department of Energy and the Treasury would simply be looking at the sale to draw lessons as "was common form in these circumstances".[17] There was no "top level" inquiry. However, the Amersham sale did lead to some soul-searching within the Treasury.

The scale of the applications for shares owed much, it seems, to unexpectedly favourable media coverage of the flotation and the case for buying the shares after the share price was set. As was later commented: "What is forgotten about [the flotation of] Amersham . . . was that it was touch and go whether it would be a success at all. It was only strong press comment which built up that mystique on which markets stags thrived, that resulted in a mad scramble for the shares."[18] Certainly the success of the sale provided a fillip to the planning of the very much larger flotation of British Telecom, which was by now underway.

With the benefit of hindsight, the decision to underwrite the offer had been unnecessary given the oversubscription for the shares. But the decision reflected a genuine difficulty in these early days of privatisation in pricing shares and judging the scale of investor interest. Also, the Government, including the Treasury, lacked experience and City advisers had the whip hand. The City sold to Government a traditional form of share sale, the underwritten fixed price offer, at more or less standard commission and fee rates for a new share issue. Arguably more attention might have been given to adopting more novel forms of selling government assets and setting lower charges. This would come only later when experience within Government and the City increased.

Individual shareholdings in Amersham International were restricted to 15 per cent to limit the scope for a takeover bid and there were restrictions on a future material disposal of the company's assets or a winding up of the company. These conditions were included in the Articles of Association and the Articles were protected from change by the special share. In effect, any change in the Articles could occur only with the agreement of Government while the share remained in being. The special share could be redeemed by the Government on or after 31 March 1988.[19] Also, each eligible employee was offered 35 free shares and one free share for every one purchased, up to 350 shares per employee. Ninety-nine per cent of employees became shareholders in the company confirming, alongside the BAe and C&W sales, the attraction of such schemes to employees.[20]

The very large oversubscription for Amersham shares did fuel concern that was already mounting after the BAe and C&W share issues about the pricing of privatisations.[21] Also, this sale demonstrated to the City, more than earlier privatisations had, how it could make substantial money out of privatisations in commissions and in the after market, making later sales easier to arrange. Lawson has since excused the large share premium for investors following the Amersham sale: "The serious underpricing of Amersham, although in no sense deliberate, may have been no bad thing. The enormous publicity given to the profits enjoyed by subscribers to the issue conveyed the clear message to the general public that investing in privatisation issues was a good thing."[22] But attracting the public to privatisation by an under-priced share sale produced a tide of criticism at the time. Afterwards, the Chancellor of the Exchequer proposed that for each future privatisation the sponsoring Minister should, in consultation with the Treasury, prepare a paper identifying the Government's key objectives and the options for achieving them, including the size and method of sale and the use of underwriting, with a view to heading off future criticism. Within Government, after Amersham, there was a feeling that the benefits of any share premium following a privatisation flotation would have to be spread more widely to keep privatisation politically acceptable.[23]

## The National Freight Corporation

The National Freight Corporation's (NFC) origins lay in the transport and storage facilities nationalised by the Labour Government in 1950. The Conservative administration from 1951 reversed a number of the state acquisitions in road transport, leaving a rump of companies. In the Transport Act 1968 the NFC was established to manage the road freight businesses left in the public sector, including those previously controlled by the railways, and to co-operate with British Rail to provide an "integrated" system for freight transport services. In practice, transport integration was not pursued and during the mid-1970s the NFC ran up large financial losses. After 1968 the road haulage licensing system was liberalised and the NFC struggled to find a new role for its basic road haulage operations. In response, the Conservative's Election Manifesto in 1979 promised "We aim to sell shares in the National Freight Corporation to the general public in order to achieve substantial private investment in it."[24]

The NFC had concentrated during the 1970s on developing its road haulage subsidiaries, the best known of which were Pickfords, British Road Services, Roadline and National Carriers Ltd (NCL). By the late 1970s the Corporation accounted for about seven per cent of the country's road haulage industry and employed some 36,000. Large financial losses in the mid-1970s led to a financial restructuring under the 1978 Transport Act, which reduced the Corporation's debt to the Government to £100 million and provided for grant funding to help NCL. However in spite of this, NFC's profit levels by 1979 were only just sufficient to cover the interest on its remaining debts.[25] Any privatisation of the NFC would involve providing the Corporation with an improved capital structure.

Norman Fowler, Secretary of State for Transport, wrote to Nigel Lawson at the Treasury on 29 June 1979 setting out his plans for the NFC. The sale of the NFC was to be his Department's main contribution to the Chancellor's public asset sales target announced in the Budget.[26] On 17 July Fowler confirmed that it was his intention to set up a successor company to the Corporation "as soon as I have powers to do so", which he envisaged would be in the spring of the following year when the Transport Bill should have completed its Parliamentary passage and NFC's 1980 financial results would be available.[27] He had already ruled out a break-up of the NFC except as a last resort.[28] Once the new Transport Bill was on the statute book Fowler's intention was that the NFC should be wound up and its assets transferred to a new National Freight Company Ltd. The objective would then be to sell the NFC as one unit through a flotation of most or all of the equity in the new company. A break up would almost certainly leave the biggest loss making parts of the Corporation with the Government and a break-up was opposed by the NFC management and trade unions.

To achieve a successful sale, the Department of Transport concluded that some of the NFC's debt would need to be converted into equity and around £100 million of debt would have to be cancelled. Fowler believed that incorporation with a 100 per cent equity structure would increase the chances of a successful flotation whenever it occurred and would ease the Corporation's cash position. The Government would also need to deal with the substantial deficiencies in the NFC's pension funds, especially if union opposition to a sale was to be reduced. The deficits in the Corporation's various pension schemes were historic, the origins dating back to the days before the NFC was formed. Fowler intended that the new company should adopt a pension scheme more in line with those common in the private sector road haulage industry. This would involve closing the existing index-linked (inflation proofed) pension scheme to new entrants. He was also minded to remove government loan guarantees and access to the National Loans Fund in the run-up to a disposal.

The immediate effect of these plans on the public finances meant that there would be the loss of the interest on the debt written off and there would be the cost of making good the pension fund deficiencies. The cost was put at £30–40 million, which would only be partly offset by dividends on the shares whilst still held by the Government. On the sale of the shares, a very preliminary estimate suggested that the receipts might be £60 million if the sale took place in 1981. This would provide a "modest contribution" only to the Treasury finances once the costs were subtracted, although Fowler stressed that "in the longer run we could be saved very much more by getting rid of the contingent liability to guarantee the NFC's losses".[29]

On 26 July 1979 the Minister's proposals were considered in E(DL). Some concerns were raised about the reaction of the trade unions, especially the railway unions who were likely to be very hostile to a transfer of the NFC to the private sector. The railway unions functioned in NFC as a legacy from the days when certain road haulage activities had been under the control of British Rail. There was also some concern voiced that "there was a risk that Government control [of the organisation] would be reduced by the legislation, and yet the discipline of a private shareholding would not be achieved." However, in spite of such reservations, the Sub-Committee backed the Minister's plans with the Chancellor stressing that the aim should be to have a short period only during which the Government held the 100 per cent shareholding in the new company.[30]

Following the E(DL) meeting the planning of the sale of NFC began in earnest. However, the "modest contribution" to the Exchequer predicted by the Secretary of State for Transport visibly dulled the Treasury's enthusiasm for a sale.[31] Although there was the Election Manifesto commitment on NFC to fulfil, there was now no real political pressure on the Secretary of State from his Cabinet colleagues to achieve privatisation within any particular period. In March 1980, in discussions with the PM, it was clear that the Treasury considered that the sale of the NFC was not of great importance to them because it was "unlikely to raise any net revenue".[32] It also seems that some civil servants in the Department of Transport were dubious about the merits of a sale, particularly given the state of the Corporation's finances. Certainly, the Corporation's trading performance was causing increasing concern. Indeed, so seriously had the NFC's performance deteriorated as the economy plunged into recession that by the early summer of 1980 the financial advisers to the flotation for the Department of Transport, J. Henry Schroder Wagg & Co. (Schroders), were advising that it might not be possible to float the business until 1981, at the earliest.[33] As the economy continued to deteriorate, the prospects for a flotation of the NFC receded further.[34] To make matters worse NFC lost its most important single contract, representing seven per cent of its turnover. In June 1980 the Government decided to back a decision of British Rail to close its express parcel service run in conjunction with the NFC. The service made losses for British Rail, but for the NFC had been profitable.

Nevertheless, on 23 July 1980 Fowler wrote to Sir Geoffrey Howe, the Chancellor of the Exchequer, proposing an early incorporation of the NFC as a concrete step towards eventual privatisation. However, establishing a company to replace the NFC and in effect replacing debt with equity would have the immediate effect of reducing the flow of income to the Exchequer, which would otherwise have been due in the form of interest payments on the Corporation's debt. Schroders estimated that the size of the sale receipts would not be increased by the full amount of the likely interest that the Exchequer would forego. If vesting occurred on 1 October 1980 and flotation was delayed until the following May, Schroders reckoned that the interest foregone would be £6.3 million and the likely increase in the sale proceeds would be £2–4 million. If the flotation was delayed beyond May the loss to the Government would be even greater. Understandably, these figures did not meet with a sympathetic reception in the Treasury. Nevertheless, Fowler was "firmly of the view that our overall policy objective of early flotation justifies accepting a loss". In his opinion the incorporation would boost morale in the company and by ending the £9 million a year that the Exchequer took in fixed interest payments from NFC, the new company would be able to switch funds to repaying some of its indebtedness to banks and leasing companies. In return Fowler intended to reduce the Corporation's EFL bid for the next financial year which would help the PSBR, commenting: "I see no difficulty at all about an amicable agreement with the NFC Board on this".[35]

The NFC could be expected to welcome the relief from interest payments, but the Treasury was dismayed. Fowler's suggestion produced a very negative response from the Financial Secretary. While Nigel Lawson acknowledged the desirability of moving towards privatisation as soon as possible, he did not agree that this necessitated early incorporation of the business at a cost to the Exchequer. In his opinion early incorporation would provide few advantages while leading to an effective subsidy from the taxpayer to the company, concluding: "If the Corporation is in need of such financial assistance, then I would not choose to give it in this sort of open-ended way that has the effect of reducing our control over its less than strong financial position . . . We have always envisaged giving NFC an appropriate capital structure at the time of sale." Lawson considered that there was a need to keep extremely tight control over the company's finances while the NFC remained publicly owned. It was unclear how this would be achieved under the Minister of Transport's proposal.

Moreover, Lawson was sceptical about the possibility of early privatisation of the NFC given the Corporation's current lack of profitability and the substantial deficiencies in its pension funds: "If, as seems quite likely, these deficiencies exceed the expected proceeds, it is difficult to see how a sale could take place in the foreseeable future . . . It seems inconceivable that we should take the step you propose without waiting to satisfy ourselves that this major potential obstacle to a sale is resolved." While he could understand why an early incorporation on a wholly equity basis would be welcomed by the NFC management, because it removed interest payments on the cancelled government debt, in his view planning for privatisation should not become an excuse for relaxing financial discipline. That the NFC Board could be expected to reach an "amicable agreement" on the EFL bid was, he commented, unsurprising because under the Secretary of State's plan the EFL became irrelevant once the new company succeeded the NFC. The new company would be able to borrow in its own right unless Treasury controls continued. Lawson concluded that vesting should wait until definite sale arrangements were in hand.[36]

With the Secretary of State for Transport and the Financial Secretary at loggerheads on the timing of the incorporation of the NFC, on 5 August 1980 the matter was considered by E(DL). E(DL) agreed on balance to the Minister of Transport's proposals for early incorporation, but did sympathise with a number of the arguments raised by the Financial Secretary.[37] Immediately following the meeting Fowler wrote to the Chancellor of the Exchequer pressing the importance of making quick progress, presumably in the hope that he might overrule the Financial Secretary. Fowler still hoped to be able to make an early statement on incorporation of the NFC to the House of Commons.[38]

The Chancellor replied the following day pointing to the need to think clearly about the risks from incorporation. In particular, the potential loss of control of NFC's borrowings could be greatly to the detriment of public expenditure control and the PSBR. While he made it clear that he would not stand in the way of early incorporation of NFC given the support for this in E(DL), he stressed that it would be important following vesting and prior to a sale of the company to maintain Treasury controls over investment and borrowing identical to those that existed for public corporations. It was therefore essential that such controls were put in place in the company's Articles of Association or through a legally binding Memorandum of Understanding with the NFC Board. The company should also be expected to pay a dividend to the Government on its 100 per cent shareholding, in lieu of the interest lost on the government debt in the company if the flotation was delayed.[39]

Lawson's and Howe's concerns were borne out. Earlier hopes that a sale of shares might occur in the spring of 1981 quickly evaporated as the NFC's business environment continued to deteriorate and indeed it soon became doubtful whether the company would be floated at all in the current Parliament.[40] The National Freight Company Ltd took over the assets and liabilities of the public corporation on 1 October 1980, but soon Schroders were forecasting that a flotation might not be possible for two to three years. In response, Fowler asked them to explore alternative ways to bring about a disposal. In the late spring of 1981 an alternative unexpectedly arose. On 10 June Fowler wrote to the PM about "a potentially exciting new development concerning our efforts to put the NFC into the private sector".[41] Quite independently to Schroders' consideration of alternative ways of introducing private capital into the company in the absence of a share flotation, the senior management of NFC had responded to the prospect of an indefinite postponement of a sale by considering the prospects for a management-employee buyout. In June 1981 they informed the Department of Transport that they definitely wished to develop a takeover bid for the company.

The idea of a buyout seems to have originated within the senior management of NFC during 1980, after the company was valued at around £60 million or less. A number of the management judged that this was a surprisingly low figure, perhaps reflecting their inside knowledge of the business opportunities that existed once in the private sector, including the scope for selling off or redeveloping the Corporation's extensive holdings of land and buildings. The postponement of a flotation in the spring of 1981 encouraged the management to begin to explore more seriously the buyout option, especially as some management feared that the Government might otherwise decide to sell off the profitable parts of the NFC separately.[42] The senior management were opposed to a break-up of the Corporation. A buyout received backing from the NFC Board in March 1981.[43] On first hearing of the idea Fowler was sceptical as to whether the management would be able to raise the necessary funding to finance a serious bid, but by early June Barclays Merchant Bank had agreed to back the scheme, which made it a real possibility, provided that the management could raise a minimum of £2.5 million themselves. Fowler was informed that a conference involving the top 120 managers in NFC had enthusiastically supported the buyout proposal and had committed to raise the money. The idea would now be put to the NFC's management more widely and then to other employees. Fowler accepted that he would need to discuss the proposal with colleagues in E(DL) and obtain a new valuation of the Corporation to set the sale price. However, he was hopeful of reaching an agreement for a management takeover of NFC within a few weeks.[44]

On 11 June 1981 Fowler received a letter from Peter Thompson, Chairman of the NFC, and a leading light in driving through the buyout, confirming that the management, with employees, were willing to purchase the ordinary share capital at par value. In addition, they would arrange to discharge the outstanding pension obligations, which would otherwise fall to be covered out of the sale proceeds. The management estimated that the total value of their offer was between £51 million and £53 million. However, only £5 million would relate to payment for the issued share capital with the funding of the pension fund deficits accounting for the remainder. To protect the Government from the potential political damage if subsequent to the buyout the management was quickly to mount a public share flotation and benefit from a large capital gain, the Articles of Association of the new company would contain provisions designed to ensure that for the first five years of its existence the company would remain in its present form. In particular, it was agreed that there would not be an intention to seek a stock market listing during that time.[45]

The following day Fowler wrote excitedly to Sir Keith Joseph at the Department of Industry with copies to the PM and members of E(DL) stating that "events have been moving faster than expected." He favoured supporting the offer. Although the Government would receive only a net £5 million for the shares, he argued that this "would be of the order we have always envisaged" and should be accepted. He reminded Ministers that the company was not a particularly attractive proposition to other investors at the present time and that the management-employee buyout was the only serious proposal on the table. Also, he judged that the proposed takeover would be a good way of motivating management and employees. The proposal included an intention that all staff would be able to buy shares, an outcome consistent with the Government's objective of widening the ownership of industry. He concluded that while there was a possibility of inviting competitive bids for the company, which "could conceivably produce a marginally better return for the Exchequer", there were great risks in doing so, including reducing the commitment and morale of the management and delaying the sale. To keep up the momentum, Fowler sought approval to make a public announcement of the buyout within the next few days.[46]

The request brought an immediate positive response from Lawson who believed that the amount to be paid for the company was acceptable and that the management's offer was preferable to delaying a sale in the stock market until 1982 or 1983. Whatever the misgiving that the Treasury might have about the sale price, disposing of the troublesome Corporation was now a priority. Moreover, he too had decided that the transfer of control of a state enterprise to the present management and employees, "would further our policy of encouraging employee share ownership in privatisation cases".[47] There was also strong support from other Ministers. On 18 June Fowler announced in the House of Commons that a buyout bid had been launched, although he warned that the proposal was still at an early stage lest the plan later collapsed.[48]

Following finalisation of the legal and financial negotiations, on 16 October 1981 David Howell, who had moved from the Department of Energy to Transport replacing Fowler during the September ministerial reshuffle, reported to the PM that agreement had now been reached on the sale of NFC to a management and employee consortium. The Department of Transport had felt required to continue the search for other possible buyers until the last minute because of the prospect of criticism from the Public Accounts Committee that it had not achieved the highest possible sale price. But there had been no interest from other purchasers except for indication of one alternative bid. Schroders advised against pursuing it because a complete consortium of buyers had not been formed.[49] On 16 February 1982 Howell was able to confirm that the management and employee consortium had been able to raise the necessary funds and that the sale could be completed within the next week or so.[50]

The final agreed price was £53.5 million of which around £47 million would be devoted to making up deficiencies in the pension funds, leaving a slightly larger residual to the Government than earlier estimated, of £6–7 million.[51] The success of the buyout relied on bank loan financing including, unusually, some unsecured lending. The loans totalled around £120 million. Barclays Merchant Bank lent £40 million and £5 million to fund pension deficiencies. The banks also provided an overdraft facility of up to £25 million to fund working capital. In addition, the directors of NFC were required by the banks who loaned most of the capital for the buyout to invest at least £25,000 each. The amount subscribed in total by NFC staff and management was £7 million with management and staff subscribing on the same terms and with a minimum subscription of £100. This gave the employees (including some NFC pensioners) a total of 82.5 per cent of the equity. The remaining shares were held by banks.[52] A legal difficulty arose over the buyout team's original idea to secure bank loans on the company's assets. Section 54 of the 1981 Companies Act prevented loans from being secured against properties owned or leased by NFC subsidiaries. A new Companies Act became law in November 1981 reducing this restriction and waiting for this was one of the reasons the buyout was delayed until early the following year.

The sale of NFC through a management-employee buyout was not a unique event in British privatisation – there were some later buyouts of businesses, for example in the motor and steel industries, shipyards, bus operations, the coal industry and the railways – but the NFC was the first and the most important. The PM called it "an imaginative scheme which reflects confidence in the future of the company, particularly by its workforce".[53] The buyout had the virtue of addressing the Treasury's two principal objectives at this time for privatisations, of raising funds for the Exchequer, albeit as it turned out a very small amount, and more importantly in this case, widening share ownership. Indeed, a management-employee buyout was arguably more consistent with the objective of widening ownership than a share flotation. It was also to be expected that the result would be good for labour relations. However, a buyout was not feasible for later, larger, privatisations because of the amounts that had to be raised to buy and finance the companies. In these cases a share flotation or a trade sale to an existing company with access to large amounts of capital for investment were the only feasible solutions.

The financial performance of NFC strengthened after privatisation with the same management as had existed under state ownership. Employment also rose.[54] Management and employees were now motivated by their share ownership and new bonus schemes (15 per cent of pre-tax profits were regularly set aside for paying bonuses).[55] Also, new channels of communication had been opened up between workers and management during the planning of the privatisation, enabling more staff input into decision making. For the first six years after privatisation the company achieved a compound growth in profits before tax in excess of 40 per cent a year.

The company had been privatised with an extremely high debt to equity ratio and the management was keen to reduce the amount of debt financing. It set about removing some of the operating inefficiencies that had been around since the Corporation was established, including running down the heavily loss making parcels division and rationalising the use of property. This allowed the sale of surplus land and buildings to raise cash to pare down debt.[56] Property sales accounted for a part of the profit growth in the early years after privatisation. Whether the management had been aware of the full potential to capitalise on property sales at privatisation and kept this from the Government and whether the Government's financial advisers should have spotted this potential, remain moot points. It does seem that senior civil servants in the Department of Transport approached the Secretary of State just before the sale pointing out that under the terms of the buyout, the management and employees might very well make large financial gains in future years and that perhaps the sale should be halted to give time to renegotiate. These objections were waived aside. The political priority was to sell the Corporation without further delay.

What is unquestionable is that the NFC quickly developed a remunerative activity in property sales and development. Another important factor in NFC's success in the private sector was the country's general economic revival from 1982, which led to a recovery in the road freight market. The NFC responded by moving upmarket from heavy general haulage to higher value warehousing and distribution for major retailers like Marks & Spencer. Capital expenditure, regularly capped at £25 million a year when in the public sector, increased fourfold. The company also took advantage of its new freedom from state control to expand operations overseas, in the US, Australia, New Zealand and the Far East, although as it turned out with mixed fortunes.[57]

The Transport and General Workers' Union had opposed the privatisation of NFC and recommended to its members not to buy shares. Many heeded the union call and shunned the buyout offer. More than half the workforce did not participate in the buy out, although some of these did later obtain shares. Nevertheless, the offer was over-subscribed by £800,000 and applications had to be scaled back. By 1986 the number of employee share-holders had risen from around 10,000 at privatisation to 19,500. For those workers who did buy into the company at privatisation enormously large capital gains were recorded. The investments multiplied in value a hundred times during the 1980s.[58] For the senior management that had arranged the buyout and had the largest individual investments in the NFC the financial rewards were huge.

Over time the company would abandon the characteristics of employee share ownership. Annual additions to the share capital to meet the needs of new employees, bonuses, a rights issue and a listing on the stock market in February 1989 diluted the employee stake, so that by 1995 it stood at less than ten per cent compared with 82.5 per cent at the time of privatisation.[59] Nevertheless, the NFC example remains unique in the history of British privatisations. It is the only case of an entire public corporation privatised through a buyout by the existing staff. Importantly, it had occurred only because the City had got cold feet about a share flotation during the depths of the 1980/1 economic recession. The form of privatisation of the NFC was a product of economic pragmatism and management opportunism rather than political ideology. However, the result fitted with the Conservatives' belief in widening property ownership. During the 1980s the NFC was continuously cited by Government Ministers as a shining example of the success of privatisation and the "property owning democracy". In so doing they demonstrated considerable ex post facto opportunism.

## Associated British Ports

The privatisation of the ports had not featured as a policy objective in the Conservatives' Election Manifesto. Nevertheless, like Cable and Wireless it quickly emerged as a candidate for disposal. The state-owned British Transport Docks Board (BTDB) was the single largest port owner in Britain operating 19 ports including some of the country's largest. It accounted for some 25 per cent of the country's port industry by capacity and volume of traffic. The state had acquired a number of ports on the nationalisation of the railways. Britain's other ports were owned in the private sector, by trusts or by companies owned by municipalities. Table 6.1 provides a summary of the Board's financial record from 1973 to 1978. At privatisation BTDB was renamed Associated British Ports (ABP).

The BTDB was likely to be attractive to private investors. It had a good profit record during the 1970s, better than a number of the country's other port undertakings, indeed it had been steadily increasing its profitability. Unlike some public corporations it had been able to finance all of its own capital investment from revenue. However, set against this, the ports had an unenviable industrial relations record and it was expected that the dock unions would strongly oppose any suggestion of privatisation. Also, manning in a number of ports was regulated by the National Dock Labour Scheme (NDLS) aimed at ending casualisation of the labour in the industry. The Scheme, which dated back to the 1940s and was strengthened in 1972 by the Heath Government to facilitate the ending of a national dock strike, effectively guaranteed employment for dock workers for life in Britain's ports that employed "registered dock workers". Until the Scheme was ended the scope to raise labour productivity in the BTDB would be restricted.[60] Meanwhile, the BTDB ports lost business to ports that were outside the NDLS, notably Felixstowe, which expanded rapidly.

*Table 6.1* British Transport Docks Board: financial record 1973–8 (£m, outturn prices)

|  | 1973 | 1974 | 1975 | 1976 | 1977 | 1978 |
|---|---|---|---|---|---|---|
| Surplus after replacement cost depreciation but before interest and tax | 10.1 | 8.5 | 8.4 | 19.1 | 22.0 | 21.1 |
| Capital investment | (8.8) | (8.7) | (11.1) | (6.9) | (10.2) | (9.2) |
| Interest paid to the government | (6.8) | (7.0) | (6.7) | (6.8) | (6.8) | (6.5) |
| Repayments of capital debt to the government | – | – | – | (5.5) | (5.5) | (5.4) |
| Total payments to the government | (6.8) | (7.0) | (6.7) | (12.3) | (12.3) | (11.9) |
| Corporation tax paid | – | – | – | – | – | (2.4) |
| Outstanding capital debt (face value) at year end | 124.7 | 124.5 | 124.5 | 118.0 | 111.6 | 105.2 |
| Reserves at year end | 11.7 | 15.4 | 20.6 | 32.9 | 47.4 | 62.5 |

*Source*: E(DL)(80)1.

In the summer of 1979 the Department of Transport considered but initially ruled out privatisation of BTDB on the grounds that port sell-offs were likely to provoke strike action. In the Treasury too the attitude of the workforce was seen as a barrier to a sale.[61] Instead, the Department focused on extracting more cash from the BTDB than it was currently providing through repayment of National Loans Fund debt.[62] However, with the Treasury pressing the Department for more candidates to achieve the Chancellor's disposals target for 1980/1, in a paper to an E(DL) meeting scheduled for 18 February 1980 the Minister of Transport proposed the introduction of private capital and sought authority for more detailed discussions with the Board. In his paper Norman Fowler acknowledged that: "The British Transport Docks Board is undoubtedly amongst the most efficient parts of the docks industry." Clearly, at this time the grounds for privatisation were primarily financial rather than related to concerns about efficiency.[63]

Fowler had already begun informal discussions with the Chairman of BTDB, Sir Humphrey Brown, who had confirmed that it should be possible to devise a workable scheme for conversion to company status. The senior management of BTDB, including Brown and his successor as Chairman from May 1982, Keith Stuart, welcomed the prospect of breaking free from Treasury controls over investment, which they felt restricted the business. However, it would be important to convince potential investors that there would be no serious opposition from the unions. Brown advised Fowler that "the Board could persuade the union not to oppose a privatisation scheme provided the enterprise was maintained as a single management unit". In other words, there should be no attempt to break up the BTDB. It would also be important if the unions were to be placated that the Government maintained a substantial shareholding. Certainly the dock unions consistently opposed privatisation throughout the planning, but the Chairman's conditions would ensure that there was no serious strike action. They also ensured that the Corporation would transfer to the private sector intact, something certain to appeal to the existing senior management.

In all privatisations it would prove important to have the support of senior management if the sale was to proceed smoothly. Sir Denis Rooke at British Gas was already demonstrating the additional difficulties that Government faced if the management were opposed, or at best lukewarm, to a sale. Fowler supported providing assurances to the BTDB on both of the points raised by the Chairman. In his opinion selling ports separately "would seriously weaken the commercial and industrial relations benefits that flow from a strong and unified management". Moreover, the effect could be to reduce the total market value earned from a sale, an argument that was likely to clinch matters with the Treasury. However, although the BTDB Board had advised him that the Government would need to retain at least a 51 per cent shareholding to pacify the unions, he considered that it would be best not to commit on the actual size of the government holding at this stage. In principle, he wanted to keep the residual shareholding as low as possible, especially as the Department's financial adviser, Schroders, was warning that to facilitate a smooth flotation the Government would probably need to give an undertaking that there would be no further share sales for around five years.[64] Without this guarantee investors would be wary that the remaining shares might be suddenly offloaded onto the market, leading to a sharp decline in the share price (similar warnings were given during the sale of BAe and C&W, as we have seen).

Fowler also made it clear that he had been advised that the best price for the shares would probably be obtained in the summer of 1981, after publication of the Board's 1980 results. This was so, provided that the Corporation's performance did not deteriorate in the meantime. The market value of BTDB was estimated by Schroders at between £70 million and

£120 million and he intended to plan for a sale midway through 1981. However, he stressed that there should be no public announcement of the decision to sell BTDB until the Board had had a chance to consult with the unions.[65] Fowler also noted that the Chairman of one of the trust ports had suggested to him that it might be feasible to introduce equity capital into the more profitable of the trust ports. The trust ports were independent public sector statutory bodies and operated in a number of mainly smaller ports around the country. While he had found this an interesting suggestion, the amounts that would be raised would be less attractive than from the sale of BTDB and selling trust ports at the same time could interfere with the marketing of the BTDB securities. It was also likely to increase union opposition. He had therefore decided to rule out the privatisation of these ports. A sale of the trust ports would not begin until the early 1990s.

The E(DL) meeting scheduled for 18 February 1980 was postponed and therefore a collective decision on the Secretary of State's proposal was delayed. However, the Chancellor responded to Fowler's paper with a letter of support.[66] So did John Nott, Secretary of State for Trade, who wrote to Fowler on 27 February giving his full backing to privatisation of the BTDB, but calling for reconsideration of the decision to privatise the Corporation as one unit. He pointed out that the shipping industry wanted more commercial flexibility and diversity in the choice of ports and the efficiency of the ports was important to the country's trade. It would be better, therefore, if the Secretary of State could find it possible to introduce some competition, "such as dividing the Board's present operation into three or more separate units, each with a smaller market share".[67] However, like Fowler other Ministers were nervous that privatisation of the ports could lead to serious conflict with the dock unions and a division of BTDB would be almost certain to inflame industrial unrest and alienate the management. A national dock strike was something the Government was keen to avoid because of the potential economic damage and because private investors in BTDB were likely to be repelled by serious industrial strife. The Government decided to delay a decision on the details of the privatisation until the Board had tested out the unions on the subject.

On 8 July 1980 Fowler re-presented his proposals to E(DL). He was able to say that the BTDB Board had now consulted with the unions and while they had disagreed with the principle of privatisation, which was to be expected, he was pleased to report that the Board had "managed to achieve a measure of agreement with them" provided the BTDB was sold as one unit. He expected to include provisions to privatise the Corporation in a Transport Bill to be introduced in the current parliamentary session and probably by November. Early advice suggested that because of the complex number of laws relating to the BTDB ports detailed legislation would be needed. The privatisation of BTDB would require the creation of a company with the usual provisions of the Companies Act, but modified to take account of the Board's existing statutory powers and duties, which resulted from numerous pieces of legislation relating to the ports, including private Acts of Parliament.[68]

Fowler explained that it was his intention to take powers in the forthcoming Transport Bill to create a two-tier structure for the ports. This would involve creating a holding company and a subsidiary. The subsidiary company would inherit all of the BTDB's existing statutory powers and obligations and would operate the ports. Fowler had been advised that this structure "would simplify the drafting of the legislation, and should be more attractive to investors than a single tier statutory company". Consultation had confirmed that the plan would be supported by BTDB and would have "the acquiescence of the unions". But this was so only if the Government retained a minimum 51 per cent shareholding in the holding company and no attempt was made to dispose of the ports separately. He therefore confirmed his earlier decision to sell BTDB as one unit and with the Government retaining a majority shareholding, possibly for at least five years. While the Government would retain majority ownership, he would "make it clear that the Government did not intend to exercise any commercial control", appoint directors to the Board or provide any guarantees of the borrowings. He was hopeful that this would mean that the company could be classified as in the private sector for public expenditure purposes. This is a similar argument to that mounted by the Secretary of State for Industry during the privatisation of Cable and Wireless. As part of the sale process, Fowler intended to promote employee participation in the public offer for sale to "encourage a positive attitude" amongst the workforce towards the move into the private sector. He concluded that if the legislation was enacted by July 1981, he would aim to sell the shares in the ports later that year or early in 1982 "depending on trading conditions." The total receipts might be around £90 million. Set against this, in subsequent years there would be a small annual net reduction in cash flow to the Exchequer "because dividends from the new company would be less than the present flow of funds from the BTDB".[69]

The fear of a future hostile takeover bid for the ports, especially from the users, the shipping companies, lay behind the Board's support for the Government retaining a majority share ownership. The BTDB now made representations to Fowler requesting that individual port users be debarred from holding more than, say, five per cent, of the shares so as to avoid having an undue influence on dock policy. The unions also attached importance to such a safeguard. However, Fowler was reluctant to concede the point. He was advised that it would have the effect of depressing the share price. Another issue that he was struggling with at this time was the transfer of the index-linked pension rights of BTDB's 6,000 employees to the new company. At the last valuation of the relevant pension schemes they had showed a deficiency of about £7 million, which was being funded by annual payments from the BTDB's profits. He did not believe that this was an insuperable problem, provided an updated valuation due in August did not reveal that the deficiency was now extraordinarily large. He expected a privatised BTDB to continue to make up the deficiency. This was important because any attempt to renege on the index linked pension "would cause major industrial problems and possibly prejudice the whole privatisation exercise".[70]

In discussion in E(DL) on 8 July 1980 there was some continuing dissent about the desirability of the Government retaining a 51 per cent shareholding and to any commitment to continue to hold these shares for at least five years. However, the outcome of the meeting was an agreement that the Minister of Transport should proceed as he had suggested, although he was asked to consider allocating shares for an employee share ownership scheme out of the 51 per cent holding and reducing the period of the Government commitment to hold the remainder of the shares, mirroring the same sort of discussion as went on during the planning of the British Aerospace and Cable and Wireless sales. It was agreed that the Department of Transport should consult closely with the Treasury to ensure that the company was classified as being in the private sector following a flotation if the Government were to retain a majority of the issued shares.[71]

After the meeting Fowler considered whether some of the proposed government holding of 51 per cent could be used to provide shares to employees, thereby stealthily reducing the remaining government holding to under 50 per cent. However, he concluded that any departure from the commitment that the Government should maintain a majority shareholding would prejudice the Board's support and the acquiescence of the unions to privatisation.

In his view the safest approach to removing the Government's majority holding would be to wait until the company needed to issue more share capital. Kleinworts was now advising that a commitment to maintain the Government's shares for three years might be sufficient to prevent the share price being depressed at privatisation and he hoped that this would go some way towards pacifying the Treasury. Also Fowler offered to review the whole issue of the Government's shareholding in the light of market conditions nearer the time of the flotation.[72] But this set of suggestions did not satisfy Treasury Ministers, who continued to press for a Government commitment to dispose of more than 50 per cent of the shares and thereby clearly take the BTDB out of the public sector.

The enabling powers to restructure and sell shares in BTDB were contained in the Transport Act, which became law on 31 July 1981.[73] By November the Department of Transport had firmed up its proposal to have a holding company with a subsidiary, following further advice. There would definitely be a holding company and a statutory corporation to inherit BTDB's statutory powers.[74] However, the plans for the privatisation of BTDB had by this time been adversely affected by a downturn in BTDB's financial performance, reflecting the economic recession. In March 1981 the forecast was for BTDB's EFL, originally set at minus £10 million (a cash repayment), to be positive, raising public borrowing. This led to an immediate Treasury request that the BTDB achieve efficiency savings.[75] Fowler replied anxiously to a letter from the new Chief Secretary to the Treasury, Leon Brittan, that such action might precipitate a damaging cutback in investment, "which could impair the operation of their ports and affect the prospects for BTDB's privatisation".[76]

During the summer of 1981 BTDB's finances continued to deteriorate in the face of the economic recession and it became clear that a flotation that year was now no longer possible, just as, as we have seen, the state of the economy at the time ruled out a flotation of the NFC. On 27 October 1981 the new Secretary of State for Transport, David Howell, wrote to Patrick Jenkin, now his opposite number at the Department of Industry, confirming that his Department was hoping to float BTDB in the following year. But a flotation now depended on resolution of a serious dispute that had erupted between the BTDB and one of its customers, the British Steel Corporation (BSC). BSC was itself facing a torrid time in its markets due to an oversupply of steel and uncompetitive costs.[77] Under a 25 year agreement dating from 1970, iron ore was unloaded at Port Talbot in South Wales for the Llanwern steelworks for a fixed payment plus an amount based on tonnage, both indexed each year to reflect inflation.[78] BSC was now refusing to honour the agreement arguing that it was excessively profitable for BTDB at a time when BSC needed to make urgent economies. It began to withhold some payments while trying to secure more favourable terms. BSC offered to pay half the agreed amount under the contract, which BTDB rejected. BTDB responded with legal action, fearing that if it conceded to a contract change with BSC it would face a tide of similar demands from other businesses for which port facilities were supplied on similar terms. Given that port investments involved high sunk costs, it was normal practice for the BTDB to enter into long–term contracts before investing in new facilities. By the autumn of 1981 the total sum due from BSC amounted to over £4 million, which, compared to BTDB's net profit of £0.3 million for the first 34 weeks of 1981, was not an inappreciable sum.[79]

The BTDB had issued a writ to recover the lost amount in February 1981. But the case was not expected to come before the courts until the following year, threatening to delay the BTDB sale. Alternatively, the Government would have to undertake the sale with an important legal dispute pending, which could be expected to deflate the sales receipts.

To resolve the argument between two state corporations out of court the Department of Industry suggested the appointment of an "honest broker". This was rejected by the BTDB. Howell sympathised with the Board that they should not be expected "to take part in arbitration proceedings which would imply a readiness to make concessions". In his letter to Jenkin he pressed the Secretary of State for Industry to put pressure on the Chairman of BSC, Ian MacGregor, to bring the dispute to an end.[80] However, Jenkin was mindful of the effect of any settlement on BSC's already crippled finances. Nor was it clear that BSC would respond positively to any overtures that he might make. MacGregor considered the contract "unfair".

With no early resolution of the dispute in sight and with the economic recession continuing to depress traffic through the ports, and an industrial dispute in BTDB's Southampton docks now underway, in November 1981 Howell advised the Chancellor of the Exchequer that a sale of BTDB in the immediate future "would be completely impracticable. Potential purchasers would be deterred because they would think that the Government saw no real prospect of improvement and had decided to raise what they could as soon as possible". If the shares were sold at a cheaper price to reflect this, "the Government would be rightly criticised for selling the public assets too cheaply and Opposition threats of renationalisation would inevitably follow." Kleinworts' valuation of the business, which had been £90 million or more in 1980 had by now fallen to a mere £20–30 million. This compares with the book value of BTBD's assets, which were stated at £170 million. Howell offered to undertake "a substantive review" of the prospects for privatisation with the next realistic opportunity for flotation being May of the following year.[81]

Howell's decision to postpone the sale provoked Nicholas Ridley at the Treasury to express deep disappointment. The decision was considered "most unwelcome since we had hoped for a contribution from sale of the Board to the 1981–82 disposals target". There was also a need "to keep up the current momentum of the privatisation programme". While welcoming the Secretary of State for Transport's commitment to "a substantive review", Ridley suggested that as part of the process consideration should be given to selling the BTDB to a single corporate buyer. This might lead to a better sale price than a share flotation and might be more achievable at the present time.[82]

Howell replied to Ridley on 30 November 1981 agreeing that if a meeting with the Board and the Department's merchant bankers, scheduled for December, decided that a market flotation in May 1982 was likely to be impracticable then he would consider the possibility of negotiating a sale to a single buyer. However, he made it clear that he would need first "to discuss with my colleagues some of the problems I might encounter in handling such a proposition with the Board and their unions." The Board had pressed for a sale of under 50 per cent of the equity because of the industrial relations risk and because of "great concern that a significant block of shares might be acquired by a major shipping line" or consortium of lines, "which would then be in a position to exercise pressure on management to favour its own interests in particular ports". While he considered that the fears were exaggerated, he did not feel he could ignore the strength of the Board's objections. The Government would need their co-operation to complete a successful flotation or sale. Also, it was his view that "we can ascribe the lack of real opposition from the unions (and indeed of any industrial action related to privatisation) to our commitment, frequently stated in the House, to retention of 51 per cent of the equity."[83]

Treasury Ministers now renewed their opposition to the Government keeping a majority holding in any future share flotation should a trade sale be ruled out by the opposition of the

Board and the unions. Ridley suggested that there had been unease in E(DL) over the 49 per cent sale and while he was aware of the reasons for the decision, there were "important counter arguments" especially if the flotation was in any case to be delayed. It was also his opinion that the decision not to split up the BTDB before privatisation should be revisited. The break-up of the BTDB could create beneficial additional competition in the ports. Ridley also wanted to resurrect the matter of the possible privatisation of the trust ports.[84]

On 23 December 1981 Howell responded by agreeing that alternative approaches to the disposal of BTDB other than a share flotation should not be ruled out. However, he repeated the importance he attached to maintaining the co-operation of the unions and the Board: "The strengths of BTDB are the attractive mix of ports, good management and relatively sound industrial relations. The current policy of selling BTDB's undertaking as a single manage-ment unit and retaining 51 per cent of the equity is geared to preserving those strengths. I would certainly oppose any suggestion that BTDB's undertaking should be divided." In any case, the Transport Act 1981 empowering privatisation was now on the statute book and the legislation, he explained, "is not appropriate for a break-up of BTDB at the point of sale".[85]

On 18 January 1982 Howell wrote to the Chancellor of the Exchequer and other members of E(DL) confirming that he had carried out his promised substantive review. As part of it, Kleinworts had concluded that there was a reasonable prospect of achieving some £25–30 million from the sale of 49 per cent of the share capital of BTDB, an expectation little different to the previous November, although there still needed to be further examination of whether it would be necessary to fund the whole or part of the Corporation's pension and other liabilities, notably the right of some staff to free rail travel. This might amount to £23 million. Offsetting this, it might be possible to sell some of the Board's debt, raising up to £20 million. Regarding Ridley's suggested alternative to a flotation of a sale to a trade buyer, Howell had concluded that he could not see how this would raise more money for the Exchequer, while he believed it certainly risked serious strife with the unions.[86] In effect, within the Department of Transport any possibility of a trade sale had been dismissed.

Both Kleinworts and the BTDB considered that it would be better to go for a flotation in June rather than in May because this would allow better account to be taken of any uplift in port traffic in the early part of the year. However, the prospect of a successful flotation in the immediate future still depended upon the performance of the ports and settlement of the dispute with the BSC over contractual payments. The Department of Transport continued to prepare for a flotation in June, but in April 1982 Howell had to advise the Chancellor, reluctantly, that a sale would have to be postponed to the autumn. Obtaining a satisfactory price remained a priority and to do so would be difficult at present given "significant industrial trouble and a disappointing [performance] record in the last two years".[87] On 24 June 1982 Howell wrote again to Jenkin at the Department of Industry regarding the dispute with BSC. He had discussed the matter with Ridley at the Treasury and Norman Lamont, Minister of State at the Department of Industry, on 16 March, when it had been agreed that there should be a further approach to the Chairmen of BSC and BTDB to seek a resolution to the conflict. The Chairman of BTDB, Keith Stuart, had subsequently met his opposite number, Ian MacGregor, on 26 April but little progress had seemingly been made. Howell's letter made it clear that the interest on the amount owing to BTDB would be around £8 million by July and that the failure to settle the dispute was jeopardising the sale of the ports.[88] This letter was backed up by one from Ridley calling on the Secretary of State for Industry to settle the matter, either through negotiation or by issuing a specific Direction to the BSC Board.[89]

On 22 July 1982 Lamont was able to reply that there had been a number of exchanges between BSC and BTDB aimed at breaking the deadlock. BSC had now informed him that they had made a payment of £4 million, representing about a half of the amount in dispute. In return BTDB had agreed to enter into negotiations for a new agreement with BSC. BSC expected that the new agreement would take account of the difficult financial climate in which its South Wales steel works was operating.[90] It seemed that the dispute was coming to an end and that the privatisation of BTDB, now scheduled for the following January, might be achievable. But the dispute had not been settled. On 20 October 1982 Howell complained again to Patrick Jenkin that BTDB had been attempting to resolve the deadlock with BSC, "but so far with a total lack of success . . . it has now become extremely urgent to settle the dispute if flotation is to be practicable in January next, as we plan". He repeated that the concessions already made by BTDB would lead to a saving of £1.3 million for BSC in the first year and savings later depending on the tonnage handled. This was likely to reduce the value of the BTDB business by at least £5 million. Nevertheless, BSC was continuing to press for a very different agreement with BTDB. This would "reduce the total value of the business to an extent that would put the possibility of any flotation at all at risk. Put simply, Kleinworts advise me that we cannot hope to proceed with a successful flotation until this dispute has been resolved . . . In my view, and despite all the other graver issues facing the BSC, it has now become a political priority that Ian MacGregor should be persuaded to settle this matter, more or less on the basis already offered by BTDB".[91]

Howell and Jenkin met on 1 November 1982 to try once again to find a way forward. Following the meeting Howell discussed with the Chairman of the BTDB whether any further ground might be given by the Board to achieve a quick settlement. On 5 November he reported to Jenkin that his discussion had produced no compromise, while City advisers Kleinworts and Cazenove remained unequivocal that there could be no flotation until the dispute was ended. As far as the BTDB was concerned, to offer further concessions on the Port Talbot agreement would have serious consequences for the Board's other and similar long-term contracts.[92]

On 11 November at E(DL) Howell made a last-ditch attempt to save the flotation. He suggested that if BSC was unwilling to accept the BTDB's offer under the existing contract, then the best course would be for BSC to make a one-off payment to obtain a new contract. In his view the minimum payment would need to be in the range of £15–30 million. If BSC was unable to afford this amount, the sum should be provided out of taxpayer funds since the taxpayer would then benefit from the sales revenues from the flotation of BTDB.[93]

After some discussion with the Treasury, the suggestion of a one-off payment from BSC was agreed in the absence of an alternative solution to put the ABP sale back on track, despite the fact that it would require some taxpayer input. The result was that BSC bought out the 25 year contract from ABP with financial support from the Government. The amount BTDB received was around £25 million, consisting of £20 million to terminate the contract and £5 million to meet the outstanding payments due, payable at £2 million per annum. The Corporation was able to use the sum received to meet the pension fund deficit and to compensate employees who received free rail travel. Those members of the BTDB staff who had been employees at the time of the British Transport Commission, that is to 1962, when the Commission was disbanded, had been given privileged travel arrangements on the railways. In effect, through the settlement with BSC, the BTDB was able to remove two liabilities – the pension deficit and the free travel costs – cleaning up its finances ahead of the flotation.

With the dispute with BSC now ended, in January 1983 arrangements were complete for the sale of 49 per cent of BTDB, and the new group was renamed Associated British Ports (ABP). Schroders still recommended postponing the sale for six or twelve months to allow for better economic conditions and so that a better sale price might be achieved. However, the difficult preceding months had left neither the Secretary of State for Transport, the Secretary of State for Industry, nor Treasury Ministers with the stomach to risk a further flotation postponement. The suggestion was rejected. The view was taken that there was just as much chance that trading conditions would deteriorate as improve in the future.

On 31 January John Sparrow, now head of the Central Policy Review Staff in the Cabinet Office following the departure of Sir Robin Ibbs, advised the PM that the flotation price suggested by Schroders seemed reasonable and recommended that the PM approve an early sale.[94] On the same day Howell wrote to the PM stressing that "The whole company is poised to go and the stock market is expecting the sale to take place. Long delay would do no good to the whole momentum of our privatisation programme".[95] Later on the 31st the PM agreed to the sale going ahead as planned.[96] As part of the sale it was agreed that £56 million of debt would be extinguished at the time of the flotation.

The sale involved 49 per cent of the issued share equity so as to meet the commitment to the Board and the port unions that a majority of the company would not be transferred to the private sector. However, quietly 2.5 per cent of the Government's remaining holding was transferred to an employee share scheme. Employees were offered 53 free shares and a one-for-one matching issue for up to 225 shares per employee.[97] The transfer left the Government with effectively slightly under 50 per cent of the shares while only floating 49 per cent. This was a skilful solution to the Treasury's concerns and the Board and the unions did not react. The Government could say that it had relinquished ownership of the company, removing its borrowings from the PSBR, while the Board could console itself that the Government and employees still held over 50 per cent of the share capital, preventing an unwelcome takeover bid. The unions were not expected to take industrial action over shares bought by their members. Dock workers enthusiastically took up the free shares and the matching offer despite union opposition.

The offer for sale closed on 9 February 1983 with the price per share fixed at 112p, payable in full on application. The offer was 34 times oversubscribed, which contrasted with some problems experienced immediately before the sale with the sub-underwriting. The flotation was underwritten only with difficulty, reflecting the poor image of ports and dock unions in the City and the recent Britoil undersubscription, which had left the underwriters with most of the shares.

Like the sale of BAe, this was not a privatisation that satisfied the Chancellor's objective of raising significant sums for the Exchequer. The sale grossed £22 million. However, as £56 million of debt was extinguished, on one calculation the flotation led to a *net cost* to the Exchequer of some £34 million.[98] Another calculation, taking into account funds extracted from ABP as part of a debt reissue during the capital reconstruction immediately ahead of the sale, puts the net benefit to Government at around £46 million.[99] More importantly, the sale did succeed in removing from the state sector a large part of an industry in which there was a history of difficult labour relations and one where there was always the threat that the Government would be forced into making a capital injection if a port failed. The Government prepared for criticism if the share price rose when trading began on 15 February 1983, as was to be expected, but felt that a sensible judgement on the sale could only be made when the share price settled down in a month or so.[100] Howell had commented immediately prior to the sale that, "This is unlikely to be seen as a highly attractive growth stock, given the miserable history of many of our ports and the terrible industrial relations of the past."[101] Cazanove, who were one of the two stockbrokers to the offer, had been sceptical of getting the ABP shares away successfully given the recent financial difficulties of the Mersey Docks and Harbours Board. It seems that the popularity of the offer took the Government and some sections of the City genuinely by surprise. The shares went to a 23 per cent premium by the end of the first day of trading. The Government concluded that there had been "very heavy stagging" of the issue (buying the shares on flotation to sell quickly for a profit).

The Government's residual holding of 48.5 per cent of the ordinary share capital in ABP was sold on 17 April 1984 through a tender issue with a striking price of 270p per share and with encouragement to small investors to apply for up to 1,000 shares at the striking price. Again preferential treatment was given to applications from employees.[102] However, as was becoming the norm for privatisation issues, this second sale of shares did not attract the benefits of free or matching shares. To encourage small investors the share price was payable in two instalments, 100p on application and 170p on 13 July 1984.

The sale of the residual holding grossed receipts of £52.4 million (£50 million net) and therefore this time the Exchequer did benefit. The sale had occurred 14 months after the first disposal and well before the two year period that in earlier privatisations had been considered the minimum period necessary to wait before selling more shares. As in the cases of the sales of British Aerospace and Cable and Wireless, the Government had been advised that the remaining shares it held would act as an "overhang" in the stock market threatening to deflate the share price on issue and therefore there should be a commitment not to sell a further tranche of shares for some time. By 1984 the City was becoming more accustomed to absorbing privatisation issues. Also, by 1984 the objections of the Board to a complete disposal of the Government's shareholding had dissolved because of the evident advantages to management of operating in the private sector free of government controls. At the same time, the power of the trade unions had waned in the face of new industrial relations laws and unemployment. Their opposition could be more safely ignored.

*　*　*

By April 1984 the privatisation of ABP was complete. The 1962 Transport Act had effectively limited the BTDB to using its assets for the purpose of running ports. Privatisation removed this legal constraint and allowed ABP, like the NFC, to sell off surplus land and buildings and diversify into property development. For example, in 1987 ABP bought into Grosvenor Square Properties, which was heavily involved in property development in London and the South East. In the years after privatisation, economic and financial performance including labour productivity and capital investment rose, as manning contracted and restrictive working practices and trade union dominance in the industry were tackled.[103] The fact that the Government was able to sell the second and final tranche of ABP shares in April 1984 at over twice the price obtained during the first sale in February 1983 attests to the immediate rise in performance after privatisation and growing investor confidence in the management, which continued in subsequent years. By 1987 the company was valued at £550 million or over twelve times its value in February 1983.

# 7

# THE FIRST FOUR YEARS

## A retrospective

By the spring of 1983 the privatisation programme was growing in momentum. In 1979/80 and 1980/1 asset sales had been less than the Chancellor of the Exchequer's targets. However, in 1981/2 the sum raised came in at close to target, at £494 million,[1] and in 1982/3 the figure was almost the same, £488 million. In 1983/4 the amount raised from disposals would jump to £1,161 million (Table 7.1).[2] Also, shares in a number of major corporations had been sold, namely BP, British Aerospace (BAe), Cable and Wireless (C&W), Amersham International, the National Freight Corporation (NFC), Britoil and the British Transport Docks Board/Associated British Ports (ABP), and planning was underway for the sale of British Telecom. There had also been the sale of some smaller enterprises, notably Amersham International, that went on to thrive in the private sector, and businesses such as Drake and Skull Holdings and Suez Finance. At the October 1982 Party Conference in Brighton, the PM could claim, with some justification, "already we have done more to roll back the frontiers of socialism than any previous Conservative Government."[3]

During the first Thatcher administration an ideological drive to substitute markets for state provision had combined with Treasury pressure on Ministers to identify assets to sell. Throughout the life of much of the first Thatcher Government the economic recession compounded the Government's budgetary problems inherited from Labour. For a time it seemed that the credibility of the MTFS and indeed of the Government's entire macroeconomic strategy was at serious risk. The privatisation receipts provided a welcome third leg of public funding, alongside taxation and borrowing, especially since cutting public spending proved to be so difficult at a time of economic recession. It is interesting that although the first Conservative Government talked a lot about the importance of cutting public spending, unlike the previous Labour Government it failed to achieve total real cuts.

The introduction of private capital into British Aerospace and the NFC was not driven by the financial imperative, but rather the political commitment given in the Conservatives' General Election Manifesto. But as further evidence of the importance more generally of raising funds for the Exchequer as a motive in these first years of privatisation, in a letter of 23 April 1982 the Chancellor of the Exchequer, Geoffrey Howe, commented on one proposed sale:

"I assume that you are not suggesting here that ensuring a wide spread of holdings should be the dominant objective in the sale . . .. there is a basic conflict between this objective and the objective of obtaining the best possible price for HMG as vendor. I suggest that if any objective is to be dominant in our planning for the sale then it should be our desire to maximise sale proceeds, subject only to the need to

*Table 7.1* Special sales of assets 1979/80–1983/4

|  | 1979/80 | 1980/1 | 1981/2 | 1982/3 | 1983/4 |
|---|---|---|---|---|---|
| Amersham International | – | – | 64 | – | – |
| Associated British Ports | – | – | – | 46 | – |
| British Aerospace | – | 43 | – | – | – |
| British Petroleum | 276 | – | – | – | 543 |
| Government's Nil-Paid BP Rights | – | – | 8 | – | – |
| British Sugar Corporation | – | – | 44 | – | – |
| Britoil | – | – | – | 334 | 293 |
| Cable & Wireless | – | – | 182 | – | 263 |
| Crown Agents | – | – | 7 | 16 | 2 |
| Cwmbran Development Corporation | – | – | – | 1 | – |
| Drake & Scull Holdings | 1 | – | – | – | – |
| Forestry Commission | – | – | 7 | 14 | 23 |
| Land Settlement Assoc. | – | – | – | – | 2 |
| Motorway Leases | – | 28 | 19 | 4 | 1 |
| British Technology Group | 37 | 83 | 2 | – | – |
| National Freight Company | – | – | 5 | – | – |
| New Town Devt. Agency | 26 | 52 | 73 | – | – |
| North Sea Oil Licences | – | 195 | – | 33 | 19 |
| Property Services Agency | 5 | 4 | 1 | – | – |
| Regional Water Authorities | 3 | – | – | – | – |
| Sale of Oil Stockpiles | – | – | 63 | 33 | 4 |
| Sale of Commodity Stocks | – | – | 19 | 7 | 11 |
| Suez Finance Company | 22 | – | – | – | – |
| **Special Sales of Assets Total/ Privatisation receipts to the Exchequer** | **370** | **405** | **494** | **488** | **1161** |
| Advance Oil Payments | 622 | –49 | –573 | – | – |
| Stamp Duty & VAT | 7 | – | – | – | – |
| **Total after advanced oil payments** | **999** | **356** | **–79** | **488** | **1161** |
| NCB Subsidiaries | – | – | – | – | 7 |
| BR Subsidiaries | – | – | – | 40 | 17 |
| International Aeradio Ltd | – | – | – | 60 | – |
| HMSO Gateshead Press | – | – | – | – | 2 |
| **Total Privatisation Receipts including net oil payments** | **999** | **356** | **–79** | **588** | **1187** |

*Notes*:
1 All figures to the nearest £ million.
2 Figures for the final year are provisional

*Source*: "Privatisation Programme 1983–84 to 1987–88: Progress Report July 1984. Note by the Treasury", in E(DL) Part 10.

sell sufficient shares to effect a transfer of the Company to the private sector during this Parliament. In short, the first step is to decide the method of flotation which maximises proceeds; only then should one move to consider the measures which might be adopted to secure a wide spread of holdings under that method of flotation."[4]

To some extent significant privatisation had always been a possibility – the Conservatives were never natural allies of nationalisation – but in May 1979 large-scale sell-offs were far from being inevitable. Thatcher comments in her autobiography, "I came into 10 Downing Street with an overall conception of how to put Britain's economy right, rather than a detailed plan: progress in different areas would depend on circumstances, both economic and political."[5] In May 1979 some in the Cabinet, notably Joseph, Howe, Lawson and the PM favoured a programme of denationalisation, although Thatcher appears to have been initially sceptical and cautious regarding the political feasibility of mounting it.[6] Nigel Lawson in particular played a key role in promoting the case for privatisation during the first Thatcher Government, and later.[7] However, Thatcher was concerned that policy promoted by her Governments should not run too far ahead of public opinion. From the outset she was concerned about the performance and cost to the Exchequer of the nationalised sector, but she started with limited ambitions regarding possible privatisations, focusing largely on divesting some subsidiary businesses and restructuring the rest. Only later, and especially towards the end of her first Government were the prospects of a major privatisation programme born. By then it was clear that there were investors waiting to buy state-owned industries and, although the public never showed great enthusiasm for privatisation, privatisation was unlikely to be a serious political liability.

By the June 1983 General Election a programme that had begun slowly and hesitatingly had become a major policy initiative in its own right. When the sale of British Aerospace was planned in 1979/80, in Whitehall privatisation was not seen as a long-term or permanent programme. This came later. Thatcher confirms in her autobiography that the programme of disposals was "far more extensive than we had thought would ever be possible when we came into office only four years before".[8] The importance of the programme was evidenced by the fact that by 1983 the term "privatisation" had entered the popular public vocabulary. Both "dries" and "wets" in the Government shared a desire to find the means to permit the promised tax cuts. The sales of BAe and the NFC were heralded in the Conservatives' 1979 Election Manifesto, but other sales were not. The impetus for advancing these sales was financial. It is ironic, therefore, that a number of the first privatisations in the end raised relatively little net funding for the Exchequer once capital injections, debt write-offs and other costs were accounted for, disappointing the Treasury. Indeed, on one set of calculations the disposals of both the BTDB and BAe led to a net cost to the Exchequer and the sale of the NFC raised very little, £5 million, after funding a pension fund deficit. The large sums from privatisation sales would come after 1983, not before.

Alongside raising funds for the Exchequer, from the outset a dominant objective of privatisation was spreading property ownership more widely. However, any suggestion of issuing free or heavily price discounted shares – like the "mass privatisations" seen later in parts of Central and Eastern Europe – was dismissed on the grounds that, as voiced by the Prime Minister, people who did not pay for their property did not respect it. Also, and more pragmatically, issuing free shares was inconsistent with raising funds for the Exchequer.

Only in the case of the highly successful sale of council homes was a partial exception made, in the form of deeply discounted sales. Even in this case, however, the PM was hesitant initially about its merits.

It soon became clear that the privatised industries generally performed well financially after transfer to the private sector, as reflected in the returns to shareholders. By February 1983 the price of British Aerospace shares had risen by 45 per cent compared with a rise of 36 per cent in the FT all-share index over the same period. The comparable figure for Cable and Wireless shares was 140 per cent compared with 36 per cent, Amersham International 92 per cent compared with 29 per cent, and Associated British Ports 23 per cent compared with minus 1 per cent.[9] But during the first Thatcher administration raising economic efficiency was not so obviously an articulated motive for privatisation, as it became later. Admittedly, the Official Committee on Nationalised Industry Policy based in the Treasury, at one of its early meetings in June 1979, recorded the aims of "denationalisation" as "improving efficiency by increasing management motivation and external discipline" alongside "raising money for revenue purposes, spreading share ownership and reducing the public sector".[10] Also, some nationalised industries were believed to be inefficient and unresponsive to consumer demands. But the first privatisations were of BP, Amersham International, Cable and Wireless, BNOC, British Gas oil and gas fields operated in co-operation with the private sector, and ABP. At the time within Government these businesses were considered, correctly or not, to be fairly efficiently operated. Even though the Conservatives had opposed the creation of BAe in 1977, it is far from evident that the result was viewed as being a very inefficient corporation. Indeed, a promise at the time of national-isation to sell the individual aerospace firms that made up BAe back to their previous owners was dropped in 1979 in favour of retaining BAe as one unit, reflecting evidence of economic benefits from combining the businesses. Moreover, the economic success of all of these enterprises first privatised was one important reason why the Government felt that they could be sold – they would be attractive to investors. The only major exception to this argument is the NFC; its dubious financial prospect was the reason that this sale involved a management-employee buyout rather than a City flotation.[11] Only much later were the large loss making businesses such as the National Coal Board and the railways considered to be serious privatisation candidates. During the first Thatcher Government, privatisation of the inefficient, loss making nationalised industries was not on the agenda.

One result of the first privatisations that seems to have surprised Ministers was the interest there was amongst small investors, including first time investors, in buying the offered shares. A total of 88,300 workers in BP, BAe, C&W, Ferranti and Amersham International held shares in their companies after privatisation, although this figure includes free shares.[12] The successful flotation of Amersham International, in particular, revealed the potential attractiveness of privatisation issues to small investors. Marketing shares to the public was not a key objective during the disposal of BAe but grew so after the sale of Amersham. Under the next Conservative Government a determined effort would be made to ensure that the small investor benefited from each of the major flotations. This had the advantage of raising more capital to buy the shares on offer, but it also meant that there would be a greater chance that privatisation would prove to be a vote winner rather than a vote loser. Certainly any talk by the Labour Party of renationalisation without compensation was almost certain to meet with the deep disapproval of the new league of small investors.

At the same time, the first privatisations also revealed how difficult it was for the Government to set a share price at flotation which cleared the market without leading to large oversubscription and "stagging" gains. The first issues were fixed price offers for sale that were to varying degrees oversubscribed, including the 24 times oversubscription for Amersham shares. When trading in the shares began, those fortunate enough to have received shares were able to sell them quickly at a substantial profit. This contributed to a quick decline in share registers. The number of shareholders in BAe fell from 158,000 initially to 27,000, C&W from 150,000 to 27,000 and Amersham International from 63,000 to 10,000 in the months following flotation. This in turn led to growing criticism in the media and Parliament of the sale prices and the "stagging gains". In 1982 the House of Commons Public Accounts Committee published a disapproving report on the early share sales and especially of the sale of BAe, commenting:

"to get privatisation off to a good start, the price of the British Aerospace sale was in practice set at an unduly cautious level. The rising demand for the two subsequent sales [C&W and Amersham International] suggest that the cautious approach continued."

Also, picked out for criticism were the costs of underwriting the share issues.

Overall commission payments paid by Government during these early sales totalled £21.3 million and no shares were left with the underwriters.[13] The Public Accounts Committee recommended that serious consideration should be given in future government flotations to adopting higher priced share offers and sales by tender, even if this raised the risk of undersubscription. The Committee also questioned the need for the underwriting of issues. However, when in response to such criticism sales by tender were tried to better match the demand for shares to the supply available, in the cases of the privatisation of Britoil in 1982 and Enterprise Oil in 1984, the issues flopped.

More satisfactory proved to be the effort to encourage employees in the privatised companies to buy shares. For each of the privatisations a procedure developed under which, typically, employees received priority when applying for shares, some free shares and a matching offer, and an entitlement to buy other shares at a privileged price. In all cases shares obtained free or at a price discount were held in an employee trust account for at least two years to benefit from tax relief.[14] This procedure would be continued in later privatisations. During the privatisation of BAe the Treasury expressed serious reservations about the need for an employee share scheme mindful that it would diminish the sales receipts, but was overruled by Ministers more sensitive to the political advantages of employee shares, especially the potential benefits in terms of defusing trade union opposition to privatisation amongst the workforce.

Much learning occurred within Government in these first four years, but initially barriers to privatisation were also experienced. Firstly, there was a lack of experience in departments and industries about how best to bring about privatisation. Civil servants and the corporations' managements had no experience of how to sell off assets on any appreciable scale, including especially the selling of whole state industries. In particular, within Government in the early days there was a lack of familiarity with the technicalities of corporate finance, company valuations, underwriting and methods of sale. This had to be gradually learnt, assisted from time to time by the secondment of people from the City and by the publication of Treasury guidance. Inexperience did cause delays and some mistakes. Matters were not assisted by the use of different teams of officials, sometimes in different departments, to handle each sale. There was also the complication of arranging the timing of flotations so as not to be affected by the regular round of government financial statements, especially the Autumn Financial Statement and the Budget speech. This too caused some difficulties.

In March 1982, in an attempt to achieve smoother sell-offs it was agreed that Ministers should prepare a paper for E(DL) for each proposed disposal, identifying the key privatisation objectives and the options for achieving them. This would include the size and method of sale, employee and small investor shareholding preferences, the possible need for underwriting and the share allotment policy. The paper was to be prepared in close consultation with the Treasury.[15] Although each sponsor department was responsible for the privatisation of the nationalised industries that it oversaw, from the earliest days the Treasury assumed responsibility for bringing some coherence to the privatisation programme, in terms of methods of sale, the appointment of advisers, commissions and fees paid, and so on.[16] Guidance to departments was issued and in early 1982 the Public Enterprises Analytical Unit (PEAU) with accounting and economic skills was established within the Treasury.[17] Initially privatisations were dealt with by industry desks within the Treasury. The PEAU's main function was to oversee the finances of the nationalised industries as an input into developing the Government's spending plans, but it quickly launched out into promoting and overseeing privatisations. Another body that input into privatisation policy in these years was the Official Committee on Nationalised Industry Policy. It had interdepartmental representation but operated from the Treasury and shadowed the activities of the Cabinet Sub-Committees on Nationalised Industries (E(NI)) and disposals (E(DL)).

Secondly, during the first privatisations it became clear that privatisation would be much more difficult to achieve unless there was co-operation from the management. The record of the Department of Energy in its battle with the Board of British Gas over the sale of its oil interests was a particularly acute example of the delays and difficulties that an obstructive management could introduce. This led over time to Government action to replace recalcitrant chairmen and other board members who were known to be uncomfortable with the prospect of privatisation with those known to be more sympathetic. New board members were brought in with private sector experience, such as in British Airways. To a degree the same applied to the civil service. John Hoskyns, the successful computer entrepreneur who headed up the Policy Unit at No. 10 between 1979 and 1982, had little time for the government machinery, believing that it obstructed his work. It has been suggested that Thatcher judged that civil servants could be overly cautious and a barrier to her plans.[18] She is said to have particularly harboured reservations about some senior officials in the Treasury and even more so in the Foreign Office.[19] However, Thatcher soon came to rely on her own officials at No. 10 and it is not apparent that she saw the Civil Service as a major obstruction, especially as she was able "to mould the Civil Service to her liking" by making suitable promotions.[20] Over time the PM was able to appoint new senior civil servants. By 1986 she had appointed 43 Permanent Secretaries and 138 Deputy Secretaries.

Department officials had understandable reservations about a cavalier attitude to selling public assets. Civil servants were used to working with the industries' boards and shared some of their apprehension about an overly quick transfer to the private sector without full consideration of the implications. For example, Department of Energy officials were used to negotiating with nationalised industry management and had spent their days ensuring that the country's energy supplies were guaranteed. They were understandably concerned that a rushed and poorly planned denationalisation of oil and gas could put all this at risk. But this is very different to saying that the Civil Service was a barrier to reform. It was certainly not a barrier to a determined Minister, as Lawson demonstrated when he took over as Secretary of State for Energy in September 1981.[21] Howe comments on the impression he had when entering the Treasury of his Permanent Secretary, Sir Douglas Wass, that he "was sceptically eager, along with most of his colleagues, to join in a genuinely fresh and determined onslaught on the 'British disease' with which they had grappled in vain for so long".[22] This sentiment after the economic debacle of the 1970s seems to have been more widespread in Whitehall than simply in the upper echelons of the Treasury.

Thirdly, progress in completing privatisations was slowed because disposals usually required some financial restructuring and the passage of primary legislation. In the early months of the new Government the policy emphasis was on tackling the severe economic crisis inherited in May 1979. But even after the economic pressures abated a little, each proposed privatisation needed to be negotiated with the management of the industries concerned and the legislation drafted and then fitted into a crowded Parliamentary timetable. Also, in a number of cases there had to be a restructuring of the industries ahead of sale, including capital injections to improve balance sheets or to fund pension fund deficits. This took time and planning. The Government chose to privatise each public corporation using primary legislation rather than an omnibus privatisation bill to empower Ministers to sell the corporations at their discretion.[23] This took up Parliamentary time and tended to mean that only two or three disposals could be completed each year, adding to delay. At the same time, the decision to use dedicated legislation for each privatisation was sound given the peculiar issues that faced each sale. In any case, an omnibus privatisation bill would have been extremely contentious because of the wide powers it would have transferred to Ministers. It might not have obtained Parliamentary approval.

Fourthly, in the early days there was a lack of clarity about how the state-owned monopoly industries might be privatised, if at all. In a speech to the Institute of Directors in London on 23 February 1983 the PM gave her explanation of what had gone wrong with the socialist "utopian dream", "I will tell you in a word: Monopoly – monopoly power. That's where the root of the evil lies."[24] But during the early years of the first Thatcher Government it was far from clear how state-owned monopolies could be transferred to the private sector successfully. On the face of it privately-owned monopolies were not an attractive proposition. Economists and others were drawing attention to the need for privatisations to be designed to maximise consumer benefits rather than stock market proceeds and this implied an emphasis on restructuring and regulating monopoly industries to promote future competition.[25] It was in the autumn of 1982 at the time of the CPRS report on natural monopolies that a way forward began to emerge, involving promoting competition wherever possible and privatising the monopoly elements as regulated businesses. The actual role of this report in changing opinion within Government is unclear, but it was certainly timely. By then planning had begun for the privatisation of BT and during that privatisation much additional learning about how to privatise monopolies would occur.

Finally, plans were laid initially for partial disposals of shares in state-owned enterprises with the Government retaining a majority or certainly some ownership. For example, the Conservatives' 1979 Election Manifesto promised "to sell shares in the National Freight Corporation to the general public in order to achieve substantial private investment in it". During the passage of the Civil Aviation Act 1980 the Government envisaged a 49 per cent sale of British Airways (BA).[26] In other words the commitment in 1979 was to introduce private capital into the nationalised industries to supplement their funding but not necessarily to denationalise them completely. There was some doubt at the time about both the practicality and wisdom of transferring firms to the private sector. It was unclear that private investors would want to buy them and there were reservations within Government about giving up control or at least influence over major industries with national security implications, such as BAe and C&W, or what were seen as national champions, such as BA. This sentiment was particularly evident in the discussions on the future of BNOC's oil assets and BP shares, where the PM had clear concerns about a loss of state control over North Sea oil. Also, there was in these early days uncertainty about the proportion of shares that would need to be sold to take an industry's loans out of public sector borrowing. It was following discussion with the Central Statistical Office that the Treasury concluded that if the Government retained a majority holding in a corporation its borrowings were likely to remain classified as part of the PSBR. This was because the Government would be perceived as still having possible control over the management. Guidance to departments along these lines was issued in 1981 and again in later years.

Gradually the Treasury was able to win over departments to a sale of a majority shareholding and a commitment not to intervene in the management of the enterprises after an initial share issue. Even so, in the main privatisations of the first Thatcher administration, the Government retained almost 50 per cent of the shares at first and in the case of C&W 50 per cent plus one share after deducting shares committed to employee share schemes. Leaving aside the sale of subsidiary businesses of corporations such as the National Enterprise Board, British Rail and British Steel, only in the case of Amersham International and the NFC were there complete disposals. Amersham was a relatively small enterprise and the NFC was a management buyout. However, with growing confidence in the benefits of privatisation, the PM and the Treasury insisted that the remainder of the shares should be disposed of and from 1983 the state's residual holdings in the companies were sold.

Alongside this development, "special shares" were invented as a solution to the Government's wish to maintain some influence over some of the companies' futures. Special shares introduced at privatisation protected conditions in the Articles of Association aimed at preventing individuals, or individuals acting in concert, from gaining a significant, usually 15 per cent, interest in a privatised company without the Government's consent. This included protecting against foreign ownership where national interests were deemed to be at issue, such as in aerospace. The PM and a number of other Ministers shared a preference to see the privatised firms British-owned, although the Government had to navigate carefully because of the EEC rules on not discriminating against investments from other member states. Equally, had the industries been sold to foreigners this would certainly have played into the hands of the vocal opponents of privatisation, who would have undoubtedly condemned the policy as "a national sell out". Throughout there was some uncertainty within Government about whether the use of special shares would be legally challenged within Europe, and if a credible takeover bidder emerged, whether they would be effective if the takeover had other shareholder backing. Could the Government reasonably oppose the wishes of the vast majority of shareholders?

\* \* \*

On 9 May 1983 the PM informed her Cabinet colleagues that she would be seeking the Queen's approval for Parliament to be dissolved.[27] The General Election was held on 9 June. The Conservatives' Election Manifesto identified British Telecom, British Airways, substantial parts of the British Steel Corporation, British Shipbuilders and British Leyland, plus the offshore assets of British Gas, as privatisation candidates for the next Government.

By contrast, the Labour Party went into the Election promising more nationalisation – along with higher public spending, more power for the trade unions, withdrawal from the EEC and unilateral nuclear disarmament. The Labour Party Election Manifesto has been described as "the longest suicide note in history".[28]

The Conservatives swept back into power winning 397 seats, the largest number for any party since the War. Thatcher later described the result as "my smoothest general election victory".[29] Although the Conservatives' share of the vote fell slightly on 1979, the Labour Party was hopelessly divided with four of its prominent figures having in March 1981 deserted to form a new party, the Social Democrats. The Liberal Party and the Social Democrats formed an electoral alliance in 1983 which took votes from both Labour and the Conservatives, although it never really threatened to displace either. The Conservatives also benefited during the election campaign from the economic recovery and "the Falklands effect". In April 1982 the Argentinians had invaded the Falkland Islands in the South Atlantic and the Government had despatched a naval task force and expelled the invaders. After the Falklands War the PM basked in the glory of victory. In retrospect the Election result was a foregone conclusion.

# 8

# INTO THE HEARTLANDS
# OF THE PUBLIC TRADING
# SECTOR

## Privatisation and the 1983–7
## Thatcher Government

Under the second Thatcher Government privatisation became a dominant economic policy with the privatisation of major nationalised industries notably British Telecom and British Gas and the initial planning for the privatisation of the water industry. Between 1979 and 1983 the policy had developed, cautiously at first. From 1983 it was extended into the heartlands of the nationalised sector in a seemingly unbounded fashion. There appeared to be no industry that could not be privatised including those with substantial market power, even if in a number of cases the corporations had to be made more efficient before they could be successfully sold. As part of the process often new management was brought into the nationalised industries, including management from overseas, notably Ian MacGregor (a Scot with a career in the US, brought in first to British Steel in 1980 and later, in 1983, to the National Coal Board) and Graham Day (a Canadian, first to British Shipbuilders in 1983 and then to British Leyland in 1986). This chapter details the general evolution of privatisation as government policy during these years while providing relevant information on the political and economic environment. Later chapters provide more detailed coverage of each of the main privatisations completed during the second Thatcher administration.

In the June 1983 General Election the Conservatives achieved an overall majority in the House of Commons of 144 seats, despite capturing only 42.4 per cent of the votes cast.[1] The Conservatives benefited from a divided opposition and also from an economy that had been recovering since 1981. The economic recovery continued after the Election with the years from 1983 to 1987 seeing GDP grow by around three per cent per annum. Inflation, which had peaked at 21.9 per cent during 1980, fell to around 2.5 per cent in 1986 (Figure 8.1) and with the improved economic environment profitability rose. The gross return recorded by industrial and commercial companies increased from a record low of 4.8 per cent in 1981 to 9.1 per cent by 1988, by which time it was back to a level similar to that of the early 1970s.[2] Less satisfactory, due in part to rising labour productivity and a growing population of working age, was the record on unemployment. Unemployment in September 1984 still stood at 14 per cent before falling to 12 per cent by 1987. Also, Britain had a rapidly growing trade deficit in manufactures and manufacturing output did not recover to 1979 levels until 1987, reflecting the damage inflicted on industry by the deep recession of the early 1980s.[3]

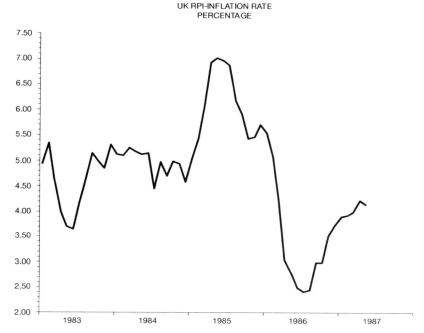

*Figure 8.1* UK inflation 1983–7 (%)

*Source*: Office for National Statistics.

## Economic and political developments

The Government continued to pay some lip service to monetarism. But since 1981 a more pragmatic approach to macroeconomic management ruled. After the election the new Chancellor of the Exchequer, Nigel Lawson, began to target the exchange rate as a means of macroeconomic control in the belief that a stable pound on the foreign exchanges would keep inflation under control. Interest rates were raised or lowered to influence exchange rate movements. Targeting sterling M3, the favoured monetary measure in the Government's 1980 Medium Term Financial Strategy, was downgraded initially in favour of a narrower monetary aggregate, M0, and finally abandoned in 1987.[4] A plunge in the value of sterling in July 1984 and in early 1985 to almost parity with the US dollar seems to have converted Lawson to the idea that Britain should join the European Exchange Rate Mechanism; but this met with firm opposition from the PM.[5] After some recovery in value, especially in late 1986, the pound dropped sharply again against the dollar. By early 1987, in a salute to Germany's greater success in achieving a stable currency, Lawson was concentrating upon sterling shadowing the Deutschmark as an instrument of macroeconomic control.[6]

Trade union legislation passed in 1980 and 1982 had tackled secondary picketing and the closed shop. The legal constraints on union action were further tightened by the Trade Union Act of 1984, which removed the unions' immunity to prosecution if a ballot had not been held to ratify strike action. Also, the decline in traditional heavy manufacturing and the movement to a service-led economy reduced employment in those areas where unionisation was prevalent. By 1987 48.5 per cent of the workforce was unionised, compared to 57.4 per cent in 1979.[7] The number of man days lost through strikes improved, falling from 822,000 in the final quarter of 1983 to 381,000 in the final quarter of 1986, although it rose sharply in 1984/5 due to the miners' strike. During these years weakening the influence of the trade unions was an important rationale for privatisation within the Conservative Party.

In 1981 the Government had backed down over pit closures in the face of threatened industrial action by the National Union of Mineworkers (NUM). Afterwards the Government planned for a future strike by building up large coal stocks at the power stations. The catalyst for the strike which broke out in March 1984 was the National Coal Board's announcement of the closure of the Cortonwood pit in Yorkshire. Arthur Scargill, the militant leader of the NUM and from the Yorkshire coal fields, rejected the NCB's argument that Cortonwood and a number of other pits in line for closure were uneconomic. On three occasions before March he had attempted to call a strike over pit closures, but had failed each time to achieve the necessary level of support in union ballots.[8] This time the strike was called without a national vote, although some branches of the union held ballots, with only one result suggesting the stomach for a strike. Called at the start of a summer period when the demand for coal was falling, from the miners' perspective the strike was fatally ill-timed.

In the event the dispute dragged on for 12 months before those miners remaining on strike drifted back to work. For both Thatcher and Scargill this was above all a political dispute, about who should rule the country. The union resorted to flying pickets to close pits still working and to prevent the movement of coal stocks, as it had done successfully at the time of the Heath Government in early 1974. But this time the union met with determined and nationally co-ordinated police action. The Government used its new legal powers against secondary picketing and the failure to call a strike ballot led to the union's funds being seized, in October 1984, cutting off strike pay to the miners. The final development which doomed the strike was the creation of the breakaway union, the Union of Democratic Mineworkers, in the Nottinghamshire coal fields, which had largely defied the strike call.[9] After the miners' strike the unions were no longer the political and economic threat to government that they had seemed since the late 1960s. However, the defeat of the NUM came at a cost. The strike added an estimated £2.75 billion to public expenditure, reduced economic output by one per cent and led to a sharp fall in the value of the pound on the foreign exchanges.[10]

In the early 1980s the economic priority was to bring the Government's finances back under control. The Government feared that it would be unable to fund the PSBR without cripplingly high interest rates. The Treasury's frantic search for state assets to sell from the summer of 1979 was a product of this concern. However, by 1983 the PSBR was falling and the gilt-edged market was absorbing all of the issued stock, assisted by the introduction of indexed-linked gilts in 1981. Nevertheless, public spending remained a matter of tension within the Government between the Treasury and spending departments.[11] Shortly after the 1983 Election an emergency budget was assembled to reduce a forecast overspend of £3 billion[12] and in November 1985 the Cabinet agreed to freeze the real level of public expenditure for three years with the aim of reducing its share of GDP from around 45 per cent to 42 per cent by 1988/9.[13] Each autumn government spending plans were the subject of tough bilateral discussions with the Star Chamber (officially known as the Cabinet special committee Misc 62), an ad hoc grouping of Ministers chaired by William Whitelaw,[14] invoked to settle differences between the Treasury and departments. In October 1985 public expenditure was still three per cent higher as a percentage of GDP than it had been when the Government took office in May 1979 and tax revenue was over five per cent higher. This was a disappointing result for an administration that preached public spending restraint and was committed to cutting taxation. Nevertheless, the fiscal position was not as precarious after 1983 as it had been during the first Thatcher administration. In 1986/7 with the economy and tax receipts expanding, public spending as a proportion of GDP finally fell below the May 1979 level, and without invoking the radical cuts in public spending advocated by free market organisations such as the Institute of Economic Affairs and the Adam Smith Institute.[15]

One small but politically significant contribution to the improvement in the public finances resulted from the negotiations which led, in June 1984, to a permanent reduction in Britain's contribution to the European Community budget. In 1979 Britain had been the second largest net contributor of financing to the EEC after Germany. During her first Government the PM had obtained a temporary reduction in Britain's contribution, but in 1983 she was determined to win a larger and permanent rebate, even at the cost of alienating the leaders of the other EEC member states. In June 1984, after much obstinacy by the PM, at a summit at Fontainebleau Britain was granted a 66 per cent budget rebate.[16]

Public expenditure had an upward momentum because of demand-led social security spending, local authority expenditure and borrowing by the nationalised industries, as had been the case before 1983.[17] The improvement in the public finances was largely attributable to higher tax revenues alongside slowing the growth in, but not actually cutting, public spending. A major source of political controversy was local government expenditure. In an attempt to rein back local authority spending, between 1980 and 1986 the value of central government funding to local government was cut from 60 per cent of local authority income to 49 per cent and a system of expenditure targets was established. Under these expenditure targets cuts in government grant were imposed when spending exceeded agreed levels. However, instead of responding with significant reductions in their spending plans, many local authorities compensated for the loss of central finance by raising their rate charges (the local property tax). This led to howls of protest from both domestic residents and businesses about the "rate burden". Under the 1984 Rate Act the Government took powers to impose "rate-caps" or a limit on rate rises in England and Wales (rate-capping had already been introduced in Scotland).[18] In 1985/6 18 local authorities were rate-capped, all but two of which were Labour controlled.[19] The Labour council of Liverpool, under the influence of the militant left-winger Derek Hatton, in open defiance of the Government, waited until the very last moment before reluctantly setting a legal rate. Meanwhile concerns over the "rate burden" would rumble on within central government, culminating in the Conservatives' politically disastrous decision later in the decade to introduce a per capita Community Charge to replace the local authority domestic rate. A more immediate demonstration of central government impatience with the activities of left-wing Labour councils was the decision announced in the Conservatives' 1983 Election Manifesto to abolish the Greater London Council (GLC) and the metropolitan councils, removing a tier of local administration. A main focus was the Greater London Council. Between 1981 and 1986 the Labour leader of the GLC, Ken Livingstone, raised expenditure by 170 per cent and made contributions to "good causes", such as one-parent families and peace campaigners, in a barely veiled challenge to Thatcherism.[20] In 1986 the GLC and the metropolitan councils were abolished, but not before Livingstone had draped a defiant banner across County Hall opposite Westminster.

The very deep divisions on economic policy within the Cabinet seen in 1980 and 1981 were not repeated after 1983. The Cabinet reshuffle of September 1981, the Falklands victory and the outcome of the 1983 Election meant that the PM's position was much more secure.

In the immediate post-election Government Nigel Lawson was promoted to Chancellor of the Exchequer, replacing Geoffrey Howe, and there were posts for Leon Brittan, Cecil Parkinson (until October 1983 when he resigned following revelation of an extramarital affair[21]) and Normal Tebbit, all reliable Thatcherites. The Cabinet also included Thatcherite stalwarts like Nicholas Ridley, from September 1984 Lord (David) Young and from 1986 John Moore. A prominent "wet" in the previous Government, Francis Pym, was sacked as Foreign Secretary after the Election and replaced by Geoffrey Howe. Pym had compounded his deficiencies in the eyes of the PM by remarking during the Election that a landslide victory for the Conservatives would not be a good thing. In the autumn of 1984 the last definite "wet" in the Cabinet, Jim Prior, stood down as Secretary of State for Northern Ireland, announcing his intention to leave politics and pursue a business career. In the mid-1980s the Cabinet was therefore more clearly Thatcherite than ever before. However, this did not last. In May 1986 Thatcher's economic mentor, Sir Keith Joseph, decided to leave the Government[22] and with the appointments of Malcolm Rifkind and Paul Channon to the Cabinet plus the promotions of Douglas Hurd, Kenneth Baker and Kenneth Clarke, by the summer of 1987 the Cabinet had begun to take on a more consensual appearance again.

Nevertheless, there was no division on the principle of privatisation. Privatisation had not been a serious cause of division amongst "wets" and "dries" before 1983 and there remained during the second Thatcher administration agreement amongst Ministers on the desirability of the policy. As Francis Pym wrote in 1984, "I do not agree with all aspects of the Government's approach to industry, but I believe that most of the privatisation programme has been sensible and will prove an enduring success."[23] Any differences in views between Ministers were concerned with matters of detail, such as the timing and form of particular asset sales. After the May 1983 General Election the Departments of Trade and Industry were combined to recreate the Department of Trade and Industry which had existed under the Heath Government in the early 1970s – the incoming Labour Government in March 1974 had separated the Department into a Department of Trade and a Department of Industry. There were possibly a number of reasons for this restructuring, but occasional disagreement between the two separate departments over their responsibilities during the first Thatcher administration was no doubt a factor.

The second Thatcher Government did have its share of political difficulties. There were a number of poor by-election results, for example in the summer of 1985 the Conservatives came third in the Brecon by-election and the Party was behind both Labour and the Alliance in most opinion polls during much of 1985 and 1986.[24] In May 1986 there were two further disappointing by-election performances and the Conservatives suffered a net loss of 705 seats in council elections that year. There were political rows over the banning of trade unions at the General Communications Headquarters (GCHQ) and over the decision in April 1986 to allow American F-111 aircraft to use bases in Britain to bomb Libya. In September 1985 renewed rioting broke out in the poorer areas of London, Birmingham and Liverpool, refuelling claims that Thatcherism was dividing Britain into a nation of "haves" and "have nots". Also, there was political embarrassment over the October 1983 US invasion of Grenada, a Commonwealth country, which occurred without the PM being forewarned by her friend and ally President Reagan. But two events in particular shocked the Government.

The first was the IRA bomb that exploded in October 1984 at the Conservative Conference hotel in Brighton killing five people and seriously injuring two members of the Cabinet, Norman Tebbit and John Wakeham. The PM escaped physically uninjured but the event illustrated the ever present terrorist threat in Britain. The second was the Westland Affair, which had a damaging effect on the PM's standing in Government and outside. Westland was Britain's only major helicopter manufacturer but by late 1985 it was in financial difficulty and the Board including the new Westland chairman, Sir John Cuckney, decided in favour of a merger with the US manufacturer, Sikorsky. However, the Secretary of State for Defence, Michael Heseltine, was keen to see Europe maintain its own defence capability and favoured the ailing firm joining a consortium of European arms manufacturers.[25] The affair culminated in Heseltine walking out of the Cabinet on 9 January 1986, after an argument with the PM following a disputed leaking from No. 10 of a letter from the Solicitor General. In this letter the Solicitor General claimed that there were "material inaccuracies" in earlier correspondence by Heseltine to the press on the future of Westland.[26] Heseltine's departure was immediately followed by the resignation of Leon Brittan, the Secretary of State for Trade and Industry, who had favoured the Sikorsky proposal and been implicated in leaking the letter. Mrs Thatcher escaped official censure for the leak in a subsequent parliamentary inquiry, but only just. Westland would prove to be the worst personal crisis in Margaret Thatcher's years in Downing Street "for she lost what had hitherto been her most priceless asset, her reputation for integrity".[27] As confirmation, in April Thatcher's personal popularity rating fell to its lowest point since 1981, at 28 per cent. The Government also suffered a by-election defeat in Fulham. Perhaps most importantly, Heseltine from the back benches would cast a shadow over Thatcher's future leadership of the Party. However, when in 1985 Francis Pym formed the Centre Forward group of Conservative MPs, in an open challenge to Thatcherism, it attracted little support and quickly sank into obscurity.

In his Mais lecture in 1984 Lawson set out the Government's approach to economic policy – using macroeconomic policy to suppress inflation and microeconomic policy to improve economic growth and employment.[28] There was much interest in the mid-1980s amongst economists in the microeconomics of what was popularly known as "supply-side economics".[29] As part of this policy thrust, the Government set about promoting competition and deregulating in a number of areas. Lord Young's Enterprise Unit promoted the deregulation agenda,[30] but it was also taken forward by government departments. In particular, under the Administration of Justice Act 1985 the solicitors' monopoly of property conveyance work was broken and in March 1985 restrictive practices on the part of opticians prescribing optical aids were ended under the 1984 Health and Social Security Act. Broadcasting was opened up to more competition with the planning of cable and satellite services, following the earlier founding of Channel 4. But the reforms which had arguably the greatest immediate economic significance were in financial services. The system by which building societies had effectively agreed interest rates on mortgages was abandoned in 1983 and under legislation in 1986 they were permitted for the first time to diversify away from their traditional function of providing home mortgages. Following an Office of Fair Trading investigation into share trading in the City, new dealing systems were introduced. In particular, broker-dealers replaced the old broker – jobber structure in the Stock Exchange and fixed commissions on share dealing were abolished.[31] The dual capacity broker-dealer system was introduced for international equities in 1984 and extended to domestic equities and gilt-edged securities, in what became known as "Big Bang", in October 1986.[32]

In addition to deregulation, important in supply-side economics was the creation of incentives to work and save through tax reforms. After the June 1979 Budget the first Thatcher administration had deferred further tax cutting because of the poor budgetary position, but from 1983 a number of tax cuts were introduced. This continued in the 1987 Budget, which reduced the basic rate of income tax from 29 per cent to 27 per cent. Another, central, component of supply-side economics during the second Thatcher Government was privatisation.

## Privatisation policy

Privatisation receipts continued to be treated in the public accounts as negative public spending and provided a useful, if relatively small, contribution to the Chancellor's balancing of the books. The net income to the Exchequer from privatisations never amounted to the equivalent of more than around three per cent of public spending and was usually less. Nevertheless, the Treasury remained keen to see an annual flow of receipts from privatisations, even though sales receipts were no longer the fiscal priority they had been in 1979.[33] The income from privatisation sales was not an irrelevance as far as the Treasury was concerned, but whereas under the first Thatcher administration budgetary considerations had greatly encouraged the privatisation programme, at least at the outset, now the emphasis in ministerial statements was on the benefits of privatisation for competition, economic efficiency and economic growth. The PM told the House of Commons in February 1983, "Privatization, through exposing former State-owned companies more fully to the disciplines and opportunities of the market . . . improves the efficiency of businesses that are crucial to our overall economic performance. As such it forms an important part of the Government's overall strategy for long-term economic growth."[34] In the November the Financial Secretary, John Moore, stressed the importance of promoting competition as the privatisation programme "moves into the heartlands of the public sector . . . No state monopoly is sacrosanct".[35]

Initially the Government had been unclear about what to do about state monopolies, but from 1982 the notion of privatising them and introducing dedicated regulatory structures developed, first for the privatisation in November 1984 of British Telecom (BT). A lack of competition was now not necessarily a barrier to privatisation. As Moore observed: "Where competition is impractical privatisation policies have now been developed to such an extent, that regulated private ownership of natural monopolies is preferable to nationalisation."[36] Moore, as Economic Secretary between June and October 1983 and then Financial Secretary until May 1986, when he briefly became Secretary of State for Transport and then Secretary of State for Health and Social Services, was a strident advocate of privatisation and, in effect, the unofficial Minister of Privatisation in the mid-1980s. An additional significant development was the appointment, in August 1983, of John Redwood, another champion of the selling-off of state industries, as Head of the No. 10 Policy Unit.[37] Redwood appears to have been instrumental in persuading the PM to appoint John Moore to the Treasury to lead the programme of privatisation during her second Government and in encouraging her to believe that an extensive programme was achievable. However, when in July 1984 Redwood pressed the PM to intensify pressure on Ministers to keep up the rate of privatisations, it was felt that a progress chasing meeting was only likely to irritate Ministers.[38] There would remain some tension within Government between the more gung-ho privatisers, such as Moore and Redwood, and those Ministers who took a more cautious line, wishing to plan each privatisation with great care.

Whereas in 1979 there had been only limited reference to denationalisation measures in the Conservatives' Election Manifesto, the 1983 Manifesto promised extensive privatisation. Commitments were made to sell 51 per cent of the shares in BT, a privatisation delayed by the calling of the General Election, the disposal of Rolls-Royce, British Airways and "substantial parts" of the British Steel Corporation, British Shipbuilders and British Leyland, and the completion of the sale of state-owned oil businesses through the disposal of the offshore oil interests of British Gas. There was also a promise that "as many as possible of Britain's airports, shall become private sector companies" and that private capital would be introduced into the National Bus Company. In addition, there was reference to seeking to increase competition and attract private capital into the gas and electricity industries. The Manifesto also acknowledged the importance now attached to promoting competition, stating that: "Merely to replace state monopolies by private ones would be to waste an historic opportunity."[39]

On 16 June 1983, at the first Cabinet meeting following the General Election, it was agreed that the Queen's Speech on the opening of the new Parliament should refer specifically to privatisation of telecommunications and a disposal not mentioned in the Manifesto, the Royal Ordnance Factories, was added. The speech would also leave open the possibility of other privatisations.[40] It was recognised that the resulting legislative programme would be crowded and challenging because of the privatisation measures, along with the Bill to scrap the GLC and the metropolitan councils. There was also legislation proposed to enable the Trustee Savings Banks (TSB) to become an independent group of banks in the private sector. Not technically a privatisation because the state did not own the TSBs – indeed an issue that arose during the planning of the sale was uncertainty over who did own them – broadly they were a form of trust – the TSBs would be floated in the stock market in September 1986. Buoyed up by the experience of earlier privatisation issues, small investors were attracted to the TSB sale anticipating yet again a quick capital gain. The offer was seven times oversubscribed.[41] The crowded legislative timetable meant that proposals for legislation to advance the privatisations of the National Bus Company and British Airways had to be shelved.

During the 1983–87 Government large numbers were attracted for the first time to buy and hold shares by privatisation issues and the flotation of the TSB, and later of the Abbey National building society in 1987, another mutual.[42] Thatcher first used the term "popular capitalism" in February 1986 to describe the result,[43] with Lawson resorting to the same emotional descriptor in his Budget speech a month later.[44] Spreading share ownership had been an important goal in May 1979 and remained so. However, as before 1983, the enthusiasm for small shareholding did not extend in the Treasury to providing the public with free shares. A letter from Sir Emmanuel Kaye, Chairman of the company Lansing Bagnall, to Lawson on 7 July 1986, suggesting that BT and other privatisation shares might be freely distributed to extend property ownership, met with a firm rejection, again on the grounds that those who do not pay for something fail to value it.[45]

There was also the point that free shares produced no revenues. The Treasury continued to set targets for asset sales and took these targets into consideration when planning the public finances. In July 1983, during the Chancellor's review of public spending to tackle an expected £3 billion overspend, Lawson was looking "to increase the programme of disposals of public sector assets with a view to raising a further £500 million".[46] In the autumn new disposal targets were set of £1.5 billion in 1984/5 and £500 million in 1985/6. Beyond 1986 Treasury Ministers proposed to keep expenditure plans on target by assuming higher, although they believed attainable, asset sales in 1986/7 and 1987/8.

As part of the annual debates within Government about the acceptable level of public expenditure, the EFL claims submitted by the nationalised industries were cut back. The demands imposed on the Government's finances by the investment programmes of the nationalised industries continued to be a factor in promoting privatisation within Government.[47] Equally, the industries' managements increasingly appreciated that privatisation would bring with it freedom to raise further capital without Treasury controls. In the second half of 1984 the Government consulted the nationalised industries on their future relations and contemplated legislation sponsored by the Treasury to set common financial obligations and duties on the nationalised industries, to clarify the statutory backing for setting financial targets, to replace the existing different pieces of legislation relating to the industries, and to allow Ministers to hire and fire nationalised industry chairmen and board members more easily.[48] The chairmen of the industries could be a serious barrier to a smooth privatisation, as Sir Denis Rooke had demonstrated at British Gas during the Government's planning of the disposal of the Corporation's oil interests. Certainly replacing the chairman and sometimes other members of the board with people more sympathetic to privatisation and with experience attractive to City investors was not infrequently a prerequisite for a successful sale. The intended legislation would also have allowed Ministers to order the nationalised industries to set up subsidiaries under the Companies Act and to transfer assets to Ministers so that they could be more easily and quickly sold off.[49] In a real sense the proposed Bill was the nearest Britain came to having a general Privatisation Authorisation Act to speed up sales. Sales would have been achieved by affirmative order rather than individual bills, although the disposal of complete industries would have still required primary legislation. However, the proposals, which formally appeared in a Treasury consultative paper in December 1984, met with a predictably frosty reception in the industries and from some Ministers. The Nationalised Industries Chairmen's Group argued that it would undermine the authority of the Boards and involve Ministers in the detailed running of the industries;[50] while the Secretaries of State for Energy and Trade and Industry were sceptical of the value of the Bill, seeing it as an erosion of the industries' commercial freedom. The Whips Office warned that such an omnibus Bill would be subject to a host of amendments and would have a difficult passage.[51] Within a year the legislation had been abandoned.[52]

In July 1983, the Chancellor of the Exchequer wrote to the PM on the challenges now facing a privatisation programme:

> "Hitherto the companies we have sold have mainly been profitable and operating in competitive environments. Preparing them for privatisation, although time-consuming in terms of legislation and preparation for flotation, has involved relatively little change to that structure. But from now on we are increasingly working in the heartland of the public trading sector, where we shall have to deal both with the giant utilities and unprofitable companies."[53]

The Government continued to press the nationalised industries to hive off those businesses which could be sold immediately and to make more use of the private sector, in areas such as project management.[54] It also pressured a number of the industries to improve their management and accounting practices and to raise prices significantly. Encouraging the nationalised industries to be more efficient, less of a financial burden, and more ready for privatisation was a theme of Treasury management during the 1983-7 Government. A Treasury report in 1986 on improving economic accounting for new and existing assets in the industries encouraged the use of current cost accounting. This had the by-product of putting industry accounts on to a better basis ahead of a sale.[55] Concerns had surfaced during some of the early privatisations over the proper value of the industries' assets, which made setting an appropriate sale price difficult, while higher prices for the industries' products meant greater profitability and industries therefore more attractive as privatisation candidates.[56] By 1989 the remaining nationalised sector was generating an overall surplus to the Exchequer. Meanwhile, the Public Enterprises Analytical Unit (PEAU) within the Treasury identified possible privatisation candidates and oversaw the Government's privatisation timetable.[57]

In October 1983 Lawson had set out the advantages of privatisation for improved economic performance and this became a major theme of his Chancellorship.[58] He requested that Ministers prepare and submit regular privatisation plans and timetables.[59] The Financial Secretary held bilateral discussions with departments to identify new privatisation candidates. However, Lawson was not entirely satisfied with the responses received. He was particularly concerned about the need to accelerate the programme and to plan privatisations carefully to prevent major bottlenecks in the Government's legislative programme and in the equity market.[60] Also, he was concerned that insufficient attention was being given by departments to promoting competition in the plans submitted, having earlier concluded, "This is an area where strong political leadership is essential if our objectives are to be achieved. There is little evidence that officials in Departments, left to their own devices, will drive the programme forward."[61] Promoting competition would be a particularly important goal of the second Thatcher Government's privatisation programme.

The Chancellor of the Exchequer returned to this theme in E(A) Sub-Committee in January 1984 when he discussed the importance of deregulation and increasing competition, remarking: "Outside commentators increasingly, and rightly, were judging the success of the programme by reference to these yardsticks."[62] The Financial Secretary, John Moore, was authorised to oversee the privatisation with competition programme to produce more progress. By now privatisation was attracting much critical attention in the media[63] and amongst academic economists. In July 1983 in the *Lloyds Bank Review* Professors Stephen Littlechild and Michael Beesley suggested that privatisation could be extended to include 80 per cent of the nationalised industries, including electricity, the Post Office, the NCB and British Rail.[64] Both were heavily involved as advisers to the Government, particularly during the privatisation of BT. Their study and studies by other academics emphasised the importance of extending competition over maximising sales receipts when planning privatisations, and introducing effective regulation where monopoly powers continued to exist.[65] This was taken up with fervour by the PEAU within the Treasury which promoted the privatisation with competition agenda, providing a series of papers on how competition might be extended.[66] A paper on competition and privatisation in July 1983 argued that the introduction of effective competition would often involve restructuring and privatisation of parts of an industry and, where monopoly continued, effective state regulation.[67]

By early 1984 E(A) Sub-Committee was contemplating the sale of a large part of the nationalised industries, including gas, electricity, coal, the Post Office and the railways (Table 8.1), although it should be understood that a number of these, including electricity, coal and British Rail, were long-term prospects rather than realistic propositions during the current Parliament. Also, planning for the privatisation of British Rail and coal involved at this time mainly the selling-off of subsidiary businesses not the whole enterprises. In E(A) Sub-Committee in the spring of 1984 Lawson re-stressed the importance of ensuring that the privatisations planned were phased so as to fit with the Parliamentary timetable and to ensure that the cash calls on the stock market were not too large at any one time.[68] It was also important, he emphasised, to monitor the programme continuously "to ensure that slippage

*Table 8.1* Main privatisation candidates January 1984

Royal Ordnance Factories
British Gas Corporation
Wytch Farm
Gas Appliance Retailing
British Nuclear Fuels Ltd
Electricity (England and Wales and Scottish Electricity Boards)
Enterprise Oil
National Coal Board
British Leyland
British Shipbuilders
British Steel Corporation
British Technology Group Holdings
British Telecom
Post Office and National Girobank
Rolls-Royce
British Airports Authority
British Airways
British Rail
CAA Scottish Airports
National Bus Company
Sealink
Short Brothers
Scottish Transport Group

*Source*: E (A) (84) 3, 16 January 1984. Also, "Privatisation Programme 1983–84
to 1987–88. Progress Report – July 1984. Note by the Treasury", E(DL) Part 10.

does not occur and that repercussions between sales are minimised". Another matter that concerned him was ensuring that the privatisation legislation was properly drafted and presented to Parliament. The Telecommunications Bill to privatise BT had encountered difficulties in the House of Lords, which had been put down to poor drafting and rushing the legislation through the House of Commons under guillotine.[69] A number of amendments had to be introduced during the Bill's passage to command support in the Lords.

Lawson was also keen to refute recent comment in the media that had suggested that the Government Ministers had retained residual shareholdings in privatised companies "as a deliberate act of policy" so that they could continue to exert influence over the companies. He therefore proposed that the Government's residual shareholdings in Associated British Ports and British Aerospace, currently held by the sponsoring departments, the Department of Transport and the DTI respectively, be transferred to the Treasury.[70] Excluded from the transfer would be any "special shares", which would remain with departments, and any shares retained by Departments to fulfil future bonus issue commitments under share sale incentive schemes. The expectation was that the transfer "would allow the Government's portfolio to be consistently managed and would emphasise that ordinary shareholdings had not been retained to further sectoral policies". But no doubt a further objective was to ensure that the Treasury would be able to guarantee that the residual holdings were sold as quickly as possible. The proposal met with some opposition, on the grounds that it would not be right "for Treasury Ministers to be able to take a unilateral decision to dispose of shares in a particular company even if disposal might be contrary to the interests of the company". Nevertheless, the Sub-Committee agreed to the transfer, subject to Treasury Ministers consulting departmental Ministers before disposing of any shareholdings. The decision was announced during the March 1984 Budget debate.[71] From 1984 the Treasury was responsible for the residual shareholdings in privatised industries and not the sponsoring departments.

In addition to continuing the disposal of surplus land and buildings and encouraging nationalised industries to sell off subsidiary businesses, the 1983–87 Government introduced a number of important privatisations of state-owned industries. During the first year of the new Parliament legislation authorising the sale of BT was passed, along with a law to introduce private finance into the Royal Ordnance Factories.[72] A majority of shares in BT were sold in November 1984 and two years later British Gas was privatised. The Government also oversaw the selling-off of the Wytch Farm onshore oil facilities owned by British Gas in May 1984 and Enterprise Oil was successfully floated in the following month. December 1983 saw the second issue of Cable and Wireless shares with a third and final issue occurring in December 1985. Rolls-Royce was privatised in May 1987, the National Bus Company in 1986/7 and British Airways in February 1987. In May 1985 the Chancellor of the Exchequer presented another report to E(A) on privatisation including an attached report from the Financial Secretary detailing an ambitious programme of current and prospective disposals.[73] The Sub-Committee reaffirmed the importance of pressing ahead with privatisation with Ministers to inform the Chancellor of the Exchequer of their plans before the summer recess.[74]

By the autumn of 1985 the Government's future programme included measures to introduce private capital into BAA and steps to require larger local authority airports to be formed into companies, and to introduce commercial management into the Naval Dockyards.[75] In addition, serious planning began during this second Thatcher Government of the sale of the water industry, although this privatisation required especially long and careful consideration because of its complexity. A plan to sell the regional water authorities was added to the privatisation programme in the spring of 1985[76] and was announced publicly in February 1986, but in July the decision was taken to postpone a sale until after the next election, mainly due to difficulties over the regulation of environmental issues. The privatisation of electricity would also have to await the next Conservative administration. Privatisation of gas, water and electricity in the same Parliament was ruled out because of the excessive pressure that would have been imposed on parliamentary time.[77] Another privatisation with a long gestation period was BA, whose sale had been announced as early as June 1979. The financial state of the Corporation and later a legal dispute relating to the collapse of the Laker airline meant that BA was not privatised until February 1987. Similarly, the privatisation of the National Girobank, a subsidiary of the Post Office, was contemplated in 1985/6 but delayed until 1990 due to the complexities of arranging a successful sale. Another privatisation planned but delayed involved the British Steel Corporation, which underwent considerable restructuring before it was successfully sold. It would not be privatised until the third Thatcher Government. Equally, the disposal of the British Airports Authority was planned during the 1983–7 Government but not completed until immediately after the June 1987 General Election.

The Conservatives' Election Manifesto in 1979 had promised the denationalisation of shipbuilding. But the financial and economic state of British shipbuilding was such that a disposal of the Corporation was out of the question before the mid-1980s. Under the 1983–87 Government progress was made in selling off a number of the yards including those involved in warship building. There were also after 1983 disposals of the Government's remaining shareholdings in Associated British Ports in April 1984, British Aerospace in May 1985, and Britoil in August 1985. The events surrounding the privatisations of Wytch Farm, Britoil, Enterprise Oil, British Aerospace, Associated British Ports and Cable and Wireless were detailed in chapters 4, 5 and 6 above. The privatisations of British Airways, Rolls-Royce, shipbuilding including the Royal Dockyards, the National Bus Company, and the Royal Ordnance Factories are discussed in chapters 9 and 10. Detailed study of the privatisations of BT and British Gas is deferred to chapters 11 to 15. Both were very large privatisations and require separate, detailed coverage.

Alongside these large privatisations under the second Thatcher Government there were a number of smaller sales, such as of Associated Heating Services and Sankeys, both subsidiaries of the NCB, and some of the assets of the British Technology Group (BTG), which had incorporated the remaining assets of the National Enterprise Board. This included BTG's investments in INMOS, the loss making silicon chip manufacturer, which was sold to Thorn/EMI in July and August 1984 for £95 million.[78] The British Rail cross-channel ferry subsidiary, Sealink, was sold in July 1984 to a trade buyer Sea Containers Ltd for £66 million, and early in 1987 British Transport Advertising passed almost unnoticed to the private sector through a buyout by eight senior managers supported by institutional investors. The sale grossed £50 million. Where subsidiaries of nationalised industries were sold the receipts went to the parent corporation not the Exchequer, for example in the case of Sealink to British Rail. However, the Government could take the receipts into account when setting the industry's EFL, thereby benefiting the PSBR.[79]

The disposal of the main vehicle assembly activities of British Leyland, Austin-Morris, Rover and Land Rover, had to wait until after the 1987 General Election. In 1986 there was an opportunity to sell these activities to Ford or General Motors, but the PM was unable to convince sufficient of her parliamentary colleagues to support the proposals. The idea floundered in the face of opposition shepherded by the former Conservative Party leader Edward Heath and involving particularly Conservative MPs from Midland seats.[80] Vehicle manufacturing was highly concentrated in the Midlands region of England and there was an understandable fear that Ford and GM might rationalise their existing production facilities in Britain and those acquired from BL leading to major job losses. Some MPs also opposed the sale of BL to "foreigners", in the conviction that BL should remain "British" owned.[81] Nevertheless, a number of other parts of BL were sold between 1983 and 1987. The Jaguar cars assembly subsidiary was floated in July 1984 with 15 per cent of the issued share capital reserved for applications from Jaguar and BL employees and BL shareholders, and with the Government retaining a special share.[82] Adopting what by now had become the conventional approach to a privatisation flotation, the sale was arranged as a fixed price offer, at 165p, and raised £294 million for the Government. As was now also commonplace the offer was oversubscribed, by 8.3 times. Setting the share price so as to avoid large oversubscription and stagging gains for those investors fortunate to receive shares remained a real difficulty for the privatisation programme. Also, the Jaguar sale was accompanied by some controversy over multiple applications and applications in bogus names. Hill Samuel, the receiving bank, identified 25,000 multiple applications but the British Leyland Board maintained that there was evidence of the existence of a much larger number of bogus applications to benefit from the priority given to small investors when allocating the shares.[83]

Unipart, the parts division of BL, was sold to a management team in January 1987 for £30 million with additional future payments linked to a profits target and a possible stock market flotation (perhaps this reflected the large returns made by management and employees of the National Freight Corporation privatised through a buyout in 1981 and where no facility was included for the Government to share in either the subsequent unexpectedly high profits or the results of a future stock market offer).[84] Leyland Bus was sold in the same month to a consortium involving management, employees and banks, for £4 million (but in this case with apparently no facility for Government to share in future profits; perhaps the Government judged, correctly, that there was less scope for big profits in bus production). In April 1987 British Leyland Trucks was merged with the Dutch vehicle manufacturer DAF with BL continuing to hold 40 per cent of the new company. Also, May 1987 saw a Danish bus manufacturing subsidiary of BL, DAB, sold off through a management buyout for £7 million, and in June there was the disposal of the computer services business of BL, Istel for £26 million, again through a management buyout.[85]

During the 1983–7 Government there were also further sales of the Government's holding of shares in BP. The first sales had occurred in 1977 and 1979, reducing the Government's shareholding to 46 per cent. In September 1983 the Government sold a further seven per cent of the shares, lowering its holding further from 39 per cent to 32 per cent (a rights issue not taken up by the Government in June 1981 had reduced its holding from 46 per cent). The offer was a tender issue and the offer was 1.3 times oversubscribed at the striking price of 435p per share. The sale raised £566 million. Tender issues are less prone to under-pricing because of the mechanism by which the share price is set, as discussed earlier, chapter 4, pp.96–7. However, the Government continued to prefer fixed price offers, especially where it was keen to attract large numbers of small investors, as did the City.

An area of growing sensitivity for the Government concerned the amounts paid to advisers, including merchant banks, underwriters and stockbrokers. This led the Treasury in February 1984 to issue formal guidance to departments on the appointments procedure. The guidance stressed the need for "satisfactory competition" for advisory posts, including inviting those interested to make their interest known by announcements in the financial press, the drawing up of shortlists in consultation with the Treasury and the Bank of England, and the use of competitive interviews.[86] The Government also turned to new methods for selling shares to City institutions and in arranging underwriting terms to maximise revenues and reduce flotation costs, as detailed in later chapters.

Table 8.2 summarises the main privatisations undertaken from May 1979 until June 1987 and the amounts raised.[87] When sales of government land and buildings are included (but excluding the sale of council homes), the total revenue to the Exchequer from asset disposals amounted to around £28.5 billion. However, privatisation policy during the second Thatcher Government did not simply embrace the sale of assets, it also included the extension of competitive tendering for public services.

## Competitive tendering

As Lawson confirms in his memoirs, "there were never any plans for the wholesale transfer of public services to the private sector".[88] However, the idea of competitive tendering for a range of government activities continued after 1983. Competitive tendering involved "market testing" public sector provision by requiring the in-house provider to compete periodically for the service contract. The result might be that the winning bid was submitted by a private

*Table 8.2* The major privatisation sales 1979–87

| | Date of sale | Method of sale | Remaining government shareholding* | Net proceeds (£ million) |
|---|---|---|---|---|
| Amersham International | Feb 1982 | Fixed price offer 100 per cent | Nil[a] | 64 |
| Associated British Ports | Feb 1983 | Fixed price offer 51.5 per cent | 48.5 per cent | 46 |
| | Apr 1984 | Tender offer 48.5 per cent | Nil | 51 |
| British Aerospace | Feb 1981 | Fixed price offer 51.6 per cent | 48.4 per cent | 43 |
| | May 1985 | Fixed price offer 48.4 per cent | Nil[a] | 346 |
| British Airways | Feb 1987 | Fixed price offer 100 per cent | Nil | 871 |
| British Petroleum | Oct 1979 | Fixed price offer 5 per cent | 46 per cent | 276 |
| | Jun 1981 | Sales of government rights in a rights issue | 39 per cent | 8 |
| | Sep 1983 | Tender offer 7 per cent | 31.7 | 543 |
| British Telecom | Nov 1984 | Fixed price offer 50.2 per cent | 49.8[a,b] | 3,693[b] |
| Britoil | Nov 1982 | Tender offer 51 per cent | 49 per cent | 627 |
| | Aug 1985 | Fixed price offer 49 per cent | Nil[a] | 426 |
| Cable and Wireless | Oct 1981 | Fixed price offer 49 per cent | 50 per cent[c] | 182 |
| | Dec 1983[d] | Tender offer 22.3 per cent | 23 per cent | 263 |
| | Dec 1985 | Fixed price offer 22.7 per cent | Nil[a] | 580 |
| Enterprise Oil | Jun 1984 | Tender offer 100 per cent | Nil[a] | 380 |
| National Enterprise Board assets | From 1979 | Private sales | n/a | n/a |
| National Freight Co. | Feb 1982 | Management-led buyout | Nil | 5 |
| Rolls-Royce | May 1987 | Fixed price offer 100 per cent | Nil[a] | 1080[i] |
| **Subsidiaries**[e] | | | | |
| *British Airways' subsidiaries:* | | | | |
| International Aeradio | Mar 1983 | Sold to Standard Telephone & Cables | Nil | 60 |
| British Airways Helicopters | Sep 1986 | Sold to SDR Helicopters | Nil | 14 |

| | | | | |
|---|---|---|---|---|
| British Gas Corporation's Wytch Farm onshore oilfield | May 1984 | Sold to a group of bidders | Nil | 82 |
| *British Rail subsidiaries:* | | | | |
| Hotels | Mar 1983 and thereafter | Private sale | Nil | 45 |
| Sealink | Jul 1984 | Sold to British Ferries | Nil[a] | 66 |
| British Shipbuilders' warship yards | May 1985 to Mar 1986 | Private sales[f] | Nil | 75 |
| British Steel Corporation's rationalisation and disposal programme | 1980 onwards | Private sale and establishment of joint ventures with private sector | Nil[g] | 592 |
| National Bus Company subsidiaries | Aug 1986 onwards | Each subsidiary sold separately *f* | Nil | n/a |
| *Rover Group subsidiaries* | | | | |
| Jaguar[h] | Jul 1984 | Fixed price offer 100 per cent | Nil[a] | 297 |
| Unipart | Jan 1987 | Private sale | Nil | 30[i] |
| Leyland Bus | Jan 1987 | Private sale | Nil | 4[i] |
| Leyland Trucks | Apr 1987 | Private sale | Nil | 0 |

*Key*

a  The Government retained a special share.

b  Residual shareholding also included £750 million of preference shares and £2,750 million of loan stock.

c  45 per cent from March 1983 when government waived any entitlement to new shares in a rights issue.

d  An issue of new shares in February 1983 reduced the Government's shareholding from 50.6 per cent to 45 per cent.

e  Proceeds of sales of subsidiaries were normally retained by the parent company.

f  Subsidiaries were retained by the parent company for a time until sold.

g  The Corporation retained a share in a number of the joint ventures established with the private sector.

h  Rover Group was known as BL at the time of sale.

i  Gross receipts.

*Note:*

* Excluding any shares held to meet bonus issue commitments under share purchase investor schemes.

sector company – in which case the service was "contracted out" – but it was also possible that the in-house provider retained the work by lodging the most competitive bid. In this case the service remained publicly provided but typically at a lower cost.

Putting more government services out to competitive tender had begun during the 1979–83 Government, largely to reduce costs and cut the number of public sector workers.[89] Under the Local Government Planning and Land Act 1980, local authority direct labour organisations (DLOs) were required to bid for a proportion of their work in competition with the private sector. The outcome was that staff numbers in DLOs fell, by 11 per cent. In addition, 16 local authorities, led by Southend, Ealing and Wandsworth voluntarily put a number of other services out to tender. By 1985 Conservative-controlled Wandsworth in London had privatised 13 services, starting with street cleaning.[90] However, Labour-controlled councils generally remained strongly opposed to competitive tendering for public services. Also, under the first Thatcher Government departments were pressured to outsource more of their operations and in the NHS a series of pilot experiments on contracting had begun in each Regional Health Authority. In 1982/3 about £160 million of work was contracted out in the NHS with building and engineering maintenance accounting for £110 million.[91]

One impediment to the expansion of contracting out in the NHS and central government (although not local government) in the first half of the 1980s was the payment of VAT on bought-in services but not on in-house operations. This tended to make in-house provision more cost-effective.[92] A measure to rectify this was dropped from the 1983 Finance Bill with the calling of the General Election and instead the Treasury enabled VAT refunds to be claimed by extra statutory concession. The concession was given statutory authority in the 1984 Finance Act, levelling the VAT position for outsourced and in-house services.

Another obstacle was the Transfer of Undertaking (Protection of Employment) Regulations 1981 (TUPE), which derived from an EEC's Acquired Rights Directive. Under the regulation employees' employment rights were protected where the ownership of an undertaking was transferred. This extended to continued enjoyment of the existing terms and conditions of employment after a transfer. The regulation had already raised some difficulties regarding the sale of government establishments, such as research laboratories, to the private sector during the first Thatcher administration. It became an issue again immediately after the 1983 General Election, during the planning of the sale of heavy goods vehicle testing to the private sector. In June Tom King, Secretary of State for Transport, alerted the Chancellor of the Exchequer to "a nasty problem that has just arisen, which could cause problems for our plans for privatisation of civil service activities". In this case it seemed that the civil servants who transferred would need either to be offered large cash sums to voluntarily agree to transfer to the private sector on new terms of employment or be guaranteed civil service conditions of employment, including redundancy terms, for the remainder of their careers. A private sector company was most unlikely to be willing to offer civil service terms.[93] Initially, the first Thatcher Government had adopted the stance that the provision did not apply to government services contracted out. But by now it was clear that this was open to legal challenge.[94] The scope of TUPE would continue to create some uncertainty during the development of the Government's strategy on the outsourcing of public services during the second half of the 1980s, especially where private contractors were likely to want to impose lower rates of pay and change working conditions such as hours of work and holiday entitlement.

The Cabinet turned to the issue of contracting out immediately after the 1983 General Election.[95] From October 1983 local authorities were required under the 1980 Act to seek tenders for at least half of their building and maintenance work.[96] In February 1984 Patrick Jenkin, the Secretary of State for the Environment, provided a paper to E(A) Sub-Committee which included the possibility of legislation to compel local authorities to contract out more services "by withdrawing their power to provide the service themselves". However, he recognised that this "would be a controversial political step and provocative to local authorities". Also, the employers' body, the CBI, indicated that they were opposed to compelling local authorities to contract out to the private sector because of the ill-feeling towards private firms that might result within local government. Another alternative would be a statutory right for private firms to tender for local authority services, an option favoured by the Institute of Directors. But this proposal faced "administrative problems . . . and it might be difficult to draw up a satisfactory legal framework". Therefore Jenkin favoured a third option and one which would build on the approach adopted under the 1980 Local Government Act. This would require competitive tendering for more specified services provided by DLOs.[97]

The proposal met with an enthusiastic reception in the No.10 Policy Unit, but the PM was hesitant about introducing legislation, recognising that it would prove highly contentious and that some Conservative councillors might resent the loss of local discretion. In a further paper by Jenkin sent to the Chancellor of the Exchequer in February of the following year, 1985, again proposals were put forward to extend compulsory competitive tendering in local government, along with measures to ensure that councils did not unfairly favour bids submitted by their DLOs.[98] The PM now supported taking forward the proposal.[99] However, the necessary legislation would not be passed until after the 1987 General Election.

The 1983–7 Government did renew attempts to raise the level of contracting out in the NHS.[100] From September 1983 all health authorities were asked to draw up programmes to implement compulsory tendering for cleaning, catering and laundry work in hospitals; though in the NHS progress was obstructed by the suspicions of many health authorities and the opposition of the health sector unions.[101] There were also efforts to encourage central government departments to tender competitively for work traditionally undertaken in-house. On a number of occasions between 1983 and 1987 the Government announced initiatives aimed at the award of more contracts by government departments to private sector firms. For example, on 14 January 1985 the Chief Secretary, Peter Rees, put forward proposals aimed at ensuring that central government offered more work to the private sector.[102] The new initiative was announced to the House of Commons a little later, on 4 March, during a debate on public expenditure. Five services were singled out for what was now increasingly referred to by Ministers as "market testing", namely cleaning, laundry, catering, security and some kinds of maintenance work. Following this announcement, detailed guidance was issued to government departments, which were expected to draw up plans to subject most of the specified services to competitive tendering by April 1987. On 31 July 1985 the Chief Secretary was able to report to the PM that for the five listed services, an estimated £176 million or 46 per cent of the total spend would be contracted out by the year end.[103] However, a subsequent note from No. 10 to the Treasury expressed disappointment that the average cost saving resulting from competitive tendering was surprisingly low.[104] In 1984/5 an estimated £3.7 million only was saved through contracting out, although there may have been some additional savings when services were subjected to competitive tender but remained in-house.[105] Table 8.3 confirms that only a modest annual contribution was made by competitive tendering to reducing central government costs between 1980 and 1986.

*Table 8.3* Savings in central government from competitive tendering 1980–6 (£ million)

|            | 1980/1 | 1981/2 | 1982/3 | 1983/4 | 1984/5 | 1985/6 |
|------------|--------|--------|--------|--------|--------|--------|
| Actual     | 0.6    | 7.5    | 4.5    | 3.6    | 3.7    | 2.1    |
| Cumulative | 0.6    | 8.1    | 12.6   | 16.2   | 19.9   | 22.0   |

*Source*: "Using Private Enterprise in Government: Report of a multi-departmental review of competitive tendering and contracting for services in Government Departments", August 1986, in E(DL) Part 14. A detailed breakdown of competitive tendering savings in each government department can be found in "Draft Cabinet Paper on Contracting Out: Using Private Enterprise in Government. Memorandum by the Chief Secretary, Treasury", E(DL) Part 10.

On 19 December 1985 John MacGregor, who had replaced Peter Rees as Chief Secretary to the Treasury in September, wrote to Ministers in charge of departments noting that "we need to do more". A multi-departmental review was commissioned led by the No. 10 Efficiency Unit, which reported to the PM on 4 August 1986.[106] The results of the study revealed that Departments had so far concentrated on introducing contracting out in the five services.[107] However, for substantial savings to occur, the report concluded that the scope of the policy would need to be widened. It also confirmed a continuing "widespread prejudice in the civil service against the use of contractors".[108] There was a perception in at least some parts of the civil service that contracting out would lead to poorer quality services.

The report was circulated to departments in mid-September 1986[109] and the Government's Central Unit on Purchasing (CUP) issued detailed guidelines on competitive tendering and contracting out.[110] However, successful mass picketing by TGWU members at the Huyton local health and social security office in Liverpool in April 1986 over the award of a cleaning contract to a company which paid lower wages than the public sector, confirmed that determined unions could seriously hinder implementation. In spite of Government support, the contractor withdrew. The PM demanded that immediate steps be taken to prevent another successful union action, including using the full legal powers open to Government to prevent mass picketing.[111] Elsewhere progress in putting new activities out to tender proved slow in spite of Treasury exhortations. In October 1987 a report from the CUP, updating progress on using private enterprise in government, showed that only 19 out of 44 departments reported any new market testing during 1986/7, with the largest single amount being accounted for by the Ministry of Defence.[112]

Meanwhile, the Treasury was reporting slow progress with contracting out in local government and while in the NHS just over a half of health authority support services had now been subjected to competitive tendering, annual savings there were estimated at a mere £52 million, split between £22 million where outside contractors were used and £30 million when the in-house unit won the work.[113] In other words, competitive tendering expanded the scope of privatisation during the second Thatcher Government, but its impact remained limited by especially the attitude of government officials, Labour councils and the trade unions to resorting to the private sector for the provision of public services. After the 1987 General Election a renewed attempt would be made to expand "market testing".

## The welfare state

A clear no-go area for privatisation during the second Thatcher Government, as during the first, was the welfare state. A group of right-wing MPs published a document called

*No Turning Back* at the end of 1986, in which they called for the extension of the free market to health and education, and the Institute of Economic Affairs and the Adam Smith Institute lobbied for a more radical approach to the reform of the welfare state. The ASI published its so-called OMEGA file in 1983, which detailed the possibilities for market-led reforms in every area of government.[114] Also, the Treasury believed that slimming down the welfare state was necessary if there was ever to be a low tax economy and a number of academics waded in pointing to inefficiencies and inequities within the existing welfare system.[115] But there was little response from Government.[116] The PM's promise to maintain the NHS, following the leaked CPRS report to the Cabinet in September 1982, had removed any real prospect of radical measures in health care, beyond competitive tendering and the continued selling-off of surplus land and buildings. Rather the Government focused on deflecting continuing public concern about the Government's long-term intentions towards the NHS by claiming to spend more on the NHS than ever before. During the 1987 General Election campaign the PM boasted about spending £15 billion on health compared to £8 billion in 1979, an increase of around 30 per cent in real terms.[117] Thatcher would have liked to have seen a greater reliance on private health care, but her political antennae told her that running down the NHS was certain to lose her vast numbers of votes. Norman Fowler, Health and Social Security Secretary from September 1981 to June 1987, summed up a wider belief amongst Cabinet Ministers that "the National Health Service should remain at the centre of the health-care system and that politically we would reap the whirlwind if we could be portrayed as moving away from it".[118]

Instead of privatisation, efforts were made to modernise the management of the NHS and economies were sought without damaging front-line services; for example in November 1984 a number of branded drugs were taken off prescription. In early 1983 Roy Griffiths, the Chief Executive of the grocer retailing group Sainsbury's, agreed to head an inquiry into the management of the NHS. His report called for a devolvement of decision making and the introduction of professional management across the service. Subsequently a middle tier of management was removed. But being one of the world's largest employers and riddled with political sensitivities, managing the NHS would remain a formidable challenge even for the most seasoned of professional managers. Victor Paige, earlier at the National Freight Corporation, became the first chief executive officer of the NHS following the Griffiths Report, but resigned in frustration in 1986. In the same year a Green Paper was published on the provision of primary services which envisaged making it easier for patients to change doctors and changes in the way doctors were paid. This formed the basis for legislation after the 1987 Election.

There was also to be no serious encroachment of market forces into state education. Sir Keith Joseph, Secretary of State for Education until he retired from the Government in May 1986, favoured the introduction of education vouchers, as did Thatcher.[119] This was an idea promoted by the monetarist economist Professor Milton Friedman and involved the Government giving parents a voucher to pay for all or part of their children's education. Schools would then compete to attract pupils and their vouchers. The intention was that the result would be real choice for parents of the schools their children attended. At the 1981 Party Conference Joseph confirmed his interest in introducing educational vouchers to promote parental choice. However, the Department of Education and Science was not enthusiastic and the idea was strongly opposed by the teaching unions.[120] At the Conservative Party Conference in the autumn of 1983 he announced that the idea was "dead", much to the dismay of his free market supporters.[121] When Joseph later suggested that contributions towards the education of university students should be increased from better off parents, middle-class mums and dads protested and more than half the Parliamentary party eventually voted against the proposal.[122] However, the universities and students did not escape cuts in Government funding per student. This led to protests from academics about the damage to higher education. In January 1985 Margaret Thatcher was proposed for an honorary degree at her alma mater, Oxford University, but the dons voted to withhold it in retaliation for her policies. Thatcher never forgave the snub. Sometime after leaving No. 10 she retaliated by donating her personal papers to Cambridge, not Oxford.

In July 1985 Joseph proposed a scheme for a small number of government-maintained primary schools to be set up by charitable trusts or sponsored by entrepreneurs and which would be able to charge modest fees. This too came to nothing.[123] Also, quickly forgotten was a suggested scheme to make payments to local education authorities based on the level of educational attainment.[124] The 1980 Education Act had introduced the Assisted Places scheme to enable a small number of bright children from poor backgrounds to go to independent schools and in 1986 a new Act established governing bodies for schools to bring about more management autonomy from local authorities.[125] At the Conservative Party Conference in the autumn of 1986 the Education Secretary who replaced Joseph when he retired from the Government the previous May, Kenneth Baker, announced the establishment of around 20 City Technology Colleges with enhanced state funding. However, in most respects state education continued much as before between 1983 and 1987 with comprehensive schools remaining the dominant mode of state secondary education. Reform was generally limited to replacing the school leaving certificates GCEs and CSEs with a new one, the GCSE, changes to teacher training, the introduction of a new technical and vocational education initiative (TVEI) to address the lack of vocational skills training for the young, and more parental involvement in the management of schools. Also, the reforms that did occur have to be set alongside the changes in state spending on education which occurred between 1979 and 1986. Total expenditure on schools rose in real terms when expressed as spending per pupil. The result was a fall in the pupil-teacher ratio from 19.1 in 1979 to 17.6 in 1986. However, shortly after Joseph resigned as Education Secretary the ninth annual report of Her Majesty's Inspectorate of Schools revealed that around a quarter of schools were suffering from inadequate resources and that 30 per cent of lessons were unsatisfactory.[126]

During the first Thatcher Government pensions had been indexed to prices rather than earnings to reduce the growing financial burden placed on the welfare state caused by people living longer. Following the 1983 Election the Treasury pressed for more expenditure savings and the outcome was a reappraisal of the social security system including pensions led by the Secretary of State for Social Services, Norman Fowler. This took the form of four separate reviews of different parts of the system and included Ministers, officials and some outsiders. The review was heralded by the Government as the most substantial examination of the social security system since the Beveridge report 40 years earlier and within Government was overseen in its later stages by a specially convened Cabinet Committee, MISC 111, chaired by the PM. But in reality its scope was heavily constrained by commitments given by Ministers during the 1983 General Election campaign not to cut old age pensions, widows' benefits, industrial injury benefits and invalidity payments – amounting to about 60 per cent of the social security budget.[127] Also, the Chancellor of the Exchequer refused to allow the review to consider funding issues because taxes and national insurance were a matter for the Treasury. This led to a number of turf rows between Fowler and Lawson.[128]

During the review and just before Fowler's proposals were about to be presented to Cabinet, Treasury Ministers became interested in the prospect of significant savings in the social security budget; savings of up to £2 billion became the objective. However, Fowler was more concerned about improving the targeting of welfare benefits. The review had identified overlapping purposes and different entitlement conditions in the state welfare system. The review quickly centred on the future of pensions, support for low income families and the special payments system, under which welfare beneficiaries could make claims to buy emergency items such as cookers.[129] The product was the Social Security Act 1986, which was fully implemented in 1988. The Act ended the Death Grant (payable to assist funeral costs), replaced emergency grants to the poor with loans, cut back housing benefit and replaced supplementary benefit and family income supplement with income support and family credit. The aim was to better target benefits to where they were most needed; but subsequently both family credit and income support would suffer from a disappointing level of take up. There were some financial savings, mainly due to changes to housing benefit, but the overall result of the Act was to trim a mere £750 million or so from the social security budget of £36 billion and much less than the Treasury had hoped for. By 1988 social security spending had risen since 1979 by about 30 per cent in real terms, driven largely by higher unemployment and invalidity benefits (the long-term unemployed not infrequently registered as too sick to work as the eligibility for unemployment pay was tightened), increased numbers of pensioners and more lone parents.

In addition to reforming social security, the Fowler reforms attempted to address the future of old age pensions. Around ten million people relied only on state provision and had no additional pension funds. In the Green Paper in June 1985 (*The Reform of Social Security*, Cmnd. 9517), in which he set out his proposed changes to social security, Fowler proposed the abolition of the State Earnings Related Pension Scheme (SERPS). SERPS had been introduced by the Labour Government in 1975 to help those who did not benefit from an occupational pension, but it threatened to become unaffordable without a sharp rise in taxation as the number of pensioners rose. By the mid-1980s there were 625,000 more pensioners than five years earlier and it was forecast that the number of pensioners was set to rise from nine million to over 12 million by 2025. Fowler proposed replacing SERPS with personal pensions to which employees and employers would be required to contribute, an idea the PM initially promoted.[130] However, the Treasury baulked at the potential cost of compulsory private provision not least to the Exchequer in terms of the tax relief on pension contributions.[131] Also, opposition came from representatives of employers concerned about the costs of compulsory contributions, as well as from the unions who wanted to keep SERPS.[132] In the event, widespread opposition to the abolition of SERPS both inside and outside Government meant that the scheme was simply scaled back. The proportion of earnings on which the pension was based was reduced from 25 per cent to 20 per cent and incentives were provided to "contract out" of SERPS. As a carrot to contract out, the Treasury agreed to a two per cent national insurance incentive to those employees who set up a personal pension voluntarily – which further diminished the prospects that the Fowler review would bring about fiscal benefits. The new pensions regime took effect in January 1988.[133] However, the problem of funding adequate pensions did not go away and in the 1990s controversy would erupt over the mis-selling of personal pensions by over-enthusiastic insurance companies.

Elsewhere the Government continued to intervene to provide special job creation measures including training and assistance for the unemployed. For example, the Youth Training

Scheme (YTS) was introduced to offer training to those who did not proceed from school to university or college and other measures were adopted with the objective of encouraging the unemployed off the dole. Noteworthy was the so-called Restart programme, which tightened up the basis on which unemployment benefits were paid and paved the way for the later Job Seekers Allowance.[134] But such changes, even when successful, were not the hallmarks of an out-and-out reform of the welfare state. When John Moore was promoted to Secretary of State for Health and Social Security following the June 1987 General Election, he believed that Thatcher wanted him to adopt a radical approach to the welfare state, as he had done towards the nationalised industries when Financial Secretary. Whether this is really what Thatcher had in mind must be uncertain given her cautious position on welfare reform, but in any case, like his predecessors, Moore quickly became swamped by day-to-day administration and would later succumb to ill health.

Between May 1983 and June 1987 the Thatcher Government was a benevolent steward of the welfare state, just like the Conservative administrations before it. At a time when privatisation was proceeding rapidly in industry, the welfare state remained out of bounds. This would continue to be the position after June 1987.

\* \* \*

The 1983–87 Conservative government saw privatisation entrenched as a central component of the Government's economic strategy. While raising revenue for the Government remained an important objective and annual disposal targets were part of budgetary policy, the importance of raising economic efficiency was now more evident as a primary rationale for privatisation than it had been under the first Thatcher Government. Also, not only were state industries operating in competitive markets lined up to be sold off, as before, but the Government embarked on the privatisation of the big state monopolies. This necessitated the creation of new regulatory structures.

The following chapters deal in detail with the main privatisations between 1983 and 1987, of British Airways, Rolls-Royce, shipbuilding and the Royal Dockyards, bus transport, the Royal Ordnance Factories, British Telecommunications and British Gas.

# 9

# PRIVATISING BRITISH AIRWAYS, ROLLS-ROYCE, SHIPBUILDING AND THE ROYAL DOCKYARDS

The previous chapter provided an overview of privatisation activity between 1983 and 1987. In this and the following chapter a more detailed account is provided of a number of the major privatisations undertaken by the second Thatcher Government, namely British Airways, Rolls-Royce, shipbuilding including the naval dockyards, and bus transport and the Royal Ordnance Factories. Each of these privatisations involved specific challenges and difficulties. For example, the sales of the shipyards and the Royal Dockyards and the privatisation of bus services were particularly drawn out and not completed until after the 1987 General Election.

The privatisations of British Airways, Rolls-Royce, bus transport, shipbuilding and the Royal Dockyards, and the Royal Ordnance illustrate how each privatisation faced its own set of problems, which had to be addressed before a sale could be completed. The disposal of the Royal Ordnance factories, in particular, emphasises how the initial privatisation plans had to be materially altered in the face of practical problems in selling the business. However, each privatisation provided useful learning experience, although as pointed out earlier, the use of different teams of civil servants across different departments within Government to privatise each industry inevitably reduced the extent to which this experience was shared across Government to the benefit of later privatisations. The Treasury provided some continuity, but as the NAO commented on the Royal Ordnance sale: "While we accept that departments are responsible for arranging privatisations, the Treasury should in future do more to ensure that experience gained and lessons learned from past privatisations are passed on to departments."[1]

The privatisations reviewed in these two chapters were important milestones in the evolution of privatisation as policy in the 1980s. But they are overshadowed in any assessment of privatisation during the second Thatcher administration by the sales of British Telecom in November 1984 and British Gas in November 1986, which are the subjects of later chapters.

## British Airways

British Airways (BA) was established in 1972 through a merger of the two state-owned airlines, British Overseas Airways Corporation and British European Airways. But the merger was plagued with difficulties and by the late 1970s the Corporation had an unenviable reputation for poor service quality and reliability. The Corporation's financial difficulties were compounded by the high costs of flying the supersonic aircraft, Concorde, which BA had been required by the Government to buy in the early 1970s.[2]

The possibility of denationalising BA had not featured in the Conservatives' Election Manifesto in May 1979. But immediately after the General Election the Secretary of State for Trade, John Nott, commissioned a study of the possibility of introducing private sector capital. Immediately before the Election he had speculated on the possibility of selling some shares in BA, including to employees.[3] BA had embarked on a major programme of fleet replacement and expansion, which was likely to cost £2.4 billion over the following five years. The airline therefore became an immediately attractive candidate for disposal. It was intended that selling shares in BA should remove its future borrowings from the PSBR. There were also Ministers that took the view that BA was a commercial organisation and should therefore be in the private not the public sector, while private sector airlines, notably British Caledonian, complained about competing against a state-backed BA.[4]

The future of the Corporation was first discussed at Cabinet level in E(DL) Sub-Committee in late June 1979 and then in July, when the Trade Secretary John Nott suggested that a sale of shares in BA would both help contribute to the Chancellor's funding target and "in developing a successful commercial organisation".[5] The objective at this time was to sell up to 49 per cent of the shares in a new company created out of the public corporation with some shares distributed to the airline's employees to meet the Government's objective of widening share ownership. The Government was to retain a majority, 51 per cent, holding, but at the same time the aim would be to disengage the state from intervention in the airline as far as possible so as to facilitate its commercial management.[6] A sale of a majority shareholding to the private sector was ruled out because it "would more likely be seen as 'denationalisation' and attract a hostile reaction".[7] It seems that Nott's position was that BA was the national flag carrier and should remain under state control. This is consistent with the tentative approach adopted to other privatisations in the early months of the first Thatcher Government, when it was uncertain how the City, the unions and the public would react to the selling of state industries. It was also the case that BA's Chairman, Ross Stainton, had urged that to reduce union opposition to the plan the Government should retain a majority of the shares and "it should not involve dismemberment of the airline". There should be no breaking up of BA.[8] However, it soon became clear that Treasury Ministers preferred that no definite decision should be reached on the proportion of the shares to be sold off until the effect of retaining Government control of the company on the treatment of the Corporation's finances and the PSBR was clarified.[9]

Parliament was informed of the Government's decision to sell shares in BA on 20 July 1979, making BA the first privatisation to be announced.[10] The following year the Civil Aviation Act was passed empowering the Government to transfer BA's assets and liabilities to a new company, British Airways Limited.[11] The intention remained to sell only a minority of BA's shares in the first instance – possibly 49 per cent – with the Government retaining the rest. Whether a majority of the shares would eventually be sold remained uncertain.[12] But in any case the plan to proceed quickly to a share flotation collapsed during the 1980 economic recession. In November 1980 the airline recorded a loss of £2 million and by early 1981 revenue was forecast to be some £400 million below that which BA had originally budgeted.[13] At the same time, the Treasury's view strengthened that a majority of the shares in a state enterprise would have to be transferred to the private sector to remove its borrowings from the PSBR.

The economic state of BA meant that an immediate sale of shares was out of the question. Nevertheless, during the autumn of 1981 Nicholas Ridley, Financial Secretary to the Treasury, called on the Department of Trade to bring forward the flotation of the airline, "even if that meant we were selling it rather cheap".[14] However, the Department's financial advisers, Hill Samuel, argued that privatisation was unlikely to be feasible until BA's profitability was restored. The Corporation's debt burden was so unsatisfactory that it was unlikely privatisation could occur before there was a major capital reconstruction including the writing off of older aircraft, notably the Lockheed Tristar fleet.[15]

In an attempt to turn around the airline's fortunes, in February 1981 Sir John King was recruited by the Government as the new Chairman of BA to replace Ross Stainton, who was retiring.[16] King had business experience, most recently as chairman of Babcock and Wilcox, and arrived with a brief to prepare BA for privatisation (he was elevated to the peerage in 1983). Shortly after his arrival he restructured the BA Board removing nine of its 14 existing members including the sole trade union representative and recruiting replacements from the private sector. In 1983 Sir Colin Marshall, with a background in Hertz and Avis, was brought in by King as BA's Chief Executive, along with other new management with experience in consumer marketing.[17]

The first objective of the new management team was to stem the airline's losses. By 1982 its workforce had already shrunk to 41,000 compared with 56,000 in 1980 and in that year a radical restructuring plan was announced, involving further job losses, reduced capital expenditure and asset sales, including the sale of aircraft to plug the yawning gap in the airline's finances and to rationalise the fleet.[18] In January 1983 another round of redundancies was announced to shrink the airline's employment by a further 2,000.[19] Also, during that year the airline was reorganised around eight profit centres, based on geographic regions and businesses and King set about improving the airline's marketing and reversing its lamentable reputation for poor customer service. All staff were required to attend a "Putting the Customer First" training programme, 51 new and more cost efficient aircraft were purchased or leased and the rest of the fleet was refurbished, catering was upgraded and new staff uniforms, airline livery and corporate logo were introduced to mark a break with the past. The emphasis was put on competing in terms of quality of service rather than price and a new advertising campaign was mounted to change perceptions of the airline, under the guidance of a marketing group created within BA.[20] In 1983 the airline returned to profit-ability.[21] In the spring the Cabinet was informed that a new Civil Aviation Bill would be brought forward in the 1983/4 Parliamentary Session to provide the powers for a capital reconstruction, as a prelude to the airline's privatisation.[22] However, this prospect was immediately overtaken by the calling of the 1983 General Election.

Following the General Election the Government began to plan for the privatisation of BA to take place in the autumn of 1984. However, the Treasury was keen that nothing should be done to deflect attention away from the sale of BT that was scheduled for around the same time. On 11 November 1983 the Chancellor of the Exchequer, Nigel Lawson, wrote to Nicholas Ridley, who became Secretary of State for Transport in October, expressing concerns about stories appearing in the press, "apparently largely inspired by members of the BA Board", which were promoting BA's privatisation at the expense of BT's sale. Lawson noted "I need hardly say that such comments are very unhelpful." While under-standing the Board's desire for an early privatisation in the light of the airline's improved financial results, he asked Ridley to "have a word with John King to dissuade him and his Board from pursuing this line".[23]

In mid-November Ridley circulated a memorandum to members of E(DL) Sub-Committee setting out proposals for the flotation of BA. The proposals were aimed at ensuring that a sale could go ahead the following autumn should the privatisation of BT be postponed for any reason, otherwise it would have to occur later. Statutory provision to establish BA plc already existed under the 1980 Civil Aviation Act and Ridley was keen to make progress by setting 1 April 1984 as the vesting day for the new company.

However, although BA's finances were recovering, with expected profits of £150 million in 1983/4 after interest and tax, the Corporation still had a negative net worth of £1.2 billion. In the absence of a capital reconstruction before privatisation, the state of the airline's balance sheet would rule out any real prospect of a successful flotation.[24] Ridley hoped that BA would go ahead with a revaluation of its assets and possibly repair its balance sheet with some further voluntary asset sales. There was also always the possibility of the airline issuing some new shares at flotation to repay some of its debt. But Ridley also considered applying to the Companies' Court for a write-down of BA's capital, leaving the Government with less than a 50 per cent shareholding. However, there were concerns in No. 10 that this action would be heavily criticised in Parliament as privatisation by the back door.[25]

Ridley's ultimate aim was a disposal of BA's entire share capital, but the advice from his financial advisers was that such a flotation could not go ahead without a significant capital reconstruction first. Also, a further obstacle to an early sale had now emerged involving a legal dispute over the collapse of Laker Airways. The British entrepreneur Freddie Laker had set up an airline offering cut-price air fares on cross-Atlantic routes in the 1970s, which had collapsed in February 1982.[26] The allegation was that BA and certain other airlines had acted unfairly to force Laker out of the market. Anti-trust law suits had been mounted against BA and the other airlines in the US courts. As the seriousness of the legal challenge became apparent – with the possibility of treble damages and penalties in the US in excess of $1 billion – plans to privatise BA had to be put on hold.[27] There was also another potentially serious obstacle to a sale at this time, the issue of future competition on air routes from the UK.

Under the 1980 Civil Aviation Act, the Civil Aviation Authority, (CAA) the country's air traffic regulator, was required to have regard to ensuring "that British airlines compete as effectively as possible with other airlines in providing air transport services on international routes".[28] As it became clear that the Government was committed to privatising BA, the CAA became concerned about the competitive threat that the privatised airline would pose given its dominance of air routes between the UK and a number of international destinations. In particular, BA held a large share of the landing slots at Heathrow, Britain's and one of Europe's most popular airports. The Chairman of BA's main domestic rival, the airline British Caledonian (BCal), was also very concerned. Sir Adam Thomson made it known that while he welcomed the prospect of BA transferring from state control, he was troubled by the idea of competing with BA privatised with a greatly strengthened balance sheet following a capital reconstruction. He suggested that BCal should be compensated by being allowed to take over certain of BA's routes.[29] Governments had pursued a "second force" policy in the airlines industry since the Edwards Report in 1969 on the future of British aviation[30] – encouraging the development of BCal as a second UK airline to BA – and in effect Thomson was arguing that this was now at risk. The idea of route transfers to benefit BCal received some support within Government. In particular, the PM and Ridley were sympathetic so as to build up BCal as a more viable second force to BA in the British airline sector. However, he had no powers to bring about route changes except to try and persuade BA to offer them. It seems that Ridley hoped to trade some amendment of routes for agreeing to the capital reconstruction BA considered it needed.[31]

E(DL) Sub-Committee considered Ridley's privatisation proposals on 24 November 1983. After discussion it was agreed that he should announce a date for BA's privatisation of early 1985, although this might be advanced if the sale of British Telecom slipped. Vesting day would be 1 April 1984 and meanwhile BA should be encouraged to restructure its balance sheet voluntarily. In addition, E(DL) confirmed that it was unwilling to sanction an approach to the courts for a capital write-down because it would be likely to be "seen as a device for avoiding Parliamentary scrutiny and as doubtful financial practice". There was also some opposition to the idea of engineering route transfers from BA to BCal because it was felt that one powerful British airline would be able to compete more successfully with international competitors than two UK airlines. Also, some Ministers feared that forcing through route transfers could damage morale within BA. It was agreed that the Secretary of State should explore the possibility of route transfers to BCal with Sir John King, but there could be no question of compelling BA to divest routes or of making privatisation contingent on such transfers. It was decided that route transfers were properly a matter for decision by the CAA.[32] Under the Civil Aviation Act 1980 the CAA was responsible for route licensing.

The decision in E(DL) on 24 November to reject a compulsory capital write-down through the courts led John Redwood in the No. 10 Policy Unit to complain that, "One way or another, in order to sell British Airways the balance sheet has to be reconstructed."[33] In his view waiting for the balance sheet to be turned around through profit accumulation could only delay privatisation. This led the PM to suggest that further work should be done on the question of a capital reconstruction.[34] Meanwhile the Treasury hoped that the matter could be settled through a revaluation of BA's assets, which Treasury Ministers considered would be necessary anyway before preparing a prospectus for sale.[35] The decision on vesting and the plans for privatisation were announced by the Secretary of State in the House of Commons on 12 December 1983. However, the statement referred in passing only to the possible need for a capital reconstruction of the airline, with Ridley commenting "I have reached no firm decision about this". The statement reflected uncertainty within Government about how best to proceed.[36]

In line with the decision in E(DL) that the future of airline routes should be a matter for the CAA, the Government asked the CAA to review the implications of privatisation for competition in air travel.[37] The CAA did not report until 16 July 1984. When published its report called for additional competition on intercontinental routes, airlines other than BA to operate from regional airports, action against any future predatory pricing or other anti-competitive practices on the part of BA, and wider licensing powers.[38] The most difficult issue in the report for the Government was a recommendation that BA should be required to relinquish certain air routes. The Government had mistakenly expected that the CAA would not recommend an immediate transfer of routes from BA, but rather some change in the criteria for awarding future route licences. The routes singled out by the CAA for transfer were out of Manchester and Birmingham airports to a large number of destinations in Western Europe, between Glasgow and Paris, between Heathrow and Saudi Arabia, between Heathrow and Harare, and between Gatwick and destinations in Spain, Portugal, Gibraltar, Italy and Scandinavia. With the exception of the Manchester and Birmingham routes, which would go to smaller airlines, the likelihood was that the services would be awarded by the CAA to BCal. The CAA estimated that these transfers would cost BA about seven per cent of its revenue and about £30 million in profits, but considered that without such transfers BCal would have an inherently weak route structure which would prevent it from becoming a serious competitor to BA.[39]

E(A) Sub-Committee considered the report two days after it was published. Some Ministers objected to the short time given to study the CAA's proposals before arriving at a decision, but nevertheless a majority of the Sub-Committee were in favour of accepting the recommendations, except, importantly, for those relating to the route transfers.[40] Ridley was opposed to the route transfer recommendations because he feared they would delay the privatisation of BA and because he was well aware that they would be strongly resisted by the BA Board. However, a meeting of the full Cabinet the following day effectively overturned the decision of E(DL), when it was agreed that the best outcome would be a negotiated compromise in which BA would agree at least some route transfers to BCal.[41] Therefore, over the next few days discussions occurred between the Government and BA over the possibility of offering some route transfers to BCal, although King and the BA Board proved resistant.[42] King was already lobbying hard against the CAA report arguing that it would cost BA heavily in terms of profits and jobs and would certainly jeopardise a privatisation of the Corporation. In an open letter to MPs he raised earlier Government assurances "that there will be no arbitrary reallocation of routes" and that no part of BA "should be broken up or sold off".[43] He equated route transfers with a reneging on this commitment. Reports appeared in the press that if King was forced to agree to route transfers, he would resign.

Discussion resumed in Cabinet on 2 August. Ridley observed that King "showed an arrogance which boded ill for the unrestrained exercise by the airline of its market power after privatisation". Nevertheless, in Ridley's opinion, to give the CAA authority to order reallocations would give the body "too much power . . . and they might well delay or harm the sale of British Airways".[44] The Department of Transport's advisers, Hill Samuel, had warned that the transfer of the Saudi Arabia route might delay privatisation by up to two years because the market would want to see the impact of the transfer on the Corporation's profits. Ridley also believed that the divestment of the Birmingham and Manchester routes for the benefit of smaller international operators should be rejected because of the potentially negative impact on BA's finances.[45]

Ridley met with Sir Adam Thomson to explore what would be the minimum transfer of routes from BA which would be acceptable to BCal. It was established at this meeting that for BCal the most important route was the one to Saudi Arabia, with an estimated profit for 1985/6 of £30 million. It seems that Sir Adam Thomson was much less interested in the other route transfers mentioned in the CAA report, including routes out of Birmingham and Manchester and possibly certain destinations served from Gatwick.[46] Ridley reported to Cabinet that Sir Adam had threatened "that if he got no transfers at all, he would seek to merge with BA". If this merger was then referred to the Monopolies and Mergers Commission and they found against it, Sir Adam had warned that "BCal would decline and eventually be forced out of business". Ridley concluded that to some extent this was a bluff, but the threat clearly worried him.[47] In conclusion, he suggested that it might be possible to proceed with the privatisation of BA as planned if the airline would concede the transfer to BCal of the Gatwick-Iberia routes and possibly the route to Harare. However, it was still the case that King and the rest of the BA Board "were absolutely opposed to [any] transfer". Ridley saw little prospect of convincing them to change their position.

For Ridley the Government now faced a stark choice, either to reject the route transfers recommended by the CAA "and argue that they would add nothing to creating competition in the airline industry" or insist on the transfer of sufficient routes from BA to strengthen

BCal's competitive position in the face of complete opposition from the BA Board. To reject all of the route transfers recommended by the CAA would in all likelihood mean that BCal would seek to merge with BA and if this was blocked it might go out of business. The result would, he concluded, be very undesirable as it would "reduce the pressure on BA to be efficient, and make it harder to liberalise air transport in Europe". At the same time, Ridley recognised that to insist successfully on sufficient route transfers from BA to maintain BCal's competitive position would depend both upon BA's co-operation and BCal agreeing that any route transfers offered were adequate. It was unclear how far the Government had the power to issue a direction to the BA Board to relinquish routes. The Board might refuse to accept such an instruction if they believed that it would entail them breaching their statutory duties. Ridley had concluded the matter could only be put beyond doubt by inserting an appropriate provision in BA's Articles of Association, but this would undoubtedly be highly contentious. It was unlikely, but not inconceivable, that the BA Board would resign over the matter.

In Cabinet there was real concern about the implications of all this for both the privatisation of BA and future competition in the UK airline market. In the end the Cabinet divided on the advisability of forcing BA to transfer routes to BCal and over which routes should be included. To give time for further consideration, the PM suggested that Ministers should return to the issue after the summer recess.[48]

The Cabinet returned to the subject at a meeting on 11 September 1984. Here it was agreed that legislation to force BA to relinquish routes would be undesirably contentious and arguably in breach of undertakings given by the Secretary of State for Trade in July 1979 not to break up BA. The meeting therefore encouraged Ridley to pursue a negotiated "route swap" between BA and BCal and urged him to strengthen the safeguards against future predatory behaviour on the part of BA.[49]

Ridley renewed his difficult discussions with King and Thomson. He was able to report to Cabinet on 4 October that he had with "the greatest of difficulty . . . prevailed upon BA to agree to the transfer of their routes to Saudi Arabia to BCal in exchange for BCal's route to Atlanta in the southern United States and a number of other routes mainly to Latin America". BA had estimated that the deal would reduce its profitability by around £20 million a year in the short run and increase BCal's profits by about £17 million. This could be expected to have an effect on the proceeds from privatising BA of between £80 million and £100 million if the Government were to sell 100 per cent of the shares.[50] However, the route transfers now contemplated were much less favourable to BCal than those proposed by the CAA and BCal indicated that they were unhappy to lose the Atlanta route because it generated some two-thirds of their profits. The Cabinet meeting concluded that Ridley should try and persuade BA to transfer the Saudi Arabia route to BCal while allowing BCal to retain the Atlanta service. If BA were to resist then the only way to force BA to do the deal would be to introduce legislation, even though this would involve "serious drawbacks".[51]

The legislative option was most unattractive and risked BA Board resignations and a serious postponement of the BA privatisation. Ridley therefore continued to try and broker a deal between King and Thomson. The result after some further discussions with the airlines was a compromise arrangement under which BA, albeit reluctantly, withdrew from the UK-Saudi route and in return accepted BCal's South America, Denver and Morocco destinations instead of the Atlanta service. In effect, the agreement left both King and Thomson dissatisfied and sealed the fate of BCal.[52] These transfers were less than the ones recommended by the CAA and subsequent events were to prove that the compromise agreement was insufficient to maintain BCal as a competitor, especially since shortly after the arrangement was put into effect traffic on the Saudi route turned down. In 1986/7 BCal made a loss of £19.3 million. At least one senior Minister had already voiced doubts about the strategy of trying to maintain two viable "national champions" in what was an increasingly competitive international airline industry. In October 1983 Norman Tebbit, the Secretary of State for Trade and Industry, had privately advised Thomson of BCal that once BA was privatised a takeover bid of one by the other was likely to secure a sounder flag carrier.[53] In April 1988 BA bought BCal.[54]

Once the matter of the allocation of routes had been decided and published in a White Paper – albeit without assuring the future of BCal – attention shifted back to finalising the plans for the privatisation of BA. The firm aim in Government was now a flotation of 100 per cent of the airline's equity, reflecting the Government's growing confidence in the privatisation agenda, although there was some nervousness that the stock market might not be able to absorb all of the BA shares in "one bite". There was also the matter of BA's balance sheet still to repair. Ridley warned that to achieve a debt-equity ratio at which BA would be saleable, "we shall have to leave perhaps as much as £400 million of the gross proceeds of perhaps £800–£1,000 million, with the airline to repay debt." This reflected BA's heavy losses in the past. But there were concerns that critics of the privatisation would call it a handout to the airline.[55] In addition, the privatisation could not go ahead until the legal actions in the US over Laker were concluded.[56] Meanwhile, King and the Board of BA had become extremely frustrated by the series of delays to the airline's privatisation.[57] The original intention had been to privatise in 1980 or 1981 and then in the autumn of 1984. In March 1986 King offered to mount a management buyout of BA rather than wait much longer for an eventual flotation. The Government immediately rejected the idea.

In March 1983 Thatcher had written to President Reagan asking him to intervene to speed up a settlement of the legal actions in the US against BA. He had been reluctant to become involved, but following his re-election in November 1984 and a meeting with Thatcher at Camp David in Maryland in December,[58] Reagan was successful in having a grand jury criminal investigation called off and in the following year he persuaded the leading US creditor in Laker to drop its civil action. Subsequently, BA's lawyers in the US achieved an out of court settlement to bring all of the legal actions against the airline to an end. Also, through negotiations with the US Government on the Bermuda 2 agreement, which regulated transatlantic air traffic, the threat of future civil anti-trust actions against BA in the US was reduced.[59] The agreement also removed uncertainty about the future of BA's transatlantic routes. In September 1986 the new Secretary of State for Transport, Paul Channon, was able to inform the Cabinet that the legal problems which had delayed the BA flotation had now been resolved and that he intended to proceed with the privatisation of the airline early in the New Year.[60]

The flotation of BA occurred in February 1987, when almost the company's entire share capital was sold by the Government at a fixed price of 125p per share,[61] raising gross proceeds of £900 million.[62] However, prior to the sale there was a capital reconstruction which involved debt write offs totalling some £160m.[63] Also, a new pension scheme was introduced which would apply to all new employees and which would no longer offer a guarantee of inflation-proofing. This was intended to head off concerns amongst investors about potential future pension liabilities. Three main markets for the shares were identified, UK institutions, UK retail investors and overseas markets (more specifically, Switzerland, Canada, Japan and the USA). Overseas demand was intended to increase the actual scarcity of shares available to UK investors and to create the perception of such a scarcity. This would encourage institutional investors, in particular, to bid for the shares rather than wait to acquire them in the aftermarket.[64]

Payment for the shares was in two instalments (65p payable on application and 60p on 18 August 1987) to make the shares more attractive to small investors. In addition, individuals buying shares were eligible for a loyalty bonus of one share for every ten held continuously until 28 February 1990 (subject to a maximum bonus of 400 shares). The aim was to discourage investors from quickly selling their shares and pocketing a capital gain. At the time there was some uncertainty within Government as to whether attracting individual investors to buy BA shares was sensible, given the fluctuating financial fortunes of airlines, and in the end the Government did not mount a large marketing campaign aimed at small investors. Nevertheless, with the experience of previous privatisation offers and large capital gains, many small investors did apply for shares. Also, and as by now was the norm in privatisations, there was an issue of free shares to employees and preferential arrangements for employees to buy further shares.[65] BA proposed a highly attractive scheme, which the Department of Transport trimmed back on cost grounds. The Department's proposal was in turn trimmed back by the Treasury, to ensure that the employee share ownership scheme was comparable to schemes offered in other privatisations.[66] To meet the requirements of national laws separate arrangements were made for employees in the USA and Canada. The Government was becoming increasingly sensitive to criticism of selling shares in privatisations too cheaply, but once again it got the company's valuation badly wrong.[67] The BA issue was almost 11 times oversubscribed and the shares sold on a partly paid basis at 65p were valued at 109p by the end of the first day of stock market trading.[68] However, in its defence the Government could point to the fact that this flotation occurred at a time when stock markets were volatile.[69]

More successful were the Government's efforts to economise on primary underwriting costs. The sales of a third tranche of Cable and Wireless in December 1985 and British Gas shares in November of the following year had seen the introduction of competitive bidding for underwriting privatisation issues. This was repeated for the sale of BA and commission rates fell to as low as 0.111 per cent.[70] However, after the sale it was decided that the underwriters were investing institutions that were bound to buy shares in what would be a FT100 company and therefore the need for secondary underwriting was questionable. This would influence thinking in later privatisations.[71] Another feature of privatisation issues was now priority applications. This occurred during the privatisation of BA with 48 per cent of the shares on offer placed firm with institutions at 0.5 per cent commission and 12 per cent provisionally placed at 1.257 per cent commission.[72] The provisionally placed shares were subject to "clawback terms", under which a proportion of the shares issued were provisionally placed with financial institutions in Britain and overseas, but could be clawed back where there was an oversubscription of the remaining shares on offer.[73] The objective of clawback was to ensure that there were sufficient shares to satisfy applications by small investors, in line with the Government's objective of widening share ownership. The clawback terms were triggered in the BA flotation.

As was common to a number of the privatisation flotations, the Government introduced terms in the company's Articles of Association to prevent more than 25 per cent of the company's shares being owned by non-UK nationals. In addition, no one person or persons acting in concert was permitted to hold more than 15 per cent of the issued shares. However, in the case of the privatisation of BA there was no "special share". At the time the view in Government was that the EEC would accept special shares allowing the Government to block unwelcome takeover bids where there was a legitimate issue affecting national security, such as in the case of British Aerospace and British Telecom. It was much more difficult to mount a national security argument for retaining a special share in the case of a commercial airline. It was also judged that the terms of international Air Services Agreements on ownership and control meant that in practice BA would be safe from takeover by non-UK nationals. Under these agreements BA had to be "substantially owned and effectively controlled" by UK citizens. However, the result was a somewhat more complex regime to restrict foreign ownership than existed for other privatisations.

## Rolls-Royce

Rolls-Royce (RR) had become a 100 per cent government-owned company under the Heath Government in 1971, following a financial collapse caused by serious cost overruns during the development of the RB211 aero engine. The aim of the Heath Government was to return Rolls-Royce to the private sector as soon as was practicable, but from 1974 denationalisation was not on the agenda of the then Labour Government. Instead, RR was placed under the supervision of the new National Enterprise Board (NEB).

By the late 1970s roughly 40 per cent of RR's turnover came from military aircraft engines, 40 per cent from civil aircraft engines, 12 per cent from industrial and marine engines, 5 per cent from helicopter engines and 3 per cent from nuclear engines for submarines.[74] The company was therefore highly dependent on defence and civil airline orders. Following the May 1979 General Election the new Conservative Government received a proposal from Sir Arnold Weinstock at GEC to buy the whole of RR and then sell back to the Government the aero engine business, which GEC offered to manage under contract. GEC was not interested in owning the aero side of the business because of the large cash injections needed to develop new engines.[75] However, after careful consideration of the offer, the Government decided to retain RR in the state sector for the time being. There was concern about how well the company would fare under GEC control.[76] At the time the option of public flotation was also dismissed because RR was not considered ready for launching on the stock market. There were also pending decisions on military contracts involving the company. Instead Sir Frank McFadzean, a former Chairman of Shell, was appointed as the new Chairman of RR in place of Sir Kenneth Keith, who had been Chairman since 1971, and the decision was taken in November 1979 to remove the supervision of RR from the NEB. McFadzean insisted that RR be withdrawn from the NEB, something the Government had already been minded to do on the grounds that it did not seem efficient for the RR Board to report to another board. Relations between the Board of RR and the NEB were poor. However, removal of RR led to an angry reaction within the NEB and the resignation of its Board including its Chairman, Sir Leslie Murphy.[77]

McFadzean's strategy involved maintaining a strong competitive position in civil as well as military aero engines, believing that this was the only way to prevent a loss of key engineering skills and retain competitiveness in military work. However, a decline in civil aircraft engine orders and orders for spare parts in the post-1979 economic recession, alongside unfavourable exchange rate movements and restructuring costs, plunged RR into deep losses. Employment in RR fell by 13,500 or 24 per cent between 1981 and 1983.

Sir William Duncan was appointed in the spring of 1983 from ICI as the successor to McFadzean and objectives for the company agreed with the new Chairman included "that the company should be managed in such a way that it can be returned to the private sector during the course of the next Parliament and no later than 1988". One of Sir William's first actions was to reorganise the top management structure and strengthen the Board. He also commenced a complete review of RR's product strategy and began to develop collaborative arrangements with other manufacturers.[78] Sir William died suddenly in November 1984 and was replaced temporarily by Sir Arnold Hall until a permanent Chairman could be found, Sir Francis Tombs.

The objective of privatising RR was confirmed in the Conservatives' Election Manifesto in 1983 and was reconfirmed immediately afterwards in a statement by the PM in the House of Commons on 21 July. In 1984 the company returned to profitability after recording large losses in 1982 and 1983. Between 1984 and 1986 annual profits rose from £20 million to £110 million and turnover from £1.4 billion to £1.9 billion.[79] However, it was considered that privatisation was unlikely before 1987 because of the need to demonstrate to the stock market a consistent trend of profitability.[80] Another difficulty involved negotiating the appropriate level of financial aid the Government would continue to offer RR to assist with the development of new aero engines. It was conventional practice in aero engine production, as in a number of other areas of the aerospace industry, for the Government to offer "launch aid", which was effectively a preferential loan to offset some of the upfront development costs of new products, repayable by a levy on their sale. In July 1983 RR applied for launch aid of £96 million to help develop a derivative of the RB211 engine, the RB211–535 E4. The Secretary of State for Trade and Industry, Cecil Parkinson, supported the application and reported that, "The company had made substantial improvements in efficiency and productivity and were on course for further improvements."[81] However, the proposal met with opposition from the Treasury. The Treasury considered that the project did not offer sufficient prospects of viability.[82] The Chief Secretary of the Treasury, Peter Rees, pointed out that the company had already received over £200 million in launch aid since 1978 and the outcome had been very disappointing, concluding: "Very few of these engines would be sold; and the money was effectively lost."

In discussion in E(A) Sub-Committee mixed views were expressed. While there was some sympathy for the Chief Secretary's position when the Government was trying to control public spending, fears were voiced that if RR failed then the US would be granted an effective monopoly of the production of aero engines – the other two main aero engine manufacturers were General Electric and Pratt and Whitney, both based in the US. The debate was so closely balanced that the Committee invited Parkinson to negotiate with the company the minimum possible launch aid, while not committing the Government at this stage to give any financial assistance. Later, in private discussion with the PM, Parkinson was able to agree funding for the new Rolls-Royce engine. The decision to provide £70 million in launch aid was announced on 17 November 1983.[83]

Nevertheless, the issue of launch aid would continue to cast a shadow over the privatisation of RR because without preferential government financing the company's borrowings and cash flow were likely to be such that it would be much less attractive to investors. The subject resurfaced the following February when RR applied for help with development of the V2500 aero engine, designed to suit the Airbus A320 and other aircraft. This was being built in co-operation with partners from the US, Japan, Germany and Italy. Again there was a division between the Department of Trade and Industry and the Treasury on the amount of launch aid that should be granted. RR asked for 50 per cent of the total costs of the development to be advanced, or some £137 million. Norman Tebbit, now the Secretary of State for Trade and Industry, was willing to offer somewhat less, up to £96 million, while the Treasury wished to limit the commitment to a mere £45 million.[84] In the opinion of the DTI this sum would not allow the company to reduce its borrowings to the extent necessary to establish itself on a sound financial footing.

The PM concluded that the Secretary of State should initially offer £45 million, but he was permitted to raise the sum to £60 million if this proved necessary.[85] Sir William Duncan threatened in a subsequent letter to the PM that the failure to award the launch aid RR had requested could threaten the company's privatisation.[86] In the event RR received more than £60 million to develop the V2500 engine, obtaining £72 million between 1984 and 1987.[87] Although the Government was keen to separate the award of launch aid from consideration of the privatisation of RR in its public statements, it is difficult to escape the conclusion that the Government was always minded that without adequate launch aid RR would either have to cancel technological investments or resort to more loan financing, with a potentially damaging effect on its level of gearing. Either course would prejudice a successful privatisation of the company.

In the summer of 1985 the Samuel Montagu bank was appointed by the DTI to provide preliminary advice on the disposal of RR.[88] Its report at the end of September concluded that a flotation of the company would be feasible sometime between September 1986 and June 1987, provided that the company's financial position continued to improve. The DTI and Treasury Ministers agreed in October 1985 to proceed with preliminary work in preparation for privatisation.[89]

The plans to privatise RR were confirmed in E(A) Sub-Committee on 20 March 1986.[90] Paul Channon reported that there should be sufficient evidence of continual improvement in RR's finances by September for the privatisation to take place at any time thereafter. Channon had replaced Leon Brittan as Secretary of State for Trade and Industry after the latter's resignation during the Westland affair (see chapter 8, p.171). Brittan had replaced Tebbit in September 1985 when Tebbit was appointed Conservative Party Chairman. Channon's preference was to privatise immediately. However, the Treasury advised that this would not be possible because of the pending British Gas flotation.[91] Therefore, he began to plan to sell RR during the first two months of 1987. Channon considered a possible trade sale of RR to another company instead of a public flotation, but to maximise the sales receipts Samuel Montagu confirmed that the most appropriate route was a share sale. It was felt that the only British company likely to be interested in purchasing RR would be GEC or a GEC-led consortium and it was considered unlikely that they would be willing to pay a sum approaching the amount that could be raised in the stock market. Sale to a foreign company was out of the question; it was agreed that a privatised RR should stay under British control given its importance for national defence. During the flotation foreign shareholdings were limited to a total of 15 per cent of the company's issued voting shares indefinitely and the same limit was applied to British investors until 1 January 1989; a special share was created to prevent this restriction being removed from the Articles of Association without Government agreement.[92] However, in the case of RR, because of the company's strategic importance, further protection of the national interest was introduced through a condition that at least 75 per cent of the directors, including the Chairman and Managing Director, should be British citizens.[93]

Although no one person would be allowed to have an interest in over 15 per cent of the voting shares until 1 January 1989, to prevent a politically embarrassing early takeover of RR, in the longer term the Government expected that the company might need to form an association with another company or companies to fund future developments. The Secretary of State warned that, "In the medium and longer term commercial pressures on Rolls-Royce may well develop to amalgamate with a larger grouping, very possibly involving overseas companies. In the event, we might not wish to prevent such a move, especially if the alternatives were increased Government financial support."[94] In other words, the DTI appears to have concluded that RR might not remain for long after privatisation as an independent company given the costs of aero engine development. Therefore, it must have contemplated not using its special share and hence its power of veto. However, as matters turned out this would not be tested. After privatisation RR went on to become a highly successful, independent company in the private sector.

The sale proceeds were expected to be in the range of £625–750 million. To facilitate a successful flotation and raise a larger sum Samuel Montagu advised that a substantial capital injection would be needed. Under what was known as the "Cranley Onslow assurance", RR's debts were guaranteed by the Government in the event of liquidation. With privatisation this assurance would cease and the improved capital base would be needed to offset this. In the event the Government made a £283 million capital injection in the form of a subscription for additional shares, which then formed part of the public offer for sale.[95] The major proportion of the proceeds was used to repay most of RR's borrowings.[96] On 1 May 1986 RR was re-registered as a public limited company. On 18 December Channon announced in the House of Commons that, subject to market conditions, the Government intended to return the company to the private sector in April or May of the following year.[97]

RR was floated in the stock market in May 1987. The offer for sale was on a fixed price basis of 170p per share payable in two instalments (85p on issue and 85p on 23 September 1987) and the sale raised net cash for the Government of £1.08 billion after the £283 million capital injection to bolster the balance sheet.[98] As usual, there were special arrangements for employees to obtain a number of free shares and others at a discount[99] and, as in the case of BA, competitive underwriting bids were used, resulting in a commission rate as low as 0.061 per cent and significantly lower than had been paid in earlier privatisations, including BA three months earlier.[100] Even more so than in the case of BA, the Government had decided that RR was probably not a suitable investment for small shareholders because of the economic and technological risks faced by the company, as reflected in its record of fluctuating profitability. There was much debate about the nature and scope of the marketing campaign and especially whether there should be any TV advertising. In the end TV advertising was used and RR, like BA, did attract a large number of small investors. This in turn led to an embarrassing shortage of share application forms and resulting criticism in the media. With two million applications lodged, shares were allocated in favour of smaller applications and once again clawback terms affecting shares placed with the financial institutions were triggered, to satisfy the unexpected demand from the retail market.[101] The flotation price was announced on 7 May and between then and the closure of applications, 20 May, the stock market rose. The RR flotation illustrated, like other privatisations in the 1980s, the difficulties created by setting the share price around two weeks before applications had to be submitted. At the end of the first day of trading in the shares on the London stock market, the price had risen from the partly paid price of 85p to 143p.

## Shipbuilding

### *British Shipbuilders*

In 1950 42 per cent of the world's new ships were built in British yards. By 1978 the figure had shrunk dramatically to only 4.5 per cent in the face of growing foreign competition and outmoded working practices in British yards. The bulk of the British shipbuilding industry had been nationalised by the Labour Government in 1977, when in total 27 companies involved in shipbuilding, ship repair and marine engineering in Britain were merged to create a new public corporation, British Shipbuilders (BS), leaving only small, specialist yards in the private sector. The Prime Minister of the time, James Callaghan, argued that this was "The only way to ensure secure, long-term employment" in the industry.[102] However, the disruption caused by nationalisation contributed to a fall in labour productivity in the ship-yards between 1976 and 1978 of nine per cent, which further damaged the industry's competitiveness.[103] British shipyards had been temporarily assisted in the 1970s by rising government subsidies and North Sea oil work but were badly affected by the worldwide excess capacity in shipbuilding after 1978.

Nationalisation of the industry was strongly opposed by the Conservative Party in Opposition and in the Party's Election Manifesto in 1979 a commitment was made to denationalise BS with, seemingly, preference to be given to bids from the previous owners. However, following the election victory this commitment was quietly dropped[104] and in any case privatisation of BS was prevented by the losses being made in British shipyards, as they struggled to compete in the face of world overcapacity in shipbuilding. At an early meeting of E(DL) Sub-Committee in the summer of 1979 the Secretary of State for Industry, Sir Keith Joseph, concluded that given the financial state of BS its denationalisation would have to be deferred.[105] In 1979 BS recorded an overall loss of £110 million and although its financial position later improved a little due to cost cutting – between December 1979 and March 1983 employment in BS fell from 75,900 to 61,900[106] – in 1982/3 only the warship building business was profitable. At the same time, warship building yards had failed to achieve export sales for many years and were totally dependent on orders from the Royal Navy. The other main activity of BS, merchant shipbuilding, recorded an £85 million loss (see Table 9.1).

Although a separate sale of the profitable warship yards seemed possible,[107] the possibility of a sale was complicated in the early months of the 1979 Thatcher Government by an on-going legal dispute with the previous private sector owners over the shipbuilding national-isation compensation terms.[108] The problem arose because the 1977 Act which nationalised the industry (and aerospace) set the compensation to the private sector owners using the national stock market value of the companies in a six month reference period ending on 28 February 1974. Fourteen of the nationalised companies, whose value declined between that period and the time of nationalisation, accepted the compensation terms. But six companies whose profits rose substantially before nationalisation disputed them.[109] After this legal dispute was largely settled, one previous owner continued to strongly contest the compen-sation, Sir William Lithgow.

On 23 July 1979 the Secretary of State for Industry made the following brief comment after announcing his plans for the sale of British Aerospace: "I have also considered whether a comparable financial reconstruction might be made for British Shipbuilders. In principle I should have liked to introduce private sector finance to this industry at the same time. I have concluded, however, that in light of the particular problems

*Table 9.1* Results for British Shipbuilders 1982/3

|  | Turnover (£000) | Trading profit/ (loss) (£m) | Average number employed (March 1983) |
|---|---|---|---|
| Merchant Shipbuilding Division | 395,759 | (85) | 17,200 |
| Warship Building Division | 428,387 | 47 | 27,000 |
| Engineering Division (including engine building) | 71,372 | (16) | 7,900 |
| Ship Repair Division | 53,189 | (5) | 2,900 |
| Offshore Division | 134,769 | (77) | 6,900 |

*Source*: Turnover figures from "Brief on nationalised industries and privatisation for the Debate on the Address", 9 November 1982, Conservative Research Department, in E(DL) Part 6 and profit/loss and employment figures from E(A)(85)48, "British Shipbuilders: Corporate Plan 1985/86–1987/88. Memorandum by the Secretary of State for Trade and Industry", 16 July 1985.

of the industry, and the consequent difficulty of predicting its future size . . . this is not the right time. The Government have therefore decided not to bring forward measures at the moment to introduce private sector finance to the shipbuilding industry."[110]

The merchant bank NM Rothschild was asked to prepare a report on the possible value of disposal of parts of BS, which was submitted in June 1980.[111] However, when the future of British shipbuilding was discussed in Cabinet and E Committee in the summer and early autumn of 1980, it was agreed that there could be no early sale of any of the major shipyards.[112] The Chairman of BS had made it clear that selling the profitable warship business perhaps back to the previous owners "would render the prospect of returning to viability the remaining part of the industry unlikely of achievement". Without the profits from the warship yards, BS's losses would be greater as would, therefore, the amount of government subsidy needed. When in June 1981 defence cuts reduced naval orders the prospects of any early sales receded further. In 1980/1 Government provided financial assistance to the British shipbuilding industry totalling almost £300 million, in the form of public dividend capital and subsidies from the Intervention Fund. The Intervention Fund was established under the Industry Act 1972 to assist BS to compete for orders against yards overseas.[113] Under the terms of the Intervention Fund, Government could pay grants to shipbuilders up to 20.5 per cent of the contract price of a ship (in Northern Ireland up to 25.5 per cent) to match prices quoted by foreign yards. Also, Joseph was aware that if the Government forced a sale of the yards there were likely to be immediate Board resignations and a withdrawal of union co-operation. Consequently, while a Bill was introduced in 1982 in fulfilment of the 1979 Election Manifesto promise to denationalise, which included providing powers to the Secretary of State to direct the Corporation to dispose of particular assets, in reality there remained very little prospect of appreciable privatisation in the short term.[114]

### The warship yards

By 1983 the Government had provided some £700 million of financial assistance to the British shipbuilding industry and had raised BS's borrowing limit from £500 million to £800 million. But the industry remained in a parlous state.[115] After the 1983 General Election the Government turned again to the possibility of privatising some of the shipbuilding yards.

*Table 9.2* The five large warship builders July 1984

| Yard | Description | Current employment | Completion of current order book |
|------|-------------|--------------------|----------------------------------|
| Cammell Laird | Merseyside: Frigates<br>Offshore rigs | 1704* | Dec 84 |
| Swan Hunter | Tyneside: Frigates<br>Merchant Ships | 3530<br>3800 | Jan 88 |
| Vosper Thorneycroft | Southampton: Frigates &<br>GRP (glass reinforced plastic)<br>vessels, such as minesweepers<br>Merchant Ships | 3800<br>630 | Mar 85 |
| Yarrow | Glasgow: Frigates & GRP vessels | 5520 | Dec 87 |
| Vickers | Barrow: submarines<br>Engineering | 8220<br>4200 | Building Trident Subs into 1990s |

*Note*: *On completion of current round of redundancies.
*Source*: C(84)19.

The most attractive to private investors were the warship building yards, the main ones being Cammell Laird at Birkenhead, Swan Hunter on the Tyne, Vosper Thorneycroft in Portsmouth and Southampton, Yarrow on the Clyde and Vickers in Barrow-in-Furness (Table 9.2). All except Vickers undertook some commercial work such as offshore rigs and merchant ships, but all relied heavily on Royal Navy orders.

Under the Bill introduced in 1982, which became the British Shipbuilding Act 1983, the Government directed BS, in July 1984, to dispose of its warship building yards by 31 March 1986. However, it was by now clear that there were unlikely to be sufficient such orders to sustain all of these yards, particularly once the naval losses sustained in the Falklands War two years earlier were made good. Only Vickers could be confident of its future given its contract for Trident submarines into the 1990s. Also, although warship building was profitable overall, the profitability of each of the yards varied and therefore so did their likely attraction to the private sector. Vickers was profitable and Vosper Thorneycroft was just profitable; it was felt that both might be sold separately. But the prospects for Swan Hunter and Cammell Laird were much bleaker.

Swan Hunter's commercial work was due to cease around the end of the year when orders ran out and it would then be dependent solely on defence contracts. These were expected to keep the yard partially employed only until 1987 or early 1988.[116] The future for Cammell Laird was even more precarious. Its current order book would run out at the end of 1984. In a search for new work it bid to build two Type 22 frigates required by the Royal Navy, one to replace a loss in the Falklands, offering a lower price than Swan Hunter. However, the bid was based on a figure for overheads which many considered unrealistic. Also, the yard had been subject to some militant union action, including a sit-in over redundancies, and there was continuing concern about working practices there. This coloured the attitude of a number of Government Ministers towards their bid.[117] A new Chairman of BS was appointed with effect from 1 September 1983, Graham Day. Day was given a mandate to continue the rationalisation of production and work towards the eventual privatisation of the industry.[118] He quickly made it known that in his view Cammell Laird could not survive as an independent yard and presented a plan to merge it with Vickers.

In May 1984 the Secretary of State for Trade and Industry, Norman Tebbit, favoured placing the two Type 22 orders with Swan Hunter and closing Cammell Laird.[119] But the Secretary of State for Defence, Michael Heseltine, disagreed.[120] Cammell Laird was the third largest local employer on Merseyside and in his opinion its closure "would have serious social and political repercussions". He offered instead to place an order for one of the Type 22s with Cammell Laird, leaving a decision on the placement of the second order until the yard had demonstrated its ability to build the first frigate efficiently.[121]

On 19 July 1984 the entire future of the warship building yards was debated in Cabinet. Tebbit maintained that all of the yards would have to be privatised, as bidders would be reluctant to buy yards which then competed for MoD orders with warship building yards still under state ownership. At the same time, selling all of the yards as one unit would mean that the MoD would face a monopoly supplier of naval ships. The yards would therefore have to be sold off individually or in small groupings. Tebbit recommended proceeding with the planning of individual sales, but at the same time taking steps to prepare for a possible flotation of the warship building yards as one unit as a fall-back position. The detailed task of negotiating sales would be passed to Graham Day with the goal of making substantial progress towards completing the sales by March 1985, or the end of 1985 in the case of a public flotation.[122] Summing up the discussion, the PM confirmed Cabinet approval for Tebbit's proposals for the warship building yards and for a further round of bidding for the Type 22 orders. The PM made it clear that whether Cammell Laird eventually secured the orders depended "not only on the details of their tender but on whether they and their trade unions were able to give satisfactory assurances regarding productivity and working practices".[123] However, subsequently Day instructed Cammell Laird to rebid for only one of the frigate orders, while allowing Swan Hunter to bid for both.[124] As all of Cammell Laird's overheads would now fall on the costing for one ship, it was clear to an irritated Heseltine that "This was effectively the end of Cammell's chances."

Heseltine continued to be unhappy about the prospect of the closure of Cammell Laird but faced opposition elsewhere in Government.[125] In January 1985 he complained in Cabinet that "Tebbit had deliberately fixed the rules in order to ensure that Swan won" and that this was an unacceptable interference in his Department's tendering procedures. Following the Cabinet meeting the PM instructed Sir Robert Armstrong, the Cabinet Secretary, to broker a solution. He telephoned the MoD permanent secretary, Sir Clive Whitmore, and in discussions involving Heseltine it was decided that an acceptable solution would be to give one order to Swan Hunter and the other to Cammell Laird. To placate Swan Hunter, the second order for the Type 23 anti-submarine frigate would be placed with the yard "as soon as this can sensibly be done".[126] The first order for this next generation frigate to the Type 22 had gone to Yarrrow.[127] Dividing the frigate orders provided an uneasy but costly resolution to the dispute.[128] The estimate at the time was that there would be extra costs to the defence budget of £7 million and the cost to BS was put at some £40 million or more.[129]

Following the agreement on the Type 22 sales, negotiations for the sale of the yards stepped up a gear. Yarrow Shipbuilders Ltd in Glasgow with a book value of £20 million was sold in June 1985 for £34 million to GEC, with BS agreeing to accept a small contingent liability should redundancies subsequently arise. After competitive bidding Vosper Thorneycroft was subject to a management buy-out in November 1985 for £18.5 million plus one per cent of the value of certain contracts, compared with its book value of £23.4 million.[130] Swan Hunter was also sold to its management, in January 1986, and for a mere £5 million after a cash injection from BS of some £3.5 million.[131] The low figure reflected the fact that the yard was heavily loss making and its balance sheet showed a £71 million deficiency.[132]

In spite of the frigate order, no one was likely to be particularly interested in buying Cammell Laird, so in the summer of 1985 the yard became effectively a subsidiary of Vickers at Barrow-in-Furness. Two bids were then received for the new combined entity, one from Trafalgar House (TH) plc and another from an employee consortium backed by local residents. The value of the TH bid was, broadly, slightly over £82.5 million, but this sum was conditional on the MoD committing itself to buy the first Trident submarine before 25 February 1987.[133] By contrast, the employee consortium (EC) bid involved a lower £60 million initial consideration, alongside a profit sharing arrangement which might produce further payments of between £10 million and £40 million in total in 1992 and 1993. The central estimate was that the TH offer was likely to be the better of the two in straight financial terms. However, the EC bid had strong support from the workforce and local residents. An Early Day motion in the House of Commons in its favour was sponsored by the MP for Barrow-in-Furness and signed by 100 MPs. After some heated discussion, with Ministerial views divided, the Government agreed to accept the EC bid, even though it seems that BS's preference may have been to sell to TH.[134] Vickers, along with its loss making subsidiary Cammell Laird, was sold in March 1986 to a management-employee buyout supported by Lloyds Merchant bank. The sum paid was £60 million plus deferred payments of £40 million dependent upon future profits and payable in 1992/3. Vickers Shipbuilding and Engineering Employee Consortium (VSEL) plc was formed and 20 per cent of the ordinary share capital of the company offered to employees and residents of Barrow and Birkenhead.[135] The offer was twice subscribed with 82.3 per cent of the 14,000 employees and over 5,000 local residents applying for shares. Each employee was given access to a £500 interest free loan to purchase equity, repayable out of future wages. Also, free shares were offered to employees who subscribed for 200 shares or more. The net book value of the assets acquired by the new company was £42 million after a £86 million debt write-off by BS.[136]

However, in spite of such capital restructuring it was clear from the outset that each of the privatised warship building yards, including VSEL, would face a difficult future. A report of an ad hoc Cabinet committee on the Shipbuilding Industry (MISC 127) in July 1986 concluded that there was no long-term requirement for retention of all the recently privatised yards.[137] Matters were made worse by a Long-Term Costing exercise undertaken in the Ministry of Defence, which led to a decision that the number of naval orders over the next few years would be less than the industry was expecting. In the following years the privatised warship building yards struggled for work in spite of Government action to advance some naval orders.[138]

### Merchant shipbuilding, engineering and ship repair

The sale of the warship building yards in 1985–6 still left the Government with the problem of disposing of a number of BS's other businesses, including merchant shipbuilding. Some smaller concerns had already been sold off. Between September 1983, when Graham Day became Chairman, and the summer of 1985 BS had sold or closed 15 businesses, including all the peripheral engineering companies and all but one of the Corporation's ship repair yards, the sale of which was under negotiation.[139] For example, the Scott Lithgow shipbuilding, ship repairing and offshore engineering facilities were sold to Trafalgar House in 1984 for £20 million but at a net cost to the taxpayer of more than £71 million after restructuring costs.[140] At the same time, production in the main merchant shipbuilding yards had been further rationalised, employment falling from 13,400 in March 1984 to 8,400 in May 1985.[141] Over the same period BS had restructured its main engineering operations down from five main sites to two, with employment falling from 1,100 to 900, and had attempted to improve cost effectiveness through a regionalisation of activities. There had also been substantial job cuts at Austin and Pickersgill, Smiths Dock and Appledore and some ship repairing facilities had been either sold or offered for sale.[142] The overall effect was that BS's total losses had fallen. A trading loss of £117 million in 1982/3 had declined to £25 million by 1984/5.[143] Nevertheless, by July 1984 the industry had received close to £1.2 billion in financial assistance from the Exchequer since nationalisation in 1977.[144]

The future of the remainder of BS was reviewed in E(A) Sub-Committee on 23 July 1985 when the Corporation's corporate plan for 1985/6 to 1987/8 was discussed.[145] In July 1984 E(A) had agreed to set BS on a continuing downward glidepath for merchant shipbuilding from an annual order equivalent to 230,000 compensated gross tonnes (cgt) in 1984/5 to 115,000 cgt in 1987/8. Merchant shipbuilding capacity had stood at 600,000 cgt at nationalisation.[146] The outcome was expected to bring BS closer to commercial viability, although it was also expected that the industry would still need some continuing subsidy for the foreseeable future. The Secretary of State for Trade and Industry, Norman Tebbit, now informed his colleagues that he proposed to tell BS that it should plan on the assumption that there would be an elimination of all government subsidies by the end of 1990. The PM summing up the discussion stated that "it was hardly conceivable that the United Kingdom's merchant shipbuilding capability should disappear completely", and that a continuing glidepath reduction in capacity was the right way forward.[147]

At the time continuing world overcapacity continued to damage BS's merchant shipbuilding competitiveness. On 8 May 1986 the new Secretary of State for Trade and Industry, Paul Channon, reported to E(A) Sub-Committee that the prospects for BS were bleak given the depressed state of the global shipbuilding market.[148] The BS Board were looking at various scenarios but had concluded that even with a reasonable degree of success in winning new orders, they would have to close their Wallsend Engine Works with a loss of 400 jobs, Smith's Dock with 1500 jobs, and the Ferguson-Ailsa yard at Troon in Scotland with 400 jobs lost. In addition, they were seeking to introduce "economic manning" in the remaining yards, which would bring the total number of redundancies in the current financial year to around 3,500, of which 2,500 would be in the North East. Even with these measures there would still be overcapacity and it was likely that the eventual outcome would include the closure of the Austin Pickersgill yard at Sunderland, employing 1,500, and the Ferguson yard at Port Glasgow, employing 400. Later that year Austin and Pickersgill merged with Sunderland Shipbuilders to create a new BS subsidiary North-East Shipbuilders Limited.

Channon proposed supporting BS's objective of maintaining employment in the Corporation at broadly 6,500, provided sufficient orders could be won. However, there was general agreement in E(A) that there was no strategic or industrial case for continuing to support merchant shipbuilding where this was not cost-effective. In the middle of the decade BS was achieving little more than ten per cent of the orders it had forecast in its corporate plan and a number of contracts won were loss making. By 1988, of the £1.8 billion spent by

Government on BS only £250 million had been used to win orders; most of the rest had been eaten up by losses on existing contracts.[149] An internal Government report in June 1986 concluded: "The picture is a sombre one. The prospects for merchant shipbuilding world-wide are poor; ships and shipbuilding capacity are in over-supply and orders are hard to come by even at today's exceptionally depressed prices. Without significant orders soon, BS could go out of business by 1988."[150]

A further review of British Shipbuilders took place in E(A) on 19 March 1987.[151] BS was reported to be responding to the difficult financial situation with further structural changes to control costs. These included tightening control over the large shipbuilding yards and grouping responsibility for small shipbuilding, engineering and engine building businesses. However, it seemed that even after these measures, the only way that BS would be able to remain close to the financial limits agreed with the Government the previous year would be to close its Govan and Clark Kincaid facilities. The Appledore Shipbuilders and North-East Shipbuilders had work until at least 1989, but work would run out at Govan on the Clyde at the end of March and at the engineering works at Clark Kincaid at Greenock much sooner.

By the autumn of 1987 BS's prospects for financial viability were so poor, despite the heavy Government financial support in subsidies and soft loans, that there was discussion at a senior level in Government of the desirability of closing most of the remaining facilities. In October and November Kenneth Clarke, the Chancellor of the Duchy of Lancaster, lobbied the PM recommending closure of BS and a number of other Ministers felt this was inevitable, especially given a new Directive from the EEC aimed at limiting Government financial assistance to shipyards. It was felt that this would make it even more difficult for BS to win orders.[152] Another note at the time to the PM, on the current competitive position of BS in merchant shipbuilding, concluded dismally that: "As the rest of our economy grows, activities such as shipbuilding are increasingly shown up as dinosaur industries with an uncompetitive cost structure. When this endogenous problem is compounded by gross world over-capacity the prospect of any ultimate permanent return to profitability is hopeless . . . Even Korean shipbuilders are currently making losses."[153] The Chancellor of the Exchequer is reported to have said in a meeting of Ministers on 27 October 1987 that, "British shipbuilders had no future, and the nettle of closure should now be grasped".[154] However, following protests especially from the Secretary of State for Scotland where many of the yards at threat were situated, as well as other areas of high unemployment, the PM drew back from liquidating BS.[155]

In the event, the Govan yard was saved by an order for ships from China, secured with the help of a 60 per cent government subsidy. But a final nail was hammered into the coffin of North-East Shipbuilders Limited (NESL) when an order to build 24 ferries for a Danish buyer ran into serious difficulties. In December 1988 the Government announced the closure of NESL following a failure to attract a viable alternative buyer. A little later four organ-isations bid for the yard, but by then its rundown was well advanced and the Treasury was reluctant to have the matter reopened.[156] After some deliberation, controversially the Government decided to reject the bids which might have kept the yard open despite vocal support locally and in Parliament.[157] The Government judged that its plans for urban renewal in Sunderland and bringing in non-shipbuilding jobs were superior to any attempt to sustain shipbuilding in the area, which it concluded had no long-term future.

The Harland and Wolff (H&W) yard in Belfast was a mixed yard involved in shipbuilding and repair, the manufacturing of marine engines and engineering products. It had come into public ownership in 1975 to avoid closure at a time of great political unrest in Northern Ireland, but had never become part of BS, remaining a separate company under the Companies Act owned by the Northern Ireland Department of Economic Development. By early 1987 the yard employed 3,900. Although employment had declined sharply since the mid-1970s it had been saved from some of the more draconian measures, including closure, meted out to other British shipyards in the early 1980s because of the continuing political troubles and high unemployment in the province.[158] On 6 March 1986 E(A) Sub-Committee considered a memorandum from the Secretary of State for Northern Ireland, Tom King, on H&W's Corporate Plan.[159] The Secretary of State reported that H&W was not a viable company in what was a highly competitive world shipbuilding market. In discussion, it was pointed out that the costs of keeping H&W operating amounted to nearly £10,000 a year per job, a sum roughly twice as high as for BS as a whole. However, closure was not an attractive option given the political difficulties and high unemployment in Northern Ireland. The outcome of the discussion was that King was asked to bring forward proposals by the summer on how best to reduce the yard's overheads and improve labour flexibility.

King presented his proposals in July 1986 and they included a new redundancy and capacity reduction programme.[160] However, in March 1987 the Government felt the need to agree to further financial support to H&W in return for another round of rationalisation of production. The aim was now to bring employment in the yard down to around 2,300.[161]

The Government considered the future of H&W and what was left of BS on 10 May 1988 in a meeting of E(A) Sub-Committee. Here it was decided that in the light of the shipyards' continuing losses a clear policy was now needed on their future. The Sub-Committee agreed that the priority should be to transfer all of the remaining BS shipyards and H&W to the private sector. This would spare the Exchequer further substantial losses on contracts and other financial support. However, there was to be no general announcement of Government policy on selling the shipyards at the present time; instead progress would be made by selling the yards one by one, in effect continuing the policy that had operated since 1983.[162] The Govan yard on the Clyde had already been sold to Kvaerner, a Norwegian company, for £1.3 million a month earlier. On 30 June 1988 King announced in Parliament that he was seeking bids from the private sector for H&W[163] and in November he reported to E(A) Sub-Committee that his officials had held discussions with three possible buyers. The possibility of a management-employee buy-out had also surfaced.[164]

Subsequently, the management-employee buy-out, supported by Fred Olsen, a Norwegian with extensive shipping interests, became the favoured option.[165] H&W was sold in March 1989 to a new company owned by the management and employees and Olsen for £10.3 million. However, the deal involved a large net cost to the taxpayer, including £422 million in debt written off.[166] Indeed, privatising H&W may have led to a charge to the Government that exceeded the net receipts from the sale of all of the BS shipyards put together.

By December 1989 the long and painful disposal and closure of British shipbuilding was in its last stages. Following the sale of H&W attention turned to the disposal of Clark Kincaid in Greenock and of the Appledore yard in North Devon. Negotiations for the sale of the Ferguson yard at Port Glasgow were also underway, while Marine Design Consultants was sold to a team led by its managing director.[167] In summary, five operating subsidiaries were sold between June 1988 and April 1989, two through management buyouts with the proceeds retained by BS. By the end of the 1980s BS was a shell corporation with its shipbuilding activities either sold or closed down.

Perhaps unsurprisingly, given the growing competition in shipbuilding from countries with cheaper labour and more flexible working practices, a number of the sell-offs subsequently suffered from major problems. For example, by 1992 Swan Hunter was in serious financial difficulty and VSEL had decided to put its Cammell Laird yard up for sale.[168] Brooke Marine, Vosper ship repair and Hall Russell fell into the hands of administrators. In 1999 the Kvaerner Group decided to withdraw from shipbuilding worldwide, plunging the future of the Govan yard into doubt once more. In 2000 the Ailsa Troon yard closed when its owner decided to cut its losses.[169] The privatisation of the shipyards, like nationalisation in 1977, failed to stem the unremitting decline of the British shipbuilding industry.

## The Royal Dockyards

In the early 1980s the Royal Dockyards suffered some slimming down with the closure of the Chatham dockyard in 1981 and the rundown of facilities at Devonport in Plymouth.[170] By the mid-1980s the main facilities remaining were at Devonport and Rosyth in Scotland. These yards carried out around 80 per cent of the work of refitting and maintaining the Royal Navy's fleet. The remaining 20 per cent, consisting largely of Royal Fleet Auxiliary ships and minor warships, was refitted and maintained under contracts placed by competitive tender for which other yards could bid. By the mid-1980s the core of the Royal Dockyards' work involved the refitting and refuelling of nuclear-powered submarines, including the Polaris submarines, the core of the country's frontline nuclear deterrent. The Polaris submarines were serviced exclusively at Rosyth, which employed around 6,300. The Devonport yard was larger, employing some 13,000. Together the Royal Dockyards had a combined turnover of around £400 million per annum.

Concerns had been mounting for some time within the Royal Navy and the MoD that the dockyards were not operating as efficiently as they might. There were cost overruns and cases of late delivery of refits and repairs. Overmanning was widely suspected and there was concern about the lack of a proper customer-supplier relationship between the Navy and the dockyards. The lack of a commercially structured accounting system made it difficult to ascertain the true costs of refitting and maintaining naval ships and compounded concerns. To input commercial management into the yards, consideration was given both to setting up a trading fund for the Royal Dockyards and full privatisation. Both options faced problems, however. It was felt that a trading fund, under which the Dockyards would remain under Government ownership and the workers would remain Government employees, would not guarantee commercial management; while full privatisation would necessitate separating out the assets that the MoD would need to retain from those to be sold off. In addition, establishing companies in the Royal Dockyards and selling them would take time. Also, the Government was nervous about losing all control of the naval refitting and maintenance programme if there was full privatisation of the dockyards.

After the 1983 General Election Michael Heseltine, Secretary of State for Defence, invited Peter Levene, his Special Adviser on procurement practices, to take a fresh look at the organisation of the dockyards.[171] Levene recommended changes, which were said to be similar to those adopted in the US and known as "Government Owned, Contractor Operated". Following a competitive tender, under his plan a private contractor would employ the workforce and rent the dockyard facilities from the Government. The Admiralty Board was in favour of this proposal and while officials in the MoD drew attention to the possible complexity of operating an effective contracting regime, on balance they considered it workable.[172] The term "contractorisation" was invented to describe it – later substituted by the less awkward term "commercial management". Although the MoD acknowledged that some savings might be achieved by changing working practices under the existing ownership arrangement, it was expected that contracting out the management of the yards to the private sector would lead to greater savings.[173]

The future of the Royal Dockyards was discussed at meetings of E(A) Sub-Committee on 30 January and 21 March 1985. Here Heseltine set out the options, including full privatisation of the Devonport and Rosyth dockyards at one end of the spectrum and, at the other, the creation of a trading fund. At this meeting he also explained why he was opposed to full privatisation. To begin with there was Rosyth's importance to the maintenance of the country's nuclear deterrent, hence in his view full privatisation "would be going further than was desirable". Also, this solution would still leave the Navy with a monopoly supplier rather than competition for ship repair and shipfitting. Moreover, he argued that there was a practical problem of valuing the dockyard assets so as to sell them at a price to the private sector which reflected their true value, given the current lack of proper asset valuations. Finally, he felt that full privatisation would be a complex process and unlikely to be completed within the current Parliament.

At the same time, Heseltine was not favourably disposed to the introduction of trading fund status either, as this would in his opinion not expose the Dockyards to competition, would leave the workers as Government employees, and would not bring about the necessary changes to working practices and conditions of employment to ensure an improvement in performance. He therefore recommended the option of "contractorisation".

Under his favoured scheme, the management of each Royal Dockyard would be open to competition every four years. The four-yearly contracting exercise would, Heseltine believed, overcome the monopoly supplier problem to the Navy which existed under state management and which would also exist if the yards were simply sold off to one buyer.[174] The fixed equipment in the yards would remain in public ownership and be available for use by the successful contractor – this would overcome the difficulty of transferring the assets from one contractor to another at the time of a contract rebidding, a problem that confronts all periodic competitive tendering where there are appreciable sunk costs. The workforce would be transferred to the successful bidder and would thus cease to be civil servants. However, to conform to the Transfer of Undertakings (Protection of Employment) Regulations and to avoid industrial action, Heseltine suggested that they should transfer with their existing terms and conditions of employment and an equivalent index-linked pension to the one they benefited from in the Civil Service. There would be redundancies, but in his view this was inevitable whatever the future ownership of the dockyards. Heseltine calculated that there were likely to be around 3,000 lost jobs, largely concentrated at Devonport. Employment at Rosyth would be maintained because of the recently announced Government decision to refit the new Trident nuclear submarines there.

Heseltine's preference was to have the new arrangements in place before April 1987, which would necessitate primary legislation in the 1985/6 session. In addition to legal authority to move to "contractorisation" the next step would be to value the Royal Dockyards' assets, after which two separate companies would be established, one at each of the yards. These companies would pay a rent for the assets and employ the workforce. Competitive tenders would then be invited from contractors to take over the running of the yards. The specified work programme would comprise perhaps 70 per cent of the expected total naval requirement and the contractors would have to offer fixed rates for the use of the labour and dockyard facilities to undertake a further ten per cent of naval work whose incidence could not be predicted. The final 20 per cent of the naval requirement would be subject to competitive tender by the dockyard contractors and private sector ship repairing companies. At the same time, the Royal Dockyard companies would be free to tender for private sector ship repairing work. While Heseltine anticipated some opposition to his plan, especially given Rosyth's role in servicing the country's nuclear deterrent, he concluded that the prospect of annual savings of between £20 million and £30 million in return for a once and for all restructuring cost of £50–60 million "should make it possible to meet these criticisms". However, he agreed that if the contractorisation proposal failed, then the introduction of trading fund status should be reconsidered.[175]

In discussion in E(A) it was felt to be important to ensure that the contractors paid the full market price for the Dockyards' capital stock so as not to put them in an unfairly favourable position when bidding against other private sector companies for ship repairing work. There was also concern that commercial management might not bring about greater savings than could be secured through improvements in working practices under continued Government ownership, especially when the contractors' profit margins were taken into account. In addition, there was concern that fresh competition for the contracts every five years or so might prove impracticable. There were also fears expressed about the ability of contractorised dockyards to respond flexibly to defence needs should there be another Falklands-type emergency.[176] Nevertheless, the Sub-Committee endorsed contractorisation as the most promising option for the future of the Royal Dockyards. It was agreed that the Secretary of State for Defence should initiate a consultation process leading to its implementation. However, the PM, perhaps a little disappointed that full privatisation had been ruled out by the Secretary of State, commented that in endorsing this route the Sub-Committee "were not definitely ruling out full privatisation at any stage". She concluded that contractorisation "might in the end be only a half-way house on the road to full privatisation, but in the meantime it offered the earliest possible prospect of putting the Royal Dockyards operations on a fully commercial basis".

On 17 April 1985 Heseltine outlined his plan to the House of Commons and by the summer a consultation document had been issued. Also, preliminary discussions had begun with companies that might be interested in bidding for the contracts.[177] On 16 July Heseltine informed the PM that he had completed the consultation exercise. He had received views from the House of Commons Public Accounts Committee, the House Defence Committee, the trade unions, local authorities and industry, and advice from the Navy Board. There had been much support for "contractorisation" but unsurprisingly the unions were opposed. More worryingly perhaps, the Public Accounts Committee had expressed concerns about the MoD's costings, suggesting that the savings would be only £40 million over a ten year period, compared with costs to the Government of £60 million to implement. However, Heseltine seems to have shrugged off such criticism.[178]

On 23 July 1985 he announced in the House that contractorisation was the preferred option of both the Government and the Royal Navy. Also, he confirmed that there had already been much interest in bidding for the contracts from a number of industrial concerns, including Babcocks, Balfour Beatty, Costain, Plessey, STC, Trafalgar House and the Weir Group. The intention would be to introduce as early as possible the necessary legislation with the intention of introducing commercial management no later than 1 April 1987. The Secretary of State's announcement was heavily criticised by Denzil Davies for the Opposition, who accused Heseltine of ignoring the advice of the Public Accounts Committee, and by Dr David Owen, the MP for Plymouth Devonport in whose constituency many of the affected workers lived.[179]

Concerns continued over the following months while the planning of contractorisation proceeded within the MoD, that the MoD's initial costings might be inaccurate. The concerns were seemingly confirmed when a note in July 1986 to the PM from George Younger, who had replaced Heseltine as Secretary of State for Defence after his resignation over the Westlands affair in January, suggested that the contractorised dockyards were likely to cost the Exchequer £34 million a year and the MoD £67 million initially.[180] This led to a tetchy letter from John MacGregor at the Treasury to Younger asking for an explanation of why the net savings from commercial management set out earlier had been superseded by forecasts of additional costs.[181] Moreover, by this time there were also concerns about the implications of an amendment in the House of Lords to the Dockyard Services Bill that had been introduced into Parliament the previous November. During the House of Lords stage of the Bill the trade unions had persuaded Lord Denning to propose an amendment which would give them a right to go to the High Court before any dockyard transfer could take place if they felt that they had not been properly and fully consulted. The Treasury was concerned that this might set a precedent for future privatisations. MacGregor stressed: "I very much hope that it will be generally accepted that the dockyards must be treated as a peculiar case requiring special treatment so that this concession does not affect other privatisations."[182]

Bidding documents were issued in April 1986 with a closure date for bids for Rosyth of 1 August and for Devonport of 29 August, and by July there were three established bidding teams for Rosyth (Babcock International/Thorn EMI, Balfour Beatty/Weir Group, and Press Offshore). Also, a management team at the Devonport dockyard had proposed a buyout of the yard. However, they faced difficulty in obtaining the necessary financial support to mount a serious bid. Other potential bidders for the Devonport contract were Foster Wheeler, a US firm that had formed a bid group with VSEL and A & P Appledore, but their firm proposals were still awaited, and a late entrant, Brown and Root (a subsidiary of Halliburton Corporation in the USA), which had expressed interest and was given, along with the other bidders, an extra month to prepare a bid. Brown and Root had yet to secure adequate British participation in the management, as required by the "foreign control" provisions in the draft contract. Meanwhile, the MoD had been developing models of a government-owned plc operation at each of the dockyards to provide a baseline for assessing commercial bids and as a fall-back if the commercial bids proved unacceptable. Whatever happened job reductions were certain to occur. Coopers and Lybrand made broad estimates of redundancies of 2,000 to 2,500 at Devonport and 500 to 1,000 at Rosyth in the early years of the contract, and contrary to Heseltine's earlier prediction that employment at Rosyth would be broadly maintained.

On 18 September 1986 Younger wrote to the PM confirming that information on the contracts would now need to be provided to the unions under the Dockyard Services Act, as a result of Lord Denning's amendment. The unions remained implacably opposed to privatisation and had refused to be part of the Dockyard Planning Team since July 1985. They were hoping to exploit the opportunity for delay opened up by Lord Denning's amendment, perhaps until after the next general election. In addition, all of the Devonport bidders had now made it clear that they were not prepared to carry the responsibility of announcing redundancies.

Meanwhile, bids for Rosyth had been evaluated in the MoD and contract negotiations were expected to start in the following two weeks. The target was to complete them by early November so that the management contract could be signed by the end of that month. This would permit the contractor to start a period of parallel operation in early December through to April 1987, when the formal transfer of responsibility would take place.[183] On 24 November 1986 Younger informed the PM that there had been good progress on the contractual front, although there had been a slight slippage. For Rosyth he was now expecting to receive a submission early the following week reporting the outcome of negotiations with Babcock/Thorn with a view to contract signature. For Devonport the three bids had been fully evaluated and contract negotiations had begun with the two commercial consortia – Devonport Operations Ltd, led by Foster Wheeler, and Devonport Management Ltd, led by Brown and Root.[184]

On 1 December 1986 Younger was able to confirm that he was now in a position to enter into a contract for the operation of Rosyth with Babcock/Thorn. The contract included a profit sharing arrangement so that the Government could benefit from subsequent improved performance, but would require the Government to underwrite the effects of any major industrial disputes in the yard costing more than £4 million until 30 June 1988.[185] The bidders insisted upon this guarantee to protect their cash flow in the face of union opposition to the proposed contract. Overall, the MoD still estimated that the total return to the Exchequer from the seven year contract would be around £38.5 million compared with £15.2 million from a government-owned plc over the same period. Slightly offsetting this, for the first four or five years, would be costs to the MoD of additional annual payments into the employees' pension fund. The agreement with Babcock/Thorn was finalised and announced in the House of Commons on 27 January 1987.[186]

On 19 January 1987 Younger was able to inform the PM that he was now in a position to contract for the operation of Devonport with Devonport Management Ltd. This was announced in Parliament two days later.[187] Savings of up to £123 million over the seven years of the contract were forecast. However Younger conceded that the figures were less well substantiated than in the case of Rosyth "because neither of the two Devonport bidders has as good an understanding of the cost structure".[188] Also, the contract indemnified the contractors against the financial effects of strike action with a lower threshold for payments from the Government to the contractors than under the Rosyth contract, to reflect "the greater risk of strike action" given the size of the manpower cuts planned. The contract was finalised on 23 February 1987 and the terms announced to the House of Commons on the 24th.[189]

\* \* \*

Over the following months the MoD allocated the bulk of its refit and repair work to the dockyards at Rosyth and Devonport under the contractor arrangements, and despite reduced manning the quality and timeliness of refits and repairs improved.[190] In 1993 the MoD decided that the country now needed only one nuclear submarine refitting base and this was to be Devonport. After some initial concern that Rosyth might have to close, the Government decided that it should be favoured for all future non-nuclear refits. In October of the same year the MoD announced its intention to move to full privatisation by selling the dockyards.

The rationale was to allow the yards even greater flexibility to operate in a commercial environment and encourage private sector investment in dockyard infrastructure. It was also hoped that this final stage in the privatisation of the dockyards would lead to even more cost savings for naval repair and refit work. However, the sale of the Royal Dockyards proved to be something of a disappointment.

The MoD advertised for buyers, but received bids only from the existing management companies. Also the sums offered were around 50 per cent lower than the Department's valuation of the yards. Nevertheless, the sales went ahead early in 1997. When allowance is made for the sale costs and to compensate for the workers' loss of redundancy entitlement following privatisation, there was an estimated net outflow from the MoD as a result of the sales of £9 million, with future contingent net outflows amounting to a further £24 million.[191] The National Audit Office produced an unflattering report. In particular, it was critical of the basis of the MoD's earlier assessment of the likely cost savings from full privatisation. The privatisation of Rosyth and Devonport also disappointed over the longer term in terms of creating rivalry for naval work. In 2007 the two yards were united under Babcock's ownership.

# 10

# PRIVATISING BUS
# TRANSPORT AND THE ROYAL
# ORDNANCE FACTORIES

Since 1930 bus services in Britain had been subject to a system of licensing administered by quasi-judicial Traffic Commissioners. Each bus operator required a licence, which was granted by the Commissioners only when they were satisfied that the service would be in the public interest. Existing transport operators (including British Rail) could and did object to applications for new bus services and would often point to the need to restrict competition to enable the cross-subsidisation of less popular routes to continue, such as in rural areas. As people increasingly turned to using cars in the post-war period, the number of bus users fell and local bus operations became gradually more dependent on state subsidy. In 1982 subsidies amounted to £490 million in revenue support, £235 million to fund concessionary fares, and £93 million in the form of the fuel duty rebate, which reduced fuel taxes on public transport. However, in spite of the heavy subsidy and rebate, fares rose and the volume of bus passenger journeys continued to fall, by 30 per cent over the ten years to 1982.[1]

In the early 1980s there were some 70,000 buses and coaches operating in Great Britain, some 40,000 owned by public sector bus operators and the remainder by the private sector. The largest provider was the state-owned National Bus Company (NBC) operating in England and Wales with 14,600 buses, followed by the public sector Passenger Transport Executives (PTEs), which were responsible for the provision of passenger transport services in the English metropolitan areas and the Strathclyde region of Scotland, with 9,600 vehicles.[2] The next largest operator was the London Transport Executive (renamed London Regional Transport in June 1984), which owned 5,600 buses and provided transport in the capital. Municipal authorities (district councils and in Scotland regional councils) were responsible for a further 5,300 buses and the Scottish Bus Group (SBG) for 3,100.[3] The SBG, a subsidiary of the state-owned Scottish Transport Group, provided services in Scotland outside the main cities.

The NBC had been established by the Transport Act 1968 and by the early-1980s had a holding company structure with 40 regional operating subsidiaries, employing some 50,000 staff. The company provided intercity coach travel through its subsidiary National Express, coach holidays through a company called National Holidays, and contract and private hire services. But its largest business was the provision of stage carriage (local) bus services in rural and some urban areas. The stage carriage market accounted for around 85 per cent of the NBC's operations. The company made losses in 1975 and 1980 but was often profitable. For example in 1982 it made a trading profit of £39.5 million on a turnover of £655 million. However, nearly £175 million of this came from government subsidies, including rebated fuel duty.[4]

## The deregulation of bus services

The Government had committed itself in its 1979 General Election Manifesto to relaxing the Traffic Commissioner licensing regulations and enabling new bus services to develop including encouraging new private operators.[5] Also, Norman Fowler, the Secretary of State for Transport from May 1979 to September 1981 was keen to deregulate the industry. However, he recognised that this could only be done gradually because of fears within the industry that deregulation might lead to a loss of some services. As a first step, in 1980 the Government removed licensing restrictions on entry into bus and coach services with a minimum passenger journey length of 30 miles ("express coaches"). In response, a number of new operators entered the market to compete with National Express. However, British Coachways, a consortium of private sector coach operators launched as the principal competitor to National Express, collapsed within a year.[6] British Coachways was unable to compete against the large incumbent operator with its national coverage and better access to key bus terminals, including the important Victoria Coach Station in London. Also, National Express matched the cheaper fares introduced by British Coachways within a week.[7]

Another part of the 1980 legislation involved local (stage) bus services, where regulation was relaxed including the removal of fares control except where it was necessary to protect the public from monopoly abuse. From 1980 the criteria for the grant of road licences was amended so that licences for new local bus services would be granted unless the Traffic Commissioners were satisfied that to do so would be against the public interest. However, the result proved not to be a substantial change because, while the licensing authority was now required to grant a licence unless this would be against the public interest, this arrangement still tended to favour existing operators, who usually had more resources to fight their case. In three small "trial areas" licensing of stage carriage services was removed entirely in 1981, although only in one of these, the town of Hereford, did significant new competition develop.[8]

In 1980 deregulating and privatising local bus travel was considered a step too far. Public transport was still seen as something that should be provided largely by the public sector. Moreover, as Fowler commented in a letter of 21 June 1979, because many bus routes were loss making they were unlikely to be attractive to private investors.[9] Investors would be nervous of buying into an industry so heavily dependent on state subsidy and because of the prevalence of cross-subsidies. Typically, low use routes, often in rural areas or offpeak, were cross-subsidised by more highly used urban and peak services. Fowler retained the view that there was little prospect of a successful sale of shares in any of the NBC's stage carriage operations. However, by the summer of 1981 he did think that it might be possible to attract private capital into National Express.[10] One possibility would be to vest all of the assets of National Express, mainly coach stations and coaches, in a new company. Shares in the company could then be sold to private investors. Among the assets to be transferred to National Express from the NBC would be "non-operational property" plus some "developable operational property", so as to make the business more attractive to the private capital market. At the same time, Fowler believed that it would be necessary to permit the NBC "to retain a minority shareholding, say 30 per cent, and thus a stake in the future profits of the business" to win the Board's support for the sell-off.[11]

The PM gave her approval for Fowler to discuss the possibility of privatising National Express with the Chairman of the NBC, Lord Shepherd.[12] But Nigel Lawson at the Treasury, while content for discussion to occur, wanted to see the NBC retain a shareholding of less than 30 per cent so that the new company could be unambiguously classified as in the private sector.[13] Fowler maintained that he would be unlikely to persuade the NBC to accept this.[14] In the end Lawson backed down, reluctantly agreeing to privatisation proceeding with the NBC retaining a 30 per cent shareholding if this was necessary to retain Lord Shepherd's support.[15]

The resulting Transport Act 1982 empowered the Secretary of State to request the sale of part of the NBC business, including National Express. However, developments under the Act were interrupted by the calling of the 1983 General Election.[16] Meanwhile, a Monopolies and Mergers Commission inquiry in 1982 into four bus companies concluded that cost savings were achievable but that removing parts of the NBC Group and transferring them to other bodies would be damaging to efficiency and not in the interests of passengers. The report also found no evidence that the bus companies abused their monopoly positions.[17] Buses faced competition from rail and car. These were interesting findings in the light of the Government's later decisions on both bus deregulation and the break-up of the NBC.

The Conservatives' 1983 General Election Manifesto pledged to introduce private capital into the NBC, while another Manifesto commitment to abolish the metropolitan county councils meant that their bus operations would need to be reorganised too. In the October following the election a Cabinet reshuffle saw Nicholas Ridley appointed as Secretary of State for Transport, someone clearly sympathetic to wide-scale privatisation.[18] Ridley had been a champion of denationalisation since the 1960s. In October 1983, on his last day at the Treasury, he had learnt about proposals in the Department of Transport to privatise NBC as one unit, something seemingly favoured by his predecessors as Secretary of State and supported by Lord Shepherd. He reacted strongly against the idea, believing that the company should be divided up because a company of the NBC's size would deter other bus operators from competing. Creating competition implied deregulating and breaking up the large state-sector companies in the bus industry. At the same time, there were some in Ridley's new Department who were sceptical about the whole prospects for sustained competition in bus services.[19] Nevertheless, Ridley got his way.

Ridley immediately submitted a memorandum to E(DL) Sub-Committee recommending that the Government privatise the NBC. By this time the Corporation's financial advisers, Barclays Merchant Bank, had put forward a plan for a bank supported management buy-out of the company, an idea that had found favour with the NBC Board and the plan had been endorsed by the Department of Transport's financial advisers, S.G. Warburg. Barclays had estimated that the management buyout could provide immediate receipts of £130 million. However, Ridley was not persuaded by it, especially as it was likely that the banks financing the buyout would require that their loans should rank above any remaining government loan stock in the company and because he expected that the Government would have to step in and support the company if it got into financial difficulty. Moreover, Ridley was still keen to promote competition in local bus transport and essentially the plan envisaged retaining the existing structure of the NBC.

At the same time, Ridley's preference to break up the NBC faced a number of difficulties. To begin with, separating off National Express would be difficult because many of its coaches were used for part of the day or week on stage carriage services and bus station facilities were shared. Also, introducing a number of separate bus operators into the stage carriage market would require deregulation of the bus industry and it was feared that deregulation would endanger rural bus services, which currently benefited from cross-subsidisation by more highly used urban services. Moreover, deregulation could make privatisation of the

NBC impossible until investors were sure that the new pattern of operation was financially sound.[20] Finally, Ridley's proposals seem to have met with a mixed response in the Treasury, in the No. 10 Policy Unit and amongst some Ministers where there was a preference for a more limited restructuring.[21] The PM also harboured reservations. There was concern that if subsequent to a large-scale break-up of the industry bus services were withdrawn, the Government would get the blame.[22]

As it turned out, time was made available for further contemplation by the fact that there was no prospect of including the necessary privatisation legislation in the current session of Parliament.[23] On 18 November 1983 Ridley and the PM agreed that the privatisation should not be rushed and that there should first be a review of the whole regime of regulation and subsidy, "rather than turning over NBC ... into a regulated, subsidised and unionised regime".[24] Meanwhile, the Cabinet agreed that Ridley should plan to include a Public Transport Bill in the 1984/5 Parliamentary session.

It was the following spring before Ridley was ready to put forward detailed proposals to E(A) Sub-Committee.[25] London was excluded from the planning ostensibly because the London Regional Transport Act had recently transferred responsibility for the London Transport Executive from the Greater London Council to the Secretary of State. This Act had provided for the greater involvement of the private sector in the provision of services by requiring the new London Regional Transport to contract out work wherever suitable. It was felt that it was too soon to unleash a further wave of reform in the capital. No doubt Ridley was also concerned about the political reaction to altering substantially the organisation of bus transport in the capital. But for the rest of England and Wales, the proposals Ridley had formulated over the winter and which he now put to E(A), involved the major restructuring of bus services that he had favoured all along.

The plan involved abolishing road service licensing, replacing the duties of county councils to plan and co-ordinate public passenger transport with a power simply to ensure provision of necessary transport not supplied by the market, and changing the payment of subsidies to bus transport. In place of cross-subsidisation and direct subsidies to favoured bus operations, local authorities would be required to seek competitive tenders for contracts to run subsidised bus services. The proposals also involved the breaking up and privatising of the NBC and the transferring of municipal and PTE bus undertakings to smaller, specially established, companies. Also, as an alternative transport to buses on routes with low usage, there were provisions to consult on expanding minibus services and to relax the restrictions on the number of taxis. Bus operators would remain registered with the Traffic Commissioners to prevent disorderly entry and exit of services, and quality control including the safety of buses would continue to be vigorously enforced, but in other respects the industry would be deregulated. The intention from the outset was that these reforms would apply in due course also to Scotland.[26]

Ridley recognised that his proposals involved risks in terms of resulting higher prices on some routes, reduced rural services, redundancies and congestion on roads caused by competing bus operators. He acknowledged that some bus services currently sustained through cross-subsidies might disappear unless local authorities agreed to subsidise them. The experience of the three trial areas introduced in 1980 had revealed examples of bad behaviour between competing operators, such as buses racing to get to bus stops first. But he felt that these problems could be addressed and should be judged alongside the prospects for greater efficiency in bus operations and therefore lower fares overall.[27] There would also be the advantage of better targeted state subsidies. Where subsidies continued they would now be transparent and linked to winning competitive tenders to operate bus services. [28]He also expected his proposals to ease the adverse effects on bus fares of the planned abolition of the metropolitan counties, by reducing inefficiency in the industry. Some of the metropolitan councils, such as South Yorkshire, had heavily subsidised their bus services and there was a fear in Conservative ranks that the Government would be blamed once the councils were abolished and fares rose. To help retain bus services in rural areas, Ridley proposed easing the restrictions on running buses for community services and providing a small "pump-priming grant", of perhaps £1 million per year initially, to help rural communities start services to replace lost buses.

However, when the plans were circulated amongst Government Ministers in late April 1984[29] there was a clear division on the proposals between those who believed that bus deregulation and privatisation would be both good for passengers and good for the Exchequer, by reducing subsidies without necessarily reducing services, (a commonly quoted figure at this time was that private sector bus services were around 30 per cent less costly than public sector services) and others, notably Patrick Jenkin, the Secretary of State for the Environment, Michael Jopling at the Ministry of Agriculture, Fisheries and Food and the Secretary of State for Wales, Nicholas Edwards, who were concerned about the impact of the measures on rural bus routes.[30] The worry was also shared by George Younger at the Scottish Office. Jenkin claimed in E(A) that: "the proposals are not simply controversial; they are potentially explosive". While not against the principle of deregulation, he called for rural bus services to be excluded from the reform or, at the very least, for the deregulation to be carefully staged in rural areas. Jenkin was also worried that his Department's plans for Passenger Transport Joint Boards to oversee public transport once the metropolitan councils were abolished would be disrupted by the Ridley proposals.[31] Younger was content to accept Ridley's plan, provided that there was no expectation that the Scottish Transport Group would be privatised and that he was given "local flexibility" in applying bus subsidies in Scotland. He seems to have been especially worried about the implications of deregulation for the future of the Strathclyde PTE bus operation serving the Glasgow region.[32] The Secretary of State for Wales also pitched in noting that "our opponents will be quick to claim the proposals [by the Secretary of State for Transport] as proof of a supposed indifference on our part to the future of these [rural] areas."[33]

After discussion in E(A) it was agreed that on balance there was sufficient support for the principle of deregulating local bus services for planning to continue, but that presentation of the policy would need very careful handling. Ridley was authorised to prepare a draft White Paper, but Ministers would need to satisfy themselves that the policy could be presented to the public in a way that was politically acceptable before it was published.[34] In other words, no final decision on deregulation had yet been made.

At E(A) Sub-Committee on 28 June 1984 concerns arose again, particularly in the context of some of the content of the draft paper's annexes that had been circulated.[35] In particular, it was feared that an annex that pointed out that Sunday, early morning, late evening and rural bus services were often unprofitable, raised the prospect of service deterioration after liberalisation, providing "a positive goldmine for our opponents". Equally, an annex dealing with the results of deregulation in the three trial areas suggested that only in Hereford had there been substantial gains from deregulation and even here the eventual outcome was unpredictable. This was not considered helpful either.[36] It was agreed that the paper's drafting needed to be much more positive.[37] In response the Department of Transport agreed to make some changes to the document, while remarking that they did not agree that the annexes should avoid dealing with material that could be useful to the policy's opponents: "Their purpose is precisely to demonstrate that the Government has fully considered the issues and to put the arguments of those who oppose competition in proper perspective."[38]

In early July a draft of the White Paper was circulated by the Department of Transport to Ministers. It stressed the benefits of liberalisation in terms of a reduction in costs, a better use of buses and a rationalisation of the industry. The paper rejected the notion of keeping the NBC together on grounds of economies of scale in bus transport, an argument that had been put forward by some in the industry, claiming that the scope for economies of scale in bus transport was very limited.[39] It also dismissed objections based on the need to cross-subsidise some routes.[40] To meet the anxieties expressed in E(A) about the possible effects of deregulation on rural areas and to head off opposition in his Party – many Conservative MPs represented rural constituencies – Ridley now formally proposed the introduction of a public transport grant of £1 million a year and a special grant for rural services payable for three years (later raised to four years) to operators in rural areas. The estimated cost was £20 million in the first full year. The grant had been agreed with the Treasury "to cover the period before the full benefits of greater efficiency flow through".[41] The paper also advocated retention of the fuel duty rebate to hold down bus fares and empowered local authorities to continue concessionary fares.

Nevertheless, a number of Ministers still harboured serious concerns about the impact of the proposals on rural areas and disadvantaged groups such as pensioners;[42] while the No. 10 Policy Unit and the PM questioned the need to retain the fuel rebate because of its cost.[43] Ridley, however, held firm on its retention, emphasising that while he was no advocate of large indiscriminate subsidies of this kind, the rebate was particularly important for bus services in rural areas and its removal "could be a particular blow to small private operators, many of whom have sought to avoid dependence on local authority subsidy and all the paperwork that entails".[44]

The finalised White Paper (*Buses*, Cmnd 9300) was presented to the House of Commons on Thursday 12 July 1984. Alongside it a complementary consultation paper from the Welsh Office was published called "Local Choice in Public Transport". The proposals met with a predictably hostile reception from the Opposition Labour benches with John Prescott leading the protests, claiming: "The White Paper means nothing less than a return to a Beeching policy on the buses. The Tories chopped the railways in the 1960s and they are taking the Beeching axe to the buses in the 1980s."[45] There was also opposition from a number of councils, unions and the staff of NBC, bus manufacturers and parts of the media. Some Conservative MPs harboured doubts.

In this environment the resulting Bill had a difficult passage through Parliament. A report from the House of Commons Transport Select Committee in early March 1985 recommended that the Government should abandon its proposals for deregulation and instead adopt a policy of comprehensive competitive tendering for bus services.[46] However Ridley was dismissive of this suggestion, arguing that this proposal "would make the bus transport market more restrictive than it is now, and I reject it absolutely".[47] The Committee had been divided on the Government's plans with three Conservative MPs siding with the Opposition.

In an attempt to steady nerves within the Conservative Party, in December 1984 a briefing note was produced by the Department of Transport in an endeavour to counter what the Government saw as a gross distortion of its plans in some of the media comment: "Some opponents, for example, have even stooped to frightening the elderly by saying that concessionary fares will end, and that rural dwellers will be cut off from their bus services."[48]

221

A letter to *The Times* from an angry member of the public claiming that rural areas would be left high and dry once bus deregulation came in, led to a quick riposte from the Department of Transport to the paper's editor in an attempt to put the record straight.[49] Nevertheless, a by-election at Ryedale in May 1986 revealed continuing public disquiet about the Government's plans.[50]

In spite of the controversy inside and outside Parliament, the Transport Bill eventually received the royal assent and on 18 October 1986 the Secretary of State for Transport, now John Moore – Ridley having moved to the Department of the Environment in May to front the privatisation of water – was able to inform the Cabinet that the deregulation of bus services would start from Sunday 26 October. To ensure an orderly transition to the new competitive regime, there would be a freeze on the withdrawal or introduction of most bus services until 26 January 1987. Thereafter services could be varied with six weeks notice given to the Traffic Commissioners.[51] Publicity and advertising had been arranged particularly emphasising the opportunities for small businesses to enter the industry and provide new services. He expected that any difficulties experienced would be confined to isolated incidents and would be short-lived. On the eve of Deregulation Day Moore commented that: "We are deregulating not for any kind of ideological reasons but for benevolent ones . . . Tomorrow will see the bus industry in a position to serve its customers with efficiency and innovation for years to come."[52]

## Selling the National Bus Company

Meanwhile the planning of the sale of the NBC had been progressing. The Transport Act required the Board of NBC to submit to the Secretary of State a programme for disposing of all of its operations and to implement the agreed programme by January 1989. The Board favoured privatisation mainly as a single unit, while pursuing the divestment of some subsidiaries on commercial grounds. It believed that a fragmentation of the NBC would take too long to arrange and result in small, unviable bus companies. However, privatisation of the NBC en bloc or in just a few large groupings was ruled out by Ridley who was keen to promote competition. Nevertheless, the Board continued to oppose the break-up of the NBC.

In his memoirs Ridley comments that his insistence on breaking up the NBC met with "violent opposition but with, I believe, wholly beneficial results".[53] Two successive chairmen, Lord Shepherd and Robert Brook who took over in 1985, both objected to the Government ignoring the Board's preferences. Shepherd eventually retired and Brook, who had earlier been Chief Executive Officer, felt compelled to resign. In February 1986 the Board bowed to Government pressure but only after it requested that the Government issue it with a formal Ministerial Direction.[54] This was only the second time that a Minister had recourse to the use of a Direction to get his way during a privatisation, the first involving British Gas and its Wytch Farm oil field (see chapter 4, p.104). The Board then reluctantly agreed to a break-up of the NBC into 70 to 80 separate companies. To allow time for planning and capital raising, each would be sold over up to a three year period. Competitive bidding would be used, which had the advantage of letting the market set the sale prices in the absence of valuations for the new entities. In each case the Department of Transport intended that adjacent bus operations should be placed under different ownership to promote competition.

However, the Direction did not end tensions between the Government and the Board over the appropriate form of privatisation. At a meeting with Ridley and Department of Transport officials on 13 November 1985, the Board argued that if the break-up plan went ahead and bids were invited there should be "some price preference to [management and employee] buy-out offers over third-party offers". Following the meeting Brook wrote to Ridley commenting: "We think the best outcome all round will be arrived at by our proposing a programme to which we can commit ourselves wholeheartedly."[55]

The Government was keen to see employees invest in the success of the bus companies. As part of its wider shareholding agenda it had placed in the Transport Act (Section 48(4)) a requirement that the NBC should take such steps as might be practicable to ensure that the employees were afforded a reasonable opportunity of acquiring a controlling interest in the equity share capital of their companies. The Board saw management and/or employee buy-outs (MEBOs) as the appropriate response. Ridley certainly had no objections to privatisation through buy-outs, but insisted that to ensure a fair sale price (and maximise receipts) other, outside, bidders should be invited to bid whenever a company was sold. The NBC then complained that its managers and employees would be reluctant to sink funds into mounting bids which they might not win.

Subsequently, the Secretary of State agreed that NBC could meet a proportion of the fees and expenses of mounting a MEBO, up to a limit of £42,000 per bid.[56] In December 1985 the Secretary of State had commissioned the Bankers Trust Company to undertake a feasibility study to establish whether MEBOs of NBC subsidiaries would be a viable way of achieving the goals of privatisation.[57] The bank was also requested to develop syndicated loan facilities and seminars were commissioned from Price Waterhouse to educate bus managers on mounting buyouts. Once it became clear that MEBOs were a practical route to privatisation, the Department of Transport agreed that in making a decision on competitive bids a price preference in favour of a MEBO of up to five per cent would be permitted. Also, management and employees would be able to consider mounting bids for their businesses well before they were advertised in the press, providing an advantage in terms of time for planning.

The NBC was divided into a number of operating companies in April 1986 and the management was restructured, including the abolition of a tier of regional management. In the same month a new Chairman of the NBC was appointed, Rodney Lund, following Brook's resignation and while the change of chairman delayed final agreement on the disposal programme, it became obvious within the NBC that the break up was going to occur and that further resistance was futile. Over the following two and a half years the NBC was privatised as 72 separate companies.[58] To further assist the success of MEBOs, and placate the NBC Board, no disposal to a third party was recommended until a MEBO team had been given reasonable time to lodge a bid. The overall sale process was controlled by a "task force" made up of NBC senior management, advisers including lawyers, and civil servants from the Department of Transport. In general, the sales went through fairly smoothly with only a few criticisms of the tendering process. At first businesses were sold at proportionately lower prices than later businesses, reflecting initial inexperience of valuing bus companies and of the open tendering process. Later as experience developed, sales increasingly took the form of sealed tender bids. The Department was advised, unusually, not by a merchant bank but by accountants Price Waterhouse, on the grounds that accounting expertise was particularly relevant to this privatisation, which involved creating a large number of viable companies out of the NBC. The Department also employed six independent consultants as negotiators to help arrange the sales by liaising between the subsidiaries and potential buyers, although the actual sales were handled by the NBC. There was only one serious hiccough, when, in October 1987, the sale of six companies was reopened after criticism of the bidding process.[59]

Pension rights proved to be a tricky issue with the Government refusing to guarantee the industry's pension fund after privatisation. The NBC had never provided a formal guarantee, but in any event the Government was keen during privatisations to avoid giving such guarantees (the privatisation of British Telecom being a notable exception, see chapter 13, p.304). After some difficult negotiations, it was agreed with the unions that on the dissolution of the NBC any deficiencies in the fund based on an actuarial valuation would be made good by the NBC. Transfer values would then be agreed from the fund to new industry pension schemes to be established (or at the employee's discretion to a personal pension provided by an insurance company). Existing employees had their existing pension rights protected.[60] As it turned out the actuarial valuation revealed a surplus in the pension fund and £120 million was eventually paid over to the NBC. Through the sale of the NBC, the sum effectively flowed to the Exchequer.

The first major disposal from the NBC was of National Holidays to the Pleasurama Group in July 1986.[61] This was followed the following month with the first of the local bus operations, Devon General. Between the summer of 1986 and late 1988, the NBC was sold through 40 MEBOs (most involving management groups, including some with a proportion of the shares for employees) and 32 sales to other interests (including eight management buy-ins).[62] After the first sales succeeded, there was more interest in bidding and therefore generally higher sale prices were achieved. The dominance of MEBOs reflected not only the price preference given to management bids but the superior knowledge of the management about the prospects for their companies when valuing the businesses. Under Section 47 of the Transport Act the NBC had three years to implement an agreed disposals programme with the Secretary of State. The programme was completed ahead of time. The last disposal was of the Victoria Coach Station, which, as a critical asset in terms of coach competition, the Government decided to retain in the public sector. It was sold to London Regional Transport in October 1988.

The NBC's companies were reorganised as free-standing units in January 1986 and their balance sheets were reinstated with a view to making each viable as an independent company. This made a number of the companies more attractive to private investment than would otherwise have been the case. But investor interest in the companies was also assisted by the fact that NBC (like the NFC and ABP earlier) owned a large number of sites that might after privatisation be sold profitably to developers of shopping precincts and for other commercial uses.[63] That private investors might be more interested in buying the companies to strip out undervalued land and buildings rather than run bus services did not evade the Government. The NBC's freehold properties were revalued in the first part of 1986 and non-operational properties were transferred to a separate company, National Bus Properties Ltd, which was later sold as essentially a property business for £44 million. There remained the prospect that the privatised businesses might later sell operational properties such as city centre bus terminals to be developed as shopping centres. Therefore, after the first few sales an arrangement was introduced under which the NBC could benefit from future development profits within an agreed time scale of ten years.[64] Nevertheless, scope for investors to benefit from development gains remained. The fact that some properties were sold with clawback terms helped protect the taxpayer's interest, raising in due course a further £6 million. However, the National Audit Office later argued that clawback could have been applied more widely, judging "we do not feel that the taxpayer's interest has been fully protected."[65] Only 28 out of 1,500 properties subsequently sold were subject to clawback. The profitability of bus operations after privatisation lay in part in the efficiency improvements achieved in terms of staffing, management and bus utilisation, as the Government intended, but also in the gains from selling surplus land and buildings, which were not necessarily fully reflected in the purchase prices paid. Typically the sale price of an NBC subsidiary was based on its earning capacity as a bus company and the forecast cash flow rather than the book (or sale) value of the assets.[66]

The gross receipts from the disposal of the entire NBC totalled £324 million. The net receipts to the Exchequer, after costs of sale, repayment of loans and other expenses and including a surplus on the pension fund, amounted to some £165 million.[67] This was a creditable achievement. As a result of restructuring before and following privatisation there were some labour redundancies, working practices including overtime arrangements were altered, and over time local wage bargaining replaced national labour agreements. The deregulation of the bus industry and the break-up and sale of the NBC substantially changed the provision of bus transport in England and Wales. But arguably before privatisation the Government should have taken more action to reduce the potential for windfall gains after privatisation from selling land and buildings.

## The Scottish Transport Group

At the same time as the future of bus transport in England and Wales was being decided within Government, there had been a parallel consideration of its future in Scotland. The Scottish Transport Group (STG) was established in 1968 and by the mid-1980s had a staff of about 11,000, a turnover of around £184 million, and operated through 12 subsidiary companies including the Scottish Bus Group (SBG). SBG was Scotland's largest provider of bus services outside the country's four main cities, where bus services were the responsibility of PTEs.[68] STG was also responsible for two shipping businesses providing ferry services in the Clyde and the west coast of Scotland (known as Caledonian MacBrayne or CalMac for short), and a road haulage company serving the Highlands and Islands (called MacBrayne Haulage).

In early 1983 the Secretary of State for Scotland, George Younger, asked the Chairman of the STG to commission a study to consider the potential for privatising all or part of the Group. The report, undertaken by the British Linen Bank (the merchant banking arm of the Bank of Scotland), concluded that "one important subsidiary company of the Group should probably be privatised". However, the report advised that for the present time there should be no privatisation of the Group's two principal activities, buses and shipping services. The report concluded that STG could only be privatised at a very substantial discount to its book value and that rural bus services would be reliant on continued government subsidy, which was likely to make them unattractive to private investors. Younger acknowledged that "In certain respects, the study has been carried out with less depth than I would wish . . . For the most part, however, I do not quarrel with its main conclusions."[69]

Although the Treasury remained keen to see some privatisation of STG's activities, in subsequent months it remained Younger's firm position that the privatisation of SBG contained too many risks in terms of damage to rural bus services and the Conservatives' political standing in Scotland. He concluded that it would be prudent for the NBC in England and Wales to be privatised first so that the practicality of bus privatisation was demonstrated before the policy was seriously contemplated north of the border.[70] To placate his critics, Younger proposed that there should be a Monopolies and Mergers Commission inquiry into Scottish bus services. However, later he withdrew the suggestion after Ridley complained that a MMC inquiry would be a hindrance to bus deregulation and privatisation in England and Wales.[71]

In the bus deregulation White Paper of July 1984 the Government had stated that it did not intend for the time being to change the ownership of the SBG. But on 29 October 1986 Ridley, who had moved from being Secretary of State for Transport to Secretary of State for the Environment in May, wrote to Malcolm Rifkind, now Secretary of State for Scotland, requesting some early progress. With the Scottish bus market subject to deregulation under the 1985 Transport Act, he feared that the SBG would stymie the development of true competition in Scotland.[72] Although SBG had given assurances that cross-subsidisation would not occur, in his view these were flimsy promises given that subsidies could be easily hidden within the accounts. Moreover, he was concerned to learn that SBG was now planning a large increase in its manpower, by 400, over the next two years. In his view this confirmed that the Corporation intended to flood the market with services to damage competitors. Meanwhile, the Scottish Office had agreed to a new financial target for SBG including a five per cent real reduction in operating costs per mile by 1990, stating that this was a tough target. Ridley flatly disagreed.[73]

Rifkind replied by reminding Ridley that the SBG was changing, in particular the Board was being restructured and the Group had reorganised its bus subsidiaries, increasing the number from six to 13. Financial targets were being applied to each of the subsidiaries separately thus limiting the scope for cross subsidisation. Contrary to Ridley's conclusion, Rifkind maintained that the five per cent real reduction in operating costs was a tough target, particularly because it implied holding wage increases for bus workers below the rate of inflation.[74] However, Ridley was not placated[75] and Norman Tebbit, Chancellor of the Duchy of Lancaster, the new Secretary of State for Transport, John Moore, and John MacGregor, Chief Secretary to the Treasury, added to the pressure on Rifkind. Tebbit suggested "that there should now be a collective reconsideration of whether the time has now arrived to privatize the Scottish Bus Group."[76] On 16 March 1987 the PM intervened adding her support for such a review and requesting that the Secretary of State for Scotland "bring forward proposals for collective consideration before too long".[77]

Following this intervention, the Scottish Office agreed to a discussion of the privatisation of the STG in the Cabinet's nationalised industries committee, E(NI), on 6 May. However, Rifkind then changed his mind and decided that he did not want to come to a decision on privatisation until after the summer. His reason seems to have been a fear of the electoral consequences in Scotland ahead of a general election.[78] Rifkind's position is best summarised as supportive of privatisation in principle but doubtful of the practicality in this case. The PM also appears to have had second thoughts, probably for the same political reasons, and agreed to the postponement.

Although it was still expected that the Scottish Office would progress plans for the privatisation of STG after the 1987 General Election, it was not until 14 January 1988 that Rifkind wrote to the PM confirming that he now proposed to seek approval for the introduction of legislation in the 1988/9 Parliamentary session, which became the Transport (Scotland) Act of 1989. The aim was to privatise SBG in late 1989 or early 1990. However, Rifkind continued to worry particularly about the effects on bus services in rural areas and therefore on local communities and businesses. Also, he understood that competition would be best created by splitting up the SBG, as had happened to the NBC, but in his view this could leave Scotland with small and unviable bus companies. There was also the fact that the Board of STG, like the NBC before it, favoured privatisation as a single company. He therefore wished to take advice before deciding on what precise form privatisation should take. He also commented that he was reconsidering the future of CalMac, the ferry company. However, this business was loss making and in his view was not an obvious candidate for early privatisation.[79]

Rifkind's note to the PM led to a speedy intervention from the Treasury, opposing the sale of the SBG as one unit. Norman Lamont, Financial Secretary to the Treasury, pressed for no further delay in planning the privatisation and for Rifkind to agree that privatisation would take place through a number of separate sales.[80] The Secretary of State for Transport, Paul Channon, added his weight to the case for privatising SBG in a broken up form to stimulate competition.[81] However, the PM considered that the form the sale should take could not yet be decided and needed to be "talked through further. We have to take S of S [Secretary of State for Scotland] along with us".[82]

Following financial advice and with continuing pressure from the Treasury, Rifkind finally came round to the view that the SBG could be successfully divided into around ten separate units, including nine companies based on local areas served and Citylink providing cross-country services.[83] The decision was announced in the House of Commons on 24 May 1988.[84] By November the fine details had been agreed to dispose of the SBG as nine regional companies, Scottish Citylink express coaching, and a company containing the engineering activities. It was felt that this would create enterprises strong enough to compete on equal terms with the local authority and PTE bus operators, notably in Strathclyde.[85]

During the passage of the legislation privatising the SBG the Opposition tabled a number of amendments placing a stronger requirement on the Secretary of State to achieve MEBOs. In dealing with these amendments, the Government made clear that it was still its wish to see MEBOs succeed, as it had been during the sale of the NBC, but that this could not take place regardless of the price offered. Meanwhile, a number of local authorities in England and Wales had begun to dispose of their bus undertakings by means of negotiated sales to management and employees. This meant that these bus services were being sold through negotiated sales, while the SBG was to be sold through competitive bids. This led to complaints of unequal treatment from the SBG's management and employees.[86]

In response, on 4 July 1989 Rifkind circulated proposals to encourage MEBOs. Following the disposal of the large number of small bus companies formed out of the NBC, already there had been a number of mergers and takeovers and large private sector bus companies were forming. Rifkind feared that these companies might be able to outbid the MEBO teams in Scotland in a competitive auction. His proposal, therefore, was to give MEBO bids extra preferred status in the bidding process. This would permit negotiated sales to take place provided a satisfactory price could be obtained, and only if this was not successful would the bidding be opened to third parties. If this was not acceptable then Rifkind offered the alternative of a substantial price preference for MEBO bids to give them a distinct advantage. In his view the minimum price preference should be five per cent, as applied during the NBC sale, but with larger discounts of up to ten per cent in individual cases. He asked for Ministerial support for his proposals, warning: "There is, in Scottish terms, a major political prize to be grasped and won here – and a significant political price to pay if we fail to do so."[87]

On 11 July 1989 Paul Channon at Transport advised the Financial Secretary, Norman Lamont, that of the two options put forward by Rifkind to promote MEBOs he favoured the price preference. He agreed with Rifkind that the arrival of a number of big bus groupings and the development of a market in bus companies, both absent at the time of the NBC privatisation, meant that it might now be more difficult for MEBOs to win competitive tenders. However, any departure from a competitive tendering process would be against the Government's policy on open market sales of public assets. While single tender sales to management and employees had been allowed for some local authority bus operations, after independent valuations by outside financial advisers, this had occurred because it had been the only way to get reluctant Labour councils to agree to dispose of their bus services. Channon was also reluctant to see price preferences for MEBOs significantly above the five per cent given in the case of the NBC and in local authority bus sales.[88] The Treasury was also troubled by Rifkind's proposals, arguing that the price preferences for MEBOs given at the time of the sale of the NBC had been introduced to stimulate competition in the tenders. Now that competition was established in the bus industry in England and Wales, "we can look forward to it to provide welcome competition in the SBG sales." A five per cent preference was acceptable, as in the case of the NBC sales, but not more.[89]

With disagreement now existing between the Scottish Office, and the Department of Transport and the Treasury over the terms of the privatisation of the SBG, the PM noted that she preferred to let them "fight it out" rather than personally intervene, although she was willing to make it known that she tended to think "that a 5 per cent preference is sufficient".[90] Rifkind continued to press for MEBO teams to be given preferred status in bids and if this was not acceptable price preferences of up to ten per cent. He also wanted to see a ruling that no buyer would be allowed to buy more than one bus company: "I believe that any outcome in Scotland where, in the short or medium term, companies based south of the border take over any substantial number of Scottish Bus Group companies would be extremely damaging politically."[91] The Treasury continued to argue that there should be no departure from the Government's policy of competitive tendering and that a five per cent price preference was the maximum they were willing to concede. The Treasury maintained that any political gain in Scotland from giving an advantage to MEBOs had to be set against the difficulty that would result from having a different ceiling on the price preference than was being applied at the time by local authorities.[92]

Rifkind informed the House of Commons of his intention to privatise SBG on 27 January 1989.[93] Under the Transport Act (Scotland) 1989 the SBG was sold by competitive tender between August 1990 and October 1991. Relations had been smoothed over with the Treasury and Rifkind had agreed to accept a limit of a five per cent preference on MEBO bids to keep the sale on track. Also, preference was given to third party bids which contained proposals for at least 25 per cent of the shares to be offered to employees. Thirty-six final bids were received from 23 different organisations and six companies received four or more bids. In the case of all ten companies management and employee bids were submitted. In five cases these were successful. The gross proceeds from the sale totalled £103.1 million with total sale costs of £2.3 million.[94]

The disposal terms prohibited purchasers from buying companies operating in adjacent areas and, reflecting Rifkind's worry that the sale would attract the large bus operators from south of the border, purchasers were restricted to the acquisition of not more than two companies (excluding Citylink). Mirroring the NBC disposal, 21 non-operational properties were transferred into Group ownership for separate sale and individual clawback terms were introduced in relation to 31 operational properties (proportionately more than in the case of the NBC disposal, probably reflecting NAO criticism after that sale).[95] Pension transfer terms were agreed on the lines of those agreed earlier for the NBC. In preparation, an actuarial valuation of the funds was undertaken at 1 April 1991. This revealed a surplus of some £75 million, which accrued to the Group before being surrendered to the Treasury.

## Local authority bus services and London buses

The Transport Act 1985 had provided for other local authority bus operations, including those operated by the PTEs, to be formed into separate companies to stimulate competition. Forty-six companies were created. Also, local authorities were required to register those services they were prepared to operate without subsidy and put loss making services out to competitive tender. Nevertheless, suspicions remained that local authorities favoured their own operations and private operators continued to complain about unfair competition.[96]

The Government encouraged local authorities and PTEs to consider privatisation but had no powers to force councils or PTEs to sell their bus operations. The case for requiring local authorities to privatise their bus services had been agreed in principle in E(A) Sub-Committee in 1988 and later legislation was considered for introduction in the 1991/92 Parliamentary session, but was then dropped for lack of time in a crowded legislative schedule.[97] However, with bus services now operating according to market rules and local authorities having lost effective control over bus operations in their areas, local authorities became more receptive to privatisation proposals. In some cases employees judged that their futures including their pensions might be better protected by supporting a sale. Also, in 1993 John MacGregor, Secretary of State for Transport, provided an added impetus when he directed that local authorities should complete their disposals by 31 December of that year if they wished to keep the entire sales proceeds. After that date 50 per cent of proceeds would be used to reduce local government debt. By mid-1991 nine bus companies had been sold voluntarily, eight through MEBOs.[98] Later others were sold leaving just 17 bus companies still formally owned by local councils. Privatisation was also voluntarily undertaken by the PTEs. Privatisation began in October 1988 with the sale of Yorkshire Rider and was completed in March 1994 with the sale of bus services in Greater Manchester.[99]

The bus services of London Regional Transport were sold between January 1994 and January 1995. This resulted in proceeds of £233 million, well above the valuation put on the assets by the financial advisers, BZW.[100] Initially it had been planned that privatisation would take the form of 14 to 16 separate companies each with between 200 and 400 buses. However, this idea was revised later and eventually eleven bus operating subsidiary companies were created (one disbanded before privatisation as the result of losing a significant amount of its tendered work). Three of the sales were in the form of management buyouts, three employee buyouts and the rest trade sales.

## Bus privatisation: an assessment

The deregulation and privatisation of bus services from 1985 led to a major change in the way that public transport was provided in Britain. The level of public subsidy fell and some new services were introduced including minibus services,[101] vindicating the Government's reform.[102] Some large savings from tendering for bus subsidies were recorded with initial savings of 70 per cent in Lancashire and West Sussex and 50 per cent in Surrey. In total, financial support for local bus transport in England fell from £911 million in 1984/5 to £263 million by 1993/4. Also, bus mileage rose considerably, aided by the use of more mini buses. However bus fares rose in real terms over the same period, the actual rise varying across the country reflecting the extent to which subsidies had previously been paid by local authorities, but averaging 19 per cent. Intense price competition occurred only spasmodically when one or another bus company sought to force a competitor out of the local market or a new provider

*Table 10.1* Bus passenger journeys 1985/6 to 1993/4

|  | % change to 1993/4 |
|---|---|
| London | −3.0 |
| Metropolitan Areas | −35.5 |
| English Shires | −20.2 |
| Scotland | −21.6 |
| Wales | −20.2 |
| *Average outside London* | *−27.4* |

Source: Transport Committee (1995), p.xliii.

entered. Passenger journeys in England continued to fall especially outside London, between 1985/6 and 1993/4 by an average of 27.4 per cent (Table 10.1). Similar results were recorded in Wales.[103] In Scotland, as in England (Table 10.2), operating costs fell per vehicle kilometre due to a rationalisation of depots and manning reductions and the number of bus operators expanded at first. However, bus usage also continued to decline.[104] Across England, Wales and Scotland there was evidence of fewer buses operating in the evenings and weekends and on more sparsely used routes, while in general earnings, pensions and holiday pay for employees fell relative to other manual workers (Table 10.3).[105]

In so far as performance rose, this was probably more down to the results of competition than privatisation. Also, and contrary to Ridley's expectation at the time of the 1985 White Paper, neither liberalisation nor privatisation reversed the long-term decline in bus journeys in Britain. Nor was the move to competition an obvious long-term success in England and Wales or in Scotland when measured by the number of separate bus operators. In spite of terms during the sale of the NBC and SBG under which purchasers were not allowed to

*Table 10.2* Local bus services: operating costs 1985/6 to 1993/4

*Operating costs per vehicle kilometre (pence) excluding depreciation at 1993/4 prices*

|  | London | English Metropolitan areas | English shire counties | England |
|---|---|---|---|---|
| 1985/86 | 238 | 165 | 117 | 151 |
| 1986/87 | 220 | 146 | 102 | 133 |
| 1987/88 | 206 | 117 | 90 | 114 |
| 1988/89 | 203 | 108 | 86 | 108 |
| 1989/90 | 193 | 103 | 82 | 105 |
| 1990/91 | 190 | 101 | 80 | 103 |
| 1991/92 | 180 | 98 | 79 | 101 |
| 1992/93 | 167 | 90 | 77 | 95 |
| 1993/94 | 150 | 85 | 72 | 89 |

*Note*: costs adjusted using GDP deflator.
*Source*: Transport Committee (1995), Table 2, p.xxv.

*Table 10.3* Average earnings of bus and coach drivers 1975 to 1994

*£ per hour at April 1994 prices*

| | Bus and coach drivers | All manual workers | Bus and coach as % of manual |
|---|---|---|---|
| 1975 | 5.51 | 5.38 | 102 |
| 1976 | 5.30 | 5.34 | 99 |
| 1977 | 4.83 | 4.95 | 98 |
| 1978 | 5.00 | 5.14 | 97 |
| 1979 | 4.78 | 5.34 | 90 |
| 1980 | 5.06 | 5.37 | 94 |
| 1981 | 5.16 | 5.35 | 96 |
| 1982 | 5.27 | 5.37 | 98 |
| 1983 | 5.58 | 5.59 | 100 |
| 1984 | 5.48 | 5.61 | 98 |
| 1985 | 5.48 | 5.60 | 98 |
| 1986 | 5.70 | 5.80 | 98 |
| 1987 | 5.34 | 5.91 | 90 |
| 1988 | 5.44 | 6.08 | 89 |
| 1989 | 5.27 | 6.07 | 87 |
| 1990 | 5.18 | 6.09 | 85 |
| 1991 | 5.08 | 6.18 | 82 |
| 1992 | 5.17 | 6.29 | 82 |
| 1993 | 5.09 | 6.37 | 80 |
| 1994 | 5.03 | 6.31 | 80 |

*Note*: Figures deflated by the RPI.

*Source*: Transport Committee (1995), Table 3, p. xxvi.

acquire more than a certain number of the subsidiaries on the market and were not allowed to purchase two contiguous subsidiaries, over time there was a reconsolidation of the industry. Within a few years a number of the newly independent bus companies merged or were taken over. In particular, in most cases those bus companies bought through MEBOs were sold on to the large bus groups that formed in the 1990s. Management and employee ownership was a transitory phenomenon. The prospect of a large capital gain by selling shareholdings proved too tempting to the new owners. For example, when Yorkshire Rider was sold to Badgerline in March 1994, three senior managers received over £3 million each and long-serving employees a windfall of around £10,000 each.[106]

Of the 72 companies created out of the NBC, by 1995 all but 14 were part of large groups and over 30 per cent of turnover in the British bus industry was accounted for by the four largest bus groupings – National Express, FirstGroup, Stagecoach and Arriva (formerly Cowie) – owning almost 22,000 buses between them. By 1998 their share of the market had risen to 60 per cent. At the same time, there were frequent complaints about the activities of a number of bus operators, including poor timetabling, concentration of competition on the most popular routes and rival bus operators racing to bus stops. There were also instances of alleged predatory pricing to drive out competitors. Between 1986 and 1994, 541 complaints about either anti-competitive practices against bus operators or bus mergers were investigated by the Office of Fair Trading or the MMC.[107] In the mid-1980s the Department of Transport had played down the importance of economies of scale in bus provision. The merger of the industry into large private sector groupings was justified by management in terms of lower costs, for example in terms of economising on workshop facilities and administration and benefits in terms of procurement. Suspicion remains that the main motive was to remove competition.

In London bus journeys rose during the 1990s.[108] But here fares were regulated and services were secured from public and private sector operators under a system of competitive tendering. This is an approach to the provision of public transport that the Government at the time of the 1985 Transport Act had rejected for the rest of Britain, on the grounds that it did not amount to true competition. Starting in 1985 bus services in London were progressively put out to tender and by 1994 a half of the network was contracted, of which around 50 per cent of the contracts had been won by London Buses Ltd, a subsidiary of London Regional Transport, and the rest by private operators. In time, individual companies within London Buses were permitted to compete with one another for contracts.[109] Arguably more trials should have been undertaken across the country of different forms of competition before bus liberalisation was enforced in the mid-1980s. The 1985 Transport Act imposed what was in effect a "one size fits all" policy to bus service provision outside London. By default, London was a trial area or benchmark for a different type of market liberalisation – competition "for routes" rather than "on routes".

In summary, bus deregulation and privatisation produced uneven results and consequently debate continues about whether public transport is best state planned and delivered or left to the market. In the Transport Act 2000 the new Labour Government, supported by many local authorities, introduced "quality partnerships" and "quality contracts", in effect reintroducing what some see as an element of regulation and control of bus services by local government.[110]

## The Royal Ordnance factories

The Royal Ordnance (RO) factories made ammunition, explosives, small arms and fighting vehicles, primarily for the British Army. Historically, the RO manufactured equipment to Ministry of Defence (MoD) requirements, the products often having been developed in MoD research establishments. By the mid-1980s the RO had a turnover of some £500 million and employed around 16,500 workers at 16 plants across Britain (Table 10.4), although plans existed to reduce this number to 12,000 as part of a drive to raise efficiency. The RO was profitable; in 1985 it made profits of £26 million after tax, although some parts of the RO were more profitable than others. Nevertheless, in general the RO was likely to be of interest to the private sector.

In 1974 the RO had been reconstituted as a trading fund at arm's length from the MoD in an attempt to introduce a more commercial approach to its management. A trading fund has its own accounts and is expected to operate in a more businesslike manner than a government department but remains part of the Government. Its assets remain government assets and the permanent staff are civil servants. However, concerns continued within the Government about the efficiency of the RO's operations. In 1982 the Government decided that the business should operate under the Companies Act and intended to introduce legislation when the Parliamentary timetable allowed.[111] The Queen's Speech on the opening of Parliament following the May 1983 General Election referred to a possible sale of the RO and by 1985 planning was underway in the MoD for privatisation.

*Table 10.4* The Royal Ordnance factories 1985

| Factory | Product | Number of employees at 31 December 1985 |
|---|---|---|
| *Weapons and Fighting Vehicles Division* | | |
| Leeds | Main battle tanks | 1514 |
| Nottingham | Large guns, vehicles, mortars | 1213 |
| *Ammunition Division* | | |
| Birtley (Newcastle) | Ammunition components, mainly for Chorley and Glascoed | 1282 |
| Patricroft (Lancs) | Ammunition components, mainly for Chorley and Glascoed | 1461 |
| Blackburn (Lancs) | Fuzes | 2077 |
| Chorley (Lancs) | Assembly and filling of ammunition | 1740 |
| Glascoed (South Wales) | Assembly and filling of ammunition | 1848 |
| Featherstone | Armour piercing components | 196 |
| *Explosives Division* | | |
| Bishopton (Glasgow) | Explosives and propellants | 1784 |
| Bridgwater | Explosives and propellants | 567 |
| Westcott (Bucks) | Rocket motors R&D | 795 |
| Summerfield (Worcester) | Rocket motors R&D | 657 |
| Waltham Abbey | Explosives R&D | (included in Westcott total) |
| *Small Arms Division* | | |
| Enfield | Small Arms | 1010 |
| Radway Green | Small Arms Ammunition | 2239 |
| Powfoot (Dumfriesshire) | Propellant | 188 |

*Source*: E (A) (86) 40 "Privatisation of Royal Ordnance Plc. Memorandum by the Secretary of State for Defence", 17 July 1986.

Initially, consideration was given to selling some or all of the factories to existing private sector companies. But the Department's preference was to keep the RO as one unit. The MoD was concerned that any suggestion of dividing it up could cause a serious loss of morale within the organisation. Also, it was felt that there were some good commercial reasons for keeping the RO together because of significant inter-factory trading.[112] In particular, the Explosives and Ammunition Divisions relied heavily on orders from each other. Finally, the MoD argued that the sales receipts from selling the various components of the RO were likely to be less than selling the organisation as one concern, especially as the bits left unsold might well have to be shut, leading to closure costs. When approaches to possible trade buyers, particularly Lord Weinstock at GEC and Lord Hanson of Hanson Trust, came to nothing, the Government decided to enact legislation to enable corporatisation and a share flotation. The Ordnance Factories and Military Services Act 1984 created the Royal Ordnance plc. In January 1985 this new company took over the assets of the former RO trading fund, together with some related R&D facilities owned by the MoD.

During the planning for privatisation new relationships and dividing lines were agreed between the MoD and RO. Previously the two had been highly integrated with information readily exchanged and a "preferred source" policy for procuring supplies from the RO operated. Now something more akin to a normal commercial, arm's length, relationship was established. The new relationship included the transfer of certain intellectual property rights to manufacture equipment to the RO from the MoD, agreement over access rights to MoD research establishments, and the provision of some product development capability. However, from the point of view of the MoD the negotiations proved more difficult than expected with the RO submitting a series of demands.

A new Chairman of the RO, Bryan Basset, was appointed in August 1985, but it seems that his performance failed to impress. In April 1986 a new Chief Executive, Roger Pinnington, was appointed and was seen within Government as being more satisfactory. Changes in management methods and new financial control systems were introduced into the RO and the RO Board became committed to a flotation. But after his arrival Pinnington expressed doubts about the company's readiness for transfer to the private sector. N. M. Rothschild & Co. (Rothschilds) advising the Government also concluded that flotation in 1986 would be premature unless the remaining negotiations over matters such as the ownership of intellectual property rights in the products produced by the RO were settled. Lord Young recounts in his memoirs "long, fraught meetings" during the planning of the sale with those sceptical of the case for privatisation preferring the sale as one company "for that way it would be more difficult to sell the whole. So the more cynical of us thought."[113]

The flotation of the RO had been provisionally scheduled for 16 July 1986. The idea at this time was to place a large majority of the shares, around 75 per cent, with the financial institutions. This would leave 25 per cent of the shares for public subscription and allocation or sale to the RO's employees. But given the quality of the company's financial controls, it was considered unlikely that the company would be able to include a formal profits forecast in its prospectus. A failure to do so could be expected to depress interest in the share issue. Moreover, it had been estimated that £50 million would be needed by way of a capital injection to construct a balance sheet sufficiently attractive to the private sector. This would leave net sale proceeds of about £100 million, a figure less than the book value of the assets, which was put at over £200 million. The Government feared that a sale for £100 million would attract the critical attention of the House of Commons Public Accounts Committee.

Most threatening to the planned flotation, however, was a dispute that had broken out over MoD tank orders. In June 1984 the MoD had awarded a contract for 64 Challenger tanks for the British army's 5th Tank regiment to the RO without competition. The RO's chief domestic competitor, Vickers plc, which had recently invested in its tank manufacturing factory in Newcastle, protested and sought assurances that this would not happen again. Later Sir David Plastow, Managing Director and Chief Executive of Vickers, would claim that an assurance had been given, something MoD officials denied. A year later an order for a further 18 Challenger tanks for the 6th tank regiment was given to the RO's Leeds factory, again under a non-competitive contract. This time Vickers was mollified by the award of a contract for the development and initial production of a batch of Challenger Repair and Recovery Vehicles. Nevertheless, Vickers remained irritated about what it saw as the un-level playing field for military contracts. Once the RO was privatised Vickers demanded that it should not be given preferential treatment when MoD orders were allocated.

In the autumn of 1985 an announcement was made that another tank order would be placed, this time for the 7th tank regiment. Once again the order was placed with the RO non-competitively, although the price was negotiated downwards by ten per cent in real terms on the price agreed with the RO for the earlier tanks. The contract was expected to secure the future of RO's Leeds tank factory until 1989, which otherwise was at risk of closure. Placing the order with RO was in part justified on the grounds that the MoD would have had to pay for redundancies at Leeds had the order gone elsewhere. However, Vickers still made strong representations about their exclusion from the contract. The placing of this MoD order non-competitively had been agreed by Michael Heseltine, the Defence Secretary, to keep the flotation on track, prior to him walking out of the Cabinet in January 1986 over the future of Westland, the British helicopter manufacturer. Plastow pressed for a meeting with the new Secretary of State for Defence, George Younger, to discuss his concerns.

After the meeting Vickers was still not satisfied and continued to lobby for equal treatment. Vickers' anger was further fuelled by revelation that the design rights for the Challenger, Chieftain and Centurian tanks had been transferred by the MoD to the RO. Vickers feared that this might mean that it would be unable to compete for battle tank work in the future except as sub-contractors to the RO. This was felt to be contrary to an assurance the company had received in December 1984 that intellectual property rights granted by Vickers under an earlier contract and vested in the MoD would not be transferred. It was Vickers that in 1960 had designed the turret used for the Chieftain tank and on which the Challenger's turret was based. Plastow threatened that Vickers would seek a legal remedy to compensate for the potential damage to the company, including the impact on the company's credibility in overseas markets.[114] On 30 May 1986, Plastow demanded "immediate assurance" that the next contract for Challenger tanks would be open to competitive tender and not awarded directly to the RO.[115]

Meanwhile, with this dispute casting a serious shadow over the RO's privatisation, the protracted negotiations between the MoD and RO management lumbered on. During the discussions RO demanded that the MoD agree to place with it all of the Government's requirements for explosives and propellants for at least seven years.[116] Acceding to such a demand would inevitably annoy Vickers and possibly other potential suppliers. This and other new demands resulted in an angry reaction within No.10, as evident in an internal memorandum:

"The RO have now presented a final list of demands and are insisting that the MOD concedes them in full if privatisation is to proceed. The list goes from the absurd (the unprivatised atomic weapons 'Royal Ordnance factories' must be renamed immediately) to the impossible (the MOD should settle a contract dispute between Royal Ordnance and Hunting). On the substantive issues they want legally binding agreements on access to MOD ranges and research establishments, to be effectively a sole supplier to the MOD in some equipment areas, and to renegotiate the arrangements on intellectual property. Although there may be some room for compromise, (the MOD has already bent over backwards), it cannot possibly give way in toto."

In an attempt to find a way forward Younger held what was described as a "final crunch meeting" with the RO's management to try to settle the differences. It seems that Younger was on the point of recommending that the privatisation be cancelled. As the internal No. 10 memorandum concludes, "This must be right – the long term cost of conceding the RO terms must outweigh the proceeds from the sale, and in any event it would be an unfortunate precedent to give in to such naked blackmail."[117]

However, after further discussion with the RO, Younger decided that the flotation should continue. He was conscious of the political damage that could arise if the privatisation was withdrawn and he was keen for the RO to operate in the private sector to raise its efficiency.[118] But the concerns over the award of the latest contract for the Challenger tanks to the Leeds factory continued. Within Government it was agreed that the matter would need to be resolved before privatisation could occur.[119]

The MoD and the Treasury judged that placing the tank order with the RO was still essential if a flotation of the company was to attract a sufficient number of investors. But the Trade and Industry Secretary, Paul Channon, now sided with Vickers expressing concerns about non-competitive procurement. This threatened a highly damaging division in the Cabinet not long after the Westland affair and again on policy towards defence procurement. Moreover, it was felt that to push ahead with the planned flotation might trigger adverse publicity over job losses at the Vickers factory in Newcastle.

Younger wished to continue with the privatisation and the Chancellor of the Exchequer was willing to agree, "though most reluctantly", but serious reservations still existed within No. 10. Matters then took a further twist. On 4 June 1986 Vickers wrote to the MoD stating that the company wished to enter into serious negotiations to purchase the RO plants in Nottingham and Leeds. The offer was subject to the order of Challenger tanks for the 7th regiment being negotiated with the new combined, Vickers owned, undertaking.[120] The alternative of breaking the company up and selling off the individual factories was now a real possibility, but the Government was conscious of the risk of being left with an unsaleable rump of assets.[121] At the same time, the MoD was aware that there were unlikely to be sufficient defence orders in the future to sustain the UK's four military vehicle manufacturers – RO, Vickers, Alvis (Coventry) and GKN-Sankey. In this context Vickers' proposal to purchase the RO's tank manufacturing plants and then rationalise production had clear attractions. But the MoD still preferred to see RO sold off as one unit. Also, Vickers was now signalling that if, despite its protests, the RO was given priority for the next Challenger orders, it would definitely seek compensation from the MoD.

A meeting of Ministers, including the Secretaries of State for Defence and Trade and Industry, the Chancellor of the Exchequer and the Financial Secretary, was called by the PM for the afternoon of Wednesday 11 June 1986 to try to thrash out a solution. In preparation for the meeting a briefing paper from the Cabinet Office warned, in the light of the Westland debacle, of "the makings of another nasty and embarrassing row (with familiar ingredients – DTI and MOD in dispute over a medium sized defence contractor)". It concluded that a postponement of the flotation might be the sensible option.[122] Regarding the future for the remainder of the RO, if Vickers took over the Leeds and Nottingham factories, the paper suggested that the explosive and propellant facilities of the RO might be attractive to other companies, such as ICI and IMI, and the Enfield small arms plant might also be attractive to a trade buyer. Dismemberment of the RO as a route to privatisation was therefore once more an option, but it would require a more co-operative management. The PM was therefore advised that this option was not likely to be worth pursuing further unless the Government was willing to put new management into the RO. The conclusion of the No. 10 Policy Unit was that, "On balance the commercial arguments are probably against privatisation and the political ones in favour. It is a difficult choice, but having gone so far, it may be best to carry on with the flotation."[123]

At the meeting on 11 June the acceptability of placing the latest order for Challenger tanks with the RO generated much heat. Following the meeting the PM seems to have been very doubtful about the wisdom of proceeding with the flotation and the MoD promised a paper on the consequences of not privatising. The Government feared a flotation flop, just prior to the much more important privatisation of the British Gas Corporation scheduled for November. Advice within No. 10 to the PM was that unless this promised piece from the MoD was very compelling, the PM should stop the sale: "Public opinion is already very sceptical about the sale of BGC and water. To sell RO on the present basis would hand the Opposition a tremendous weapon to attack the entire policy."[124]

The MoD's response came in two letters. Both made an impassioned plea not to give up on the flotation. The MoD argued that even in the absence of a sale of RO it would still wish to proceed with the contract for the Challenger tanks and that building the tanks at Leeds was the quickest way of fulfilling the contract. To embark now on a competitive bidding process for the contract would impose an unwelcome delay of up to 12 months. In addition, the MoD reminded Ministers that without the order large redundancies would occur at the Leeds tank factory and probably the factory would close, leaving Vickers as the only domestic supplier of tanks. There would also be other difficulties for the Government if the flotation did not go ahead. These included the prospect of continuing state financing and, if the Leeds and Nottingham factories were sold to Vickers, regrouping the rest of the business to make it attractive to buyers, which "would, at best, take a couple of years" even if the management co-operated. In total the contents of the two MoD letters amounted to a determined attempt to prevent the flotation from being pulled.[125]

Within No. 10 there appears to have been some disagreement on how best to proceed, with some believing that the planned flotation should continue,[126] but with the No. 10 Policy Unit preferring that the Challenger contract be placed with Leeds and then the Leeds and Nottingham factories sold to Vickers.[127] The Treasury agreed to delay the flotation by a week to allow a final decision to be made. However, it stressed that to do so tended to edge the Government nearer to cancelling the sale because of the need if the sale went ahead to adjust the Government's timetable for other privatisations. Meanwhile Younger asked to see the PM to re-stress the problems a cancellation of the flotation would produce, while Vickers added to the Government's discomfort by, it appears, briefing the press. On 15 June Plastow was quoted in *The Sunday Times* as stating that if the tank order went to RO "that will be totally indefensible". On 16 June *The Daily Telegraph* reported on Vickers' opposition to the RO sell-off. The future of the RO and the related tank orders was now blowing up into a highly public row and one that could prove as politically damaging as Westland.[128]

Another Ministerial meeting was called for 17 June. Ahead of the meeting, Norman Tebbit, Chancellor of the Duchy of Lancaster, counselled the PM that the flotation should be abandoned because it would be unfair to Vickers "and constitute a travesty of our commitment to competition in defence procurement . . .. No amount of effective presentation can make this story palatable".[129] At the same time, the Government had come to the view that provided the MoD could demonstrate that the placing of the order with the Leeds factory was not connected with the privatisation sale, then a legal challenge from Vickers was unlikely to succeed.

On the morning of 16 June the PM met with Younger and voiced her preference for abandoning the planned flotation, placing the 7th regiment Challenger order with the Leeds factory, selling the Leeds and Nottingham factories to Vickers, and floating the rest of the RO later. It seems that Younger did not demur but wished to consult with the Financial Secretary. Meanwhile, opposition to giving the Challenger contract to Leeds before the factory was sold off was hardening within the Treasury because this would prevent competition for the contract and possible financial savings.[130] At a meeting of Ministers the following day under the PM's chairmanship the arguments for and against flotation were again aired, the PM finally concluding that the flotation should not go ahead in July. The decision was to be described publicly as a "deferral" of the sale. But it was recognised that a lengthy "deferral" would effectively make the flotation of RO impossible during the present Parliament because of the Government's crowded legislative timetable and because the order book at the Leeds factory was due to dry up by the end of 1989.

Following the meeting the MoD was invited to prepare a paper on the future options for the RO and the Challenger tank contract.[131] On 20 June 1986 Lord Trefgarne, Minister of State for Defence Procurement, in an effort to revive the sale, wrote to Plastow formally inviting him to make a proposal for the purchase of the Leeds factory. His letter also noted that the new Challenger order would be placed immediately after the terms of a sale to Vickers had been agreed. In the absence of an agreement, the Challenger order would be placed with the Leeds factory by the end of July. A short deadline for a decision, of 4 July, was imposed and the MoD made clear that the RO's Nottingham factory would not be included in the sale negotiation, although it might become available later.[132]

Vickers responded with an initial offer for the RO's tank building assets at Leeds of £3 million, which the Government considered too low. The Government threatened that the 7th regiment contract would definitely go to Leeds whether Vickers bought the factory or not. Vickers then agreed to increase its offer to around £11 million, closer to the book value of the assets of around £15 million. In addition, Vickers arranged to match the RO's prices for the 5th and 6th regiments' Challenger tanks and to improve slightly the terms of the contract for the tanks for the 7th regiment. Vickers' plan involved keeping both the Leeds factory and its existing Newcastle tank factory open and the company offered to invest £13 million in the Leeds operation to ensure its survival. The MoD's advisers, Rothschilds, judged that the offer was a fair one and the MoD agreed to support the proposal, even though it would effectively make Vickers a monopoly supplier of UK made tanks to the Government. This had been something the MoD previously had been keen to avoid. But the Department consoled itself that, given its current order book, in the absence of the deal the Leeds factory would have closed in 1990 also leaving Vickers as the sole domestic supplier.

On 22 July 1986 at E(A) Sub-Committee Younger confirmed that a provisional agreement had been reached with Vickers to purchase the Leeds factory for around £11 million. No other company had shown interest in buying the facility. Younger stressed that the deal made possible the elimination of excess capacity in the fighting vehicle industry with the rationalisation costs falling on Vickers rather than the Government or the RO. He went on to comment that although the outcome would eliminate competition between UK suppliers of tanks to the armed forces, this was not after all of such great concern because there was no prospect of further tank orders for a considerable time, while the next generation of tanks was likely to be produced through international collaboration.[133] The Sub-Committee endorsed the proposal. Two days later Younger informed the full Cabinet that he would be making a statement that afternoon in the House of Commons on the sale of the RO factory in Leeds to Vickers and the decision not to proceed with a flotation.[134] The statement to the House included the Government's plan to sell the remainder of RO as a single entity to a trade buyer, if practicable. The Opposition responded by criticising the creation of a private monopoly in main battle tank provision.[135]

The disposal of tank production to Vickers was completed in October 1986 with Vickers making an initial payment of £11.2 million for the Leeds factory with the final price to be determined by formula based on the audited net asset value. This left the Government with the challenge of disposing of the remainder of the RO, consisting of manufacturing and R&D centres involving weapons, explosives and ammunition. It was decided that if possible the remainder should be sold to a trade buyer as one entity.[136] In October a memorandum was issued to prospective buyers. In early April of the following year, Younger was able to inform the House that firm bids had been received from two companies, British Aerospace (BAe) and GKN, for the remainder of the RO and that the Government had decided to sell to BAe for £190 million. In accordance with the Government's aim of widening share ownership, shares in BAe would be made available to employees of RO.[137] Also, provision was made for the transfer of staff under the Transfer of Undertakings (Protection of Employment) Regulations (TUPE) with the effect that the terms and conditions of work were protected. A new pension scheme was established to which existing employees could transfer or remain in their current civil service scheme. The new scheme provided broadly the same benefits (with some improvements), including the index-linking of future pensions and was funded by a lump sum transfer paid by Government. However, a 12 per cent inflation cap was placed on the index-linking because it was anticipated that potential investors would be unwilling to accept an open-ended commitment to inflation proof pensions if very high inflation ever returned.[138] The beneficial pension rights did not extend to workers newly employed after the sale. These provisions followed the precedents set by earlier privatisations.[139]

*   *   *

The Government succeeded in disposing of the RO, but the overall result was to consolidate more of Britain's defence manufacturing in Vickers and BAe, an outcome inconsistent with the Government's stated preference for more competition and one which at the outset the MoD had been keen to avoid. Also, and as the Treasury observed at the time, following the disposal of the RO benefits to the taxpayer would depend upon whether the MoD was able to procure supplies of comparable quality more cheaply.[140] It is not clear that follow up studies were ever performed to check whether these benefits materialised. The purchase of the RO by BAe was followed by a rationalisation of production. However, some of the rationalisation and reduction in production facilities in the 1990s resulted from the decline in MoD orders following the end of the "cold war" rather than from the privatisation of the RO.

# 11

# PRIVATISING BRITISH TELECOM

## The decision to privatise

The privatisation of British Telecommunications (BT) in November 1984 was arguably the most important of all of the privatisations of the 1980s. It was the first involving an enterprise which had a monopoly position in the country and the privatisation required the design of a regulatory system to prevent the exploitation of market power after transfer to the private sector. It was also by far the largest privatisation to date, indeed at the time the largest stock market flotation ever, with a flotation value of about £3.9 billion. There was considerable uncertainty over whether the capital market would be able to absorb such a large share issue. The privatisation of BT built up experience and confidence in privatising large state enterprises, which the Government would tap into later, especially when it undertook the sales of British Gas, the water and sewerage industry, electricity and the railways.

Given the importance of the sale of BT for the entire privatisation programme, the discussion is spread across three chapters. This chapter is concerned with the origins of the Government's decision to privatise BT and the resulting Telecommunications Bill and BT's licence. The next chapter details the design of the new regulatory office for telecommunications in Britain and the price cap mechanism, which together provided the model for the regulatory regimes created during the later privatisations of gas, airports, water, electricity and the railways, and for telecommunications and other industries in many other parts of the world. The third chapter deals specifically with the flotation of BT in November 1984 and the difficulties that had to be overcome. The chapter also includes the conclusions on one of Britain's biggest privatisations.

## Background to the decision to privatise

The telephone service in Britain developed in the late nineteenth century as a mixture of state and private sector provision but with much of the operation undertaken by the General Post Office (GPO). In 1896 the private sector trunk service was taken over by the GPO and in 1912 the GPO absorbed all of the telecommunications providers with the exception of the service in the City of Kingston-upon-Hull, which remained under local authority ownership. Henceforth, until 1969, telecommunications services in Britain apart from Hull were the responsibility of the Postmaster General. In 1969 the Post Office became a public corporation and in July 1977 an official committee, the Carter Committee recommended that the two functions of post and telecommunications be separated.[1] Following the May 1979 General Election, the new Conservative Secretary of State for Industry, Sir Keith Joseph, announced a review of the telecommunications sector and the Government's intention to transfer telecommunications to a new public corporation, British Telecommunications (BT). BT took over the telecommunications business from the Post Office corporation (PO) on 1 October 1981.

By the late 1970s it was clear that telecommunications would need large investment owing to a combination of a growing demand for telecommunications services and technological change. The arrival of digitalisation and the prospect of transmitting computerised data as well as voice calls necessitated replacing much of the existing capacity, especially since 89 per cent of connections from telephone exchanges to subscribers in Britain were still accounted for by Strowger mechanical switching equipment.[2] Investment in telecommunications had risen sharply since the mid-1970s, from £816 million in 1976–7 to £1,898 million in 1981/2 and future plans suggested a continuing rise, with a planned total for 1982/3 of £2,380 million.[3] Telecommunications had been largely self financing between 1977 and 1981, but the investment programme needed to digitalise exchanges and provide the infrastructure needed to satisfy the growing demand for telecommunications services, it was believed would necessitate external financing.[4]

The issue was how to achieve the necessary level of investment without a sharp rise in the Corporation's external financing limit (EFL). Although in 1979/80 and 1980/1 the telecommunications side of the PO had failed to achieve its five per cent target rate of return, because of the economic recession and rising costs, in general the business was financially sound, as confirmed by the figures in Table 11.1. BT's first annual report and accounts as an independent corporation, published in September 1982, showed a profit of £458 million on a turnover of £5.7 billion, business growth of six per cent, and a 2.1 per cent annual reduction in real unit costs.[5] Under private sector operation, especially given the organisation's monopoly position, access to loan finance would not have been a problem. But when in July 1980 PO telecommunications put in a bid to the Treasury for future external financing there was great alarm in E Committee, given the Government's macroeconomic objective of reducing the PSBR.[6] The management announced that to install the planned electronic exchanges and a multi-purpose digital network, around £2 billion would need to be invested in 1981/2 with a resulting increase in its borrowings limit of approximately £500 million. Meanwhile they indicated that the level of investment and external funding requested would need to be repeated in future years.[7]

In addition to anxiety about the level of borrowing needed to sustain the investment programme, the Treasury and No.10 were concerned about the level of cost efficiency in BT and especially what were perceived to be excessive pay settlements. Telecommunications was prone, like the rest of the PO, to bouts of poor industrial relations. The election of the new Conservative Government coincided with a major strike by computer and administrative staff. This disrupted telephone billing between April and September 1979 and cost the organisation £110 million in delayed revenues.[8] In August 1979 the PM reluctantly agreed to an increase in telecommunications charges to customers, largely to meet the higher labour costs.[9] The following July the PO offered the Post Office Engineering Union (POEU) a further 18 per cent increase in basic pay plus three per cent for unspecified productivity improvements. It then followed this up with a demand for another rise in telephone charges, of around 20 per cent, and threatened an additional surcharge on subscribers to stay within its EFL.[10] E Committee expressed deep concern and particularly opposed any idea of a surcharge on subscribers. But the Government was caught between wanting to hold down telephone charges and avoiding demands from BT for a rise in its EFL.[11]

*Table 11.1* The finances of PO Telecommunications/BT 1973–82

| | 1972/3 | 1973/4 | 1974/5 | 1975/6 | 1976/7 | 1977/8 | 1978/9 | 1979/80 | 1980/81 | 1981/82 |
|---|---|---|---|---|---|---|---|---|---|---|
| Profit/loss for year (£m) | −9.7 | −61.4 | −194.5 | 154.7 | 365.4 | 326.6 | 336.4 | 129.1 | 123.9 | 457.8 |
| Fixed assets net expenditure (£m) | 625.5 | 696.4 | 787.2 | 915.9 | 834.6 | 844.6 | 996.5 | 1240.8 | 1304.8 | 1456.1 |
| Financed: | | | | | | | | | | |
| Internal resources (£m) | 240.8 | 298.0 | 368.7 | 641.9 | 841.9 | 1039.5 | 1110.0 | 1070.3 | 1102.2 | 1630.9 |
| External borrowing (£m) | 375.5 | 293.4 | 535.9 | 270.0 | 208.2 | −48.1 | −172.9 | −178.4 | −75.4 | 127.6 |
| Self-financing ratio (per cent) | 38.6 | 36.9 | 39.8 | 92.4 | 109.2 | 113.9 | 106.1 | 79.2 | 111.9 | 88.8 |
| Return as per cent of capital employed at replacement cost | | | | | | | | | | |
| Government target | – | – | – | – | 6.0 | 6.0 | 6.0 | 5.0 | 5.0 | 5.0 |
| Achievement | – | – | – | – | 7.6 | 6.1 | 6.9 | 4.6 | 4.4 | 6.5 |

*Source*: Post Office Annual Report and Accounts (various); Harper (1977), p.151.

Sir George Jefferson, who had been in charge of the Dynamics Division of British Aerospace, became BT's first chairman having joined the Post Office as Deputy Chairman in 1980. He set about instilling commercial attitudes into the organisation. One of Jefferson's first acts was to restructure BT into four main trading divisions – Inland[12], International, BT Enterprises, and Development and Procurement – and reorganise BT's regional and local area units as individual profit centres. Subsequently, three joint ventures were planned with the private sector and reductions in manpower were authorised, but these changes could not be expected to arrest the need for more external financing. In 1980/1 and 1981/2 real unit costs rose rather than fell as might be expected in an industry benefiting from technological change and economies of scale.[13] In July 1981 the PM was incensed when she discovered that Jefferson had proposed a further round of telecommunications price increases, to take effect sometime between November and the following May to cover the higher costs. Jefferson also revealed that BT was likely to exceed its agreed 1981/2 EFL of £380 million by around 30 per cent.[14]

The scale of the tariff increases introduced by BT in the early 1980s led, unsurprisingly, to a wave of consumer complaints.[15] When a BBC programme suggested that Britain had some of the highest telephone charges internationally the PM demanded an explanation.[16] Large wage rises in the face of union threats, leading to higher telephone charges and demands for a bigger EFL, played no small part in concentrating the minds of Ministers on what to do next with BT after it was separately incorporated, precipitating what became the policy of privatisation. The Government was also aware of developments in the USA, where telecommunications were already privately owned and where promoting competition was high on the political agenda. At the time, planning was underway for the incumbent operator, AT&T, to be broken up into seven independent regional holding companies providing only local services, with AT&T continuing to operate long-distance and international calls.[17]

The Government's first stab at reform occurred in the Telecommunications Bill introduced in 1980. In this Bill, which authorised the creation of BT as a separate public corporation, BT was granted a continuation of most of its monopoly of telecommunications in Britain. But, importantly, the Act introduced some limited competition in a number of areas. In particular, it liberalised the supply and maintenance of telecommunications apparatus, opened up PABX (Private Automatic Branch Exchange)[18] maintenance to competitive supply by 1987 and permitted the licensing of value added network services (VANS), such as electronic funds transfer, on BT's network.[19] It also gave the Secretary of State power to license new operators and to require BT to form subsidiaries and eventually dispose of them wholly or in part.[20] At the time, ancillary services of BT such as Prestel (a text information service) and Radiopaging were seen within Government as possible candidates for divestment to the private sector.

One result of the liberalising of apparatus supplies was that subscribers were no longer required to rent their telephones from BT. The opening up of equipment supplies to competition was phased in over three years with the intention of giving British apparatus manufacturers time to respond to competition from imports.[21] Even so, the proposals met with fierce opposition from British manufacturers and equally predictably the Labour Party and the trade unions.[22] There were also some early signs of restlessness on the Government's own back benches about the possible effects of market liberalisation on services, especially in rural areas.[23] The Secretary of State for Industry, Sir Keith Joseph, had toyed with the idea of including in the Bill terms to require the resale of leased capacity from BT. However, in the face of hostility from the PO to the idea, which claimed it would lead to a disastrous loss of revenue, in September 1980 Joseph commissioned Professor Michael Beesley of the London Business School to carry out a study of the scope for value-added services. This quickly widened into a study of the economic implications of a wider liberalisation of the use of BT's network, including resale and the possibility of competition through other operators constructing their own facilities.[24]

Beesley reported in January 1981 and focused on network competition and competition in the resale of telecommunications services. In particular, he envisaged that competition with BT in transmission and switching would come from the resale of capacity leased from BT.[25] He therefore concluded that there should be no restriction on the freedom to offer services to third parties over BT's network and that there should be easy access to BT's network for resale operators, subject to certain conditions mainly relating to pricing.[26] Beesley was also in favour of liberalising the use of BT's international circuits and the licensing of additional networks. However, while the report seems to have been well received in the Department of Industry, and was published with only minor changes in April 1981, its recommendations were strongly opposed by BT.[27] Also, the Home Office had reservations about the creation of rival telephone service operators to BT using its network because this might interfere with the interception capability of the security forces.[28] The Home Office warned as early as July 1980 that deregulation of telecommunications might create a potential risk to the country's "intelligence gathering capacity".[29] In consequence, the Government did not invoke a number of Beesley's recommendations. There was agreement to license private operators to use BT circuits to supply services, but this freedom was not extended to simple resale to third parties of capacity on circuits leased from BT. Resale was permitted only for private networks, mainly networks owned by companies for their own use. This meant that competition through the use of existing capacity rather than the creation of new capacity was effectively prevented, except for VANS. There was also to be no liberalisation of international services at the present time. Meanwhile, the Government concentrated instead on the setting up of a rival telecommunications network operator, Mercury Communications Ltd. [30]

## The coming of competition: Mercury Communications

The 1981 Telecommunications Act paved the way for the establishment of Mercury as a rival network operator to BT. The Government was keen to reduce the monopoly power of BT and thereby the power of the trade unions, especially the Post Office Engineering Union (POEU). Mercury Communications was founded in June 1981 by a consortium of Cable and Wireless (C&W), BP and Barclays Bank, but only after David Young, Sir Keith Joseph's special adviser on privatisation, helped broker this deal and from the outset Cable and Wireless was nervous about the possible cost. Later first Barclays and then BP withdrew from the venture, leaving C&W as the sole owner.[31] To allow Mercury to build up its business and avoid fragmenting the market and due to security concerns, Mercury was licensed as the only competitor to BT in fixed-line public networks for at least five years, introducing what became known as the "duopoly policy" in British telecommunications.[32] The new company's objective was to build a fibre-optic digital network based on a figure of eight configuration linking 30 cities, including London, Birmingham, Manchester, Liverpool and Bristol. The company also planned to offer international telecommunication links via its own earth stations, but would be severely restricted in terms of offering international services if interconnection with the BT network was prevented or heavily restricted. This became a source of friction between Mercury, BT and the Government over subsequent months.[33] The first

Mercury services were planned to be launched in April 1983 and it was anticipated that in the early years Mercury would compete for around three per cent of BT's revenues. This was a purposely modest figure to ensure that BT's finances were not seriously damaged.

At the outset the Government expected Mercury to develop an alternative nationwide fixed-line network in time capable of rivalling that of BT. However, the future of Mercury remained very much in the balance in its first months of existence because of the costs of installing the new network, concerns within C&W about the viability of the project and doubts among potential customers about the company's ability to provide a credible competitive service. In response, efforts were made, but without success, to attract a major overseas telecommunications company, such as AT&T in the USA, to join the consortium building Mercury.[34] By the summer of 1984 Eric Sharp, the Chairman of C&W, made clear to the Government that Mercury was unlikely to mount an effective challenge to BT for anything like the foreseeable future. To prevent the Mercury project from collapsing as costs mounted, under a revised licence issued that year the company's brief was diluted to extending telecommunications facilities in a way that was "practicable and consistent with the sound commercial development of its network". Any attempt at this time by the Government to force Mercury to build a national telephone network within a specified period, as originally intended, would almost certainly have led the investors to withdraw and the fledgling venture to collapse. This would have severely damaged the Government's telecommunications liberalisation policy, causing considerable political embarrassment.

In addition to authorising Mercury as the fixed-line competitor to BT,[35] in June 1982 the Government licensed two cellular radio network operators, which began providing services in January 1985. Also, an inquiry was established into the future for cable technology and its use for entertainment and other services. A White Paper resulted in April 1983, *The Development of Cable Systems and Services*.[36] Although the Treasury wanted to see cable companies permitted to develop their own telecommunications services independently of BT and Mercury to increase competition, the Department of Industry plan for services to be in association with BT and Mercury prevailed. BT and Mercury would provide the telecommunications services down the cable, preserving the "duopoly".

On 17 November 1983 the Minister made a bullish statement to the House of Commons on the Government's plans for competition in telecommunications.[37] By early 1984 the Government was planning to issue 11 cable TV system franchises and associated telecommunications licences, alongside developing Mercury and cellular telephone systems. Clearly the telecommunications industry was changing. However, it was equally clear that BT's dominance of Britain's telecommunications would continue at least for some time, especially because it could be expected that BT would react aggressively to the arrival of competition. Indeed, BT responded to the threat with tariff rebalancing and an accelerated capital investment programme to modernise its network, including planning to install over two million new so-called System X exchange lines to carry digital signals and new fibre-optic and microwave systems. The Telecommunications Bill gave powers to the Government to designate cable TV operators as "public telecommunications systems", potentially competing with BT. But as a defensive strategy, by March 1984 BT had already invested in five of the 11 cable franchises allocated.

One area of particular contention within BT was the subject of *interconnection*. Interconnection concerns the arrangements under which a subscriber to one telephone operator can make telephone calls to a subscriber on another company's telephone network. If Mercury was to thrive then it needed interconnection with BT's network, otherwise people would be reluctant to sign up to Mercury because they would be unable to connect to BT's subscribers. BT recognised that it would be futile to oppose interconnection completely, as this would suggest a fundamental objection to competition and would be likely to result in legislation. Instead, over the first years of Mercury's life BT attempted to negotiate an interconnection agreement with Mercury that would limit the damage to its business.[38]

There are different levels of interconnection and four levels were under discussion. Level 1 was to involve Mercury laying a cable that would connect to a PABX on a business customer's premises. Level 2 involved Mercury leasing a BT line from its own network to the customer's premises. Then came two forms of level 3 connection: 3L involved Mercury in laying cable to a point of interconnection within the area covered by the BT local exchange serving the customer that wanted the Mercury service. The customer would dial a special number to be connected over their normal BT exchange line; and 3J involved Mercury in building out to points of interconnection at the next level up in BT's hierarchy – the junction network. Using 3J Mercury would be able to access customers in each of the areas surrounding trunk exchanges into which it built its new network. When C&W obtained the original licence under the 1981 Act, the expectation was that Mercury would build its own long-distance network, interconnecting with BT only to gain local access through level 3 interconnection – agreed with BT in 1982.[39] Mercury wanted to go further and Level 4 would have enabled Mercury simply to connect to BT's trunk network and thereby to resell switched capacity over the whole of BT's national network. In February 1983, the Government announced an easing of the restrictions on Mercury from providing international services and also stated that BT should provide interconnection to competing networks on appropriate, non-discriminatory terms. That implied Level 4 interconnection with customers free to select least cost options between the rival carriers for any long-distance national call.[40] Sir George Jefferson believed that allowing Mercury such access without the need to build much of its own alternative infrastructure would be unfair competition.[41] Sir George, part of whose role was holding the ring between BT's unions and the Government, felt this so strongly that, when he met with Kenneth Baker, the Minister of Information Technology on 15 June 1983, he threatened to resign from chairing BT if the Government insisted upon level 4 interconnection.[42]

A new Telecommunications Bill envisaged BT being licensed and being obliged to interconnect with Mercury but, ahead of that licensing, the Government could not oblige BT to accept a higher level of interconnection with Mercury. The Government hoped that a new interconnection agreement could be achieved through negotiation, as had occurred in 1982.[43] But as far as BT management was concerned, Mercury's pursuit of high-level interconnection confirmed that it had abandoned any idea of providing a competitor national network and that Mercury simply intended to invest to attract business on certain international routes and through a number of local loop by-pass connections to BT's high profit customers.[44] Immediately prior to the June 1983 General Election Mercury was informally requested by the Government not to press the matter of the terms of interconnection with BT until after the election. This was so as to avoid any politically embarrassing spats between BT and Mercury during the election campaign. But the issue would not go away. On 2 April 1984 Baker met Sharp of C&W to discuss the DTI's concern that the notion of national coverage, accepted by C&W when the first licence was issued to operate Mercury, seemed to be slipping away. Sharp replied that the planned figure-of-eight optical fibre network would cover 65 per cent of subscribers, but that it was unrealistic to expect investors to put more money into the venture given the uncertainties regarding interconnection and what he considered to be anti-competitive behaviour by BT. The fact that a number of government departments had turned down the opportunity to use Mercury rather than BT for their telecommunications services underlined the uphill struggle Mercury faced to become established.[45]

BT's licence, issued in June 1984, required the company to connect Mercury to its network, with the new industry regulator left to arbitrate between BT and Mercury should they not be able to agree terms. This was an outcome that left a degree of continuing uncertainty and one with which neither BT nor Mercury was entirely happy.[46] On 21 May 1984 Sir Douglas Lowe, the Chairman of Mercury Communications Ltd, followed up the meeting between Baker and Sharp by writing to Baker expressing concern that, as currently drafted, BT's licence did not sufficiently deter BT from predatory pricing and other activities to drive out competition following privatisation. In a weakly veiled threat, he warned that the way in which such behaviour was handled by the Government would affect Mercury shareholders' "commercial judgement as to whether it makes business sense to continue the venture and accept a new Mercury licence".[47]

Another area of dispute between BT and Mercury concerned international services. Mercury was prohibited from access to public switched networks abroad, which meant that its international calls could only link with individual customers.[48] Mercury came to an agreement with BT under which it would be able to provide its customers with private leased lines. But this was a small market and would not on its own yield an adequate return on Mercury's planned investment in international facilities. Mercury also needed access to BT's network for the distribution of incoming international calls. The Government pressed BT to ease the restrictions on Mercury's supply of international services, but the Corporation was extremely reluctant given that international calls were the source of high profits. These profits were used within BT to subsidise the losses incurred on domestic line rentals.[49]

## The Buzby Bond

While the Government slowly worked through the difficulties of establishing competition in the telecommunications market and fostering the difficult birth of Mercury in particular, it continued to consider ways of financing BT's investment programme without the Corporation breaking through its EFL. There was general agreement that new investment was needed. The Bank of England and the City had made it known that the future of London as an international financial centre was at risk unless the quality of telecommunications services greatly improved. A National Economic Development Office working party stressed the case for finding new ways of financing the nationalised industries so as to enable them to invest while not undermining the Government's macroeconomic strategy (see chapter 3, p.79)[50] and in 1981 John Hoskyns in the No. 10 Policy Unit and David Young at the Department of Industry were lobbying hard for a more flexible approach from the Treasury to investment in telecommunications.[51] At the request of Sir Keith Joseph, early in 1981 the Central Policy Review Staff in the Cabinet Office undertook a study into BT's long-term investment and financing needs. This broadly supported the case for more funding.[52] Extra funding for BT also won the backing of the PM, who concluded "that it would be indefensible to require BT to start cancelling investment orders".[53]

Over the following months the Department of Industry put forward a number of different methods of financing for BT which might get around the Treasury's strict rules on EFLs and the PSBR. These included the possible issue of a convertible bond (convertible to equity in some future privatised BT trading subsidiary; the full privatisation of BT was not yet

Government policy) and a "consumer bond", which subscribers could buy and in return receive a reduction in their telephone bills. Joseph also proposed that BT should make greater use of equipment leasing rather than outright purchase.[54] But each of these suggestions was in turn rejected by the Treasury, as either more expensive than financing through traditional government borrowing or because it would not necessarily take the financing out of the PSBR. Instead, Treasury Ministers were keener to see a reduction in BT's operating costs to free up internal funds for investment. They particularly favoured an independent investigation of BT's working practices. The idea that Government might put management consultants into BT was floated by Treasury Ministers, but already the accountants Coopers & Lybrand were reviewing BT's accounting systems and McKinseys BT's organisational structure. Joseph concluded that the introduction of even more consultants would amount to overkill.

The differences between the Department of Industry and the Treasury continued with Joseph preferring serious consideration of new modes of financing for BT and the Treasury lukewarm and favouring efficiency gains.[55] At a meeting on 24 March 1981 Treasury Ministers refused to approve BT's bid for additional investment funding, which involved an increase in its EFL for 1981/2 of £450 million.[56] However, any reduction in BT's investment programme would delay the improvement of telecommunications services demanded by the City. Reduced investment would also impact adversely on British manufacturers of telecommunications equipment. So at a further meeting on 7 April, the Treasury reluctantly agreed to sanction the extra finance. Shortly afterwards the Chancellor of the Exchequer remarked that, "Many of our problems in financing BT's investment programme would disappear to the extent that the Corporation's assets could be transferred to the private sector."[57]

The one suggestion for a new source of funding that received the most serious consideration within Government during 1981 was the idea of direct bond financing to supplement the traditional financing of BT through the National Loans Fund (NLF). The idea originated with BT's financial advisers Warburg & Co (Warburgs) and was initially welcomed by Sir George Jefferson.[58] The idea of a North Sea oil bond had been considered in 1980 when Ministers were discussing alternatives to the privatisation of BNOC (chapter 4, p.100 above). The return on the bond would have been linked to the revenues from BNOC's oilfields. However, the Treasury and the Bank of England had opposed the idea, on the grounds that it would be a more expensive way of raising finance than the Government issuing gilt-edged stock.[59] Warburgs' bond proposal had similarities to the North Sea oil bond.

Initially, Warburgs floated the idea of a "revenue bond" with the return on the bond dependent on the growth in BT's revenues. But as revenues are a function of allowed prices as well as the volume of services, if investors were to be attracted to the bond there would need to be a visible and binding formula to restrict Government intervention in BT's future pricing. Warburgs suggested as a solution that any tariff increase should be based on the RPI less an allowance for higher efficiency in BT. This effectively introduced into British telecommunications the concept of an "RPI – X" formula, as discussed further in chapter 12.[60] At a meeting with the Treasury on 17 February 1981 Warburgs were asked to produce a detailed proposal for their revenue bond. But by early March the Treasury had concluded that the return on a revenue bond would not provide a sufficient incentive for BT to improve its efficiency, the Treasury's continuing concern. Instead, the Treasury proposed that if there was to be a bond the return on it should depend either on BT's unit costs or its profits. Michael Valentine, one of Warburgs' representatives in the discussions on the bond, has since commented on the Treasury's attitude, sardonically:

"The Treasury produced a set of ten or so criteria, each of which its officials said would need to be met before the bond could be issued. I remember commenting at a meeting with them that the criteria had been written so that if nine were met, then automatically the other one would not be."[61]

The Treasury's coolness towards the idea of the revenue bond was compounded by the fact that they had a proposal in the forthcoming Budget to introduce new financing for government borrowing through the issuing of index-linked gilts. The Treasury appears to have worried that the BT bond might deflect investor attention away from this innovation in the gilts market.

In July 1981 Warburgs circulated a revised proposal under which the bond would carry a dividend as a fixed proportion of BT's annual profits. Baker referred to this bond as a "preference share" to help sell the idea to the Treasury. It would be redeemable at BT's option after ten years, would hold no voting rights, and the proportion of profits paid in dividends would remain constant. Warburgs suggested that the bond might carry a coupon of around five per cent.[62] Again, to protect investors, BT's future price rises would be set by a formula linked to the RPI plus or minus an "X" efficiency factor.[63]

The proposal was received with foreboding by BT management, who were alarmed by the notion of an efficiency-linked cap on price rises. The BT Board eventually suggested that if there was to be an X factor it should be limited to 1.5 per cent. However, the Treasury was looking for something closer to three per cent, which it considered was more consistent with the declining trend in BT's unit costs.[64] In response, the Department of Industry began to consider different formulations of X, including which BT products should be covered by the price formula.[65] However, the Treasury then dealt what would prove to be a serious blow to the whole proposal by refusing to give any assurance that the additional funding obtained from the new bond would be treated as additional to BT's borrowings under its agreed EFL. The Treasury's rigid stance resulted from their view that the bond financing would fall to be included in the PSBR. With uncertainty over how much additional net funding might result from the scheme, BT's interest in the bond understandably diminished.

By late July 1981 the Treasury and the Department of Industry had agreed that the bond – now known as the "Buzby Bond" after the cartoon crow, Buzby, then used in BT's TV advertising campaigns – might raise £150 million if issued in the autumn of 1981. While the Department of Industry now accepted that the funds raised would have to be part of BT's EFL, Baker hoped that the Treasury would agree to raise the size of the EFL, at least partially, to reflect the revenue from the bond.[66] At the Conservative Party annual conference in Blackpool on 14 October 1981 Patrick Jenkin, who had taken over as Secretary of State for Industry from Sir Keith Joseph in the Cabinet reshuffle the previous month, confirmed that more money was needed to finance BT's modernisation programme and that he hoped to "announce something soon". However, it was increasingly clear during the second half of 1981 that the bond might not be sufficient to fill the gap in BT's long-term funding needs, especially if all of the revenue generated was not additional to the EFL. Also, Treasury Ministers remained much keener on pursuing proposals to raise cost efficiency within BT.[67] If they were to agree to the bond, Treasury Ministers were insistent that it should be irredeemable to ensure that the investor bore some capital risk, that the price cap should be RPI – 2 per cent and that BT should give a commitment on cost reductions. Another option they were promoting was to sell off some of the Corporation's activities to the private sector.[68] In late 1981 Sir George Jefferson wrote to his staff calling for improved efficiency and a goal of a 25 per cent reduction in running costs over three years. This target was subsequently rejected by the BT Board and later, in discussion with Government, Jefferson explained that he had never intended it to be a real target but rather a device to shock the workforce into accepting changes in working practices. Nevertheless, the document played into the hands of the Treasury, who were now more convinced than ever that there was scope for cost savings within BT to replace the need to raise borrowing.

At the beginning of 1982 the Chancellor of the Exchequer agreed, seemingly somewhat reluctantly, that planning for a bond issue should continue and the Government's decision to issue a BT bond was announced in his March 1982 Budget.[69] The initial bond issue would raise £50 million or less but might be quickly followed by further issues to raise up to £150 million, depending on market conditions. The Treasury conceded that some but by no means all of the financing could be additional to BT's borrowings under the EFL. But by now serious discussion had begun under Jenkin's leadership within the Department of Industry on the prospects for the privatisation of BT.

## Privatise instead

In his memoirs Kenneth Baker states that he and David Young had supper with Sir Keith Joseph on 5 July 1981 to persuade him to privatise BT.[70] After some initial doubts Joseph, who had favoured introducing competition into telecommunications and letting this bring about changes for a few years before privatisation was seriously considered, became enthusiastic. Joseph saw Thatcher after the supper meeting and gained her support to investigate the potential for privatisation. At a meeting with Treasury Ministers on 28 July the objective of privatising BT was endorsed, but there was to be no public announcement. There was recognition that much careful planning would be needed before privatisation could proceed and in particular decisions would have to be taken on whether to sell BT as a single entity or not and the nature of a suitable regulatory regime.[71] Therefore, the possibility of privatisation was under consideration. However, no detailed plans for a sell-off were in Patrick Jenkin's in-tray when he took over as Secretary of State in September 1981. It was Jenkin who put into effect a thorough internal review within the Department of Industry of the prospects for privatisation. The new Secretary of State for Industry was keen to see the private sector play a bigger role in the future development of the country's telecommunications and this was an ambition shared by Sir George Jefferson at BT, frustrated by Treasury restrictions and other government controls.

Over the following months the privatisation of BT would be championed by Jenkin and his successors as Secretary of State, Cecil Parkinson and then Norman Tebbit, and by Kenneth Baker, Minister of State for Information Technology in the Department. The idea also had Jefferson's enthusiastic backing throughout, although by no means all of the BT Board agreed.[72] Also, privatisation would be championed in the face of considerable reservations within Parliament and outside. In particular, many in the City doubted whether it would be feasible. On 4 March 1982 Jenkin sent outline proposals on the prospects for the private sector to play a full "partnership" role in BT's investment programme to the membership of E Committee.[73] Jenkin informed his Ministerial colleagues that he had decided that the "main aim should be the conversion of BT as a whole into a Companies Act company, BT Ltd, and the subscription by the private sector of as much new capital as the market would bear." He expected that this would initially be between 10 per cent and 25 per cent of the total equity. At the time a majority sale of BT was considered unlikely because of the size of the share flotation that would be needed. To make the idea of privatisation more palatable to the unions, Jenkin suggested that the Government should use the term "partnership" between BT and the private sector rather than the term "privatisation". However, once the policy became public, the term partnership quickly disappeared in favour of privatisation.[74]

Jenkin asked E Committee for approval to introduce the necessary legislation in the next Parliamentary Session, 1982–83. He also noted that it would not be appropriate for a private sector company to regulate its competitors. Therefore, there would have to be consideration of removing BT's regulatory powers, for example over the approval of attachments to networks and the licensing of value-added networks, and their transfer to a separate regulatory body.[75] On 16 March 1982 the Committee agreed to plans being drawn up for the privatisation of BT, although no final decision was reached given the difficult issues that would need to be resolved before a start could be made on drafting the legislation, notably the precise scale of the flotation and the nature of the new regulatory regime.[76] The PM made it known that she was sympathetic to the idea of privatisation provided it was combined with promoting more competition in telecommunications.[77]

Jenkin's request to be allowed to explore the prospects for privatising BT was received sympathetically in E Committee, although it was also agreed that planning for a bond issue should still continue. Warburgs reported that preparation of the prospectus for a Bond would cover much of the same ground as the prospectus for a share issue and therefore the effort would not be wasted. Moreover, if the bond issue went ahead first this would enable the stock market to become familiar with BT and for a "rating" of the enterprise to be established before the actual share issue occurred. Warburgs was now enthusiastic about the idea of a bond convertible to equity at some stage in the future.[78] The privatisation proposal was discussed with the Treasury with Jenkin keen that some of the sales proceeds should be retained by BT to fund its investments. Jenkin also felt this would help overcome the expected trade union opposition to a share sale. However, in discussion with Leon Brittan, Chief Secretary to the Treasury, Jenkin was left in little doubt that the Treasury expected to receive all or the greater share of any flotation proceeds. The Treasury was adamant that the sale of BT should not reverse the by now established principle that the revenue from the sale of nationalised industries, after sale costs, went to the Exchequer.[79]

In the winter and early spring of 1982 rumours that the privatisation of BT was being seriously contemplated within Government began to circulate in the press. In response Jefferson felt the need to brief his senior managers and union officials on the Secretary of State's plans, while stressing that no decision had yet been reached.[80] The unions within BT responded by stating that they were totally opposed to the idea. There were also some reservations within BT's management.[81] In the House of Commons on 22 March John Wakeham from the Department of Industry confirmed that the Government was looking into how to introduce private capital into BT, with an emphasis on "partnership" with the private sector. In reply to questioning, he conceded that the long-term plan might include full privatisation.[82] Meanwhile Jefferson made it known that disposal of parts of BT would be more difficult to sell to the unions than privatising BT as one unit. From the outset the BT Board was determined that there should be no break-up of BT before or at privatisation and the Government quickly agreed. Joseph had favoured a break-up to increase competition but had been persuaded to drop the idea by Baker and Young, on the grounds that it would greatly delay a sale. His attention had shifted instead to the creation of Mercury as a competitor to a privatised BT. After September 1981 neither Jenkin nor Baker in the Department of Industry favoured a break-up. As Nigel Lawson comments in his memoirs on the attitude in

Government, "Our original preference had been to split up British Telecom . . . But Jefferson was insistent that his empire should remain intact . . . the trade unions . . . were bitterly opposed to privatization and were making all manner of threatening noises. We felt that we could scarcely afford to have the management against us as well, if we were to achieve a successful privatization."[83]

There would be potential difficulties in mounting an initial public offering (IPO) involving a majority of shares in the entire BT, given the size of the issue needed and the capacity of the London stock market. However, Treasury officials were of the view that a sale of a minority of the shares would also be problematic. In their view it would be unlikely to bring about the necessary changes within BT in terms of improved efficiency and higher investment. In addition, the Treasury warned that private investors might not be attracted to a minority equity investment and if they were it could be an expensive form of finance. The Treasury was also concerned that if BT was only partially privatised, it might prove very difficult to exercise effective control over BT's future investments and borrowings.[84] In certain earlier privatisations, such as Cable and Wireless (chapter 5), the Treasury had expressed concerns that a company with a majority of its shares still owned by Government might fall outside the nationalised industry financial controls. The result would be a state-owned body without Treasury oversight of its finances. In consequence, Jenkin was requested by E Committee to prepare a more detailed strategy for the disposal of BT shares.[85] Meanwhile, the Central Policy Review Staff (CPRS) in the Cabinet Office responded to Jenkin's proposal on the sale of BT by agreeing with the principle of privatisation, but stressing that it should not go ahead until the regulatory problems of preventing a dominant BT abusing its market power were overcome.[86] The Home Office expressed reservations about the privatisation of BT on security grounds.[87]

To take matters forward, following the meeting of E Committee on 16 March 1982 a small group was established to review Government policy on telecommunications and report back.[88] Over the following weeks the Official Committee on Telecommunications Policy (E(TP) Committee), chaired by the PM, thrashed out many of the details that would go into the new Telecommunications Bill. At its first meeting on 22 April 1982 there was recognition that privatising BT and establishing the necessary regulatory structure "would be a very difficult undertaking".[89] Also, earlier privatisations had involved relatively small share issues, for example the sale of Cable and Wireless had raised £224 million and British Aerospace £150 million. The BT issue would be very much larger, depending on the proportion of the share capital sold. Given that the annual value of total new share issues and the total flows of institutional funds into the equity market were put at close to £1.75 billion and around £2.5 billion respectively, the Sub-Committee concluded that with a BT issue valued at over £1 billion, "It is hard to see how a single issue of this size could be made on a conventional basis". The Committee felt that a majority sale would almost certainly have to proceed in two, or possibly more, tranches.[90] Shortly afterwards the Bank of England made it known that it too had deep concerns about the effect of a large BT share sale on financing to the private sector. A flotation of BT might crowd out other investment through the stock market for the weeks around the BT sale.[91]

Meanwhile, the Department of Industry had continued to plan for the issue of the Buzby bond with Jenkin of the view that a bond issue in December 1982 and a follow-up issue some months later would be needed to meet BT's funding gap ahead of any privatisation.[92] But now three further difficulties arose. Firstly, BT's current profit level was felt to be too low to get a good rate for the bond, Secondly, given that the Government was now planning a possible privatisation of BT, it was decided that under stock market rules it would not be possible to issue the new bond without revealing these plans to investors. At the same time, Government was keen to keep the details of the privatisation under wraps until they were sorted out and the final decision to go ahead with privatisation had been made at Cabinet level.[93] Thirdly, the Finance Bill in the spring of 1982 included a clause to close a tax avoidance loophole involving a type of bank loan. Unintentionally, the clause was drafted so widely that it made the Buzby bond potentially much less attractive to investors.

However, the final nail in the coffin of the Buzby bond was the unexpected state of BT's finances.[94] BT's EFL had been raised under pressure from management by £200 million in 1981/2, but it now seemed that this had been unnecessary. BT would under-spend its EFL by some £130 million. Much of this underspend resulted from delays in the delivery of telecommunications equipment to BT by manufacturers rather than from a true downturn in BT's investment plans. Nevertheless, the Treasury and the Department of Industry decided that a Buzby bond issue later in the year would not now be needed, to which BT agreed.[95] The Treasury was particularly keen to prevent BT from getting its hands on surplus cash, believing that this would only encourage its management to run the business even less efficiently, including being even more willing to agree to inflationary pay rises.[96] Although Jenkin suggested that a bond issue might still be necessary in future years if EFLs remained tight and privatisation did not proceed,[97] by the summer of 1982 the Buzby bond was effectively dead.

## The 1982 Telecommunications Bill

When in April 1982 the serious planning of the privatisation began, there was no certainty that legislation would be ready for introduction by the beginning of the next Parliamentary session, as Jenkin hoped.[98] During the spring and early summer of 1982 the deliberations on telecommunications policy continued within Government with the size of the share issue and the future regulation of telecommunications especially thorny issues to be resolved.[99] There was also the matter of the standing of BT's debt in terms of the PSBR if less than 50 per cent of the shares in the new company were sold to the private sector initially.[100] At a meeting of E(TP) on 30 June 1982, proposals to transfer all of BT's assets and liabilities to a new company and to dispose of an indefinite number of the company's shares were agreed. The Department of Industry's financial advisers Kleinwort, Benson (Kleinworts) advised that special guidelines to set parameters for borrowing and a statement of non-intervention in BT's commercial decisions might be sufficient to satisfy minority investors should there be less than a majority share disposal. Also, once BT became a company its directors would have a common law duty to act in the best interests of the enterprise as a whole. In addition, the minority shareholders would have a right to petition the courts for redress under Section 75 of the Companies Act 1980 if the directors acted in a way that was "unfairly prejudicial" to their interests. Nevertheless, the Treasury remained nervous and observed that it would need to retain some control over BT's borrowing, reflecting its stance in earlier privatisations, given that there was no certainty as to how long Government would remain the majority shareholder.[101]

Meanwhile, Jenkin and BT wanted the Corporation to achieve freedom to borrow in the capital market once privatisation occurred even if the Government retained a majority of the shares. In particular, they feared that continuing Treasury controls would limit BT's ability to invest and therefore undo the advantages of privatisation. There was also the possibility that investors would be unwilling to buy BT equity if they felt that the company's finances were still under Government control. Kleinworts confirmed that if the Treasury retained control over BT's borrowings privatisation might not be feasible. One possible solution, brokered between the Department of Industry and the Treasury, was for the Government to give investors a firm commitment as to BT's permitted borrowing levels for a two year period following a flotation, by which time it was hoped a majority of the shares would be in the private sector and the Treasury's controls could be removed.[102] However, the Treasury was aware that with the expected intervention of a general election and the possible return of a Labour Government, there could be no certainty that either any, let alone a majority, of the shares would eventually be floated or whether any commitments given would hold. To meet the Treasury's concerns, it was decided that between "vesting day" when the Corporation's assets and liabilities would be transferred to the new company BT plc, and a share flotation, an exchange of letters between the DTI and BT might be arranged setting out the terms under which the company could borrow.[103] It was accepted, however, that if the flotation was delayed for long, more formal arrangements with the Treasury would be needed.[104] At the same time, there remained concern that continued Treasury oversight of BT's borrowings could be difficult to sell to investors.

The difficulty of reconciling the Treasury's desire to maintain control over BT's finances while the Government remained the majority shareholder and giving management commercial freedom to manage the business was a main reason why, during the summer of 1982, the privatisation planning changed. It shifted from the possible first sale of a minority of the shares, to finding a means to enable the sale of a majority holding. Also, during the summer a challenge to the Department of Industry's planning from the Central Policy Review Staff was seen off. Ahead of a meeting of E(TP) sub-committee on 30 June the CPRS recommended that "competition and regulation should precede privatisation". This would mean that a final decision on privatisation would be postponed until after a general election, expected sometime in 1983.[105] The CPRS appears to have been of the view that after privatisation occurred it would be more difficult for Government to put in place effective competition and regulation. However, Ministers were not keen to delay a sale. In E(TP) there was agreement to introduce in the 1982–83 session of Parliament a Telecommunications Bill. The aim would be to pass the legislation before the dissolution of Parliament even though the actual share sale would be unlikely to occur until after a general election. Jenkin was authorised to make an announcement to Parliament shortly before the summer recess and to begin consultations with the BT Board, the unions and other interested parties. There was recognition that the Telecommunications Bill would have to be drafted quickly to meet this timetable. There was also an expectation that the Bill's passage "was likely to be long and contentious". [106]

On 19 July 1982 in the House of Commons Jenkin promoted the privatisation of BT in terms of freeing the Corporation to raise finance from the capital market and improving efficiency:

"As a nationalised industry BT does not have direct access to financial markets. Its borrowing is controlled by Government and counts against the PSBR. To bring inflation under control these borrowings have been subject to strict limits. But external finance is only part of the picture. In the past monopoly power has enabled BT to raise prices to finance investment without doing all that could be done to increase efficiency. Around 90 per cent of BT's investment programme, about

£1,200 million this year, has been self-financed. By 'self-financed' I mean of course 'customer financed'; BT's charges to customers not only cover current running costs, but are also paying for 90 per cent of new investment. As a result, charges have risen steeply while investment is still not enough. Unless something is done radically to change the capital structure and ownership of BT and to provide a direct spur to efficiency, higher investment would mean still higher charges for the customer. The Government and the general public would find that unacceptable. We need to free BT from traditional forms of Government control . . .

". . . We will therefore take the earliest opportunity to introduce legislation which, while keeping BT as a single enterprise, will enable it to be converted into a Companies Act company, 'British Telecommunications plc'. The legislation will allow the sale of shares in that company to the public. It is our intention after the next election, to offer up to 51 per cent of the shares on the market in one or more tranches . . ... BT will be in a position to provide better services which are more responsive to customer needs like those provided by the privately-owned telephone companies in the United States."[107]

A White Paper was issued by the Department of Industry to coincide with this statement, which set out in more detail the case for privatisation and the Government's plans.[108] However, the Treasury immediately complained that it had not seen the final draft of the White Paper and would have liked there to have been more reference to BT's inefficiency as the rationale for privatisation and less implied criticism of the Treasury's tight financial control.[109] BT responded to the Secretary of State's announcement welcoming the prospect of full consultation on the details of the sale.[110]

Over the following weeks the legislation was drafted and its details were finally agreed in E(TP) on 16 November 1982. An attempt by the Chancellor of the Exchequer and the Secretary of State for Trade, Lord Cockfield, to refer BT to the MMC as part of the annual programme of referrals of nationalised industries, announced by Nicholas Ridley in the House of Commons on 30 November 1981, was successfully quashed. The idea won some support at a meeting of E(NI) on 26 July 1982 and the Chancellor of the Exchequer's concerns about the management of BT were aggravated when BT's likely investment underspend for 1982/3 was revealed.[111] But the Department of Industry argued successfully that a MMC inquiry would delay privatisation and might even damage the prospects of a successful sale if major management weaknesses were exposed.[112] The PM agreed, commenting unequivocally, "I take the view that denationalisation must *not* be jeopardised" (emphasis in the original).[113]

The Telecommunications Bill was introduced into Parliament on 19 November 1982, although it was expected that a sale of shares would occur after the next general election. The election would have to be called by May 1984 and a successful share flotation in the months immediately before an election would be difficult to achieve because of political uncertainty. The Bill provided both for the privatisation of BT and the appointment of a Director General of Telecommunications (DGT) to head up a new regulatory office. It also gave powers to the Government to designate cable TV operators as "public telecommuni-cation systems" and removed BT's effective control over competition in telecoms through its licensing powers. All operators, including BT, would now be licensed by the Secretary of State or, with his consent, the new Director General. The aim was to achieve royal assent to the Bill by the end of July 1983.[114] However, the hasty process by which the legislation had been drafted during the summer and autumn of 1982, so as to enable its passage before a general election, meant that the Bill would have a particularly difficult Parliamentary voyage. Jenkin acknowledged at the time that the Bill "has been prepared in some haste [and] will require amendment".[115]

## An uneasy passage and union and industry concerns

Towards the end of June 1982 Jefferson had lunched with David Young and confirmed that he wanted to see BT privatised. Within BT's senior management there was support for the principle of privatisation, but anxiety too about what might be in the Bill and the operating licence, especially concerning the regulatory regime, the precise form of the sale and the financial arrangements. The Board complained about the haste with which the Bill had been prepared and what it saw as a lack of consultation on the details. BT went so far as to suggest that its introduction to Parliament should be delayed to permit time for further consideration. In response, the Department of Industry blamed Jefferson for not attending a number of scheduled meetings and concluded that delaying the Bill's first reading would make its passage by July 1983, as planned, too difficult to achieve. Meanwhile, lower down in the management of BT there was much nervousness about what privatisation might mean for jobs, pay and working conditions. There was also concern about the workload in preparing for privatisation, given the other changes underway in telecoms. BT's concerns about the details of the privatisation and the regulatory system would continue over the following months.[116]

The Government's decision to privatise had been made known to the BT Board on a confidential basis on 13 July 1982, immediately before the announcement in Parliament. At this meeting Jenkin gave a commitment to sell BT as a single unit. This commitment was repeated in the House of Commons in his statement on the 19th. The commitment was considered essential to ensure the important support of Jefferson for privatisation, but it would later restrict the Government's freedom of manoeuvre. In terms of the Department of Industry's objectives at the time, enabling BT to operate commercially in an increasingly competitive telecommunications market was of the uppermost concern and when designing the terms of the flotation spreading share ownership was also an important consideration. However, as in previous privatisations the Treasury was also keenly interested in the potential sales receipts.[117]

As had been the case in previous privatisations, the Opposition Labour Party totally opposed the sale. More worrying, however, for the Government was the attitude of some Conservative MPs and peers. A number of Conservatives voiced reservations especially about the possible implications of the privatisation of BT for rural and emergency telephone services.[118] There were also some misgivings within Government about a number of the details of the Bill. In particular, in November 1982 Lord Cockfield at the Department of Trade voiced reservations about the powers of the proposed industry regulator and the possibility of conflict between the new regulator and the existing competition regulators, the Office of Fair Trading (OFT) and the MMC, which came under his Department.[119] Differences between the Department of Trade and the Department of Industry over the regulation of BT and certain other issues appear to have been one reason why, after the 1983 Election, the departments were merged.

Outside Parliament the trade unions had mounted a determined campaign against the Bill. There were six trade unions within BT but the POEU was the largest and most vocal. The union dismissed the idea of lower prices and better services following privatisation, claiming instead that the beneficiaries would be "short-term stock market speculators, overseas manufacturers, British importers, our principal international competitors and, of course, the Government's ideological backers".[120] On 20 October 1982 a first "Day of Action" was arranged against the Government's plans and in early April 1983 the POEU began a programme of official industrial action on a selective basis, starting in London.[121] The unions co-ordinated their opposition to the Bill under an umbrella organisation called the British Telecommunications Union Committee.

Mindful that strikes were unlikely to win votes for the Labour Party, BT's unions called off their industrial action during the May 1983 General Election. However, with the return of a Conservative Government selective industrial action was renewed, the POEU targeting government departments and other key buildings. The aim was to create the maximum economic inconvenience at a minimum cost to the union and its members. For a time it seemed that the action might prove successful; especially the Government feared that the POEU might switch off phone lines in the City of London, leading to substantial economic damage. The Government countered by contemplating what offsetting action it might take. [122] One possibility seriously considered was a publicity campaign setting out the advantages of privatisation to counter union claims. However, the idea was dropped when it was pointed out by officials that this would be treated as "political" campaigning and as such could not be legitimately financed from public funds.[123]

The decision of the PM on 9 May 1983 to dissolve Parliament and seek the Government's re-election meant that the Telecommunications Bill fell after completing its third reading in the House of Commons and a second reading in the House of Lords.[124] The Bill would be reintroduced immediately after the election. The Conservatives' Election Manifesto promised to sell off 51 per cent of BT's shares during the next Parliament.[125] Immediately after the election, BT management wrote to staff warning that with the Government's renewed mandate and the commitment to privatise BT, any industrial action "would be damagingly mistaken . . . [and] will be seen now as defying the will of Parliament and the electorate . . . .".[126] The warning seems to have had little effect. At its annual conference in June 1983 more left-wingers were voted on to the POEU executive and the action against privatisation continued. On 20 June 1983 Cecil Parkinson, the new Secretary of State for Trade and Industry following the election, met with officials of the POEU in an attempt to defuse opposition. In an unfortunate coincidence, on the same day two engineers were suspended by BT for refusing to work on interconnection with Mercury.

The suspension of the two engineers exacerbated the difficult climate of industrial relations within the Corporation. The unions objected to the arrival of Mercury and the possibility that it would "cream skim" the profitable telecommunications business, notably lines to the City, leaving BT with shrinking revenues and job losses.[127] The opposition to Mercury was compounded when the new company refused to recognise the POEU for its own staff. The POEU instructed its members within BT not to co-operate in interconnecting Mercury to BT's lines.

With the boycotting of interconnection work, Mercury issued a writ against the POEU alleging that the union was illegally interfering with the company's lawful contracts with BT. Much to the Government's anguish, on 21 October 1983 the High Court decided that the POEU was engaged in a genuine trade dispute about the protection of jobs and conditions of employment and therefore it had immunity against legal action. However, the decision was quickly overturned in the Court of Appeal where an interlocutory injunction was issued. This restrained the POEU from taking further steps to block the interconnecting of Mercury lines.[128] Nevertheless, although the Government had seen off this particular union challenge, there was deep apprehension that industrial action would continue to disrupt the privatisation. The Telecommunications Bill included a clause, Clause 45, which was intended to make interference with the transmission or reception of a telephone call a criminal offence. In principle, this would allow the Government to take action against the union if there was an attempt to interfere with services. But there was concern within the DTI that the Clause was heavy-handed and might prove unusable against union members because of the political controversy that would result, echoing the failure of the Heath Government's Industrial Relations Act.

In February 1984 Norman Tebbit, who took over as Secretary of State for Trade and Industry in October 1983 when Parkinson stepped down, decided that it would be safer to substitute Clause 45 with civil remedies. The civil remedies would be against any union which prevented BT from complying with an order of the Director General to implement a licence condition. This would put the unions' funds at threat rather than criminalise individual union members.[129] However, as matters turned out the Government's resolve was not tested. By the early spring of 1984 it was increasingly apparent to the union leadership that the privatisation of BT was unstoppable. The strategy of the POEU and the other BT unions turned to one of ensuring the best outcome for their members.[130] Later there would be some industrial stoppages in protest at restructuring and changes in working practices within the company, but no determined action against the decision to privatise.

In addition to the reaction of the trade unions, the prospect of a privatised BT worried a number of other groups. These included the National Farmers' Union, who were concerned that a profit maximising BT might disadvantage rural areas,[131] and consumer groups such as the National Consumer Council and POUNC,[132] the official consumer body for the Post Office and telecommunications, who were worried that there might be inadequate protection for consumers post-privatisation.[133] Also, the Department of Industry, No. 10 and MPs received a large number of letters from the public concerned about the future of services and employment in BT, although some of this was undoubtedly orchestrated by the BT unions. There were also letters from individual BT employees genuinely fearful that privatisation would put their future pensions at risk, in spite of reassurances from the Government that the Bill would include safeguards protecting the pension rights of existing employees.[134]

In part the concern about pensions arose from a deficit in BT's pension fund. This went back to a decision in the 1970s by the Post Office Board to charge all the then deficit in the fund to the telecommunications side of their business. Telecommunications was more profitable than postal services and was therefore deemed more capable of meeting the costs; this in spite of the fact that around 45 per cent of the deficit related to the pension liabilities of postal workers. By the early 1980s BT was paying interest on the deficit of around £185 million per annum and payments under covenant to remove the deficit were scheduled to start in 1985.[135] To allay investor fears about the impact of this future liability on profits, Jenkin suggested that the Government should agree to fund the pension deficit. In his view the deficit would have to be addressed before the privatisation could go ahead.[136] However, the Treasury objected to the use of public funds to write off the debt or to the deficit being paid off directly or indirectly from the revenue raised from a BT share issue.[137] Instead, it argued that the deficit should be reassigned between the Post Office and BT to reflect its origins.[138]

Another group particularly exercised by the privatisation of BT was the domestic telecommunications equipment manufacturers. Under state ownership British manufacturers had benefited from, in effect, privileged access to BT for all major orders. As a public corporation BT had sourced mainly from domestic suppliers. Although Jenkin in November 1982 said publicly that he saw "no reason why this should change", not everyone within or outside Government was as confident.[139] Lord Weinstock, the Chairman of GEC, a major supplier to BT, became a particularly vocal critic of the Government's plans fearing the impact on his company if after privatisation BT was to switch orders abroad. Also, he questioned the ability of any regulatory system to protect suppliers from BT exploiting its dominance in the telecommunications market. [140] In October 1983 he went so far as to suggest that at privatisation GEC should be allowed to become a major investor in BT to protect its interests.[141] In the House of Lords he joined with a number of other peers to disrupt the passage of the Telecommunications Bill.

Other manufacturers harboured similar concerns. Immediately after the 1983 General Election the President of the Telecommunications Engineering and Manufacturing Association (TEMA) wrote to the Secretary of State suggesting that there must be reciprocity overseas for British telecommunications manufacturers, if after privatisation foreign manufacturers were allowed to access the British telecommunications market. The Association commissioned a report from Professor Stephen Littlechild of Birmingham University – a report which has since attracted little attention, unlike Littlechild's report to the Government on price regulation the previous January, discussed in chapter 12. This concluded that BT would be able post-privatisation to squeeze equipment manufacturers. Littlechild's remedy was to break BT up into a number of separate companies and to prohibit it from extending its own manufacturing capacity.[142] However, the Government was already committed to selling BT as one company and BT was already a small-scale manufacturer, employing around 4000, mainly in equipment refurbishment work and the small-scale production of handsets. Littlechild's proposals were swiftly rejected by Ministers.

Nevertheless, to allay fears a measure was introduced that required BT to set up a separate subsidiary for the manufacture of telecommunications equipment by 1 July 1986, in an effort to prevent anti-competitive cross-subsidisation, and the Government also acted to prevent BT diversifying its business in ways which might reinforce its market dominance ahead of privatisation. For example, on 17 December 1982 Jefferson approached Jenkin with a request to be allowed to bid to buy International Aeradio Ltd, a company that the Government was planning to hive off from the cash-strapped British Airways. Jenkin was in favour of allowing the purchase to go ahead, believing that the acquisition would help strengthen BT's international business. But others, notably Lord Cockfield the Trade Secretary and Leon Brittan at the Treasury, were staunchly opposed on competition grounds, even after BT offered to bring in a private sector partner, Racal.[143] Another proposal from BT that the Government also rejected was put forward immediately before privatisation, in October 1984. This involved BT and IBM establishing a new joint venture to exploit the opportunities offered by the convergence of telecommunications and computer technology.[144] The Government concluded that this alliance, linking BT with the world's largest computer manufacturer, would be a serious threat to competition.

The concerns of domestic equipment manufacturers were well-founded. In his memoirs Norman Tebbit comments: "I was worried . . . about the future of GEC and Plessey. I had set my heart on bringing these two companies to realise that their continued obstinate rivalry in the production of main telephone exchanges, sharing the British market between them and gaining almost no business elsewhere in the world, would end with loss of British business too and that rationalisation would have to come."[145] BT was keen to diversify away from its domestic suppliers because it had suffered a history of delays in the delivery of new equipment, most recently the important new digital switching system, "System X", which replaced the ageing Strowger electro-mechanical switches.[146] System X had been designed, like all earlier UK switching systems by the PO/BT, most recently at its Martlesham Laboratories. UK manufacturers were entirely dependent on this technology, leaving their own R&D to atrophy. System X worked in the laboratory but caused real problems in production. The development of System X was dogged by delays, which the manufacturers blamed on BT requiring overly exacting technical standards and BT on mistakes made by manufacturers.[147] In an attempt to address the problem ahead of privatisation, the Government intervened with a rationalisation plan. This involved making one of the three manufacturers, Plessey, lead developer of the System and responsible for its delivery, with GEC acting as a subcontractor. The third manufacturer, Standard Telephone and Cables, was required to leave the development consortium and was compensated by orders for other exchange equipment. The intention was to put relations between BT and the manufacturers on to a more normal commercial basis than had existed in the past.[148] However, prior to privatisation the Government could not afford the political embarrassment of BT switching its orders from the domestically invented System X to an alternative. So when Jefferson requested in the spring of 1983 to be allowed to contract with Thorn-Ericsson, an Anglo-Swedish consortium, for an alternative digital system, System Y, to complement the supply of System X, the request was politely but firmly refused. Similarly, the Government acted to prevent BT ahead of privatisation from placing orders for computer equipment with IBM rather than Britain's national computer company ICL. Free competition in telecommunications supplies would have to await the sell-off of BT.[149] In 1985, after privatisation, BT placed its first order for System Y.[150]

The calling of the General Election in May 1983 delayed BT's privatisation. But what was essentially the same Bill was reintroduced into Parliament after the Election, receiving a new first reading on 27 June 1983. With the Bill's reintroduction the Treasury drew the attention of the DTI, which had taken over the management of the privatisation from the Department of Industry, to the overriding objective of achieving an effective privatisation, followed by the need to maximise revenue. The third objective of widening share ownership should be considered, in the words of one Treasury official, to be "very much in a tertiary position".[151] Once again the Opposition attempted to derail the legislation resorting to speeches of up to five hours in length in an attempt to filibuster. As a result, after 110 hours of debate the Bill had not progressed beyond Clause 3 and the Government felt that it had no real option but to resort to the unpopular procedure of the "guillotine" to limit further debate.[152] In the House of Lords the Bill was subjected to a battery of amendments, many inspired by the so-called Telecommunications Liberalisation Group, headed by Lord Orr-Ewing, who wanted to see more competition and more effective regulation of BT.[153] On 2 February 1984 the Lord President of the Council reported to Cabinet that he and the Chancellor of the Duchy of Lancaster were attempting to keep the changes to the Bill in the Lords to a minimum. However, the Lord President conceded that this was proving difficult.[154] A month later the Lord Privy Seal commented, "The difficulties now being encountered with the Telecommunications Bill in the House of Lords were an example of what could happen when legislation had to be rushed through the House of Commons under guillotine."[155]

One matter of deep concern was the implications of privatisation for national security, especially the provision of essential telecommunications services at a time of a national emergency. The union lobby against privatisation played on this fear by arguing that BT might at some future date become foreign owned. Baker responded by suggesting that BT's Articles of Association should contain terms to prevent BT falling into foreign hands. During the privatisation of Cable and Wireless in October 1981 its Articles of Association had been amended to limit individual private sector shareholdings to 15 per cent of the shares and later, in December 1983 when a further tranche of shares was sold, this was extended to include a requirement that the chief executive be a British citizen. At the time, there had been concerns in the Foreign Office that to go further than this might lead to a successful legal challenge in the European Court of Justice, on the grounds that the restrictions on ownership were contrary to the free movement of workers and capital under the provisions of the EEC Treaty. On 4 November 1983 the Foreign Secretary reported that terms in BT's Articles of Association similar to those inserted into the Articles of C&W might be successfully defended on the grounds of national security. However, any suggestion of extending the restrictions on nationality to all or a majority of BT's directors, as was then being contemplated within the DTI, would create a "significant risk" of a legal challenge. Such restriction would be likely to be seen as disproportionate to the security needs identified. Baker responded that he thought it might be worth taking the risk, but other Ministers were not convinced.[156] Eventually Baker settled for requirements that mirrored those for C&W, namely that the company's chief executive should be a British citizen and that no one person may hold 15 per cent or more of the voting shares. The BT Board pressed, but unsuccessfully, for an even lower limit of ten per cent, to provide even more protection from hostile takeover bids.[157] The Government also retained a "special share" to prevent these restrictions from later amendment, as was introduced for C&W, and the Bill contained powers for the Secretary of State to make directions to any telecommunications operator in the interests of national security.

When the decision had been taken in the spring of 1982 to privatise BT some consideration had been given within the Department of Industry to the possibility of breaking up the Corporation and selling it off in separate parts. Sir Keith Joseph had initially favoured the idea, but had been convinced by officials and advisers that the necessary restructuring of BT to bring this about would greatly delay a sale, probably for many years, and would be strongly opposed by the BT Board and the trade unions. BT was managed as a unitary concern and there were no separate accounts for the different parts of the business. Also, disposing of the profitable parts of BT separately could be expected to make the sale of the remainder of the Corporation more difficult and might diminish the overall value of a sale.[158] In addition, the example of AT&T in the USA, where a break-up was occurring, was dismissed as not relevant to the UK with its smaller market and geographical area. Therefore, when Patrick Jenkin announced his decision to privatise in Parliament on 19 July 1982 he committed the Government to the sale of BT as one unit.

Nevertheless, in the autumn of 1982 the issue was briefly revisited when the PM suggested that dividing BT into a number of regional or local telephone companies should receive serious reconsideration. Her belief that this might lead to better monopoly control and more incentives to innovate seems to have resulted from lobbying by David Young and her personal economic adviser Alan Walters, who were both in favour of a break-up.[159] Young favoured splitting BT into a number of regional and trunk and international telecommunications companies along the lines planned in the US.[160] The PM asked the CPRS to look into the possibility.[161] But Jenkin and Baker remained flatly opposed to the idea, as did the BT Board. On learning that a break-up of BT was being considered within No. 10, Jefferson countered that this would be incompatible with BT's integrated telecommunications network and would seriously damage services. He also warned that any threat of a break-up might well precipitate a national strike by the trade unions.[162] Baker harboured the same concerns and warned that a major restructuring would wreck the entire privatisation timetable.[163]

To head off the possibility that No. 10 might conclude in favour of splitting up BT, the Department of Industry countered that the same benefits could be achieved more simply by having separate profit centres and devolved management. This was not a major concession. Jefferson was already in the process of devolving management within BT and was introducing new management accounts into BT's businesses at regional and local levels. The Department also suggested that if by the end of the decade BT was still a sluggish monopoly, the Government would be able to refer the matter to the Monopolies and Mergers Commission. If the MMC should then consider that it was in the public interest to order a restructuring, this would be a reason to do it. This would coincide with the time of a possible government review of the future of competition in telecommunications. The Department was already contemplating after five years or so a review of the BT-Mercury duopoly.[164]

With the Department of Industry and BT united against a break-up, at a meeting on 9 November 1982 the PM backed down. While she said that she did not agree with a number of the arguments that had been put forward, she accepted that restructuring BT now would "set back privatisation to an unacceptable extent". Nevertheless, it seems clear that she regretted that the issue had not been more thoroughly explored at an earlier stage in the planning.[165] At privatisation the Government settled for the promise of accounting separation within BT by 1987.[166] No public statement was to be made about the possibility of a MMC inspired break-up of BT at a later date; indeed, it was agreed that there should be no hint of such a possibility. To have done so would have alarmed potential investors. BT's future behaviour on cross-subsidisation and bundling services to customers would be left to be sorted out by the new industry regulator.[167] Meanwhile, Ministers pressed BT on the need to set up separate subsidiaries for the different parts of its business to reduce the scope for anti-competitive cross-subsidisation. A report from the Conservative Party's Centre for Policy Studies immediately after the 1983 General Election attempted to resurrect discussion of a possible break-up of BT into regional companies, but the report was quietly ignored.[168]

### Negotiating the BT licence

When eventually the Telecommunications Bill received royal assent, on 12 April 1984, it had spent 320 hours in Parliament. But there was not simply the matter of achieving the passage of the Bill; both BT and Mercury needed operating licences under the new Act setting out their services and responsibilities. Agreeing the terms of BT's licence proved complex and time-consuming. Under pressure from backbenchers, the Government had agreed to allow Parliament to vote on BT's licence before it took effect. The licence would therefore need to be drafted and available to Parliament by the House of Commons Committee stage. This deadline put pressure on the whole privatisation timetable. There was also a real threat that Parliament might, when it saw the terms of the licence, vote it down, removing the prospect of a flotation during 1984.

The BT draft licence was published in late October 1983. Like the Telecommunications Bill it was prepared in a hurry and was far from being in final form. It covered BT's obligations to provide a comprehensive telephone service (the "universal service obligation", including the provision of rural services, public call boxes, emergency services and directory enquiries), restrictions to prevent BT abusing its dominant position (including a price control formula) and requirements on separate accounting for the apparatus supply business. Separate accounting for local, trunk and international services was not a requirement under the licence, because BT's accounting systems did not, as yet, permit the production of such information; although within the DTI there was certainly the view that it would have to be developed for future regulation to be effective. The licence also permitted the introduction of an access charge by BT on other operators using BT's network, to cover the costs of BT's loss making public services under its universal service obligation.[169] The level of the access fee would be a matter left for determination by the new industry regulator.[170] Over the following months a number of changes were made to the draft licence, to fill gaps and in response to criticism from BT and from other organisations, including Mercury.[171]

Throughout the negotiations between the DTI and BT on the draft licence, BT attempted to protect itself from continuing Government controls by pointing to the need for a national telecommunications champion and its past track record in telecommunications innovation. Also, Jefferson opposed the DTI's proposal for a fixed term licence of 25 years, after which BT might lose the right to operate telecommunications in Britain. He argued for at least a 15 years' notice period. If this was unacceptable the Board wanted the Government to agree to buy BT's assets at their residual value if the licence was terminated.[172] However, it quickly became evident that the 25 years was a notional period only and after further discussion a ten year notice period was agreed, to cover the very unlikely possibility that at any time in the future the Government should decide that BT was no longer a fit provider of telecommunications services.

Of more real importance were proposed terms requiring BT to notify the Government on purchasing and R&D decisions and negotiations on joint ventures. BT resisted these conditions, which it saw as being an unacceptable intervention in its commercial decision making. In the end the restrictions were removed or watered down. BT also worried about losing legal privileges that had protected it from liabilities in tort and under the Consumer Credit Act. It particularly opposed a Government idea of legal contracts between BT and its consumers, defining the precise services they should expect. Also, BT worried about the new regulatory regime it would face. The Treasury had proposed the inclusion of performance targets for BT, such as planned cost reduction targets. BT was strongly against this, even while a majority of its shares remained government owned. Initially the Telecommunications Bill contained provisions for the setting of performance targets but these were later deleted.[173] Also, in a meeting on 5 October 1983 on the licence terms, Baker pressed Jefferson on the need to maintain standard and uniform pricing for installation, line maintenance and rental charges, perhaps for ten years to assuage the fears of the rural lobby. However, Jefferson replied that BT should have the freedom to rebalance its tariffs immediately to address the new competition.[174] Jefferson was adamant that privatisation implied commercial freedom and not on-going state regulation.

Another difficult subject was the "resale" of leased circuits, the idea endorsed by Professor Beesley in his earlier report. Treasury Ministers tended to be in favour of competition through resale as well as network competition from Mercury, but the Department of Industry was opposed.[175] After the 1983 Election John Moore, Financial Secretary to the Treasury, lobbied for permitting resale of telephone lines by BT and Mercury believing that this would lead to the most efficient development of telecommunications services.[176] In his view competition would develop more quickly if competitors were able to lease lines from BT, and possibly in time from Mercury, and sell telecommunication services to customers. However, BT was intractably against granting resale fearing that it would take away its profitable trunk and international businesses – it was especially opposed to allowing international leased circuit resale. BT was also opposed to a suggested increase in the permitted number of organisations able to communicate across a leased private circuit.[177] Private circuits were allowed for businesses and other organisations with large inter-office or factory telecommunications. BT feared that expansion of the facility might provide a backdoor method to set up a rival telecommunications network.[178] Meanwhile, the PM was concerned that Mercury should have time to establish itself as a viable competitor to BT before competition was expanded.[179] A reseller using BT's facilities might be able to create a form of national telecommunications network, undermining the competitiveness of not just BT but of the fledgling Mercury. In the end it was agreed that there would be no resale of leased lines until at least 1987 and there would be no licence issued for a further public carrier before 1989. The intention was both to allow Mercury to become established and to ensure a more orderly development of competition.[180]

The original plan had been for the DTI and BT to settle all outstanding licence issues by Easter 1984. However, this deadline slipped as BT negotiated hard over interconnection terms and resale competition in particular. In a letter to Baker on 13 April 1984, Jefferson threatened that "the competition regime, together with other bits of the licence, with whatever agreements on price control and financial matters we may reach, is a key element in the package of arrangements which the Board will have to consider before it agrees to accept the package and sign the Prospectus."[181] There was now real concern within the DTI that BT's failure to finalise the provisions in the draft licence would wreck the entire privatisation timetable. There was also a suspicion that Jefferson was aware of this and that it was strengthening his refusal to compromise. If the disagreements continued the licence would not be ready to keep to the timetable of 1 July 1984 for BT's vesting day. If Jefferson was not bluffing and the Board did refuse to sign the prospectus, there would be no prospect of privatisation that year.[182] However, by mid-May 1984 BT had been persuaded by the Government to shift its position and accept the principle of allowing Mercury to interconnect on the trunk side of local exchanges (broadly Level 4 interconnection), although a number of differences still existed. The actual terms of the interconnection would remain a source of conflict between BT and Mercury after privatisation.[183]

By mid-May, albeit later than originally planned, BT was able to agree to the remaining licence terms at issue. The licence was published in June 1984 and came into effect on 5 August. As finally drafted, the licence required BT to provide services throughout the UK (excluding Kingston-upon-Hull), 999 services, services for the disabled, directory enquiry services, maritime services and public call boxes. The licence also included the price control conditions and a requirement on BT to publish standard terms for providing certain services. For a limited period there would also be a requirement to make a uniform charge for the maintenance of exchange lines for premises served by a single line and to apply a published scale of charges for installing residential exchange lines. The licence terms ensured that charges for the maintenance of exchange lines and for installation would remain common across the UK for at least five years. This condition was introduced to placate the rural lobby in particular. Moreover, under the licence BT would not be permitted to show undue preference to or discriminate against others for services it was required to provide or to favour unfairly any part of its own business, adopt exclusive dealing arrangements on supplies, or to impose linked sales to consumers. There were also conditions restricting cross-subsidies and relating to the liberalisation of services, including the connection of other service providers. In addition, the licence required BT to provide the new regulator with information to monitor its compliance with the licence and to maintain segregated accounts for certain parts of its business.[184]

The final licence differed from the draft one published the previous October due to pressure from interested parties and changes to the Bill in Parliament. The main changes related to directory information, publication of charges and prohibition of undue preference and undue discrimination, all of which were expanded in scope. Other changes related to the price regulation, connection terms, prohibition of cross-subsidies, separation of BT's accounts and the establishment of a separate company for BT's apparatus production, and prohibitions on linked sales and exclusive deals. There were also some new terms introduced into the final draft relating to numbering arrangements, intellectual property rights, testing requirements, installation and maintenance arrangements, international services, and circuits for resale.[185]

\* \* \*

The agreement on the terms of the Telecommunications Bill and BT's operating licence had involved a long, negotiated set of compromises between the DTI, the Treasury and BT.[186] Similar difficulties faced the design of an agreed regulatory structure for BT – of which the licence was a part. From the earliest days in the planning of the privatisation of BT the Department of Industry recognised that because of the Corporation's dominance of the country's telecommunications market its prices and outputs would need to be regulated. This is the subject of the next chapter.

# 12

# PRIVATISING
# BRITISH TELECOM
## OFTEL and regulating profits
## or prices

The liberalisation of telecommunications services from 1981 meant that BT no longer had a legally enforceable monopoly in any part of its business except switched international services. Nevertheless, BT could be expected to dominate a large part of the telecommunications market for some considerable period. On 30 March 1982 officials within the Department of Industry concluded that, given the strategic importance of telecommunications it would have to be "an administered market" with continued regulation by the Government for some time.[1] A paper to the Official Committee on Telecommunications, E(TP), in June 1982 similarly concluded that "a high degree of market dominance . . . will continue for a long period", necessitating the creation of an effective regulatory regime.[2] Privatisation would go ahead with market liberalisation, but in turn this would require a regulatory structure to protect telephone users from monopoly abuse until competition developed and to protect new entrants from BT's market power. A paper to the same Committee from the Secretary of State, Patrick Jenkin, warned:

> "a comparison with the USA is salutary. After 13 years of liberalisation, AT&T and GTE (General Telephone and Electronics) still dominate some 94 per cent of the US market between them. Telecommunications remain essentially administered markets in all countries and the dominance achieved by the national telecommunication operator over history cannot be unscrambled in a decade, let alone overnight."[3]

In departmental papers telecommunication services are commonly referred to as a "natural monopoly".[4] Today this view has been challenged because of the arrival of wireless technologies and cable service providers. There has also recently been "local loop unbundling", which allows rival companies to make the last mile connection (from the subscriber's premises to the first switch). But in 1982 the judgement that BT had a major economic advantage in telecommunications that would diminish the prospects for competition for a long time was perfectly understandable. As one Treasury official recorded at the time:

> "From the Government's point of view privatisation of telecommunications would be a major step in reducing the size of the public sector. But the privatisation would be of an ideological rather than of a practical kind. Because of the continuation of

monopoly the industry would not be put into the market in any real sense, and because of the absence of competition would do little or nothing to promote efficiency."[5]

This was a particularly sceptical conclusion but one more widely shared.[6] Therefore the objective of the Department of Industry and the Treasury over the following months was to find a method of regulating BT once privatised to ensure no monopoly abuse and to impose efficiency incentives. This should have regard, according to one early internal report at the time, to economic principles, administrative practicality and political constraints and without incurring excessive bureaucratic costs.[7] In planning a new regulatory regime for BT the Government purposely attempted to distance itself from the form of regulation that existed in US telecommunications. This was judged to be overly bureaucratic, subject to regulatory capture and reliant on lengthy and expensive court cases.[8] It was also associated with over-investment to increase the regulatory asset base.[9]

The previous chapter reviewed the terms of BT's operating licence, which lies at the heart of the regulation of BT. This chapter is primarily concerned with the establishment of a new regulatory office and decisions on the regulation of profits and prices.

## Founding the Office of Telecommunications

The Department of Industry first approached the regulation of BT in the spring and summer of 1982 by considering the possibility of control through existing competition policy. Competition policy in the UK was administered by the Office of Fair Trading (OFT) and the Monopolies and Mergers Commission (MMC). However, it was quickly concluded that the existing competition legislation would be inadequate to the task of controlling BT's market power and, as a compounding factor, the OFT and the MMC were judged to lack expertise in telecommunications questions. For example, the Official Committee on Telecommunications Policy (E(TP)) decided in June 1982 that current competition law would be inadequate and too slow working to regulate BT adequately. Equally, it seems that the OFT was not keen to take on the burden of regulating the industry believing that without considerably more resources its other competition work would be jeopardised. The MMC also expressed strong reservations when first approached by the Department of Industry about becoming involved in the regulation of BT, especially if the MMC was to be left to decide on the adequacy of BT's profits.[10] There was the prospect that regulating BT could "swamp the other work of the OFT and MMC".[11] E(TP) therefore recommended establishing a separate structure for the regulation of BT's services and tariffs, although it was expected that the competition authorities would play some role in the regulation. At the time the Treasury was keen to see BT referred to the MMC for periodic efficiency studies, especially while the Government retained a majority of the company's shares.

The outcome during the summer of 1982 was a decision to remove from BT all of the regulatory powers over the UK telecommunications market that it had inherited from the Post Office and to create a new dedicated regulatory office for BT, modelled on the OFT and headed by a Director General of Telecommunications (DGT).[12] The new office would be responsible for monitoring BT's performance in terms of its operating licence and carrying out for the Secretary of State such functions as he might delegate. This would include monitoring monopoly abuses in services and apparatus supply. The intention was that DGT would be able to issue orders for licence infringements by BT (and in time any other licensed operators) and seek a civil remedy through the courts.[13] BT's behaviour would be set down in its operating licence agreed between the Department and the Corporation.

In particular, the Government decided to remove from BT its existing power to license competitors. Instead, under the new regulatory regime they would be authorised by the Secretary of State in consultation with the DGT. One reason for concentrating the licensing powers in the Secretary of State was the desire to preserve a universal telecommunications service, which might be threatened by free competition. Another reason was security issues. The DGT would be able to alter a licence condition, but if the licensee objected the matter would be referred to the MMC. If the MMC concluded that the change was desirable in the public interest, the DGT would then be able to make the variation. An early proposal involved the Secretary of State having the final say on licence amendments, but the Department's financial advisers, Kleinworts, suggested that without some clear distancing of the decision from political control, a successful flotation was unlikely to be achieved. Therefore the referral mechanism to the MMC was established. It was specifically designed so as to provide an alternative to recourse to the judiciary to settle disputes.[14] In the USA regulatory disputes went to the courts, but it was recognised that this was costly and time-consuming. In the UK the regulatory structure was designed so that only "due process" (essentially the process and rationality of the regulator's decision) became a matter for adjudication by the courts, not the facts on which the DGT's decision was made. In addition, it was intended that there should be referrals to the MMC whenever there was a suggestion of a competition law infringement under existing competition law.[15]

For a time the Department of Industry considered the possibility of transferring all of the OFT's powers relating to competition matters in the field of telecommunications to the DGT, but the Department of Trade was opposed to this. [16] Lord Cockfield, Secretary of State for Trade, was determined to ensure that the powers of the existing competition authorities were not diminished.[17] After discussions between the Department of Industry and the Department of Trade, it was agreed that the DGT would oversee concurrently with the OFT the application of the Fair Trading Act 1973 and the Competition Act 1980, as they applied to telecoms. Interestingly, within the Department of Industry and the Treasury it was suggested that at some time in the future it might be desirable to merge the Office of Telecommunications (OFTEL) into the OFT. This possibility has never been pursued. Meanwhile, Kleinworts warned that ideally the new regulatory regime should operate for at least nine to 12 months prior to a flotation, to reassure investors as to its nature.[18] This meant that the regulatory system would need to be agreed quickly.

The constitutional status of the new regulatory office was an early subject of debate within the Department of Industry. In June 1982 it was agreed that the new regulatory office should be "a non-Ministerial government department" to remove its decisions from direct political interference – something private investors were almost certain to insist upon. Consideration was given to the establishment of a non-departmental public body like the Civil Aviation Authority, on the grounds that this would be more obviously independent of political control. Also, its employees might not be civil servants, which would permit more flexibility in terms of staffing and salaries. However, within the Department of Industry there was a fear that the regulatory agency might become too independent, leading to conflict over telecommunications policy between the DGT and the Minister.[19] Also, the Home Office wished to ensure on security grounds that the industry remained controlled within government. It was believed that interception and other security issues would be better facilitated if there was a non-Ministerial body staffed by civil servants.[20]

In consequence, the new regulatory office was designed to ensure that the regulator had a degree of independence from political control to satisfy investors, while remaining ultimately accountable to the Secretary of State and Parliament. Kleinworts advised that if BT remained regulated by Government department, potential investment would be discouraged because investors would fear decisions being made for political rather than economic reasons. However, compared to the suggestion so often made since by commentators on UK regulatory policy that the creation of the Office of Telecommunications (OFTEL) heralded the arrival of "independent regulation" in Britain, from the early planning stage there was recognition that the regulator's independence would have to be tempered to minimise the risk of any possible conflict between Ministerial policy on telecommunications and that of the regulator. As a result, it was agreed that a non-Ministerial department was established but clearly within Government, on the lines of the OFT. OFTEL would be a statutory body and staffed primarily by civil servants[21] and the Secretary of State would be able to give general directions on considerations to which the DGT should have particular regard. The DGT would report annually to the Secretary of State and his reports would be laid before Parliament. Later, following criticism of a lack of consumer representation in the proposed regulatory structure, it was agreed that the DGT would be advised by user committees for England, Northern Ireland, Scotland and Wales and by other committees representing the specific interests of the elderly and disabled and small businesses appointed by the Secretary of State.

The Department of Industry had in mind that the DGT should be able to attract to the new regulatory office experts in telecommunications and that this might necessitate pay levels above those in the civil service, a view shared by the Central Policy Review Staff (CPRS) in the Cabinet Office.[22] However, the Civil Service Management and Personnel Office opposed the idea. The Treasury was also suspicious, being keen to maintain control over salaries and the Office's other running costs. It was finally agreed, therefore, that the staff should be civil servants but that additional payments could be made where necessary for the discharge of essential tasks. Also, outside experts could be brought in on special contracts from time to time.[23] Initially an office of around 10 to 20 people was envisaged. Later the number was revised upwards to around 50 with a budget of some £1.5 million a year, as the importance and extent of the necessary regulation of telecommunications became clearer. Perhaps not entirely coincidentally, this number was broadly similar to the number of civil servants then monitoring BT in the DTI, who it was intended would transfer in the main to OFTEL when it was established. At the same time, officials questioned whether the number would be sufficient. As one Treasury civil servant commented: "the general view was that several hundred, say 300 – would be required to do a decent job" and that obtaining people with the necessary technical skill would be difficult.[24] Others may have felt that this was a pessimistic assessment, but there was wider concern in the Treasury that unless competition developed quickly OFTEL would need far more than the 50 staff proposed.[25]

BT responded to the creation of a new regulatory regime, which had primarily the objective of controlling its commercial behaviour, with considerable suspicion.[26] On 5 August 1982 Sir George Jefferson wrote to Jenkin expressing deep concern about suggestions from his Department that BT's operating licence should include special terms going beyond normal competition legislation. Also, BT wanted the activity of licensing operators to be removed from the Government, something the Government rejected, because of the broad policy issues involved.

As the intended powers of the proposed regulatory office began to evolve, including control over service levels and profits or prices, BT became even more concerned. Before privatisation the Corporation was subject to almost no significant regulation by the Department of Industry of its prices and services. BT had to meet a minimum rate of return on investment target and would be enjoined to observe pay guidelines, which were often ignored. Government would use persuasion when prices were being adjusted. But the proposed regulation suggested that BT might face more not less intervention in its business than had existed under nationalisation. On 10 November 1982 Jefferson left with Jenkin a written list of complaints about the proposed regulatory structure, concluding: "The Board cannot over-emphasise the gravity of its concern over the position which seems to have evolved. The regimes proposed or implied are repressive and unrealistic. They are diametrically opposed to the Government's stated aim of removing BT from the web of Government interference and control."[27]

BT management were especially worried that while the Government remained the majority shareholder, and in 1982 it was by no means clear that a majority flotation of BT could be successfully achieved in the short term, the company would face dual control. That is to say, BT would face the traditional controls over a nationalised industry of the Treasury and the Department of Industry, alongside controls imposed by the new regulatory office. BT was therefore very much against the establishment of OFTEL ahead of privatisation.[28] When the Telecommunications Bill was presented to Parliament on 19 November 1982, BT issued a press release welcoming the Government's intention, while stressing "that regulation must not spin a new web of bureaucracy over telecommunications or stifle investment".[29]

In late January 1983, using headhunters, the Department of Industry short-listed eight possible candidates for the post of DGT. The aim was to recruit someone with an accountancy or financial background who would have sufficient authority in the telecommunications sector. At the same time, it was seen as important that the person selected was not from the telecommunications industry itself and especially BT, to ensure objectivity. However, considerable delay then ensued as Ministers focused on getting the Telecommunications Bill passed. It was therefore the end of the year before interviews for the post were held. Three people were interviewed and Professor Bryan Carsberg from the London School of Economics was selected. Carsberg had already been involved in the privatisation of BT, inputting into the Government's deliberations on market liberalisation under the 1981 Telecommunications Act.[30]

In the DTI's discussions with the Treasury on the appropriate seniority for the position of the DGT, the Treasury initially maintained that the DGT would have less responsibility and fewer staff than the Director General of the OFT. Treasury officials suggested that an appropriate grade might be equivalent to that of the Chairman of the Traffic Commissioners or under-secretary grade, although it did not necessarily object to a higher rate of pay.[31] However, following DTI representations that no one of suitable calibre could be recruited at this level, the Treasury reluctantly relented. It was agreed that the DGT should be appointed at a level equivalent to a Second Permanent Secretary, comparable with the seniority of the Director General of the OFT and the Chairman of the MMC.[32] Even then the Department still felt that it might be very difficult to attract someone of the right calibre.[33] Also, the DTI favoured the creation of a post of Deputy Director at under-secretary level. Again the Treasury opposed the idea but eventually gave way.[34]

The Treasury originally proposed a salary of some £45,000 for the post of Director General. This led some of the eight candidates initially short-listed and with more lucrative salaries outside Government to withdraw their interest in the job. Following the decision to appoint Carsberg, it seemed that the salary would be insufficient to attract him too.[35] The DTI requested permission to offer a higher amount given Carsberg's current earnings, but the Treasury procrastinated. Indeed, it took considerable argument between the DTI and the Treasury and an approach by the Secretary of State to the PM before, in March 1984, a marginally improved salary of £50,000 was agreed. It was felt that Carsberg might find this just acceptable. But when Carsberg was offered the post he responded that he no longer felt he was in a position to accept the appointment. The reason was his failure to persuade his employers, the London School of Economics, to give him a five year secondment. But perhaps he was also irritated by the long delay in obtaining formal confirmation of his appointment. Norman Tebbit notes: "At one stage I almost lost Professor Carsberg whom I wanted to appoint as Director General of OFTEL . . . because approval of his contract was delayed."[36] The result was an urgent telephone call to Carsberg, who by this time was in America giving a lecture, to persuade him to accept the offer and agreement to an initial three year appointment, equivalent to the maximum sabbatical leave he could arrange from the LSE. The higher salary was also confirmed.[37] Carsberg now agreed to the accept the appointment, but subject to the additional condition of being allowed to continue to work for one day a week for the Institute of Chartered Accountants. The Chancellor of the Exchequer expressed some misgivings about these terms, especially the day a week to be spent on Institute business.[38] Carsberg first took up office at the DTI on a part-time contract before transferring to OFTEL in July 1984.[39]

## Regulating profits or prices?

In addition to the appointment of the regulator, the issue of how precisely to regulate BT's prices or profits needed to be decided. As a nationalised industry the Government did not set BT's prices, although the Government did influence them through both moral suasion and by setting financial targets and the EFL. Also, the Secretary of State's authorisation was sought when prices were raised. In the planning of the privatisation there was therefore the immediate question as to whether after the sell-off there should still be similar Ministerial oversight of pricing.

It soon became clear from City advice "that if Ministers could in any way interfere with the tariff setting process then BT could not be sold". Shareholders would need assurance "that no pressure for political reasons could be placed upon the tariff recommendations of BT and the supervisory process which would examine them".[40] There was also the point that price controls were associated with prices and incomes policies, which the PM had been anxious to disown on coming to office in May 1979. Therefore officials quickly rejected the prospect of direct Government regulation of BT's prices. It was also decided that it would not be sensible for BT to be required to seek the approval of the DGT whenever a tariff change was envisaged. This similarly might undo much of the potential benefit from allowing BT to operate commercially in the private sector.[41] On 30 June 1982 E(TP) discussed establishing a maximum rate of return for either the whole or individual parts of BT's business. However, Kleinworts argued that if BT was set what was in effect a more or less fixed rate of return then the City would view BT shares as equivalent to a dull, fixed interest stock, reducing potential interest in the forthcoming flotation. The Secretary of State was therefore invited by E(TP), in consultation with the Department of Trade, the No. 10 Policy Unit and the CPRS, "to consider the respective merits of a single maximum rate of return for BT, a two-tier maximum rate of return and a profits tax, and to report".[42]

During the summer of 1982 officials in the Department of Industry responded by exploring possible ways of regulating BT's profitability, including imposing a maximum rate of return for BT as a whole. On 1 September 1982, to advance matters, a Working Group was established to consider the options, involving mainly economists from the Department of Industry, the Department of Trade, the Monopolies and Mergers Commission and the Office of Fair Trading, along with David Clementi from Kleinworts. External economic advice was sought from Professor Michael Beesley of the London Business School.[43] The Group held its first meeting on Tuesday 7 September. It was given a very tight timetable for its work, being asked to report by the 23rd of the month. Throughout its deliberations, the Group was hampered by a lack of accurate figures from BT on the profitability of the Corporation's different activities.[44]

The Group considered the idea of having some form of "sliding scale rate of return", which would essentially involve a fixed rate of return and a graduated excess profits tax. Any profits earned above the target rate would either be taxed or in some other way partially removed from the company. Such a scheme was in use in some parts of the USA with the amounts taken away applied to a trust fund to pay bonuses to staff and management, pay rebates to consumers, or pay for additional investments. The Department contemplated BT's excess profits being returned to consumers through a reduction in their telephone bills.[45] The scheme which eventually won the day was similar and based on a proposal from the economics section of the Department of Industry (and one of its economists, Bruce Laidlaw, in particular) and involved setting a two-tier rate of return.[46] Under the proposal there would be a minimum and a maximum rate of return for BT's regulated services. It was felt that the maximum return might be around six per cent, although this would be a matter for Ministers to decide. When BT exceeded the permitted maximum, it would be required to pay back to consumers a percentage of the excess profit. The percentage might start at 50 per cent but would rise according to the extent to which the permitted rate of return was exceeded. BT would also be required to take action, notably through a price freeze or price cuts, to prevent a repetition of excess profits in the following year. As there were large profit differences across BT's businesses, there might be a separate maximum rate of return for the local, trunk and international businesses, to discourage cross-subsidisation, as well as for BT as a whole. The minimum rate of return was intended to provide a profit guarantee to investors. It would also address the requirement in Clause 3 of the Telecommunications Bill for BT to be allowed to achieve a return on capital sufficient to finance its services.

The permitted maximum and minimum rates of return would be reassessed every five years. A five year period was felt to be a suitable length of time given the pace of technological change and changes in telecommunications services, although there is no evidence that the choice was a scientific one. The change in the rates of return would take the form of a licence amendment, but there would also be provision for the DGT to adjust the maximum return up or down by up to ten per cent, to reflect improvements and deteriorations in service quality or other measures of efficiency agreed in any year and to overcome any incentive for BT to cut costs by reducing service quality.[47] After five years the DGT would have the power to refer the allowed maximum and minimum rates of return to the MMC, to judge whether they needed to be reset. The DGT would also be empowered to limit the level of tariffs if excess profits were made and to refer BT to the MMC at any other time to review the company's efficiency.[48]

It was expected that the guarantee of a minimum rate of return would be welcomed by the capital market, while the maximum rate of return was intended to protect consumers from excess profit making. However, any form of rate of return regulation was open to criticism because of the known incentives for management to pad costs. Rate of return limits were used in the regulation of US privately-owned utilities and were associated particularly with what economists referred to as "the Averch-Johnson effect". Whenever the allowed rate of return exceeded the cost of capital there would be an incentive for the firm to invest to increase the regulated assets base, on which the allowed rate of return was based.[49] The outcome would be over-investment. The effect had been first postulated in 1962 by two American economists and was known to the economics section of the Department of Industry. Research in regulatory economics in the USA had also identified other possible inefficiencies from rate of return regulation, including a failure to restrict operating costs if any cost increases could be passed on to consumers in higher prices to maintain the allowed return. More generally, the regulatory economics literature suggested that the difficulty of rate of return regulation lay in the regulator having insufficient accurate information on the firm's efficient levels of operating costs, capital costs and revenues, so as to set profitability at a level which was neither excessive, leading to monopoly profits, or inadequate, leading to the firm having difficulty raising capital in the market. Either way, rate of return regulation was associated with bureaucratic information gathering with the objective of setting the "right" rate. Contemporary reports from the US Federal Communications Commission (FCC), which regulated telecommunications in the USA, circulated within the Department of Industry during the autumn of 1982. The reports illustrated the difficulties of regulating profits in telecommunications without creating disincentives to operate efficiently and how the FCC "has largely abandoned its efforts to establish the effective rate and profit regulation".[50]

The idea of a two-tier rate of return scheme was promoted within the Department of Industry on the grounds that it would be less likely to lead to cost padding than setting a single fixed rate of return.[51] However, the Treasury was uneasy that the scheme might have little impact on prices and that a specific provision on price control might also be needed.[52] The Treasury also pressed for a condition to be included in BT's licence requiring it to conduct its affairs efficiently and for there to be value for money audits by independent consultants with the results going to the DGT. This was strongly opposed by the Department of Industry, on the grounds that it would constitute an unacceptable level of interference in BT's management of its business. Also, the Department dropped a plan to give the DGT powers to set BT performance targets following hostility from BT management.[53] Strengthening the opposition to rate of return regulation was the point that Kleinworts wished to avoid BT stock being seen by investors as equivalent to a bond with a more or less fixed rate of return. Also, and decisively, Professor Alan Walters, the PM's special economic adviser, canvassed against rate of return regulation. He criticised the excessive bureaucracy that would result from the need to set and police the allowed return. He also argued that the prospect when the permitted rate of return was greatly exceeded of up to a 100 per cent "profit tax" was "the stuff that socialists are made of", a comment that was no doubt intended to raise the PM's hackles. Walters championed instead an idea of his own for an "output-related profit levy" (ORPL) – also referred to as the "output-related profit tax" (ORPT).[54]

The ORPL scheme involved the regulator fixing an agreed level of output growth for BT in advance for a given period. With the level set at, say, five per cent per annum growth, the profits would be taxed at a rate of, say, 50 per cent with the receipts going to the Exchequer. But if BT's output growth fell below the target then the rate of profits tax would rise.

Importantly, and crucially different to the Department of Industry's proposal, if output rose above target, the rate of profit tax would fall. The idea behind the scheme was that BT would therefore have an incentive to expand its output beyond the monopoly level. By providing management with the incentive to raise output, Walters' scheme directly addressed the tendency for monopolists to restrict supply below competitive levels. In turn this could be expected to bring prices down. Also, Walters' proposal was intended to encourage BT to cut prices not output when demand fell, as output reductions would be penalised. This contrasted with the general experience under nationalisation of firms raising prices to protect their revenues in a recession. To head off criticism that his scheme might not provide incentives for BT to diversify into new activities, Walters suggested that the regulator could choose output weights to encourage the growth in desirable new services.

The interdepartmental Working Group studied Walters' proposal but found against it.[55] The Group had been set up to find a method of preventing a privatised BT from making monopoly profits and its members were concerned about the likely political reaction if BT were allowed to earn high profits when output rose, something that could occur under Walters' scheme.[56] They also took the view that the proposal would be difficult to implement for a multi-product firm like BT and where outputs were affected by external influences over which management had no control.[57] Contrary to Walters' claim, the Department of Industry was unconvinced that the ORPL would require less regulatory bureaucracy than the two-tier rate of return proposal.[58] They also had other objections to Walters' proposal, including the difficulty of setting an output target for five years ahead. Kleinworts too were suspicious of the idea, warning that investors in BT's shares would be unfamiliar with such a novel and untested method of regulation and that this might reduce significantly the prospects for a successful flotation. Investor nervousness would not have been irrational. Under Walters' scheme, a lower output growth due to lower than expected sales would have led to a higher profit levy, leading to a doubly damaging effect on BT's share price.

Another objection to the Walters' proposal related to the expected price elasticity of demand for telecommunications services. While it was to be expected that the elasticity would vary across different services, overall there would have to be an elastic demand for BT to have the necessary incentive to raise output and reduce prices. With a price elastic demand the percentage rise in output would be greater than the percentage fall in prices leading to BT earning higher revenue. By contrast, a price inelastic demand would lead to a proportionately larger fall in prices than the gain in output and therefore lower revenue. Walters argued that the demand for telecommunications services was price elastic, but economists within the Department of Industry were sceptical. They believed that local and business calls, in particular, might be price inelastic. However, given Walters' continued lobbying and his closeness to the PM, Professor Beesley was asked to review the ORPL including the price elasticity issue. Beesley concluded that he preferred the Walters' scheme to the one favoured by the Department of Industry, but he doubted whether either would achieve its regulatory objectives. Instead, Beesley preferred price control via MMC inquiries, with the MMC able to implement remedies including rolling back price rises.[59] On the question of the price elasticity of demand for local calls, where BT would have the clearest monopoly, Beesley concluded that the elasticity was low. This suggested that in this important part of the telecommunications market at least, Walters' adjustment mechanism might not work. Beesley was also concerned that the Walters' scheme carried a particularly serious risk of penalising BT if the rate of growth of output did not come up to expectation, perhaps for reasons independent of the efforts of the management. However, he did believe that the proposal would require less collection of information by the regulator than would rate of return setting. He also concluded that, while both schemes could result in regulatory capture, on balance rate of return regulation was the more vulnerable because of its greater information needs.[60] In summary, Beesley's report failed to come down conclusively in favour of either the inter-departmental Group's or Walters' proposal.

The interdepartmental Working Group's report with its recommendation and Beesley's paper as an annex were discussed in the Department of Industry on 6 October 1982. In the light of Beesley's equivocal endorsement of Walters' scheme, it was rejected. The Depart-ment endorsed two-tier rate of return regulation, with the DGT having discretion to control prices once BT exceeded its allowed rate of return. There would also be a facility for periodic monopoly references to the MMC on efficiency grounds which might also trigger a price adjustment, a possibility that it was expected would be welcomed by the Treasury. Although some officials felt that an interval of five years between regulatory reviews might be too long, it was agreed that this provision was probably necessary so as to reassure investors. However, it was felt that the DGT should be able to initiate an earlier profit review if he had good grounds.[61]

Walters, however, refused to accept the decision, and to placate him a meeting was called with Baker and officials from the Department of Industry on 20 October. Here the arguments for and against rate of return regulation and the ORPL were aired once again. At the meeting Walters conceded that his proposal was not fully worked up, reflecting some of Beesley's concerns, but he maintained that the Department's objections to his scheme "applied more strongly to the Department's proposals". At the meeting, the Secretary of State concluded, perhaps mindful of Walters' standing within No.10, that he saw some attractions in his scheme.

The outcome of the meeting was a decision to commission Professor Littlechild of Birmingham University, a former student of Walters, "to work up Professor Walters' scheme in more detail" and compare it with the Working Group's proposal. Meanwhile, the Telecommunications Bill would be drafted for introduction into Parliament including mention of a rate of return regulatory regime, but with the Secretary of State reserving the right to introduce a new clause to replace or supplement it with one based on Walters' proposal, in the light of Littlechild's report.[62] Outside the meeting Jenkin revealed his own confusion over the merits of the two different proposals: "I believe that officials who have been grappling with this problem for several months now are assuming that those people (like me) who have not been doing so nonetheless understand what they (the grapplers) are talking about. I fear I don't."[63] It seems that Jenkin hoped that Littlechild's deliberations might provide him with the necessary clarity. If so, he may well have been disappointed. Littlechild's early deliberations took the form of detailed economic analysis, which officials in the Department of Industry and at Kleinworts struggled to comprehend.

On learning of Professor Littlechild's appointment, BT complained that it had not been consulted on the terms of reference. As Littlechild's recommendations would have a major effect on the Corporation's future performance, BT insisted that he should at least spend some time with the Corporation before reporting.[64] This did not occur, although he did have a meeting over dinner with Jefferson and Michael Valentine and Michael Fry of Warburgs.[65] Littlechild was under considerable time pressure to report. His report was commissioned on 28 October 1982 for delivery on 14 January 1983 at the latest, with an instruction to present a draft report within 6 to 7 weeks. Meanwhile, disagreement continued within and outside Government about the appropriate form of regulation. In particular, in November the Central

Policy Review Staff came out against the ORPL, while also confirming the difficulties experienced abroad with rate of return regulation.[66] Later in the same month, Sir William Barlow, former Chairman of the Post Office, made it known that he was not convinced that a maximum rate of return for BT would adequately protect Mercury from BT's market power.[67] Also, the MMC injected the view that its "economists would still prefer to see less emphasis on rate of return control. Whereas Professor Walters' scheme may suffer in many ways, we feel that the regulatory framework should shift more perceptibly towards his plan".[68]

Some initial comments were provided by Littlechild on 24 November. In what was a highly technical paper, almost certainly incomprehensible to the non-economist, Littlechild suggested that an ORPL could accentuate the cyclical fluctuation in profits after tax in an economic recession, although the outcome was not entirely clear. Also he questioned the practicality of calculating the appropriate weights to apply to the output target so as to address the differing price elasticities issue, especially given the large number of different outputs produced by BT. Overall, Littlechild concluded that "The ORPT is evidently a rather complex phenomenon".[69]

On hearing of Littlechild's initial conclusion, Walters suggested that Littlechild had successfully established the possibility of his scheme. This was a charitable interpretation; certainly it was not the conclusion drawn in the Department of Industry. A commentary on Littlechild's paper from one Departmental economist concluded that, "while interesting to economists, development of a rationale for Professor Walters' idea does not lead to the conclusion that a scheme consistent with the theory can be made to work." On Littlechild's conclusion that the ORPL could be effective in increasing output, the comment ends tellingly, "I cannot reproduce his algebra and do not accept his conclusion."[70]

Littlechild followed up his initial observations in another paper on 29 November, this time concerned with rate of return regulation. In this study Littlechild criticised the information demands that rate of return regulation would require and the difficult judgement that would have to be made about what was a reasonable rate of return for BT.[71] He also singled out the scope for bureaucracy, mistakes and regulatory capture, as evidenced by experience of operating rate of return regulation in the USA. These were all criticisms raised earlier by Walters. In effect, Littlechild had concluded that neither the ORPL nor rate of return regulation was free from serious shortcomings, echoing the conclusions of Professor Beesley.

Littlechild later commented in terms of Walters' and the DTI's proposals: "Unfortunately, I could not immediately think of anything better, other than a variant of the working group scheme that I called the profit ceiling scheme . . . without enthusiasm I submitted my draft report."[72] Littlechild had been asked to produce a draft report by 17 December. In it he rejected both the Working Group's proposal for a two-tier control on the return on investment and the ORPL advocated by Walters. Instead, he proposed determining a real rate of return on capital employed that would be reasonable for BT to earn. Price controls would then be used to ensure that BT did not persistently exceed this level.

This proposal was described by Littlechild as a variant on the Department of Industry scheme. If the profit ceiling was breached, BT would be required within four months to reduce its general level of tariffs to get its profits back below the ceiling. Three breaches within six years would incur the penalty of an automatic reference to the MMC. However, as a free market economist of an "Austrian" persuasion Littlechild was instinctively against controlling profits. His report suggested that the profit ceiling should only exist until competition developed. To speed up its arrival, Littlechild recommended that competition should be further encouraged by new entry from cable and cellular radio operators and through more liberal use of the radio spectrum, permitting resale of BT lines, and permitting competition for international calls.[73] In the meantime BT's efficiency would be overseen by periodic references to the MMC, the Treasury's preference. As the profit control would be temporary until competition developed sufficiently, he argued that it could be fixed by political judgement with the cost of capital or other economic criteria subordinate. This was intended to reduce the possible bureaucracy and costs associated with the detailed regulation of profits.

Kleinworts and Warburgs were favourably disposed to Littlechild's proposal on the grounds that it would be readily sellable to investors. But the report was not well received in the Department of Industry. The Department concluded that it provided a weak form of control over profits because there might be little or no intervention by the DGT, depending upon the level at which the profit ceiling was set. There was also concern within the Department about Littlechild's suggestion that the profit ceiling be determined by political judgement rather than economic considerations. This was considered naïve. In addition, the idea of moving quickly to further deregulation of telecommunications, on the lines suggested by Littlechild, was judged to require "radical changes in the direction of our policy". Officials judged that to produce the level of deregulation recommended by Littlechild would require permitting free market entry into telecommunications, separation of basic and enhanced services, a break-up of the BT monopoly, maintenance of price controls in monopoly services, and prohibition of BT from manufacturing.[74] These changes were considered to be politically infeasible, although it was felt that Littlechild's report had "provided a new set of negotiable trade-offs with BT". That is to say, BT might be persuaded to acquiesce to more competition in its international and trunk services in return for allowing some headroom for general tariff increases.

A Departmental economist closely involved in the privatisation of BT concluded that, "Professor Littlechild has written the kind of report that can be expected from someone committed to de-regulation. He has probably buried Professor Walters' intervention, but his scheme seems to offer little improvement over our own proposal."[75] At the same time, the Department of Industry had begun exploring the possibility that "there might be merit in considering giving users direct protection in the form of a specific real price objective for licensed services. BT could be required to keep the tariffs for these services falling in real terms by, say 2% per annum with the objective being reviewed every five years." The concept of a price control linked to inflation, adjusted to reflect efficiency gains within BT, was a throwback to earlier discussion within the Department on price setting at the time of the Buzby bond, chapter 11, pp.248–9. A favoured version of the bond proposal had provided for an RPI – 2% cap.

Kenneth Baker, Minister for State, responded to Littlechild's report with the comment that: "I am attracted to the Littlechild idea – it's simple. But in the absence of widespread effective competition, BT will have a heyday – it would certainly make BT more marketable." He too saw attraction in the idea of a high overall profit ceiling coupled with some form of price control, perhaps based on a RPI – 2% formula.[76] At a meeting with BT on 22 December 1982, Department officials suggested a compromise between the Department's two-tier rate of return regulation and Littlechild's proposals, "namely an overall rate of return . . . to be ended as soon as effective competition was established in the market – ie; probably by 1992 – and some formula on domestic tariffs such as the RPI – 2% agreed for the Buzby Bond". In other words, even before Littlechild's final report was submitted recommending the use of some form of price cap, the Department of Industry had already begun to consider the idea of a formula for domestic tariffs along the same lines. In addition, in return for relaxing the rate of return control, BT would be expected to make a number of further concessions on competition.[77]

At a meeting on Wednesday 5 January 1983, involving Department of Industry and Treasury officials and representatives from Kleinworts and the CPRS, Littlechild was left in no uncertainty about the Department of Industry's difficulties with his December proposals.[78] The Treasury was also concerned, concluding that the report had "killed off the MRR [maximum rate of return] scheme" but that the suggestion that there need only be a weak regulatory system "is not helpful" given that the competition faced by BT was only likely to develop slowly. There remained sympathy in the Treasury for some variant of the ORPL.[79] But by now it was almost certain that this would not be adopted, given the reservations of Beesley, the Department of Industry and Littlechild. The following day Littlechild met Walters. Walters repeated that he still felt that his scheme was the best available, but conceded that it needed much more work to make it operational. At this meeting, aware of the interest within the Department of Industry of linking price rises in some way to the RPI, Walters expressed some support for the idea of (what is now known as) a price cap mechanism.[80] Meanwhile, BT management made clear again that they did not see the need for regulation of profits or efficiency. They submitted a paper which was described within the Department of Industry as, "the minimum they think they can get away with rather than a coherent statement and should be regarded as a try-on".[81]

Littlechild's final report was delivered on 18 January 1983.[82] It was basically the draft report but with an important additional final chapter, seemingly written sometime in early January.[83] The addition of the final chapter indicated some serious second thoughts compared to the draft report of the previous month, reflecting the Department of Industry's lack of enthusiasm for the conclusions of the earlier paper. Littlechild confirmed that further consideration of Walters' proposal had unearthed too many doubts for it to be considered practical. But he also emphasised that while a ceiling rate of return was still an option, it would share many of the drawbacks of US-style rate of return regulation. That is to say, it would be burdensome to BT, reduce incentives for efficiency and market entry, and distort investment decisions. Also, a control on BT's overall rate of return would cover the whole of BT's licensed activities instead of focusing on those services where monopoly power was likely to be of greatest concern, notably local calls and line rentals. Instead, therefore, Littlechild proposed setting a price formula for BT's local services.

Michael Valentine, one of Warburgs' advisers to BT and who had been involved in designing the price formula for the Buzby bond, claims credit for having explained the idea of the price cap to Littlechild over dinner at BT's company flat in Howland Street, London.[84] However, Littlechild's price control differed from that contemplated during the planning of the Buzby bond. Under that scheme, with BT still in the state sector, its prices would have remained subject to Government approval. Also, the RPI – 2% might have acted as a floor rather than a cap on price rises, to satisfy investors in the bond rather than protect consumers.[85] The Secretary of State would have been permitted to grant larger price rises on application from BT. In Littlechild's final report a so-called "Local Tariff Reduction Scheme" was proposed to apply to the services provided by BT's Local Areas. The Local Tariff Reduction Scheme was intended to protect particularly residential subscribers and small businesses, whose services could not be expected to be opened up to competition in the foreseeable future, from monopoly pricing. Included were call box charges and excluded were trunk calls and international services where competition was expected to develop quickly. Two alternative methods of implementing the Scheme were put forward: (1) specifying in BT's licence the services to which the real price objective would apply individually, for example rentals and local call charges, and (2) preparing a "basket" of services to which the objective would apply collectively. Littlechild explained that method 1 would give greater assurance to consumers that charges for local services were regulated. But method 2 would allow for the inclusion of other but perhaps important monopoly services, such as directory enquiries, and would leave BT with greater freedom to set and rebalance its tariffs in response to competition. To protect against any deterioration in service quality due to the price control, Littlechild suggested that BT's licence should include a commitment not to reduce the quality of service, backed up by the threat of an MMC reference on the recommendation of the DGT. Also, under Littlechild's proposals there would be an automatic reference to the MMC after five years to reconsider the coverage and future need for the Local Tariff Reduction Scheme.

## "A substantial degree of risk and uncertainty"

The real price objective was not intended to be demanding or difficult to achieve. Littlechild envisaged it being somewhere in the range of two per cent to five per cent and set by negotiation with BT. This reflected Littlechild's desire to avoid overly formal methods of setting the X factor and the creation of a regulatory bureaucracy. Also, and interestingly in the light of the way that the X factor was later used by successive DGTs, Littlechild's purpose was to check the abuse of monopoly power until competition developed. As he emphasised in his report, "Profit regulation is merely a 'stop-gap' until sufficient competition develops" and "Regulation is essentially a means of preventing the worst excess of monopoly; it is not a substitute for competition. It is a means of 'holding the fort' until competition arrives." The main focus was not to set up a long-term system of regulation to force BT into making efficiency gains over time through the setting of the X factor. Littlechild saw scope for BT to become more efficient, but expected this to be addressed by competition rather than through the price cap. Also, he was of the view that: "Prevention of excessive profits to shareholders is *not* (emphasis in the original) a relevant consideration, since expected profits will be reflected in the price of BT shares at flotation, so shareholders will not earn an excessive return on their investment."[86] BT would repeatedly refer back to this observation over the following weeks as the Department of Industry and the Treasury shifted the focus of the price cap on to profits and efficiency incentives.

The final recommendations from Professor Littlechild were a major advance on those put forward almost a month earlier. They incorporated a price cap mechanism for which the Littlechild report has since become justifiably celebrated. However, the report is a continuation from the December one to the extent that Littlechild was still of the view that competition would be more effective than regulation in protecting consumers. He still wanted to see Government action to increase competition in the resale of capacity on leased lines, easing restrictions on the supply of international services by competitors including Mercury, allowing cable companies and others to compete, and action to enable competing networks to interconnect with the BT network. [87]

Walters judged the report to be a "very good" one and fully endorsed its conclusions, commenting that "the local tariff guaranteed reduction scheme now offers the best way forward". However, he still wanted his ORPL idea to be developed further on the grounds that, "I can foresee that there will be other instances where such a concept would be more appropriate than the present case".[88] The response in the Department of Industry to the Littlechild report was much more equivocal. An internal Departmental memorandum on 24 January 1983 noted "that both the OFT and Treasury economists are a bit uneasy at the road Littlechild is pushing us down. They query the efficacity(sic) of the price objective and competition being adequate controls on BT".[89] Another internal note commented that until effective competition material-ised, "it could be argued that the removal of any profit control would be premature". Also, it was felt that price control would be "inconsistent with the Government's general philosophy of non-intervention in the determination of prices and incomes". [90]

John Sparrow in the CPRS gave Littlechild's proposals support while noting that it would be important to remove the restraint on competition, especially in the areas not covered under the tariff reduction scheme.[91] However, this was likely to be difficult given the Government's already published plans for the gradual opening up of telecommunications to competition. Littlechild's report received a cautious response from Kleinworts who explained that while the City would have confidence in rate of return regulation, of which there was the experience in the USA to draw on, "They will be suspicious of the RPI minus x one(sic) formula". In addition, Kleinworts went on to warn, with much prescience, that agreeing the appropriate level of X with BT "will prove immensely difficult".[92] Economists in the Department of Industry also concluded that they did not believe that a price formula "will be easy to agree or prove wholly satisfactory". Accounting practices in BT made accurate cost allocation a formidable challenge and there would be a need to select the basket of regulated services very carefully given BT's desire to rebalance its tariffs.[93]

Littlechild had discussed his ideas with Professor Beesley and was aware that Beesley now favoured some form of price cap.[94] Beesley's solution now involved having more competition in telecommunications, alongside a negotiated rate of real price reduction on the services included in the bill of BT's median residential consumer.[95] Use of the median residential bill was intended to address the issue that a small number of heavy telephone users would cause an upward bias in an alternative measure, the average telephone bill. Subsequently, the Government would conclude in favour of a wider price control than the one proposed by Littlechild, although not one based on the median residential consumer's bill. This was at least in part because BT reported that it was unable to supply data on the median bill.

In spite of reservations amongst officials, Littlechild's report was apparently more warmly received by Ministers – probably because it offered a way out from the impasse over Walters' ORPL without upsetting him unduly. When officials discussed the Littlechild report with Kenneth Baker on 24 January, Baker was minded to publish it almost unchanged. He had come around to Walters' view that rate of return regulation would require a major increase in OFTEL's manpower and considerable probing of BT's accounts and therefore it might be difficult to carry through. Nonetheless, although Baker favoured the Littlechild proposal, he did feel that the basket of services to be price controlled would probably have to be widened from local services to include all of BT's inland tariffs, if BT was to be regulated effectively. This would bring the price control closer to Beesley's suggestion of one based on the bill of the median subscriber.[96] Meanwhile, BT management responded to Littlechild's proposal that they were open-minded about it. They would accept Littlechild's price reduction scheme provided that it could be worked up satisfactorily. However, there was some doubt at the time as to whether a practical scheme could be designed. A particular area of difficulty would be determining the appropriate level of the X term.

At meetings over three days at the start of February 1983 between Baker, Department of Industry officials and BT management, including Jefferson, BT expressed concerns about the level at which the X factor might be set. In particular, Jefferson doubted whether he could commit BT to X being negative, which implied real price reductions. BT was also anxious about Littlechild's suggestion that there should be increased competition in other areas of their business over and above the levels currently planned by the Government. Jefferson warned "of a severe danger to the future of both BT's and Mercury's public switched network if this further opening of competition were carried out without a great deal of thought".[97]

With Baker supporting the Littlechild proposal, in principle at least, officials in the Department of Industry swung round to support it too; albeit it seems in a number of cases without complete enthusiasm. In particular, officials did not wish to preclude continued discussion of other alternatives, including the two-tier rate of return. A Departmental draft note for E(TP) Committee at the end of January recommended that further work should be undertaken on the Littlechild proposal "and on alternatives that might achieve the same ends".[98] The Departmental view was that if detailed study over the next two to three months disclosed insuperable difficulties with Littlechild's scheme, the Government should remain free to insert a different form of price or profit control in BT's licence.[99] There was scepticism the price control should be restricted only to local services, as recommended by Littlechild, given the lack of effective competition in other parts of the telecommunications market.[100]

On 3 February 1983 the PM gave permission for Baker to publish the Littlechild report.[101] In his statement to the House four days later, Baker announced the Government's support for price control on the lines suggested by Littlechild and a further initiative to promote competition in apparatus supply. He also confirmed that he would be considering the case for more competition elsewhere, including reducing restrictions on the resale of capacity on private telecommunications circuits leased from BT and other public telecommunications operators. However, he stressed that this was a matter for further discussion.[102] In the end the Government backed away from the more radical measures for opening up the telecommunications market to competition canvassed by Littlechild. The following months were spent agreeing the details of the price control scheme, including the appropriate level of X.

Littlechild had suggested that X could be fixed by political judgement. But no one in Government appears to have taken this suggestion seriously, given that the level of X could be expected to have a material effect on BT's revenues and the sale price of BT's shares. Over the decade to 1981 BT had achieved an average reduction in real unit costs of 1.7 per cent per annum, and up to 2.4 per cent annually more recently. It had kept tariff rises to an average of 2.8 per cent below the RPI.[103] However, Department of Industry officials were well aware that historic trends under nationalisation might be an inadequate basis for setting efficiency targets once BT was privatised. Privatisation was intended to provide management with more incentive to improve efficiency. On 10 February 1983 at a meeting with Department of Industry staff, Treasury officials expressed the view that Ministers should obtain an "authoritative and independent" report on the scope of price regulation and the ability of BT to reduce real prices.[104] The Treasury suggested that the MMC might undertake the work. The Treasury was still keen for there to be some provision for regular efficiency audits of BT, of which this might be the first.[105] However, the Department of Industry preferred to use outside consultants with accounting, economic and telecommunications expertise. The decision was taken by the Department to commission a six month study, beginning on 1 March. It was considered unlikely that the work could be completed satisfactorily in a shorter period.[106]

Too low an X factor could mean insufficient incentives for BT management to pursue cost savings.[107] But there was also concern within the Department of Industry, and more

281

especially BT, that X might be set too high, damaging BT's finances and the prospects for a successful flotation. There was also continuing anxiety within the Department as to whether the RPI – X formula alone would provide sufficient control over BT's profits for a five year period. The Department hankered for some kind of "correction mechanism" to the RPI– formula. In the words of one official, "if, as is virtually certain, we get X wrong" some kind of correction to the X would be needed within the first five years if BT were not either to earn excessive profits or find itself with insufficient capacity to raise new funding for investment.[108]

On learning that outside consultants were to be brought in to help set the X factor, Jefferson responded nervously. His reading of Littlechild's report suggested that the RPI – X formula was there only as a "safety net" to reassure customers that they would get a fair deal. It was certainly not intended to be a draconian measure to constrain profits and pressurise management to make significant cost savings. In terms of some of Littlechild's wording this was not an entirely unjustified interpretation. However, based on the Department's draft terms of reference for the consultants, BT concluded that it did seem that the Department of Industry and the Treasury were bent on making the formula a tough objective, which would be achievable only "by making rapid . . . improvements in efficiency". Jefferson concluded that the inevitable outcome would be the tight regulation of BT that Littlechild had judged undesirable. It would be a level of regulation that the BT Board could not agree to. Jefferson was also at pains to point out that in the view of his Board the level of X could not be agreed until the capital structure of BT had been settled. This was because the level of gearing at privatisation would have implications for the level of revenue needed to meet interest charges.[109] Over the following months of what would prove to be difficult, indeed painful, negotiations Jefferson would attempt to trade off concessions on the level of X for a lower opening gearing in BT's post-privatisation balance sheet.

Wrangling between the Department of Industry and BT over who should undertake the study into the desirable level of X continued with BT reluctant to accept outside consultants, especially given the Department's proposed terms of reference. In the end, to placate BT the Department of Industry agreed that the report should be undertaken within Government rather than outside. As a result the RPI – X Study Team was set up in April 1983. Its brief was to examine the scope for real price reductions by BT. It included three members each from BT and the Government (two representatives from the Department of Industry and one from the Treasury), Professor Bryan Carsberg as an independent member,[110] and Roger Davis of Coopers & Lybrand, BT's auditors, as its chairman. The decision to drop the idea of using outside consultants and to give BT a direct input into the setting of X had been taken by Ministers reluctantly. Jenkin warned Jefferson, "I could only go along with this approach on the understanding that your people engage on this work with real commitment to unearth the most important factors that will be relevant to the very difficult decisions to be made in this area."[111] From the outset there was scepticism within the Department of Industry about how quickly and successfully the study would proceed given BT's hostility to using the level of X as an efficiency lever, alongside the need for information from BT on its future costs and revenues if X was to be set appropriately. Also, Carsberg made it known that he would be able to devote an average of only one day a fortnight to the task. This did not assist the pace with which the Study Team went about its work over the following months.

The Treasury was of the view that it was important to have a thorough study rather than a rushed one. But at the same time, the Government recognised that delay in determining the price formula could delay the entire privatisation of BT.[112] It would be necessary to have

1 The Winter of Discontent, February 1979

2 The National Freight Management
Buy Out, February 1981

3
Launching the 1983
Conservative
Manifesto

4 Government Front Bench, November 1986

5 Thatcher and the oil industry "Will our oil stay British?" July 1980

# YOU HAVE ONLY 5 DAYS TO GET YOUR APPLICATION IN FOR BRITISH GAS SHARES.

## YOU'LL FIND PROSPECTUSES AND APPLICATION FORMS IN BANKS, POST OFFICES, GAS SHOWROOMS AND THE PRESS.

Postal applications must be received by 10am next <u>Wednesday, December 3rd</u>. Use first class post and allow at least 2 days for delivery.

Alternatively, hand in your application at any UK branch of NatWest, Bank of Scotland or Ulster Bank before close of business next <u>Tuesday, December 2nd.</u>

## Hurry if you want to apply for a share of the shares.

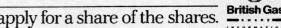

ISSUED BY N M ROTHSCHILD & SONS LIMITED ON BEHALF OF H M GOVERNMENT.

**British Gas**
■ S H A R E ■
I N F O R M A T I O N
■ O F F I C E ■

**UP AGAINST TIME** by Jeanne Willis and Trevor Melvin

6  British Gas – "5 days to go", November 1986

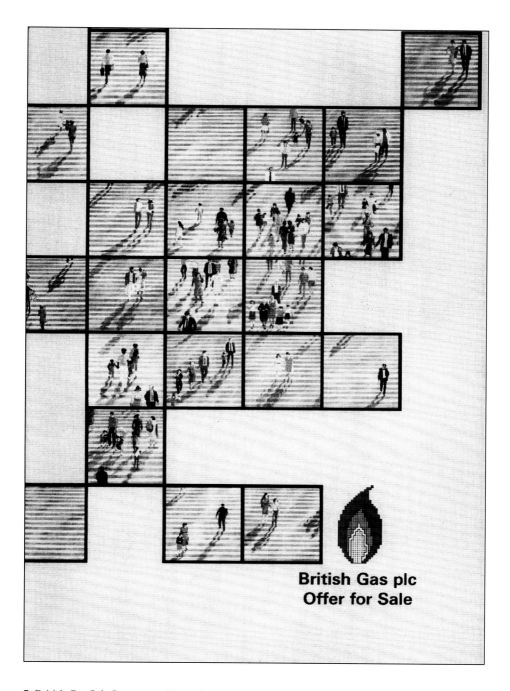

**British Gas plc**
**Offer for Sale**

7 British Gas Sale Prospectus, November 1986

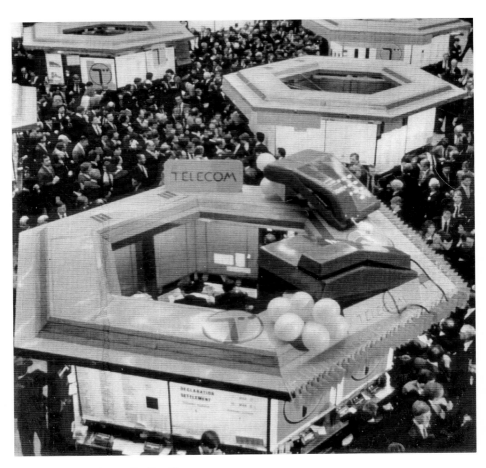

8  BT – Stock Exchange Trading Floor,
   December 1984

9  "Now everyone can share in British Telecom's future", November 1984

10  Telecommunications Act 1984

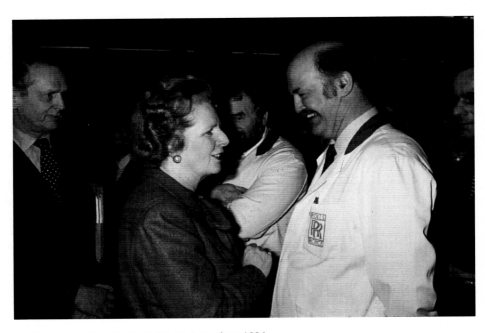

11 Thatcher visiting the Rolls-Royce Aero plant, 1986

the price formula in place before the flotation, otherwise investors might be unwilling to invest. It was agreed that unlike the Littlechild report, which was published in March in a slightly edited form, the report of the Study Team should remain unpublished. Parliament was simply informed that detailed work was underway into the setting of the price formula.

There was concern from the outset that the work of the Study Team would become yet another "ongoing departmental-BT haggle".[113] The Government hoped that the report would be an agreed outcome with BT and might be completed by August.[114] But with a general election intervening and in the face of BT's lack of enthusiasm for the whole project, the Study Team did not meet for the first time until 27 June 1983. At this time the report was timetabled for 1 October.[115] In fact, the work of the Team went on for much longer. The history of the Study Team's deliberations confirmed that Littlechild's price control, seemingly straightforward on paper, would be far from straightforward in reality. The Study Team did conclude quickly that Littlechild's idea was in principle workable and could serve a useful purpose. But difficulties were equally quickly identified in terms of implementing it, especially given that currently BT's tariffs for individual services did not reflect the costs of provision and would need rebalancing with the coming of competition. This complicated the issue of which services to include within the price cap. Alongside this, BT proved slow and difficult in terms of providing the necessary data to allow revenue projections to be made for the different possible levels of X and for the different possible service baskets that might be covered by the price formula.

BT wanted minimal price control so that it could rebalance its tariffs to face up to competition, which it was expected would come first in trunk and international services. This would involve, in particular, higher charges for line rentals and local calls to fund price reductions for the services facing competition. Line rentals especially did not at present cover the costs of their provision. But the Treasury, while seeing the economic case for tariff rebalancing to bring prices for individual services closer to their marginal costs of supply, was mindful of the political consequences if charges to the general public rose in real terms after privatisation. Government statements justifying the privatisation of BT had suggested that consumers could expect tariff reductions due to higher efficiency, not higher bills. The Treasury believed that an important objective of RPI – X should be realising cost reductions for the benefit of customers and not sanctioning higher prices and profits. However, this view remained an anathema to BT's management. The management believed that comforting customers that BT would not be inefficient or make excess profits should be "more in the nature of a reassurance objective rather than a precise regulatory objective". After all, after privatisation BT would be a private sector company facing competition and with commercial goals. Competition would determine prices and profits.

In consequence, within the Study Team there was soon a noticeable gap between what the Treasury believed should be the level of X and the level that was likely to be acceptable to BT. The Treasury was of the view that X should be set somewhere between 3% and 5% and perhaps as high as 7.5%, while BT felt it should be zero or at most 1%. One calculation in the Treasury suggested that BT should be able to achieve annually from 1% to 2% real price reductions due to technological progress, 3.5% by reducing overmanning and excess pay, and 2% from the benefits of increasing output to meet demand.[116] Meanwhile, Department officials endeavoured to broker a compromise, concerned to ensure that X should not be set in such a way as to damage the prospects of a successful flotation, but while at the same time ensuring that BT should not make huge monopoly profits.

The RPI – X Study Team continued to meet through the summer of 1983, but their discussions made little progress. One Departmental attendee observed that even when BT was not there, "it was very difficult to identify any point on which more than three participants round the table agreed."[117] The implication is that when BT attended the proceedings they were even less fruitful. Michael Valentine, who represented Warburgs in other meetings relating to the privatisation of BT, blamed prevarication on a lack of "joined-up government" and the partisan attitude of civil servants:

"It would be tedious to chronicle the endless series of meetings that went on from August 1982 to November 1984, particularly as so many of these were inconclusive and unproductive . . . .. meetings were normally held in an atmosphere of competitive rancour, departmental partisanship and lack of frankness. All sides would dig in and yield nothing . . . Exacerbating the total absence of 'joined-up government' was the attitude of the Treasury. It . . . would refuse to be drawn on what the Treasury's view on any proposal would be, so that there was further delay and uncertainty pending the completion of its drawn-out second-guessing processes. Decisions were all too often taken by inadequately briefed ministers at bad tempered meetings held late in the evening, habitually long after the agreed timetable indicated they were due."[118]

This may be an extreme view but it reflects the frustration felt by others about the speed of decision making.

The Study Team had not been asked to set the final size of X or determine the actual basket of services to include within the price formula, which would be for Ministers to decide. But it was expected to set out the options available in a considered way. This meant that it needed to gather and analyse data on BT's costs, international price comparisons, competition, technological change, and any other factors that might enter into a decision on the setting of X and the basket of services to be included. [119] At the same time, BT continued to maintain, not unreasonably, that the issues could not be settled until its financial structure and especially the level of debt in its balance sheet were agreed.

By September 1983 it was clear that the Study Team would not complete its work by 1 October as planned. BT had still not provided much of the information that the Team considered it needed to come to a decision, in particular cost projections for the next three to five years. An interim report was issued in September in which the Study Team pointed to both the novelty of RPI – X regulation, which "must inevitably carry a substantial degree of risk and uncertainty" and the possibility that it might lead to unexpected and undesirable financial pressures on BT. The report particularly singled out as a concern that it might be difficult to extricate BT from the price formula arrangement once it was set, even if this proved desirable. The report also confirmed that: "While the concept of the RPI – X formula is a simple one, we have shown that it gives rise to issues of considerable complexity."[120] In October 1983 the Department of Industry concluded that a decision on the level of X was unlikely to be made until the second quarter of 1984.[121] A decision on the price formula would have to await decisions on BT's financial restructuring. Meanwhile, in evident frustration at the slow pace of the Study Team's deliberations, the Treasury concluded that "because . . . there are growing doubts about the effectiveness of RPI – X", it would be important to press ahead with promoting competition in telecommunications.[122]

In October the Study Team was being pressed to report by the end of February 1984, so that the level of X could be set in April and included in BT's draft licence in time for the flotation to proceed as planned in November. In a meeting on 6 October 1983 Baker agreed with Jefferson that the Team's deliberations on the choice of the alternative baskets of services to be included within the cap should be reduced from the six currently under consideration to three, to better focus the discussions.[123] DTI officials were sceptical that competition would occur quickly in local services and perhaps in trunk services too. They therefore concluded that there would be a need for effective regulation of both sets of services, both to protect consumers and stimulate BT to raise its efficiency. But the DTI also worried that if the price cap was set to cover a wide basket of services, BT would rebalance its tariffs within the cap. This would mean higher charges for local calls and line rentals that were currently loss making. The higher prices would fall disproportionately on low telephone users, who were often low income consumers. The result could be politically embarrassing.

Following the meeting between Baker and Jefferson on 6 October, the work of the Team centred on the three options of a price formula applying to a local services basket, a basket comprising all inland telephone services, and one based on the telephone bill of the average residential user (but excluding payments for apparatus and international calls). All three service baskets would include connection charges and charges for relevant calls made from public call boxes, but would exclude charges for operator connected calls.[124]

By January 1984 some progress had been made, but the Study Team was still struggling to meet the new February deadline for its report. This was because of a continuing lack of data from BT to permit useful simulations of the effect on BT's finances of different possible levels of X and different service baskets. BT excused the failure on its staff being fully stretched coping with preparing other aspects of the forthcoming privatisation. Within the DTI news that the report might not be ready by February was considered "catastrophic to BT and catastrophic to the Government". John Rickard, an official in the Treasury heavily involved in the privatisation of BT, responded by criticising the meetings of the Study Team over the previous months for "amiable drift". Carsberg was singled out for special criticism because of his absence from a number of the Team's meetings.[125]

Faced with mounting concern, BT suggested that agreement should be reached on the RPI – X formula without waiting for the Study Team to complete its work. BT was happy simply to negotiate X, in the spirit of Littlechild's original suggestion. However, the DTI was reluctant to agree, believing that the Team's report was necessary to identify the main issues that should be considered in setting the price formula.[126] At two difficult meetings between BT and DTI officials on 16 and 17 January 1984, BT objected to expanding RPI – X from protecting local services, as recommended by Littlechild, to trunk services. Also, BT once again objected to the use of the price formula to stimulate efficiency gains, which, as for any other commercially-oriented company, it believed should be a matter for its customers and shareholders not Government. To expedite matters, it was agreed during these meetings that the Study Team should proceed on the basis of including a local basket of services only and with a reporting deadline of the end of February. It was recognised that inclusion of trunk calls would take much longer to agree.[127] Meanwhile, Kleinworts warned that the later a decision was made on the coverage of the price formula, the more difficult it would be to undertake the necessary educational task in the City to sell the regulation ahead of a share flotation.

On 6 January 1984 a DTI briefing paper on the work of the Study Team had noted that, "The most noteworthy conclusion is the remarkably small degree to which the group even now have the data needed to ensure that a report can be given which matches the group's terms of reference." Frustrated by the continuing lack of progress, the Treasury criticised the Team for being "mesmerised" by the need for cost data from BT which it could not or would not supply.[128] Shortly afterwards, at yet another meeting of the Study Team, BT confirmed that they were unable to produce quantitative projections for the whole five years to be covered by the price formula. A lesser simulation had been provided by BT and had been considered unsatisfactory. It was now clear that it would be futile to await further information from the Corporation.[129]

A DTI briefing note for Ministers on 9 February 1984 concluded that, "the absence of authoritative BT cost projections for three of the next five years and our inability to judge BT's absolute level of efficiency, make precise quantification impossible."[130] Despairing of obtaining useful computer simulations from BT of the effects of different possible levels of X on the Corporation's finances, the DTI turned to its own simulations.[131] These suggested that compared with an X of 3% an X of 1% raised profits by the end of five years by £186 million, while an X of 5% reduced profits by £193 million.[132] However, the results depended upon the services included in the price cap. In January it had been decided to focus on price control for local services only, but now Ministers were not convinced that this would be adequate. This led to consideration as to whether there should be a separate RPI – X control on line rentals, which might be needed to protect residential consumers from the effects of fast tariff rebalancing.[133] Currently line rentals did not meet the costs of installing and maintaining the lines. The Government recognised that too quick a switch to higher line rentals post-privatisation could be politically damaging. However, the Treasury had some concerns about a separate control over domestic rental charges and there was a reluctance in the DTI to pre-empt the findings of the Study Team.[134]

Meanwhile, the Study Team continued to fail to reach agreement on what were reasonable cost reduction forecasts for BT. Complicating matters was guidance to the Team's Chairman, Roger Davis, on 1 February 1984 from the DTI that it would be prudent for the Team to supplement its work on a local basket with work on one including trunk services, effectively reversing the decision in January. Officials had hoped that Ministers would have given clear guidance by now on the coverage of the price formula, but this had not been forthcoming and was unlikely before mid-February, at the earliest. On hearing this news, predictably BT objected to the continuing uncertainty. Davis was also unhappy.[135] Ministers were warned that the end of February deadline for the Team's report was now unlikely to be met.

As a solution to the impasse, on 9 February DTI officials recommended that Roger Davis be asked to report on the price formula on a personal basis by mid-March. The intention was to bypass the disagreements within the Study Team.[136] Aware that the whole flotation timetable was at risk, Baker saw Davis on 15 February and requested that he "cut through some of the tangle" that had occurred. Davis's terms of reference were to review and report on the three tariff basket options left open since October, consulting other members of the team only as required. He was to report by the tight deadline of 29 February.[137] In the event, Davis reported quickly and with little or no consultation with other members of the Study Team, which was disbanded. Although he confirmed that BT was projecting, with certain qualifications, a 5% annual reduction in real unit costs, he came down in favour of an X of around 3%, and a price formula covering a wider basket of services than the local services recommended by Littlechild.[138] It was not coincidental that 3% was the figure favoured by DTI Ministers. Davis had warned Baker that with only three weeks to report the result would be pragmatic rather than scientific. He was aware that the Departmental view was that around 3% was the most appropriate figure.

## Finalising X=3%

Unfortunately, Davis's recommendation did not end disagreement. Warburgs had already made clear that in their view an X of 3% would be an insuperable barrier to a successful flotation because it would unduly restrict BT's future revenue growth and profitability. Hoare Govett and Kleinworts were also concerned. In a meeting on 23 March 1984 Baker speculated that the X factor might be 3% or 4%, depending upon which services were included in the basket.[139] At a further meeting, between Norman Tebbit, the Secretary of State for Trade and Industry appointed in October 1983, and Jefferson on 28 March 1984, Tebbit attempted to smooth matters by suggesting that the DTI's modelling of the level of X implied that within the range under discussion the precise level would not have a huge effect on BT's profits. This conclusion is difficult to understand given the results of the DTI's and the Treasury's simulations.[140] Even a 1% difference in X might be expected to have a significant effect. Unsurprisingly, it does not seem that Jefferson's fears were diminished. Jefferson was now intent on trading off his agreement to a higher level of X for a more generous write-off by the Government of debt in BT's balance sheet. The DTI wanted to see a high gearing rate because a lower one meant issuing more equity and therefore potentially a lower share price at flotation.[141] But Jefferson continued to protest that a higher X, and especially the 5% favoured by the Treasury (in fact privately 4% was now the target figure in the Treasury[142]), would be incompatible with achieving a financially sound BT in the private sector unless much of the Corporation's debt was written off. BT also feared that by including trunk calls in the basket the DTI might be going back on an earlier commitment to allow BT to rebalance its tariffs to meet competition. In addition, BT was opposed to a separate cap for line rentals, also on the grounds that this would reduce its ability to rebalance its tariffs.

At a meeting on 9 April 1984 BT offered a small concession, an X of 1.5%. At the same meeting Baker conceded that an X of 5% would be unfavourably received in the City. On 10 April in a meeting with Baker, Nigel Lawson and John Moore from the Treasury, Tebbit concluded that it might be possible to sell an X factor of 3% to the market. However, at the same time he pointed out that this might not be easy because he had been informed by the financial advisers that the market was expecting 2%. In return the Government would have to come up with an attractive capital structure. In a meeting between Baker and Jefferson two days later, Jefferson protested about a leak in the *Daily Telegraph* that morning which had mentioned an X of 3%. With Jefferson trying to dictate terms, Baker threatened that unless BT adopted a more realistic position it would be necessary to postpone the whole flotation timetable.[143]

In a further meeting between Baker and Jefferson on 17 April, with two further short meetings on the two following days, agreement on BT's capital structure was hammered out.[144] Earlier the Chancellor had supported a capital structure that would leave BT with a gross annual borrowing requirement to fund its investment programme of £500 million. But the Corporation's financial advisers Warburgs judged that with an X of 3% a figure of £300 million a year was more realistic. Otherwise it was felt that the debt to equity ratio would quickly become excessive after privatisation, as BT tapped the capital market for loans. At the same time, the Treasury remained suspicious of BT's forecasts of its future capital needs because of recent experience. In 1982/3 BT's profits had fallen by £93 million but the Corporation had not used any of its EFL of £310 million, indeed its external borrowing was a negative £323 million.[145] Details of the final capital restructuring agreed are provided in chapter 13 (p.303 below); suffice to say here that the restructuring was one which Jefferson felt he could live with.

Agreement on BT's capital structure opened the way for a final decision on the level of X.[146] Warburgs was still advising BT against accepting an X of 3%. Nevertheless, Jefferson offered to agree to 3% if he could add international call charges to the tariff basket. As these prices were falling anyway, this amounted to an effective X of about 2.5%. Baker declined the offer. Instead, in April 1984 the option of having an X set at 3% but at 2% if the national inflation rate fell to 3% or below was floated by Baker, subject to Treasury approval.[147] Jefferson felt this would help him sell the price cap to his Board because price rises to increase revenue and the ability to keep real wage costs down became more difficult with low inflation. Expecting opposition to the idea from the Treasury, the Secretary of State arranged to see the PM to win her backing to this compromise deal. It was vital to have the draft licence completed so that the privatisation timetable remained on course.[148] On 18 April, with a continuing lack of agreement on the appropriate level of X, Jefferson threatened to force a postponement of the sale. He may have had in mind withdrawing future co-operation or even recommending to his Board not to sign the sale prospectus.

On hearing news of the latest DTI proposal Nigel Lawson, the Chancellor of the Exchequer, on his way to holiday in Crete phoned Baker on the afternoon of 19 April. He objected strongly to the 2% concession, making it clear that he would only agree to it if BT was willing to surrender £100 million of the debt to equity conversion already agreed. Baker responded by warning that as the whole flotation timetable was at risk the Chancellor should reconsider. He also pointed out that his concession to BT was probably worthless since it was most unlikely that the RPI would fall below 3% in the next five years.[149] But in the absence of the Chancellor on holiday, in two phone calls to Tebbit from John Moore, the Financial Secretary, on 25 April, the Treasury's opposition to the concession was repeated.[150] Faced with no other choice, Tebbit reluctantly informed Jefferson, ahead of the BT Board meeting to discuss the concession, that he had failed to get the Treasury's agreement to it and that consequently the offer was no longer on the table.

Fortunately in reality BT management was not keen to see the privatisation delayed. In effect, the Treasury had called Jefferson's bluff. Jefferson's response was that while the Board still had serious reservations about 3% and felt that it could jeopardise BT's future and therefore the flotation, it would be willing to accept it "subject to an acceptable resolution of all outstanding issues". While still apprehensive about his Board's reaction to an X of 3%, Jefferson advised that they might be able to live with it given the capital restructuring negotiated and if the proposed initial dividend to be paid by BT plc was reduced to ease any possible cash flow problems.[151] He was also probably aware that he would be unlikely to wring any further concessions out of the Government. At the same time, Jefferson felt that the matter should be explored informally with City institutions as the 3% figure was more than the City was expecting.[152] Baker responded by pointing out that Kleinworts and Hoare Govett now felt that they might be able to present the result to the City as equivalent to an X of about 1.5% if a narrower basket of services had been adopted. [153]

Although Jefferson had now agreed to the 3% X, subject to conditions, Tebbit advised Lawson that the Board's reluctant agreement might have adverse implications for the flotation. He concluded that the Chancellor's unwillingness to accept an X of 2% if inflation fell to 3% or below was unfortunate: "I remain of the view that a relatively minor concession of this kind would have secured BT's full commitment to the package."[154] On 2 May 1984 the House of Commons was informed of the RPI – 3% price formula, to be applied to a weighted average of BT's local calls, business and residential line rentals and trunk calls.[155] A separate constraint would be placed on line rentals of RPI + 2 %. Jefferson had managed to negotiate this up from the 1% originally proposed. Nevertheless, Jefferson commented that the price formulae would represent "a challenge" for BT's management and staff.[156] BT's licence was laid before Parliament on 26 June 1984 containing the price caps. The licence also included conditions requiring separate accounting of services to counter anti-competitive cross-subsidies and BT agreed to continue its practice of giving rebates to low users of telephones. A limitation on fast tariff rebalancing by BT after privatisation, which the Government was keen to see for political reasons, was contained in an exchange of letters between Ministers and Jefferson.

The Treasury, which had started by asking for an X of 5% concluded that BT had got a good deal with 3%, especially given the capital restructuring agreed. In addition to the debt conversions and write-offs, the pension fund deficit inherited from the Post Office was left with the Government.[157] Also, only in 1975/6, 1979/80 and 1980/1 BT had in recent years increased its prices by more than the RPI, and taking BT's average real charges in 1969/70 as 100, the level stood at 73.4 in 1979/80.[158] Moreover, BT's Medium Term Plan of 1982 had forecast real price reductions of between 4.7 per cent and 7.8 per cent for the years to 1986/7.[159] What is indisputable is that after privatisation BT proved to be highly profitable. In reality, the 3% figure did not prove especially challenging. At the first scheduled opportunity available to the DGT to change the price cap, in 1989, it was raised by 50 per cent to RPI − 4.5%.[160]

*   *   *

On 8 October 1984 BT announced price rises within the new RPI − 3% formula with rentals rising by almost the full 2% limit above inflation allowed. The effective price of peak standard rate trunk calls, the service most immediately vulnerable to competition from Mercury, was reduced. Also, call box charges were increased. In other words, BT implemented almost the maximum tariff rebalancing permitted under its licence. The result was renewed alarm within the DTI that the price formula would be insufficient to prevent excess profits, a view that a number of officials had held since the time of the Littlechild report.[161] Meanwhile, although BT would continue to say publicly that it had accepted a tough X settlement, more quietly BT's Deputy Chairman, Deryk Vander Weyer, reassured prospective investors that, "We regard our regulatory environment as relatively mild and favourable to our growth."[162] He also commented on a comparison made between BT and AT&T by Morgan Stanley that, AT&T's "return on capital constraint is more burdensome than the tariff restraint on part of our business".[163] It is perhaps fair to conclude that from BT's perspective the regulatory settlement could have been much worse.

The appointed day when OFTEL took over the regulatory duties from BT and the vesting day for BT plc, when the assets and liabilities were transferred from the public corporation to the new company, were brought together as adjacent days in July 1984. This was done to address BT's fears about a possible "web" of regulatory controls applied by OFTEL and the DTI. With the regulation in place, the path was now open for the flotation of BT in the stock market, in November.

# 13

# PRIVATISING
# BRITISH TELECOM

## The flotation and repercussions

The Telecommunications Bill received royal assent on 19 April 1984 and the licence defining BT's duties was published on 26 June. At the start of August, BT plc was established and the DG OFTEL took up his duties. The Department of Industry had set out the Government's principal objectives for the flotation of BT in its early planning as: (1) an overall perception that the flotation had been successful, requiring BT to be a financially sound, free-standing enterprise, (2) disposal of the Government's controlling shareholding as soon as possible, (3) maximum net proceeds from the sale, (4) correct pricing of the issue to avoid extensive profit making by stock market stags, and (5) the achievement of broadly based share ownership, including employees and telephone subscribers.[1] The Department was aware that achieving each of these objectives would require some compromises, for example between disposing of a controlling shareholding as soon as possible and maximising the net proceeds from the sale.

The Department of Industry had invited five leading merchant banks to tender for the role as its financial adviser for the BT sale. Following a "beauty contest" Kleinwort, Benson Ltd (Kleinworts) had been chosen.[2] Following a similar procedure, Hoare Govett was appointed as the lead stockbroker adviser and later Scrimgeour Kemp Gee and de Zoete and Bevan were also appointed to assist the flotation. Kleinworts was appointed as advisers in August 1982 and the stockbrokers in December 1983. BT appointed its own financial advisers, Warburg & Co. The sale of BT posed considerable challenges because of the Corporation's dominance in the telecommunications market and the need to put in place a regulatory structure acceptable to both BT and investors. There was also the issue of the potential size of the share offer. Hambros bank had undertaken in June 1981 a preliminary valuation of BT for the Department of Industry and using a price-earnings (P/E) ratio of 8.5, derived from the P/E ratios of US quoted telecommunications companies, had come up with a figure of around £4–4.5 billion.[3] This would mean that a sale of a half of the equity implied a value for BT of around £2 billion in the capital market. Later, in the summer of 1983, Kleinworts would take a more bullish view and suggest that with careful marketing a half of the equity might conceivably raise closer to £4 billion.[4] Even the lower figure of £2 billion dwarfed the previous largest sum raised by an initial public offering (IPO) internationally, including the earlier privatisation sell-offs.[5] There was therefore understandable concern within Government and its financial advisers that the issue, whatever its precise valuation, would be difficult for the stock market to digest. Warburgs produced an early report suggesting that there was no possibility of floating off BT as a whole. The capacity of the market for all new issues was judged to be in the region of £1 billion to £2 billion a year and the largest privatisation flotation so far had involved BP shares in September 1983, which had raised a comparatively modest figure of £566 million. A report from de Zoete and Bevan in the late summer of 1983 concluded that raising over £2 billion through the sale of BT shares "could cause disruption in the market".[6] During the passage of the Telecommunications Bill through Parliament, a number of MPs similarly queried whether a successful sale in the stock market would be possible.[7] Nigel Lawson reports in his memoirs a dinner with leading merchant bankers from the City, where all but with one exception declared that the privatisation of BT would be impossible, "the capital market was simply not large enough to absorb it."[8]

## Early planning

Given the potential size of the flotation, from the outset there was recognition that any chance of success would turn upon tapping sources of finance that were not usually reached by a conventional stock exchange issue.[9] In June 1983 Hambros bank provided a report which suggested that BT might be established as a Companies Act company with a market capital-isation of £3 billion, of which £1.5 billion would be shares created by the conversion of existing BT debt to the National Loans Fund into equity. The Government could then sell 51 per cent of this equity raising around £750 million, which the market should be able to absorb. The remaining £1.5 billion of capitalisation would be in the form of government held convertible preference shares, which could be sold at a later date.[10] However, given the Government's large continuing holding in the company, after some initial interest in the idea the Treasury judged that the scheme would not remove BT's borrowings from the PSBR.[11]

Another idea considered within the Department of Industry in the summer and autumn of 1982 was to have a small first issue of shares, possibly aimed at residential telephone subscribers and employees.[12] However, Kleinworts cautioned that there would be no certainty of an adequate take-up of the shares and this might lead to a depressed share price for the second stage public issue. Also, again the proposal failed to remove BT from the public finances until some uncertain date in the future when the state might dispose of a majority holding. On 15 September 1982 the Central Statistical Office confirmed that there were two basic criteria for deciding whether a partial privatisation took an enterprise out of the public sector. The first involved the Government relinquishing all control after the sale of a first tranche of shares and, secondly, a commitment to sell further tranches of shares in a short time period ("say six months") to result in a minority government holding.[13]

Through 1983 and into 1984 the Government explored a number of other possibilities, with each in turn eventually rejected. One possibility, advanced by Hoare Govett, involved a bond issue convertible into BT equity on preferential terms at a later date,[14] while the Treasury explored the possibility of using loan stock to help achieve a majority disposal.[15] A variant on these proposals involved an issue of shares with the possibility of an option to convert the shares at some later date into gilt-edged stock. It was felt that the option of conversion to a fixed interest return might make the shares more attractive to small investors.[16] Another suggestion involved the resort to a "tap" issue, as used for gilt sales (a tap issue involves stock being "dripped" onto the market). But this was rejected because of the likely institutional reaction to the prospect of the sale of further blocks of shares and because of the costs that would be incurred each time an issue of shares was made.[17] Other possibilities included the issue of equity with warrants giving an option to purchase more shares in the future.[18]

The objective behind all of these proposals was to ease BT's transfer to the private sector without overstraining the stock market. Meanwhile, Kleinworts worried about the logistics of dealing with large numbers of share applications and BT harboured serious concerns about being privatised through some untested route, which might fail. Management also worried about the costs of distributing annual reports and accounts to hundreds of thousands of shareholders and the feasibility of accommodating large numbers of shareholders at Annual General Meetings (AGMs).[19]

One idea explored particularly seriously within the DTI in the summer of 1983 was to have a unit trust scheme. Under this proposal the public would subscribe for units in the trust rather than for BT shares directly. Amongst other things, this would address BT's objections about the costs of servicing hundreds of thousands of individual shareholders and accommodating them at its AGMs. The Treasury was sympathetic to the proposal. However, a snag with the idea was that the trust would have to have a high level of liquidity to allow repayment of investments to those who wished to sell their units at any time.[20] There was also the objection that this form of investment was not true small share ownership, something the Government was keen to encourage.[21] Moreover, BT was not sympathetic to the idea, again judging it to be untested. Nevertheless, the unit trust proposal was not entirely abandoned within the DTI until January 1984, when it was agreed that there would be serious difficulties in implementing it.[22]

With the rejection in turn of each of the various ideas proposed within the DTI, the Treasury and by Kleinworts and Warburgs, the proposal that became the favoured option was to have a normal issue of ordinary shares. However, to ease pressure on the capital market, protect the sale price and not undermine the gilt market by extracting too much cash from the City, a particular Treasury concern, the issue would be split into two or more tranches.[23] At first the Department of Industry contemplated an initial sale of less than 50 per cent of the shares, which raised the thorny issue of what financial controls the Treasury should retain until the sale of a majority holding was completed. The Treasury was unwilling to permit BT full financial independence while its borrowings remained part of the PSBR – it had held a similar position in earlier privatisations, as we have seen. One idea seriously discussed involved the Treasury agreeing BT's borrowing limits in advance for a period of two or three years and having a formula by which the borrowing limits would be determined automatically in subsequent years if a majority of BT's shares had not by then been sold. This would provide some certainty for investors, but the Treasury resisted agreeing to any such commitment.[24] Instead, by the summer of 1983 discussions with financial institutions had led the Government to conclude that a single sale of 51 per cent of the shares might be possible, provided that payment for the shares was staged in instalments.[25]

The proposal for payment in instalments emerged from discussions between the DTI, Kleinworts and the Treasury and was taken forward by the interdepartmental Working Group on the Methods of Flotation of BT, which held regular meetings from June 1983.[26] The Treasury preferred a short period between the instalment payments, within one year to reduce the possibility of a successful challenge to the notion that BT was now in the private sector and that BT's borrowings were removed from the PSBR. But Kleinworts warned that if the instalment scheme was to succeed in attracting sufficient investment into BT without overstraining the capital market, the instalments would need to be phased over at least two years and possibly three given the unprecedented size of the issue.[27] By March 1984 the decision had been taken in favour of a majority share issue paid in three instalments. The first instalment would be payable on flotation and the other two instalments at a later date.

In the event, the payments were just under 40 per cent of the issue price on 28 November 1984 (50p), submitted with the application for shares, a further 30 per cent (40p) on 24 June 1985, and the final 30 per cent (40p) on 9 April 1986. Assuming a £4 billion share sale and a first instalment payment of nearly 40 per cent of the issue price, the flotation would require raising £1.6 billion in the capital market at the time of the issue. In March 1984 Hoare Govett confirmed that this should be fundable.[28]

The use of instalment payments in a privatisation was not new. It had already been used during the sale of shares in BP in November 1979, Britoil in November 1982 and Cable and Wireless in December 1983 and would be used for the sale of Associated British Ports and Enterprise Oil shares in April and June 1984, respectively. However, in these cases the time between the two instalment periods was limited to less than five months. In the case of BT, given the size of the issue they would need to be spaced over a much longer period. This raised a number of legal issues. In particular, until after the final payment, normally shares carried no voting and dividend rights. Investors had not been unduly deterred from investing on these terms in the previous privatisations because of the short time before achieving full shareholder status. But for BT the lack of voting and dividend rights over a number of years could be expected to be a serious deterrent to investing. Therefore, it was decided that investors should have full voting and dividend rights from the payment of the first instalment.[29] This was an innovation in the UK stock market and it had the incidental effect of raising the effective yield on the shares. For example, if the price of the BT shares at flotation in November 1984 was set at 130p (which was the eventual issue price) but with only 50p payable initially, a future dividend of, say, 13p per share would provide a ten per cent yield on the full share price but a much higher 26 per cent yield on the partly paid price. It is not clear that the DTI or Treasury fully appreciated this effect when the instalment programme was planned. But in the weeks before the flotation the Treasury would question the need to provide other incentives to investors to invest, such as bonus shares and bill vouchers, given the very healthy potential yield on the partly paid shares. An underestimation of the partly paid yield effect in the planning of the privatisation may well be an, at least partial, explanation of the degree of the flotation's unexpected success.

During 1983, however, it was felt there would need to be a major marketing campaign to ensure sufficient interest in the offer. In the summer of 1982 a survey of City opinion by Kleinworts had suggested a low level of understanding of BT's business, and subsequent surveys confirmed a worrying lack of confidence in its management and prospects.[30] Initially, Kleinworts were unfavourable to the idea of trying to market BT shares to small investors. But it soon became clear that, apart from the fact that the Government favoured extending share ownership, this would be necessary to ensure a successful flotation.[31] Creating the perception that there would be a "scarcity" of shares for institutional investors became a key component of Kleinwort's flotation strategy. A healthy demand for shares from the retail sector could be expected to bolster interest from City institutions. A target of achieving a sale of £1 billion of shares to small investors was provisionally set. But it was recognised that attracting that level of funding from small investors would "require an unconventional approach" to marketing the shares.[32]

The "unconventional approach" that Kleinworts designed was based around an unprecedented marketing campaign. This had two broad thrusts: the first to raise awareness of BT's prospects in the fast developing telecommunications market and portray it as a successful growth stock; the second to stress the benefits to the public of investing in the shares. In early 1984 there were only 1.8 million individual investors in shares in the UK and only around one million had shares in more than one company. The percentage of shares in the stock market held by individuals had fallen from 51 per cent in 1963 to 25 per cent in 1981. Previous privatisations had attracted small investors but not on the scale that would be needed to raise £1 billion. The thrust of much of the marketing was therefore directed at attracting small and in many cases first time investors. In the very early planning a minimum investment of £2,000 was contemplated, but the figure was eventually set much lower to attract the maximum interest.

In 1982 merchant bank advice had suggested that a sale of a majority of the shares in BT might just be possible between September and November 1983. The management of BT were keen to have an early flotation to remove uncertainty about the future and to minimise the opportunity for the trade unions to mount an effective opposition to the sale.[33] But the calling of the General Election in May 1983 and the consequent delay in passing the Telecommunications Bill meant that a share sale before the autumn of 1984 became impractical.[34] Moreover, it was felt that the flotation could go ahead then only provided that no other large share issues were scheduled around the time of the BT offer. In particular, there should be no other privatisation sales around the same time.[35] Kleinworts were particularly nervous about the sale of Enterprise Oil shares scheduled for June 1984 and the flotation of Jaguar planned for July.[36] In each case, the concern was not simply a matter of the possible diversion of capital into these alternative share offerings, but that if one or more of these privatisation issues flopped, leaving shares with the underwriters, City sentiment might turn fatally against the BT flotation. In the event the Jaguar sale was successful, although the Enterprise Oil issue, based on a tender offer, did leave shares with the sub-underwriters.

Also, before a flotation could occur there was the matter of BT's finances to sort out. Under the Stock Exchange Yellow Book on the admission of securities for listing, an opinion from the auditors on whether the accounting information provided a "true and fair view" was required. The Post Office telecommunications accounts had been qualified for 13 years due to the lamentable state of the accounting systems within the Post Office. For example, in 1979/80 and 1980/1 they were qualified because of industrial action, which prevented the keeping of proper records, and because of weaknesses in the accounting procedures for fixed assets. In particular the Corporation lacked a proper register of the properties it owned. In 1981/2 and 1982/3 BT's first accounts were qualified, this time for a number of accounting irregularities including inadequate stock control.[37] When Jefferson took over as the first Chairman of BT there was a lack of qualified accountants in the organisation.[38] Further accountants were employed, including Douglas Perryman who was brought in from the NCB as Finance Director in 1981, and BT's auditors, Coopers and Lybrand, worked with BT management in a determined effort to improve the accounting systems. Nevertheless, fears remained that the 1983/4 accounts, when published, would be qualified. This might jeopardise a flotation in 1984.[39] In the event the accounts were not qualified. The fact that qualifying the accounts would have disrupted BT's flotation appears to have had a bearing on the auditors' decision not to qualify them.[40] Certainly there remained weaknesses in BT's control systems until well after privatisation.

## Organising the sale and investor incentives

The public relations consultants Dewe Rogerson, who had acted during the Cable and Wireless privatisation, were selected in September 1983 to oversee the marketing campaign for the BT share issue from a short list of four firms.[41] Advertising for the sale was handled by Dorland Advertising and marketing research was undertaken by MORI (Market & Opinion Research International).[42] Printing work was undertaken by Barrup Mathieson who had handled the printing work for the earlier British Aerospace and Cable and Wireless privatisations. To organise the flotation, a Steering Group and a number of interdepartmental committees were established. For example, a Prospectus Committee was formed including representatives from the DTI, Treasury, BT, Kleinworts and Warburgs (later it also included representatives from Coopers and Lybrand, Hoare Govett and the legal firm Linklaters and Paines[43]) to be responsible for the arrangements for the sale and drafting the flotation prospectus. It held its first meeting on 28 July 1983. A Flotation Marketing Sub-Committee, including Kleinworts, Warburgs, Dorland Advertising, Dewe Rogerson and representatives from the DTI and the Treasury, and a Public Relations Sub-Committee, composed of representatives from BT, the DTI, Kleinworts, Warburgs and Dewe Rogerson, were also formed.[44] Another important committee was the Flotation Committee with representatives from BT, DTI, Warburgs, Treasury, Kleinworts, Dewe Rogerson, Dorland Advertising and stock brokers Hoare Govett and Cazenove & Co. This managed the flotation in the months leading up to the sale. In addition, there were from time to time a number of ad hoc working groups that reported to these committees, including the Working Group on Methods of Flotation. Also, immediately before the flotation a group to develop the BT Privatisation Information Pack for investors was established.[45] A planning document called "The Critical Path" was used to co-ordinate the activities and timetables of the different committees and working groups. Table 13.1 summarises the main decisions and events during the privatisation of BT that these committees and working groups addressed.

The lead in the flotation planning was undertaken by the Department of Industry and, after the May 1983 General Election, its successor the Department of Trade and Industry (DTI). However, the Treasury insisted on being consulted on all major decisions and its interest in the sale increased as it became clearer that the flotation would produce a large revenue to the Exchequer.[46] In January 1984 it was agreed that meetings between Kenneth Baker and John Moore, the Financial Secretary, and their officials should occur at least once a month in the run-up to the flotation. The Secretary of State for Trade and Industry, Norman Tebbit, was adamant that the DTI should retain control of the sale.[47] But the serious injury to Tebbit in the Brighton bombing in the autumn of 1984 meant that the Chancellor of the Exchequer took more of a leadership role in the remaining weeks before the flotation.[48]

In December 1983 Dewe Rogerson had reported worrying evidence that public opinion was moving against the privatisation of BT, reflecting anti-privatisation lobbying by the unions and some hostile press reporting.[49] At the end of 1983 two of eight leading stock-broking firms consulted by Kleinworts doubted whether a single sale of 51 per cent of the shares would be feasible, even with instalment payments.[50] Also, between November 1983 and January 1984 Kleinworts interviewed 88 institutional fund managers and 19 tele-communications and new technology stockbroking analysts. The interviews confirmed that attitudes to BT were at best neutral and that BT's management was rated mainly "average" or "below average".[51] There would be much work to do if the sale was to succeed.

In February 1984 Kleinworts produced confidential and detailed proposals for the flotation aimed at winning over both the City and small investors. These were contained in a document known as "Odyssey" prepared by David Clementi of Kleinworts. A key feature of the document was the need to attract an adequate number of potential investors so as to reassure the

Table 13.1 Timetable of main decisions and events in the BT flotation

| Date | Marketing | | Other | |
|------|-----------|--|-------|--|
| Feb 1984 | Preliminary discussions with institutions | | | |
| March | Regional brokers appointed | | | |
| April | Principle and level of selling commissions agreed | | (1st) | British Telecommunications plc incorporated |
| | | | (12th) | Telecommunications Act received royal assent |
| May | (2nd) | Details of employee share offer, and plans for a subscriber incentive announced | (2nd) | Outline capital structure of BT plc and RPI − X announced |
| | (24th) | Form of incentive for BT subscribers (the vouchers) and preferential application scheme for BT pensioners announced | | |
| May/July | BT sales train (with "privatisation coaches") | | | |
| June | Second round of discussions with institutions Share Information Office set up | | (26th) | BT's licence published |
| July | (2nd) | Circulation of bill stuffer began (running over succeeding 3 months) | (2nd) | OFTEL established Decision taken to keep open option of a North American sale |
| Aug | (1st) | Details of small shareholder incentives (vouchers and bonus shares) announced | (5th) | BT's licence came into effect |
| | | | (6th) | Transfer Date − BT's business vested in BT plc |

| Month | Date | Event |
|---|---|---|
| | (20th) | Advertising campaign began (continued until late in Offer period) |
| Sept | | Cheap dealing facility for small shareholdings in place |
| Oct | | Further institutional soundings |
| | (6–13th) | Japanese Roadshow |
| | (26th) | Pathfinder Prospectus published and press conference |
| | (29th to 21st Nov) | UK Roadshows |
| | | Broad method of sale agreed (including overseas offers) |
| | | Issues registered in US, Canada and Japan |
| | | Bids for priority applications sought from institutions |
| Nov | (5–13th) | North American Roadshow |
| | (16th) | Impact Day |
| | (20th) | Prospectus and mini prospectus printed in national press available at the banks and post offices and in letter boxes of most Share Information office enquirers |
| | (14th to 16th) | Price agreed |
| | | Impact Day – UK offer underwritten by merchant banks |
| | | Priority applications submitted |
| | (28th) | Close of offer period (10.00 am) |
| | | Overseas underwriting agreements signed |
| Dec | | |
| | (2nd) | Basis of allocation announced |
| | (3rd) | Start of share dealings in UK and overseas |
| | (10th) | Letters of Acceptance posted |

Source: BT/A/61 Part 3.

City that the flotation was unlikely to be a failure. This would involve the sale of shares in the UK institutional market, overseas and in the UK retail market. To stimulate adequate demand, especially in the retail market, Kleinworts advocated extensive advertising and marketing of the issue and special incentives to attract and retain the small shareholder. The use of incentives was not unique, for example a private sector new issue involving European Ferries included the offer of discounted ferry fares for investors. Also, an investor incentive was provided during the privatisation of Britoil, in the form of a loyalty bonus of one free share for every ten held for three years, for those purchasing up to 2,000 shares.[52] However, in the case of the sale of BT, Kleinworts was of the view that an unprecedented two million private investors would probably need to be attracted to achieve the £1 billion target figure.[53] There would also be a need to ensure that investors did not dispose of their shares immediately after the flotation. Any prospect that this might happen would damage City interest in the offer because it would increase the likelihood of a share price fall after the issue rather than a price rise. If a price fall was anticipated, City investors could purchase the shares they needed more cheaply in the after market rather than at issue.

To provide an incentive for large numbers of small investors to participate in the flotation and not to resell their shares quickly, in February 1984 the DTI and Kleinworts settled on the idea of a novel voucher scheme. Earlier the Government put to BT the idea of giving out phone box call cards or reducing the cost of installing and running BT's Prestel information system as incentives to invest, but BT was keen on neither and they were not pursued. Other ideas explored included the possibility of subscribers paying for the shares via their telephone accounts and receiving their dividends in the form of reduced telephone bills. However, this possibility was abandoned when BT reported that its billing system would be unable to cope. In discussions within the DTI and BT the possibility of offering incentives to small investors such as free telephone calls and free telephones and sockets were considered, but in turn again rejected. There was concern within BT about the complexity of administering free calls; and it was recognised that an offer of telephones or sockets would not be of interest to those who already had telephones and sockets installed.[54] Under the voucher proposal, small investors would receive vouchers covering the cost of up to four of BT's quarterly rental charges.[55] As an alternative to the vouchers, investors would be able to opt for a one for ten free share offer, subject to a maximum eligibility of 400 bonus shares. The decision to offer two alternative incentives reflected research by MORI, which revealed high interest amongst potential investors in having a choice between bill vouchers and bonus shares.

The incentive scheme won the support of Ministers and an outline was provided by Kenneth Baker in the House of Commons on 25 May 1984, although at the time a number of the details had still to be thrashed out.[56] The full details of the voucher and bonus schemes would not be announced to Parliament until 1 August.[57] Baker had hoped that BT might be able to give the voucher credit against telephone bills directly, but BT concluded, once again, that its billing system was not up to it.[58] This meant that an alternative mechanism had to be created to handle the vouchers with credit given when telephone bills were paid. Telephone bills were often paid through a bank or at the local Post Office. As bank and Post Office staff would need to check that the name on the voucher accorded with the name on the telephone bill and the banks and the Post Office would then have to process the vouchers, it was reasonable to expect that they would insist upon payment to undertake the work.[59] Also, BT suggested that the voucher scheme would impose costs upon them, in terms of collecting and accounting for the vouchers, which it initially estimated at up to 35p per voucher.

BT insisted that the Government should bear these costs as well as those of the banks and the Post Office.[60]

In an effort to reduce the expense of the voucher scheme, the idea of a "supervoucher" was contemplated. Instead of BT manually counting the vouchers, they would be sent to Lloyds Bank to be computer read. Another possibility considered involved Lloyds Bank issuing the vouchers in the form of quasi-cheques, made payable to BT and drawn on the Government. The cheques would then be cleared through the normal bank clearing system. However, in both cases it was concluded that the mechanisms would be too expensive. Also, the Bank of England reported that it might be difficult to obtain agreement from the clearing banks to handle the quasi-cheques.[61]

Throughout the discussions on incentives for investors, the Treasury grew increasingly concerned about the potential costs. John Moore had been an architect of the Britoil loyalty bonus, but in February 1984 he questioned whether it might be better in the case of BT to aim for a smaller-scale flotation, say of 40 per cent of the shares, than become embroiled in providing expensive inducements to potential investors.[62] This suggestion was surprising given the Treasury's usual desire to see majority control transferred to the private sector to remove the company's borrowings from the PSBR. The DTI responded, alarmed that any reversal of the decision to sell a majority of the shares in the first tranche would be interpreted by political opponents as "a political defeat for the Government".[63] The discussions continued through the first half of 1984. By July Baker was pressing the Treasury for final agreement on the voucher and shareholder bonus schemes.[64] By now the cost of the incentives was put at £3.5 million in administrative charges and around £72 million in telephone bill discounts, assuming that there were 1.4 million eligible investors. Baker reasoned that this was a relatively small price to pay to attract £1 billion in share subscriptions. But the Treasury remained concerned, although in the end Moore relented after Baker warned that further delay in reaching an agreement was no longer an option if the flotation was to proceed to timetable. On 30 July Moore agreed to Baker's proposals. Each bill voucher would have a face value of £18 and the maximum number receivable would be 12 vouchers, based on an individual buying 2,400 or more shares, and one voucher for purchases of 200 to 399 shares. The allocations would only apply if the shares were held by the original investors for specified periods, varying according to the total investment. By now the decision had been taken that the minimum number of shares that could be subscribed for at flotation would be 200. This figure was a compromise between encouraging the maximum number of small investors and the costs of administration, including issuing the letters of allotment to successful applicants.[65] The bonus shares would be one extra for every ten held continuously by an investor to 30 November 1987.[66] The Government would bear the full costs of the bill vouchers and the bonus shares, including the administration costs.

In spite of this agreement, in correspondence with Baker, Moore complained that on his reckoning the share sale to small investors would bring in about 25 per cent of the total proceeds from the flotation but account for about 50 per cent of the total flotation costs. He concluded that, "it would not be right to subordinate our objective of maximising proceeds to our objective of wider share ownership."[67] Consistent with its attitude during earlier privatisations, the Treasury was keen to ensure that achieving healthy net sales receipts for the Exchequer remained an important objective of the privatisation, even if this was not so evident in the Government's public statements, which stressed advantages in terms of lower telephone bills, more choice and better services.

## Marketing the sale

The marketing campaign for the sale of BT was the first initial public offering (IPO) in the UK in which there was a co-ordinated effort comprising TV, press, poster and radio advertising and travelling road shows and videos. The campaign even featured a special train that chugged around the country visiting 17 cities from May 1984 promoting the issue. In the past BT had commissioned a special train to market its services. This was adapted for the marketing of the share issue.[68] The road shows involved the senior management of BT making presentations to regional stockbrokers, accountants and bankers across Britain and in Paris, Amsterdam and Frankfurt. The use of TV advertising during a privatisation was not new – it had been adopted during the last stage of the privatisation of Cable and Wireless in response to a threatened national newspaper strike. But TV advertising had never been used before on the scale adopted during the privatisation of BT. The sale of BT also made use of more market research to gauge investor sentiment and over a longer period than in any earlier privatisation.

The planning for the marketing started in the autumn of 1983 with a review within BT of the steps that would need to be taken. In November 1983 BT began a corporate advertising campaign using TV and the press, managed by Dorland Advertising. The campaign started by reassuring BT's customers of the Corporation's continuing commitment to public service, to counter a contrary claim by the unions. From the start of 1984 the campaign moved up a gear, to projecting BT as a highly successful enterprise operating in a growth sector of the economy. By the spring it was focusing on BT's position as a leader in communications innovation, under the slogan "The Power behind the Button".[69] BT spent nearly £50 million on its campaign. On no occasion was there explicit reference to the forthcoming share issue, which would have violated stock market rules. Pre-prospectus advertising was new and had to be handled very carefully to avoid legal problems. Instead, the focus was on improving the public image of BT. With the ending of BT's corporate marketing, on 20 August 1984 a substantial Government funded advertising campaign began, although again to avoid legal difficulties ahead of the publication of the sale prospectus the advertisements were billed as "Presented by Kleinwort Benson" rather than HM Government. This campaign was targeted at raising interest in the share flotation specifically. The expenditure had become legally possible once the Telecommunications Bill had become law. However, in conformity with stock market rules, the Government had to be careful not to be seen to be advocating that people should necessarily buy the shares.[70] This required careful vetting of all of the marketing literature and broadcasts, including ministerial statements. Dewe Rogerson also produced in conjunction with the Stock Exchange a booklet on "Buying and Selling Shares" to provide basic information on share transactions for novice investors.

The Government's marketing campaign involved ensuring that everyone realised that they would have an opportunity to invest in BT. There were four phases, designed by Dewe Rogerson. The first, known as "Alert", dealt with raising public awareness of the forthcoming sale of BT. The second, "Maintenance", was concerned with building awareness of the ability to buy the shares. The third, "Action", explained the share application process. The final phase, "Prospectus", involved the issue of a Pathfinder prospectus (see below) and later full and mini prospectuses along with share application forms, which were made available through banks, Post Offices and in newspapers.[71] As part of the initiative financial inducements were provided to stockbrokers, accountants and bankers, that is to say, agents who would be closely involved in advising clients on whether or not to purchase the shares.[72] The selling commission for BT shares was set at two per cent for stockbrokers (with 1.25 per cent re-assignable to solicitors and accountants) and 1.5 per cent for banks. Previous government sales had provided no such commission, but Kleinworts had advised that it would be import-ant to the success of the BT sale that brokers, accountants, banks and solicitors encouraged their clients to invest in the issue. In addition, cheap dealing rates for the BT shares after the flotation were negotiated, as low as £5, to cater for individuals who did not have access to an existing stockbroker. If small shareholders were given a cheap and easy means of selling their shares, it was to be expected that this would encourage their interest in the offer. The BT sale also saw the development of a network of regional brokers to co-ordinate the sale in their territories.[73]

In July 1984 leaflets started to go out with BT's quarterly telephone bills in what was referred to as the "bill stuffer" to raise awareness of the pending flotation.[74] Dewe Rogerson had been keen for the main marketing campaign to begin in June. However, Baker was aware of the Treasury's growing concerns about the costs of the flotation and in any case it was unlikely that BT's licence terms would be finalised in time for a marketing campaign to start then.[75] Also, Jefferson lobbied against a June start because it would coincide with a POEU conference on privatisation.[76] On 30 April 1984 Dewe Rogerson estimated that the necessary marketing and communication spend to achieve a successful flotation might need to be in the range of £16.6 million to £21.6 million, excluding VAT. But much of the specifics of the campaign had yet to be settled.[77] In the face of Treasury concerns, the Government eventually approved a much smaller marketing budget, of up to £8 million. This was close to the revised figure of £8.8 million that Dewe Rogerson and Dorland had finally recom-mended under pressure from the DTI to keep down the costs.[78] In late August the advertising began including the strap line "You can share in BT's future".[79]

Attracting a big number of investors would necessitate the printing and distribution of large numbers of the prospectus, at potentially a huge cost.[80] Under the 1948 Companies Act it was a requirement to issue a full prospectus to all investors. To reduce costs, at the House of Lords stage of the Telecommunications Bill a clause was inserted to enable the Secretary of State to send out public application forms for BT shares without having to issue the full prospectus.[81] This move raised eyebrows in the City. The Government was providing a special exemption for its own share issue that was not available to companies in general. However, the move did enable the Government to substitute an eight page mini prospectus for the 62 page full BT prospectus.[82] This was much cheaper to print and distribute and was more likely to be read by the small investors that the Government was keen to attract. In preparation for the sale nearly seven million mini prospectuses and 400,000 full prospectuses were produced, along with share application forms designed to be comprehensible to the first-time investor. The prospectus and an application form were also reproduced in a selection of newspapers.[83] One particular innovation during the privatisation of BT was the use of a "red herring" prospectus. The idea and that term came from the USA and in the BT sale took the name of the Pathfinder prospectus. Although a Pathfinder prospectus was used for the sale of Jaguar in the summer of 1984, it was planned first for BT.[84] In the case of the BT offer it was issued some three weeks before the full prospectus and was similar except that it excluded the sale price and related data such as the forecast yield on the shares. These were yet to be agreed. The objective of the Pathfinder was to raise interest in the offer for sale and help get firm commitments to purchase shares from the City. The tactic proved to be very successful.

The Government's decision to try and attract two million shareholders necessitated the creation of an administration to handle potentially very large numbers of share enquiries and applications.[85] A telephone enquiry handling office and information centre, the BT Share Information Office, was established in Bristol. This made use of the "Telecom Tan" computer-aided telephone answering service developed by BT.[86] All of this was costly, and in June 1984 the Treasury warned that if the marketing costs of the issue continued to rise there would be a need to reconsider providing a facility for potential investors to phone in with their enquiries.[87] On 9 August again the Treasury complained, this time about the mounting expenditure on marketing when the idea of a video specifically to guide bank staff on processing share applications was proposed. The Treasury concluded that, "There is at present no effective mechanism which forces the PR agencies to consider priorities and the costs of their suggestions. The general practice has been for the marketing committee to endorse virtually every suggestion put to it."[88] By 13 September Dorland Advertising had spent almost £7 million (including VAT) on advertising.[89] The direct marketing costs of the BT flotation would eventually come to £14 million (excluding selling commission and fees to advisers).

## Structuring the flotation

By late July 1984 agreement had been reached on the main structure of the flotation. Kleinworts focused their sale efforts on 35 first-line City institutions and to a lesser extent on another 250 investing bodies. The institutions stressed that their interest in the offer would partially depend upon a high level of retail and overseas sales. However, as late as August 1984, the Government had still not decided whether to offer shares overseas.[90] The reason was concern about the costs of achieving a successful overseas sale and the possibility of a flowback of stock to the UK immediately after the flotation.[91] A flowback of shares might seriously depress the share price in the after market. In the end the shares were separately offered in the USA, Canada and Japan.[92] In another first, this meant that the BT issue involved an offer of equity shares on a co-ordinated basis in more than two national financial markets. The aim was to raise about £3.5 billion in the November with £2 billion raised from UK institutional investors, £0.5 billion from overseas investors, and £1 billion from domestic private investors.[93]

One particular matter that needed to be settled before a flotation could safely proceed was the state of BT's accounts. BT was keen to undertake a number of accounting changes including shortening the life of some of its fixed assets in preparation for transfer to the private sector and the arrival of competition.[94] BT argued that these events constituted a fundamental change in its operating environment justifying an immediate write-off of asset values. Initially the DTI had resisted the idea, fearing that the proposed changes might give BT an unfair advantage against future competitors. Also, the fixed assets write-down would lower profits ahead of the flotation and might depress the offer price.[95] However, in early 1984 Coopers and Lybrand, BT's auditors, agreed to the accounting changes proposed by BT's management. This left the Government with little alternative but also to consent.[96] Nevertheless, there remained some important financial issues still to be settled. Historically, BT like other nationalised industries had been funded by debt raised through the National Loans Fund (NLF). BT management were keen to have a gearing level on flotation that would allow them to borrow easily in the capital market after privatisation, to fund their capital programme. Jefferson's main reason for wishing to escape state ownership was the freedom to raise finance for investment without the shackles of Treasury controls. BT claimed that it would be trapped into profitless growth by the advent of competition and the imposition of the

RPI – X price cap unless it could diversify its business. It was therefore concerned that BT's NLF debt should not be simply converted into loan stock because this would leave BT with high gearing (a high debt to equity ratio) and therefore less scope to borrow to finance diversification.[97]

The appropriate level of gearing for BT at privatisation was discussed as early as September 1982, but no decision was reached.[98] Kleinworts felt that the highest gearing credible for BT was 50 per cent. But BT, supported by Warburgs, was lobbying for a level of 40 per cent, or less, to provide even more headroom for borrowing once in the private sector.[99] Later the DTI and the Treasury made known that they preferred a gearing ratio of around 80 per cent.[100]

Two principal forms of financial restructuring at privatisation were considered. The first involved a government write-off of some or all of BT's NLF debt; the second a conversion of some or all of the debt into equity.[101] BT management was solidly against any suggestion that the debt owed to the NLF should be sold in the market, on the grounds that this would reduce the company's ability to raise loan financing post-privatisation. BT was looking for what the Treasury calculated would amount to a debt write off of £2.4 billion.[102] After much discussion, the Treasury agreed to a somewhat smaller debt write-off, the issue of £500 million in 11.95 per cent cumulative preference shares and a re-couponing of the remaining debt.[103] Outstanding balances of the Corporation relating to advances from the NLF, totalling £2.79 billion, would be cancelled by the Secretary of State and replaced in large part by debenture stock. BT's existing debt to the NLF, with its lumpy profile of repayments, was extinguished and replaced with debt having a smooth maturity profile over 25 years. However, a tax change in the 1984 Budget reduced capital allowances on the purchase of "plant and machinery" and therefore the tax allowances that BT could claim against taxable profits for capital expenditure. It was immediately recognised that this could have a large, negative, effect in the short term on BT's finances because the change meant that a tax charge was more likely.[104] Owing to continuing investment, BT had not paid Corporation Tax on its profits in recent years. To offset the effects of the tax change, the conversion of BT's debt to preference shares was increased to £750 million, alongside the conversion of £250 million of debt to ordinary shares.[105] It is unclear whether the Treasury had considered the impact on BT when planning the tax change, which was aimed at closing a tax loophole used by banks.

The capital structure of the privatised BT was revealed to the House of Commons on 2 May 1984 by the Secretary of State for Trade and Industry, at the same time as the decision to impose a price cap of RPI – 3%. As discussed in chapter 12, the reluctant agreement of BT's Board to an X of 3% had been heavily contingent on achieving an acceptable capital restructuring. The Government had originally intended that the net present value (NPV) of the new company's initial debt burden, comprising its liabilities in respect of debentures, preference shares and foreign loans, should equal the NPV of the corresponding liabilities of the previous Corporation. However, because of the debt for equity conversion that was finally agreed there was a reduction in NPV, in the order of £370 million.[106] There was also a moratorium agreed on debt repayments for a period ahead, an alteration in the interest payable, and an agreement that BT would not declare an interim dividend payment for the financial year 1984/5.[107] On 14 November 1984 the authorised share capital of the company was increased from £1.25 billion to £2.625 billion by the creation of an additional 5,500 million new ordinary shares with a face value of 25p each. At flotation BT's debt to equity ratio was about 60 per cent, or 77 per cent if BT's preference capital of £750 million is included with the long-term debt. This was well above the UK industrial average of 20 per cent, but interest charges were well covered by expected earnings, at around five times. The City's response to the share issue indicates that investors were content with the resulting balance sheet.[108]

As part of the financial restructuring, particular attention had to be paid to BT's pension fund deficit relating to service before 1969 amounting to £1.25 billion and which BT had inherited from the Post Office.[109] BT was under an obligation to make good the pre-1969 deficiency by 1992, by means of payments under a deed of covenant.[110] Kleinworts expressed concern as early as November 1982 at the implications of this obligation for a successful flotation of BT's shares if the liability was transferred to BT plc. But the Treasury was not keen for the Government to pick up the cost and favoured flotation with all the pension liabilities remaining with BT. Alternatively, it suggested that the liability should be transferred back to the Post Office, something the DTI resisted not least because of its impact on the Post Office's finances.[111] BT favoured the Government taking over the liabilities or using some of the share receipts to fund the costs. Faced with continuing argument from Kleinworts that the flotation would be damaged, the Treasury eventually gave way.[112] On 6 August 1984 the Corporation transferred its business to the new company, British Telecommunications plc, with the company bearing a debt to the Government in the form of debentures totalling £2.75 billion. Some of these debentures were assigned to the residual Corporation to meet the liabilities under the deed of covenant in respect of the pension fund deficiency.[113] Also, a cut-off date of April 1986 was set after which new BT employees would not have the guarantee of an index-linked pension although existing employees retained the benefit. The effect of all of this financial restructuring was effectively to write off £1.29 billion of BT debt. In addition, part of the arrangement involved the Government agreeing to a contingent liability, under which should BT go into liquidation the pensions of BT employees would be guaranteed. This was the only privatisation in which the Treasury conceded such a guarantee and this appears to have resulted from the peculiar circumstances surrounding the BT pension fund. At the time the concession was not considered to be overly important. There was no anticipation of the large pension fund deficits in the British economy that materialised 20 years later.

In the planning of the privatisation there were numerous legal issues to confront. In particular, there was the need to ensure that stock market rules on flotations and the marketing of new issues in the UK, North America and Japan were not accidentally flouted. Selling shares simultaneously in more than one national market produced an inevitable complexity. For example, Sections 13 and 14 of the Prevention of Fraud (Investments) Act 1958, relating to distributing documents inviting persons to subscribe for securities and the making of misleading statements, caused some difficulty. The planned marketing campaign included promotional material relating to the offer going out with telephone bills (the "bill stuffer"). It was important that this and other information relating to the flotation were consistent with stock market rules and national laws in the countries in which the shares were sold. Lawyers within and outside the DTI worked long and hard to ensure conformity with all of the many legal provisions. It was also up to the lawyers to translate economic decisions, including the RPI – X formula, into wording of the licence in a way that was legally unambiguous.[114] One particular issue that arose was whether the price cap formula should be specified in the licence. There was a view that this might cause difficulties. Another potential difficulty related to the US Securities Act "margin rules" that restricted the sale of shares on credit. It was discovered that part-payment for BT shares might infringe the rules. However, after discussion the US authorities decided that the terms of the BT sale meant that the margin rules were not breached after all.[115]

In addition to concern about legal issues and the cost of the share incentive scheme and the marketing campaign, the Treasury grew worried about the fees to be charged by the clearing banks to handle the share issue. It leaned on the DTI to reduce them. Six clearing banks were appointed as the receiving bankers for the issue and initially the idea was to appoint two of them, Lloyds and the NatWest, as temporary registrars. The registrars would handle the instalment payments. After February 1986 Lloyds would become the permanent registrar administering the share register. However, the Stock Exchange objected to there being two registrars and therefore Lloyds was solely appointed.[116] It had been expected that local Post Offices would be involved in the flotation work, but the Post Office informed the DTI in February 1984 that this could cause trouble with its unions. The Post Office also named a high price for administering the issue, of 80p for each voucher handled.[117] The banks put a much lower figure on the cost.[118] The banks therefore obtained the work and using the banks rather than the Post Office helped to keep costs down. Nevertheless, by early August 1984 the clearing banks' charges were estimated at around £20 million or, in the words of one Treasury official, if there were around 1.5 million applications "a staggering £13.28 per applicant . . . I find it hard to square this with the banks' repeated assertion that this business is, at best, only marginally profitable".

The Treasury became especially irritated when the banks tried to raise their fees claiming that this was necessary to cover their rising costs. NatWest at one point threatened to withdraw from the issue arguing that the costs it would incur were not adequately reflected in the fees the Government was willing to pay. The main point of friction concerned the fixed costs of setting up the administration to handle the issue. Baker planned for a maximum of two million applications and the banks were to be paid per application handled. The banks, however, also insisted on a commitment from the Government that if the applications fell well short of the intended two million, the Government would bear the fixed costs which otherwise might not be met from the fees received. The fixed costs mainly related to computer equipment, temporary premises, staff wages and training costs.[119]

In August 1984 Baker advised John Moore at the Treasury that, while some of the sale costs were still uncertain, he expected the total to come to around seven per cent of the yield from the sale, or around £250 million. Marketing, selling commissions and fees to advisers would account for almost £39 million, bank costs £20 million, an employee share scheme (discussed below) £31 million and underwriting costs £70 million.[120] In an effort to reduce the costs to the Exchequer, the DTI invited BT to make a contribution. However, BT had spent £16 million on its own corporate advertising campaign and countered by suggesting that Government should make some contribution to this expense. At a meeting on 7 June 1984 BT backed down a little and agreed to contribute £1 million towards the Government's advertising expenses. In past privatisations the companies had paid a half of the cost of the sale prospectus. Baker argued that the same should apply to the issue of the BT prospectus. He also wanted to see BT contribute to the overseas sales expenses and all of the costs relating to the employee share scheme.[121] But BT maintained that as these costs arose from the Government's decision to privatise and as the company would receive no direct financial benefit from the expenditure, it would not be proper for BT to contribute.[122] Meanwhile, DTI officials became frustrated with what they saw as the Treasury's "penny pinching attitude". In their view the costs, while mounting, were trivial when compared to the intended sales receipts of up to £4 billion.[123]

As discussed in earlier chapters, the Government had been criticised in the past for its policy on the pricing of privatisation shares and the underwriting of privatisation issues. Concerns were exacerbated when City institutions during the Britoil issue seemingly preferred to pick up the shares they needed through their sub-underwriting commitment or in the aftermarket rather than through subscribing during the tender offer.[124] With the objective of reducing the scope for underpricing of the shares, the Britoil issue had been the first privatisation to use a sale by tender rather than a fixed price offer for sale. The sale had flopped (chapter 4, p.111). In the light of this experience and soundings in the City, which suggested a majority of institutions were against a tender issue for BT, and given the size of the flotation and uncertainty about the likely investor interest, in the summer of 1984 Kleinworts advised in favour of a fixed price offer. It was also felt that, as in previous privatisations, a tender offer would not be as attractive to small investors who might find it complex to understand. Some consideration was given to an idea put forward by the Treasury to have a fixed price issue to the retail market and a tender issue to the institutions at above this price. But it was decided that this might create a major stagging opportunity. The Treasury did explore the possibility of the Government taking on the sub-underwriting risk, but the size of the issue weighed against the idea. In the end, the Treasury agreed to an underwritten fixed price offer, but stressed that this would put extra pressure on Ministers to determine the appropriate offer price.[125]

The size of the BT flotation and the political necessity to minimise the risks that the flotation would fail had ruled out not underwriting the offer. However, Kleinworts and Hoare Govett devised a novel approach to the underwriting. City institutions entered into a commitment to take, on an actual or contingent basis, the equity being offered for sale, up to 60 per cent on a "firm placing" basis and the remainder as "commitment" shares if the public did not take up all of the remaining offer. The agreement was concluded with 15 primary underwriters in the City led by Kleinworts (a listing is provided in Table 13.2), under which they underwrote the 2,597 million shares on offer in the UK for a commission of 0.375 per cent.[126] The placing shares benefited from a commission rate of 1.5 per cent and the commitment shares 1.25 per cent. This unconventional sub-underwriting arrangement would be later copied in a number of subsequent privatisations and some private sector share issues.

For political reasons overseas markets could only be tapped to a limited degree. It was considered too politically risky to be seen to be transferring too much of BT into foreign ownership. In any event, Government Ministers and not least the PM were keen to have a "British" British Telecom. The result was that only 415 million shares or 13.8 per cent of the shares on offer were allocated for flotation overseas. About 2,000 institutional investors together with a Swiss corporation acting on behalf of a syndicate of Swiss banks were invited to apply for these shares on a priority basis.[127] The Department concluded separate underwriting agreements with US, Canadian and Japanese syndicates, at commission rates of between 2.5 per cent and 3.5 per cent. At the same time, the Department reached an agreement with the Bank of England under which its Issue Department undertook to purchase any of the overseas allocation not taken up by overseas underwriters, for a commission of 1.25 per cent. Unlike in Britain, US underwriters did not commit to buying shares until immediately before the closing date for applications.[128] The role of the Bank of England would be to take up unsold shares in the USA if the financial institutions there refused to provide sufficient underwriting capacity when the time came to commit.

*Table 13.2* The BT underwriters

| |
|---|
| Kleinwort, Benson Limited |
| S G Warburg & Co Limited |
| Barclays Merchant Bank Limited |
| Baring Brothers & Co Limited |
| Charterhouse Japhet PLC |
| County Bank Limited |
| Robert Fleming & Co Limited |
| Hambros Bank Limited |
| Hill Samuel & Co Limited |
| Lazard Brothers & Co Limited |
| Lloyds Bank International Limited |
| Samuel Montagu & Co Limited |
| Morgan Grenfell & Co Limited |
| N M Rothschild & Sons Limited |
| J Henry Schroder Wagg & Co Limited |

Source: BT/C/47.

The precise date of the flotation was influenced by the timing of the Chancellor's Autumn Statement. The Autumn Statement detailed the Government's expenditure plans and its economic forecasts for the coming year and was scheduled for 12 November 1984. Kleinworts advised that the Autumn Statement should not occur between "Impact Day", when the share price was announced and applications started, and the closure of applications for shares, lest the Chancellor said something that unnerved the stock market.[129] In addition, there was a potential legal difficulty because if the offer preceded the Statement and the Statement then contained something that adversely affected the share price, those who experienced a loss might have grounds to sue the Government. The grounds would be that the matter had not been revealed in the prospectus but must have been known to the Government at the time the prospectus was published.[130] There was also the need to ensure that the flotation did not occur during the US presidential election, when it was to be expected that the US stock market might be unsettled. This might adversely affect the planned flotation in North America. The date eventually chosen for the "Impact Day" was therefore 16 November – after the US election and the Autumn Statement.

## The share flotation and setting the issue price

In late August the market research company commissioned by the Government, MORI, reported that 630,000 people were "certain to buy" and 3.9 million' were "likely to buy" BT shares at the flotation. By early September over 300,000 requests had been made to the Shareholder Information Office for further information, in response either to the leaflet included with telephone bills or to the media advertising.[131] Nevertheless, while the DTI was encouraged by such reports of investor interest in the issue, officials still believed that "our big problem is going to be to get a million or two people to invest a substantial sum rather than excess demand".[132] Similarly, Kleinworts still believed that there was as much a risk of undersubscription as oversubscription. The marketing campaign was judged to be going well, but there were also some worrying signs. In particular, there was a constant stream of letters from members of the public to the media, MPs, BT and the DTI objecting to the privatisation. This suggested a number of people would not apply for the shares, although in the event some of the objectors may still have applied, the prospect of a capital gain overriding their principles – the scale is unknown.[133] Meanwhile, some potential investors raised concerns about what might happen to their investment if Labour got back into power.[134] The Labour Party Annual Conference in October 1984 passed a resolution calling for the renationalisation of BT with compensation paid on the basis of "no speculative gain". A warning to that effect therefore had to be contained in the prospectus. Even so, worrying news was received from Warburgs that lawyers were being retained in the USA to try and prevent the registration of the BT Prospectus there. The possible action was based on the contention that the prospectus did not reveal the true extent of the threat to investors from renationalisation without adequate compensation.[135] In the event the threat came to nothing.

Also, during the summer of 1984 some City reporting on the pending flotation was not especially favourable. A report on BT produced by stock brokers de Zoete and Bevan in June suggested that there would be a low growth of profits after privatisation. In this respect, the profit figures published by BT in its 1983/84 accounts, released in July 1984, were not considered helpful. They revealed a fall in retained profit.[136] In August an industrial dispute at Thames TV disrupted the TV advertising campaign and there was a fall in the value of the stock market between May and July, which threatened to unnerve investors. When a BBC TV current affairs programme, Panorama, on 29 October made a number of unfavourable comments about BT's business practices, Jefferson protested to the BBC's Board of Governors concerned about a negative impact on the flotation.[137] Moreover, the disappointing Enterprise Oil issue in June 1984 did, as Kleinworts had feared, lead to some concerns among City institutions about privatisation sales.[138] It was clear that investor interest would turn on the flotation price.

The Pathfinder prospectus was issued on 26 October 1984. During the Pathfinder period there was an almost continuous feedback of institutional views on the appropriate price for the shares. Establishing the appropriate selling price was, as in previous and later privatisations, a matter of judgement rather than science. Kleinworts advised that there were no other UK companies with which BT could be directly compared, to assist in establishing the share price. Kleinworts' approach to the pricing of the shares was therefore based primarily on taking account of the views of City investors, although the views of the City could hardly be considered disinterested. Kleinworts and the four lead stock brokers – Hoare Govett, Cazenove & Co., de Zoete and Bevan, and Scrimgeour Kemp-Gee & Co. – carried out a wide survey of attitudes in the City to BT shares starting in January 1984, with a visit to 35 major investment institutions. In the Spring of 1984 another 50 institutions were visited. By the early summer of 1984 120 core institutions had discussed their views on BT and the offer. Further City institutions were consulted in the October, leading to a total of 250 institutions visited during the year. These represented the vast majority of the institutional investment that would be required.

There was no telephone company against which to benchmark BT in the UK. US telephone companies provided some gauge as to the appropriate financial multiples, but Kleinworts pointed out that the US regulatory system was different from that being created in the UK and was established with a track record. Consultation in the City suggested that investors would be likely to compare BT's projected performance with that of UK industry as a whole. However, even though the Government had decided in favour of price over profit regulation, there was still a risk that the City would view BT as simply a dull utility and therefore not worthy of a "growth stock" rating, notwithstanding the expected rate of innovation in telecommunications. Therefore, Kleinworts' promotion of the shares in the City focused on the stock's growth potential and on the overall expected yield. Following an initial valuation in June 1984, in October Kleinworts expected that by the end of 1985 the yield on the FT all-share index might rise. This indicated a desired yield for BT shares in the order of eight per cent and a price range for the issue of 119p to 124p per share. On this basis, a 50 per cent share sale would raise some £3.2 billion to £3.5 billion. Kleinworts had suggested that a lower yield figure, of around possibly 7.75 per cent, should be used at the Pathfinder prospectus stage, to gauge the reaction of fund managers before setting the final figure.[139]

The prospective dividend yield became the key determinant of the offer price in the UK and in overseas stock markets.[140] In May 1984 Morgan Grenfell, appointed to lead the issue in the USA, argued that a nine per cent yield would be needed to attract investors there.[141] At the time this was in line with the average yield on US telephone utility shares, which was around 8.5 per cent to 9.5 per cent.[142] It was also recognised that the sentiment of investors in overseas stock markets would depend upon their expectation of whether the issue was likely to succeed in the UK. [143]

As a check on the share valuation proposed by Kleinworts, the DTI commissioned the City firm Phillips & Drew to give a second opinion. Phillips & Drew was chosen after a number of other City institutions were ruled out because they were already actively involved in the issue as potential investors.[144] Phillips & Drew was involved in the share sale as a broker introducing priority institutional applicants and as a fund manager, but was willing to provide an assurance that internal arrangements would be put in place to ensure that the advice it gave Government was produced on an independent basis. Phillips & Drew reported on 22 October 1984, favouring valuation on the basis of the expected price-earnings (P/E) ratio once trading in BT's shares had settled down after the issue. The judgement was that BT merited a P/E of 9.3, which was close to but below the UK stock market average. This suggested a share price of 134p, from which Phillips & Drew recommended that there should be a 15 per cent discount to get the flotation away successfully. This produced a share price of 114p. This was not much different to the price proposed by Kleinworts using the alternative method of the expected yield, of 116p.[145]

Kleinworts' strategy in the weeks leading up to the flotation was to keep the capital market hungry for BT's shares by giving the City institutions the impression that they might not receive all of the shares for which they applied. But considerable uncertainty remained that the strategy would work. The share valuations put forward by Kleinworts and Phillips & Drew were dependent upon both no sudden deterioration in City opinion towards the BT sale and a high demand from private investors for the shares. Private investors would be influenced by the type of press coverage the flotation received once the share price was announced.[146] Even though there was growing evidence that the marketing campaign had gone well and at the time BT was making bullish predictions of its future performance and dividends, at a meeting with the Chancellor of the Exchequer on 23 October 1984 Kleinworts reported that the issue was still unlikely to be stagged to any significant degree.

It was only following the issue of the Pathfinder prospectus that the possibility of a large oversubscription began to be seriously discussed within Government. Following the issue of the Pathfinder prospectus there was very favourable press coverage and City comment.

On 1 November brokers Grenfell & Colegrave circulated their clients suggesting that the Government was likely to decide on a share price of around 125p and given the dividend yield, boosted by part-payment and bonus shares or bill vouchers, BT's modest gearing and its growth prospects, the offer was "an unparalleled and unique investment opportunity".[147] On 2 November, and after a slight rise in the stock market and favourable reporting of pending flotation in the media, Phillips & Drew revised its proposal on the share price upwards, to 124p, On the same day another section of the same merchant bank, from behind "Chinese walls", recommended that its clients should apply for the shares, predicting a profit growth of 60 per cent over the following two years.[148] On 9 November stock broker Fielding, Newson-Smith suggested to its clients that even based on a fully paid offer price as high as 130p, the opening price premium might be at least 20p.[149]

On 3 November *The Daily Telegraph* had commented that at a share price of 125p there would be little premium to justify stagging and that undersubscription was a real possibility. However, by 10 November the same newspaper was predicting a premium when share dealing began of up to 20p on an offer price of 128p, implying a 40 per cent return on the partly paid price of 50p. In the following week forecasts of premiums of 10p to 20p or more appeared regularly in the press. The favourable coverage had the desired effect for the Government. By mid-November, MORI was reporting that the numbers of people "certain to buy" BT shares had risen sharply to 3.3 million. Also, the average amount they would be willing to invest had increased to £900, compared with £487 in late August. Strong interest from small investors was confirmed when it was revealed that 900,000 people had asked for copies of the pre-launch brochure. Nor was the enthusiasm for the offer limited to the UK. On 20 November Morgan Stanley, who in the past had been pessimistic about the prospects for the flotation in North America, contacted the DTI to say that the US demand for BT shares was now "out of control".[150] In the event, the 415 million shares reserved for sale in the USA, Canada and Japan were fully subscribed.

On 8 November the Flotation Committee heard that the current provision of lines and operators at the Shareholder Information Centre was inadequate given the level of enquiries. It was agreed that a further 25 lines and staff to cover them should be provided.[151] On 12 November, a number of regional stockbrokers reported that there was an insufficient quantity of BT prospectuses to meet the demand.[152] In the face of evidence that the retail demand for BT shares could possibly exceed any previous expectation, both Kleinworts and Phillips & Drew revised their recommendation on the issue price. On 16 November Phillips & Drew raised its expectation to 125p and just before "Impact Day" to 127p or 128p.[153] By then Kleinworts was recommending an offer price of 130p.[154] As prospects for a successful retail sale continued to improve, the firm placing arrangements were reduced from 60 per cent to the minimum 55 per cent allowed under the terms of the agreement with the City institutions, to free up more shares for the retail sector. Some thought was given to reducing the percentage to 50 per cent but this was rejected because it would have meant reneging on the earlier understanding with the City and would have left the institutions with far fewer shares than they expected.

A meeting to discuss the appropriate share price for the fixed price offer was held in the Chancellor of the Exchequer's room at the Treasury on 9 November 1984. Here the Chancellor pressed for a high price to maximise the sales proceeds, while Kleinworts still canvassed caution. Kleinworts reported that the City had now developed an expectation that the issue price would be around 125p and that any larger figure might well discourage purchasers. After discussion it was agreed that the price would be likely to be in the range of 123p-128p, but that a decision should be postponed to closer to the "Impact Day".[155]

The final meeting to determine the issue price occurred on 14 November and involved the DTI, the Chancellor of the Exchequer, the Financial Secretary and representatives from Kleinworts and Hoare Govett. A day earlier the Secretary of State for Trade and Industry, still recovering from the Brighton bomb blast, had expressed the view "that it would be better to be crucified for . . . [a premium in the aftermarket] than for losing small investors' money and therefore there could be no question of agreeing to a risky price".[156] It was now evident that a price of above 125p would not be unduly risky. At the meeting Kleinworts recommended the price of 130p a share, which it considered was the maximum the City would accept. This price implied a yield on the shares of 7.14 per cent. After some discussion, the price was agreed. It was publicly announced two days later, emblazoned on a banner at the top of Kleinworts' City building. At 8am the underwriting began and within three hours 2.6 billion shares had been underwritten or sub-underwritten by a wide spread of City institutions.

The sale prospectus was published on 20 November and, consistent with the objective of encouraging small investors, an eight day application period was confirmed.[157] It was felt that new investors would need longer than seasoned investors to complete and return the application form. At a sale price of 130p Kleinworts' expectation was for a modest opening premium of between 10p and 20p per share when initial dealings in the shares began on 3 December. It was felt that the prospect of this premium would be sufficient to get the flotation away. It was conventional at the time for IPOs[158] to be sold in London at a price that was likely to generate a ten per cent or so premium to promote investor interest in the issue. On a fully paid basis Kleinworts' forecast for the BT share was consistent with this norm. However, immediately after 14 November it became clear that the premium for the BT issue could be much larger.[159] There was also the important point that the BT shares were being sold on a partly paid basis. In the offer period the stock market hit a record high, in part helped by a lowering of interest rates, and there was a dramatic surge in retail demand for BT shares in response to the enthusiastic media coverage.[160] The *Financial Times* reported that "From Tokyo to Toronto, investors scramble for shares", while the mass circulation newspaper, *The Sun*, reported, more speculatively, that the "Queen joins rush for BT sell-off".[161] At an after privatisation party of those chiefly involved in the BT sale, the PM is reported to have commented, in response to a suggestion that the Government had been lucky in selling the shares so successfully, that she and the Chancellor of the Exchequer had made sure of the success by reducing interest rates in the weeks before the flotation. Interest rates had risen to 12 per cent in the summer of 1984 before falling back.[162] However, while lower interest rates helped the stock market, they were not decisive in terms of determining the outcome of the BT share sale. Neither Margaret Thatcher nor her Chancellor Nigel Lawson in their memoirs make any reference to the interest rate change ahead of the BT sale. The remark by the PM at the party is best interpreted as an acidic response to the suggestion that her Government had been "lucky".

With favourable City comment and journalists advising their readers to buy the shares, by 3 December the general forecast in the press was for an opening premium of 30p to 40p. Only now did Kleinworts feel that they could advise confidently "that the issue would be significantly oversubscribed".[163] People who had pre-registered their interest in the offer with the Share Information Office received application forms for the shares automatically. Those who had not were able to obtain them from banks, at the local Post Office or from newspapers.

On 27 November Kleinworts reported that there had already been 1.5 million applications for the shares and that the final number could be up to 3 million.[164] The prospect of a large-scale oversubscription now led to concern about whether the banks would be able to cope with the unexpectedly big number of applications. Lloyds Bank indicated that it was prepared to deal with up to 2.5 million applications, or a half a million more than its contractual responsibility. But this still left the possibility that the system set up would be unable to cope. Contingency planning therefore began to arrange for advertising to inform investors that their Letters of Acceptance might be delayed.[165] At the same time, TV advertisements scheduled to promote investor interest in the offer immediately before the closing date for applications were scaled back. Also, the prospect of large oversubscription meant that thought had to be given to how best the available number of shares might be rationed out. The usual method in the City when there was an oversubscription for an IPO was to apportion the available shares amongst the applicants by ballot. However, the Government was not keen on this method for the BT issue because of the political damage that would be likely to result if many applicants received no shares. Moreover, the Government wanted to favour the small investor over large investors as part of its widening shareholding agenda, something a ballot could not guarantee.

Applications for shares closed at 10am on 28 November and two days later a meeting between Ministers, officials and Kleinworts was called to discuss how to allocate the shares To avoid disappointing many small investors, Kleinworts proposed a scaling back under which allocations for 200 and 400 shares would be allotted in full. There would be a maximum of 800 shares for larger applications but applicants for over 100,000 shares would receive no allocation. A number present at the meeting were hostile to the idea predicting that it would greatly upset the big City investors, which might in turn damage the prospects for future privatisation sales. It seems that discussion was protracted, but it was finally agreed that the Kleinworts' proposal was the best means of minimising an adverse public reaction and ensuring that small share ownership was maximised. The full details of the scaling back were announced in Parliament on 3 December and are reproduced in Table 13.3.[166] The reason for excluding the very large applications was not simply a matter of wishing to favour small investors. Had large applications been accepted the cheques with the application forms would have needed to be processed. The Government would cash the cheques and there would be a delay before refunds were issued. It was judged that large investors would probably prefer that their cheques were simply returned and not cashed at all.[167]

The BT flotation had proved to be an enormous success. Over two million applications were received from the public, of which almost one half were met in full. Apart from the shares separately floated in the USA, Canada and Japan, 49.5 million shares were sold in Switzerland and 100 million to institutions in countries other than Switzerland where offers for sale were not formally made. These sales formed an integral part of the UK portion of the offer. The overseas sales cost £30 million and looking back were unnecessary given the large oversubscription at home. However, at the time they had been considered necessary to help create the perception of a likely shortage of shares for investors.

BT ended up with 2.15 million investors with some two-thirds of the applicants choosing the bonus shares incentive over the alternative of telephone vouchers.[168] Of these, around 920,000 held on to their shares until 30 November 1987 and therefore qualified for the bonus issue.[169] Some 500,000 chose the alternative bill voucher incentive but because the share allocations were averaged down nobody received more than four vouchers. Nevertheless, the cost of the voucher scheme was quite significant in relation to the take up, amounting to some

*Table 13.3* BT: The share allocation under the public and employee offers

**Public offer**

| Number of shares applied for | Number of shares allocated |
|---|---|
| 200 | 200 |
| 400 | 400 |
| 800 | 500 |
| 1200 | 600 |
| 1600–100,000 | 800 |
| Over 100,000 | None |

**Employee offer**

Applications on preferential forms from BT employees and pensioners were allocated in full up to 20,000 shares. All larger applications were scaled down to 20,000 shares.

**Overall allocation of shares**

| | Shares million | % of total offer | Value £ million (fully paid) |
|---|---|---|---|
| *Institutions* | | | |
| Institutional placing | 1378.9 | 45.8 | 1792.4 |
| Swiss Bank Corporation | 49.5 | 1.6 | 64.3 |
| *Retail* | | | |
| Public | 1024.0 | 34.0 | 1331.2 |
| Employees | 114.8 | 3.8 | 149.2 |
| Pensioners | 22.3 | 0.7 | 29.2 |
| *Overseas* | | | |
| USA | 180.0 | 6.0 | 234.0 |
| Japan | 180.0 | 6.0 | 234.0 |
| Canada | 55.0 | 1.8 | 71.5 |
| Float | 7.5 | 0.2 | 9.8 |
| **Total** | **3012.0** | **99.9\*** | **3915.6** |

*Note*: * Does not equal 100 due to rounding to one decimal place.
*Source*: BT/A/91 Part 3.

£25 million in administration and postage. The majority who chose the bonus shares probably did so because of media advice that the capital appreciation in the share value was likely to be a more valuable concession than the bill vouchers.[170]

Following the flotation the Government was left holding 49.8 per cent of BT's equity (plus a small amount of shares to satisfy erroneous application rejections and the bonus issue). The aim was to sell the remainder of the shares once the circumstances of the company and market conditions permitted. In a letter to Jefferson on 16 November 1984, Tebbit had offered a more specific commitment than that given in previous privatisations. This involved promising not to dispose of further BT shares before 9 April 1988. The intention was to remove any fear the City might have of an early further flotation which might depress the share price. Tebbit had also confirmed that in the meantime, "HM Government does not intend to use its rights as an ordinary shareholder to intervene in the commercial decisions of British Telecom. It does not expect to vote its shareholding on resolutions moved at general meetings, although it retains the right to do so."[171] The commitment was repeated in the prospectus. In addition, the Government retained a "special share" in BT. The company's Articles of Association were written so that no one person or group of persons was allowed to hold 15 per cent or more of the equity and the Chief Executive Officer had to be a British national. The 15 per cent limit was judged for BT, as in earlier privatisations, to be compatible with the EEC requirement for "free transferability" of shares between member states, especially as telecommunications was judged to be a service with national security considerations and therefore subject to the special treatment under Article 223 of the Treaty of Rome.[172] The special share carried no voting rights but through the Articles of Association entitled the Secretary of State to appoint two directors to the Board. Also, the permission of the holder of the special share was needed to alter the Articles of Association, including the one limiting the size of shareholdings and the nationality of the Chief Executive.[173] Only in July 1997 was the special share in BT relinquished, as part of the Government's abandonment of special shares in the face of hostility to them from the European Commission. The European Commission considered the restriction on investment enforced through the special share to be contrary to the free movement of capital under the European Treaty. This was something that the Foreign Office had warned during the 1980s might occur. Fortunately for the British Government, the legal ruling in the European Court came after Britain's privatisation programme was largely completed.

As in a number of previous privatisations employees were favoured. Up to ten per cent of the share issue was reserved for BT employees provided that they had worked for at least 16 hours a week and been in continuous employment with BT since 2 April 1984.[174] BT and the DTI were both keen to encourage employee shareholding, in part to reduce the opposition of trade union members within BT to the privatisation. BT had initially proposed issuing free shares to each eligible employee to a value of £120 and providing a matching offer of £240 of shares for £80 of shares purchased.[175] However, the Treasury was opposed to moving outside its guidelines on shares for employees that had been applied in other privatisations. In the end a figure of just over £70 for free shares was agreed or more precisely 54 shares based on the eventual 130p issue price. This was consistent with the guidelines. But in the case of the matching offer a limit was set at two shares for each one bought, up to a maximum for each eligible employee of 150 shares. This was the first occasion on which employees were offered a "matching" offer on a more generous basis than the "one for one" recommended in the Treasury guidance. The BT privatisation was also the first privatisation in which, additionally, employees were able to buy shares at a discount to the offer price. Kenneth Baker particularly championed this concession. Employees were allowed to buy shares on a priority basis at a price discount of ten per cent, up to a limit of 1,600 shares each.[176] It was also the first in which pensioners of the privatised company were able to participate alongside employees in a priority application scheme. This was conceded after representations from BT.

In total the change in the matching share allocation and the price discount meant that the BT sale involved a modest advance on the total value given to each employee permitted in previous privatisations.[177] The Treasury had attempted to limit the cost of the employee concessions to £40–45 million with a free share allocation of no more than £50 per employee, but had given way. The total cost came to around £56 million. Some 222,000 employees or about 96 per cent of those eligible to do so became shareholders, 84 per cent took part in the matching offer and 26 per cent of employees applied for the discounted shares. The figure of 96 per cent was higher than for any previous privatisation with the exception of Amersham International, where the number of employees was relatively small. Even so, the ten per cent of shares set aside for employees and pensioners was not fully taken up. In spite of this, it was judged indefensible to allow BT employees with large applications (in one case for up to 700,000 shares) to be granted a full allocation when applications from members of the public were to be scaled back to a maximum of 800 shares. In the end, employees were treated much more generously than the general public, being limited to 20,000 shares each.[178]

BT had proposed in early October 1984 the establishment of a share option scheme for 200 of its most senior managers and an employee "share save scheme" for its other employees. The schemes would have been based on the offer for sale price and have given the most senior 200 managers in BT the option to invest an amount of up to four times their salaries in BT shares, to be exercised between three and ten years after the flotation. The DTI immediately protested about what it saw as the casual way in which BT had proposed the scheme and to the "substantial political and presentational problems" that would be created if it became public knowledge. The Treasury objected to the precedent that would be created.[179] The Government had resisted such schemes in previous privatisations, preferring instead that the offer for sale prospectus simply stated that the directors intended to recommend to shareholders after privatisation that such a scheme be set up. This left the decision with the shareholders and not the Government. However, the British Leyland Board had agreed a management share option scheme during the sale of Jaguar cars, much to the administration's embarrassment. The Government had been unable to prevent it because it was granted by the BL Board, as owner of Jaguar, not the Government. Following the Jaguar sale Ministers had reconfirmed that such schemes should only be put in place after privatisation, by the new shareholders. Also, it had been agreed that they should not operate on the offer for sale price, for fear of criticism that the Government was placing large potential benefits in the hands of a small number of senior executives.[180] Nevertheless, a precedent existed.

In the case of BT the financial advice was that having an executive share option scheme would assist the flotation and achieve a better price for the shares. Investors would conclude that BT management would now have a direct incentive to manage the business efficiently and improve the share price. After much debate within Government, the Chancellor of the Exchequer agreed to the setting up of such a scheme prior to the privatisation provided that the option was not granted at the offer price for the shares but at a price at a later date, to be agreed.[181] It was accepted that making this concession for BT would probably make it very difficult to resist similar executive share option schemes in future privatisations.[182]

Dealing in the BT shares commenced in the UK stock market on Monday 3 December 1984 at 3pm, to coincide with the opening of the market in the USA, and the share price closed at the end of the day at 93p, giving a premium of 96 per cent on the partly paid share price of 50p, or 33 per cent on the full offer price of 130p.[183] The large premium resulted because institutional investors had received far fewer shares than they had applied for and because BT was 6.5 per cent of the *Financial Times* (FT) all-share index. The decision by the FT to give BT shares a full weighting in its FT 100 and all-share indices, even though the Government's retained 49.8 per cent holding was non-tradeable, increased the upward

*Table 13.4* Estimated receipts from and costs of sale of shares in British Telecom plc

|  | £ million | £ million |
| --- | --- | --- |
| Value of shares included in offer (at selling price) |  | 3,916 |
| Shares given to employees under free and matching offers | 51 |  |
| Employee discounts | 5 |  |
| Premium from later sale of retained shares | (3) | 53 |
| **Total sale proceeds** |  | **3,863** |
| Costs in respect of UK offer (excluding incentives) |  |  |
| Underwriting, placing and commitment commissions | 74 |  |
| Selling commission | 13 |  |
| Clearing bank costs including registration | 20 |  |
| Marketing costs | 14 |  |
| Fees to advisers | 6 |  |
| Total costs in respect of UK offer | 127 |  |
| Total costs in respect of overseas offers | 30 |  |
| Total costs (excluding incentives) | 157 |  |
| Receipts to be netted against costs |  |  |
| Contribution from BT | (1) |  |
| Interest on application money | (4) |  |
| Net costs (excluding incentives) | 152 |  |
| Incentives for small shareholders |  |  |
| Bill vouchers (a cash cost) | 23 |  |
| Bonus shares (a non-cash cost) | 88 |  |
| Net costs (including incentives) |  | 263 |
| **Net proceeds** |  | **3,600** |

*Note*: The calculations were made in 1985. The incentives for small shareholders were maximum figures and assumed that all those eligible would continue to hold their shares and receive the benefits. The cost of bonus shares is based on the issue price of 130p per share.

*Source*: BT Flotation: NAO Report July 1985.

pressure on the share price. The institutional investors found themselves seriously underweight in the stock. Moreover, as BT's share price rose, demand for the shares from the financial institutions grew because of the additional underperformance of their portfolios that resulted. Tightening the market further was the fact that small investors had an incentive not to sell their shares because of the promise of future bill vouchers or bonus shares, although the situation was eased a little by the flow back of shares from overseas.[184] Three-quarters of the shares issued in North America and up to one half of the shares allocated to other foreign investors had flowed back to the UK by the end of January 1985, confirming earlier fears.[185] It appears that the shares offered in the US proved to be too small in number to allow institutions to build up large enough allotments to be worth holding longer term. This was an issue addressed during the later sale of British Gas shares in North America. Nevertheless, due to continuing high domestic demand, by 23 January 1985 the partly paid BT share price still stood at 82p.

Table 13.4 provides a summary of the receipts from the BT flotation and the sale costs. The single largest cost related to underwriting and related commissions, which amounted to £74 million. Immediately after the flotation the DTI asked Phillips & Drew to prepare a paper on the behaviour of the share price after flotation, conscious of likely criticism, yet again, of under pricing of a privatisation from the Public Accounts Committee and the National Audit Office. The resulting paper from Phillips & Drew put the result down to the inevitable uncertainty about the retail demand at flotation and setting the share price two weeks before share applications closed.[186]

## "A good result"

The privatisation of BT had been a formidable challenge and had involved a flotation on a scale never seen before. The issue was six times larger than any previous UK issue. Not only was BT safely transferred to the private sector but the sale had been successful in attracting around 2.15 million investors, although some of these sold their shares for a quick capital gain when stock trading began. During the first fortnight of trading in BT equity, over 700 million shares passed through the UK exchange and a further 280 million were traded in American Depository Receipts (ADR) form in New York. The first three days saw the majority of this activity with individuals' net sales totalling 27 million shares. US investors sold around two-thirds of their initial allocation of 120 million shares in the first fortnight, leading to the flowback of shares to the UK referred to earlier. About three per cent of the issued share capital was transferred to the large institutions in the first two weeks.[187] Nevertheless, by March 1985 about 75 per cent of the investors still held their shares, an outcome that the DTI judged to be "a good result".[188] Over twenty years later BT still had 1.6 million shareholders, over 650,000 of them owning only 400 shares each.

At the same time, like other newly publicly quoted companies the majority of BT's shares were held by the institutions from day one. The final allocation of shares had been to UK and Swiss institutions 47.4 per cent[189], BT employees and pensioners 4.5 per cent, overseas investors 13.8 per cent, and other investors (UK individual investors) 34 per cent.[190] Also, over time as more small shareholders gradually cashed in their shares, the grip of the institutions strengthened. Today BT still has more small shareholders than a typical plc on the London Stock Exchange, but the small shareholders exercise little or no influence in terms of corporate governance. BT had worried ahead of privatisation about how it would house its shareholders at its AGMs. In fact, BT need not have worried. Its first AGM was held at the large National Exhibition Centre in Birmingham and two halls were hired, in anticipation that many thousands of investors might attend. In the event, around 4,000 arrived and one hall was not needed. The privatisation of BT did not noticeably advance the ownership of British industry by small shareholders. Selling shares to small investors was critical in getting the BT flotation away successfully, but it did not reverse the trend in British capitalism towards a growing concentration of ownership in powerful financial institutions. "Popular capitalism" was always more political rhetoric rather than economic reality.

Also, one initiative to promote future mass shareholding explored during the privatisation of BT never really developed. Ministers had been keen to see share shops offering low cost share trading facilities as part of the wider share ownership agenda. It was felt that if shares could be traded more cheaply then this would encourage individuals to become more active investors. There were some share shop experiments around the time of the BT sale and immediately afterwards, but none was particularly successful. It is highly questionable whether the sale of BT, and the later privatisations of companies such as British Gas, did much to promote active share ownership amongst the public.[191] Most small shareholders who held on to their BT shares after the first few weeks of trading tucked them away in a drawer. Even in the first months after the sale of BT, when enthusiasm for the shares was running high, only around five per cent of those who had purchased BT equity were estimated to have bought shares in other companies.[192]

The gross proceeds from the BT sale to Government were £3.863 billion and the costs of the sale around £263 million. Added to this, between 1985/6 and 1990/1 the Government incurred a further £19.7 million in expenses in respect of the administration of the share instalment and bonus and bill voucher schemes.[193] The flotation of BT had involved the use of novel methods of marketing, including small shareholder incentives costing around £110 million.[194] The total costs of the sale represented 6.8 per cent of the proceeds.[195] This was a higher percentage than in all but one of the six previous sales of government shares, where costs on a comparable basis averaged 3.3 per cent of proceeds – ranging from 11.2 per cent for the sale of ABP to 2.8 per cent for the disposal of Enterprise Oil.[196] Moreover, the planning and implementation of the sale of BT involved civil service resources not separately accounted for. The maximum staffing for the flotation in the DTI included a large proportion of the time of one Under Secretary and his Personal Secretary and the whole of the time of one Assistant Secretary, two Principals, two Higher Executive Officers, two Personal Secretaries and one Clerical Assistant. To this can be added some time of four more civil servants at Higher Executive Officer rank or lower and inputs from time to time from the Department's solicitors, economists and the Accountancy Services Division. At very busy times one Deputy Secretary and the Permanent Secretary also became involved, although in the early days of planning the sale, in 1982 and 1983, the staffing commitment was much smaller. It is a matter of judgement as to whether this level of staffing was appropriate, but given the size and importance of the sale it does not appear that it was excessive.

What is certain is that even allowing also for the costs of the capital restructuring pre-sale, the disposal of BT produced a windfall to the Exchequer. The sale of BT confirmed that privatisation sales could make some, if always marginal, contribution to the public finances. As we have seen in earlier chapters, the Treasury had already shown a keen interest in privatisation sales receipts to help balance the Government's books, but the privatisation of BT reinforced this tendency. This was notwithstanding that during the planning of the privatisation the Treasury was keen to see more competition in telecommunications and effective regulation, a result that could be expected to diminish the eventual sales receipts because an unregulated monopoly would be more attractive to investors.

A key to the success of the BT flotation had been the unprecedented marketing campaign. Over 38 million brochures, fact sheets, leaflets and prospectuses had been printed and distributed, including 1.5 million corporate brochures, 20 million telephone bill leaflets, 100,000 BT brochures, 1.4 million stock exchange leaflets and one million BT fact sheets. In addition, over 70 different advertisements had been created and published in newspapers, magazines, posters and on TV and radio. Over 100 presentations had been made by BT management and the financial advisers to thousands of analysts, brokers and other intermediaries and editorial contact had been achieved with almost every national and regional newspaper and radio broadcasting station. The result had been over 1.4 million enquiries to the BT Share Information Office and at the flotation five per cent of the adult population had bought shares. In addition, even in the face of opposition to the privatisation from the unions within BT, BT employees were caught up in the frenzy to purchase in the days before the offer closed.

The offer was oversubscribed three times.[197] In spite of worries in late November 1984 that the banks might be unable to cope with such a level of applications, the letters of acceptance and the return of un-cashed cheques were achieved by the receiving banks by the deadline of 10 December, thereby avoiding a conflict with the Christmas mail, something the Post Office was keen to see.[198] The oversubscription led to predictable criticism of the privatisation issue for being under-priced in Parliament and in some sections of the media.[199] Every penny extra on the share price above 130p would have contributed another £30 million in revenue. However, the flotation had been high risk both financially and politically. It had proven very difficult to judge the likely level of investor interest. Equally, failure of the BT issue would have led to great political embarrassment and could well have brought the Government's entire privatisation programme to a halt. Following the Enterprise Oil share flop in the June, when 63 per cent of the issue was left with the underwriters, a failure of the BT flotation might well have fatally dented City confidence in privatisation issues for a number of years and perhaps permanently. Moreover, it was not just government new issues at this time that resulted in oversubscription. The sale of shares in the private-sector company Iceland Frozen Foods in October 1984 was 113 times oversubscribed and the premium at the end of the first day's trading was 51 per cent. The flotation of the insurance company Abbey Life in June 1985 was oversubscribed 19 times and went to an opening price premium of 29 per cent.[200] Pricing new issues is always a hazardous venture, prone to error. There is no evidence that the Government did not attempt to maximise the sale price of BT shares, subject to the overriding need to ensure that the flotation was successful.

Small investors had been attracted by the prospect of a capital gain and by the bill vouchers and bonus shares. The prospect of vouchers or bonus shares also succeeded in preventing a large sell-off of the shares immediately after the flotation, as had occurred, for example following the sale of British Aerospace and Jaguar cars. The incentives also helped to ensure that investors paid the later instalments. For example, fewer than 2,000 shareholders defaulted on the second payment for BT shares in June 1985.[201] Two-thirds of investors had opted for the bonus share option and were likely to continue to hold their shares until the bonus issue became due, in November 1987.

Nevertheless, the incentive schemes were expensive and triggered some controversy both before and after the sale. The Treasury questioned the cost of them in the run-up to the flotation, while the eligibility for the voucher scheme was narrowly worded and led to complaints from MPs, investors and the media when the first bill vouchers were issued, in July 1985.[202] Recipients could use only one voucher per telephone bill and under the terms of the voucher scheme, the vouchers expired within nine months of issue. The expiry date for the first issue was 25 April 1986. In a number of cases, such as where husbands and wives had bought shares, recipients complained that they would be unable to use all of their vouchers, until BT responded by issuing interim telephone bills. Also, some people received vouchers but the telephone bill was not in their name. For example, some people had applied for shares and vouchers even though they did not have a telephone, expecting to give the vouchers away to friends and relations. Small traders had their vouchers rejected when the telephone bill was in a business name (although a concession was introduced to cover this later). Some lost the right to bonus shares because they had altered the arrangements under which their shares were held, for example following the death of a spouse.[203] A background departmental note reviewing the episode reveals that the DTI had not anticipated the difficulties: "With hindsight we probably underestimated the difficulties to which the voucher scheme would give rise – both in terms of people's understanding (people new to shareholding and to prospectuses) and administratively."[204] Apart from a few concessions, in general the DTI decided to stand firm on the terms set out in the Prospectus; although during the later privatisations of gas, water and electricity similar schemes were more generously worded to avoid the same problems.[205] Meanwhile, the Government benefited by around £1 million when five per cent of the bill vouchers issued to shareholders were not used by the expiry dates.[206]

There were also 30,000 enquiries and complaints from those whose applications for shares had been rejected or not processed, mainly because their application forms had been completed incorrectly.[207] In addition, there were some fraudulent applications including multiple applications. The Government had taken a low profile on multiple applications ahead of a sale uncertain whether they would want to prosecute.[208] After the flotation a number of fraudulent applications were unearthed by accountants Pete Marwick and Mitchell, who were appointed at the end of October 1984 to audit the applications. In the weeks after the flotation the Labour MP Bryan Gould was particularly vocal in making allegations of malpractices. A number of alleged cases were referred to the Director of Public Prosecutions and there were ten successful prosecutions.[209] A separate trade union investigation of BT's share register claimed that two Conservative MPs had obtained BT shares using different versions of their names or different addresses.[210]

## Results and later developments

Problems with the voucher scheme and cases of fraud are now lost in the mists of time. In their memoirs the key Ministers involved are unequivocal in their praise of the privatisation and make little or no reference to these difficulties. The Chancellor of the Exchequer, Nigel Lawson, hails the sale of BT as marking "the birth of people's capitalism".[211] Kenneth Baker, who had steered the privatisation until he was replaced by Geoffrey Pattie as Minister of State immediately before the flotation, concludes that the sale was an undoubted success and a landmark: "The successful privatization of BT made possible all the other public utility sales of the 1980s. We showed it could be done and that the benefits to the country were enormous."[212] Margaret Thatcher is equally gushing in her praise:

> "The consequences of privatization of BT were seen in a doubling of its level of investment, now no longer constrained by the Treasury rules applying in the public sector. The consequences for consumers were just as good. Prices fell sharply in real terms, the waiting list for telephones shrank and the number of telephone boxes in operation at any particular time increased. It was a convincing demonstration that utilities were better run in the private sector."[213]

The judgement of the National Audit Office, which issued a report into the BT privatisation in July 1985, was more measured. The report found that the Department had correctly sought advice on pricing, considered alternative methods of sale and acted consistently within its objectives. But it also drew attention to the costs of the restructuring of BT's balance sheet ahead of the sale and especially the reduction in debt income to the Exchequer. In addition, the report drew attention to the commissions and other expenses paid during the sale, which the NAO noted were high in comparison with earlier, but admittedly much smaller, privatisations. [214] The House of Commons Public Accounts Committee had previously criticised a number of privatisation sales for underpricing and reported on the BT sale in December 1985. The Committee noted that its earlier recommendations on methods of sale had not been overlooked. Nevertheless, the Committee was curious as to why the DTI had not foreseen a high share premium as UK institutions rushed to buy the shares in the aftermarket, the institutions being short of shares given BT's weighting in the FT all-share index. It also questioned whether BT could have been sold in smaller tranches to reduce the effects of under-pricing and judged that the underwriting commissions were too large given the risks involved. In addition, the PAC's report raised questions about the need for overseas sales of the shares and the inducements to buy in the form of the bill vouchers and bonus shares. In total it concluded that all this "raises the question whether the Government objective of maximising net sale proceeds has been met".[215]

However, compared with some of the earlier privatisations, overall the criticism from the NAO and PAC was more muted. The DTI and Treasury shrugged off the criticism of a majority sale because a smaller disposal would not have achieved the Government's objective of a transfer of BT to the private sector, and of the underwriting, overseas sales and share incentives, which they argued had only been shown to be unnecessary after the over-subscription was achieved. But in a conciliatory gesture the Government did concede that it: "has always accepted that experience gained in sales should influence the conduct of future offers and it notes the Committee's views that there are lessons to be learned from the BT sale".[216] After the privatisation of BT the Government would in particular continue to reassess how the share flotations might be best underwritten.[217] Meanwhile, the sale of BT had provided a major boost to the City in the form of payments, commissions, experience and reputation. The City subsequently capitalised on the BT sale by developing a very lucrative business advising overseas governments on their privatisation programmes.

Following the privatisation of BT a duopoly existed in British telecommunications with Mercury Communications as the only other licensed network operator. In particular, BT and Mercury had sole rights to provide trunk (long-distance) telephony services and there was virtually no direct competition for BT in the local telephony network, in which Mercury showed little interest, preferring to concentrate on the trunk and international market. At privatisation the expectation was that competition for BT would come primarily from Mercury and perhaps in the future other licensed networks. However, this did not occur on any great scale, at least outside the big cities and especially London. Competition was not assisted by continuing wrangling between BT and Mercury over interconnection terms. At privatisation a Heads of Agreement had been reached between the two companies; however, Mercury quickly contended that this should not constrain the eventual terms negotiated. In 1985 BT and Mercury failed to agree on whether the Heads of Agreement was legally binding and the matter went to the High Court. Mercury was successful but the subsequent negotiations proved inconclusive. In October 1985 the DGT was forced to make a determination. BT and Mercury signed an agreement on interconnection in March 1986.[218]

Under the terms of this agreement Mercury was able to use BT's network to connect Mercury's network to customers on either local or trunk routes. This meant that Mercury was able to concentrate on competing for high density traffic and high volume customers, principally business users.[219] This put more pressure on BT to abandon its previous policy of cross-subsidising local call charges. With BT threatening to rebalance its tariffs quickly, which would have had an adverse impact on the charges to those who mainly made local calls, commonly low users of telephones on poorer incomes, the DGT felt the need to intervene to slow down the tariff rebalancing. However, as an unintended effect, this reduced the scope for profitable competition at the local level. As a consequence, residential subscribers and small businesses continued to rely mainly on BT's local network. The Government's policy to develop a competing fixed-line network faltered. By June 1990 Mercury had a market share of only five per cent.[220] In the mid-1990s its operations and staffing were cut back and an attempt to capture some of the residential telephone market and to provide public call boxes abandoned. Under the banner of its parent company, Cable and Wireless, from the mid-1990s it concentrated on international and business services.[221]

More effectively than competition in the form of a rival fixed-line network, competition for BT developed in terms of value-added services and resale using BT and Mercury lines.[222] In 1987 value-added and data services were fully liberalised, permitting resale of capacity leased from BT and Mercury for all services except voice and realtime telex. In July 1989 competition through the "simple resale" of surplus capacity on circuits leased from BT and Mercury to third parties was permitted, although restrictions on international calls and international private leased circuits remained until 1997. As with competition from Mercury, BT responded by rebalancing its tariffs, leaving less scope for profitable price competition from new entrants. Nevertheless, rival services developed. Also, two mobile telephone operators had been set up in the mid-1980s, Racal Vodafone and Cellnet (a Securicor joint venture with BT in which BT had a 60 per cent stake), and in July 1991 the UK became the first country in the world to issue licences for a new generation of mobile phones, the so-called Personal Communication Networks (PCNs). Three PCNs were licensed. Therefore, in the 1990s wireless communications would provide some competition to BT's fixed-line services, although usually subscribers treated them as complements. Most subscribers to mobile telephone networks retained their fixed line services, which were particularly necessary for data transmission.

The BT-Mercury duopoly was reviewed in 1990. On 21 June 1990 E(A) Committee met to consider the future of the duopoly with the Secretary of State for Trade and Industry, Nicholas Ridley, keen "to adopt a pro-competitive approach to the review, while keeping an open mind on the options".[223] However, although when the PM had reopened the issue of a possible break-up of BT ahead of privatisation in the autumn of 1982 it had been suggested that the matter might be revisited at the end of the decade, Ridley showed little enthusiasm. He pointed out that BT was now a private sector company and to break it up would require either primary legislation or a MMC reference with an uncertain outcome. Moreover, any attempt to break up the company might provoke a messy legal challenge, and any talk of the possibility could be expected to depress BT's share price. The Government still held 49.8 per cent of the shares and therefore still had an interest in maintaining a high price. In addition, he concluded that to raise the question of a break-up now might "suggest that the Government had reached the wrong conclusion originally." However, if the matter of a break-up were raised during the review by others, he noted that the Government would "be free to deal with this as we think best if it becomes a significant issue".[224] The possibility of a break-up was therefore not entirely ruled out, but equally it was not to be promoted by Government. During the following duopoly review the Government remained keen to avoid a dispute with BT that might trigger a MMC inquiry. The Government was planning to sell its remaining shareholding in BT and a MMC inquiry could be expected to delay a sale.[225]

In March 1991 the Government published a telecommunications White Paper ending the duopoly policy, whereby BT and Mercury were the only licensed public fixed-link telecommunications networks.[226] New applicants were now allowed to come forward for licences to run trunk and local telecommunications systems, although there were to be no new international operating licences in the short term.[227] By October 1991 over 30 companies had expressed an interest in applying for licences for a range of services and geographical areas. After 1991 it became possible for competitors to install their own exchanges and linking transmission facilities. New networks, such as Energis based on running a fibre-optic network along existing electricity cables, were established to provide long-distance facilities alongside Mercury and specialist operators such as Colt tapped into the business market. Competing providers of private networks in Britain were now free to resell circuits leased from BT and Mercury and sustained their businesses through marketing, value-added services and price competition. The result of the duopoly review was to open up almost all of the telecommunications market to competition, but not by dividing up BT which remained intact. Some submissions to Government mentioned the possibility of a break-up, but no one appears to have considered it a serious prospect. New operators were licensed to offer services such as CT2 and Telepoint, however these were slow to develop and ultimately unsuccessful. Another initiative surrounded by much publicity was Ionica, which used radio links rather than fixed lines to transmit calls. It was established in the mid-1990s to compete with BT for subscribers, and quickly failed. As late as 2001/2, BT still accounted for 82 per cent of lines and 61 per cent of call revenues, reflecting the company's success in meeting the competition.

Another field of competition where there were initially high hopes but which proved difficult to establish was cable. Local areas were franchised to cable companies and by the late 1980s cable television operators were installing new networks for television services on which telephone calls could be made with limited additional investment. Twelve cable operators were set up, some involving investment by BT, but each struggled financially when the number of subscribers fell well below expectation and the costs of installing cable connections per subscriber escalated. The development of cable was stunted because the operators could only act as agents of BT or Mercury. Cable TV networks were not allowed to connect to each other and therefore calls outside their localised franchise areas had to go along BT or Mercury lines. Government feared in the run up to the duopoly review in 1989 that if the cable firms proved too successful in attracting subscribers for telephone services, the result could undermine BT and endanger the universal service obligation. In the event, cable did not prove to be much of a threat to BT's dominance, even after a number of restrictions were later removed. Cable attracted investment especially from the USA but its future remained insecure because of high costs. By the early 1990s cable had only around 50,000 telephone subscribers. A Broadcasting White Paper in November 1988 committed the Government to consider at the same time as the duopoly review the recommendation of the Peacock Committee that public telecommunications operators should be allowed to carry entertainment services over their main networks. When BT lobbied to be allowed to offer entertainment services over its telephone lines during the duopoly review, the Government rejected the idea for at least another ten years, fearing that this would further undermine the economics of cable.[228]

Littlechild had forecast when he had put forward his idea of a Local Tariff Reduction Scheme that under it "The DGT does not have to make any judgements or calculations with respect to capital, allocation of costs, rates of return, future movements of costs and demand, desirable performance, etc."[229] This might have proved true had price regulation only existed for five years or so. But once it became clear that the price cap would last for much longer (it was not finally removed from residential calls until August 2006) the prospects of simplicity diminished. Under Bryan Carsberg's stewardship OFTEL demonstrated laudable independence from government and went about policing BT's behaviour with some gusto.

There was never any question of regulatory capture, a dread of Walters and Littlechild. But OFTEL was drawn into demanding growing amounts of information from BT, including accounting and operational data, and responding to public pressure as the scope and expectations of regulation increased. In 1988 Walters, now in Washington, complained about price control being extended to more of BT's services rather than fewer, as he and Littlechild had intended.[230] When the price cap was reset in 1989 no detailed explanation of how the new cap was determined was published by OFTEL. However, it seems that the rate of return BT needed to earn to cover its cost of capital played an important part, alongside estimation of BT's funding needs for operating expenditure and its capital investment programme.[231] These were very much the same considerations as those taken into account when US telecommunications regulators set allowed rates of return in America, contrary to Littlechild's intention.[232] State ownership had been replaced by state regulation of a nature and on a scale not anticipated in 1984.

BT made large profits after privatisation even though occasionally it set its prices below the permitted maximum under the RPI – X formula. The high profits led to customer and media complaints, to which the regulator was not immune. In response, in 1989 OFTEL raised the X factor from 3% to 4.5% and then in August 1991 to 6.25 per cent and widened the basket of services included. The original RPI – X covered 55 per cent of BT's total revenues. After the 1989 review this rose to 73.5 per cent. The RPI + 2% placed on residential line rentals at privatisation was widened to include business line rentals and a separate price cap was applied to installation and connection charges. In the face of complaints about international call charges, these were added to the regulated services in the same year. Following representations from competitors and potential competitors about interconnection charges and other alleged anti-competitive behaviour by BT, OFTEL was also pulled into regulating many of BT's wholesale as well as retail services. As the regulatory net widened, new accounting practices were introduced alongside strict codes of practice relating to marketing and commercial practices, policed by the regulator.[233] BT had been successful before privatisation in resisting the introduction into its licence of legal liabilities for service quality. After privatisation there were occasional complaints about poor services. For example, the conversion of two exchanges in the City to digital operation was badly handled, causing service difficulties for a number of weeks, mainly due to delays in equipment supplies, and in 1987 the state of poor repair of public call boxes became a matter of national concern.[234] The regulator responded to such complaints by increased monitoring of BT's service quality and the setting of explicit quality targets.[235] After privatisation BT abandoned its policy of publishing quality of service figures, but this was reinstated following pressure from the regulator.

Littlechild had suggested in his report to the Secretary of State in January 1983 that the regulator would be "holding the fort" until the competition arrived. The wooden fort fast became a stone castle. The birth of OFTEL announced the arrival of a whole new regulatory industry in Britain that would become on the one hand highly admired around the world and on the other increasingly intricate and demanding on the regulated companies in terms of compliance costs. Regulation did not turn out to be "light touch". The managerial freedom that BT expected with privatisation was compromised by regulation, as Jefferson had feared. Bryan Carsberg proved to be a very determined and effective regulator, sometimes cajoling BT to fall into line with a threat of a referral to the MMC. When, shortly after privatisation, BT approached the Secretary of State, Normal Tebbit, to put pressure on Carsberg to change his attitude, the Secretary of State refused to intervene. In some respects OFTEL imposed a more detailed oversight of BT's operations than had existed previously under direct departmental control. Littlechild had projected OFTEL having costs of £1.5 million a year and a staff of 50. By 2001/2 the Office's expenditure totalled £17 million and its staffing had risen to 230, well above the levels of staffing devoted to overseeing BT in the DTI before privatisation.

The privatisation of BT did lead to lower charges and improved services. Business customer bills did not increase at all from privatisation to 1988, while domestic bills rose by eight per cent compared with an inflation rate over the same period of 17 per cent. Between 1984 and 1991 prices fell overall by more than 20 per cent in real terms. However, prices had been falling as a long-term trend before privatisation, due to technological change and economies of scale. Also, telecommunications prices fell in the 1980s and 1990s in other countries where the operator remained state-owned. Waiting lists for the installation of telephones were removed after privatisation, although again they had been declining sharply ahead of privatisation. BT's waiting lists had fallen from 122,000 in 1981 to 2,000 in 1984.[236] There had been improvements in the response time for repair requests in the early 1980s – in September 1984 a DTI official noted "the time taken to repair faults had fallen dramatically" – and this continued after privatisation.[237] Arguably it was the price freeze imposed by the Labour Government in the late 1970s, at a time of growing demand for telephone connections, rather than state ownership per se that had led to the long waiting lists and many of the difficulties with repairs.[238] In other words, it is uncertain to what extent privatisation was followed by lower prices and better service than that which would have come about in any case, especially with the arrival of competition. At the same time, it is the case that privatisation did provide more managerial freedom for BT to respond to customer needs and this was reflected in management changes and organisational restructuring within the company. Equally, competition might not have developed – or developed to the same extent – had BT remained state-owned. The experience in continental Europe in the 1980s and early 1990s demonstrates how reluctant governments can be to allow state-owned telephone enterprises to be put under real competitive pressure and how easy it is to claim that technological advance is best achieved by the state's national champion.

Privatisation saw significant changes in management personnel and practices. Beginning before privatisation but continuing afterwards there was a move towards more devolved management with the move from a regional to a district structure and the establishment of new profit centres and operating subsidiaries with a high degree of managerial independence. BT had been unionised almost up to board level and management had spent much of its time placating the unions under state ownership. This now changed. The influence of the unions declined and BT was able to introduce performance-related pay and personal contracts for senior managers and a less generous pension scheme was introduced for new employees to reduce costs. Staff promotion became less a matter of the number of years served and more a matter of merit.[239] As part of the change process, new management with private sector experience was brought in both to provide the necessary skills required and as part of a "culture change" programme, which also involved retraining of existing staff.[240] As a monopoly BT had not needed a marketing capability, this now had to be developed. Whether the changes and the pace of change would have been possible without privatisation remains a moot point. Unequivocally it is the case that pay differentials within BT widened after privatisation, as remuneration was linked to individual performance and market rates. Nowhere was this more apparent than at Board level. The rise in senior management pay, at a time of rising profits within BT, engendered public criticism. However, prior to privatisation top salaries in BT, as elsewhere in the nationalised industries, compared most unfavourably with those paid in the private sector for comparable jobs.

After privatisation the annual rate of spend on renewal and expansion of the network rose, by 35 per cent. Between 1984 and 1991 BT invested £15 billion. By 1988 the creation of a fully digital trunk network had been completed and 1,200 of BT's 6,000 local exchanges had been digitalised.[241] Large programmes were also underway to bring fibre-optic transmission links directly to major business customers in London and other cities. Two new national networks were constructed by BT, one for cellular telephony and one for '0800' free phone services. However, the growth in investment was part of a longer-term trend necessitated by increasing demand for telecommunications services and technological change. BT had doubled its investment between 1978 and 1982 and therefore it remains also uncertain how far higher investment and technological innovation after 1984 were the result of privatisation.[242] State-owned telecommunications operators on the continent similarly invested in renewing their networks. It is the case that privatisation freed BT from Treasury financial controls and enabled the company to access the capital market directly. Jefferson had been keen to ensure that BT had a balance sheet that would permit more borrowing after privatisation to fund investment. However, it was 1996 before BT felt the need to access the capital market for loan financing to finance the acquisition of fixed assets. This suggests that access to the private capital market was not critical in determining the scale of BT's investment programme after privatisation and that the reduced gearing conceded by the Treasury in 1984 may have been unnecessary.

Other changes within BT after privatisation involved the development of commercial relationships with suppliers from overseas, outsourcing of non-core activities, and developing an international strategy involving acquisitions and joint ventures. In March 1985 BT announced its intention to purchase up to £100 million of digital electronic local telephone exchanges known as System Y from Thorn Ericsson Telecommunications Ltd, something it had been prevented from doing before privatisation.[243] BT's Martlesham research facility, which had developed the rival System X in the 1970s, was used increasingly on a customer-client basis and BT turned to the international market place for expansion opportunities.[244] One of BT's earliest acquisitions following privatisation was the Mitel Corporation in Canada.[245] Mitel designed, developed and manufactured a family of microprocessor controlled switching equipment (private automatic branch exchanges) and items such as telephone sets, and had an active UK manufacturing subsidiary. The result of the merger reawakened fears during the passage of the 1984 Telecommunications Act that BT intended to become a major manufacturer of equipment in its own right to the detriment of the existing domestic manufacturers, something prevented under state ownership.[246] However, like a number of other ventures entered into by BT in the early years post-privatisation, the Mitel purchase struggled to make a sound financial return. Meanwhile, the development of microelectronics and digital computing continued to lower entry barriers into the terminal equipment market and microwave did the same for the private long-distance calls market. More intense competition and a global strategy meant that over time BT did turn away from its traditional domestic supply base. This and management mistakes made within the telecommunications manufacturing businesses meant that by 1996 only one major UK-based telecommunications supplier survived – GPT – and this was 40 per cent owned by Siemens of Germany.[247] Weinstock's fears for British manufacturing during the passage of the Telecommunications Bill were confirmed.

In the months immediately before privatisation the unions within BT had changed tactics, from opposing the sale of the Corporation to endeavouring to protect their members from its harmful effects. Following privatisation, from time to time the unions did take industrial action to oppose changes in organisation of the business and working practices. In particular, at the beginning of 1987 there was a national strike of engineering and some clerical workers in BT. However, in the early years after privatisation the concerns of the unions were diminished by rising employment, some of it necessitated by work on restructuring, inter-connection and developing a consumer focus. Employment in BT rose from around 238,000 in 1984 to 248,000 in 1990, in spite of increased outsourcing. However, after the duopoly review the greater threat from competition necessitated more radical changes within BT, in terms of its processes and offerings to consumers. Numbers employed fell to around 149,000 by 1995.

Lower employment and increasing output was associated with higher labour productivity. Labour productivity had been growing under nationalisation, immediately before privatisation by around 6.9 per cent per annum. After privatisation the growth rate fell to between four per cent and six per cent annually, reflecting increased employment within BT, before climbing sharply to around 15 per cent a year in the early to mid-1990s as employment declined.[248] In other words, productivity growth in BT may have fallen or certainly not risen after privatisation until competition began to bite in the 1990s and BT responded with restructuring to reduce costs and preserve its business.[249] As one commentator has concluded on the effects of privatisation, the productivity gains from privatisation are "too often presented in black-and-white terms, as a sudden transformation from incompetent, Civil-Service-dominated management on one day to thrusting commercialism on the next. What is forgotten is the extent to which, in some cases, the period before and after privatization showed a high degree of continuity. This is particularly true of telecommunications . . ."[250]

The public expenditure effects of privatising BT are also far from straightforward. BT's EFL was negative in the years immediately before privatisation (1982/3 –£323 million; 1984/5 –£225 million and 1984/5 around –£350 million) due to better cost control and delays in investment. In addition, BT paid interest to the NLF on its debt of £300 million per annum in 1982/3 and 1983/4. By contrast, around £1,500 million was paid over annually to the Government in Corporation Tax, loan servicing and dividends on the Government's remaining holding of BT shares in the years immediately after privatisation. The sale proceeds also saved the Government from the interest on gilts that would otherwise have had to be issued to fund government borrowing.[251] The sale raised £3.86 billion or £2.6 billion allowing for the pension liability which effectively stayed with the Government. Overall, the Treasury estimated that in 1985/6 and 1986/7 the Exchequer received in dividends, payments on government loans and tax receipts £1,330 million compared with a likely counterfactual if BT had remained state-owned of £1,233 million, or a net gain, albeit relatively small, of almost £100 million.[252]

The Government had agreed at privatisation not to dispose of more of its BT shares before April 1988, except for those shares required under the bonus share scheme. It had also agreed to sell none of its holding of loan stock in BT before November 1989. In December 1991 the Government sold around a half of its remaining holding of BT's share capital, reducing its holding to 21.8 per cent, having previously obtained £92 million from the sale of BT loan stock in 1989/90.[253] The share sale was delayed after 1988 by the need for the Government to determine the duopoly review and because of Treasury concerns that there should not be another large Government share flotation during the privatisations of water, in 1989, and electricity, in 1990/1. A minor share sale had been contemplated in 1989 and rejected as too costly in relation to the probable receipts.[254] The decision to sell a tranche of BT shares ahead of the 1992 General Election was in part motivated by Labour's pledge at that time to renationalise the company by the cheap route of purchasing only two to three per cent of the shares. This would have taken the Government's holding to over 50 per cent. In July 1993 virtually all of the Government's remaining shares were sold. During the sale OFTEL became a very significant player with BT wishing to renegotiate aspects of its regulation with OFTEL to reassure the City as to its long-term future.

* * *

The privatisation of BT was driven by both practical and ideological objectives. The practical objective was concerned with the difficulty of funding BT's investment needs and stimulating effective competition in telecommunications while the Corporation remained state-owned. Privatising BT seemed to be the only way to finance the necessary investment in telecommunications while achieving the Government's macroeconomic objectives – at the same time it proved to be the case that BT self-financed its investments until the 1990s. Equally, the privatisation of BT was consistent with the Conservative Government's ideological objective of transferring state enterprises to the private sector, where they would be managed more effectively. Privatisation of BT was promised in the Conservatives' 1983 General Election Manifesto. However, it is an intriguing question as to whether, without the incorrectly forecast external funding imperative, the Government would have continued to pursue this most complex and controversial sale to a successful conclusion, given the problems faced.

BT was sold with much of its dominance in the market place as yet unaffected by competition and after 1984 Mercury struggled to develop a viable competing network. This along with the sale two years later of British Gas as more or less the sole gas provider, turned opinion within Government and outside against the further privatisation of monopoly state-owned enterprises without major restructuring into competing units. As Cecil Parkinson, briefly the Secretary of State responsible for the sale of BT in the summer and early autumn of 1983, concludes in his memoirs: "For my part, my experiences with BT made me determined, should I ever get another opportunity to privatize a state-owned monopoly, that I would not do so as a single regulated monopoly."[255] Parkinson played a leading role in the later privatisation of the electricity industry. The view that a possible mistake had been made in privatising BT and later gas without more radical surgery to promote competition would have a profound effect on government policy some years later, during the privatisations of electricity and the railways. This was notwithstanding that structurally separating telecommunications horizontally or vertically is arguably much more challenging than in gas or electricity supply because of the highly integrated nature of the system. And, as discussed earlier, any attempt to break up BT ahead of privatisation would have meant postponing the sale perhaps for a number of years. But in any event, by the end of the 1990s BT was facing extensive competition.

Finally, the sale of BT introduced many challenges, but the civil servants chiefly involved in the Department of Industry and then in the DTI provided enthusiastic support to Ministers throughout. There is no evidence of any obstruction of government policy on the future of telecommunications on the part of the government machinery. The opposition to privatisation came from outside Government, from the Labour Party, the trade unions, domestic equipment manufacturers and even some Conservative MPs and peers fearful of the effects on rural areas. The learning built up during the planning of the flotation of BT within Government and the City would be capitalised upon in later privatisations. There was also the continuity in privatisation planning which by 1984 was being provided by the Treasury. But once again, knowledge within Government was partially lost after November 1984 as individual civil servants within the DTI moved on to new tasks. Although briefings were provided by the DTI to civil servants in the Department of Energy, now planning the privatisation of British Gas, this disposal would be undertaken by a new set of officials, who embarked upon their own steep learning curves.

# 14

# PRIVATISING BRITISH GAS

## The decision to privatise and designing an appropriate regulatory regime

The gas industry in Britain developed from the nineteenth century as a mixture of private and later mainly municipal services. The industry was nationalised in 1948 as a collection of regional operations. Over 1,000 separate gas businesses were taken over and formed into 12 Area Boards, overseen by a Gas Council. In 1972 the Gas Act was passed vesting all of the component parts of the state-owned industry in the new British Gas Corporation (BGC) consisting of a headquarters and 12 regions, following the conversion of Britain's mains gas supply from "town gas" to "natural gas". The BGC was given a monopoly position in the British Gas market derived from legal powers stretching back over many years. Although there was some competition between gas companies for customers in the first half of the nineteenth century, an official inquiry in 1847 had concluded that "Competition between companies is never long lived." Nor did the inquiry find competition necessarily beneficial to consumers. By the end of the nineteenth century the gas industry had consolidated into geographic monopolies and "sliding scale" regulation had been imposed, in which the payment of higher dividends than the permitted amount to shareholders meant passing on the advantage in lower prices to consumers.[1]

From the earliest days of North Sea oil and gas development, BGC had been given first offer position on gas landed in the UK from the North Sea, with Ministers interceding only where there was disagreement over the price.[2] BGC was therefore effectively the only buyer of gas from Britain's gasfields; the only organisation allowed to transmit gas through pipelines onshore; and the only seller of gas to final customers. By the early 1980s BGC's gas supplies came mainly from two types of fields: the older Southern North Sea Basin gasfields and early associated gasfields and more costly newer oil-and gasfields mainly in other parts of the North Sea.[3] Through its purchasing monopoly BGC had a large amount of control over the price it paid for gas.[4] Also it tended to use average cost pricing to consumers instead of reflecting in prices newer and more costly supplies, despite earlier guidance to the nationalised industries to adopt long-run marginal cost pricing.

In return for its legal privileges BGC had a duty "to develop and maintain an efficient, co-ordinated and economical system of gas supply for Great Britain, and to satisfy, so far as it is economical to do so, all reasonable demands for gas in Great Britain". It had five main businesses: namely the purchase of gas from independent oil companies; the transmission and distribution of gas from the beachhead to consumers' meters; the exploration and production from offshore and onshore gasfields (BGC's business extended upstream to onshore and offshore oil and gas exploration and production); retailing of gas appliances through showrooms (which also handled servicing arrangements and bill paying); and the installation and servicing of appliances. BGC's gas supply business produced around 90 per cent of the Corporation's total revenues. Some 60 per cent accrued from gas sales to "tariff" customers (i.e. domestic and small commercial/industrial consumers) and the remaining 30 per cent from gas sales under contracts to larger commercial and industrial consumers.[5] By 1985 BGC accounted for just over 32 per cent of the UK's energy market. This compares with as little as six per cent in 1965. The sharp growth reflected increased gas usage associated with the introduction of natural gas, a relative rise in electricity and oil prices and more efficient and marketable gas appliances.

BGC was required to supply all customers within 25 yards of a main who did not consume more than 25,000 therms a year (in practice all domestic and smaller business customers).[6] In the year to 31 March 1985, the Corporation distributed gas to over 16 million domestic customers or 78 per cent of households in Britain. Its gas to larger industrial and commercial consumers was provided using either "firm contracts", where the Corporation guaranteed continuous supply, or "interruptible contracts", where supply could be interrupted during periods of peak demand at BGC's discretion for up to 90 days a year.[7] These customers generally had back-up fuel supplies of oil or coal. The remainder of revenues came from the sale of gas burning appliances (four per cent) and installation and contracting services (three per cent). The sale of oil and condensates to third parties earned revenues of £5.5 million (less than 0.1 per cent of revenues). Although BGC faced competition from other fuels, gas was increasingly the first choice fuel for domestic and industrial use aided by prices set below long-run marginal cost. In the 1970s, under pressure from Government to hold down prices, domestic customers were effectively cross-subsidised by industrial and commercial users. Also, the Government concluded that natural gas was a premium fuel which should be conserved. This ruled out its use in power stations. Table 14.1 provides fuller details of the change in gas sales per sector from the mid-1970s. Figure 14.1 illustrates the strong growth in the proportion of the UK energy market accounted for by gas.

By 1984 the Corporation employed around 99,000 workers and operated 144,200 miles of gas mains, making it one of the world's largest integrated gas operations. In 1984/5 the total turnover of BGC amounted to £6.9 billion, generating an operating profit before interest and tax of £651 million on the current cost accounting (CCA) basis preferred by the management or £930 million on an historic cost (HCA) basis. BGC remained profitable in spite of periodic ministerial intervention in pricing and the purchasing of gas to protect national energy security. For example, in February 1985 the Government vetoed the Sleipner contract negotiated by BGC to obtain gas from a Norwegian field so as to favour supplies from the UK Continental Shelf (UKCS).[8] Reflecting its profitability, BGC had paid off loans so that by the early 1980s it was almost debt free. The Corporation had a negative EFL in 1980/1 of £400 million and £87 million in 1982/3.[9] Whereas Treasury concern about the potential costs to the Exchequer of funding new investment in telecommunications was a motivation in the privatisation of BT, in the case of BGC, which had already completed the massive conversion of the country to natural gas, future investment needs were much less of a consideration.

## Early measures

At the time of the May 1979 General Election, the Conservatives were committed only to consideration of "some modification" in the arrangements relating to the Government–owned

*Table 14.1* Gas sales by sector 1975–85

|  | Domestic sector | | Commercial sector | | Industrial sector | |
|---|---|---|---|---|---|---|
|  | Volume billion therms | Market share (%) | Volume billion therms | Market share (%) | Volume billion therms | Market share (%) |
| 1975 | 5.9 | 40.1 | 1.3 | 18.8 | 5.5 | 25.0 |
| 1976 | 6.2 | 42.6 | 1.5 | 23.2 | 6.1 | 26.8 |
| 1977 | 6.6 | 43.8 | 1.6 | 23.0 | 6.3 | 27.8 |
| 1978 | 7.3 | 47.2 | 1.7 | 25.1 | 6.4 | 28.4 |
| 1979 | 8.2 | 49.7 | 2.0 | 25.0 | 6.6 | 28.4 |
| 1980 | 8.4 | 53.2 | 2.1 | 28.0 | 6.3 | 33.0 |
| 1981 | 8.8 | 55.6 | 2.1 | 28.4 | 6.0 | 33.1 |
| 1982 | 8.7 | 55.8 | 2.2 | 29.7 | 6.0 | 34.5 |
| 1983 | 8.9 | 57.4 | 2.3 | 31.1 | 6.0 | 35.5 |
| 1984 | 8.9 | 59.3 | 2.3 | 30.7 | 6.2 | 37.6 |
| 1985 | 9.7 | 58.1 | 2.6 | 33.3 | 6.4 | 38.1 |
| *Growth % pa* | *5.1* | – | *7.2* | – | *1.4* | – |

Source: Department of Energy.

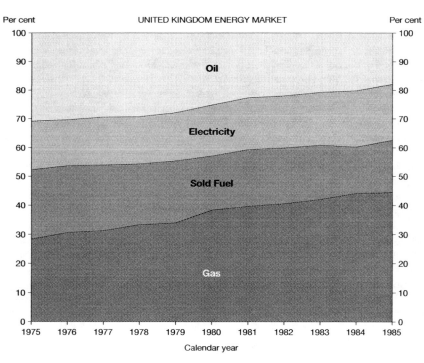

*Figure 14.1* Changes in the UK energy market 1975–85
*Source*: Department of Energy Digests of UK Energy Statistics.

energy sector.[10] Following the May 1979 General Election, policy towards the gas industry including the BGC's monopoly rights to purchase gas in the North Sea was reviewed under the chairmanship of Norman Lamont. In December 1979 the Official Committee on Nationalised Industry Policy in the Treasury reported that BGC was a profitable company making a major contribution to the PSBR and that "In developing any proposals for major structural changes in the industry it would be necessary to move very carefully so as to avoid risking the dissipation of these advantages."[11] The Government's first priority was to remove the underpricing of domestic gas that had occurred under the previous Labour Government, in part the result of prices and incomes policies. The higher prices would reflect higher energy prices in world markets and reduce the overuse of gas that occurred due to gas prices remaining low. Importantly, the higher prices would also permit the setting of a bigger negative EFL for BGC at a time when the Government was struggling to achieve its PSBR targets.

In the autumn of 1979 the Secretary of State for Energy, David Howell, recommended that domestic gas prices should increase in real terms by an average of ten per cent a year for the following three years or so.[12] The Government did not have the legal power to require a nationalised industry to impose a particular level of charges, but Howell intended to achieve the result through discussion with the BGC Board and by establishing a financial target for the Corporation that necessitated its agreement to the rise. Some Ministers were fearful that higher gas prices might increase inflation and provoke a negative public reaction. Nevertheless, on 25 October 1979 the Cabinet agreed to raise gas prices the following April in line with inflation followed by a further ten per cent increase in the autumn.[13] The Chancellor of the Exchequer welcomed the additional funding that consequently could be creamed off from the BGC.[14] BGC was very irritated, felt that the increase was unnecessary and publicly blamed the Government for the price rise. Relations between the new Government and BGC got off to a bad start.

This move to raise gas prices was followed in February 1980 by agreement in E Committee to introduce a new Gas Levy on BGC's purchases of North Sea gas. The Levy was introduced in 1981. The aim was to capture the rent accruing to the BGC from purchasing gas under long-term contracts exempt from Petroleum Revenue Tax (PRT) and signed before the recent sharp rise in fuel prices.[15] In the early months of the new Government BGC was seen as a useful "cash cow"; but the possibility of privatising the entire Corporation, as against disposing of a few of its assets, did not surface as a serious proposition. There was concern in the Department of Energy that a privately-owned BGC with its privileged buyer position for gas supplies would be unacceptable to both the oil industry which produced much of the gas as a by-product, and Parliament.[16] One possible solution to BGC's monopoly position would be to promote competition in supplies by allowing imports and exports of gas without regulation. But this went against the Department of Energy's policy of wishing to maintain security of supplies in the national interest.[17]

Howell and some ministerial colleagues, notably the Financial Secretary Nigel Lawson, were keen to see more competition introduced into domestic gas supplies and Lawson would replace Howell as Energy Secretary in the Cabinet reshuffle of September 1981. A memorandum to E Committee from Howell in July 1981 argued that competition would lead to more "internal efficiency and the proper allocation of resources".[18] In particular, the Secretary of State flagged the misallocation of resources caused by BGC pricing gas below long-run marginal cost. This had led to a buoyant demand in the domestic sector, "whilst many industrial companies have over the past few years been denied supplies". Moreover,

BGC's activities in gas exploration and production had discouraged private sector activity with some licensees "unwilling to proceed with development of their discoveries". The same argument applied to gas manufacturing (e.g. the production of synthetic natural gas) and to the importing of liquefied natural gas. The Secretary of State's proposals were intended to produce an improvement in the efficiency of BGC, an increase in gas exploration and production, and a better deal for the industrial gas customer.

Howell's proposals involved removing BGC's privilege of having the first option on the purchase of gas landed from the UKCS "and to break their monopoly over sales to industrial consumers and possibly larger commercial consumers". The aim was to free manufacturing industry to purchase gas without BGC acting as a necessary intermediary. BGC would also be expected to dispose of its offshore oil assets. Under powers derived from the 1972 Gas Act, the Secretary of State could direct BGC to cease activities and dispose of assets, but only if he was satisfied that he would not thereby impede the proper discharge of the Corporation's duties. Moreover, even if he felt able to proceed with a Directive, this would not require BGC to pass the proceeds from the asset sales to the Government.[19] It was therefore important to obtain new legal powers to arrange that particular assets were transferred to a subsidiary company of the Corporation, in which shares could later be offered to the public, and to claw back the proceeds of sale to the Exchequer. However, Howell was at pains to stress that the monopoly of supply to non-industrial, including domestic, users should be preserved, "because in this case the existence of a monopoly supplier confers genuine advantages (security of supply, safety, lower costs from economies of scale and avoidance of duplicate facilities)". Also, there was no intention of removing the need to obtain the Secretary of State's consent for the use of gas for non-fuel industrial purposes, "as the Government will need to satisfy itself that this finite national resource is not used wastefully".[20]

The proposals were therefore cautious and modest. They also raised a series of problems that would need to be addressed. The requirement that all gas from the UKCS had to be landed in the UK was already vulnerable to attack as incompatible with the terms of the Treaty of Rome and the requirement for free trade amongst European Community Member States. Ending BGC's monopoly of gas purchases would not in itself directly affect the issue. However, within the Department of Energy there was concern that some private sector licensees might take the opportunity to seek approval to export gas, leading to challenges under the Treaty. Also, there was the issue of encouraging competing gas suppliers to BGC when the Corporation owned the gas transmission and distribution system. How would the independent suppliers get their gas to the customer? Howell intended "that the private sector should have greater freedom under the new regime to build its own onshore pipelines", but recognised that in practice this would usually be uneconomic. To promote effective competition, the new suppliers would need access to BGC's network.

Under Howell's proposals an obligation would be imposed on BGC not to refuse unreasonably to carry private sector gas. This still left open the prospect of BGC seeing off the competition by either charging high prices for gas transmission or claiming that it had insufficient capacity at any given time to transport the additional gas supplies. To address these possibilities, Howell recognised that a form of regulation would be needed. Within the Department of Energy the idea of an independent regulatory agency was briefly considered but rejected on the grounds that it was difficult or impossible to forecast the amount of regulatory work that would be needed. Howell recommended that the new regulatory powers he envisaged should be vested in the Department, at least initially. They might later be transferred to a separate agency if the volume of work justified the move.[21]

A Bill to enact Howell's proposals was agreed in E Committee. However, its introduction into Parliament was delayed by the need to draft the various clauses. Also, BGC was unco-operative. In particular, BGC's Chairman, Sir Denis Rooke, refused to sanction the disposal of the Corporation's production and exploration assets, on the grounds that to do so "would seriously impair the performance of the Corporation's statutory duties and would not be in its commercial interests". This has been discussed in detail in chapter 4 above. In July the Cabinet urged Howell to speed up the drafting of the Bill. But on 24 September it conceded that it was unlikely that the legislation would now be ready for introduction into Parliament until later in the 1981–82 session.[22]

The Bill was published on 17 December 1981 and included proposals to address BGC's monopoly position and allow the sale of subsidiary businesses. It reduced the Corporation's monopoly of gas supplies by allowing independent producers of gas to sell directly to large gas customers without first offering the gas to BGC. There would be freedom to supply customers consuming more than 25,000 therms a year, subject to meeting certain safety requirements. BGC retained its monopoly over supply to those consuming below 25,000 therms, namely domestic users and businesses with lower demands for gas. Also, under the Bill BGC was required to allow new gas suppliers to use its pipelines. In effect, BGC was required to take on a "common carrier" function, carrying competitors' gas supplies down its transmission and distribution system. If a supplier and the Corporation were unable to agree terms for transporting the gas, there could be an appeal to the Secretary of State, who then had the power to determine the carriage charge. Sir Denis Rooke particularly objected to this provision, arguing that as BGC had built the pipelines it was unreasonable to allow them to be used by competitors.

The resulting Oil and Gas (Enterprise) Act was passed in 1982 and permitted competition in larger gas supplies for the first time. But it proved to have a negligible effect on BGC's control of the country's gas supplies.[23] Large gas users needed assurance that there would be back-up supplies in the event of a gasfield shutting down for maintenance and repair, something smaller gas producers could not necessarily give. Potential independent producers of gas faced much more difficulty than BGC in matching demand for gas with the supply available. In other words, BGC's access to large gas resources and adequate back-up supplies left it at a considerable advantage in negotiations with large gas consumers for industrial contracts. Over time this might change if BGC was restricted in terms of new exploration activities (in the 8th round of North Sea licensing in 1982/3 its applications were confined to areas of proven gas prospectivity). But in the short term the effect would be slight because BGC had already contracted for virtually all of the gas from fields currently in production within the UKCS.

## The gas showrooms: a privatisation failure

One potential asset sale under the 1982 Act proved especially controversial. This related to the forced sale of BGC's gas showrooms. BGC accounted for over 90 per cent of retail sales of gas cookers, fires and water heaters through 800 or so showrooms situated in most of Britain's towns and cities. Also, some 60 per cent of BGC's customers (9 million people), many being of low income or pensioners, paid their gas bills through the showrooms.[24] At the time, discount appliance retailers were making fast inroads into domestic electric equipment retailing. The Government decided that a similar development in the supply of gas appliances would be assisted by hiving off BGC's retail outlets to the private sector.

The Government's plans for gas appliance retailing stemmed from one of the first Monopolies and Mergers Commission (MMC) inquiries to report adversely on a nationalised industry following the Competition Act 1980, which extended the MMC's scope to the nationalised industries. In a report published in July 1980, the MMC concluded that BGC's domination of the gas appliance retail market acted against the public interest. The Commission alleged that BGC was able to demand advantageous terms from suppliers and subsidised appliance sales from profits made from its gas supply business. Moreover, there was evidence that the manufacturers' close relationship with BGC had reduced the competitive pressure on them to increase their efficiency. The MMC put forward two preferred remedies: ending retailing by BGC or allowing continued retailing but with controls to prevent anti-competitive cross-subsidies from BGC's other businesses.[25]

Sally Oppenheim, responsible for competition and consumer affairs at the Department of Trade, responded to the report by obtaining the agreement of her Ministerial colleagues to a disposal of the showrooms, starting in 1983. However, it was clear immediately that the measure would be fiercely resisted by the BGC Board and the gas unions. Some Conservative backbenchers were also far from happy, fearing a hostile public reaction to the possible loss of the facility to pay gas bills through the showrooms. As Lawson comments in his memoirs: "Few of us realized what a storm would be unleashed over what could scarcely be called one of the commanding heights of the economy ... The Government's opponents were remarkably successful in portraying the privatization of the state-owned chain of shops ... as an ideologically inspired attack on the British way of life. The heart of every community, it seemed, was neither the church nor the pub, but the local gas showroom."[26]

Two of the major unions in the gas industry, NALGO (the National and Local Government Officers Association) for white collar staff and the GMBATU (the General and Municipal Boilermakers and Allied Trade Union) for blue collar workers mounted a particularly effective campaign against the sale, predicting showroom closures and job losses. The threat was not unfounded. Howell privately estimated that "at least 250" gas showrooms were at risk of closure. However, another part of the unions' campaign warning of a threat to public safety was more speculative although effectively endorsed by BGC. The gas unions supported by the TUC and the Labour Party lobbied local authorities, and a number of Labour councils responded with letters to MPs in which job losses and safety concerns loomed large. An umbrella organisation for the gas industry unions, called GUARD, was set up to co-ordinate the opposition and a one day strike was held in July 1981. This would prove to be the only national strike successfully called by the gas unions against privatisation in the gas industry. Later strike ballots would fail to obtain the required level of support. The unions were joined in their lobbying by the National Gas Consumers' Council, the Consumers' Association and the National Consumer Council, who all came out against the sale. There was also apprehension amongst domestic manufacturers of gas appliances. They feared that private retailers might source from overseas. The Secretary of State for Industry, Sir Keith Joseph, commented to the PM that the manufacturers were "probably excessively influenced by their present cosy relationship with BGC". But he did concede that following the opening of the market to competition, "there would almost certainly be some increase in import penetration, though this could perhaps be reduced by specifying appropriate technical standards."[27]

The future of the gas showrooms was discussed in E(DL) Sub-Committee on 10 June 1981. Three proposals were tabled. The first required BGC to withdraw from gas retailing over five years with a disposal of a half of its showrooms within two years, a quarter in the following year, and the remaining quarter in the final two years. The second would entail the hiving off of the Corporation's retail activities into a separate Companies Act subsidiary, to be sold to the private sector but only once it had developed into a viable business. The third involved BGC disposing of 75 per cent of its showrooms over five years with the remaining 25 per cent held in a new BGC subsidiary, which would be privatised as soon as possible. Howell favoured the second option believing that this would produce the least opposition from the BGC Board and the gas unions. It conveniently postponed having to reach a definite decision on privatisation until a later date. However, while option 3 was effectively rejected in E(DL), there was no clear agreement on either options 1 or 2. During the meeting a number of Ministers supported in principle BGC's exit from the retail market, but voiced concern about the strength of union opposition and the reaction of public opinion, especially given the unions' assertions on public safety. All domestic appliances sold by BGC were covered by BSI standards and by the strict standards of BGC's own Approval Division. Neither standard was mandatory and with the transfer of some or all gas appliance retailing to the private sector, there was a perceived risk of some unapproved appliances reaching the market. It was agreed that whatever option was finally selected, it would be necessary to strengthen the arrangements for ensuring that private suppliers observed safety standards. This was necessary in its own right and to reduce the force of the unions' arguments.[28]

Discussions were renewed on 23 June, this time in E Committee. Howell again advocated option 2.[29] He stressed that both manufacturers and consumers were opposed to the Corporation withdrawing from the market and that legislation would be needed to address public fears about safety standards. This would take time to arrange.[30] Also, he was opposed to forcing through a measure in the face of management opposition. However, some Ministers considered this option to be too much of a concession to the unions and BGC. Sally Oppenheim recommended that the Corporation be required to withdraw from gas retailing preferably within three years, but failing that over a period of five years. In her opinion, "The Government could not defend, particularly to its own supporters, any less robust response to the MMC's highly critical report." She argued that the case against disposal, notably safety concerns and the handling of gas bill queries in showrooms, was exaggerated and reminded the Committee that BGC already successfully sub-contracted 92 per cent of its work on central heating installation to registered private sector firms.

In discussion the Committee including the PM sided with Oppenheim. It also criticised the BGC for coming close to using public money for political purposes by campaigning against the sale of the showrooms. To address the concerns of domestic manufacturers, it was suggested that "technical standards could be introduced which, though in harmony with European Community requirements, gave British manufacturers the best possible chance of competing successfully with foreign imports of gas appliances."[31]

The Government's decision in favour of a sale of the gas showrooms was announced on 8 July 1981. Ministers agreed that the necessary powers to dispose of them should be included in the Oil and Gas (Enterprise) Bill, but drafting the necessary clauses, especially to address the concerns about public safety, proved time consuming.[32] To assuage public concern and counter the BGC and trade union campaign, the Government gave a commitment that gas safety standards would be maintained. Although the new Secretary of State for Energy, Nigel Lawson, was "determined to speed up rather than slow down the pace of privatization", in the face of opposition from the BGC Board, the trade unions and the Labour Party, and the worries of some Conservative backbenchers, the proposal continued to face difficulties.[33]

In May 1982 the Government suffered a defeat in the House of Lords during the Committee Stage of the Bill on an amendment that had the effect of making the disposal of any BGC assets, including the gas showrooms, subject to challenge in the courts.[34]

It became increasingly obvious to Ministers that the Government would be unable to begin the disposal of the gas showrooms ahead of the next general election, expected some time in 1983. The Government's position became even more tenuous when BGC submitted a counter proposal to change its gas appliance retailing business to meet the criticisms in the MMC's report without the need for an outright sale. Under the plan the retailing business would be made a separate and clearly identifiable subsidiary, both managerially and financially. There would be separate audited accounts and those showrooms that under the revised accounting procedures were shown to be uneconomic would be closed to avoid unfair competition with private sector retailers. In addition, BGC offered to make its wholesaling service, covering appliances and spare parts, including the Corporation's installation and contracting service, available to the private sector on comparable terms to those available to its own appliance retailing business. BGC would also seek to encourage competition in appliance purchasing and manufacturing by "undertaking not to indulge in any unfair competitive practices".

On 10 February 1983 E Committee agreed to shelve the idea of a forced sale of the showrooms. Lawson advised that the BGC's proposals should be accepted as an interim measure until after a general election. This was an embarrassing climb down for the Government and one of only a small number of occasions in the 1980s when Government failed to push a privatisation through and had to go back to the drawing board. Lawson feared that accepting the BGC plan "would be regarded as a BGC/union victory over the Government and would undermine our plans to increase BGC's efficiency and to reduce their monopoly in other areas".[35] Similarly, the Secretary of State for Trade, Lord Cockfield, expressed concern that acceptance of the proposals, even as an interim measure, "would represent a reversal of previously announced Government policy". It was agreed in E Committee that "nothing should be said or done which might prejudice the ability of the Government to move towards the privatisation of BGC's appliance retailing, wholesaling, and installation business in the next Parliament."[36] However, there seemed little prospect of resurrecting a disposal under the 1982 Act.

## The decision to privatise British Gas

The Government's bruising in the face of the BGC and union campaign against the disposal of the gas showrooms and the failure of the 1982 legislation to lead to an immediate interest amongst independent gas supply companies in competing against BGC led to new thinking. A report from the Treasury in August 1982 on progress in introducing private capital into the public sector had commented that, given that the Department of Energy's plans to sell BGC's onshore and offshore oil interests and dispose of the appliance retailing business had created so much opposition from the Corporation's Chairman, the Department of Energy believed "there is nothing to be gained from an effort to find ways of involving private finance in the main business of gas supply."[37] However, the Conservatives' 1983 General Election Manifesto was less timid and carried a pledge to seek the "means of increasing competition in, and attracting private capital into, the gas and electricity industries".[38] Lawson claims that he secured the PM's agreement to include the commitment.[39]

Prior to the May 1983 General Election a committee of officials from the Department of Energy and the Treasury had met to discuss the future of British Gas, but had not got very far. Following the Conservatives' landslide result, during the summer the Treasury's Public Enterprises Analytical Unit explored possible ways of introducing private capital into gas supply by extending the powers introduced in the Oil and Gas (Enterprise) Act. Consideration was given to imposing an obligation on the BGC to buy and sell gas from any supplier using a Bulk Supply Tariff scheme, similar to the one operating in the electricity sector.[40] Independent gas producers would have the right to compete for large gas consumers by selling gas into the BGC pipeline grid at scheduled prices. However, no serious consideration was given to introducing competing supplies to domestic consumers. This was still considered economically infeasible. Individual domestic customers bought relatively small amounts of gas that, it was felt, would not produce a revenue sufficient to offset the costs of introducing competing supplies.[41]

In October 1983 Walker, who had taken over as Secretary of State for Energy after the election, was invited by E(A) Committee to put forward options for the future of the gas and electricity industries. By now the privatisation of British Telecom (BT) was at an advanced stage of planning and the possibility of selling a state monopoly to the private sector seemed less absurd than it had seemed one or two years earlier. It was agreed that the privatisation of both BGC and the electricity industry was worth exploring, but that legislation for both could not be squeezed into the current Parliament. Also, it was likely that the plans for gas would be ready before those for electricity. However, from the outset, in the Department of Energy's Gas Division there was recognition that significant questions relating to the industrial structure and monopoly regulation would need to be addressed before BGC could be privatised.

Staff from the Gas Division explored the scope for introducing private capital into the Corporation during the autumn of 1983. But by November no definite decision had been reached on whether the potential difficulties could be overcome.[42] The Treasury was particularly sceptical about the advantages of selling BGC as an unrestructured monopoly. Nigel Lawson, now Chancellor of the Exchequer, canvassed the break-up of the BGC into separate regional companies so that benchmarking of performance could occur or into separate gas distribution and retailing businesses. However, Walker was sceptical of the advantages of such major restructuring and believed that splitting the Corporation into regional companies would do little to produce effective benchmarking of performance given varying cost structures in the different regions. It would be difficult to make useful comparisons of performance across companies which served different geographical areas.[43] Over the following months Walker would side with the BGC's vociferous Chairman, Sir Denis Rooke, in favouring the retention of a large integrated gas company in Britain with supposedly world-beating qualities. Eventually, after a number of Ministerial discussions that made little progress, Lawson agreed to the planning of the privatisation of BGC as one unit, provided that Walker proceeded without further delay.[44] The final decision to sell BGC without major restructuring was taken at a meeting between the PM, Peter Walker, Nigel Lawson and John Moore on Tuesday 26 March 1985. In her memoirs, Margaret Thatcher explains the decision not to break up BGC at privatisation in the following terms: "there were a number of considerations which argued against fundamentally restructuring or breaking up of the business. The most important of these, curiously enough, was lack of parliamentary time." She acknowledges that her Energy Secretary and the BGC "were determined to privatize BGC as a whole and their full co-operation was essential if it were to be achieved as I wanted during our second term. There was much to be said for using the model of British Telecom rather than trying to come up with a fundamentally different one under these conditions".[45]

Within the Treasury the decision to agree to a sale without a restructuring of BGC had been made reluctantly. Serious reservations remained about privatising without more effort to promote competition and these reservations continued right up to the time of the sale, in November 1986.[46] It is clear that Treasury Ministers would have liked to have seen more competition built into the privatisation planning. By contrast, Walker's position remained throughout that BGC could not be won over to the idea and that in any case there would be competition for gas from other fuels. However, a number of Ministers remained dissatisfied. For example, Nicholas Ridley, Secretary of State for Transport, was concerned that BGC might price discriminate after privatisation and cross-subsidise any competitive parts of its business from its monopoly activities. As late as November 1985 he wrote to the PM warning that, "the dangers of the abuse of the gas supply monopoly are not figments dreamed up by opponents of privatisation in principle – they are events which we must expect to happen unless the appointed watchdog has the power to initiate action to prevent them."[47] But by this time the planning of the privatisation of BGC was well underway and Walker responded, "We are well past the point where breaking up BGC into many separate companies is an option." In his view Ridley's proposal "would risk precipitating a showdown with the unions. This is precisely what our opponents would like to see".[48] Instead, regulation with separate accounting for the different businesses of the Corporation would have to suffice to protect the customer from monopoly abuse.[49]

The disposal of BT was smoothed by having a Chairman of the Corporation, Sir George Jefferson, who favoured privatisation. Rooke, a long time British Gas man, and a number of others on the BGC Board, were opposed or lukewarm to the idea. The privatisation of BGC and the introduction of a new regulatory regime would take place in the face of scepticism or at best indifference from Rooke and the BGC Board.[50] Rooke was particularly opposed to conceding much on competition, believing that BGC had become a world-leading gas supplier as a monopoly state enterprise. The Treasury would complain about "the lack of commitment to privatisation at senior levels within BGC. This leads them to take unrealistic positions and to try and treat everything as a grudging negotiation".[51] Walker comments on an early meeting with Rooke on the possible privatisation of BGC:

"I then called in Sir Denis Rooke, the Gas Board chairman, and told him that I understood his opposition to privatization, but I wanted it to go ahead. I could either do it with guess-work from the outside or he could give me, from the inside, all the information I wanted. If he did co-operate, my decision was likely to be of a better quality than if he did not. He was persuaded that he would prefer me to know all the facts and details . . . Sir Denis Rooke realized that though British Gas had worked well and been profitable as a nationalized enterprise, privatization would mean an end to interference and long meetings in Whitehall. He was going to be able to make his own decisions and fix his own capital investment programme. From being genuinely opposed to privatization, he and the top managers, with one or two exceptions, changed their attitude and collaborated enthusiastically."

This greatly overstates Rooke's conversion. In public Rooke adopted the position that ownership was a political matter and that he could work under any form of ownership the Government chose. In private he continued to question the need for privatisation.[52]

There was also another important difference to the privatisation of BT. Ministers in charge of the Department of Industry (later the DTI) responsible for privatising BT, Sir Keith Joseph followed by Patrick Jenkin, were keen supporters of privatisation. By contrast, Peter Walker at Energy was on the so-called "wet" wing of the Conservative Party. Walker was not opposed to privatisation (although a number of his Ministerial colleagues and the PM suspected that his heart might not be entirely in it), but took the view that the sale of BGC needed very careful planning and should not be rushed, a view more widely held in his Department.[53] He also sympathised with Rooke's view that the country benefited from having a large, world-beating, gas enterprise, in the shape of the BGC. Walker was a prominent Minister in the 1970–74 Heath Government, which on industrial restructuring had taken a "corporatist" or "big business" stance. But while he and Margaret Thatcher had very different ideological positions on many issues and a difficult personal relationship, the PM was of the view that she could not afford to lose Walker to the back benches. During the privatisation of BGC, whenever the PM interceded in arguments between Walker and Treasury Ministers over the terms of the sale, she would usually side with Walker. Walker won most of the arguments in Cabinet and Cabinet Committee because the PM feared that he might choose to resign rather than lose the argument. Another interpretation is that Thatcher feared less Walker's resignation than that of Sir Denis Rooke, with whom she was on bad personal terms. By keeping Walker on board, the risk of Rooke resigning were diminished. Walker and Rooke had a good relationship. If Rooke had resigned the privatisation of BGC might well have been seriously disrupted. Probably she feared both resignations. It is not unfair to say that Walker exploited this power and that the failure to produce effective competition at privatisation resulted from the PM's reluctance to confront him. In turn, Walker was reluctant to confront Sir Denis Rooke. Treasury officials complained about "an unwillingness on Mr Walker's part to take on Rooke on a series of difficult and complex issues".[54]

### Imports, exports, oil production and the miners' strike

In addition to the difficulty within Government in obtaining unanimity about the best strategy for privatising the gas industry to benefit customers, there was concern in the Department of Energy about the possible effects on the security of the country's energy supplies. The Department considered that it had a primary duty to ensure adequate fuel supplies and that privatisation could be expected to lead to a decline in the Government's influence over gas purchasing and supply. The Department harboured particular concerns about the implications of privatisation for gas imports and exports.[55] The Government's powers to control imports of gas derived from the Petroleum and Submarine Pipelines Act 1975, which required authorisations from the Secretary of State for the development of new fields and the construction and use of pipelines on the UKCS. Also, it had been the practice for the BGC to consult the Government over new gas sourcing. Consideration was given to whether Government should take formal powers to approve major gas supply contracts after privatisation. Some officials felt that the Government should retain control over gas supply sourcing, especially from politically sensitive areas such as Russia and the Middle East (which supplied liquid natural gas, LNG). Meanwhile, others in the Department of Energy were keen to see BGC have freedom to source as it wished once privatised, seeing this as a logical outcome of freeing BGC from state ownership.[56]

There was recognition within Government that the present controls over gas imports might need to change with privatisation.[57] BGC's privileged purchasing rights for all gas landed in the UK had been compromised by the 1982 Oil and Gas (Enterprise) Act, which permitted alternative gas suppliers. But in practice BGC retained an almost totally dominant position. In discussion in E(A) in June and July 1985 it was suggested that if gas exports and imports were not regulated, the need for any supervision of BGC's gas supply contracts would be much reduced. At the same time, there was concern that if BGC was able to import gas freely, it might then be in a position to dictate low prices to UKCS gas suppliers and this could prejudice the future development of the UKCS and the tax revenues arising. Also, if UKCS licensees were free to export gas, BGC and therefore UK consumers could face much higher gas prices, which in turn might damage public support for privatisation. There was also concern that potential investors in BGC might judge BGC's operating environment to be more risky after the removal of import and export controls.[58] The Secretary of State for Energy was invited to address these concerns and bring proposals on gas exports and imports to E(A) Sub-Committee in the autumn.[59]

The issue of gas imports was the focus of an E(A) meeting on 9 December 1985. Walker explained that contracts were already in place assuring sufficient gas supplies to the UK and continental Europe until well into the 1990s.[60] However, some new imports were likely to be needed by the UK before the turn of the century. In his view there was a risk that a privatised BGC might seek to revive the Sleipner project to source gas from the Norwegian oilfields, which he had recently vetoed, or make another import deal, the effect of which might also be to discourage development of the UKCS. Walker went on to argue that the best outcome would be one in which BGC purchased all the available UKCS gas and relied on imports only to the extent that UKCS supplies fell short of demand. The Sub-Committee agreed that the Secretary of State should secure an appropriate assurance from BGC that after privatisation it would still consult the Government before proceeding with any major gas import deal.

On the subject of gas exports, Walker appears to have been initially predisposed towards allowing exports once BGC was privatised, but became more hesitant. He worried that if there were unrestricted exports multinational companies who were UKCS licensees would prefer to send their gas to the continental utilities in search of higher revenues, leading to higher gas prices for UK customers. By contrast, John Moore, Financial Secretary to the Treasury and the nearest the Government came to having a Minister for Privatisation, strongly favoured extending the competitive market in gas supply by permitting gas exports. He dismissed the notion that security of supply would be put at risk and BGC damaged, concluding "There is no reason to believe that BGC will not be able to buy all the gas it needs."[61]

In discussion in E(A) the issue was raised as to whether the imposition of quantitative restrictions on imports and exports of gas could be sustained under the Treaty of Rome and it was agreed that there would be a need to clarify that contracts to purchase North Sea gas were not vulnerable under EC law after BGC was privatised. Overall, there was some support for the introduction of a more liberalised gas export regime in E(A) Sub-Committee.[62] However, the PM seems to have been nervous about putting at possible risk the nation's energy supplies, something that always weighed heavily with her in debate on the future of the Government's oil and gas interests.[63] Walker suggested a possible solution, "where the

Government held the ring between the privatised BGC and UKCS gas suppliers, keeping open the options of permitting individual gas imports and exports on their merits". But with no final decision made in E(A), it was agreed that the Secretary of State should avoid saying anything during the pending second reading of the Gas Bill on gas trading which might prejudice the Government's further consideration of the issue. We return to the issue of gas imports and exports later in the chapter.

Another sensitive matter was BGC's activities in oil exploration and production. By the autumn of 1983, following forced divestments, the Corporation had been left with only a few small onshore oil interests and supplied only six per cent of its own gas needs.[64] The Corporation was keen to be allowed to re-enter oil and gas exploration and production if privatisation occurred and the Department of Energy's financial adviser on the BGC sale, N. M. Rothschild & Sons (Rothschilds), supported the ambition.[65] Rothschilds confirmed that a sale of BGC would be assisted by re-entry into oil and gas exploration. It would help in projecting the BGC to investors as a dynamic company rather than a dull utility.[66] The ability to re-enter oil and gas exploration and production was also seen as a "carrot" to the BGC Board and its Chairman to support the idea of privatisation and the Treasury advised that it was not opposed, provided that the Corporation was sold.[67]

In December 1983 Walker planned to put papers to E(A) Sub-committee early the following February setting out his views on the future of the gas and electricity industries. However, by now it was clear that the privatisation of electricity posed too many major problems to be undertaken in the current Parliament, including sorting out the future of the nuclear power stations and the relationship between the coal and electricity industries. Privatising gas would be simpler. Walker intended that a gas privatisation Bill should be included in the 1984–85 Parliamentary session "with a view to beginning a sale in, say, the early part of 1986". However, to achieve privatisation in the current Parliament Walker warned that "the timing is quite tight."

The Secretary of State's proposals on privatisation were welcomed within No. 10 by John Redwood who agreed that proposing a sale of gas before coal and electricity made sense because "the problems are less intractable".[68] However, he encouraged the PM to impress on Walker that it was vital to introduce as much competition as possible into the gas industry.[69] Similarly, John Moore emphasised the importance of privatising gas "to bring as much competition into the industry as possible and to enable gas prices to be determined in the market place".[70] But the tightness of the timetable now played into the hands of Walker and Rooke who still preferred modest reform.[71]

The planning for the privatisation had to be undertaken discreetly at first so as not to upset the unions and management. So sensitive did Walker believe the subject to be that as late as early 1985 he was reluctant to see gas privatisation discussed in open session within the Cabinet.[72] Hence, it was particularly embarrassing to him when in January of that year the *Financial Times* and *The Daily Telegraph* published reports claiming that the Government had committed itself to selling off state assets worth £10 billion over the following five years, but that the distribution networks for gas and electricity were seen as natural monopolies that should remain in the public sector. The reports also claimed that there had been agreement that BGC should not be sold off as one block in its present form.[73] The fact that both reports were inaccurate compounded the Secretary of State's discomfort. Rooke and the gas unions could be expected to react angrily to suggestion that the Government was planning a break-up of the Corporation. Walker sent an irate note to the PM demanding an investigation into the source of the journalists' briefings.[74] An inquiry was started in No.10

and one of the journalists involved implicated the Department of Energy, although its press office denied any involvement.[75] The source of any leak was not discovered.

Progress in planning the sale was slowed not only by the BGC Board's absence of a strong commitment to privatisation but during 1984 by the attention the Government, and especially the Department of Energy, had to give to tackling the miners' strike. The strike began in March of that year and would go on for almost 12 months.[76] Walker decided that privatisation of gas was not possible while the miners' strike continued to preoccupy him and his Department. Walker took a very active role in leading the Government's campaign against the National Union of Mineworkers. Also, it would certainly have been unwise to have risked the gas unions coming out on strike at a time when coal supplies were disrupted. While some limited background work on the privatisation did continue within the Department, it was 25 April 1985 before Walker put the matter again to E(A) Committee. At this meeting he confirmed that with the coal strike settled, and the successful sale of BT achieved the previous November, "there was now an opportunity to begin moving the energy utilities into the private sector" starting with gas.[77] Within the Department of Energy there was now a new momentum, with a view to having a privatisation Bill ready in November.[78]

## The introduction of the Gas Bill

Walker considered that the immediate prospects for the gas industry were good and while BGC did not have BT's advantages of a growing market and the same scope for the application of new technology, some parts of BG's activities – and especially the opportunity to participate in further exploitation of the UKCS – could be attractive to investors. There was also the prospect of BGC diversifying into other profitable new businesses once privately owned. Under his privatisation plans BGC would operate under a licence setting out its duties and obligations and other gas supply operators would be licensed "in appropriate circumstances". Gas appliance retailing would be liberalised. However, Walker once again scotched any notion of serious competition in gas supplies to domestic consumers stating that, "private sector competition for the supply of gas was not a realistic possibility". Instead, BGC would be regulated to protect customers with no choice of supplier from monopoly abuse. He emphasised that the privatisation of BGC would be complex and demanding and that policy decisions on the details of the regulatory structure and gas imports and exports would be needed before instructions could be given to Parliamentary Counsel to prepare the necessary legislation. There would also be a need to restructure the Government's legislative programme to fit in what would be a politically controversial Bill. So contentious was the measure expected to be that the final decision on privatisation was left to a meeting of the full Cabinet.

The Cabinet considered the matter on 2 May 1985. Here Walker successfully saw off arguments for a break-up of BGC into a series of regional utilities before privatisation, once again on the grounds that this would delay a sale by several years. He also pointed out that the introduction of a regional-based structure would create the politically unwelcome prospect of higher prices in regions where gas distribution costs were relatively high.[79] His conclusion that, "The residual [offshore] BGC assets have a disproportionate importance as one of the few areas of interest and potential to which we can point investors in writing the prospectus for the new company"[80] was ironic, given previous Government policy requiring BGC to sell off its assets in oil and gas exploration and production.

Walker's proposals for privatisation were welcomed, although some Ministers were still anxious that the Government was creating a dominant, private sector gas supplier. They believed that at the very least there should be some change in the regime regulating gas imports and exports. There was also concern that the parliamentary timetable for the Bill might be too tight if it was to receive royal assent before the summer recess in 1986, so that BGC could be sold before the likely date of a next general election. However, at the end of the debate the Cabinet endorsed the objective of privatising the gas industry within the timescale set down by the Secretary of State. The decision annoyed the Lord President of the Council responsible for overseeing the legislative programme. Two Bills would need to be removed to make space for a gas Bill. He immediately complained "that it was most undesirable that changes should be made to the agreed [legislative] programme at such a late stage. To do so imposed great strains on Departments and Parliamentary Counsel." The suggestion was made that the Nationalised Industries Bill and the Northern Ireland (Emergency Provisions) Bill might be postponed. This in turn angered the Secretary of State for Northern Ireland.[81]

On 7 May 1985 Walker announced in the House of Commons the Government's decision to privatise the BGC, commenting:

"Major progress has been made with the Government's privatisation programme. Management and enterprise have been freed from bureaucratic intervention in industries as diverse as aerospace, the ports and cross-Channel services, the oil industry and British Telecom.

"The Government have decided that the time has come for a further major step in the transfer of state industry to the private sector. I propose to introduce legislation at the earliest opportunity to provide for the transfer to a new private sector company of all the assets of the British Gas Corporation, and for appropriate regulation of monopoly aspects of the gas supply business . . .

"This change, like the earlier ones, will remove state intervention and substitute realistic tests of performance for bureaucratic or political ones. It will create a real public ownership by the public and employees in place of a nominal public ownership of the nationalisation statute. It will place new emphasis on efficiency for the benefit of consumers and give employees a new stake in the business . . .

"I believe that today's announcement will mark a new and long period of successful development into which the management and all who work in the industry can bring their present talents and link them with new freedoms in the interests of the nation."[82]

At E(A) on 31 July 1985 Walker was able to confirm that most of the provisions required for a new gas Bill had now been finalised following discussions with other Departments. To meet the timetable for a sale well before the next election, which at the latest would have to be in May 1988, it was agreed that the Bill would need to be ready for introduction by very early in the 1985–86 session. Instructions had been sent to Counsel to begin the drafting of the Bill in early July. The objective would be to sell shares in BGC in the autumn of 1986. However, there was recognition that the privatisation planning would need to be handled very carefully so as to ensure that there was sufficient support inside and outside Parliament to allow the privatisation to be carried through successfully. Once more the argument for restructuring the BGC into separate businesses or on regional lines was raised, and dismissed.[83]

By 14 November 1985 Walker was able to report to E(A) that the drafting of the Gas Bill was now virtually complete.[84] Walker received support for the Bill to be introduced and it received its first reading on 28 November.[85] Predictably the Labour Party and the trade unions immediately announced their total opposition to the measure. NALGO and the GMBATU mounted a concerted campaign against the sale, as they had done earlier against the plan to dispose of the gas showrooms. The campaign once more centred on safety risks to the public, as well as reduced employment. The Labour Party and the unions also predicted that privatisation would bring about higher gas prices. Councils were again lobbied and a number of Labour local authorities once more responded with letters of protest to local MPs and Ministers.[86] But it was not just the predictable response of the unions, the Labour Party and Labour Councils that the Government confronted. In Parliament concerns were voiced by some Conservative MPs and peers about the likely extent of competition in gas supply after privatisation and the possible impact of privatisation on customers. Some believed that the industry would remain largely a monopoly whatever the new measures the Government proposed in the Bill to facilitate competition.[87] Sir Terence Beckett of the CBI lobbied on behalf of his members reflecting similar concerns and the possible effects on British industry of BGC's future pricing policy. Reflecting such concerns, some amendments were incorporated into the Gas Bill during its Parliamentary passage, especially relating to regulatory issues, as discussed below. However, essentially the Act passed was very similar to the Bill first published. This contrasts with the fortunes of the earlier Telecommunications Bill privatising BT, which was more substantially altered and reflects the much greater care that went into the preparation of the Gas Bill compared to the more rushed telecommunications legislation. This may be considered to vindicate Walker's cautious approach to the planning of the Bill.[88]

The Bill ran to 64 Clauses and eight Schedules and allowed for the transfer of BGC to a registered company and the sale of its shares to the public. It was divided into three parts: Part I dealing with gas supply generally and setting the legal framework post-privatisation; Part II effecting the transfer of BGC's undertaking to a new private sector company; and Part III containing miscellaneous general provisions. Included in the Bill were powers to appoint a regulator for the industry heading a new regulatory office. All public gas suppliers, starting with BGC, would be licensed detailing their duties and obligations. The intention was to achieve a second reading of the Bill before Christmas with the Committee Stage early in the New Year. Royal assent could then be achieved by the target date of the summer 1986 Parliamentary recess.

## The regulatory regime

The decision to privatise BGC without major restructuring to promote competition in the gas industry placed an added onus on establishing an effective regulatory structure to protect consumers. The approach to regulation adopted borrowed heavily from the experience of the BT privatisation. This included establishing a new dedicated regulatory body, the Office of Gas Supply (OFGAS), and a system of price regulation similar to that used for BT, which was based on a RPI − X formula (retail price index to reflect inflation less an efficiency adjustment). The decision to regulate from a government agency rather than the Department of Energy was founded on the belief, as in the case of the privatisation of BT, that investors would need assurance that Government could no longer meddle in the management of BGC. Sir Denis Rooke also strongly supported the move, to confirm BGC's new status as an independent private sector company. The possible structure of the regulatory regime was discussed a few months prior to the introduction into Parliament of the Gas Bill, in E(A)

Sub-Committee, on 11 June 1985.[89] Walker explained that the aim would be to regulate gas supply involving the transmission and distribution of gas from the beachhead to customers' meters. BGC would have a licence (termed an "authorisation") setting out its duties and responsibilities. Areas of BGC's activities where there was scope for competition would be subject to normal competition law, as administered by the OFT and the MMC. The monopoly gas supply business would be ring-fenced to exclude cross-subsidisation of the more competitive markets and BGC would be required to publish separate accounts for its different activities.[90]

There was some discussion in E(A) as to whether it might be better to create one regulatory body able to regulate all of the privatised utilities including BT, but the preliminary view was taken that "a single regulatory body covering several privatised industries might prove unwieldy". Within the Department of Energy consideration was given to setting up a combined regulatory office for telecommunications and gas or possibly for gas and electricity, in anticipation of a later sale of the electricity industry. This might ensure sufficient work for the regulator, but it was considered that there was very little chance of gaining the necessary political support for such a move, especially ahead of the privatisation of electricity. While it was agreed in E(A) that it "would be premature a this stage to decide between these alternative approaches", there was nevertheless a presumption that OFGAS would be a separate body from OFTEL. There was also recognition that safety arrangements in a privatised gas industry would be "a particularly important and emotive issue" and that it would be important to ensure that the provisions were adequate to forestall public fears. The trade unions had already mounted the successful campaign against privatisation of the gas showrooms stressing the risks to public safety. Regarding the role of Consumer Councils to represent customer interests, it was agreed that any arrangements would have to be such that investors were not deterred. No decision was taken on what form consumer representation should take in the regulatory arrangements.

At a further meeting of E(A) Sub-Committee on 31 July 1985 Walker confirmed that the regulatory body would be a stand-alone non-ministerial department along the lines of the OFT and OFTEL under its own Director General.[91] The Director General Gas Supply (DGGS) would be appointed by the Secretary of State for a term not exceeding five years in the first instance[92] and would, in turn, appoint "such staff as he thinks fit" and be responsible for the day-to-day regulation of the industry, including the price control formula. Between them the Secretary of State for Energy and the DGGS would have certain statutory duties, such as the duty to ensure that gas demand is met where this is economic, that public gas suppliers "operate efficiently and economically", and that licensees are able to remain financially viable ("able to earn a reasonable return and are not forced into bankruptcy"[93]). They would also be expected to protect the interests of consumers "and ensure fair competition". There would also be provision for the DGGS to take account of the need for R&D, public safety and metering requirements and the efficient and economic use of gas. Walker noted that his Department was examining the scope for reducing the obstacles to private supplies of gas to industry experienced since the passage of the 1982 Oil and Gas (Enterprise) Act.[94]

Within the Department of Energy there was some uncertainty about the workload that would fall on the new office. As one official commented on the draft list of functions, "Whilst the list may look impressive, I suspect there is little of real substance in it. Many of the issues are those which in the past have been handled by Gas 1 [division in the Department] and first guess is that the package is hardly sufficient to occupy a full branch." However, he went on to emphasise that "we need to create an office of sufficient size to be credible and which will superficially appear to be on par with OFTEL."[95] The initial expectation was that the Office would have a headcount of 20, which was considered to "be a publicly credible minimum size". Later this was revised to 32. The staff would be made up mainly of secondees from the Department of Energy but perhaps with the addition of a business adviser from an accountancy firm.[96] The budget for the Office was to start at around £1 million but would be raised quickly to £3 million. There was an expectation that the annual cost might be as high as £6 million by 1986/7.[97] The early experience of running OFTEL suggested that the numbers of staff needed would increase as therefore would the Office's operating costs. The costs would be recouped from the annual authorisation fee paid by BGC and in time other public gas suppliers.[98]

The DGGS would be a crown appointee independent of the Secretary of State, although appointed by him. The DGGS could be removed from office during his term of office only on grounds of incapacity or misbehaviour and only in certain limited circumstances would the Secretary be able to give him general directions. It was suggested that the initial appointment should be for less than the five years so as to avoid a change in the DGGS occurring at the time of the first gas price review. But the appointment could occur only once a Commencement Order had been laid following the royal assent to the Gas Bill. Royal assent was not expected until the summer of 1986 and the candidate would have to be chosen well before this date. The DGGS was responsible for appointing the OFGAS staff and it would be important to have the office up and running by the time of the privatisation.

The Department of Energy concluded that the post of DGGS "whilst demanding high public visibility will be less demanding than the post of Director-General of Telecommunications". This was because the latter was responsible for regulating BT and overseeing the development of competition in telecommunications. The Department of Energy doubted whether competition would develop to anything like the same extent in gas supply. Also, BGC was resisting any suggestion that the DGGS should have similar powers to the Director General of OFTEL (DGOFTEL) to promote competition. The draft Bill included no such measure. At the same time, it was felt that "it is essential that the Director enjoys a status approximately equivalent to his OFTEL counterpart" if someone of the right calibre was to be attracted. The Government concluded that, "The ideal candidate will be of recognised standing, is likely to be aged 50 or over and with skills in finance/accountancy." But it was felt that the more limited tasks of OFGAS would reduce the appeal of the job to potential applicants. [99] It was judged unlikely that a candidate "as vigorous" as Bryan Carsberg at OFTEL could be recruited.

In deciding on a site for OFGAS the Department favoured somewhere in Victoria in London. Offices south of the Thames would be cheaper but it was felt that this "could deter attracting a suitable Director". The salary for the position of DGGS would need to be agreed with the Treasury, although it was not anticipated that there would be the same conflict with the Treasury as had occurred over the appropriate salary for the DGOFTEL. The salary for the DGOFTEL had now set a benchmark. Nevertheless, the Department was aware that the Treasury might still be smarting from the results of the salary negotiations for the appointment of Carsberg, who had been employed at a salary some 40 per cent above that of a Deputy Secretary. A list of 23 possible candidates for the position of DGGS was drawn up culled from the original DGOFTEL trawl and other suggestions. This was reduced to a short list and from this James McKinnon was formally appointed as the first Director General of OFGAS on 18 August 1986. McKinnon was previously Finance Director of Imperial Group plc and a former President of the Institute of Chartered Accountants for Scotland. He would prove to be an effective and determined regulator, much to BGC's chagrin and despite earlier departmental fears that no one of the right calibre might be found.

Under nationalisation, Gas Consumers' Councils operated in each of the gas regions and at the national level in the form of the National Gas Consumer Council (NGCC). The Councils handled thousands of customer complaints about BGC's services each year. Nevertheless, the decision was taken to wind up the existing structure of consumer representation because it was felt that it "would not fit easily" alongside the duties of OFGAS and, importantly, would deter investors by creating uncertainty about the extent to which the Councils would influence the content of the regulation. The decision quickly led to criticism inside and outside Parliament about the lack of consumer representation in the proposed regulatory structure. The decision was therefore taken to replace the Gas Consumers' Councils with a single body with a chairman and members appointed by the Secretary of State for Trade and Industry. This was to be known as the Gas Users Council (GUC), a title suggested by the Department's public relations advisers, Dewe Rogerson.[100] Later the title was amended to the Gas Consumers' Council.

The GUC would be a body independent of OFGAS and its main function would be the investigation of complaints from both tariff and industrial consumers, except those relating to the enforcement of licence conditions, which lay with the DGGS. The Council would also advise the Director on any matters that it thought appropriate or which the Director referred to it for investigation. It would make an annual report to the Director and to the Secretary of State which would be published. The new Council would also have greater powers than the earlier National and Regional Gas Consumers' Councils to obtain information from BGC. However, some members of these Councils remained unhappy that the provisions for consumer protection following privatisation did not go far enough in terms of protecting gas users from higher prices and a poorer quality of service.[101] In response, on 17 March 1986 the Government tabled an amendment at the report stage of the Gas Bill extending the scope of the GUC to deal with complaints about cookers, boilers and heaters, as well as installation, servicing and the safety of gas appliances. This helped placate some but not all critics. BGC strongly resisted any suggestion that the scope of the new Council should be widened further.

The Department of Energy originally proposed that the GUC should be staffed by civil servants seconded from OFGAS. But the existing NGCC and the CBI and BGC joined in protest that this might be seen to compromise the Council's independence from the regulator. The Council was therefore given power to appoint its own staff. There then followed a brief tussle between the Department and the DTI over funding and responsibility for the new organisation. The Department of Energy suggested that oversight and funding of the new consumer council should lie with the DTI, given its wider responsibility for consumer protection. However, the DTI worried that an independent Council with its own staff, as planned, might cast in a poor light the arrangements for consumer representation it had put in place a few months earlier for BT, where consumer representation was channelled through OFTEL. The adequacy of the arrangements put in place for consumer representation in telecommunications regulation was already drawing criticism.[102] Also, the DTI was reluctant to bear the costs of funding the Council.[103] However, once BGC offered to meet the costs in its authorisation fee, the DTI's opposition subsided. BGC's motive was to head off the possibility of the GUC becoming an agency of the industry regulator.[104]

## The nature of the regulation, competition and the problem
of cross-subsidy

Much of the relevant text on regulation in the Gas Bill mirrored that in the earlier 1984 Telecommunications Act and BT's licence. "Public gas suppliers", of which BGC would be the first authorised, would have a statutory duty to maintain an efficient and economic gas supply and avoid undue preference when supplying customers. BGC would also have a continuing duty to supply customers within 25 yards of a distribution main and requiring fewer than 25,000 therms a year. Later the DGGS's primary duties were firmed up to include ensuring that all reasonable demands for gas were met where this was economic. Also, there was a duty on the DGGS to keep himself informed of gas supply matters and give information and advice to the Secretary of State or the Director General of Fair Trading. The DGGS would have power to obtain information and to publish information provided it did not damage the interests of individuals or bodies. He would also have an obligation to make an annual report to the Secretary of State, which would be laid before Parliament. BGC would continue to be required to produce a code of practice for people facing difficulties in paying their bills. In addition, BGC would be required to continue to provide a 24 hour a day emergency service and special services for the elderly and disabled.[105]

Authorisation to be a public gas supplier would be granted by the Secretary of State after consulting the DGGS and would apply to a specific geographical area. For the successor to BGC this would initially be the whole of Great Britain, and the authorisation would run for at least 25 years, "but will be progressively reduced if other suppliers are granted authorisations in respect of areas not already supplied by BGC".[106] After 25 years BGC's authorisation would be revocable if the Secretary of State gave ten years' notice. The Secretary of State would also be able to revoke the authorisation with 30 days' notice if BGC could no longer carry on its gas supply business due to insolvency or cessation of business or following non-compliance with enforcement orders made by the DGGS or the Secretary of State for Trade and Industry under certain provisions of general competition law. It was recognised that this was an ultimate sanction and was very unlikely to be invoked. Revocation would also be permitted where BGC agreed; for example to allow for a major restructuring of the company. The terms were similar to those for BT under its licence.

The DGGS would be empowered to make modifications to the authorisation where he and the company agreed at any time (provided the Secretary of State did not object). In the event of a disagreement the Director could make a reference to the MMC. The DGGS could also refer to the MMC any matters relating to the supply of gas to tariff customers. On receipt of the MMC's report on whether the matters referred operate, or may be expected to operate, against the public interest, the DGGS would be required to modify the authorisation in such a way as "he believes to be necessary to remedy or prevent the adverse effects identified by the MMC".[107] In addition to a reference to the MMC, the DGGS's decisions would be challengeable in the Courts on procedural grounds or because the Director was considered to have exceeded his powers. Authorisation conditions would be enforced through orders issued by the Director enforceable by the Courts. Failure to comply with an order would make the gas supplier open to civil damages by third parties suffering a loss.

The market for gas totalled 19 billion therms and was divided into a tariff market representing 62 per cent of the total market for gas, a firm contract market representing 18 per cent and an interruptible supplies market accounting for the remainder. The tariff market included all customers using fewer than 25,000 therms per year (the average household used around 600 therms; the rest of the tariff market was businesses except those using large amounts of gas). The Department of Energy was keen to limit the scope of OFGAS to regulating the supply activities of public gas suppliers in the tariff area of the market and to prevent regulation extending into the contract market and upstream into gas exploration and production, including gas purchases. It was judged that regulation in these markets might undermine competition and damage the development of the UKCS gas and oil fields. The aim, therefore, was to keep OFGAS out of the contract market. In October 1985 Alick Buchanan-Smith, Minister of State for Energy, commented: "If OFGAS could *both* initiate an investigation of this market *and* broaden its own regime following an investigation then we really do have a recipe for empire building" (emphasis in the original).[108] BGC was also insistent that there should be no role for the regulator in the contract market on the grounds, legally correct but at the time in practice fictitious, that following the Oil and Gas (Enterprise) Act industrial supplies of gas were competitive. One implication of limiting the scope of regulation was that the regulator would not be empowered to intervene to ensure that BGC bought its gas at the lowest possible price. This was considered to be potentially bureaucratic, would be opposed by the oil companies, and might deter exploration for new gas if US experience was anything to go by. In the USA regulation of gas purchases had forced down prices to the point where exploration activity had virtually ceased.[109]

A dominant BGC might attempt to cross-subsidise its competitive activities in the contract market, gas appliance retailing and servicing and installation from its monopoly business supplying gas to the tariff market.[110] Alternatively, BGC might raise its prices in the contract market reflecting the lack of competition so far in that sector to offset profits lost in the tariff market due to price control.[111] In the case of BT cross-subsidisation had been addressed by an explicit licence condition. The Treasury wanted to see this applied to BGC. But the BGC Board maintained that this was not feasible because of the extent to which resources were shared across the Corporation, including the staff used for safety and emergency purposes, and once more Walker conceded. BGC agreed instead to an initial cost allocation exercise to apportion costs across its different activities, along with separate accounts reporting for the different businesses. BGC's authorisation would require publication of separate accounts for gas supply and separate accounts for offshore operations and retail and ancillary services would be maintained.

The cost allocation was to be settled between the Department of Energy and BGC. The new DGGS would only become involved if in the future BGC decided to change the allocation, which would require his agreement. BGC had a long history of separate accounting, which had not existed for BT, but the accounting practices were such that there was the potential for many areas of disagreement. In particular, servicing, installation and contracting was an area of concern in the Department of Energy and the Treasury, where BGC calculated the costs on a marginal cost basis because gas staff undertook this work at times when they were not needed elsewhere in the gas supply business. This practice was accepted by the Corporation's accountants, Touche Ross, but challenged by the Treasury who realised how difficult it was, as a result, for private sector companies to compete on price for gas servicing and installation. The Treasury feared that any cost allocation decided before privatisation could prove anti-competitive in the future. Its preferred option was to have the cost allocation agreed between the DGGS and BGC, making the situation more similar to that which existed for BT.[112] However, Walker and the BGC wanted the cost allocation agreed before OFGAS would be established. This would mean that the financial projections needed for the sale Prospectus were not delayed; also, BGC was nervous about leaving the allocation to be decided with an unknown quantity, the DGGS. In any case, Walker concluded that a privatised BGC would have a commercial incentive "not to set prices at uneconomically subsidised levels" and if this did occur it would fall foul of competition legislation. Under the monopoly provisions in the Fair Trading Act 1973, a reference could be made by the Government, through the OFT, to the MMC to investigate any anti-competitive practices.[113]

However, by no means everyone in Government was reassured that competition law would prevent anti-competitive practices in a privatised gas industry. In particular, Leon Brittan at the DTI concluded that competition law would be insufficient especially to protect consumers in the contract market: "I think the outside world would see it as counter to common sense to set up a special regulator because of worries about monopoly power but to exclude the regulator from part of the market where that power is held."[114] BGC had already been able to undercut a potential competitor in the contract market on price because of its access to cheap Southern Basin gas from the North Sea. When Hamilton Oil of the USA tried to use the Gas and Oil (Enterprise) Act to sell gas from one of its North Sea fields directly to the industrial company ICI, BGC was able to see off the challenge. BGC priced its gas at average costs rather than at the higher long-run marginal costs which resulted from accessing production from more costly parts of the UKCS. The Treasury wanted to see BGC move closer to long-run marginal cost pricing, which implied higher prices. BGC resisted. Also, the oil companies complained that BGC's gas purchasing department obtained substantial geological and economic information about individual UKCS gasfields from companies operating the fields, which could be of great value to BGC's gas supply operations after privatisation. Discussions occurred with a range of businesses and the CBI was invited to examine any problems that might arise from the proposed arrangements for large and smaller contract customers. The CBI endorsed the Secretary of State's view that an appropriate balance would be struck by a combination of voluntary assurances on uncompetitive practices by BGC, including the exploration and production business agreeing not to transfer confidential information to the gas supply business, backed up by existing legislative safeguards against monopoly abuse.[115]

In E(A) in June and July 1985 another concern was voiced, that a privatised BGC might abuse its monopoly by taking over other oil and gas companies, thereby reducing competition. At the same time there was general agreement amongst Ministers that excessive constraints on management entering into future merger discussions would be incompatible with the operation of BGC as a successful private sector business. Walker considered that voluntary assurances plus the threat of a referral to the MMC would act to ensure good behaviour. If BGC embarked on mergers to tighten its control over the gas industry, something oil companies understandably feared, normal competition law existed to check the company's growth. However, there remained apprehension within Government that there would be insufficient competition in the contract market to prevent monopoly abuse by a privatised BGC and that takeovers by BGC could make matters worse.[116] John Moore at the Treasury complained that earlier he had understood that BGC's authorisation would incorporate provisions against discrimination and undue preference in the offshore and contract markets, but Walker was now simply proposing that the licence would require BGC to publish some assurances.[117]

A meeting was held on 21 November 1985 between Walker, Leon Brittan and John Moore to look at ways of heading off concerns about the lack of current and future competition in the industrial market.[118] Following this meeting it was agreed that the task of initiating control of the contract market should be placed with the OFT and not the DGGS, "who will have a vested interest in expanding his area of influence and control". The Gas Bill therefore provided for the DGGS to make references to the MMC for licence changes relating to tariff consumers only. The DGGS would not have power to make a Fair Trading reference under competition law. This remained the prerogative of the OFT or Ministers. The price for gas in the contract market would be a matter for individual negotiation, but under pressure from the Department of Energy BGC did agree to publish a schedule of its maximum contract prices. Also, BGC entered into a commitment not to increase prices by more than the rate of inflation for three years after privatisation, subject to there being no significant changes in oil prices and exchange rates. Over the same period it would continue to set prices for interruptible supplies in relation to the prices for competing fuels and would not unduly differentiate prices without good commercial reasons. By the end of three years the Department hoped that competition would be sufficiently developed in the contract market to protect against monopoly pricing, although there were deep reservations amongst some officials as to whether this would be the case. The concessions were announced during the second reading of the Gas Bill. It was agreed that future mergers and takeovers by BGC should be policed by the MMC under existing competition legislation.

Nevertheless, worries about possible monopoly abuse by a privatised BGC were revived when the Corporation suggested that it intended to include maintenance and installation services within the definition of its gas supply business. Treasury Ministers were unhappy that Walker was willing to concede that the costs of these services should be included in gas supply. Treasury calculations suggested that BGC could be losing some £120 million on a turnover of £275 million on these activities. Showroom costs for collecting bills and promoting the sale of gas were another area of controversy, as was the accounting for R&D expenditures, especially the costs incurred in undertaking research into substitute natural gas. BGC also allocated these costs to gas supply. Moreover, Condition 2 of BGC's authorisation required the presentation of separate accounts for BGC's gas and oil businesses. However, gas supply was an integrated business so that accounting apportionment between the tariff and industrial contract markets was deemed too difficult.[119] There was, therefore, concern that BGC might find ways around the common carriage conditions. At the Committee stage, under backbench pressure, the Government relented and to head off a major revolt amongst backbenchers accepted an amendment giving the DGGS a duty "to enable persons to compete effectively in the supply of gas through pipes at rates which, in relation to any premises, exceed 25,000 therms a year".[120] This went someway towards meeting some of the concerns. The absence of such a clause in the original Bill was an act of commission rather than omission. Department officials had suggested the inclusion of a duty on the DGGS to promote competition in the non-tariff market, but Walker had opposed it. When he conceded to the amendment, Rooke was furious.[121]

Walker appears to have concluded that worries about future monopoly abuse by a privatised BGC were exaggerated and that any threat could be tackled through a combination of the proposed regulatory structure and competition law.[122] But Walker was also mindful throughout the preparation of the Bill and the authorisation of not "derailing" Rooke, who was totally opposed to any extension of the regulatory net to the contract market and gas purchases. The possibility of BGC being required to set up subsidiary companies to make the scope for cross-subsidisation more difficult was raised in E(A) but not pursued. Walker considered that such reorganisation of the Corporation would not guarantee an end to cross-subsidisation and in any case it would take too long to arrange. Establishing subsidiary companies would set back the privatisation timetable, especially as restructuring was unlikely to receive the co-operation of BGC management. Rather timidly, the Department concluded that while the structure they proposed might lack transparency, "it could be justified on the grounds that unfair trading practices outside the gas supply business are properly a matter for the OFT, and hidden cross-subsidy between appliance retailing and exploration and production is a matter for the company."[123] The Treasury remained far from convinced. It would later complain that in the exercise to set the cost allocations BGC had "shown no readiness to do anything other than stick to the existing allocation".[124] Meanwhile, Rooke continued to oppose any suggestion that the new regulator should become involved.

### Common carriage

Under the 1982 Oil and Gas (Enterprise) Act the Secretary of State was responsible for setting the terms of any common carriage deals in the gas industry where agreement could not be reached between the BGC and an independent supplier. In fact, there had been few deals negotiated so far and the Secretary of State had not been required to intervene. Under the new Gas Bill, this power was transferred to the DGGS and the terms for common carriage were strengthened with the intention of promoting competition in the contract market. Walker still saw no real scope for competition in the supply of gas to the tariff market. In a speech at a Sixth Form Conference for Economics students he confirmed: "It has long been accepted that competition in supplies to ordinary customers does not make sense. It would be absurd on safety practical and economic grounds to duplicate existing gas pipes under the street. I have therefore decided to retain the British Gas's monopoly in supplies to tariff (mainly domestic) consumers."[125]

BGC sought assurances about the discretion that the DGGS would have when setting common carriage charges and pressed the Government to provide a statement of pricing principles to guide the DGGS in the future. The Corporation sought agreement that the DGGS would only intervene in determining the charges if negotiations between the BGC and independent gas suppliers broke down. It was also concerned that the charges should reflect full cost recovery and not be determined on an incremental cost basis, which would be lower. However, the Department of Energy believed that this would unduly restrict the DGGS's discretion, especially since there could be circumstances where prices should be set below average costs, as occurred in competitive markets.[126] As a compromise, the Department concluded that the DGGS should take into account an "appropriate proportion" of all costs when setting the charges. This would mean that BGC could recover depreciation and overheads not directly related to the volume of business. Nevertheless, BGC remained concerned that the DGGS might set common carriage charges to promote competition that did not fully reimburse the Corporation for the full costs of conveyance.

Also, BGC objected to a new duty introduced to provide back-up supplies. One reason why there had been so little competition in the contract market following the 1982 legislation was because third party suppliers were unable to offer potential customers the same degree of supply reliability as BGC, especially as their supplies might come from a single gasfield. The Department responded with the suggestion that BGC should both provide back up supplies for third parties to improve the security of supply and offer to purchase residual volumes of gas from gasfields where the bulk of gas had been sold to another party.[127]The BGC Board was hostile. After some initial signals that the Corporation might be willing to take residual gas on the same basis as other gas on offer at the time, management indicated that they were not willing to offer anything in this area. BGC was prepared only to allow third parties to use its storage facilities to provide the kind of back-up needed for a supplier to achieve a higher standard of security of supply.

On this issue BGC's objections were eventually overridden, largely because of industrial lobbying and back-bench pressure. An amendment to the Bill introduced at the report stage meant that BGC would be obliged to provide gas supplies where a third party could not get gas from other sources, providing this did not prejudice BGC's obligations to its own consumers. BGC would be obliged to provide back-up supplies of gas on "reasonable terms" as decided by the DGGS and to buy in surplus gas when demand was seasonally low.[128] In this respect, the common carrier provisions in the Gas Bill represented a major strengthening of the ability of UKCS producers to transport their gas to their own customers economically using BGC's distribution system. But Rooke fought hard and with some success to prevent these concessions resulting in serious damage to BGC. In particular, he was successful in requiring that detailed limits be agreed to the DGGS's discretion in setting common carriage charges. The overall result of the measures was to create a greater prospect of effective competition in the contracts market than existed under the 1982 Oil and Gas (Enterprise) Act. At the same time, the principles to be taken into account when the DGGS determined the common carrier charges went well beyond those laid down for the DGOFTEL. The Treasury would have preferred to have left much more discretion to the DGGS.[129]

Within the Department of Energy too there was some unease. Walker judged that the concessions extracted from BGC were about the most that could be obtained while keeping the privatisation on track. Yet some officials in the Department reflected that the resulting terms would still be heavily criticised by the independent oil companies and that they were "most unlikely to result in many, if any, direct deals". Fears were enhanced when BGC published sample contract prices. These were much higher than those that existed in the USA.[130] Meanwhile, BGC complained that as a result of the new arrangements it would face competition in both the buying and selling ends of the gas market. Third party gas suppliers would compare the option of a sale of gas to the Corporation with that of a direct sale to customers. Where there was a direct sale, this would be at the expense of a loss of market to BGC. Also, any profits lost in the contract market might not be recoverable through higher prices in the tariff market because of the price cap. Right up to the day of the flotation, BGC complained about the prospect of losing a substantial share of the contract market while having gas purchase contracts in place. BGC was already contracted to take gas from fields and management feared that with a loss of market share to competitors, the result would be an over-contracted position from the early 1990s. The damaging effects were unlikely before then because of the lead time needed to bring forward new gas supplies.[131] Nevertheless, BGC judged rightly that the effect could be very damaging to profitability in the longer term, especially as a number of the contracts were on a "take or pay" basis.[132]

Discussion of the privatisation plans and regulatory structure returned to E(A) Sub-Committee on 14 November 1985. Walker repeated his position that it would be wrong for the regulator to be given powers to intervene in BGC gas purchases because this might conflict with the Government's policy of encouraging exploration and development on the UKCS.[133] In his view the company's competitiveness would be steadily eroded if gas costs rose unnecessarily and therefore "it has obvious commercial incentive to contain them." Regulatory intervention at the wellhead would "impose a bureaucratic and potentially meddlesome system which works to no clear advantage. It would be resented by the oil industry and, if US experience is anything to go by, might actively deter exploration for new gas, disbenefiting consumers in the longer term." Moreover, he warned that: "There was a genuine risk that, if the Government insisted on the Regulator having specific powers to intervene in the industrial contracts market, BGC managements' (sic.) support for privatisation would be prejudiced."[134] However, the private oil companies were not satisfied. They worried about BGC's effective monopoly over gas purchases and the prospect of a privatised BGC being allowed to build up its oil exploration activities again. The CBI and other industrial lobby groups, notably the Energy Intensive Users' Group, were content with the position on interruptible gas but pressed for lower firm gas prices, citing lower prices in some other countries. Ministers responded by maintaining that prices were a matter for users to negotiate with the BGC.[135]

## Mounting criticism

By the end of November 1985 the details of BGC's authorisation were well advanced, although with the terms of BGC's assurances on the industrial market still subject to finalisation.[136] The Financial Secretary, John Moore, was far from satisfied. While conceding that some progress had been made, he remained of the view that under the current proposals "the privatised gas industry would be subject to a more passive and relaxed form of regulation than Telecommunications." He concluded that this "would be hard to justify in an industry whose monopoly position was likely to prove more enduring than that of British Telecom". Once the licence of the privatised gas company was published, parallels would be quickly drawn between the roles of the Director of OFTEL and the Director of OFGAS. If the regulatory regime was perceived to be much less stringent for gas, in his opinion the reputation of privatisation in the eyes of the public would be damaged, making future privatisations much harder to accomplish. He had six specific concerns. Firstly, the proposals envisaged no role for the regulator in BGC's gas purchases. Secondly, the Financial Secretary was anxious, even after the agreement of the CBI to Walker's plans, that medium-sized firms might be alarmed at the proposals for the industrial contracts market. Thirdly, that it would be insufficient to rely on the DGOFT to make a reference to the MMC under competition legislation. Fourthly, the Financial Secretary was still concerned that at present the regulator's role was confined to changes in the initial cost allocations for gas supply agreed by BGC and the Department of Energy. In his view the regulator should participate in setting the initial allocations. Fifthly, there needed to be separate accounts for the tariff and non-tariff sectors. Finally, in his view "there was nothing in the present proposals to prevent cross-subsidisation", for instance of gas appliance retailing from the non-regulated industrial gas business.

Relations between the Department of Energy and the Treasury were clearly tense. In response, as usual the PM gave her backing to Walker's proposals but she made it clear that if there was criticism in Parliament of the arrangements proposed "there may have to be an amendment to the Bill at the Committee stage."[137] In the same month BGC caused further irritation in the Treasury when it raised concerns that its gas supply contracts might infringe the Restrictive Trade Practices Act. The Government reluctantly agreed to ensure that the contracts fell outside the scope of the legislation by making an appropriate Order.[138] This did little to dampen worries in parts of Government and in the private sector oil and gas industry about potential monopoly abuse by BGC after privatisation.[139]

There was a particular concern that BGC might buy its own gas at a different price than independently sourced gas. Independent oil companies, such as Saxon Oil plc and Premier

Oil, wrote to the Department arguing that it would be in the national interest to limit BGC to purchasing, distributing and marketing natural gas in the UK. They feared that if BGC was allowed to expand its exploration and production activities again, it would unfairly favour its own supplies or favour imports to squeeze the profitability of the independent oil companies. The independent oil companies also tended to favour freedom for producers to import and export oil and gas (perhaps subject to residual powers to control exports in the national interest where necessary). These views were widely held by BRINDEX (The Association of British Independent Oil Exploration Companies), which wanted to see potential predatory practices in the gas market by BGC controlled and the UK and European gas markets integrated.[140] The large oil companies were concerned too. BP raised the prospect of a privatised BGC abusing its monopoly powers in gas purchases and thereby damaging future gas exploration and development.[141] The Anglo-Dutch oil multinational Shell similarly expressed concerns about BGC abusing its market power by giving preference to its own supplies through its pipelines, making it difficult for others to compete for industrial contracts.[142] The Society of British Gas Industries (SBGI) also harboured worries.[143] However, the view in the Department was that BGC would be a more attractive proposition to investors with an exploration and production arm. As one official commented in a briefing to the Secretary of State ahead of a meeting with representatives from the smaller British oil companies, "BGC has much to gain from integrating these activities."[144]

To placate the private sector oil companies, Clause 61 of the Gas Bill allowed the Secretary of State to give directions to a public gas supplier to restrict the supplier's use of information obtained while negotiating gas purchase contracts. A "Chinese wall" would be agreed within BGC to protect information that might give BGC's gas supply business an "unfair commercial advantage" when competing with independent suppliers for business. Although BGC believed that there was no need for a Chinese wall, the Corporation responded by supplying a draft text of a confidentiality undertaking.[145] Also, the Department of Trade and Industry argued that existing competition legislation would offer some further protection against significant cases of preference or discrimination by BGC in its acquisition of gas from the UKCS. At the same time there was recognition that MMC inquiries could take up to two years, by which time much damage might have been done.[146]

One radical solution to reduce the threat of monopoly abuse would be to allow unrestricted imports and exports of gas from the UKCS, a step that was winning more support in Parliament.[147] As introduced earlier in the chapter, the Treasury was keen to see restrictions on gas exports lifted. But the Department of Energy retained its belief that the trading of gas from the UKCS still needed to be controlled to maintain security of supply. Also, the Department's financial adviser, Rothschilds, reported that the success of the flotation might be damaged if imports were controlled but exports were not. On 22 October 1985 Alick Buchanan-Smith wrote to Phillips Petroleum Co UK Ltd, in response to their concerns and suggestions on gas trading, stating: "The UK Government's policies regarding development of the UKCS will be unaffected by the decision to privatise the gas industry. We have no intention of letting the privatised industry have decisive control over development of the UKCS. That is properly a function of Government, and with Government it will remain."[148]

However, debate continued inside and outside Government through the autumn and winter of 1985 on the future for gas imports and exports with Walker seemingly opposed to any relaxation of the restrictions on BGC's monopoly of gas landed in the UK. There was some embarrassment when the differences in opinion within Government were leaked to the press.[149] After a series of articles appeared in the *Financial Times* reporting disagreements amongst Ministers, Walker protested to the PM that "stories circulating in the City strongly suggest that the Treasury is the source of today's leaks."[150] By the early spring of 1986 Walker had been pressured to relent to a degree and permit some exporting of gas. He announced that he would be prepared, on a case by case basis, to consider applications from UKCS producers for waiver of the requirement to land gas in the UK. But this occurred only after the Department of Energy calculated that it would be the 1990s before exports became significant because of BGC's existing gas contracts. There was also a proviso that the Secretary of State would take into account the security of the UK's gas supplies in reaching a decision. The Department of Energy needed to balance the suggestion that competition in gas supplies should increase after privatisation with the need to attract investors during the forthcoming flotation of BGC. Investors could be expected to favour buying shares in a monopoly business. This helps explain a number of the Department's decisions and statements at the time, although they did sometimes trigger a nervous response from the Treasury, which was keen to see more competition. On 10 March 1986 the Financial Secretary wrote to Walker complaining about a recent Departmental statement which "gives rather a gloomy picture of the potential".[151]

Another unhappy party was the nationalised electricity supply industry. The Electricity Council complained about the possible effects of competition from a privatised BGC for large fuel users, especially given the continuation of the existing financial targets set for the electricity industry. A meeting between Walker and T.P. Jones of the Electricity Council occurred on 1 December 1985. Jones claimed that the electricity supply industry would be put at a competitive disadvantage once BGC was privatised and that therefore there should be stricter regulation of the industrial gas market. Walker rejected the idea concluding that it would be absurd to subject a privatised BGC to more detailed control than when it was nationalised. In any event, he explained to Jones that he expected the industrial market to become competitive.[152] Some concessions to placate the electricity industry were contemplated within the Department of Energy, including giving greater freedom to set connection charges, the provision of electricity outside the bulk supply tariff, accounting changes and changes to the industry's financial targets and EFLs, but all these possibilities raised considerable difficulties, including the likely opposition of the Treasury.[153] Instead, the electricity industry would have to await its own liberalisation from government control, and this could not occur before the next general election.

The trade unions and the Labour Opposition played the safety card again to drum up public support against the privatisation, as they had done earlier in the fight over the ownership of the gas showrooms. In response the Government went out of its way to emphasise the existing and new arrangements for gas safety. Safety monitoring was strengthened by bringing the main gas safety regulations into line with the general requirements of health and safety legislation and increasing by 60 per cent the amount of time Health and Safety Executive staff would spend on gas safety inspection. Legally backed training standards were set for gas installers and a new independent body was set up to promote safety in gas installation. In July 1986 BGC agreed to provide certain essential and safety services free to customers or at agreed prices.[154]

Finally, gas equipment manufacturers and their employees continued to worry that a privatised BGC would seek to diversify its supplies procuring more equipment from overseas. The Government tried to placate the industry by pointing to its success in winning orders in the past. In a letter to the union leader Eric Hammond, Walker responded:

"we must all applaud BGC's excellent buy British record. Their policy is of course self-imposed and I have every confidence in their management's future judgement here. I do not believe however it would be in the long term national interest to impose a buy British policy irrespective of whether the goods involved were competitive. The technology of the British gas industry is however as good as that of any other country and I can see no reason why British Gas' record on procurement should be affected by privatisation."[155]

Sir Keith Joseph's earlier admission to the PM that some decline in purchases from UK manufacturers was to be expected after privatisation was not made public.[156]

## The price cap

By early 1986 there had been progress in formulating BGC's price control. At the time of the privatisation of BT direct profit regulation had been rejected, on the grounds that it would not provide adequate incentives for management to reduce costs. Also, it was felt that profit regulation might deter investors from buying the shares. In the autumn of 1983 Department officials reviewed international practice and some thought was given to adopting US-style rate of return regulation. But officials recognised the potential superiority of adopting a price cap like the one designed for BT. Therefore, during the privatisation of BGC there was little of the soul-searching that had occurred in the case of BT about the best way of protecting consumers from excessive pricing. It was acknowledged that the price cap, while not without problems, was so far "proving practical in BT's case" and should be adopted for gas for the regulated tariff market. The details of the price control formula to be included in BGC's authorisation were established by the Department in negotiation with management and the financial advisers from the summer of 1985, following an initial Departmental paper to the Secretary of State on 19 July.[157]

In the case of gas the price formula would be RPI − X + Y. The formula provided that gas prices would not rise faster than inflation less "a performance target X for reducing onshore costs within the company's direct control" plus a Y factor to cover costs of offshore gas purchases.[158] The Y factor would apply to costs arising from payments to third parties under contracts for gas delivered at the terminal of entry and for gas produced by the company itself (based on the valuation of the gas for tax purposes). It was felt necessary to allow a cost pass through for gas input costs as they accounted for almost a half of BGC's cost structure and the price paid was determined by factors such as oil prices and exchange rates, which were considered to be outside the control of the BGC management. Concern was raised in E(A) about allowing a 100 per cent cost pass through because this might remove the incentives on management to seek out the cheapest gas supplies and the Department of Energy did review the case for having explicit incentives for BGC to minimise its gas purchase costs, including the possibility of regulating the price paid to North Sea producers. But again the Department concluded that the regulator should not be drawn into policing gas purchases from the UKCS. Instead, and perhaps rather limply, the Department concluded that BGC had a well-established track record as a strong gas purchaser and would "have clear commercial incentives to keep its costs down". There would be a need to maintain a competitive price for gas supplies against other fuels in the contract market.[159] Giving BGC an obligation in its licence to minimise gas costs passed through to consumers, was "unnecessary and would lead to a burdensome and interventionist form of regulation".[160]

Nevertheless, some apprehension remained in the Department of Energy and in the Treasury about allowing BGC to pass through all of its gas purchase costs.[161]

The price formula would be averaged across the tariffs charged by BGC in the tariff market and would be backed up with a duty not to discriminate between consumers, reinforced by separate accounting for the gas supply business. The price control would run for a minimum of five years. Whereas the BT precedent allowed for the price control to lapse after five years because of a presumption that growing competition could by then have rendered such control redundant in telecommunications, in the case of gas the possibility of continuing price control was left open. From 1 April 1992 the price control could be modified or terminated by agreement between BGC and the regulator or, in the absence of agreement, after the intervention of the MMC.[162] However, neither in the legislation nor elsewhere was it set down how the price control might be best reset. This was intentional. Within the Department of Energy it was judged "that there should be maximum flexibility . . . depending on the circumstances at the time."

The BT price formula involved samples of the price at fixed points during the year as well as at the time of any increase. For BGC the price ceiling would be set for the year ahead based on forecasts of the cost of gas and the RPI. As the forecasts might be inaccurate – in particular gas costs could fluctuate significantly – a "correction factor" was introduced, which allowed for any over or under-charging in one year to be corrected subsequently. Also, the DGGS was given power to intervene to set prices if the average price actually charged exceeded the maximum allowed by the formula by more than four per cent once the correct gas cost and inflation figures were known. There were also terms for the DGGS to intervene if the average price charged was significantly lower than the maximum allowed. In effect, the objective was to create an incentive for BGC to supply accurate forecasts.[163]

Detailed computer modelling was adopted to simulate the results of the price formula on BGC's finances. It was agreed in E(A) that the figure for X would need to be "both realistic and attainable, yet one which keeps the company on its toes and forces it to eliminate wasteful expenditure". It was also recognised that there was a need "to strike a balance between setting a tough discipline to improve the company's efficiency and making it so demanding as to undermine the interests of potential investors".[164] By late October 1985, based on the modelling work undertaken by the Department of Energy, its advisers and British Gas, the workability of the proposed formula was confirmed: "the results so far suggest that the privatised company, provided it is efficient, should achieve financial results of at least the same order of magnitude as the existing public sector Corporation." On a turnover approaching £8 billion, the simulations suggested that the Corporation might expect to earn a historic cost operating profit, before tax and interest, of some 11–12 per cent on net assets, assuming an X factor of between 2% and 3%. Higher and lower X factors would lead to lower or higher profits. The Department of Energy judged that the overall result "should provide the company with a significant incentive to maintain and improve its commercial performance . . . [although] it would be foolish to pretend that the overall system is perfect. It walks the tightrope between under and over-regulation".

The price cap formula was set out in BGC's authorisation, just as it was specified in BT's licence. But at the time the draft authorisation was prepared the precise value of X had still not been fixed. The Treasury appears to have favoured an X of 3%, which it considered was consistent with BGC's recent performance in reducing operating costs. But BGC and Rothschilds favoured a lower figure of 1%, and 2% as a maximum. BGC did not believe that a target of 3% was achievable and Rothschilds was keen to ensure the success of the pending flotation. BGC had projected declining real operating costs consistent with an X of 2% or 3%, but now suggested that the price cap should be set so that shareholders benefited as well as customers from any cost savings.[165] Equally, BGC was reluctant to agree to a price cap figure until negotiation of its balance sheet structure and debt financing at privatisation were complete (as discussed further in chapter 15, p.380). Rothshilds believed that the X factor should be set so as to achieve a growth rate in profits of five per cent to ten per cent a year in money terms or three per cent to four per cent in real terms concluding that, as BGC did not have access to new technology to reduce costs and widen its market, "we do not see, therefore, RPI – 3 applied to British Telecom as setting any reasonably precedent for British Gas."[166] The Department of Energy's preference was for a figure of around 2%.

To assist in setting the precise figure for X, Brian Pomeroy of Touche Ross was appointed in December 1985 to undertake an independent study into BGC's scope for efficiency gains. The original deadline for his report was the end of March 1986, but in the event his study was obstructed by BGC's delays in providing necessary financial and operating information – in part because the Corporation genuinely had difficulty in supplying the information and in part because of game playing. Close to the March deadline the Department wrote to BGC in frustration formally requesting its co-operation in providing the information that Pomeroy had requested and which he still needed to complete his study.[167] As a result of the delay, Pomeroy delivered his report later than intended, on 8 May 1986. In it he concluded in favour of a value for X in the range of 1.75% to 2.75%, which encompassed the Department's earlier working assumption that 2% might be appropriate.[168] In June, after Rothshilds re-confirmed that in their opinion this figure was probably the maximum the business could stand, an X of 2% was agreed with the Chancellor of the Exchequer.[169] There would also be a separate control on the level of standing charges and a condition requiring publication of the principles by which connection charges were to be made. A rapid rise in standing charges (a fixed charge for access to gas) would increase small consumers' bills disproportionately and there were fears that a price capped BGC might attempt to recoup revenues by charging excessive charges for new gas connections. The increase in standing charges was limited to the rate of inflation as measured by the RPI.[170] The terms of the price control were announced to the House on 18 June 1986, Walker commenting: "After careful examination, I have decided that the appropriate value for the initial five year period of the regulatory formula will be two . . . The formula will set a demanding discipline for the company to meet while leaving opportunities for a profit-oriented management to work for still better performance."[171] However, given the profits BGC would later record, arguably the price cap was set too low. The level of X was raised to 5% once the regulator was able to change the cap, in 1992.

## A regulatory dwarf?

The draft authorisation was prepared by the legal firm Slaughter and May and published on 9 December 1985.[172] It was subjected to a number of amendments, especially to reflect commitments made by the Government during the Committee stage in the House of Lords and to address a number of technical issues. BGC was given an obligation under its authorisation to publish tariffs and not unduly discriminate between consumers, a requirement to publish separate accounts for the gas supply business, to provide the regulator and the new Gas Consumers' Council with information, and a condition requiring BGC to consult the DGGS and the Council on the efficient use of gas and then publish the information for tariff consumers.[173]Also included were the price cap formula for tariff customers, the terms on standing charges and connection charges, the conditions of pricing for the conveyance of third party gas to contract customers, and codes of practice on emergency services, services for the elderly and disabled, and the payment of bills. In addition, BGC agreed to give an assurance that it would continue to supply gas to customers in remote areas on the current basis of pricing until at least 31 March 1991.[174] The final draft of the authorisation was published on 18 August 1986. It came into effect along with the regulatory framework under the Gas Act five days later.

After much negotiation the regulatory package had been accepted by the BGC Board, although they retained a number of reservations on the details. At the same time, there was some unease at the result within the Department of Energy. The Conservative Election Manifesto in 1983 had stated: "In the next Parliament, we shall seek other means of increasing competition in, and attracting private capital into, the gas and electricity industries . . . Merely to replace state monopolies by private ones would be to waste an historic opportunity. So we will take steps to ensure that these new firms do not exploit their powerful positions to the detriment of consumers or their competitors."[175] One Department of Energy official concluded during the privatisation planning that this commitment had been neglected as a result of Treasury pressure to sell BGC to fund tax cuts. He wrote, "the quest for the highest possible sale price for BGC has meant that the Manifesto's objectives have been forgotten and the co-operation of Sir Denis Rooke has been bought at a price that negates the initial stated objective . . . I have no doubt that future commentators and other pundits looking back will point to this as the single most important factor which either limited the success of the privatisation or sowed the seeds for its failure."[176] This official was particularly worried that BGC would be able to adopt discriminatory pricing in the contract market. However, the reality was that the commitment to competition was watered down by Peter Walker under pressure from Sir Denis Rooke, and not the Treasury. The Treasury favoured competition. Indeed, within the Treasury concerns lingered about the details of the regulation and the real prospects of effective competition in industrial gas supplies given the regulatory structure imposed.

Meanwhile, BGC complained too. BGC's worries centred on the common carriage terms, even though the perception in the Department of Energy was that BGC had got off lightly: "The fact of the matter is the BGC have got away with a common carriage regime that is likely to lead to very few direct sales."[177] In spite of his public opposition to the common carriage terms, before the Select Committee on Energy on 10 December 1985 Rooke conceded that the use of the grid by competitors would be limited due to technical factors.[178] The eventual Offer for Sale document stated similarly, "it is unlikely that common carriage developments could take place before 1990 because of the lead time required to bring forward new supplies and British Gas intends to compete effectively in the supply of gas."[179] Admittedly, in the months running up to the sale the Government walked a tight rope between calming fears about BGC's monopoly power and ensuring that investors were attracted to buying BGC shares by the prospect of healthy returns. But it does appear that the concerns within Government about the ability of the regulatory regime to keep BGC's monopoly powers in check after privatisation were real. They increased in July 1986 when the DTI expressed alarm, following complaints from industry, about BGC's pricing of fixed and interruptible gas supplies. These were designed to get consumers to switch to fixed supplies so that they would not then be able to switch quickly to using alternative fuel suppliers later. This was judged to be "a prima facie abuse of monopoly power".[180]

Publication of the details of the regulatory structure ignited critical comment outside Government. In sections of the press the powers of OFGAS were criticised as inadequate.

For example, *The Economist* called the Office "a regulatory dwarf".[181] Irwin Stelzer, formerly a director of Rothschilds in New York, caused embarrassment early in 1986 when he published a piece in *The Sunday Times* newspaper criticising the proposals for the regulation of BGC, particularly singling out BGC's ability through setting prices to deny access by competitors to its pipeline grid, the possibility of anti-competitive cross-subsidies to the industrial market, and his opinion that the price cap formula would not act as a sufficient spur for efficiency in BGC. He also scotched any notion that electricity would provide effective competition for gas supplies. In the absence of competition and with the existence of what he saw as inadequate regulation, his conclusion was that the privatisation of BGC was merely a money-raising exercise.[182] When the House of Commons Energy Select Committee reported on gas privatisation and regulation in January 1986, it raised similar concerns. The Committee concluded that the Government's privatisation plan appears to be "dominated by the revenue-raising aim" and that "privatisation without market liberalisation would be unlikely to benefit consumers". The Committee recommended that the national gas transmission and local distribution networks be established as completely separate businesses and privatised separately or retained in the public sector. The Committee doubted whether regulation could be an adequate alternative to competition in supplies.[183]

* * *

The weaknesses inherent in the regulatory regime introduced for BGC, along with the failure to restructure the Corporation to prevent anti-competitive practices, would be left for the regulator and the MMC to address after privatisation. These weaknesses stemmed from a perceived need to win over the management of BGC, and especially its Chairman, to privatisation, Peter Walker's belief that it was important to maintain a strong British Gas with world-beating qualities, and the PM's unwillingness to confront her Secretary of State. Walker was sceptical as to the extent to which real competition could be introduced into gas supply, especially for smaller gas customers.[184] It is telling that he vetoed the inclusion of a duty on the DGGS to promote competition against the advice of his officials when the Gas Bill was being drafted. The duty was introduced only later under pressure within Parliament and outside and then as "enable" competition.

More positively, since lessons had been learned from the privatisation of BT, the Gas Bill suffered much less amendment in Parliament than the earlier Telecommunications Bill (although the Government had to resort once again to the Parliamentary guillotine to prevent the Labour Opposition disrupting the privatisation timetable). This was because the Bill was better drafted, in part because of the BT example. In particular, the drafters of the Bill and the authorisation could call on the content of the Telecommunications Bill and BT's licence for models. The regulatory structure created for BT was adjusted to apply to the gas industry, including the terms of the appointment of the DGGS and the price formula.[185] But credit should also go to Peter Walker for insisting on careful preparation.

With the Gas Bill having passed through Parliament and the terms of the regulation settled, the necessary prerequisites for a successful sale of BGC had been put in place. The next chapter discusses the actual flotation.

# 15

# PRIVATISING BRITISH GAS

## The flotation and aftermath

With the Gas Bill drafted, the principles on which the offer for sale would be made needed to be settled. In November 1985 an action plan and marketing programme for a flotation sometime in the autumn of 1986 was put together with October 1986 the favoured month for the sale.[1] As in the case of the flotation of British Telecom (BT), it would be important to ensure that no other large share issues occurred immediately before the BGC sale so as not to overstretch the capital market. When it was suggested that the Treasury might try to squeeze in another privatisation before the end of the year, Rothschilds responded anxiously that this could well endanger a successful sale of BGC.[2] There was also worry that there might be a large competitive private sector offer and that the TSB share issue, already planned for mid-September 1986, might detract from a successful flotation of BGC.[3] Walker requested that the TSB issue be stopped, but the Chancellor of the Exchequer responded that there could be no question of the Government prohibiting other firms' access to the capital market.[4] As it turned out, the TSB sale was very successful and probably assisted in further raising interest amongst small investors in the BGC offer.

In the case of the flotation of the BGC there was the complicating issue of the major restructuring of the functions of the Stock Market scheduled for 27 October 1986. The changes involved a new market trading system including the ending of the separation of stockbrokers and stockjobbers who did the actual stock trading. It was to be expected that the reform, known popularly as "Big Bang", could lead to teething problems in terms of speedily handling and recording share purchases and sales. It would therefore be important not to schedule the flotation of BGC too close to 27 October. Friday 10 October appeared as a possible flotation date in a number of early outline timetables and Walker preferred the issue to be planned for October lest slippage postponed a planned November sale into early the following year and too close to a general election.[5]

It would also be important to avoid a flotation date near to the Chancellor of the Exchequer's autumn Financial Statement, usually made in mid-November setting out the Government's fiscal plans. Flotation immediately before the Statement was out of the question because of the need to disclose in the sale prospectus any fiscal changes the Chancellor was planning that could impact on BGC.[6] It was also possible that press speculation about public expenditure levels, taxation and public borrowing ahead of the Statement could unnerve the stock market. The Treasury favoured flotation sometime before the autumn Statement so as not to constrain the Chancellor on his choice of a date to make his announcement.[7] This meant having the flotation in September or early October at the latest. But Dewe Rogerson concluded that this would not leave sufficient time to market the issue effectively. The likely

364

date for the royal assent to the Gas Bill meant that the mass marketing campaign could not begin until the end of July.[8] Cazenoves weighed in pointing out that an early autumn flotation would mean generating institutional demand when many City professionals were away from their desks taking summer vacation.[9] It was therefore decided that the sale would have to occur after the autumn Statement, pushing the flotation date into the second half of November, despite Walker's reservations.[10]

From February 1986 either 21 or 28 November were the favoured dates. However, this would mean, as in the case of the BT sale, that share allotment letters confirming the share allocation to each investor would be posted out just before Christmas. To avoid exacerbating the Christmas mail rush and overwhelming the ability of the Royal Mail to deliver the allotment letters before trading in BGC shares officially began, it would be essential that the letters went out very early in December. This added to the pressure to devise a share application process that could handle the expected large number of share applications speedily.

## Planning the sale

An early decision was taken to attempt to sell 100 per cent of the Corporation in one tranche. While selling the shares in more than one tranche might raise the total sales revenue by reducing the strain on the capital market and by being able to sell later tranches of the shares at the going market price, it would not be possible to sell a second tranche of BGC's shares until after the next general election. This left open the prospect that an elected Labour Government might be able to take the company back into public ownership by buying only a small percentage of the shares. It was felt that this possibility was politically undesirable and would unnerve investors. The decision was therefore taken to sell all of the equity. At privatisation BGC would have just over four thousand million shares of which 97 per cent were to be offered for sale, the Government retaining three per cent of the shares to satisfy applications by employees and pensioners under free and matching offers and to accommodate a share bonus scheme. To be able to sell such a large issue at an appropriate price, Rothschilds advised that it would be necessary to issue the shares on a partly paid basis, as had occurred in some earlier privatisations including that of BT.[11]

Rothschilds was appointed as the issuing house and lead underwriter, following previous convention in privatisations to appoint the Department's financial adviser on the sale to this position.[12] This was in spite of lobbying from Kleinwort Benson, the financial adviser to BGC, to be joint lead issuing house. Following the BT model, there would be overseas share sales to reduce the number of shares that would need to be sold in the domestic market. Goldman Sachs, Wood Gundy, Nomura and Swiss Bank Corporation International were appointed as financial advisers and then lead managers for the overseas sales in the US, Canada, Japan and Europe, respectively[13]. Linklaters and Paines were the solicitors to the underwriters and Herbert Smith for the new company, which took over the property rights and liabilities of the Corporation on 24 August (British Gas plc was incorporated on 1 April 1986 but did not trade until 24 August). Slaughter and May acted as solicitors for the Department of Energy. Touche Ross were accountancy and tax advisers and Price Waterhouse auditors and reporting accountants. A beauty contest was held in the autumn of 1985 for specialist brokers for the BGC offer. Cazenoves was appointed for the Government and Wood Mackenzie, Hoare Govett and James Capel, with strengths in energy research, were selected by BGC. A fuller listing of the advisers during the BGC disposal is provided in Table 15.1.[14]

*Table 15.1* Advisers during the British Gas Disposal

| Company | Function |
| --- | --- |
| N.M. Rothschild and Sons Ltd | Financial advisers to the Department |
| Kleinwort Benson Ltd | Financial advisers to British Gas |
| Slaughter and May | Solicitors to the Department |
| Herbert Smith | Solicitors to British Gas |
| Linklaters and Paines | Solicitors to the Underwriters |
| Touche Ross & Co. | Accountancy and Tax adviser |
| Price Waterhouse | Auditors and reporting accountants |
| Cazenove & Co. | Stock brokers (lead broker) |
| Wood Mackenzie & Co. Ltd | Stock brokers |
| James Capel & Co | Stock brokers |
| Hoare Govett Ltd | Stock brokers |
| ERC Energy Resource Consultants Ltd. | Petroleum consultants |
| National Westminster Bank PLC | Registrars and receiving bank |
| Dewe Rogerson Limited | PR consultants |
| Young & Rubicam Ltd. | Advertising agency |
| Goldman Sachs International Corp. | US financial adviser |
| Swiss Bank Corporation International Ltd. | European financial adviser |
| Nomura Securities Company Limited | Japanese financial adviser |
| Wood Gundy Ltd | Canadian financial adviser |
| Sullivan & Cromwell | US legal adviser |
| Anderson, Mori and Rabinowitz | Japanese legal adviser |
| Blake, Cassels & Graydon | Canadian legal adviser |

*Source*: Hansard, 16 June 1986, column 408; N.M. Rothschild & Sons Ltd, *British Gas Share Offer: A Background Briefing*, 6 November 1986, p.16.

The entire privatisation planning in the Department was overseen by John Guinness, Deputy Under Secretary, and a Gas Privatisation Team was established in the Department of Energy headed by Derek Davis.[15] In addition, a number of interdepartmental committees were formed to work on different aspects of the sale. An important committee was the Key Issues Group. This included representatives from the Department of Energy, the Treasury, the Bank of England, Rothschilds and Cazenoves and met from 3 February 1986. Matters covered included the method of sale and underwriting. Another important committee was the Issuing House Progress Group, chaired by Tony Alt from Rothschilds, which organised the privatisation of BGC through working groups. Initially seven groups were set up to work on financial, legal, employee, prospectus, overseas offerings and registration issues (details in Figure 15.1). The secretary of the Group was responsible for a "Privatisation Masterplan" designed to ensure that the sale kept to timetable.[16] The first meeting of the Issuing House Progress Group occurred on 21 January. There was a BGC Steering Group and a Joint Privatisation Promotion Committee (JPPC), which organised and monitored all matters relating to the sale promotion, including the marketing roadshows, the Share Information Office, advertising and market research. An Offer for Sale Co-ordinating Group was formed and held its first meeting on 14 January 1986.[17] This included representatives from the

Department of Energy, BGC, Kleinwort Benson, Slaughter and May, and Rothschilds.[18] Its purpose was to co-ordinate work on preparing for the flotation.[19] Also, in the weeks immediately leading up to the sale Walker held weekly meetings with the BGC Chairman, Sir Denis Rooke. But during the BGC sale there was surprisingly limited contact between the officials planning the sale within the Department of Energy and those officials in the DTI who had earlier privatised BT. This resulted from the culture of departmental boundaries within the Civil Service.[20]

In the autumn of 1985 Rothschilds and Cazenoves had estimated that with reasonable market conditions and a successful marketing campaign promoting BGC as a successful, dynamic business with a rising profit profile, it should be possible to raise between £6 billion and £8 billion from the flotation through a combination of equity and debt. By the following April Rothschilds had revised its estimate and now suggested a wider valuation range of between £3.3 billion and £8.9 billion, depending upon the oil price at the time of the flotation, BGC's operating profit, debt level, and the expected dividend payout.[21] The Key Issues Group tasked Rothschilds with preparing a report on the strategy for the sale and the choice between a tender or fixed price offer.[22] The Treasury, as usual, was keen to see high sales receipts, but during this flotation, not coincidental with the improved state of the Government finances, also adopted a particularly aggressive stance on efficiency and the consumer interest. The Treasury harboured concerns about whether the regulatory system for the tariff market and competition in the contract market would be adequate to ensure that BGC operated efficiently after privatisation and customers were properly protected from monopoly abuse, as discussed in the previous chapter. Even so, to ensure a healthy sale price, the Treasury favoured in the months leading up to the flotation keeping open the option of a 51 per cent sale in the event of bad market conditions or a failure to reach agreement with the Corporation on the details of the Prospectus, especially the profit and dividend forecasts. Rothschilds had advised that the profit and dividend forecasts would be very important in attracting sufficient investment. However, in the Department of Energy the view was taken that to sell a bare majority of the shares would signal that something had gone wrong with the sale. The Government had already indicated publicly a preference for a total disposal. It was agreed in the Key Issues Group that only if it became absolute necessary would less than a 100 per cent sale occur.

The Key Issue Group's report in August 1986 was prepared on the basis that the Government's objectives in privatising BGC were "to secure the successful transfer of the company to the private sector", "maximise net sales proceeds", "achieve widespread shareownership" and "avoid an excessive premium in the aftermarket". The risk of the latter would be reduced by having a tender issue, but Rothschilds was against the idea favouring a fixed price offer on the grounds that this was more likely to appeal to the small investor – an argument that had held sway in a number of the earlier privatisations including BT. After deliberation, the Group agreed. Rothschilds and Cazenoves did submit a paper in late February 1986 proposing a partial tender/fixed price mechanism, but it was felt that this could damage the success of the sale.[23] The Key Issues Group also concluded that the shares should be fully underwritten, in spite of criticism from the Public Accounts Committee and others of some of the underwriting terms in earlier privatisations. The underwriters were many of the same banks and acceptance houses as in the sale of BT two years earlier.[24] However, during the sale of BGC the overall commission rate was successfully negotiated down to below the rate paid during the BT issue. To reduce the underwriting costs a two tier structure was chosen, involving a normal fixed price offer to the general public with part of the offer

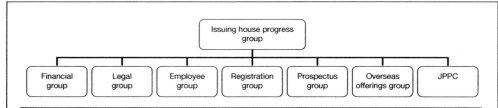

## Issuing House Progress Group

To be responsible for liaison with the Department of Energy/BGC Offer for Sale Co-ordinating Group and for the planning, co-ordination and delegation of work to Working Groups; to receive and consider reports from Working Groups; to resolve matters that cannot be resolved within individual Working Groups; to act as arbiter between Working Groups in the event of a conflict of interests arising; to maintain a privatisation Masterplan and to ensure that work is progressed by Working Groups in accordance with the time constraints imposed by the Masterplan; to monitor expenditure of the Working Groups.

## Financial Group

To consider detailed capital structure points referred to the Group by the principals; to produce all necessary financial information so as to enable BGC plc to meet the Listing Requirements of the London Stock Exchange; to ensure that whatever additional financial information as is required to enable Overseas Offerings of BGC plc to be made in USA, Canada, Japan and Europe is also available, the Financial Group to be advised of such additional requirements by the Overseas Offerings Working Group; to monitor the procurement of all appropriate clearances from the Inland Revenue.

## Legal Group

To oversee the Vesting of British Gas plc and the finalising of the Memorandum and Articles of Association; to ensure that all necessary verification and due diligence is undertaken (other than Prospectus verification); also to act as a forum for the debate on any legal matter which cannot be accommodated within any other Working Group (such as underwriting agreements).

## Employee Group

To co-ordinate arrangements, including communications, for BGC employees and pensioners to be allocated shares in BGC plc and to subscribe for additional shares; to ensure that the Issuing House Progress Group is kept informed of areas of particular concern to BGC employees including pension rights and staffing levels; to liaise with the printers on the production of all associated documents.

## Registration Group

*(full title, Registration and Logistics Group)*
To co-ordinate arrangements with the Receiving Banks, including collection of completed application forms; to

establish means of detecting multiple applications; to co-ordinate arrangements for the establishment of a permanent Register; to liaise with British Gas over the establishment of any Customer Shareholder Register; to oversee arrangements for the establishment of the Employee Share Register; to provide guidance as to the possible design and layout of application forms; to organise the national distribution of the prospectus, liaising with the Prospectus Working Group on this task; and to draw up and advise on the tax consequences of the necessary Instalment and Incentive Agreements.

## Prospectus Group

To co-ordinate the drafting of the Mini Prospectus and Prospectus, including all necessary verification, Report on Title and Material Contracts; to liaise with the Stock Exchange; to oversee all printing arrangements relating to the Prospectus and its immediately associated documents; to compile information on BGC's programme of exploration and development in the run-up to privatisation; and to co-ordinate the production of a report from petroleum consultants.

## Overseas Offerings Group

To co-ordinate the timing of overseas offerings; to advise on overseas offer terms; to co-ordinate the production of overseas prospectuses; to organise the promotional effort necessary to ensure the success of overseas offerings; to ensure that BGC plc meets the necessary legal requirements of overseas offerings to be made in the USA, Canada, Japan and Europe.

## Joint Privatisation Promotion Committee (JPPC)

To organise and monitor all matters relating to the promotion of BGC plc including:

- Familiarisation visits for advisers, brokers and investment analysts
- Roadshows
- Share Information Office and literature produced by it (including legal vetting)
- Corporate advertising
- Pre-flotation advertising
- Offer for Sale advertising
- Market Research
- Design and layout of all Offer for Sale literature
- Introduction of brokers to the company
- Drafting of the Share Information Office corporate brochure in close liaison with the Prospectus Group.

*Figure 15.1* BGC privatisation – Issuing House Progress Group organisational structure February 1986

Source: G800/49/14 Part II.

placed with the institutions first.[25] Rothschilds agreed to a commission rate of 0.175 per cent for arranging the underwriting.

A programme of lunches with City institutions began in May 1986 to raise interest in the issue. More formal meetings with the institutions began at the end of September.[26] The method of flotation was designed by Rothschilds to meet the objectives of the Key Issues Group and to achieve a ten per cent premium on the offer price in the aftermarket, to get the sale away successfully. Rothschilds argued that BGC would be valued in the City on the basis of its earnings, both historic and forecast, and on the basis of the dividend yield on which the shares would be offered, rather than on the basis of the underlying net asset value of the company. The tighter the regulation, the more investors would pay attention to the level of dividends that would be paid rather than the forecast earnings and the more like a dull utility business BGC would seem.

In the Department of Energy there was understandable concern that as in previous privatisations the underwriters would try to bid the share price down. Rothschilds did contemplate persuading institutional investors to accept a premium price over the public offer price in return for receiving a sizeable allotment of shares. But by late September 1986 the bank had decided that this was unlikely to be advantageous.[27] Nevertheless, as in the case of the BT sale a percentage of the shares was allocated firm to the financial institutions. Each institution was offered a package of shares some of which were placed firm, some placed subject to clawback if the UK public offer was heavily over-subscribed, and the remainder using conventional sub-underwriting. UK institutions would receive 3,230 million shares, 30 per cent as "firm placing shares" at a commission rate of 0.5 per cent and 20 per cent as "provisional placing shares" at a commission rate of 1.25 per cent. The balance of the shares were "commitment shares", placed with the underwriters if the UK public offer was not fully subscribed, also with a commission rate of 1.25 per cent. But if retail demand was very high in the UK, the provisional placing shares would be subject to "clawback" to ensure priority allocation to small investors. The clawback would also apply to shares provisionally allocated to overseas buyers. Clawback served not only to ensure a priority allocation of sufficient shares to small investors but would tend to make the institutions short of BGC shares in the UK and overseas and thereby raise the likelihood of a successful aftermarket.[28] The institutions would be asked to pay a premium of five per cent to ten per cent over the basic offer price for the firm shares, to reflect the certainty of receiving them. Rothschilds and Kleinwort Benson were precluded from taking part in the tender to avoid a conflict of interest.[29]

The BGC privatisation was the first involving a fully synchronised sale across different countries. In October 1985 Rothschilds reported that following a number of informal discussions with overseas banks it was their opinion that 40 per cent of the shares could be placed overseas.[30] Later the New York office of Goldman Sachs, the Government's financial advisers in the US, reported that they expected "strong US demand for British Gas shares in both the institutional and retail markets".[31] Even so, to favour the domestic market the overseas allocation was restricted to a maximum of 20 per cent. The Department of Energy did contemplate whether BGC should seek a "triple A" rating to help ensure that the flotation in America was successful, but BGC objected to diverting management time into the effort. The Department wondered whether this reflected the Corporation's lukewarm attitude to the whole idea of an overseas offer. This led to a comment in the Department that "You can lead a horse to water but rhubarb must be forced!"[32] Norman Lamont at the Treasury was not satisfied and also argued that BGC should be pressured to seek the rating.[33]

However, Goldman Sachs and Rothschilds saw only marginal benefit for the float in the US, and Cazenoves none for the UK. It was decided not to pursue the matter.[34]

The 20 per cent for the overseas market was expected "to give a good impression of scarcity and so as to avoid a high degree of flowback".[35] Walker was keen that BGC shares sold in the US should not be resold quickly and flow back to the UK, as had happened immediately after the flotation of BT. He believed that if this happened again, "it would pose a very serious question mark over the placing of any further privatisation issues in the United States". However, Goldman Sachs assured him that this was not likely to occur this time.[36] During the sale of BT it seems that the flowback from the US immediately afterwards was exacerbated by the fact that the US institutions were unable to build up big enough share allotments to be worth holding longer term.[37] It was intended that the gas offer would address this problem. Also, after the privatisation of BT there had been concern that the local managers of the share offer in the US had unduly favoured themselves through the share allocation. During the privatisation of BGC, efforts were made to better monitor the share sale to prevent this happening.[38] Also, reflecting the fact that the Government decided that it would be possible to sell shares into the US through Wood Gundy in Canada, leaving out US banks if necessary, the US institutions agreed to follow UK practice and commit to the offer from the beginning. This did away with the need, as during the BT flotation, to organise for the Bank of England to step in if the offer was not fully underwritten in the US.[39] Also, the commission rates for the overseas share sales had been considerably higher than for the domestic sales in the BT flotation, something commented upon by the PAC in its report on the sale. For example, Morgan Stanley in the US received 3.5 per cent compared with UK rates of 1.5 per cent for placement shares and 1.25 per cent for commitment shares. This time the overseas commission rates were negotiated down to 1.65 per cent.[40]

The plan became to aim for a public oversubscription of 1.25 times the shares on offer. Following the successful BT precedent, a Pathfinder prospectus was to be issued, on Friday 31 October. This would confirm a provisional allocation of 40 per cent of the shares on offer to UK institutions, 40 per cent to UK retail investors and around 20 per cent to overseas markets, subject to clawback.[41] If the domestic public offer was approximately twice oversubscribed then some of the shares intended for the overseas markets and UK institutions would be clawed back, raising the allocation to the public from 40 per cent to up to 60 per cent.[42] When the Government became aware that a small number of wealthy individuals might obtain sizeable allotments of firmly placed shares by making special arrangements with City institutions with which they were connected, a letter was sent to potential priority applicants requesting a warranty that they would not transfer any of the benefit of their applications to individuals or funds held by individuals.[43]

BGC was worried about the prospect after privatisation of a hostile takeover bid, especially from one or more oil companies or gas equipment suppliers. Within the Department of Energy too there was some nervousness about a possible future ownership of BGC that could put the country's energy supplies at risk. While it was recognised that BGC's size and the threat of an MMC inquiry would act as some barrier to an undesirable takeover, additional powers were considered necessary. In accordance with privatisation precedents, including BT, Rothschilds recommended that a 15 per cent limit be placed on any individual shareholding in the company's Articles of Association. In the case of BT the Stock Exchange had judged this level to be compatible with the EC rules, which required that shares be "freely negotiable". The risk of a successful legal challenge to a 15 per cent shareholding limit in the case of BGC was therefore judged to be small. However, BGC pressed for a much lower limit, at one time as little as one per cent, and when this was rejected by the Government as clearly unacceptable, no higher than ten per cent.[44] Rothschilds advised that a ten per cent limit might seriously depress the flotation proceeds, while the Treasury concluded that with limited prospects for effective competition in gas supply, the takeover threat was necessary to provide a stimulus to efficiency within the company.[45]

The Treasury suggested as a solution the introduction of a special share, which would permit the Secretary of State to gain temporary voting control of the company if someone attempted to obtain more than a given percentage of the voting rights. This left the door open to allow takeovers that were considered acceptable to the Government. However, the Department of Energy opposed the idea believing that it would be entirely inappropriate for the Secretary of State to take control of the voting of the company just because someone had built up a particular shareholding.[46] Rothschilds suggested alternatively including special restrictions on holdings of BGC shares by competitor oil companies, but the Department of Energy concluded that providing a legally tight definition of an "oil company" would be too difficult. Instead, the Department preferred to rely on imposing a maximum 15 per cent shareholding limit, plus the possibility of an OFT/MMC merger review under competition law if a takeover bid occurred. It continued to argue that it would be too risky under EC rules to go below a 15 per cent limit on individual shareholdings.[47] The limit would be backed up by a special share held by the Government to prevent the removal of the limit from the Articles of Association. The special share would be redeemable at some unspecified future date at the Government's request.

BGC was still not content and proposed that the company should have a veto over the future redemption of the special share and that the limitations on shareholdings should be enshrined in the company's Memorandum of Association rather than its Articles. This would make the share limit more difficult to remove in the future. This proved quite unacceptable to the Treasury and the Department of Energy.[48] In February 1986 Walker and Sir Denis Rooke were still unable to agree on the terms of the restriction on individual shareholdings and the special share.[49] At the same time, it was increasingly urgent to get the matter settled so that BGC's Articles and Memorandum of Association could be published and made available to Parliament. There was protest at the Committee stage of the Bill regarding the delay.[50] In the end Rooke backed down, at a time when both the Government and BGC were having to make compromises on the terms of BGC's regulation and financial structure. The 15 per cent limit was confirmed, along with a special share redeemable by the Government. It was decided that there should be no nationality requirements for directors, as existed for BT, where the CEO had to be British. This was because of a perceived threat of a possible successful challenge from the European Commission. In the case of BT, the Government had reckoned that it would be able to see off a legal challenge on the grounds that telecommunications was a strategically important asset. The same argument was not thought to be valid for the gas industry.

As in previous privatisations a Memorandum of Understanding between BGC and the Secretary of State setting out the relationship between the company and the Government in the interim period before flotation was agreed, including restrictions on new debt financing. The Treasury made clear that if the flotation was delayed beyond the end of November 1986, it would feel obliged to impose on the new company nationalised industry style EFLs and financial and performance targets.[51]

## The marketing campaign

It was clear from the outset of the privatisation that given the size of the company there would have to be a major marketing initiative to ensure that BGC could be successfully sold. The BGC offer was likely to be around double the value of the BT sale and the objective became to attract around an unprecedented four million retail investors as well as the usual City interest. At the same time, it was recognised that BGC might be less attractive to investors than BT. BT was a profitable and expanding business, while there was a risk that potential investors would view BGC to be a relatively boring utility with limited prospects.[52]

In the autumn of 1985 Dewe Rogerson undertook an initial assessment of the marketing that would be needed, on behalf of the Joint Privatisation Promotion Committee. It reported that there was considerable public opposition to the privatisation of BGC and that while the Corporation had a good image with potential investors, this was not as strong as BT's at a similar stage of the marketing campaign.[53] In the run-up to the privatisation of BT there had been public concern about the possible effects of privatisation on customer service. Dewe Rogerson reported that its preliminary research indicated a similar concern surrounding the sale of BGC. BGC's corporate advertising campaign began, therefore, with TV commercials to reassure viewers that BGC was "committed to service" and "committed to its customers". From February 1986 the corporate campaign shifted to project BGC as a dynamic leader in energy supplies.[54]

The sale of BGC involved an advertising budget larger than that used for BT, in part reflecting higher TV advertising costs. The campaign was directed by Young & Rubicam, who were appointed in July 1986 from a short list of four firms.[55] With Dewe Rogerson, they had already been involved in designing the corporate advertising.[56] The marketing of the issue in the City was planned by representatives from the Department of Energy, BGC, Cazenoves, Rothschilds, Kleinworts, Dewe Rogerson, Hoare Govett, Wood MacKenzie and James Capel and fell into two parts. The initial part of the programme consisted of a series of site visits, lunches and dinners, at which senior investment managers from financial institutions were introduced to BGC's senior management team. The aim was to improve the image of BGC in the City and the programme commenced in mid-May 1986. The second part involved the publication of brokers' research from Wood MacKenzie, James Capel and Hoare Govett concentrating on key aspects of BGC's business.[57]

Seventeen regional co-ordinators were appointed shortly after Easter 1986 covering the whole country to assist in marketing the issue to retail investors and financial intermediaries such as accountants and bank managers. In addition, the beginning of August saw the start of the largest ever single mailing to take place in the UK. Over a number of days letters went out with details of the share offer to BGC's 16 million or so customers along with their gas bills, in what was referred to as the "bill stuffer". Four million registrations were received as a result of this mailing.[58] A separate "solus mailing" to customers was also undertaken, handled by Burrup Mathieson & Co who had been responsible for printing work during the privatisation of BT, in the form of a letter signed by Sir Denis Rooke. In addition, Burrup Mathieson was responsible for the mailing of prospectuses and offer guides to nearly 7.7 million people in mid-November.[59] Another part of the marketing campaign included road-shows (as used during the sale of BT and of the residual shareholdings in Britoil, BAe and C&W) to alert financial intermediaries – stockbrokers, accountants, bank managers and others – to the attractiveness of the offer. The roadshows were undertaken in two stages, both before and immediately after the issue of a Pathfinder prospectus. However, BGC objected to being involved in the roadshows until the Gas Bill had received its royal assent. As a result, the roadshows did not begin until July.[60] In July and August there were 16 roadshows around the country. Overseas roadshows were also mounted, especially in North America.[61] However one suggestion, to encourage share applications by allowing payment by credit card, came to nothing. The Treasury objected to the idea on the grounds that it would encourage share stagging and the credit card companies, Access and Barclaycard, declined the invitation to be involved in the sale.[62] Another marketing idea, also quickly aborted, was put forward by Dewe Rogerson. This involved issuing a special postage stamp to promote the sale. The Department of Energy judged this to be a non-runner. The measure would have required the co-operation of the Post Office and the Post Office unions and this could not be guaranteed.[63]

The marketing strategy was very similar to that pursued during the sale of BT, namely to create a strong retail demand for the shares in Britain in part to stimulate greater institutional and overseas interest in the offer because of the prospect of a shortage of shares. One obvious group to target was BGC's customers. Rothschilds came up with a special scheme for gas customers under which they would pre-register for shares and be guaranteed a minimum allotment and preferential treatment for applications above this minimum. The customer share register would be kept separate from the main share register until after the flotation.[64] Walker was sympathetic to the idea, but Lawson and Moore argued that the proposal would be discriminatory. The 22 per cent of the public that were non-gas users would not be able to take advantage of the scheme and importantly many were Conservative voters living in rural areas with no access to mains gas. They also felt that the scheme would deplete the number of shares available for the main share offer.[65] Meanwhile, Rooke pointed out that in implementing any special arrangements for customers, BGC's billing records were not necessarily accurate because people moved home without informing the Corporation. In addition, records for prepayment customers were so incomplete that they would need to be excluded from any preferential scheme. As prepayment gas consumers were often the poorest households, excluding them from the benefits would be very politically controversial.[66]

A specially constituted working party of the Registration and Logistics Group put forward a number of proposals for a customer share scheme in a report on 21 February 1986. The scheme finally selected involved BGC's domestic gas consumers who registered their interest by 14 November being guaranteed the right to buy at least 200 priority shares. Apprehension remained within the Treasury about the risk that the Government would not be able to honour the guarantee of shares to all those customers who applied and about the possible costs. But in discussions between Walker, Lawson and the PM at No. 10 on 29 May 1986 it was agreed that the customer share scheme should go ahead, "bearing in mind the importance of the sale and the great value of securing the widest possible spread of share ownership".[67] Gas customers would also be able to apply by telephone to the Share Information Office. Although one MP objected that some of his constituents using a gas fired district heating system would be unable to benefit, as it turned out the scheme proved to be a big success.[68]

The BT sale had involved a minimum investment of £260, but with only £100 payable on application. Rothschilds and Dewe Rogerson were of the view that it would be even more important in the BGC flotation than in the earlier privatisations to have a low minimum price for each share to generate sufficient interest from small investors. It would be important to attract a substantial number of individual investors to meet the Government's shareholding agenda and reduce the strain on the City and overseas markets. There was still some concern, although much more muted than during the privatisation of BT, that the sum to be raised might overstretch the capital market.[69] The Department of Energy and the Treasury initially had in mind for BGC a minimum investment of £200, with a first payment of around 80p per share. Rothschilds advocated a lower figure of £135 to £150 and an initial outlay of 50p. Dewe Rogerson was even more cautious, canvassing at one point a minimum investment of only £50 and later around £100. Its research had shown that a lack of sufficient cash was the main reason why some of those who had expressed an interest in buying BT shares had failed to do so.[70] Also, Rothschilds advised that to attract sufficient small investors the part payment for the shares at flotation should be no higher than 40 per cent of the fully paid up price.[71] However, the Treasury with its eye on its privatisation revenue target for the year wanted to see a first instalment payment of no lower than 45 per cent.[72] In the end it was agreed that the initial payment required would be £50 for a minimum investment of 100 shares. Meanwhile, BGC expressed concern that the share register should not go greatly over the four million level because of the costs of administration. The Board favoured a minimum investment of around £200.[73] In spite of the unnecessary worries of BT management two years earlier that they would not be able to accommodate all of their investors at company meetings, BGC management raised the same issue and proposed to limit attendance via a ticket. The Treasury rejected the idea.

Other schemes to attract small investors were introduced mirroring those used in the BT sale, including lower than normal commission rates for share purchases and special dealing facilities for the resale of the shares after flotation.[74] But as during the BT offer, the most important carrots for the small investor were payment by instalments and the benefit of bonus shares or bill vouchers. It was judged early on that the terms for the bonus shares and vouchers would have to be at least as generous as those offered during the sale of BT to prevent media criticism of the Government for meanness. In fact, the Department of Energy wished to go even further and was keen to improve on the BT scheme, where vouchers of a maximum value of £216 or up to 400 bonus shares had been on offer. A working group came up with two schemes, one involving special terms for all investors and the other limited to BGC's 16 million customers. But given the BT precedent it was quickly judged to be out of the question to limit the benefits to customers.[75] Rooke did put forward the idea of "super vouchers" to provide even greater rewards to gas users, but the Department of Energy was hostile on the grounds that the vouchers were there to ensure a successful flotation not to reward past customers for buying gas. The Department concluded that if there was to be a "super voucher" the cost should be met by BGC. On receiving this news, BGC seems to have lost interest in the proposal.[76] Another idea, this time from the Department of Energy, that the vouchers might be convertible into premium bonds to broaden the appeal to non-gas users, also seems to have quickly disappeared.[77]

The incentives scheme chosen was designed by the Department, the Treasury and Rothschilds in consultation with BGC. Bill vouchers worth £10 would be issued for every 100 shares allotted and retained for three years, to discourage early selling of the shares, subject to a maximum for each shareholder of £250 in vouchers. The vouchers would, of course, only appeal to BGC customers. Other share purchasers would opt for the bonus issue. However, there were some changes to the voucher scheme adopted during the BT sale to make the incentive more attractive and to prevent some of the complaints that had dogged the BT issue. In particular, husbands and wives would be able to use their vouchers against the same bill (vouchers could be used against a gas bill in another person's name provided that the gas was supplied, at least in part, to the holder's home) and voucher holders would be allowed to keep their vouchers for a period rather than being obliged to use them against the first available gas bill. This would help ensure that the full advantage of the voucher was not lost, something that had led to particular criticism following the BT sale.[78] In addition, the voucher entitlement would be arranged so as to avoid a skewing of applications for shares, as had occurred during the privatisation of BT in favour of the number of shares which provided the greatest yield from the incentives.

During the privatisation of BT there were a relatively small number of share bands that investors could apply for, in part constrained by the provisions of the voucher system. This led to some problems for the receiving banks when people applied for invalid numbers, for example 500 shares. In the BGC flotation the vouchers would not limit the share bandings in the same way. Agreement was reached between Rothschilds, the National Westminster Bank and the Treasury for bands of 100 to 1000 shares in multiples of 100 and 1,000 to 2,500 shares in multiples of 500.[79] One voucher worth £10 would be awarded for every multiple of 100 shares bought in the offer for sale and held continuously to qualifying dates between 31 December 1987 and 31 December 1989. The maximum value of the bill vouchers a person could receive would be obtained by purchasing 2,500 shares. The voucher arrangements therefore represented an improvement on the BT scheme in terms of value, usage and flexibility. At the same time, the Treasury had questioned the need for a bill voucher incentive scheme and had been determined to keep down the cost.[80] One official commented that the vouchers should be as generous as in the case of BT but no more: "I think it is agreed that vouchers and bonus shares are not a cost effective way of generating applications (or retaining shareholder loyalty)."[81]

As an alternative to the bill vouchers, applicants would be able to choose bonus shares.[82] Bonus shares would be of benefit to non-gas users in particular and would be granted on the basis of one share for every ten purchased in the offer and held until 31 December 1989.[83] The maximum number of bonus shares per investor was capped at 500.[84] BGC was initially sensitive about the relative yield on the vouchers and the bonus shares. Rooke felt that it would be dishonest to steer his customers towards vouchers when the bonus shares were likely to be more valuable in the longer run.[85] However, within the Department of Energy it was felt that the BT sale had created an expectation that bill vouchers would be on offer as well as bonus shares.[86] Following experience during the BT sale, the expectation was that most investors would opt for the bonus shares, although it was hoped that the simplifications introduced to the BGC scheme might generate more interest in the vouchers.[87]

The marketing campaign was accompanied by disagreement between BGC, the Department of Energy and the Treasury over who should meet the various costs. The Department maintained that the expense of the corporate advertising campaign should be met fully by BGC, albeit that in private it conceded that in helping to ensure a successful flotation, "The campaign, after all, is more in our interests than theirs".[88] Also, the Department of Energy under pressure from the Treasury requested that BGC pay £4 million of the other pre-flotation advertising costs. BGC responded hostilely but agreed to provide £1 million as a goodwill gesture.[89] The Treasury remained keen to see BGC pick up more of the expense. Meanwhile, as during earlier privatisations, the Treasury tried to rein back the overall expense of the sale. At one point it insisted that £650,000 of the costs should be offset by savings elsewhere in the Department of Energy's budget. This led to an angry reaction from Walker who accused the Treasury of adopting a "short-sighted line" given the "miniscule" costs compared to the potential sales revenue.[90]

Aware of the deal BT had negotiated with the DTI over the allocation of the total costs of the sale, Rooke dug in arguing that as it was the Government that wanted the privatisation it should bear the costs other than those BGC had already agreed to bear.[91] After some weeks of sometimes tetchy negotiation, during which there were fears that delay in agreement might set back the entire privatisation timetable, BGC agreed to meet a further proportion of the expense.[92] However, the issue erupted again, in October 1986, when Rooke suggested that the Government should meet BGC's full flotation costs, estimated then at some £13 million, on the grounds that this cost would be more than recouped through a higher sale price. Whereas in the private sector flotations costs were typically treated as an extraordinary item, "below the line", BGC proposed to follow the BT example and treat them as an ordinary trading cost. If the Government met the cost, the reported profits would be higher. Rooke's suggestion won some support from Rothschilds and John Guinness in the Department of Energy. However, while the Treasury indicated that it would not necessarily oppose the proposal provided it could be shown definitely to lead to higher sales proceeds, it was reluctant to change what had now become established practice in privatisations that corporations paid their own expenses.[93]

In the end the Corporation paid for its own advisers, corporate advertising, registrar's fees, and the administration costs of the employee share offer. The Government paid for its advisers, underwriting commissions, the registrar's setting up fees, the vouchers and bonus shares, and the free shares for employees. The costs of Price Waterhouse, Dewe Rogerson and the overseas banks who provided advice to the Department and BGC were split equally. Certain other costs, for example the flotation and Prospectus advertising, PR consultants and roadshows, were also shared.[94]

## The employee share offer

BGC's employees and pensioners were offered shares on especially favourable terms so as to help neutralise union opposition to the sale within the Corporation and to meet the Government's agenda of encouraging employee share ownership. In E(DL) Sub-Committee in June 1980, on the suggestion of the Treasury, an upper limit on free offers to employees during privatisations had been agreed of around £70 per employee. Free offers in subsequent privatisations had been worth between around £50 and £70.[95] There had also been matching offers where employees could buy additional shares on privileged terms, limited to one free share for each one purchased with an upper ceiling on the total value. The BT scheme was more complex than the other flotations, involving free shares worth some £70, a two for one matching offer for up to 77 shares purchased and a ten per cent discount on purchases of up to 1,600 further shares. The discount was deducted from the final instalment payable in April 1986, although by then many employees had sold their shares and therefore they lost this advantage.

BGC initially requested a share offer package for its employees and pensioners that would be more costly per employee than in the case of the earlier sales, including that of BT.[96] The BGC proposal was for a free offer of shares worth around £70, as adopted during the BT sale, but with a further increment of shares based on the length of service. There would also be a matching offer worth up to £400 and a discount offer of £250. Immediately the Treasury objected on grounds of cost and precedent. Lawson and Moore were not keen to go beyond what had been offered during the BT sale.[97]

However, there was some sympathy for the BGC proposal within the Department of Energy. Although more expensive per employee than the BT offer, the Department agreed that because of the much larger size of the BGC flotation the BGC proposal would account for a lower percentage of the total sales receipts. Also, the Department felt that a generous scheme was needed "to carry the workforce with us" and to encourage management to support the flotation. The Department responded with a proposal that attempted to sidestep the £70 free offer limit set in E(DL) Sub-Committee. The proposal was for an additional £2 worth of free shares for each year of service and a matching offer of two shares for each purchased, up to a maximum of £300. There would also be a discount offer of ten per cent on purchases of up to a further £2,000 worth of shares. Overall, the Department's scheme involved a maximum value of shares per employee of £745. Later, due to objections from the Treasury that this was far too generous, the value was reduced to £700 and then to £600.[98]

By February 1986 the proposal on the table was for a matching offer giving employees £400 of shares for a contribution of £200. However, if the value of the discount scheme was added to the matching offer, this would rise to £650 of shares for a contribution per employee of £325.[99] By now the Treasury was opposing any offer that amounted to more than a maximum value of shares per employee of £530.[100] Rooke was still looking for a deal worth £750 per employee.[101] Another source of friction was the proposed treatment of BGC pensioners. The BGC was keen to see the Corporation's pensioners benefit too with perhaps up to £75 per head of free shares, but the Treasury objected that giving pensioners shares during a privatisation would be unprecedented.[102] For example, pensioners did not receive free shares during the BT flotation. In any case, the Treasury argued that such an incentive for pensioners was unnecessary because the aim of the employee scheme was not to reward previous service to BGC, but rather to provide encouragement for future improved performance.[103] As seemingly a bargaining ploy, Walker agreed to settle for a £50 limit on free shares to pensioners provided the employee scheme devised by the Department went through.[104]

In a meeting between Walker, Lawson and the PM on 29 May designed to break the deadlock, the PM conceded to Walker's request for a more generous employee scheme to the one favoured by the Treasury. The PM concluded that the expense was "tiny" in relation to the potential revenue from the flotation and also leant towards generosity for BGC's pensioners. The Chancellor of the Exchequer's objections were overridden. Each person employed continuously by BGC from 1 May to 13 November 1986 and contracted to work more than 16 hours per week would be offered 52 free shares, plus £2 worth of shares for every year of continuous employment in BGC at 31 May 1986. Qualifying employees would also benefit from a two for one matching offer for up to 111 shares purchased, and up to around £2,000 worth of shares (1,481 shares) at a ten per cent price discount, provided that the shares were still held at 19 April 1988, the date of the final instalment under the partly paid share scheme. Pensioners would benefit from up to 56 shares free each, worth up to £76, and both pensioners and current employees could take advantage of a priority application scheme for further shares.[105] As in past privatisations, the free and matching shares would be vested in an employee profit sharing scheme for a minimum of two years to obtain favourable tax treatment.[106]

The terms of the proposal followed the BT precedent but with the innovation of an entitlement to free shares based on the length of service and the total package had a value above the Treasury's target figure.[107] Rothschilds warned that a discount offer of shares to employees might encourage employees to buy shares to stag the offer and indeed at the flotation some banks did offer loans to BGC employees to help them buy more shares.

BGC allowed employees to opt out of the scheme, but in the event relatively few chose to do so.[108]

## Profitability, the balance sheet and accounting practices

Early on it was recognised that BGC was a potentially attractive investment in terms of cash flow. The Corporation had invested nearly £3.6 billion in fixed assets over the five years before privatisation and had still been able to repay all but £250 million of its debt – and had accumulated cash and short-term monetary investments of nearly £1 billion.[109] Nevertheless, Rothschilds stressed that a successful sale of BGC would depend upon the reporting of a rising profit trend and forecasts of increasing profits and healthy dividend payments, otherwise the company would be seen by investors as a dull utility stock. Investors were unlikely to treat claims for future profit growth as credible if current growth trends were flat or declining. They advised, therefore, that the goal should be a forecast of a ten per cent profit increase in 1986/7,[110] the year of the flotation. However, profits for 1981/2 and 1982/3 had risen following the Government's decision to increase domestic gas prices by ten per cent above the rate of inflation and this would make achieving the rising profit trend in the following years more difficult. Also, from 1983/4 to 1985/6 BGC kept price increases at or below the rate of inflation despite a rise in gas input costs because it was on course to meet its financial targets set by Government. Domestic gas prices, which accounted for the largest part of BGC's revenues, rose by an average of only four per cent in 1984/5 and four per cent in 1985/6.[111] The prospects of flat or even perhaps falling profitability in 1986/7, when BGC was to be floated, were increased by the fact that profit growth in 1985/6 had benefited from exchange rate movements and by a cold spell in the winter, which had boosted gas sales.

In November 1985 Walker was planning that BGC should achieve a pre-tax profit in the current year of nearly ten per cent higher than in the previous year and a further ten per cent rise in profits in 1986/7. However, this rosy picture assumed continued good trading conditions and a further rise in gas tariffs. The Treasury was pressing for a five per cent to six per cent price increase or possibly more; the Department for at least four per cent.[112] Rothschilds estimated that a six per cent rise in gas prices in 1986 would raise the price/earnings (P/E) ratio on which BGC would be valued and could add around £3 billion to the sales proceeds. But BGC was unwilling to sanction the sort of price rise suggested by the Department, let alone that preferred by the Treasury. BGC decided to raise gas tariffs in 1986/7 by an average of only 1.7 per cent, arguing that a larger increase was unjustified given the Corporation's financial target of a four per cent return on its current cost assets over the four years to 31 March 1987, which it was already achieving, and price competition from other fuels.[113] Also, BGC management adopted the strategy that the profit recorded in 1986/7 should not be greater than that achievable in later years, to avoid investors having profit expectations after privatisation that could not be met. Furthermore, BGC also made it known that they were not prepared to offer to pay out a high percentage of profits as dividends to attract investors.

The disagreements between the Department and BGC on prices, profits and forecast dividends were not assisted by a suspicion within Government that BGC had hidden profits for years to prevent the Treasury getting its hands on them. The suspicion appeared to be confirmed when in one meeting on the flotation Rooke is said to have claimed that he could produce some further profits if needed. Meanwhile, the Government considered that ensuring a successful sale overrode setting prices to achieve the Corporation's financial target.[114]

There were also other sources of friction over finances between the Corporation and the Government in the run-up to the privatisation. One related to the reporting of financial information in the Prospectus using historic cost accounting (HCA). BGC used current cost accounting (CCA) for its annual reports which, given the higher current replacement cost of assets, led to lower reported profits than on a HCA basis. The Government took the view that HCA was the more normal approach to financial reporting in share sale prospectuses. Also, Rothschilds confirmed, following soundings with stockbrokers, that it would be the HCA figures on which investors would judge the company and higher reported profits would lead to higher flotation receipts.[115] After lengthy discussions during which BGC management remained adamantly committed to CCA, they did reluctantly give some ground. Parallel HCA and CCA figures were published in the sale Prospectus.[116]

Another subject of disagreement was the appropriate level of gearing at privatisation. BGC was opposed to the introduction of new debt capital. Management argued that the company would need to borrow after privatisation to fund a necessary diversification programme because of the slow growth in its core gas supply business. It should therefore start life in the private sector with no debt.[117] Officials from Rothschilds gave their preliminary views on a privatised BGC's capital structure in October 1985. While noting that in their opinion, "Relative to the important consideration of establishing an environment in which BG plc can be seen to grow, the precise details of capital structure are of relative second-order importance", they suggested that an opening position in negotiations with Rooke should be a debt level of £2.5 billion, but with a fall back of a minimum of £2 billion. This could raise the flotation receipts by up to £1.5 billion because the introduction of debt would reduce the size of the equity issue needed. Moreover, it would help ensure healthy dividends per share post-privatisation for any overall growth in profitability, which would be attractive to equity investors.[118] The Treasury went further canvassing that the Government's opening position should be a debt level of closer to £3 billion or £3.5 billion, especially as it might be negotiated downwards by BGC. The Department replied that any such figure would be "unnegotiable with Sir D. Rooke."[119]

The new debt would take the form of British Gas loan stock held by the Exchequer.[120] With a debt of £2.5 billion the result would be a gearing level at privatisation of around 35 per cent. The Government believed that this would still leave BGC with ample scope to raise further loan capital to finance diversification after privatisation.[121] Also, the Government was willing to agree that the substantial cash reserves of £600 million which BGC had built up should remain in the business. This was because it was decided that the market might perceive the company to be more attractive with a large cash balance; also there was concern that Rooke would react very adversely to having the cash taken away.[122] In addition, the Government agreed to assume responsibility for the servicing and redemption of existing BGC three per cent stock, which arose from the nationalisation of gas in 1949.[123]

In a meeting with the Financial Secretary and Rothschilds on 21 November 1985 Walker agreed that he should aim to negotiate a debt of £2.5 billion, although £2 billion might be workable in extremis.[124] This was expected to lead to a valuation of the equity of around £6.2 billion.[125] However, Rooke remained strongly opposed to a debt of anything near such levels. He was looking for something closer to £1 billion, at most (although around the same time Chris Brierley, Managing Director Economic Planning at BGC, mentioned that up to £1.75 billion might be acceptable).[126]BGC worried about the combined cost of paying dividends and interest on the new debt after privatisation. The Corporation argued that it could only make available each year some £365 million to cover both dividends and interest because of the need to retain profits to expand the business. It produced its own analysis of the cash flows of selected large UK corporations with the objective of achieving a better financial settlement.[127] The Department countered that BGC could cover a cost of £490 million in the first year and still have plenty of cash to diversify. It pointed to the success of BT and BP both with higher levels of gearing than those proposed for BGC (the Department calculated that at privatisation BT had a comparable net gearing of 70 per cent).

On 2 December Walker wrote to Rooke in an attempt to persuade him to accept at least £2.5 billion of debt. Based on advice from Rothschilds he dangled the carrot that the capital servicing costs to BGC in cash flow terms over the first three years after privatisation would be over £110 million greater if the company had no debt as against having £2.5 billion of debt because interest charges would be less than dividend costs. Also, with the lower dividend payments implied by the higher debt figure he suggested that BGC would be better placed to finance acquisitions using its own debt. Government calculations suggested that BGC should be able to make modest extensions to its business by borrowing and still be able to reduce its gearing to 25 per cent by 1989/90.[128] Rooke replied on 12 December still refusing to agree to the proposed debt level. He adopted the strategy, also followed by BT's management, of holding back from agreeing the level of post-privatisation gearing until the X factor in the price formula had been set. [129] Rooke also wanted to see the Gas Levy, introduced in 1981 to extract additional revenues from BGC, removed or reduced at privatisation. By contrast, Rothschilds argued in favour of the retention of the Levy because removing it would raise the value of BGC and therefore the potential size of the share flotation needed.[130] In the end the Levy was retained but with a Government commitment that the rate would be fixed at the current level of four pence per therm until 1992.

A final area of friction over finances related to BGC's conservative practice of expensing all of its replacement expenditure. Each year BGC spent around £300 million to £350 million on replacing gas mains, pipes and meters. Rothschilds suggested that if this expenditure was capitalised the resulting higher reported profit might add between £500 million and £1 billion to the sales proceeds.[131] Rothschilds and Touche Ross advised that it would be appropriate for such expenditure to be capitalised in BGC's accounts and the Treasury demanded that the accounting policy be changed.[132] But BGC's auditors, Price Waterhouse, disagreed, arguing that expensing the replacement expenditure was the correct accounting treatment because the assets were a recurring cost in maintaining the Corporation's infrastructure.[133]

By January 1986 the Treasury was alarmed at the slow pace in finalising BGC's financial structure and was holding back from agreeing the terms of the employee share offer in apparent retaliation.[134] Officials in the Department of Energy were of the view that BGC was deliberately withholding information and obstructing the process: "we are up against a deeply obstructive attitude . . . In summary I see little sign of co-operation or movement on BGC's side on accounting practices, profit forecasts, or debt . . . Generally I believe BGC are deliberately seeking to thwart progress for motives wholly inconsistent with the Government's legitimate interest in obtaining a full and proper valuation of the company."[135] Moreover, falling energy prices threatened to reduce the sales receipts. Oil prices were now down to under $18 a barrel (the price of Brent crude fell from just over $18 a barrel in January 1986 to a low of $6 by July: see Figure 15.2), which affected the price of gas, a competitor fuel.[136] By early February the prospects for fuel prices were such that BGC reported that it expected to fail to achieve its 1985/6 profit target by £25 million and that the expected profit performance in 1986/7 could be even worse, profits falling by a further £100 million.[137] One possible offset would be a reduction in BGC's annual contributions to its pension schemes.

*Figure 15.2* Movements in oil prices in 1986 (Brent crude in US $ per barrel)
*Source*: Department of Energy.

But BGC were reluctant to use pension fund revaluations to achieve the Government's desired profit profile. In any case, Rothschilds advised that the effects of the one-off revaluations would be discounted heavily by investors when assessing the underlying profit trend.[138] The Government decided not to press BGC to revalue its pension funds.

Concerned by the falling energy prices and the effects on BGC's profits, Department officials reviewed the choices open to them, including changing the flotation strategy to present BGC as a utility with little growth prospects. This would be consistent with having less equity and more debt, but it was not an appealing option given that it would mean a reversal of the marketing strategy followed so far. The Department anxiously asked Rothschilds to advise on the prospects for the flotation if oil prices in the autumn continued at their current lower levels, while hoping that OPEC would "get their act together" and raise oil prices to $18 or $19 a barrel.[139] Meanwhile, Rooke was making it known that BGC might not be saleable if oil prices remained at their current level. He urgently commissioned an internal study of BGC's profit profile with different oil prices and exchange rates.

In March BGC provided the Department with its latest profit forecasts and the sensitivity analysis turning on the price of oil and the exchange rate. The forecasts suggested that CCA profits in 1986/7 might be as low as £400–500 million. However, the Board still proposed only a 1.7 per cent increase in gas tariffs, arguing that competition in the industrial market from cheaper fuel oil ruled out a larger rise. Such an increase would go nowhere near to restoring the level of profitability that Rothschilds maintained was necessary to achieve a successful flotation. Irritated by BGC's resistance to at least a four per cent price rise, let alone the six per cent it had pressed for earlier, the Treasury queried whether a 100 per cent sale that autumn was still sensible. It even voiced the possibility of postponing the entire sale of BGC, perhaps until after the next general election. Consequently, within the Department of Energy there was anxiety that the flotation of 100 per cent of the company or even perhaps of 51 per cent might now be in jeopardy. A Department of Energy official concluded that: "A decision to go for 1.7 per cent [price rise] rather than 4 per cent would put the flotation at serious risk."[140]

The Department contemplated whether, through accelerating purchases of new assets or substituting expensive gas for cheap gas at the end of the 1985/6 year, profits might be moved between years, so as to artificially create the upward profit trend that Rothschilds placed so much store on. However, officials concluded that such profit massaging was unlikely to be sufficient to produce the intended effect and in any event investors might see through it.[141] The pressure was clearly on to get Rooke and the rest of the BGC Board to change their stance on gas prices. On 24 March 1986 the Chancellor of the Exchequer wrote to Walker requesting that he speak to Rooke and convince him of the need for at least a four per cent price rise to make the sale a success.[142] On 17 April he followed this up by expressing deep concerns about the forthcoming privatisation. He believed that the prospects for the flotation were now very different to those of the previous autumn when the sale had been planned and that there was a case for postponing the sale or for selling only 51 per cent of the equity and increasing the debt injection to above £2.5 billion:

> "It is important to ensure that, in any sale, we would get proper value for the company. The PAC [Public Accounts Committee] would almost inevitably examine the handling of any sale and we must avoid any criticism from that quarter.
>
> "Obviously deferral of the sale would be unwelcome but it would have some attractions. There are several other companies which are pressing hard for early privatisation. I would be able to let them use the gaps in the queue which would be released by deferring BGC. In addition deferral would give us the opportunity to improve BGC's regulatory regime and to improve the quality and balance of BGC's board."[143]

Rothschilds was now similarly warning that with the disappointing profit trend, BGC might only be sellable on the dividend yield basis appropriate for a utility business with limited growth prospects and that a 51 per cent sale might be preferable. Rothschilds concluded that the total equity proceeds with a $12 oil price, a £2.5 billion debt and a low rise in gas prices could be a mere £1.3 billion if there was an attempt to sell all of the Corporation.[144] In spite of some counterbalancing considerations, including a cold spell in April 1986 and gas input costs falling faster than BGC had expected earlier in the year, Rothschilds' earlier vision of selling a growth company to raise up to £8 billion was now considered "dead", even with an X factor in the price formula set towards the lower end of any recommended range. At most the proceeds might be "a derisory . . . £4 billion". Heated discussions between the BGC, the Department of Energy and the Treasury and with the financial advisers continued as pressure mounted on Rooke to agree a price increase that would assist a 100 per cent flotation in the autumn and one supportive of the marketing strategy for a growth stock. Rooke continued to be reluctant to raise gas prices as oil prices fell.

To prevent a postponement or collapse of the sale, in May Walker reached what he called a "concordat" with Rooke over the financial forecasts to be included in the forthcoming sale prospectus. This followed agreement on an X factor for the price cap of a modest 2%. The concordat involved the Corporation confirming that it could pay out around 80 per cent of its CCA profits as dividends taking one year with another. Rooke also reluctantly agreed to accept £2.5 billion of debt financing. However, this may not have been such an important concession as Rooke maintained at the time. In a due diligence meeting with BGC in September, Rothschilds were informed by BGC that they had no expectation of higher debt financing over the next five years and no real plans for diversification other than modest additional expenditure on exploration and production.[145] It seems that the debt issue, while reflecting Rooke's genuine objection to BGC assuming debt obligations without adequate financial compensation, was a useful bargaining ploy by BGC to negotiate financial concessions elsewhere, including the size of the price cap. In April the BGC Board confirmed its decision to opt for only a very small rise in gas prices of 1p per therm and a reduction in standing charges of £1 a quarter, and the Government gave way on the Corporation's conservative practice of expensing replacement expenditure.[146]

The concordat and price settlement involved a compromise between the Government and BGC and still left uncertain the terms of the flotation. When in June Rooke pressed Walker for a final commitment to sell 100 per cent of the shares, the Department wished to reserve the final decision until closer to the proposed sale date in the autumn.[147] There were concerns that a collapse in the value of sterling or another fall in oil prices could still disrupt the sale. Nevertheless, progress on BGC's finances had now been made, although there was still the problem of settling BGC's figures for the forecasts of profits and dividends for 1986/7 to go into the prospectus. In July BGC was suggesting profits would be in the range of £610–800 million (on a CCA basis) as against the £800 million that Rothschilds had originally suggested was needed for the prospectus. This was somewhat better than the dire forecasts earlier in the year because oil prices had stabilised and from the end of the month recovered from $6 to nearly $10 a barrel. Also, BGC's sales volumes had not fallen by as much as the Corporation had earlier forecast. Moreover, in September there was some cold weather early in the month which raised the demand for gas. By the middle of the month the Department was arguing that BGC should now be able to table for the prospectus profits £200 million to £250 million higher than the Corporation had previously suggested. The figures currently tabled suggested a valuation for BGC of £4.5–5 billion. But it was believed that a valuation of £6 billion or perhaps more might still be possible if more buoyant profit figures could be wrung out of BGC.[148]

Equally there was suspicion that BGC could still be planning to suppress profit figures by rearranging its gas purchases, increasing costs and pushing profits into later years. It was in the interests of management to postpone profits so that the profit performance after privatisation would satisfy investors. The Department pressed BGC to find more cost savings to boost profitability ahead of the sale. The Department also wanted to see the Board move from its preference to limit dividend payments to around 80 per cent of CCA profit. When BGC proposed that dividends should be paid well after the end of the company's accounting year, the Department did not consider this helpful in generating investor interest in the issue.[149] Meanwhile, the assets and liabilities of BGC were vested in British Gas plc on 24 August.[150]

In September Cazenoves complained that full profit forecasts were unlikely to be available before mid-October and therefore in time for the beginning of its approach to the financial institutions, which was scheduled to begin in late September.[151] Both Rothschilds and Cazenoves stressed that to get the desired provisional commitment to buy shares from City institutions, they would need to give a rough indication of the overall structure of the sale and a specific impression of the profit levels and valuation.[152] Cazenoves confirmed that lower profits than the previous year would call into question the whole strategy developed to sell shares to the financial institutions.[153] Similarly, James Capel & Co grumbled about the continuing uncertainty over the profit figures commenting, we "are still very unhappy about publishing a report without specific profit forecasts ... it could be positively counter-productive".[154]

In response to the mounting pressure, BGC put out a statement that there was a "good chance" that profits for 1986/7 would be at least as good as in 1985/6 and Cazenoves confirmed that this represented a sufficient minimum basis for proceeding with the first phase of the institutional marketing. But on 10 October Rooke wrote to Walker still protesting that the Government's expectations of prices and profits were unrealistic, given the recent trend in fuel prices and the company's costs. Rooke warned: "The price levels now apparently being suggested by your officials are totally unrealistic and if pressed would not only give rise to significant loss of business but also, in my view, create political repercussions." He concluded: "The Directors are mindful of the responsibilities attaching to the profit forecast in the prospectus and will not wish to give assurances to prospective shareholders which cannot be sustained."[155] Department of Energy officials were unsympathetic, believing that Rooke was being overly pessimistic about both future fuel prices and other costs. They believed that if necessary some adjustments should be made between 1986/7 and 1987/8 to ensure that this year's profit level was at least as high as in the previous year.[156] At the same time, Walker pressed Rooke to agree to profits for 1986/7 at the top end of the £610 million to £800 million range discussed in the summer, especially as the profits for the first part of the year were already some £240 million better than budgeted.[157]

In early October 1986 the Department was still looking for BGC to offer in the prospectus £100 million more in profits in 1986/87 and £60–80 million more in dividends, pointing to better contract prices for gas than BGC had forecast earlier and an ability to trim costs and shift gas purchases between accounting years.[158] A meeting between Rooke and Walker on 6 October made little headway with Rooke rejecting any suggestion that the Company was artificially padding its costs or minimising its revenues. The most Rooke would offer was a rise in the historic cost profit forecast from £980 million to £990 million.[159] Walker responded by writing to Rooke requesting a rethink so that the Prospectus could still show some improvement on last year's profitability, especially since BGC had been more successful than earlier feared in holding on to existing customers and regaining volumes, notably in the interruptible market: "It does seem to me that taking all present indications into account, we should have the basis for fixing a figure towards the top end of the £610–£800 million range [on a CCA basis] we identified in the summer."[160]

At a meeting between the Department of Energy and BGC officials on 22 October the Department remained highly critical of the company's assumptions about future price trends, volumes of sales and profitability, and there was disagreement over the course of future oil prices. In addition, the Department questioned BGC's grounds for forecasting rising manpower costs when they felt that labour costs should be falling due to lower employ-ment.[161] BGC had cut its workforce, from 106,000 employees in 1980/1 to 95,600 in 1984/5 and 91,900 in 1985/6 and further cuts were planned. In return, BGC rejected any suggestion of extrapolating forward the improved financial position in the first half of the year, which management put down to the unexpectedly cold weather at the time.[162] Chris Brierley of BGC indicated that he was prepared to agree the publication of a HCA profit of £1,030 million and a CCA profit of £795 million for 1986/7 in the Prospectus, but he explained that this would involve some accounting manipulation and the figures were higher than the BGC Board wished to sanction. He stressed that it had been "reached for" only in response to pressure from the Secretary of State. Also, BGC was nervous about the Department of Energy's intention to state in the prospectus that the company would pay a dividend of around 80 per cent of its after-tax CCA profit. On receiving this news Walker reacted by writing to Brierley to remind him of the terms of the May "concordat" and pointing out that the dividends forecast "will have an impact upon our ability to obtain a proper value for the flotation out of all proportion to the impact it will have on the Company itself".

The Secretary of State was looking for a dividend forecast of at least £300 million to support the flotation, but the Board was reluctant to endorse anything over £270million, still pointing to the servicing of the £2.5 billion debt as an obstacle to a higher figure.[163] Walker emphasised that a report by BGC's auditors, Price Waterhouse, on working capital had confirmed a healthy position, while lower gas costs suggested that profits would rise substantially in 1987/8.[164] Brierley responded negatively by pointing out that much of the purpose of the privatisation was to enable the development of a business outside the utility area and this necessitated BGC having the ability to readily raise additional financing after privatisation. He also argued that it would be irresponsible to pay higher dividends in 1986/7 on the expectation of higher profits from lower fuel prices in the following year. He concluded that BGC's computations suggested a worsening cash position from December 1987.[165]

Walker replied to Brierley's latest letter on 29 October, repeating his contention that dividends of at least £300 million would be reasonable and requesting that Brierley place his figures before the Board.[166] Following the Board meeting, Rooke telephoned Walker to confirm that a forecast dividend of £270 million was the maximum the Board would sanction and that it would be irresponsible to give investors the impression that profits in the future would be higher than they were likely to be.[167] Meanwhile, the company's merchant bank advisers, Kleinworts, and one of the possible underwriters of the offer, Barclays de Zoete Wedd, provided some indirect support for BGC management by reporting that it was essential that the forecast dividend be covered at least twice by forecast profit. A lower coverage would be interpreted by the City as an excessive squeeze on the company. This, they concluded, could depress the sale proceeds by more than the effect of proposing a lower dividend.[168]

BGC's financial projections continued to disappoint the Government right up to the time of the publication of the sale prospectus. The Government concluded that the profit and dividend forecasts were unnecessarily conservative and the cost forecasts too high. They particularly considered that BGC had not factored in sufficiently the recent improvement in the oil market.[169] In October the Chancellor of the Exchequer again raised the issue of whether a 51 per cent sale might still be preferable if Rooke refused to revise upwards his profit forecasts. While he still favoured a 100 per cent sale in principle, he hoped that the prospect of a 51 per cent sale might shake Rooke into coming forward with better figures. However, raising the matter of a 51 per cent sale at this advanced stage of the flotation clearly irritated Walker.

It is interesting that with only one month to go before the planned sale of BGC, the profit and dividend figures to go into the Prospectus were yet to be finalised and that a less than 100 per cent sale of the company had still not been entirely ruled out.[170]

## Other difficulties

The run-up to the flotation faced other potential difficulties. In March 1986 NALGO balloted its members on industrial action against the privatisation. On a turnout of around 40 per cent the strike call was rejected. More disruptive was legal action taken by NALGO against Thames Water for alleged ultra vires expenditure on preparing for water privatisation. [171] In the House of Commons the Secretary of State for the Environment conceded that the legal right of the water authorities to plan and prepare for privatisation was "not entirely without doubt". The issue related to what was known as the Littman Opinion on ultra vires expenditure by corporations. Boards of public corporations might not have legal powers to spend on preparing for privatisation, ahead of the royal assent to the privatisation legislation, because the expenditure did not relate to the corporation's existing statutory duties. In earlier privatisations the matter had not been raised or had been ignored within Government. But by now the trade unions had become aware of the issue and saw it as a convenient vehicle to derail sales. In the case of the privatisation of water, which was at a much earlier stage of planning, the problem could be addressed through the passage of a paving Bill giving the boards of the water authorities the necessary legal protection. However, in the case of gas, where BGC had already incurred expenditure on preparing for the flotation, the matter was more difficult. It was considered that introducing a change in the Gas Bill at this late stage to permit the expenditure retrospectively would be too controversial. There was also the point that if the Government was seen to be reacting to a possible legal challenge during the sale of BGC, this could suggest that the Government acknowledged the possibility of illegal expenditure during earlier privatisations, including that of BT. To head off the threat, quietly the Department decided to meet certain of BGC's costs. [172]

Another problem related to tax changes. The Finance Bill in March 1986 made some proposals for changes to stamp duty and to the taxation of ADRs, [173] which the Department of Energy did not feel were helpful. [174] Changes were subsequently made to the Bill to reduce some of the negative impacts on the BGC sale, but at the time there was anger in the Department of Energy about the Treasury's lack of consultation before preparing the changes. There was also the problem of the European Regional Development Fund (ERDF) grants used by BGC in areas of high unemployment such as Scotland, Wales and the North East of England. This issue had been of limited importance during the privatisation of BT, but BGC was a much bigger beneficiary of the scheme. The Department of Energy applied to the European Commission for funding to continue once the Corporation was in the private sector. But there was much uncertainty at the time as to whether privatised firms could benefit from these grants, which were principally aimed at meeting costs borne wholly or in part by public authorities. The Government had already tested the ground with the privatised ports and the European Commission had provisionally ruled that the privatised ports were eligible, although some socialist members of the European Parliament still hoped to reverse the ruling with the intention that this would dissuade European governments from pursuing privatisations. The loss of the grants to BGC would be more than a political embarrassment to the Government. Britain already had a relatively small share of the amounts granted in the EC under the scheme and the share would fall even further if BGC were excluded.

There was a further complication. If BGC continued to benefit from ERDF grants, under the conditions of the scheme the Government would have to continue to provide matching funding. The Treasury advised the Department of Energy that it would not provide further financing. This meant that in the future the Department would have to produce public

386

expenditure savings in other areas of an equivalent amount to the matching funding, expected to be around £5 million per annum. Walker protested on the grounds that it was unreasonable for his Department to meet costs arising from the operations of a private sector BGC without additional Exchequer support. Nevertheless, the Treasury refused to alter its position because of the bigger consequences for the public finances when the water industry was privatised. The water industry was an even larger beneficiary from the scheme.[175]

The prospectus had to carry a warning about Labour Party policy towards future re-nationalisation. In its Election Manifesto the Labour Party had committed itself to "return to public ownership the public assets and rights hived off by the Tories, with compensation of no more than that received when the assets were denationalised". During a debate on the Gas Bill on 10 December 1985, speaking from the Opposition Front Bench, the Rt Hon Stan Orme confirmed that a Labour Government would reacquire the assets of BGC. The following October the Labour Party Annual Conference passed a resolution committing a future Labour Government to a policy under which companies such as BT and BGC would be acquired under the umbrella of a new state holding company.[176] The Government attempted to address this threat by stressing how unlikely it was that the commitment would be carried out. But there was still concern that investors might be discouraged from investing, especially if only 51 per cent of the enterprise was sold initially, which would enable a future Labour Government to take the company back into state control by purchasing only an additional two per cent of the shares. Related to this, as during some earlier privatisations, Sir William Lithgow, who was still aggrieved by the terms of the compensation he had received during the nationalisation of the aircraft and shipbuilding industries in 1977, argued that the Government was underemphasising the risk to investors from renationalisation. There was concern within the Department of Energy that he might contact the US Securities and Exchange Commission with the aim of disrupting the BGC sale in America.[177]

In May 1986 Peter Walker advised the PM that the flotation was on course to realise a capital value around the top end of the £6 billion to £8 billion originally envisaged.[178] However, this figure did depend upon trading conditions at the time, agreeing the profit and dividend forecasts, remaining committed to floating 100 per cent of the company, and a successful marketing campaign, involving no adverse media comment or other disruption to the sale. The start was not propitious. In April and May Dewe Rogerson produced assessments of the prospects for the flotation noting that more people opposed the privatisation of BGC than supported it (45 per cent against and 35 per cent in support) and that in several respects the sale programme was lagging behind that of BT at a similar stage. In particular, awareness of the forthcoming share sale was 20 points lower than for BT at around the same stage of the marketing campaign and potential investors rated BGC worse than BT in terms of being a good company to invest in. So far the corporate advertising campaign appeared to have failed to shift attitudes.[179] A survey in the City confirmed a lack of knowledge about the abilities of BGC's management, a perception of poor communication by BGC, and limited knowledge of the forthcoming offer. There was also apprehension amongst potential investors about continuing government regulation. In this context, both Rothschilds and Kleinwort, Benson expressed alarm when Professor Carsberg, DGOFTEL, published his first annual report including statements which they felt might be interpreted by investors as suggesting an "apparent change in philosophy from price control to rate of return control" in telecommunications. It was felt that this would be unhelpful to the BGC share offer.[180] There were also concerns within Government about the enthusiasm with which the senior management of BGC, including particularly Rooke, would support the offer during the final marketing period, including the roadshows.[181] In July 1986 the Financial Secretary complained to the Department of Energy about Rooke's "unsatisfactory" and "weak" commitment to the privatisation "and sometimes positively unhelpful actions". The complaint appears to have been triggered by a suggestion that Rooke was refusing to sign a letter promoting the sale to go out to gas customers over the summer.[182]

During the summer the prospects for a successful sale improved as the main marketing campaign got fully underway and BGC, albeit reluctantly, revised upwards its earlier disappointing profit and dividend forecasts to be included in the sale prospectus. Also, Dewe Rogerson reported that the Corporation's monopoly position would be a major strength in getting the flotation away successfully.[183] Its public opinion survey in early July showed that awareness of the flotation had risen by 12 per cent to 59 per cent, although balanced against this the image of BGC had deteriorated as had interest in investing in BGC shares.[184] Later Rooke proposed an increase of ten per cent in the salaries of the members of the Corporation backdated to 1 April. This was considered most unhelpful in terms of improving the public's image of the Corporation and under pressure from the Government the rise was reduced.[185] The Government also suggested to the Board that bullish comments on future senior management remuneration should be avoided in the run up to the sale![186] Nevertheless, figures in the Offer for Sale document issued in November confirmed that the annual remuneration of directors including the chairman would rise on privatisation by around 87 per cent.[187] In addition, the company intended to introduce an executive share option scheme, although under Government pressure its implementation was postponed until after the flotation. The company did establish at privatisation an employee profit sharing scheme operated in conjunction with the offer for sale and a savings-related share option scheme.

## "Tell Sid"

In late June stockbrokers James Capel produced a favourable report for investors on BGC's prospects, concluding: "The proposed regulatory and capital structure will leave British Gas in a strong and flexible position, while providing safeguards for consumers where necessary. They will allow the company plenty of scope to achieve growth in the future. We believe that the company will have widespread appeal both to institutional investors and private individuals."[188] By early August the Department of Energy was contemplating two opposite scenarios: the first that there might be large-scale over-subscription for the shares "with resulting logistical chaos" and the other that a 51 per cent sale might still be all that could be achieved.[189] The outcome of the flotation remained uncertain.

In early September, after an OPEC inspired rally which saw Brent crude prices return to over $10 a barrel, world oil prices slipped once more and there were renewed worries about the profit figures that would appear in the prospectus.[190] The City bank Morgan Grenfell issued a report to its clients which concluded that BGC's operating profits could fall by 20 per cent in 1986/7 due to a loss of part of the interruptible market to cheaper fuel oil and the need to cut prices to non-tariff customers. The bank was also critical of BGC's reliance on gas supplies with only around 9 per cent of turnover due to non-gas distribution business, concluding: "This only emphasises the extent to which BGC must be viewed as a utility."[191] This implied a valuation of the company on a dividend yield basis and a lower sale price. There was also depressing news from America when the US advisers became concerned about the failure of BGC to make available certain documentation needed to discharge its due diligence responsibilities.[192] At the same time the BGC Board was nervous about accepting legal responsibility for statements about the company made in overseas prospectuses, even though the Government, as in previous privatisations, offered the Board an indemnity.[193]

The start of September saw the beginning of the pre-flotation advertising campaign with the lighting of gas beacons across the country and TV advertisements inviting everyone to participate in the share offer. Around the same time the Share Information Office for the offer became fully functional. By the end of the first week in September the Office was already receiving about 15,000 calls a day using the "hotline" number given at the end of each media advertisement of the BGC sale.[194] By mid-September a million enquires had been received and a backlog of unanswered queries had built up. Steps were taken to reduce it.[195] On 18 September Walker was able to inform the Cabinet that the flotation of BGC was attracting considerable public interest, on a scale comparable to that shown during the flotation of BT.[196] A report from Dewe Rogerson showed that awareness of the share issue amongst adults now stood at 74 per cent.[197] Later, with six weeks to go before flotation, there had been more than two million enquiries about buying shares.

The television and press advertising for the flotation occurred under the slogan "Tell Sid" about the British Gas sale, which is now immortalised in the history of the British advertising industry. The campaign was very successful with "Sid" passing into popular mythology. So successful was the campaign in convincing the public that Sid actually existed, Walker raised the question as to what would be Sid's fate when the campaign ended. On 20 November the advertising agency responsible, Young & Rubicam replied to the Department of Energy that "the finest and most witty point of departure for our hero" should be the aim![198] The final TV advertisement had a camera focused on a mountaineer (Sid?) going through clouds at the peak of a mountain while reminding viewers not to forget the date of the share issue.

Details of the share offer were issued in late September with the announcement that the minimum investment level would be for 100 shares with an initial payment of only £50 to encourage the maximum number of investors. The bill voucher and bonus share schemes were also announced. British Gas's domestic customers were guaranteed the right to a minimum allocation of 200 shares each, provided they registered their interest by contacting the British Gas Share Information Office by 14 November.[199] On 16 October Dewe Rogerson was able to confirm that there was "massive public interest" in the issue. This had now been buoyed up by the success of the TSB flotation in mid-September and which earlier some in Government had worried might divert interest from the BGC sale. Since the TSB flotation, interest in the BGC issue had risen by over one third to 5.5 million people. Awareness of the offer was now at 85 per cent of adults and ahead of the BT figure at a similar stage of the sale process, while those certain to buy shares stood at 10.3 per cent (4.2 million people). The best current estimate was that there would be around eight million applications for shares, but possibly over 10 million.[200] By 24 October enquiries at the Share Information Office had risen to six million, while public opinion surveys suggested that 45 per cent of adults now supported the privatisation with only 29 per cent against. Even one in four Labour Party supporters were said to favour the privatisation.[201] However, there was still no complacency within Government. With a month still to go before the flotation the Department of Energy remained cautious lest something still should happen to disrupt the sale.[202] In particular, the stock market was proving volatile, registering an unhelpful fall in September, and there was recognition that much would still turn on retaining favourable media coverage of the offer once the Pathfinder prospectus was issued and the share price announced.

However, given the mounting evidence that the flotation should be a great success unless there was an unexpected sudden loss of confidence in the issue, the Treasury raised with the Department of Energy the matter of whether more than eight million share applications could be handled. The Treasury also questioned whether the firm placing element of the issue with the underwriters and the overseas issues should be removed or reduced to provide more shares for the domestic retail market.[203] Within the Department too there was some nervousness about whether such a large number of applications could be processed in time before trading in the shares was due to begin.[204] On 4 November Brierley at BGC wrote to the Department of Energy canvassing that with registrations now standing at over seven million, planning should start to consider how an application level of up to 15 million might be handled, although he considered it most unlikely that this number would be reached.

The receiving banks collected the applications, counted them, processed the cheques and implemented the instructions on the allocation of shares. This involved a significant amount of work – in the case of BT it had involved the use of 5,000 staff. The National Westminster bank had been appointed the lead receiving bank and the share registrar for the BGC offer (the registrar administered the final share register) and had initially agreed to handle three million applications and later up to around 6.5 million– or twice the capacity that had previously been achieved for a share flotation in the UK.[205] But the Department had concluded in June that with the possibility of a much larger number of applications extra capacity should be brought in as an insurance policy. Ravensbourne, a subsidiary of Barings bank, was employed, raising the processing capacity.[206] The Government also had in mind that trading in BGC shares would take place only six weeks after the Stock Market "Big Bang" reforms. Given the fragility of the new settlement systems of the Stock Exchange established on 27 October, there was trepidation that dealings in BGC shares might overwhelm the stock market and cause it to grind to a halt. The Government was therefore eager to guide investors towards "approved" dealing arrangements, where transactions would be consolidated before passing them to the market. Therefore, there was concern when de Zoete and Bevan, the regional co-ordinator for London and the South East for the BGC issue, warned in the last week of November that it might not be able to handle the selling orders once share dealing started. To head off this possibility, banks were directed to place share sales with other brokers.[207]

## The Pathfinder prospectus and setting the share price

The Pathfinder prospectus was issued on Friday 31 October, the day after Walker gave the final go-ahead for a 100 per cent disposal.[208] At the Press Conference British Gas was presented as "a strong, efficient and profitable company with an impressive track record and we believe that it represents an excellent investment opportunity". The Government had made some concessions on accounting policy in negotiation with BGC over the previous weeks and subtly the message was put out during the flotation that the accounts were highly conservative. Swallowing remaining reservations and putting behind him the past dis-agreements with Government, Rooke commented at the press conference: "My colleagues and I welcome the new challenges that privatisation will bring, and particularly the wider commercial opportunities presented by freedom from Government control." He concluded on the extension of the common carriage facility under the new Gas Act to facilitate competition that the sale of significant amounts of gas directly to consumers by competitors was "unlikely . . . [to] take place before the 1990s". [209] This statement was intended to placate investors and proved to be correct, yet it was a view very much at odds with Rooke's earlier protests against market liberalisation. The forecast profit for 1986/7 was put at £836 million on a CCA basis (before tax) as against £782 million in the previous year, achieving the upward profit trend which had always been the Department's goal but which had been at risk in the spring and summer. The pro forma earnings implied a capability to pay dividends that fell a little short of what the Government had been pursuing as a minimum. However, the forecast dividend of 9.2p per share inclusive of tax credit was generally favourably received in the City, although the first dividend to be paid in October 1987 would only be a net four pence per share to help achieve this. BGC's debt level and the price cap formula had already both been "well received in the market". [210]

Following its failure to bring its members out on strike against privatisation the previous March, the trade union NALGO balloted its members in October on strike action over a wage claim. There were immediate worries that this might damage the prospects for the flotation. But again NALGO was unable to obtain the required 50 per cent support for action – perhaps many employees feared delaying the flotation and losing their benefits from the employee share offer. [211] By 13 November Dewe Rogerson was reporting that 87 per cent of the public were aware of the flotation and Rothschilds confirmed that in extremis the receiving banks might be able to process just over eight million share applications, if needed. [212] BGC share information packs and enquiry registration cards were distributed through the banks with the Prospectus available from bank branches from 25 November. [213] The full prospectus was also published in *The Times*, *The Daily Telegraph* and the *Financial Times*, but not in *The Independent* or *The Guardian*. Market research had shown that a much smaller percentage of these papers' readers, especially of *The Guardian* with its left of centre editorial policy, were interested in the offer than amongst the population as a whole. [214]

Within Government attention now turned to setting the share price. During the summer in discussions between No. 10 and the Department of Energy it was felt that the sale figure might be set so as to achieve £5.5 billion in revenues from the equity sale, alongside the £2.5 billion from debt financing. However, the Treasury still hoped for a higher total figure, of closer to £9 billion. [215] On 9 September Rothschilds advised that its valuation figure had not changed appreciably since its earlier estimates. BGC was likely to sell for around £6 billion with the P/E ratio and the dividend yield methods both entering into the valuation. [216]

BGC would form part of the oil and gas sector in the FT all-share index and it was considered that investors would take the existing majors in the oil and gas sector as a benchmark for BGC. Between May and September the all-share index had risen by four per cent, while the major oil companies, such as BP and Shell, had seen their stock prices rise by much more. In early September Cazenoves and Hoare Govett approached the FT Actuaries' classification sub-committee to discuss the possibility of BGC being placed in a new, separate, sector on the grounds that BGC was not a normal oil company. They worried that comparisons with companies such as BP and Shell might depress the sale receipts. [217] However, they then changed their minds on the grounds that the inclusion of BGC in the Oil and Gas sub-sector could lead to institutions being underweight in that sector, leading to greater interest in buying BGC shares. [218]

Every one penny extra negotiated on the share price was estimated to be worth around £40 million in additional receipts to the Government. [219] At the same time, the Department of Energy was aware that in terms of setting the share price, "whilst a technical approach to valuation will have its uses, it cannot be ultimately used to set the price which . . . is principally a matter of long hard negotiations."[220] In this context, there were concerns that analysts might talk the price down tactically. It was also felt that current media speculation that the issue price would be 130p was not helpful, possibly reducing the Government's freedom of manoeuvre on price.[221]

The Public Accounts Committee had commented favourably on the Government obtaining a second opinion before setting the BT issue price, something also adopted for other privatisation flotations since 1981. For BT this had been obtained from Phillips and Drew. But the Chancellor of the Exchequer now judged that no City firm could be truly independent and suggested that it would be best to appoint someone who had recently retired from the City. In mid-October Walker decided to appoint Godfrey Chandler to provide independent advice, with effect from 7 November.[222] Chandler had recently retired from the stock-brokers Cazenoves.[223] The first meeting on setting the share price was held at the Department of Energy on Thursday 13 November, at which Chandler was present. [224] At this meeting Rothschilds recommended a price of 130p per share. On 18 November Rothschilds supported by Cazenoves moved to 135p, but emphasised recent unfavourable movements in the US and UK stock markets for not going higher. Chandler recommended a price of 138p to 140p, although it seems that this was partly a tactical measure to keep Rothschilds and Cazenoves on their toes. Rothschilds and Cazenoves were asked to reconsider their valuations.

The opening share premium at the end of the first day of trading in BT shares, of 43p a share or a 96 per cent gain on the partly paid price of 50p, had led to claims that the Government had sold off the corporation too cheaply and failed to maximise the sale receipts. Given this background, Tony Blair, one of the Labour Party's Treasury team, wrote to the Chancellor of the Exchequer anticipating underpricing of the BGC shares and a loss to taxpayers.[225] To head off criticism, the Chancellor pressed his officials to ensure that there would be no runaway share premium once trading in BGC shares began.[226] Michael Richardson, a leading figure in the Rothschilds team, thought the objective should be to achieve an opening share price at a ten per cent premium on the fully paid issue price, although this would mean a much higher effective premium given that shareholders would only have paid the first instalment, expected to be 50p. BGC management supported by their financial advisers, Kleinwort, Benson, favoured a higher target premium to ensure a successful sale.

The share price was eventually determined at a meeting on 19 November including the Secretary of State, the Financial Secretary to the Treasury, representatives from the financial advisers, officials from the Department of Energy and the Treasury, and Godfrey Chandler. At this meeting BGC, Kleinworts and Hoare Govett canvassed that they preferred a price close to 130p and stressed that they would be most worried if the price was set above 140p. Chandler suggested a price of 135p or 136p per share.[227] However, it was Richardson from Rothschilds who carried the day. He explained that a fall in the Wall Street market had adversely affected the UK stock market and that a price above 135p would now be too risky. It was also important that the price should be a multiple of five pence following the convention of previous privatisations, chosen so as to minimise the chance of small investors making mistakes when calculating the amount to submit with their applications and completing their cheques.[228] This implied that if the price was set above 135p, it should be set at 140p. He concluded that a price of 140p would be far too ambitious, while 135p was likely to lead to sufficient demand in the domestic retail market to trigger the clawback provision "which would be a key indicator of the success of the issue". The price should also produce the necessary underwriting interest; discussions with the UK underwriters had begun on 10 November. After discussion, during which it appears that there was no serious disagreement, the price of 135p per share was agreed.[229] The anticipated proceeds would be around £5.5 billion.[230] On learning of the 135p share price, Rooke expressed satisfaction.[231] The underwriting of the issue took place successfully on 19 and 20 November.

## The flotation achieved

On 21 November 1986 Rothschilds issued a press release setting out the terms of the offer for sale. 4,025.5 million ordinary shares would be available at 135p per share, capitalising the company at £5.6 billion. Payment would be in three instalments with 50p per share payable on application, 45p on 9 June 1987 and 40p on 19 April 1988. As with the partly paid BT shares, purchasers would be free to sell them in partly paid form. At 135p the resulting price-earnings multiple was 9.7 on a pro-forma earnings basis, comparing well with other major oil and gas companies quoted in the London market, and with the forecast dividend the gross yield was projected at 6.8 per cent. However, the addition of the gas bill vouchers and payment in instalments led to a forecast return to retail investors of over 20 per cent, or 11 per cent a year for three years for those investors choosing the bonus shares over the bill vouchers. Such prospective returns were intended to make Sid a happy man and were deemed sufficient to ensure continued favourable coverage of the BGC sale in the media and recommendations to newspaper readers to buy the shares.

The prospectus and application forms appeared in newspapers from 25 November. Copies of the prospectus were also made available at bank branches, Post Offices and BGC showrooms, as well as at the offices of the brokers and regional co-ordinators for the offer.[232] All those who had registered their interest in the offer with the British Gas Share Information Office were sent a mini prospectus including an application form.[233] By the end of November market research suggested that those certain to buy had risen to 14.7 per cent or six million people and awareness of the offer had risen to 98 per cent of adults, providing concrete evidence of the success of the "Tell Sid" campaign.[234] With journalists now suggesting a possible 30 per cent plus return to small investors and the share price in the grey market already standing at 62p, there was satisfaction within the Department of Energy that the Government was on course to achieve the most popular offer for sale ever in the country's history.[235] Applications for shares closed at 10am on Wednesday 3 December.

The BGC share sale raised £5.434 billion for the Government, although because of the instalment payments not all of this accrued immediately. The flotation was an undoubted success with almost twice as many people applying for BGC shares as had applied during the BT offer – over 4.5 million applications were received, leaving BGC with the largest number of shareholders of any company in the world.[236] The offer was over three times subscribed, although the number of applicants finished up well short of the up to eight million at one time suggested.[237] Also, two million investors had bought shares for the first time during the flotation, making the BGC sale a major success for the Government's policy of widening share ownership.[238] Because of the success of the flotation the share allocations had to be scaled back. As in the case of earlier over-subscribed privatisations, the Government was keen to avoid a ballot to allocate the shares as this was likely to disappoint many smaller investors.[239] Instead, preference was given to applications from BGC customers and employees and, as during the BT sale, smaller applications. The basis of the share allocation was announced on 8 December. All those with applications for 400 shares or fewer received their application in full. The rest received fewer than they had applied for with the largest applications receiving only seven per cent of the number of shares requested. Around 85,000 of BGC's employees or some 99 per cent of those eligible also became shareholders, along with BGC pensioners.[240]

As the offer was more than twice oversubscribed the clawback terms for the provisionally placed shares with UK underwriters and the overseas markets were triggered. After clawback, some 64 per cent of the total share offering was made available to the British public. The number of shares made available to UK institutions fell from 1,615 million to 969 million and for overseas investors from 795.5 million to 477.3 million.[241] The final overseas allocation was 11.8 per cent of the shares with 4 per cent going to investors in the USA, and the remainder going equally to investors in Europe, Japan and Canada. All four markets reported demand substantially above their allocations.[242] In particular, there was strong demand for the shares in Japan, including in the aftermarket, and there was no net flowback from the US immediately after the flotation as had occurred during the sale of BT. Indeed, there was net purchasing of shares from North America. By 19 December there had been a 64 per cent increase in BGC ADRs outstanding in the US.[243] Similarly, there was no net flowback from Europe where there was also a strong aftermarket in the shares.[244] This helped keep the share price buoyant in the London market. After one month the share price stood at 65p for the partly paid share.

## Conclusions and aftermath

The whole of BGC had been sold except for a special share retained by the Government and the shares retained to satisfy the later bonus issue. The share application and processing went well with all applications handled and allotment letters issued before share trading began.[245] In spite of improvements to the terms of the bill voucher scheme compared with that adopted for the BT disposal, more investors again opted for the bonus shares rather than the vouchers, steered by media coverage emphasising the greater yield. Margaret Thatcher concluded on the sale that "the privatization was a resounding success."[246] Undoubtedly it had been an enormous achievement to sell the entire Corporation in one tranche, involving the world's largest ever flotation and in the face of some obstruction or at least indifference on the part of the BGC Board and especially its chairman. Not only did the Government rid itself of another nationalised industry, it obtained net receipts of £7.7 billion including the debt finance and advanced its small shareholder programme. By the autumn of 1987 the number of BGC shareholders had fallen by 1.5 million as people cashed in their investments for a capital gain. But this still left about two-thirds of the original holdings retained.[247]

There were some mishaps during the final stages of the flotation. Unfortunately, Ravensbourne Registration Services, responsible for sending out some of the allotment letters, incorrectly sent them out to applicants whose applications had been rejected, for example where the cheque with the application was not honoured.[248] Also, there was a repeat of the fraudulent (alongside accidental) multiple applications for shares that had occurred during the BT sale. These were unearthed by accountants Touche Ross, appointed to identify fraudulent and multiple applications. In addition, there was an incident during the printing of allotment letters by a Woolwich based printer, in which a child requesting scrap paper obtained some seven hundred allotment letters printed as test issues. The child's mother notified *The Sun* newspaper. The resulting embarrassment led to an urgent review of security in contractor firms.[249] Also embarrassment was caused when the British Gas Share Offer

Terms and Conditions, largely drafted by the law firm Slaughter and May, was awarded a Golden Bull statuette for gobbledygook by the Plain English Campaign. One Departmental official judged it to be "a fairly easy target".[250]

But this is relatively trivial stuff and cannot detract from the success of the sale. John Campbell in his biography of Margaret Thatcher comments on the flotation of BGC that the shares were "Once again . . . deliberately under-valued".[251] Certainly the partly paid share price jumped by 25 per cent on the first day of trading, but this was fully consistent with the ten per cent premium on a fully paid basis that had been Rothschilds target and it met the Chancellor's objective that there should be no repeat of the premiums seen in some previous privatisations, including BT. Once again the difficulty was setting a market clearing price in the absence of full information on the likely demand for shares. The Government and its advisers naturally erred on the safe side when setting the issue price, to get the privatisation away successfully and avoid the political embarrassment that a privatisation failure would undoubtedly have caused. But in the case of BGC, and unusually for a privatisation, the Government saw the target aftermarket share premium achieved.

Reflecting this and after some stinging comments on earlier privatisations, the National Audit Office (NAO) report on the BGC sale was relatively benign. Also, the Public Accounts Committee had criticised some of the costs incurred during the sale of BT and the Department of Energy was successful during the disposal of BGC in reducing some fees considerably below those paid for BT. The total costs of the BGC sale were estimated at £360 million. This was around 4.4 per cent of the proceeds including new debt, compared to costs equivalent to 6.8 per cent of the proceeds for the BT flotation.[252] The sale had been at least as successful as the BT disposal in attracting investor interest and at a relatively lower cost. The NAO report on the BGC sale especially complimented the Department of Energy for achieving significant reductions in the normal rates of underwriting commissions, especially where shares were placed with priority applicants, although it questioned whether it had been really necessary to pay the 0.5 per cent sub-underwriting commission in respect of the firmly placed shares. The Department responded that the payment was justified to help achieve the maximisation of sale proceeds. Also, the NAO questioned the developing practice of setting the share price of privatisation issues in multiples of five pence, which it judged, correctly, reduced flexibility when setting the issue price. While the NAO did not consider that this procedure had disadvantaged the BGC flotation, it did request that the Government reconsider the practice for future privatisations.[253]

The Exchequer gained from the privatisation immediately and customers gained later. In terms of economic performance post-privatisation, employment in BGC fell from over 91,000 in 1985/6 to under 70,000 ten years later, leading to higher labour productivity.[254] The average annual rate of return on capital employed on a CCA basis averaged between four per cent and five per cent pre-privatisation and over six per cent afterwards. Reflecting the improved economic performance but also movements in international fuel costs, by 1994 average gas prices had fallen by 20 per cent in real terms since privatisation with industrial prices falling the most steeply. However, the public's view of the post-privatisation record of BGC was tainted by argument over top salaries. Management remuneration rose, inflated by a share option scheme adopted in BGC after privatisation. The wider controversy over "fat cat" management salaries in privatised firms became a crescendo in November 1994 when the press reported that Cedric Brown, the Chief Executive of British Gas, was to receive a pay rise of 75 per cent. The unions went so far as to take a 30 stone pig, named Cedric, to the company's AGM. With other cases of large increases in remuneration for senior executives in privatised companies exposed at the time, this undoubtedly damaged the public image of privatisation.[255]

Also, the privatisation of BGC left the problem of monopoly power to be tackled by the industry regulator and the competition authorities. By the early 1990s competition in gas had developed only slowly, although in part this was because BGC cut its prices in the contract market, the only market open to new suppliers, to forestall competition. BGC still controlled around 90 per cent of this market in 1990, appearing to confirm concern in the Department of Energy and the Treasury at the time of privatisation that the concessions on common carriage and competition, painfully extracted from the BGC Board, might not have gone far enough. The Director General of Fair Trading and the DGGS did attempt to address this. The DGGS ensured that BGC provided appropriate accounting and other information to regulate more effectively and the Office of Fair Trading secured an MMC inquiry in 1988. The OFT proved rather more vigorous than the BGC might have expected in bringing competition law to bear on the contract market after privatisation in response to complaints from large gas users. The MMC report found that BGC was in a position to undercut potential competitors by discriminatory pricing. The result was that BGC was required to publish price schedules,[256] with a view to removing the ability to price discriminate, and the company agreed that at least ten per cent of all gas from new fields should be made available to other gas suppliers.[257] But it would be the 1990s before more appreciable steps were taken to address the structural failings not tackled at privatisation.

In 1991 an OFT review of the industry led BGC to give undertakings designed to reduce further its share of the non-tariff market for gas and in the following year the Government announced the removal of the remaining controls on the import of gas.[258] Also, from 1992 the threshold for monopoly gas supplies (the tariff market) was reduced sharply from 25,000 therms to 2,500 therms.[259] In the same year the Government announced the intention to review this limit in the future and extend choice in gas supplies to domestic consumers. In 1993 an MMC inquiry recommended the physical separation of gas transmission and distribution from gas supply and a release of a proportion of BGC's contracted gas.[260] It also recommended that the monopoly threshold be reduced to 1,500 therms in 1997 and in the early 2000s be abolished altogether.[261] After some internal debate the Government decided to give priority to accelerating the introduction of competition in the tariff market rather than to an enforced break-up of BGC (which the company opposed, although it did agree to a voluntary internal separation of its trading and transportation activities). In 1995 a new Gas Act amended the duties of the regulator from "enable persons to compete effectively" (in the above 25,000 therms market only), as set out in the 1986 legislation, to "to secure effective competition" in gas supplies.[262] Full competition in gas supplies was phased in regionally from 1996. The effect was that by 1998 domestic and business customers in England, Wales and Scotland could choose from alternative gas suppliers and BGC therefore faced effective competition for all of its gas customers for the first time.

By the mid-1990s BGC's share of the contract market had fallen to 35 per cent. Under the pressure of falling gas prices, along with what BG plc management considered to be an increasingly hostile regulatory environment, the company then changed its mind and reversed its previous opposition to a break-up. In 1997 the storage and transportation parts of BGC were separated from the trading activities. In other words, it was in the mid-1990s that BGC's fears at the time of privatisation, that given the existence of long-term gas purchase contracts competition would undermine its finances, became reality. This was so even though the successor company, Centrica, was successful in renegotiating a number of them.

The BGC privatisation has been criticised for inadequate restructuring of the industry before the sale to create scope for extensive competition.[263] It is true that the sale of BGC had involved no break-up of the Corporation and later ideas of separating gas supply from transmission and distribution and having full retail competition were not considered serious possibilities in 1984. Walker consistently ruled out competition for smaller gas users and more or less everyone at the time agreed.[264] There was also the Government's objective of selling off the total Corporation ahead of a next general election to consider. Restructuring would undoubtedly have caused a serious delay. It is also fair to say that without privatisation, the break-up of the company which occurred during the late 1990s would probably not have happened, because it was privatisation that brought about effective regulation to promote competition. Moreover, by the end of the 1990s competition was extensive in gas, vindicating those who placed more emphasis at and following privatisation on promoting competition rather than restructuring BGC. Nevertheless, mounting criticism immediately after 1986 of the terms of the BGC privatisation was instrumental in leading to a more determined effort within Government and Parliament to restructure to create immediate competition when the electricity industry and the railways were later sold.

* * *

In 1997 investors in BGC were given one share each in three new companies: Centrica (which took over the retail gas supply and servicing businesses), Transco (which became owner of the gas pipelines and storage facilities) and British Gas (to concentrate on international exploration and production and the ownership of gasfields[265]). In 2000 British Gas demerged its Transco pipeline and in 2002 National Grid took over Transco, renamed Lattice. As the energy economist Dieter Helm has concluded: "History has not been kind to this privatization – its structures have not survived, nor was its regulation smooth."[266] However, in spite of the postponed major restructuring of the industry following privatisation and the potential loss of economic gains that earlier effective competition might have produced, the 1986 privatisation was an undoubted success for investors. By 2006 the stock market value of what had been the BGC had risen from £4.4 billion to £44.2 billion, composed of £23.1 billion for British Gas, £12.6 billion for Centrica and £8.5 billion for Lattice (a 43 per cent stake in National Grid).

# 16

# NATIONALISATION AND PRIVATISATION 1970–87

## An overview and conclusions

The Conservative Government under the leadership of Edward Heath was elected in 1970 on a manifesto of smaller government. However, between 1970 and 1974 only minor denationalisation occurred, of a small brewery in Carlisle and the travel agent Thomas Cook. Indeed, during the Heath Government public spending rose and in a number of respects the intervention of government in the economy in the form of industrial policy became more intrusive. After the defeat of the Government in the February 1974 General Election, during a "who rules Britain" confrontation with the National Union of Mineworkers, a new Labour administration extended state ownership with the nationalisation of aerospace and shipbuilding, the establishment of the National Enterprise Board and the creation of the British National Oil Corporation (BNOC). In February 1975 Margaret Thatcher replaced Edward Heath as leader of the Conservative Party. However, this did not necessarily signal an immediate change in Conservative policy towards state-owned industry. In two Party policy documents in 1976 and 1977, *The Right Approach* and *The Right Approach to the Economy,* there was little sign of a major shift in party thinking on nationalisation. This was also the case in the Manifesto on which the Conservatives won the May 1979 General Election. This Manifesto proposed limited denationalisation, mainly focused on reversing the recent privatisations of aerospace and shipbuilding and introducing some private capital into the National Freight Corporation.

In 1979, including central and local government and the National Health Service as well as the public corporations, around 7.45 million or 29.3 per cent of the labour force was employed in the public sector.[1] The UK was truly a mixed economy. Taking the state-owned industries alone, in 1979 they accounted for about ten per cent of the UK's Gross Domestic Product (GDP), 14 per cent of total investment in the economy and ten per cent of the Retail Price Index and employed some 1.5 million people or eight per cent of the country's workforce. The nationalised industries dominated a number of sectors of the economy, notably energy, communications, shipbuilding, public transport and steel and were major suppliers of outputs and purchasers of inputs from the private sector. If the industries were run as inefficient bureaucracies, unresponsive to market forces, then the impact across the economy was potentially very damaging. The 1970s was a particularly bad period for state industries with losses increasing and productivity growth declining. By 1979 the public sector corporations had debts of some £27 billion and the borrowings and losses of state-owned industries were running at about £3 billion a year.[2]

The Conservative Government elected in May 1979 wanted to make public administration and the nationalised industries more efficient and reduce taxation. The term "rolling back the frontiers of the state" came to typify the policy direction. But leaving aside a Manifesto commitment to give council house tenants a "right to buy" their homes, the policy stance was not seen at the time as implying a fundamental review of state ownership. Few, if any, within the Conservative Party or outside anticipated what was to come. Major denationalisation, or what from the early 1980s became known as privatisation, was at best a twinkle in the eye of a few of the members of the shadow Cabinet, notably Sir Keith Joseph and Geoffrey Howe and more questionably Margaret Thatcher. Many Ministers neither expected it nor saw it as a policy priority, given the pressing problems of inflation, economic recession and the trade unions.

Margaret Thatcher's position on the future of the nationalised industries in May 1979 is particularly enigmatic. She was a politician who in the past had demonstrated hostility to big government and state ownership. But in her first senior ministerial position as Education Secretary, between 1970 and 1974, she had overseen one of the Government's biggest spending departments and had shown no inkling of a wish to see her department's spending cut. In her first months as Prime Minister, while no friend of nationalisation, she was hesitant and cautious about a denationalisation agenda, especially in the energy sector, and left the final decisions on sales to the Ministers of the relevant sponsor departments. The sponsor departments were those that were responsible for overseeing the performance of each of the nationalised industries. Later she became more obviously actively involved and began to champion privatisation publicly. The explanation for the change seems to lie in her concern in 1979 that successful denationalisation might be difficult to achieve and might provoke the wrath of the trade unions, who had brought down the previous Conservative administration in 1974. In the early days she also appears to have harboured deep reservations about the voters' acceptance of selling "public" assets – would privatisation be a vote loser? By 1982 it had become clearer that the unions would not be able to mount a serious opposition to sales and that privatisations would not be an obvious political liability. The Prime Minister was now more clearly in favour of pushing forward with privatisations than she had been three years earlier, but she was still unsure how far the policy could be pursued. It was only in late 1984 with the privatisation of British Telecom (BT) that it became clear that even the largest of the nationalised industries with considerable monopoly powers might be successfully sold. Kenneth Clarke, a junior minister before 1987, but to become Chancellor of the Exchequer from May 1993, was typical of most Conservatives, including the PM, in coming around to privatisation as practical politics when it was demonstrated that the policy was successful:

"I had always believed in free market economics but I combined it with what I thought was sensible pragmatism – the R.A. Butler art of the possible. When Nick Ridley first started advocating that you took great state industries out of state control I think most people regarded it as completely mad. When we first started privatising, the main aim was to get private-sector capital into industries previously deprived of it. I was never sold on rolling back the frontiers of the state, all this stuff. But as time went on, I became persuaded that not only did you get rid of all the politics out of it, and put private capital in, but you raised the performance of the company. But if you'd asked me that in 1979, I would have regarded it as all a bit ideological."[3]

During the early 1980s in Britain a new orthodoxy developed in favour of private ownership replacing state ownership. This was a product of repeated government wrestling with the challenges of running large sectors of the economy efficiently and effectively and at a time of macroeconomic turbulence brought on, not least, by a sharp rise in energy prices. But the new orthodoxy was also consistent and in tune with a movement in economics away from state planning, Keynesianism and the concept of a "welfare state" towards market liberalisation, monetarism and the concept of consumerism during the 1970s. In this the economics of public choice and agency theory played the important role of providing an intellectual rationale for why private ownership should be more efficient than state ownership. This economics came largely from the USA, but was championed in Britain by right-wing think tanks such as the Institute of Economic Affairs and the Adam Smith Institute. Margaret Thatcher and other leading Conservatives had links with these organisations. The ideas also had an influence on Conservative Party thinking through Party organisations, notably the Centre for Policy Studies established by Sir Keith Joseph in 1974.

Privatisation gained an intellectual rationale which offered the prospect of industries being managed more efficiently and effectively. But more pragmatically, privatisation provided the new Conservative Government with the means of closing the yawning gap between public spending and tax revenues. What really kick-started the privatisation programme after May 1979 was the demand from Treasury Ministers that state assets should be identified for sale. The search for candidates for disposal within Government after May 1979 was driven principally by budgetary pressures. Privatisation receipts were netted off against public expenditure in the UK's public finances and therefore had the bonus of appearing to reduce the size of public spending as a proportion of GDP, an outcome consistent with the Government's macroeconomic agenda. At first the disposals programme mainly took the form of sales of surplus land and buildings and small shareholdings in organisations with some state ownership due to historical accident, such as BP and Suez Finance (the previous Labour Government had already sold some of the state's shareholding in BP and for the same reason, to raise cash). As Ministers concentrated upon identifying "special asset sales", as they tended to be termed in the public accounts, this led in time to interest in the possibility of selling entire nationalised industries – and growing confidence that it would be possible. As Thatcher comments, "we got bolder and we learned as we went along."[4]

By June 1987 the programme of privatisation was an established component of Government economic policy. During the first Thatcher administration, from May 1979 to May 1983, British Airways was lined up for the introduction of some private capital, but not necessarily full denationalisation – but in any case the sale had to be delayed; British Aerospace was transferred back to the private sector, fulfilling a Manifesto commitment; and the National Freight Corporation was sold, going further than the Manifesto, which had raised only the possibility of introducing private capital. In addition, a number of other sales occurred such as Amersham International and Cable and Wireless, largely as a response to Treasury pressure for sales receipts.

But it was after the May 1983 General Election that privatisation entered the heartlands of the nationalised industries with the privatisations of British Telecom and later British Gas. Ministers such as Ian Gilmour and Jim Prior on the so-called "wet" wing of the Conservative Party had departed from the Cabinet and within the Civil Service it was becoming increasingly plain that career success was linked to accepting and preferably enthusing about the Government's privatisation programme. After the success of the sale of British Telecom, which in the early days of its planning appeared to be very ambitious given the unprecedented size of the sale, £3.9 billion, the climate became even more favourable for privatisation within Government and outside, including the City. Meanwhile, the trade unions were a dwindling force due to high unemployment, the drastic shrinking of the country's traditional manufacturing base, in which unionisation was concentrated, and new government laws that reduced the scope for trade union action.

As successive privatisation successes were notched up, the Government expanded the field of possible candidates for disposal. Experience of how to privatise, lacking at the outset of the first Thatcher administration, was built up in government departments and in the City. As each privatisation occurred it became clearer that the potential obstacles could be addressed, such as tapping the capital market for larger and larger sums, overcoming employee and union resistance and successfully regulating monopolies transferred to the private sector. The Civil Service was understandably cautious that sales should not occur without full consideration of the implications for the future of the industries and the wider economy. But there is no evidence that the Civil Service actively worked to undermine privatisations. By the mid-1980s any friction between sponsor departments and the Treasury related mainly to the details of a sale, such as the size of the employee share scheme or the degree of capital restructuring needed, rather than issues of major principle. Over time a cadre of Permanent Secretaries, Deputy Secretaries and Under Secretaries were appointed across departments who shared, or at least paid lip service to, the PM's belief in privatisation. But even before this, reflecting the principle in the British Civil Service that civil servants carry out the policies of the Government of the day, the senior Civil Service supported Ministers planning each of the various privatisations. The privatisation of oil interests proceeded slowly within the Department of Energy from the summer of 1979, but the replacement of David Howell as Secretary of State for Energy by the champion of privatisation in the Treasury, Nigel Lawson, in September 1981, effectively removed the logjam. Once civil servants in the Department were given a clearer sense of direction on privatisation, they pursued the policy with vigour. The Civil Service would warn when they felt that a particular ministerial decision might have unfortunate results, which is their role, but in other respects they saw their duty as one of ensuring that Government policy was accomplished.

Not that it was all smooth sailing. Given the need to pass legislation and carefully plan the sales with financial advisers from the City, the Government found that only two or three privatisations a year were possible, leaving aside the sale by nationalised industries of subsidiary businesses, which were generally much less demanding in terms of parliamentary time. Each privatisation threw up its own set of challenges and difficulties, and sometimes delays occurred because of circumstances outside the control of Government, such as the crash in the world steel and shipbuilding markets in the early 1980s and the Laker lawsuit that dogged the privatisation of British Airways (BA) in the mid-1980s. Equally, the order under which privatisations were undertaken was largely pragmatic and evolved around meeting the Treasury's annual disposal targets, set out each year in the Budget speech. Throughout the 1980s the Treasury set annual targets for "special asset sales", which entered into the planning of the public finances. In response government departments put forward assets for disposal. Where public corporations sold off assets, including subsidiary businesses, generally the sale receipts stayed with the corporations. But the Treasury would achieve a benefit by revising the corporation's external financing limit (EFL) downwards to reflect the receipts. Another important consideration in the selection of industries to sell off was their likely appeal to investors. This meant that the sales involved essentially the profitable nationalised industries not the loss making ones.[5] Only in the mid-1980s was a serious start made on the loss making industries, with the first privatisations of shipbuilding. The sale of the loss making coal industry and the railways still appeared a far distant prospect, if a prospect at all. More generally, privatisation was delayed where industries were judged to need substantial restructuring to restore them to profitability or at least reduce their losses before they could be successfully sold. A good example of this is the steel industry but also British Airways. Those nationalised industries which were already profitable were the most obvious early candidates for sale; in this sense the Government privatised the easiest ones first.

Also, nationalised industries that were dominant in their markets, and in some cases monopoly suppliers of important public services, were difficult to contemplate for disposal in the early days. It was for this reason that the Central Policy Review Staff (CPRS) paper of October 1982 was such an important landmark, as it set out how monopolies might be privatised as regulated businesses. This was followed by the privatisation of BT, which was a watershed because it established that the ideas encapsulated in the CPRS report were practical. This privatisation demonstrated that monopoly suppliers could be successfully sold off, with the consumer protected by a new dedicated regulatory regime at arm's length from political control until adequate competition developed. However, the sale of the monopoly businesses of BT and British Gas (BGC) needed much careful planning and the passage of the legislation to permit both sales proved controversial and time consuming.

The general objectives of privatisation policy evolved during the 1980s to become a combination of raising revenues, widening share ownership, increasing competition and consumer choice, raising efficiency and reducing the power of trade unions, but with each privatisation having its own particular agenda. For example, the sale of BGC had four stated key objectives, as set out by the sponsor department, the Department of Energy. These were to secure a successful transfer to the private sector, to maximise net sale proceeds, achieve widespread share ownership, and to avoid an excessive premium in the aftermarket.[6] In some cases, such as BT, there were additional reasons for privatisation such as finding a source of new capital for investment in the private sector. Cento Veljanovski is correct when he talks about privatisation having "a multiplicity of objectives"[7] and says that "the goals of privatisation evolved gradually and the emphasis given to each of these goals has been different for each privatisation".[8] At the same time, diverse objectives were not always readily compatible and from time to time one had to give way to another. In particular, the existence of different objectives meant that disagreements broke out from time to time within Government, notably between the sponsor department and the Treasury, over the cost of incentive schemes to small investors and employees and the extent to which competition should be promoted over other goals. Sometimes this would extend to tension within a department. For example, during the sale of BT, within the Treasury there was a desire to see more competition introduced into telecommunications but at the same time healthy sales receipts. More generally, securing a successful transfer to the private sector was always taken to be the overriding goal. A privatisation failure would be a political embarrassment and risk a fatal loss of confidence in the City in the privatisation programme. Without continuing investor support, the privatisation programme would be lost.

In the early days, what the economist Christopher Foster has referred to as "the power of certain more or less questionable macroeconomic arguments in the difficult economic circumstances of raging inflation and high unemployment at the start of the 1980s"[9] provided the catalyst for Treasury pressure on departments to find assets to sell. He had in mind, amongst other things, the effect of public borrowing on the money supply and inflation. At the same time, suggestion that privatisation was "a policy which was adopted almost by accident"[10] and "a policy in search of a rationale"[11] is very misleading. In particular, any suggestion that the promotion of wider share ownership became a declared objective of privatisation only from 1984, and after it had become a reality, is simply wrong. Widening share ownership was a Government objective from the outset, albeit that in the early days it was unclear to Ministers whether the public would respond positively and buy the shares on offer. Moreover, there was a tension between widening share ownership by introducing incentives for small investors to subscribe for shares and maximising sales receipts.

In the first months after the May 1979 General Election raising receipts for a hard pressed Exchequer was a primary consideration, certainly for Treasury ministers. However, not all sales were financially driven. The denationalisation of BAe was a Manifesto commitment, as already noted. Also, this sale and the sales of the National Freight Corporation (NFC) and Associated British Ports (ABP) in the end raised precious little net sums for the Exchequer, once the costs of financial restructuring including debt write-offs, pension fund deficits and sale costs were deducted. This was reflected at the time in dwindling interest in these particular sales amongst Treasury Ministers.

In any case, sale receipts became less important as a driver of the privatisation programme by the mid-1980s because the state of the public finances had improved considerably by then. Also, over time rather than pricing shares "to the last penny", the benefits of maximising proceeds over the longer term by raising the public's enthusiasm for privatisation became a more obvious feature of government policy.[12] At the same time, sale receipts never became an irrelevant issue, at least as far as the Treasury was concerned. This was especially so once the large sums that could be raised from selling major public corporations like BT and BGC became evident. After 1983 the disposals targets set out annually by the Chancellor of the Exchequer became much larger and ambitious. Privatisation receipts remained necessary to make the budgetary figures add up.[13] Even though privatisation receipts never amounted to much more than 2.6 per cent of government expenditure in any year up to 1987, and were usually much less (Table 16.1), they provided a useful supplement to tax revenues.

## Managing the privatisation process

By the June 1987 General Election the scale of the Government's achievement in terms of dismantling state industry was truly astounding. BP, BAe, Cable and Wireless (C&W), Amersham International, Britoil (the oil exploration and production assets of BNOC), ABP, Jaguar motors, BT, BGC (including separately its oil interests in the form of Wytch Farm and Enterprise Oil), BA, Rolls-Royce (RR) and the assets of the National Enterprise Board (NEB) had all been privatised, along with various smaller businesses. By June 1987 around £12.5 billion had been raised from privatisation sales with another £16 billion from the disposal of government land and buildings.[14] In addition, some 600,000 employees had been transferred from state-owned industries to the private sector. Annual privatisation receipts had risen from £377 million in 1979/80 to around £4.5 billion in 1986/7 (the annual figures are provided in Table 16.1). Of the total privatisation receipts between May 1979 and June 1987, by far the largest part, £10.9 billion, was raised during the second Thatcher Government, in other words between May 1983 and June 1987. It was during these years that privatisation moved into the heartlands of the nationalised industries with the disposals of BT and BGC in particular. At the time these were the largest initial public offers (IPOs) ever mounted in any capital market anywhere in the world.

Each privatisation spawned its own legislation, except where subsidiary businesses were sold by nationalised industry boards. Drafting the legislation and then achieving a smooth

*Table 16.1* Privatisation proceeds 1979 to 1987

|  | £ million | % of government expenditure |
|---|---|---|
| 1979/80 | 377 | 0.4 |
| 1980/1 | 210 | 0.4 |
| 1981/2 | 493 | 0.4 |
| 1982/3 | 455 | 0.4 |
| 1983/4 | 1,139 | 0.8 |
| 1984/5 | 2,050 | 1.4 |
| 1985/6 | 2,706 | 1.7 |
| 1986/7 | 4,458 | 2.6 |
| Total | 11,888 | |

*Source*: HM Treasury (1992) *Her Majesty's Treasury Guide to the UK Privatisation Programme*, June, London: HM Treasury, Appendix C; Marsh (1991), Table 2, p.471.

sell-off was never straightforward, partly because there was limited precedent to call upon within government departments or City firms and partly because of particular legal issues that arose in each case, such as the Port Talbot contract during the sale of Associated British Ports and the Cranley Onslow assurances during the privatisation of Rolls-Royce. Privatisations were delayed by the need to introduce accounting changes (such as in the case of BT), to remove losses so that the enterprise was a going concern (a good example is shipbuilding, albeit with very mixed results), and to deal with regulatory and social issues. Regulation and social issues bulked large during the sales of BT and BGC, but also featured during the liberalisation of the bus market that preceded the sale of the National Bus Company (NBC).

The timetabling of each privatisation was a significant consideration to prevent gaps in the programme and the opposite of legislative and stock market bottlenecks. By 1987 a sale process or sequencing had evolved which, while not exactly a rigid template, broadly applied to each of the privatisations. This encompassed an initial feasibility study of the prospects for a privatisation, the Ministerial decision to proceed, the selecting of advisers, designing and passing the appropriate enabling legislation where necessary, determining the privatised firm's capital structure (including gearing, interest cover and reserves, dividend capacity, and in a number of cases addressing pension fund deficits), choosing the method of sale and the target investors (including in some cases the use of investor incentives such as bonus issues and bill vouchers, and tapping overseas stock markets), timing the vesting of the assets and liabilities into the new company (and arranging the terms of the continued Government oversight of the finances of the business until a majority of the company's shares were sold), marketing the sale including the advertising campaign, determining the nature of the share sale, the flotation date and arranging a stock market listing, valuing the business and setting the sale price, arranging the publication of the sale prospectus and underwriting, and finally handling the share applications and allocating the shares. Because there were concerns during the sale of the larger enterprises, notably BT and BGC, that the UK capital market might have insufficient capacity to absorb the share issue, shares were also sold in some overseas markets, notably North America and Japan. But this added to the complexity of some privatisations. One objective during all sales was to create a competitive tension between the different investor markets, i.e. institutional and retail investors in the UK and between UK and international investors, so as to reduce the risk of under-subscription and maximise the share price.

Figure 16.1 is a flow chart summarising each of the stages of a typical privatisation.[15] In the case of MEBOs and trade sales the privatisation process as set out in the Figure was similar with the main differences relating to the final stages; in particular, negotiations with the management and bankers replaced the share flotation stage including the publication of

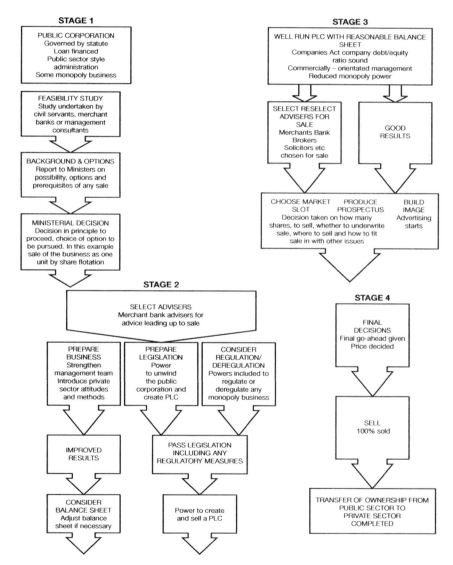

*Figure 16.1* Outline of the typical steps to privatisation
*Source*: HM Treasury (1992).

a prospectus. The timing of each flotation depended upon careful planning of the privatisation timetable. In particular, in all cases departments had to plan the disposal dates around the timing of the Chancellor of the Exchequer's autumn Financial Statement and his spring Budget speech. Government expenditure and tax changes could affect the financial prospects of a company to be privatised and would have to be acknowledged in the sale prospectus. But to do so would breach the secrecy that surrounds the Government's financial plans ahead of a formal statement by the Chancellor. At the same time, sometimes delays occurred because of extraneous factors, for example in the case of ABP a legal dispute with British Steel. In the case of the state-owned airline BA, exceptionally the delay between the decision to proceed with an introduction of private capital and the eventual privatisation lasted for almost seven years, due to a combination of economic factors and legal disputes.

The UK Government did not opt for the passage of an omnibus Privatisation Bill empowering Ministers to sell a range of industries, as occurred in some countries. For example, the French adopted enabling legislation which permitted the Government to sell any of a list of companies or assets. Legislation giving Ministers general denationalisation powers would have done away with the need to pass separate privatisation Acts and would therefore almost certainly have speeded up the process of selling, allowing more industries to have been privatised more quickly. At the same time, however, empowering the privatisation of a number of different industries through one piece of legislation would certainly have concentrated opposition to privatisation in Parliament and outside, with perhaps fatal effects. Such a Bill might well have had a very difficult Parliamentary passage, as MPs and peers raised objections to different potential sales and outside interests including the various trade unions combined in opposition. The legislation might well have been lost. The Government did consider introducing a law in 1984 that would have empowered Ministers to require nationalised industry boards to divest and sell off subsidiary businesses, as part of a wider piece of legislation to consolidate the statutory controls of the nationalised sector. But this Bill was withdrawn following strong objections, especially from nationalised industry chairmen. There was also concern within Government that it marked an unfortunate reversal of the policy of Government distancing itself from the management of the industries. In any case, under this proposal, where a whole nationalised industry was to be sold there would still have been the need for separate primary legislation.

Although passing numerous privatisation bills was time consuming, it did have the benefit of permitting individual provisions to be introduced to meet the needs of each industry. It also enabled a learning process to occur within government departments with improvements to the process introduced over time. At the same time, the arrangement did have the by-product of introducing some differences in the details of each privatisation and in the regulatory regimes introduced for the monopoly sectors; for example, there were some differences between the regulatory powers of the Director Generals of OFTEL and OFGAS.[16]

Various methods of privatisation were adopted, namely initial public offers (IPOs), followed by secondary share sales some months or even years later where less than a 100 per cent share sale had first occurred; trade sales, where a business was sold to an existing private sector company or one created to purchase the business; management and employee buyouts (MEBOs); and competitive tendering/contracting out schemes. However, in terms of the scale and total value of assets sold, IPOs dominated. Trade sales and MEBOs were confined to smaller businesses, such as British Rail hotels and ferry services and subsidiaries of BA, the National Coal Board (NCB) and British Steel. Bus companies were sold through a combination of MEBOs and trade sales. The largest single MEBO involved the NFC in

February 1982, a buy-out that resulted only after City advice against a public flotation in the difficult economic conditions of 1981/2. Contracting out/competitive tendering was used for certain services, such as cleaning, catering and security, within central government and the National Health Service, where in-house staff competed with the private sector for time limited contracts to provide the services. It was also made compulsory for some activities in local government in 1980. However, the big expansion of competitive tendering for local services did not come until after 1987, when legislation was introduced extending the scheme. Contracting out/competitive tendering led to some reduction in public sector employment and some reductions in public spending, but the effect was always small in relation to the total activities of Government.

Most important were the IPOs. The Stock Exchange expected that a company coming to the market would have a track record of past performance, normally a satisfactory run of results over the previous three years with the most recent accounts published usually within the previous six months. Accountants would early in the sale process prepare a "long-form report" covering all aspects of the business including production, accounting systems, employees and management and marketing. This and a later "short-form report" would form the basis for the financial information that went into the sale prospectus. In the meantime, before the prospectus could be finalised, preparing the many volumes of documents and legal agreements required to float on the London stock market, and sometimes overseas stock markets, proved painstaking for government departments and their advisers.

Each flotation required that assets and liabilities were valued to produce an opening balance sheet and that an appropriate capital structure was put in place. This sometimes meant that part of the sale proceeds was needed as a capital injection into the company, notably in the cases of British Aerospace, Cable and Wireless and Rolls-Royce. In a number of instances receipts had to be set aside to meet deficits in pension funds. The corporation boards were keen to see balance sheets repaired ahead of sale and this frequently led to a capital restructuring immediately before privatisation. Inevitably this involved some difficult negotiations between the corporation boards, Departments and the Treasury over the cost to the public finances. During the sales of BT and BGC the negotiations over capital restructuring were subsumed into a wider set of negotiations over future price controls or the RPI – X price caps. Occasionally, the discussions over the appropriate balance sheet gearing, interest cover and dividend yield after privatisation became so fraught that there were fears that the board would be unwilling to sanction the sale prospectus and the planned flotation date would be missed.[17]

Closer to the time of the flotation a sale prospectus for the enterprise was drawn up and issued and arrangements for the underwriting of the sale were concluded. As part of this exercise, the share price was determined. Sometimes this was preceeded by a Pathfinder prospectus, omitting the share price. The share price was set the day before the issue of the full prospectus and immediately before the underwriting was agreed. Sometimes, as in the case of BT, debt would also be sold. When shares were over-subscribed, as was commonly the case, a method of share allocation was adopted to favour the small investor. To counter the threat of multiple applications by the same investor, to get around the limit on shares allocated to each applicant, applications had to be carefully checked to prevent fraud. Some legal actions resulted.

Each privatisation of a nationalised industry was executed within its sponsoring department. As John Redwood commented at the time: "It is easiest to review privatization progress department by department – as departmental culture is deeply embedded in the Whitehall machine and each act of privatization is seen as a departmental rather than a governmental problem."[18] At the same time, nationalised industry policy was always the responsibility of the Treasury in the post-war period, with policy statements covering more than one industry presented to Parliament by Treasury Ministers. This central co-ordinating role of the Treasury carried over into the privatisation programme of the 1980s. In particular, the Treasury was responsible for co-ordinating and timetabling the various privatisations planned across government and overseeing the terms of each sale, in consultation with the Bank of England.[19] The Bank of England's primary role was to monitor the stock market, including other planned share issues, and to advise on whether and when the market would be best able to absorb the privatisation issues (however, in the cases of the sale of BP shares in November 1979 and September 1983 and the second issue of C&W shares in December 1983 the Bank also acted as a financial adviser).[20]

Typically each privatisation involved a team of departmental officials from the sponsor department, representation from the Treasury (and sometimes from other departments with an interest in the outcome of the sale and the Bank of England) and outside financial advisers. The outside advisers were typically composed of the merchant bank (later alternatively referred to as the investment bank) advising the government department on the sale, the lead stock broking firms, solicitors and public relations and marketing advisers. The public corporation being sold would obtain advice from its own merchant bank and broker and from its accountants and specialist advisers, for example on pensions and property valuation. The government department also sought the help of such specialist advisers from time to time. Committees and working groups would be set up drawing from the Civil Service and the outside advisers to the Government to deal with different aspects of the sale, including legal and accounting issues, financial restructuring, marketing, designing the flotation prospectus, and regulatory issues when relevant.

Civil servants within departments were encouraged to share their experiences with others. At the end of each privatisation the main civil servants involved reflected on their experience, sometimes preparing a written report. Also, departments did capitalise on earlier experience directly, for example within the Department of Energy up to five civil servants and two support service employees were occupied during the Enterprise Oil sale in 1984. Of these, two had worked on the earlier Britoil sale and one on the sale of Amersham International. However, with privatisations occurring in different government departments (between 1979 and 1987 the Department of Trade, the Department of Industry – later combined as the Department of Trade and Industry – the Department of Energy, the Department of Transport and the Ministry of Defence were all involved in one or more privatisations), the opportunity did not exist to achieve full economies of scale and learning economies by centralising privatisation skills. Moreover, different teams of officials could be involved in different privatisations even when carried on within the same department. Some experience and continuity must therefore have been lost.

Within the Treasury the development of privatisation skills was assisted by the establishment of the Public Enterprises Analytical Unit (PEAU) within the department's Public Enterprises Group at the end of January 1982. The creation of the PEAU was part of a reform of the oversight of the nationalised industries, triggered by a CPRS report in July of the previous year (see chapter 3, p.79). The Unit's initial brief was to monitor and improve the performance of the nationalised industries. But it quickly became involved in championing the privatisation policy, including agreeing the annual sales target which fed into the PSBR calculations and harassing government departments on the desirability of promoting competition during privatisations. In this it was aided by consultants brought in from the City and academia by the Treasury and departments. Paralleling this, a body of expertise developed in the City which passed from privatisation to privatisation, but, as in the case of expertise within Government, from a very low base in 1980/1.

A lack of expertise within Government, exacerbated when civil servants left for more lucrative posts in the private sector, told against the achievement of a more equal balance in negotiations between Government and the City advisers. Certainly in the early years civil servants were "green" with little knowledge of public flotations and the pricing of shares. In particular, in 1979 there was a lack of experience of corporate finance, including asset valuation and asset sales, across Whitehall, including in the Treasury. Government seems to have accepted with little questioning the form of sale and the sale price as recommended by their financial advisers from the City. However over time, as experience in the Treasury and sponsoring departments increased, so did the confidence to challenge City advice.

In defence of the approach adopted, where especially in the early days departments handled each privatisation as essentially a unique event often using different officials, no two industries were identical and fresh perspectives to each sale could bring advantages. In any case, each Minister had his own privatisation agenda and this operated against establishing some kind of definite blueprint for sales within Government. Nevertheless, it is certainly the case that staff changes, departmental boundaries and the decentralised way in which privatisations occurred weighed against capitalising on experience within Government. It might be argued that the speed and smoothness of privatisations would have been better served by centralising the privatisation work and building up a body of civil servants dedicated to privatising state industry. However, to have established something akin to a Ministry for Privatisation to handle all of the privatisation work (as occurred in some countries) would have meant first transferring responsibility for the nationalised industries from the sponsor departments. The sponsor departments had knowledge of each industry and its particular problems and challenges and the Ministry of Privatisation would have lacked this. This might have led to less successful privatisations. Moreover, the sponsor departments were responsible for agreeing EFLs and investment programmes and dealing with a range of other issues relating to the nationalised industries, which presumably would not have transferred to a privatisation ministry. Also, establishment of a Ministry of Privatisation would almost certainly have been vigorously opposed by the Treasury, which has a history of preventing matters of important economic policy slipping from its grasp.

The alternative would have been to transfer all privatisation work to the Treasury. But without major restructuring and new resources the Treasury would not have been able to cope with the workload. Certainly the transfer of power from departments to a Ministry of Privatisation or the Treasury would have meant a substantial upheaval of the oversight of the nationalised industries and would have generated considerable opposition from the sponsor departments and possibly the nationalised industries. It would have diverted Civil Service effort for some time into restructuring government rather than preparing the industries for sale, thereby delaying the privatisation programme.

There is no evidence that such a restructuring was ever contemplated. Instead, from the earliest days the Treasury adopted a co-ordinating role, in an endeavour to ensure a reasonable level of consistency across government departments. Over time the Treasury provided guidance to departments and this extended to the way that the disposals were mounted and to ensuring that the disposal receipts were not dissipated, for example by the granting of overly generous employee share schemes (although this did not guarantee that departments always followed the guidance). The Cabinet Sub-Committee on disposals (E(DL)) also provided an oversight of the privatisation programme in the early years and this too may have led to greater consistency in the approaches adopted.

There was some criticism of the method of appointment of the advisers used in early disposals, in which departments used their own discretion. Later there was more emphasis on ensuring proper competition for posts. As John Moore, Financial Secretary to the Treasury between 1983 and 1986, and the unofficial Minister of Privatisation, was to comment later:

> "In the initial stages [of privatisation], we felt very much at the mercy of bankers and brokers and wondered if they were giving us the best possible service. To make sure they were, we turned to the traditional mechanism for improving performance: competition. We required banks and brokers, much to their annoyance, to bid for government privatization business."[21]

In November 1983 the PEAU published criteria for departments relating to the choice of financial and other advisers during privatisations, the methods of sale and the marketing of disposals, and the methods of company valuation that should be adopted. The document confirmed that the objective should be "obtaining the best available advice at the lowest appropriate cost". Previously the practice had been for departments and corporations to choose their financial adviser from a short list of banks who had been involved in previous privatisations. The result was a concentration on a small number of advising firms. By the autumn of 1983, J. Henry Schroder Wagg (Schroders) and Kleinwort, Benson (Kleinworts) had been involved in five privatisations each and S.G.Warburg (Warburgs) and N.M. Rothschild & Sons (Rothschilds) in two each. Less than half of the merchant banks involved had been appointed after competition. In some cases bank appointments to conduct preliminary evaluations led to reappointment to carry through the sale. For example, Kleinworts was invited to carry out a feasibility study of the sale of BAe and was then appointed by the Department of Industry as the merchant bank for the disposal. Barings and Rothschilds carried out feasibility studies into the sale of C&W and in the first instance Barings was then appointed by the Government. In the case of the NFC, Schroders, which handled the privatisation, was already advising the Corporation.

Following the introduction of Treasury guidance this changed; merchant banks and stockbrokers were appointed after a departmental announcement in the financial press of the Government's intention to commission work, followed by a short-listing, and then a presentation and interview, referred to within Government as a "beauty parade" or "beauty contest". The successful bidder was chosen on the basis of competence to undertake the work and the price quoted.[22] Typically, the Treasury would have a representative on the selection panels. In all cases the Treasury and the Bank of England were notified of the outcome to retain oversight and ensure consistency in the appointments process. At the same time, the Treasury developed a list of recognised advisers based on experience in previous privatisations and their wider reputation.[23] No formal procedures were set down for appointing other advisers (e.g. stockbrokers, public relations consultants, underwriters, solicitors and printers), but the presumption was that some form of competition would be adopted. The Department of Transport and the Department of Trade and Industry (DTI) at first opposed the use of competition for appointments, arguing that the process would increase the workload on departments, but such objections were waived aside. The Departments fell into line.[24]

In all cases the imposition of what the Treasury perceived as best practice in the selection process had the objective of avoiding "over concentrating the [privatisation] programme as a whole on too few advisers".[25] Similar guidance on fees to advisers was issued by the Treasury fifteen months later, in February 1985, again to ensure competition and with the intention of reducing costs.[26] The fees at issue were those paid to merchant banks, underwriters and stockbrokers, solicitors, accountants, receiving banks and public relations advisers. The guidance stressed that "The prestige and scale of privatisation business is such that the Government expects to command the finest rates when commissioning advice". In a barely veiled criticism of previous departmental practice, the guidance went on to stress: "Although fees charged for earlier privatisations may provide a guide to subsequent negotiators, Departments should be wary of attempts by advisers to seek to be paid at the maximum levels conceded in previous sales." Henceforth the Treasury expected to be consulted before fees for advisers were agreed, with the view of the Bank of England also sought in appropriate circumstances.[27]

The rates to advisers and the City were typically based on a fixed sum or a fixed sum per period plus a commission related to the sale proceeds, although there were some variations from privatisation to privatisation and dependent upon the nature of the work. During the second Thatcher Government the Treasury took a more active role in overseeing the process of fee setting. Reflecting recognition that City firms benefited from contracting for the privatisation work in terms of future work and privatisation work overseas, Treasury guidance made clear that "the Government does not expect to pay normal City rates either for preliminary advice or for conducting a sale."[28] This applied to all City work including underwriting fees. Over time the commission rates were pushed down from the levels paid during the first privatisations. In particular, in the early 1980s the standard commission for underwriting new privatisation issues in the City was up to two per cent, split 0.5 per cent to the lead underwriter, 0.25 per cent to the broker or brokers to the issue and 1.25 per cent to the sub-underwriters.[29] Later primary underwriting rates fell sharply following the introduction of competition, as discussed more fully below.[30] Similarly, stockbrokers' fees as low as 0.07 per cent were achieved and departments were henceforth encouraged to seek rates of below 0.125 per cent. The Treasury's objective was to ensure that departments achieved the keenest prices.[31]

The cost of privatisations in terms of advisers' fees, marketing costs and underwriting and other commissions paid varied. The official estimated figures as a percentage of the sales receipts between 1979 and 1987 (ignoring reorganisation and restructuring costs including capital and loan write-offs) averaged around 4.2 per cent and ranged from a low of 1.3 per cent for the tranche of BP shares sold in September 1983, 2.2 per cent for the sale of Rolls-Royce, 2.8 per cent for Enterprise Oil, 3.1 per cent for the first C&W issue in 1981, 3.1 per cent for the first Britoil flotation, 4 per cent for the first tranche of BAe shares, 4.4 per cent for the sale of British Gas, 4.7 per cent for the disposal of BA, 4.8 per cent in the case of the privatisation of Amersham International, 6.8 per cent for the sale of BT, and a large 9.1 per cent during the sale of ABP.[32] Table 16.2 provides further detail of the costs to Government of each of the major sales.[33] From late 1983, when the Treasury injected more competition into the process of appointing merchant banks, other advisers and the primary underwriters, in general the costs were brought down. However, the costs of a sale also reflected the complexity of the privatisation. Understandably, the costs tended to be higher when shares issues were particularly targeted at small retail investors because of the additional marketing and advertising costs incurred, the expense of handling large numbers of applications (and enquiries before the sale) and the cost of any share incentive schemes.

*Table 16.2* The cost of sales

|  | Year | Total costs of sale to Government including VAT, excluding incentives to investors |
|---|---|---|
|  |  | £thousands |
| British Aerospace | 1981 | 5,600 |
| Cable and Wireless | 1981 | 8,900 |
| Amersham International | 1982 | 2,900 |
| Britoil | 1982 | 12,600 |
| National Freight Corporation | 1982 | 300 |
| Associated British Ports | 1983 | 2,600 |
| British Petroleum | 1983 | 22,760 |
| Cable and Wireless | 1983 | 12,500 |
| Associated British Ports | 1984 | 1,400 |
| Enterprise Oil | 1984 | 10,700 |
| Jaguar | 1984 | n/a* |
| Sealink | 1984 | 100 |
| Wytch Farm | 1984 | 98 |
| British Telecom | 1984 | 183,000 |
| British Aerospace | 1985 | 17,800 |
| Britoil | 1985 | 23,300 |
| Cable and Wireless | 1985 | 21,400 |
| British Gas | 1986 | 175,000 |
| British Shipbuilding warship yards | 1986 | 55,500 |
| British Airways | 1987 | 33,900 |
| Rolls-Royce | 1987 | 41,600 |

Note: * Sale conducted by the parent company, BL (British Leyland).

Source: HM Treasury papers, PE2 Division, 1998.

An appendix to this volume provides information on the financial advisers used and the primary underwriters, legal advisers, auditors and stockbrokers for all of the main privatisations between 1979 and June 1987.

Privatisation also imposed less obvious but real costs in terms of Civil Service and Ministerial time spent on planning and arranging each disposal. It is not possible to put any definite figures on these costs; again they reflected the size and scope of a sale. But to take one example: towards the end of the sale of Enterprise Oil one Assistant Secretary, three Principals, one Executive Officer and two support service employees were working wholly or largely on the disposal. In addition, some staff time will have been taken up in the Treasury. Earlier in a sale, typically the commitment from departmental officials and the Treasury was less.

The Treasury guidance on fees set out in general terms which costs of sale should fall on the nationalised industry that was being privatised (typically the cost of the corporation's own advisers, corporate image advertising and public relations, and listing and registration costs) and those that should fall on the sponsoring department. The issuing of this guidance reflected early argument between Government and the management of corporations over who should bear which costs. However, the guidance was worded in very general terms only, reflecting the difficulty of being prescriptive when the circumstances of each sale differed. This meant that disagreement between Government and the corporations continued, as evidenced in 1986 during the sale of BGC (chapter 15, p.375).

At first, as in the case of the sale of BAe shares in February 1981 and C&W shares in October 1981, the same merchant bank advised the government department and the public corporation. But in later privatisations separate advisers were appointed, along with separate broking, legal and other advice. This change reflected the fact that, while the interests of the Government were generally in maximising the sales receipts, the management of the corporations could be expected to prefer the strongest balance sheet and dividend and new debt capacity post-privatisation. Equally, a lower share price at flotation would help ensure a substantial share price appreciation after the sale, for which the management could claim credit from grateful investors. The difference in the objectives of management and Government over the balance sheet and sale price was compounded by the introduction of share option schemes, either during or immediately after a privatisation, which meant that management had a personal interest in ensuring a speedy and significant share price rise. The appointment of separate advisers led to some disagreements over the advice to the department and to the corporation on such matters as financial reconstructions, the valuation of the companies and the flotation price, but it almost certainly led to a better outcome than relying on only one recommendation. Also, the advisers could identify difficult issues and suggest solutions when the industries and Government were unable to agree. There were bound to be disagreements, but generally the corporations drew back from serious confrontation with Government.

A share flotation involved an initial marketing of the enterprise to the public and the City, drawing attention to its exciting long-term prospects. This was followed by a later marketing of the offer, once the Government was empowered to undertake this following passage of the relevant privatisation legislation – prior to the passage of the legislation the Government had to steer clear of promoting the forthcoming share issue. In 1986 a trade union challenged the legal authority of corporation boards to spend on preparing for privatisations ahead of the passage of the legislation authorising each sale. It seemed that the legal duties of the board might not extend to preparing for the termination of the public corporation. In response, after 1987 the Government would turn to passing first an enabling Act, ahead of the main privatisation legislation, to permit the public corporation to undertake the preparatory work. It seems that at least some of the spending entered into by public corporations during the privatisations earlier in the 1980s may have been ultra vires. Fortunately for Government, these earlier sales were not challenged in the courts.

Obtaining the backing or at least the acquiescence of the corporation boards to privatisation continued to be of great importance to the success of any privatisation, as Sir Denis Rooke, the Chairman of BGC, demonstrated during the protracted sale of the Corporation's oil and gas assets between 1979 and 1984. The Government preferred to avoid the use of Ministerial directives to bring rebellious boards into line because of the possible political embarrassment that might result and the threat of board-level resignations. Typically, the boards wanted privatisation with no major restructuring of their industries and especially without a break-up of the existing corporation. The management got their way in most cases, including during the privatisations of the NFC, ABP, BT and BGC (in large part), but not, notably, in the case of the NBC, which was dismembered to promote competition despite the opposition of its Board.[34] In the case of the NBC and the hiving-off of Wytch Farm from BGC, this occurred only after Ministers took the unusual step of resorting to a directive to the Board. More often, where board members were a barrier to privatisation, a new chairman and sometimes other board members were appointed that were known by Ministers to be supportive of privatisation. In a number of cases they were given express briefs to prepare their corporation for sale, such as with the appointment of Sir John King at BA, Graham Day at British Shipbuilders and Sir William Duncan and later Sir Francis Tombs at Rolls-Royce.[35] Nevertheless, even this did not necessarily prevent lengthy negotiations with Boards over the terms of the sale.

It seems clear that the boards and their chairmen were acutely aware that their brinkmanship might pay dividends when faced by a Government unprepared to let the sale date slip. Government was reluctant to let the timetable slip because of flotation cancellation costs, the need to meet Treasury annual privatisation receipt targets, and the political embarrassment that would result from having to announce a delay. Also, postponement of a sale, or worse a cancellation, might produce potential difficulties in terms of the oversight of the finances and particularly the borrowings of the company. On vesting day, when the assets of the public corporation were transferred to the new company in preparation for a share sale, the sponsor department and the Treasury lost the control over financial decision making in the business which existed while it was a public corporation. Usually a Memorandum of Understanding was agreed between the board and the Treasury, which provided for some continued Ministerial oversight until the share flotation. But it was considered that this semi-informal arrangement would be unsatisfactory if the period between vesting day and flotation proved to be lengthy.

Balanced against this, generally management of the nationalised industries became more enthusiastic about privatisation as they became increasingly aware of its advantages in terms of breaking free from the Treasury straitjacket on borrowing and other bureaucratic constraints. Moreover, senior management in the early privatised corporations obtained large salary rises, bonuses and share option schemes, raising their incomes closer to those common for similar responsibilities in the private sector. This was probably not an irrelevant factor in altering the attitude of management in the nationalised sector towards a sell-off. In turn, the media and the unions attacked such gains, which were labelled "fat cat". Certainly what happened to management pay tarnished the public's perception of privatisation.

### Setting the share price, underwriting the issues and the use of instalment payments

The sale price for a privatised business was set on the advice of the Government's financial adviser and the Minister of the sponsor department in consultation with the Treasury. The Bank of England might also input into the process. Also, after the privatisation of British Aerospace in 1981 sponsor departments adopted the practice of appointing an independent adviser immediately before the sale price was finally set to give a second opinion. This would be someone not engaged in the underwriting or marketing of the issue. Where there was a public flotation the share price was typically set on a price-earnings basis and to a lesser degree the prospective dividend yield, with cognisance taken of the price-earnings ratios or dividend yields in comparable organisations quoted on the London stock market or stock markets overseas. The resulting valuation could differ widely from the net book value of the assets in the corporation's latest accounts, reflecting the extent to which accounting valuations and economic valuations differed.

Two broad methods were adopted for public flotations, namely a fixed price offer, where the share price was published when applications were invited, and a sale by tender, where the share price was set after the applications were received based on demand. Within the Government, including the Treasury, in the early days of privatisation there was a clear preference for adopting a fixed price offer for sale.[36] Fixed price offers were the norm in the City for big public issues. Later as criticism from the House of Commons Public Accounts Committee and the National Audit Office mounted, there was an experiment with sales by tender. In addition, later mixed fixed price and tender issues were used, including a fixed price offer for individual investors and tenders for the financial institutions in the UK and overseas. There was also the placing of shares with financial institutions immediately before the main flotation, which was adopted for the first time during the sale of BT in November 1984 and would progress into book building[37] during privatisation sales in the 1990s. Table 16.3 details the method of sale for each of the major privatisations between May 1979 and June 1987, indicating the method of disposal, any remaining government shareholding and the gross proceeds raised.

Throughout the first two Thatcher Governments the administration wrestled with the difficulty of pitching the sale price at a level that would encourage investors, including small shareholders, to apply for shares, while providing against an overly large share price premium when the shares first traded in the stock market. Possibly the City advisers should have been given more obvious incentives to achieve better prices (and lower costs) than those achieved, to overcome their innate conservatism.[38] But in the early days there was a lack of understanding both in Government and the City about the prospects for privatisation sales. During IPOs it is advisable to pitch an offer for sale towards the lower end of the expected market price for the shares to ensure the success of the offer. Also, a discount to the market price compensates investors for the time between them putting up their money to buy the shares and the time at which dealing in the shares first begins in the stock market. For privatisation issues this was up to around two weeks, to allow time, especially for smaller investors, to apply for shares. However, the discounts were particularly large for a number of the privatised enterprises (although interestingly not out of line with the pricing of the 67 million BP shares sold in June 1977 by the then Labour Government, which opened at an initial premium of 68p or 23 per cent above the partly-paid issue price).[39]

Table 16.4 details the resulting share price appreciation as at the end of the first day of trading in the shares in the stock market and at one week after trading commenced for the early privatisations using IPOs. The capital gain for investors varied between three per cent and 86 per cent by the end of the first day of trading and averaged 26 per cent, ignoring the sale by tender offers. This contrasts with the five per cent to 15 per cent discount more typical of private sector IPOs at the time, although sometimes private sector IPOs produced much larger gains.[40] In other words, for a number of privatisations there was a much bigger discount on the offer price than was typical for other IPOs.[41] The explanation is that, while there is no evidence that Government intentionally under-priced offers significantly, after all the Treasury was intent on maximising the sales receipts whenever possible, privatisations were associated with particular difficulties in setting an accurate share price so as just to clear the market. The issues tended to be large in value and there were often few if any comparable firms quoted on the London stock market to provide a share price benchmark. Also, the challenge for government departments after 1979 was to price the shares at the highest possible levels, while avoiding a politically embarrassing flotation failure. Sometimes this was successful, notably for the sale of BGC shares in November 1986. The Government's

Table 16.3 The major privatisation sales May 1979–June 1987

| | Date of sale | Method of sale | Remaining government shareholding[a] | Gross proceeds (£ million) |
|---|---|---|---|---|
| Amersham International | Feb 1982 | Fixed price offer 100 per cent | Nil | 71 |
| Associated British Ports | Feb 1983 | Fixed price offer 51.5 per cent | 48.5 per cent | 22 |
| | Apr 1984 | Tender offer 48.5 per cent | Nil | 52 |
| British Aerospace | Feb 1981 | Fixed price offer 51.6 per cent | 48.4 per cent | 149 |
| | May 1985 | Fixed price offer 48.4 per cent | Nil | 551 |
| British Airways | Feb 1987 | Fixed price offer 100 per cent | Nil | 900 |
| British Gas | Dec 1986 | Fixed price offer 100 per cent | Nil | 5,434 |
| British Petroleum | Oct 1979 | Fixed price offer 5 per cent | 46 per cent | 290 |
| | Jun 1981 | Sales of government rights in a rights issue | 39 per cent | 8 |
| | Sep 1983 | Tender offer 7 per cent | 31.7 | 566 |
| British Telecom | Nov 1984 | Fixed price offer 50.2 per cent | 49.8 | 3,863 |
| Britoil | Nov 1982 | Tender offer 51 per cent | 49 per cent | 549 |
| | Aug 1985 | Fixed price offer 49 per cent | Nil | 449 |
| Cable and Wireless | Oct 1981 | Fixed price offer 49 per cent | 50 per cent[b] | 224 |
| | Dec 1983 | Tender offer 22.3 per cent | 23 per cent | 275 |
| | Dec 1985 | Fixed price offer 22.7 per cent | Nil | 933 |
| Enterprise Oil | Jun 1984 | Tender offer 100 per cent | Nil | 392 |
| National Enterprise Board assets | From 1979 | Private sales | n/a | n/a |
| National Freight Co. | Feb 1982 | Management-led buyout | Nil | 7 |
| Rolls-Royce | May 1987 | Fixed price offer 100 per cent | Nil | 1,363 |
| Royal Ordnance Factories | Jul 1986/ Apr 1987 | Private sales | Nil | 201 |

**Subsidiaries:**

*British Airways' subsidiaries:*

| | | | | |
|---|---|---|---|---|
| International Aeradio | Mar 1983 | Sold to Standard Telephone & Cables | Nil | 60 |
| British Airways Helicopters | Sep 1986 | Sold to SDR Helicopters | Nil | 14 |
| British Gas Corporation's Wytch Farm onshore oilfield | May 1984 | Sold to a group of bidders | Nil | 80 |

*British Rail subsidiaries:*

| | | | | |
|---|---|---|---|---|
| Hotels | Mar 1983 & thereafter | Private sale | Nil | 45 |
| Sealink | Jul 1984 | Sold to British Ferries | Nil | 66 |
| British Shipbuilders' warship yards | May 1985 to Mar 1986 | Private sales | Nil | 75 |
| British Steel Corporation's rationalisation & disposal programme | 1980 onwards | Private sales & establishment of joint ventures with private sector | Nil[c] | 592 |

| | | | | |
|---|---|---|---|---|
| *National Bus Company subsidiaries* | Aug 1986 onwards | Each subsidiary sold separately | Nil | n/a |

*Rover Group subsidiaries:[d]*

| | | | | |
|---|---|---|---|---|
| Jaguar | Jul 1984 | Fixed price offer 100 per cent | Nil | 294 |
| Unipart | Jan 1987 | Private sale | Nil | 30 |
| Leyland Bus | Jan 1987 | Private sale | Nil | 4 |
| Leyland Trucks | Apr 1987 | Private sale | Nil | 0 |

*Note:* Gross proceeds are before any debt write-offs and other capital injections and before the costs of sale.

*Key:*

a  Excluding, in particular, any shares held to meet bonus issue commitments under share purchase investor schemes and special shares.

b  45 per cent from March 1983 when government waived any entitlement to new shares in a rights issue.

c  The Corporation retained a holding in a number of the joint ventures established with the private sector.

d  Earlier BL (British Leyland).

*Table 16.4* The share price appreciation following privatisation: examples

| Company | Offer/ minimum tender price (pence) | First trading day | Share price appreciation at end of 1st day (per cent) | Share price appreciation at end of 1st week (per cent) | Times over- subscribed |
|---|---|---|---|---|---|
| *Offers for sale* | | | | | |
| British Petroleum[2] | 363 | 12.11.79 | 3 | 6 | 1.5 |
| British Aerospace[1] | 150 | 20.02.81 | 14 | 15 | 3.5 |
| Cable and Wireless[1] | 168 | 06.11.81 | 17 | 15 | 5.6 |
| Amersham International | 142 | 25.02.82 | 32 | 35 | 24 |
| Associated British Ports[1] | 112 | 16.02.83 | 23 | 28 | 34 |
| Jaguar | 165 | 10.08.84 | 8 | 8 | 8.3 |
| British Telecom[1] | 130 | 03.12.84 | 86 | 91 | 3 |
| British Aerospace[2] | 375 | 14.05.85 | 22 | 19 | 5.4 |
| Britoil[2] | 185 | 12.08.85 | 22 | 22 | 10 |
| *Tender Offers* | | | | | |
| Britoil[1] | 215 | 23.11.82 | −19 | 21 | u.s. (0.27) |
| British Peroleum[2] | 435 | 26.09.83 | 3 | 3 | 1.3 |
| Cable and Wireless[2] | 275 | 05.12.83 | −2 | −3 | u.s. (0.7) |
| Associated British Ports[2] | 250 | 19.04.84 | 2 | −2 | n/a |
| Enterprise Oil | 185 | 02.07.84 | 0 | 2 | u.s. (0.37) |

*Notes*:
Share price appreciation after end of 1st week is relative to market movements.
u.s. = undersubscribed (figure in parenthesis is the proportion of the shares on offer for which applications were received).
1  1st share issue
2  2nd share issue

*Source*: Price Waterhouse (1987); Mayer and Meadowcroft (1985), Table 2, p.45.

financial adviser, Rothschilds, planned for a ten per cent premium in the immediate after-market, and this was achieved. But more often than not, a large oversubscription for the share issues resulted, which in turn meant big capital gains in the stock market for lucky investors. In turn the large immediate capital gains attracted more investors to later privatisation issues. Whether encouraging the public to invest on this basis and "stag"[42] share flotations was sensible must be questionable; it certainly did not assist the agenda of creating long-term shareholding. Criticism continued during the 1980s of the large oversubscriptions for shares followed by an immediate sharp appreciation in the share price.

However, there was never a deliberate policy of setting giveaway prices. The underpricing reflected the difficulty of valuing the privatised companies accurately. This difficulty was compounded by the nationalised industries' archaic accounting practices. Oddly enough, the interdepartmental Official Committee on Nationalised Industry Policy in October 1982 judged "that nationalised industry accounts were of a high standard and compared favourably with private sector equivalents".[43] This proved to be a naïve view and was not borne out by experience. Often nationalised industry assets were poorly accounted for in terms of their true economic value. The large share price premiums in the aftermarket also reflected the fact that the privatised companies became some of the most highly capitalised companies in the stock market. Their shares entered into the FT100 share price index and this meant that the institutional investors felt obliged to hold the shares broadly in proportion to their weighting in the index. If they could not obtain shares at flotation, they were required to purchase them in the aftermarket, putting further upward pressure on the share price.

Typically, fixed price offers for sale led to large oversubscriptions. By contrast, this was not true of sales by tender. Under the sale by tender method, a minimum offer price is set and prospective purchasers bid for the shares at or above this price. According to one contemporary study, the average fixed price offer for sale in the private sector was reported to have a discount of around 12 per cent but with sales by tender typically having lower average discounts, of some seven per cent.[44] Sales by tender, therefore, appeared to have the advantage over a fixed price offer of reducing the underpricing of shares. But when the Government experimented with sales by tender in 1983 and 1984 for the flotations of Britoil, C&W (second tranche) and Enterprise Oil, all failed to attract sufficient investors, leaving stock with the underwriters.

Part of the reason for these undersubscriptions was the City's coolness towards the sale by tender method. It offered less prospect of a sizeable share premium in the aftermarket and therefore capital gains for investors. Also, while sales by tender were used in gilt-edged stock sales and in some private sector flotations – 40 per cent of newly-quoted private sector companies' offers between 1980 and 1984 are said to have been by tender[45] – it seems that they had not been used before for flotations of the size of many of the privatisation issues. The City therefore faced greater uncertainty about the outcome than for a fixed price offer for sale. There was also a technical reason why sales by tender tended to underperform. This related to the underwriting. If during a sale by tender the sub-underwriters concluded that the shares on offer might not be fully subscribed, there were advantages in them not applying for shares and relying on acquiring them through the underwriting commitment. In turn, this behaviour raised the likelihood of an undersubscription. Such a sequence of events seems to have occurred during the Britoil, C&W and Enterprise Oil tender sales.

There were benefits to sub-underwriters in behaving this way. To begin with the shares acquired through the underwriting commitment were paid for later than the shares applied for on flotation. In addition, there was the possibility that if there was an undersubscription, underwriting institutions that also applied for shares on their own account during the offer could end up with more shares than they wished to hold. Where an issue was undersubscribed, the unsold shares (called the "stick") were apportioned to the sub-underwriters. An underwriter could end up with its application in full plus a proportion of the stick.

The resulting lack of City enthusiasm for privatisations by sales by tender meant that they were invariably much less successful than the fixed price offers. This limited their use, especially as the Government was then criticised for overpricing. When the sale by tender of Britoil in November 1982 led to undersubscription, the Government was once again attacked for getting the share price "wrong". The Government could have been excused for concluding that it could not win. A final reason why sales by tender tended not to be favoured and why fixed price offers were generally preferred was that sales by tender were considered more complex for unsophisticated investors to understand. In a fixed price offer the applicant knows the price they will have to pay for shares; this is not the case when applying in a sale by tender. The financial advisers and Government therefore judged that sales by tender would be less attractive to small investors, which the Government was keen to encourage to apply for shares. In an effort to ameliorate this effect, the Government did permit in tender issues small investors simply to write on their application forms their agreement to pay the "striking price" for their shares. This meant that they undertook to subscribe for shares at the lowest price which resulted from the tender exercise rather than having to stipulate a particular offer price.[46] It also meant that with payment by instalments for the shares, the amount of the first instalment could be fixed in advance. The small investor could then send the correct cheque with the application form.

Turning specifically to the underwriting of the privatisation offers, an almost standard procedure for underwriting developed with the merchant bank advising the government department on the share issue also taking the lead role in the underwriting. This would continue until the privatisation of British Steel in 1988, when the activities would be separated. The trigger for the change was the BP share issue in October 1987, which coincided with a collapse of the stock market. This episode is discussed in Volume 2 of this *Official History*, which deals with the privatisations after the June 1987 General Election. Suffice to say here that arguably the roles should have been separated earlier, given that the merchant bank, as lead underwriter, had an evident conflict of interest when advising on the flotation price. Underwriters have an incentive to press for a lower sale price to avoid being left with unsold stock, whereas the Government's objective was to achieve a high price.[47] While there is no evidence in the official files of a financial adviser persuading the Government to set a low sale price against its better judgement – Ministers too were keen for the flotation not to flop and therefore also tended to err on the safe side when setting the sale price – the arrangement under which the financial adviser was also the lead underwriter clearly created the prospect of conservative pricing.

There is also a question surrounding the whole logic of the underwriting of privatisation issues: firstly, because in the absence of underwriting the costs of unsold shares left with the Government would have been spread, in effect, across all taxpayers through lower flotation receipts, without the cost of underwriting. Secondly, underwriting exists to protect the company against a flotation failure and if the Government felt that it needed to underwrite offers it could have acted as its own underwriter, through the Bank of England (as it did temporarily for the issue of BT shares in the USA before American underwriting took effect) or the Government Broker, to mop up unsold shares.

The oversubscription for privatisation issues alongside the underwriting of issues drew criticism from the House of Commons Public Accounts Committee as early as 1982.[48] In response, the Government agreed to keep the case for underwriting under review. Nevertheless, the Government continued to maintain that it was necessary to avoid being left with unsold shares. The undersubscription in the cases of the Britoil issue in 1982 and the C&W Enterprise Oil flotations in 1983/4, and a further undersubscription involving the sale of the Government's remaining shareholding in BP, which occurred shortly after the 1987 General Election, suggested that this fear was not entirely unfounded (although before the BP issue there were no cases of undersubscriptions where fixed price offers were used). Many flotation failures would certainly have undermined City confidence in future privatisation offers and therefore the future of the Government's entire privatisation programme. Failures would also have led to considerable political flack which the Government was keen to avoid.

In the late spring of 1982, six leading firms in the City were asked to comment on a Treasury paper reviewing the arrangements for privatisation sales. The suggestion to consult the City came from E(DL) Sub-Committee and Nicholas Ridley, the Financial Secretary, in response to criticism of the method of privatisation adopted from inside and outside Parliament. While the result was some recognition in the financial community of the case for examining new approaches to the share issues, there was a clear resistance to going outside the City's "comfort zone".[49] In particular, the notion of using an idea from the USA of having a Red Herring Prospectus ahead of the full Prospectus, to drum up interest in an issue, was considered by most of the banks to be inappropriate. The banks argued that it was resorted to in America because of the size of the country and the resulting difficulty in getting information to all potential investors simultaneously. The same circumstances did not hold in the UK. However, one of the banks consulted, Kleinwort, Benson, did see merit in the idea. Under the title of a Pathfinder prospectus, it was introduced by this bank into UK privatisations during the planning of the flotation of BT two years later.

During the consultation exercise in the City there was also a clear consensus amongst the banks approached against the use of competitive tendering for primary underwriting. Under competitive underwriting, syndicates of City institutions would bid to underwrite an offer based on an unpriced prospectus. The winning bid would be that which offered the highest net proceeds (gross proceeds less underwriting commission). The successful bidder would then arrange the sub-underwriting in the normal way. The Treasury was keen for underwriting costs to be reduced, especially given the Public Accounts Committee's criticism, and competitive bidding appeared to offer the prospect of lower commission charges. But the City institutions consulted flatly opposed the idea. Firstly, they contended that competitive underwriting would not work for privatisation share sales because, they argued, close familiarity with the company issuing the shares and direct access to the management was needed by the lead underwriter. This was linked to the lead underwriter needing to exercise due diligence, including examining the sale prospectus. Competitive underwriting would disrupt this process. Secondly, they suggested that it would be more difficult to keep the likely flotation price confidential ahead of a formal announcement if competitive bids for underwriting were sought.

In total, the banks concluded that if competitive underwriting was introduced, the result would be that at least some City firms would refuse to underwrite future privatisation offers. The outcome would be a damaging reduction in the Government's capacity to have an offer fully underwritten. As a possible compromise, the banks suggested that if the Government was determined to introduce competitive underwriting, against their better judgement, it should be limited to at most two syndicates bidding and preferably be used only for small secondary share sales, of less than £100 million in value. This, in effect, ruled out its use for most privatisation IPOs. After considering the advice, the Treasury decided that "the practical limitations [of competitive underwriting] are such that it is not easy to envisage it being adopted for a government sale."[50] The conclusion once again reflected the extent to which the City had the upper hand in negotiations with Government over privatisation flotations in the early years.

However, during the second Thatcher Government, departments and the Treasury would become tougher negotiators with the City, including of underwriting fees. Starting with the third C&W share issue in December 1985 and then the BGC flotation the following year, the Government reversed its earlier decision and began to seek competitive bids for primary underwriting. This helped to reduce the commissions paid. However, competition was not extended to sub-underwriting. The argument at the time was that a large number of sub-underwriters operated in the London market and might wish to enter bids and this was not compatible with the limited time period available to arrange the underwriting.[51]

In the early days of privatisation, sales were treated very much as one-off transactions, but later a degree of co-ordination was introduced and innovations to reduce costs and ensure a successful sale were encouraged. In particular, the Government moved during flotations to placing some of the shares firm and others provisionally with City institutions to ensure that a proportion of the shares had buyers identified ahead of the public float. This was particularly useful for the large flotations, notably of BT and BGC, where there was a question mark over whether all of the shares would be taken up. The procedure also reduced the underwriting commission on the public issue. For example, during the BT sale in November 1984 61 per cent of the shares were placed with financial institutions and overseas interests immediately ahead of the public flotation. These were largely institutions which would otherwise have underwritten that portion of the offer.

Some of the provisionally placed shares were subject to clawback to ensure that there was still an adequate number of shares available to satisfy applications from the public for the shares, to meet the Government's widening ownership goal. The first sale using clawback was the third issue of C&W shares in December 1985. However, clawback had an important limitation in that it threatened to leave the institutional investors even more short of shares when trading started, leading to a potentially larger demand for shares in the immediate aftermarket and therefore a greater likelihood of a sharp price premium.[52]

In a document issued to departments in February 1985 the Treasury reviewed the underwriting process, in the light particularly of criticism of the cost. Given that in London share sales were nearly always underwritten, it was felt that not to do so for privatisation offers "would clearly indicate that something was wrong". Therefore underwriting was to continue and during the hugely important BT flotation three months earlier there was no serious discussion of the case for moving away from a traditional underwriting of the offer. At the same time, periodic criticism continued against the costs of underwriting the privatisation issues. Table 16.5 provides details of the underwriting commission rates for each of the main privatisation issues between 1979 and June 1987. Underwriters are estimated to have obtained gross fees of around £179 million from privatisations between 1979 and 1987 with costs relating to the few under-subscriptions, "on the most pessimistic assumptions", of only £16.5 million.[53]

As experience within government developed and new methods were gradually adopted, sale costs fell. Whereas in the early days of privatisation underwriting commissions of 1.375 per cent to 1.75 per cent were common, out of which 1.25 per cent was paid to sub-under-writers, later the commissions declined. Within government departments there was a growing recognition that underwriting fees had been unduly generous. At the same time, the option of dispensing with underwriting did not appeal to the Government. Being left with unsold stock risked political embarrassment, which underwriting insured against. As a possible alternative the Government might have reduced the risk of being left with unsold shares and have reduced the risks of a "wrong" flotation price by selling a small tranche of the shares first. This first sale would have established a market price as a guide for setting the share price when further flotations came later. An extreme version of this approach to privatisations would have been some form of "tap issue" with stock drip-fed onto the market over time, which was briefly considered but rejected during the planning of the BT sale. The National Audit Office suggested something similar in a report in 1988.[54] The NAO argued that proceeds would be maximised by staging sales. However, during the Treasury's consultation exercise in 1982, referred to above, a number of possibilities were tested by the Treasury on the City, including selling shares using a tap issue and more use of sales by tender. Again, neither idea met with much support. Only one bank strongly supported the use of a tender offer, to maximise sale proceeds, and there was no enthusiasm at all for tap issues.[55]

*Table 16.5* Underwriting commission rates May 1979–June 1987

| Flotation | Date | Total commission (per cent ) | UK primary underwriting commission rate[1] (per cent ) | UK sub-underwriting commission rate (per cent ) |
|---|---|---|---|---|
| BP | November 1979 | 1.375 | 0.125 | 1.25 |
| British Aerospace | February 1981 | 1.75 | 0.5 | 1.25 |
| Cable and Wireless | October 1981 | 1.75 | 0.5 | 1.25 |
| Amersham International | February 1982 | 1.688 | [2] | 1.25 |
| Britoil | November 1982 | 1.55 | 0.3 | 1.25 |
| Associated British Ports | February 1983 | 1.675 | 0.425 | 1.25 |
| BP | September 1983 | 1.375 | 0.125 | 1.25 |
| Cable and Wireless | December 1983 | 1.375 | 0.125 | 1.25 |
| Associated British Ports | April 1984 | [3] | [3] | 1.25 |
| Enterprise Oil | June 1984 | 1.55 | 0.3 | 1.25 |
| British Telecom | November 1984 | [4] | [4] | 1.25 |
| Jaguar | July 1984 | 1.625 | 0.5 | 1.25 |
| British Aerospace | May 1985 | [5] | [5] | 1.25 |
| Britoil | August 1985 | [6] | [6] | 1.25 |
| Cable and Wireless | December 1985 | [7] | [7] | 1.25 |
| British Gas | December 1986 | [8] | [8] | 1.25 |
| British Airways | February 1987 | [9] | [9] | 1.25 |
| Rolls-Royce | May 1987 | [10] | [10] | 1.25 |

*Notes*:
1  Out of the primary underwriting commission brokers' fees were sometimes payable.
2  In the case of the sale of Amersham International the shares were sold to N. M. Rothschild and Morgan Grenfell, who received fees totalling £1,287,000. They then offered the shares for sale paying the underwriting commissions and brokers' fees.
3  All shares were underwritten at a commission rate of 0.525 per cent of the striking price, 1.25 per cent of the minimum tender price.
4  Up to 55 per cent of the UK shares were offered to priority applicants as firm placing shares at a commission of 1.5 per cent and the balance of commitment shares at a commission rate of 1.25 per cent. Provisionally allocated shares were underwritten at a commission rate of 0.375 per cent. Overseas offers were underwritten by the Bank of England at a commission rate of 1.25 per cent. There were also underwriting agents in the US, Canada and Japan who received rates of 2.5 per cent to 3.75 per cent.
5  All shares underwritten at a commission rate of 0.425 per cent out of which brokers' commissions of 0.125 per cent were paid. Firm placing shares at a commission rate of 1.5 per cent and the balance of commitment shares at a commission rate of 1.25 per cent.
6  The UK portion of the shares was underwritten at a commission rate of 0.425 per cent out of which brokers' commissions of 0.125 per cent were paid. Firm placing shares at a commission rate of 1.5 per cent and the balance were offered as commitment shares at a commission rate of 1.25 per cent. Overseas commission rate 1.8 per cent.
7  Competitive bids for underwriting introduced for the first time and resulted in a commission rate of 0.2625 per cent. Firm placing shares at a commission rate of 0.5 per cent and provisional placing shares (subject to clawback) and commitment shares at a commission rate of 1.25 per cent. Commission rates overseas were either 1.8 per cent or 2.5 per cent depending upon the country.
8  Firm placing shares at a commission rate of 0.5 per cent. Provisional placing shares (subject to clawback) and the balance as commitment shares at a commission rate of 1.25 per cent. Overseas commission rate 1.65 per cent.
9  Competitive underwriting bids resulted in a commission rate of 0.111 per cent. Firm placing shares at a commission rate of 0.5 per cent, provisional placing shares (subject to clawback) and the balance as commitment shares at a commission rate of 1.25 per cent. Overseas commission rate 1.575 per cent.
10 Competitive bids for underwriting resulted in a commission rate of 0.061 per cent. Firm placing shares by priority applicants at a commission rate of 0.25 per cent. Provisionally placed shares (subject to clawback) and the balance as commitment shares at a commission rate of 1.25 per cent.

*Source*: Offer for Sale documents; Price Waterhouse (1987).

In any event, in reality the Treasury had a major objection to small, staged share sales. Until 51 per cent of the shares were sold the Government would not have given up control of the business and the companies and their borrowings would therefore still have been treated as part of the public sector. A majority share sale was a political and budgetary imperative. Also, and in defence of the attitude adopted within Government, a trial sale or staging sales might not have established a reliable guide to the price for future issues, as intended. External events might have pushed the share price up or down between a trial sale and a full sale. Also, the City might have been unwilling to display the extent of its appetite for a privatisation issue in response to a trial sale, preferring to engage in a bit of strategic game playing to depress the share price ahead of the full flotation.

At first, such as in the planning of the sales of BA, BAe as well as C&W, minority share sales were contemplated. At the time the Government lacked confidence that majority sales would be easy to achieve or perhaps even desirable. There was considerable uncertainty about how much investor interest there would be in investing in former public corporations. Equally, Government was unsure whether it wished to give up control of the enterprises and there was no previous experience of an extensive denationalisation programme in Britain to draw upon.

However, the attitude quickly changed. Firstly, there was pressure from the Treasury to dispose of majority holdings and give up control over the enterprises, so as to ensure that their borrowings were removed from the PSBR figures. Secondly, the first sales demonstrated that with the appropriate marketing large share issues could be successful. In the event, the first tranche of shares sold during privatisations always involved at least 51 per cent of the shares – the only exception being the sale of the first tranche of shares in C&W in October 1981. In this case it was not a question of establishing a market price for the shares that determined the size of the sale, but rather the views of overseas governments in the countries in which C&W operated. These governments were initially reluctant to see C&W privately controlled. In the very early privatisations majority sales – but usually bare majorities or 51 per cent disposals (British Aerospace, Britoil, ABP[56]) – were the norm, except for smaller businesses such as Amersham International or where exceptionally management mounted a bid for the whole corporation, as in the case of the NFC. The sale of 51 per cent or more of the shares addressed the concern about enterprises remaining in the public sector, but not an argument for selling all of the shares outright, that a residual government shareholding would create an "overhang" in the market, possibly depressing the share price because of the prospect of a further share sale. To address this, the Government typically gave a commitment at the time of the first share sale not to sell further tranches of a company's shares for at least two years.

Equally, selling only 51 per cent of the shares made future renationalisation by an incoming Labour Government a real possibility. A 51 per cent sale meant that a future Labour Government would need to buy less than two per cent of the shares to bring the enterprise back under majority state control. The possibility that a future Labour administration might renationalise at least some of the privatised businesses was a real one up to 1987. After 1951 the steel industry passed backwards and forwards between public and private ownership with changes of Government, with arguably damaging effects on management and investment programmes. The Conservatives were keen to see no repeat of this experience.

Therefore, after the very first privatisations the practice moved to favouring 100 per cent share flotations, except where the enterprises were so large, notably in the case of BT, that it was felt that the stock market would struggle to absorb a 100 per cent sale in one tranche successfully. Once the enterprise was fully in the private sector, cost became a formidable deterrent to an incoming Labour administration bent on renationalisation. Long-term privatisation was secured. At the same time, to reduce the strain on the capital market, during the large privatisations payment for the shares by instalment evolved. This was used very successfully during the BT and BGC privatisations in particular. Payment by instalments reduced the immediate cash outlay that investors had to make.

In the first privatisation issues using instalment payments, the payments tended to be close together,[57] typically the second and final instalment was paid within six months of the application for shares. But to encourage large numbers of small investors to apply for the BT and BGC shares and reflecting the size of these offers, the part payments were spread over almost 17 months. To overcome the usual disadvantages of partly paid shares in the market, notably a lack of full shareholder rights and restrictions on share trading in partly paid form, these limitations were removed. An inability to fully trade in the shares for many months would have depressed interest in the flotation. Technically the shares were deemed to be fully paid but partly subscribed. The shares therefore also benefited from full dividend rights, which had the advantage for investors that the shares effectively had a higher yield. Initial part payment for the shares but with full dividend entitlement proved understandably attractive to investors. When the effective yield on the shares plus the bonus issues or bill vouchers provided in a number of the privatisations are taken into account, it is self-evident why the shares were highly sought after by small investors, as well as by City institutions.

Other innovations introduced over time into privatisation share sales included the issuing, as already mentioned, of a Pathfinder prospectus before the main prospectus to create interest in the offer, and the publishing of mini prospectuses to go to smaller investors. Both were first introduced during the BT sale. The mini prospectus was designed so that it would be easily comprehensible to the novice investor and cheaper to print and distribute.[58] Interestingly, a number of the techniques introduced for privatisations, sometimes developed by civil servants, were received cautiously in the City. They would later be adopted by the private sector for public offers and in time were exported by City banks to other countries around the world.

However, although innovations were introduced, there is no real evidence that the ability of Government and its advisers to determine the "correct" flotation price improved over time. There was also a problem of pricing where businesses were sold through MEBOs, like the NFC and some bus companies. In these cases management had the advantage of insider knowledge of the true value of the businesses and especially the potential development value of underutilised land and buildings. While clawback terms were introduced during the sale of the bus companies to recoup for Government some of the windfall gains from a later sale of assets, a number of managers went on to make appreciable sums from disposing of their investments, some when they sold out profitably to bigger bus groups in the 1990s. In the case of the NFC, one cause of its financial success after 1981 was the disposal or redevelopment of land and buildings. ABP shareholders also benefited from the development and sale of surplus properties. It appears that such potential gains were not properly appreciated within Government when the firms were privatised. In some cases the financial advisers might have given better advice.

In summary, the Government was on a steep learning curve and from a low base when it came to dealing with the City (and management) during the first privatisations. Equally, the City institutions were on a steep learning curve too, having at the outset no experience of privatisation issues. Large capital gains were made by investors and at a cost to taxpayers in terms of lower sales receipts. As Buckland and Davis commented in 1984, in an early critique of the Government's policy on share sales: "on their past record and by the lessons of research, privatisation methods to date have been costly even when applied in the most propitious of conditions."[59] However, in defence of the Government, getting the sale price right was always going to be extremely difficult given the unprecedented nature of the privatisations – earlier denationalisations had been on a much smaller scale or had occurred in the 1950s. For Government the priority was to transfer state assets into private hands and remove the firm's debts from public borrowing. As Nicholas Ridley states in his memoirs, somewhat tersely: "My conclusion is that it is impossible to get the sale price of a privatization right; it is far more important to get it off the public books. Sniping at the Government for selling it too cheap only proves that it is the only aspect of privatization which its opponents still felt strong enough to criticize."[60] In the same spirit, it might be argued that criticisms levied by the Public Accounts Committee and the National Audit Office showed insufficient regard for the magnitude of the challenges and surrounding uncertainties involved in achieving successful privatisations. Critics can be expected to say that the sale price was set too low (over-subscription) or too high (undersubscription). But it is difficult to put an accurate commercial value on a business that has not operated in the private sector and sometimes has few if any comparators quoted in the domestic stock market.

## The special share

In some industries, notably aerospace, energy and telecommunications, there is a perceived requirement to protect companies from undesirable future ownership on public interest grounds. Also, the Government was aware at the time of privatisation that if privatised firms were acquired at flotation or for some years afterwards by other companies – effectively taken over – this might well damage the public image of the policy. Moreover, wherever possible the Prime Minister was keen to ensure that privatisation did not lead to foreign ownership, although the terms of the Treaty of Rome limited the extent to which the Government could prevent foreign shareholdings overtly.

In a number of privatisations, therefore, the companies' Articles of Association were adapted prior to flotation to limit future ownership arrangements. The restrictions varied from enterprise to enterprise, in part reflecting the particular nature of the company and, it seems, due to the simple fact that the terms were drawn up by different officials over time. Typically, however, the Articles ensured that no more than 15 per cent of the shares might be acquired by one investor or investors acting in concert[61] and in some cases that the Chairman or Chief Executive Officer or other directors should remain British citizens. However, Articles of Association could be changed if a 75 per cent majority of the shareholders agreed to an amendment. To prevent the Articles from amendment, during the first privatisations planned, BA, BAe and C&W, Government contemplated retaining at least 25 per cent of the shares to block an undesirable ownership change. But the permanent retention of a large block of shares would have ruled out a complete transfer of the enterprises to the private sector and left the Government as the largest or at least one of the largest shareholders in the business. No matter what assurances the Government might give about not interfering in the management of the company, this would not be binding on any future Government and this was likely to make potential investors nervous, depressing the sale price.

Another possibility to prevent a future change in the Articles of Association would have been to have protected against changes without Government agreement in the primary legislation that authorised each of the sales. However, this would have introduced rigidity into the legal protection, in the sense of preventing the Government from repealing its powers quickly should it feel this necessary. Also, it would certainly have meant that a number of privatised firms would have had different statutory provisions from other private sector companies.

With the Government and especially the Treasury keen to see majority or even total privatisation of state industries, the special preference share, sometimes later known as a "golden share", was created. Nigel Lawson as Energy Secretary has claimed credit for the idea of creating the special share, which was first introduced during his Department's sale of Amersham International in February 1982. The special share offered an alternative and less objectionable form of preventing what Government saw as unwanted changes to the Articles of Association.[62] Special shares were introduced for a number of later privatisations; a full listing up to June 1987 is provided in Table 16.6. In some cases the special share lapsed after a given period, such as five years, and therefore protected against unwelcome takeover bids during the first few years after privatisation. The temporary protection was designed to give the management time to adjust to operating in the private sector. For example, a time protection factor was written into Amersham's Articles stipulating that the company could not be taken over for at least six years. Amersham was the only company in the world supplying certain radioactive medical and industrial products and many people were worried about a possible immediate takeover. In other cases, such as BAe, Britoil and BT, national security concerns meant that the special share was not time limited but redeemable at the Government's discretion.[63]

The special shareholder was permitted to attend company general meetings but not vote or speak except on matters relating to the special share. The special share meant that in effect the Government's permission was required for there to be a change in the control of the business. In addition to the restrictions listed in Table 16.6, it was also usual for the special share to protect against a voluntary winding up of the company and sometimes a material disposal of assets without the Government's consent.[64] Moreover, it was usual for the consent of the special shareholder to be required for the creation of further shares with different voting rights from the ordinary shares.

Not for the public record but evident from Government papers was the agenda of preventing foreign ownership of a number of the privatised concerns. For example, during a review of the future of the special shares in BT and C&W in 1991, Peter Lilley, Secretary of State for Trade and Industry, noted:

"A limit on the equity holding in each company is an important means of ensuring its independence. It helps to avoid any potential conflict between the objectives of national security and the potential interests of a major shareholder. Such a conflict could become particularly apparent were an overseas company to acquire a significant holding. While there may be circumstances in which we might be prepared to consider a UK company having a share of more than 15 per cent, this could create a difficult precedent in the event of a similar approach from another Member State of the EC or, albeit to a lesser extent, from a company outside of the EC."[65]

The Government considered that restrictions on the foreign control of a privatised company were permissible under Article 223 of the Treaty of Rome on grounds of public security. The Article stated that, "Any member state may take such measures as it considers necessary for the protection of the essential interests of its security which are connected with the production of or trade in arms, munitions and war material". However, the scope of Article 223 in relation to privatisations was not entirely clear and blocking a takeover from a company outside of the EEC (later EC) remained legally simpler.

*Table 16.6* The special shares created, May 1979–June 1987

| Company | Expiry date | Major restriction |
| --- | --- | --- |
| Amersham International | Redeemable on or after 31 Mar 1988 at the Government's discretion | 15% limit on individual shareholdings |
| Britoil | No time limit | Temporary majority voting rights to the special shareholding in the event of one person controlling over 25% of the voting rights |
| Cable and Wireless | No time limit | 15% limit on individual shareholdings |
| Jaguar | Redeemable by the company at par on 31 Dec 1990 | 15% limit on individual shareholdings |
| Enterprise Oil | Redeemable by the company at par on 31 Dec 1988 | Special shareholder has no voting rights unless one person controls over 50% of the voting rights, when the special shareholder can then out vote all of the other shareholders |
| Sealink | No time limit | Restrictions on the winding up of the business, disposal of assets and availability of the fleet to the Government in an emergency |
| British Telecom | No time limit | 15% limit on individual shareholdings |
| British Aerospace | No time limit | 15% limit on foreign shareholdings |
| VSEL Consortium | No time limit | 15% limit on individual shareholdings |
| British Gas | No time limit | 15% limit on individual shareholdings |
| Rolls-Royce | No time limit for the foreign ownership restriction Domestic ownership restriction until 1 Jan1989 | 15% limit on foreign shareholdings and a 15% limit on other individual shareholdings |

*Note*: British Airways' Articles of Association included a 25% limit on share ownership by non-UK nationals and a limit of 15% on any individual shareholding. However, these restrictions were not protected by a special share.

*Source*: Minute from the Chancellor of the Exchequer to the PM, 12 May 1988, E(DL) Part 16; supplemented by information from the Offer for Sale documents.

From the outset the Foreign and Commonwealth Office was worried that the European Commission might attempt to challenge the legality of special shares under the EC principle of no discrimination against member states. At the time, the effectiveness of the special share remained untested in the courts and in any case there was uncertainty about how the Government would respond in terms of using the powers bequeathed by the special share should a takeover bid for a privatised company be mounted.[66] The share gave the Government discretion to veto takeovers, it did not rule them out.

This issue came to a head in December 1987 after BP made a bid for Britoil based in Scotland. After negotiations between BP and the Government – and in the face of an Opposition in Parliament that attempted to make political capital out of the potential embarrassment to the Government of Britoil's loss of independence – the Government decided not to exercise its rights. However, it was able to use its threat to veto the bid to obtain BP's agreement to maintain Britoil's headquarters in Glasgow and to transfer certain research and development activities there. This helped to defuse the hostile political reaction in Scotland to Britoil's loss of independence. BP also agreed to Britoil not disappearing but becoming a subsidiary of BP and to new appointments to the board.[67] The special share in Britoil was then redeemed by the Government in 1990. Similarly, the Government chose not to use its special share when the board of Jaguar accepted a takeover bid from the US motor manufacturer Ford, in 1989. In this case the Government judged that the takeover would best secure the company's long-term existence. In both cases the Government was influenced by the fact that the other shareholders were strongly in favour of the takeovers.

Following the BP takeover of Britoil, the Chancellor of the Exchequer commissioned an internal review of the 12 special shares in existence for privatised firms to see what lessons could be learned. This included the 11 special shares listed in Table 16.6 plus the special share created when the British Airports Authority (BAA) was privatised immediately after the 1987 General Election. The European Commission had already begun privately to question the legitimacy of the 15 per cent share limits applying to BAe and Rolls-Royce, and had made it known that it would prefer a higher limit.[68] Nevertheless, the existence of the special shares in these two cases, and the special share for VSEL Consortium which manufactured nuclear submarines, were not thought to be at risk because of Article 223. But the special share for Sealink was considered more problematic and less easy to defend. It was introduced because the Government would wish to secure the requisition of the company's cross-channel ferries should there be a national emergency requiring the movement of large numbers of troops and materials to the Continent. At the same time, the Government had no such share interest in other private sector ferry companies, whose vessels would in all likelihood also be requisitioned. The special shares in BT and BGC were seen as justified because they were "classed as monopoly utilities".[69]

The Government decided that the special share in Amersham International should be redeemed, and this was announced in July 1988.[70] It was also decided that the special share in C&W should be retained on national security grounds, subject to review in five to seven years' time. But these were matters of detail. The review led to no change of substance in Government policy. The key recommendation from the review was that in future privatisations there should be a standard form for a special share, including the now conventional 15 per cent limit on the shares held by one person or a group acting in concert. Any additional restrictions, such as on the nationality of Chairmen and Chief Executives, were to be limited to industries in which security issues were deemed important. Both of these conditions reflected existing policy.

Leaving aside the possible legal questions that surrounded the whole use of special shares, there is a possible economic argument against their use. This is that protection from takeover diminishes an important incentive on management to strive for efficiency after privatisation. The threat of takeover by new management is a pressure imposed by a competitive capital market to keep existing management on its toes. In addition, preventing takeover bids (or making their outcome uncertain, depending upon whether Government chooses to invoke its share) might also be expected to reduce the attractiveness of the shares to investors, by precluding takeover bid premiums after flotation. Typically, shareholders of firms that are being taken over benefit from an offer for their shares at a price well above the level in the stock market immediately before the bid is announced. However, the Official Committee on Nationalised Industry Policy in the Treasury concluded in 1984 that "There is no evidence to date that investors have been deterred by appropriate special share provisions. In certain cases, these may even have reassured some customers of the independence of the company and thus indirectly added to the attractions of the privatisation."[71] Also, the fact that the Government decided not to invoke its veto during the takeovers of Britoil and Jaguar may be taken as evidence that the capital market pressures on management were not necessarily diminished, to any appreciable degree, by the existence of special shares. At the same time, the innovation of the special share did away with the need for Government to retain a large shareholding in an enterprise to protect its future ownership, opening up the prospect of 100 per cent sales. Without the creation of the special share, it is possible that Government would not have contemplated the total sale of industries with strategic importance to the economy – in the defence sector, energy industries and telecommunications. This would have significantly reduced the scale of the UK's privatisation programme.

## Widening property ownership

Throughout the 1980s an important privatisation policy objective remained of spreading share ownership or selling shares to investors who might never in the past have owned shares. When the first Thatcher Government was elected in May 1979 only around seven per cent of the adult population held shares in companies. The level of small shareholding had fallen almost continuously during the post-war period, reflecting the rise of shareholdings by financial institutions, such as pension funds, insurance companies and investment trusts. This in turn reflected the preference of individuals to invest their savings elsewhere, such as in unit trust linked policies marketed by insurance companies and building society accounts. This development was encouraged by a tax regime that favoured institutional savings.

To advance the Government's small shareholder agenda, or "popular capitalism" as it was sometimes termed after 1983, a number of special schemes were created. This was necessary both to ensure that there was sufficient retail demand for the shares in privatised companies, and therefore prevent an undersubscribed issue, and to fulfil the Government's widening share ownership agenda. Also, selling shares to the public, along with the provision of shares to employees, discussed below, defused trade union opposition to sales and made renationalisation more difficult for any incoming Labour Government, at least without fair compensation terms. It may also have made the return of a Labour Government less likely. A MORI poll in 1987 found that shareholders were one and a half times more likely to vote Conservative – although this leaves open whether Conservative voters were more likely to buy shares or whether those buying shares switched allegiance to the Conservative Party.[72]

Due to the success of Conservative Governments after 1979 in selling privatisation stock to small investors, and a resulting new interest amongst the public in buying shares, by 1987 around 8.5 million people or 19 per cent of the adult population held equity with ownership significant across most socio-economic groups. Over 3.5 million were first time shareholders attracted by privatisation sales and over a million were in employee share schemes. By 1988 there were some 1,300 all-employee share schemes in operation (i.e. where all employees were eligible to join) compared to 30 in 1979, a development encouraged by generous tax treatment.[73] Small investors were attracted to privatisation shares through extensive marketing and advertising campaigns and the wide distribution of prospectuses and application forms. In addition, depending upon the particular privatisation, the Government also used privileged share trading arrangements, the phasing of payments for shares, bonus shares and bill voucher incentive schemes, and permitted bids at the striking price when tender issues were adopted.

The use of shareholder incentives was especially in evidence during the privatisations of BT and BGC. Incentives were used previously in a few private sector flotations, but they became something of the norm for the very large privatisations to attract a sufficient number of investors. The incentives were also intended to reduce the flow back of shares on to the aftermarket. When shares are floated at a discount there is always a risk that investors will "stag" the issue, buying the shares and then immediately selling them for a capital gain. The flow of shares into the stock market immediately after issue then depresses the share price. In turn the prospect of a depressed share price in the aftermarket creates an incentive for institutional investors to reduce their share purchases at flotation, preferring to buy at a lower price later. Investors could take advantage of bill voucher and bonus share schemes only if they held on to their shares for some time.

As investors began to experience the benefits from buying privatisation stock, which usually quickly appreciated in value, more first-time investors dived into buying shares, sometimes into companies where the Government had neither expected nor particularly encouraged them to do so. Especially during the privatisations of Rolls-Royce and British Airways a number in Government did not feel the shares were appropriate for small investors with limited share portfolios. The companies had a history of fluctuating financial performance and in the case of Rolls-Royce a heavy reliance on defence orders, at a time when defence budgets were under review. Nevertheless, large numbers of small investors still applied for the shares.

The Government was understandably proud of its achievement in widening share ownership. But the success in attracting large and growing numbers of small investors owed much to a combination of a bull market for shares during the 1980s, which meant that shares bought were more likely to be saleable later at a profit, keen pricing of the shares, attractive incentives to buy shares in the forms of bonus issues and bill discounts, priority allocation and instalment terms. The cost of the incentive schemes was significant; for example in the BT sale bill vouchers and bonus shares cost £111 million. In 1988 the National Audit Office concluded that: "it must be seriously questioned whether the costs of these incentives are necessary to the achievement of certain of the sales objectives". The Treasury responded by promising to consider their use in the future on a case by case basis to ensure that they represented value for money.[74] Also, the failure to use sales by tender, which might have reduced the stagging gains, was partly a response to the widening shareholding agenda, as discussed earlier.[75] Tender issues were considered to be more complex for new investors to understand. Certainly, short-term stagging gains tended to be higher when shares were targeted at the small investor.[76] At the same time, small investors gained only modest sums individually because of the small share allocations applied for, and received, and they faced relatively higher dealing costs as a proportion of the receipts when the shares were eventually sold. The big capital gains were made in the City.[77]

It is also important to recognise that while the percentage of individuals holding shares grew during the 1980s, largely as a result of the privatisations (and the public flotation of a mutual bank and a building society, i.e. the TSB in 1986 and the Abbey National in 1989), so did the investments of the financial institutions. The fact is that even in the most highly promoted of the privatisations to the small investor, the vast bulk of shares on offer were bought by the City. "Sid", immortalised as the archetypal small investor in the British Gas sale campaign on TV, and his friends never were the majority owners. By the late 1980s the financial institutions controlled over 75 per cent of share capital in the UK, a larger proportion than a decade earlier.[78] In other words, while privatisation did appear on the face of it to widen property ownership, it did not reverse the concentration of financial muscle in the City. Attempts by Government to build on the success of privatisation issues in attracting small investors, by encouraging investment in private sector companies through the development of cheaper and more convenient share dealing services, generally failed.

In addition to not widening their investment portfolios by investing in private sector companies, many small investors sold their privatisation stock, sometimes very quickly, to take advantage of a windfall financial gain. For example, within a year of privatisation the number of shareholders in BAe had fallen from 158,000 to 27,000 and in C&W from 157,000 to 26,000.[79] Amersham International initially had 62,000 shareholders, but the number had fallen by 10,000 within one month of the flotation. Following the Jaguar sale of July 1984 the company started with 125,000 shareholders but only 49,000 remained by May 1985.[80] BA was privatised on 6 February 1987 with an initial share register of 1.2 million, but the number had declined rapidly to 450,000 within three months. In the cases of Amersham International and Britoil around 90 per cent of the original shareholders had sold their shares by 1989. By contrast, in the case of British Gas the numbers of small investors that sold out was appreciably less, at only 33 per cent within five years. Overall, the average percentage of the original shareholders who still retained their shares in privatised companies by 1989 was estimated to be around 40 per cent.[81]

Importantly, whether selling shares to large numbers of small investors, who either sold their shares for a quick gain or put them in a drawer and forgot about them, was a sensible policy objective remains questionable. Equally, whether it was sensible from the perspective of corporate governance to encourage large numbers of small investors in the privatised companies, given that large investors have more incentive to monitor management behaviour given the size of their individual holdings, also remains a matter for debate. Even when small investors did take a continuing interest in their privatised shareholdings, the very small holding each had at stake made it most unlikely that they would trouble management to account for their actions. As Letwin concludes: "Revenues for the Exchequer could have been increased, and very possibly the management of the privatized industries made more efficient, if the shares had been sold to major, existing, private-sector entities rather than to 'Sid' . . . and his five million friends."[82]

Certainly the wider share ownership agenda led to some huge share registers, which worried management in terms of the cost of servicing investors (dividend payments and circulation of annual reports and accounts) and accommodating all of the investors at company annual general meetings, although the latter concern proved to be unwarranted because the vast majority of small investors chose not to attend. The privatised companies were fearful of the costs of administering large share registers. Meanwhile, within Government doubts were expressed from time to time about the wisdom of enticing small investors to buy shares instead of investing in diversified portfolios through unit and investment trusts and the like. In 1988 the National Audit Office suggested that: "it would be advantageous for departments to define in advance of sales the broad assumptions which underlie their objectives in relation to numbers of shareholdings held by individuals, employees, and by institutions. They should then systematically review how these assumptions have turned out in practice."[83] There is no evidence, however, that departments were willing to investigate seriously the costs and benefits of what was essentially a politically-driven policy commitment on the part of Ministers to widen share ownership.[84]

Much more successful in terms of permanently widening property ownership was the separate policy of selling council homes and promoting house buying. Prior to 1980 the sale of council homes was at the discretion of local authorities. Sales had peaked in 1972 at 45,878.[85] The 1980 Housing Act replaced the discretionary policy with a "right to buy" under which councils were required to permit tenants to purchase their homes and at a price discount. The discount started at 33 per cent for council tenants of three years' standing plus a one per cent discount for every subsequent year of tenancy, rising to a maximum discount of 50 per cent. Later the terms were made even more generous. Between 1979 and 1987 around one million council houses were sold and the proportion of people in public sector housing fell from over 40 per cent to 27 per cent. Home ownership was also encouraged by rising council house rents, resulting from Government policy to cut housing subsidies, and the continuation of interest relief against income tax for mortgage payments. In spite of the argument of economists that the tax relief served to raise the demand for and therefore the price of housing, in 1983 the Government raised the ceiling on mortgage tax relief from £25,000 to £30,000. The amount spent by Government on tax relief to home buyers rose by 200 per cent in real terms during the 1980s and was costing the Exchequer £4.8 billion a year by 1987/88.

By 1987 there were 2.5 million more home owners in Britain and owner occupation had risen from 55 per cent of the population in 1980 to 64 per cent, boosted by the one million council home sales. It was housing sales rather than the privatisation of nationalised industries which had the most lasting effect on widening property ownership in the country. By 1992 1.7 million homes in the public sector housing stock had been sold, raising over £24 billion, making this the single largest privatisation scheme by far. At the same time new council house building was reduced, aggravated by a restriction imposed by Government on the amount of the receipts from home sales local councils could spend. This started at 50 per cent but had fallen to 20 per cent by 1985/6. In 1987 21,000 new council homes were built compared with 112,300 in 1978.[86] This meant that by the end of the second Thatcher Government, for the 25 per cent of the population still dependent upon living in public sector homes, the average quality of the housing stock available to rent had declined. It was generally the better quality homes that were the most attractive for tenants to buy, not the council flats and houses on sink estates, which were left for council tenancy.

Nevertheless, the sale of council homes was a major political success and particularly a vote winner for the Conservatives amongst working-class voters in the 1983 General Election. The policy was hugely popular amongst lower-income voters because they now had the prospect for the first time of getting on to the private sector housing ladder, and sharing in the house price appreciation. In Britain by the 1980s buying a home was seen as a sure-fire way of making money over the longer term. When some homes bought from councils originally built by non-traditional methods were subsequently discovered to have defects that made them virtually un-resaleable, the Government acted speedily to head off what might have been a public relations disaster. The Housing Defects Act was passed to provide financial compensation to the new owners.

The Labour Party opposed the sale of council homes in the election of 1983, but in its General Election Manifesto of 1987 reversed position and promised "to maintain the right to buy". The sale of council homes remains one of the lasting legacies of the Conservative Governments of the 1980s, and arguably one of the most controversial.

## Employee shareholdings and pension arrangements

In addition to promoting shareholding to the wider public, the Government was intent upon encouraging employees to own shares. It was felt that this would improve industrial relations in Britain – where in the 1970s there was a huge "them and us" culture in industry – and weaken the power of the trade unions. There was the additional point that the trade unions invariably opposed each privatisation, but if the workforce could be won over through the prospect of being provided with shares on privileged terms, strikes to disrupt privatisations might be avoided. In general, the policy was successful. Employees proved to be enthusiastic to own shares even when advised by their unions to shun the offer – for example, 89 per cent of eligible employees in BAe, 90 per cent in ABP and 99 per cent in Amersham International and C&W took advantage of the preferential terms to obtain shares. The take-up of free offers in privatisations varied from between 89 per cent and 99 per cent and of matching offers from 41 per cent to 99 per cent. The most successful schemes were arguably those for BT and BGC, where 96 per cent and 99 per cent respectively, of eligible employees applied for and were allotted shares.

Employee free and matching schemes applied only to the original public offer and not to any subsequent sales of the Government's residual holdings of shares. Also, they applied to "eligible employees", who were normally those who had worked for the enterprise for a minimum period (such as 12 months). The schemes did not necessarily apply to part-time workers and overseas employees (the position regarding overseas employees varied; in some instances they received their own preference schemes tailored to the tax treatment in their countries of residence). In Britain, to qualify for tax relief the shares had to be held by the trustees of an Inland Revenue approved profit sharing scheme for at least two years, except in the case of an employee's death, redundancy or other special circumstances.

Employee share schemes helped to win over employees to supporting or at least not actively opposing a transfer to the private sector. There were very few strikes against privatisations, and none was successful. However, there were other reasons too why industrial action was infrequent. In particular, where employees were made redundant before privatisation this was usually on a voluntary basis with generous compensation. Also, for those workers who transferred to the new private sector company, their working conditions were protected by the European Community Directive that was implemented in the UK in the form of the Transfer of Undertakings (Protection of Employment) (TUPE) regulations. Therefore, the extent to which the share schemes headed off industrial action is difficult to assess accurately, although they must have assisted. Certainly, the use of employee share schemes helped portray privatisation as more than the sale of underpriced assets to City friends – they therefore had a propaganda value. The Government was sensitive to this criticism coming from the Labour movement and some sections of the media and it was for this reason that the Government also attempted to prevent the commencement of executive share option schemes until after privatisation. A number of privatisations included the setting up of long-term share-based profit sharing schemes; but the Government was keen to ensure that they did not take effect until after transfer to the private sector, when the decision whether to go ahead and the final terms would be a matter for the private sector shareholders. However, when British Leyland sold Jaguar in July 1984 it did permit an executive share option scheme alongside a long-term share-based profit sharing scheme for other employees to be set up ahead of the sale. As the sale was undertaken by a corporation board and not the Government directly the Government was unable to prevent the move. As the Government had feared, this set a precedent for succeeding privatisations.

For public flotations the nature of the incentives to employees to buy shares evolved and generally became a little more generous over time. For example, the offer of BP shares in 1979 did not include a free offer to employees, while the BT sale was the first to add a discount on the price of shares employees applied for, in addition to the free and matching offers. By the mid-1980s the special arrangements to encourage employees to participate in public flotations took the form of employees pre-registering for shares. The schemes typically took the form of an offer of free shares, an offer of shares given free in proportion to shares bought by employees (known as "matching" shares), and a special application form giving employees priority in the allocation of shares they applied for in addition to the free and matching shares. Table 16.7 provides a summary of the terms of each of the employee share schemes introduced during the main privatisations between May 1979 and June 1987. In the case of the C&W sale, shares were provided over a period of time as part of an employees' profit sharing scheme. However, this method did not prove popular and therefore was not repeated.

Throughout the Treasury was keen to ensure that the cost of employee schemes did not become excessive. Treasury approval for each scheme was needed, ostensibly to ensure consistency across different departments' privatisations but in reality also to cap the cost. Indeed, initially the Treasury seems to have been very sceptical of the need for free and matching share schemes for employees, as evidenced by its attitude towards them during the sale of BAe in 1981 (chapter 5, p.122). Scepticism was also evident during an early meeting of the Official Committee on Nationalised Industry Policy at the Treasury, when it was concluded that it was difficult from the limited evidence available to draw any definite conclusions about the effects on industrial relations of promoting workers' shareholdings.[87]

To cap the cost and ensure that the employee schemes did not escalate in generosity, as early as 20 July 1980 the Treasury recommended a formal limit of five per cent of expected gross proceeds that could be devoted to encouraging employee shareholdings. In practice the Treasury went on to encourage a lower limit.[88] The five per cent figure was less than allowed for under Stock Exchange rules on employee shareholdings, which generally limited the percentage of shares set aside for employees in a public offer to ten per cent .

Free shares were limited by the Treasury to around £50 per head at first, although this was raised to £60 during the Britoil sale and then to £70 by the mid-1980s, mainly to reflect inflation. Matching share offers were capped too, although the limit varied more widely.[89] In summary, the employee shareholdings were modest in scale. Different in terms of the degree of employee shareholding were the management and employee buyouts (MEBOs), of which the most important by far in terms of size was the sale of the NFC in 1981. But these were exceptional. Leaving aside MEBOs, employee shareholdings never accounted for

Table 16.7 Employee participation in privatisation share sales May 1979–June 1987

| Company | Date of sale | Per cent of total workforce that participated | Maximum value per employee of free, matching and discount offers (£) | Free offer (£) | Matching offer (£) (Free/bought) | Discount offer (per cent) | Cost as per cent of proceeds (approx.) |
|---|---|---|---|---|---|---|---|
| British Petroleum | November 1979 | 43 | 497.00 | None | 497.00 (1:1) | None | N/A |
| British Aerospace | February 1981 | 89 | 499.50 | 49.50 | 450.00 (1:1) | None | 4.38 |
| Cable and Wireless | October 1981 | 99 | 300.00[1] | 50.00 | 250.00 (1:1)[2] | None | 1.29 |
| Amersham International | February 1982 | 99 | 546.70 | 49.70 | 497.00 (1:1) | None | 0.58 |
| National Freight Consortium[2] | February 1982 | 36 | £200.00 (interest free loan for share purchase) 36% of employees participated in the management/employee buyout | | | | |
| Britoil | November 1982 | 72 | 457.95 | 58.05 | 399.90 (1:1) | None | 0.15 |
| Associated British Ports | February 1983 | 90 | 311.36 | 59.36 | 252.00 (1:1) | None | 2.5 |
| Enterprise Oil | June 1984 | 71 | (No free, matching or discount offers) | | | | |
| Jaguar | July 1984 | 19 | (No free, matching or discount offers) | | | | |
| British Telecom | November 1984 | 96[3] | 478.20 | 70.20 | 200.00 (2:1) | 10 per cent discount on up to £2080 of further shares | 1.3 |
| British Gas | December 1986 | 99 | 569.90 (minimum) | 70.20 (minimum) | 299.70 | 10 per cent discount on up to £2000 of further shares | 0.8 |
| British Airways | February 1987 | n/a | 595.00 | 95.00 | 300.00 | 10 per cent discount on up to £2000 of further shares | 2.4 |
| Rolls-Royce | May 1987 | n/a | 568.90 | 69.70 | 299.20 | 10 per cent discount on up to £2000 of further shares | 1.6 |

Notes:
1 Government made the preferential terms available initially and over the life of the company's profit sharing scheme. In all of the privatisations it was normal for employees also to be given preference in applications for other shares at full price.
2 £200 interest free loan to employees to buy shares provided by the company.
3 In addition, 2.4 per cent of BL employees made preferential applications for 0.9 per cent of the issued share capital.

Source: Offer for Sale documents; Price Waterhouse (1987). Costs as per cent of proceeds, own estimates.

more than 4.3 per cent of the shares issued (ABP) and in one case was as low as 0.1 per cent (Britoil). Also, following privatisation some employees sold their shares to benefit from a capital gain. Like the small shareholder agenda, the employee share schemes introduced made very little, if any, long-term difference to the ownership of British industry.

In the case of a number of the privatisations it was discovered that the employees' pension funds were in deficit. During the early planning of the privatisations of the NFC and what became Amersham International, for example, it was feared that extra funding to the pension schemes prior to privatisation to make them actuarially sound might well swallow up a large percentage of the expected proceeds, much to the Treasury's alarm.[90] In a number of sales, sorting out the pension funding took much time and effort and involved a capital injection (although in the case of the bus industry pension schemes the funds were found to be overfunded and the Government obtained an indirect capital gain). Typically public sector pension schemes were generous, based on defined benefits rather than contributions made. That is to say, broadly, pension payments were based on a formula that took into account the final salary at retirement and the number of years of service. Also, the schemes often included some form of index-linking of future pensions to retain their real value in the face of inflation. Merchant bank advice during early privatisations was that the existence of such generous pension entitlements would impact negatively in terms of achieving successful sales.[91]

The usual outcome at privatisation was that existing employees and pensioners retained their current pension rights. New employees, those that joined the firm after privatisation, were typically put into a new and less generous pension scheme; that is to say, one more characteristic of schemes found in the private sector. This was true, for example, during the privatisation of BA, when a separate pension scheme not offering a guarantee of inflation-proofing was set up for new recruits. Where necessary Government contributed a lump sum to the pension fund (by one means or another) to meet the future expected liabilities, based on an actuarial valuation ahead of the privatisation. At the same time, in most cases Government avoided entering into providing a future guarantee of pension liabilities.

This is the general picture, but the terms of public sector pension schemes varied and therefore so did the precise pension arrangements at privatisation. Indeed, in the case of Britoil the pension scheme did not provide for index-linking and this was unchanged by privatisation. In the case of ABP two-thirds of employees were covered by a pension scheme that provided for full index-linking, but the pension scheme for the remaining one-third, who were registered dock workers covered by the National Dock Labour Board scheme, required pensions to be increased by three per cent per annum. Again these arrangements continued at privatisation. In C&W the pension scheme similarly provided for a three per cent increase per annum for pensions and with further increases at the discretion of the company and the trustees. The scheme was retained at privatisation.[92]

The NFC pension scheme provided for full pension index-linking under state ownership and this continued after 1982. The Government's future liability was limited to deficiencies in the pension fund at the date of sale and to any emerging costs of certain pensions in relation to ex-British Rail workers, who had transferred to the employment of the NFC in 1968. Turning to Amersham International employees, they were members of the UK Atomic Energy pension scheme which was a notionally funded public sector scheme. They remained in the scheme after privatisation. For employees of British Aerospace the position was more complicated. The pension scheme was unaffected by privatisation, providing for a four per cent increase in pensions per annum. But the British Aerospace Act 1980 provided that the

Government would stand behind all liabilities transferred to the company on privatisation in the event of a future liquidation (reflecting earlier Government assurances; see chapter 5, pp.114–15). While this arrangement was introduced with trading liabilities in mind, it was also considered to extend to meeting any deficiencies in the company's pension fund in respect of past or future service of current employees at the time of privatisation. However, no liability was anticipated given the strength of the pension fund.

Finally, in the case of BT the DTI took the BAe precedent and decided that if the company was ever to go into liquidation, the Government should agree to pay its debts in respect of obligations which were formally obligations of the public corporation and which were vested in the successor company. Given that BT was a nationalised industry where there was a contractual obligation to make good any deficiency in the pension fund, a by-product was to place a contingent liability on the Government in respect of any pension fund liabilities. The Government was advised that this contingent liability existed in respect of employees at the time of privatisation, in respect of their service before and after privatisation, and also covered BT's existing pensioners on similar terms. The practical effect was that if BT was ever to get into financial difficulty and have a deficient pension fund, the Government would be required to make good that part of the deficiency which could be attributed to the service of employees and BT pensioners at the time of privatisation. Later the Treasury would oppose repeating this protection; for example it successfully opposed its extension to the pensions of Royal Ordnance Factory workers.

## Economic regulation

The privatisation of monopoly industries that began with the sale of BT in November 1984 and continued with the disposal of BGC two years later led to the creation of new regulatory structures and industry-specific regulatory bodies to prevent monopoly abuse, namely OFTEL and OFGAS. The regulatory structures operated alongside and complemented existing competition policy, which continued to be policed by the Office of Fair Trading and the Monopolies and Mergers Commission (MMC). In general terms, regulatory duties and powers were divided between the Government Minister, who granted licences to firms operating in the industry and the industry-specific regulatory office headed by a Director General, who enforced and kept under review the licence conditions and who was also consulted by the Minister on grants of licences. When the regulator proposed to amend the terms of the licence and the regulated company objected, the matter was referred to the MMC. The MMC's report was addressed to the regulator, who was expected to amend the licence in accordance with the MMC's findings.

BT and BGC, and in the future new suppliers as they entered the telecommunications and gas industries to compete, were required to operate under licences (in the case of the gas industry termed an "authorisation"). These licences regulated the quality of service, enforced special terms relating to the dominant incumbent operator (such as the universal service obligation and network access), set out the framework under which prices would be regulated, and laid down other terms and conditions with which operators were required to conform. Conformity with the licence was policed by OFTEL and OFGAS. The decision was taken early in the planning of the sale of BT, in the summer of 1982, that continued regulation by Government department would deter investors, who would fear continued Ministerial control of the company. Central to the new regulation, therefore, was the establishment of the largely independent offices free from the day-to-day influence of Ministers. The regulatory offices were technically non-ministerial departments of government, which appointed their own staff and developed their own management structures. Although the core staff were civil servants and came initially largely from the section of the sponsor department responsible for the industry, the offices quickly gained a separate legitimacy within public administration in Britain. The first DGs appointed, Bryan Carsberg at OFTEL and James McKinnon at OFGAS, must be given much credit for ensuring that regulatory independence was truly achieved and maintained during these early years. Both proved to be highly effective regulators and over time became vigorous in promoting competition in their respective industries.

The new regulatory structures came with a new regulatory tool, the "price cap", promoted by Professor Stephen Littlechild in January 1983. This drew upon a proposal put forward by Warburgs for the ill-fated "Buzby bond" some months earlier. The price cap mechanism involved linking future price rises in BT, and later also BGC, to the national inflation rate (measured by the retail price index) less an "X" efficiency factor. The X-efficiency factor reflected the expectation of productivity gains in the company over and above the average national productivity gains reflected in the RPI. Although the price caps were leniently set at privatisation, and both BT and British Gas at first seem to have found little difficulty in raising profits while maintaining prices within their caps, the price cap system provided an effective means of regulating public utility prices without direct control of profit levels. Rate of return regulation in the USA was associated with inefficient investment and "cost padding". The price cap was intended to be a better alternative, which would remove the disincentives for management to pursue higher productivity and cost reductions inherent in rate of return control. At the same time, the price cap would ensure that consumers were not exploited through excessive charges. The price cap method, suitably adapted to reflect the special features of different industries, would subsequently be adopted for later privatisations involving state industries with substantial market power, namely the larger airports, the water and electricity industries, and the railways. It would also be taken up in a number of countries across the globe for their monopoly utilities.

The Government recognised that the problem of monopoly needed careful handling so as not to bring privatisation into disrepute.[93] The development of the new regulatory offices enabled industries with some natural monopoly characteristics, as found in fixed-line telephone systems and gas transportation and distribution, to be privatised. Following the apparent success of OFTEL and then OFGAS, private ownership with state regulation of monopolies was increasingly viewed as superior to direct state ownership. Under state ownership, Government faces a potential conflict of interest between regulating the industry and bearing the consequences and costs of regulatory decisions. As Norman Tebbit, Secretary of State for Trade and Industry at the time of the privatisation of BT, later commented: "A government free from ownership is freed from the conflict of interest inevitably posed with regulation and whilst ownership is not the business of the state, regulation directly by approved agencies certainly is."[94]

The new regulatory offices were able to enforce new standards of service, limit price rises through the price cap mechanism and promote competition. It is very questionable whether any of these results would have been so effectively achieved had BT and BGC remained under state ownership. Arm's length regulation removed political interference in the management of the telecommunications and gas industries and, as a Treasury document later judged, "The regulators provide a level of protection that the consumer never enjoyed before privatisation."[95] It is doubtful whether competition would have developed as quickly and extensively in telecommunications and later gas supply had the Government remained the owner of the incumbent suppliers, especially in the face of the inevitable trade union opposition to any threat to jobs.

However, regulation did bring some unintended effects. In his report to Government in January 1983 Littlechild talked about regulation being temporary and "holding the fort" until competition arrived in the industry (chapter 12, p.279). Regulation was supposed to be light-handed and to wither over time. However, the regulatory structures created would prove to be much more permanent than expected, with OFTEL and OFGAS effectively still existing down to the present day, albeit now absorbed into wider regulatory agencies concerned with communications (OFCOM[96]) and energy markets (OFGEM[97]). This applies also to the RPI minus X price cap. If anything, regulation became tighter and more detailed (less "light-handed") over the first few years after privatisation with the price cap moving closer to a form of rate of return regulation with a time lag.[98] Later, especially after 2000, as competition became more firmly established in telecoms and gas supply, some aspects of regulation were relaxed and a number of the price controls were abolished. For example, the price cap on BT's retail prices was removed in 2006. But much of the regulatory structure remains.

Neither Ministers nor their civil servants during the privatisation of BT and BGC appear to have foreseen the enduring nature of the regulatory structures that they were creating.[99] They did not foresee the offices growing greatly in size and taking on new powers, as occurred. By the late 1990s a new industry of regulation had been created in Britain, with supporting university training courses, university regulation research units (such as the Centre for the study of Regulated Industries at the University of Bath[100]), conferences and seminars, and management consultancies with regulation specialists. None of this was anticipated. It is interesting to speculate whether the regulatory arrangements first introduced in the mid-1980s would have been different if all of this had been foreseen.

In addition, in many respects regulation of BT and BGC (and later water, electricity and the railways) evolved rather than being planned. What was developed for BT was adapted for other industries. But OFTEL was created without a large amount of prior research and its powers had to be altered over time – and not simply to reflect new developments but also to address perceived deficiencies in the regulatory powers provided at the time of privatisation. This was also true for the gas industry, where under the 1986 Gas Act OFGAS's powers were almost entirely restricted to the tariff market. After privatisation concerns were raised about predatory pricing and other anti-competitive activities by BGC in the large-user ("contract") market, but the regulator was greatly constrained from intervening.[101]

However, in spite of some failure in the regulatory systems established at privatisation, in both telecoms and gas, full retail competition did come in the longer run. Although BT and British Gas started life in the private sector facing limited competition (BT from Mercury and later cellular telephones and cable and British Gas only in the contract market), later competition became increasingly effective. During the 1990s both BT and British Gas faced the introduction of real competition across wide areas of their businesses for the first time. One result in the case of British Gas was a substantial restructuring of the company in 1997 with the establishment of separate gas supply and pipeline companies. Competition therefore did develop, vindicating those who had planned for it at the time of privatisation. Nevertheless, the perceived failure to do enough initially to promote competition, especially in gas supply, led to a more determined effort to restructure ahead of privatisation during the planning of the disposal of the electricity industry, after the June 1987 General Election.

440

## Privatisation and economic performance

A full review of the evidence on the effects of privatisation on economic performance is deferred to Volume 2 of this *Official History*; in other words, until the privatisations between 1987 and 1997 have been studied. However, some initial comment is appropriate here.

The belief that privatisation would lead to a significant improvement in the performance of the industries concerned – and in turn of the British economy – grew during the 1980s. As the pressing need to raise funding for a hard-strapped Exchequer receded after 1982, the notion that nationalisation was inefficient and private ownership efficient, and therefore privatisation was crucial to achieving productivity gains and cost reductions, became a prominent theme of Ministerial speeches. On average, in the nationalised sector pre-tax returns on investment had lagged behind those found in the private sector and after 1972 were never significantly above zero during the rest of the 1970s; although at least some of this result can be put down to governments limiting price rises in the industries as part of an ill-judged anti-inflation policy at the time. The case for privatisation on efficiency grounds was summarised by the PM in the House of Commons in February 1986:

> "Privatisation, through exposing former state-owned companies more fully to the disciplines and opportunities of the market . . . improves the efficiency of businesses that are crucial to our overall economic performance. As such, it forms an important part of the Government's overall strategy for long-term economic growth . . . further reinforcing the enterprise culture that is essential for economic success."[102]

Ministers were confident that privatisation worked. Commenting in July 1984, John Moore, the Financial Secretary, claimed: "The acid test of the success of privatisation policy is the performance of those companies which have already been privatised." He was in no doubt that privatisation had led to a dramatic improvement in the performance of the firms concerned, referring explicitly to BAe achieving record sales in 1983, Britoil, C&W and Amersham International recording much higher profits in the private sector, and the management and employees of the NFC enjoying a six-fold increase in the value of their shares since mounting their buyout. Also, in his view the prospect of privatisation had led to substantial improvements in the services provided by BT and BA with waiting lists for telephones falling from 250,000 in 1979 to around 2,000 and BA achieving an average annual improvement of nine per cent in labour productivity.[103] Moreover, where competitive tendering had been introduced for services, such as cleaning and cleansing in central and local government and the NHS, contemporary studies suggested that in general cost savings of around 20 per cent were being achieved.[104] Also, employees were judged to have benefited from share schemes and more involvement in the management of their industries, notably in the case of the MEBO in NFC. A study into privatisation and "cultural change" completed somewhat later, in 1990, found that the former nationalised industries had become more customer-focused, management had been strengthened by new recruits from outside, performance incentives had been introduced for employees, and there had been significant beneficial restructuring of the businesses.[105] However, the study was partly based on discussions with senior management within the privatised companies, and therefore the possibility of exaggeration cannot be discounted.

There were some large gains in profitability and in some other efficiency measures in the run-up to privatisations and afterwards. At the same time, the Treasury, while a keen promoter of privatisation, never stopped to commission a serious study of the actual effects on economic performance. Some civil servants would have liked to have seen such a study undertaken, but it was not in their interests to push the matter, in the face of ministerial hostility or indifference. As far as Ministers were concerned, it was axiomatic that privatisation succeeded and therefore a study was redundant.

Interestingly, while Government Ministers in the mid-1980s trumpeted that privatisation had made inefficient firms efficient, this was not necessarily the expectation at the time of the first privatisations. These privatisations usually involved reasonably successful state-owned businesses, where at the time the case for disposal was not argued on efficiency grounds. In particular, there was very little or no attempt made to sell the case for privatising the oilfields, BP, BAe, Amersham International, C&W and ABP in terms of inefficiency under state ownership. Rather, these enterprises were sold because they were seen as successful and therefore easily sellable. The enterprises sold were doing reasonably well before privatisation, "otherwise they could not have been sold off to the private sector", as one former head of a nationalised industry observed.[106] The main possible exceptions to this argument are the National Freight Corporation and some of the subsidiaries of the National Enterprise Board, British Steel, and British Rail. The rationale for these sales was to relieve the Exchequer from future costs or, putting this alternatively, to transfer the costs of future restructuring, redundancies and possible closure to the private sector. Nevertheless, only with the disposal of shipbuilding from the mid-1980s was a serious attempt made to sell a major loss making industry.

Equally, there is the difficulty in taking the statistical evidence on performance improvements cited by Ministers, including profitability after privatisation, at face value. This is because of the counterfactual – or what would have been the industries' performances had they remained state-owned? The poor performance of nationalised industries in the 1970s coincided with poor economic performance across the British economy as a whole. By contrast, after 1981/2 when the first major privatisations were underway or being planned, macroeconomic conditions improved.[107] At least some of the better performance of businesses after privatisation was probably a product of better economic times.

Moreover, a number of state-owned firms restructured and improved performance significantly in the 1980s without privatisation. For example, the economic performance of the coal industry, the railways and the Post Office improved sharply. The borrowings of the nationalised industries rose in the early 1980s, but fell from £1.1 billion in 1984 to a positive contribution to the public finances of £1.35 billion by 1987. By 1988/9 the deficits of the remaining nationalised industries had been turned into an overall surplus of about £400 million. The planning total or net claim upon the Treasury imposed by state-owned industries, composed mainly of grants, subsidies and borrowings less profits extracted, fell from £3.8 billion in 1984/5 to around £355 million in 1987/8. Consistent with this view of better performance in state industry, the big improvements in productivity and profitability in privatised industries, such as BA and British Steel, occurred ahead of privatisation. The results in one statistical study of performance pre- and post-privatisation suggest that in a number of cases after privatisation productivity growth actually slowed down.[108] Whether the large improvements ahead of privatisation were a product of preparing for the private sector and the appointment of new industry chairmen, such as Ian MacGregor and Sir John King, with briefs to prepare the industries for sale, or the setting of more commercial objectives for the nationalised industries by the Thatcher Governments of the 1980s, remains a matter of conjecture.

Certainly, during the 1980s the remaining nationalised industries were made to operate under the tighter governance regime introduced in 1981/82, involving annual corporate plans finalised each spring and agreed with Ministers based on figures set out in each industry's Investment and Financing Review (IFR). Regular comprehensive annual assessments of the major nationalised industries occurred, including consideration of their corporate plans drawn up by the boards and a performance review for each enterprise produced by the sponsoring department. The results of this exercise then fed into the annual IFR. To assist forward planning, capital programmes were agreed for up to 100 per cent of the investment in the year ahead, up to 85 per cent in the second year and up to 70 per cent in the third year. In addition, EFLs still operated as an important financial control, alongside financial targets and other performance goals set for each industry, usually in the form of cost reduction targets and sometimes quality of service standards.[109] Each month returns were submitted by the industries to sponsor departments and the Treasury under what was known as the Nationalised Industries Financial Information System. In other words, during the 1980s state enterprises were better managed and controlled by Government than they had been in the 1970s.

It is important also to recognise that not all of the privatisations were obviously successful. A number of businesses ran into financial difficulties after privatisation, notably a number of the shipbuilding and ship repair facilities sold were closed or seriously shrank their operations in the following years. By 1989 Jaguar cars, hived off from British Leyland in 1985, was in need of major investment and was taken over by the US car manufacturer Ford. After privatisation and especially in the 1990s C&W struggled to find a coherent business model, having failed to make a success of its Mercury telecommunications operation in the domestic market and following a series of other disappointing investments. Moreover, BT never became the internationally dominant player that the Secretary of State, Norman Tebbit, expected at the time of privatisation. As one commentator concluded in 1989 in the face of Ministerial enthusiasm and enthusiasm in large sections of the media for privatisation: "The clear cut picture of the advantages of privatization as often presented by ministers is naïve and over-simplified."[110] Sir Colin Marshall, Chief Executive of BA, also added a word of caution in spite of BA's success in the 1980s in shaking off bureaucracy, raising profit and finding better ways to compete:

> "I assure you that it is not merely the act of moving from the public to the private arena which may cause these things to happen. It requires long hard work at every level of the company to ensure they do. Becoming private is in itself no immediate guarantee of improvement. In fact, if unaccompanied by anything else it may well result in additional travail, since quite often the personnel of public corporations find themselves ill-equipped to move efficiently into sections of business that are very different."[111]

Turning to the effects of privatisation on the public finances and taxpayers, these are complex and certainly more difficult to summarise than was sometimes suggested at the time, when Ministers simply stressed the financial savings in terms of calls on the Exchequer by the nationalised industries. Provided that the capitalisation rate for income from shares sold in privatised companies is the same as the interest rate on government borrowing, there is no effect on the Government's net financial position. The sale of shares means that the Exchequer loses a stream of future revenue, but an equal amount borrowed would have committed the Treasury to make future interest payments of the same amount. However, the cost of raising government finance through privatisations is not necessarily the same as through the sale of gilts. Moreover, although the Exchequer receives higher tax revenues if the profits of the companies rise after privatisation, through Corporation Tax receipts, the Government foregoes the returns that would have accrued to the Exchequer from the nationalised industries.[112]

Also to be considered is how public expenditure and taxation would have changed in the absence of privatisation receipts, which is ultimately an unknown. A reasonable assessment is that privatisation receipts proved to be an easier way politically of reducing the total of public expenditure (in British public sector accounts they are treated as negative public spending) than cutting actual spending on education, health, social security etc. Or putting this another way, without the receipts, and given the Government's determination to cut tax rates, some difficult spending cuts would have had to be made. In effect, the taxpayer was compensated for the asset sales by public spending (say on education or health care) without either a corresponding tax hike or more government borrowing and therefore a higher national debt to service.

The former Conservative Prime Minister, Harold Macmillan, talking to the Tory Reform Group in November 1985 caused the Government some embarrassment when he was reported in the press to have complained that privatisation was like a once wealthy family "selling off the family silver". This criticism was taken up by critics of privatisation. But in fact Macmillan did not intend his comments to be an attack on the policy of privatisation, instead he merely intended to flag his concerns that the sums raised through privatisation sales should not be treated as Government income to be spent in a profligate manner on current consumption.[113] Privatisation involves a transfer of resources from the private sector to the public sector in the form of sales receipts, just as will normal government borrowing in the form of the sales of gilts. In so far as Government did use the receipts from privatisations to fund current Government consumption or tax cuts to consumers, there was something in Macmillan's warning. However, provided that the sales receipts represented a fair value for the assets sold, the taxpayer neither gained nor lost. The taxpayer gave up the "asset" of the nationalised industry, but the Exchequer obtained equivalent cash receipts in return.

The question is was the taxpayer adequately compensated? Did the sale receipts represent fair value? As commented above, the privatisation programme was associated with difficulties in setting a market clearing share price. A number of the sales were associated with large oversubscription and big share premiums when share trading began. One set of estimates suggests that had the privatisations between 1979 and 1987 been achieved with only a ten per cent price discount, the Government and hence the taxpayer would have received receipts some £595 million greater than actually received. Had the shares been sold in smaller tranches to permit an initial share price to be set – secondary sales typically sell at a much smaller or negligible discount – an extra £1.3 billion might have been raised.[114] In so far as there was underpricing of state assets, privatisation involved wealth redistribution from taxpayers to shareholders, some of whom were resident overseas.

Moving to the effects of privatisation on wider social welfare, these are also complex to assess, requiring an analysis of the impact on consumer surplus (prices and outputs), producer rents (profits) in the privatised firms and the effects on input suppliers (including of course the labour force). A more detailed appraisal will be provided in Volume 2 of this *Official History*; but briefly here, in so far as privatisation leads to a harder budget constraint on management this may reduce rents and rent dissipation within enterprises. As an example of this, privatisation was associated with some job losses. At the same time, there were some job gains. Employment expanded in some industries and declined in others, as enterprises adjusted to market changes. Also, there appears to have been no clear pattern in terms of the effect on average wages in the industries. However, where competitive tendering in central and local government and the NHS was introduced jobs were lost and sometimes inferior wages and working conditions were imposed.[115]

A definite result was the reduction in unionisation in the 1980s. Trade union membership fell between 1979 and 1987 from 30 per cent to 22 per cent of the workforce, although by no means was privatisation the sole cause. The reduction mainly reflected the decline of traditional manufacturing in Britain. Nevertheless, in privatised industry, while unionisation was often tolerated amongst middle-ranking and lower-level employees, amongst management grades it was not. Unionisation in management was replaced after privatisation by share option and profit sharing schemes. Fixed salary scales disappeared to be replaced by payment by results and promotion was now more clearly on merit rather than years of service. There were also changes to pension schemes especially for new employees, leading to reduced benefits, as summarised earlier in the chapter.[116]

In terms of the effects on consumers, privatisation led to changes in product pricing and the provision of particular products and services, for example removing previous cross-subsidies. Some consumers were also investors in the privatised industries and shared in the capital gains. What can be concluded is that privatisation did have an effect on income and wealth distribution; but it occurred at a time of wider economic and social change, which challenges any notion of separating out the effects of privatisation alone. During the 1980s, mainly as a result of employment trends, the decline of traditional manufacturing industry and tax and social security changes, income and wealth distribution became more unequal. On average unemployed and employed low-income families saw some real improvement in income during the 1980s, reflecting economic growth, but higher income groups saw much greater gains. In real terms the single childless unemployed person was worse off in 1989 than 1979.[117] It is difficult to believe that selling shares in privatised companies did other than exacerbate the gap between the fortunes of the poor and the rest and between the more and less prosperous regions of Britain.

However, none of this is intended to suggest that privatisation was a failure or a mistake. The Treasury has a short-termist, revenue maximising and budget minimising attitude and Government in the UK is simply not attuned to the evaluation of investment risk and return that is at the heart of commercial management. A number of industries prospered after privatisation and employment and incomes rose. There was a widespread underestimation of the possible productivity gains achievable after privatisation, even amongst those who championed the programme. The fact that the value of ABP rose from £44.5 million at flotation on 1 March 1983 to £550 million in 1987 reflects an ability to run the ports more profitably in the private sector (although also the advantages of inheriting an undervalued land bank that could be sold off for development purposes). NFC's profits in 1987 were seven times those achieved in 1982 and the valuation of its stock rose 26 fold after privatisation. In the NHS savings of an estimated £93 million a year were generated from the introduction of competitive tendering in the mid-1980s, mainly in domestic, catering and laundry services, some of this as a result of in-house operators becoming more cost efficient.[118]

In the 1970s nationalised industries were associated with low sometimes negative returns on capital, poor labour relations, inefficiency, low productivity, high costs, and poor customer service. Political priorities too often took precedence over commercial ones. Political timeframes based around periodic elections were much shorter than those needed for sound business investment.[119] Under nationalisation industries were prevented from tapping the external capital market and queued for funding alongside Government investments in education, health, roads etc. Market signals were diminished and there was an underpinning of state financing and therefore the lack of an effective bankruptcy constraint. Management deferred to Government rather than the City and consumers.

In the 1980s privatisation ended all of this. Privatisation allowed managers to manage the industries free from the threat of Ministerial intervention and with accountability for results to an independent capital market. Privatisation removed the underpinnings of state finance and reintroduced the possibility of bankruptcy and liquidation into industries that for 40 years or more had rested on the comfortable mattress of taxpayer funding. The result was that prices and outputs were set more according to market conditions than political imperatives. Unions and management were free to negotiate wages, working conditions and employment levels in a commercial rather than a political environment. Employees were permitted to invest and take a stake in the success of their employers. Through employee shareholding and widening small share ownership, some view privatisation as having introduced a true form of "public ownership" in the place of "state ownership". Perhaps above all, with the beginnings of the privatisation of the big state monopolies, starting with telecommunications and gas, choice was introduced to customers. This would continue after the June 1987 Election with the privatisation of electricity supplies.

A theme of the nationalisations of the 1940s was to bring competing firms under the umbrella of one management, so that industries could be planned and rationalised. Economies of scale rather than competition were the mantra of the time. Later it was discovered that a lack of competition led to inefficiency. In the absence of competition there was no direct benchmark for judging the performance of management, no means by which customers could express their dissatisfaction about prices and the quality of service by changing to another supplier, and no means for taxpayers, the ultimate financiers of the industries, to judge whether the industries were providing good value for money. In some cases, such as steel and vehicle production, there was the option of buying imported substitutes, and in transport consumers could switch to other transport modes. But privatisation came with a greater commitment in public policy to raising the level of consumer choice. Under public ownership, where the Government guarantees the industries' finances and there is a trade union agenda of preserving jobs, there is an inherent tendency for Government to be very cautious about encouraging competition.

## Conclusions

In 1992 John Moore summed up the achievements of the privatisation programme as follows:

"Begun as a radical experiment, privatization works so well that it has become a practical process by which a state-owned industry can join the free market with visible, often dramatic gains for the industry, its employees, its customers, and for the citizens who set it free by purchasing its shares. More important, privatization has become an educational process by which the people of a country can grasp the fundamental beliefs and values of free enterprise."[120]

State industries had been established, nationalisation had occurred, because the champions of the policy in the 1940s (and after) believed sincerely that state ownership would lead to improved goods and services for consumers and better working conditions for workers. Nationalisation was a political act linked to an ideological belief in socialism; but in addition it involved a pragmatic response to the lack of adequate provision of healthy supplies of water and sewerage, power and transport found in the nineteenth and first part of the twentieth centuries. In other cases, notably steel, Rolls-Royce, British Leyland and shipbuilding, state ownership was a response to economic failure. The aim was to invest public funds and rationalise production to produce "national champions" in the face of growing foreign competition.

However, from the 1950s it became increasingly clear that state-owned industries faced intractable problems in terms of industry-government relations, objectives, labour relations and management incentives. The nationalised industry White Papers of 1961, 1967 and 1977 were attempts to set more demanding financial and economic targets for the industries, above and beyond the usual breakeven "taking one year with another" requirement laid down in the nationalisation statutes. The National Economic Development Office reports of 1976/7, alongside other studies, underlined that much had not gone to plan and highlighted the difficulties of managing the industries efficiently and effectively.

The nationalised industries were found to suffer from two opposing weaknesses: Ministerial interference in their management and resulting political over commercial decision making, on the one hand, and a lack of accountability, on the other. Ministers would from time to time interfere in a range of management decisions, involving investment planning, the location of new plant, sourcing of supplies, wage settlements and redundancy programmes, and pricing policies. This came to a head during the difficult economic years of the 1970s, when a number of the industries for a time became, in effect, a tool of macroeconomic policy. But equally, the sponsor departments within government, responsible for overseeing the industries, suffered from what economists refer to as "information asymmetries". Management held the information on costs and revenues needed to determine optimal prices, outputs and investments. Management not civil servants were best able to judge whether financial losses were the result of external market forces or internal incompetence. In other words, government departments were unable to act as effective "principals", overseeing and holding to account the actions of their "agents", the industry boards.

This put the public as taxpayers – the ultimate "owners" of the industries – at great risk. It is not an exaggeration to say that some of the nationalised industries appear to have been run as fiefdoms of the chairmen and their boards; Sir Denis Rooke at British Gas comes immediately to mind in this respect. Rooke deeply resented Government interference in British Gas and actively opposed Ministers selling off the Corporation's oilfield assets. As Geoffrey Howe, the Chancellor of the Exchequer, commented in July 1981:

"The Morrisonian constitution grants our nationalised corporations a degree of autonomy which is probably unique in the Western World. In the strict sense of the word they are constitutionally 'irresponsible'. And they are better shielded from Ministerial control than the complaints of Government interference may suggest . . . The Government's only real weapon is the threat to reduce or cut off external funds. This is far too drastic to be effective. It is like equipping traffic wardens with anti-tank guns but depriving them of the right to leave parking tickets."[121]

Herbert Morrison, a leading Labour Minister in the post-1945 Labour Government, and often acknowledged to be the architect of the public corporation, in his book *Socialisation of Transport* published in 1933 expected that nationalisation would lead to improved quality of service and lower charges, that production would "be more efficiently and economically conducted" and that "The board [of the industries] and its officers must regard themselves as the high custodian of the public interest." By 1979 this expectation lay in tatters. Production was often inefficiently and uneconomically conducted and the boards and senior management were too often demoralised and either too distanced from or too subservient to their sponsoring departments. Management faced conflicting commercial, political and social objectives. In modern parlance, "corporate governance" was something of a shambles.

Since the mid-1960s the total return on capital employed in the nationalised industries had been significantly and consistently below that recorded by private sector manufacturing, even after state subsidies and debt write-offs. During the 1970s, overall the nationalised industries achieved aggregate returns on capital of around zero. By 1987 recognition of the weaknesses of state ownership in practice and the potential benefits from privatisation was not simply confined to the UK. A number of other countries in Europe, glancing over their shoulders to the UK, had embarked on their own disposals of state-owned industries, while the World Bank and other international donor agencies were taking an interest in privatisation as a policy to promote economic development in some of the poorest parts of the world. More and more countries became interested in privatisation and the corollary, market liberalisation.

Government departments, the Treasury and organisations such as the Adam Smith Institute in London became hosts to government officials and advisers from overseas, eager to learn tips from Britain about why and how to privatise. The PM boasted as early as 1986 that people were "queuing up to obtain the new British cure" of privatisation and at the Conservative Party Conference at Bournemouth later that year concluded: "So popular is our policy that it is being taken up all over the world. From France to the Philippines, from Jamaica to Japan, from Malaysia to Mexico, from Sri Lanka to Singapore, privatisation is on the move."[122]

Certainly the City banks and management consultancy firms benefited from a new British export, lucratively providing advice on how best to privatise. By the late 1980s Britain was the leading provider of professional advice on privatisation internationally, including the regulation of monopoly utilities. By the early 1990s revenues in the City of London from advising on privatisations overseas began to outweigh those from advising within the UK. The City was a major beneficiary of privatisation, in terms of commissions and other earnings, through the greater capitalisation of the stock market produced by privatisation flotations, and by the forms of flotation and debt financing developed for privatisation sales, which were later used for private sector flotations. Privatisation played a part in the City of London cementing its position as a global financial centre during the 1980s and 1990s. Meanwhile, internationally the disposal of state property was seen as essential for the existence of a free society with individual responsibility. This came to a head in Central and Eastern Europe in 1989.

Throughout the 1980s opinion polls in Britain suggested that a large section of the public remained sceptical of the case for privatisation (although council house sales were always popular). As Gerry Grimstone, one of the Treasury officials responsible for overseeing the privatisation programme in the early to mid-1980s, commented later: "Privatizations differ from all other public offerings, particularly in terms of political sensitivity, size, investor interest, and the complexity of objectives. The luxury of treating them as purely financial transactions is not available."[123] Grimstone believes that in the early days not enough was done to explain the benefits of privatisation as a coherent programme in terms of efficiency, spreading ownership and raising finance.[124] There was indeed a duality, indeed a contradiction, in the public's reaction to privatisation – a questioning of the need for sales while at the same time applying in droves to buy the stock. In the sense that actions speak louder than words, privatisation was in tune with the times, no matter what the opinion polls suggested. After 1987, Labour Party and Trades Union Congress annual conferences made continuing but essentially ritualistic attacks on privatisation. The prospect that the privatisations would be reversed was relegated to the political margins.

Although the Labour Party still remained wedded to Clause 4 of its constitution until the 1990s, and therefore to the historic commitment to common ownership of the means of production, distribution and exchange, in December 1985 the Labour leader, Neil Kinnock, confirmed that renationalisation was "well down the list of Labour priorities".[125] At the Party's annual conference in 1987 he went on to stress to the nationalisers in the Party: "if this movement pretends, for instance, that a few million people owning a few shares each will not make a difference to their perception of their economic welfare then this movement will be fooling itself . . . and the result of it is that our policies are going to have to take account of that reality."[126] The Party's criticism of privatisation now focused less on the principle of privatisation and more on the way that the nationalised industries were being sold and on the large management salaries that resulted.

\* \* \*

Throughout the 1980s and 1990s privatisation in Britain was more than the child of political ideology, although the role of ideology in the Conservative Party, which is traditionally free-market oriented, should not be ignored. That privatisation was more than simply a product of blinkered ideology is evident in the fact that, domestically and internationally, left of centre Labour-oriented governments, as well as more traditional market-oriented political parties, embraced what became, in effect, the new economic and political orthodoxy of privatisation.

On 11 June 1987 Margaret Thatcher achieved her third successive General Election victory. Privatisation had already entered into the heartlands of the public sector through the sale of British Telecom and British Gas. In the third Thatcher Government the policy was extended further, notably into water and sewerage services and electricity supply. It appeared that there was no nationalised industry beyond the limits of privatisation.

The story of privatisation after June 1987 is the subject of Volume 2 of this *Official History*.

# Appendix

# THE PRIVATISATIONS
# MAY 1979–JUNE 1987
## A listing of the principal advisers

### *Amersham International 1982*

| | | |
|---|---|---|
| **Merchant Bank** | Government | N. M. Rothschild & Sons (Rothschilds) |
| | Company | Morgan Grenfell & Co |
| **Broker to HMG** | | Cazenove & Co. (Cazenove) |
| **Underwriters** | | Rothschilds |
| | | Morgan Grenfell |

**Other advisers**

| | |
|---|---|
| Independent adviser on price | W. Greenwell & Co. (Greenwells) |
| Solicitor to Government | Slaughter & May |
| Solicitor to Company | Linklaters & Paines |
| Auditor & Reporting Accountant | Coopers & Lybrand (AI's auditors) |
| Receiving Bank | NatWest |
| Registrar | Lloyds Bank |
| Printer | Williams Lea |
| Public Relations | Streets |
| Actuary | R Watson & Sons |

### *Associated British Ports (Formerly BTDB) 1983, 1984*

**Advisers for the 1983 and 1984 share sales were the same unless otherwise indicated.**

| | | |
|---|---|---|
| **Merchant Bank** | Government | J Henry Schroder Wagg & Co (Schroders) |
| | | (Kleinwort, Benson gave initial advice – until November 1982 and were joint underwriters in 1983) |
| | Company | Kleinwort, Benson (Kleinworts) |
| **Brokers to the Issue** | | Greenwells (Lead) |
| | | Cazenove |
| | | Kitcat & Aitken (1984 only) |
| **Underwriters** | | Schroders |
| | | Kleinworts (1983 only) |

**Other advisers**

| | |
|---|---|
| Independent adviser on price | Greenwells (1983) |

| | | |
|---|---|---|
| Solicitors to Vendor | | Freshfields |
| | | Slaughter & May initial adviser until |
| | | November 1982 |
| Solicitor to Offer | | Linklaters & Paines |
| Solicitor to Company | | Slaughter & May |
| Reporting Accountant | | Price Waterhouse |
| Public Relations Agent | | Extel |
| Receiving Bank | | Lloyds |
| Printer | | Burrup Mathieson |
| Property Valuation | | Healey & Baker (1983) |

## British Aerospace 1981, 1985

**1981 share sale**

| | | |
|---|---|---|
| **Merchant Bank** | Government | Kleinworts |
| **Brokers to the Issue** | | Hoare Govett (Lead) |
| | | Cazenove |
| | | Greenwells |
| **Underwriters** | | Kleinworts (Lead) |
| | | Morgan Grenfell |
| | | Schroders |
| | | Hill Samuel |

**Other advisers**

| | |
|---|---|
| Solicitor to Government | Slaughter & May |
| Solicitor to Company | Linklaters & Paines |
| Reporting Accountant | Peat Marwick Mitchell |
| Receiving Bank/Registrar | Lloyds |
| Public Relations | Charles Barker |
| Printers | Burrup Mathieson |

**1985 share sale**

| | | |
|---|---|---|
| **Merchant Bank** | Government | Lazard Brothers (Lazards) |
| | Company | Kleinworts |
| **Brokers** | Government | Cazenove |
| | Company | Hoare Govett |
| **Underwriters** | | Lazards/Kleinworts (Joint Lead) |
| | | Morgan Grenfell |
| | | Schroders |
| | | Hill Samuel |

**Other advisers**

| | |
|---|---|
| Solicitor to Government | Slaughter & May |
| Solicitor to Company | Linklaters & Paines |
| Solicitor to Underwriters | Freshfields |
| Reporting Accountant | Peat Marwick Mitchell |
| Receiving Banks | Lloyds |
| | NatWest |
| | Midland |
| | Barclays |
| | Royal Bank of Scotland |
| Public Relations | Streets |
| Advertising Agent | Davidson Pearce |
| Printer | Burrup Mathieson |

**Regional Coordinators**

| | |
|---|---|
| London | Hoare Govett |
| | Cazenove |
| Aberdeen | Parsons |
| Belfast | Wm F Coates |
| Birmingham | Albert E Sharp |
| | Smith Keen Cutler |
| Bristol | Stock Beech |
| Cardiff | Lyddon |
| Edinburgh | Bell, Lawrie, Macgregor |
| Glasgow | Penney Easton |
| Leicester | Hill Osborne |
| Liverpool | Tilney |
| Manchester | Henry Cooke, Lumsden |
| Middlesbrough | Stancliffe Todd & Hodgson |
| Newcastle | Wise Speke |
| Plymouth | Westlake |

*British Airways 1987*

| | | |
|---|---|---|
| **Merchant Bank** | Government | Hill Samuel |
| | | Salomon Bros (US) |
| | Company | Lazards |
| | | Goldman Sachs (US) |
| | Joint | Wood Gundy (Canada) |
| | | Swiss Bank Corp (Europe) |
| | | Daiwa (Japan) |
| **Brokers** | Government | Cazenove |
| | | Wood Mackenzie |
| | Company | Rowe & Pitman |
| | | Phillips & Drew |
| **Underwriters** | | Hill Samuel |
| | | Lazards |
| | | Barings |
| | | County |
| | | Robert Fleming |
| | | Kleinworts |
| | | Lloyds |
| | | Samuel Montagu |
| | | Morgan Grenfell |
| | | Rothschilds |
| | | Schroders |
| | | Standard Chartered |
| | | S.G. Warburg & Co. (Warburgs) |

**Other advisers**

| | |
|---|---|
| Solicitor to Government | Slaughter & May |
| Solicitor to Company | Linklaters & Paines |
| Solicitor to Underwriters | Allen & Overy |
| Reporting Accountant | Ernst & Whinney (BA's auditors) |
| Multiple Applications Investigator | Peat Marwick Mitchell |

| | |
|---|---|
| US Legal Advice | Davis, Polk & Wardwell Wald |
| | Harkrader & Ross |
| Canadian legal advice | Blake, Cassels & Graydon |
| PR Consultant to Government | Valin Pollen |
| PR Consultant to Company | Broad Street Associates |
| Advertising Agent to Government | Allen, Brady & Marsh |
| Advertising Agent to Company | Saatchi & Saatchi |
| Advice on Pricing | Greenwells |
| Valuation Advice | Gerald Eve & Co |
| Printer | Williams Lea |
| Advice on consequences of foreign ownership | McGill University Centre for Research on Air & Space Law |
| Receiving Banks | Lloyds (Lead) |
| | Barclays |
| | NatWest |
| | Bank of Scotland |
| Response handling house | Teledata |

**Regional Coordinators**

| | |
|---|---|
| London and South East | de Zoete & Bevan |
| Aberdeen | Parsons |
| Belfast | Wm F Coates |
| Birmingham | Albert E Sharp |
| | Smithkeen Cutler |
| Bristol | Stock Beech |
| Cardiff | Lyddon |
| Edinburgh | Wood Mackenzie |
| Glasgow | Penney Easton |
| Leeds | Rensburg |
| Leicester | Hill Osborne |
| Liverpool | Charterhouse Tilney |
| Manchester | Henry Cooke Lumsden |
| Newcastle | Wise Speke |
| Norwich | Margetts & Addenbrooke |
| Plymouth | Westlake |

## *British Gas Corporation 1986*

| | | |
|---|---|---|
| **Merchant Bank** | Government | Rothschilds |
| | Company | Kleinworts |
| | Joint | Goldman Sachs (US) |
| | | Wood Gundy (Canada) |
| | | Swiss Bank Corp (Europe) |
| | | Nomura (Japan) |
| **Brokers** | Government | Cazenove |
| | Company | Wood Mackenzie |
| | | James Capel |
| | | Hoare Govett |
| **Underwriters** | | Rothschilds |
| | | Kleinworts |
| | | Barclays de Zoete Wedd |

Barings
Charterhouse
County
Robert Fleming
Hambros
Hill Samuel
Lazards
Lloyds
Samuel Montagu
Morgan Grenfell
Schroders
Warburgs

**Other advisers**

| | |
|---|---|
| Independent adviser on price | Godfrey Chandler |
| Solicitor to Government | Slaughter & May |
| Solicitor to BGC | Herbert Smith |
| Solicitor to Underwriters | Linklaters & Paines |
| Tax & Accountancy (Government) | Touche Ross |
| Multiple Applicant Investigator | Touche Ross |
| Reporting Accountant | Price Waterhouse |
| Joint PR Adviser to Government & Company | Dewe Rogerson |
| Joint Advertising Agent to Government & Company | Young & Rubicam |
| Reporting Petroleum Consultant | ERC Energy Resource Consultants |
| Receiving Banks | NatWest (Lead) |
| | Lloyds |
| | Midland |
| | Bank of Scotland |
| | Royal Bank of Scotland |
| | Ravensbourne |
| Printer | Burrup Mathieson |

**Regional Coordinators**

| | |
|---|---|
| London | de Zoete & Bevan |
| Aberdeen | Parsons |
| Belfast | Wm F Coates |
| Birmingham | Albert E Sharp |
| | Smith Keen Cutler |
| Bristol | Stock Beech |
| Cardiff | Lyddon |
| Edinburgh | Bell Lawrie |
| Glasgow | Penney Easton |
| Leeds/Middlesbrough | Stancliffe |
| Leeds/Newcastle | Wise Speke |
| Leicester | Hill Osborne |
| Liverpool | Charterhouse Tilney |
| Manchester | Henry Cooke Lumsden |
| Norwich | Margetts & Addenbrooke |
| Plymouth | Westlake |
| Winchester | Cobbald Roach |

## British Petroleum, 1979 and 1983

The Bank of England handled the sales of BP shares for the Government in 1979 and 1983 (and in 1977). The Bank was responsible for the appointment of the underwriting banks, brokers, receiving banks and solicitors to the offer. Warburgs advised the Bank in the preparation of the offers.

**Brokers to the Issues (1979, 1983)**  Mullens (Lead Broker)
Cazenove
Hoare Govett
Rowe & Pitman
Scrimgeour
**Underwriters (1979, 1983)**  Warburgs (Lead)
Kleinworts
Lazards
Morgan Grenfell
Robert Fleming
Schroders

**Other Advisers (1979, 1983)**
Solicitor to Government  Freshfields
Solicitor to Company  Linklaters & Paines
Receiving Banks  Bank of England
Barclays
Lloyds
Midland
Royal Bank of Scotland (1983 only)
NatWest
Auditor to the Company  Ernst & Whinney
Registrar  BP
Printers  British Printing Corporation (1979)
Metcalfe Cooper (1983)
US Lead Manager  Morgan Stanley (1979)
Morgan Guaranty (1983)

## British Rail Hotels 1983

**Merchant Bank**  Samuel Montagu advised the Government on the feasibility of selling BR's non-rail subsidiaries generally. No advisers retained specifically for the sale of hotels by HMG
British Rail  Morgan Grenfell

## British Shipbuilding Warship Yards 1985–86

**Merchant Bank**  Government  Schroders
BS  Lazards
Falmouth Shiprepair  Morgan Grenfell
**Other advisers**
Solicitor to BS  Ashurst Morris Crisp
Reporting Accountant  Touche Ross

## *NEB/British Technology Group various dates*

**(i) Sales of Subsidiaries**

| | | |
|---|---|---|
| **Merchant Bank** | Company | Lazards |
| | | Morgan Grenfell |

**(ii) Privatisations**

| | | |
|---|---|---|
| **Merchant Bank** | Government | Varied |
| | Company | Lazards |

## *British Telecom 1984*

| | | |
|---|---|---|
| **Merchant Bank** | Government | Kleinworts |
| | Company | Warburgs |
| | Joint | Morgan Stanley (US) |
| | | McLeod Young Weir (Canada) |
| | | Swiss Bank Corp (Europe) |
| | | Nomura (Japan) |
| **Brokers** | Government | Hoare Govett |
| | | de Zoete & Bevan |
| | | Scrimgeour |
| | Company | Cazenove |
| **Underwriters** | | Barclays Merchant Bank |
| | | Barings |
| | | Charterhouse Japhet |
| | | County Bank |
| | | Hambros |
| | | Hill Samuel |
| | | Kleinworts (joint lead) |
| | | Lazards |
| | | Lloyds Bank International |
| | | Morgan Grenfell |
| | | Robert Fleming |
| | | Rothschilds |
| | | Samuel Montagu |
| | | Schroders |
| | | Warburgs (joint lead) |

**Other advisers**

| | |
|---|---|
| Adviser on price | Phillips & Drew |
| Solicitor to Government | Linklaters & Paines |
| Solicitor to Company | Slaughter & May |
| Solicitor to Underwriters | Herbert Smith |
| Accountant | Coopers & Lybrand |
| Joint PR Adviser to Government & Company | Dewe Rogerson |
| Joint Advertising Agent to Government & Company | Dorlands |
| Printer | Burrup Mathieson |
| Multiple Applicant Investigator | Peat Marwick Mitchell |

| | |
|---|---|
| Receiving Banks | Lloyds (Lead) |
| | Bank of Scotland |
| | Barclays |
| | Midland |
| | NatWest |
| | Royal Bank of Scotland |
| Adviser on Economic Regulation | Professor S Littlechild |

**Regional Coordinators**

| | |
|---|---|
| Aberdeen | Parsons |
| Belfast | Wm F Coates |
| Birmingham | Albert Sharp, Smith Keen Cutler |
| Bristol | Stock Beech |
| Cardiff | Lyddon |
| Edinburgh | Wood Mackenzie, Bell Lawrie |
| | MacGregor |
| Glasgow | Penney Easton |
| | Speirs & Jeffrey |
| Lincoln | Hill Osborne |
| Liverpool | Tilney |
| London | Hoare Govett |
| | Cazenove |
| | de Zoete & Bevan |
| | Scrimgeour |
| Manchester | Henry Cooke, Lumsden |
| Middlesbrough | Stancliffe Todd & Hodgson |
| Newcastle | Wise Speke |
| Plymouth | Westlake |
| Reading | Heseltine Moss |
| South East | Quilter Goodison |

## *Britoil 1982, 1985*

### 1982 Sale

| | | |
|---|---|---|
| **Merchant Bank** | Government | Warburgs |
| | Company | Rothschilds |
| Brokers to the Issue | | Rowe & Pitman (Lead) |
| | | Hoare Govett |
| | | Cazenove |
| | | Wood Mackenzie |
| | | Greenwells |
| **Underwriters** | | Barings |
| | | Kleinworts |
| | | Schroders |
| | | Rothschilds (joint lead) |
| | | Warburgs (joint lead) |
| | | Morgan Grenfell |

**Other advisers**

| | |
|---|---|
| Solicitor to Government | Freshfields |
| Solicitor to Company | Herbert Smith |
| Solicitor to Underwriters | Ashurst, Morris, Crisp |
| Reporting Accountants | Thomson McLintock |
| Public Relations | Charles Barker |
| Receiving Banks | Lloyds (lead) Royal Bank of Scotland, Bank of Scotland |
| | |
| Independent Adviser on price | Fielding Newson Smith |

**1985 Sale**

| | | |
|---|---|---|
| **Merchant Bank** | Government | Lazards |
| | Company | Rothschilds |
| | Joint | Wood Gundy (Canada) |
| | | Swiss Bank Corp (Europe) |
| **Brokers** | Government | Hoare Govett |
| | Company | Cazenove |
| | | Wood Mackenzie |
| **Underwriters** | | Lazards (joint lead) |
| | | Barings |
| | | Schroders |
| | | Kleinworts |
| | | Rothschilds (joint lead) |
| | | Warburgs |
| | | Morgan Grenfell |

**Other Advisers**

| | |
|---|---|
| Solicitor to Government | Slaughter & May |
| Solicitor to Company | Herbert Smith |
| Solicitor to Underwriters | Freshfields |
| Reporting Accountant | Thomson McLintock |
| Public Relations | Dewe Rogerson |
| Advertising Agent | Dewe Rogerson |
| Printer | Burrup Mathieson |
| Registrar | NatWest |
| Receiving Banks | NatWest (Lead) |
| | Barclays |
| | Bank of Scotland |

**Regional Coordinators**

| | |
|---|---|
| London | Hoare Govett |
| | Cazenove |
| Aberdeen | Parsons |
| Belfast | Wm F Coates |
| Birmingham | Albert E Sharp |
| | Smith Keen Cutler |
| Bristol | Stock Beech |
| Cardiff | Lyddon |
| Edinburgh | Wood MacKenzie |

| Glasgow | Penney Easton |
| Lincoln | Hill Osborne |
| Liverpool | Tilney |
| Manchester | Henry Cooke, Lumsden |
| Middlesbrough | Stancliffe Todd & Hodgson |
| Newcastle | Wise Speke |
| Plymouth | Westlake |

## *Cable and Wireless 1981, 1983, 1985*

In 1981 Kleinwort, Benson was the Issuing House; in 1983 the Bank of England was the Issuing House in conjunction with Kleinworts.

### 1981 Sale

| **Merchant Bank** | Government | Kleinworts |
| | Company | Kleinworts |
| **Feasibility Study** | | Rothschilds |
| | | Barings |
| **Brokers to the Issue** | | Cazenove (Lead) |
| | | James Capel |
| | | Rowe & Pitman |
| **Underwriters** | | Kleinworts (Lead) |
| | | Barings |
| | | Schroders |

### Other advisers

| Independent Adviser on Price | Greenwells |
| Solicitors to Government | Linklaters & Paines |
| | Slaughter & May (Hong Kong) |
| Solicitors to Company | Speechly Bircham |
| | Johnson Stokes & Master (Hong Kong) |
| Reporting Accountant | Deloitte, Haskins & Sells (Deloittes) |
| Registrar/Receiving Bank | NatWest |
| Insurance Adviser | Willis Faber |
| Printer | Burrup Mathieson |
| Public Relations | Dewe Rogerson |

### 1983 Sale

| **Merchant Bank** | Government | Kleinworts |
| | Company | Kleinworts |
| Brokers to the Issue | | Mullens (Lead) |
| | | Cazenove |
| | | James Capel |
| | | Rowe and Pitman |
| **Underwriters** | | Kleinworts (Lead) |
| | | Barings |
| | | Schroders |
| | | Morgan Grenfell |

**Other advisers**

Solicitor to Government — Freshfields
Solicitor to Company — Speechly Bircham
Solicitor to Underwriters — Linklaters and Paines
Reporting Accountant — Deloittes
Registrar — NatWest
Receiving Banks — Bank of England / Bank of Scotland / Barclays / NatWest

Printer — Burrup Mathieson
Advertising Agents — Streets

**1985 Sale**

**Merchant Bank** — Government: Schroders; Company: Kleinworts; Joint: Dominion Securities Pitfield (Canada), Nomura (Japan)

**Brokers** — Government: Rowe and Pitman; Company: Cazenove

**Underwriters** — Schroders / Kleinworts / County Bank / Morgan Grenfell

**Other advisers**

Solicitor to Government — Freshfields
Solicitor to Company — Speechly Bircham
Solicitor to Underwriters — Linklaters & Paines
Reporting Accountant — Deloittes
Registrar — NatWest
Receiving Banks — NatWest (Lead) / Barclays / Midland / Bank of Scotland

Printer — Williams Lea
Public Relations (jointly) — Financial Strategy
Advertising Agents (jointly) — Collett, Dickenson Pearce – assisted by: Addison Design / Roundel Productions

**Regional Coordinators**

Belfast — Wm F Coates
Birmingham — Albert E Sharp / Margetts & Addenbrooke
Bristol — Stock Beech
Cardiff — Lyddon
Edinburgh — Bell, Lawrie MacGregor

| | |
|---|---|
| Glasgow | Penney Easton |
| Leicester | Hill Osborne |
| Liverpool | Tilney |
| London /SE | Rowe & Pitman |
| | Cazenove |
| Manchester | Henry, Cooke, Lumsden |
| | Pilling Trippier |
| Middlesbrough | Stancliffe, Todd & Hodgson |
| Newcastle | Wise Speke |
| Plymouth | Westlake |

## *Enterprise Oil 1984*

| | | |
|---|---|---|
| **Merchant Bank** | Government | Kleinworts |
| | | (Preliminary Advice) Warburgs |
| | British Gas | Lazards |
| **Broker to the Issue** | | Cazenove |
| | | de Zoete & Bevan (Joint) |
| **Underwriters** | | Morgan Grenfell |
| | | Schroders |
| | | Warburgs |
| | | Kleinworts |
| **Adviser on price** | | Wood Mackenzie |
| **Other advisers** | | |
| Solicitors to Government | | Freshfields |
| | | Allen & Overy (preliminary) |
| Solicitor to BGC | | Linklaters & Paines |
| Solicitor to Enterprise Oil | | Slaughter & May |
| Reporting Accountant | | Peat Marwick Mitchell |
| Accountant to BGC | | Price Waterhouse |
| Accountant to Enterprise Oil | | Peat Marwick Mitchell |
| Receiving Bank | | Barclays & Lloyds |
| Printer | | Williams Lea |
| Public Relations | | Streets |
| Management Recruitment Consultant | | Webb Bowen International |

## *International Aeradio 1983*

| | | |
|---|---|---|
| **Merchant Bank** | Government | Hill Samuel |
| | Company (BA) | Warburgs |

## *Jaguar 1984*

| | | |
|---|---|---|
| **Merchant Bank** | Government | Schroders |
| | BL | Hill Samuel |

| **Brokers to the Issue** | | Cazenove (Lead) |
| | | Laing & Cruickshank |
| **Underwriters** | | Hill Samuel |
| | | Kleinworts |

**Other advisers**
Solicitor to Vendor (BL)      Linklaters & Paines
Solicitor to Offer      Slaughter & May
Solicitor to Company      Coward Chance
Reporting Accountant      Coopers & Lybrand

## *National Bus Company 1986–87*

| **Principal Advisers** | Government | Warburgs (preliminary advice) |
| | | Price Waterhouse |
| | | Bankers Trust |
| | Company | Barclays de Zoete Wedd |
| **Other advisers** | | |
| Company Auditors | | Ernst & Whinney |
| Property advice | | Richard Ellis |

## *National Freight Consortium 1982*

| **Merchant Bank** | Government | Schroders |
| | Consortium | Barclays Merchant Bank |

**Other advisers**
Solicitor to Consortium and to offer      Ashurst, Morris Crisp & Co
Solicitor to NFC Group      Freshfields
Receiving Bank/Registrar      Lloyds Bank
Agent for Consortium      Barclays Merchant Bank (distributed
     prospectus to employees/pensioners)
Auditor & Reporting Accountant      Ernst & Whinney

## *Naval Dockyards Commercial Management 1986–87*

| **Merchant Bank** | Government | Samuel Montagu |
| **Other Advisers** | | |
| Accountant | | Coopers & Lybrand |
| Consultants | | Touche Ross |
| | | Fuller Peiser |
| | | Hay MSL |
| Independent Advisers | | John Ager |
| | | Tony Pott |

## *Rolls Royce 1987*

| | | |
|---|---|---|
| **Merchant Bank** | Government | Samuel Montagu |
| | Company | Rothschilds |
| **Brokers to the Issue** | Government | James Capel |
| | Company | Hoare Govett |
| **Underwriters** | | Samuel Montagu |
| | | Rothschilds |
| | | Barclays de Zoete Wedd |
| | | Barings |
| | | Charterhouse |
| | | County |
| | | Robert Fleming |
| | | Guinness Mahon |
| | | Hill Samuel |
| | | Lloyds |
| | | Morgan Grenfell |
| | | Schroders |
| | | Standard Chartered |
| | | TSB |

**Other advisers**

| | |
|---|---|
| Accountant | Coopers & Lybrand |
| Solicitor to Government | Linklaters & Paines |
| Solicitor to RR | Freshfields |
| Solicitor to Underwriters | Herbert Smith |
| Joint PR Adviser to Government & Company | Valin Pollen |
| Joint Advertising Agent to Government & Company | Collett Dickenson Pearce |
| Response handling house | Air Call Teledata |
| Printer | Oyez Press |
| Registrar | NatWest |
| Receiving Banks | NatWest (Lead) |
| | Barclays |
| | Midland |
| | Royal Bank of Scotland |
| Multiple Applications Investigator | Touche Ross |

**Regional Coordinators**

| | |
|---|---|
| Devon & Cornwall | Westlake |
| Avon, Somerset, Dorset, Wiltshire & Gloucestershire | Stock Beech |
| Dyfed, Glamorgan, Gwent & Powys | Lyddon |
| West Midlands, Warwickshire, Oxfordshire | Albert E Sharp |
| Staffordshire, Shropshire & Hereford & Worcester | Smith Keen Cutler |
| Nottinghamshire, Lincolnshire, Leicestershire & Northamptonshire | Hill Osborne |
| Suffolk, Norfolk & Cambridgeshire | Margetts & Addenbrooke |
| Merseyside, Cheshire, Clwyd, Gwynedd & Isle of Man | Charterhouse Tilney |

463

| | |
|---|---|
| Greater Manchester, Derbyshire & Lancashire | Henry Cooke Lumsden |
| North, West & South Yorkshire & Humberside | Rensburg |
| Tyne & Wear, Northumberland, Cumbria, Durham & Cleveland | Wise Speke |
| Strathclyde & Dumfries & Galloway | Parsons |
| Lothian, Fife, Central Scotland & Borders | Bell Lawrie |
| Grampian, Highlands & Islands & Tayside | Parsons |
| Northern Ireland | Wm F Coates |

## Royal Ordnance Factories 1987

| | | |
|---|---|---|
| **Merchant Bank** | Government | Rothschilds |
| | | Kleinworts (initial study) |
| | Company | Lazards |
| **Brokers to the Issue** | Government | Hoare Govett |
| **(appointed, but flotation** | Company | Cazenove |
| **not carried out)** | | Kleinwort Grieveson |
| **Other advisers** | | |
| Solicitor to Government | | Herbert Smith |
| Solicitor to Company | | Coward Chance |
| Accounting Adviser & Auditor | | Coopers & Lybrand |
| Consulting actuary | | R Watson & Company |
| Public Relations adviser (Joint) | | Granfield Rork Colins |
| Corporate Designer | | Wolff Olins |

## Sealink 1984

| | | |
|---|---|---|
| **Merchant Bank** | Government | Hill Samuel |
| | British Rail | Morgan Grenfell |

## Unipart 1987

| | | |
|---|---|---|
| **Merchant Bank** | Government | Samuel Montagu |
| | Company (BL) | Hill Samuel |
| **Brokers to the Issue** | | Laing & Cruickshank |
| **(appointed, but flotation** | | Cazenove |
| **not carried out)** | | |
| **Other advisers** | | |
| Accountant | | Coopers & Lybrand |
| Solicitor to Government | | Slaughter & May |
| Solicitor to BL | | Linklaters & Paines |
| Solicitor to Company | | Clifford Turner |

### *British Gas Wytch Farm 1984*

| | | |
|---|---|---|
| **Merchant Bank** | Government | Warburgs |
| | Company | Lazards |
| **Brokers to Issue & other advisers** | | Not applicable |

*Source*: From Official Committee on Nationalised Industry Policy, "Directory of Advisers Appointed in the Privatisation Programme", 29 February 1988, HM Treasury papers NIP(88)2.

# NOTES

## 1 NATIONALISATION TO PRIVATISATION: 1945–1979 – THE GENESIS OF A POLICY IDEA

1   P.F. Drucker (1969) *The Age of Discontinuity*, New York: Harper & Row; P.F. Drucker (1985) *Innovation and Entrepreneurship*, London: Pan Books, p.167.
2   David Howell (2000) *The Edge of Now: New Questions for Democracy in the Network Age*, London: Macmillan, p.34, suggests that a Conservative Political Committee document which he helped prepare, *A New Style of Government*, published in April 1970, was the first political publication in Britain to mention the word privatisation. Also on the origins of the term see D.Yergin and J.Stanislaw (1998) *The Commanding Heights: The Battle between Government and the Marketplace that is Remaking the World*, New York: Simon & Schuster.
3   M.Thatcher in London, 10 November 1986, in Collins, C. (ed.) *The Complete Public Statements of Margaret Thatcher 1945–1990 on CD Rom*, Oxford: Oxford University Press; also cited in E.H.H.Green (2006) *Thatcher*, London: Hodder Arnold, p.100.
4   M.Thatcher (1993) *The Downing Street Years*, London: HarperCollins; M. Thatcher (1995) *The Path to Power*, London: HarperCollins.
5   A. Smith (1910 ed.) *The Wealth of Nations*, vol. 1, London: J.M.Dent & Sons Ltd, p.306.
6   R. Millward (2000) "State Enterprise in Britain in the Twentieth Century", in P. Toninelli (ed.) *The Rise and Fall of State-Owned Enterprises in the Western World*, Cambridge: Cambridge University Press, p.159.
7   Ibid., p.165.
8   J. Foreman-Peck and R. Millward (1994) *Public and Private Ownership of British Industry 1820–1990*, Oxford: Clarendon Press, pp.41–61.
9   J. Foreman-Peck and M. Waterson (1984) "The Comparative Efficiency of Public and Private Enterprise in Britain: Electricity Generation between the World Wars", *Economic Journal*, conference papers, supplement to vol.95, pp.83–95; R. Millward and R. Ward (1987) "The Costs of Public and Private Gas Enterprises in late 19th Century Britain", *Oxford Economic Papers*, vol.39, pp.719–37.
10  Sir N. Chester (1975) *The Nationalisation of British Industry 1945–51*, London: HMSO, p.384.
11  L.J. Tivey (1966) *Nationalization in British Industry*, London: Jonathan Cape, p.46.
12  H.S. Morrison (1933) *Socialisation and Transport*, London: Constable, p.149.
13  G.N. Ostergaard (1954) "Labour and the Development of the Public Corporation", *Manchester School*, vol.22, pp.192–226. E.E. Barry (1965) *Nationalisation in British Politics: The Historical Background*, London: Jonathan Cape.
14  Chester, op.cit., pp.458–9.
15  Ibid., p.461.
16  L.Gordon (1938) *The Public Corporation in Great Britain*, London and New York: Oxford University Press, p.3.
17  Chester, op.cit., p.386.
18  Liberal Party (1928) *Britain's Industrial Future* (The Liberal Yellow Book), London: Liberal Party.

19  L.Hannah (1979) *Electricity before Nationalisation*, London: Macmillan; Foreman-Peck and Millward, op.cit., pp.282–3.
20  Chester, op.cit., pp.12–18.
21  Ibid., p.392.
22  As another example, the aircraft manufacturer Short Brothers in Northern Ireland succumbed to full state ownership during the War. The company became state-owned after a failure to meet production targets.
23  D. Greasley (1995) "The coal industry: Images and realities on the road to nationalisation", in R, Millward and J.Singleton (eds.), *The Political Economy of Nationalisation in Britain, 1920–50,* Cambridge: Cambridge University Press.
24  Labour Party (1945) *Let us Face the Future: A Declaration of Labour Policy for the Consideration of the Nation*, London: Labour Party.
25  Chester, op cit., p.19. At this juncture it is appropriate to observe that nationalised industries took on the public corporation form but that not all UK public corporations were nationalised industries and while the term public corporation describes a specific legal term of organisation, the term "nationalised industry" is not a legal term. In this Official History the terms used are interchangeable unless the distinction is significant.
26  Ibid., p.389.
27  Ibid., p.90.
28  Ibid., p.39.
29  The election of the Conservatives stopped a further nationalisation, of the sugar industry, planned by Labour.
30  The exception was where companies already existed prior to privatisation, as in the case, for example, of Cable and Wireless.
31  Ibid., p.270.
32  Coal Industry Nationalisation Act, 1946, cited in M.G. Webb (1973) *The Economics of Nationalized Industries*, London: Nelson, p.14.
33  Chester, op cit., p.645. The new Transport Commission was asked to progress the principles of a future rate structure for consideration by the Minister. In the meantime, the existing structure of charges on the railways continued; Chester, p.667.
34  Ibid., p.387.
35  W.A. Robson (1962) *Nationalized Industry and Public Ownership*, 2nd ed., London: Allen and Unwin. Admittedly, performance-related pay for senior management was less prevalent in the private sector in the 1940s and 1950s than it became later.
36  Chester, op cit., p.509.
37  D.Winchester (1983) "Industrial Relations in the Public Sector", in G.S.Bain (ed.) *Industrial Relations in Britain*, Oxford: Basil Blackwell.
38  Chester, op cit., pp.1025–6.
39  Ibid., p.450.
40  Ibid., pp.562–3.
41  Ibid., p.1024.
42  The industries remained funded by loan capital on which interest payments were made. In 1966 the capital structure of BOAC was divided into loans with fixed interest and Exchequer Dividend Capital (later renamed Public Dividend Capital) with payments based on financial performance. In 1969 this scheme was extended to the British Steel Corporation. The rationale for this (slight) movement away from a reliance on fixed interest loans was to help cushion industries especially subject to fluctuations in revenues from the effects of fixed interest payments. In reality, most of the nationalised industries remained dependent on internally generated funds for their capital investment programmes.
43  Chester, op cit., p.648.
44  Ibid., p.641 & 652.
45  Ibid., p.1043; A.H.Hanson (1954) "Labour and the Public Corporation", *Public Administration*, vol.32, pp.203–9. Tivey (1966), op cit.; L.J. Tivey (1973) "British Nationalization in the 1960s", in (ed.) L.J.Tivey *The Nationalized Industries since 1960: A book of Readings*, London: Royal Institute of Public Administration/George Allen & Unwin.

46    Chester, op.cit., pp.1036–7.
47    Ibid., p.958.
48    Ibid., p.1036.
49    D. Coombes (1971) *State Enterprise: Business or Politics?* London: Allen and Unwin;
      C.D.Foster (1971) *Politics, Finance and the Role of Economics: an essay in the control of public
      enterprises*, London: Allen and Unwin.
50    Webb, op cit., p.9.
51    Chester, op cit., p.1038.
52    The Minister of Fuel and Power to the Chairman of the NCB, in ibid., p.807.
53    Ibid., pp.922–3.
54    Ibid., pp.848–56.
55    Labour Party (1945) *Let us Face the Future: A Declaration of Labour Policy for the
      Consideration of the Nation*, London: Labour Party.
56    Chester op cit., p.973.
57    Ibid., p.640.
58    Although this did not appear to dim his optimism about the future of public ownership; R. Jenkins
      (1963) "Foreword" in M. Shanks (ed.) *The Lessons of Public Enterprise*, London: Jonathan Cape.
59    Ibid., p.8.
60    Select Committee on Nationalised Industries (1967–8) *Ministerial Control of the Nationalised
      Industries*, H.C.371, London: Her Majesty's Stationery Office.
61    HMSO (1961) *The Financial and Economic Obligations of the Nationalised Industries*,
      Cmnd.1337, London: Her Majesty's Stationery Office, para.2.
62    In reality, the pricing rule is more complicated than this because of possible externalities (external
      costs and benefits) and "second best" pricing in the private sector.
63    Correctly, the existence of a higher risk of default by the private sector than by government
      should mean that on average the cost of raising capital will be lower in the state sector.
64    HMSO (1967) *Nationalised Industries: a review of economic and financial objectives*,
      Cmnd.3427, London: Her Majesty's Stationery Office.
65    R. Millward (1976) "Price Restraint, Anti-inflation Policy and Public and Private Industry in
      the UK", *Economic Journal*, vol.86, pp.226–42.
66    NEDO was the administrative office of the National Economic Development Council with
      representation from unions, management and government, established in 1962 to act as a forum
      for discussions on national economic issues. NEDO would be abolished in 1992.
67    NEDO (1976–7) (National Economic Development Office) *A Study of UK Nationalised
      Industries: their role in the economy and control in the future*, London: Her Majesty's Stationery
      Office.
68    HMSO (1978) *The Nationalised Industries*, Cmnd.7131, London: Her Majesty's Stationery
      Office.
69    Ibid., 1978, para.68.
70    A.Nove (1973) *Efficiency Criteria for the Nationalised Industries*, London: Allen and Unwin;
      R.Kelf-Cohen (1973) *British Nationalisation 1945–73*, London: Macmillan; C. Harlow (1977)
      *Innovation and Productivity under Nationalization*, London: Allen and Unwin; D. Heald (1980)
      "The Economic and Financial Control of UK Nationalised Industries", *Economic Journal*, vol.90,
      pp.243–65. J.Redwood (1980) *Public Enterprise in Crisis: the Future of the Nationalised
      Industries*, Oxford: Basil Blackwell.
71    Webb, op cit., p.151.
72    Millward, op cit., p.174.
73    NEDO (1976) *A Study of UK Nationalised Industries: their role in the economy and control in
      the future*, Background Paper 3 "Output, Investment and Productivity", London: Her Majesty's
      Stationery Office.
74    R. Pryke (1971) *Public Enterprise in Practice: The British Experience of Nationalisation over
      Two Decades*, London: MacGibbon and Kee. A later study by Robert Millward on the
      performance of the nationalised industries between 1950 and 1985 has also suggested that
      productivity growth was as good as, if not better than, that achieved by the private manufacturing
      sector in Britain at the time, Millward, 2000, op cit. Other studies suggesting a more favourable

picture of the performance of the nationalised industries than commonly portrayed include Foreman-Peck and Millward, op cit., pp.309–11; and most recently C.H. Iordanoglou (2001) *Public Enterprise Revisited: A Closer Look at the 1954–79 UK Labour Productivity Record*, Cheltenham: Edward Elgar. The results are clearly sensitive to the performance measure used with the record of the nationalised industries much improved by using productivity measures rather than financial results.

75  N.M. Hamilton (1971) *Pricking Pryke: the Facts on State Industry*, London: Aims of Industry; G. Polanyi (1968) *Comparative Returns from Investment in Nationalised Industries*, London: Institute of Economic Affairs; G. Polanyi, and P. Polanyi (1971) "The Ailing Giants", in R.Boyson (ed.) *Goodbye to Nationalisation*, London: Churchill Press; G. Polanyi and P. Polanyi (1972) "The Efficiency of Nationalised Industries", *Moorgate and Wall Street Review*, spring, pp.17–49; G. Polanyi and P. Polanyi (1974) *Failing the Nation: the Record of the Nationalised Industries*, London: Fraser Ansbacher.

76  One account suggests an even weaker position for the nationalised industries with earnings before interest and tax estimated to have ranged between –0.4% and 1.1% in the period 1972–82; S. Brittan (1984) "The Politics and Economics of Privatization", *Political Quarterly*, vol.55, p.128.

77  R. Pryke (1981) *The Nationalised Industries: Policies and Performance since 1968*, Oxford: Martin Robertson; R. Pryke (1982) "The Comparative Performance of Public and Private Enterprise", *Fiscal Studies*, vol.3, no.2, pp.68–81.

78  MMC (Monopolies and Mergers Commission) (1980a) T*he Inner London Letter Post: a Report on the Letter Post Service in the Area Comprising the Numbered London Postal Districts*, HC 515, London: Her Majesty's Stationery Office; MMC (1980b) *Domestic Gas Appliances: A Report on the Supply of Certain Domestic Gas Appliances in the United Kingdom*, HC703, Session 1979–80, London: HMSO; MMC (1981) *Central Electricity Generating Board: a Report on the Operation by the Board of its System for the Generation and Supply of Electricity in Bulk*, HC 315, London: HMSO; MMC (1983) *National Coal Board: a Report on the Efficiency and Cost in the Development, Production and Supply of Coal by the NCB*, Cmnd. 8920, London: HMSO.

79  This point has been reiterated by many who lived through this period interviewed during the writing of this History.

80  G. Howe (1981) *Privatisation: The Way Ahead*, pamphlet based on a speech given to the Selsdon Group 1 July 1981, London: Conservative Political Centre and quoted from in the brief on nationalised industries and privatisation for the Debate on the Address, 9 November 1982, in E(DL) Part 6.

81  D. Healey (1989) *The Time of My Life*, London: Michael Joseph, p.580. In the 1945–51 Labour Governments Clement Attlee was Prime Minister.

82  A. Shleifer (1998) "State versus Private Ownership", *Journal of Economic Perspectives*, vol.12, pp.133–50.

83  F.A.Hayek (1948) *Individualism and Economic Order*, Chicago: University of Chicago Press, p.79.

84  F.A. Hayek (1944) *The Road to Serfdom*, London: Routledge

85  She wrote later, *The Road to Serfdom* was "the most powerful critique of socialist planning and the socialist state which I read at this time [the late 1940s] and to which I have returned so often since"; Thatcher, 1995, p.50. She went on to say that the full implication of Hayek's argument was fully grasped only in the mid-1970s "when Hayek's works were right at the top of the reading list given me by Keith Joseph".

86  Cited in R. Cockett (1994) *Thinking the Unthinkable: Think Tanks and the Economic Counter Revolution, 1931–1983*, London: Harper Collins, pp.173–5. Also see J. Campbell (2001) *Margaret Thatcher, Volume One: The Grocer's Daughter*, London: Pimlico, p.60.

87  Thatcher (1995) op cit., p.254; Cockett, op cit., p.173; Campbell, op cit., p.372. Ralph Harris helped to write some of Mrs Thatcher's speeches in the 1970s.

88  J.M. Buchanan (1972) *Theory of Public Choice*, Michigan: University of Michigan Press; J.M. Buchanan (1978) "From Private Preference to Public Philosophy: The Development of Public Choice", in J.M. Buchanan et al., *The Economics of Politics*, IEA Readings 18, London:

Institute of Economic Affairs; G. Tullock (1965) *The Politics of Bureaucracy*, Washington, DC: Public Affairs Press; G. Tullock (1976) *The Vote Motive*, London: Institute of Economic Affairs; W.A. Niskanen (1971) *Bureaucracy and Representative Government*, Chicago: Aldine; D.C. Mueller (1976) "Public Choice: a Survey", *Journal of Economic Literature*, vol.14, no.2, pp.395–433; C.B. Blankart (1983) "The contribution of public choice to public utility economics: a survey", in ed. J. Fissinger *Public Sector Economics*, London: Macmillan; and W.C. Mitchell (1988) *Government As It Is*, Hobart Paper 109, London: Institute of Economic Affairs for good overviews of the theory.

89  Niskanen (1971) op cit., p.38.

90  S.C. Littlechild (1978) *The Fallacy of the Mixed Economy: An 'Austrian' critique of recent economic thinking and policy*, Hobart Paper 80, London: Institute of Economic Affairs; R.E. Caves (1990) "Lessons from Privatization in Britain: State Enterprise Behavior, Public Choice, and Corporate Governance", *Journal of Economic Behavior and Organization*, vol.13, pp.145–69.

91  A. Dunsire, K. Hartley, D. Parker and B. Dimitriou (1988) "Organisational status and performance: a conceptual framework for testing public choice theories", *Public Administration*, vol.66, no.4, pp.363–88; A. Dunsire and C. Hood (1989) *Cutback Management in Public Bureaucracies: Popular Theories and Observed Outcomes in Whitehall*, Cambridge: Cambridge University Press; P. Dunleavy (1991) *Democracy, Bureaucracy and Public Choice: Economic Approaches in Political Science*, London: Harvester-Wheatsheaf; H.G. Rainey (1991) *Understanding and Managing Public Organizations*, San Francisco, CA: Jossey-Bass; L. Udehn (1996) *The Limits of Public Choice: a sociological critique of the economic theory of politics*, London: Routledge; J.Willner and D.Parker (2007) "The Performance of Public and Private Enterprise under Conditions of Active and Passive Ownership and Competition and Monopoly", *Journal of Economics*, vol.90, no.3, pp.221–53.

92  For example, G. Yarrow (1986) "Privatisation in Theory and Practice", *Economic Policy*, vol.2, pp.319–78; J. Vickers and G. Yarrow (1988) *Privatization: An Economic Analysis*, Cambridge, Mass.: MIT Press; M. Boycko, A. Shleifer and R.W. Vishny (1996) "A Theory of Privatisation", *Economic Journal*, vol.106, March, pp.309–19.

93  S.A. Ross (1973) "The Economic Theory of Agency: the Principal's Problem", *American Economic Review*, vol.62, pp.134–9.

94  D.E.M. Sappington and J.E. Stiglitz (1987) "Privatization, Information and Incentives", *Journal of Policy Analysis and Management*, vol.6, no.4, pp.567–82; Vickers and Yarrow, op cit., ch.2; C. Shapiro and R.D. Willig (1990) "Economic Rationales for the Scope of Privatization", in E.N. Suleiman and J. Waterbury (eds.) *The Political Economy of Public Sector Reform and Privatization*, Boulder, Colorado: Westview Press; A. Shleifer and R. Vishny (1994) "Politicians and Firms", *Quarterly Journal of Economics*, vol.109, pp.995–1025.

95  H.G. Manne (1965) "Mergers and the Market for Corporate Control", *Journal of Political Economy*, vol.73, pp.110–20; E.G. Furubotn and S. Pejovich (1972) "Property Rights and Economic Theory: a Survey of the Recent Literature", *Journal of Economic Literature*, vol.10, pp.1137–62; E.G. Furubotn and S. Pejovich (1974) *The Economics of Property Rights*, Cambridge, Mass.: Ballinger; M. Jensen and W.R. Meckling (1976) "Theory of the firm: managerial behaviour, agency costs and ownership structure", *Journal of Financial Economics*, vol.3, pp.305–60; E.F. Fama and M.C. Jensen (1983) "Separation of Ownership and Control", *Journal of Law and Economics*, vol.26, pp.301–25.

96  A.A. Alchian (1965) "Some Economics of Property Rights", *Il Politico*, vol.30, pp.816–29; L. De Alessi (1980) "The economics of property rights: a review of the evidence", *Research in Law and Economics*, vol.2, pp.1–47; D. Bös (1991) *Privatization: a Theoretical Treatment*, Oxford: Clarendon Press.

97  A recent paper has suggested that "extrinsic motivations" in the public sector, such as the award of titles, medals and other honours, may be effective in promoting good performance; B.S.Frey and M.Benz (2005) "Can Private Learn from Public Governance?", *The Economic Journal*, vol.115, November, pp.F377-F396. However, whether such incentives can ever be as powerful as the profit motive remains questionable.

98  Dunsire, et al., op cit.

99    A. Singh (1971) *Takeovers, their Relevance to the Stock Market and the Theory of the Firm*, Cambridge: Cambridge University Press; A. Singh (1975) "Takeovers, Economic Natural Selection and the Theory of the Firm: Evidence from Post-war UK Experience", *Economic Journal*, vol.85, pp.497–515; T. Jenkinson and C. Mayer (1994) *Hostile Takeovers: Defence, Attack and Corporate Governance*, London: McGraw-Hill.

100   For example, see K. Cowling, P. Stoneman, J. Cubbin, J. Cable, G. Hall, S. Domberger, and P. Dutton (1980) *Mergers and Economic Performance*, Cambridge: Cambridge University Press; Jenkinson and Mayer, op cit.

101   S. Grossman and O.D. Hart (1980) "Takeover bids, the free-rider problem, and the theory of the corporation", *Bell Journal of Economics*, vol.94, pp.691–719.

102   Of course, if public sector firms resort to state subsidies when damaged by competition then the efficiency incentives are further dulled. Some would argue that Government is unlikely to allow a public enterprise to fail. Equally, however, large private sector firms may be bailed out by government because of the serious effect of their collapse on economic activity and social conditions.

103   S. Martin and D. Parker (1997) *The Impact of Privatisation: Ownership and Corporate Performance in the UK*, London: Routledge, chapter 1.

104   The term is named after Vilfredo Pareto, an Italian economist.

105   W.W. Sharkey (1982) *The Theory of Natural Monopoly*, Cambridge: Cambridge University Press.

106   G. Stigler (1971) "The theory of economic regulation", *Bell Journal of Economics and Management Science*, vol.2, no.1, pp.3–21; S. Peltzman (1976) "Toward a more general theory of regulation", *Journal of Law and Economics*, vol.14, August, pp.109–48; G. Becker (1983) "A theory of competition among pressure groups for political influence", *Quarterly Journal of Economics*, vol. 98, pp.371–400.

107   The exception is regulation to promote competition or "competition policy". In 1980 the new Conservative Government would augment the powers of the Monopolies and Mergers Commission especially in relation to the nationalised industries. Competition policy involves "ex post" regulation by penalising anti-competitive conduct rather than "ex ante" regulation, which involves establishing detailed rules of business behaviour. The deregulation agenda is more compatible with ex post than ex ante regulation.

108   H. Averch and L.L. Johnson (1962) "Behavior of the Firm under Regulatory Constraint", *American Economic Review*, vol.52, pp.1052–69.

109   E.E. Bailey (1973) *Economic Theory of Regulatory Constraint*, Lexington: D.C.Heath & Co.

110   W.J. Baumol (1982) "Contestable Markets: an uprising in the theory of industry structure", *American Economic Review*, vol.72, no.1, pp.1–15; W.J. Baumol, J.C. Panzar and R.D. Willig (1982) *Contestable Markets and the Theory of Industry Structure*, New York: Harcourt Brace and Jovanovich.

111   Contestable market theory also contributed to deregulation, for example of airline travel.

112   H. Demsetz (1968) "Why Regulate Utilities?" *Journal of Law and Economics*, vol.11, no.1, pp.55–65.

113   J.M. Keynes (1936) *The General Theory of Employment, Interest and Money*, New York: Harcourt Brace.

114   An important development in the evolution of monetarism from the 1970s was "rational expectations theory" in which economic agents respond rationally to economic phenomena including price rises. This theory helped discredit the prevailing view that governments could trade off lower unemployment against higher inflation.

115   M. Friedman and R. Friedman (1980) *Free to Choose*, London: Secker & Warburg.

116   R.W. Bacon and W.A. Eltis (1976) *Britain's Economic Problem: Too Few Producers*, London: Macmillan.

117   J.A. Kay and D.J. Thompson (1986) "Privatisation: a policy in search of a rationale", *Economic Journal*, vol.96, March, p.19.

## 2 THE CONSERVATIVE PARTY, NATIONALISATION AND THE 1979 GENERAL ELECTION

1   H. Macmillan (1938) *The Middle Way: A Study of the Problem of Economic and Social Progress in a Free and Democratic Society*, London: Macmillan.

2   Richard Austen Butler, invariably referred to as Rab.

3   The Bow Group was founded in 1950 and took its name from the Bow & Bromley Constitutional Club where its first meeting was held. It was established to be the focus for new ideas within the Conservative Party.

4   S. Ball and A. Seldon. (eds.) (1996) *The Heath Government 1970–74: a reappraisal*, London: Longman, pp.143–6.

5   A. Denham and M. Garnett (2001) *Keith Joseph,* Chesham: Acumen Publishing Ltd, p.167.

6   Ibid..

7   N. Ridley (1991) *'My Style of Government': The Thatcher Years,* London: Hutchinson, pp.3–4.

8   Conservative Party (1970) *A Better Tomorrow*, London: Conservative Party.

9   The Labour Government had introduced a National Port Corporation Bill which fell with the calling of the General Election. The Bill would have nationalised the trust ports and the Port of London and merged them with the state's existing ports run by the British Transport Docks Board.

10  Ball and Seldon, op cit., p.13.

11  P. Cosgrave (1978) *Margaret Thatcher: A Tory and her Party,* London: Hutchinson, p.81.

12  Campbell (2001) p.201. In September 1969 an earlier meeting of the Conservative leadership had occurred at Sundridge Park to discuss future economic strategy. However, the Selsdon Park meeting is the one that attracted the most public attention. David Howell reveals on these meetings that, "The results were mixed. Most shadow ministers clearly received the message, with varying shades of enthusiasm, that the public sector had to be reduced. . . . Most future ministers also seemed to grasp that this was not going to be a simple matter . . ."; D. Howell (2000) *The Edge of Now: New Questions for Democracy in the Network Age,* London: Macmillan, p.339.

13  M. Thatcher (1995) *The Path to Power*, London: HarperCollins, p.160; J. Campbell (1993) *Edward Heath: A Biography*, London: Jonathan Cape, pp.264–5.

14  D. Young (1990) *The Enterprise Years: A Businessman in the Cabinet*, London: Heedline, p.15.

15  N. Tebbit (1988) *Upwardly Mobile,* London: Weidenfeld and Nicolson, p.94.

16  E. Heath (1998) *The Course of My Life: My Autobiography*, London: Hodder & Stoughton, p.329.

17  Ibid., p.330.

18  The Conservative Manifesto in 1970 stated bluntly "Labour's compulsory wage control was a failure and we will not repeat it" (Conservative Party, 1970).

19  J.Bruce-Gardyne (1984) *Mrs Thatcher's First Administration*, London: Macmillan, p.79

20  Ball and Seldon (ed.), op cit., pp.148–9.

21  Heath, op cit., p.343.

22  Ibid., pp.585–6.

23  Campbell (1993), p.301.

24  Tebbit, op cit., pp.101–3; Campbell (1993), op cit., p.330.

25  Campbell (1993), p.418.

26  Campbell (1993), pp.460–4.

27  Heath, op cit., p.329.

28  Ibid., p.342; Ball and Seldon eds. (1996), p.149.

29  Heath, op cit., p.343.

30  Ibid., p.339. DTI (Department of Trade and Industry) (1973) *Rolls-Royce Ltd and the RB211 Aero-engine*, Cmnd. 4860, London: Her Majesty's Stationery Office.

31  Heath, op cit., p.341.

32  Ibid., p.340. Campbell (1993), p.332.

33  Thatcher, op cit., p.207.

34  Tebbit, op cit., p.103.

35   Campbell (1993), p.443.
36   Heath, op cit., p.348.
37   Thatcher, op cit., p.215.
38   Heath never accepted that the Government did a U-turn on industrial policy during his years as Prime Minister (Heath, op cit., p.330), although few appeared to agree with this assessment at the time, or since.
39   Heath, op cit., p.348.
40   Ibid., p.400.
41   Ball and Seldon (1996), p.142.
42   Cited in Ball and Seldon (1996), p.140.
43   Heath, op cit., pp.400–1.
44   Ball and Seldon, op cit., pp.156–7. Heath made his famous remark in 1973. From the 1960s Tiny Rowland transformed Lonrho into a major corporation with international mining interests but was criticised for running the company as a personal fiefdom. A boardroom row and an unsuccessful attempt to dislodge him ensued.
45   The total cost of the modernisation programme was expected to be around £3bn over 10 years.
46   Campbell (1993), p.455.
47   Heath, op cit., pp.413–5.
48   Ridley, op cit., p.5.
49   Heath, op cit., p.400.
50   Ridley, op cit., p.4.
51   K. Baker (1993) *The Turbulent Years: My Life in Politics,* London: Faber & Faber, p.36.
52   Heath, op cit., p.416.
53   R.Lewis (1975) *Margaret Thatcher: A Personal and Political Biography,* London: Routledge & Keegan Paul, Chapter 11. Also standing against Heath was Hugh Fraser a right-wing backbencher but he was never a serious contender. The real contest in the first ballot was between Heath and Thatcher.
54   The other candidates in the second round were Sir Geoffrey Howe, Jim Prior and John Peyton.
55   Thatcher, op cit., p.261.
56   W. Keegan (1984) *Mrs Thatcher's Economic Experiment,* Harmondsworth: Penguin Books, p.52.
57   Heath, op cit., p.520.
58   R. Skidelsky (1988) "Introduction", R. Skidelsky (ed.) *Thatcherism,* London: Chatto & Windus, p.14.
59   Baker, op cit., p.42.
60   Ibid.
61   Thatcher, op cit., p.239.
62   Ibid., p.251.
63   Thatcher, op cit., pp.165–93; Campbell (2001), pp.227–8.
64   Cited in Cosgrave, op cit., p.95.
65   Campbell (2001), pp.77–8, 82.
66   D. Kavanagh (1987) *Thatcherism and British Politics: The End of Consensus?,* Oxford: Oxford University Press, p.10.
67   K. Harris (1988) *Thatcher,* London: Weidenfeld and Nicolson, p.41.
68   B. Arnold (1984) *Margaret Thatcher: A Study in Power,* London: Hamish Hamilton, p.38. The idiosyncratic psychological study of Thatcher by Abse (1989, p.112) attributes her views to "inner insecurities" in her childhood. However, there is no serious evidence to back up the claim. The suggestion should be dismissed.
69   Campbell (2001) op cit., p.179.
70   Ibid., p.91. "No politician since Churchill has appealed so emotionally to British nationalism", ibid., p.409.
71   Ibid., p.182.
72   Ibid., pp.245–6.
73   Thatcher, op cit., p.196.
74   M. Thatcher (1993) *The Downing Street Years,* London: HarperCollins; Thatcher (1995), op cit.

75  Lord Carrington (1988) *Reflect on Things Past: The Memoirs of Lord Carrington*, London: Collins, p.276.

76  S.R. Letwin (1992) *The Anatomy of Thatcherism*, London: Fontana, pp.88–9.

77  D. Butler and D. Kavanagh (1979) *The British General Election of 1979*, London: Macmillan, p.13.

78  HM Treasury (1976) *Cash Limits in Public Expenditure*, Cmnd.6440; Healey, op cit., pp.429–30; D.Wass (2008) *Decline to Fall: The Making of British Macro-Economic Policy and the 1976 IMF Crisis*, Oxford: Oxford University Press, pp.290–304.

79  J. Callaghan (1987) *Time and Chance*, London: Collins, p.426. Not that this prevented the Labour Party Conference from passing resolutions in favour of even more public spending. Keegan (1984, pp.89–91) has questioned the sincerity of Callaghan's speech, seeing it as an attempt to placate the financial markets that were in a state of panic at the time and especially the US Treasury whose support was needed to obtain further funding from the IMF.

80  Lord Blake (1976) "A Changed Climate", in Lord Blake and J. Patten (eds.) (1976) *The Conservative Opportunity*, London: Macmillan, p.7.

81  A. Clark (1998) *The Tories: Conservatives and the Nation State, 1922–1997*, London: Weidenfeld & Nicolson, p.385.

82  Harris, op cit., p.59. Also, as one of her earliest biographers noted: "To a considerable extent, when the predominantly male composition of the Conservative Parliamentary Party elected her as their leader, they changed history in a way in which the majority of them did not fully understand at the time." E. Money (1975) *Margaret Thatcher – First Lady of the House*, London: Leslie Freewin Publishers.

83  Thatcher (1995), pp.442–56. However, in her autobiography covering her period as Prime Minister, Thatcher generously pays tribute to Thorneycroft for helping her win the 1979 Election; M. Thatcher (1993) *The Downing Street Years*, London: HarperCollins, p.152.

84  At the press conference on 11 February 1975 after winning the leadership contest, Thatcher acknowledged that she was "pledged to offer Mr. Heath a place [in the shadow Cabinet] if he wishes to have it"; M. Thatcher (1975) Press Conference after winning Conservative leadership, 11 February 1975, Conservative Central Office, http://www.margaretthatcher.org/speeches/displaydocument.asp?docid=102487. But the pledge was not sincere – "In fact, I privately hoped that he would not take up my offer at all" – and was received by Heath with equal ill will; Thatcher, op cit, pp.282–3.

85  A. Seldon and D. Collings (2000) *Britain under Thatcher*, Harlow: Longman, p.5.

86  Thatcher (1995, p.291) states that by ensuring that the shadow "Treasury team . . . shared my and Keith's views on the free-market economy, [this] shifted the balance of opinion within the shadow Cabinet as a whole somewhat in my direction". The emphasis should be placed on "somewhat".

87  Howe is on record as believing that the IEA was very important in determining the direction of Conservative Party policy after 1979; for example, G.Howe (2006) "Influence at arm's length: Arthur Seldon's Influence on policy making and politicians", *Economic Affairs*, June, p.76. Dr Rhodes Boyson in his memoirs pays tribute to Ralph Harris and Arthur Seldon at the IEA for helping to shape his ideas (Boyson, 1995, p.91,119). In May 1978 he wrote a book, *Centre Forward: A Radical Conservative Programme*, which called on the next Conservative Government to pursue full-scale denationalisation, lower government expenditure, lower taxation, strengthened law and order, and the end to all trade union legal privileges. Earlier, in 1971, he had edited a volume with the provocative title, *Goodbye to Nationalisation*.

88  Cockett, op cit., p.163, 167.

89  Ibid., p.176.

90  Ibid., p.158.

91  P. Cosgrave (1978) *Margaret Thatcher: A Tory and her Party*, London: Hutchinson, pp.87–8.

92  Denham and Garnett, op cit., p.322.

93  The Selsdon Group was formed as a fringe group of the Conservative Party in September 1973 and projected what would later be described as a Thatcherite free market agenda; Cockett, op cit., p.213.

94 Thatcher, op cit., p.265. One of its members, John Nott, attributes the development of what became known as Thatcherism as much to this Club as to the better known Centre for Policy Studies; J. Nott (2002) *Here Today, Gone Tomorrow: Reflections of an Errant Politician,* London: Politico's Publishing, p.138. Other members were "sound money men" such as Jock Bruce-Gardyne and John Biffen.
95 Nott, op cit., p.173.
96 One study has claimed that economic liberalism was championed in the 1970s by around 50 people, mostly males; Cockett, op cit., pp.3–4.
97 Thatcher, op cit., p.221.
98 Denham and Garnett, op cit., pp.239–41; Thatcher, op cit., p.252.
99 Cited in Cockett, op cit., p.238.
100 However, Sherman's influence was short-lived. His blunt and critical manner alienated many who worked with him; Ridley, op cit, p.7. Thatcher more gently criticises his otherworldliness: "He was more interested, it seemed to me, in the philosophy behind policies than the policies themselves"; Thatcher, op cit., p.251.
101 K. Middlemas (1991) *Power, Competition and the State volume 3, The End of the Postwar Era: Britain since 1974*, London: Macmillan, p.198, 219.
102 Young, op cit., p.29.
103 Lord Blake (1976) "A Changed Climate", in Lord Blake and J. Patten (eds.) (1976) *The Conservative Opportunity*, London: Macmillan, p.12.
104 Ridley, op cit., pp.13–14.
105 "I never felt much affection for *The Right Approach to the Economy*. Unlike *The Right Approach* of 1976, it made little impact either on the outside world or on the policy we would pursue as a Government"; Thatcher, 1995, p.404.
106 J. Redwood (1976) "Managing the Economy" in Blake and Patten (eds.) op cit., p.75.
107 Conservative Party (1976) *The Right Approach – A Statement of Conservative Aims*, London, p.10, 18.
108 Ibid., p.33.
109 Conservative Party (1977) *The Right Approach to the Economy*, London, p.34,47.
110 M.Heseltine (2000) *Life in the Jungle: My Autobiography,* London: Coronet Books, pp.163–75.
111 M.Thatcher (1979a) Article for *Western Mail* "The kind of society I would most like to live in . . .", 1 May, http://www.margaretthatcher.org/speeches/displaydocument.asp?docid=104057. M.Thatcher (1979b) General Election Press Conference, 2 May, Conservative Central Office, http://www.margaretthatcher.org/speeches/displaydocument.asp?docid=104069.
112 Heseltine, op cit., p.176.
113 Butler and Kavanagh (1979), p.78.
114 Heseltine, op cit., pp.176–7. Thatcher skirts over the row in her memoirs; Thatcher (1995), p.300.
115 F. Pym (1984) *The Politics of Consent*, London: Hamish Hamilton, p.6.
116 Denham and Garnett, op cit., p.304.
117 P. Junor (1983) *Margaret Thatcher: Wife, Mother, Politician*, London: Sidgwick & Jackson, p.117.
118 The views are articulated in Ian Gilmour's book *Inside Right* published in 1977. Ian (later Lord) Gilmour served in Heath's Cabinet as Defence Secretary and would serve in the first Thatcher Government as Lord Privy Seal from 1979 until September 1981.
119 Campbell (2001) op cit., p.325.
120 Ibid., p.367.
121 Lord Gowrie (1976) "Industrial Relations", in Blake and Patten (eds.), op cit., p.139.
122 Thatcher, op cit., pp.421–2.
123 Ibid., p.414.
124 Harris, op cit., p.76. S. Blake and A. John (2003) *The World According to Margaret Thatcher*, London: Michael O'Mara Books Ltd, p.38.
125 Conservative Party (1979) *Conservative Party General Election Manifesto*, London.
126 Seldon and Collings, op cit., p.6.
127 Closed shop agreements restricted the employment of labour to union members and sometimes new recruits to applicants endorsed by the industry union or local union officials.

128    Campbell (2001) op cit., p.439.
129    Heath, op cit., p.523.
130    Baker, op cit., p.41.
131    Thatcher (1995), op cit., p.246.
132    Nott, op cit., p.185.
133    J. Prior (1986) *A Balance of Power*, London: Hamish Hamilton, p.112.
134    Lord Hailsham (1990) *A Sparrow's Flight: The Memoirs of Lord Hailsham of St Marylebone*, London: Collins, p.406.
135    P. Sinclair (1976) "The Economic Roles of the State", in Blake and Patten (eds.), op cit., p.63.
136    J. Redwood (1976) "Managing the Economy", in Blake and Patten (eds.), p.75.
137    Aims (1978) *Still more Galloping Nationalization*, London: Aims, The Free Enterprise Organisation.
138    Ridley, op cit., pp.15–16. Consistent with his 1968 report, Ridley again suggested that privatising gas, electricity and water supply would be impractical. Ridley did stress the desirability of breaking up many of the nationalised industries into smaller units before they were sold off. In a number of the later privatisations this did not occur.
139    N. Lawson (1992) *The View from No.11: Memoirs of a Tory Radical*, London: Bantam Press, p.199.
140    Conservative Research Department, *The Campaign Guide*, 1979, London. A further briefing from the Conservative Research Department on the Party's 1979 Manifesto confirmed the very limited commitment to denationalisation, conceding: that even for aerospace and shipbuilding we "are not committed unequivocally to denationalisation" (p.61); that the National Freight Corporation would have to become profitable before it could be denationalised (p.62); that while profitable enterprises currently under the NEB's control (e.g. Ferranti) should be sold, "We have not said we will abolish the NEB" and that there was a case for retaining a body to nurse back to health enterprises in temporary trouble (pp.64–5). Also, the briefing reminded that the Party had made no commitment on the future ownership of British Leyland and Rolls-Royce (p.68); and that while the future of BNOC would be reviewed on taking office, there was no pledge to abolish it (p.83); Conservative Research Department (1979) *"Tory Pledges Briefs": Briefing on the Conservative Manifesto* 1979, London, 5 April.
141    Thatcher (1979b), op cit..
142    Campbell (2001) op cit., p.438.
143    Ibid., p.387.
144    "We have made absolutely no statement about BP and we shall leave our hands completely open. We have no intention of just selling the lot off just like that, no intention whatsoever."
145    Interview with Lord Howe, 3 December 2006.
146    Butler and Kavanagh, op cit., p.338.
147     Keegan, op cit., p.111.
148    Skidelsky, op cit..
149    Butler and Kavanagh, op cit., p.340.
150    R. Behrens (1980) *The Conservative Party from Heath to Thatcher: Policies and Politics 1974–1979*, Farnborough: Saxon House
151    Ridley, op cit., p.13.

## 3 BALANCING THE BOOKS: PRIVATISATION AND THE 1979–83 GOVERNMENT

1    Privatisation: the UK Experience, Chancellor of the Exchequer's speech in Paris 15 December 1988, E(DL), Part 16. E(DL) files are the papers of the Cabinet Sub-Committee on Disposals. Also see footnote 3.
2    Thatcher (1993) *The Downing Street Years*, London: HarperCollins. p.45.
3    C(83)5, "Economic Strategy Memorandum by the Chancellor of the Exchequer", 1 February 1983. C indicates Cabinet meeting paper, the figure in parenthesis is the year, and the final figure is the paper number. A similar convention applies to E Committee and E(DL) Sub-Committee papers in this and subsequent chapters. Burton and Parker (1991), "Rolling Back the State? UK

Tax and Government Spending Changes in the 1980s", *British Review of Economic Issues*, vol.13, no.31, p.40, give slightly higher figures for taxation as a percentage of GDP but the same trend.

4    In correspondence on 9 and 10 May 1979 Joseph and Howe privately agreed that the earlier report from the Party policy group chaired by Nicholas Ridley in 1978 should form the framework for future reform of the nationalised industries; Policy towards the Nationalised Industries, Nationalised Industries files, Cabinet Office, Part 1. However, it was far from clear at this time that the view of Howe and Joseph would hold sway in the Cabinet. In any case, the report included some denationalisation but had also been concerned with how best to manage the nationalised industries. The shadow Cabinet had largely ignored it, see chapter 2, p.49.

5    As one of the Ministers, Norman Tebbit, remarks: "just as she balanced her original shadow Cabinet with due respect to her former colleagues in Ted Heath's Cabinet, so her first Cabinet was largely its shadow given substance." N. Tebbit (2005), "On the inner culture of the Tories" in S. Roy and J. Clarke (eds.) *Margaret Thatcher's Revolution: How It Happened and What it Meant*, London and New York: Continuum, p.20.

6    Lawson (1992), p.199. He concludes: "privatization was a central plank of our policy right from the start." This conclusion may be coloured by subsequent policy developments. In any case, there is no claim that the *scale* of the subsequent privatisations was anticipated. Lawson includes David Howell and John Nott in his list of Ministers who were enthusiasts for privatisation. Howell's subsequent performance as Secretary of State for Energy suggests that his enthusiasm was too easily subdued when faced with the realities of privatising assets, as detailed below and in chapter 4.

7    Interviews with former Ministers.

8    Conservative party, Ministerial Dossiers, 1979, Treasury, p.5, Transport, p.3. I would like to thank Sir Adam Ridley for providing me with access to his collection of these dossiers. The point is also made in some ministerial memoirs, e.g. D. Howell (2000) *The Edge of Now: New Questions for Democracy in the Network Age*, London: Macmillan, p.84.

9    C(79)1, "The Queen's Speech on the Opening of Parliament", 8 July 1979.

10   E(DL)(79), 2nd meeting, 20 June 1979, E(DL) Part 1; E(DL)(79), 6th meeting, 4 October 1979.

11   Green (2006), p.98.

12   C(79) 2nd meeting conclusions, 17 May 1979; C(79)4, "Public Expenditure: Scope for Cuts. Memorandum by the Chief Secretary, Treasury", 14 May 1979.

13   C(79)4.

14   C(79) 2nd meeting conclusions; H. Stephenson (1980) *Mrs Thatcher's First Year*, London: Jill Norman Ltd., p.47; Thatcher (1993), p.50.

15   Extract from Treasury letter of 23 May 1979, in E(DL)1st meeting papers.

16   C(79) 2nd meeting conclusions.

17   C(79)4th meeting conclusions, 31 May 1979.

18   Ibid.

19   Nor was the issuing of a Direction to require an asset sale to take a specific form problem free. This is discussed where relevant in later chapters. NIP (79) 42, "Power of Specific Direction: Report by the Official Committee on Nationalised Industry Policy", HM Treasury papers, Filefolder 11271559.There would be continuing uncertainty within Government about Ministerial powers to force through asset sales over the following months.

20   Ibid.; C(79)13, "Public Expenditure Reductions 1979–80. Memorandum by the Chief Secretary, Treasury", 29 May 1979.

21   Its title became the Ministerial Steering Committee on Economic Strategy, Sub-Committee on Economic Affairs.

22   In this Official History Margaret Thatcher's papers (PM Papers) have been used when accessing E Committee and E(DL) Committee proceedings. These files not only include the usual minutes and memoranda but associated correspondence and the PM's comments.

23   Apart from the Chancellor of the Exchequer, E(DL) membership included the Chief Secretary to the Treasury and the Financial Secretary; it was Treasury dominated. Thatcher has been

criticised for conducting economic policy outside a full Cabinet meeting, including in breakfast meetings with a favoured few; Prior (1986) *A Balance of Power*, p.133. There were Thursday Breakfast Group meetings at No. 10 ahead of the Cabinet meeting including an inner circle of Ministers, notably Howe, Ian Gow her private parliamentary secretary, Wolfson the chief of staff in her Political Office within No. 10, Joseph, Nott, Biffen and Howe; G. Howe (1994) *Conflict of Loyalty*, London: Macmillan, p.147. Given the divisions in Thatcher's first Cabinet, which erupted from time to time on the direction policy should take, such gatherings were to be expected. However, there is still a good deal of discussion of economic matters in the E and E(DL) committee papers, from which much of the information in this chapter draws.

24 E(79), 1st meeting, 14 May 1979.
25 E(79) 5th meeting, 17 July 1979.
26 E(79)35, "Nationalised Industries' Cash Limits and Performance Targets for 1980/81. Memorandum by the Chancellor of the Exchequer", 17 September 1979. The EFL was the difference between a state-owned firm's profits plus depreciation charge minus capital expenditure and any change in working capital. The EFL set governed the amount of grants and borrowing, including leasing, the firm could arrange in any year.
27 E(79) 5th meeting, 17 July 1979.
28 Ibid..
29 E(79)35. The tight squeeze on public sector wages would continue in 1980 when the Government set public sector financing on the basis of a 6% ceiling on wage rises. At the time the nationalised industries' pay settlements were averaging around 20%.
30 E(79) 5th meeting, 17 July 1979.
31 E(DL)1st meeting, 5 June 1979.
32 BNOC earned royalties on oil from North Sea fields; see chapter 4.
33 E(DL)2nd meeting, 20 June 1979.
34 Stephenson (1980), pp.36–7; Gamble (1988) *The Free Economy and the Strong State: The Politics of Thatcherism*, London: Macmillan, p.104.
35 A. Denham and M. Garnett (2001) *Keith Joseph*, Chesham: Acumen Publishing Ltd, p.343.
36 J. Campbell (2004) *Margaret Thatcher, Volume Two: The Iron Lady*, London: Pimlico, p.98.
37 A. Halcrow (1989) *Keith Joseph: A Single Mind*, London: Macmillan; Thatcher (1993), p.151 notes that "Keith Joseph had told me that he wished to move from industry." But it is likely that he would have been moved anyway. For critical comments on Joseph's stewardship of the Department of Industry see N. Ridley (1991) *'My Style of Government': The Thatcher Years*, London: Hutchinson, p.6; A. Sherman (2005) *Paradoxes of Power: Reflections on the Thatcher Interlude*, Exeter: Imprint Academic, p.100.
38 E(DL)79 1st meeting, 5 June 1979; E(DL)(79)2, "Disposals of Public Sector Trading Assets. Memorandum by the Financial Secretary", 4 June 1979.
39 Stephenson (1980), p.106; Holmes (1984) *The First Thatcher Government*, p.42; Denham and Garnett (2001), p.346. Within a few months Knight stood down for personal reasons and was replaced by Sir Freddie Wood from Croda International.
40 *Hansard*, columns 235–264, http://www.margaretthatcher.org/speeches/displaydocument.asp?docid=109497. Gamble (1988), p.99.
41 Memorandum from the Chancellor of the Exchequer to the PM, 22 June 1979, in E(DL) Part 1.
42 Letter from David Hunter to the Chancellor of the Exchequer, 23 May 1979, reply by the Chancellor on 22 June 1979, and associated internal memoranda; in E(DL) Part 1.
43 E(DL)(79)3, "Disposal of BP Shares and NEB Holdings. Memorandum by the Financial Secretary", 18 June 1979, in E(DL) Part 1.
44 E(DL)(79)9, "Disposals in 1980/81. Memorandum by the Financial Secretary", 17 July 1979, in E(DL) Part 1.
45 G. Howe (1981) *Conflict of Loyalty*, London: Macmillan, p.128.
46 K. Baker (1993) *The Turbulent Years: My Life in Politics*, London: Faber & Faber p.77.
47 E(79)24, "Strategy: Note by the Central Policy Review Staff".
48 Letter from the Financial Secretary, Treasury to Sir Keith Joseph, Secretary of State for Industry, 19 June 1979, included with E(DL) 2nd meeting minutes.

49  "Financing of British Airways", Department of Trade and Industry", June 1979; E(DL)(79)4, "Financing of British Airways – Share Issue. Memorandum by the Secretary of State for Trade", in E(DL) Part 1.

50  Official Committee on Nationalised Industry Policy, NIP (79) 9th meeting, 25 September 1979, HM Treasury Filefolder 11271561.

51  "Financial Aspects of Disposals", Official Committee on Nationalised Industries paper NIP(79)23, HM Treasury Filefolder 11271558.

52  E(DL)(79)3rd meeting Minutes, 5 July 1979; E(DL)(79)5, "Disposal of Assets. Memorandum by the Financial Secretary, Treasury", 2 July 1979; both in E(DL) Part 1.

53  Contents of letter mentioned in E(DL)(79)3; E(DL)2nd meeting, 20 June 1979, in E(DL) Part 1.

54  E(DL)(79)5, "Disposal of Assets. Memorandum by the Financial Secretary, Treasury", 2 July 1979, in E(DL) Part 1.

55  The Government owned nearly 8% of the equity in the French registered company, a holding that originated from the former Suez Canal Company in which the British Government had a stake.

56  The British Sugar Corporation had been established in 1936 as a result of the merger of a number of sugar beet producers, D.Swann (1988), *The Retreat of the State: Deregulation and Privatisation in the UK and US*, London: Harvester Wheatsheaf, p.192. The Government held 14.5m shares in British Sugar or around 11% of the voting capital. Subsequently the sale was slowed by an on-going dispute between the Corporation and another sugar supplier, Tate & Lyle.

57  The Government's financial year ran from 1 April to 31 March.

58  E(DL)(79)5.

59  Letter from Nigel Lawson to Sir Keith Joseph at the Department of Industry, 16 July 1979 in E(DL) Part 1.

60  Letter from E.C.Flanagan, Private Secretary (PS), Department of Transport to T.P.Lankester, PS to the PM, 6 July 1979, in E(DL) Part 1.

61  Correspondence in E(DL) Part 1.

62  Note for the Record, PM's Meeting with Gordon Pepper. Discussion on the Budget and Monetary Policy, 18 May 1979, PM Papers Box no.220.

63  Letter with E(DL)1st meeting papers.

64  Letter from Heseltine to Howe, 6 June 1979, in E(DL)2nd meeting papers.

65  Letter from Howe to Heseltine, 8 June 1979, with the minutes of E(DL)2nd meeting.

66  C(79)13, "Public Sector Reductions 1979–80. Memorandum by the Chief Secretary, Treasury", 29 May 1979; "Disposal of Public Sector Trading Assets. Note by Officials", HM Treasury, with E(DL)1st meeting minutes.

67  Papers with E(DL)2nd meeting minutes.

68  Letter from D.Brereton, Principal PS, Department of Health and Social Security, 20 November 1979. The PM's comment is written on the letter. The PM's conclusion was transmitted to Brereton in more measured language on 26 November: "She is very pleased that there has been some progress on this front"; note to Don Brereton; all in E(DL) Part 2.

69  E(DL)(79)10, "Disposal of Surplus Land and Buildings in the Public Sector. Memorandum by the Secretary of State for the Environment", 16 July 1979, in E(DL) Part 1.

70  E(DL)5th meeting 26 July 1979, in E(DL) Part 2.

71  Ibid.

72  Memorandum from Sir Kenneth Berrill, CPRS, to T.P.Lankester, 19 July 1979, in E(DL) Part1.

73  Personal Minute from the Prime Minister to Heseltine, 24 July 1979, in E(DL) Part 2.

74  E(DL)(79)17, "Disposal of New Town Assets. Memorandum by the Secretary of State for the Environment", 30 October 1979; letter and report by Healey & Baker, 13 September 1979 in E(DL) Part 2.

75  Note from D.A.Edmonds, PS at the Department of the Environment, 3 December 1979, 5 December, in E(DL) Part 2.

76  Letter from Nigel Lawson to George Younger with a copy to Nicholas Edwards,15 August 1979, in E(DL) Part 2.

77 Letter from Younger to Lawson, 28 September 1979, in E(DL) Part 2; letter on behalf of the Financial Secretary and signed by his PS, P. Diggle, to Younger, 11 October 1979, in E(DL) Part 2.

78 Letter from Lawson to Peter Walker, Minster of Agriculture, 16 July 1979, in E(DL) Part 1.

79 Letter from Younger to Lawson, 18 July 1979, in E(DL) Part 1.

80 Letter from Edwards to Lawson, 19 July 1979, in E(DL) Part 1.

81 Note from T.P.Lankester, PS No. 10, to J.S. Wilson, Scottish Office, 30 July 1980, in E(DL) Part 3.

82 Note from the Secretary of State for Scotland to the PM, 31 July 1980, in E(DL) Part 3.

83 E(79)31, "Disposal of Public Assets in 1979–80. Memorandum by the Chancellor of the Exchequer", 7 September 1979.

84 E(DL)(79)13, "Drake and Skull Holdings Ltd (DSH). Memorandum by the Secretary of State for the Environment", 23 July 1979, in E(DL) Part 2.

85 E(DL)(79) 5th meeting, 26 July 1979, in E(DL) Part 2.

86 "PSBR and Public Corporations Sales of Assets and the Injection of Private Capital. Note by the Treasury", 18 July 1979, in E(DL) Part 2.

87 The Government's power to intervene and the exclusion of loans from the PSBR were set down in memoranda of understanding with the companies.

88 Minute from the Central Statistical Office to HM Treasury 15 September 1982, HM Treasury papers JA/1760/01 Part B. The guidance was further reviewed and revised in July 1984, NIP(84) 10, Public/Private Sector Clarification: Note by HM Treasury and the Central Statistical Office, Official Committee on Nationalised Industry Policy, HM Treasury papers, A/301/01.

89 E(DL)(79) 6th meeting, 4 October 1979.

90 E(DL)(79)7th meeting, 17 October 1979; E(DL)(79)16, "Privatisation of British Aerospace, British Airways, and the National Freight Corporation. Note by the Secretaries" (P.Mountfield, G.D.Miles and A.S.D.Whybrow), 15 October 1979.

91 C(79) 9th meeting conclusions, 12 July 1979; C(79)25, "Public Expenditure 1980–81 to 1983–84: The Scope for Reductions. A Report by the Public Expenditure Survey Committee".

92 Lady O. Maitland (1989) *Margaret Thatcher: The First Ten Years*, London: Sidgwick & Jackson p.61; J.Cole (1987) *The Thatcher Years: A Decade of Revolution in British Politics*, London: BBC Books, p.44.

93 Prior (1986), p.134. Ian Gilmour, another "wet", has stated: "The first Thatcher Cabinet, with its complement of wets, dries and those who were too intelligent, cautious, fearful or uncommitted to be either, was palpably not a happy and united body"; I.Gilmour (1992) *Dancing with Dogma: Britain under Thatcherism*, London: Simon & Schuster, p.3.

94 C(79)37, "Nationalised Industries' Investment and Financing Review: 1981–82 to 1983–84. Memorandum by the Chancellor of the Exchequer", 10 September 1979.

95 C(79)15th meeting conclusions, 13 September 1979; C(79)18th meeting conclusions, 25 October 1979.

96 Bruce-Gardyne (1984) *Mrs Thatcher's First Administration*, p.58.

97 "Brief on nationalised industries and privatisation for the Debate on the Address", 9 November 1982, in E(DL) Part 6. Part of this could be attributed to the unwinding of subsidies used by Labour to massage prices down ahead of the 1979 Election; Howe (1981), p.4.

98 Letter from Peter Walker to Nigel Lawson, 6 August 1979, in E(DL) Part 2.

99 E(79)31, "Disposals of Public Assets in 1979–80. Memorandum by the Chancellor of the Exchequer", 7 September 1979.

100 E(79) 6th meeting, 24 July 1979.

101 E(79) 7th meeting 10 September 1979; E(79)31.

102 E(DL)(79)8th meeting, 19 December 1979.

103 E(79)7th meeting, 10 September 1979.

104 C(79)20th meeting conclusions, 8 November 1979; Thatcher (1993), pp.54–5.

105 A. Walters (1986) *Britain's Economic Renaissance: Margaret Thatcher's Reforms 1979–1984*, Oxford: Oxford University Press, p.78.

106 Campbell (2001), p.49.

107    C(79)21st meeting conclusions, 15 November 1979; C(79)25th meeting conclusions, 13 December 1979; C(79)61, "The Economic Outlook and Public Expenditure. Memorandum by the Chancellor of the Exchequer", 10 December 1979.
108    C(79)25th meeting conclusions; C(79)61; C(80) 3rd meeting conclusions, 24 January 1980; C(80)3, "Public Expenditure. Memorandum by the Chancellor of the Exchequer and the Chief Secretary, Treasury", 21 January 1980.
109    C(79)18th meeting conclusions, 25 October 1979; C(79)46 "White Paper on Public Expenditure 1980–81. Memorandum by the Chief Secretary, Treasury", 22 October 1979.
110    C(80)2nd meeting conclusions, 17 January 1980.
111    C(80)4th meeting conclusions, 31 January 1980: C(80)9, "Public Expenditure. Memorandum by the Chancellor of the Exchequer", 29 January 1980; Stephenson (1980), pp.108–9.
112    *Hansard*, 26 March 1980, columns1439–91, http://www.margaretthatcher.org/speeches/display document.asp?docid=109498; Thatcher (1993), pp.96–7; Lawson (1992), p.68.
113    Abolition was advocated by the guru of monetarism, Professor Milton Friedman, and by Mrs Thatcher's personal economic adviser, Professor Douglas Hague of the Manchester Business School. However, the possibility had not been mentioned in the Conservatives' Election Manifesto and the decision took most Ministers by surprise.
114    C(80)35, "The Economic Prospect. Memorandum by the Chancellor of the Exchequer", 1 July 1980; C(80) 28th meeting conclusions, 10 July 1980.
115    E(80)64, "The Nationalised Industries: 1980 Investment and Financing Review. Memorandum by the Chief Secretary, Treasury", 3 July 1980.
116    C(80)27th meeting conclusions, 3 July 1980.
117    C(80)28th meeting conclusions, 10 July 1980; C(80)38, "Report by the Public Expenditure Survey Committee. Note by the Chief Secretary, Treasury", 3 July 1980; C(80)39, "Public Expenditure: Main Issues. Note by the Chief Secretary, Treasury", 3 July 1980; C(80)40, "Public Expenditure, 1981–82 to 1983–84. Memorandum by the Chief Secretary, Treasury", 4 July 1980.
118    G.C.Peden (1991) *British Economic and Social Policy: Lloyd George to Margaret Thatcher*, second edition, London: Philip Allan, pp.197–220; K.Middlemas (1994), "The Party, Industry, and the City", in A. Seldon and S. Ball (eds.) *Conservative Century: the Conservative Party since 1900*, Oxford: Oxford University Press, p.488.
119    Holmes (1985), p.156; Harris (1988), *Thatcher*, (1993), p.105; E.J. Evans (1997) *Thatcher and Thatcherism*, second edition, London: Routledge, p.21.
120    A. Seldon and D. Collings (2000) *Britain under Thatcher*, Harlow: London, p.15.
121    S. Blake and A. John (2003) *The World According to Margaret Thatcher*, London: Michael O'Mara Books Ltd, p.49.
122    J. Hoskyns (2000) *Just in Time: Inside the Thatcher Revolution*, London: Aurum Press, p.326.
123    C(80)38th meeting conclusions, 4 November 1980; C(80)39th meeting conclusions, 6 November 1980; C(80)40th meeting conclusions, 13 November 1980; C(80)41st meeting conclusions, 19 November 1980; C(80)64, "Public Expenditure Changes. Memorandum by the Chancellor of the Exchequer and the Chief Secretary, Treasury", 29 October 1980.
124    C(80)72, "Public Expenditure: Memorandum by the Chancellor of the Exchequer", 17 November 1980. F. Pym (1984) *The Politics of Consent*, London: Hamish Hamilton p.105, confirms that he would have resigned if the defence cuts had gone through.
125    Howe (1994), pp.189–190. Some abatement of social security benefits was included, C(80)41st meeting conclusions.
126    C(80)72; J.Bruce-Gardyne (1984) *Mrs Thatcher's First Administration*, London: Macmillan, pp.89–91; Lawson (1992), p.90; Thatcher (1993), p.128.
127    Biffen moved to the Department of Trade to take Nott's place. Nott moved to the Ministry of Defence. A few weeks earlier Biffen had made known his lack of enthusiasm for the MTFS. As Thatcher (1993, p.130) states on her decision to move him: "some ministers were trying to discredit the strategy itself. This could not be allowed to continue." On St. John-Stevas she comments: "He had a first class-brain and a ready wit. But he turned indiscretion into a political principle". Angus Maude, the Paymaster General, also left the Cabinet in January 1981 but seemingly voluntarily.
128    E(DL)(79)8th meeting, 19 December 1979.

129   Letter from the Chancellor of the Exchequer, 28 January 1980, in E(DL) Part 3.
130   Letter from Joseph to Howe, 12 February 1980, in E(DL) Part 3.
131   Letter from Heseltine to Howe, 7 February 1980, in E(DL) Part 3.
132   Letter from David Howell to Howe, 4 February 1980.
133   Letter from Norman Fowler to Sir Geoffrey Howe, 18 February 1980, in E(DL) Part 3.
134   Letter from M.A.Hall, PS, Treasury, to Tim Lankester, at No.10, 4 March 1980, in E(DL) Part 3.
135   No.10 briefing note, "Meeting with the Chancellor Thursday, 6 March 1980"; a note to the PM prior to the meeting accused the Secretary of State for Energy of being "unco-operative"; both in E(DL) Part 3.
136   Note for the Record of the meeting between the PM and the Chancellor of the Exchequer 6 March 1980, in E(DL) Part 3.
137   "Disposals Programme in 1980–81", memorandum to the PM from Howe, 12 March 1980, in E(DL) Part 3.
138   T.P. Lankester, PS to the PM, to W.J. Burroughs, Department of Energy, 18 March 1980, in E(DL) Part 3.
139   David Howell did bring in, in 1980, David Maitland as the Department's Permanent Secretary from the Foreign and Commonwealth Office to try and change departmental views and over time attitudes did change, assisted also by other changes in the departmental personnel.
140   E(81)102 "Gas Legislation. Memorandum by the Secretary of State for Energy", 19 October 1981. Section 7(2) of the Gas Act 1972 required the Secretary of State to take the Corporation's views into account when framing a Directive. BGC's principal statutory duties were set out in the Act as: to develop and maintain an efficient, co-ordinated and economical system of gas supply and to satisfy, so far as it is economical to do so, all reasonable demands for gas. The Board might argue successfully that a directive impeded these duties. Lord Denning's judgment on Tamlin vs Hannaford in 1950 supported the notion that the assets of a public corporation belonged to the corporation and not to the Government. Therefore, the proceeds from their sale accrued to the corporation not to the Exchequer.
141   Memorandum from the Secretary of State for Energy to the PM, 20 March 1980, in E(DL) Part 3.
142   Emphasis in the original. Another disappointment around the same time was a report from Leo Pliatzky. Pliatzky had just retired as Permanent Secretary to the Department of Trade and was asked by the Government to formulate ideas on privatisation. He reported in secret in 1980 and suggested either: (i) a single vast state holding company for the nationalised industries, in which shares might later be sold; or (ii) the issuing of a new type of government security valued by capitalising future revenue streams to raise more capital for the nationalised industries without privatisation. The report was dismissed by Treasury Ministers and quietly shelved; Lawson (1992), p.205.
143   E(DL)(80)3, "Reducing the Public Sector and Promoting Competition. Memorandum by the Parliamentary Under Secretary of State for Industry" (Michael Marshall, MP), 7 May 1980, in E(DL) Part 3; E(DL)(80) 2nd meeting, 12 May 1980.
144   "Disposals in 1980/1. Memorandum by the Financial Secretary, Treasury", 7 May 1980, in E(DL) Part 3; E(DL)(80) 2nd meeting.
145   "Progress with Privatisation. Note by the Secretaries", 20 October 1980, E(DL)(80)18, in E(DL) Part 3.
146   E(DL)(80)20, "Progress with Disposals in 1980–81. Note by the Secretaries" (D.J.L. Moore, G.D. Miles and W. Moyes), 8 December 1980, in E(DL) Part 4.
147   E(DL)(81) 1st meeting, 18 February 1981; E(DL)(81)2, "Prospects for Disposals in 1981–82. Memorandum by the Financial Secretary", 23 January 1981, in E(DL) Part 4.
148   On 22 January Ministers agreed to sell oil from the Government's stockpile to assist meeting the disposals target for 1981/2. The result was sales valued at £63m (with disposals totalling £33m in 1982/3 and £4m in 1983/4).
149   E(DL)(81)6, "Royal Mint and Bank of England Printing Works. Memorandum by the Financial Secretary", 16 February 1981, in E(DL) Part 4.

NOTES

150 E(DL)(81) 3, "The Crown Agents. Note by the Minister of State, Foreign and Commonwealth Office", 16 February 1981; E(DL)(81) 1st meeting, 18 February 1981. Both in E(DL) Part 4.

151 Walters (1986), p.85. Walters' proposals were supported by Professor Jurg Niehans of the University of Berne, who had been called in on the recommendation of Walters to provide an independent assessment of economic policy; Cosgrave (1979), p.116; and by Professor Douglas Hague of the University of Manchester, the part-time economic adviser to the PM; Thatcher (1993), p.126. Also, see Minford (2005 )"Inflation, unemployment and the pound", pp.52–3.

152 Lawson (1992), ch.9; Howe (1994), pp.203–4. Thatcher (1993), pp.134–6 reveals how perilously close the Government came to raising the basic rate of income tax.

153 C(81)8th meeting conclusions, 24 February 1981; C(81)10, "1981 Public Expenditure Survey. Memorandum by the Chancellor of the Exchequer", 19 February 1981.

154 Walters (1986), p.90.

155 Thatcher (1995) *The Path to Power*, p.569.

156 Prior (1986), p.140.

157 Harris (1988), p.109.

158 Bruce-Gardyne (1984), pp.95–6; J. Hillman and P. Clarke (1988) *Geoffrey Howe: A Quiet Revolutionary*, London: Weidenfeld and Nicolson, p.147; Campbell (2004), p.112.

159 *The Times*, 30 March 1981. Walters' (1986, p.88) response to the letter was dismissive: "Academic economists had sunk so low in both ministerial and, I believe, popular esteem that the conjunction of so much academic opposition was taken as some faint confirmation that the policy must be right – or at least not obviously wrong."

160 T. Congdon (2006) "Why the 1981 Budget mattered: the end of naïve Keynesianism", in P. Booth (ed.) *Were 364 Economists All Wrong?*, Readings 60, London: Institute of Economic Affairs, p.29.

161 A broad definition of the money supply, including cash and bank deposits.

162 Later research would highlight the problem of targeting any one monetary measure. Howe (2004), p.13, comments with the benefit of hindsight: "In truth, at a time of economic volatility it was to prove practically impossible to establish any single monetary indicator as consistently the "right" one."

163 Peden (1991), p.214.

164 Thatcher (1993), p.132.

165 Thatcher (1993), pp.143–7; Campbell (2004), pp.113–4.

166 One concrete result of the riots was to add to the urgency within government to come up with measures to restore economic prosperity in deprived areas. Between 1981 and 1983 the Government introduced 24 so-called Enterprise Zones in economically depressed areas with a package of financial incentives and exemptions from certain regulations to encourage business start-ups, in spite of the prevailing agenda to cut public spending. In 1984 six free ports with their own package of incentives would be established near airports or ports, again to encourage new enterprise. On Merseyside, particularly badly affected by economic decline, Michael Heseltine set up the Merseyside Task Force to promote and co-ordinate public and private sector regeneration efforts and a new urban development grant scheme was established.

167 Bruce-Gardyne (1984), p.104.

168 Booth ed. (2006) "Were 364 Economists All Wrong?"

169 C(81)18th meeting conclusions, 17 May 1981.

170 C(81)29th meeting conclusions, 23 July 1981; J. Nott (2002) *Here Today, Gone Tomorrow: Reflections of an Errant Politician*, pp.196–7; Gilmour (1992), p.5; Howe (1994), pp.222–3; Harris (1988), p.111; Lawson (1992), p.108;Thatcher (1993), p.149.

171 Thatcher (1993), p.148.

172 M. Heseltine (2000) *Life in the Jungle: My Autobiography*, London: Coronet Books, pp.229–30.

173 *Observer*, 25 February 1979, cited in Campbell (2001), p.325.

174 Soames was blamed by Thatcher for mishandling a strike by civil servants in 1981. In return he felt that the PM had mishandled the dispute; Campbell (2004), pp.103–4; Lawson (1992), p.107. In late July Thorneycroft had publicly questioned the direction of economic policy, admitting to "rising damp"; Thatcher (1993), p.150. Carlisle was politically left of centre and Thatcher claimed (1993), p.151 "had not been a very effective Education Secretary".

175   He also held the post of Paymaster General in the Cabinet.
176   See chapter 4 below. Howell was of the Thatcherite tendency in the Conservative Party when in Opposition, but he does not appear to have cultivated a good working relationship with the PM in Cabinet. Lawson (1992), p.132 describes him guardedly as "a gown-man and not a sword-man" – a thinker rather than a doer. According to Howell the move in September 1981 was at his own request, but there is no evidence that Thatcher tried to dissuade him. The move was seen as a demotion.
177   Lawson (1992), p.123.
178   Albeit after the intervention of a special group of Ministers, the Ministerial Group on Public Expenditure (MISC 62) chaired by the Home Secretary, William Whitelaw. The Group held discussions with Ministers in an attempt to overcome remaining differences; C(81)57, "Public Expenditure. Memorandum by the Secretary of State for the Home Department", 24 November 1981. The arrangement of a small group of Ministers arbitrating on spending with the Home Secretary in the chair was used on a number of occasions during the 1980s when the Treasury Ministers and departmental Ministers could not at first agree. The grouping became popularly known as the "Star Chamber".
179   C(81)33rd meeting conclusions, 20 October 1981; C(81)38th meeting conclusions, 26 November 1981; C(81)50, "Economic Policy and Public Spending. Memorandum by the Chancellor of the Exchequer", 14 October 1981; C(81)51, "Public Expenditure. Memorandum by the Chief Secretary, Treasury", 14 October 1981. The result included an acceptance by the Treasury of some increase in the nationalised industries' EFLs to reflect their economic problems.
180   Memorandum from the Chancellor of the Exchequer to the PM, 10 March 1981, in Nationalised Industries files, Part 4.
181   Memorandum from Robert Armstrong to the PM, 13 March 1981, in Nationalised Industries files, Part 4. Ibbs had been recruited from the chemicals firm ICI. The CPRS had been established within the Cabinet Office to provide policy advice to Ministers during the Heath Government and had been retained by Labour. Sir Kenneth Berrill was its head in May 1979 but was replaced within a year by Sir Robin Ibbs. Ibbs held the post for two years before returning to ICI. He was replaced by John Sparrow, a merchant banker; D. Kavanagh and A. Seldon (2000) *The Powers behind the Prime Minister: The Hidden Influence of Number Ten*, London: HarperCollins, p.168. The No. 10 Policy Unit had been established in March 1974 under the previous Labour Government to provide policy advice to the PM. From May 1979 it was headed by John Hoskyns and also included another adviser from Thatcher's period as Leader of the Opposition, Norman Strauss, seconded from Unilever. The Unit also included one civil servant, Andrew Dugoid, from the Department of Industry. Hoskyns resigned from the Policy Unit in March 1982 over what he considered to be the slow pace of change. He later became head of the Institute of Directors; Hoskyns (2000). Hoskyns was replaced as head of the Policy Unit by Ferdinand Mount, the political editor of the *Spectator* magazine.
182   Memorandum from John Hoskyns in the Policy Unit at No. 10 to the PM, 17 March 1981, and note to Sir Robert Armstrong by T.P. Lankester, 17 March 1981, in Nationalised Industries files, Part 4.
183   Note of a meeting between the PM and the Chancellor of the Exchequer, 18 March 1981, in Nationalised Industries files, Part 4.
184   Note by T.P. Lankester, 20 March 1981 and note from Sir Robert Armstrong to T.P. Lankester, 24 March 1981, in Nationalised Industries files, Part 4.
185   Memorandum from the Chancellor of the Exchequer to the PM, 9 July 1981, in Nationalised Industries files, Part 4.
186   Note from J.R. Ibbs to T.P. Lankester, 15 July 1981, in Nationalised Industries files, Part 4.
187   Note from T.P. Lankester to A.J.Wiggins at the Treasury, 20 July 1981, in Nationalised Industry files, Part 4.
188   Howe (1981), p.4. Howe (1981) *Privatisation: The Way Ahead*, pamphlet based on a speech given to the Selsdon Group 1 July 1981, London: Conservative Political Centre. In the speech Howe also considered the approach adopted for the control of public utility monopolies in the USA, a subject that was beginning to be discussed within Government.
189   C(79) 2nd meeting conclusions, 17 May 1979.

190 Public Expenditure White Paper, Cmnd.8494–11, pp.74–8. "Brief on nationalised industries and privatisation for the Debate on the Address", 9 November 1982, in E(DL) Part 6. Also, see Howe (1994), p.154; S. Jenkins (1983) "Government Policy Towards the Nationalised Industries" ", in T.J.G. Hunter (ed) *Decision Making in a Mixed Economy*, Milton Keynes: Open University Press; Swann (1988), p.236.

191 *Hansard*, column 740, 9 March 1982.

192 As the name suggests, the Group was the forum for nationalised industry chairmen to meet and exchange views. It met on a regular basis.

193 "Record of a Meeting between Ministers and the Nationalised Industries Chairmen's Group" 20 February 1980; letter from the Secretary of State for Energy to the Chancellor of the Exchequer 28 February 1980; letter from the Secretary of State for Scotland to the Chancellor of the Exchequer 28 February 1980; all in Nationalised Industries files Part 2.

194 "Nationalised Industry Financing", memorandum by J.R.Ibbs to T.P.Lankester 22 January 1981, in Nationalised Industries files Part 3.

195 Handwritten note on the memorandum from J.R.Ibbs, ibid.

196 The National Economic Office was the administrative arm of the National Economic Development Corporation established in 1962 as a tripartite (Government, industry and unions) forum to agree national economic strategies.

197 The Ryrie Rules dominated thinking on the use of private capital in Government in subsequent years, especially for public sector projects. The rules included the proposition that where the ultimate risk of a project stayed with Government, the project remained in the public sector and the funding remained part of the PSBR. The Treasury expected a substantially higher degree of private sector initiative and management than could be achieved if the project was publicly funded, leading to higher benefits to at least offset the higher funding cost. HM Treasury papers L/1821/01 Part C.

198 "The Relationship between Government and the Nationalised Industries: A Report by the Central Policy Review Staff"; note of a meeting held 10 Downing Street on Tuesday 4 August 1981; and Personal Minute M11/81 from the PM to the Secretary of State for Trade, 4 August 1981; all in Nationalised Industries files, Part 4.

199 Minutes of the Sub-Committee on Nationalised Industries, E(NI)(81)1st meeting, 2 November 1981.

200 The CPRS had proposed the creation of a new audit unit within Government to investigate the efficiency of the nationalised industries, but this idea was successfully opposed by the Department of Trade (on the grounds that it would be too difficult to get the co-operation of the industry boards) and the Department of Energy and the Department of Industry (on the grounds that it would make recruiting top quality senior management even more difficult); NIP(80) 3rd meeting, 6 November 1980, HM Treasury Filefolder 11271674. The Department of Trade also worried that such work would conflict with the work of the MMC now able to investigate the nationalised industries. However, the Official Committee on Nationalised Industry Policy based in the Treasury concluded that management consultants could usefully complement MMC inquiries and their use should not be ruled out; NIP(81)2nd meeting, HM Treasury papers H/1579/1000/01 Rev NIP/4. The Treasury continued to favour value for money audits in the nationalised industries despite opposition from sponsor departments; NIP(82)3, "Value for Money Audit". Note by the Treasury", 6 December 1982, H/1579/1000/01 Rev NIP/413.

201 Lawson (1992), p.204; note by Sir John Hoskyns to the PM, 20 April 1982, in Nationalised Industries files Part 6. The performance reviews were prepared by the sponsor department and the corporate plans by the industry boards.

202 NIP(82)11 "Review of Nationalised Industries' Performance Reviews and Corporate Plans in 1982", H/1579,1000,01, Rev NIP/413. Also, "Note by the Treasury", 17 November 1982, ibid.

203 Note from the Chancellor of the Exchequer to the PM, 6 April 1982, in Nationalised Industries files, Part 6.

204 "A Study of the State Monopolies by the Central Policy Review Staff", 21 October 1982, in Nationalised Industries files, Part 7.

205 Ibid., Annex "A Review of Regulatory Agencies".

206 Ibid., main body of the report.

207    Ibid., Annex.

208    Ibid., main body of the report.

209    Brief on nationalised industries and privatisation for the Debate on the Address, 9 November 1982, from the Conservative Research Department, in E(DL) Part 6.

210    "Government Policies towards Nationalised Industries. Report by the Official Committee on Nationalised Industry Policy", NIP(79)43, 21 December 1979, HM Treasury papers Filefolder 11271559.

211    Similarly, John Redwood, who was a leading champion of privatisation in the Conservative Party in the early 1980s wrote in 1980, "Nor is it realistic to suppose that the nation's economy would necessarily benefit or withstand a major change in state monopoly undertaken too hastily and without sufficient political support across the spectrum of debate. It is therefore necessary to propose certain other methods of dealing with monopoly regulation." He offered no alternative of substance and it seems that, like Ridley, at the time he saw little scope for selling off the big monopoly utilities.

212    *Hansard*, 5 November 1981, vol.12, cols.440–1.

213    The £600m disposals figure is in cash terms (equivalent to £500m at 1979 Survey prices). In fact, the actual sales total turned out to be somewhat less, at £494m. Public borrowing would be affected that year by an unwinding of the advance oil payments that had done much to fill the gap in the Chancellor's Budget figures in 1979/80. Oil prices had started to fall and the state of the oil market effectively ruled out further large forward sales; E(DL)(81)17, "Prospects for Special Disposals. Memorandum by the Financial Secretary, Treasury", 20 November 1981; E(DL)(81)4th meeting, 27 November 1981; both in E(DL) Part 5.

214    C(82)1, "Economic Strategy. Memorandum by the Chancellor of the Exchequer", 26 January 1982.

215    *Hansard*, 15 March 1983, columns 134–58, http://www.margaretthatcher.org/speeches/display document.asp?docid=109500. Some of this favourable fiscal outcome had arisen because oil prices and therefore North Sea tax revenues had not fallen by as much as expected at the time of the 1982 Budget; C(83)5, "Economic Strategy. Memorandum by the Chancellor of the Exchequer", 1 February 1983.

216    Ibid.; C(82)28, "Public Expenditure: Objectives for 1982 Survey. Memorandum by the Chief Secretary, Treasury", 8 July 1982.

217    C(82)46th meeting conclusions, 2 November 1982; C(82)38, "Public Expenditure Survey 1982. Memorandum by the Chief Secretary, Treasury", 27 October 1982.

218    Economic Subsidies to Nationalised Industries, HM Treasury papers, Loss Makers: PEAU Project, AD/982/1514/01. REV NIEA/132.

219    Bruce-Gardyne (1984), p.80.

220    The sale of Sealink was delayed by a Monopolies and Mergers recommendation against the purchase by its rival on cross-channel routes, European Ferries. The MMC also set conditions on the takeover of British Rail Hovercraft Ltd and Hoverlloyd Ltd. The Government was not always able to reconcile its desire to see more competition with its desire to sell off state assets as these cases, and a joint venture entered into by British Steel with Guest, Keen and Nettlefolds, illustrate. This joint venture led to a rationalisation of production but some diminution of competition.

221    Memorandum from Heseltine to the PM, 18 February 1982. Also, letters from Heseltine to Nicholas Ridley, 9 and 22 March 1982, in E(DL) Part 5. Letter from Patrick Jenkin to Howe, 30 September 1982, in E(DL) Part 6.

222    Letters from Nicholas Ridley to Michael Heseltine, 26 February 1982 and 17 and 25 March 1982, in E(DL) Part 5.

223    International Computers Ltd. The shares were purchased by STC International Computers Ltd.

224    "Privatisation Present Situation and Prospects. Report by the Secretary of State for Industry", 13 September 1982, paragraphs 12–13, in E(DL) Part 6; Middlemas (1991), pp.357–9; Denham and Garnett (2001) *Keith Joseph*, p.347.

225    Letter from Patrick Jenkin to Nicholas Ridley, 22 April 1983, in E(DL) Part 7. The English Industrial Estate Corporation and the Welsh Development Corporation had also sold some properties. Plus the NCB sold a small subsidiary, Associated Heat Services. British Shipbuilders'

Scott Lithgow rig-building yard was sold to Trafalgar House and there was a small management buyout at Brigham and Cowan, also owned by British Shipbuilders. However, the main merchant shipbuilding yards could not be sold because of the parlous economic state of the industry, see chapter 9.

226    Note from Howe and attached paper to the PM, 3 December 1982, in E(DL) Part 6. The paper, after slight revision, became C(82)41, "Using Private Enterprise in Government. Memorandum by the Chancellor of the Exchequer", 10 December 1982.

227    C(82)53rd meeting conclusions, 16 December 1982. Note from Ferdinand Mount to the PM 13 December 1982, and annotated comment by the PM, in E(DL) Part 6.

228    Cabinet Office File 236/25, Government Research and Development: Scope for Privatisation; Campbell (2004) *Margaret Thatcher, Volume Two: The Iron Lady*, p.39.

229    From the outset the Government welcomed local authorities experimenting with the use of private contractors, Conservative Research Department *General Election 1979: Questions of Policy*, p.122.

230    Letter from Heseltine to Howe with attached memorandum, 19 October 1982, in E(DL) Part 6.

231    C(79)1st meeting conclusions, 10 May 1979. However, when the House of Commons Public Accounts Committee initiated a move to extend the scope of the Exchequer and Audit Department to oversee the nationalised industries this was rejected by Government.

232    Heseltine (1987) *Where There's a Will*, p.21.

233    Heseltine (2000), p.190; Campbell (1993), pp.314–15.

234    Another factor in the case of gas was that new gas suppliers were likely to obtain gas at higher prices than British Gas, which benefited from older, lower-priced contracts; chapter 14 below.

235    Baker (1993), pp.75–8.

236    *Hansard*, columns 399–400, 3 December 1981. The legal action was taken by Norwich council after the Department of the Environment set up an office in the city to sell council homes in response to the Labour controlled council's dilatory approach to sales; M. Crick (1997) *Michael Heseltine: A Biography*, London: Penguin Books, p.200; Heseltine (2000), p.196.

237    *Hansard*, column 729, 26 April 1983; correspondence in PM Papers Box no 533 Policy on Sale of Council Houses; S. Edgell and V. Duke, (1991) *A Measure of Thatcherism*, London: HarperCollins, p.140; S.R.Letwin (1992) *The Anatomy of Thatcherism*, London: Fontana, pp.179–80.

238    House of Commons, *Second Report from the Environment Committee, Council House Sales, Volume 1*, Session 1980–81, HC 366-I, London: HMSO. The number of council houses built each year in Britain fell from 85,000 in 1979 to 15,000 by 1990. The number of homes built for rent by housing associations also fell sharply; Gilmour (1992), p.145. In later years the Treasury further restricted the percentage of housing receipts that councils could spend.

239    T. Raison (1990) *Tories and the Welfare State: A History of Conservative Social Policy since the Second World War*, Houndsmill: Macmillan, pp.111–12; M. Drakeford (2000) *Privatisation and Social Policy*, Harlow: Longman, p.87. In early 1983 pensions and social security and housing benefits were linked to the immediate past increase in prices in the economy rather than forecast prices. But this again was tinkering with the welfare state.

240    Hillman and Clarke (1988), p.149.

241    *The Economist* 18 September 1982. It may even have had the initial backing of the PM; Young (1993), p.301.

242    Cole (1987), pp.92–3; Howe (1994), p.259.

243    Thatcher (1993), p.277.

244    Speech to the Party Conference 8 October 1982, http://www.margaretthatcher.org/speeches/displaydocument.asp?docid=105032.

245    Gilmour (1992), p.151.

246    In 1981 Arthur Seldon of the IEA did publish a pamphlet, *Wither the Welfare State*, and the Centre for Policy Studies offered some ideas for reform, including a move to private insurance, but such ideas for replacing the state by markets were unlikely to appeal to any government needing assurance of re-election.

247    Thatcher (1993), p.30.

NOTES

248  C(82)36, "The Queen's Speeches on the Prorogation of Parliament and the Opening of the New Session".
249  PM's Personal Minute M6/82, emphasis in the original.
250  E(DL)(82)8, "Privatisation: Sustaining the Momentum. Note by the Financial Secretary, Treasury", 18 October 1982.
251  Ernst & Young (1994) *Privatisation in the UK: The facts and figures*, Table 18, p.32.

## 4 PRIVATISING OIL

1  Letter from David Howell to the Chancellor of the Exchequer, 4 September 1979, in E(DL) Part 2.
2  Ibid.
3  *Hansard*, columns 891–2, 26 July 1979.
4  Letter from T.P. Lankester, Private Secretary (PS), No. 10 Downing Street, to P.C.Digggle, HM Treasury, "Disposal of Public Sector Trading Assets. Note by Officials", HM Treasury, 4 June 1979, in E(DL) Part 1.
5  E(DL)(79)3rd meeting, 5 July 1979; "Disposal of Public Sector Trading Assets. Note by Officials", HM Treasury; E(79)6th meeting, 24 July 1979.
6  Note from the Chancellor of the Exchequer dated 20 July 1979 attached to the minutes of E(79) 6th meeting.
7  "Disposal of Public Sector Trading Assets. Note by Officials", HM Treasury.
8  Lawson (1992), p.217.
9  "BNOC Review: Disposal Options" dated 31 May 1979, in E(DL) 2nd meeting papers; letter from the Secretary of State for Energy to the Prime Minister, 18 July 1979 and note from the Chancellor of the Exchequer, 20 July 1979 both in E(DL) Part 2.
10  "Disposal of Public Sector Trading Assets. Note by Officials", HM Treasury.
11  Note from the Chancellor of the Exchequer dated 19 July 1979 on David Howell's letter to the Prime Minister, in E(DL) Part 2.
12  E(DL)(79)3, "Disposal of BP Shares and NEB Holdings. Memorandum by the Financial Secretary", 18 June 1979. These figures include BP shares held by the Bank of England since the collapse of Burmah Oil in the mid-1970s but which at the time were subject to a legal dispute. The dispute ended in October 1981 when Burmah Oil announced that they would not be appealing against a High Court decision in favour of the Bank of England's ownership of the shares. The 311m BP shares held by the Bank were then transferred to the Treasury; minute from the Chancellor of the Exchequer to the PM, 19 October 1981, in PM Papers, Box no.309, Part 5.
13  Ibid. On 14 June 1979 Patrick Sergeant in the *Daily Mail* newspaper put forward an idea that seems to have originated with the chairman of Orion Bank, David Montagu, of issuing a new government loan stock convertible into BP shares rather than selling the Government's holding of BP shares directly, which he argued might depress the share price ("How a BP convertible would save us £737m", *Daily Mail*, 14 June 1979). This received some support in Parliament (*Hansard*, 19 June 1979), but not in the Treasury. However, the idea of a bond secured against oil assets did resurface during the long debate in Government on the privatisation of BNOC, as discussed below.
14  E(DL)(79)3.
15  Unsigned internal No. 10 memorandum to the PM, 22 June 1979, in E(DL) Part 1.
16  Letter from T.P. Lankester to A.M.W. Battishill, HM Treasury, dated 25 June 1979, in E(DL).
17  Note for the Record, 25 June 1979, in E(DL) Part 2. It seems that a plan to sell BP shares in New York and Frankfurt, as well as London, played a part in the PM's decision to stop the sale and consider alternative options.
18  Letter from Peter Walker, Minister of Agriculture, Fisheries and Food, 25 June 1979, in E(DL).
19  PM Papers, Box no 308, The Future of BNOC: Proposed Sale of BP Assets, Part 1.
20  Telegram from Lord Carrington, 27 June 1979; letter from T.P. Lankester to Martin Hall at the Treasury, dated 27 June 1979, in E(DL); "Note for the Record: Disposal of Government Assets", 25 June 1979; also, handwritten note by the PM, 24 June 1979 headed "Disposal of Assets". All in E(DL) Part 1.

21    Note from the Chancellor of the Exchequer, 19 July 1979 in response to David Howell's letter to the PM, in E(DL) Part 2.

22    Minute from Sir Kenneth Berrill, Central Policy Review Staff, to T.P. Lankester, PS No. 10, PM Papers, Box 308, The Future of BNOC: proposed sale of BP Assets, Part 1. There was a further consideration: there was some evidence that OPEC countries increasingly preferred to do business on a government-to-government basis. This too told in favour of retaining the oil trading business of BNOC in the public sector; minute from T.P.Lankester to the PM, 11 December 1979, PM Papers, Box no.308,The Future of BNOC: Proposed Sale of BP Assets, Part 2.

23    Conservative Party Election Manifesto May 1979. This was echoed in the Ministerial Dossier on Energy produced by the Conservative Research Department in 1979; Conservative Research Department (1979) *Ministerial Dossier: Energy*, p.10.

24    J. Redwood (1976) "Managing the Economy" in Lord Blake and J. Patten (eds,) *The Conservative Opportunity*, London: Macmillan, p.183.

25    Minute from David Howell to the PM, July 1979, in PM papers, Box 308, The Future of BNOC: Proposed Sale of BP Assets, Part 1.

26    E(79) 6th meeting 24 July 1979; E(79)20, "Securing the UK's Oil Supplies: Role of BNOC. Memorandum by the Secretary of State for Energy", 13 July 1979; E(79)21, "BNOC: Implications of Disposal of Assets. Memorandum by the Secretary of State for Energy", 13 July 1979; E(79)22, "BNOC: Future Strategy. Memorandum by the Secretary of State for Energy", 13 July 1979.

27    E(79) 21, "BNOC: Implications of Disposal of Assets. Memorandum by the Secretary of State for Energy", 13 July 1979.

28    A sentiment echoed in a paper from Howell: E(79)21, "BNOC: Implication of Disposal of Assets. Memorandum by the Secretary of State for Energy", 13 July 1979.

29    Letter from Howell to Lawson, 4 September 1979, in E(DL) Part 2. On 24 June in E(DL) it had been noted that the BGC Board would oppose a separate sale of Wytch Farm.

30    Under the Act the Secretary of State was empowered to direct BGC to discontinue any activity either wholly or to a specified extent, but only after consulting with the Corporation. The Act required the Secretary of State to take the Corporation's views into account when framing a Direction. It was unclear whether this section permitted the Secretary of State to enforce a privatisation of any of the Corporation's activities that the Board opposed.

31    "Disposal of Public Sector Trading Assets. Note by Officials", HM Treasury.

32    E(79)7th meeting, 10 September 1979; E(79)36, "BNOC Disposals. Memorandum by the Secretary of State for Energy", 7 September 1979.

33    Ibid.

34    Later the Treasury would take the view that Howell had been over pessimistic about the likely receipts from a sale in the short term; minute from the Chancellor of the Exchequer to the PM, 14 November 1979, PM Papers, Box no.308, The Future of BNOC: Proposed Sale of BP Assets, Part 2.

35    E(79)7th meeting, 11 September 1979; E(79)36.

36    E(79)7th meeting. £622m would be raised from advance oil payments in 1979/80; "Privatisation Programme 1983–84 to 1987–88: Progress Report – July 1984. Note by the Treasury", in E(DL) Part 10.

37    Minute from Sir Kenneth Berrill to T.P. Lankester, 10 September 1979, PM Papers, Box no.308, The Future of BNOC: Proposed Sale of BP Assets, Part 2.

38    The main costs were merchant bank, broking and underwriting fees. Underwriting is the process by which financial institutions, in return for a commission, commit themselves in advance to take up shares in a public offer for sale in the event of an offer not being fully subscribed. It effectively insures the seller of the shares against the risks of a flotation failure and being left with unsold shares. In the UK in the 1980s lead underwriters typically laid off the risks from underwriting the offer to sub-underwriters. The lead underwriter (often the issuing house for the shares) was paid an overall commission out of which stock broking and sub-underwriting commissions were paid. The residual percentage accruing to the lead underwriter or underwriters

was known as "the overrider". In the BP share sale the underwriting commission rate was 1.375% out of which 1.25% was paid for sub-underwriting.

39   The merchant bank S.G.Warburg & Co advised the Bank of England in the preparation of the offer. The Bank of England had handled the sale of BP shares in 1977 and did so again in 1983.

40   "UK Employee Participation in Sale of BP Stock: A Note by the British Petroleum Company Limited", 21 June 1979, in E(DL) Part 1.

41   Unlike in a number of later privatisations the preferential terms for employee share purchases were modest. Price Waterhouse (1987) *Privatisation: The Facts*, pp.37–8. The allocation to the trust scheme was necessary if the employee was to benefit from the preferential tax regime for employee shares introduced in the Finance Act 1978. Employee trust share schemes were set up to hold shares allocated on preferential terms in all subsequent privatisations. Provided that the shares were held by trustees for at least two years, the value of preferential shares allocated was not subject to full Income Tax on the employee. The longer the shares were held in the trust the more favourable the tax treatment with no tax liability after seven years.

42   This had been guaranteed for a number of years by what was known as the "Bradbury letter", which was required by the Securities and Exchange Commission to permit BP shares to be traded in New York.

43   In June 1981 the Government had not taken up a BP rights issue so as to avoid its shareholding increasing. This reduced the Government's holding in the company from 46% to 39%.

44   E(79) 15th meeting, 26 November 1979; E(79)67, "BNOC – Future Structure and Private Sector Participation. A Memorandum by the Secretary of State for Energy", 21 November 1979.

45   E(79)67, Annex 3, "The British National Oil Corporation – Privatisation: an Interim Report" by Philip Shelbourne, Samuel Montagu & Co. Ltd., London. In British Columbia a Conservative administration had come to power and wanted to sell off a public corporation established by the previous administration. To deflect criticism that the public were being asked to buy something they already owned, albeit indirectly (the same point was made from time to time in the UK), the decision was taken to offer the public free shares with an option to buy additional shares. The scheme was successful.

46   Unfortunately, the Committee minutes do not identify who raised the objections, but it is reasonable to assume that it was Treasury Ministers.

47   Minute from T.P.Lankester to W.J.Burroughs, Department of Energy, 14 November 1979 and minute from Howell to the PM, 30 December 1979; both in PM Papers, Box no.308, The Future of BNOC: Proposed Sale of BP Assets, Part 2.

48   Howell's proposals received a critical reception in No. 10; minute from T.P.Lankester to the PM, 11 December 1979, PM Papers, Box no.308, ibid.

49   E(79)67, annex, "The British National Oil Corporation – Privatisation: an Interim Report" by Philip Shelbourne, Samuel Montagu & Co. Ltd., London.

50   E(79)67.

51   E(79)68, "The Privatisation of BNOC: Note by the Central Policy Review Staff", 22 November 1979.

52   E(79), 19th meeting 12 December 1979; E(79)80, "BNOC: Future Structure and Private Sector Participation. Memorandum by the Secretary of State for Energy", 7 December 1979.

53   E(80)9th meeting, 11 March 1980; E(80)22, "BNOC: Private Sector Participation. Memorandum by the Secretary of State for Energy", 6 March 1980.

54   E(80)22.

55   The Department of Energy was meantime arguing that it could see no advantages other than receipts to the Exchequer from the restructuring and sale of BNOC. The Official Committee on Nationalised Industry Policy based in the Treasury noted at a meeting on 3 December 1979: "The Department of Energy saw no substantial benefits in terms of greater efficiency by [BNOC] Operating as a result of the split and removal of Government controls"; NIP(79)12th meeting, HM Treasury Filefolder 11271561. Also, the Department of Energy continued to worry about the implications for oil supplies. Related to security of supply was the Department's view that the depletion of the North Sea fields should be regulated. Howell (2000), pp.84–5, has since written, "I saw my task while serving as Secretary of State for Energy as being to parcel up and

prepare the state's vast possessions in the energy sector, so that they could then be floated as properly working and potentially profitable corporations, attracting the widest possible investor interest. Treasury officials had a different and quite disruptive view. They wanted sales of assets to start forthwith, beginning with the sale of oil-and-gas field interests, which looked to them like fat and ripe fruit on the state tree waiting to be plundered . . .. My perspective may well have seemed overly idealistic and even procrastinating. But it was based on a perfectly solid strategy and in the end, of course, it broadly prevailed."

56  Note for the Record, 23 April 1980, PM Papers, Box no.308, The Future of BNOC: Proposed Sale of BP Assets, Part 3.
57  "Disposals Programme in 1980–81", memorandum to the PM from the Chancellor of the Exchequer, 12 March 1980, in E(DL) Part 3.
58  Note from T.P.Lankester, PS No.10 to Bill Burroughs, PS, Department of Energy, 18 March 1980, in E(DL) Part 3.
59  E(80)30th meeting, 6 August 1980; E(80)81, "Disposal of BGC oil assets. Memorandum by the Secretary of State for Energy", 30 July 1980.
60  E(80)30th meeting; briefing note to the PM from Robert Armstrong, Cabinet Secretary, 12 September 1980, in E(DL) Part 3.
61  E(DL)(80)2nd meeting.
62  E(DL)(80)6, "Public Participation in British Gas. Memorandum by the Secretary of State for Energy, dated 13 June 1980.
63  E(DL)(80)3rd meeting, 24 June 1980.
64  E(80)81, "Disposal of BGC's Oil Assets. Memorandum by the Secretary of State for Energy", 30 July 1980.
65  Letter from the Secretary of State for Energy to the Secretary of State for Industry, dated 24 July 1980, in E(DL) Part 3; E(80)81, "Disposal of BGC Oil Assets. Memorandum by the Secretary of State for Energy", in E(DL) Part 3.
66  Letter from Howe to Howell, 1 August 1980, in E(DL) Part 3.
67  Note from Howe to the PM, 1 August 1980, in E(DL) Part 3.
68  E(80)29th meeting 4 August 1980; E(80)80, "BNOC: Private Sector Participation. Memorandum by the Secretary of State for Energy", dated 30 July 1980.
69  Quoted in E(80)80. It seems that officials in the Department of Energy expected that the Treasury would oppose the idea and were sceptical as to whether it would ever come to fruition.
70  E(80)32nd meeting 10 September 1980; E(80)95, "BNOC Revenue Bonds Scheme. Memorandum by the Secretary of State for Energy", 5 September 1980. Minute from T.P.Lankester to J.West, Department of Energy, 14 July 1980, PM Papers, Box no.309, The Future of BNOC: Proposed Sale of BP Assets. Petroleum and Continental Shelf Bill, Part 4.
71  The Secretary of State's memorandum makes reference to a third scheme, which is briefly described as a hybrid of the other two schemes. This Scheme does not appear to have been considered in detail; E(80)95.
72  E(80)80.
73  Various correspondence in PM Papers, Box no.309, The Future of BNOC: Proposed Sale of BP Assets. Petroleum and Continental Shelf Bill, Parts 4 and 5.
74  Letter from Howell to the Chancellor of the Exchequer, 14 May 1981; PM Papers, Box no.309, The Future of BNOC: Proposed Sale of BP Assets. Petroleum and Continental Shelf Bill, Part 5.
75  BGC's principal statutory duties were set out in the Gas Act 1972 (for details see endnote 140, chapter 3). The Board judged that disposing of its oil assets was inconsistent with these duties and the best interests of the Corporation.
76  Letter from Sir Denis Rooke to Howell, 23 July 1980, with E(80)(80). Also in E(DL) Part 3.
77  Letter from Howell to Rooke, 14 August 1980, with E(80)(80). Also in E(DL) Part 3.
78  The request was made in discussion but later in the year Lawson refers to it as a commitment made by the Secretary of State, see below.
79  Letter from Rooke to Howell, 27 August 1980, in E(DL) Part 3.

80  E(80)97, "British Gas Corporation – Disposal of Oil Assets. Memorandum by the Secretary of State for Energy", 10 September 1980, in E(DL) Part 3.
81  E(80)33rd meeting, 15 September 1980.
82  Note from Howell to the PM, 8 October 1980, in E(DL) Part 3.
83  Note from Lawson to the PM, 16 October 1980, in E(DL) Part 3.
84  Memorandum from Joseph to the PM, 27 October 1980, in E(DL) Part 3.
85  Letter from T. Lankester, PS, No. 10, to Ian Ellison, Department of Industry, 29 October 1980, in E(DL) Part 3.
86  Memorandum from Lawson to the PM, 16 October 1980, in E(DL) Part 3.
87  Note from Howell to the PM, 22 October 1980, in E(DL) Part 3.
88  Memorandum from D.J.Wright, No. 10, to the PM, 24 October 1980, in E(DL) Part 3; letter from T. Lankester, PS No. 10, to J.D.West, Department of Energy, 27 October 1980, in E(DL) Part 3.
89  Memorandum from Howell to the PM, 27 April 1981, in E(DL) Part 4.
90  Annotated note on ibid.
91  Note from Lawson to the PM, 6 May 1981, in E(DL) Part 4.
92  PM, 30 July 1981, *Hansard*, column 1159. http://www.margaretthatcher.org/speeches/display document.asp?docid=104697.
93  Lawson (1992), p.214.
94  Notes of the Secretary of State's meeting with the Dorset Group, 17 January 1983, in E(DL) Part 9.
95  As one civil servant in the Department of Energy at the time commented during the preparation of this chapter, "once the department had an effective Minister in Nigel Lawson, civil servants were only too delighted to vigorously drive through his clear agenda. The sense of purpose and direction under Lawson were a different world from the ineffectiveness and lack of achievement under Howell." However, to be fair to Howell, Lawson inherited the planning that Howell had put in place.
96  Note of the Secretary of State's meeting with the Board of the British Gas Corporation, 30 March 1983, and letter from Lawson to Rooke following the meeting, in E(DL) Part 9. BP was the largest single investor in Dorset with a 50% interest.
97  Letter from Rooke to Lawson, Secretary of State for Energy, 10 March 1983, in E(DL) Part 9.
98  Letters from Walker to Rooke, 2 and 17 November 1983, in E(DL) Part 9.
99  Letter from Rooke to Walker, 7 November 1983, in E(DL) Part 9.
100  Letter from Rooke to Walker, 26 March 1984, in E(DL) Part 9.
101  Briefing note to the PM from Sir Robert Armstrong, Cabinet Secretary, 5 April 1984, in E(DL) Part 9.
102  Note from Andrew Turnbull, PS to the PM, 5 April 1984, in E(DL) Part 9.
103  Note from David Pascall in No. 10 to Turnbull, 9 April 1984, in E(DL) Part 9.
104  "Wytch Farm", memorandum from the Secretary of State for Energy, 7 April 1984, in E(DL) Part 9.
105  Note of the PM's meeting to Michael Reidy, Department of Energy, 9 April 1984, in E(DL) Part 9.
106  Memorandum from the Secretary of State for Energy to the PM, 2 May 1984, in E(DL) Part 9.
107  Note from Armstrong to Turnbull, 3 May 1984, in E(DL) Part 9.
108  Note from Walker to the PM, 4 May 1984, in E(DL) Part 9.
109  Annotated note on ibid. BGC would also receive 40% of production profits after Dorset had recovered its investment and production had reached 23m barrels.
110  The Direction was issued by the Secretary of State on 4 August 1982 under Section 11(1) of the Act.
111  Similarly, on 1 November 1983 BGC's prospective exploration assets were transferred to a separate BGC subsidiary, which was transferred to Holdings, now called Enterprise Oil, on 23 December 1983. Some consideration was given to selling the businesses separately, but this was ruled out because of the higher value that was likely to arise from a combined sale.
112  The Board's co-operation with the sale increased after the Election with the change in Secretary of State – Lawson and Rooke had been at loggerheads – and the fact that the return of a Conservative Government made privatisation inevitable.

113 Holdings (later Enterprise Oil) decided not to appoint its own advisers believing that it had sufficient skills in its new management team to handle the sale. However, the company appointed Schroder Wagg (Schroders) after the flotation to advise on the RTZ bid, see below.

114 There was also the point that a trade sale might have been to an American company. In privatisations the financial adviser was a City merchant bank and was later also known as the investment banking adviser.

115 Operating agreements relating to offshore oil assets provided for preferred purchasing rights for BGC's co-licensees in the event of a sale of licence interests, but not in the event of a change in the ownership of the company owning the interests.

116 The reason was that once the corporation became a company it stepped outside the usual Treasury controls over a nationalised industry's finances. This is discussed in more detail in the review of a number of other privatisations in later chapters.

117 Letter from Nigel Lawson, Secretary of State for Energy to the Chancellor of the Exchequer, 10 May 1983, in E(DL) Part 7; Letter from the Chancellor of the Exchequer to Lawson, 18 May 1983, in E(DL) Part 7.

118 Letter from Alick Buchanan-Smith, Minister of State, Department of Energy, to John Moore, Economic Secretary, Treasury, 17 August 1983 and the reply 22 August 1983 from the Chancellor, both in E(DL) Part 7.

119 Department of Energy (1984) *Enterprise Oil: A report on the Privatisation of Enterprise Oil*, London.

120 House of Commons, Session 1981–82, *Tenth Report from the Committee of Public Accounts. Department of Industry. Sale of shares in British Aerospace; Sales of Government Shareholdings in other publicly owned Companies and British Petroleum Limited*, HMSO, 1982.

121 Department of Energy (1984), pp.21–3.

122 Cazenove & Co and de Zoete & Bevan acted as stockbrokers. Wood Mackenzie provided independent advice to the Government on the pricing of the offer.

123 Note to the Prime Minister from the Secretary of State for Energy, 13 June 1984, in E(DL) Part 10.

124 Note to the PM from the Foreign Secretary, 18 June 1984, in E(DL) Part 10.

125 The issue was valued mainly on a dividend yield basis. The sale price implied a dividend yield of 5.41%.

126 In this issue there were no free shares or matching offers for employees, as used in many other privatisations, because the company had few employees. Thirty four employees applied under the preferential application scheme for a total of 61,250 shares.

127 *The Times, Guardian, Daily Telegraph, Financial Times* Lex column, all 20 June 1984, press cuttings in E(DL) Part 10.

128 In tender issues the share price finally set reflected the demand and supply of shares on offer, which reduced the prospect of an under-pricing of the sale.

129 Department of Energy (1984), op cit., p.30.

130 Letter from Lord Rothschild, 27 June 1984, in E(DL) Part 10.

131 Letter from Callum McCarthy, PS, Department of Trade and Industry, to David Peretz, PS/Chancellor of the Exchequer, 28 June 1984, in E(DL) Part 10.

132 CC(84)24th meeting conclusions, 28 June 1984.

133 Later it appears that the limit was raised further to just over 29%. Note to the PM from Andrew Turnbull, 27 June 1984, in E(DL) Part 10.

134 Secretary of State for Energy's statement to the House 28 June 1984, *Hansard*, column 1167; Price Waterhouse *Privatisation: The Facts*, p.61.

135 Out of the 1.55%, the lead underwriter took 0.3% and the sub-underwriters 1.25%.

136 For essentially political reasons the company was registered in Scotland, making it the largest Scottish registered company.

137 Background note on Britoil's Oil Interests, 25 November 1985, Department of Energy files, G63/602/14, Part 1.

138 "Gas Privatisation: Upstream Matters", G.63/602/14, Part 1.

139 In effect, Warburgs and Rothschilds became joint managers of the offer but with Warburgs in the lead. The brokers to the offer were Rowe and Pitman, Cazenove & Co, Wood Mackenzie,

Hoare Govett and W. Greenwell & Co. Freshfields acted as solicitors. By now the Treasury was insisting on "beauty contests" (competition) when departments appointed advisers for a sale. However, the Department of Energy was permitted to appoint Warburgs without competition because the firm had already been advising the Department on the sale of BNOC.

140 In this case Freshfields.
141 In addition, profit sharing and share option schemes were introduced. Consideration was given to providing employees that had remained with BNOC following the separation of the Operating arm with free and matching shares on the grounds that they too had helped build up the business. However, the benefits would have been taxable and the idea was abandoned.
142 In this privatisation involving a public offer, as in later privatisations, the shares for employees came out of the Government's remaining holding. Also, in this and other privatisations, employees were permitted to decline the free and matching share offers. This was because a share offer to employees on different terms to other potential shareholders was likely to be classified as a separate offer for sale. This would have led to additional costs. Also, to ensure that gains from the shares were treated as capital gains and not income for tax purposes, the shares had to arise from the offer for sale not from the employment.
143 The terms did differ, however, from those introduced by the Department of Energy for the special share in Amersham International sold in February 1982 (see chapter 6), in which a shareholding of more than 15% was effectively prohibited. As mentioned elsewhere, in these early days of privatisation how special shares would work, if at all, was not entirely clear. There was some experimenting with the terms.
144 The rationale was the same as in the later tender sale of shares in Enterprise Oil, to make the application process simpler and more predictable for small investors; Lawson (1992), p.220. Interestingly in the light of the subsequent undersubscription for the shares, City institutions complained about the special terms for small investors on the grounds that it could leave them having to pay a higher price.
145 Individuals who applied for up to 2,000 shares could take advantage of the loyalty bonus.
146 Minute from Nigel Lawson to the Chancellor of the Exchequer, 25 October 1982, PM Papers, Box No. 309, The Future of BNOC: Proposed Sale of BP Assets, Part 5.
147 Note from M.C.Scholar, PS No. 10, to J.West, Department of Energy, 29 October 1982, ibid.
148 Lawson (1992), p.210.
149 Minute from N.L.Wicks, 5 November 1982, PM Papers, Box no.309, Part 5, op cit. Independent advice on the oil price was provided by brokers Fielding Newson-Smith.
150 The adviser was Dundas Hamilton, a distinguished stockbroker.
151 Department of Energy (1982) *Britoil: Departmental history of the share offer*, London; Price Waterhouse *Privatisation: The Facts*, p.46. The final decision to proceed with a sale by tender was made on 5 November. As in the case of Enterprise Oil, the total underwriting commission paid was 1.55%, with 0.3% to the lead underwriter and 1.25% to sub-underwriters. Serious consideration was given to undertaking the sub-underwriting first before the lead underwriter committed with a view to reducing the commissions payable. If the sub-underwriting succeeded there would be no need to undertake and pay for the lead underwriting function. However, Warburgs, the prospective lead underwriter, feared that they would be left with a large underwriting commitment if the sub-underwriting failed, opposed the idea and argued that they should be paid a higher main underwriting commission to bear the risk should it go ahead. The idea was dropped.
152 Even so, 35,000 small investors ended up with shares.
153 *Hansard*, column 305, 13 March 1985.

## 5 PRIVATISING BRITISH AEROSPACE AND CABLE AND WIRELESS

1 E(DL)(79)4th meeting, 19 July 1979; E(DL)(79)8, "British Aerospace: Sale to the Private Sector. Memorandum by the Secretary of State for Industry", dated 13 July 1979; both in E(DL) Part 1.

2   Official Committee on Nationalised Industry Policy, NIP(79) 2nd meeting, HM Treasury Papers, Filefolder 11271561.
3   E(DL)(79)8; E(DL)(79)4th meeting.
4   Letter with draft Statement from Peter Mason, Private Secretary (PS), Department of Industry, to Martin Hall, PS/Chancellor of the Exchequer, 19 July 1979, in E(DL)(79) Part 1.
5   *Hansard*, 23 July 1979, columns 30–39.
6   Conservative Research Department (1979) *General Election 1979: Questions of Policy*, p.121.
7   E(DL)(79)14, "British Aerospace: Introduction of Private Sector Capital. Memorandum by the Secretary of State for Industry", dated 2 October 1979, in E(DL) Part 2.
8   In other words, there were certain contingent liabilities that might arise if BAe went bust. Official Committee on Nationalised Industry Policy, NIP(79)9th meeting, 25 September 1979, HM Treasury papers Filefolder 11271561.
9   The main exception was the sale of the first tranche of shares in Cable & Wireless, which was already at an advanced stage of planning when the BAe sale was completed.
10  Article 223 states: "Any member state may take such measures as it considers necessary for the protection of the essential interests of its security which are connected with the production of or trade in arms, munitions and war material; such measures shall not adversely affect the conditions of competition in the common market regarding products which are not intended for specifically military purposes."
11  E(DL)(79)7th meeting, 17 October 1979.
12  E(DL)(79) 6th meeting, 4 October 1979, in E(DL) Part 1.
13  Note from the Chairman of Vickers Ltd to T.P. Lankester, PS in the PM's Office, 23 April 1980, in Nationalised Industries files Part 2. The dispute also extended to the nationalisation terms for shipbuilding and related to setting the compensation by reference to the value of the securities to be acquired, with the valuations based on the average share price during a six month period prior to the nationalisation. Critics argued that the share prices were depressed at this time and the valuations therefore too low. In Opposition Sir Keith Joseph had been highly critical of the compensation terms, but after becoming Secretary of State for Industry, in August 1979 he announced that no acceptable way could be found to alter the terms, on the grounds that those who had already accepted them would be adversely affected if the terms were now improved. In the following months agreement was reached on a number of the outstanding compensation claims. However, some former owners applied to the European Court arguing that the compensation terms were in breach of the European Convention on Human Rights; BT/C/30, Part 2 (BT files relate to the privatisation of BT and are held by the DTI/BERR). Sir William Lithgow, the largest single shareholder in Kincaid, one of the shipbuilding companies nationalised, was a leading appellant and for a number of years continued his legal action. The issue of the compensation terms arose during a number of the privatisations, including British Telecom, when Lithgow demanded a stronger statement on the threat of nationalisation by a future Labour Government and possible financial loss in the sale prospectus.
14  The Bank did handle the later sale of BP shares in 1983 and would continue to be consulted on other privatisations as part of the Bank's oversight of the timing of new issues in the Stock Market.
15  Henry Benson, one of the most eminent accountants of the time, was an adviser to the Governor of the Bank of England and a former director of Hawker Siddley, one of the constituent companies of BAe at nationalisation. Benson believed that BAe's balance sheet was too weak to survive in the private sector and the company was too dependent on government contracts. It seems that his views influenced the Bank into judging that a privatised BAe might be a financial failure. Although Kleinworts continued as advisers to the sale, they too worried about the effect on their reputation if the sale flopped.
16  E(DL)(80)5th meeting, 5 August 1980; E(DL)(80)10, "British Aerospace. Memorandum by the Minister of State, Department of Industry", 30 July 1980, in E(DL) Part 3. The Government had pulled out of the Airbus project in the late 1960s and re-entered in 1978 with an agreement that the Government would stand behind BAe's financial participation in the project.
17  E(DL)(80)10.
18  *British Aerospace Act*, chapter 26, London: HMSO.

19  E(DL)(80)6th meeting, 14 October 1980; E(DL)(80)15, "British Aerospace: Timing of Vesting in a Successor Company. Memorandum by the Minister of State, Department of Industry, 10 October 1980; both in E(DL) Part 3.

20  E(DL)(80)6th meeting. E(DL)(80)4, "British Aerospace: Prospects for Sale of Shares in 1980/1: Memorandum by the Minister of State for Industry", 8 May 1980.

21  Letter from A.J. Wiggins, HM Treasury, to T. Lankester, No. 10, 17 October 1980, in E(DL) Part 3.

22  Memorandum from Joseph to the PM, 23 October 1980, in Nationalised Industries files Part 3.

23  E(DL)(80)7th meeting, 23 October 1980.

24  Letter from Pym to Joseph, 20 October 1980, in E(DL) Part 3.

25  Letter from Joseph to Pym, 7 November 1980, in E(DL) Part 4.

26  Letter from Pym to Joseph, 24 November 1980, in E(DL) Part 4.

27  This followed a review of the accounts and forecasts of Airbus Industrie.

28  MISC 11, 16 July 1979 during Public Expenditure Survey discussions.

29  Letter from Biffen to Joseph, 18 December 1980, in E(DL) Part 4.

30  Letter from Butler to Biffen, 2 January 1981, in E(DL) Part 4.

31  E(DL)(80)15, 10 October 1980.

32  E(DL)(80)19, "British Aerospace Vesting in the Successor Company and Flotation. Memorandum by the Minister of State for Industry", 9 December 1980, in E(DL) Part 4.

33  E(DL)(80)8th meeting, 11 December 1980.

34  E(DL)(80)5th meeting; letter from PS/Chancellor, to T.Lankester, PM's Office, 15 December 1980, in E(DL) Part 4.

35  For details of the debt write-off see footnote 39 below.

36  Letter from Jenkins to Lankester, 15 December 1980, in E(DL) Part 4.

37  E(DL)(80)15, "British Aerospace: Timing of Vesting in a Successor Company. Memorandum by the Minister of State, Department of Industry", 10 October 1980, in E(DL) Part 4.

38  E(DL)(80) 8th meeting, 11 December 1980, in E(DL) Part 4.

39  Draft written answer in E(DL) Part 4. BAe's liability in respect of commencing capital of £158.7m and public dividend capital of £110m was extinguished, but outstanding National Loans Fund advances and other liabilities were transferred to the new company.

40  Letter from Butler to Lawson with a copy to the PM, 16 December 1980, in E(DL) Part 4.

41  Memorandum from Norman Tebbit, Minister for State at the Department of Industry, to the PM, 7 January 1980, in E(DL) Part 4.

42  Letter from Lawson to Tebbit, 8 January 1981, in E(DL) Part 4.

43  Annotated note to the PM from T. Lankester on the memorandum from John Nott, below. Also, note to the PM from the Chancellor, 19 January 1981, in E(DL) Part 4.

44  Memorandum from Nott to the PM, 16 January 1981.

45  Memorandum from Joseph to the PM, January 1981 (the precise date is not given it but was probably the 19th), in E(DL) Part 4.

46  Notes of the meeting, letter to Brian Norbury, Ministry of Defence, from Clive Whitmore, Principal PS, No.10, 19 January 1981. The Foreign and Commonwealth Secretary attended because of concerns about the impact of the announced defence cuts on relations with allied governments and especially the US government; memorandum from Sir Robert Armstrong to the PM, 19 January 1981. Both documents in E(DL) Part 4.

47  Price Waterhouse *Privatisation: The Facts.* The stockbrokers to the offer were Hoare Govett, Cazenove & Co, and W.Greenwell & Co.

48  House of Commons, Session 1981–82, *Tenth Report from the Committee of Public Accounts.*

49  Minute by G.M.A.Lambert, DTI, to T.Tarkowski, HM Treasury, 31 May 1985, British Telecom privatisation files, BT/A/61 Part 4.

50  The flotation was underwritten incurring a total commission of 1.75%, out of which the sub-underwriters received 1.25% and brokers' fees were paid.

51  House of Commons, Session 1981–82, *Tenth Report from the Committee of Public Accounts*, paragraph 14.

52    HM Treasury (1982) *Treasury Minute on the Seventh, Ninth to Eighteenth and Twentieth to Twenty-Ninth Reports from the Committee on Public Accounts*, Session 1981–82, Cmnd. 8759, London: HMSO.

53    Ibid., paragraphs 16–17. E(DL)80, 1st meeting, 10 March 1980.

54    Letter from the Secretary of State for Industry to the PM, 13 March 1980, PM Papers, British Aerospace: Shares for Employees, Cabinet Office.

55    This was set out in a letter from the Chancellor of the Exchequer on 28 July 1980.

56    Letter from the Chancellor of the Exchequer to the PM, 18 June 1980, ibid.

57    "Privatisation Present Situation and Prospects. Report by the Secretary of State for Industry", 13 September 1982, in E(DL) Part 6. Memorandum of understanding sent by Joseph to Sir Austin Pearce, Chairman of BAe, 3 February 1981, in E(DL) Part 4. Kleinworts had been against retention of government directors in case this acted as a disincentive to private investors.

58    Note from Joseph to Sir Peter Carey, 20 February 1981, in E(DL) Part 4.

59    Letter from Secretary of State for Industry to the PM, 23 March 1983, PM Papers, British Aerospace: Shares for Employees.

60    After the June 1983 General Election the Departments of Industry and Trade were combined.

61    Letter from Lazard Brothers & Co, Ltd. and attached report, 28 November 1984, in E(DL) Part 11.

62    Letter from the Chancellor of the Exchequer to the Secretary of State for Trade and Industry, 9 January 1985, in E(DL) Part 11.

63    *Hansard*, 15 January 1985, columns 185–91. Late during the planning of the sale of the second tranche of shares the issue of MoD procurement again raised its head. The issue was whether BAe was going to get a particular new contract. The MoD was pressed to make an exception to its developing policy on the use of competitive tendering and declared in advance that BAe would win the contract, so that the sale would not be disrupted.

64    After £188m raised for the company for restructuring. PM Papers, Aerospace, Part 3. As this was a second issue, setting the flotation price should have been less hazardous because there was already a market price for the company's shares. However, there was a suspicion within Government that the City deliberately marked down the BAe share price the day before the sale of the second tranche of shares so that the issue price would be set low. The costs of the issue to the Government were £18m and to the company around £8m. The underwriting commissions were set lower than for the first issue, at 0.425%; out of which brokers' commissions of 0.125% were paid; Price Waterhouse *Privatisation: The Facts*, pp.21–2. The second share sale coincided with a BAe rights issue.

65    DTI internal note, "British Aerospace: Offer for Shares", in BT/A/61, Part 4.

66    Statement to the House by Geoffrey Pattie, Minister for Information Technology, *Hansard*, 13 May 1985, column 40.

67    Correspondence in PM Papers, Box 4, British Aerospace: Possible Merger Between British Aerospace and Thorn-EMI or GEC. *Hansard*, columns 361–2, 16 May 1984.

68    Again, the Government took advantage of Article 223 of the Rome Treaty.

69    Letter from Tebbit to Lawson, 14 January 1985, in E(DL) Part 11.

70    Tebbit (1988) *Upwardly Mobile*, p.177.

71    Chester (1975), p.453.

72    Also, its debt was never treated as part of public sector borrowing.

73    The company was formed following the merger of the international cable and wireless companies Eastern Telegraph and Marconi Wireless.

74    Ibid; Baglehole (1970) *A Century of Service*; *Cable and Wireless plc Offer for Sale of Ordinary Shares by Kleinwort Benson Ltd on the instructions of the Lord Commissioners of HM Treasury and the Secretary of State for Industry*, 1981, pp.2–3.

75    E(DL)(79)5, "Disposal of Assets. Memorandum by the Financial Secretary, Treasury", dated 2 July 1979, in E(DL) Part 1.

76    E(81)27, "Cable and Wireless. Memorandum by the Secretary of State for Industry", dated 3 March 1981.

77    Barings and Rothschilds carried out initial feasibility studies of a C&W sale in 1979 and Barings was chosen to advise the Government. C&W engaged Rothschilds but after Sharp became

Chairman of the company (see below) Kleinworts was appointed because of the bank's previous experience of privatisation sales. Kleinworts also became the Government's advisers in the summer of 1980 because of cheaper fees than Barings and because C&W was unwilling to work with Barings.

78   Ted Short became Chairman of C&W in 1976, six months after retiring as Labour's Deputy Prime Minister, providing an example of how state-owned firms were susceptible to politically-inspired senior appointments.

79   E(DL)(80)11, "Cable and Wireless: Sale of Shares. Memorandum by the Minister of State, Department of Industry", 25 July 1980, in E(DL) Part 3.

80   E(DL)(80)5th meeting, 5 August 1980.

81   E(DL)(80)16, "Cable and Wireless: Sale of Shares. Memorandum by the Minister of State, Department of Industry", 21 October 1980, in E(DL) Part 3.

82   Ibid.

83   Ibid.

84   In his memoirs, David Young, involved in the sale of C&W, comments on the attitude of senior management in the company, that they were concerned with managing decline rather than expansion; Young (1990) *The Enterprise Years*, p.51.

85   E(DL)(80)16.

86   Ibid.

87   Ibid.

88   E(DL)(80) 7th meeting, 23 October 1980.

89   Ibid; E(DL)(80)16.

90   E(DL)(80)7th meeting.

91   E(DL)(81)1, "Cable and Wireless. Memorandum by the Minister of State, Department of Industry", 26 January 1981.

92   Ibid.

93   E(81) 9th meeting, 5 March 1981; E(81)27, "Cable and Wireless. Memorandum by the Secretary of State for Industry", 3 March 1981.

94   Reported in a note from N.J.Sanders, PS to the PM, to J.C.Hudson at the Department of Industry, 23 February 1981, in Nationalised Industries files Part 3.

95   Draft statement in E(DL) Part 4, along with PM's annotated comment.

96   E(81)27, paragraph 2; letter from S.A.J. Locke, PS at the Treasury, to J.C.Hudson, PS/Minister of State for Industry, 27 February 1981, in E(DL) Part 4.

97   Annotated note to the PM on a letter from L.Riley, PS, Department of Industry, to Sanders on 27 February 1981, in E(DL) Part 4.

98   Note from T.P.Lankester, PS No.10, to L. Riley at the Department of Industry, 2 March 1981.

99   Letter from David Young to Lankester, 2 March 1981, with E(81)27.

100   E(81)27, paragraph 10.

101   Letter from Riley to Sanders, 27 February 1981.

102   Correspondence in E(DL) Part 4. E(81)27, para. 10

103   E(81)27, para. 10.

104   Briefing for the PM by the Cabinet Secretary, 4 March 1981, in E(DL) Part 4.

105   Letter from PS/Lord Privy Seal to Sanders, 27 February 1981, in E(DL) Part 4.

106   Note from J.R.Ibbs to Lankester, 4 March 1981, in E(DL) Part 4.

107   E(81) 9th meeting, 5 March 1981; Baker (1993) *The Turbulent Years*, p.76.

108   Note from T.P. Lankester to J.C.Hudson at the Department of Industry, 9 March 1981, in E(DL) Part 4.

109   E(DL) (81) 13, "Cable and Wireless: Post Flotation Ownership and Control. Memorandum by the Minister of State, Department of Industry", 17 July 1981; E(DL)(81)3rd meeting, 23 July 1981; both in E(DL) Part 4. The Minister of State was Kenneth Baker.

110   E(DL)(81)3rd meeting.

111   Cable and Wireless Offer for Sale document, p.20. Meanwhile, Government retained the right to appoint not more than two non-executive directors.

112   Following a 'beauty contest' the Treasury engaged W. Greenwell & Co for a second opinion on the price advised by Kleinworts. As in the setting of the share price in other privatisations,

the forecast dividend yield and the price-earnings ratio were both taken into account when determining the price. The advisers came up with a range of prices of between 165p and 170p. The number 168 was considered to be a lucky number in the Chinese community and it has been suggested that this had an influence on the final price chosen given the simultaneous flotation in Hong Kong. When pronounced in Chinese Mandarin, 168 sounds like the phrase "making money all the way". The stockbrokers to the offer were Cazenove & Co, James Capel & Co, and Rowe and Pitman.

113  Press release from Kleinwort Benson Ltd., 2 November 1981, in E(DL) part 5.

114  In this privatisation the free shares were made available over a period as part of a company employee profit-sharing scheme. In subsequent privatisations the free shares were allotted immediately after the flotation to employees, albeit to be held in trust. This resulted from the experience of the C&W share offer, where employees were found to prefer an obvious personal benefit at the time of privatisation. The reason for the trust scheme was again fiscal, to benefit from tax concessions for employee share schemes under the 1978 Finance Act. Shares were also allocated for overseas employees and in these cases the terms reflected local tax laws.

115  The largest part, £4.7m, represented underwriting fees; G.M.A.Lambert, DTI, to T.Tarkowski, HM Treasury, 31 May 1985, BT/A/61 Part 4. The underwriting commission was 1.75% out of which 1.25% went to the sub-underwriters and brokers' fees were also paid.

116  Letter from Patrick Jenkin to Francis Pym, Lord President of the Council, 9 October 1981, in E(DL) Part 4.

117  Memorandum from Jenkin to the PM, 4 November 1981, in E(DL) Part 5. Jenkin replaced Joseph as Secretary of State for Industry in September 1981.

118  Letter from Sir Geoffrey Howe to Jenkin, 9 November 1981, in E(DL) Part 5.

119  Letter from the PM to Jenkin, 17 November 1981, in E(DL) Part 5.

120  Letter from the Chancellor of the Exchequer to the PM, 25 October 1983, in PM Papers E(DL) Part 7.

121  In early 1983 Hong Kong Land, a shareholder in the Hong Kong telephone company, Telco, decided to dispose of some of its holding. Eager to prevent another operator such as AT&T from buying the shares, C&W offered to acquire them. The C&W Board financed the acquisition by the allotment of some 30m previously unissued C&W shares to Hong Kong Land, who immediately renounced them in favour of pre-arranged UK institutional purchasers. The Foreign Office favoured the Government taking up its entitlement in the new issue to avoid possible objections to a lowering of the Government's shareholding in C&W to under 50% from overseas governments. However, the Treasury opposed the expenditure, which would have amounted to some £50–60m to acquire the shares. The PM backed the Treasury. Letter from M. O'Mara, PS Treasury, to M.C. Scholar, PS No. 10, 23 March 1983 and PM's annotated agreement, in E(DL) Part 7.

122  *Hansard*, column 437, 27 October 1983.

123  Letter to Andrew Turnbull from M. O'Mara, HM Treasury 25 November 1983 and accompanying background papers, in E(DL) Part 8.

124  Note by John Redwood, Policy Unit, to Turnbull, 6 December 1983, PM Papers E(DL) Part 7.

125  Letter from the Chancellor of the Exchequer to the PM, 30 August 1985, PM Papers E(DL) Part 10.

126  Building on experience in earlier privatisations, a number of performance incentives were built in, including merchant bank fees linked to reducing the pricing discount and lower underwriting commissions; Cable and Wireless Share Sale 1985: Points of General Interest. Note by HM Treasury, NIP (85)18, 18 December 1985, HM Treasury papers A/06 Part 4.

127  146m shares were sold in the UK, including 43.5m new shares offered by the company. In addition, 13m shares were sold simultaneously in Japan and Canada through a private placement.

128  Young (1990) p.60.

129  Cable and Wireless plc Report and Accounts 1986. Figures are for years ending 31 March.

## 6  PRIVATISING AMERSHAM INTERNATIONAL, THE NATIONAL FREIGHT CORPORATION AND ASSOCIATED BRITISH PORTS

1  E(DL)(81)15, "Disposal of Amersham International Limited. Memorandum by the Secretary of State for Energy", 17 November 1981, in E(DL) Part 5.

2    E(DL)(81), 4th meeting, 27 November 1981, in E(DL) Part 5.

3    E(DL)(80), 2nd meeting, 12 May 1980.

4    Ibid.

5    E(DL)(81)15.

6    Ibid.

7    Ibid., and attached "The Disposal of the Secretary of State for Energy's Interest in Amersham International. Note by the Department of Energy", in E(DL) Part 5.

8    This contrasts with the view held in the Department of Industry during the sale of the first tranche of C&W shares that a public flotation was beneficial to obtain an accurate valuation of the company; see p.127 above.

9    E(DL)(81)16.

10    E(DL)(81)15.

11    E(DL)(81)4th meeting, 27 November 1981, in E(DL) Part 5.

12    In addition, the company raised a further £7.3m by the sale of new shares.

13    *Hansard*, column 298, 16 March 1982. The price was near to the mid-point of the range of prices suggested by the independent adviser W. Greenwell & Co. Greenwells had acted as independent adviser to the Government on the flotation price during the C&W sale and also advised on the Amersham share price.

14    Ridley (1991) *'My Style of Government': The Thatcher Years*, p.59.

15    Lawson (1992), p.209.

16    *Hansard*, column 261, 16 March 1982.

17    Letter from Ingham to Chipp, 26 February 1982, in E(DL) Part 5.

18    Minute from J.M.Sterling to the Secretary of State for Trade and Industry, 31 December 1983, BT/A/26 Part 3.

19    The share was redeemed on 27 July 1988.

20    The shares were held in a Share Participation Scheme established by the company, again for tax reasons.

21    House of Commons, Session 1981–82, *Tenth Report from the Committee of Public Accounts*, paragraph 23.

22    Lawson (1992), p.210.

23    Letter from Howe to Jenkin, 30 March 1982; also "Methods of Privatisation. Memorandum by the Financial Secretary, Treasury"; both in E(DL) Part 5.

24    Conservative Party (1979).

25    McLachlan (1983) *The National Freight Buyout*; Thompson (1990), *Sharing the Success*.

26    Letter from Fowler to Lawson, 29 June 1979.

27    E(DL)(79)12, "Sale of Shares in the National Freight Corporation. Memorandum by the Minister of Transport", 17 July 1979, in E(DL) Part 1. The Minister of Transport's proposals also included an amendment to the 1968 Transport Act to remove the concept of integrated freight transport and repeal powers to set up a special licensing scheme for long distance road transport. However, the idea of a planned and integrated freight transport system had more or less already died in the 1970s.

28    Letter from Fowler to the Chancellor, 6 June 1979, with E(DL)2nd meeting papers.

29    E(DL)(79)12.

30    E(DL)(79)5th meeting, 26 July 1979, in E(DL) Part 2.

31    McLachlan (1983), pp.87–8.

32    "A Note for the Record", 6 March 1980, in E(DL) Part 3.

33    Letter from Fowler to Howe, 23 July 1980, in Nationalised Industries files, Part 2.

34    Thompson (1990), p.17.

35    Ibid.

36    Letter from Lawson to Fowler, 1 August 1980, in Nationalised Industries files, Part 2.

37    E(DL)(80)5th meeting, 5 August 1980, in E(DL) Part 3.

38    Letter from Fowler to Howe, 5 August 1980, in E(DL) Part 3.

39    Letter from Howe to Fowler, 6 August 1980, in E(DL) Part 3.

40    Thompson (1990), p.74.

41    Note from Fowler to the PM, 10 June 1981, in E(DL) Part 4.

42 McLachlan (1983), pp.4, 31–2. However, there is no evidence that the Government seriously considered this alternative. Being left with the unprofitable bits of NFC was unlikely to be attractive to the Treasury.
43 Ibid., p.29.
44 Note from Fowler to the PM, 10 June 1981, in E(DL) Part 4.
45 Letter of offer from P.A.Thompson to Fowler, 11 June 1981, in E(DL) Part 4.
46 Letter from Fowler to Joseph, 12 June 1981, in E(DL) Part 4.
47 Letter from Lawson to Fowler, 16 June 1981, in E(DL) Part 4.
48 Thompson (1990), p.11.
49 Note from Howell to the PM, 16 October 1981, in E(DL) Part 4.
50 Thompson (1990), pp.109, 128–31.
51 Letter from Howell to Howe, 16 February 1982, in E(DL) Part 5.
52 McLachlan (1983), p.57. Some 1,300 NFC pensioners took part in the purchase buying an average of 700 shares each.
53 The PM in the House of Commons 20 October 1981, *Hansard* column 161, http://www. margaretthatcher.org/speeches/displaydocument.asp?docid=104718
54 Thompson (1990), p.137 & 151.
55 Sir P. Thompson (1988) 'The Buyout at National Freight' in E.Butler (ed.). *The Mechanics of Privatization*, London: Adam Smith Institute.
56 Ibid., ch.6.
57 Ibid., p.126.
58 There were four unions in the NFC, three gave the buyout varying degrees of support. The TGWU, however, had the largest membership within the company. Ibid., pp.97–9, 164; McLachlan (1983), pp.63–5.
59 At privatisation the company had committed itself not to seek a stock exchange quotation for at least five years. When the company listed in 1989 it had a market capitalisation of £900m, compared to the buyout price of £54m; Thompson (1990), p.168.
60 The NDLS was reviewed in March 1984 when there was a call for it to be abolished to help save the financially embarrassed Port of London Authority. However, the fear of a national dock strike at a time when a serious dispute with the mine workers had just broken out meant that the proposal did not meet with much support in Government; E(A)(84)9th meeting, 20 March 1984. The scheme would not be abolished until 1989.
61 Official Committee on Nationalised Industry Policy, NIP(79)2nd meeting, HM Treasury papers Filefolder 11271561.
62 Letter from Fowler to Lawson, 21 June 1979, in E(DL).
63 E(DL)(80)1, "British Transport Docks Board: Introduction of Private Capital. Memorandum by the Minister of Transport", 7 February 1980.
64 The Government appointed separate financial advisers to Kleinwort, Benson who were advising the Corporation, reflecting the Government's new concern to prevent a possible conflict of interest when the same banks advised the Government and the Corporation. During the planning of the BTDB sale understandably the company wanted the strongest balance sheet going forward and the Government suspected that the advice being provided by Kleinworts on the appropriate capital restructuring was being compromised by Board pressure on Kleinworts. Both sets of advisers were appointed after expressions of interest were canvassed in the City and tenders for the work were invited.
65 Ibid.
66 Letter 21 February 1980 from Howe to Fowler, 21 February 1980, in E(DL) Part 3.
67 Letter from Nott to Fowler, 27 February 1980, in E(DL) Part 3.
68 E(80)4th meeting, 8 July 1980; E(DL)(80)9, "Introduction of Private Capital to British Transport Docks Boards (sic.). Memorandum by the Minister of Transport", dated 4 July 1980.
69 E(80)4th meeting.
70 Ibid.
71 Ibid.
72 Letter from Norman Fowler to Keith Joseph, Secretary of State for Industry, 17 July 1980, in E(DL) Part 3.

73 The Act also enabled British Rail to sell off subsidiary businesses, such as Sealink ferries and hotels.

74 Letter from Fowler, 7 November 1980, in E(DL) Part 4.

75 Letter from Leon Brittan to Fowler, 5 March 1981, in E(DL) Part 4.

76 Letter from Fowler to Brittan, 1 April 1981, in E(DL) Part 4.

77 Letter from Howell to Jenkin, 27 October 1981, in E(DL) Part 5; letter from Howell to Howe, 3 November 1981, in E(DL) Part 5.

78 It seems that no written contract was ever signed between BSC and the BTDB; letter from Nicholas Edwards, Secretary of State for Wales, to Howell, 8 November 1982, PM Papers, Nationalised Industries. The Steel Industry, Part 11.

79 E(DL)(82)10, "Privatisation of the British Transport Docks Board: Dispute with the British Steel Corporation. Memorandum by the Secretary of State for Transport", 11 November 1982, in E(DL) Part 6.

80 Letter from Howell to Jenkin, op cit.

81 Letter from Howell to Howe, 3 November 1981, in E(DL) Part 5.

82 Letter from Ridley to Howell, 18 November 1981, in E(DL) Part 5.

83 Letter from Howell to Ridley, 30 November 1981, in E(DL) Part 5.

84 Letter from Ridley to Howell, 7 December 1981, in E(DL) Part 5.

85 Letter from Howell to Ridley, 23 December 1981, in E(DL) Part 5. On the issue of the trust ports, Howell responded to Ridley that while he would look at the prospects for privatisation in the context of a general review of ports policy, the ports were "statutory bodies with statutory obligations which could not be sold in their present form". Primary legislation would be needed to create a structure similar to that set up for the BTDB. Also, he argued that it was by no means obvious that the trust ports would be attractive to private investors and the financial benefits for the Treasury from their sale were unclear. The ports had not made any applications for NLF loans for over a year and were already relying on private capital for investment, although the Government remained the lender of last resort.

86 Letter from Howell to Howe, 18 January 1982, in E(DL) Part 5.

87 Letter from Howell to Howe, 30 April 1982, in E(DL) Part 5.

88 Letter from Howell to Jenkin, 24 June 1982, in E(DL) Part 5.

89 Letter from Ridley to Jenkin, 2 July 1982, in E(DL) Part 5.

90 Letter from Lamont to Howell, 22 July 1982, in E(DL) Part 5.

91 Letter from Howell to Jenkin, 20 October 1982, in E(DL) Part 6.

92 Letter from Howell to Jenkin 5 November 1982, in E(DL) Part 6.

93 E(DL)(82)10, "Privatisation of the British Transport Docks Board: Dispute with the British Steel Corporation. Memorandum by the Secretary of State for Transport", 11 November 1982, in E(DL) Part 6.

94 Note from Sparrow to the PM, 31 January 1983, in E(DL) Part 7.

95 Memorandum from Howell to the PM, 31 January 1983, op cit.

96 Confirmed in writing on 1 February 1983, in E(DL) Part 7.

97 In addition, preference was given to employee applications to buy shares, up to a total of 3% of the shares on offer less those purchased under the matching offer.

98 Price Waterhouse (1987), p.9, there were also sale costs incurred by the Government of £3m and by the company of £0.25m. At 112p per share the company was effectively valued at £44.5m or around 25% of the value of the assets in the company's books. The financial restructuring including the write-off of debt in the balance sheet required detailed negotiation with the Inland Revenue over the tax consequences.

99 'Privatisation Programme 1983–84 to 1987–88. Progress Report – July 1984. Note by the Treasury', E(DL) Part 10.

100 Letter from R.Bird, Private Secretary (PS) Department of Transport, to M.C. Scholar, Economic Affairs PS No. 10, 14 February 1983, in E(DL) Part 7.

101 Memorandum from Howell to the PM, 31 January 1983, in E(DL) Part 7.

102 Memorandum from Ridley to the PM, n.d. April 1984 and Draft Press Release, 9 April 1984, both in E(DL) Part 9.

103 Sir K. Stuart (1988) "Making the ports private", in Butler (ed.), pp.45–7.

## 7 THE FIRST FOUR YEARS – A RETROSPECTIVE

1  Including £82m in sales of oil stockpiles and commodity stocks.
2  All figures exclude council home sales. The figures given in the text exclude small amounts, in the bottom section of Table 7.1, which relate to the sale by nationalised industries of subsidiaries and where the Exchequer did not benefit from the receipts directly. The advance oil payments, introduced as an emergency measure in 1979/80 when it became clear that the Chancellor of the Exchequer would be unable to meet his £1bn budget target for asset sales, were unwound in 1980/1 and 1981/2.
3  Speech to the Conservative Party Conference, 8 October 1982, http://www.margaretthatcher. org/speeches/displaydocument.asp?docid=105032
4  Letter from Howe to Nigel Lawson, 23 April 1982, in E(DL) Part 5.
5  Thatcher (1995) *The Path to Power*, p.569.
6  Campbell (2004) *Margaret Thatcher, Volume Two*, p.95.
7  Howe (1994), p.257.
8  Thatcher (1993) *The Downing Street Years*, p.284.
9  *The Times*, 18 February 1983.
10  NIP(79)3rd meeting, 12 June 1979, HM Treasury papers filefolder 11271561.
11  Minor exceptions include some British Rail subsidiaries in need of new investment and some of the assets of the National Enterprise Board.
12  Letter from John Butcher, Parliamentary Under Secretary of State at the Department of Industry, 21 September 1982, in BT/A/12, Part 1.
13  House of Commons, Session 1981–82, *Tenth Report from the Public Accounts Committee*. The quotation is from paragraph 25. The report deals with the sale of BP, BAe, C&W and Amersham shares.
14  The big exception was, of course, the NFC where employees were offered the opportunity to participate in the buyout by subscribing directly for shares.
15  Letter from Howe to Patrick Jenkin, 30 March 1982, in BT/A/52, Part 1.
16  As part of this, from the early days it was usual to provide that the Secretary of State could dispose of the shareholding in the enterprise only with the consent of the Treasury. The formal consent was usually given shortly before the issue of the prospectus (or pathfinder prospectus where this was issued). Given that the Treasury was generally consulted throughout the sale process and was represented on the relevant interdepartmental committees organising the sale, this process of seeking permission was a formality.
17  NIP(82)4th meeting, 18 November 1982, H1579/1000/01 Rev NIP/43. The Unit was established within the Treasury's Public Enterprise Division and was led by Herbert Christie and included teams of economists and accountants. From the earliest days the economists were led by Dr John Rickard and the accountants by Graham Houston. Initially there were three economists and three accountants. Shipbuilding, British Leyland (BL) and Rolls-Royce remained outside the Unit's responsibility and were overseen separately by a dedicated economic adviser within the Treasury, Dr Kosmin; HM Treasury Office Notice, ON(82)13, 28 January 1982; memorandum from H.Christie to Sir Douglas Wass, MH Treasury, 15 December 1982.
18  "She took office with a deep distrust of the Civil Service"; Campbell (2004), p.22. Hoskyns resigned in 1982 in part because he had failed to get what he saw as the PM's support for a more radical economic agenda; Hoskyns (2000).
19  Harris (1988), p.96.
20  Campbell (2004), p.44.
21  At the same time, civil servants were keen to remain in the picture. Young (1990, p.55) notes that a suggestion by him to Sir Keith Joseph that they should have a series of dinners with the Chairmen of the nationalised industries without department officials being present "went down like a lead balloon in the Department and over the next few weeks all kinds of ingenious suggestions were made for introducing officials". Alfred Sherman at the Centre for Policy Studies canvassed in vain for the establishment of an army of advisers across government departments to weaken the influence of the civil service and for the creation of a separate PM's department, populated with "carefully selected" civil servants; Sherman (2005), p.103. In spite of such advice,

Thatcher introduced few changes in the structure of No. 10, Whitehall or of the Cabinet Office: "She made few institutional innovations, but broadly accepted the structures and practices of the Whitehall village as she found them: and though she remained suspicious of civil servants as a class, she quickly came to trust the key individuals who served her far more than she did her political colleagues." Campbell (2004), p.23; also, see Kavanagh and Seldon (2000) *The Powers Behind the Prime Minister*, p.149. In her memoirs Thatcher pays tribute to the "professionalism" of the civil service; Thatcher (1993) *The Downing Street Years*, p.18. Such praise did not, however, prevent the occasional difficulties, including an awkward dinner with Permanent Secretaries from various ministries in May 1980. The Permanent Secretaries unwisely chose the occasion to raise complaints about Government policy; ibid., p.48.

22  Howe (1994), pp.125–6. In March 1983 Wass was succeeded by Peter Middleton who even more obviously supported the Government's economic strategy; Holmes (1985), p.204. Kavanagh and Seldon (2000), p.166, argue that Thatcher remained suspicious of the Treasury especially while Wass remained its Permanent Secretary. However, at the time her relations with the Chancellor of the Exchequer were cordial and this probably counterbalanced any doubts she may have had about Treasury loyalty.

23  The sale of subsidiary businesses by the boards of the public corporations, but not the Government directly, usually could be undertaken without the taking of new legal powers. Where the board resisted, as in the case of British Gas and the sale of oil and gas fields, the Minister could issue (or threaten to issue) a Directive. The legal scope of a Directive to sell depended upon its wording and the relevant wording in the industry's nationalisation statute.

24  http://www.margaretthatcher.org/speeches/displaydocument.asp?docid=105260

25  E.g. M.E. Beesley and S.C. Littlechild (1983) "Privatization: Principles, Problems and Priorities", *Lloyds Bank Review*, July, pp.1–20. Reproduced in Beesley (ed.) 1997, ch.2.

26  E(DL)(19)4, "Financing of British Airways – Share Issue. Memorandum by the Secretary of State for Trade", in E(DL) Part 1.

27  C(83)16th meeting conclusions, 9 May 1983.

28  A comment attributed to the Labour MP Gerald Kaufman.

29  Thatcher (1995), p.567.

## 8  INTO THE HEARTLANDS OF THE PUBLIC TRADING SECTOR: PRIVATISATION AND THE 1983–7 THATCHER GOVERNMENT

1  D. Butler and D. Kavanagh (1984), *The British General Election of 1983*, London: Macmillan p.119.

2  C. Johnson (1991) *The Economy under Mrs Thatcher 1979–1990*, London: Penguin, p.200.

3  D. Kavanagh (1987) *Thatcherism and British Politics*, p.236.

4  N. Lawson (1992) *The View from No11*, ch.36.

5  Lawson (1992) pp.138, 461–70, 488–99. R. Harris (1991) *Good and Faithful Servant: The Unauthorised Biography of Bernard Ingham*, London, Faber and Faber, p.125.

6  The chief objective was to prevent the pound falling below three Deutschmarks to the pound. C.F. Pratten (1987) "Mrs Thatcher's Economic Legacy", in K.Minogue and M.Biddiss (eds), *Thatcherism: Personality and Politics*, London: Macmillan, p.73; Lawson (1992) pp.654, 682–3; E.Dell (1996) *The Chancellors: A History of the Chancellors of the Exchequer 1945–90*, London: Harper Collins, ch.16.

7  Johnson (1991), p.312.

8  In part this probably reflected the generous redundancy package for the miners the Energy Secretary, Peter Walker, teased from the Treasury.

9  M. Crick (1985) *Scargill and the Miners*, Harmondsworth: Penguin; M. Adeney and J. Lloyd (1986) *The Miners' Strike 1984–85: Loss Without Limit*, London: Routledge; I. MacGregor (1986) *The Enemies Within: the Story of the Miners' Strike 1984–85*, London: Collins; Thatcher (1993) *The Downing Street Years*, pp.139–43 and Ch.13; Campbell (2004) pp.355–69.

10  Lawson (1992) p.160.

11  C(84)5th meeting conclusions; C(84)7, "Capital and Current Expenditure. Memorandum by the Chief Secretary, Treasury", dated 3 February 1984; C(84)25th meeting conclusions, 5 July 1984. C(84)30th meeting conclusions, 13 September 1984.

12  There was a particular need to rein back spending in the autumn of 1983, which had risen in the run-up to the Election; C(80)30th meeting conclusions, 20 October 1983.However, the reduction agreed was only £1bn reflecting the continuing difficulty in reining back public spending, and involved a half in the form of genuine spending cuts and the other half as funding from a further sale of BP shares. The revenue from which, as was the convention in public sector accounting, was treated as negative public spending; Lawson (1992) pp.282–4. Also, Thatcher (1993), p.316; Seldon and Collings (2000) *Britain under Thatcher*, p.26.

13  Holmes (1989), p.28.

14  Whitelaw held the Cabinet post of Lord President and Leader in the House of Lords.

15  D. Kavanagh (1987) *Thatcherism and British Politics*, p.98.

16  C(84)24th meeting conclusions, 28 June 1984; Thatcher (1993), pp.538–44, Campbell (2004), pp.305–6.

17  For important discussions on public spending during the second Thatcher administration, C(84) 5th meeting conclusions, 9 February 1984; C(84)5, "Economic Strategy. Memorandum by the Chancellor of the Exchequer", 3 February 1984; C(84)6, "Public Expenditure and Taxation in the Longer Term. Memorandum by the Chancellor of the Exchequer", 3 February 1984; C(84)36th meeting conclusions; E(A)(84)17th meeting, 3 July 1984; C(84)32nd meeting conclusions, 9 October 1984; C(84)29, "Public Expenditure Survey 1984. Memorandum by the Chief Secretary, Treasury", 3 October 1984; C(85)28th meeting conclusions, 3 October 1985; C(85)31st meeting conclusions, 7 November 1985; C(86)22, "Public Expenditure Survey 1986. Memorandum by the Lord President of the Council"; C(86) 36th meeting conclusions, 6 November 1986; C(86)17, "Economic Prospects. Memorandum by the Chancellor of the Exchequer", 14 July 1986; C(86)18, "1986 Public Expenditure Survey. Memorandum by the Chief Secretary, Treasury", 15 July 1986; C(86) 28th meeting conclusions, 17 July 1986.

18  J. Baker (1993) *The Turbulent Years*, p.113; Campbell (2004), p.212.

19  E.J. Evans (1997) *Thatcher and Thatcherism*, p.60.

20  S.R. Letwin (1992) *The Anatomy of Thatcherism*, p.177.

21  C. Parkinson (1992) *Right at the Centre: an autobiography*, London: Weidenfeld and Nicholson, p.253.

22  A. Denham and M. Garnett (2001*) Keith Joseph*, p.405.

23  F. Pym (1984) *The Politics of Consent*, p.13.

24  Cole (1987), p.136.

25  CC(85)37th meeting conclusions, 19 December 1985.

26  CC(86)1st meeting conclusions, 9 January 1986. J. Critchley (1987) *Heseltine*, London: Andre Deutsch, pp.143–56; W. Whitelaw (1989) *The Whitelaw Memoirs,* p.225; R.Harris (1991), pp.128–33; B. Ingham (1991) *Kill the Messenger*, pp.335–7; J. Critchley (1992) *Some of Us: People who did well under Thatcher,* pp.110–12; Thatcher (1993), pp.425–37; M. Crick (1997) *Michael Heseltine: A Biography*, London: Penguin Books, pp.283–8; Heseltine (2000) *Life in the Jungle*, ch.15.

27  Campbell (2004), p.496.

28  Lawson (1992), p.9.

29  The term did not have official sanction; Lawson (1992), p.32 footnote, explains that Thatcher hated the expression.

30  Lord Young (1990) *The Enterprise Years*, pp.146–9.

31  D. Swann (1988) *The Retreat of the State*, p.280; Lawson (1992), pp.398–402, 627.

32  Swann (1988), pp.281–2. The original impetus for "big bang" was a Labour Government decision to prosecute the Stock Exchange for activities considered to contravene the Restrictive Trade Practices Act. The case never came to court and in July 1983 the Chairman of the Stock Exchange instead reached agreement with Cecil Parkinson, then Secretary of State for Trade and Industry, to reform the stock market to remove the identified restrictive practices.

33  C(85)28th meeting conclusions, 3 October 1985; C(85)23, "Public Expenditure Survey 1985. Memorandum by the Chief Secretary, Treasury", 1 October 1985.

34 Cited in K. Harris (1988) *Thatcher*, p.187.
35 HM Treasury (1983) "The Financial Secretary Speaks out on Privatisation", 1 November, London: HM Treasury Press Release 190/83. For similar statements see HM Treasury (1984a) "Financial Secretary Reviews Privatisation Achievements", 16 July, London: HM Treasury Press Release 122/84; Moore (1986) "The Success of Privatisation" in J. Kay, C. Mayer and D. Thompson (eds.) *Privatisation and regulation: The UK experience*, Oxford: Clarendon Press.
36 J. Moore (1985) "The Success of Privatisation", Treasury Press Release 107/85.
37 D. Kavanagh and A. Seldon (2000) *The Powers Behind the Prime Minister*, p.193. From 1983 the No. 10 Policy Unit dominated as the source of policy advice at the heart of Government. Following the General Election the Central Policy Review Staff was disbanded and in the autumn of 1983 the Centre for Policy Studies was brought totally under the Government's control. It would not again be the power house of economic ideas that it had been earlier.
38 Note from John Redwood to the PM, 19 July 1984, and note from Andrew Turnbull to the PM, with the PM's annotated agreement, 20 July 1984; both in E(DL) Part 10. Nevertheless, John Redwood continued to put his weight behind injecting a new impetus into the privatisation programme fearing that it was "in danger of losing its way"; memorandum from John Redwood to Ferdinand Mount, No. 10. Policy Unit, 20 October 1983, E(DL) Part 8.
39 Conservative Party Election Manifesto 1983, p.7.
40 C(83)19th meeting conclusions, 16 June 1983; C(83)19, "Legislative Programme 1983–84. Memorandum by the Lord President of the Council", dated 30 June 1983; C(83)20, "Summary of Bills Proposed for the Legislative Programme 1983–84. Note by the Lord President of the Council", dated 30 June 1983.
41 M. Holmes (1989), p.64. The sale of the TSB was delayed for a number of months by a legal dispute over its ownership, which went as far as the House of Lords. Also, the fact that the receipts from the sale stayed within the bank created a circularity in the sale process because the sale value added to the bank's value. Unsurprisingly, therefore, investors found the issue attractive. Lawson (1992) p.229 notes: "Fortunately, neither the Press nor the Opposition tumbled to the conceptual and practical problem involved in his circularity." However, some investors did spot it. Government plans to sell off another organisation with an odd legal arrangement, the Horserace Totalisator Board (the Tote), were abandoned due to legal difficulties and the fact that the Treasury lost interest when it became clear that the Government would not gain from the sale financially; miscellaneous correspondence in PM Papers Policy Towards the Nationalised Industries. Financial Control, Part 11.
42 The Abbey National sale attracted the largest number of investors, around 4m.
43 Interview with Sir Robin Day, BBC, 17 February 1986, *Thatcher CD-ROM.*
44 Ibid. Lawson (1992) p.224 claims that he coined the term "people's capitalism", which was changed to "popular capitalism" by Thatcher who felt that the expression "sounded Communist, reminding her of expressions like 'people's republic'". In addition to promoting wider share ownership through privatisations, the Government provided tax incentives for companies to adopt share schemes for their employees and management, following an initial measure introduced in 1980. This altered the value of shares firms could allocate to each employee every year without attracting tax and brought in tax relief for savings-related share option schemes. Later measures included the extension of tax relief for senior management share schemes in 1984 and, in the 1986 Budget, further tax measures aimed at promoting share ownership. By 1987 there were over 1,200 approved employee share schemes, compared to a mere 30 in 1979, covering over 1.25m employees.
45 Letter from Lawson to Sir Emmanuel Kaye, 14 July 1986, in E(DL) Part 14.
46 C(83)22nd meeting conclusions, 7 July 1983; C(83)21, "Public Expenditure in 1983–84. Memorandum by the Chancellor of the Exchequer", dated 5 July 1983.
47 E(A)(83)2nd meeting, 14 July 1983; E(A)(83)4, "Nationalised Industries' 1983 Investment and Financing Review (IFR). Memorandum by the Chief Secretary, Treasury", 8 July 1983.
48 There was also discussion of including a requirement for regular value for money audits for the industries, a particular Treasury favourite. "Desirable Changes in Nationalised Industry Statutes. Note by HM Treasury", 18 July 1984; PM Papers Nationalised Industries. Financial Control,

Parts 9 and 10. Official Committee on Nationalised Industries, "Desirable Changes in Nationalised Industry Statutes. Note by HM Treasury", 18 July 1984, HM Treasury papers A/301/01. The Public Accounts Committee had already criticised the large reserves held by a number of the nationalised industries and there was broader recognition that the traditional breakeven financial constraint on the industries after paying interest on government loan stock was an insufficient financial control because of the declining importance of debt in the balance sheets of a number of the nationalised industries. At nationalisation most of the firms were given debt liabilities equal to their net assets and interest payments on the debt were considered an adequate reflection of the opportunity cost of capital. Over the years inflation had wiped out most of the firms' initial debt. The PAC criticised the Government for failing to develop a mechanism to collect the mounting cash surplus in some of the industries. The Bill would have facilitated a capital restructuring of the industries using a mixture of public equity capital, loans and reserves. The equity might have taken the form of ordinary shares or cumulative preference shares. A rate of return target on capital employed plus dividend targets on the share capital would have introduced a new form of financial control; Official Committee on Nationalised Industries, HM Treasury papers NIP(84)3rd meeting, 25 September 1984, REV NIP/809; "Desirable Changes in Nationalised Industry Statutes", 3 August 1984, NIP(WG)(84)5; "Nationalised Industries Legislation: Consultative Proposals. Note by HM Treasury", 14 November 1984, NIP(WG)(84)7; and NIP(85)6, 29 March 1985, A/06.

49   Note from John Redwood to Turnbull, 31 May 1994, in Nationalised Industries Part 5. John Redwood was strongly supportive of the Bill so as to speed up privatisation and improve the monitoring of the performance of the nationalised industries; minute from Redwood to Andrew Turnbull, 18 April 1985, PM Papers, Nationalised Industries. Financial Control, Part 10.

50   E(NI)(85)3, "Nationalised Industry Legislation. Note by the Chief Secretary, Treasury", 3 April 1985.

51   Letter from John MacGregor, Chief Secretary, Treasury, to the PM, 22 October 1985; letter from MacGregor to Sir Robert Haslam, Chairman, Nationalised Industries Chairmen's Group, 12 November 1985; minute from Andrew Turnbull to the PM, 28 June 1984; in PM Papers Nationalised Industries: Financial Control, Part 10.

52   E(NI)(83)5th meeting, 26 April 1983; E(NI)(84)1st meeting, 17 January 1984; E(NI)(84)3rd meeting, 29 June 1984; CC(84)8th meeting; E(NI)(84)14, "Nationalised Industries Bill. Note by Chief Secretary, HM Treasury". The decision to defer the introduction of the Bill until after the 1984/85 Parliamentary Session was made on 3 October 1984, E(NI)(84)6th meeting. Left open was the option of introducing it at a later date, but in reality the Bill was dead. Holmes (1989), pp.62–3; Swann (1988), p.261; S. Jenkins (1995) *Accountable to None: The Tory Nationalisation of Britain,* London: Hamish Hamilton, p.29.

53   Minute from the Chancellor of the Exchequer to the PM, 25 July 1983, HM Treasury papers, Competition and Privatisation: PEAU Exercise, AD/1790/01, Part C. Rev NIEA/53.

54   A report, "The Overseas Role of the Nationalised Industries" (the Ewebank Report), produced by a working party of the British Overseas Trade Board's Overseas Project Board, recommended that the nationalised industries contract out more project management to the private sector. The report received the Government's backing; letter from the Chancellor of the Exchequer to the Secretary of State for Trade and Industry, 7 May 1985, PM Papers Nationalised Industries: Financial Control, Part 10.

55   It was also important in ensuring that the industries' required rates of return, a principal financial target since 1978 (see Chapter 2, p.15), were appropriately calculated. HM Treasury (1986b) *Accounting for Economic Costs and Changing Prices; A Report by HM Treasury and Advisory Group,* London: HMSO.

56   E(A)(83)6th meeting, 27 October 1983. Letter from John MacGregor, HM Treasury, to Paul Channon, Secretary of State for Trade and Industry, 17 February 1986, PM Papers Nationalised Industries: Financial Control, Part 10.

57   HM Treasury papers, Loss Makers: PEAU Project, AD/982/1514/01 Rev NIEA/132. The PEAU promoted privatisation in government and externally through briefings to sympathetic journalists. Grimstone wrote a number of Treasury Ministers' speeches on privatisation in the mid-1980s.

58   C(83)33rd meeting conclusions.
59   E(A)(83)13, "Competition & Privatisation. Memorandum by the Chancellor of the Exchequer", dated 19 October 1983.
60   E(A)(83)13.
61   Speaking Note, July 1983, HM Treasury papers, Competition and Privatisation: PEAU Exercise, AD/1790/01, Part D.
62   E(A)(84)3 "Competition and Privatisation. Memorandum by the Chancellor of the Exchequer", 16 January 1984.
63   For example, see "Selling state fossils", *The Economist*, 23 February 1985, pp.15–16. *The Economist* was a supporter of the Government's privatisation programme, as were most of the national newspapers, but was critical of some of the detail.
64   M. Beesley and S. Littlechild (1983) "Privatization: Principles, Problems and Priorities", *Lloyds Bank Review*, July, pp.1–20. Beesley and Littlechild volunteered to prepare a paper on natural monopoly and its solutions; minute from J.H. Rickard to I. Byatt, HM Treasury papers, Competition and Privatisation: PEAU Exercise, AD/1790/01, Part B, REV NIEA/52.
65   Other studies at the time stressing the importance of competition include, D. Heald and D. Steel (1982) "Privatizing Public Enterprise: An Analysis of the Government's Case", *Political Quarterly*, July, pp.333–49; R. Millward and D. Parker (1983) "Public and Private Enterprise: comparative behaviour and relative efficiency", in R.Millward, D. Parker, L. Rosenthal, M.T. Sumner and N. Topham (eds.) *Public Sector Economics*, London: Longman; J. A. Kay and D.J. Thompson (1986) "Privatisation: a policy in search of a rationale", *Economic Journal*, vol.96, March, pp.18–32.
66   For example, immediately after the 1983 Election the PEAU produced papers on energy pricing, competition and privatisation, and on generating comparable financial pressures in public and private enterprises.
67   HM Treasury papers, PEAU Paper on "Competition and Privatisation" and Nationalised Industry Policy. Note by the Deputy Chief Economic Adviser, S/1295/02 REV NIP 591 & AD/1790/01 Part A, REV NIEA/51.
68   E(A)(84)3, "Competition and Privatisation. Memorandum by the Chancellor of the Exchequer", 16 January 1984.
69   C(84)8th meeting conclusions, 1 March 1984.
70   The Treasury already held the residual shares in Britoil and Cable & Wireless for historical reasons. E(A)(84), 25 January 1984, 2nd meeting; E(A)(84)3, "Competition and Privatisation. Memorandum by the Chancellor of the Exchequer", dated 16 January 1984.
71   Peter Rees, Chief Secretary, Treasury, *Hansard*, 14 March 1984, column 420. Minute from G.E. Grimstone, 23 January 1984, HM Treasury papers, Competition and Privatisation: PEAU Exercise, AD/1790/01 REV VNIP/591.
72   E(A)(84)2nd meeting; "Privatisation Programme 1983–84 to 1987–88: Progress Report – July 1984. Note by the Treasury" in E(DL) Part 10.
73   E(A)(85)26, "The Privatisation Programme. Memorandum by the Chancellor of the Exchequer", 8 May 1985.
74   E(A)(85)10th meeting, 15 May 1985. For the record, on the evening of 30 September 1984 the Bank of England launched a rescue package to save the Johnson Matthey Bank from collapse to prevent a wider banking crisis. Loans advanced by Johnson Matthey had turned bad and exceeded the bank's capital. The bank was purchased for the princely sum of £1 with the Bank of England absorbing its large debts. However, this did not in any real sense represent an extension of state ownership. The arrangement was part of a wider rescue package in the City and resulted from the Bank of England's responsibility to maintain the security of the financial system.
75   C(85)24, "The Queen's Speeches on the Prorogation of Parliament and the Opening of the New Session. Note by the Secretary of the Cabinet" (Lord Armstrong), dated 22 October 1985.
76   E(A)(85)26, "The Privatisation Programme. Memorandum by the Chancellor of the Exchequer", 8 May 1985.
77   E(A)(83)6th meeting, 27 October 1983.

78  E(A)(84)27, "Disposal of INMOS. Memorandum by the Secretary of State for Trade and Industry", dated 15 May 1984; E(A)(84)38, "INMOS. Memorandum by the Secretary of State for Trade and Industry", dated 4 July 1984; E(A)(84)18th meeting, 10 July 1984. HM Treasury (1984b) *Treasury Minute on the Thirteenth to Eighteenth Reports from the Committee of Public Accounts*, Session 1983–84, Cmnd. 9325, London: HMSO, p.3. What remained of the British Technology Group was put onto a statutory footing in the British Technology Group Act, 1991, with the Treasury as a sole shareholder. In March 1992 a management buyout from the Government was arranged and in 1995 the company was floated on the London stock market; National Audit Office (1993) *The Sale of the British Technology Group*, HC59 Session 1993/94, London: Stationery Office.

79  National Audit Office (1985) *Report by the Comptroller and Auditor General. Department of Energy, Trade and Industry and Transport: Sales of Subsidiary Companies and Other Assets by Nationalised Industries*, London: HMSO, January.

80  Norman Fowler, representing a Birmingham constituency, led the opposition in Cabinet.

81  M. Holmes (1989) *Thatcherism: Scope and Limits, 1983–87*, London: Macmillan.

82  As in the case of all special shares, the objective was to provide for a Government veto should there be an attempt at any time to change the company's Articles of Association to permit a winding up of the company or a takeover of the business which the Government considered undesirable. There was a fear that Jaguar would be quickly taken over. However, when it was taken over by Ford in 1989, at a time when it was struggling to survive as an independent company, the Government decided not to invoke its special share. The Government also retained a special share in Sealink because of the importance of cross-channel ferries for the movement of troops at a time of national emergency.

83  Letter from A.R.W.Large, Company Secretary, British Leyland, to Sir Nicholas Goodison, Chairman, Stock Exchange, 25 September 1984, in DTI British Telecommunications privatisation papers, BT/A/12 Part 5.

84  In Unipart the employees were allocated 12% of the shares and management were given the right to raise their stake from 10% to 20% if certain performance targets were met.

85  Price Waterhouse (1987) *Privatisation: The Facts*, pp.80–1.

86  "Arrangements for Appointing Advisers to Work on the Privatisation Programme. Note by HM Treasury", 23 February 1984, in E(DL) Part 10.

87  The table draws from various sources.

88  Lawson (1992), p.240.

89  C(84)16, "Using Private Enterprise in Government. Memorandum by the Chief Secretary, Treasury", 29 June 1984; MISC 14(80)5th meeting; "Contracting Out Public Sector Functions. A progress report by the Central Policy Review Staff" and letter to the Chancellor of the Exchequer, 13 July 1981, in E(DL) Part 4.

90  Letwin (1992), p.178; Evans (1997), p.61.

91  Letter from W.S. Ricketts Private Secretary (PS) No. 10 to D. Clarke, Department of Health and Social Security, in E(DL) Part 7; "Statement on Contracting Out in the NHS", in E(DL) Part 7; *Hansard*, 17 February 1983. K. Ascher (1987) *The Politics of Privatisation: Contracting out Public Services*, Houndsmill: Macmillan.

92  C(82)41, "Using Private Enterprise in Government. Memorandum by the Chancellor of the Exchequer", 10 December 1982.

93  Letter from Tom King to Nigel Lawson, 30 June 1983, E(DL) Part 7.

94  Letter from Peter Rees to William Whitelaw, 16 December 1983, in E(DL) Part 9.

95  C(83)24th meeting conclusions, 21 July 1983; C(83)24, "Civil Service Numbers after 1984. Memorandum by the Chief Secretary, Treasury", 18 July 1983; C(83)25, "Using Private Enterprise in Government. Memorandum by the Chief Secretary, Treasury", dated 18 July 1983.

96  C(83)25, "Using Private Enterprise in Government. Memorandum by the Chief Secretary, Treasury". 18 July 1983, copy in E(DL) Part 7.

97  E(A)(84)10, "Contracting out in Local Government. Memorandum by the Secretary of State for the Environment", 22 February 1984, in E(DL) Part 9. E(A)(84)52, "Contracting out Local Authority Services. Memorandum by the Secretary of State for the Environment", 27 September 1984.

98  Letter from the Secretary of State for the Environment to the Chancellor of the Exchequer, 5 February 1985, and attached draft paper, "Competition in the Provision of Local Authority Services", in E(DL) Part 11.

99  Note from Andrew Turnbull, PS No. 10, to John Ballard at the Department of the Environment, 7 February 1985, in E(DL) Part 11.

100  C(83)25, op cit.

101  C(84)16, op cit.

102  Note from Andrew Turnbull to Richard Broadbent, HM Treasury, 26 February 1985, in E(DL) Part 1; memorandum from the MoD to the PM, 4 February 1985, in E(DL) Part 11. Also, see C(84)25th meeting conclusions, 5 July 1984; C(84)16, "Using Private Enterprise in Government. Memorandum by the Chief Secretary, Treasury", dated 29 June 1984 and "Cabinet Paper on Contracting Out: Using Private Enterprise in Government", July 1984, in E(DL) Part 10.

103  Memorandum from Peter Rees, Chief Secretary, Treasury, to the PM, 31 July 1985, in E(DL) Part 12.

104  Letter from Andrew Turnbull to Richard Broadbent, HM Treasury, 5 August 1985.

105  "Using Private Enterprise in Government: Report of a multi-departmental review of competitive tendering and contracting for services in Government Departments", August 1986, in E(DL) Part 14.

106  Ibid., paragraph 1.

107  Ibid., paragraph 9 and Note 2, p.18.

108  Ibid., paragraph 26.

109  Covering letter from John MacGregor to Departments, 23 September 1986, in E(DL) Part 14.

110  "Competitive Tendering & Contracting Out Management Overview", Central Unit on Purchasing (a Cabinet Office-Treasury joint unit), December 1986, in E(DL) Part 15.

111  Various correspondence in E(DL) Part 13.

112  Centre Unit on Purchasing, Using Private Enterprise in Government: Progress Report – 1986/87, October 1987, in E(DL) Part 16.

113  "Competitive Tendering in Government: Progress Report 1985–86. Note by RCM division HM Treasury", n.d., in E(DL) Part 14.

114  R. Cockett (1994) *Thinking the Unthinkable*, p.305.

115  Cole (1987) p.109. For critical papers by academics see J. LeGrand and R.Robinson (eds.) (1984) *Privatisation and the Welfare State*, London: George Allen & Unwin.

116  The Conservative Minister Nicholas Ridley would later conclude that the Government's caution was mistaken and that health and education should have benefited from the privatisation broom, Ridley (1991), pp.82–3, 257.

117  N. Fowler (1991) *Ministers Decide,* p.198.

118  Fowler (1991), pp.184–5.

119  Thatcher (1993), p.278 & 578

120  R. Boyson (1995) *Speaking my Mind*, pp.164–6.

121  Cockett (1994), p.309.

122  Holmes (1989), pp.97–8; Raison (1990), p.121. Joseph also suggested student loans in place of maintenance grants, something adopted much later; C(85)16, "Review of Student Support. Memorandum by the Secretary of State for Education and Science". In Cabinet it was agreed that this would be too politically unpopular. The PM concluding: "In the circumstances the proposals for student loans . . . should be neither published nor pursued " CC(85)24th meeting conclusions, 1 July 1985.

123  As did another of Joseph's ideas billed as "privatising the current public arrangements for educating children below the compulsory school age"; letter from the Department of Education and Science to the Treasury, 25 September 1985, E(DL) Part 12.

124  Baker (1993), pp.162–3.

125  Raison (1990), pp.131–3.

126  Raison (1990), p.146; Denham and Garnett (2001), p.404.

127  Cole (1987), p.110; Raison (1990), pp.133–6; Lawson, (1992), p.587.

128  Lawson (1992), p.596.

129    C(85)27, "Review of Social Security: Final Decisions. Memorandum by the Secretary of State for Social Services," 25 November 1985.

130    The case for personal pensions had been made in a CPS paper in 1981; Centre for Policy Studies (1981) *Personal and Portable Pensions for All*, London: CPS. It seems that the PM was instrumental in requiring that the personal pension contributions were compulsory, something that Fowler (at first) and Lawson appear to have opposed; Lawson (1992), p.590. Fowler's reform also addressed the difficulties employees faced when they changed employers and left behind their pensions in "frozen" accounts. These pensions would now be revalued each year or transferred to the leaver's new pension scheme with the objective of reducing a barrier to the willingness to change jobs.

131    Lawson (1992) p.589. Lawson was particularly angered by the fact that when he first inquired about the PSBR costs, he discovered that no one had made the calculation.

132    C(85)27.

133    CC(85)34th meeting conclusions, 28 November 1985; N. Fowler (1991), pp.206–23.

134    P. Minford (2005) "Inflation, unemployment and the pound", p.55.

## 9 PRIVATISING BRITISH AIRWAYS, ROLLS-ROYCE, SHIPBUILDING AND THE ROYAL DOCKYARDS

1    NAO(1989), paragraph 37. This was the first MoD sponsored privatisation and the MoD had no departmental experience to draw on.

2    A. Reed (1990) *Airline: the Inside Story of British Airways*, London: BBC Books. Seven Concordes were sold to BOAC with £160m of public dividend capital provided by the Government to fund the purchase. In February 1979, following a review that concluded that BA could not operate the aircraft at a profit, the Government decided to write off the public dividend capital. In return BA agreed to pay the Government 80% of any future operating surpluses from flying Concorde. This continued until 1983/4, when BA paid the Government a total of £16.5m for the aircraft and spares.

3    Nott had stated in a speech, "We have no plans to sell off parts of British Airways or breaking up the company in any way  . . . The possibility of employees being enabled to have a financial stake in the future of British Airways, the chance of offering some of its shares to pension funds and individuals and of British Airways being able to raise equity in the market – perhaps along the lines of British Petroleum – is certainly an idea we might consider with management and employees following a Conservative victory." Conservative Research Department (1979) *General Election 1979: Questions of Policy*, London, p122.

4    *Hansard*, 21 July 1979, column 2188.

5    The Department of Trade was the sponsoring department for aviation until the 1983 General Election when the function was transferred to the Department of Transport.

6    E(DL)(79)4, "Financing of British Airways – Share Issue: Memorandum by the Secretary of State for Trade", dated 29 June 1979; E(DL)(79)4th meeting, 19 July 1979.

7    Department of Trade, "Financing of British Airways", June 1979, second part, p.7.

8    E(DL)(79)4.

9    Letter from Nigel Lawson, Financial Secretary, to John Nott, 18 July 1979, in E(DL) Part 1.

10    Statement "Financing British Airways", 20 July 1979, in E(DL)(79) Part 1; *Hansard*, 20 July 1979, column 2184.

11    *Civil Aviation Act 1980*, Chapter 60, London: HMSO.

12    Tebbit (1988), p.165. During the Second Reading of the Civil Aviation Bill on 19 November 1979 John Nott stated, "At the appropriate time the Government will sell a minority of the shares in British Airways", *Hansard*, column 39. By 30 June 1980 this was being interpreted in Parliament as selling up to 49% of the new company; *Hansard*, column 1088.

13    Letter and accompanying draft answer to a Parliamentary question from N. McInnes, Private Secretary (PS) Department of Trade to Mike Pattison, PS No.10, 8 January 1981, in E(DL) Part 4.

14    Letter from Nicholas Ridley to John Biffen, 8 October 1981. Biffen replaced Nott as Secretary of State for Trade in the January 1981 Cabinet reshuffle.

15 Letter from Biffen to Ridley, 21 October 1981. The financial advisers to BA were Lazard Brothers & Co.
16 King had joined the Board of BA in late 1980.
17 D. Campbell-Smith (1986) *Struggle for Take-Off: the British Airways Story,* London: Coronet; C. Marshall (1988a) "British Airways", in R.Nelson (ed.) *Turnaround: How Twenty Well-Known Companies came back from the Brink,* London: Mercury Books.
18 Nevertheless, economic weaknesses remained, as identified in a report commissioned by BA from Price Waterhouse; "British Airways: Report by Price Waterhouse", March 1982, in PM Papers, The Future and Structure of British Airways, Part 1. The report suggested that the Government should take over £812m of BA's debt to strengthen its balance sheet. This received a dismissive response from Professor Alan Walters, advising the PM, who felt that it amounted to another bail out of a nationalised industry; minute from Walters to Michael Scholar, ibid.
19 In the main redundancies were achieved on a voluntary basis and involved a severance package agreed with the trade unions. Within BA there were 17 different unions and it is a major achievement that the downsizing was realised without serious industrial action. To avoid pay disputes in the run-up to privatisation, two-year pay settlements were negotiated.
20 BA, *Annual Report and Accounts 1982/83,* p.9; Lord J. King (1987) "Lessons from Privatization", *Long Range Planning,* vol.20, no.6, pp.18–22; M. Batt (1990) "Putting a Brand on British Airways", *Marketing Business,* April, pp.14–15; A. Campbell, M. Devine and D. Young (1990) *A Sense of Mission,* London: Economist/Hutchinson.
21 Lord King (1987) "The Lessons of Privatisation", The Institute of Directors Annual Lecture, 18 June, in E(DL) part 16; A.Corke (1986) *British Airways: The Patch to Profitability,* London: Macmillan; K. Shibata (1994) *Privatisation of British Airways: Its management and politics 1982–1987,* Florence: European University Institute.
22 C(83)12th meeting conclusions, 14 April 1983.
23 Letter from Lawson to Ridley, 11 November 1983, in E(DL) Part 8.
24 Letter from Michael Scholar, PS No. 10, to John Rhodes, Department of Trade, 9 November 1982, in PM Papers The Future and Structure of British Airways, Part 1.
25 Note to Andrew Turnbull from David Barclay within No. 10, 11 November 1983, in E(DL) Part 8.
26 R.Eglin and B.Ritchie (1981) *Fly Me, I'm Freddie!,* London: Futura.
27 E(DL)(83)8, "Sale of British Airways. Note by the Secretary of State for Transport", 18 November 1983, in E(DL) Part 8. Correspondence including details of the legal actions in the US against BA and other airlines and the response of the British Government can be found in PM Papers, The Future and Structure of British Airways, Parts 3 and 4.
28 S(23A)(1), Civil Aviation Act 1980.
29 Letter from D.A. Nichols, PS, Department of Transport, to D. Barclay, PS to the PM, 13 December 1983, in PM Papers, The Future and Structure of British Airways, Part 1. Another proposal was for BCal to be allowed the use of Heathrow airport in London, something BA was certain to oppose.
30 HMSO (1969) *British Air Transport in the Seventies: Report of the Committee of Inquiry into Civil Air Transport* (Edwards Committee), Cmnd. 4018, London: HMSO.
31 Minute from the No. 10 Policy Unit to the PM, 21 February 1984, ibid. Letter from Andrew Turnbull to D.A. Nichols, Department of Transport, 18 November 1983, reporting the main conclusions of the PM's meeting with the Secretary of State, in E(DL) Part 8.
32 E(DL)(83) 1st meeting, 24 November 1983, in E(DL) Part 8.
33 Note from John Redwood to the PM, 28 November 1983, in E(DL) Part 8.
34 Memorandum from Andrew Turnbull to the PM with the PM's annotated comment, 28 November 1983 and letter from Andrew Turnbull to John Kerr, HM Treasury, 30 November 1983, both in E(DL) Part 8.
35 Letter from M. O'Mara, PS HM Treasury, to Andrew Turnbull, 2 December 1983.
36 Statement on British Airways Privatisation, 12 December 1983, in E(DL) Part 6.
37 M. Ashworth and P. Forsyth. (1984) *Civil Aviation Policy and the Privatisation of British Airways,* IFS Report 12, London: Institute for Fiscal Studies; Ashworth and Forsyth (1986) "British Airways: Privatization and airline regulatory procedure" in J. Kay, C. Mayer and D. Thompson (eds) *Privatisation and Regulation: The UK Experience,* Oxford: Clarendon Press.

38 Civil Aviation Authority (1984) *Airline Competition Policy, Final Report*, July, London: CAA. CAA Report "Summary of Main Conclusions and Recommendations" in C(84)27, 1 October 1984. Another important proposal was to cease regulating domestic air fares.

39 C(84)27, 1 October 1984, Annex A. Letter from D.A. Nichols to Andrew Turnbull, PS No. 10, 5 March 1984, in PM Papers, The Future and Structure of British Airways, Part 2.

40 E(A)(84) 19th meeting, 18 July 1984; E(A)(84)44, "Civil Aviation Review. Note by the Secretary of State for Transport", 13 July 1984.

41 C(84) 27th meeting conclusions, 19 July 1984.

42 C(84)28th meeting conclusions, 26 July 1984.

43 John Nott, *Hansard*, 19 November 1979, column 48. Letter from Lord King to all Members of Parliament, 17 July 1984, in PM Papers, The Future and Structure of British Airways, Part 2.

44 C(84)29th meeting conclusions, 2 August 1984; C(84)21, "Civil Aviation Review. Memorandum by the Secretary of State for Transport", 30 July 1984.

45 C(84)21, "Civil Aviation Authority Review. Memorandum by the Secretary of State for Transport", 30 July 1984.

46 Ibid.

47 Ibid.

48 C(84)29th meeting conclusions.

49 C(84)22, "Civil Aviation Authority's Review of Competition in Air Transport. Memorandum by the Secretary of State for Transport", 7 September 1984. C (84)32nd meeting conclusions, 4 October 1984.

50 Even during the preparation of the sale prospectus BA proved reluctant to reveal the precise profits made on different routes, arguing that this was commercially sensitive information. It therefore seems that the Government had to take BA's estimate of the profit and loss from the routes transfer at face value.

51 C(84)32nd meeting conclusions; C(84)27, "Airline Competition Policy. Note by the Secretary of State for Transport", 1 October 1984.

52 Sir C. Marshall (1986) "How British Airways was privatised", in Butler (ed.), pp.33–8. R. Bailey and R. Baldwin (1990) "Privatisation and Regulation: The Case of British Airways", in (ed.) J.J. Richardson, *Privatisation & Deregulation in Canada and Britain*, Aldershot: Institute for Research on Public Policy.

53 Tebbit (1988), p.215.

54 In July 1987 a friendly takeover bid for BCal by BA was announced, followed by a rival bid for BCal from Scandinavian Airlines Systems (SAS). SAS operated no routes in competition with BCal and the proposal seemed less objectionable on competition grounds than the bid by BA. However, the Government reacted with hostility to the idea of the airline becoming foreign-owned. After review by the MMC, the merger with BCal went ahead in November subject to concessions, including the loss of routes from Gatwick and the surrender of some licences operated by the merged airline; CC(87)24th meeting conclusions, 16 July 1987; Monopolies and Mergers Commission (1987) *British Airways PLC and British Caledonian Group PLC: A Report on the Proposed Merger*, Cm. 247, London: HMSO. C(87)36th meeting conclusions, 10 December 1987; L. Marriott (1997) *British Airways*, Shepperton: Ian Allan Ltd, p.14.

55 C(84)21, op cit.

56 Miscellaneous correspondence in PM Papers, The Future and Structure of British Airways, Part 3.

57 Ridley (1991) *My Style of Government*, p.45.

58 At this meeting Thatcher complained that the prospect of up to triple legal damages "put her government in great difficulty particularly with regard to plans to denationalize British Airways." *www.margaretthatcher.org/archive/displaydocument.asp?docid=109185*

59 Memorandum from Nicholas Ridley to the PM, 4 April 1985, in E(DL) Part 12; memorandum from Geoffrey Howe, Foreign Secretary, to Nicholas Ridley, 29 April 1985, in E(DL) Part 12.

60 C(86)31st meeting conclusions, 18 September 1986.

61 The Government retained some shares to fulfil the loyalty bonus arrangements. A pathfinder prospectus was issued on 8 January and the sale prospectus was issued on 30 January. The closing

date for the offer was 6 February. The share price was set on 27 January, but only after a protracted pricing meeting where there was some disagreement over the appropriate price. The price was set largely on a dividend yield basis using forecast dividends.

62    The costs of the sale to the Government were estimated to be £29m. In addition, the costs borne by BA were around £8m. As in other privatisations, the BA Board was reluctant to meet more costs of the sale on the ground that the decision to privatise was a Government one. Prior to the flotation, in September 1986 British Airways Helicopters had been divested and sold to SDR Helicopters for £13.5m. The sum was retained by BA.

63    Like other privatised companies, BA was keen to start life in the private sector with a strong balance sheet. There was disagreement between BA and the Government over debt write-offs. But fortunately this was resolved after BA found that it was able to arrange a large financing facility for its proposed capital programme.

64    Up to 20% of the shares were allocated to overseas markets. There were public offerings in the USA and Canada and private placings in Japan and Switzerland.

65    The intention to provide BA employees with shares had been announced by John Nott as early as July 1980, *Hansard*, 23 July 1980, column 542.

66    Letter from Ridley to the Chancellor of the Exchequer 7 June 1984 and reply from the Chancellor 15 June 1984, in PM Papers, The Future and Structure of British Airways, Part 2. The agreed scheme provided each eligible employee with 76 shares free of charge and a two for one matching offer up to 120 shares per employee. Also, BA employees (and BA pensioners) benefited from priority application and a 10% price discount if the shares were held until the final instalment was paid.

67    During the sale of BA Hill Samuel advised on the price. At the time the Treasury was concerned that the shares were being priced too cheaply.

68    As was becoming usual in privatisation issues, preference in the share allocation was given to smaller applications. All applications for over 100,000 shares were rejected.

69    National Audit Office (1987a) *Department of Transport: Sale of Government Shareholding in British Airways plc*, HC 37, Session 1987–88, London: HMSO.

70    However, the Department of Transport decided that it was not possible to use competition for sub-underwriting, a decision questioned in a subsequent National Audit Office report; National Audit Office (1988a) *Department of Transport – Sale of Government Shareholding in British Airways plc*, HC37, July 1988.

71    Prior to the BA sale the case for underwriting privatisation issues was already under scrutiny within the Treasury. Hill Samuel had advised the Government that the BA issue should be underwritten because if it was not this might be interpreted by investors as suggesting that there had been a lack of City interest in the offer.

72    The balance were commitment shares at a commission rate of 1.25%; Price Waterhouse (1987) *Privatisation: The Facts*, p.25. Of the 720.2m shares issued, 147.7m were allocated to the US, Canada, Japan and Swiss markets. These shares were underwritten at a rate of 1.575%.

73    The clawback occurred if the public offer was three or more times oversubscribed.

74    "Rolls-Royce – the Factual Background", in the PM's papers, The Future of Rolls Royce: Industrial Policy, Part 2.

75    Memorandum from Sir Geoffrey Howe to the PM, 13 July 1979; "Ministerial Group on Rolls Royce: Future Arrangements for Rolls Royce. Memorandum by the Secretary of State for Industry", 4 October 1979; and MISC2(79) 1st meeting minutes both in the PM's papers; all in The Future of Rolls Royce: Industrial Policy, Part 1. At this time an ad hoc Ministerial group, MISC 22, oversaw policy on the future of RR.

76    The reason seems to have involved concerns about the capacity of GEC management to takeover the running of RR, future plans for the nuclear industry in which GEC would have an important role, and fears that the takeover would be interpreted as a second collapse of RR; MISC 2(79), 2nd meeting minutes, 18 October 1979, in The Future of Rolls Royce: Industrial Policy, Part 2.

77    MISC2(79) 3rd meeting minutes, 5 November 1979, in The Future of Rolls Royce: Industrial Policy, Part 1.

78 "Privatisation Present Situation and Prospects. Report by the Secretary of State for Industry", paragraphs 15–16, 13 September 1982, in E(DL) Part 6.
79 E(A)(86)13, "Rolls Royce Privatisation. Memorandum by the Secretary of State for Trade and Industry", 10 March 1986.
80 Documents in the PM's papers, The Future of Rolls Royce: Industrial Policy, Part 2.
81 E(A)(83)3rd meeting, 27 July 1983; E(A)(83)5, "Rolls Royce RB211–535 Engine Programme. Memorandum by the Secretary of State for Trade and Industry", dated 20 July 1983.
82 E(A)(83)5.
83 Hansard, vol.44, columns 518–9. Parkinson (1992), p.252 suggests that a figure of £80m was agreed with the PM, but £70m was the figure subsequently announced.
84 BAe was competing with RR for launch aid relating to the A320 aircraft. The Treasury was understandably keen to keep down the total cost. In the end BAe received £150m.
85 E(A)(84) 3rd meeting, 2 February 1984; E(A)(84)6, "Rolls Royce: V2500 Project/GE Deal. Memorandum by the Secretary of State for Trade and Industry", dated 25 January 1984. Also, correspondence from Norman Tebbit and Peter Rees to the PM dated 31 January and 1 February 1984 respectively, in PM Papers, The Future of Rolls Royce: Industrial Policy, Part 3. The figure of £60m was announced in Parliament on 1 March 1984, Hansard, vol.55, columns 403–8.
86 Letter from Sir William Duncan to the PM, 26 March 1984, in The Future of Rolls Royce: Industrial Policy, Part 2.
87 Documents in the PM's papers, The Future of Rolls Royce: Industrial Policy, Part 3.
88 N.M. Rothschild & Sons acted as RR's financial advisers.
89 E(A)(86)13, "Rolls Royce Privatisation. Memorandum by the Secretary of State for Trade and Industry", 10 March 1986, para.2.
90 E(A)(86)19th meeting, 20 March 1986; E(A)(86)13.
91 Note from Peter Warry, No. 10 Policy Unit, to the PM, 19 March 1986, in The Future of Rolls Royce: Industrial Policy, Part 3.
92 A restriction was also placed on the disposal of more than 25% of the company's assets or of significant assets used in nuclear work. Such disposals would require permission of the special shareholder, i.e. the Government.
93 As in the case of BAe, the Government was of the opinion that in this case a special share did not infringe EC rules and was permitted under the defence exemption in Article 223 of the Treaty of Rome. The Articles of Association also required the consent of the Government, as holder of the special share, to any disposal of a material part of the business. This was defined as 25% or more of the net asset value or average profits attributed to the company of either the Group as a whole or its nuclear business; Rolls-Royce plc. Offer for Sale document, Samuel Montagu on behalf of HM Government, 1987.
94 E(A)(86)13, para.9. Also, note from J.B. Unwin to the PM, 19 March 1986, in "The Future of Rolls Royce: Industrial Policy", Part 3.
95 The capital injection was a slightly higher figure than the £220m that Samuel Montagu had earlier suggested, but this figure had been calculated before detailed discussion with the Chairman of RR. Following this privatisation the NAO concluded that in the future capital injections should be kept to a minimum, notwithstanding the Treasury's valid argument that injections were recovered through a higher sale price – capital injections should have a neutral effect on net proceeds unless investors think the management will waste the injected capital; National Audit Office (1988b) Department of Trade and Industry – Sale of Government Shareholding in Rolls-Royce plc, HC243 Session 1987–88, London: HMSO; National Audit Office (1988c) Sale of Government shareholdings in British Gas plc, British Airways plc, Rolls-Royce plc and BAA, HC211 Session, London: HMSO
96 Rolls-Royce plc Offer for Sale document, 1987.
97 Hansard, column 607, 18 December 1986.
98 The gross proceeds were £1.363bn.
99 Eligible employees (those with at least 12 months service) were offered a minimum of 41 shares free of charge and there was a two-for-one matching offer for up to 88 shares per employee. All such shares were placed in the Rolls-Royce Profit Sharing Scheme. Up to 5% of the issued share capital was reserved for priority applications from employees and RR pensioners of up to 5,882

shares per person. The first 1,176 shares per employee purchased under the priority arrangement were offered at a 10% discount if held until the last instalment was paid.

100 Also, priority applicants were invited to apply for shares and were allocated 50% of their application as firm placing shares at a commission of 0.25%, 10% as provisional placing shares subject to "clawback" at a commission of 1.25% and the balance as commitment shares at a commission of 1.25%; Price Waterhouse (1987) *Privatisation: The Facts*, p.69.
101 For example, applicants for 400–1,000 shares were awarded 150.
102 In "British Business", 8 July 1977, cited in the brief on nationalised industries and privatisation for the Debate on the Address, 9 November 1982, from the Conservative Research Department, in E(DL) Part 6.
103 Ibid.
104 As it was similarly dropped for British Aerospace, chapter 5, p.114.
105 E(DL)(79)4th meeting, 19 July 1979; E(DL)(79)11, "British Shipbuilders: Sale to the Private Sector, Memorandum by the Secretary of State for Industry", 16 July 1979.
106 E(A)(85)48, "British Shipbuilders: Corporate Plan 1985/86 – 1987/88. Memorandum by the Secretary of State for Trade and Industry", 16 July 1985.
107 Conservative Research Department (1979) *General Election 1979: Questions of Policy*, London, April, p.102.
108 C(80)31st meeting conclusions, 31 July 1980; C(80)49, "Compensation and Privatisation of Shipbuilding. Memorandum by the Secretary of State for Industry", dated 29 July 1980.
109 Miscellaneous correspondence in PM Papers, Nationalised Industries: Shipbuilding Policy, Part 2.
110 *Hansard* 23 July 1979, column 30.
111 NM Rothschild & Sons Ltd, "Memorandum for the Department of Industry on Possible Values Arising from Disposal of Interests in Certain Subsidiaries in British Shipbuilders", 30 June 1980.
112 C(80)49; C(80)31st meeting conclusions; C(80)32nd meeting conclusions, 7 August 1980; C(80)51, "Compensation and Privatisation of Shipbuilding. Memorandum by the Secretary of State for Industry", dated 5 August 1980; C(80)52, "Compensation and Privatisation of Shipbuilding. Memorandum by the Lord Chancellor", dated 5 August 1980; C(80)51; C(80)49. E(80)103, "British Shipbuilders Finances. Memorandum by the Secretary of State for Industry", 12 September 1980; E(80) 34th meeting 17 September 1980; E(80)112, "British Shipbuilders Strategy and Finance. Memorandum by the Secretary of State for Industry", 16 October 1980; E(80)38th meeting 22 October 1980.
113 E(A)(85)48, op.cit.
114 "Privatisation Present Situation and Prospects. Report by the Secretary of State for Industry", paragraphs 7–10, 13 September 1982, in E(DL) Part 6.
115 Conservative Research Department (1983) *Questions of Policy: General Election 1983*, London, p.71.
116 Note from Peter Warry, No. 10 Policy Unit, to Andrew Turnbull, 24 October 1984, in E(DL) Part 11.
117 Heseltine (2001), p.277.
118 Letter from the Secretary of State for Industry to the Financial Secretary, 22 April 1983, in E(DL) Part 7.
119 E(A)(84) 11th meeting, 10 May 1984; E(A)(84)23, "Warshipbuilding. Memorandum by the Secretary of State for Trade and Industry", 3 May 1984.
120 E(A)(84) 11th meeting; E(A)(84)24, "Cammell Laird Shipbuilders Limited. Memorandum by the Secretary of State for Defence", 3 May 1984.
121 E(A)(84) 11th meeting, 10 May 1984.
122 C(84)19, Annex A; C(84)27th meeting conclusions, 19 July 1984; C(84)19, "Warshipbuilding Privatisation. Memorandum by the Secretary of State for Trade and Industry", 16 July 1984.
123 C(84)27th meeting conclusions.
124 The impetus for this Heseltine says came from Tebbit, Heseltine (2001), p.278.
125 Letter from the Secretary of State for Defence to Norman Lamont, 27 November 1984, in E(DL) Part 11. Minute from P.Wary to A.Turnbull, 4 December 1984, and minute from Heseltine to the PM, 18 December 1984, both in PM Papers, Nationalised Industries: Shipbuilding Policy, Part 7.

126 *Hansard*, 28 January 1985, columns 21–2.

127 C(85)4th meeting conclusions, 31 January 1985; Heseltine (2001), p.278.

128 It has been claimed that Heseltine threatened to resign if Cammell Laird did not receive at least one Type 22 order; Crick (1997), pp.271–72.

129 "Order for Frigates. Note by the Secretary of the Cabinet", January 1984, in PM Papers, Nationalised Industries: Shipbuilding Policy, Part 2; C(85)3, "The Order for Type 22 Frigates 13 and 4. Note by the Secretary of State for Trade and Industry", 22 January 1985.

130 Letter from M.Gilbertson, PS/DTI, to T.Kuczys, PS/Chancellor of the Exchequer, 28 October 1985, in PM Papers, Nationalised Industries: Shipbuilding Policy, Part 8.

131 In addition, the buy-out team refused to offer the usual financial guarantees to the MoD should the yard close and orders not be fulfilled. Consequently, the MoD effectively took on a contingent liability.

132 Letter from Leon Brittan, Secretary of State for Trade and Industry, to the Chancellor of the Exchequer, 8 January 1986, in PM Papers, Nationalised Industries: Shipbuilding Policy, Part 8. Also, some smaller warship building facilities were successfully sold including Brooke Marine Ltd in Lowestoft, which was subject to a management buy-out for £100,000 in May 1985 – the book value of the net assets sold was around £1.9m reflecting the extent to which balance sheet values had departed from economic reality – and Hal Russell Ltd, in Aberdeen, which was sold to a company especially formed to buy the business, Aberdeen Shipbuilders Ltd, in March 1986 for £2.1m but with net costs of £3.1m. This sale occurred after BS received two other less attractive offers; letter from M.McHardy, DTI, to R.Broadbent, PS/Chief Secretary, 3 March 1986, in PM Papers, Nationalised Industries: Shipbuilding Policy, Part 9.

133 Miscellaneous correspondence in PM Papers, Nationalised Industries: Shipbuilding Policy, Part 9. Vickers was the monopoly supplier of nuclear submarines to the navy. Uncertainty concerned how many Trident submarines would eventually be ordered. This probably reduced interest from potential bidders.

134 E(A)(86)8th meeting, 7 March 1986. Miscellaneous correspondence in PM Papers, Nationalised Industries: Shipbuilding Policy, Part 9. *Hansard*, 7 March 1986, column 596.

135 In addition, Lloyds Merchant Bank and brokers Hoare Govett arranged for the underwriting and subscription of £28m of ordinary shares and £40m of loan stock. The Government acquired one special share.

136 Letter from R.C.G.Fortin, Executive Director Lloyds Merchant Bank, to the PM, 26 March 1985, in PM Papers, Nationalised Industries: Shipbuilding Policy, Part 9. Price Waterhouse (1987) *Privatisation: The Facts*, pp.72–74.

137 Reported in E(A)(86)18th meeting, 2 July 1986. Also, minute from J.O'Sullivan, No. 10 Policy Unit, to the PM, 18 November 1987.

138 E(A)(86)18th meeting, 2 July 1986; E(A)(86)32, "Type 23 Frigate Orders. Memorandum by the Secretary of State for Defence", 30 June 1986.

139 Minute from P.Warry to the PM, 19 July 1985, in PM Papers, Nationalised Industries: Shipbuilding Policy, Part 8.

140 Three ship repair yards were sold between February 1984 and September 1985, two through management buy-outs. The proceeds totalled £54m, which was retained by BS; HM Treasury (1992) *Her Majesty's Treasury Guide to the UK Privatisation Programme*, June, London: HM Treasury, p.12. The net cost of the Scott Lithgow sale was inflated by compensation paid to Trafalgar House relating to the completion of an oil rig contract for BP.

141 E(A)(85)48, "British Shipbuilders: Corporate Plan 1985/86–1987/88. Memorandum by the Secretary of State for Trade and Industry", 16 July 1985,Table 1. Closures included three small merchant shipbuilding yards at Goole, Leith and on Tyneside.

142 Letter from Norman Lamont, DTI, to the PM, 25 September 1984, in PM Papers, Nationalised Industries: Shipbuilding Policy, Part 7.

143 Ibid., Table 2.

144 Note in PM Papers, Nationalised Industries: Shipbuilding Policy, Part 7, 7 July 1984.

145 E(A)(85) 15th meeting, 23 July 1985; E(A)(85)48.

146 "Report of the Official Group on the Shipbuilding Industry", interdepartmental report, June 1986, in PM Papers, Nationalised Industries: Shipbuilding Policy, Part 10.

NOTES

147 E(A)(85) 15th meeting.

148 E(A)(86)15th meeting, 8 May 1986.

149 E(A)(88)26, "British Shipbuilders. Memorandum by the Chancellor of the Duchy of Lancaster", 6 May 1988.

150 E(A)(86)31, "Future of the Shipbuilding Industry. Note by the Chairman of the Official Group on the Shipbuilding Industry", 24 June 1986.

151 E(A)(87)5th meeting, 19 March 1987; E(A)(87)12, "British Shipbuilders. Memorandum by the Secretary of State for Trade and Industry", 16 March 1987.

152 Minute from Kenneth Clarke, Chancellor of the Duchy of Lancaster, to the PM, 29 October 1987, and note by David Norgrove, PS No. 10, 27 October 1987, both in Nationalised Industries files, Part 15. Minute from Clarke to the PM, 9 November 1987, in PM Papers, Nationalised Industries: Shipbuilding Policy, Part 13. The Directive was the Sixth Directive. Clarke had spent some months trying to find buyers for the yards. At one point a Japanese company showed interest, but withdrew when it discovered the poor state of working practices in the yards and the state of the order books. This failure led him to conclude that closure of BS was inevitable.

153 Internal No. 10 memorandum from George Guise to the PM, 23 October 1987, in Nationalised Industries files, Part 15.

154 Note by David Norgrove, PS No. 10, in Nationalised Industries files, Part 15.

155 Minute from Malcolm Rifkind to the PM, November 1987, in PM Papers, Nationalised Industries: Shipbuilding Policy, Part 13. Also, Kenneth Clarke who had been pushing for the liquidation of BS was replaced by Tony Newton in July 1988. Newton was initially against a speedy closure of the industry. This delayed some of the shutdown of yards for a number of months.

156 E(A)(89)18, "North East Shipbuilders Limited (NSEL). Memorandum by the Chancellor of the Duchy of Lancaster", 2 June 1989. Letter from Tony Newton, Chancellor of the Duchy of Lancaster and Minister of Trade and Industry, to John Major, Chief Secretary, Treasury, 19 May 1989, and Major's reply, 22 May 1989, both with E(A)(89)18. Newton and Major met on 24 May 1989 but were unable to agree on the best approach to the future of North-East Shipbuilders, Major preferring not to reverse the closure decision, letter from Newton to Major 26 May 1989, with E(A)(89)18; E(A)(89)5th meeting, 6 June 1989.

157 E(A)(89)7th meeting, 12 July 1989; *Hansard*, 13 July 1989, columns 1148–57.

158 E(A)(87)11, "The Warshipbuilding Industry. Memorandum by the Secretary of State for Defence", 11 March 1987, Annex A.

159 E(A)(86)7th meeting, 6 March 1986; E(A)(86)10, "Harland and Wolff Plc. Memorandum by the Secretary of State for Northern Ireland", 14 February 1986.

160 E(A)(86)42, "Harland and Wolff Plc. Memorandum by the Secretary of State for Northern Ireland", 24 July 1986.

161 E(A)(87)10, "Harland and Wolff: Corporate Plan. Memorandum by the Secretary of State for Northern Ireland", 16 March 1987; E(A)(86)11th meeting, 17 September 1986; E(A)(87)30, "Harland and Wolff. Memorandum by the Secretary of State for Northern Ireland", 16 March 1987; E(A)(87)5th meeting, 19 March 1987.

162 E(A)(88) 7th meeting, 10 May 1988; E(A)(88)26, "British Shipbuilders. Memorandum by the Chancellor of the Duchy of Lancaster", 6 May 1988.

163 E(A)(88)10th meeting, 13 July 1988; E(A)(88)35, "Memorandum by the Secretary of State for Northern Ireland. Harland and Wolf Plc", 7 July 1988; letter from King to Moore at the Treasury, 29 June 1988, attached to E(A)(88)35.

164 E(A)(88)50, "James Mackie and Sons Ltd, Harland and Wolff, Short Brothers Plc. Memorandum by the Secretary of State for Northern Ireland", 25 November 1988.

165 E(A)(89) 4th meeting, 2 March 1989; "Harland and Wolff and James Mackie. Memorandum by the Secretary of State for Northern Ireland", 27 February 1989.

166 On announcing the sale, Tom King, Secretary of State for Northern Ireland, put the cost to the Exchequer around £100m, *Hansard,* 22 March 1989, columns 1089–90. But this does not appear to have included all of the debt write-offs.

167 *Hansard*, 14 November 1988, columns 745–6 and 7 December 1988, columns 315–16.

518

168 Letter from Malcolm Rifkind, Secretary of State for Defence, to Michael Heseltine, President of the Board of Trade, 4 December 1992, in PM Papers, Nationalised Industries: Shipbuilding Policy, Part 16.

169 M. Bellamy (2001) *The Shipbuilders: An Anthology of Scottish Shipyard Life*, Edinburgh: Birlinn, p.209 & 214.

170 Nott (2002) *Here Today, Gone Tomorrow*, p.237. Portsmouth was reduced to a stand-by facility.

171 Levene was Chairman of United Scientific Holdings (USH), a leading MoD contractor. He was appointed on secondment from USH and in 1985 was promoted to chief of Defence Procurement. The appointment was controversial given USH's role as a supplier to the MoD and because Levene was appointed on a salary twice that paid to the Permanent Secretary of the MoD, Sir Clive Whitmore; Crick (1997), pp.269–70.

172 Heseltine (2000) *Life in the Jungle*, p.271.

173 E(A)(85)1, "The Future of the Royal Dockyards. Memorandum by the Secretary of State for Defence", 7 January 1985.

174 E(A)(85)1; E(A)(85)3rd meeting, 30 January 1985; E(A)(85)7th meeting, 21 March 1985; E(A)(85)15, "The Royal Dockyards – Open Government Document. Memorandum by the Secretary of State for Defence", 14 March 1985, and briefing notes for the PM, 20 March 1985, in E(DL) Part 11.

175 E(A)(85)3rd meeting.

176 Internal No. 10 memorandum from Nicholas Owen, No. 10 Policy Unit, to Andrew Turnbull, 30 January 1985, in E(DL) Part 11.

177 C(85)19th meeting conclusions, 6 June 1985.

178 Public Accounts Committee (1986) *Control of dockyards operation and manpower, Twenty-first report from the Committee of Public Accounts*, Session 1985–86; Memorandum from the Secretary of State for Defence to the PM, 16 July 1985, in E(DL) Part 12.

179 *Hansard*, 23 July 1985, columns 867–88. Owen, who had been a founder of the Social Democrats that had split away from Labour, stood as an Alliance candidate in the 1983 General Election. He attempted, although unsuccessfully, to obtain an emergency debate on the Government's plan by moving an adjournment of the House.

180 "Commercial management of the dockyards", minute to the PM from George Younger with covering note, 22 July 1986, in E(DL) Part 14.

181 Letter from John MacGregor, HM Treasury, to George Younger, 5 August 1986, in E(DL) Part 14.

182 Ibid. Subsequently, the unions decided not to take part in consultation meetings with officials and went to court in an endeavour to disrupt the Government's plans, where they were defeated.

183 Minute from Younger to the PM, 18 September 1986, in E(DL) Part 14.

184 Minute from Younger to the PM, 24 November 1986, in E(DL) Part 15.

185 Minute from Younger to the PM, "Commercial Management in the Royal Dockyards", 1 December 1986, in E(DL) Part 15. With Treasury approval, only the Chairman of the Public Accounts Committee was informed. Correspondence between George Younger and John MacGregor, 9 and 20 January 1987, in E(DL) Part 15.

186 *Hansard*, 27 January 1987, column 183.

187 *Hansard*, 21 January 1987, columns 891–6.

188 Minute from George Younger to the PM, 19 January 1987, in E(DL) Part 15.

189 *Hansard*, 24 February 1987, column 139.

190 Heseltine (2000), p.271.

191 National Audit Office (1998) *Report by the Comptroller and Auditor General: Sales of the Royal Dockyards*, HC748 Session 1997–98, London: HMSO.

## 10 PRIVATISING BUS TRANSPORT AND THE ROYAL ORDNANCE FACTORIES

1 Memorandum by Robert Young, Policy Unit, to the PM, 26 April 1984, in E(DL) Part 9; J.A. Birks (1990) *National Bus Company, 1968–89: A Commemorative Volume*, Glossop: Transport Publishing; K. Lane (2004) *National Bus Company: The Early Years*, Shepperton: Ian Allan Ltd.

2    Four PTEs were established in England under the 1968 Transport Act – in Greater Manchester, Merseyside, Tyne and Wear and the Midlands. In 1973 a PTE was established for Greater Glasgow and the following year for West Yorkshire and South Yorkshire. Each PTE was accountable to a Passenger Transport Authority (PTA) made up of elected representatives from local authorities and Department of Transport nominees.

3    Draft Bus White Paper, 3 July 1984, in E(DL) Part 10.

4    "Introduction of Private Capital into the National Bus Company: Note by Officials", Department of Transport October 1983, in E(DL) Part 8. For a short summary of the history of bus service regulation and provision see J. Hibbs (2005) *The Dangers of Bus Re-regulation and Other Perspectives on Markets in Transport*, Occasional Paper 137, London: Institute of Economic Affairs, ch.2.

5    Conservative Party (1979) *Conservative Party General Election Manifesto*.

6    S.Jaffer and D.Thompson (1986) "Deregulating Express Coaches: A Reassessment", *Fiscal Studies*, vol.7, no.4, pp.45–68; Birks (1990), p.461, 493–6.

7    D.Thompson and A.Whitfield (1995) "Express Coaching: Privatization, Incumbent Advantage, and the Competitive Process", in M.Bishop, J.Kay and C.Mayer, *The Regulatory Challenge*, Oxford: Oxford UP. National Express also hit back with a new Rapide service including toilets, video and hostess services.

8    All local authorities were invited to consider trial areas but only three chose to do so. The other two areas were in Norfolk and rural Devon. Later a few local authorities, such as Cardiff, experimented with some competition in stage transport.

9    Letter from Fowler to Nigel Lawson at the Treasury, dated 21 June 1979, in E(DL).

10   Letter from Fowler to Sir Keith Joseph at the Department of Industry, 8 July 1981, in Nationalised Industries files, Part 4.

11   Ibid.

12   Handwritten note on the letter from Fowler to Joseph, 8 July 1981, ibid.

13   Letter from Lawson to Joseph, 13 July 1981, in Nationalised Industries files, Part 4.

14   Letter from Fowler to Lawson, 22 July 1981, in Nationalised Industries files, Part 4.

15   Letter from Lawson to Fowler, 27 July 1981, in Nationalised Industries files, Part 4. Lord Shepherd was an ex-Labour minister.

16   Birks (1990), p.130.

17   MMC (1982) *Bristol Omnibus Company Limited Cheltenham District Traction Company City of Cardiff District Council Trent Motor Traction Company Limited and West Midlands Passenger Transport Executive: A Report on Stage Carriage Services supplied by the Undertakings*, HC442, 1981–82, London: Monopolies and Mergers Commission.

18   Ridley replaced Tom King who had replaced David Howell as Transport Minister in June 1983. King became Secretary of State for Employment. Howell had become Transport Minister in September 1981 when Fowler moved to become Secretary of State for Health and Social Security. The October 1983 reshuffle was triggered by the resignation of Cecil Parkinson, chapter 7, p.170.

19   Ridley (1991), p.61. Professor Michael Beesley had presented the case for bus deregulation to the Department of Transport in December 1982; Beesley (1997), ch.10 "Bus Deregulation".

20   E(DL)(83)5, "National Bus Company: Privatisation. Memorandum by the Secretary of State for Transport", 11 October 1983, in E(DL) Part 8.

21   Note from Andrew Turnbull, Private Secretary (PS) No. 10, to John Kerr, HM Treasury, 18 October 1983, in E(DL) Part 8. In October 1983 John Moore in the Treasury stated that deregulation should come before privatisation of the NBC and favoured some restructuring, but serious plans had not been formulated; Minute from D.C.W. Revolta to J. H. Rickard, 20 October 1983, H M Treasury papers, Competition and Privatisation: PEAU Exercise, AD/1290/01 Part C. REV NIEA/53.

22   Note from Robert Young, No. 10 Policy Unit, to Turnbull, 17 October 1983, in E(DL) Part 8. C.D.Foster (2005) *British Government in Crisis or The Third English Revolution*, Oxford: Hart Publishing.

23   Note to Turnbull from David Barclay in No. 10, 11 November 1983, briefing note for the PM for her meeting with Ridley by Barclay, 17 November 1983, both in E(DL) Part 8.

24 Letter from Turnbull to Dinah Nichols, Department of Transport, 18 November 1983, reporting the main conclusions of the PM's meeting with the Secretary of State, in E(DL) Part 8.
25 C(84)8th meeting conclusions, 1 March 1984.
26 Draft White Paper, "A Better Way for Public Transport", and accompanying Note to the PM 14 June 1984, in E(DL) Part 10. Bus deregulation was not to apply to Northern Ireland, reflecting the particular political difficulties in the province at the time.
27 E(A)(84)21, "The Bus Industry. Memorandum by the Secretary of State for Transport", 27 April 1984, "Public Road Passenger Transport Report", Department of Transport, both in E(DL) Part 9.
28 Ridley would have ideally liked to have seen a phasing out of state subsidies, but this was never a serious practical proposition unless the Government was willing to endorse a significant contraction of services.
29 E(A)(84)21.
30 Memorandum by Robert Young, Policy Unit, to the PM, 26 April 1984, in E(DL) Part 9. Letter from Michael Jopling to the PM, 15 May 1984, in E(DL) Part 9.
31 E(A)(84)26, "The Bus Industry. Memorandum by the Secretary of State for the Environment", 9 May 1984.
32 E(A)(84)25, "The Bus Industry. Memorandum by the Secretary of State for Scotland", 9 May 1984.
33 Memorandum from Nicholas Edwards to the PM, 15 May 1984, E(DL) Part 9.
34 E(A)(84)12th meeting, 16 May 1984. The Secretary of State for Scotland was asked to prepare a separate draft White Paper setting out how the proposals might best be applied there, alongside a paper that the Secretary of State for Wales was already preparing. Following the meeting the Secretary of State for Scotland changed his mind about preparing a separate paper and on 31 May the PM agreed to there being one White Paper on bus deregulation; note from David Barclay, PS No. 10, to John Graham, Scottish Office, 31 May 1984, in E(DL) Part 9.
35 E(A)(84)16th meeting; also note from Ridley to members of E(A) Sub-Committee, 3 July 1984, in E(DL) Part 10.
36 In Hereford bus competition developed but services soon consolidated under one operator, an experience that would be repeated in a number of areas following national bus deregulation.
37 Memorandum from Chris Butler, Special Adviser, to the Private Secretaries, Secretary of State and Minister of State for Transport, 4 July 1984, in E(DL) Part 10.
38 Letter from H.C.D. Derwent, PS/Department of Transport, to Colin Jones, PS/Secretary of State for Wales, 9 July 1984, in E(DL) Part 10.
39 The idea that economies of scale were limited in bus transport was promoted by the Department of Transport's economic adviser, Professor Michael Beesley.
40 Draft Bus White Paper, 3 July 1984, in E(DL) Part 10.
41 It had also been endorsed in E(A) Committee on 28 June 1984; E(A) 16th meeting.
42 Letter from the Secretary of State for the Environment, 21 June 1984, and from the Secretary of State for Education, 22 June 1984, to the Secretary of State for Transport, in E(DL) Part 10.
43 Note from Robert Young, No. 10 Policy Unit, to Turnbull, 18 June 1984, in E(DL) Part 10; letter from Turnbull to Nichols, Department of Transport, 19 June 1984, in E(DL) Part 10.
44 Note to the PM from Ridley, 26 June 1984, in E(DL) Part 10.
45 *Hansard*, columns 1381–2, 12 July 1984; letter from Nicholas Edwards to Ridley, 11 July 1984, and the accompanying consultation paper, in E(DL) Part 10.
46 *Financing of Public Transport Services: The Buses White Paper. Second Report from the Transport Committee*, House of Commons, Session 1984–85. Report and Minutes of Proceedings (CHC-38-I), Cmnd 9300, HMSO, 1985.
47 Letter from Ridley to Lawson, 28 May 1985, and attached draft paper replying to the Select Committee to be issued before the Committee Stage in the House of Lords on the Transport Bill; also briefing note from John Wybrew to the PM, 7 June 1985; all in E(DL) Part 12.
48 "The Buses Proposal: Better Prospects for Passengers", December 1984, in E(DL) Part 11.
49 Correspondence 6 February 1985, in E(DL) Part 11.
50 Memorandum from John Wybrew, No. 10 Policy Unit, to the PM, 13 June 1986, in E(DL) Part 13.

51     Letter from John Moore, Department of Transport, to the PM with supporting briefing notes entitled "Deregulation of Local Bus Services", in E(DL) Part 14.

52     Speech by John Moore to the Greater London Areas Conservative Political Centre at International House, Saturday 25 October 1986, in E(DL) Part 14.

53     Ridley (1991), p.56.

54     Birks (1990), p.270. In early 1986 the Board of NBC notified the Department of Transport that it could not recommend a disposal programme based on the sale of individual subsidiaries because of its statutory duties and asked the Secretary of State to give them a Direction to do so; letter from Ridley to Lawson, 13 March 1986, in E(DL) Part 13.

55     Letter from Brook to Ridley, 21 November 1985, in E(DL) Part 12.

56     Letter from Ridley to Lawson, 13 March 1986, in E(DL) Part 13.

57     Copy of draft letter to Bankers Trust Company, 13 December 1985, and Bankers Trust Press release, 18 December 1985, both in E(DL) Part 13.

58     National Bus Company (1986) *Disposals Programme*, London: NBC. Mulley and Wright (1986) "Buy-outs and the Privatisation of National Bus", *Fiscal Studies*, vol.7, no.3, pp.1–24. The original intention had been for the NBC to produce a disposal programme by 6 April 1986. The deadline was extended and the programme was approved six weeks later, on 19 May.

59     Birks (1990), p.676–7.

60     Members of the pension scheme with fewer than five years of qualifying service were entitled to reclaim their contributions instead and many did so; NAO (1991), pp.24–5.

61     The small NBC Computer Services had been sold earlier; Birks (1990), p.676.

62     Ernst & Young (1994) *Privatization in the UK: The facts and figures*, p.29. In the majority of cases between 10% and 40% of the share capital was set aside for employee purchase, although there were at least two cases where complete sales were to employees, Birks (1990), p.683. In the case of outside purchases, the NBC encouraged the buyers to offer some shares to employees.

63     Birks (1990), p.270.

64     Birks (1990), p.151 & 680.

65     National Audit Office (1991) *Sale of the National Bus Company*, HC119 Session 1990–91, London: HMSO, paragraph 2(viii).

66     "Privatisation of the National Bus Company", Department of Transport report, February 1987, E(DL) Part 15.

67     National Audit Office (1990a) *Department of Transport: Sale of the National Bus Company*, HC43 Session 1990–91, London: HMSO.

68     E(DL)(83)1, "Scottish Transport Group: Privatisation. Memorandum by the Secretary of State for Scotland", 14 February 1983, in E(DL) Part 7.

69     Ibid.

70     Ibid.

71     Letter to the Secretary of State for Trade and Industry from Younger, 12 June 1984; letter from the Secretary of State for Trade and Industry to Younger, 5 July 1984; letter from Younger to the Secretary of State for Trade and Industry, 26 July 1984; all in E(DL) Part 10. Letter from Ridley to the Secretary of State for Trade and Industry, 2 August 1984, in E(DL) Part 11.

72     SBG's behaviour in the Glasgow area was already causing particular concern.

73     Letter from Ridley to Rifkind, 29 October 1986, in E(DL) Part 14.

74     Letter from Rifkind to Ridley, 19 November 1986, in E(DL) Part 15; letters from Rifkind to Lawson, 21 October 1986, and with an accompanying objectives statement for SBG, 20 November 1986, in E(DL) Part 15 and PM Papers, Policy Towards the Nationalised Industries: Financial Control, Part 11.

75     Letter from Ridley to Rifkind, 24 November 1986, in E(DL) Part 14, emphasis in original.

76     Letter from Tebbit to Rifkind, 27 November 1986; Letter from John MacGregor, HM Treasury, to Malcolm Rifkind, 1 December 1986, letter from John Moore to Rifkind, 1 December 1986; all in E(DL) Part 15. Letter from Moore to Rifkind, 17 November 1986, in PM Papers, Policy Towards the Nationalised Industries: Financial Control, Part 11.

77     Letter from David Norgrove, PS No. 10, to Robert Gordon, Scottish Office, 16 March 1987.

78     Letter from Gordon to Norgrove, 24 April 1987, in E(DL) Part 16.

79     Minute from Rifkind to the PM, 14 January 1988, letter from Rifkind to Lamont, 31 October 1988, and letter from Lamont to Rifkind, 14 November 1988, all in E(DL) Part 16. The possible

privatisation of CalMac was reconsidered periodically in the Scottish Office over the following years, but on each occasion the idea was similarly rejected. Under the 1989 Act and the resulting winding up of the STG in 1994, CalMac became the responsibility of the Scottish Office. Letter from Ian Lang to Francis Maude, Financial Secretary to the Treasury, 20 December 1991 and letter from Maude to Lang, 8 January 1992, both in E(DL) Part 19.

80    Letter from Lamont to Rifkind, 18 January 1988, in E(DL) Part 16.
81    Letter from Paul Channon to Rifkind, 20 January 1988, in E(DL) Part 16.
82    Annotated note from the PM, 19 January 1988, on a note summarising the differences between Rifkind and the Treasury, in E(DL) Part 16.
83    Minute from Paul Gray to the PM, 13 May 1988, in E(DL) Part 16. One of the nine area companies was formed by the merger of two loss making businesses Kelvin with Central and Western and Clydeside. It was felt that neither would be easily sellable separately. Quayle Munro was the financial adviser to the Scottish Office and Coopers and Lybrand to the STG.
84    *Hansard,* 24 May 1988, column 201.
85    Letter from Rifkind to Lamont, 22 November 1988, in E(DL) Part 16.
86    *Hansard*, 14 December 1988, column 1003 et seq.
87    Letter from Rifkind to Lamont, 4 July 1989, with supporting paper from the Scottish Office, "Scottish Bus Group: Management Employee Buy-Outs", June 1989, in E(DL) Part 17.
88    Letter from Channon to Lamont, 11 July 1989, in E(DL) Part 17.
89    Letter from Peter Lilley, Financial Secretary to the Treasury, to Malcolm Rifkind, 26 July 1989, in E(DL) Part 17. Lilley replaced Lamont as Financial Secretary in July 1989.
90    PM's annotated comments on a briefing note from Paul Gray, 28 July 1989, in E(DL) Part 17.
91    Letter from Rifkind to Lilley, 28 July 1989, in E(DL) Part 17.
92    Reply from Richard Ryder in Lilley's absence, 4 August 1989, in E(DL) Part 17.
93    *Hansard*, 27 January 1989, columns 311–12.
94    These are National Audit Office estimated figures in July 1993 and are made up of pre-sale dividends less debt write-offs and capital injections of £56.4m; company sale proceeds of £39.8m; and profits from the separate disposal of bus company properties transferred into Group ownership in advance of the sales of £6.9m; National Audit Office (1993) *Sale of the Scottish Bus Group,* HC97 Session 1993–94, London: HMSO, p.3.
95    The clawback provisions applied for seven years at 50% of any gain from a property sale made within five years, 40% in the sixth year and 30% in the seventh year (in the case of one property considered very likely to be sold quickly, a rate of 75% applied for the first two years); ibid.
96    Letter from Malcolm Rifkind to Norman Lamont, Chancellor of the Exchequer, 14 March 1991, in E(DL) Part 17.
97    Letter from Francis Maude, Financial Secretary to the Treasury, to Malcolm Rifkind, Secretary of State for Transport, 4 April 1981, and reply by Rifkind 19 April 1991, both in E(A)(91) Part 18.
98    Ernst & Young (1994) *Privatization in the UK: The facts and figures*, p.29.
99    The Transport Act gave the Secretary of State powers to force each PTE to be broken up into smaller units. This power was used only once, in Greater Manchester, when the bus services were divided into two in December 1993 prior to their privatisation.
100  National Audit Office (1996) *Sale of London Transport's Bus Operating Companies*, HC251.
101  The number of minibuses run by former NBC subsidiaries rose from 1,000 to 4,000, Birks (1990), p.670.
102  C(86)33rd meeting conclusions, 16 October 1986.
103  P.J. White (1990) "Bus Deregulation: A Welfare Balance Sheet", *Journal of Transport Economics and Policy*, vol.24, no.3, pp.311–32; W.J. Tyson (1990) "The Effects of Deregulation on Service Co-ordination in the Metropolitan Areas", *Journal of Transport Economics and Policy,* vol.24, no.3, pp.283–95; P.J.Mackie, J.M.Preston and C.A.Nash (1995) "Bus Deregulation: Ten Years on", *Transport Reviews,* vol.15, no.3, pp.229–51; B. Colson (1996) "UK Bus Deregulation: a qualified success with much still to offer customers and society at large", *Transport Reviews,* vol.16, pp.301–11; D.Bayliss (1997) "Bus Privatization in Great Britain", *Proceedings of the Institution of Civil Engineers,* vol.123, May, pp.81–93.

104   P.M.Heseltine and C.Mulley (1993) *The Effects of Privatisation of the Scottish Bus Group and Bus Deregulation: A Consultants Report by the Transport Operations Research Group, University of Newcastle upon Tyne*, Edinburgh: The Scottish Office Central Research Unit Papers, November.

105   House of Commons Transport Committee (1995) *The Consequences of Bus Deregulation, First Report*, Session 1995/96, London: HMSO; W.P.Bradshaw (1996) "Ten Turbulent Years – the Effects on the Bus Industry of Deregulation and Privatisation", *Policy Studies*, vol.17, no.2, pp.125–36; P.White (1997) "What Conclusions Can Be Drawn about Bus Deregulation in Britain?" *Transport Reviews*, vol.17, no.1, pp.1–16; D.Bayliss (1999) "Buses in Great Britain: Privatisation, Deregulation and Competition", mimeo.

106   At the time of the privatisation of the NBC there were reputedly a number of officials in the Department of Transport and the Treasury who very much doubted whether the fragmented structure created was sustainable. They anticipated future consolidation.

107   For example, MMC (1995) *The Supply of Bus Services in the North East of England*, Cmnd.2933, London: HMSO; MMC (1996) *Stagecoach Holdings plc and Chesterfield Transport (1989) Ltd: a Report on the Merger Situation*, Cmnd.3086, London: HMSO.

108   House of Commons Public Accounts Committee (2006) *Delivery chain analysis for bus services in England, Forty-third Report of Session 2005–6*, HC851, London: HMSO.

109   D.Kennedy (1995) "London bus tendering: an overview", *Transport Reviews*, vol.15, pp.253–64.

110   J.R.Hibbs (2005) *The Danger of Bus Re-regulation*, London: Institute of Economic Affairs.

111   Conservative Research Department (1983) *Questions of Policy: General Election 1983*, p.154.

112   Similar concerns had surfaced within the Treasury, Royal Ordnance Factories, Annex to Minute from J. H. Rickard to G. Grimstone, HM Treasury papers, Competition and Privatisation: PEAU Exercise, AD/1790/01 Part C. REV NIEA/53.

113   D. Young (1990) *The Enterprise Years*, p.46. A committee within the MoD oversaw the planning of the privatisation. Young's frustration was directed at the slow pace of this committee's work and what he saw as deliberate obstruction by some MoD officials.

114   Letters from Sir David Plastow to George Younger, 24 January 1986, 4 March 1986 and 14 May 1986, all in E(DL) Part 13.

115   Letter from Plastow to Younger, 30 May 1986 in E(DL) Part 13.

116   Minute from Lord Trefgarne, Minister of State for Defence Procurement, to the PM, 10 June 1986, in E(DL) Part 13.

117   Minute from Peter Warry, No. 10 Policy Unit, 4 June 1986, in E(DL) Part 13.

118   Minute from Lord Trefgarne to the PM, 10 June 1989, in E(DL) Part 13.

119   Cabinet Office minute from J.B.Unwin, 9 June 1986, in E(DL) Part 10.

120   Letter from Gerald Boxhall, Chairman and Chief Executive Vickers Defence Systems, to Peter Levene, Chief of Defence Procurement MoD, 4 June 1986 and letter from Plastow to the PM, 9 June 1986, both in E(DL) Part 13.

121   Minute from David Norgrove to the PM, 10 June 1986, in E(DL) Part 13.

122   Briefing paper from J.B. Unwin to the PM, 10 June 1986, in E(DL) Part 13.

123   Two minutes by Peter Warry, No. 10 Policy Unit, to the PM, 11 June 1986, in E(DL) Part 13.

124   Minute from David Norgrove to the PM, 11 June 1986, in E(DL) Part 13.

125   Letters from Richard Hatfield, Acting PS/Secretary of State for Defence to David Norgrove in No. 10, 11 June 1986, in E(DL) Part 13.

126   Note from Norgrove to the PM, 11 June 1986, in E(DL) Part 13.

127   Minute from Warry to the PM, 13 June 1986, in E(DL) Part 13.

128   Press cuttings in E(DL) Part 13.

129   Minute from Tebbit to the PM, 16 June 1986, in E(DL) Part 13.

130   Memorandum to Lawson from P.J. Kitcatt, 16 June 1986, in E(DL) Part 13.

131   Letter from Norgrove to John Howe, Ministry of Defence, 17 June 1986, in E(DL) Part 13.

132   Letter from Trefgarne to Plastow, 20 June 1986, in E(DL) Part 13.

133   E(A)(86)20th meeting, 22 July 1986. The Secretary of State's proposals were set out in detail in E(A)(86)40, "Privatisation of Royal Ordnance Plc. Memorandum by the Secretary of State for Defence", 17 July 1986, circulated before the meeting.

134   C(86)29th meeting conclusions, 24 July 1986.

135 *Hansard*, 24 July 1986, columns 618–28.
136 Minute from Younger to the PM and briefing notes to the PM from J.B.Unwin and P. Warry, all 21 July 1986, in E(DL) Part 14; E(A)(86)20th meeting, 22 July 1986; E(A)(86)40.
137 *Hansard*, 2 April 1987, column 1238. Subsequently there was some criticism that the development value of the sites acquired by BAe might be well in excess of the price the company had paid for the assets. However, the National Audit Office gave the sale a clean bill of health concluding that the RO's assets had been sold competitively. The NAO did suggest that in the future where there was the potential for development gains, thought should be given to the use of clawback facilities under which government would receive a percentage of the gains when assets were later sold. This was applied during the sale of the bus corporations, NBC and SBC, as discussed above. National Audit Office (1987b) *Ministry of Defence – Sale of Royal Ordnance plc*, HC162 Session 1987–88, London: HMSO. National Audit Office (1989) *Ministry of Defence: Further Examination of the Sale of Royal Ordnance plc*, HC448 Session 1988–89, London: HMSO; National Audit Office (1990b) *Ministry of Defence: Further Examination of the Sale of Royal Ordnance plc*, HC352 Session 1988–89, London: HMSO.
138 "Royal Ordnance Factories: Guarantee for Pensions after Privatisation. Note by HM Treasury" and letter from the Secretary of State for Defence to the Chancellor of the Exchequer, 14 August 1984, both in E(DL) Part 11. During the early planning of the sale of the RO, Michael Heseltine did press the Treasury to agree to some form of commitment that the Government would stand behind the RO pension fund after privatisation. The Chancellor of the Exchequer resisted, as he did in other privatisations except BT. Giving such an assurance would have implied an on-going contingent liability for the Exchequer. Main Privatisation Candidates, Annex, Royal Ordnance Factories, January 1984, HM Treasury papers, Competition and Privatisation: PEAU Exercise, AD/1790/01. Part D. REV NIEA/53. Heseltine cited the BT case as a precedent for some level of continuing Government guarantee.
139 The lump sum transfer was intended to meet all future liabilities under the pension scheme. Only in the case of the privatisation of British Telecom did the Government effectively provide employees with an actual pension guarantee, see chapter 11.
140 National Audit Office (1987) *Ministry of Defence – Sale of Royal Ordnance plc*, HC162 Session 1987–88, London: HMSO.

## 11 PRIVATISING BRITISH TELECOM: THE DECISION TO PRIVATISE

1 HMSO (1977) *Report of the Post Office Review Committee*, Cmnd. 6850, London: HMSO.
2 E(TP)(82)2, "Future Telecommunications Policy. Note by the Chairman of the Official Committee on Telecommunications Policy", 16 April 1982. Letter from Lord Weinstock, GEC, to Joseph with a copy to the PM, 16 March 1981, PM Papers, Post and Telecommunications, Part 3.
3 Brief on nationalised industries and privatisation for the Debate on the Address, 9 November 1982, in E(DL) Part 6.
4 Letter from H.P.Brown, DOI, to J.K.Glynn, General Secretary Society of Post Office Executives, BT/A/18 Part 2.
5 BT Press Release, September 1982, PM Papers, Post and Telecommunications, Part 4.
6 E(80)65, "Investment and Financing Review: Telecommunications. Memorandum by the Secretary of State for Industry", 7 July 1980. For the buildup, letter from Joseph to John Biffen, Chief Secretary Treasury, 23 October 1979 and replies from Biffen to Joseph, 29 October 1979 and 7 November 1979, all in PM Papers, Post and Telecommunications, Part 1.
7 1981–82 External Financing Limit, n.d., BT/A/1 Part 3. British Telecommunications, undated note in HM Treasury papers JA/1760/01 Part A.
8 *Daily Telegraph*, "Phone Bill Pay Deal Rejected", 7 August 1979.
9 Letter from Joseph to John Biffen, Chief Secretary Treasury, with copy to PM and PM's annotated comments, 6 August 1979, and letter from Biffen to Joseph, 30 August 1979, all in PM Papers, Post and Telecommunications, Part 1.

10  Note from Joseph to the PM, 23 July 1980, PM Papers, Post and Telecommunications, Part 2. In response some Ministers pressed for telecommunications to be referred to the MMC for an efficiency study, but Joseph opposed this believing it would divert effort from the forthcoming separation from the Post Office and the liberalisation measures planned; various correspondence in ibid.

11  E(80)28th meeting, 28 July 1980; E(80)79, "Post Office: Pay Financing and Prices. Memorandum by the Secretary of State for Trade and Industry".

12  In 1983 the Inland division was split into two.

13  British Telecommunications Organisation, n.d., BT/C/17 Part 1. Letter from Jenkin to Ridley, Financial Secretary, 12 February 1982, BT/A/3 Part 1. British Telecom Performance Review 1977/78–1981/82, n.d., PM Papers, Post and Telecommunications, Part 5. E(NI)(82)22, "British Telecommunications Corporate Plan. Memorandum by the Secretary of State for Industry", 19 July 1982.

14  Memorandum from Joseph to the PM, 10 July 1981, and PM's annotated comments, PM Papers, Post and Telecommunications, Part 3.

15  "Buzby coins it in – and pips the world", *Sunday Times*, 25 July 1982.

16  Note by the PM, 20 August 1982, and reply from Department of Industry, 7 September 1982, both in PM Papers, Post and Telecommunications, Part 5.

17  The break up of AT&T went ahead on 1 January 1984.

18  A Private Automatic Branch Exchange (PABX) is a telephone exchange dedicated to a particular business or office, as opposed to one that a telephone company operates publicly.

19  Note of Press Conference 12 September 1979 and note from Joseph to Norman St. John-Stevas, Chancellor of the Duchy of Lancaster, 14 November 1979, both in PM Papers, Post and Telecommunications, Part 1. "British Telecommunications Bill", briefing document, Conservative Research Department, 28 November 1980, PM Papers, Post and Telecommunications, Part 2; British Telecommunications. Section 1: The History and Present Business of BT. Report to Kleinwort, Benson Ltd and S.G. Warburg Ltd, by Coopers and Lybrand, November 1983, BT/C/6 Part 4. VANS are lines leased from a common carrier (initially BT and later Mercury, see below) by an operator who adds special terminal equipment or "conditions" to the line to provide a specialised service. A VANS general licence potentially introduced a significant amount of competition in the use of private leased circuits provided by BT.

20  BT had inherited from the Post Office the duty to issue licences to private and public bodies which had telecommunication systems for their own use.

21  *Hansard*, 2 December 1980, column 214. "British Telecommunications Bill", briefing note, Conservative Research Department, 27 March 1981, PM Papers, Post and Telecommunications, Part 3. The same Bill provided for the Treasury to dispose of its shares in Cable & Wireless and allowed the Secretary of State to license alternative letter services, L(80)64, "British Telecommunications Bill 1980. Memorandum by the Secretary of State for Industry, 12 November 1980, Cabinet Legislation Committee, in MT841 Post and Telecommunications papers Part 2. IT(81)23 "BT Bill: Implications for Information Technology. Note by the Department of Industry", 5 March 1981, and IT(81)24, "BT Bill: Powers of the Secretary of State. Note by the Department of Industry", 5 March 1980, IT(81)27, "Liberalisation of Telecommunications Subscriber Equipment. Note by the Department of Industry", all in MT841 Post and Telecommunications papers Part 3.

22  Letter from D.H.Pitcher, Managing Director, Plessey Telecommunications and Office Systems Ltd, to John Hoskyns, Policy Unit No. 10, 19 November 1980, and letter from Joseph to Hoskyns, 22 December 1980, both in PM Papers, Post and Telecommunications, Part 2.

23  *Hansard*, 30 July 1981, columns 1172–3.

24  *Hansard*, 21 July 1980, columns 29–30. M.E.Beesley and B.Laidlaw (1993) *International Review of Comparative Public Policy*, vol.5; reprinted in Beesley (1997), chapter 16, see especially p.331.

25  HMSO (1981) *Liberalisation of the use of British Telecommunications Network, Report to the Secretary of State for Industry*, London: HMSO, January; reprinted as chapter 14 in Beesley (1997). As a result of the report Beesley became an economic adviser to the Department of Industry during the privatisation of BT and by February 1984 had produced 24 working papers

for the Department on the future of the Corporation. BT would conclude that some of the suggestions made in these papers were unduly hostile to the Corporation and it is fair to say that relations between BT and Beesley became icy.

26   Note in BT/A/25 Part 1.
27   "Note by the Department of Industry", 5 March 1981, Memorandum from Joseph to the PM, 3 April 1981, all in PM Papers, Post and Telecommunications, Part 3.
28   Letter from J.F.Halliday, Home Office, to N.J.Sanders, DTI, 7 April 1981, and Memorandum from Whitelaw to Joseph, nd., both in PM Papers, Post and Telecommunications, Part 3. The Government's initial idea in response to Home Office concerns about maintaining the surveillance capability of the security forces was for BT to retain a monopoly of the maintenance of PABXs. However, it soon became clear that there was support in Parliament to liberalise this activity, if over time; letter from Joseph to the Home Secretary, William Whitelaw, 13 February 1981, PM Papers, Post and Telecommunications, Part 2; minute from Whitmore, Principal Private Secretary No. 10 to John Hallsday, Home Office, 19 March 1981, PM Papers, Post and Telecommunications, Part 3.
29   Minute from Home Secretary, William Whitelaw, to the PM, 7 July 1980, PM Papers, Post and Telecommunications, Part 2 and note to the PM from Whitelaw, 16 March 1981, PM Papers, Post and Telecommunications, Part 3.
30   Minute from Bruce Laidlaw, economist in the Department of Industry, to Private Secretary (PS)/Kenneth Baker, 31 March 1983, BT/A/20 Part 4.
31   C&W purchased BP's 50% interest in Mercury Communications on 14 August 1984.
32   While by early 1983 the Government had assured investors in Mercury that it would be the only licensed telecoms operator alongside BT for some time, the "duopoly policy" was not formally announced until November of that year to continue until at least 1989. IT(81)31, "Additional Networks. Note by the Department of Industry", 5 March 1981, and minute from Joseph to William Whitelaw, Home Secretary, 18 June 1981, both in PM Papers, Post and Telecom-munications, Part 3. Note of a meeting with BT on international telecommunications, 20 July 1983, BT/A.21 Part 3. There was also a view within the Department of Industry that unlimited competition in telecommunications would be undesirable because it would prevent the continuing cross-subsidisation of rural services; note by I.K.C. Ellison for ministerial meeting with the Chancellor of the Exchequer on the Telecommunications Bill, 25 October 1982, BT/A/8 Part 2. E(TP)(82)5, "Scope for Further Liberalisation of Telecommunications. Memorandum by the Secretary of State for Industry", 4 June 1982, PM Papers, Post and Telecommunications, Part 4. Minute from J.H. Rickard, HM Treasury, to the Economic Secretary, 14 October 1983, BT/A/20 Part 4.
33   Mercury was also prevented from providing public call boxes lest this undermined BT's ability to provide a national call box service. From 1988 Mercury was permitted to install them, found them unprofitable, and later withdrew from the call box business.
34   Miscellaneous correspondence in PM Papers, Post and Telecommunications, Part 7. Letter from Lansley to Turnbull, 28 June 1984, PM Papers, Post and Telecommunications, Part 8.
35   The first licence was awarded to Cable and Wireless. An amended licence in the name of Mercury Communications was issued in 1984.
36   *Report of the Inquiry into Cable Expansion and Broadcasting Policy* (Hunt Report), PM Papers, Post and Telecommunications, Part 6. The Carter Committee in 1977 had foreseen the potential of cable for telecommunications as well as entertainment services. Cable was also already well established in the USA. Government policy towards cable in Britain was overseen by the Information Technology Advisory Panel situated in the Cabinet Office.
37   *Hansard*, 17 November 1983, columns 681–7.
38   The City of Hull with its own telephone service negotiated its own interconnection agreement separately.
39   M.E. Beesley and B. Laidlaw (1992) "The British Telecom/Mercury interconnect determination: An exposition and commentary" in Beesley (1997), chapter 15. I am also thankful to Adam Scott for help in the drafting of this discussion of interconnection.
40   Letter from R. de L. Holmes, Secretary, Mercury Communications, to I.K.C. Ellison, DTI, 6 October 1983, BT/A/23 Part 1. Minute from Andrew D. Lansley, PS/Secretary of State for Trade

and Industry, to PS/Baker, 22 May 1984, BT/A/26 Part 1. Letter from Jefferson to Sir Douglas Love, Chairman, Mercury Communications Ltd, 14 June 1985, BT/A/23 Part 2.

41  BT's Approach to Mercury Interconnect, 30 May 1984, BT/A/9 Part 6. Note of Secretary of State's Meeting with Sir George Jefferson and other Representatives of BT, 11 October 1983, BT/A/23 Part 2.

42  Note of a meeting with BT to discuss privatisation and POEU action, 15 June 1983, BT/A/21 Part 3.

43  Note of a Meeting on Interconnect, Resale and Related Issues, 12 July 1983 and letter from Baker to Jefferson, 3 October 1983, both in BT/A/9 Part 4.

44  Interconnect position, BT paper, n.d., BT/A/9 Part 6.

45  Meeting with Mercury Shareholders on 2 April 1984, BT/A/9 Part 6. Note of a Meeting with Mercury and BT on Interconnect, 21 May 1984, BT/A/9 Part 6.

46  "British Telecom Licence Conditions: Chairman Responds", BT Press Release 25 October 1983, BT/A/23 Part 2.

47  Letter from Lowe to Baker, 21 May 1984, BT/A/9 Part 6.

48  BT retained the exclusive privilege to supply switched international services.

49  Minute from Jenkin to the PM, 6 June 1983, PM Papers, Post and Telecommunications, Part 7.

50  *Hansard*, 26 March 1981, column 385.

51  Minute from David Young, Special Adviser to PS/Secretary of State, 17 March 1981, and note from Hoskyns to the PM, 6 March 1981, both in PM Papers, Post and Telecommunications, Part 3.

52  Note from J.R.Ibbs, CPRS Cabinet Office, to the Chancellor of the Exchequer, 6 March 1981, and "Telecommunications in the UK: Investment and Financing. A Report by the CPRS", 19 June 1981, both in PM Papers, Post and Telecommunications, Part 3.

53  Note from T.P.Lankester, PS No. 10, to A.J. Wiggins, HM Treasury, 11 March 1981, MT841 Post and Telecommunications, Part 3.

54  Letter from Joseph to Howe, 5 March 1981, in PM Papers, Post and Telecommunications, Part 3.

55  Letters from Joseph to Howe, 8 May and 11 May 1981 and from Leon Brittan to Joseph, 21 May 1981, all in PM Papers, Post and Telecommunications, Part 3.

56  Minute from R.H.F.Croft, Deputy Secretary Department of Industry, to Young, Department of Industry, 18 March 1981, in MT841 Post and Telecommunications papers Part 3.

57  Letter from Howe to Joseph with copy to E Committee members including the PM, 10 April 1981, PM Papers, Post and Telecommunications, Part 3.

58  Letter from the Department of Industry to P. Jenkins, PS/Chancellor of the Exchequer, 28 January 1981, in Nationalised Industries files, Part 3.

59  Memorandum from J.S.Neilson, Department of Energy, to H.P.Brown, DTI, 15 September 1983, BT/A/31 Part 3. Advice to the Treasury from Warburgs suggested that the additional cost of the bond financing over gilts in the case of BT might be around 4%.

60  The formula was apparently devised by Andrew Smithers of Warburgs assisted by his colleague Michael Valentine, M. Valentine (2006) *Free Range Ego*, London: Valentine, p.131. Had the BT bond gone ahead there would have been a provision for BT to request the Secretary of State to allow a price rise outside of the RPI − X cap in exceptional circumstances.

61  Ibid., p.128.

62  Points arising from the meeting at the Department of Industry, 29 October 1981, BT/A/1 Part 2.

63  Issue of profit-related securities, S.G. Warburg & Co. Ltd, 4 November 1981, BT/A/1 Part 2.

64  Letter from Jefferson to Croft, 9 November 1981, BT/A/1 Part 2; note of a Meeting 25 November 1981, BT/A/1 Part 3.

65  Minute from Solomon to Sharp and minute from Brown to Solomon, 4 December 1981, both in BT/A/1 Part 3. Brief for possible meeting with the Chancellor of the Exchequer, 9 November on the BT bond, by T.Sharp, 6 November 1981, BT Bond: Department of Industry Price Assurances, n.d., and BT Bond: Formula for Price Rises, by H.P. Brown, all in BT/A/1 Part 2.

66  Letter from P.S.Jenkins, PS HM Treasury, to Ian Ellison, PS Department of Industry, 24 July 1981, MT841 Post and Telecommunications papers Part 3.

67    Letter from Patrick Jenkin to the Chancellor of the Exchequer, 28 January 1982, minute from T.U. Burgner to the Chancellor of the Exchequer, 4 February 1982, and letters from the Chancellor of the Exchequer to Patrick Jenkin, 9 and 19 February 1982, all in HM Treasury papers JA/1760/01 Part A.

68    Record of a meeting held in HM Treasury, 31 July 1981, and note of a meeting held in the Chief Secretary's office, 22 September 1981, both in BT/A/1 Part 1; minute from D.L.Willets, 8 February 1982, HM Treasury papers JA/1760/01 Part A.

69    Letters from Howe to Jenkin, 9 and 18 February 1982, BT/A/1 Part 3. *Hansard*, 9 March 1982, column 740.

70    Baker (1993), p.78.

71    Note of a meeting held in the Chancellor of the Exchequer's room, House of Commons 5.50pm on Tuesday 28 July 1981, HM Treasury papers JA/1760/01 Part A.

72    However, Jefferson was adamant that BT must not be broken up and sold off piecemeal.

73    E(82)23, "Future Policy on Telecommunications. Memorandum by the Secretary of State for Industry", 4 March 1982.

74    Note of the Secretary of State's meeting with the Chancellor, 24 February 1982, and note of a Meeting between Baker, Wakeham, Jefferson and their officials, 8 March 1982, both in BT/A/3 Part 1.

75    E(82)23.

76    E(A)(82)9th meeting, 16 March 1982.

77    Campbell (2003), p.166; minute from J.P.Spencer, PS/Secretary of State, to Solomon, 17 March 1982, BT/A/1 Part 4.

78    Letter from M.R.Valentine, S.G. Warburg, to F.D. Perryman, BT, 9 June 1982, BT/A/1 Part 4.

79    Letter from Jenkin to Leon Brittan, 12 March 1982, BT/A/3 Part 1.

80    Correspondence in BT/C/17 Part 1.

81    Letter from Bryan Stanley, General Secretary POEU, to Jenkin, 2 February 1982, BT/A/3 Part 1.

82    *Hansard*, 22 March 1982, columns 242, 679. John Wakeham was Parliamentary Under Secretary of State in the Department of Industry.

83    Lawson (1992), p.222.

84    Minute from J.M.M.Vereker to John Hoskyns, No. 10 Policy Unit, 8 March 1982, PM Papers, Post and Telecommunications, Part 3.

85    E(82)6, "Future Policy on Telecommunications. Memorandum by the Chief Secretary Treasury", 9 March 1982.

86    E(82)29, "Telecommunications Policy. Note by the Central Policy Review Staff", 11 March 1982.

87    Minute from P.L.Gregson to the PM, 15 March 1982, PM Papers, Post and Telecommunications, Part 3.

88    E(82)9th meeting, 16 March 1982. Minute from Solomon to PS/Secretary of State, 11 March 1982, draft memorandum to the Chief Secretary, 11 March 1982, minute from Solomon to Ellison and Sharp, 1 March 1982, minute from H.P.Brown to Sharp, 8 March 1982, and memorandum from I.K.C.Ellison to the Secretary of State, 12 July 1982, all in BT/A/3 Part 2.

89    E(TP)(82) 1st meeting, 22 April 1982, PM Papers, Post and Telecommunications, Part 4.

90    E(TP)(82)2, "Future Telecommunications Policy. Note by the Chairman of the Official Committee on Telecommunications Policy", 16 April 1982.

91    Memorandum from P.L.Gregson to the PM, 20 April 1982, PM Papers, Post and Telecommunications, Part 4.

92    Letter from Jenkin to the Chancellor of the Exchequer, 24 January 1982, HM Treasury papers JA/1760/01 Part A.

93    Letter from Howe to Jenkin, 9 February 1982, BT/A/3 Part 1.

94    Note of a Meeting between Baker, Wakeham, Jefferson and their officials, 8 March 1982, BT/A/3 Part 1.

95    A report by accountants Coopers & Lybrand to the Treasury in October 1982 confirmed this conclusion. It reported that there was no evidence that BT had so far been restricted from investing by Treasury controls; Coopers & Lybrand Report on British Telecommunications,

30 December 1982, HM Treasury papers, Privatisation: British Telecommunications, AQ/1760/01. The Treasury does not appear to have dwelt on the corollary that this weakened the case for privatisation of BT on financial grounds.

96    Letter from Howe to Jenkin, 20 April 1982, PM Papers, Post and Telecommunications, Part 4.

97    Letter from Jenkin to Howe, 28 June 1982, and reply from Howe, 2 July 1982, both in PM Papers, Post and Telecommunications, Part 4.

98    C(82)19th meeting conclusions, 22 April 1982.

99    TP(0)(82)5th meeting, 4 June 1982.

100   Minute from H.P.Brown, PT2, to Solomon, 11 January 1982, BT/A/3 Part 1.

101   TP(0)(82)10, "British Telecom Privatisation: The Length and Nature of the Interim Regime. Joint Note by the Department of Industry and Treasury", 1 June 1982, BT/A/5. A further possible complication was the prospect of a minority shareholder successfully challenging a Government decision on BT's borrowing on the grounds that it was not in the best interests of the company; minute from F.D. Perryman, Finance Director BT, to PS/Secretary of State for Industry, 25 October 1982, BT/A/17 Part 1.

102   Letter from Sharp to R.H.Wilson, HM Treasury, 25 November 1982, BT/A/8 Part 3.

103   Letter from D.C. Clementi, Kleinworts, to T. Sharp, Department of Industry, 13 September 1982, letters from Sharp to R.H. Wilson, HM Treasury, 13 and 28 September 1982, and letter from Jefferson to Jenkin, 6 October 1982, all in BT/A/8 Part 2. The control system would be set out in S.67 of the 1984 Telecommunications Act should BT remain majority state-controlled for some time. However, once the decision was taken to sell 51% of the shares, the Government's powers over BT plc until the share flotation were confirmed by the informal process of an exchange of letters between the Minister and BT.

104   Correspondence in BT/A/30. Minute from Solomon to PS/Baker, 21 April 1983, BT/A/9 Part 3. Letters from Jefferson to Jenkin, 6 and 20 October 1982, BT/B/54; minute from J.B.K.Rickford to Robson, Department of Industry, 28 October 1982 and other miscellaneous correspondence in BT/A/8 Part 2.

105   E(TP)(82)9, "Future Telecommunications Policy. Note by the Central Policy Review Staff", 28 June 1982, PM Papers, Post and Telecommunications, Part 4.

106   E(TP)(82)8, "Future Telecommunications Policy. Memorandum by the Secretary of State for Industry", 24 June 1982; E(TP)(82)2nd meeting, 30 June 1982, both in PM Papers, Post and Telecommunications, Part 4.

107   *Hansard*, 19 July 1982, columns 23–4.

108   Department of Industry, *The Future of Telecommunications in Britain*, July 1982, Cmnd. 8610.

109   Letter from Jill Rutter, HM Treasury, to David Saunders, PS/Secretary of State for Industry, 20 July 1982, BT/A/3 Part 3. Letter from Howe to Jenkin, 15 July 1982, PM Papers, Post and Telecommunications, Part 4.

110   BT Response to the Secretary of State's Announcement, n.d., BT/A/3 Part 2.

111   Letter from Lord Cockfield to Jenkin, 2 December 1982, PM Papers, Post and Telecommunications, Part 6.

112   E(NI)(82)33, "Monopolies and Mergers Commission Efficiency Investigation. Memorandum by the Secretary of State for Trade and Industry", 15 December 1982.

113   Note from Ferdinand Mount, No. 10 Policy Unit, to the PM, 17 December 1982, and her annotated comment, PM Papers, Post and Telecommunications, Part 6.

114   The Bill amended a number of earlier Acts including the Telegraph Acts of 1863 to 1916 and the Wireless Telegraphy Acts of 1949 and 1967. E(TP)(82)16th meeting, PM Papers, Post and Telecommunications, Part 6. L(82)93, "Telecommunications Bill 1992. Memorandum by the Secretary of State for Industry", 1 November 1982, PM Papers, Post and Telecommunications, Part 6. "Telecoms Bill will benefit all says Patrick Jenkin", DOI Press Release 19 November 1982, BT/A/18 Part 2.

115   Letter from Jenkin to Cockfield, 29 November 1982, PM Papers, Post and Telecommunications, Part 6.

116   Note of the Secretary of State's meeting with the Board of BT, 13 July 1982, and Telecoms Bill: Note of a Meeting at BT Headquarters, 14 July 1982, both in BT/A/3 Part 3. Letter from Jefferson

to Jenkin, 19 July 1982, BT/A/17 Part 1. Letter from Jenkin to Jefferson, 21 July 1982, and BT response to Secretary of State's announcement, both in BT/A/3 Part 3.

117 Minute from I.K.C.Ellison to Berry, n.d., BT/A/52 Part 1.

118 However, there were also some MPs who felt that the Bill did not go far enough in introducing competition and dismantling BT's market dominance.

119 Letter from Lord Cockfield to Jenkin, 11 November 1982, PM Papers, Post and Telecommunications, Part 6. Minute from Baker to Jenkin, 23 February 1983, BT/A/9 Part 3. Letter from Lord Cockfield to Jenkin, 3 December 1982, PM Papers, Post and Telecommunications, Part 6.

120 POEU Press Release 3 November 1982, BT/A/18 Part 2.

121 Baker (1993), pp.81–2.

122 Minute from Nicklen, PS/Secretary of State, to Solomon, BT/A/21 Part 3.

123 Correspondence in BT/C/17 Part 1. Government convention required that government publicity should be relevant to Government responsibilities, objective and explanatory, not tendentious or polemical and should not be liable to misrepresentation as being party political. Nor should Government publicity assume or anticipate Parliamentary approval of legislation. These and other principles were formerly set down later in a memorandum submitted to the Widdicombe Committee of Inquiry into Local Authority Business. The inquiry was held in 1985; PM Papers, Government Machinery: Presentation of Government Policies Part 2, C(P)87, December 1997.

124 C(83) 16th meeting conclusions, 9 May 1983.

125 *Conservative Party Election Manifesto 1983.*

126 Letter from Jefferson to all BT staff, June 1983, BT/A/21 Part 3.

127 Various correspondence in BT/A/18 Part 1.

128 Minute from Solomon to Croft, 24 October 1983, BT/A/21 Part 3.

129 Letter from Tebbit to Tom King, Secretary of State for Employment, 3 February 1984, BT/A/9 Part 5.

130 Miscellaneous correspondence, union publications and letter from Jefferson to all staff in BT, n.d, letter from Jefferson to Tebbit on the legal position, 24 October 1983, and reply by Tebbit, 14 November 1983, and reply from Jefferson, 17 November 1983; from Jefferson to Baker, 31 October 1984, on the unions' campaign; and from Len Murray to Tebbit, 25 November 1983, and reply by Tebbit, 4 January 1984; all in BT/C/12 Part 1.

131 Letter from Sir Richard Butler, President NFU, 17 January 1983, BT/A/18 Part 2.

132 The Post Office Users National Council. POUNC was to be abolished under the Telecommunications Bill.

133 Letter from Shanks to Jenkin, 22 December 1982, BT/A/18 Part 2. Note of a meeting between Department of Industry officials and POUNC, 4 October 1982, BT/A/18, Part 1.

134 Various letters in BT/A/18 Part 2. *Hansard*, 19 July 1982, column 24, and correspondence in BT/A/18 Parts 4, 5, 6 and 7.

135 The Post Office Pension Fund Pre-1969 Deficiency, BT/A/17 Part 1.

136 Letter from David Clementi, Kleinwort, Benson, to H.Brown, Department of Industry, 21 October 1982, BT/A/17 Part 1.

137 Note of a meeting between Howe and Jenkin, 25 October 1982, BT/A/17.

138 Letter from Leon Brittan to Jenkin, 20 October 1992, BT/A/17 Part 1.

139 Notes for Press Conference 19 November 1982, BT/A/18 Part 2.

140 Minute from R.C.Dobbie to PS/Baker, 17 January 1983, and minute from S.Nicklen, PS/Secretary of State, to Solomon, 17 June 1983, both in BT/A/21 Part 3.

141 Minute from P.L.Bunn to MacDonald, 19 October 1983, BT/A/9 Part 4.

142 Letter from D.E. Pitcher to Parkinson, 13 June 1983, along with a copy of Littlechild's report, *Preventing Abuse of a Dominant Position in the Telecommunications Terminal Equipment Market*, 2 June 1983, and note of an internal DTI meeting on the Littlechild report, all in BT/A/18 Part 3. Note from P.L.Gregson to the PM ahead of the E(NI) sub-committee meeting to discuss the BT's Corporate Plan, 23 July 1982, PM Papers, Post and Telecommunications, Part 5. E(NI)(82)6th meeting, 26 July 1982. Minute from J.H.M.Solomon, DTI, to PS/Ministers, 10 October 1983, BT/A/23 Part 1. It is interesting that Littlechild was now recommending a break-up of BT, something that did not feature in his January 1983 report to the Government on economic regulation (chapter 12, pp.276–7). The absence of a recommendation on break up in

this report no doubt reflected the terms of reference but also recognition that this was contrary to Government policy of maintaining a unitary BT.

143 Letter from Jefferson to Jenkin, 17 December 1982, PM Papers, Post and Telecommunications, Part 6. Letter from Jefferson to Jenkin, 28 January 1983; letter from Jenkin to Cockfield, 6 January 1983, reply from Cockfield, 11 January 1983, and a further letter from Jenkin to Cockfield, 4 February 1983; letter from Brittan to Jenkin, 12 January 1983; letter from Sparrow to Cockfield, 3 February 1983; letter from Brittan to Jenkin, 4 February 1983; letter from Cockfield to Jenkin, 4 February 1983; all in PM Papers, Post and Telecommunications, Part 6.

144 DTI Press Release, 15 October 1984, BT/A/12 Part 6. Letter from Sir Edwin Nixon, IBM UK, to the PM, 22 October 1984, BT/A/11 Part 5. Also, correspondence in PM Papers, Post and Telecommunications, Part 9.

145 Tebbit (1988), p.241.

146 "BT Bill: Position of UK Suppliers. Note by the Department of Industry", IT (81)25 Cabinet Official Committee on Information Technology, PM Papers, Post and Telecommunications, Part 3.

147 Speech by Jefferson to the Telecommunications Engineering and Manufacturing Association, 17 March 1983, BT/A/25 Part 2. J. Harper (1997) *Monopoly and Competition in British Telecommunications: The Past, the Present and the Future*, Pinter London, ch.12.

148 E(TP)(82)3, "System X and the UK Telecommunications Industry.Memorandum by the Minister of State for Trade and Industry", 16 April 1982; E(TP)(82) 1st meeting, 22 April 1982; note from Kenneth Baker to the PM 30 March 1982; and letter from BT to GEC, Plessey and STC, 18 May 1982, all in PM Papers, Post and Telecommunications, Part 4. Notes from Jenkin to the PM, 23 July 1982 and 15 September 1983; note from Baker to the PM, 29 September 1982; letter from Howe to Baker, 4 October 1982; all in PM Papers, Post and Telecommunications, Part 5.

149 Note of a meeting on 27 July 1983 with BT to discuss Licence issues, BT/A/23 Part 1. Secretary of State's meeting with Sir George Jefferson, 28 March 1984, BT/A/52 Part 2. DTI note 12 April 1984, BT/A/61 Part 2. How fast procurement of telecommunications equipment would become much more competitive after privatisation was a matter of some uncertainty during the planning of the BT sale.

150 BT's Procurement of Digital Exchanges: A Report by the Director General of Telecommunications and letter from Lansley to Turnbull, 25 July 1985, both in MT Part 9. Correspondence in BT/C/4 Part 4 especially letter from Jefferson to Cecil Parkinson, Secretary of State for Trade and Industry, 7 October 1983. Miscellaneous correspondence in PM Papers, Post and Telecommunications, Part 7.

151 "Objectives" document, 21 July 1983, T1, BT/A/12 Part 3. Letter from R.H. Wilson, HM Treasury, to H.P.Brown, DTI, 18 July 1983, BT/A/12 Part 3.

152 Various correspondence in BT/A/25 Part 2. The parliamentary guillotine places a limit on the length of a debate.

153 Correspondence in BT/A/62 Part 1.

154 CC(84)4th meeting conclusions, 2 February 1984.

155 CC(84)8th meeting conclusions, 1 March 1984.

156 Letters from Howe to Tebbit, 4 November 1983 and 14 November 1983, and Tebbit to Howe, 9 November 1983 and 21 November 1983, all in BT/B/155.

157 Note of a Meeting with BT on 1 October 1984, BT/A/38 Part 1. Letter from Kenneth Baker to Andrew Rowe, MP, 15 November 1983, in E(DL) Part 8.

158 "Privatisation: Present Situation and Prospects. Report by the Secretary of State for Industry", 13 September 1982, E(DL) Part 6.

159 Note from Walters to Scholar, 14 October 1982, PM Papers, Post and Telecommunications, Part 5.

160 Young (1990), p.51. Later Young conceded that the accounting systems in BT were such that it would take many years for his preferred restructuring to be achieved; ibid., p.52.

161 Minute from E.E.R.Butler, Principal Private Secretary No. 10, to Sparrow, CPRS, 1 September 1982, PM Papers, Post and Telecommunications, Part 5.

162 Minute from S. Nicklen, PS/Secretary of State, to Solomon, 21 June 1983, BT/A/21 Part 3.

163 Note from Michael Scholar to John Sparrow, 8 September 1982, PM Papers, Post and Tele-communications, Part 4. Minute from Croft to PS/Jenkin, 8 November 1982, and minute from Ellison to PS/Jenkin, November 1982, both in BT/A/21 Part 1. Note from Sparrow, CPRS, to Scholar, 18 October 1982, PM Papers, Post and Telecommunications, Part 5. Baker (1993), p.81.

164 Letter from J.P.Spencer, PS/Secretary of State for Industry to Michael Scholar, PS to the PM, 13 October 1982, and Department of Industry paper, The Scope for Breaking in British Telecommunications in the Light of American Experience, 11 October 1982, both in PM Papers, Post and Telecommunications, Part 5.

165 Minute from M.C.Scholar, PS No. 10, to Jonathan Spencer, DOI, 9 November 1982, PM Papers, Post and Telecommunications, Part 5. Note from Scholar to Jonathan Spencer, DOI, 9 September 1982, MT841 Post and Telecommunications papers Part 4. Given the importance of the privatisation of BT, it takes up surprisingly little space in Margaret Thatcher's memoirs (Thatcher, 1993, p.680) – one page. In particular there is only the briefest of comments on the controversy over whether BT should be broken up at or before privatisation: "But if we wanted to go further and break up BT into separate businesses, which would have been better on competition grounds, we would have had to wait many years before privatization could take place. This was because its accounting and management systems were, by modern standards, almost nonexistent. There was no way in which the sort of figures which investors would want to see could have been speedily or reliably produced." There is no discussion of the other controversies that surrounded the sale.

166 Minute from Ellison to PS/Baker, 26 July 1983, BT/A/9 Part 4.

167 Minute from J.H.M.Solmon, HD/T, DTI, to PS/Ministers, 10 October 1983 and Minute from I.K.C.Ellison to PS/Kenneth Baker, both in BT/A/23 Part 1. Note of Secretary of State's meeting with Sir George Jefferson and other representatives of BT, 11 October 1983; Ministerial Group on BT Flotation: Policy Issues Concerning the BT Licence. Note by Department of Trade and Industry Officials, 14 October 1983; both in BT/A/23 Part 2. Note of a meeting on 27 July with BT to discuss Licence issues, 3 August 1983, BT/A/23 Part 1. Note in BT/A/23 Part 1.

168 Note of the Secretary of State's meeting with Jefferson, 17 July 1983, BT/A/21 Part 3. The new Secretary of State for Trade and Industry after the Election, Cecil Parkinson, was very keen in principle on breaking up BT to foster competition. He notes in his autobiography that he had been "unhappy about the original bill" that had fallen at the General Election, preferring to see more competition introduced (Parkinson, 1992, *Right at the Centre: an autobiography*, p.241). However, in his brief period in office there were no noticeable changes in policy towards the privatisation of BT. It appears that he recognised that it was too late or too difficult to achieve a break-up. Parkinson did make some changes to the Bill, but these were matters of detail relating, for example, to the Secretary of State's and the DGT's statutory duties and BT's public service obligations.

169 BT Flotation Joint Steering Group, agenda for meeting on 1 August 1983, BT/A/51. Draft letter to John Moore, Financial Secretary to the Treasury, from Kenneth Baker, 9 November 1983, BT/A/20 Part 5.

170 Access Fees, by Bruce Laidlaw, DOI, 31 March 1983, BT/A/20 Part 4.

171 Minute from M.C.McCarthy, PS/Secretary of State for Trade and Industry, to Ellison, 26 October 1983, BT/A/9 Part 4. Note of meeting with Eric Sharp 25 October 1983, BT/A/18 Part 3.

172 Note from Jonathan Phillips, DTI, 8 September 1983, BT/A/23 Part 1.

173 Letter from Jenkin to Cockfield, Department of Trade, 29 November 1982, PM Papers, Post and Telecommunications, Part 6. Note from I.K.C. Ellison to Bradbury, 26 January 1983, BT/A/20 Part 3. Minute from J.H.Rickard, HM Treasury, to the Economic Secretary, 14 October 1983, BT/A/9 Part 4. Minute from Ellison to PS/Jenkin, 9 November 1982, BT/A/21 Part 1.

174 Note of a meeting held on 5 October 1983 with BT on the Licence, BT/A/23 Part 1.

175 Minute from R.H.Wilson to J.H.Rickard, 23 December 1982, HM Treasury papers N/1368/1399/01 Part B.

176 Letters from Moore to Tebbit, 8 November 1983, and from Moore to Baker, 10 November 1983, both in PM Papers, Post and Telecommunications, Part 7.

177 Resale: BT Position Paper, 10 October 1983, BT/A/9 Part 4.
178 Minute from MacDonald to Croft, 12 March 1984, and minute from McMillan to Macdonald, 21 May 1984, both in BT/A/9 Part 6.
179 Letter from Andrew Turnbull, PS No. 10, to M.C.McCarthy, 7 November 1983, BT/A/9 Part 4. Mercury was not in favour of unrestricted resale of BT circuits, which it saw as a possible threat to its business. Later Mercury would change its mind.
180 Note of a Meeting on Interconnect, Resale and Related Issues, 12 July 1983, and letter from Baker to Jefferson, 3 October 1983, both in BT/A/9 Part 4. Letter from John Moore, Financial Secretary to the Treasury, to Kenneth Baker, 24 November 1983, BT/A/20 Part 5.
181 Letter from Jefferson to Baker, 13 April 1984, BT/A/9 Part 6.
182 Minute from MacDonald to PS/Secretary of State, 28 February 1984, minute from McMillan to Croft, 2 March 1984, letter from Baker to Lord Cockfield, 2 March 1984, all in BT/A/9 Part 5.
183 Note by Andrew Lansley, PS/Secretary of State for Trade and Industry, 12 April 1984, BT/A/26 Part 3.
184 BT Prospectus, p.17, BT/A/18 Part 6. Mercury's licence was broadly equivalent but without the universal service obligations placed on BT.
185 Telecommunications Act: British Telecom's Licence, draft press notice, n.d., BT/A/23 Part 2.
186 Note by MacDonald, Head T Division, 15 June 1984, BT/A/26 Part 4.

## 12 PRIVATISING BRITISH TELECOM: OFTEL AND REGULATING PROFITS OR PRICES

1 Note from J.H.M.Solomon, HD/PT, to Croft, 1 April 1982, BT/A/5.
2 E(T)(82)6, "Regulation of Telecommunications. Note by the Chairman of the Official Committee on Telecommunications Policy", 18 June 1982, PM Papers, Post and Telecommunications, Part 4.
3 E(TP)(82)5, "Scope for Further Liberalisation of Telecommunications. Memorandum by the Secretary of State for Industry", 4 June 1982, PM Papers, Post and Telecommunications, Part 4. BT also started out by claiming that telecommunications was a natural monopoly on grounds of economies of scale, as evidenced in Professor Beesley's report to the Secretary of State on telecommunications liberalisation in January 1981; HMSO (1981), Appendix 2.
4 E.g. "Telecommunications Regulation: The Options for the Regulatory Instrument", September 1982, paragraph 2, BT/A/20 Part 1.
5 Minute from T.U.Burgner to W.S.Ryrie, 3 July 1981, HM Treasury papers JA/1760/01 Part A.
6 Minute from A.N.Ridley to the Chancellor of the Exchequer, 16 November 1982, HM Treasury papers N/1368/1399/01 Part A.
7 Report of the Inter-Departmental Group on Rate of Return Regulation in Telecommunications – Reply by DOI to Comments Thereon by Professor Walters, October 1982, BT/A/20 Part 1.
8 Draft reply from PM to Richard Shepherd, MP, 16 May 1983, BT/A/9 Part 4.
9 Associated with the Averch-Johnson effect, see below.
10 Note of a Meeting 26 August 1982 to discuss the proposed Regulatory Authority under the Telecommunications Act, BT/A/9 Part 1. Letter from N.E.D.Burton, Secretary to the MMC, to Ian Ellison, 23 September 1982, BT/A/9 Part 2. Within the Department of Industry, Ellison was the official primarily involved with regulation issues.
11 Regulation of Telecommunications: The Competition Aspects, March 1982, BT/A/9 Part 1; letter from L. Lightman, OFT, to S.G.Linstead, Department of Trade, 3 August 1982, BT/A/9 Part 1; Telecoms Regulations: Note of a Meeting, 30 September 1982, BT/A/9 Part 3.
12 Minute from E.A.Riley, Assistant Private Secretary (APS)/Baker, to Ellison, 7 June 1982, BT/A/0 Part 1.
13 Minute from Ellison to Private Secretary (PS)/Secretary of State, 27 September 1982, BT/A/9 Part 2.
14 Minute from G.M.A. Lambert, T Division, to Gunner, 15 August 1983, BT/A/21 Part 3.

15    Draft for Telecommunications Bill Part 4, July 1982., BT/A/9 Part 1. Minute from C.J.A. Chivers, 5 August 1983, and letter from Kenneth Baker to Barney Hayhoe, Minister of State HM Treasury, 22 September 1983, both in HM Treasury papers N/12/1399/01 Part C.

16    Letter from Ellison to S.Linstead, Department of Trade, 21 September 1982, BT/A/9 Part 2.

17    Minute from Croft to Solomon, n.d.; minute from Ellison to PS/Jenkin, n.d., and letter from Cockfield to Jenkin, 3 December 1982, both in BT/A/21 Part 2.

18    Letter from D.C.Clementi, Kleinwort Benson, to Dr R. Dobbie, Department of Industry, 21 September 1982, BT/A/1 Part 2.

19    Minute from M.S.Bradbury to Solomon, 18 June 1982, BT/A/84 Part 1.

20    Minute from Robert Armstrong, Cabinet Secretary, to the PM, 30 June 1982, PM Papers, Post and Telecommunications, Part 4.

21    The exception would be for specialist technical posts where different terms and conditions of employment might need to apply.

22    Letter from J.B.Stuttard, CPRS, to Ellison, 23 September 1982, BT/A/9 Part 2.

23    E(TP)(82)6, "Regulation of Telecommunications. Note by the Chairman of the Official Committee on Telecommunications Policy", 18 June 1982, PM Papers, Post and Telecommunications, Part 12. Letter from T.R.M.Simon, Management and Personnel Office, to Ellison, 6 September 1982, BT/A/9 Part 2.

24    Minute from C.J.A. Chivers, 21 July 1983, HM Treasury papers British Telecommunications Privatisation – Regulation of BT (OFTEL) N/12/1399/01 Part C.

25    Minute from A.M.White to Chivers, 3 August 1983, HM Treasury papers N/12/1399/01 Part C.

26    BT Response to Secretary of State's Announcement, n.d., BT/A/3 Part 2.

27    Aide-memoire, 10 November 1982, BT/A/9 Part 3. Minute from B.Murray to Solomon, Department of Industry, 10 March 1983, BT/A/8 Part 3.

28    Minute from R.H.Wilson, 2 March 1983, HM Treasury papers N/12/1399/01 Part C.

29    BT Press Notice 19 November 1982, BT/A/21, Part 1.

30    Carsberg was also an adviser on the issuing of a second cellular phone licence, to Racal/Vodafone.

31    Minute from Joyce Blow, MSM Division DTI, to Baker, 27 July 1983, BT/A/9 Part 4.

32    Letter from Baker to Rees, 29 July 1983, BT/A/9 Part 4.

33    Minute from Solomon to PS/Secretary of State, 31 January 1983, BT/A/9 Part 3, and minute from S.Nicklen to Croft, 17 November 1983, BT/A/9 Part 4. The Treasury all along suspected that the reason why the DTI favoured a second permanent secretary grading was that this normally automatically led to a knighthood, Minute from Chivers, 5 August 1983, HM Treasury papers N/12/1399/01 Part C.

34    Letter from Barney Hayhoe to Baker, 1 November 1983, HM Treasury papers N/12/1399/01 Part C. The Treasury was unconvinced that the post was necessary and argued that if appointed the person should be at assistant secretary level only.

35    Letter from Brian Hayes, Permanent Secretary DTI, to Sir Peter Middleton, HM Treasury, 2 February 1984, BT/A/9 Part 5. There was also difficulty over the pension arrangements.

36    Tebbit (1988), p.219.

37    It seems that Carsberg first became aware that he might be appointed when *The Times* newspaper tipped him for the post. Before leaving for the USA Carsberg wrote to Baker saying that he wanted to take the job, but could not do so on the terms set out. In his memoirs Baker says that the phone call was made in 1983, Baker (1993), p.83. This appears to be a mistake. Government records show that Carsberg was offered the job in March 1984.

38    Minute from Tebbit to the PM, 28 March 1984 and from Lawson to the PM, 28 March 1984, both in BT/A/9 Part 6.

39    By this time a "shadow" OFTEL had been established within the DTI consisting of around 30 civil servants.

40    Note from Kenneth Baker to named officials and other ministers in the Department of Industry, 5 October 1982, in BT/A/20 Part 1.

41    Working Group on BTL's Rate of Return on Capital, Note by the Chairman, 3 September 1982, in BT/A/20 Part 1.

NOTES

42  E(TP)(82)6, "Regulation of Telecommunications. Note by the Chairman of the Official Committee on Telecommunications Policy", 18 June 1982, PM Papers, Post and Telecommunications, Part 12; E(TP)(82) 2nd meeting, June 1982.

43  Working Group on BTL's Rate of Return on Capital. Note of First Meeting, 7 September 1982, BT/A/20 Part 1.

44  Letter from M.S.Bradbury, Economics Branch 1A, Department of Industry, to H. Brown in T division, Department of Industry, 1 September 1982, in BT/A/20, Part 1.

45  Minute from G.M.A. Lambert to Dr Dobbie, Department of Industry, 18 August 1982, BT/A/9 Part 1.

46  Littlechild (2003a), p.5, footnote 13.

47  Working Group on BTL's Rate of Return on Capital. Note of Fourth Meeting, 21 September 1982, BT/A/20 Part 1

48  Proposals for Controlling Monopoly Profits Earned by British Telecommunications PLC and for Promoting Greater Efficiency in its Operations, Telecommunications Division, Department of Industry internal document, 14 October 1982, and Rate of Return Regulation in Telecommunications, report of the Working Group on BTL's Rate of Return on Capital, both in BT/A/20 Part 1.

49  H. Averch and L. Johnson (1962) "Behavior of the firm under regulatory constraint", *American Economic Review*, vol.52, pp.1052–69.

50  Note from Jim Shine, EC1A Department of Industry to Members of the Working Group on Return on Capital, 7 September 1982, in BT/A/20 Part 1. The failure of rate of return regulation and tariff setting in US telecommunications is discussed in detail in "Rate of Return Regulation in Telecommunications", report of the Working Group on BTL's Rate of Return on Capital, Annex II, BT/A/20 Part 1

51  Note on the Report of the Department of Industry Group on Rate of Return Regulation in Telecommunications; also, memorandum from R.H.F.Croft, Deputy Secretary DOI, to J.P.Spencer, the PS/Secretary of State for Industry, 15 October 1982; both in BT/A/20 Part 1

52  Note of a Meeting 25 September 1982, BT/A/9 Part 3. Minute from R.H.Wilson, HM Treasury papers N/1368/1399/01 Part A.

53  Minute from R.H.Wilson to T.U.Burgner, 19 November 1982, HM Treasury papers N/1368/1399/01 Part A; minute from T.U.Burgner to R.H.F.Croft, Department of Industry, 6 December 1982, HM Treasury papers N/1368/1399/01 Part B. Nevertheless, the Treasury continued to press for there to be regular MMC inquiries into BT's efficiency.

54  Walters to Scholar, 23 June 1982, MT841 Post and Telecommunications papers Part 4. Letter from Walters to Bradbury, 1 October 1982, PM Papers, Post and Telecommunications, Part 5. Letter from Walters to Baker, 11 January 1983, BT/A/18 Part 2.

55  Working Group on BTL's Rate of Return on Capital. Note of Third Meeting, 17 September 1982, BT/A/20 Part 1.

56  Internal memorandum from Bradbury to Ellison in the Department of Industry along with a summary of the Working Group's conclusions, September 1982, in BT/A/20 Part 1.

57  Ibid., paragraph 8. Note from Walters to Scholar, 21 October 1982, PM Papers, Post and Telecommunications, Part 5.

58  Report of the Inter-Departmental Group on Rate of Return Regulation in Telecommunications – Reply by the Department of Industry to Comments Thereon by Professor Walters, October 1982, BT/A/20 Part 1.

59  Ibid., Annex 3 reporting Professor Beesley's views.

60  Ibid., main report.

61  Telecoms Regulation: Note of a Meeting held in the Department of Industry on Monday 6 October to Discuss Rate of Return, in BT/A/20 Part 1.

62  Note of a Meeting with Professor Walters on 20 October 1982, note dated 28 October, BT/A/20 Part 1. Letter from Jenkin to Lord Cockfield, Department of Trade, 29 November 1982. PM Papers, Post and Telecommunications, Part 6 Littlechild's terms of reference included to "prepare a practical scheme for an output related profits levy", "evaluate the strengths and weaknesses of an output related profits levy and of the controls on BT's profitability proposed by the

inter-departmental working group", and "consider relevant variants of [these] schemes", Regulation of BT's Profitability: Terms of Reference", HM Treasury papers N/1368/1399/01 Part B. Memorandum from J.P. Spencer, PS/Secretary of State for Industry, to R.H.F.Croft, Deputy Secretary DOI, 18 October 1982, in BT/A/20 Part 1.

63 Memorandum from Jenkin to the PM, 8 November 1982; also note from Walters to Scholar, 8 November 1982, both in PM Papers, Post and Telecommunications, Part 6.

64 Letters from Malcolm Argent, BT, to Ian Ellison, Department of Industry, 2 December 1982, BT/A/20 Part 2.

65 Littlechild later talked to them about the RPI – X idea proposed for the aborted Buzby bond. His final report states: "In preparing this Report, I have benefited from discussions with a large number of people especially at DoI, HM Treasury, CPRS, Prime Minister's Office, BT, Kleinwort Benson and Warburgs." S.C. Littlechild (1983) *Regulation of British Telecommunications' Profitability, Report to the Secretary of State*, London: Department of Industry, February.

66 Letter from John Sparrow, CPRS, to Jenkin, 15 November 1982, BT/A/21 Part 1. Letter from J.B.Stuttard, CPRS, to I.Ellison, Department of Industry, 8 October 1982, BT/A/20 Part 1.

67 Note of Mr Baker's meeting with Sir William Barlow on 30 November 1982, note dated 7 December, BT/A/20 Part 2.

68 Letter from G.T.Boon, MMC, to J.B.Stuttard, CPRS, 19 October 1982, BT/A/20 Part 1.

69 "An Output Related Profits Tax" S.C. Littlechild, 24 November 1982, BT/A/20 Part 1.

70 Memorandum from Bruce Laidlaw, Ecla, DOI, to I. Ellison, 1 December 1982.

71 "Variants of Rate of Return Regulation" by S.C. Littlechild, 29 November 1982, BT/A/20 Part 2.

72 S.C. Littlechild (2003a) "The birth of RPI – X and other observations", in I. Bartle (ed.), *The UK Model of Utility Regulation: a 20th anniversary collection to market the 'Littlechild Report' – retrospect and prospect*, Bath: Centre for the study of Regulated Industries, University of Bath, p.32.

73 "Regulation of BT's Profitability. First Draft of Report", S.C. Littlechild, December 1982, BT/A/20 Part 2.

74 Comment on Professor Littlechild's draft report, unsigned and undated, BT/A/20 Part 2.

75 Minute from Bruce Laidlaw to Ian Ellison, 20 December 1982, BT/A/20 Part 2.

76 He also favoured allowing "resale à la Beesley"; minute from E.A.Riley, APS Kenneth Baker, to Solomon and quoting Baker, 6 January 1983, BT/A/20 Part 2.

77 Minute from David Saunders to Solomon, 10 January 1983, BT/A/20 Part 2.

78 Note of a Meeting to Discuss Professor Littlechild's Draft Report on the Regulation of BT, 5 January 1983, BT/A/20 Part 2.

79 Minute from J.H.Rickard to R.H.Wilson, 20 December 1982, and reply from Wilson, 23 December 1982, HM Treasury papers N/1368/1399/01 Part B.

80 Minute from M.S. Bradbury to Croft, 7 January 1983, BT/A/20 Part 2.

81 Minute from B.H. Laidlaw, Ec 1a, to Solomon, 12 January 1983, in BT/A/20 Part 2.

82 Littlechild (1983).

83 Littlechild (2003a), p.35.

84 Valentine (2006), p.131 & p.165. Littlechild (1983, para. 13.15) briefly acknowledges the similarity of his proposal to that put forward earlier for the Buzby bond. He also draws attention in his report to a recent proposal by the MMC to control profits in the supply of contraceptive sheaths, involving price rises adjusted by less than inflation (para. 14.5). However, there is no evidence in Government papers that this report had a material influence on the decision to adopt a price cap for BT.

85 "Regulation of BT's Profitability", note from the economics section, Department of Industry, 22 December 1982, BT/A/20 Part 2.

86 Littlechild (1983), para.1.5a. The same point is repeated in paras. 4.7 and 4.8. In para.6.17 he also commented reflecting his position in the earlier draft report: "To summarise, there would be a number of significant advantages in imposing no explicit constraints on BT's profits. Efficiency and innovation would not be discouraged, the burden of regulation would be negligible, and BT's prospects would be good."

87   Regulation of BT's Profitability. Report by Professor S.C. Littlechild, note from the economics section, Department of Industry, January 1983, BT/A/20 Part 3.

88   Letter from Walters to Bradbury in the Department of Industry, 18 January 1983, BT/A/20 Part 2. In his report, Littlechild (1983, Appendix 2, para. 5) also recommended "further study . . . as there could well be other situations more favourable to the adoption of the ORPL."

89   Minute from Solomon to Croft, 24 January 1983, BT/A/20 Part 3.

90   Regulation of BT's Profitability. Note by the Department of Industry, nd (January 1983), BT/A/20 Part 3.

91   Letter from John Sparrow, CPRS, to Patrick Jenkin, 28 January 1983, BT/A/20 Part 3.

92   Minute from T.Sharp, Ti, Department of Industry, to Croft, 19 January 1983, BT/A/20 Part 2.

93   Minute from J.R.Shepherd to Croft, Department of Industry, 26 January 1983, BT/A/20 Part 3.

94   Littlechild (2003a), p.33.

95   Internal minute to Solomon, undated (January 1983), BT/A/20 Part 3.

96   Minute from N.M.McMillan, PS/Kenneth Baker, to Croft, 25 January 1983, BT/A/20 Part 3.

97   Notes of Meetings held to discuss the Government's proposed response to the Littlechild report, 1,2 and 3 February 1984, BT/A/21 Part 2. Note of a Meeting with BT to discuss Littlechild's report, 1 February 1982, BT/A/20 Part 3.

98   Tariff Reduction Scheme for British Telecommunications, economics section paper, Department of Industry, 28 January 1983, BT/A/20 Part 3.

99   Regulation of BT's Profitability. Note by the Department of Industry, January 1983, BT/A/20 Part 3.

100  Note of a Meeting held at the Treasury on 21 January 1983 to discuss British Telecommunications Privatisation, HM Treasury papers N/1368/1399/01 Part C.

101  Note 3 February 1983, PM Papers, Post and Telecommunications, Part 6 *Hansard,* 7 February 1983, columns 633–4: "Telecommunications Regulation" DOI Press Notice, 7 February 1983, BT/A/20 Part 3.

102  "Telecommunications Regulation", DOI Press Release, 7 February 1983, BT/A/9 Part 3.

103  Telecom Bond, draft Department of Industry document, 4 November 1981, BT/A/1 Part 2.

104  Coopers & Lybrands, BT's auditors, were commissioned by BT to undertake a study of the Corporation's cost structure but it seems that the Treasury wanted to see an alternative study undertaken.

105  Under the Department of Industry's maximum and minimum rate of return proposal there was provision for the MMC to undertake five yearly reviews of BT's performance, but with the rejection of the scheme this was shelved; minutes from R.H.Wilson, 19 January 1983 and 21 February 1983, HM Treasury papers N/12/1399/01 Part C.

106  Work by Consultants on Real Price Objectives for British Telecommunications, n.d. (February) and letter from A.G. Mayo, MMC, to Bradbury, Department of Industry, 17 February 1983, minute from Bradbury to Solomon, 18 February 1983, minute from Solomon to PS/Baker, 18 February 1983, all BT/A/20 Part 3.

107  Note from H.P.Brown to Sharp, Department of Industry, 11 February 1983, BT/A/20 Part 3.

108  Minute from B. Murray to Laidlaw, Department of Industry, 2 March 1983, BT/A/20 Part 3. In an early draft of BT's licence the RPI – X formula was to be set by reference to a forecast of inflation. Later this was changed on the grounds that it would be difficult to forecast inflation accurately. The price cap finally set would be based on the RPI in the previous year. If inflation was to change sharply from one year to the next this could have a serious effect (positive or negative) on BT's finances. In such circumstances the company would be able to apply to the DGT for the cap to be amended or the DGT could chose to amend the cap, subject to referral to the MMC in cases of disagreement; RPI – X License Issues, 17 April 1984, BT/A.48 Part 2.

109  Letter from Jefferson to Jenkin, 18 March 1983; minute from Croft to Solomon, 10 March 1983, letter from Croft to A.M. Bailey, HM Treasury, 25 March 1983, all BT/A/20 Part 3.

110  At this time Carsberg was being considered for the post of DG OFTEL and Baker was keen to include him in the Study Team to test him out.

111  Letter from Jenkin to Jefferson, 31 March 1983, BT/A/20 Part 3. Minute from Bradbury to Sharp, 21 April 1983, BT/A/20 Part 4.

112 Letter from R.H. Wilson, HM Treasury, to T.Sharp, 22 April 1983, BT/A/20 Part 4.
113 Letter from R.H. Wilson, HM Treasury, to Solomon, 27 April 1983, BT/A/20 Part 4.
114 Letter to Professor Carsberg, 25 April 1983, BT/A/20 Part 4.
115 Letter from Sharp to F.D.Perryman, Board Member for Finance, BT, 26 May 1983, BT/A/20 Part 4.
116 Minute from J.H. Rickard, HM Treasury, to the Economic Secretary, 14 October 1983, BT/A/20 Part 4. Minute from J.H.Rickard to R.H.Wilson, 7 January 1983, HM Treasury papers N/1368/1399/01 Part C.
117 Minute from A.J. Macdonald to Croft, 7 February 1984, BT/A/12 Part 3.
118 Valentine (2006), p.159.
119 Terms of Reference of the RPI – X Study Group, n.d.; minutes of the First Meeting of the Group, 27 June 1983; memorandum from A.J.Vardy, BT, 10 August 1983; all in BT/A/48 Part 1. Letter from John Moore, Financial Secretary to the Treasury, to Baker, 24 November 1983, BT/A/20 Part 5.
120 Interim Report of the RPI – X Study Group, 19 September 1983, BT/A/48 Part 1.
121 "RPI – X: Meeting between Mr Baker and Sir George Jefferson on 6 October 1983, BT/A/20 Part 4.
122 Minute from J.H. Rickard, HM Treasury, to the Economic Secretary, 14 October 1983, BT/A/20 Part 4.
123 Note of Secretary of State's Meeting with Sir George Jefferson and other Representatives of BT, 6 October 1983, BT/A/23 Part 2. Minutes of meeting of RPI – X Steering Group 31 October 1983, BT/A/48 Part 1.
124 The decision to include the RPI – X formula in BT's licence was confirmed at the committee stage of the Telecommunications Bill, on 22 November 1983, although a number of details were still to be settled.
125 Minute from Rickard to Wilson, 2 February 1984, BT/A/48 Part 1.
126 Minute from R.H.F.Croft, Deputy Secretary, to PS/Kenneth Baker, 13 January 1984, BT/A/20 Part 5.
127 Minutes of the Study Group meeting 16 January 1984 and meeting with DTI/Treasury on the BT Licence, 17 January 1984, both in BT/A/48 Part 1.
128 Letter from R.H. Wilson, HM Treasury, to T.Sharp, 10 January 1983, in BT/A/20 Part 5.
129 Minute from M.S. Bradbury to Laidlaw, 18 January 1984, BT/A/20 Part 5.
130 RPI – X. Note for Discussion between Financial Secretary Treasury and Minister of State DTI by Bradbury, 9 February 1984, BT/A/20 Part 5.
131 Draft DTI Paper for High Level Meeting with BT on RPI – X, 6 January 1984, minute from Bradbury to Laidlaw, 18 January 1984, both in BT/A/48 Part 1.
132 RPI – X: The Effect of Varying X, BT/A/48 Part 1.
133 Draft note by R.H.F.Croft, 17 January 1984, BT/A/20 Part 5.
134 DTI Paper for High Level Meeting with BT on RPI – X, 6 January 1984, BT/A/20 Part 5.
135 Minute from Bradbury to Croft, 2 February 1984, BT/A/48 Part 1.
136 RPI – X. Note for Discussion between Financial Secretary Treasury and Minister of State DTI by Bradbury, 9 February 1984, BT/A/20 Part 5.
137 Note for discussion between Financial Secretary Treasury and Minister of State DTI, 9 February 1984; letter from Baker to Jefferson, 13 February 1984; minute from McMillan, PS/Baker, to MacDonald, 15 February 1984; all in BT/A/48 Part 1.
138 R.O'B Davis, *Report to Minister of State for Industry and Information Technology*, draft, March 1984, BT/A/48 Part 2. The first draft of the report was more favourable to BT than the final report, suggesting that X should be no more than 1% or 2%. This was altered after discussion with the DTI and Treasury officials. The draft report was judged by DTI officials to be disappointing; Note of a meeting on 7 March 1984 to Discuss a Draft Report on RPI – X by Mr Davis; minute by M.S.Bradbury, RPI – X: Draft report by Mr Davis, March 1984; Ministerial Group on BT Flotation, RPI – X: Note by the Department of Trade and Industry, n.d.; all in BT/A/48 Part 2. In his draft report Davis repeated that "simple though the concept [RPI – X] was as envisaged, it has proved to be fraught with difficulty to decide how it should apply in practice . . . I conclude that RPI – X is going to be very imperfect and cannot substitute for competition in improving

BT's efficiency" (draft report paras. 1.9 and 10.1). It is also the case that Davis doubted whether any price cap set could survive a five year period without an interim price review (para. 10.1).

139    Minute from Andrew Lansley, PS/Secretary of State for Trade & Industry, to Croft, 23 March 1984, BT/A/26 Part 3.

140    DTI paper, The Implications of Varying 'X', n.d.; minute from B.Laidlaw to PS/Baker, 4 April 1981; both in BT/A/48 Part 2.

141    Secretary of State's meeting with Sir George Jefferson, 28 March 1984, BT/A/52 Part 2. BT objected to the suggestion from the DTI that £500m of debt be substituted by new preference shares and preferred that this debt be converted entirely into normal equity. This would have left BT with a gearing of around 35%. The DTI had started out with a target gearing of up to 80% but had now reduced this to 50%, as a concession to BT; Notes of meetings with BT on RPI − X and Capital Structure, 19 March and 6 April 1984; letter from Tebbit to Lawson, 2 April 1984; both in BT/A/48 Part 2.

142    Minute from the Financial Secretary to the Chancellor of the Exchequer, 27 February 1984, HM Treasury papers N/1368/1399/01 Part C.

143    Note of a meeting with BT on capital structure and RPI − X, 12 April 1984, BT/A/52 Part 2.

144    Notes of the meetings, BT/A/48 Part 2.

145    Letter from Leon Brittan, Chief Secretary, Treasury, to Jenkin, 29 November 1982 and reply by Jenkin, 6 December 1982, both in PM Papers, Post and Telecommunications, Part 6. Jenkin acknowledged that BT's forecasting "has contained too much fat". Letter from Jenkin to Howe, 22 March 1983, MT841 Post and Telecommunications papers Part 6. Minute from Sharp to PS/Baker, 15 July 1983, BT/A/11 Part 5.

146    Note of a meeting in No. 11 Downing Street, 10 April 1984, BT/Z/52 Part 2. Letter from Lansley, PS DTI, to Turnbull, PS to the PM, 19 April 1984, PM Papers, Post and Telecommunications, Part 8. Some of the debt was assigned to meet deed of covenant obligations under BT's pension schemes, DTI Press Release, 2 May 1984, BT/C/30 Part 2.

147    Minute from N.M. McMillan, PS/Baker, 19 April 1984; meeting on 18 April with BT to discuss RPI − X; both in BT/A/48 Part 2.

148    Brief for the Secretary of State's meeting with the PM, 25 April 1984, BT/A/48 Part 3.

149    Various correspondence, 24–25 April 1984, in BT/A/52 Part 2.

150    Minutes from Lansley, PS/Secretary of State for Trade and Industry, to Sharp, 25 April 1984, BT/A/48 Part 3.

151    Minute from McCarthy, PS/Secretary of State for Trade and Industry, to Croft, 3 May 1984, BT/A/48 Part 3.

152    Letter from Jefferson to Baker, 24 April 1984, BT/A/48 Part 2. Letter from Jefferson to Tebbit, 25 April 1984, PM Papers, Post and Telecommunications, Part 8.

153    Minute from McMillan, PS/Baker, to Croft, 25 April 1984, BT/A./48 Part 3.

154    Letter from Tebbit to Lawson, 30 April 1984, PM Papers, Post and Telecommunications, Part 8. In his memoirs, Nigel Lawson states, "In the case of British Telecom, there was a major argument as to how big the x-factor should be, with the company (supported by Norman Tebbit) arguing for 2%, while I wanted 4%. Inevitably, we eventually compromised on 3%." Lawson (1992), p.223. This is a very brief summary of the controversy.

155    Hansard, 2 May 1984, column 353.

156    BT News release, 2 May 1984, BT/A/48 Part 3.

157    Letter from F.P.Bogan, HM Treasury, to T.Flescher, PS to the PM, 25 April 1984, PM Papers, Post and Telecommunications, Part 8.

158    Note in BT/A/25 Part 2.

159    Tariff Reduction Scheme for British Telecommunications, Department of Industry, 28 January 1983, BT/A/20 Part 3.

160    In fact, the DGT did have power to pursue a change to the price cap before 1989 but chose not to exercise it.

161    Minute from Bradbury to Sharp, 8 October 1984, BT/A/20 Part 5.

162    Cited in K. Newman (1986) The Selling of British Telecom, London: Holt, Rinehart and Winston, p.12.

163    Letter from Vander Weyer to Valentine, Warburgs, 25 May 1984, BT/C/15 Part 5.

## 13 PRIVATISING BRITISH TELECOM: THE FLOTATION
## AND REPERCUSSIONS

1  British Telecom – Methods of Achieving Broadly Based Ownership, n.d., BT/A/31 Part 1.
2  The Kleinworts team on the privatisation of BT was James Rockley, Martin Jacomb and David Clementi. In charge in the Department of Industry was Roy Croft, a Deputy Secretary. Sir William Ryrie led the Treasury team. Andrew Smither, Michael Valentine and Nick Fry represented Warburgs. In BT the Directors most involved with the privatisation were Sir George Jefferson (Chairman), Deryk VanderWeyer (Deputy Chairman) and Douglas Perryman (Finance Director).
3  Undated draft note in BT/A/3 Part 1.
4  The recalculation was provoked by a back of the envelope calculation in the Treasury and was understood to be a very rough estimate. Undated note (probably July 1983) in BT/A/12 Part 3.
5  Prior to BT, the largest equity share offer anywhere in the world had been a secondary offering by AT&T in America, valued at just over US$1bn.
6  Report by Technology Group Research, de Zoete & Bevan, September 1983, BT/A/56, Part 1.
7  *Hansard*, 29 November and 14 December 1983.
8  Lawson (1992), p.222.
9  E(TP)(82)7, "Privatisation of British Telecommunications: Interim Regime. Note by the Chairman of the Official Committee on Telecommunications Policy" and the attached Official Report, PM Papers, Post and Telecommunications, Part 4. Campbell (2003), p.237 notes that John Redwood, at the time head of the No.10 Policy Unit, has claimed credit for persuading the PM of the case for selling shares directly to the public through a wide marketing campaign. The idea was also developed within the Department of Industry in conjunction with its financial adviser, Kleinworts.
10  Minutes from W.S.Ryrie, 29 and 30 June 1981 and supporting correspondence and memoranda, HM Treasury papers JA/1760/01 Part A.
11  Minute from T.U.Burgner, 3 July 1981, and minute from W.S.Ryrie, 22 July 1981, ibid.
12  Minute from Solomon to Winkett, R356 Ash, 30 July 1982, BT/A/21 Part 1.
13  Minute from R.G.Ward, Cabinet Office Central Statistical Office, to HM Treasury, 15 September 1982, HM Treasury papers JA/1760/01 Part B.
14  Letter from D.C. Clementi to Solomon, 15 October 1982, BT/A/12 Part 3. Minute from Laidlaw to Solomon, 18 October 1982, BT/A/12 Part 1.
15  Note by Ellison for meeting with the Chancellor on the Telecommunications Bill, 25 October 1982, BT/A/8 Part 2.
16  Correspondence in BT/A/12 Part 1. Note by H.P.Brown, DTI, 2 June 1983, BT/A/26 Part 4.
17  British Telecom – a Tap Issue, n.d., BT/A/91 Part 1. Methods of Sale, n.d., BT/A/91 Part 4. However, the idea won some support outside Government; e.g. Buckland and Davis (1984), p.51.
18  Kleinwort Benson paper, British Telecommunications: Preference Shares, 25 October 1983, BT/A/31 Part 3. Letter from R.H. Wilson, HM Treasury, to H.P.Brown, DTI, 18 July 1983, BT/A/12 Part 3.
19  Secretary of State's Meeting with Sir George Jefferson and BT Board, 16 March 1983, BT/A/21 Part 2; letter from D.C. Clementi to Solomon, 15 October 1982, BT/A/12 Part 3; letter from BT to J.Cazalet, Cazenove & Co., 13 September 1984, BT/A/31 Part 8. Wider share ownership and customer shareholding: the BT view, April 1983, BT/A/12 Part 3.
20  Kleinwort, Benson Ltd, British Telecommunications: Methods of Achieving Broadly Based Ownership, 17 February 1983, BT/A/12 Part 3; Share ownership by telephone subscribers, note by G.F.Heath, DTI, 8 July 1983, and letter from T.G.Barker, Kleinwort Benson, to J.B.K.Rickford, solicitor DTI, 24 June 1983; both in BT/A/31, Part 1; minute from H.P.Brown, T Division, DOI, to Solomon, 14 January 1983, BT/A/31 Part 1; letter from R.H.Wilson, HM Treasury, to Solomon, 2 November 1983, BT/A/31 Part 3.
21  British Telecom – Broadly Based Ownership. The Co-operative Scheme, n.d., BT/A/31, Part 1; letter from D.P.Savill, BT, to R.H.F.Croft, DTI, 30 November 1983, BT/A/31 Part 9.
22  Minutes of Meeting of the Joint Steering Group, 12 January 1984, BT/A/51.
23  Ministerial Group on the BT Flotation, note of the First Meeting, 22 July 1983, BT/A/52 Part 1.

24 Minute from R.H.Wilson to the Chancellor of the Exchequer, 22 October 1982, HM Treasury papers N/1368/1399/01 Part A.
25 Note by Bruce Laidlaw, Department of Industry, 17 September 1982, BT/A/12 Part 1. The Merits of an Introductory Issue of BT Shares, DTI paper, 21 July 1983, BT/A/31 Part 2. British Telecom – Methods of Achieving Broadly Based Ownership, n.d., BT/A/31 Part 1. Kleinwort Benson, British Telecommunications, Market Capacity and Related Matters, 18 April 1983, BT/A/12 Part 3. Note of a meeting at the DTI 7 November 1983 and "The British Telecom Trust: a Paper by Kleinwort Benson", November 1983, both in BT/A/31 Part 3. Letter from John Moore to Baker, 17 April 1984, BT/A/38 Part 1.
26 BT/A/12 Part 3.
27 Ministerial Group on BT Flotation. Note of the First Meeting held on 22 July 1983, BT/A/12 Part 3.
28 Letter from M.W.Jacomb, Kleinwort, Benson Ltd, to Nick Monck, HM Treasury, 27 March 1984, BT/A/12 Part 4.
29 Working Group on Methods of Flotation: Draft Report, 14 July 1983, BT/A/12 Part 3.
30 Timetable for the Telecommunications Bill, Department of Industry, 21 July 1983, BT/A/12 Part 3.
31 Minute from Laidlaw to Sharp, DTI, 23 February 1983, BT/A/31 Part 1.
32 Meeting of Interdepartmental Working Group, 6 September 1983, BT/A/31 Part 2. At the time Shell plc had the largest shareholder base with around 350,000 investors. It was clear that BT would have a much larger number. At first a figure of about 500,000 was suggested as the target but this was quickly raised to over 1m.
33 Minute from S.Nicklen, PS/Secretary of State for Industry, to Solomon, 8 April 1983; minute from H.P.Brown to Croft, 22 April 1983, both in BT/A/26 Part 2. Minute from Sharp to Solomon, 16 March 1983 and from Solomon to PS/Jenkin, 23 February 1983, both in BT/A/21 Part 2.
34 Sale of Shares in BT: Method of Sale, April 1983, BT/A/12 Part 3.
35 Various correspondence in BT/A/12 Part 3.
36 Correspondence in BT/A/21 Part 4.
37 BT's Accounts and the Flotation: Background Note, BT/A/62 Part 2.
38 Parkinson (1992), p.242. There were also other specialised skills, which had to be bought in. For example, in spite of having a huge property portfolio in 1981 BT employed only one qualified Chartered Surveyor.
39 Note of a Meeting with Coopers & Lybrand, 13 December 1983 and minute from B. Heatley to Croft, 15 December 1983, both in BT/A/11 Part 5. The Reports by the Auditors of BT Accounts 1979–80 to 1983–84, n.d., BT/A/91 Part 1
40 One former member of the Coopers & Lybrand auditing team recalls: "we could have either qualification or privatisation, but not both. We were asked whether we would like to go home and think about it. We thought about it and did not qualify after that. It was perfectly straightforward." Private information.
41 Note by T.Sharp, 12 September 1983, BT/A/31 Part 3. For a very detailed discussion of the marketing of the issue see K. Newman (1986) *The Selling of British Telecom*, London: Holt, Rinehart and Winston.
42 Letter to K.Newman from M.J.Cole, DTI, 23 August 1985, BT/A/56 Part 2.
43 Lawyers Linklater and Paines were appointed in September 1983 by the DTI. Slaughter and May acted as BT's solicitors.
44 Joint Steering Group 2nd meeting Minutes, 19 July 1983, BT/A/51. Correspondence in BT/C/17 Part 1. The Flotation Marketing Sub-Committee of the Prospectus Committee was initially chaired by Peter Young, BT's Director of Corporate Relations, and from mid-1984 by John King, newly appointed to BT's Board and responsible for marketing and corporate strategy. It met fortnightly from November 1983.
45 BT/C/17 Part 2.
46 BT flotation: note of a meeting at HM Treasury, 24 January 1984, BT/A/26 Part 3.
47 Minute from S. Nicklen, Private Secretary (PS)/Secretary of State for Trade and Industry, to Solomon, 19 December 1983, and minute from Sharp to Croft, 9 January 1984, BT/A/26 Part 3.

48 Lawson (1992), p.223.
49 Letter from Anthony Carlisle, Dewe Rogerson, to Solomon, 20 December 1983, and minute from Steve Mummery, Assistant Private Secretary (APS)/Baker, to Solomon, 13 January 1984, both in BT/C/17 Part 2.
50 British Telecom Offer for Sale, retrospective from Kleinwort Benson, 19 February 1985, BT/A/91 Part 1.
51 Memorandum from Market & Opinion Research International Ltd to Anthony Carlisle, Dewe Rogerson, 23 January 1984, BT/C/17 Part 2.
52 Given the low share purchase threshold, the benefit did not apply to large institutional investors. For the BT sale no similar share purchase limit was imposed and therefore institutional investors could benefit from the bonus issue (as could overseas investors – in the Britoil sale there was no overseas issue). Another difference between the Britoil and BT bonus schemes involved the allocation of the bonus shares. Under the terms of the Britoil sale investors eligible for bonus shares had to apply for them at the end of the three year qualifying period. In the case of BT the shares would be allocated automatically.
53 Letter from D.C.Clementi, Kleinwort, Benson Ltd to J.Solomon, DTI, 15 October 1982, BT/A/12 Part 1.
54 British Telecom/DTI Joint Steering Group on Flotation – Shareholder Concessions, report by W.P.Kember, Chief Accountant BT, January 1984, BT/A/31 Part 5. Proposals for the Issue of Shares by British Telecom: A New Strategy for Widening Share Ownership in the United Kingdom, Barclays Merchant Bank Ltd. 2 February 1984, quotation from p.11, in E(DL) Part 9.
55 Odyssey: Size and Structure of the Flotation, report by Kleinwort Benson, 6 February 1984, BT/A/26 Part 3. British Telecom – Methods of Achieving Broadly Based Ownership, n.d., BT/A/31 Part 1. Letter from R.H.Wilson. HM Treasury, to A.J.Macdonald, DTI, 15 February 1984, BT/A/12 Part 4.
56 *Hansard*, column 599, 25 May 1984. DTI Press Release, 25 May 1984, BT/A/71 Part 3.
57 *Hansard*, column 298, 1 August 1984.
58 Ministerial Group on BT Flotation. Note of the First Meeting held on 22 July 1983, BT/A/12 Part 3.
59 Correspondence in BT/A/71 Part 1.
60 Letter from J.B.Webb, Head of LCS Billing Administration BT, to J.C.W.Kent, T Division DTI, 6 July 1984, BT/A/71 Part 2. Later BT revised down the cost to 26p per voucher.
61 Bill Voucher Scheme: Mechanics, n.d., BT/A/71 Part 2; Shareholder Incentives: Summary of Administrative Costs, BT/A/71 Part 3.
62 Minute from MacDonald to PS/Baker, 21 February 1984, BT/A/52 Part 1.
63 Ministerial Group on BT Flotation, note of meeting held on 6 March 1984, BT/A/66 Part 2. Minute from A.J. Macdonald to PS/Secretary of State, 9 April 1984, BT/A/26 Part 3.
64 Letter from Baker to Moore, 12 July 1984, BT/A/71 Part 3.
65 Letter from Sharp to J.Williams, HM Treasury, 30 May 1984, BT/A/12 Part 4.
66 BT *Offer for Sale*, Part V1, A.
67 Letters from Baker to Moore, 12 July 1984 and 20 July 1984, and from Moore to Baker, 17 July 1984 and 30 July 1984, in BT/B/261.
68 Three videos were produced relating to the train tour and a video was produced to be used in the clearing banks handling the offer.
69 Paper by the Director Corporate Relations BT for the Flotation Sub-Committee meeting 23 January 1984, BT/C/17 Part 2. Briefing meetings were also arranged with MPs. A. Carlisle (1988) "Marketing privatization", in E.Butler (ed.) *The Mechanics of Privatization*, London: Adam Smith Institute. Anthony Carlisle was the director of Dewe Rogerson most closely involved in the BT sale.
70 C(84)29th meeting conclusions, 2 August 1984.
71 Dewe Rogerson, BT Case History, BT/C/17 Part 15.
72 Correspondence in BT/C/17 Part 5.
73 Correspondence in BT/A/31 Part 8.

74  BT/C/17 Part 7. The leaflet was stuffed into an envelope with the telephone bill, hence the name. Consideration was given to having in addition a separate direct mailing to customers, but the idea was dropped mainly it seems because of fears that the postal union might direct its members to refuse to handle the mailing. The union was opposed to the privatisation. During the later sale of British Gas there was an additional separate mailing to customers, chapter 15, p.372.

75  Note from C.Bridge, DTI, 29 March 1984 and note from N.M. McMillan, PS/Baker, 30 March 1984, BT/A/12 Part 4.

76  Correspondence in BT/C/17 Part 5.

77  Letter from Anthony Carlisle to Bridge, DTI, BT/C/17 Part 5.

78  Notes in BT/C/17 Part 8.

79  Miscellaneous correspondence in BT/C/8. There was poster, TV, radio and newspaper advertising.

80  Prospectuses were also published for overseas investors.

81  Telecoms Bill: Lords Briefing and Proceedings, n.d., BT/A/62. The amendment exempted the BT issue from restrictions laid down in the Companies Act 1948 and the Prevention of Fraud (Investments) Act 1958.

82  Letter from Bruce Laidlaw to David Clementi, Kleinwort Benson, 19 May 1983, BT/A/31 Part 1; British Telecom – Methods of Achieving Broadly Based Ownership, n.d., BT/A/31 Part 1. Following the success of the mini prospectus during the BT sale, New Listing Particulars came into force on 1 January 1985 under the Financial Services Act that gave the Stock Exchange the power to approve mini prospectuses for future share issues in the City, thereby removing complaint of special treatment for Government sponsored issues.

83  Note in BT/A/18 Part 7. The editor of *The Sun* newspaper, a staunch supporter of the Conservatives at the two previous General Elections, objected vociferously when he discovered that his newspaper had not been selected to carry the Prospectus.

84  In the case of Jaguar, a document had to be sent to all British Leyland's shareholders. Although BL was almost entirely state-owned, it did have a residue of private sector investors.

85  BT Flotation: Enquiry Handling, 10 May 1984, BT/C/17 Part 5.

86  There was also an office in London to co-ordinate the activity and deal with any particularly difficult enquiries.

87  Note from John Williams, HM Treasury, to Sharp, 12 June 1984, BT/C/17 Part 7.

88  Letter from J.F.Williams, HM Treasury, to Brian Heatley, 9 August 1984, DTI, BT/C/17 Part 10.

89  Dorland, BT Flotation Media Buying Report as at 13 September 1984, BT/C/17 Part 12.

90  Miscellaneous correspondence, BT/C/15 Part 5.

91  This included the cost of meeting the different legal requirements for the flotation in each of the countries in which BT shares were to be sold.

92  Shares were also marketed in Switzerland by the Swiss Bank Corporation but through the London stock market.

93  Record of a meeting held in the PM's room in the House of Commons, Monday 30 July 1984, BT/A/26 Part 4.

94  *BT, Annual Report and Accounts 1983/84*, report to the accounts paragraph 6. Full details of the changes are provided in British Telecommunications: Form of Accounts, Finance Department BT, BT/A/66 Part 1. Also, Defensive Briefing for BT Interim Accounts, n.d., BT/A/62 Part 2.

95  Note by N.M.McMillan, PS/Kenneth Baker, BT/A/66 Part 1; notes by G.F.Heath, 13 December 1983, and Laidlaw, 14 December 1983, BT/A/66 Part 1.

96  Other changes included ceasing a practice of charging supplementary depreciation to take account of the replacement cost of fixed assets and ending the capitalisation of certain assets such as telephone instruments, which would now be charged to the profit and loss account in the year of acquisition. Letter from D.C.Clementi, Kleinwort Benson, 27 February 1984 and meeting with BT on 21 February 1984 to Discuss Shortening of Asset Lives and Accounting Treatment Thereof, minutes, and "The Auditors' Assessment and BT Flotation: Accounting Treatment Proposed by BT for Asset Lives", all in BT/A/66 Part 1. Letter from Coopers & Lybrand to Baker, 29 March 1984, BT/A/66 Part 2 and in HM Treasury papers H/1760/01 Part G.

97    Letter from F.D.Perrryman, BT Board Member for Finance, to Croft, 4 November 1982, BT/A/17 Part 1.
98    Letter from D.C.Clementi, Kleinwort Benson, to H.P.Brown, DOI, 29 September 1982, BT/A/18 Part 1.
99    Minute from H.P.Brown, to Croft, 19 July 1983, BT/A/51.
100   Memorandum from A.J.Macdonald, Head T division, to PS/Secretary of State, 23 February 1984, BT/A/12 Part 4.
101   Letter from H.P.Brown, DOI, to Clementi, Kleinwort Benson, 12 October 1982, BT/A/18 Part 2.
102   Minute from R.H.Wilson to the Financial Secretary, 22 December 1983, HM Treasury papers H/1760/01 Part F.
103   The idea of issuing preference shares convertible into equity was dropped after it was pointed out that this might create a back door for future renationalisation.
104   In the longer-term the judgement was that BT might benefit, but up to 1988/89 BT reckoned that there would be an annual reduction of after tax profits of between £60m and £235m and in its cash position of between £21m and £262m a year; letter from F.D.Perryman, BT, to R.H.Croft, DTI, 21 March 1984 and minute from R.H.Wilson, 21 March 1984, HM Treasury papers H/1760/01 Part G.
105   Capital structure, briefing, n.d., BT/A/91 Part 3.
106   National Audit Office (1985) *Report by the Comptroller and Auditor General, Department of Trade and Industry: Sale of Government Shareholding in British Telecommunications plc*, London: HMSO, July, para. 19.
107   To compensate investors the final dividend was declared early, in August 1985.
108   Valentine (2006, p.163) of Warburgs during the sale of BT states that at the time the bank calculated that a higher gearing would have been acceptable to the City. The higher gearing might have raised the overall net proceeds to the Government by some £815m.Warburgs were advisers to BT and BT was in favour of lower gearing. It seems that the Government was not aware of Warburg's calculation. The level of gearing to maximise the sale proceeds would be a matter of much debate in later privatisations too; for example, see the discussions on British Gas's balance sheet in chapter 15.
109   £550m of this related to pensions for postal workers which had been arbitrarily allocated by the Post Office to the telecommunications side of the business because it was the more profitable and therefore deemed more able to bear the cost.
110   Note in BT/A/25, Part 1.
111   Minute from R.H.Wilson, 12 November 1982 and other correspondence in HM Treasury papers JA/1760/01 Part B.
112   Internal Department of Industry minute by V.A. Novarra, 2 November 1982, BT/A/18 Part 2.
113   *Hansard*, 2 May 1984, columns 353–4.
114   Miscellaneous correspondence in BT/C/17 Part 4. Letter from Ian Wrigglesworth, MP, to Geoffrey Pattie, Minister for State for Industry and Information Technology, 22 November 1984, BT/A/31 Part 9. Minute from J.B.K.Rickford to B.Hilton, DTI, BT/C/17 Part 4.
115   Fortunately the US markets regulator, the Securities and Exchange Commission, also showed a degree of flexibility when interpreting its rules on the marketing of BT shares before the issue of the Prospectus.
116   Minute from M.K. O'Shea to Sharp, 29 June 1984, BT/C/14.
117   BT Flotation, Executive Group Meeting 14 February 1984, BT/A/71 Part 1; letter from D.W.Miller, National Accounts Manager PO Counters, to J.C.W.Kent, DTI, 5 July 1984, BT/A/71 Part 2.
118   E.g. Lloyds Bank estimated the cost at £13.50 per 1,000 items for vouchers that avoided clearing bank costs and 15p per item for quasi-cheques, letter from M.Young, Manager Lloyds Bank, to J.C.W.Kent, DTI, 5 July 1984, BT/A/71 Part 2.
119   Minute from B.A.Heatley, DTI, to Sharp and PS/Baker, 13 July 1984, BT/A/12 Part 4. Letter from Baker to John Moore, Financial Secretary, 16 July 1984, and other miscellaneous correspondence in BT/C/14 Parts 2, 3 and 4. Letter from K.F.Murphy, Treasury Chambers, to B. Heatley, DTI, 3 August 1984; letter from C.J.Bailey, Bank of England, to Sharp, DTI, 9 August 1984; both in BT/C/14 Part 2.

120    Letter from Baker to Moore, 9 August 1984, BT/A/12 Part 5.
121    Minute from N.M.McMillan, PS/Baker, to Sharp, 30 May 1984, letter from Baker to John Moore, Financial Secretary, 26 June 1983 and reply by Moore, 11 July 1984; all in BT/A/12 Part 4.
122    Letter from Deryk Vander Weyer, Deputy Chairman BT, to Baker, 7 August 1984; memorandum from B.A.Heatley, T1, to Sharp and Croft, 10 September 1984; minute from Sharp to A.J.P.Macdonald, 21 September 1984; all in BT/A/12 Part 5.
123    Minute from N.M.McMillan, PS/Baker, 12 January 1984, BT/A/21 Part 3.
124    Minute from Macdonald to PS/Sir Brian Hayes, 31 October 1984, BT/A/84 Part 1.
125    BT Method of Sale; Notes of meetings held on 21 June and 17 July 1984 at HM Treasury, BT/A/84 Part 1.
126    As usual in privatisations at this time, the Government's financial adviser, in this case Kleinworts, acted as the issuing house and lead underwriter.
127    BT: Use of the Issue Department, BT/A/84 Part 2.
128    In Britain underwriting typically occurred some 12 days or so before applications from the public. In the USA, and a number of other markets, the share offer process involved "building a book" in the shares before the share was priced. During the sale of BT, Morgan Stanley insisted on being able to buy the shares at a discount of 3.25% to 3.75% below the London offer for sale price and only at least 10 days after the London underwriting agreement. This meant that the US shares would be allocated to purchasers when the London market price was known.
129    Correspondence in BT/A/84 Part 2.
130    Even with the Autumn Statement coming after the underwriting was completed, there was a fear that the underwriters might take legal action for release from their contractual obligations should there be anything in the Statement prejudicial to the offer, Lawson (1992), p.225.
131    Note by A.J. MacDonald, 6 September 1984, BT/C/17 Part 12.
132    Minute from Sharp to PS/Baker, 7 September 1984, BT/C/17 Part 12.
133    Correspondence in BT/A/18 Part 5. An example is a letter from a rector in Essex who wrote: "I am sorry that I do not have to(sic) money to purchase shares in the new privatised company, and am sorry that legislation has been passed to sell my shares of this magnificent and most successful company. I say farewell with regret", BT/A/18 Part 5.
134    Correspondence in BT/A/18 Parts 5 and 6.
135    Note of a meeting at HM Treasury, 2 November 1984, BT/A/84 Part 2.
136    de Zoete & Bevan: British Telecom, internal DTI note, 29 June 1984, BT/A/56 Part 1. Minute by T.Sharp, 5 July 1984, BT/A/66 Part 2.
137    Letter from Jefferson to Stuart Young, Chairman of the BBC Board of Governors, 31 October 1984, BT/C/30 Part 2.
138    However, this was offset by a sharp drop in capital issues by firms during the second half of 1984, probably because of the forthcoming BT issue.
139    British Telecom Valuation – a Discussion Paper, Kleinwort, Benson Ltd., 5 October 1984, BT/A/91 Part 1.
140    Minute from Bradbury to Sharp, 17 October 1984, BT/A/12 Part 6.
141    McLeod Young Weir were the advisers in Canada and Nomura Securities in Japan. Like Morgan Grenfell, they were appointed using "beauty contests".
142    Minute from A.J. Macdonald to PS/Secretary of State, 30 May 1984, BT/A/26 Part 1. The Method of Sale of BT, Its Pricing and Valuation, BT/A/84 Part 1.
143    Note of a meeting held on 23 October 1984 at HM Treasury, BT/A/84 Part 1.
144    Minute from Macdonald to PS/Pattie, 23 October 1984, BT/A/84 Part 1.
145    British Telecom, report by Phillips & Drew, 23 October 1984, BT/A/84 Part 1.
146    Pricing, n.d., BT/A/91 Part 3.
147    Circular in BT/A/84 Part 2.
148    British Telecom Report by Phillips & Drew, 2 November 1984, BT/A/91 Part 1. Phillips & Drewe note to investors, "British Telecom – It's for you", 1 November 1984, BT/A/56 Part 1.
149    Letter from D.C.Clementi, Kleinwort Benson, to Sharp, 25 February 1984, BT/A/84 Part 2.
150    Note by Macdonald, 21 November 1984, BT/C/46 Part 1.
151    Minutes of the Meeting of the Flotation Committee, 8 November 1984, BT/C/17 Part 15.
152    Note in BT/A/18 Part 6.

153 Correspondence from Phillips & Drew, 2, 9 and 14 November 1984, BT/A/84 Part 2 and The Pricing of BT: The DTI Perspective, 2 November 1984, BT/A/26 Part 4.
154 Arrangements for sale, n.d., BT/A/91 Part 1.
155 Note of a meeting at HM Treasury, 9 November 1984, BT/A/84 Part 2. Letter from T.Sharp to J.Williams, HM Treasury, 30 May 1984, BT/A/71 Part 2.
156 Minute from Edward Blades, PS/Secretary of State for Trade and Industry, to PS/Sir Brian Hayes, 15 November 1984, BT/A/26 Part 4.
157 At the time a three day application period was more normal for flotations in London.
158 Initial Public Offer.
159 British Telecom, review of the press coverage, 19 February 1985, BT/A/91 Part 1.
160 Around this time there was also growing confidence that the Government would defeat the miners' strike that had begun the previous March, as miners began to return to work in bigger numbers.
161 *Financial Times*, 26 November 1984; *The Sun*, 21 November 1984.
162 To be raised again to 14% in the face of an exchange rate crisis in January 1985.
163 File memo by B.Heatley, 4 November 1984, BT/C/46 Part 1. Note of a meeting held in the Chancellor's room, HM Treasury, 14 November 1984, BT/A/84 Part 2.
164 Note of a meeting on 29 November 1984 to discuss the possible basis of allocation of BT shares, BT/C/46 Part 1.
165 Minute from Sharp to PS/Pattie, 8 November 1984, BT/C/17 Part 14.
166 *Hansard*, 3 December 1984, column 19.
167 Ministerial Group on the BT Flotation, note of meeting 27 November 1984 and note of a meeting 30 November 1984 on the allocation of BT Shares, both in BT/A/52 Part 3.
168 Note in BT/A/38 Part 2. However, amongst BT subscribers it appears that a majority favoured the vouchers over the bonus shares. Of course, bill vouchers had no attraction for investors who were not BT subscribers and for institutional investors.
169 Briefing for PM's Question Time, November 1987, BT/A/104.
170 Letter from Neil McMillan, DTI, to Chris Morris, Department of Energy, 14 May 1986, BT/A/71 Part 12.
171 Letter from Tebbit to Jefferson, 16 November 1984, BT/A/38 Part 1.
172 See chapter 5, endnote 10, for the terms of Article 223.
173 DTI Press Release, "British Telecom Appointments", September 1984, BT/A/38 Part 1. Minute from J,.C.W.Kent, 12 August 1985, BT/A/38 Part 2.
174 The Department of Industry in late 1982 employed consultants, Copeman Paterson Ltd, to report on possible arrangements for employees. However, BT preferred to develop its own plans. The arrangements that resulted were therefore the result of BT's suggestions, as toned down by the DTI in response to Treasury concern about the costs.
175 Note of a meeting with BT on flotation – 15 September 1983, BT/A/31 Part 3. Letter from R.H.Wilson to the Financial Secretary, John Moore, 20 January 1984, and letter from John Moore to Kenneth Baker, 31 January 1984, HM Treasury papers British Telecommunications Flotation: Employee Share Holding Scheme, N/1693/1510/01 Part C.
176 Baker had initially pressed for a 15% discount but had agreed to 10% as part of the compromise deal with the Treasury. BT pensioners also benefited from the priority application scheme but without the price discount. Employee applications occurred using a "pink form". The BT sale involved different coloured application forms for different groups of investors, a method of distinguishing the applications to assist the processing of the forms adopted in other privatisations.
177 The discounted price offer was an innovation encouraged by a change in tax law in the 1984 Finance Act. This involved an amendment to Section 79 of the Finance Act 1972 and relieved BT employees of an Income Tax charge which otherwise would have arisen on the price discounted shares; minute from S.P.Ayling, Inland Revenue Policy Division, to HM Treasury, 17 February and 21 June 1984, HM Treasury papers N/1693/1510/01 Part D. As in previous privatisations, shares allotted to employees under both the free scheme and matching scheme were to be held by trustees of the Company's Employee Share Scheme for a minimum of two years to take advantage of a tax concession.

NOTES

178    *Hansard*, 21 January 1985, column 504.

179    Internal note from B.A. Heatley, DTI, 11 October 1984, BT/A/18 Part 7. Minute from H.C.Goodman, 19 October 1984, HM Treasury papers N/1693/1510/01 Part D. Nicholas Ridley, the Secretary of State for Transport, was particularly opposed to accepting the BT proposal on the grounds that it would almost certainly mean that he would have to concede something similar during the privatisation of BA; letter to the PM, 22 October 1984, PM Papers, Post and Telecommunications, Part 9.

180    Letter from Norman Tebbit, Secretary of State for Trade and Industry, to Nigel Lawson, Chancellor of the Exchequer, 28 June 1984, BT/A/22 Part 7. Memorandum from Geoffrey Pattie to the PM, 22 October 1984; letter from Pattie to John Moore, Financial Secretary, 16 October 1984; letter from Ridley to Moore, 22 October 1984, note from Nigel Lawson, Chancellor of the Exchequer, to the PM, 22 October 1984; all in BT/A/18 Part 7. Geoffrey Pattie replaced Kenneth Baker as Minister of State for Industry and Information Technology in September 1984.

181    Minute from Pattie to the PM, 22 October 1984, and minute from the Chancellor of the Exchequer to the PM, 22 October 1984, both in PM Papers, Post and Telecommunications, Part 9.

182    Letter from Pattie to the Financial Secretary, 16 October 1984, HM Treasury papers N/1693/1510/01 Part D; letter from the Chancellor of the Exchequer to the PM, 22 October 1984, HM Treasury papers Executive Share Option Schemes, L/1821/01 Part K.

183    Pricing, summary notes, BT/A/84 Part 2.

184    The Behaviour of NBT's Share Price – a comment by Phillips & Drew, 23 January 1985, BT/A/91 Part 1.

185    Overseas shareholders in BT: Background Note, T Division, 23 January 1985, BT/A/84 Part 2. Another difficulty arose with regards to the US issue. A "grey market" in trading in the shares developed. The shares in the US were not firmly allocated until the Allotment Day, which was 1 December, but trading in the shares occurred earlier. US underwriters and dealers were restricted under the underwriting agreement and selling arrangements from disposing of stock until the allotment. It seems that the grey market resulted from a leakage of shares on to the market sold "firm" to British institutions on 16 November through certain non-syndicate dealers; memorandum from Goldman Sachs & Co, 17 July 1986, in Department of Energy British Gas privatisation file G800/49/14 Part 27.

186    Note of a meeting between the DTI and Phillips & Drew, BT/A/84 Part 2.

187    The British Telecom Issue – Dealing Patterns during the First Two Weeks, 24 January 1985, BT/C/46 Part 1.

188    Note by J.C.W.Kent, 12 March 1985, BT/A/31 Part 9.

189    Swiss institutions purchased their shares through the UK stock market.

190    7.5m shares or 0.2% of the offer was retained by the DTI in the short term, for reasons explained earlier.

191    MORI survey for BT, note by J.C.W.Kent, 18 June 1985, BT/A/31 Part 10.

192    Ibid.

193    Minute from M. Dowling, DTI, 24 April 1991, BT/A/104.

194    A later estimate, in April 1991, put the total costs somewhat higher at £158.5m plus an additional £59.6m for the employee share scheme and up to £110m for the bill voucher and bonus share incentives; details in BT/A/61 Part 3 and note dated 24 April 1991, in BT/A/104.

195    The costs exclude £51m worth of shares given to employees under the employee share offers and the bonus shares for shareholders due in November 1987.

196    National Audit Office (1985) *Report by the Comptroller and Auditor General, Department of Trade and Industry: Sale of Government Shareholding in British Telecommunications plc*, London: HMSO, July, paras. 33 – 42.

197    PAC Hearing 22 July: BT Privatisation, Annex B, BT/A/91 Part 3.

198    CC(84)37th meeting conclusions, 15 November 1984; CC(84)28th meeting conclusions, 29 November 1984. Minute from Sharp to PS/Pattie, 10 December 1984, BT/A/52 Part 3.

199    Correspondence in BT/A/56 Part 2 and BT/A/84 Part 2.

200    Brief on Wider Share Ownership, July 1985, BT/A/91 Part 3.

201    Letter from Coopers & Lybrand to Kent, DTI, 11 November 1985, BT/A/71 Part 11.

202    E.g. "The £18 phone vouchers that turn out to be worthless", *Daily Mail*, 12 August 1985.

203 Correspondence in BT/A/71 Parts 10 and 11.
204 Background Note: BT Bill Voucher Scheme, DTI, 20 October 1986, BT/A/71 Part 11.
205 Following a briefing from the DTI, the Department of Energy which was planning the sale of British Gas decided upon a gas voucher scheme with no validity periods. A separate communication from the DTI stressed that the Department of Energy should expect no one to have read the Prospectus, to blame the Government for any mistakes investors might make because they had not read terms carefully, and to expect large numbers of irate calls from aggrieved investors! Letter from Neil McMillan, DTI, to Chris Morris, Department of Energy, 14 May 1986, BT/A/71 Part 12. During the sale of British Gas the voucher terms were made more liberal to reduce complaints, see chapter 15 pp.374–5.
206 Answer to question in the House of Lords, *Hansard,* columns 269–70, 22 October 1986; Background Note: BT Bill Voucher Scheme, BT/A/104.
207 Minute from J.W.C.Kent, T, to PS/Pattie, 21 January 1985, BT/C/46 Part 1. Correspondence in BT/A/18 Parts 8, 9, 10 and 11.
208 Flotation Group Meeting Minutes, 22 November 1984, BT/A/52 Part 3.
209 Miscellaneous correspondence in BT/A/91 Part 5. Background note, 21 November 1986, BT/A/104.
210 Minute from David Norgrove to the PM, 1 April 1987, PM Papers, Post and Telecommunications, Part 10.
211 Lawson (1992), p.224.
212 Baker (1993), p.84.
213 Thatcher (1993), p.681.
214 National Audit Office (1985); National Audit Office, Press Notice, 11 July 1985.
215 Public Accounts Committee (1985) *Third Report 1985–86: Sale of Government Shareholding in British Telecommunications plc,* London: HMSO, paragraph 29.
216 Sale of Government Shareholding in British Telecommunications plc, HM Treasury/DTI, n.d., BT/A/91 Part 5. Also, HM Treasury (1986) *Treasury Minute on the First to Fourth Reports from the Committee of Public Accounts,* Session 1985–86, Cmnd. 9755, London: HMSO.
217 *Third Report from the Public Accounts Committee,* London: HMSO.
218 M.E.Beesley and B.Laidlaw (1992) "The British Telecom/Mercury interconnect determination: An exposition and commentary" in Beesley (1997), chapter 15.
219 However, in 1994 another legal battle, this time between Mercury and OFTEL, broke out over interconnection costs as Mercury sought even more favourable terms.
220 Harper (1997), p.203.
221 In total Cable & Wireless through its subsidiary Mercury committed around £2bn to building a new domestic fixed-line network that proved to be a commercial disappointment.
222 For a more detailed discussion of the development of competition in British telecommunications into the 1990s, see P. Curwen (1997) *Restructuring Telecommunications: A Study of Europe in a Global Context,* Houndsmill: Macmillan, ch.11.
223 E(A)(90) 3rd meeting, 21 June 1990; E(A)(90)8, "Telecommunications Duopoly Review. Memorandum by the Secretary of State for Trade and Industry", 14 June 1990.
224 Ibid., paragraph 25. Memorandum from Nicholas Ridley to the PM, 2 May 1990, PM Papers, Post and Telecommunications, Part 12.
225 Memorandum from P.F.Owen, Cabinet Office, to the PM on Ridley's memorandum, 20 June 1990, and other miscellaneous correspondence in MT841 Post and Telecommunications papers Part 12.
226 HMSO (1991) *Competition and Choice: Telecommunications Policy for the 1990s,* Cmnd.1461, London: HMSO. Peter Lilley was Secretary of State for Trade and Industry and worked closely with the regulator, Bryan Carsberg, on the duopoly review. Lilley wanted to complete the review and sell another tranche of BT shares before a general election. A difficult issue during the review was what to do about the continuing imbalance in BT's charges. BT had not so far made much progress on rebalancing because digitalisation had raised the fixed costs of local calls. The rise in local call prices since 1984 was largely offset by this rise in fixed costs. Meanwhile, the continuing imbalance had helped Mercury build up its trunk and international businesses (incidentally, Mercury lobbied hard during the review to retain the duopoly to protect its market share). The solution brokered was an Access Deficit contribution taking the form of

a payment from Mercury to BT, based on the volume of business. At a late stage in the negotiations Carsberg decided that the terms of the payment were too favourable to BT. This led to a series of difficult meetings with Lilley, who feared that BT would object to a change in the terms of the scheme, triggering a MMC referral, which Lilley was determined to avoid. However, after conferring with the PM and the Chancellor of the Exchequer, Lilley confirmed that the Government remained committed to having independent regulation and that Carsberg should do what he considered best. After a meeting with BT that went on long into the night, Carsberg was able to convince the management of BT to accept the new terms. A referral to the MMC was avoided; private information; CM(91)26th meeting conclusions, 23 July 1991.

227  Competition and Choice: Telecommunications Policy for the 1990s, PM Papers, Post and Telecommunications, Part 13.
228  E(A)(90)8, "Telecommunications Duopoly Review. Memorandum by the Secretary of State for Trade and Industry", 14 June 1990, paragraphs 11 and 12. The DGT would be able to review the matter after seven years if circumstances had changed sufficiently to warrant it.
229  Littlechild (1983), para.13.20.
230  Letter from Alan Walters to Paul Grey, PM Papers, Post and Telecommunications, Part 11. Also, Littlechild (2003b).
231  Director General of Telecommunications (1988a) *The Regulation of British Telecom's Prices: A Consultative Document*, London: Office of Telecommunications. Director General of Telecommunications (1988b) *The Control of British Telecom's Price*, London: Office of Telecommunications. Also, see M.E. Beesley and S.C. Littlechild (1987) "The regulation of privatized monopolies in the United Kingdom", *RAND Journal of Economics*, vol.20, no.3, pp.454–72; reprinted in Beesley (1997), chapter 4
232  Beesley and Littlechild (1989); D. Parker, T. Dassler and D. Saal (2006) "Performance benchmarking in utility regulation: principles and the UK's experience", in M. Crew and D. Parker (eds.) *International Handbook on Economic Regulation*, Cheltenham: Edward Elgar.
233  Unpublished speaking notes by Sir George Jefferson, n.d. When the monopoly policy was ended in 1991, the interconnection question on what terms rivals could access BT's local network became an even greater focus of controversy. The tension would later ease as firstly BT's tariffs were rebalanced to reflect costs and secondly entry barriers, such as the lack of number portability, were tackled by the regulator. However, the arrival of broadband would later bring renewed interest in the interconnection question. In 2005 BT agreed to operational separation of its local areas infrastructure to address the problem.
234  The matter led to Sir George Jefferson's resignation as Chairman of BT. The BT Board appointed as his successor Iain Vallance, who had spent his career in the Post Office and then in BT, and who had been unenthusiastic about privatisation. The decision irritated the Government, but the Government decided that it was unable to intervene in the decision of the Board of what was now a private sector company.
235  Some of the service failure in 1987 could be put down to a strike by BT engineers early in the year, but there were also more systemic service failures which those in favour of privatisation put down to the legacy of state ownership. But part of the failure at least resulted from restructuring within BT, which was a product of privatisation.
236  Harper (1997), p.54.
237  Letter from D.J. Brown, DTI, to R.J. Goundry (a member of the public), 28 September 1984, BT/A/18 Part 5.
238  Note from S.G.Warburg to Kleinwort Benson, 20 July 1983, BT/C/17 Part 1.
239  Harper (1997), p.133–45.
240  Martin and Parker (1997), ch.9.
241  DTI Privatisation Brief: Update, 7 October 1991, BT/A/104.
242  Harper (1997), p.159.
243  OFTEL Press Notice, 6/85, 22 March 1985, BT/A/61 Part 3.
244  Note of a lunch meeting between the Secretary of State and Sir George Jefferson, 4 February 1985, BT/A/61 Part 3.
245  Another early international acquisition was ITT Dialcom, a US-based electronic mail business.
246  Minute from Lansley to Turnbull, 10 May 1985, PM Papers, Post and Telecommunications, Part 9. BT proposal to take over MITEL, background note and other correspondence in BT/A/61 Parts 3 and 4.

247 Harper (1997), p.92.
248 Martin and Parker (1997), ch.5.
249 There was similar continuity in the trend of total factor productivity which includes all inputs and not just labour; ibid.
250 Harper (1997), p.vii.
251 What are the public expenditure implications of the flotation of BT?, attached to minute from A.J.MacDonald, Head of T Division, 21 January 1985, BT/A/38 Part 2.
252 Performance of a Privatised BT, n.d. (probably 1987), BT/A/107.
253 *Hansard*, 26 July 1990, also in BT/A/104. This sale involved a novel international tender. The Government retained its special share but following the 1991 sale decided not to exercise its right to appoint a second director to the BT Board; minute from B.H.Potter to M.Stanley, DTI, 30 July 1991, E(DL) Part 19.
254 Letter from John Major, Chancellor of the Exchequer, to Nicholas Ridley, Secretary of State for Trade and Industry, 29 November 1989, PM Papers, Post and Telecommunications, Part 12.
255 Parkinson (1992), p.242.

## 14 THE PRIVATISATION OF BRITISH GAS: THE DECISION TO PRIVATISE AND DESIGNING AN APPROPRIATE REGULATORY REGIME

1 Regulation of the Gas Industry in Britain Annex 1, Memorandum by the Department of Energy to the Select Committee on Energy, 2 October 1985, G800/49/14 Part 1.
2 Section 9, Continental Shelf Act 1964.
3 Memorandum from D.R.Davis, Annex B, Department of Energy, 14 February 1986, G800/49/14 Part 11. The other significant source of offshore gas was the Morecambe Bay field in the Irish Sea.
4 Strictly, BGC had a monopsony (single buyer) privilege for gas supplies from the North Sea.
5 E(A)(85)52, "Gas Industry Privatisation: Legislation and Price Regulation. Memorandum by the Secretary of State for Energy", 26 July 1985, Annex 2, para.1.
6 Section 13, Energy Act 1976, as later strengthened by the Gas Act 1980.
7 Those receiving interruptible supplies were known as "non-premium industrial users". The chemical industry was collectively the largest business customer accounting for around 40% of industrial sales, followed by the engineering industry. There was one particularly large contract with the chemical firm ICI.
8 Lawson (1992), pp.246–7. Peter Walker, the Secretary of State for Energy, argues that the reason for his vetoing the Sleipner contract was that its financial terms meant too high a price for the gas; P. Walker (1991) *Staying Power: An Autobiography*, London: Bloomsbury, pp.192–3. But favouring UKCS fields so as to promote their development was certainly an important consideration; Gas Imports and Exports document, n.d., in HM Treasury papers, British Gas Corporation Privatisation Proposals, L/1821/01. Immediately after privatisation, British Gas announced its intention to re-open talks with the Norwegian Government for the purchase of gas.
9 E(A)(85)24, "Gas Industry Privatisation. Memorandum by the Secretary of State for Energy", 22 April 1984, Annex 3.
10 "Gas, coal and electricity are Government-owned already. We cannot, of course, make sweeping changes in the short term affecting their monopoly position. But some modification is possible in the public interest, and we shall examine the position closely." Conservative Research Department (1979) *Ministerial Dossier: Energy*, London, p.6.
11 NIP (79) 43, British Gas Corporation, 21 December 1979, in HM Treasury, Government Policies towards the Nationalised Industries. Report by the Official Committee on Nationalised Industry Policy, Filefolder 11271559.
12 E(79)51, "Gas Pricing Policy and the Financial Target for the British Gas Corporation. Memorandum by the Secretary of State for Energy", 12 October 1979. E(79)57, "Energy Pricing: Note by the Secretary of State for Energy", 15 October 1979.

13  E(79)61, "Gas and Electricity Prices and Public Expenditure 1981/82–1983/84. Memorandum by the Secretary of State for Energy", October 1979; E(79)64 "Gas Pricing Policy and the Financial Target for the British Gas Corporation. Memorandum by the Secretary of State for Energy", 9 November 1979.

14  E(79)65, "Gas Revenues. Memorandum by the Chancellor of the Exchequer", 16 November 1979.

15  It also had the effect of supporting the upward movement in gas prices. E(80)8th meeting, 26 February 1980. PRT was chargeable on a field-by-field basis on profits from the production of petroleum in UK and UKCS fields, after royalties where applicable and certain other expenses. The Gas Levy was payable by BGC on all UK gas supplies exempt from PRT, i.e. those contracts entered into before 1 July 1975 ( the southern sector fields and the UK Frigg and Brent fields). At privatisation the Levy was 4p per therm and it raised for the Exchequer between £231m and £383m net annually in the 1980s. Its importance declined with the reduction of supplies from the older fields and on 1 April 1998 the Levy was reduced to a zero rate.

16  Most gas from the North Sea was a by-product of oil extraction.

17  "Prices for North Sea Gas, Memorandum from the Permanent Under-Secretary", 8 November 1983, G63/112/1. Prices for North Sea Gas, Department of Energy draft minute, 10 November 1983, G63/112/1.

18  E(81)80, "British Gas Corporation's Monopoly. Memorandum by the Secretary of State for Energy", 22 July 1981.

19  E(81)102, "Gas Legislation. Memorandum by the Secretary of State for Energy", 19 October 1981.

20  E(81)80, Annex 1, para.3i.

21  Howell estimated that the Department of Energy would need an additional eight to ten staff in the early days, plus possibly one or two consultants in the first year, rising perhaps to 40 to 50 as the regulatory work expanded, "but at this stage we would transfer the work to a separate agency". E(81)80.

22  CC(81), 32nd meeting.

23  Only one direct producer-consumer deal was agreed and involved a very small quantity of gas supplied by the Taylor Woodrow Group from an onshore field at Hatfield to Belton Brickworks.

24  E(81)69, "The Future of BGC's Appliance Retailing Activity. Memorandum by the Secretary of State for Energy", 18 June 1981.

25  MMC (1980b) *Domestic Gas Appliances: A Report on the Supply of Certain Domestic Gas Appliances in the United Kingdom*, HC703, Session 1979–80, London: HMSO.

26  Lawson (1992), p.213,

27  Minute from the Secretary of State for Industry to the Prime Minister reporting discussions in E(DL), in E(81)68, "British Gas Corporation: Retailing of Gas Appliances. Note by the Secretaries", dated 17 June 1981. The Secretaries were Robert Armstrong, P. Le Cheminant and D.J.L.Moore.

28  Regarding appliance installation, the 1972 Gas Safety Regulations governed the installation of all gas appliances and required that only a competent person should install appliances (though the word "competent" was not defined). Transferring this work largely or entirely to the private sector would require a strengthening of controls. The Gas Safety (Rights of Entry) Regulations 1976 gave BGC power to disconnect a dangerous appliance. Private installers would not have power to disconnect unsafe appliances unless it were specifically given to them. BGC claimed that a large number of unsafe appliances were discovered during their normal servicing work. An independent and strengthened CORGI gas safety registration scheme was considered the best way forward. The CORGI (Corporation of Registered Gas Installers) scheme of voluntary registration for independent installers was at this time largely run and funded by BGC. A full discussion of gas safety issues can be found in the Annex to E(81)69.

29  E(81)21st meeting, 23 June 1981; E(81)69.

30  E(81)69. E(DL) had considered the option of issuing a British Standard under the Consumer Safety Act 1978, but by the time the matter came to E Committee the decision had been taken that this would not adequately address all of the problems, E(81)69.

31  E(81)21st meeting.

NOTES

32  The Government was advised that there was a reasonable chance that the powers under the 1972 Gas Act were adequate to allow the Secretary of State for Energy to direct the BGC Board to divest the gas appliance retailing business without further legislation. But the decision was taken that it was unlikely a firm view could be reached on this until the arguments deployed by BGC against a Directive were known. Howell judged that it was probable that BGC Board would argue that an enforced withdrawal from gas appliance retailing would impede its statutory duties and the Corporation might well challenge the Secretary of State in the courts; E(81)68; E(81)69.

33  Lawson (1992), p.213.

34  CC(82)26th meeting conclusions, 13 May 1982.

35  E(83)1 "Gas Appliance Retailing. Memorandum by the Secretary of State for Energy", 24 January 1983.

36  E(83)1st meeting, 10 February 1983; E(83)1.

37  "Private Finance: Progress Report. Note by the Treasury", paragraph 8, 19 August 1982, in E(DL) Part 6.

38  Conservative Party (1983).

39  Lawson (1992), p.226.

40  In electricity the Bulk Supply Tariff was a statutory tariff set by the Central Electricity Generating Board, which determined the charge to the electricity Area Boards for electricity supplies. The Area Boards then distributed and sold the electricity to the ultimate consumer.

41  Competition and Privatisation, paper by the Public Enterprises Analytical Unit, HM Treasury, 1 July 1983, in E(DL) Part 7.

42  Correspondence in G63/112/1 Part 2.

43  Walker (1991), p.189.

44  Lawson (1992), pp.215–16.

45  Thatcher (1993), p.681.

46  Walker (1991), p.190, discusses how an official from the Treasury spent weeks talking to Department of Energy officials and BGC and concludes, "I can only presume he went back to Nigel Lawson and said 'Dammit, Walker's right'. I was suddenly phoned up by Nigel and went round to No. 11 to be told he wanted to get on with the privatization and agreed to do it by my method." However, it is clear that Lawson remained unhappy and Treasury Ministers on a number of later occasions resurrected the case for restructuring BGC before a sale.

47  Letter from Nicholas Ridley, Secretary of State for Transport, to Peter Walker, 19 November 1985, and memorandum from Ridley to the PM, 27 November 1985, both in G800/49/14 Part 5. At the time Ridley was contemplating privatising BAA's airports by setting up separate companies for each airport or groups of airports. He felt that that something similar could be devised for BGC's different businesses.

48  Minute from Walker to the PM, December 1985, G800/49/14 Part 6.

49  Draft memorandum from the Secretary of State for Energy to the PM, 26 November 1985, G800/49/14 Part 5.

50  Rooke was appointed Chairman of BGC in 1976 and had worked in the gas industry since 1949. On 1 July 1986 he was appointed Chairman for a further three years – there was no question of sacking Rooke, despite some Ministerial instincts, a few months before the flotation. For Lawson's unflattering opinion of Rooke, see Lawson (1992), p.213. Rooke was sceptical of the case for privatisation of the gas industry in the national interest and remains so to this day. Another example of a Board member known to be lukewarm to privatisation of BGC was W.G. Jewers, who was Managing Director Finance. Aged 65 he retired at the end of 1986, just after BGC was floated. On the BGC Board in 1984 only Martin Jacomb from merchant banking and Leslie Smith from BOC plc were outsiders or not long-term BGC officers. In an attempt to address this, the Treasury pressed for a strengthening of the Board through the appointment of additional non-executive directors with private sector experience and more sympathetic to privatisation; minute from S.A.Robson, HM Treasury, to John Moore, Financial Secretary, 30 January 1986, in HM Treasury papers, British Gas Privatisation Proposals, L/1921/01 Part J.

51  Minute from Robson to Moore, 30 January 1986, op cit.

52  Walker, (1991), pp.189–91.

53  Walker (1991), p.188.

54   Minute from Robson to Moore, 30 January, op.cit.
55   Also, the Public Enterprises Analytical Unit in the Treasury raised concerns over gas storage, controlled by BGC. "Competition and Privatisation: Energy Industries", minute from S.A. Robson to the Financial Secretary, 22 February 1984, HM Treasury Paper, Competition and Privatisation: PEAU Exercise, AD/1790/01, part D. However, the implication of access to gas storage facilities for competition did not feature more widely as an important subject for discussion ahead of privatisation. Storage would become a major issue during the 1990s when competing gas supplies developed.
56   Correspondence in G63/602/14 Part 1.
57   British Gas Corporation, February 1984, HM Treasury papers, Competition and Privatisation: PEAU Exercise, AD/1790/01, Part D.
58   Department of Energy paper, Implications of Gas Privatisation: Imports Exports and UKCS Developments, n.d., G63/602/14.
59   E(A)(85)17th meeting.
60   E(A)(85)23rd meeting, 9 December 1985; E(A)(85)71, "Gas Industry Privatisation: Gas Imports and Exports. Memorandum by the Secretary of State for Energy", 5 December 1985.
61   Letter from John Moore to Peter Walker, 21 November 1985, and memorandum from John Moore to the PM, 25 November 1985, both in G800/49/14 Part 5.
62   Letter from C.J.V.Robson, Slaughter and May, to M.Reidy, Department of Energy, 1 October 1986, G800/49/14 Part 37.
63   See chapter 4.
64   Alongside this small amount, 25% of BGC's gas came from Norwegian gasfields in the North Sea and the remainder from oil companies operating on the UKCS. The BGC Offer for Sale document would note that the company still had interests in 10 petroleum discoveries where drilling had demonstrated the existence of potentially commercial reserves, seven on the UKCS and three onshore; British Gas: Offer for Sale by NM Rothschild & Sons Limited on behalf of the Secretary of State for Energy, November 1986, p.56.
65   Letter from D.R.Atkinson, Director of Finance, BG Group, to H.P.Hodges, Securities and Exchange Commission, Washington DC, 13 June 1986, G800/49/14 Part 21. As in other privatisations, Rothschilds was appointed financial adviser to the Department of Energy after a "beauty contest." Kleinwort, Benson was appointed similarly as financial adviser to British Gas.
66   The Rothschild team was led by Michael Richardson.
67   Letter from N.M.Rothschild & Sons Ltd, 2 July 1983, and other correspondence in G63/602/14 Part 1.
68   Note from John Redwood to Andrew Turnbull, 21 December 1983, in E(DL) Part 8.
69   With the agreement of the PM, Andrew Turnbull wrote to his opposite number at the Department of Energy, Michael Reidy, on 22 December confirming that the PM "was grateful for the progress he [the Secretary of State] has made in defining the programme for privatisation in the energy industries", noting the provisional bid for legislative time in 1984/5, and stressing that "While it is obviously difficult to introduce competition into the gas industry, the Prime Minister hopes that every effort will be made to do so in order to reduce the reliance that has to be placed on regulation." Letter from Andrew Turnbull to Michael Reidy, Department of Energy, 22 December 1983, in E(DL) Part 8.
70   Memorandum from John Moore, Financial Secretary, Treasury to the PM, 23 December 1983, in E(DL) Part 8.
71   Memorandum from Peter Walker to the PM, 20 December 1983, in E(DL) Part 8.
72   Note from Andrew Turnbull to the PM, 27 February 1985, in E(DL) Part 11.
73   "Five year plan for £10bn of state sales", Financial Times, Saturday 28 January 1984; "More state sell-offs planned", Daily Telegraph, 28 January 1984.
74   Note from Peter Walker to the PM, 30 January 1984, in E(DL) Part 9.
75   Memorandum from Andrew Turnbull to the PM, 30 January 1984, in E(DL) Part 9.
76   Thatcher (1993), p.681.
77   E(A)(85)9th meeting, 25 April 1985; E(A)(85)24, "Gas Industry Privatisation. Memorandum by the Secretary of State for Energy", 22 April 1985.

78    Within the Department of Energy the Bill team was headed by Dr David Evans, an Assistant Secretary. The team already had the well-drafted 1972 Gas Bill to build upon.
79    CC(85)15th meeting conclusions, 2 May 1985; C(85)10, "Gas Industry Privatisation. Memorandum by the Secretary of State for Energy", 30 April 1985.
80    C(85)10.
81    C(85)11, "Legislative Programme 1985–86: Consequences of the Inclusion of a Gas Bill. Memorandum by the Lord President of the Council", 30 April 1985. The Northern Ireland Bill was designed to help the police in Northern Ireland combat terrorism. Dropping the Nationalised Industries Bill was not a problem because E(NI) Committee decided against proceeding with the Bill on policy grounds; see chapter 8, p.174.
82    *Hansard*, 17 May 1985.
83    E(A)(85)17th meeting, 31 July 1985; E(A)(85)52.
84    E(A)(85)20th meeting, 14 November 1985; E(A)(85)65, "Memorandum by the Secretary of State for Energy", 12 November 1985.
85    *Hansard*, column 1043.
86    Briefing for the Leader of the House, n.d., G800/49/14 Part 13.
87    E.g. letter from Richard Ottawa, MP, to Walker, 4 December 1985, G800/49/14 Part 6.
88    Walker (1991), p.190: "When it came to the legislation, I insisted there should be no shoddy drafting. I did not want the bill to attract hundreds of amendments in Parliament . . . When the bill actually came to Parliament it suffered fewer government amendments than any other piece of legislation I can remember . . ."
89    E(A)(85)11th meeting, 11 June 1985; E(A)(85)30, "Gas Industry Privatisation Regulation. Memorandum by the Secretary of State for Energy", 24 May 1985.
90    Draft E(A) paper, n.d. (autumn 1985), G800/49/14 Part 4.
91    E(A)(85)17th meeting, 31 July 1985.
92    The final wording in the Gas Act was "appointment . . . shall not be for a term exceeding five years; but previous appointment to that office shall not affect eligibility for re-appointment." S(1)(2).
93    E(A)(85)52, Annex 1, para.4.
94    E(A)(85)17th meeting, 31 July 1985.
95    Minute from J.G. Wright to J.R.S. Guinness, Department of Energy, 8 November 1985, G800/49/14 Part 6.
96    Minute by J.G. Wright, Gas Division, 6 December 1985, G800/49/14 Part 6.
97    Minute from J.I.Britton, Gas Division, 26 June 1986, and minute from D.R.Davis to PS/Secretary of State, 26 June 1986, both in G800/49/14 Part 24.
98    Proposed changes to BGC's authorisation by the regulator that could not be agreed, like amendments to BT's licence, would be referred to the Monopolies and Mergers Commission for review, see below. The cost of any authorisation modification references to the MMC would also be financed by annual fees levied on companies holding authorisations to supply gas, initially BGC alone.
99    Letter from D.J.Trevelyan, Civil Service Commission, 18 January 1985, G800/49/14 Part 6. Correspondence in G800/49/14 Part 7.
100   E(A)(85)30, para.7.
101   Letter from S.P.Black, Chairman National Gas Consumers' Council, to Alick Buchanan-Smith, Minister of State for Energy, 13 December 1985, G800/49/14 Part 8. Letter from Black to Peter Walker, 13 March 1986, and related correspondence in G800/49/14 Part 13.
102   Letter from Lord Lucas of Chilworth, DTI, to D.Hunt, Parliamentary Under Secretary Department of Energy, 25 November 1985, and related correspondence, G800/49/14 Part 10.
103   Minute by W.D.Evans, Gas Division, 14 November 1985, G800/49/14 Part 5. Letter from Leon Brittan, Secretary of State for Trade and Industry, to Walker, 18 December 1985 and minute from J.I.Britton, Gas Division, 3 January 1986, both in G800/49/14 Part 8.
104   Minute by W.D.Evans, Gas Division, 1 October 1985, G800/49/14 Part 1. Letter from David Hunt, Department of Energy, to Lord Lucas of Chilworth, Parliamentary Under Secretary of State, DTI, 18 October 1985, G800/49/14 Part 5.

105 Department of Energy (1986) Authorisation granted and Directions given by the Secretary of State for Energy to British Gas Corporation under the Gas Act 1986, London: Department of Energy.
106 Ibid., Gas Bill: Summary, para.6.
107 Offer for Sale document, p.34.
108 Memorandum by Alick Buchanan-Smith, 10 October 1985, G800/49/14 Part 1.
109 Briefing paper from M.F.Reidy to the PS/Secretary of State, 14 November 1985, ahead of E(A) discussion, G800/49/14 Part 5.
110 Minute from S.Killen, PS/Minister of State, 13 March 1986, G800/49/14 Part 13.
111 Letter from N.R.Thornton, DTI, to D.Davis, Gas Division, 1 November 1985, G800/49/14 Part 4.
112 Minute from J.G.Wright, Gas Division, to PS/Secretary of State, n.d., G800/49/14 Part 12.
113 The 1980 Competition Act powers were felt to be less likely to be helpful as preference or discrimination towards gas producers might fall outside the powers under this Act.
114 Letter from Leon Brittan to Peter Walker, 20 November 1985, G800/49/14 Part 5.
115 E(A)(85)65, para.10.
116 E(A)(85)17th meeting.
117 Memorandum from John Moore to the PM, 13 November 1985, G800/49/14 Part 5.
118 Minute by M.F.Reidy, Gas Division, 21 November 1985, and memorandum from the Secretary of State to the PM, 22 November 1985, both in G800/49/14 Part 5.
119 Letter from Peter Walker to Eric Hammond, General Secretary, Electrical Electronics Telecommunications and Plumbing Union, 10 June 1986, G800/49/14 Part 20.
120 Letter from John Moore, Treasury, to Peter Walker, 25 November 1985, G800/49/14 Part 5. The clause became S(4)(2d) *The Gas Act 1986*, Chapter 44, London: HMSO. Its introduction owed much to the efforts of the Conservative MP Michael Portillo and is sometimes referred to as the Portillo amendment.
121 Minute from S.A Robson to John Moore, 30 January 1986, op cit.
122 Brief for the Secretary of State's Meeting with Sir Terence Beckett, n.d., G800/49/14 Part 13. This also applied to quality of service issues, where officials pointed out the BGC would have an incentive after privatisation to boost profits by reducing service quality.
123 Minute by M.A.Higson, Gas Division, 25 October 1985.
124 Letter from Norman Lamont, Treasury, to Peter Walker, 26 June 1986, G800/49/14 Part 27.
125 Speech: Sixth Form Conference for Economics Students on the Privatisation of British Gas, n.d. (autumn 1986), G800/49/14 Part 45.
126 Minute from W.D.Evans, Gas Division, to PS/Secretary of State, 25 October 1985, G800/49/14 Part 4.
127 Minute by W.D.Evans, Gas Division, 18 November 1985, G800/49/14 Part 5.
128 British Gas Corporation, "The Commercial Implications of Common Carriage", n.d. (March, 1986), G800/49/14 Part 14.
129 Letter from John Moore, Financial Secretary, HM Treasury, to Peter Walker, 25 November 1985, G800/49/14 Part 4.
130 Minute from J.R.S.Guinness, Department of Energy, to the Secretary of State, 27 November 1985, G800/49/14 Part 5.
131 Memorandum from British Gas to Rothschilds and the Department of Energy, 14 October 1986, G800/49/14 Part 39.
132 BGC had entered into gas contracts averaging around 25 years under which BGC agreed to pay for the gas even if it was not required. This encouraged North Sea gas development and the Corporation was able to enter into such contracts because before privatisation the risk of not needing the gas was exceptionally low given its effective monopoly position in gas supplies. Also, any costs could be passed through to captive customers.
133 E(A)(85)20th meeting, 14 November 1985; E(A)(85)65, "Memorandum by the Secretary of State for Energy", 12 November 1985.
134 Letter from BGC to D.R.Davis, Gas Division, 14 November 1985, G800/49/14 Part 5.
135 Minute by D.R.Davis, Gas Division, 13 August 1986, G800/9/14 Part 30.

136 Minute by D.R.Davis, Gas Division, 27 November 1985, G800/49/14 Part 5.
137 Memorandum from David Norgrove, PS/ No. 10, to W.G.Dart, Department of Energy, 27 November 1985, G800/49/14 Part 5.
138 Letter from John Moore to Walker, 22 November 1985, G800/49/14 Part 4.
139 Minute from W.D.Evans, Department of Energy, 13 October 1986, G800/49/14 Part 39.
140 Letters from Roland Shaw, Premier Oil plc and J.B.Healey, Saxon Oil plc, to Alick Buchanan-Smith, Minister of State for Energy, 1 and 8 August 1985 and related correspondence in G800/49/14 Part 1. Letter from R.C.Shaw, Honorary Secretary, BRINDEX, to Peter Walker, 30 October 1985, G800/49/14 Part 2. Letter from Roland C.Shaw, Secretary, BRINDEX, to the Select Committee on Energy, November 1985, in G800/49/14 Part 4.
141 Minute summarising a meeting with BP plc by J.R.S.Guinness, 29 November 1985, G800/49/14 Part 5. Letter from R.Bexon, Deputy Chairman BP plc, to Alick Buchanan-Smith, 7 January 1986, G800/49/14 Part 8.
142 Minute from J.R.S.Guinness, 6 October 1986, and attached letter from Shell dated 3 October 1986, G800/49/14 Part 37.
143 Letter from R.W.Sinden, Director SBGI, to Peter Morrison, Minister of State for Industry, 18 April 1986, G800/49/14 Part 17.
144 Briefing note for the Secretary of State's meeting on 3 October 1985, G800/49/14 Part 1.
145 Minute from D.FR.Davis, Gas Division, to PS/Secretary of State, 29 November 1985, G63/602/14 Part 1.
146 Minute from R.Woolman, Department of Trade and Industry, to D.Long, Department of Energy, 4 February 1986, G800/49/14 Part 11.
147 HM Treasury papers, L/1821/01 Part J. The Select Committee on Energy in its seventh report, Session 1984–85 (HC76–1) recommended that gas exports should be permitted when the ratio of gas reserves to production exceeded an appropriate security margin.
148 Letter 22 October 1985, in G63/602/14 Part 1.
149 *Financial Times*, "Ministers differ over privatised British Gas", 25 November 1985, p.1.
150 Minute from Walker to the PM, 9 December 1985, G800/49/14 Part 7. The articles appeared in the *Financial Times* on 25 and 26 November and 9 December.
151 Letter from Moore to Walker, 10 March 1986, in HM Treasury papers, L/1821/01 Part J.
152 Note of the Secretary of State's Meeting with T.P. Jones, 1 December 1985, G800/49/14 Part 7.
153 Minute from G.S.Dart to PS/Secretary of State, 14 October 1985, G800/49/14 Part 1. Minute from J.H.Pownall, Department of Energy, 12 February 1986, G800/49/14 Part 11.
154 Letter from Sir Denis Rooke to Peter Walker, 15 July 1986, G800/49/14 Part 27.
155 Letter from Walker to Hammond, General Secretary Electrical Electronics Telecommunications and Plumbing Union, 10 June 1986, G800/49/14 Part 20.
156 Minute from the Secretary of State for Industry to the Prime Minister reporting discussions in E(DL), in E(81)68, "British Gas Corporation: Retailing of Gas Appliances. Note by the Secretaries", dated 17 June 1981.
157 Price Regulation, Annex 2, RPI − X + Y Price Control, para.5, G800/49/14 Part 15.
158 The "allowable gas costs" or Y term would be deducted from the total price and the RPI − X applied to the remainder of the price only. Therefore, while loosely describable as RPI − X + Y, more correctly, in mathematical terms the price formula was:

$$M_t = (1 + (RPI_t - 2)/100) \times P_{t-1} + Y_t - K_t$$

$$\frac{\text{Maximum}}{\text{average price}} = \text{non-gas component} + \text{gas costs} - \text{positive or negative correction factor}$$

where non-gas component is calculated from: (factor to adjust the previous year's non-gas component by the change in the Retail Price Index less two percentage points) × (previous year's non-gas component)

and where

$M_t$ = the maximum average price per therm in year t;

$RPI_t$ = the percentage change in the Retail Price Index between that for October in
year t and that for the preceding October;

$P_{t-1}$ = the non-gas component of the price per therm in the prior financial year t–1;

$Y_t$ = the gas cost per therm in year t;

$K_t$ = the correction factor per therm to be made in year t (the correction factor will
be positive if in year t–1 the actual price charged exceeded the maximum
determined by the formula, negative if the actual price was lower than the
maximum); and

t represents the relevant financial year.

159 Ibid., para. 7.

160 Price Regulation: Key Issues. Annex 2. Nature of the Price Control Formula, October 1985, G800/49/14 Part 2.

161 Note by M.F.Reidy, Gas Division, 1 April 1986, G800/49/14 Part 15.

162 More precisely, BGC could request the disapplication of the price control with effect from a date not earlier than 1 April 1992. The price control would then cease to apply unless a reference was made by the DGGS to the MMC and the MMC concluded that cessation of the condition, in whole or in part, would or might be expected to operate against the public interest.

163 Minute from J.I.Britton, Gas Division, 26 June 1986, G800/49/14 Part 24.

164 E(A)(85)11th meeting, 11 June 1985; E(A)(85)30, "Gas Industry Privatisation Regulation. Memorandum by the Secretary of State for Energy, 24 May 1985.

165 Minute by D.R.Davis, Gas Division, 23 October 1985.

166 Letter from A.J. Alt, Rothschilds, to D.Davis, Gas Division, 11 October 1985; document "Parameters for a successful privatisation of BG plc", October 1985; and Minute by J.S. Neilson, Gas Division, 23 October 1985; all in G800/49/14 Part 2.

167 Letter with draft terms of reference from J.S.Neilson, Gas Division, to Brian Pomeroy, Touche Ross & Co, 3 December 1986, G800/49/14 Part 6. Letter from J.R.S.Guinness to C.W.Brierley, Managing Director, British Gas Corporation, 20 March 1986, G800/49/14 Part 14.

168 Letter from B.W.Pomeroy, Touche Ross Management Consultants, to M.F.Reidy, Department of Energy, 16 April 1986, G800/49/14 Part 15. Letter from Pomeroy to Reidy, 8 May 1986 and accompanying documentation, G800/49/14 Part 17.

169 Minute from D.R.Davis, Gas Division, 12 June 1986, G800/49/14 Part 21.

170 E(A)(85)17th meeting, 31 July 1985. Initially, the wording would have required BGC to use its "best endeavours" to ensure that standing charges did not rise faster than inflation. This was criticised as inadequate during the passage of the Bill and the Government agreed to frame a more clearly worded obligation during the Committee Stage in the House of Lords.

171 *Hansard*, 18 June 1986.

172 This was on the eve of the second reading of the Gas Bill.

173 Minute from J.I.Britton, Gas Division, 26 June 1986, and minute from D.R.Davis to PS/Secretary of State, 26 June 1986, both in G800/49/14 Part 24.

174 Minute from W.D.Evans, Gas Division, to PS/Secretary of State, 7 January 1986, G800/49/14 Part 8.

175 *Conservative Party Election Manifesto 1983*.

176 Minute from P.H.Agrell, EP2, 11 October 1985, G800/49/14 Part 2.

177 Minute from J.R.S.Guinness to the Secretary of State, 17 January 1986, G800/49/14 Part 9.

178 Summary of Evidence Taken Before the Select Committee on Energy, November/December 1985, Third Hearing on British Gas 10 December 1985, G800/49/14 Part 9.

179 Offer for Sale document, p.30.

180 Letter from N.R.Thornton, DTI, to M.F.Reidy, Gas Division, 4 July 1986 and minute by Reidy, 7 July 1986, both in G800/49/14 Part 26.

181 Cited in I. Stelzer (1996), "Price rip-off ahead for gas customers", *The Sunday Times*, 2 February 1986, G800/49/14 Part 11.

182 Ibid.

183 *First Report from the Energy Committee Regulation of the Gas Industry*, January 1986, HC 15, London: HMSO.

184    Privately, as was the Government's financial adviser, Rothschilds.

185    It also drew on the Gas Act 1972 regarding safety and certain other issues.

## 15  THE PRIVATISATION OF BRITISH GAS:
## THE FLOTATION AND AFTERMATH

1    Minute by D.J.W.Lumley, Gas Division, 22 November 1985, G800/49/14 Part 5.

2    Minute from J.R.S.Guinness to the Secretary of State, 14 January 1986, G800/49/14 Part 8. Minute from M.F.Reidy, Department of Energy, 5 February 1986, G800/49/14 Part 11.

3    Minute from M.F.Reidy to PS/Secretary of State, G800/49/14 Part 35. Letter from M.Richardson, Rothschilds, to J.R.S.Guinnesss, 16 May 1986, G800/49/14 Part 19.

4    Minute from J.R.S.Guinness to M.F.Reidy, 12 May 1986, G800/49/14 Part 18. Letter from Nigel Lawson to Peter Walker, 6 October 1986, G800/49/14 Part 37. On 20 May Walker wrote to the Financial Secretary requesting that the TSB issue be prevented; minute from S.A.Robson to the Chancellor of the Exchequer, 22 May 1986, in HM Treasury papers, British Gas Corporation Privatisation Proposals, L/1821/01 Part K. The extent to which the Government had any ownership rights over the TSB was so uncertain that it is very doubtful whether the Chancellor could have prevented the sale should he have so wished.

5    Secretary of State's Meeting to Discuss Timing of BGC Flotation, 16 January 1986, G800/49/14 Part 9. The large sale of BT shares had tested the stock market's dealing arrangements with the result that many deals were left un-reconciled and trading positions had been left open. With the new market arrangements largely untested, there was a fear of something similar happening again but with perhaps even more disruptive results.

6    Minute from J.L.Wheldon to J.M.Bird, HM Treasury, 14 May 1986, HM Treasury papers, British Gas Corporation Privatisation Proposals, JA/162/01 Part B.

7    Letter from Lawson to Walker, 4 March 1986, G800/49/14 Part 13.

8    Letter from A.Carlisle, Dewe Rogerson Ltd, to A.Alt, N.M.Rothschild & Sons Ltd, 17 January 1986, G800/49/14 Part 9.

9    Letter from Nigel Lawson to Peter Walker, 18 February 1986, and letter from Rothshilds, 7 February 1986, both in G800/49/14 Part 11.

10    Letter from Michael Richardson to J.R.S.Guinness, Department of Energy, 2 December 1985, G800/49/14 Part 7.

11    Department of Energy Draft Discussion Paper, British Gas Offer for Sale. The Percentage to be Sold: 100% or less, 27 February 1986, G800/49/14 Part 12.

12    And following the usual "beauty contest" (competitive bidding) for the role of financial adviser based on price and competence. The Secretary of State, Peter Walker, had been unhappy with Rothschilds' role in the Enterprise Oil sale, when the bank had bought shares on behalf of RTZ (see chapter 4, pp.108–9). However, the bank performed well in the "beauty contest" and this overcame Walker's reservations about appointing the bank.

13    Again, the appointments were made after competition.

14    Minute by L.B.Davies, Gas Division, 17 October 1985, G800/49/14 Part 1. Cazenoves were appointed on 17 July 1985.

15    The team was 14 strong and consisted of Davis, Reidy, Faiz, Nelson, Lumley, Steele, Collett, Higson, Davies, Morris and Dr Wright and Mrs Dickson, Mrs Galloway and Miss Jackson; note in G800/49/14 Part 38.

16    Structure to organise and implement the privatisation of the company, 3 February 1986, G800/49/14 Part 11.

17    Note of the First Meeting of the Offer for Sale Co-ordinating Group held at the Department of Energy on 14 January 1986, G800/49/14 Part 9.

18    Papers in G800/49/14 Part 8.

19    Correspondence in G800/49/14 Part 8.

20    However, when later the electricity industry was privatised by the Department of Energy, a number of officials involved in the gas privatisation were called upon to work on electricity.

21   Minute from M.F. Reidy, Gas Division, 29 April 1986, G800/49/14 Part 16. Walker wrote to the Chancellor of the Exchequer on 13 May noting that the Government was on course to achieve a yield at the top end of this range, of £7bn to £9n; letter in HM Treasury papers, British Gas Privatisation and Prospects, L/182101 Part K.
22   G800/49/14 Part 11.
23   Draft discussion paper, British Gas – Partial Tender, 20 March 1986, G800/49/14 Part 14. Minute from S.A.Robson to G. Grimstone, in HM Treasury papers, L/1821/01 Part J.
24   Summary and Conclusions of the Key Issues Group's Report, 4 August 1986, G800/49/14 Part 45.
25   Method of Privatisation, Rothschild, n.d., G800/49/14 Part 11.
26   Memorandum from Cazenove & Co, 19 May 1986, G800/49/14 Part 19.
27   Minute from J.R.S. Guinness to M.F.Reidy, n.d. August 1986; Premium Pricing: A Balanced Viewpoint, N.M.Rothschild & Sons Ltd, 10 September 1986; and minute from J.R.S.Guinness to Secretary of State, 26 September 1986; all in G800/49/14 Part 36. Note of the Twenty First Meeting of the Offer for Sale Co-ordinating Group held at the Department of Energy on 1 October 1986, in HM Treasury papers, N/1329/01.
28   Minute from S.Linnett, 17 November 1986, G800/49/14 Part 48. Price Waterhouse (1987), p.30.
29   British Gas Underwriting, briefing note, 13 November 1986, G800/49/14 Part 49.
30   Minute by L.B.Davies, Gas Division, 21 October 1985, G800/49/14 Part 1.
31   Letter from Goldman Sachs New York to N.M. Rothschild & Sons, 13 June 1986, G800/49/14 Part 20.
32   Letter from D.R.Atkinson, Director of Finance, BGC, 12 August 1986, G800/49/14 Part 30. Minute by L.B.Davies, Gas Division, 17 September 1986, G800/49/14 Part 35.
33   Minute from G.S.Dart, PPS/Secretary of State, 22 September 1986, and letter from Norman Lamont, Treasury, to Walker, 24 September 1986, both in G800/49/14 Part 35.
34   Letter from Peter Walker to Norman Lamont, Financial Secretary, 30 September 1986, G800/49/14 Part 36.
35   N.M.Rothschild & Sons Ltd, British Gas Corporation. Structuring the Offer: Discussion Paper for the Co-ordinating Group, 11 July 1986, G800/49/14 Part 26.
36   Secretary of State's Meeting with Goldman Sachs, 19 November 1986, G800/49/14 Part 49.
37   Minute by L.B.Davies, Gas Division, 11 August 1986, G800/49/14 Part 30.
38   Minute by C.J.Morris, Gas Division, 11 July 1986, G800/49/14 Part 26.
39   Related to this, in the US and a number of other overseas markets underwriting commitments were entered into only in the closing stages of the offer, whereas in the UK the commitment was made earlier. In London typically underwriters and sub-underwriters carried the risk of the flotation flopping for up to two weeks from agreeing to underwrite until flotation. In the US underwriters were exposed to risk for a much shorter time. During the gas privatisation US underwriters were persuaded to change their normal procedures and commit to underwriting earlier. However, as a consequence they then suffered a year later during the fourth BP share sale, which was massively under-subscribed.
40   Minute from J.R.S.Guinness to the Secretary of State, 15 August 1986, G800/49/14 Part 31.
41   Minute from J.R.S.Guinness to the Secretary of State, 22 September 1986, G800/49 14 Part 35.
42   Ibid.
43   Minute from J.S.Neilson, Gas Division, 6 November 1986, G800/49/14 Part 45.
44   Letter from C.W.Brierley to W.D.Evans, Department of Energy, 4 September 1985, G800/49/14 Part 2. Letter from Leon Brittan, Secretary of State for Trade and Industry, to Walker, 10 December 1985, G800/49/14 Part 7. Letter from Peter Walker to John Moore, 17 February 1986, and minute from M.F.Reidy, Department of Energy, both in G800/49/14 Part 11.
45   Minute by W.D.Evans, Gas Division, 6 August 1986, and letter from Walker to BGC, 8 August 1986, both in G800/49/14 Part 30.
46   Letter from Moore to Walker, 16 December 1985, and minute from D.J.W.Lumley, Gas Division, January 1986, both in G800/49/14 Part 8.
47   Minute by M.F.Reidy, Gas Division, 23 October 1985, G800/49/14 Part 2. Letter from Sir Denis Rooke to Peter Walker, 26 June 1986, G800/49/14 Part 24. Technically, the 15% applied to the

total votes attaching to the share capital. Anyone breaching the limit would be ordered to reduce their holding to less than 15% within 21 days.

48  Minute from M.F.Reidy, 28 January 1986, G800/49/14 Part 10. Minute from S.A.Robson to John Moore, 18 July 1986, in HM Treasury papers, British Gas Privatisation Proposals, L/1821/01 Part K.

49  Letter from Walker to Rooke, 26 February 1986, and reply by Rooke, 27 February 1986, G800/49/14 Part 12.

50  Letter from G.S.Dart, Private Secretary Department of Energy, to V.Life, Private Secretary to the Financial Secretary, Treasury, 28 February 1986, G800/49/14 Part 12.

51  Minute by W.D.Evans, Gas Division, to PS/Secretary of State, 11 August 1986, G800/49/14 Part 30.

52  Note by J.R.S.Guinness, Department of Energy, 10 April 1986, G800/49/14 Part 15.

53  Dewe Rogerson, The Privatisation of the British Gas Corporation: General Public Research Findings and Implications, G800/49/14 Part 6.

54  Minute by D.J.W.Lumley, Gas Division, 29 November 1985, G800/49/14 Part 5.

55  Minute from M.F.Reidy, Gas Division, 30 June 1986, G800/49/14 Part 24.

56  Notes by M.F.Reidy, Gas Division, 18 July 1986 and 20 May 1986, G800/49/14 Parts 19 and 27.

57  Minute by L.B.Davies, Department of Energy, 17 February 1986, G800/49/14 Part 11.

58  Minute from M.F.Reidy to PS /Secretary of State, 11 July 1986, G800/49/14 Part 26. Letter from Walker to P.K.Rooke, Managing Director, Burrup Mathieson & Co Ltd, 10 November 1986, G800/49/14 Part 46.

59  Minute by R.P.Steele, Department of Energy, 24 November 1986, G800/49/14 Part 49. At the time Barrup Mathieson was seen as being the only City printer with the capacity to handle printing for large privatisations.

60  Minute from L.B.Davies, Department of Energy, 12 February 1986, G800/49/14 Part 11. The Gas Bill received the royal assent on 25 July 1986.

61  Note by C.C.Wilcox, Director of Resources Department of Energy, to M.F.Reidy, 25 September 1986, G800/49/14 Part 36.

62  Minute by R.P.Steele, Gas Division, 31 July 1986, G800/49/14 Part 29.

63  Letter to D.Lumley, Gas Division, from Dewe Rogerson, 21 May 1986, G800/49/14 Part 19.

64  Minute by D.J.W.Lumley, Gas Division, 30 November 1985, G800/49/14 Part 6. N.M.Rothschild & Sons Ltd, Draft briefing note for the Secretary of State's Meeting with the Chairman of BGC, G800/49/14 Part 7.

65  Minute from S.A.Robson to the Chancellor of the Exchequer, 20 May 1986, in HM Treasury papers, British Gas Privatisation and Prospects, L/1821/01 Part K. Minute from J.R.S.Guinness to D.R.Davis, 9 January 1986, G800/49/14 Part 8. Letter from Moore to Walker, 16 May 1986, and M.Richardson, NM Rothschild & Sons Ltd, to J.R.S.Guinness, 16 May 1986, and related correspondence, all in G800/49/14 Part 18. Note by D.R.Davis, Gas Division, 28 May 1986, G800/49/14 Part 19. Minute from J.R.S.Guinness to the Secretary of State, 4 August 1986, G800/49/14 Part 45.

66  Letter from Rooke to Walker, 16 January 1986, G800/49/14 Part 9.

67  Letter from David Norgrove, Private Secretary (PS) No. 10, to G. Dart, Department of Energy, 29 May 1986, G800/49/14 Part 30.

68  Letter from J.Cartwright MP, 30 October 1986, and related correspondence, G800/49/14 Part 50.

69  Minute by A.J.Meyrick, Department of Energy, 10 November 1983, G63/112/1. As in previous privatisations, the different categories of applicants were distinguished by the use of different coloured application forms. BGC customers would apply using a green form.

70  Minute from J.R.S.Guinness to Secretary of State, 8 August 1986, G800/49/14 Part 30. As with earlier privatisations using partly subscribed shares, the shares would be tradeable in partly subscribed form.

71  "Summary and Conclusions of the Key Issues Group's Report", draft, 4 August 1986, G800/49/14 Part 29.

72 Minute from J.S.Neilson, Gas Division, 30 July 1986, G800/49/14 Part 29. The Treasury's preference was for the second instalment to be payable in August 1987 so as not to conflict with other privatisation offers during the first half of the year. Rothschilds were recommending June or July. One of the instalment payments for BT shares had been on 9 April and some investors had sent in their payments before 31 March putting the funds into a different financial year. This had caused some irritation in the Treasury because it affected the planning of annual privatisation receipts. It was to be avoided in the case of BGC by dating the instalments more carefully and not advertising for the instalment payments to be made until the "correct" financial year. Letter from S.A Robson, Treasury, to R.Steele, Gas Division, 22 September 1986, G800/623/7 Part 3. Minute from J.P.McIntyre, 15 September 1986, in HM Treasury papers, British Gas Privatisation Proposals, JA/162/01 Part B.

73 Gas Privatisation: Co-ordinating Group. Paper 1. Fixing the Minimum Application Level, G800/49/14 Part 30.

74 Dealing Arrangements for Individual Investors, note by Cazenove & Co, 7 August 1986, G800/49/14 Part 30. Letter from S.Linnett, N.M.Rothschild & Sons Ltd, to the major UK commercial banks, 23 September 1986, G800/623/7 Part 3. The brokers to the offer and the regional co-ordinators agreed to buy and sell BGC shares at preferential rates until 31 December 1988.

75 Customer Share Scheme: Guaranteed Allotment, n.d., G800/49/14 Part 13. Letter from J.R.S.Guinness to C.W.Brierley, British Gas, 4 April 1986, G800/49/14 Part 15.

76 Minute by R.P.Steele, Gas Division, February 1986, G800/49/14 Part 12. As with previous privatisations, the cost of bill vouchers and bonus shares was met by the Government.

77 Customer Share Scheme, Annex A, May 1986, G800/49/14 Part 30. One official in the Treasury commented on the proposal: "Frankly, the whole idea looks rather silly and would, I am sure, attract critical comment." Minute from T.F.Mathews to S.A.Robson, 20 May 1986, in HM Treasury papers, British Gas Corporation Privatisation Proposals, G/162/404/01 Part C.

78 Discussion Paper – Co-ordinating Group: Incentives for Small Shareholders, 29 July 1986, G800/49/14 Part 28.

79 Larger purchases took the following form: 5,000 to 10,000 in multiples of 1000; 10,000 to 50,000 in multiples of 5,000; 50,000 to 100,000 in multiples of 10,000; and over 100,000 in multiples of 50,000 shares. Different application levels applied to an employee share scheme.

80 Minute from M.F.Reidy, Gas Division, 6 August 1986, G800/49/14 Part 30.

81 Letter from S.A.Robson, Treasury, to J.R.S.Guinness, Department of Energy, G800/49/14 Part 27.

82 British Gas Privatisation: Co-ordinating Group. The Customer Share Scheme, Department of Energy, 5 August 1986, G800/49/14 Part 30.

83 They would also be preferred by residents of Northern Ireland who were not served by BGC.

84 "British Gas Share Price 135p: Company Valued at £5.6bn", Press Release, N.M. Rothschild & Sons Ltd, 21 November 1986, G800/49/14 Part 49. There were special arrangements to enable investors in the overseas offerings to obtain an equivalent to the domestic share bonus.

85 Note of the Minister of State's Meeting with Sir Denis Rooke, 4 September 1986, G800/49/14 Part 33.

86 Discussion Paper, Incentives for Small Shareholders, May 1986, G800/49/14 Part 20.

87 Minute from J.S.Neilson, Gas Division, 13 October 1986, G800/49/14 Part 39.

88 Minute from D.J.W.Lumley to D.R.Davis, Gas Division, 24 January 1986, G800/49/14 Part 9.

89 Minute from J.R.S.Guinness to M.F.Reidy, 10 July 1986, G800/49/14 Part 26.

90 Letter from Peter Walker to Peter Rees, Chief Secretary, 11 June 1985, and minute from D.J.W.Lumley, Department of Energy, 10 February 1986, both in G800/49/14 Part 11.

91 Minute by D.J.W. Lumby, 30 November 1986, G800/49/14 Part 5.

92 Minutes by C.J.R.Morris, 22 April 1986, and M.F.Reidy, 17 April 1986, Gas Division, G800/49/14 Part 15.

93 Minute from J.G.Wright, Gas Division, 15 October 1986, G800/49/14 Part 39. Minutes by J.G.Wright and C.F. Henderson, 17 October 1986, G800/49/14 Part 40. Minute from J.R.S.Guinness and letter from S.Linnett, NM Rothschild & Sons Ltd, both 22 October 1986, G800/49/14 Part 42.

94 Minute from D.J.W.Lumley, 21 March 1986, G800/49/14 Part 14.
95 The limits of the free offer per employee ranged from £49.50 during the sale of British Aerospace in February 1981 to £70.20 in the case of BT in November 1984. There was also a formal upper limit on the total value of the entire employee share scheme of 5% of the expected sales receipts from the privatisation. In practice, a much lower limit had generally applied: Privatisation: Employer Shareholdings, Note by HM Treasury, 4 February 1985, in HM Treasury Papers, British Gas Corporation Privatisation Proposals, L/1821/01, Part K.
96 Minute by J.S.Neilson, Gas Division, 8 November 1985, G800/49/14 Part 4.
97 Minute from S.A.Robson to John Moore, 30 January 1986, and letter from G.S.Dart Private Secretary, Department of Energy, to V.Life, Private Secretary to the Financial Secretary, both in HM Treasury Papers, British Gas Corporation Privatisation Proposals, L/1821/01, Part J. Minute from S.A.Robson to the Chancellor of the Exchequer, 20 May 1986 and letter from Walker to the Chancellor of the Exchequer, 13 May 1986, both in L/1821/01, Part K.
98 Minute from J.S.Neilson, Gas Division, 22 October 1985, G800/49/14 Part 1.
99 Brief for Secretary of State's meeting with the Financial Secretary, 12 February 1986; letter from G.S Dart, PS Department of Energy, to V.Life, PS to the Financial Secretary, 6 February 1986; minute from M.F.Reidy, Department of Energy, 7 February 1986; all in G800/49/14 Part 11.
100 Also, at first the Treasury indicated that it would prefer that the 10% price discount offer to BT employees was not repeated in the BGC offer for sale. It had not proved particularly attractive to employees. However, it was reinstated after Treasury officials reflected that because many employees would have sold their shares before the payment for the final instalment, when the discount applied, it would not be unduly expensive.
101 Briefing for meeting between the Secretary of State and the PM, 29 May 1986, G800/49/14 Part 19.
102 The proposal for pensioners also involved some shares based on length of service.
103 Minute from J.S.Neilson, Gas Division, 21 January 1986, G800/49/14 Part 9. Annex B, Employee Share Scheme, May 1986, G800/49/14 Part 30.
104 Letter from Walker to the PM, 19 May 1986, G800/49/14 Part 30. John Moore had indicated that the Treasury might be willing to accept this figure; minute from S.A.Robson to the Chancellor of the Exchequer, 20 May 1986, in HM Treasury Papers, British Gas Corporation Privatisation Proposals, L/1821/01, Part K.
105 Letter from David Norgrove, PS No. 10, to G. Dart, Department of Energy, 29 May 1986, G800/49/14 Part 30. Letters between J.R.S. Guinness, Department of Energy, and C.W.Brierley, BGC, 26 and 28 November 1986, G800/49/14 Part 49. Each employee could apply for up 20,000 additional shares and each BGC pensioner 18,519 shares. However, the decision was taken not to have a share offer for BGC pensioners living overseas. Legal difficulties in some countries were identified.
106 British Gas Corporation – Proposed Profit Sharing Scheme, in HM Treasury, Nationalised Industries Policy (86). Circulated Papers, Minutes etc, April 1986, A/07. Statement by Peter Walker, *Hansard*, 16 June 1986. At the time the Inland Revenue was reviewing its policy on the tax treatment of shares for employees under the 1978 Finance Act. The result was to tighten the terms to reflect the increase in the share price between the offer for sale price and the price when dealing started. The price for calculating tax on capital gains would now normally be the market value at the date of appropriation or grant if made before the commencement of dealing, which would usually be higher than the offer price.
107 Letter from Moore to Walker, 16 May 1986, G800/49/14 Part 18. Per employee the free shares were worth a minimum of £70.20, the matching offer up to £300, and the discounted shares up to £200.
108 In the case of all privatisations, it was necessary to allow employees to opt out of the preferential employee share scheme if the shares offered to employees were not to be treated as a separate share offer to the main flotation, with the associated additional costs that would have been incurred.
109 Pathfinder Roadshows – UK/Europe. Draft Script on Finance, 21 October 1986, G800/49/14 Part 42.

110 BGC's financial year was to 31 March.
111 The Treasury had encouraged Walker to press for higher increases so that a larger negative EFL could be imposed on the Corporation, but Walker had resisted; Walker (1991), p.191.
112 Briefing note from D.R.Davis, Gas Division, to the PS/Secretary of State, 4 November 1985, G800/49/14 Part 4.
113 The target rate of return was on a CCA valuation and was set in 1983 to run until the end of March 1987. There was also a target to achieve a 12% reduction in net trading costs per therm over the same period, which BGC was also on target to achieve.
114 The Privatisation of BGC, Department of Energy briefing note, March 1986, G800/49/14 Part 13.
115 Ibid.
116 During the negotiations with BGC over the provision of HCA information, the Byatt group in the Treasury published its report favouring the use of CCA. In the Department of Energy this was judged to be very bad timing and most unhelpful. As to be expected, BGC used the report to support its case for not using HCA. Letter from Walker to John MacGregor, Chief Secretary, HM Treasury, HM Treasury papers, British Gas Corporation Privatisation Proposals, L/1821/01 Part J. The Byatt report was published: HM Treasury (1986b) *Accounting for Economic Costs and Changing Prices: A Report to HM Treasury by an Advisory Group*, London: HMSO.
117 The BGC Board was also resistant to a revaluation of land and buildings in BGC's balance sheet and this did not occur.
118 The fact that there may be circumstances, depending upon the relation of interest rates to the price earnings multiple the profits will be capitalised at, when introducing debt into a company's balance sheet increases the sale proceeds, had come to the attention of the Treasury too late to alter the terms of the BT privatisation, which was in the form of equity only including preference shares.
119 Letter from V.Life, Treasury, to G.Dart, PS/Secretary of State for Energy, 27 November 1985, G800/49/14 Part 5.
120 The debt finally agreed took the form of an unsecured debenture repayable in tranches from 1987 to 1992.
121 On a HCA basis. On a CCA basis the gearing would be something over 10%.
122 Minute from J.R.S.Guinness, Deputy Secretary, to the Secretary of State ahead of a meeting with the Financial Secretary, 25 October 1985, G800/49/14 Part 2.
123 The stock would be transferred to the National Loans Fund and the Treasury demanded that BGC should compensate the Fund by handing over cash of an equivalent value, some £120–130m. Minute from S.A.Robson to the Chancellor of the Exchequer, 14 May 1986, in HM Treasury papers, British Gas Corporation Privatisation Proposals, L/1821/01 Part K. However, BGC argued that the Government should take over the stock without compensation. Later it would get the Department of Energy to agree to this in return for accepting the imposition of £2.5bn of debt. The Treasury was not in favour of this compromise, but Walker maintained that it was the best deal he could negotiate. The Gas Bill, therefore, included the necessary powers for the Government to transfer to the NLF the 3% stock with the cost met from the Consolidated Fund; minute from S.A.Robson, 16 May 1986, in HM Treasury papers, British Gas Corporation: Privatisation – Debts, G/162/404/01 Part C; minute from S.A.Robson to Sir Peter Middleton, 19 May 1986, in HM Treasury papers, British Gas Corporation Privatisation Proposals, L/1821/01 Part K; statement by Walker to the House, *Hansard*, 18 June 1986. But as one Treasury official complained on returning from leave, "There is no escaping the thought that the Treasury was well and truly conned by Energy." Minute from L.Walters, 25 June 1986, in HM Treasury papers, British Gas Corporation Privatisation Proposals, G/162/404/01 Part C.
124 Minute from G.S.Dart, PS/Secretary of State, 22 November 1985, G800/49/14 Part 4.
125 Brief for the Secretary of State's meeting with Sir Denis Rooke, Thursday 28 November 1985, G800/49/14 Part 5.
126 Minute from M.F.Reidy to PS/Secretary of State, 27 November 1986, G800/49/14 Part 5. Minute by D.R.Davis, Gas Division, 23 October 1985. The Privatisation of BGC, Department of Energy briefing note, March 1986, G800/49/14 Part 13.
127 Letter from S.Linnett, Rothschilds, 4 February 1986, G800/49/14 Part 11.

128    Minute from M.F.Reidy to PS/Secretary of State, 12 November 1985, G800/49/14 Part 4. However, at the time the Treasury was predicting pre-tax interest rates of 10% and a net dividend yield of 5% post-privatisation; minute from S.A.Robson to John Moore, 18 November 1985, in HM Treasury papers, British Gas Corporation Privatisation Proposals, L/1821/01 Part F. Equally, the Treasury preferred that any decision on the appropriate level of dividends be postponed until nearer the flotation when a better forecast could be made; minute from S.A.Robson to the Chancellor of the Exchequer, 28 April 1986, in HM Treasury papers, British Gas Corporation Privatisation Proposals, L/1821/01 Part J.

129    Letter from Walker to Rooke, 2 December 1985, G800/49/14 Part 6. Summary of reply from Rooke, in draft letter to Rooke from Walker, n.d., G800/49/14 Part 7.

130    Letter from A.J.Alt, N.M. Rothschild and Sons Ltd, to D.Davis, Gas Division, 11 October 1985; document "Parameters for a successful privatisation of BG plc", October 1985; and Minute by J.S.Neilson, Gas Division, 23 October 1985; all in G800/49/14 Part 2. Steering Brief, 28 April 1986, G800/49/14 Part 16.

131    Note by J.R.S.Guinness, 9 April 1986, G800/49/14 Part 15.

132    Minute from M.F.Reidy, Department of Energy, 7 February 1986, G800/49/14 Part 11.

133    Letter from Price Waterhouse to Touche Ross & Co, 27 February 1986, G800/49/14 Part 12. BGC also maintained that capitalising replacement expenditure would have adverse tax consequences; an argument that the Treasury discounted as unsubstantiated; BGC Privatisation, note in HM Treasury papers, British Gas Corporation Privatisation Proposals, L/1821/01 Part K. As part of the discussions on financial restructuring BGC was permitted to extend asset lives and there was a resulting release of deferred tax.

134    Minute from S.A.Robson to John Moore, 30 January 1986, in HM Treasury papers, British Gas Corporation Privatisation Proposals, L/1821/01 Part J.

135    Minute from M.F.Reidy to J.R.S Guinness, Department of Energy, 29 January 1986, G800/49/14 Part 10.

136    Prices for gas had peaked in 1981/82.

137    Minute from G.S.Dart, Department of Energy, G800/49/14 Part 11.

138    Letter from A.J.Alt, N.M. Rothschild & Sons Ltd, to M.F.Reidy, 31 January 1986, G800/49/14 Part 10. BGC's annual contribution to two pension funds was expected to fall by around £100m p.a. from April 1986 as a result of a revaluation of the fund's assets. Although the new company was to take over BGC's obligations under the schemes, the funds did not have any formal index-linking provisions similar to those that had caused problems in the BT privatisation and there would be no need to guarantee the BGC pension fund, as occurred during the BT sale; E(A(85)30, "Gas Industry Privatisation: Regulation. Memorandum by the Secretary of State for Energy", 24 May 1985. A full valuation of the BGC's pension schemes for staff and manual workers was carried out at 1 April 1985. An unfunded past service liability was revealed, which was made good by additional employer's contributions in the years ending 31 March 1986 and 31 March 1987; BGC Offer for Sale document, p.48.

139    Minutes from J.R.S. Guinness, Deputy Secretary and M.F. Reidy, Department of Energy, 3 & 7 February 2006, G800/49/14 Part 11.

140    Minute from D.R. Davis, Department of Energy, to PS/Secretary of State, 14 March 1986, G800/49/14 Part 13.

141    Capital Structure Paper 1: Cash and Profit Prospects for the Company, M.F.Reidy, G800/49/14 Part 2.

142    Letter from Nigel Lawson to Peter Walker, 24 March 1986, G800/49/14 Part 14.

143    Letter from Lawson to Walker, 17 April 1986, G800/49/14 Part 16. The threat to postpone the sale was intended to put pressure on Rooke and may not have been entirely serious, although an alternative sale of BA, BAA, Rolls-Royce or further BP shares was discussed within the Treasury.

144    Minute by J.R.S.Guinness, 25 April 1986, G800/49/14 Part 16.

145    Letter from A.J.Alt, N.M.Rothschild & Sons Ltd, to J.R.S.Guinness, 25 September 1986, G800/49/14 Part 36.

146    Note of the Seventh Meeting of the Offer for Sale Co-ordinating Group held at the Department of Energy on 8 April 1986, in HM Treasury papers, British Gas Corporation Privatisation Proposals, N/1329/01.

NOTES

147 Minute from J.R.S.Guinness, 13 June 1986, G800/49/14 Part 21.
148 Minute by J.R.S. Guinness, 24 September 1986, G800/49/14 Part 35. Minute from J.G.Wright to J.R.S. Guinness, 25 September 1986, G800/49/14 Part 36.
149 Minute from J.R.S.Guinness to Secretary of State, 29 September 1986; minute from D.R.Davis, Gas Division, to PS/Secretary of State, 30 September 1986; and minute from S.Linnett, 30 September 1986, all in G800/49/14 Part 36
150 This was one month after royal assent to the Gas Act. There was usually a two month period between royal assent and an Act coming into effect, but a dispensation was obtained in this case.
151 Letter from Cazenove & Co., 10 September 1986, G800/49/14 Part 34.
152 Minute from M.F.Reidy, 25 September 1986, G800/49/14 Part 36.
153 Minute from J.R.S.Guinness, Deputy Secretary, to the Secretary of State, 13 October 1986, G800/49/14 Part 39.
154 Letter from D.M.Gray, James Capel & Co., to S. Linnett, N.M.Rothschild & Sons, 23 September 1986, G800/49/14 Part 35.
155 Letter from Rooke to Walker, 10 October 1986, G800/49/14 Part 38.
156 Minute from D.R.Davis, Head Gas Division, to PS/Secretary of State, 10 October 1986, G800/49/14 Part 38.
157 Draft letter to Rooke, n.d., G800/49/14 Part 37.
158 Brief on Profits and Dividends for the Secretary of State's meeting with Sir Denis Rooke, 3 October 1986, G800/49/14 Part 37.
159 Secretary of State's Meeting with BGC, Monday 6 October 1986, G800/49/14 Part 38.
160 Letter from Walker to Rooke, 7 October 1986, G800/49/14 Part 38.
161 In January 1986 manual employees of BGC had received a 6% increase in basic wage rates plus improvements to other terms and conditions of work and by the time of the flotation the unions had lodged another claim for the following year. The Treasury believed that BGC was not doing enough to hold down its manpower costs.
162 Note of a Meeting on the Profit Forecast held at the Department of Energy on 22 October 1986, G800/49/14 Part 42.
163 Note of a telephone conversation between C. Brierley, BGC, and G.Dart, Department of Energy, and letter from Dart to Brierley, both 24 October 1986. Also, letter from Brierley to Peter Walker, 27 October 1986; all in G800/49/14 Part 43.
164 Letter from Walker to Brierley, MD Economic Planning BGC, 27 October 1986, G800/49/14 Part 43.
165 Letter from Brierley to Walker, 28 October 1986, G800/49/14 Part 43.
166 Letter from Walker to Brierley, 29 October 1986, G800/49/14 Part 44.
167 Minute by G.S.Dart, PPS/Secretary of State, 29 October 1986, and minute from J.R.S.Guinness, Deputy Secretary, 29 October 1986, both in G800/49/14 Part 44.
168 Memorandum from the Permanent Under-Secretary, 29 October 2006, G800/49/14 Part 44.
169 Commentary on Sir Denis Rooke's letter, October 1986, G800/49/14 Part 39.
170 Letter from Lawson to Walker, 20 October 1986 and reply by Walker, 21 October 1986, both in G800/49/14 Part 42.
171 "NALGO goes to court over Thames Water sell-off", *Financial Times*, 18 June 1986.
172 If the ultra vires claim was upheld, the BGC directors might be at risk on a personal basis. Note of a Meeting held on 9 July 1986 at the Department of Energy, G800/49/14 Part 26. Minute from S.A.Robson to John Moore, 18 July 1986, in HM Treasury papers, British Gas Corporation Privatisation Proposals, L/1821/01 Part K.
173 ADRs are American Depository Receipts and represent ownership in the shares of a foreign company trading on US financial markets. They tend to be favoured in the US because they enable Americans to buy shares in foreign companies without undertaking cross-border transactions. ADRs are denominated in dollars and issued by US depository banks. Holders of an ADR have the right to obtain the foreign stock it represents should they wish.
174 Implications of the Budget for the British Gas Offer for Sale, draft letter from the Secretary of State to John Moore, March 1986, and letter from M.Richardson, Rothschild & Sons Ltd to J.R.S.Guinness, Department of Energy, 4 April 1986, both in G800/49/14 Part 15. Letter from

Peter Walker to Nigel Lawson, 3 July 1986, and Lawson's reply, 7 July 1986, in G800/49/14 Parts 25 and 26, respectively.
175 Letters from Walker to John MacGregor, Chief Secretary, 7 February 1986 and 12 June 1986 in G800/49/14 Parts 11 and 21, respectively. Letter from John Moore, Financial Secretary, to Walker, 26 February 1986, G800/49/14 Part 12. Minute from J.G.Wright, Gas Division, 8 July 1986, G800/49/14 Part 26. Letter from MacGregor to Walker, 30 July 1986, G800/49/14 Part 29. Letter from Kenneth Baker, Department of the Environment, to John Moore, Treasury, 14 March 1986, G800/49/14 Part 13. Letter from Walker to MacGregor, 18 July 1986, G800/49/14 Part 27. It seems that the Treasury favoured adopting the same strategy for BGC as had applied to BT since its privatisation of refusing to forward any more applications for grants from the company to the European Commission; minute by J.M.Bird, HM Treasury, 12 February 1986, in HM Treasury papers, British Gas Corporation Privatisation, JA/162/01 Part B.
176 Attitude of Opposition Parties to Public Ownership, G800/49/14 Part 42.
177 Minute by G.S. Dart, PPS/Secretary of State, 24 June 1986, G800/49/14 Part 24 and miscellaneous correspondence in G800/49/14 Part 47. Following a legal challenge from Lithgow, the European Court handed down a judgement in July 1986 favourable to the Government but this did not end his objections. Lithgow's grievances related to inadequate compensation when his company's assets were nationalised and inadequate prior government consultation, which he considered contrary to the European Convention on Human Rights; letter from Lithgow to Slaughter & May, 22 October 1986, G800/49/14 Part 48; letter from Lithgow to the PM 4 August 1986, in HM Treasury papers, British Gas Privatisation Prospects, L/1821/01.
178 Letter from Walker to the PM, 19 May 1986, G800/49/14 Part 30.
179 Note by G.W.S Lumley, Gas Division, 14 April 1986, G800/49/14 Part 15. Minute by D.R.David, Gas Division, 20 May 1986, G800/49/14 Part 19.
180 Minute by G.S.Part, PPS/Secretary of State, summary of BG Privatisation Progress Meeting on 8 July 1986, G800/49/14 Part 26. Carsberg faced public criticism of BT's policy on tariff rebalancing and had responded by signalling that he would be looking into BT's activities. This caused some alarm in the City that he might be intending to intervene to reduce BT's profits. In fact, this proved not to be the case. Carsberg continued to operate a price cap regulation.
181 Minute from W.D.Evans, Department of Energy, to PS/Secretary of State, 18 February 1986, G800/49/14 Part 11.
182 Letter from John Moore to J.R.S.Guinness, Department of Energy, in HM Treasury papers, L/1821/01, Part K. Letter from S.A.Robson, HM Treasury, to J.R.S.Guinness, Department of Energy, 4 July 1986, G800/49/14 Part 25. In the event, Rooke was persuaded to sign the letter.
183 Dewe Rogerson, Memo on Gas City Survey, 2 May 1986, G800/49/14 Part 17.
184 Letter from Dewe Rogerson Ltd to D.Heslop, British Gas, 9 July 1986, G800/49/14 Part 26.
185 Letter from Peter Walker to R.Evans, Chief Executive Officer, BGC, 28 October 1986, G800/49/14 Part 43.
186 Minute by G.S.Dart, PPS/Secretary of State, 29 October 1986, G800/49/14 Part 44. Statement on Directors' Salaries, n.d., G800/49/14 Part 47.
187 BGC Offer for Sale document, p.62.
188 James Capel & Co, "British Gas", Fourth Draft 30 June 1986. The quotation is from the Draft Press Release 26 June 1986, G800/49/14 Part 24.
189 British Gas Privatisation: Co-ordinating Group. The Customer Share Scheme, Department of Energy, 5 August 1986, G800/49/14 Part 30.
190 Minute by J.G.Wright, Gas Division, 18 September 1986, G800/49/14 Part 35.
191 "British Gas – The Major Factors", Morgan Grenfell Securities, October? 1986, G800/49/14 Part 33.
192 Minute by M.A.Higson, Gas Division, 1 September 1986, G800/49/14 Part 33.
193 The indemnity applied except in cases where the Corporation was negligent or there was wilful default. BGC wanted this financial exposure to be capped in cases of negligence. Letter from C.W.Brierley, BGC, to M.F.Reidy, Department of Energy, G800/49/14 Part 38. Minutes from M.F.Reidy, Gas Division, to PS/Secretary of State, 24 and 27 October 1986, G800/49/14 Part 43.

194    Minute by C.J.R.Morris, Gas Division, 9 September 1986, G800/49/14 Part 33. Also, a smaller office in London acted as a control centre dealing with the press, financial intermediaries and with particularly difficult enquiries.

195    Note of the Nineteenth Meeting of the Offer for Sale Co-ordinating Group held at the Department of Energy on 18 September 1986, in HM Treasury Papers, British Gas Corporation: Offer for Sale Co-ordinating Group, N/1329/01. Minute by C.J.R.Morris, Gas Division, 24 September 1986, G800/49/14 Part 35.

196    CC(86)31st meeting, conclusions, 18 September 1986.

197    Draft press release from Dewe Rogerson, 2 September 1986, G800/49/14 Part 34.

198    Letter from R.Howell, Young & Rubicam Ltd., to M. Reidy, Department of Energy, 20 November 1986, G800/49/14 Part 49. In his autobiography Walker (1991), p.193, comments that the first promotional material presented to him by Young and Rubicam was "terrible . . . I said we were trying to interest millions of people who had never bought a share in their lives before. They could not understand any of the 'guff' which was being presented . . . They went away and came back with 'Sid' . . . I thought it was a good name and decided not to tell anyone my brother was called Syd."

199    Draft press release, 26 September 1986, G800/49/14 Part 36.

200    Letter from Anthony Carlisle, Dewe Rogerson Ltd, to M.F.Reidy, Department of Energy, 16 October 1986, G800/49/14 Part 39.

201    Dewe Rogerson Trading Survey Report, 16 October 1986, G800/49/14 Part 40.

202    Note of the Twenty First Meeting of the Offer for Sale Co-ordinating Group held at the Department of Energy on 5 November 1986, in HM Treasury Papers, British Gas Corporation: Offer for Sale Co-ordinating Group, N/1329/01.

203    Letter from S.A.Robson, Treasury, to J.R.S.Guinness, Department of Energy, 16 October 1986, G800/49/14 Part 39.

204    Minute from R.P.Steele, Gas Division, October 1986, G800/49/14 Part 42. Letter from Norman Lamont, Treasury, to Peter Walker, 27 October 1986, G800/49/14 Part 43. Letter from National Westminster Bank to BGC, 28 October 1986, G800/49/14 Part 44.

205    The National Westminster had been the only major bank willing to be considered as both lead receiving bank and registrar, and originally suggested that it would only be able to process 3m allotments. Letter from M. Richardson to the Secretary of State for Energy, 21 October 1985, G800/49/14 Part 1. Competition for the role of the receiving bank had come only from Barclays and for registrar only from Ravensbourne. This led to a claim in the Department of Energy that "There is effectively a City cartel in this area." Minute from L.B.Davis, Gas Division, 19 November 1985, G800/49/14 Part 4. NatWest proposed charges of £4.265m to establish the register and between £1.80 and £2.50 per shareholder in running costs per year. These charges were considered excessive by the Government and after Walker met with Lord Boardman, Chairman of the National Westminster, the bank revised up its expectation as to the number of shareholders it could register and reduced its price. The receiving bank capacity was raised through the introduction of computer processing of personalised application forms to replace manual sorting. Letter from Lord Boardman to Walker, 11 December 1985, G800/49/14 Part 7. Later this was increased again, to 6.5m.

206    Minute from J.R.S.Guinness, 4 June 1986, G800/49/14 Part 20.

207    Draft letter to the National Westminster, Lloyds and Midland Banks, n.d. (November 1986), G800/49/14 Part 49.

208    Minute by G.S.Dart, 30 October 1986, G800/49/14 Part 44.

209    Note on the Pathfinder conference and BGC Press Release, 30 and 31 October 1986, both in G800/49/14 Part 44.

210    Letter from M.Richardson, N.M.Rothschild & Sons Ltd, to J.R.S. Guinness, Department of Energy, 9 September 1986, G800/49/14 Part 33. The profit trend using HCA accounting was less favourable (£1,100m in 1985/6 and £1,071m in 1986/7). However, the pro-forma accounts, reflecting balance sheet restructuring, did show a slight upward trend for profit before taxation on both HCA and CCA bases; Offer for Sale document, p.5.

211    Minute by J.G.Wright, PS/Secretary of State, 30 October 1986, G800/49/14 Part 44. Minute from J.G. Wright, Department of Energy, to PS/Secretary of State, 26 November 1986, G800/49/14 Part 49.

212 Note in G800/49/14 Part 47. Note of the Twenty First Meeting of the Offer for Sale Co-ordinating Group held at the Department of Energy on 5 November 1986, in HM Treasury Papers, British Gas Corporation: Offer for Sale Co-ordinating Group, N/1329/01.

213 Draft Press Release, Department of Energy, 6 November 1986, G800/623/7 Part 3.

214 Minute from S.B.Dickinson, Gas Division, 10 November 1986, G800/49/14 Part 46.

215 Minute from D.R.Davis, Head/Gas, 20 October 1986, G800/49/14 Part 41.

216 Letter from M.Richardson, N.M.Rothschild & Sons Ltd, to J.R.S. Guinness, Department of Energy, 9 September 1986, G800/49/14 Part 33. Minute by J.R.S.Guinness to the Secretary of State, 3 October 1986, G800/49/14 Part 37.

217 Memorandum from Cazenove & Co to the Actuarial Classification Committee, 8 October 1986, G800/623/7 Part 3. Note for file by L.B.Davies, Gas Division, 11 September 1986, G800/49/14 Part 34.

218 Letter from A.D.Forbes, Cazenove & Co, to J.R.S.Guinness, 7 November 1986, G800/49/14 Part 46.

219 British Gas Valuation Matrix, 17 November 1986, G800/49/14 Part 48.

220 Minute from L.B.Davies, Gas Division, 10 June 1986, G800/49/14 Part 26.

221 Minute from J.R.S.Guinness to the Secretary of State, 18 November 1986, G800/49/14 Part 48.

222 Memorandum from the Permanent Under-Secretary to the Secretary of State, 4 August 1986, G800/49/14 Part 29. Minute by M.F.Reidy, Gas Division, 15 October 1986, G800/49/14 Part 47. The Pricing of British Gas plc, note by J.R.S.Guinness, 11 November 1986 and letter of appointment of G.Chandler, 7 November 1986, both in G800/49/14 Part 46. However, as one official in the Department of Energy commented on the appointment of an independent adviser from the City, 'it is stretching a point to call any one of their breed "independent"'; note by M.F.Reidy, Gas Division, 2 April 1986, G800/49/14 Part 15.

223 A couple of other people were considered but rejected.

224 Letter from J.R.S.Guinness to G.Chandler, 11 November 1986, G800/49/14 Part 47.

225 Various press cuttings in G800/49/14 Part 49. Blair also questioned the need to sell shares to foreigners, pointing out that when the Japanese Government had sold shares in the telecommunications company NTT the previous month, they had excluded foreign participation.

226 Minute from S.Linnett, 17 November 1986, G800/49/14 Part 48.

227 Letter from G.J.Chandler to Walker, 19 November 1986, G800/49/14 Part 48.

228 This is perhaps an unfortunate reflection on the competence of the general British public.

229 It has also been suggested that John Guinness was very influential in determining the share price of 135p. Some other officials in the Department of Energy, including Michael Reidy, thought this was at the top end of what could be achieved.

230 Minute from J.R.S.Guinness to the Secretary of State, 18 November 1986, G800/49/14 Part 48. Minute from J.R.S.Guinness, 3 December 1986, G800/49/14 Part 50.

231 Secretary of State's Meeting with Advisers to Discuss Pricing of the British Gas Share Issue, 19 November 1986, G800/49/14 Part 49.

232 Minute by M.Higson, Gas Division, 14 November 1986, G800/49/14 Part 47.

233 The use of a mini prospectus to reduce costs drew on the experience of the successful BT flotation.

234 Letter from C.W.Brierley to J.R.S.Guinness, 4 November 1986, G800/49/14 Part 45. Minute from D.J.W.Lumley, Gas Division, 1 December 1986, G800/49/14 Part 50.

235 Minute from D.J.W.Lumley to PS/Secretary of State, 24 November 1986, G800/49/14 Part 49. Minutes from D.J.W. Lumley and R.P.Steele, Department of Energy, to PS/Secretary of State, 28 November 1986, both in G800/49/14 Part 49.

236 Minute from R.P.Steele, to PS/Secretary of State, 4 December 1986, G800/49/14 Part 50.

237 See pp.391–2.

238 CC(86)41st meeting conclusions, 11 December 1986.

239 Minute from R.Steele and S.Linnett to the Co-ordinating Group Meeting, 12 November 1986, in HM Treasury Papers, British Gas Corporation: Offer for Sale Co-ordinating Group, N/1329/01.

240 Department of Energy Press Release 233, 5 December 1986, G800/49/14 Part 50.

241 Minute from S.Collett, Gas Division, to PS/Secretary of State, 4 December 1986, G800/49/14 Part 50.

242 British Gas Share Allocation, minute from S.Collett, Gas Division to PS/ Secretary of State, 4 December 1986, G800/49/14 Part 50.

243 Minute from E.Dobkin, Goldman Sachs, to J.R.S. Guinness, 22 December 1986, G800/49/14 Part 50.

244 Note for the record by L.B.Davies, Gas Division, in G800/49/14 Part 50

245 To ensure that the applications were processed in time some overseas facilities for processing and registration of the share issue were used. On one occasion a civil servant taking a suitcase of applications for shares to Germany for processing found that he could obtain only a standby air ticket. Colin Marshall at British Airways was telephoned to ensure that the civil servant obtained a seat on the flight even if this meant off-loading another passenger. Apparently there were still advantages to be gained from the state owning an airline after all!

246 Thatcher (1993), p.682.

247 Privatisation Briefing for use on 25 November 1987, BT/A/104.

248 Minute by R.P.Steele and letter from M.F.Reidy to Ravensbourne, both 16 December 1986, in G800/40/14 Part 49.

249 Minute from R.P.Steele to PS/Secretary of State, 8 December 1986, G800/49/14 Part 50.

250 Letter from the Plain English Campaign to Walker, 4 December 1986, and minute from M.F.Reidy, 5 December 1986, both in G800/49/14 Part 50.

251 Campbell (2003), p.238.

252 These are the figures reported by the NAO. Price Waterhouse (1987), p.28, puts the cost of sale lower at £164m with costs borne by the company at around £18m.

253 National Audit Office (1987c) *Department of Energy – Sale of Government Shareholding in British Gas plc*, 30 June, HC 22 Session 1986–87, London: HMSO.

254 Martin and Parker (1997), Tables 5.1, 6.1 and 8.1. However, labour productivity growth had also been healthy in the years preceding privatisation. For example, the number of therms sold per employee increased by nearly 32% over the five years ending 31 March 1986; N.M.Rothschild & Sons Ltd on behalf of HM Government through the British Gas Share Information Office, *British Gas Share Offer: A Background Briefing*, 6 November 1986, p.11.

255 There was also criticism when Peter Walker was appointed to the Board of British Gas as a non-executive director in June 1990, having only very recently stepped down as a Minister; http://www.spinwatch.org/content/view/248/8/. Walker defends his actions on the grounds that he had been approached by a number of oil companies to join their boards and chose BGC for other than financial reward; Walker (1991), pp.226–7. Walker served on the BGC Board until 1996.

256 The requirement for British Gas plc to publish its prices, which its competitors were not required to do, would eventually be lifted by OFGAS in mid-1995. By then there was extensive competition in the contract market.

257 MMC (1988) *Gas: a Report on the Matter of the Existence or Possible Existence of a Monopoly Situation in Relation to the Supply of Gas through Pipes to Persons other than Tariff Customers*, Cmnd.500, London: HMSO. Helm (2004), ch.13, provides an excellent review of the changes in the gas industry during the 1990s.

258 OFT (1991) *The Gas Review*, London: Office of Fair Trading.

259 Neither OFGAS nor the MMC could change the threshold defining the tariff market because this was set down in the Gas Act. Therefore, new legislation was needed, the Competition and Service (Utilities) Act 1992. This Act also gave OFGAS the power to make a reference to the MMC in relation to the conveyance and storage of gas.

260 MMC (1993a) *Gas and British Gas plc*, London: HMSO; MMC (1993b) *Gas: Volume 1 of Reports under the Fair Trading Act 1973 on the Supply Within Great Britain of the Conveyance or Storage of Gas by Public Gas Suppliers*, Cmnd.2314, London: HMSO.

261 In return for these changes BGC was compensated for the resulting loss in revenues by a reduction in the X term in the price cap from the 5% set in 1991 to 4%, to begin in 1994.

262 S(1)(4)(c) *The Gas Act 1995*, Chapter 45, London: HMSO. The 1995 Gas Act also put OFGAS on the same footing as OFTEL regarding the power to make Fair Trading Act monopoly references to the MMC.

NOTES

263   For example, Vickers and Yarrow (1988), pp.267–8, conclude: "British Gas has been transferred to the private sector with its monopoly and monopsony powers intact . . . major opportunities to improve incentives in the industry have been missed." In a similar vein, Foster (1992), p.131 comments that, "Arguably a high price was paid for securing the Corporation's agreement to privatisation".

264   Helm (2004), p.116 argues that only one academic paper, of which he was a co-author, argued at the time for a major restructuring of BGC. This suggested restructuring on regional lines but with no separation of the supply function.

265   Excluding the Morecambe Bay fields which were placed in Centrica.

266   Helm (2004), p.7.

## 16 NATIONALISATION AND PRIVATISATION 1970 – 87: AN OVERVIEW AND CONCLUSIONS

1   Letwin (1992), p.89.

2   J.Moore (1992) "British Privatisation – Taking Capitalism to the People", *Harvard Business Review*, January-February, reprinted in HM Treasury (1992) *Her Majesty's Treasury Guide to the UK Privatisation Programme*, June, London: HM Treasury.

3   Cited in M.Balen (1994) *Kenneth Clarke*, London: Fourth Estate, p.113. The reference to Nick Ridley is probably to Ridley's report on nationalised industries in 1978, which was quietly suppressed at the time by the shadow Cabinet.

4   M. Thatcher (1995) *The Path to Power*, p.574.

5   The main partial exception to this was the National Freight Corporation, which was not highly profitable. However, it was sold in February 1982 to its management and employees not external investors.

6   Statement by the Key Issue Group reported in Premium Pricing: A Balanced Viewpoint, report by N.M.Rothschild & Sons Ltd, 10 September 1986, in British Gas privatisation files, Department of Energy, G800/49/14 Part 36.

7   Veljanovski (1987), p.93.

8   Ibid., pp.7–8.

9   Foster (1992), p.116.

10   M. Bishop and J. Kay (1988) *Does Privatisation Work?* London: London Business School, p.10. R. Green and J. Haskel (2001) "Seeking a Premier League Economy: The Role of Privatization", in R.Blundell, D.Card and R.B.Freeman (eds.) *Seeking a Premier League Economy,* Chicago: University of Chicago Press, p.64, have more recently repeated the same claim: "Privatization, at least on a large scale, was in fact something of an accident."

11   Kay and Thompson (1986).

12   Grimstone (1988), p.20.

13   Even though in financial terms much more important were the tax receipts from North Sea oil.

14   The figures in Table 16.1 below are to March 1987 and show total privatisation receipts of just under £12bn. Between April and June 1987 additional receipts were obtained from the sale of the remainder of the Royal Ordnance Factories to BAe, the sale of British Leyland Trucks and the flotation of Rolls-Royce.

15   There is one important issue not specifically mentioned in the flow chart: the need prior to the finalisation of the sale prospectus for a formal trawl across government departments seeking information on anything that might need to be disclosed in the prospectus. There was usually a section in the prospectus on Government policy that might impact on the business.

16   The Office of Telecommunications and the Office of Gas Supply.

17   There were occasionally other issues to sort out too; for example, during the sale of Sealink ferries, a subsidiary of British Rail, the right of employees to travel at concessional rates on the railways had to be bought out and there were a number of contingent liability matters to address prior to the sale of British Airways.

18   J.Redwood (1986) *Equity for Everyman: new ways to widen ownership,* Policy Study no.74, London: Centre for Policy Studies.

19  The privatisations typically contained a requirement that Treasury consent was required before the Government's shareholding was sold. In practice, this was a formality because Treasury officials were consulted and some actively involved during the sale process.

20  The Bank of England might have played a more prominent role in each of the privatisations of the 1980s had it not taken the decision to reduce its role during the sale of BAe; see chapter 5, p.116.

21  J. Moore (1992), p.59.

22  Official Committee on Nationalised Industry Policy, HM Treasury papers NIP(83)10, "Arrangements for Appointing Advisers to Work on the Privatisation Programme. Note by HM Treasury", 4 November 1983, REV NIP/414, H/1579/1000/05. The arrangements were refined later, NIP(84)11, "Arrangements for Appointing Advisers to Work on the Privatisation Programme. Note by HM Treasury", 16 October 1984, REV NIP/809, H/1759/1000/05.

23  The listing was known as the "Appointment of Advisers in the Privatisation Programme" and set out the names of all those firms that could be considered for government appointments.

24  NIP(83)5th meeting, 18 November 1983, REV NIP/414, H/1579/1000/05. Where advisers were appointed by departments to provide some initial advice on a disposal, there was now to be no presumption that they would obtain the final work on the sale. However, given satisfactory performance and Treasury agreement they could be reappointed without further interview.

25  "Arrangements for Appointing Advisers to Work on the Privatisation Programme. Note by HM Treasury", 23 February 1984.

26  NIP(85)2, "Privatisation Fees. Note by HM Treasury", 8 February 1985, A/06.

27  In the case of legal fees the advice of the Treasury Solicitor was to be sought. Fees to solicitors were regulated by the Solicitors Remuneration Order 1972. In cases where nationalised industries were responsible for the sale of a subsidiary business, departments were expected to impress upon the industries the desirability of conforming to the Treasury's guidance.

28  NIP(85)2.

29  Where a placing of shares occurred generally investors would receive a commission of 0.5% .

30  After competition was introduced, essentially the primary underwriters would meet and be told the share price and the number of shares to be underwritten. They would then separately indicate how many shares they would underwrite and at what commission rate. The lead underwriter would then on the basis of these submissions determine the lowest level of commission that would clear the market.

31  Privatisation Fees. Note by HM Treasury, 4 February 1985, Official Committee on Nationalised Industry Policy files, NIP(85)2.

32  DTI Privatisation Brief August 1991, in British Telecom privatisation files, BT/A/104.

33  Using these figures in relation to the sales receipts produces different percentage figures to those just given. This probably results from the inclusion and exclusion of different costs. Vickers and Yarrow (1988), Table 7.3, p.181 also provide slightly different figures. But in all cases what is revealed is a wide variation in costs in relation to receipts.

34  NBC faced a Minister, Nicholas Ridley, who was determined to introduce competition into bus travel come what may.

35  Sometimes the chairman not the government department then dominated the sale process, as was the case during the sale of shipyards by British Shipbuilders under Graham Day.

36  NIP(79)23, "Financial Aspects of Disposals", 13 September 1979, HM Treasury papers filefolder 11271558.

37  Today book building is a process used by companies raising capital through a public share offer. During the period in which the "book" for the offer is open, generally five days, bids are collected from investors for shares at various prices, but within a price band specified by the issuer of the shares. The issue price is determined based on the demand for the shares at the various price levels. Allocation of shares is then made to the successful bidders. The process is led by a merchant bank that acts as the "book runner", nominated by the issuer of the shares.

38  City institutions, probably rightly, felt that their reputation would be more damaged by an under-subscription than an over-subscription.

39  Price Waterhouse (1987), p.33.

40    National Audit Office (1988c) *Sale of Government shareholdings in British Gas plc, British Airways plc, Rolls-Royce plc and BAA*, HC211 Session, London: HMSO.
41    R. Buckland (1987) "The costs and returns of the privatisation of nationalised industries", *Public Administration*, vol.65, no.3, pp.241–57. A number of studies around the time suggested a 10% to 12% target discount for private sector IPOs.
42    Buying shares at flotation intentionally to sell quickly at a profit.
43    NIP(82)3rd meeting, 19 October 1982, HM Treasury papers filefolder H/1579/1000/01 Rev NIP/413.
44    Cited in R.Buckland and E.W.Davis (1984) "Privatisation Techniques and the PSBR", *Fiscal Studies*, vol.5, no.3, p.47.
45    Buckland (1987), p.245.
46    Lawson (1992), p.220.
47    Mayer and Meadowcroft (1986) "Selling public assets: Techniques and financial implications", in J. Kay, C. Mayer and D. Thompson (eds.) *Privatisation and Regulation: The UK Experience*, Oxford: Clarendon Press.
48    House of Commons, Session 1981–82, *Tenth Report from the Committee of Public Accounts*, London: HMSO.
49    "Arrangements for Share Sales: Summary of City Reactions" and letter from Ridley to Geoffrey Howe, 6 August 1982, in British Telecom privatisation files, DTI, BT/A/12 Part 1.
50    Underwriting Share Sales, Note by HM Treasury, 6 February 1985.
51    National Audit Office (1988c) *Sale of Government shareholdings in British Gas plc, British Airways plc, Rolls-Royce plc and BAA*, HC211 Session, London: HMSO.
52    Technically, clawback could involve "super-clawback", under which a whole tranche of shares could be clawed back if public demand exceeded a set threshold, and simple clawback, where shares could be clawed back one-by-one to satisfy excess demand in the public offer.
53    Buckland (1987), footnote 6, p.256.
54    National Audit Office (1988c) op cit.
55    The chief objection to a tap issue was understandable concern that knowledge that shares were to be sold into the market over time might well depress the share price.
56    To be specific, for Britoil the figure was 51%, BAe 51.6% and ABP 51.5% .
57    The first "privatisation" involving partly paid shares was the sale of shares in BP in June 1977, which were issued at 845p per share with 300p payable on application and the remainder on 6 December 1977. When the new Conservative Government in November 1979 sold further BP shares, it also permitted payment in two instalments.
58    The main prospectus had to comply with increasingly burdensome disclosure requirements. The mini-prospectus was abbreviated and more user friendly. It did rely on cross-links with the main prospectus which almost certainly few small investors read.
59    Op cit., p.52.
60    N. Ridley (1991) *'My Style of Government'*, p.59.
61    The 15% limit did not apply to Government or its nominee or a trustee of an employee share scheme.
62    Under company law, rights conferred by the articles of a particular class of share can be altered if 75% of the holders of those shares agree. The special share constituted a class of shares on its own and the rights conferred by the share at flotation could not be varied in the future without the Government's consent.
63    Special Share Rights, 12 June 1984, HM Treasury Papers, NIP(84)5; Graham and Prosser (1991), pp.141–50.
64    There were restrictions on asset disposals of over 25% imposed for the sales of Amersham International, Cable & Wireless, Jaguar and Rolls-Royce.
65    Letter from Lilley to Kenneth Baker, Home Secretary, 26 July 1991, E(DL)Part 19.
66    Much later, in landmark decisions in 2002 and 2003 against the UK and four other Member States, the European Court would establish that special rights mechanisms restricted the freedom under the EC Treaty on capital movements and establishment. This meant that special shares ceased to be a reliable policy instrument.

67   *Hansard*, 23 February 1988, columns 149–50.
68   Minute from the Chancellor of the Exchequer to the PM, 12 May 1988, E(DL) Part 16.
69   The introduction of a special share for BAA was judged to be less easy to defend, but given that this privatisation had just occurred it was agreed that no changes should be made for the present time.
70   Minute from Norman Lamont, HM Treasury, to Cecil Parkinson, Secretary of State for Energy, 26 July 1988, in E(DL)Part 16.
71   Special Rights Shares, 12 June 1984, NIP(84)5, HM Treasury Papers A/301/01.
72   Harris (1988), p.189.
73   Lamont (1988), p.4. Conservative Research Department, *The Campaign Guide 1987*, p.96. The Government also promoted share ownership by halving stamp duty on share transactions in October 1986, to 0.5% .
74   National Audit Office (1988c).
75   Buckland (1987), p.255.
76   Ibid., Table 4, p.253.
77   TUC (1985a) *Stripping Our Assets: The City's Privatisation Killing*, London: Trades Union Congress.
78   P.R.Saunders and C.N.Harris (1994) *Privatization and Popular Capitalism*, Oxford: Oxford University Press.
79   C.P. Mayer and S.A. Meadowcroft (1985) "Selling Public Assets: Techniques and Financial Implications", *Fiscal Studies,*vol.6, no.4, pp.42–55.
80   Labour Research (1985), "Who Got the Lion's Share of Jaguar?", September, p.239, cited in Buckland (1987), p.254.
81   Privatisation Briefing, 25 November 1987, in British Telecom privatisation files, DTI, BT/A/104. Also, D. Marsh (1991) "Privatization Under Mrs Thatcher: A Review of the Literature", *Public Administration*, vol.69, p.474.
82   Letwin (1992), p.101.
83   National Audit Office (1988c) op cit., paragraph 60.
84   Aims of Industry (1983) *Privatisation: A Threat to Its Future*, London: Aims of Industry.
85   In 1975 the number had fallen to 2,723 but had risen again to 30,045 in 1978; R. Sillars (2007) "The Development of the Right to Buy and the Sale of Council Houses", *Economic Affairs*, vol.27, no.1, pp.52–7.
86   R. Berthoud (1989) "Social security and the economics of housing", in A. Dilnot and I. Walker (eds.) *The Economics of Social Security*, Oxford: Oxford University Press; Peden (1991), pp.235–6.
87   NIP(79)2nd meeting, HM Treasury papers filefolder 11271561.
88   NIP(85)1, Privatisations: Employee Shareholdings. Note by HM Treasury, 8 February 1985, Nationalised Industries and Policy, Circulated Papers and Minutes 1985, A/06.
89   Privatisation: Employee Participation, paper by J.Whaley, Department of Energy, in British Gas privatisation files, G63/112/1.
90   NIP(80)2nd meeting, 22 July 1980, HM Treasury papers filefolder 11271674.
91   NIP(80)9, Nationalised Industry Pension Schemes: Index Linking and Privatisation, 29 October 1980, HM Treasury papers filefolder 11271676.
92   This and other annual percentage pension increases were subject to the pension fund being "in payment". The details of each of the pension entitlements here come from Annex B: Guarantees Given in Privatisation and Contracting Out, n.d. in E(DL) Part 11.
93   Foreword by John Redwood to O. Letwin (1988) *Privatising the World: A Study of International Privatisation in Theory and Practice*, London: Cassell, p.xv.
94   N.Tebbit (1991) *Unfinished Business*, London: Weidenfeld & Nicolson, p.88.
95   HM Treasury (1992) *Her Majesty's Treasury Guide to the UK Privatisation Programme*, London: HM Treasury, p.19.
96   The Office of Communications.
97   The Office of Gas and Electricity Markets.

98 This is because the regulators took account of costs of production including the cost of capital when setting price caps. However, regulators were always keen to ensure that this should not become rate of return regulation by default and experimented with various other ways of setting the price caps, including performance benchmarking; D. Parker, T. Dassler, and D.S. Saal (2006) "Performance benchmarking in utility regulation: principles and the UK's experience", in M. Crew and D. Parker (eds.) *International Handbook on Economic Regulation*, Cheltenham: Edward Elgar.

99 This would change later with the privatisation of the British Airports Authority and the water and sewerage industry, as discussed in Volume 2 of this *Official History*.

100 Other noteworthy regulation research units in British Universities could be found at the London Business School and Hertford College Oxford.

101 The initial intervention came from the Office of Fair Trading instead; see chapter 15, p.396.

102 *Hansard,* 10 February 1986, column 311.

103 "Privatisation Achievement", speech at the Eccleston Supper Club, Eccleston Square, London, 18 July 1984, London: HM Treasury Press Office. Moore made a number of speeches in the mid-1980s, with drafting assisted by Gerry Grimstone in the Treasury, detailing the achievements of privatisation and the failure of nationalisation; for example, "Why Privatise?" 1 November 1983. I would like to thank John Moore for providing me with copies of these speeches.

104 S. Domberger, S.Meadowcroft and D. Thompson (1986) "Competitive Tendering and Efficiency: the case of refuse collection", *Fiscal Studies,* vol.7, no.4, pp.69–87; S. Domberger, S. Meadowcroft and D. Thompson (1987) "The Impact of Competitive Tendering on the Costs of Hospital Domestic Services", *Fiscal Studies,* vol.8, no.4, pp.39–54.

105 P. Walters (1990) *Privatisation: Implications for Cultural Change*, London: United Research.

106 Lord Ezra (1987) "Privatisation: A Middle Course", in J. Neuberger (ed.) *Privatisation . . . Fair Shares for All or Selling the Family Silver?*, London: Macmillan, p.47.

107 Similarly, a rising stock market was generally favourable in the 1980s and 1990s to floating off state enterprises.

108 Martin and Parker (1997). The author of this *Official History* was one of the authors of this earlier study.

109 At the same time, explicit Government agreement was still needed for large or what were considered to be contentious investments.

110 P.Riddell (1989) *The Thatcher Decade: How Britain has changed during the 1980s*, Oxford: Blackwell, p.95.

111 Sir C.Marshall (1988) "How British Airways was privatized", in E.Butler (ed.) *The Mechanics of Privatization*, London: Adam Smith Institute, p.35.

112 The results of one study of the effect of privatising BT on the PSBR in 1985/86 underlines the difficulty of making sweeping judgements about the effects of privatisation on the public finances; C.P.Mayer and S.A.Meadowcroft (1985) "Selling Public Assets: Techniques and Financial Implications", *Fiscal Studies*, vol.6, no.1, pp.42–56.

113 Campbell (2004), p.240.

114 Buckland (1987), pp.247–8.

115 Ascher (1987), pp.104–8; Martin and Parker (1997), ch.8.

116 Martin and Parker (1997), pp.186–90.

117 P. Johnson and G. Stark (1989) *Taxation and Social Security 1979–1989: The Impact on Household Incomes*, London: Institute for Fiscal Studies.

118 N. Lamont (1988) "The benefits of privatization: an overview", in E.Butler (ed.) *The Mechanics of Privatization*, London: Adam Smith Institute, p.2.

119 Moore (1992).

120 Ibid.

121 Howe (1981), p.5, and quoted in the brief on nationalised industries and privatisation for the Debate on the Address, 9 November 1982, E(DL) Part 6.

122 Cited in Conservative Research Department *The Campaign Guide 1987,* London: Conservative Research Department, p.93.

123 G.Grimstone (1988) "Organizing a privatization programme", in E. Butler (ed.) *The Mechanics of Privatization*, London: Adam Smith Institute, p.18.
124 Ibid., p.18.
125 *Daily Telegraph*, 30 December 1985, cited in Conservative Research Department *The Campaign Guide 1987*, p.97.
126 Cited in Parkinson (1992), p.302.

# REFERENCES

## Official records

Prefix BT: Department of Industry/Department of Trade and Industry papers on the privatisation of British Telecom.

Prefix C: Cabinet Committee Minutes and Memoranda.

Prefix E or E(A): E Committee (Ministerial Committee on Economic Affairs) after May 1983 E(A) Committee (Ministerial Committee on Economic Affairs. Subcommittee on Economic Affairs).

Prefix E(DL): Ministerial Sub-Committee on Disposals of E later E(A) Committee.

Prefix E(NI): Policy Towards the Nationalised Industries. Financial Control. Privatisation. Sub-committee of E Committee (later E(A) Committee) on Nationalised Industries. Also referred to as "the Nationalised Industries files".

Margaret Thatcher's Prime Ministerial files (PM papers) have been sometimes used when accessing E/E(A) Committee, E(DL) Sub-committee proceedings and E(NI) papers (see below). These files include the usual minutes and memoranda but also associated correspondence and the PM's comments. The PM files containing E(DL) minutes and memoranda are filed as Policy Towards Privatisation. Disposal of Public Assets. In the Notes to the book the abbreviation E(DL) followed by the part number is used when referring to these files.

Prefix G: Department of Energy papers on the privatisation of British Gas.

HM Treasury papers (various prefixes).

PM papers: the Prime Minister's files dealing with particular economic matters including the nationalised industries.

## Published sources

Abse, L. (1989) *Margaret, daughter of Beatrice*, London: Jonathan Cape.

Adam Smith Institute (1986) *Privatisation Worldwide*, London: Adam Smith Institute.

Adeney, M. and Lloyd, J. (1986) *The Miners' Strike 1984–85: Loss Without Limit*, London: Routledge.

Aims (1978) *Still more Galloping Nationalization*, London: Aims, The Free Enterprise Organisation.

Aims of Industry (1983) *Privatisation: A Threat to Its Future*, London: Aims of Industry.

Alchian, A.A. (1965) "Some Economics of Property Rights", *Il Politico*,vol.30, pp.816–29.

Arnold, B. (1984) *Margaret Thatcher: A Study in Power*, London: Hamish Hamilton.

Ashworth, M. and Forsyth, P. (1984) *Civil Aviation Policy and the Privatisation of British Airways*, IFS Report 12, London: Institute for Fiscal Studies.

Ashworth, M. and Forsyth, P. (1986) "British Airways: Privatization and airline regulatory procedure", in J.Kay, C. Mayer and D. Thompson (eds.), *Privatisation and Regulation: The UK Experience*, Oxford: Clarendon Press.

Averch, H. and Johnson, L.L. (1962) "Behavior of the Firm under Regulatory Constraint", *American Economic Review*, vol.52, pp.1052–1069.

BA (British Airways), *Annual Report and Accounts 1982/83*, London: British Airways.

Bacon, R.W. and Eltis, W.A. (1976) *Britain's Economic Problem: Too Few Producers*, London: Macmillan.

Bailey, E.E. (1973) *Economic Theory of Regulatory Constraint*, Lexington: D.C.Heath & Co.

Bailey, R. and Baldwin, R. (1990) "Privatisation and Regulation: The Case of British Airways", in J.J. Richardson (ed.), *Privatisation & Deregulation in Canada and Britain*, Aldershot: Institute for Research on Public Policy.

Baker, K. (1993) *The Turbulent Years: My Life in Politics*, London: Faber & Faber.

Ball, S. and Seldon, A. (eds.) (1996) *The Heath Government 1970–74: a reappraisal*, London: Longman.

Barry, E.E. (1965) *Nationalisation in British Politics: The Historical Background*, London: Jonathan Cape.

Batt, M. (1990) "Putting a Brand on British Airways", *Marketing Business*, April, pp.14–15.

Baumol, W.J. (1982) "Contestable Markets: an uprising in the theory of industry structure", *American Economic Review*, vol.72, no.1, pp.1–15.

Baumol, W.J., Panzar, J.C. and Willig, R.D. (1982) *Contestable Markets and the Theory of Industry Structure*, New York: Harcourt Brace and Jovanovich.

Becker, G. (1983) "A theory of competition among pressure groups for political influence", *Quarterly Journal of Economics*, vol. 98, pp.371–400.

Beesley, M. and Littlechild, S.C. (1983) "Privatization: Principles, Problems and Priorities", *Lloyds Bank Review*, July, pp.1–20.

Beesley, M. and Littlechild, S.C. (1989) "The Regulation of Privatized Monopolies in the United Kingdom", *The RAND Journal of Economics*, Vol. 20, No. 3 (Autumn, 1989), pp.454–72.

Beesley, M.E. (ed.) (1997) *Privatization, Regulation and Deregulation*, London: Routledge in association with the Institute of Economic Affairs, 2nd edition.

Behrens, R. (1980) *The Conservative Party from Heath to Thatcher: Policies and Politics 1974–1979*, Farnborough: Saxon House.

Bellamy, M. (2001) *The Shipbuilders: An Anthology of Scottish Shipyard Life*, Edinburgh: Birlinn

Berthoud, R. (1989) "Social security and the economics of housing", in A. Dilnot and I. Walker (eds.) *The Economics of Social Security*, Oxford: Oxford University Press.

Birks, J.A. (1990) *National Bus Company, 1968–89*, Glossop: Transport Publishing.

Bishop, M. and Kay, J. (1988), *Does Privatisation Work?* London: London Business School.

Blake, S. and John, A. (2003) *The World According to Margaret Thatcher*, London: Michael O'Mara Books Ltd.

Blake, Lord (1976) "A Changed Climate", in Lord Blake and J. Patten (eds.)

Blake, Lord and Patten, J. eds. (1976) *The Conservative Opportunity*, London: Macmillan.

Blake, R. (1985) *The Conservative Party from Peel to Churchill*, London: Fontana.

Blankart, C.B. (1983) "The contribution of public choice to public utility economics: a survey", in J. Fissinger (ed.), *Public Sector Economics*, London: Macmillan.

Booth, P. (ed.) (2006) *Were 364 Economists All Wrong?*, Readings 60, London: Institute of Economic Affairs.

Borcherding, T.E., Pommerehne, W.E. and Schneider, F. (1982) "Comparing the Efficiency of Private and Public Production: The Evidence from Five Countries", *Zeitschrift für Nationalökonomie*, vol.42, no.2 supplement, pp.127–56.

Bös, D. (1991) *Privatization: a Theoretical Treatment*, Oxford: Clarendon Press.

Boycko, M., Shleifer, A. and Vishny, R.W. (1996) "A Theory of Privatisation", *Economic Journal*, vol.106, March, pp.309–19.

Boyson, R. (1995) *Speaking My Mind: The Autobiography of Rhodes Boyson*, London: Peter Owen.

Bradshaw, W.P. (1996) "Ten Turbulent Years – the Effects on the Bus Industry of Deregulation and Privatisation", *Policy Studies*, vol.17, no.2, pp.125–36.

*British Gas: Offer for Sale by NM Rothschild & Sons Limited on behalf of the Secretary of State for Energy*, November 1986.

*British Telecom: Offer for Sale by Kleinwort, Benson Ltd on behalf of the Secretary of State for Trade and Industry*, November 1984.

Brittan, S. (1984) "The Politics and Economics of Privatization", *Political Quarterly*, vol.55, pp.109–28.

Bruce-Gardyne, J. (1984) *Mrs Thatcher's First Administration*, London: Macmillan.

Buchanan, J.M. (1972) *Theory of Public Choice*, Michigan: University of Michigan Press.

Buchanan, J.M. (1978) "From Private Preference to Public Philosophy: The Development of Public Choice", in J.M. Buchanan et al., *The Economics of Politics*, IEA Readings 18, London: Institute of Economic Affairs.

Buckland, R. (1987) "The Costs and Returns of the Privatization of Nationalized Industries", *Public Administration*, vol.65, no.3, pp.241–57.

Buckland, R. and Davis, E.W. (1984) "Privatisation Techniques and the PSBR", *Fiscal Studies*, vol.5, no.3, p.47.

Burton, J. (1987) "Privatisation: the Thatcher case", *Managerial and Decision Economics*, vol.8, pp.21–9.

Burton, J. and Parker, D. (1991) "Rolling Back the State? UK Tax and Government Spending Changes in the 1980s", *British Review of Economic Issues*, vol.13, no.31, pp.29–66.

Butler, D. and Kavanagh, D. (1979) *The British General Election of 1979*, London: Macmillan.

Butler, D. and Kavanagh, D. (1984) *The British General Election of 1983*, London: Macmillan.

Butler, D. and Kavanagh, D. (1988) *The British General Election of 1987*, London: Macmillan.

Butler, E. (ed.) (1988) *The Mechanics of Privatization*, London: Adam Smith Institute.

Callaghan, J. (1987) *Time and Chance*, London: Collins.

Campbell, A., Devine, M. and Young, D. (1990) *A Sense of Mission*, London: Economist/Hutchinson.

Campbell, J. (1993) *Edward Heath: A Biography*, London: Jonathan Cape.

Campbell, J. (2001) *Margaret Thatcher, Volume One: The Grocer's Daughter*, London: Pimlico.

Campbell, J. (2004) *Margaret Thatcher, Volume Two: The Iron Lady*, London: Pimlico.

Campbell-Smith, D. (1986) *Struggle for Take-Off: the British Airways Story*, London: Coronet.

Carlisle, A. (1988) "Marketing privatization", in E.Butler (ed.), *The Mechanics of Privatization*, London: Adam Smith Institute.

Carrington, Lord (1988) *Reflect on Things Past: The Memoirs of Lord Carrington*, London: Collins.

Caves, R.E. (1990) "Lessons from Privatization in Britain: State Enterprise Behavior, Public Choice, and Corporate Governance", *Journal of Economic Behavior and Organization*, vol.13, pp.145–69.

Centre for Policy Studies (1981) *Personal and Portable Pensions for All*, London: CPS.

Chester, Sir N. (1975) *The Nationalisation of British Industry 1945–51*, London: HMSO.

Childs, D. (2001) *Britain since 1945: A Political History*, 5th ed., London: Routledge.

Civil Aviation Act 1980, Chapter 60, London: HMSO.

Civil Aviation Authority (1984) *Airline Competition Policy, Final Report*, July, London: CAA.

Clark, A. (1998) *The Tories: Conservatives and the Nation State, 1922–1997*, London: Weidenfeld & Nicolson.

Clark, A. (2000) *Diaries: Into Politics*, London: Weidenfeld & Nicolson.

Cockett, R. (1994) *Thinking the Unthinkable: Think Tanks and the Economic Counter Revolution, 1931–1983*, London: HarperCollins.

Cole, J. (1987) *The Thatcher Years: A Decade of Revolution in British Politics*, London: BBC Books.

Collins, C. (ed.) *The Complete Public Statements of Margaret Thatcher 1945–1990 on CD Rom*, Oxford: Oxford University Press.

Congdon, T. (2006) "Why the 1981 Budget mattered: the end of naïve Keynesianism", in P. Booth (ed.), *Were 364 Economists All Wrong?*, Readings 60, London: Institute of Economic Affairs.

Conservative Party (1970) *A Better Tomorrow* (General Election Manifesto), http://www.psr.keele.ac.uk/area/uk/man/con70.htm

Conservative Party (1974) *Putting Britain First* (General Election Manifesto) http://www.psr.keele.ac.uk/area/uk/man/con74oct.htm.

Conservative Party (1976) *The Right Approach: A Statement of Conservative Aims*, http://www.margaretthatcher.org/archive/displaydocument.asp?docid=109439.

Conservative Party (1977) *The Right Approach to the Economy*, http://www.margaretthatcher.org/document/3FE9928C24064D23804B47E4879E2CF0.pdf.

Conservative Party (1979) *Conservative Party General Election Manifesto*, http://www.psr.keele.ac. uk/area/uk/man/con79.htm.

Conservative Party (1983) Conservative Party General Election Manifesto, http://www.psr.keele. ac.uk/area/uk/man/con83.htm.

Coombes, D. (1971) *State Enterprise: Business or Politics?*, London: Allen and Unwin.

Corke, A. (1986) *British Airways: The Patch to Profitability*, London: Macmillan.

Cosgrave, P. (1978) *Margaret Thatcher: A Tory and her Party,* London: Hutchinson.

Cosgrave, P. (1979) *Thatcher: The First Term*, London: Bodley Head.

Cosgrave, P. (1985) *Carrington: A Life and a Policy*, London: J.M. Dent & Sons.

Cowling, K., Stoneman, P., Cubbin, J., Cable, J., Hall, G., Domberger, S. and Dutton, P. (1980) *Mergers and Economic Performance*, Cambridge: Cambridge University Press.

Crick, M. (1985) *Scargill and the Miners*, Harmondsworth: Penguin.

Critchley, J. (1992) *Some of Us: People who did well under Thatcher,* London: John Murray.

De Alessi, L. (1980) "The economics of property rights: a review of the evidence", *Research in Law and Economics,* vol.2, pp.1–47.

Dell, E. (1996) *The Chancellors: A History of the Chancellors of the Exchequer 1945–90*, London: Harper Collins.

Demsetz, H. (1968) "Why Regulate Utilities?", *Journal of Law and Economics,* vol.11, no.1, pp.55–65.

Denham, A. and Garnett, M. (2001) *Keith Joseph,* Chesham: Acumen Publishing Ltd.

Department of Energy (1982) *Britoil: Departmental history of the share offer*, London.

Department of Energy (1984) *Enterprise Oil: A report on the Privatisation of Enterprise Oil*, London.

Department of Energy (1986) *Authorisation granted and Directions given by the Secretary of State for Energy to British Gas Corporation under the Gas Act 1986*, London: Department of Energy.

Department of Industry (1982) *The Future of Telecommunications in Britain*, July, London: HMSO, Cmnd. 8610.

Drucker, P.F. (1969) *The Age of Discontinuity*, New York: Harper & Row.

Drucker, P.F. (1985) *Innovation and Entrepreneurship*, London: Pan Books.

DTI (Department of Trade and Industry) (1973) *Rolls Royce Ltd and the RB211 Aero-Engine*, Cmnd. 4860, London: HMSO.

Dunleavy, P. (1991) *Democracy, Bureaucracy and Public Choice: Economic Approaches in Political Science*, London: Harvester-Wheatsheaf.

Dunsire, A. and Hood, C. (1989) *Cutback Management in Public Bureaucracies: Popular Theories and Observed Outcomes in Whitehall,* Cambridge: Cambridge University Press.

Dunsire, A., Hartley, K., Parker, D. and Dimitriou, B. (1988) "Organisational status and performance: a conceptual framework for testing public choice theories", *Public Administration,* vol.66, no.4, pp.363–88.

Edgell, S. and Duke, V. (1991) *A Measure of Thatcherism*, London: HarperCollins.

Eglin, R. and Ritchie, B. (1981) *Fly Me, I'm Freddie!,* London: Futura.

Ernst & Young (1994) *Privatization in the UK: The facts and figures*, London: Ernst & Young.

Evans, E.J. (1997) *Thatcher and Thatcherism*, second edition, London: Routledge.

Ezra, Lord (1987) "Privatisation: A Middle Course", in J.Neuberger (ed.) *Privatisation . . . Fair Shares for All or Selling the Family Silver?*, London: Macmillan.

Fama, E.F. and Jensen, M.C. (1983) "Separation of Ownership and Control", *Journal of Law and Economics,* vol.26, pp.301–25.

Foreman-Peck, J. and Millward, R. (1994) *Public and Private Ownership of British Industry 1820–1990*, Oxford: Clarendon Press.

Foreman-Peck, J. and Waterson, M. (1984) "The Comparative Efficiency of Public and Private Enterprise in Britain: Electricity Generation between the World Wars", *Economic Journal*, conference papers, supplement to vol.95, pp.83–95.

Foster, C.D. (1971) *Politics, Finance and the Role of Economics: an essay in the control of public enterprises*, London: Allen and Unwin.

Foster, C.D. (1992) *Privatization, Public Ownership and the Regulation of Natural Monopoly*, Oxford: Blackwell.

Foster, C.D. (2005) *British Government in Crisis or The Third English Revolution*, Oxford: Hart Publishing.

Fowler, N. (1991) *Ministers Decide: A Personal Memoir of the Thatcher Years*, London: Chapmans.

Frey, B.S. and Benz, M. (2005) "Can Private Learn from Public Governance?", *Economic Journal*, vol.115, November, pp.F377–F396.

Friedman, M. and Friedman, R. (1980) *Free to Choose*, London: Secker & Warburg.

Furubotn, E.G. and Pejovich, S. (1972) "Property Rights and Economic Theory: a Survey of the Recent Literature", *Journal of Economic Literature*, vol.10, pp.1137–62

Furubotn, E.G.and Pejovich, S. (1974) *The Economics of Property Rights*, Cambridge, Mass.: Ballinger.

Gamble, A. (1988) *The Free Economy and the Strong State: The Politics of Thatcherism*, London: Macmillan.

*Gas Act 1986*, Chapter 44, London: HMSO.

*Gas Act 1995*, Chapter 45, London: HMSO.

Gilmour, I. (1992) *Dancing with Dogma: Britain under Thatcherism*, London: Simon & Schuster.

Gordon, L. (1938) *The Public Corporation in Great Britain*, London and New York: Oxford University Press.

Gowrie, Lord (1976) "Industrial Relations", in Lord Blake and J.Patten (eds.)

Greasley, D. (1995) "The coal industry: Images and realities on the road to nationalisation", in R. Millward and J. Singleton (eds.), *The Political Economy of Nationalisation in Britain, 1920–50*, Cambridge: Cambridge University Press.

Green, E.H.H. (2006) *Thatcher*, London: Hodder Arnold.

Green, R. and Haskel, J. (2001) "Seeking a Premier League Economy: The Role of Privatization", in R.Blundell, D.Card and R.B.Freeman (eds.), *Seeking a Premier League Economy*, Chicago: University of Chicago Press.

Grimstone, G. (1988) "Organizing a privatization programme", in E.Butler (ed.) *The Mechanics of Privatization*, London: Adam Smith Institute, pp.10–23.

Grossman, S. and Hart, O.D. (1980) "Takeover bids, the free-rider problem, and the theory of the corporation", *Bell Journal of Economics*, vol.11, pp.42–64.

Grossman, S. and Hart, O.D. (1986) "The Costs and Benefits of Ownership: a theory of vertical and lateral integration", *Journal of Political Economy*, vol.94, pp.691–719.

Hailsham, Lord (1990) *A Sparrow's Flight: The Memoirs of Lord Hailsham of St Marylebone*, London: Collins.

Halcrow, A. (1989) *Keith Joseph: A Single Mind*, London: Macmillan.

Hamilton, N.M. (1971) *Pricking Pryke: the Facts on State Industry*, London: Aims of Industry.

Hannah, L. (1979) *Electricity before Nationalisation*, London: Macmillan.

Hanson, A.H. (1954) "Labour and the Public Corporation", *Public Administration*, vol.32, pp.203–9.

Harlow, C. (1977) *Innovation and Productivity under Nationalization*, London: Allen and Unwin.

Harper, J. (1997) *Monopoly and Competition in British Telecommunications: The Past, the Present and the Future*, London: Pinter.

Harris, K. (1988) *Thatcher*, London: Weidenfeld and Nicolson.

Harris, R. (1991) *Good and Faithful Servant: The Unauthorised Biography of Bernard Ingham*, London: Faber and Faber.

Hayek, F.A. (1944) *The Road to Serfdom*, London: Routledge.

Hayek, F.A. (1948) *Individualism and Economic Order*, Chicago: University of Chicago Press.

Heald, D. (1980) "The Economic and Financial Control of UK Nationalised Industries", *Economic Journal*, vol.90, pp.243–65.

Heald, D. and Steel, D. (1982) "Privatizing Public Enterprise: An Analysis of the Government's Case", *Political Quarterly*, vol.53, July, pp.333–49.

Healey, D. (1989) *The Time of My Life*, London: Michael Joseph, p.580.

Heath, E. (1998) *The Course of My Life: My Autobiography*, London: Hodder & Stoughton.

Hennessy, P. (1983) "History men wrestling with Morrison's monsters", *The Times*, 3 May.

Heseltine, M. (1987) *Where There's a Will*, London: Hutchinson.

Heseltine, M. (2000) *Life in the Jungle: My Autobiography*, London: Coronet Books.

Heseltine, P.M. and Mulley, C. (1993) *The Effects of Privatisation of the Scottish Bus Group and Bus Deregulation: A Consultants Report by the Transport Operations Research Group, University of Newcastle upon Tyne*, Edinburgh: The Scottish Office Central Research Unit Papers, November.

Hibbs, J. (2005) *The Dangers of Bus Re-regulation and Other Perspectives on Markets in Transport*, Occasional Paper 137, London: Institute of Economic Affairs.

Hillman, J. and Clarke, P. (1988) *Geoffrey Howe: A Quiet Revolutionary*, London: Weidenfeld and Nicolson.

HMSO (1956) *Report of the Committee of Inquiry into the Electricity Supply Industry* (Herbert Committee), Cmnd.9672, London: HMSO.

HMSO (1961) *The Financial and Economic Obligations of the Nationalised Industries*, Cmnd.1337, London: HMSO.

HMSO (1967) *Nationalised Industries: a review of economic and financial objectives*, Cmnd.3427, London: HMSO.

HMSO (1969) *British Air Transport in the Seventies: Report of the Committee on Inquiry into Civil Air Transport* (Edwardes Committee), Cmnd.4018, London: HMSO.

HMSO (1977) *Report of the Post Office Review Committee*, Cmnd. 6850, London: HMSO.

HMSO (1978) *The Nationalised Industries*, Cmnd.7131, London: HMSO.

HMSO (1981) *Liberalisation of the use of British Telecommunications Network*, Report to the Secretary of State for Industry, London: HMSO.

HMSO (1985–6) *Department of Energy, Transport and Trade and Industry, effectiveness of Government financial controls over the nationalised industries*, Report by the Comptroller and Auditor General, H.C.253, London: HMSO.

HM Treasury (1982) *Treasury Minute on the Seventh, Ninth to Eighteenth and Twentieth to Twenty-Ninth Reports from the Committee on Public Accounts*, Session 1981–82, Cmnd. 8759, London: HMSO.

HM Treasury (1983) "The Financial Secretary Speaks out on Privatisation", 1 November, London: HM Treasury Press Release 190/83.

HM Treasury (1984a) "Financial Secretary Reviews Privatisation Achievements", 16 July, London: HM Treasury Press Release 122/84.

HM Treasury (1984b) *Treasury Minute of the Thirteenth to Eighteenth Reports from the Committee of Public Accounts*, Session 1983–84, Cmnd. 9325, London: HMSO.

HM Treasury (1986a) *Treasury Minute on the First to Fourth Reports from the Committee of Public Accounts*, Session 1985–86, Cmnd. 9755, London: HMSO.

HM Treasury (1986b) *Accounting for Economic Costs and Changing Prices: A Report to HM Treasury by an Advisory Group*, London: HMSO.

HM Treasury (1992) *Her Majesty's Treasury Guide to the UK Privatisation Programme*, June, London: HM Treasury.

Holmes, M. (1985) *The First Thatcher Government 1979–1983: Contemporary Conservatism and Economic Change*, Brighton: Harvester Wheatsheaf.

Holmes, M. (1989) *Thatcherism: Scope and Limits, 1983–87*, London: Macmillan.

Hoskyns, J. (2000) *Just in Time: Inside the Thatcher Revolution*, London: Aurum Press.

House of Commons, Session 1980–81, *Second Report from the Environment Committee, Council House Sales, Volume 1*, HC 366-I, London: HMSO, 1981.

House of Commons, Session 1981–82, *Tenth Report from the Committee of Public Accounts. Department of Industry. Sale of shares in British Aerospace; Sales of Government Shareholdings in other publicly owned Companies and British Petroleum Limited*, London: HMSO, 1982.

House of Commons Public Accounts Committee (1985) *Third Report: British Telecommunications*, London: HMSO.

House of Commons Public Accounts Committee (2006) *Delivery chain analysis for bus services in England, Forty-third Report of Session 2005–6*, HC851, London: HMSO.

Howe, G. (1978) "Liberating Free Enterprise: A New Experiment", speech to the Bow Group in London on 26 June, reproduced in G. Howe (1988) *Enterprise Zones and the Enterprise Culture*, London: Bow publications.

Howe, G. (1981) *Privatisation: The Way Ahead*, pamphlet based on a speech given to the Selsdon Group 1 July 1981, London: Conservative Political Centre.

Howe, G. (1988) *Enterprise Zones and the Enterprise Culture: Ten Years On*, speech given to the Bow Group 26 June 1988, London: Bow publications.

Howe, G. (1994) *Conflict of Loyalty*, London: Macmillan.

Ingham, B. (1991) *Kill the Messenger*, London: HarperCollins.

Iordanoglou, C.H. (2001) *Public Enterprise Revisited: A Closer Look at the 1954–79 UK Labour Productivity Record*, Cheltenham: Edward Elgar.

Jaffer, S. and Thompson, D. (1986) "Deregulating Express Coaches: A Reassessment", *Fiscal Studies*, vol.7, no.4, pp.45–68.

Jenkins, P. (1987) *Mrs Thatcher's Revolution: The Ending of the Socialist Era*, London: Jonathan Cape.

Jenkins, R. (1963) "Foreword" in M. Shanks (ed.), *The Lessons of Public Enterprise*, London: Jonathan Cape.

Jenkins, S. (1983) "Government Policy Towards the Nationalised Industries", in T.J.G. Hunter, (ed.) *Decision Making in a Mixed Economy*, Milton Keynes: Open University Press.

Jenkins, S. (1995) *Accountable to None: The Tory Nationalisation of Britain*, London: Hamish Hamilton.

Jenkinson, T. and Mayer, C. (1994) *Hostile Takeovers: Defence, Attack and Corporate Governance*, London: McGraw-Hill.

Jensen, M. and Meckling, W.R. (1976) "Theory of the firm: managerial behaviour, agency costs and ownership structure", *Journal of Financial Economics*, vol.3, pp.305–60.

Johnson, C (1991) *The Economy under Mrs Thatcher 1979–1990*, London: Penguin.

Johnson, P. and Stark, G. (1989) *Taxation and Social Security 1979–1989: The Impact on Household Incomes*, London: Institute for Fiscal Studies.

Junor, P. (1983) *Margaret Thatcher: Wife, Mother, Politician*, London: Sidgwick & Jackson.

Kavanagh, D. (1987) *Thatcherism and British Politics: The End of Consensus?*, Oxford: Oxford University Press.

Kavanagh, D. and Seldon, A. (2000) *The Powers behind the Prime Minister: The Hidden Influence of Number Ten*, London: HarperCollins.

Kay, J., Mayer, C. and Thompson, D. (eds.) (1986) *Privatisation and Regulation: the UK experience*, Oxford: Clarendon Press.

Kay, J.A. and Thompson, D.J. (1986) "Privatisation: a policy in search of a rationale", *Economic Journal*, vol.96, March, pp.18–32.

Keegan, W. (1984) *Mrs Thatcher's Economic Experiment*, Harmondsworth: Penguin Books.

Kelf-Cohen, R. (1973) *British Nationalisation 1945–73*, London: Macmillan.

Keynes, J.M. (1936) *The General Theory of Employment, Interest and Money*, New York: Harcourt Brace.

King, Lord J. (1987) "Lessons from Privatization", *Long Range Planning*, vol.20, no.6, pp.18–22.

Labour Party (1945) *Let us Face the Future: A Declaration of Labour Policy for the Consideration of the Nation*, London: Labour Party. http://www.psr.keele.ac.uk/area/uk/man/lab50.htm

Labour Party (1950) *Let Us Win Through Together: A Declaration of Labour Policy for the Consideration of the Nation*, http://www.psr.keele.ac.uk/area/uk/man/lab50.htm.

Labour Research Department (1987) *Privatisation: paying the price*, London: Labour Research Department.

Lamont, N. (1988) "The benefits of privatization: an overview", in E.Butler (ed.), *The Mechanics of Privatization*, London: Adam Smith Institute, pp.1–9.

Lane, K. (2004) *National Bus Company: The Early Years*, Shepperton: Ian Allan Ltd.

Lawson, N. (1992) *The View from No.11: Memoirs of a Tory Radical*, London: Bantam Press.

LeGrand, J. and Robinson, R. J. (eds.) (1984) *Privatisation and the Welfare State*, London: George Allen & Unwin.

Letwin, O. (1988) *Privatising the World: A Study of International Privatisation in Theory and Practice*, London: Cassell.

Letwin, S.R. (1992) *The Anatomy of Thatcherism*, London: Fontana.

Liberal Party (1928) *Britain's Industrial Future* (The Liberal Yellow Book), London: Liberal Party.

Likierman, A. (1979) "Performance Indicators for State Industry", *Accountancy*, October, pp.91–2.

Littlechild, S.C. (1978) *The Fallacy of the Mixed Economy: An 'Austrian' critique of recent economic thinking and policy*, Hobart Paper 80, London: Institute of Economic Affairs.

Littlechild, S.C. (1983) *Regulation of British Telecommunications' Profitability, Report to the Secretary of State*, London: Department of Industry, February.

Littlechild, S.C. (2003a) "The Birth of RPI – X and Other Observations", paper presented at the UK Model of Utility Regulation Conference, London, 9 April.

Littlechild, S.C. (2003b) "Reflections on Incentive Regulation", *Review of Network Economics*, vol.2, no.1, pp.289–315.

MacGregor, I. (1986) *The Enemies Within: the Story of the Miners' Strike 1984–85*, London: Collins.

Macmillan, H. (1938) *The Middle Way: A Study of the Problem of Economic and Social Progress in a Free and Democratic Society*, London: Macmillan.

Maitland, Lady O. (1989) *Margaret Thatcher: The First Ten Years*, London: Sidgwick & Jackson.

Manne, H.G. (1965) "Mergers and the Market for Corporate Control", *Journal of Political Economy*, vol.73, pp.110–20.

Marriott, L. (1997) *British Airways*, Shepperton: Ian Allan Ltd

Marsh, D. (1991) "Privatization Under Mrs Thatcher: A Review of the Literature", *Public Administration*, vol.69, winter, pp459–80.

Marshall, Sir C. (1988a) "British Airways", in R. Nelson (ed.) *Turnaround: How Twenty Well-Known Companies came back from the Brink*, London: Mercury Books.

Marshall, Sir C. (1988b) "How British Airways was privatized", in E.Butler (ed.), *The Mechanics of Privatization*, London: Adam Smith Institute, pp.35–44.

Martin, S. and Parker, D. (1997) *The Impact of Privatisation: Ownership and Corporate Performance in the UK*, London: Routledge.

Mayer, C. and Meadowcroft, S.A. (1986) "Selling Public Assets: Techniques and Financial Implications", *Fiscal Studies*, vol.6, no.1, pp.42–56. Reprinted in J. Kay, C. Mayer and D. Thompson (eds.), *Privatisation and Regulation: The UK Experience*, Oxford: Clarendon Press.

McLachlan, S. (1983) *The National Freight Buy-Out: The Inside Story*, London: Macmillan.

Middlemas, K. (1991) *Power, Competition and the State volume 3, The End of the Postwar Era: Britain since 1974*, London: Macmillan.

Middlemas, K. (1994) "The Party, Industry, and the City", in A. Seldon and S. Ball (eds.), *Conservative Century: the Conservative Party since 1900*, Oxford: Oxford University Press.

Millward, R. (1976) "Price Restraint, Anti-inflation Policy and Public and Private Industry in the UK", *Economic Journal*, vol.86, pp.226–42.

Millward, R. (2000) "State Enterprise in Britain in the Twentieth Century", in P. Toninelli (ed.), *The Rise and Fall of State-Owned Enterprises in the Western World*, Cambridge: Cambridge University Press.

Millward, R. and Parker, D. (1983) "Public and Private Enterprise: comparative behaviour and relative efficiency", in R. Millward, D. Parker, L. Rosenthal, M.T. Sumner and N. Topham (eds.), *Public Sector Economics*, London: Longman.

Millward, R. and Ward, R. (1987) "The Costs of Public and Private Gas Enterprises in late 19th Century Britain", *Oxford Economic Papers*, vol.39, pp.719–37.

Minford, P. (1988) "Mrs Thatcher's Economic Reform Programme", in R. Skidelsky (ed.), *Thatcherism*, London: Chatto & Windus.

Minford, P. (2005) "Inflation, unemployment and the pound", in S. Roy and J. Clarke (eds.), *Margaret Thatcher's Revolution: How It Happened and What it Meant*, London and New York: Continuum.

Mitchell, W.C. (1988) *Government As It Is*, Hobart Paper 109, London: Institute of Economic Affairs.

MMC (Monopolies and Mergers Commission) (1980a) *The Inner London Letter Post: a Report on the Letter Post Service in the Area Comprising the Numbered London Postal Districts*, HC 515, London: HMSO.

MMC (1980b) *Domestic Gas Appliances: A Report on the Supply of Certain Domestic Gas Appliances in the United Kingdom*, HC703, Session 1979–80, London: HMSO.

MMC (1981) *Central Electricity Generating Board: a Report on the Operation by the Board of its System for the Generation and Supply of Electricity in Bulk*, HC 315, London: HMSO.

MMC (1982) *Bristol Omnibus Company Limited Cheltenham District Traction Company City of Cardiff District Council Trent Motor Traction Company Limited and West Midlands Passenger Transport Executive: A Report on Stage Carriage Services supplied by the Undertakings*, HC442, 1981–82, London: HMSO.

MMC (1983) *National Coal Board: a Report on the Efficiency and Cost in the Development, Production and Supply of Coal by the NCB*, Cmnd. 8920, London: HMSO.

MMC (1987) *British Airways PLC and British Caledonian Group PLC: A Report on the Proposed Merger*, Cmnd. 247, London: HMSO.

MMC (1988) *Gas: a Report on the Matter of the Existence or Possible Existence of a Monopoly Situation in Relation to the Supply of Gas through Pipes to Persons other than Tariff Customers*, Cmnd. 500, London: HMSO.

MMC (1993a) *Gas and British Gas plc*, London: HMSO.

MMC (1993b) *Gas: Volume 1 of Reports under the Fair Trading Act 1973 on the Supply Within Great Britain of the Conveyance or Storage of Gas by Public Gas Suppliers*, Cmnd. 2314, London: HMSO.

Moore, J. (1986) "The Success of Privatisation" in J. Kay, C. Mayer and D. Thompson (eds.), *Privatisation and regulation: The UK experience*, Oxford: Clarendon Press.

Moore, J. (1992) "British Privatization – Taking Capitalization to the People", *Harvard Business Review*, January.

Morrison, H.S. (1933) *Socialisation and Transport*, London: Constable.

Mueller, D.C. (1976) "Public Choice: a Survey", *Journal of Economic Literature*, vol.14, no.2, pp.395–433.

Mulley, C. and Wright, M. (1986) "Buy-outs and the Privatisation of National Bus", *Fiscal Studies*, vol.7, no.3, pp.1–24.

National Audit Office (1985a) *Report by the Comptroller and Auditor General, Department of Trade and Industry: Sale of Government Shareholding in British Telecommunications plc*, London: HMSO.

National Audit Office (1985b) *Report by the Comptroller and Auditor General. Department of Energy, Trade and Industry and Transport: Sales of Subsidiary Companies and Other Assets by Nationalised Industries*, London: HMSO.

National Audit Office (1987a) *Department of Transport: Sale of Government Shareholding in British Airways plc*, HC 37, Session 1987–88, London: HMSO.

National Audit Office (1987b) *Ministry of Defence – Sale of Royal Ordnance plc*, HC162, Session 1987–88, London: HMSO.

National Audit Office (1987c) *Department of Energy – Sale of Government Shareholding in British Gas plc*, 30 June, HC 22, Session 1986–87, London: HMSO.

National Audit Office (1988a) *Department of Transport – Sale of Government Shareholding in British Airways plc*, HC37, Session 1987–88, London: HMSO.

National Audit Office (1988b) *Department of Trade and Industry – Sale of Government Shareholding in Rolls-Royce plc*, HC243, Session 1987–88, London: HMSO.

National Audit Office (1988c) *Sale of Government shareholdings in British Gas plc, British Airways plc, Rolls-Royce plc and BAA*, HC211, Session 1987–88, London: HMSO.

National Audit Office (1989) *Ministry of Defence: Further Examination of the Sale of Royal Ordnance PLC*, HC448, Session 1988–89, London: HMSO.

National Audit Office (1990a) *Department of Transport: Sale of the National Bus Company*, HC43, Session 1990–91, London: HMSO.

National Audit Office (1990b) *Ministry of Defence: Further Examination of the Sale of Royal Ordnance PLC*, HC352, Session 1989–90, London: HMSO.

National Audit Office (1991) *Sale of the National Bus Company*, HC119, Session 1990–91, London: HMSO.

National Audit Office (1993) *The Sale of the British Technology Group*, HC59, Session 1993–94, London: HMSO.

National Audit Office (1994) *Sale of the Scottish Bus Group*, HC97, Session 1993–94, London: HMSO.

National Audit Office (1996) *Sale of London Transport's Bus Operating Companies*, HC251, Session 1995–96, London: HMSO.

National Audit Office (1998) *Report by the Comptroller and Auditor General: Sales of the Royal Dockyards*, HC748, Session 1997–98, London: HMSO.

National Bus Company (1986) *Disposals Programme*, London: NBC

National Economic Research Associates (1986) *Economic Regulation of the British Airports Authority plc: A report prepared for the Department of Transport by National Economic Research Associates*, London: Department of Transport.

NEDO (1976–77) (National Economic Development Office) *A Study of UK Nationalised Industries: their role in the economy and control in the future*, London: HMSO.

NEDO (1976) *A Study of UK Nationalised Industries: their role in the economy and control in the future. A report to the Government from the National Economic Development Office*, London: HMSO.

OFT (1991) *The Gas Review*, London: Office of Fair Trading.

Newman, K. (1986) *The Selling of British Telecom*, London: Holt, Rinehart and Winston.

Niskanen, W.A. Jr. (1971) *Bureaucracy and Representative Government*, Chicago: Aldine.

Nott, J. (2002) *Here Today, Gone Tomorrow: Reflections of an Errant Politician*, London: Politico's Publishing.

Nove, A. (1973) *Efficiency Criteria for the Nationalised Industries*, London: Allen and Unwin.

Ostergaard, G.N. (1954) "Labour and the Development of the Public Corporation", *Manchester School*, vol.22, pp.192–226.

Parker, D. (ed.) (1998) *Privatisation in the European Union: Theory and Policy Perspectives*, London: Routledge.

Parker, D., Dassler, T. and Saal, D. (2006) "Performance benchmarking in utility regulation: principles and the UK's experience", in M. Crew and D. Parker (eds), *International Handbook on Economic Regulation*, Cheltenham: Edward Elgar.

Parkinson, C. (1992) *Right at the Centre: an autobiography*, London: Weidenfeld and Nicolson.

Peden, G.C. (1991) *British Economic and Social Policy: Lloyd George to Margaret Thatcher*, second edition, London: Philip Allan.

Peltzman, S. (1976) "Toward a more general theory of regulation", *Journal of Law and Economics*, vol.14, August, pp.109–48.

Polanyi, G. (1968) *Comparative Returns from Investment in Nationalised Industries*, London: Institute of Economic Affairs.

Polanyi, G. and Polanyi, P. (1971) "The Ailing Giants", in R.Boyson (ed.), *Goodbye to Nationalisation*, London: Churchill Press.

Polanyi, G. and Polanyi, P. (1972) "The Efficiency of Nationalised Industries", *Moorgate and Wall Street Review*, spring, pp.17–49.

Polanyi, G. and Polanyi, P. (1974) *Failing the Nation: the Record of the Nationalised Industries,* London: Fraser Ansbacher.

Pratten, C.F. (1987) "Mrs Thatcher's Economic Legacy", in K.Minogue and M.Biddiss (eds.), *Thatcherism: Personality and Politics,* London: Macmillan.

Price Waterhouse (1987) *Privatisation: The Facts*, London: Price Waterhouse.

Prior, J. (1986) *A Balance of Power*, London: Hamish Hamilton.

Pryke, R. (1971) *Public Enterprise in Practice: The British Experience of Nationalisation over Two Decades*, London: MacGibbon and Kee.

Pryke, R. (1981) *The Nationalised Industries: Policies and Performance since 1968*, Oxford: Martin Robertson.

Pryke, R. (1982) "The Comparative Performance of Public and Private Enterprise", *Fiscal Studies*, vol.3, no.2, pp.68–81.

Public Accounts Committee (1985) *Third Report 1985–86: Sale of Government Shareholding in British Telecommunications plc*, HC495, Session 1984–85, London: HMSO.

Public Accounts Committee (1986) *Control of dockyards operation and manpower*, Twenty-first report from the Committee of Public Accounts, Session 1985–86.

Pym, F. (1984) *The Politics of Consent*, London: Hamish Hamilton.

Rainey, H.G. (1991) *Understanding and Managing Public Organizations,* San Francisco, CA: Jossey-Bass.

Redwood, J. (1976) "Managing the Economy", in Lord Blake and J.Patten (eds.), *The Conservative Opportunity*, London: Macmillan.

Redwood, J. (1980) *Public Enterprise in Crisis: the Future of the Nationalised Industries*, Oxford: Basil Blackwell.

Redwood, J. (1986) *Equity for Everyman: new ways to widen ownership,* Policy Study no.74, London: Centre for Policy Studies.

Reed, A. (1990) *Airline: the Inside Story of British Airways*, London: BBC Books.

Riddle, P. (1983) *The Thatcher Government*, Oxford: Martin Robertson.

Riddle, P. (1989) *The Thatcher Decade: How Britain has changed during the 1980s*, Oxford: Blackwell.

Ridley, N. (1991) *'My Style of Government': The Thatcher Years,* London: Hutchinson.

Robson, W.A. (1962) *Nationalized Industry and Public Ownership*, 2nd ed., London: Allen and Unwin.

Ross, S.A. (1973) "The Economic Theory of Agency: the Principal's Problem", *American Economic Review*, vol.62, pp.134–9.

Sappington, D.E.M. and Stiglitz, J.E. (1987) "Privatization, Information and Incentives", *Journal of Policy Analysis and Management,* vol.6, no.4, pp.567–82.

Saunders, P.R. and Harris, C.N. (1994) *Privatization and Popular Capitalism*, Oxford: Oxford University Press.

Seldon, A. (1981) *Wither the Welfare State*, London: Institute of Economic Affairs.

Seldon, A. and Collings, D. (2000) *Britain under Thatcher,* Harlow: Longman.

Select Committee on Nationalised Industries (1967–8) *Ministerial Control of the Nationalised Industries*, H.C.371, London: HMSO.

Shapiro, C. and Willig, R.D. (1990) "Economic Rationales for the Scope of Privatization", in E.N. Suleiman and J. Waterbury (eds.), *The Political Economy of Public Sector Reform and Privatization*, Boulder, Colorado: Westview Press.

Sharkey, W.W. (1982) *The Theory of Natural Monopoly*, Cambridge: Cambridge University Press.

Sherman, A. (2005) *Paradoxes of Power: Reflections on the Thatcher Interlude*, Exeter: Imprint Academic.

Shibata, K. (1994) *Privatisation of British Airways: Its management and politics 1982–1987,* Florence: European University Institute.

587

Shleifer, A. (1998) "State versus Private Ownership", *Journal of Economic Perspectives*, vol.12, pp.133–50.

Shleifer, A. and Vishny, R. (1994) "Politicians and Firms", *Quarterly Journal of Economics*, vol.109, pp.995–1025.

Sillars, P. (2007) "The Development of the Right to Buy and the Sale of Council Houses", *Economic Affairs*, vol.27, no.1, pp.52–7.

Sinclair, P. (1976) "The Economic Roles of the State", in Lord Blake and J.Patten (eds.), *The Conservative Opportunity*, London: Macmillan.

Singh, A. (1971) *Takeovers, their Relevance to the Stock Market and the Theory of the Firm*, Cambridge: Cambridge University Press.

Singh, A. (1975) "Takeovers, Economic Natural Selection and the Theory of the Firm: Evidence from Post-war UK Experience", *Economic Journal*, vol.85, pp.497–515.

Skidelsky, R. (1988) "Introduction", in R. Skidelsky (ed.), *Thatcherism*, London: Chatto & Windus.

Smith, A. (1910 ed.) *The Wealth of Nations*, vol. 1, London: J.M.Dent & Sons Ltd.

Starkie, D. and Thompson, D. (1985a) *Privatising London's Airports*, London: Institute for Fiscal Studies.

Starkie, D. and Thompson, D. (1985b) "The Airports Policy White Paper: Privatisation and Regulation", *Fiscal Studies*, vol.6, no.4, pp.30–41.

Stephenson, H. (1980) *Mrs Thatcher's First Year*, London: Jill Norman Ltd.

Stigler, G. (1971) "The theory of economic regulation", *Bell Journal of Economics and Management Science*, vol.2, no.1, pp.3–21.

Swann, D. (1988) *The Retreat of the State: Deregulation and Privatisation in the UK and US*, London: Harvester Wheatsheaf.

Tebbit, N. (1988) *Upwardly Mobile,* London: Weidenfeld and Nicolson.

Tebbit, N. (1991) *Unfinished Business,* London: Weidenfeld and Nicolson.

Tebbit, N. (2005) "On the inner culture of the Tories", in S. Roy and J. Clarke (eds.), *Margaret Thatcher's Revolution: How It Happened and What it Meant*, London and New York: Continuum.

Thatcher, M. (1975) Press Conference after winning Conservative leadership, 11 February 1975, Conservative Central Office, http://www.margaretthatcher.org/speeches/displaydocument.asp?docid=102487.

Thatcher, M. (1978) TV Interview for Granada *Bolton 500*, 30 April, http://www.margaretthatcher.org/speeches/displaydocument.asp?docid=103812

Thatcher, M. (1979a) Article for *Western Mail* ("The kind of society I would most like to live in . . .", 1 May, http://www.margaretthatcher.org/speeches/displaydocument.asp?docid=104057.

Thatcher, M. (1979b) General Election Press Conference, 2 May, Conservative Central Office, http://www.margaretthatcher.org/speeches/displaydocument.asp?docid=104069

Thatcher, M. (1993) *The Downing Street Years*, London: HarperCollins.

Thatcher, M. (1995) *The Path to Power*, London: HarperCollins.

Thompson, D. and Whitfield, A. (1995) "Express Coaching: Privatization, Incumbent Advantage, and the Competitive Process", in M. Bishop, J. Kay and C. Mayer (eds.), *The Regulatory Challenge*, Oxford: Oxford University Press.

Thompson, Sir P. (1988) "The Buyout at National Freight" in E. Butler (ed.), *The Mechanics of Prvatization*, London: Adam Smith Institute.

Thompson, Sir P. (1990) *Sharing the Success: The Story of NFC*, London: Collins.

Tivey, L.J. (1966) *Nationalization in British Industry*, London: Jonathan Cape.

Tivey, L.J. (1973) "British Nationalization in the 1960s", in L.J.Tivey (ed.), *The Nationalized Industries since 1960: A book of Readings*, London: Royal Institute of Public Administration/George Allen & Unwin.

TUC (1984) *Contractors' Failures,* London: Trades Union Congress.

TUC (1985a) *Stripping Our Assets: The City's Privatisation Killing,* London: Trades Union Congress.

TUC (1985b) *Privatisation and Top Pay,* London: Trades Union Congress.

TUC (1986a) *More Contractors' Failures,* London: Trades Union Congress.

TUC (1986b) *Bargaining in Privatised Companies,* London: Trades Union Congress.

Tullock, G. (1965) *The Politics of Bureaucracy,* Washington, DC: Public Affairs Press.

Tullock, G. (1976) *The Vote Motive,* London: Institute of Economic Affairs.

Tyson, W.J. (1990) "The Effects of Deregulation on Service Co-ordination in the Metropolitan Areas", *Journal of Transport Economics and Policy,* vol.24, no.3, pp.283–95.

Udehn, L. (1996) *The Limits of Public Choice: a sociological critique of the economic theory of politics,* London: Routledge.

Valentine, M. (2006) *Free Range Ego,* London: Valentine.

Veljanovski, C. (1987) *Selling the State: Privatisation in Britain,* London: Weidenfeld and Nicolson.

Vickers, J. and Yarrow, G. (1988) *Privatization: An Economic Analysis,* Cambridge, Mass.: MIT Press.

Walker, P. (1991) *Staying Power: An Autobiography,* London: Bloomsbury.

Walters, A. (1986) *Britain's Economic Renaissance: Margaret Thatcher's Reforms 1979–1984,* Oxford: Oxford University Press.

Walters, P. (1990) *Privatisation: Implications for Cultural Change,* London: United Research.

Wass, D. (2008) *Decline to Fall: The Making of British Macro-Economic Policy and the 1976 IMF Crisis,* Oxford: Oxford University Press.

Webb, M.G. (1973) *The Economics of Nationalized Industries,* London: Nelson.

White, P.J. (1990) "Bus Deregulation: A Welfare Balance Sheet", *Journal of Transport Economics and Policy,* vol.24, no.3, pp.311–32.

Whitelaw, W. (1989) *The Whitelaw Memoirs,* London: Aurum Press.

Willner, J. and Parker, D. (2007) "The Performance of Public and Private Enterprise under Conditions of Active and Passive Ownership and Competition and Monopoly", *Journal of Economics,* vol.90, no.3, pp.221–53.

Winchester, D. (1983) "Industrial Relations in the Public Sector", in G.S.Bain (ed.), *Industrial Relations in Britain,* Oxford: Basil Blackwell.

Yarrow, G. (1986) "Privatisation in Theory and Practice", *Economic Policy,* vol.2, pp.319–78.

Yergin, D. and Stanislaw, J. (1998) *The Commanding Heights: The Battle between Government and the Marketplace that is Remaking the World,* New York: Simon & Schuster.

Young, D. (1990) *The Enterprise Years: A Businessman in the Cabinet,* London: Headline.

Young, H. (1993) *One of Us: A Biography of Margaret Thatcher,* London: Pan Books.

# INDEX